POSTCODE ATLAS

BRITAIN

& NORTHERN IRELAND

CONTENTS

Key to map symbols ii
Structure of postcodes iii
Postcode areas iv-v
Britain maps (4.1 miles to 1 inch) 2-107
Northern Ireland map (9 miles to 1 inch) 108-109
Urban maps (1.6 miles to 1 inch) 110-122
- London (1.3 miles to 1 inch) 110-113
- West Midlands 114-115
- Manchester 116-117
- Leeds and Bradford 118-119
- Liverpool 120
- Newcastle upon Tyne 121
- Glasgow 122

London key to map pages and symbols 123
London mapping (3.2 inches to 1 mile) 124-131
Administrative areas information 132-145
Administrative areas map (19.7 miles to inch) 146-151
London boroughs map (2.6 miles to 1 inch) 152-153
Index to London street names 154-166
Index to Great Britain place names 167-223
Index to Northern Ireland place names 224

Collins
Published by Collins
An imprint of HarperCollins Publishers
77-85 Fulham Palace Road, Hammersmith, London W6 8JB

www.collins.co.uk

The postcode boundary information published in this atlas is compiled from the Postcode Address File (PAF) and reproduced with the permission of Royal Mail Group plc. The copyright and database rights in PAF are owned by Royal Mail Group plc. Details included in this atlas are subject to change without notice.

Mapping generated from Collins Bartholomew digital databases

The grid on this map is the National Grid taken from the Ordnance Survey map with the permission of the Controller of Her Majesty's Stationery Office.

Printed in Hong Kong

ISBN-13 978 0 00 722748 8
ISBN-10 0 00 722748 5 Imp 001 TV12204 RDR

e-mail: roadcheck@harpercollins.co.uk

Key to map symbols

Postcode information

PL — Area code

Area boundary

35 — District code

District boundary

Britain map symbols (pages 2-107)

M4 — Motorway

M6Toll — Toll Motorway

8, 9 — Motorway junction with full / limited access

Maidstone, Birch, Sarn — Motorway service areas (off road, full, limited access)

A48 — Primary route dual / single carriageway

A5 — 'A' road dual / single carriageway

B1403 — 'B' road dual / single carriageway

Minor road

Restricted access due to road condition or private ownership

Roads with passing places

Roads proposed or under construction

32b — Multi-level junction (occasionally with junction number)

Roundabout

Road tunnel

Steep hill (arrows point downhill)

Level crossing

Toll — Toll

Caen 6 hrs — Car ferry route with journey times

Railway line and station

Preserved railway line and station

Railway tunnel

Airport with / without scheduled services

Heliport

Built up area

Towns, villages and other settlements

National boundary

County / Unitary Authority boundary

468, 941 — Spot / Summit height in metres

Lake, dam and river

Canal / Dry canal / Canal tunnel

Beach

1:260,000 (approx)

0, 2, 4, 6, 8, 10 miles

0, 2, 4, 6, 8, 10, 12, 14, 16 km

4.1 miles to 1 inch   2.6 km to 1 cm

Northern Ireland map symbols (pages 108-109)

M1 — Motorway

5, 9 — Motorway junction with full / limited access

A28, N4 — Primary / National primary route

A29, N52 — 'A' road / National secondary route

B113, R408 — 'B' road / Regional road

Minor road

Road under construction

Multi-level junction / roundabout

Steep hill (arrows point downhill)

Car ferry route

International / domestic airport

Canal

International boundary

District / County boundary

754 — Summit height (in metres)

Built up areas

Beach

Conurbation map symbols (pages 110-122)

M73 — Motorway

M6 Toll — Toll motorway

5, 4 — Motorway junctions with full / limited access

FRANKLEY SERVICES — Motorway service area

A725 — Primary route dual / single carriageway

A4054 — 'A' road dual / single carriageway

B7078 — 'B' road dual / single carriageway

Minor road dual / single carriageway

Roundabout

Car ferry

Railway line and station

London Underground / Subway / Metro / Light rail station

Railway tunnel

Airport with scheduled services

Built up areas

Public building

County / Unitary Authority boundary

Woodland / Park

266 — Spot height in metres

Congestion charging zone

Extended congestion charging zone (from Feb 2007)

Postcodes operate at five levels.

Level 1. Areas are denoted by the first one or two letters of the code, eg GL. These areas are then divided into districts.

Level 2. Districts are denoted by the number or numbers in the first part of the postcode, eg GL52. Districts are further subdivided into sectors.

Level 3. Subdistricts are a further special division of districts and only occur in London, eg EC1A.

Level 4. Sectors are denoted by the number in the second part of the postcode, eg GL52 5.

Level 5. The final two letters of the code denote a group of houses or an individual building, eg GL52 5HH.

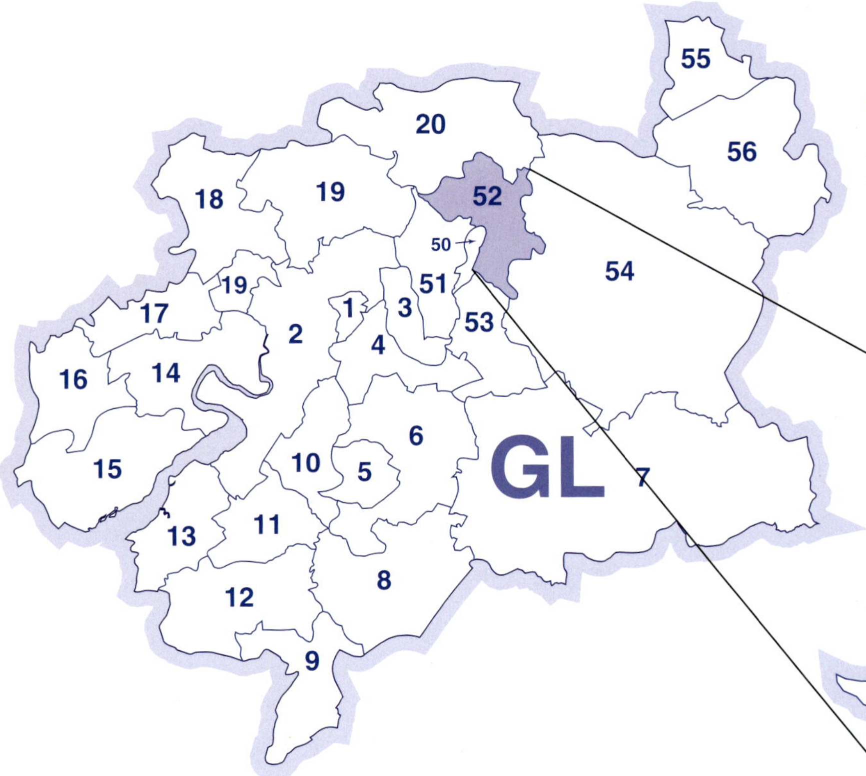

GL (Gloucester) is one of the postcode areas in the UK.

GL52 is a district within postcode area GL.

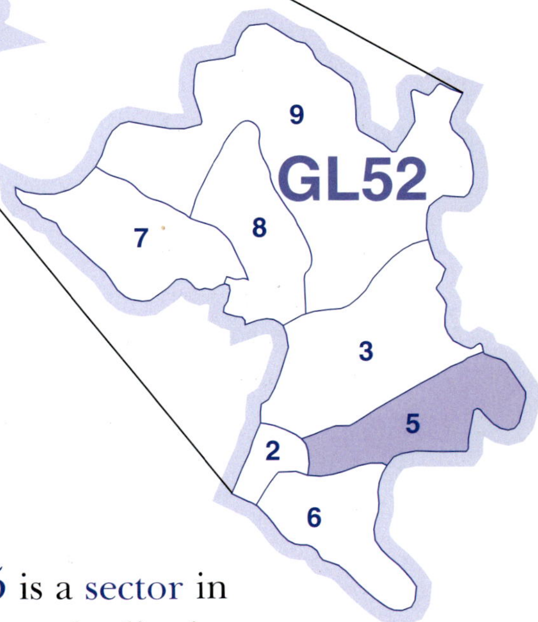

All postcode areas and districts are featured in this atlas.

Postcode subdistricts and sectors are not shown on the maps in this atlas with the exception of subdistricts and sectors in Central London.

GL52 5 is a sector in GL52 postcode district.

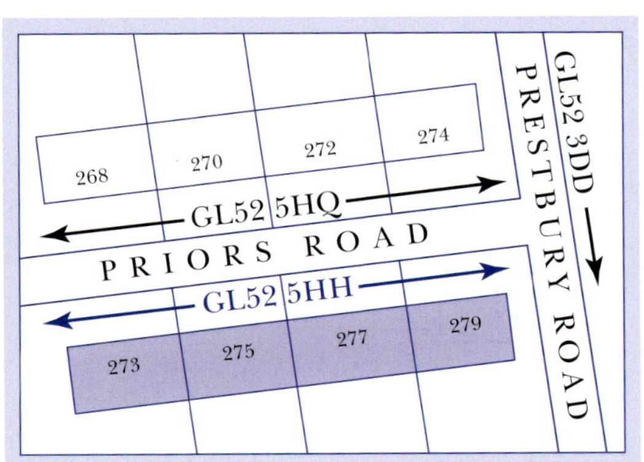

GL52 5HH is the postcode. It pinpoints a group of houses and in some cases individual business premises.

Postcode areas

Postcode	Area	Postcode	Area
AB	Aberdeen	HR	Hereford
AL	St Albans	HS	Hebrides
B	Birmingham	HU	Kingston upon Hull
BA	Bath	HX	Halifax
BB	Blackburn	IG	Ilford
BD	Bradford	IM	Isle of Man
BH	Bournemouth	IP	Ipswich
BL	Bolton	IV	Inverness
BN	Brighton	JE	Jersey
BR	Bromley	KA	Kilmarnock
BS	Bristol	KT	Kingston-upon-Thames
BT	Northern Ireland	KW	Kirkwall
CA	Carlisle	KY	Kirkcaldy
CB	Cambridge	L	Liverpool
CF	Cardiff	LA	Lancaster
CH	Chester	LD	Llandrindod Wells
CM	Chelmsford	LE	Leicester
CO	Colchester	LL	Llandudno
CR	Croydon	LN	Lincoln
CT	Canterbury	LS	Leeds
CV	Coventry	LU	Luton
CW	Crewe	M	Manchester
DA	Dartford	ME	Medway
DD	Dundee	MK	Milton Keynes
DE	Derby	ML	Motherwell
DG	Dumfries	N	London N
DH	Durham	NE	Newcastle upon Tyne
DL	Darlington	NG	Nottingham
DN	Doncaster	NN	Northampton
DT	Dorchester	NP	Newport
DY	Dudley	NR	Norwich
E	London E	NW	London NW
EC	London EC	OL	Oldham
EH	Edinburgh	OX	Oxford
EN	Enfield	PA	Paisley
EX	Exeter	PE	Peterborough
FK	Falkirk	PH	Perth
FY	Blackpool	PL	Plymouth
G	Glasgow	PO	Portsmouth
GL	Gloucester	PR	Preston
GU	Guildford	RG	Reading
GY	Guernsey	RH	Redhill
HA	Harrow	RM	Romford
HD	Huddersfield	S	Sheffield
HG	Harrogate		
HP	Hemel Hempstead		

Postcode	Area
SA	Swansea
SE	London SE
SG	Stevenage
SK	Stockport
SL	Slough
SM	Sutton
SN	Swindon
SO	Southampton
SP	Salisbury
SR	Sunderland
SS	Southend-on-Sea
ST	Stoke-on-Trent
SW	London SW
SY	Shrewsbury
TA	Taunton
TD	Galashiels
TF	Telford
TN	Royal Tunbridge Wells
TQ	Torquay
TR	Truro
TS	Teesside
TW	Twickenham
UB	Southall
W	London W
WA	Warrington
WC	London WC
WD	Watford
WF	Wakefield
WN	Wigan
WR	Worcester
WS	Walsall
WV	Wolverhampton
YO	York
ZE	Shetland

REPUBLIC OF IRELAND
Irish Sea
Isle of Man
English Channel
FRANCE
Isles of Scilly
Channel Islands
BELFAST
Stranraer
Carlisle
Middlesbrough
Lancaster
Leeds
Liverpool
Manchester
Lincoln
Nottingham
Aberystwyth
Birmingham
Norwich
Cambridge
Ipswich
Oxford
LONDON
Swansea
CARDIFF
Bristol
Southampton
Folkestone
Brighton
Exeter
Plymouth
BT
IM
SR
DH
CA
DL
TS
LA
HG
YO
BD
FY
PR
BB
LS
HU
HX
WF
L
WN
BL
OL
HD
M
DN
WA
SK
S
LL
CH
CW
LN
NG
ST
DE
TF
WS
SY
LE
PE
NR
WV
DY
B
CV
NN
IP
LD
HR
WR
MK
CB
OX
SG
CO
SA
LU
CM
GL
AL
EN
IG
HP
WD
CF
NP
HA
SS
UB
RM
SL
BS
SN
TW
BR
DA
RG
S
M
KT
CR
ME
CT
BA
GU
TA
SP
SO
RH
TN
EX
PO
DT
BH
BN
PO
PL
TQ
TR
TR
GY
JE

A
B
C
D
E
1
2
3
4
5
6
7
ISLES OF SCILLY
St Helen's
White Island
Tean
St Martin's
Old Grimsby
Lower Town
Middle Town
Higher Town
Eastern Isles
Bryher
New Grimsby
Tresco
Samson
Crow Sound
North West Channel
The Road
Hugh Town
Maypole
St Mary's
ST. MARY'S
Old Town
Crim Rocks
Broad Sound
Annet
Gugh
St Mary's Sound
Bishop Rock
Western Rocks
Smith Sound
St Agnes
21
22
23
24
25
TR
same scale as main map
Towan Head
Fistral Bay
Newquay
Kelsey Head
West Pentire
Pentire
Holywell Bay
Crantock
Penhale Point
Holywell
Ligger Pt
Cubert
Penhale Sands
Ligger Bay (Perran Bay)
6
Rose
Perranporth
Goonhavern
Bawden Rocks (Man and his Man)
St Agnes Head
Trevellas
Bolingey
St Agnes
5
Mithian
Perranzabuloe
4
Goonvrea
Goonbell
C O R
Towan Cross
Allet Common
Mount Hawke
Porthtowan
Three Burrows
Tregavethan
Blackwater
Nancekuke
Portreath
Bridge
Mawla
Chacewater
Threemilestone
Crane Islands
Illogan
Scorrier
Godrevy Island
Navax Point
Mount Ambrose
St Day
Twelveheads
TR
Baldhu
Bissoe
Carn Naun Pt
The Island
Gwithian
Coombe
Pool
Redruth
Carharrack
The Carracks
26
St Ives
St Ives Bay
Trevarnon
Kehelland
Tuckingmill
Carn Brea
Village
Pennance
Carnkie
Gwennap
Gurnard's Head
Trendrine Hill
Zennor
Towednack
Halsetown
Carbis Bay
Phillack
Connor Downs
Camborne
15
Brea
Lanner
Treen
Longstone
Hayle
Angarrack
Penponds
Barripper
14
Four Lanes
16
Perranarworthal
Devoran
Porthmeor
Amalebra
Trencrom Hill
Lelant
Bolenowe
Troon
Ponsanooth
Pendeen Watch
Nancledra
Gwinear
Carnhell Green
Penhalvean
Stithians
Lower Boscaswell
Morvah
20
New Mill
Castle Gate
27
Wall
Praze-an-Beeble
Canon's Town
St Erth Praze
Long Downs
Penryn
Bojewyan
Pendeen
Chysauster
Whitecross
St Erth
Fraddam
Crowan
Burras
Carnkie
Trewellard
Boswarthan
Kerthen Wood
Paul's Green
Leedstown
Crowan Beacon
Rame
Mabe Burnthouse
Botallack
Carnyorth
Ludgvan
Crowlas
Townshend
Releath
Porkellis
Lezerea
10
Cape Cornwall
Kenidjack
Madron
Heamoor
Gulval
Longrock
17
Relubbus
Trenwheal
Crelly
Edgcumbe
Budock Water
The Brisons
St Just
Newbridge
Tremethick Cross
Trevarrack
Chyandour
18
Marazion
Goldsithney
St Hilary
Godolphin Cross
Nancegollan
Crowntown
Wendron
Trenear
Seworgan
Treverva
Kelynack
Bosavern
Penzance
Perran Downs
Trescowe
Tregonning Hill
13
Trebarvah
11
Grumbla
Sancreed
Rosudgeon
Newtown
Germoe
Carleen
Pollardras
Lower Town
Trevenen
Brill
LAND'S END
Drift Reservoir
Buryas Bridge
Tredavoe
Newlyn
Perranuthnoe
Kenneggy Downs
Tresowes Green
Constantine
Whitesand Bay
Brane
Lower Drift
Catchall
Prussia Cove
Ashton
Sithney
Trewennack
Mawnan
Sennen Cove
Crows-an-wra
Kerris
Paul
Cudden Point
Praa Sands
Breage
Helston
Porth Navas
Durgan
Mousehole
Rinsey
Gweek
LAND'S END
Sennen
St Buryan
St Clement's Isle
Trewavas Head
Helford
Longships
Trevescan
Porthleven
Manaccan
19
Boleigh
Lamorna
Mawgan
Flushing
Trethewey
St Martin
Garras
Lamorna Cove
MOUNT'S BAY
Loe
Tregidden
Porthcurno
Treen
Berepper
Newtown-in-St-Martin
Tregarne
Gunwalloe
Tregowris
St Levan
Gwennap Head
Cribba Head
Logan Rock
Cury
Cross Lanes
Traboe
Lanarth
St Keverne
Poldhu Cove
12
PENINSULA
Poldhu Point
Goonhilly Downs
Mullion
Trelan
Mullion Cove
Penhale
Erisey Barton
Gwenter
Coverack
Mullion Island
Ponsongath
Gwendreath
Predannack Wollas
Kuggar
Black Head
Ruan Major
LIZARD
Vellan Head
St Ruan
Ruan Minor
Cadgwith
Grade
Toll
Kynance Cove
Landewednack
Lizard
Hot Point
LIZARD POINT
Wolf Rock
A30
A3071
A394
A3074
A3047
A393
A39
A3083
A3110
A390
B3306
B3315
B3283
B3311
B3309
B3301
B3302
B3280
B3300
B3297
B3293
B3296
B3304
B3277
B3285
B3284
0 2 4 6 miles
0 2 4 6 8 10 km

F
G
H
J
K
3
4
BODMIN MOOR
PL
Padstow
Wadebridge
Bodmin
Liskeard
Lostwithiel
ST AUSTELL
Fowey
Looe
Polperro
Mevagissey
TRURO
Falmouth
St Mawes
NEWQUAY CORNWALL INTERNATIONAL
N W A L L
Trevose Head
Constantine Bay
Porthcothan Beach
Park Head
St Columb Major
St Dennis
Roche
Bugle
St Blazey
Par
Grampound
Tregony
Probus
St Stephen
Polruan
Gribbin Head
Dodman Point
Nare Head
Zone Point
Pendennis Point
FALMOUTH BAY
Rosemullion Head
Nare Point
Manacle Point
The Manacles
Lowland Pt
ALDERNEY
GY
ALDERNEY
St Anne
same scale as main map
GUERNSEY
Grandes Rocques
St Sampson
St Peter Port
St Saviour
St Martin
Herm
Jethou
Sark
Brecqhou
Little Sark
Jerbourg Pt
Pleinmont Pt
Lihou
Poole 2½
Portsmouth 6½
Weymouth 2¼
Jersey 1
then St Malo 2-2¼
CHANNEL ISLANDS
location map
Alderney
Guernsey
Herm
Sark
Jersey
JERSEY
JE
Plémont Pt
St John
St Mary
St Ouen
Trinity
Rozel
St Martin
Carrefour Selous
St Peter
St Lawrence
Five Oaks
Gorey
Beaumont
St Aubin
St Brelade
ST HELIER
St Clement
Grouville
La Rocque Pt
Noirmont Pt
Guernsey 1
Poole 3-3¾
Portsmouth 10
Weymouth 3½
St Malo 1¼ hrs
1
2
3
4
5
6
7

A
B
C
D
E
1
2
3
4
5
6
7
CORNWALL
BODMIN MOOR
PL
PLYMOUTH
Launceston
Bodmin
Liskeard
Saltash
Tavistock
Callington
Camelford
Wadebridge
Lostwithiel
Fowey
Looe
Polperro
Torpoint
ST AUSTELL
Mevagissey
Tintagel
Boscastle
Holsworthy
Whitsand Bay
Eddystone
Roscoff.......................5½-8
Santander (summer only)....20½
hours
0 2 4 6 miles
0 2 4 6 8 10 km

F
G
H
J
K
1
2
3
4
5
6
7
DEVON
EX
TQ
DARTMOOR
Okehampton
Crediton
EXETER
Exmouth
Dawlish
Teignmouth
Chudleigh
Bovey Tracey
Kingsteignton
NEWTON ABBOT
Moretonhampstead
Chagford
Ashburton
Buckfastleigh
South Brent
Ivybridge
PLYMOUTH
Totnes
TORQUAY
Paignton
TORBAY
Brixham
Dartmouth
Kingsbridge
Salcombe
Modbury
Yelverton
Princetown
Topsham
Exminster
Kingsbridge
Start Bay
Tor Bay
Babbacombe Bay
Bigbury Bay
Start Point
Bolt Head
Bolt Tail
Prawle Point
Berry Head
Hope's Nose
Sharkham Point
Scabbacombe Head
Stoke Point
Mew Stone
Burgh Island
Bigbury-on-Sea
Hope
Thurlestone
Hallsands
Beesands
Torcross
Slapton
Strete
Stoke Fleming
Kingswear
Dittisham
Harbertonford
Halwell
Loddiswell
Aveton Gifford
Ringmore
Newton Ferrers
Noss Mayo
Yealmpton
Brixton
Wembury
Widecombe in the Moor
Haytor Vale
Manaton
North Bovey
Lustleigh
Ipplepen
Denbury
Kingskerswell
Abbotskerswell
Marldon
Stokeinteignhead
Shaldon
Bishopsteignton
Ideford
Kenton
Starcross
Cockwood
Kenn
Kennford
Dunsford
Drewsteignton
Cheriton Bishop
Tedburn St Mary
Whiddon Down
South Zeal
Sticklepath
Belstone
South Tawton
Throwleigh
Gidleigh
Lydford
Mary Tavy
Peter Tavy
Horrabridge
Walkhampton
Meavy
Dousland
Sheepstor
Shaugh Prior
Cornwood
Harford
Ugborough
Bittaford
Wrangaton
Avonwick
Diptford
Moreleigh
Woodleigh
Churchstow
West Alvington
Malborough
South Pool
Chivelstone
East Prawle
East Portlemouth
Frogmore
Sherford
Stokenham
Chillington
Blackawton
Cornworthy
Ashprington
Harberton
Staverton
Dartington
Landscove
Woolston Green
Broadhempston
Dean Prior
Holne
Buckfast
Poundsgate
Ponsworthy
Ilsington
Liverton
Bickington
Ogwell
Coffinswell
Combeinteignhead
Haccombe
Doddiscombsleigh
Christow
Bridford
Trusham
Ashcombe
Mamhead
Holcombe
Ide
Alphington
Shillingford St George
Whitestone
Pocombe Bridge
Exwick
Clyst St Mary
Clyst St George
Woodbury
Lympstone
Ebford
Exton
Powderham
Broadclyst
Poltimore
Stoke Canon
Brampford Speke
Thorverton
Silverton
Up Exe
Rewe
Newton St Cyres
Upton Pyne
Sandford
Copplestone
Yeoford
Spreyton
Bow
Zeal Monachorum
North Tawton
Sampford Courtenay
Exbourne
Jacobstowe
Inwardleigh
Folly Gate
Hatherleigh
Bridestowe and Sourton Common
Sourton
Meldon
Okehampton Camp
Yes Tor
High Willhays
Cawsand Hill
Great Kneeset
Sittaford Tor
Fernworthy Reservoir
Warren House
Postbridge
Bellever
Two Bridges
Rundlestone
Merrivale
Royal Hill
Ryder's Hill
Cater's Beam
Dean Moor
Harford Moor
Ugborough Moor
Penn Moor
Stall Moor
Hamel Down
Easdon Tor
Rippon Tor
Corndon Tor
Bonehill Down
Great Haldon
Little Haldon
Exeter International
M5
A30
A38
A380
A381
A379
A382
A383
A384
A385
A386
A3122
A3121
A3022
A377
A376
A396
B3212
B3357
Plymouth City
Plym Forest
Plym Bridge
Plympton
Elburton
Hemerdon
Sparkwell
Lee Mill Bridge
Ermington
Holbeton
Kingston
Ashford
Yealmbridge
Wotter
Lee Moor
Bickleigh
Clearbrook
Hoo Meavy
Cadover Bridge
Wigford Down
Gara Bridge
Topsham Bridge
Halwell
East Allington
Woodford
Capton
Galmpton
Goodrington
Collaton St Mary
Blagdon
Berry Pomeroy
Littlehempston
Rattery
Tigley
Harbourneford
Didworthy
Scorriton
Hele
Rew
New Bridge
Lower Town
Buckland in the Moor
Dunstone
Leusdon
Dartmeet
Hexworthy
Whiteworks
Sheepstor
Hollacombe
Colebrooke
Knowle
Woolsgrove
Crediton
Shobrooke
Stockleigh Pomeroy
Nether Exe
Bradninch
Killerton
Westwood
Dog Village
Sowton
Heavitree
Wonford
Countess Wear
Pinhoe
Monkerton
Clyst Honiton
Aylesbeare
Farringdon
Woodbury Salterton
Holcombe Burnell
Longdown
Nadderwater
Pathfinder Village
Oldridge
Venny Tedburn
Harford
Woodland Head
Hittisleigh
Crockernwell
Cheriton Cross
Sandypark
Easton
Murchington
Great Weeke
Doccombe
Lettaford
Sanduck
Butts
Lower Ashton
Higher Ashton
Oxencombe
Hennock
Teign Village
Chudleigh Knighton
Heathfield
Teigngrace
Preston
Sandygate
Humber
Luton
Waddon
Lower Upcott
Gappah
Olchard
Holcombe
Ringmore
Netherton
Milber
Daccombe
Maidencombe
Watcombe
Barton
St Marychurch
Babbacombe
Shiphay
Cockington
Preston
Shorton
Hollicombe
Upton
Compton
Red Post
Upthorpe
Longcombe
Sharpham House
Aish
Stoke Gabriel
Waddeton
Sandridge
Tuckenhay
Washbourne
Allaleigh
Hemborough Post
Downton
Hillhead
Woodhuish
Boohay
Kingswear
Blackpool
Bowden
Eastdown
Millcombe
Hutcherleigh
Merrifield
Coombe
Cole's Cross
Goveton
Buckland-tout-Saints
Ledstone
Venn
Bridge End
Harleston
Frittiscombe
Kernborough
Beeson
Kellaton
Bickerton
South Allington
West Prawle
Lannacombe Bay
Soar
Bolberry
Galmpton
South Huish
South Milton
Bantham
Buckland
Upton
Sutton
Woolston
Lincombe
Batson
Dodbrooke
Chillington
North Pool
Ford
West Charleton
East Charleton
Slapton Sands
Slapton Ley

A
B
C
D
E
1
2
3
4
5
6
7
North West Point
EX
LUNDY
34
Shutter Rock
Rat Island
Heddon's Mouth
Widmouth Head
Ilfracombe
Hele
Berrynarbor
Combe Martin
Trentishoe
Martinhoe
Hunter's Inn
Heale
Kemacott
Killington
Parracombe
Churchtown
Bull Point
Morte Point
Mortehoe
Lee
Slade
Mullacott Cross
Sterridge
Seymour Villas
Woolacombe
Trimstone
Cheglinch
West Down
Dean Cross
Bradwell
Berry Down Cross
Kentisbury
Blackmoor Gate
Challacombe Common
Challacombe
Swincombe
Patchole
Kentisbury Ford
Arlington Beccott
Arlington
Morte Bay
Bittadon
East Down
Clifton
Churchill
Baggy Point
Putsborough
Pickwell
North Buckland
Croyde Bay
Georgeham
Croyde
33
Knowle
Halsinger
Winsham
Boode
Lobb
Middle Marwood
Marwood
Milltown
Muddiford
Upcott
31
Higher Muddiford
Shirwell Cross
Shirwell
Kingsheanton
Prixford
Pippacott
Lower Loxhore
Loxhore
Knightacott
Bratton Fleming
Benton
Stoke Rivers
Saunton
Saunton Sands
Braunton
Heanton Punchardon
West Ashford
Ashford
Wrafton
Braunton Burrows
Chivenor
Bradiford
Pilton
Northleigh
Goodleigh
Willesleigh
Gunn
32
Stoodleigh
Charles
East Buckland
BARNSTAPLE
Bickington
Newport
Lilly
West Buckland
Yelland
Fremington
Lake
Landkey
Swimbridge Newland
Yarnacott
Riverton
Swimbridge
BARNSTAPLE BAY (BIDEFORD BAY)
The Neck
Appledore
Instow
Bickleton
Tawstock
Bishop's Tawton
St John's Chapel
Westward Ho!
Northam
Tapeley
Westleigh
Eastleigh
Horwood
Lower Lovacott
Harracott
Newton Tracey
Hiscott
Ensis
Herner
Chapelton
Cobbaton
Stowford
Chittlehampton
Filleigh
Hartland Point
Titchberry
Windbury Point
Gallantry Bower
Clovelly
Abbotsham
East-the-Water
Bideford
Gammaton
Woodtown
Alverdiscott
Gammaton Moor
Landcross
Hartland Quay
Stoke
Hartland
Sierra
Dyke
Clovelly Cross
Buck's Mills
Buck's Cross
Horns Cross
Fairy Cross
Ford
Yeo Vale
Alwington
Littleham
Fishleigh Barton
Atherington
Langridge
Umberleigh
Eastacott
Warkleigh
Hudscott
Clapworthy
Satterleigh
Milford
Elmscott
Edistone
Philham
Tosberry
Woolfardisworthy
Goldworthy
Cranford
Parkham
Parkham Ash
Buckland Brewer
Saltrens
Monkleigh
Weare Giffard
Huntshaw Water
Huntshaw
Huntshaw Cross
Langridgeford
Sherwood Green
High Bullen
High Bickington
Chittlehamholt
37
39
South Hole
Knaps Longpeak
Welcombe
Mead
Almiston Cross
Melbury
Great Torrington
Dodscott
St Giles in the Wood
Kingscott
Frithelstock Stone
Frithelstock
Taddiport
38
Roborough
Burrington
Darracott
Meddon
Woolley
Gooseham
Ashmansworthy
Fowler's Piece
Kimbledon Bridge
East Putford
West Putford
Little Torrington
Langtree
Langtree Week
Villavin
Beaford
Eastcott
East Youlstone
Dinworthy
Morwenstow
Higher Sharpnose Point
Lower Sharpnose Point
West Youlstone
Shop
Woodford
Bradworthy
Haytown
Bulkworthy
Berry Cross
Peters Marland
Winswell
Woollaton
Great Potheridge
Little Potheridge
Cottwood
Copy Lake
Riddlecombe
Ashreigney
Bridge Reeve
EX
Taylors Cross
Coombe
Kilkhampton
Alfardisworthy
Brendon
Sutcombe
Sutcombemill
Abbots Bickington
Vennggreen
Newton St Petrock
Little Marland
Merton
Heanton Satchville
Huish
Dolton
Hollacombe Town
Holcombe
Ashley
Eggesford Barton
Stibb
Thurdon
Soldon
Soldon Cross
Milton Damerel
23
Youldonmoor Cross
Youldon
Shebbear
Buckland Filleigh
North Town
Petrockstowe
Ash Barton
Dowland
19
Iddesleigh
Meeth
Wembworthy
Winkleigh
Coldridge
Poughill
Flexbury
Hersham
Bush
Grimscott
Holsworthy Beacon
Thornbury
Woodacott
Bradford
Brendon
Lashbrook
Bude Haven
Bude
Stratton
Launcells Cross
Chilsworthy
Lana
Pancrasweek
22
Sheepwash
Hele Bridge
Inglegh Green
D
E
Brushford
Broadwood Kelly
Monkokehampton
Black Torrington
Cookbury
Cookbury Wick
Middlecott
Launcells
Red Post
Derril
Rydon
Holsworthy
Brandis Corner
Dunsland Cross
Anvil Corner
Highampton
Hatherleigh
Bondleigh
Lowton
Marhamchurch
Helebridge
Bridgerule
Pyworthy
Derriton
Chasty
Whimble
Hollacombe
Graddon Moor
Lydacott
Odham
Bassett's Cross
Honeychurch
Exbourne
Sampford Courtenay
North Tawton
Widemouth Bay
Titson
Box's Shop
Yeomadon
Chilla
Halwill Forest
21
Jacobstowe
Shilstone
Coppathorne
Week Orchard
Trecott
Poundstock
Treskinnick Cross
Tregole
Whitstone
Tinney
Corfcott Green
Clawton
Halwill
Halwill Junction
Beaworthy
Whiddon
Northlew
Inwardleigh
Oak Cross
Belstone Corner
Trewint
Week St Mary
North Tamerton
CORNWALL
Trebarrow
Tetcott
Lana
Quoditch
Higher Prestacott
Broadbury
East Kimber
Ashbury
Patchacott
Folly Gate
20
Chichacott
Taw Green
Spreyton
Jacobstow
Higher Whiteleigh
Maxworthy
West Curry
Clubworthy
Luffincott
Ashwater
Henford
Germansweek
Eworthy
Thorndon Cross
Southcott
Okehampton
Sticklepath
South Tawton
South Zeal
Belstone
Whiddon Down
Trengune
Canworthy Water
Warbstow
Troswell
Bennacott
Brazacott
Boyton
Northcott
Chapmans Well
Virginstow
East Panson
West Panson
St Giles on the Heath
Hele
Yelland
Boasley Cross
Hewton
Bratton Clovelly
Meldon
Okehampton Camp
Cawsand Hill
Throwleigh
Tremaine
15
Penrose
North Petherwin
Langdon
Bridgetown
Polapit Tamar
Werrington
Broadwoodwidger
Ebsworthy Town
Sourton
Bridestowe
Yes Tor
High Willhays
Treneglos
Tresmeer
Trebeath
Three Hammers
Tregeare
Egloskerry
Ladycross
Leat
Yeolmbridge
Cross Green
Kellacott
Thrushelton
Bidlake
Southerly
Bridestowe and Sourton Common
Okement Hill
Hangingstone Hill
Gidleigh
Murchington
Chagford
Hallworthy
Cold Northcott
Badgall
Langore
Truscott
St Stephens
Newport
Dutson
PL
Launceston
Lifton
Tinhay
Sprytown
Stowford
Lewdown
Portgate
Allerford
Lobhillcross
Lewtrenchard
Shortacombe
Amicombe Hill
Great Kneeset
Whitehorse Hill
Frenchbeer
Red Gate
Downhead
Laneast
Tregunnon
Pipers Pool
Tregadillett
Trewen
Lydford
Downton
Beardon
Sittaford Tor
Black Ridge
Polyphant
Kennards House
Daw's House
Lawhitton
16
Marystow
Liddaton Green
Coryton
Cut Hill
White Ridge
Tredaule
Fivelanes
Altarnun
Trewint
Bray Down
South Petherwin
Trecrogo
Lewannick
Plusha
Badstone
Kelly
Meadwell
Chillaton
North Brentor
Brent Tor
Black Down
Willsworthy
Lynch Tor
Rough Tor
Warren House
Lezant
Felldownhead
DARTMOOR
South Brentor
Horndon
Higher White Tor
Mary Tavy
Blackdown
Cocks Hill
Dunterton
Cudlipptown
Peter Tavy
Great Mis Tor
Postbridge
Bellever
Lamerton
19
20
0 2 4 6 miles
0 2 4 6 8 10 km
4
A39
A361
A399
A386
A388
A3072
A3079
A3124
A377
A30
A395
A388

F
G
H
18
J
K
7
BRIDGWATER BAY
EXMOOR
SOMERSET
DEVON
TA
TQ
BRENDON HILLS
VALE OF TAUNTON DEANE
Lynton
Lynmouth
Porlock
Minehead
Watchet
Williton
Dulverton
Wiveliscombe
Wellington
Taunton
South Molton
Tiverton
Cullompton
Crediton
Honiton
Exeter
Exeter International
Ottery St Mary
Sidmouth
Budleigh Salterton
Topsham
Chudleigh
Bovey Tracey
Moretonhampstead
35
24
23
22
36
16
21
4
5
18
17
15
14
6
2
1
3
8
9
10
11
12
13
7

A
B
C
D
E
1
2
3
4
5
6
7
19
7
SOMERSET
DEVON
TA
EX
BRIDGWATER
TAUNTON
Glastonbury
Street
Somerton
Langport
Wellington
Ilminster
Chard
Crewkerne
South Petherton
Martock
YEOVIL
Ilchester
Honiton
Axminster
Seaton
Lyme Regis
Bridport
Beaminster
Sidmouth
Ottery St Mary
Budleigh Salterton
VALE OF TAUNTON DEANE
Blackdown Hills
LYME BAY
0 2 4 6 miles
0 2 4 6 8 10 km

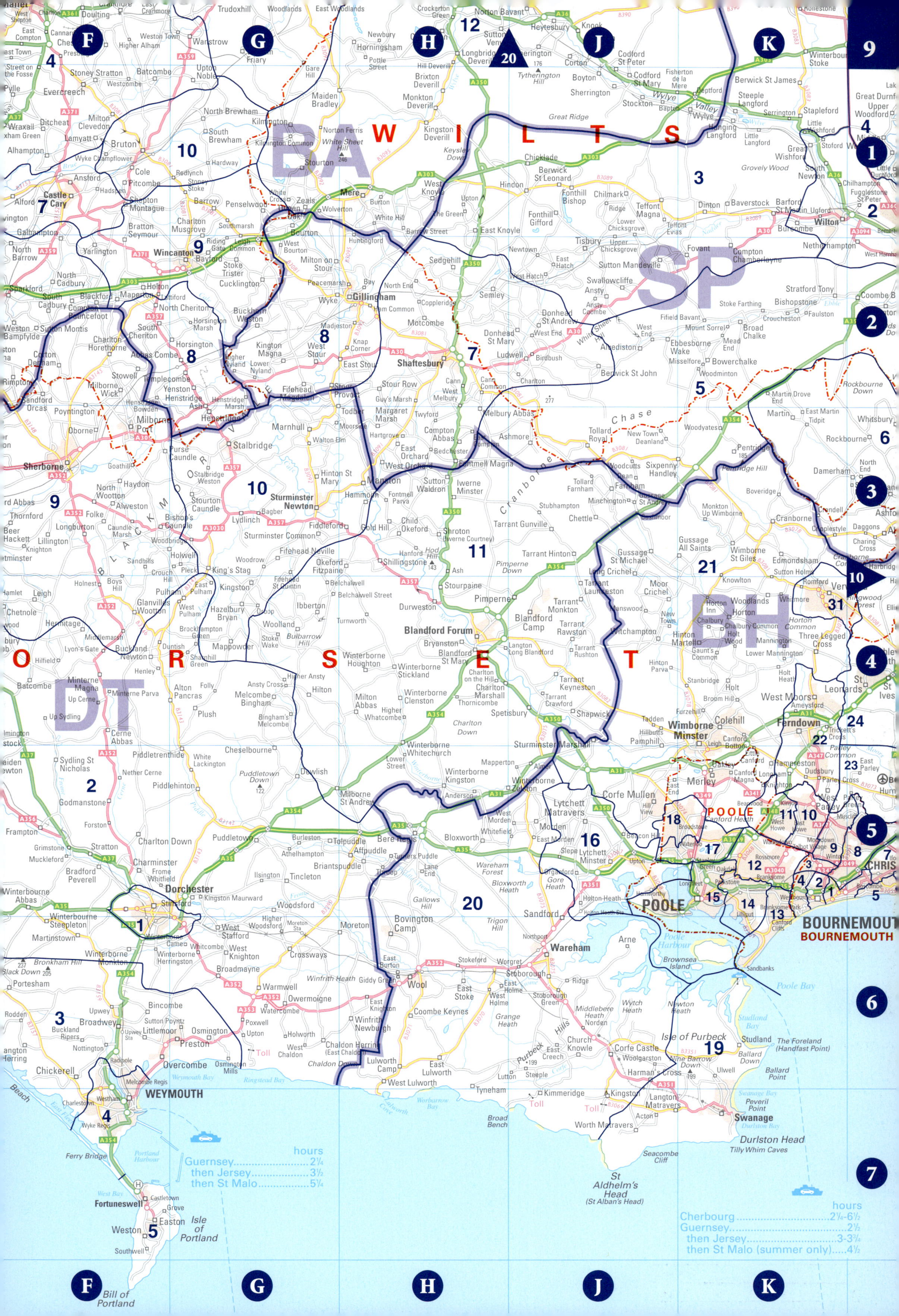

F
G
H
J
K
9
12
20
10
W I L T S
BA
SP
DT
BH
D O R S E T
Shaftesbury
Gillingham
Wincanton
Sherborne
Sturminster Newton
Blandford Forum
Wimborne Minster
Ferndown
Dorchester
Wareham
POOLE
BOURNEMOUTH
Swanage
WEYMOUTH
Fortuneswell
Isle of Portland
Bill of Portland
Isle of Purbeck
St Aldhelm's Head (St Alban's Head)
Durlston Head
Poole Bay
Brownsea Island
Poole Harbour
hours
Guernsey 2¼
then Jersey 3½
then St Malo 5¼
hours
Cherbourg 2¼-6½
Guernsey 2½
then Jersey 3-3¾
then St Malo (summer only) 4½

A
B
C
D
E
BA
SP
DT
BH
W I L T S H I R E
D O R S E T
H A M
Amesbury
Wilton
SALISBURY
Fordingbridge
Ringwood
Verwood
Ferndown
Wimborne Minster
Blandford Camp
Pimperne
Corfe Mullen
POOLE
Wareham
BOURNEMOUTH
CHRISTCHURCH
New Milton
Lymington
Milford on Sea
Brockenhurst
Lyndhurst
Totton
Romsey
Stockbridge
Swanage
Isle of Purbeck
Corfe Castle
Hengistbury Head
Christchurch Bay
Poole Harbour
Poole Bay
Studland Bay
Swanage Bay
Brownsea Island
Sandbanks
Durlston Head
Tilly Whim Caves
St Aldhelm's Head
(St Alban's Head)
The Needles
Yarmouth
Totland
Freshwater
Great Ridge
Grovely Wood
Cranborne Chase
hours
Cherbourg.........................2¼-6½
Guernsey.................................2½
then Jersey.............................3-3¾
then St Malo (summer only).....4½
0 2 4 6 miles
0 2 4 6 8 10 km

F
G
H
J
K
11
21
12
1
2
3
4
5
6
7
HAMPSHIRE
SO
GU
PO
WEST SUSSEX
SOUTH DOWNS
Proposed National Park
ISLE OF WIGHT
WINCHESTER
EASTLEIGH
SOUTHAMPTON
FAREHAM
GOSPORT
PORTSMOUTH
HAVANT
WATERLOOVILLE
CHICHESTER
NEWPORT
Alton
Bordon
Haslemere
Petersfield
Midhurst
New Alresford
Bishop's Waltham
Hythe
Fawley
Cowes
Ryde
Sandown
Shanklin
Ventnor
Selsey
Selsey Bill
Emsworth
South Hayling
The Solent
hours
Bilbao.............................35
Caen.............................5½-7
Cherbourg.......................3-5½
Guernsey...........................6½
then Jersey.........................10
Le Havre.......................5½-7½
St. Malo...........................10½

A
B
C
D
E
1
2
3
4
5
6
7
22
21
11
RG
GU
PO
KT
HANTS
NORTH DOWNS
SURREY
WEST SUSSEX
SOUTH DOWNS
CAMBERLEY
FARNBOROUGH
FLEET
ALDERSHOT
WOKING
GUILDFORD
GODALMING
Farnham
Hindhead
Haslemere
Cranleigh
Dorking
Leatherhead
Cobham
Horsham
Billingshurst
Alton
Bordon
Liphook
Liss
Petersfield
Midhurst
Petworth
Pulborough
Storrington
Steyning
Arundel
CHICHESTER
HAVANT
Emsworth
Horndean
South Hayling
Hayling Island
Thorney Island
Bosham
East Wittering
Selsey
Selsey Bill
BOGNOR REGIS
Middleton-on-Sea
LITTLEHAMPTON
Rustington
WORTHING
Lancing
SHOREHAM
Hook
Odiham
Hartley Wintney
Yateley
Sandhurst
Crowthorne
Bagshot
Frimley
Ash
Wonersh
Bramley
Milford
Witley
Chiddingfold
Fernhurst
Loxwood
The South Downs is a proposed National Park
Hayling Bay
Bracklesham Bay
0 2 4 6 miles
0 2 4 6 8 10 km

F
G
H
J
K
1
2
3
4
5
6
7
23
14
EPSOM
Banstead
Tadworth
REIGATE
Redhill
Horley
LONDON GATWICK
CRAWLEY
Caterham
Warlingham
Oxted
Limpsfield
Westerham
SEVENOAKS
Tonbridge
ROYAL TUNBRIDGE WELLS
Southborough
Edenbridge
East Grinstead
Lingfield
Forest Row
CROWBOROUGH
Wadhurst
Mayfield
Heathfield
Uckfield
HAYWARDS HEATH
Burgess Hill
Hurstpierpoint
Lindfield
Cuckfield
Lewes
BRIGHTON & HOVE
BRIGHTON
HOVE
Shoreham-by-Sea
Portslade-by-Sea
Rottingdean
Peacehaven
Newhaven
Seaford
Hailsham
Polegate
EASTBOURNE
Beachy Head
Pevensey Bay
Langney Point
Pevensey Levels
K E N T
E A S T   S U S S E X
W E S T   S U S S E X
N O R T H   D O W N S
S O U T H   D O W N S
T H E   W E A L D
Ashdown Forest
The South Downs is a proposed National Park
Dieppe (summer only) 2hrs
RH
TN
BN
BR
CR
ME

A
B
C
D
E
1
2
3
4
5
6
7
24
13
MEDWAY
DA
ME
TN
BN
K
E
N O R T H
T H E W E A L D
E A S T S U S S E X
I S L E O F S H E P P E Y
Swanley
Dartford
Gravesend
Strood
Rochester
CHATHAM
GILLINGHAM
SITTINGBOURNE
Queenborough
Minster
Eastchurch
Halstead
West Kingsdown
Kemsing
Otford
SEVENOAKS
Borough Green
West Malling
Aylesford
Snodland
MAIDSTONE
Bearsted
Harrietsham
Lenham
Charing
ASHFORD
Tonbridge
Hildenborough
Southborough
ROYAL TUNBRIDGE WELLS
Paddock Wood
Marden
Staplehurst
Headcorn
Smarden
Biddenden
Cranbrook
Goudhurst
Lamberhurst
Hawkhurst
Tenterden
Wittersham
Isle of Oxney
Rye
Camber
Winchelsea
Winchelsea Beach
Icklesham
Northiam
Robertsbridge
Battle
HASTINGS
St Leonards
BEXHILL
Wadhurst
Mayfield
Heathfield
Hailsham
Polegate
Pevensey
Pevensey Bay
Pevensey Levels
EASTBOURNE
CROWBOROUGH
Uckfield
Rotherfield
Edenbridge
Penshurst
Chiddingstone
Fairlight
Herstmonceux
Westham
Norman's Bay
Langney Point
0 2 4 6 miles
0 2 4 6 8 10 km

F
G
H
J
K
1
2
3
4
5
6
7
Warden Point
Long Nose Spit
Foreness Point
White Ness
North Foreland
Margate
Birchington
Broadstairs
Ramsgate
Herne Bay
Whitstable
Isle of Harty
Shell Ness
Seasalter
Faversham
Graveney
Goodnestone
Boughton Street
Dunkirk
Selling
Chilham
Molash
Godmersham
Challock
Wye
Brook
Hastingleigh
Brabourne
Brabourne Lees
Smeeth
Mersham
Sellindge
Stanford
Aldington
Bonnington
Bilsington
Ruckinge
Newchurch
Burmarsh
Dymchurch
St Mary's Bay
St Mary in the Marsh
Ivychurch
Brenzett
Old Romney
New Romney
Littlestone-on-Sea
Romney Sands
Greatstone-on-Sea
Lydd
London Ashford
Lydd-on-Sea
Denge Marsh
Denge Beach
Dungeness
Romney Marsh
Hythe
Lympne
Newington
Folkestone
Sandgate
Cheriton
Capel-le-Ferne
Hawkinge
Paddlesworth
Lyminge
Etchinghill
Postling
Elham
Stelling Minnis
Bossingham
Petham
Waltham
Chartham
Chartham Hatch
Bridge
Lower Hardres
Bishopsbourne
Kingston
Barham
Canterbury
Sturry
Fordwich
Blean
Tyler Hill
Littlebourne
Wickhambreaux
Ickham
Bekesbourne
Patrixbourne
Adisham
Aylesham
Nonington
Womenswold
Denton
Wootton
Lydden
Shepherdswell
Eythorne
Coldred
Ewell Minnis
Alkham
River
Temple Ewell
Whitfield
Dover
West Hougham
St Margaret's at Cliffe
South Foreland
Kingsdown
Ringwould
West Langdon
East Langdon
Guston
Deal
Walmer
Great Mongeham
Sholden
Northbourne
Tilmanstone
Elvington
Eastry
Woodnesborough
Worth
Sandwich
Pegwell Bay
Sandwich Bay
Cliffs End
Minster
Monkton
Manston
Kent International
Isle of Thanet
Acol
St Nicholas at Wade
Sarre
Chislet
Upstreet
Hoath
Herne
Reculver
Wingham
Ash
Staple
Preston
Grove
East Stourmouth
West Stourmouth
Westbere
Hersden
Broadoak
Oostende 4hrs (summer only)
hours
Boulogne...3/4
Calais...1¼-1½
Dunkerque...2
Strait of Dover
Channel Tunnel
Kent

A
B
C
D
E
1
2
3
4
5
6
7
Rosslare 1¾-3½ hrs
Cardigan (Aberteifi)
St Dogmaels (Llandudoch)
Moylgrove
Trwyn y Bwa
Dinas Head
Newport Bay
Newport (Trefdraeth)
Strumble Head
Carregwastad Point
Crincoed Point
Fishguard Bay
Pen Caer
Pen Brush
Goodwick (Wdig)
Fishguard (Abergwaun)
Penbwchdy
St Nicholas
Dinas Cross
Mynydd Melyn
Mynydd Carningli
Carningli Common
Eglwyswrw
Crymych
Ynys Deullyn
Penmorfa
Abercastle
Mathry
Trefin
Scleddau
Trecwn
Mynydd Cilciffeth
Foel Eryr
Foel Cwmcerwyn
MYNYDD PRESELI
Foel Drych
Mynachlog-ddu
Penclegyr
Porthgain
Llanrhian
Abereiddy
Carreg-gwylan-fach
Berea
Penparc
Croesgoch
Castle Morris
Letterston
Puncheston
Little Newcastle
Mynydd Castlebythe
Rosebush
Penllechwen
North Bishop
St David's Head
Whitesands Bay (Porth-mawr)
Point St John
Carreg Rhoson
Bishops and Clerks
St David's (Tyddewi)
Whitchurch
Solva
Ramsey Sound
Ramsey Island
Ynys Bery
Green Scar
Dinas Fawr
Llandeloy
Hayscastle
Wolf's Castle
Ambleston
New Moat
Maenclochog
Llangolman
Llys-y-frân Res
Llys-y-frân
Walton East
Spittal
Dudwell Mountain
Treffgarne
Penycwm
Newgale
Newgale Sands
PEMBROKESHIRE
Roch
Camrose
Clarbeston Road
Clarbeston
Llandissilio
Clynderwen
Rickets Head
Nolton Haven
Nolton
Keeston
Crundale
Wiston
ST. BRIDE'S BAY
Llawhaden
Llanddewi Velfrey
Haroldston West
Broad Haven
Haverfordwest (Hwlffordd)
Robeston Wathen
Narberth (Arberth)
Stack Rocks
Little Haven
Talbenny
Uzmaston
Templeton
The Nab Head
Garland Stone
Skomer Island
Wooltack Point
St Brides
Marloes
Mew Stone
Gateholm Island
Hooper's Point
Broad Sound
The Stack
The Head
Skokholm Island
St Ishmael's
Dale
Dale Point
Hasguard
Herbrandston
Johnston
Llangwm
Martletwy
Lawrenny
Rosemarket
Milford Haven (Aberdaugleddau)
Neyland
Pembroke Dock (Doc Penfro)
Thorn I.
MILFORD HAVEN
St. Ann's Head
Rosslare 3¾ hrs
Angle
Sheep Island
Pembroke (Penfro)
Carew
Saundersfoot
Tenby (Dinbych-y-pysgod)
Monkstone Point
St Catherine's Island
Amroth
Kilgetty
Begelly
Lamphey
Manorbier
Penally
Giltar Point
Caldey Island
St Margaret's Island
Old Castle Head
Chapel Point
Castlemartin
Linney Head
Crow Rock
Toes
Bosherston
Saddle Head
St Govan's Head
Stackpole Head
Trewent Point
Freshwater West
Cork (Mar - Dec) 10 hrs
0 2 4 6 miles
0 2 4 6 8 10 km

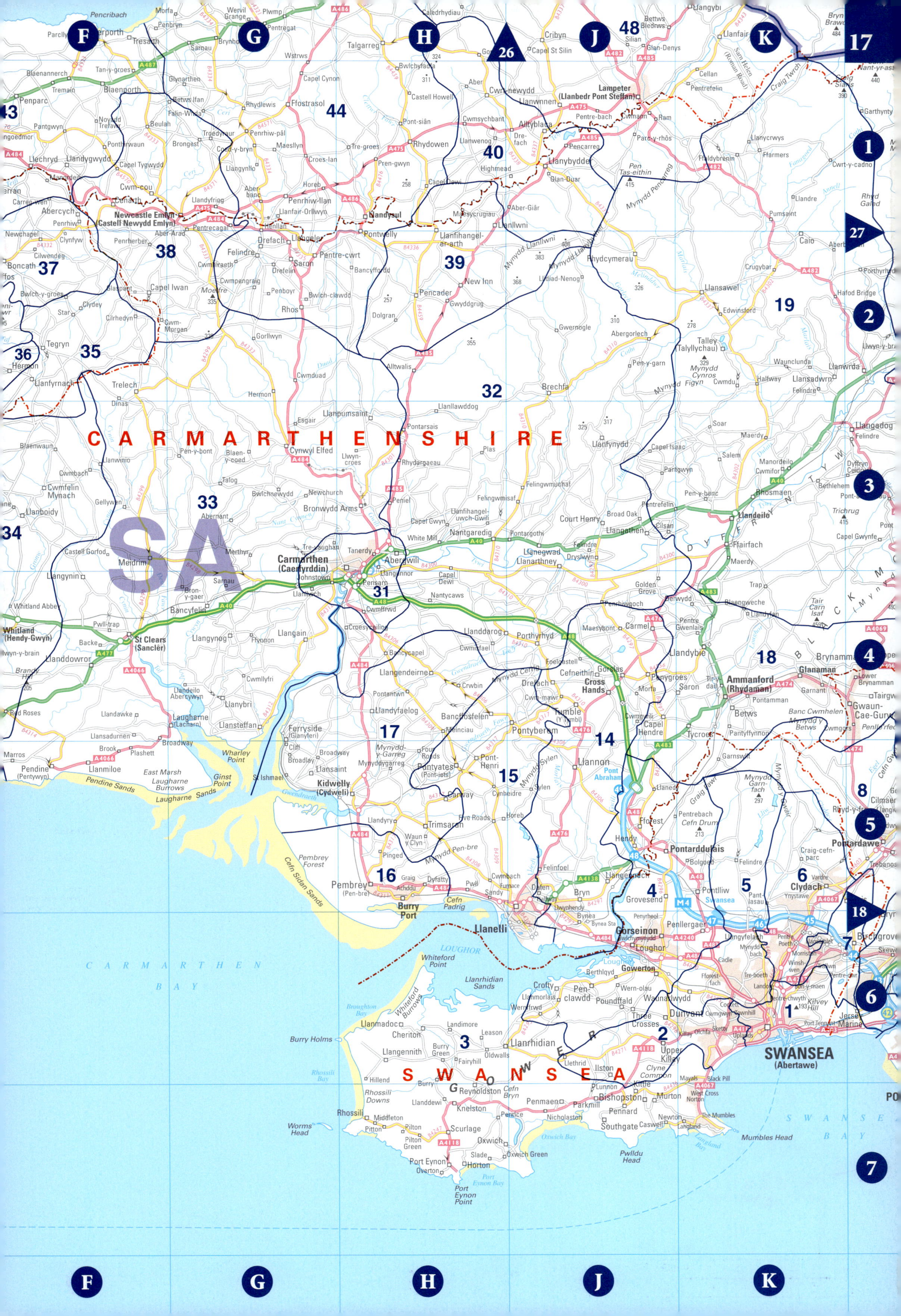

F
G
H
J
K
17
26
27
18
48
44
40
39
38
37
36
35
34
33
32
31
19
18
17
16
15
14
1
2
3
4
5
6
7
8
CARMARTHENSHIRE
SA
SWANSEA
CARMARTHEN BAY
SWANSEA BAY
Carmarthen (Caerfyrddin)
Lampeter (Llanbedr Pont Steffan)
Newcastle Emlyn (Castell Newydd Emlyn)
St Clears (Sanclêr)
Whitland (Hendy-Gwyn)
Llandysul
Llandeilo
Ammanford (Rhydaman)
Llanelli
Kidwelly (Cydweli)
Pembrey (Pen-bre)
Burry Port
Gorseinon
Pontarddulais
Gowerton
Pontardawe
Clydach
SWANSEA (Abertawe)
Laugharne (Talacharn)
Pendine (Pentywyn)
Cross Hands
Tumble (Y Tymbl)
Llandybie
Llansawel
Brechfa
Talgarreg
Llanybydder
Pencader
Ferryside (Glanyferi)
Llanrhidian
Rhossili
Port Eynon
Mumbles Head
Worms Head
Burry Holms
Pembrey Forest
Cefn Sidan Sands
Laugharne Sands
Pendine Sands
Whiteford Point
Llanrhidian Sands
A40
A48
A484
A485
A476
A483
A4138
A4118
M4

18
A
B
C
D
E
27
48
22
23
1
2
3
4
5
6
7
17
NEATH
PORT TALBOT
RHONDDA
CYNON
TAFF
MERTHYR
TYDFIL
BLAENAU
CAERPHILLY
CARDIFF
BRIDGEND
VALE OF GLAMORGAN
DEVON
EXMOOR
SWANSEA BAY
BRISTOL CHANNEL
BRIDGWATER BAY
Pontardawe
Ystradgynlais
Ystalyfera
Gwaun-Cae-Gurwen
Glynneath
Resolven
Neath (Castell-nedd)
Briton Ferry (Llansawel)
Baglan
Port Talbot
Cwmafan
Maesteg
Pyle
North Cornelly
Porthcawl
Bridgend (Pen-y-bont ar Ogwr)
Pencoed
Cowbridge
Llantwit Major
Barry
Penarth
Cardiff INT
Pontypridd
Caerphilly
Llantrisant
Tonyrefail
Treorchy
Treherbert
Ferndale
Tonypandy
Porth
Mountain Ash (Aberpennar)
Aberdare
Hirwaun
Merthyr Tydfil
Tredegar
Ebbw Vale (Glynebwy)
Rhymney
Bargoed
Blackwood
Ystrad Mynach
Nelson
Abercynon
Aberkenfig
Laleston
Ogmore-by-Sea
St Brides Major
Southerndown
Minehead
Porlock
Lynton
Lynmouth
Dunster
Watchet
Williton
Foreland Point
Sully Island
0 2 4 6 miles
0 2 4 6 8 10 km

NP
MONMOUTHSHIRE
TORFAEN
GL
GLOUCESTERSHIRE
SOUTH GLOUCESTERSHIRE
NEWPORT
CARDIFF (Caerdydd)
MOUTH OF THE SEVERN
BS
BRISTOL
NORTH SOMERSET
BATH AND NORTH EAST SOMERSET
SOMERSET
BA
WESTON-SUPER-MARE
BRIDGWATER
Chepstow (Cas-gwent)
Pontypool
Cwmbran
Clevedon
Portishead
Avonmouth
Keynsham
Wells
Shepton Mallet
Glastonbury
Burnham-on-Sea
Cheddar
Coleford
Lydney
Thornbury
Yate
Nailsea
BATH
F
G
H
J
K
1
2
3
4
5
6
7
28
20
8

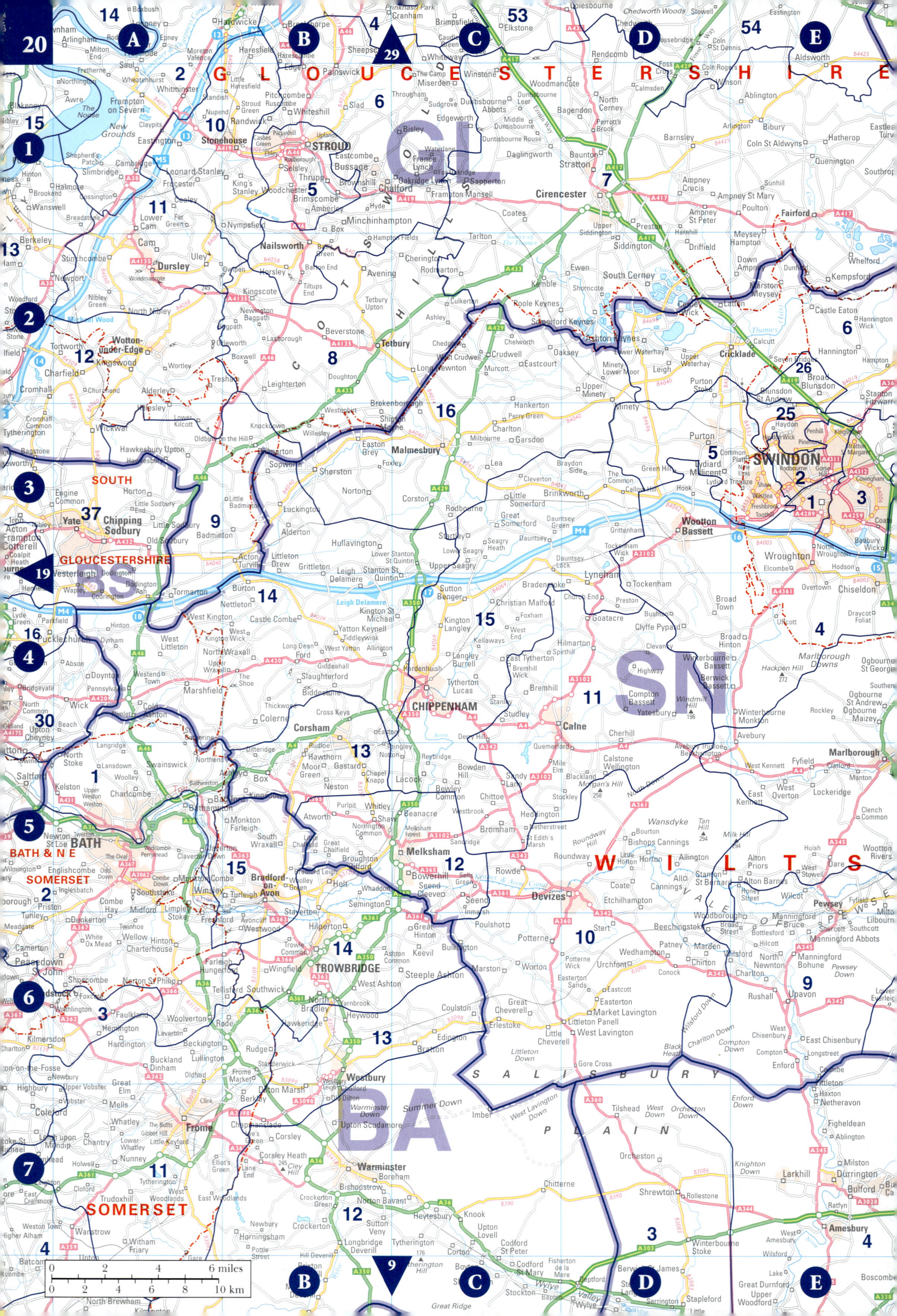
A
B
C
D
E
14
4
53
54
29
GLOUCESTERSHIRE
GL
COTSWOLD HILLS
STROUD
Stonehouse
Nailsworth
Dursley
Wotton-under-Edge
Tetbury
Cirencester
Fairford
Cricklade
Malmesbury
SWINDON
Wootton Bassett
SOUTH GLOUCESTERSHIRE
Yate
Chipping Sodbury
BS
19
CHIPPENHAM
Corsham
Calne
SN
Marlborough
BATH
BATH & N E SOMERSET
Bradford-on-Avon
Melksham
Devizes
TROWBRIDGE
WILTS
SALISBURY PLAIN
Westbury
BA
Frome
Warminster
SOMERSET
Amesbury
9
Leigh Delamere
Michael Wood
0 2 4 6 miles
0 2 4 6 8 10 km

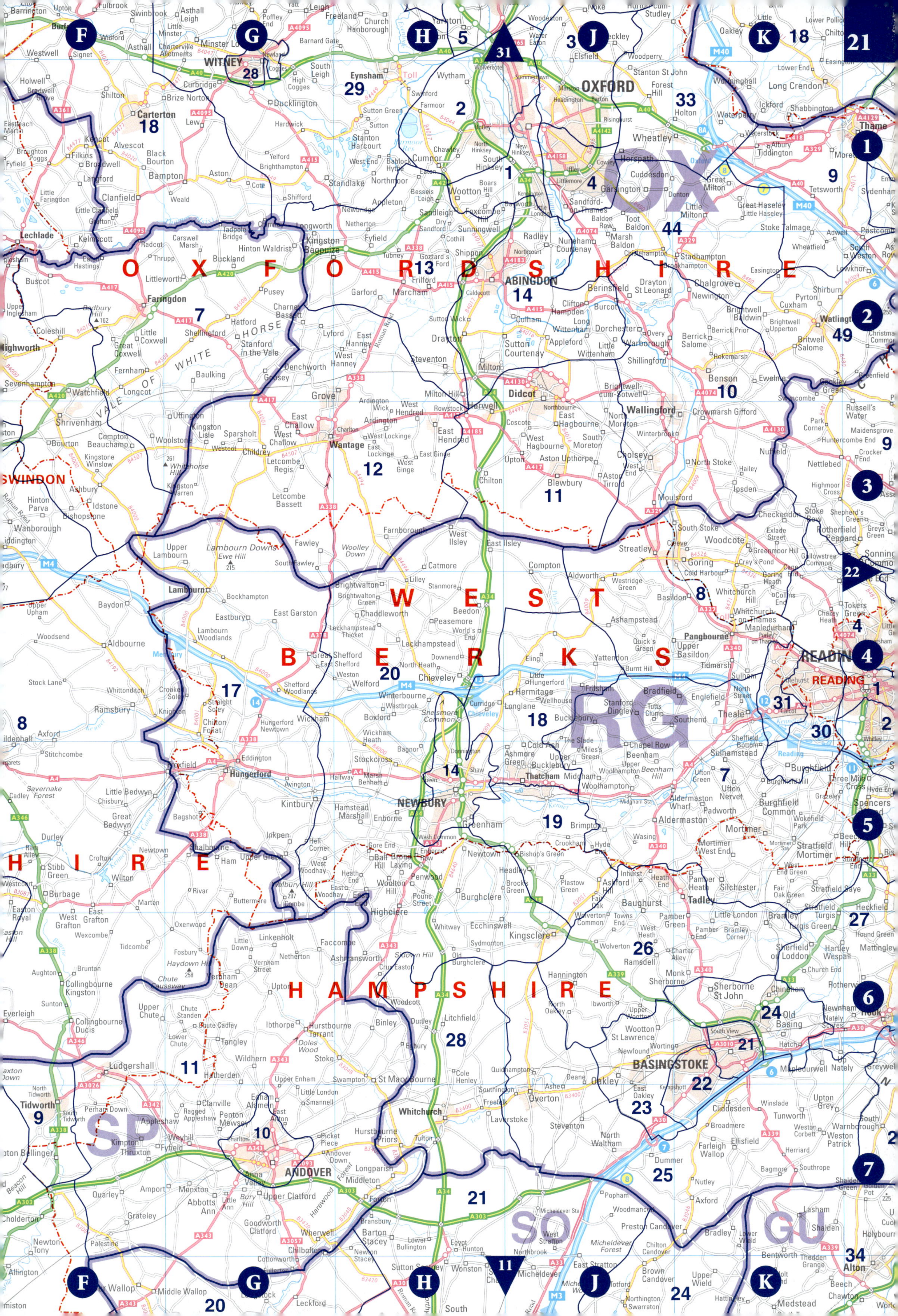

21
OXFORDSHIRE
WEST BERKS
HAMPSHIRE
OX
RG
SP
SO
GU
OXFORD
WITNEY
ABINGDON
Wantage
Didcot
Wallingford
Faringdon
Carterton
Hungerford
NEWBURY
Thatcham
READING
BASINGSTOKE
ANDOVER
Whitchurch
Tadley
Lambourn
SWINDON
Thame
Alton
M4
M40
A34
A303

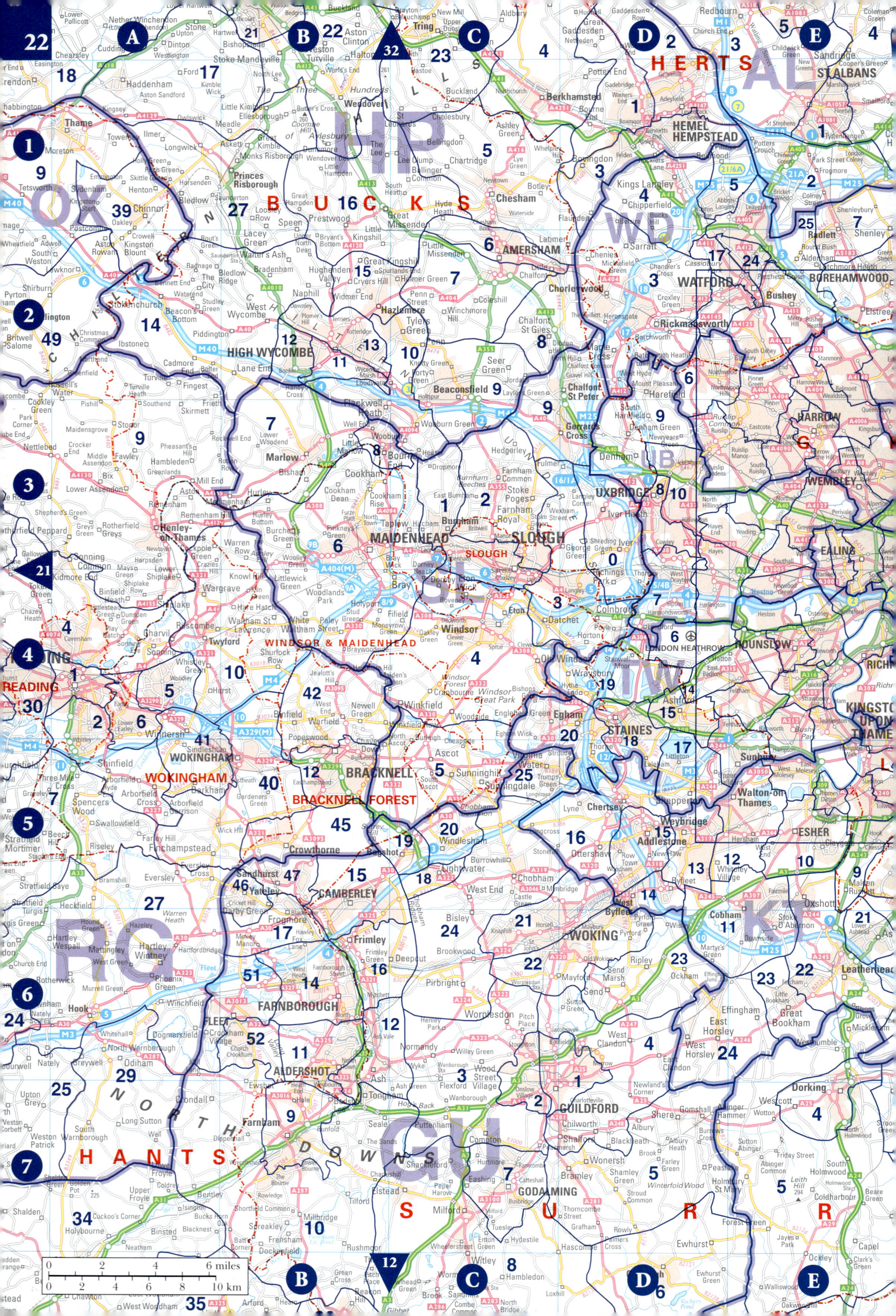
A
B
C
D
E
1
2
3
4
5
6
7
32
21
12
HERTS
BUCKS
HANTS
SURREY
ST ALBANS
HEMEL HEMPSTEAD
WATFORD
BOREHAMWOOD
Rickmansworth
HIGH WYCOMBE
AMERSHAM
Chesham
Beaconsfield
Marlow
MAIDENHEAD
SLOUGH
UXBRIDGE
HARROW
WEMBLEY
EALING
HOUNSLOW
READING
WOKINGHAM
BRACKNELL
BRACKNELL FOREST
WINDSOR & MAIDENHEAD
Windsor
STAINES
Chertsey
Weybridge
Addlestone
Walton-on-Thames
ESHER
KINGSTON UPON THAMES
CAMBERLEY
Frimley
FARNBOROUGH
FLEET
ALDERSHOT
Farnham
WOKING
GUILDFORD
GODALMING
Dorking
Leatherhead
Cobham
Thame
Princes Risborough
Henley-on-Thames
Sandhurst
Hook
Odiham
LONDON HEATHROW
NORTH DOWNS
CHILTERN HILLS
HP
SL
RG
GU
KT
TW
UB
WD
AL
OX
0 2 4 6 miles
0 2 4 6 8 10 km

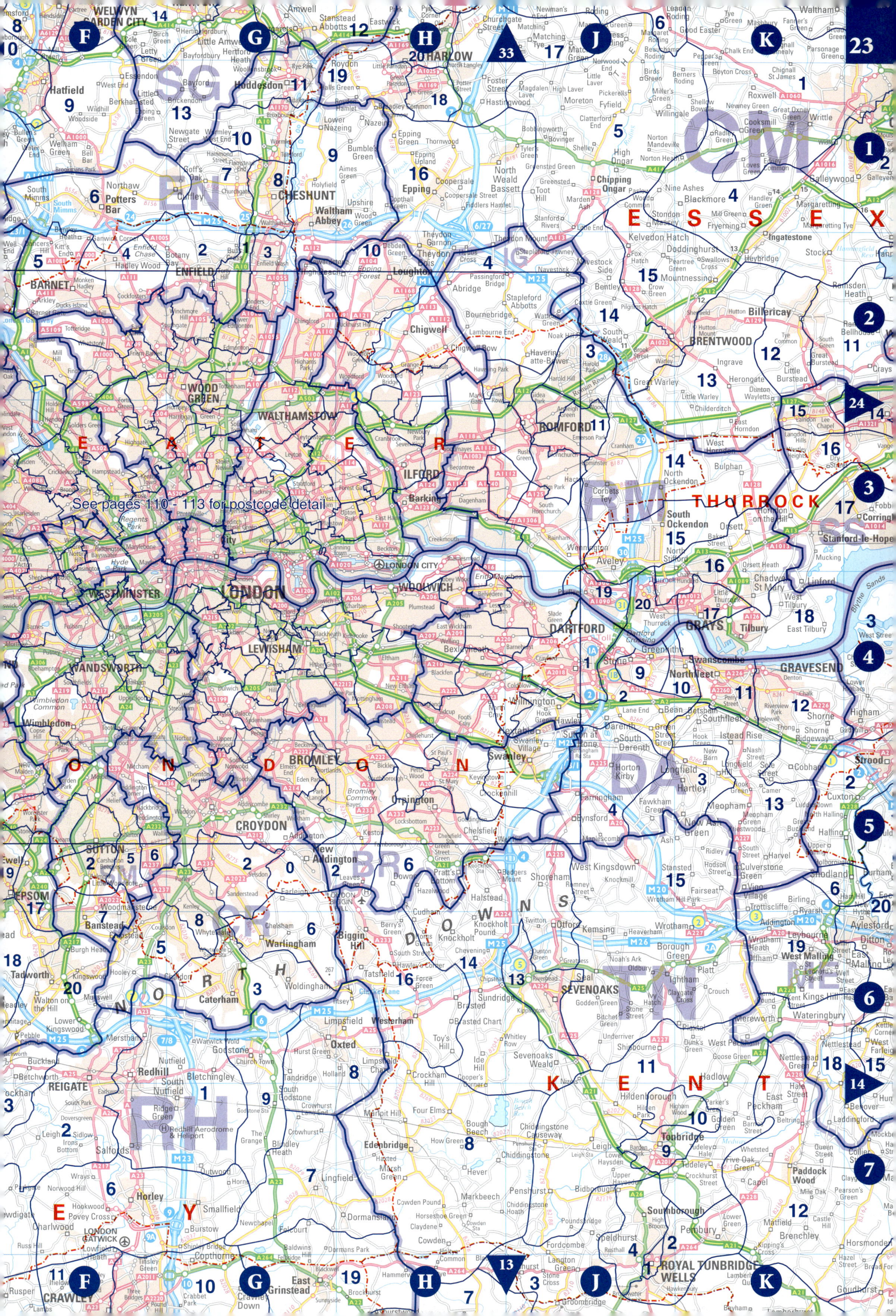

See pages 110 - 113 for postcode detail
WELWYN GARDEN CITY
HARLOW
Hatfield
Hoddesdon
CHESHUNT
Waltham Abbey
Epping
Chipping Ongar
Potters Bar
ENFIELD
BARNET
Loughton
Chigwell
BRENTWOOD
Billericay
WOOD GREEN
WALTHAMSTOW
ROMFORD
ILFORD
Barking
THURROCK
Stanford-le-Hope
WESTMINSTER
LONDON
LONDON CITY
WOOLWICH
LEWISHAM
WANDSWORTH
DARTFORD
GRAYS
Tilbury
GRAVESEND
Swanscombe
Northfleet
Wimbledon
BROMLEY
Orpington
Swanley
CROYDON
SUTTON
EPSOM
Banstead
Caterham
Warlingham
Biggin Hill
Westerham
SEVENOAKS
West Malling
Aylesford
REIGATE
Redhill
Horley
LONDON GATWICK
CRAWLEY
East Grinstead
Edenbridge
Tonbridge
ROYAL TUNBRIDGE WELLS
Southborough
Paddock Wood
ESSEX
GREATER LONDON
NORTH
SURREY
KENT
CM
EN
SG
RM
SS
DA
BR
SM
CR
RH
TN
ME

HARLOW
CHELMSFORD
Maldon
Epping
Chipping Ongar
ESSEX
BRENTWOOD
Billericay
Wickford
BASILDON
Rayleigh
Rochford
SOUTHEND
SOUTHEND-ON-SEA
Canvey Island
THURROCK
Stanford-le-Hope
ROMFORD
ILFORD
GREATER LONDON
LONDON CITY
WOOLWICH
DARTFORD
GRAYS
Tilbury
GRAVESEND
MEDWAY
Rochester
GILLINGHAM
CHATHAM
Strood
MAIDSTONE
SEVENOAKS
Tonbridge
ROYAL TUNBRIDGE WELLS
Edenbridge
BROMLEY
Orpington
Swanley
Chigwell
Loughton
Waltham Abbey
KENT
See pages 110 - 113 for postcode detail
0 2 4 6 miles
0 2 4 6 8 10 km

Tollesbury
West Mersea
Mersea Flats
Seawick
Colne Point
Cobmarsh Island
Great Cob Island
Goldhanger
Osea Island
Bradwell Waterside
Sales Point
St Peter's Flat
East End
Bradwell-on-Sea
Ramsey Island
Steeple
St Lawrence
Tillingham
Dengie
Dengie Flat
Asheldham
Mayland
Dengie Marshes
Southminster
Althorne
Ray Sand
Stoneyhills
Eves Corner
Old Montsale
Deal Hall
Burnham-on-Crouch
Foulness Sands
Foulness Point
Paglesham Churchend
Wallasea Island
Courtsend
Churchend
Paglesham Eastend
Foulness Island
Potton Island
Ballards Gore
Barling
Havengore Island
Little Wakering
Maplin Sands
Great Wakering
North Shoebury
Shoeburyness
Shoebury Ness
Sheerness
Marine Town
Mile Town
West Minster
East End
Minster
Halfway Houses
Warden Point
Eastchurch
Warden
Leysdown-on-Sea
ISLE OF SHEPPEY
Elmley Island
Eastchurch Marshes
Isle of Harty
Shell Ness
Whitstable
Kemsley
SITTINGBOURNE
Conyer
Uplees
Teynham
Rodmersham
Faversham
Graveney
Goodnestone
Lynsted
Ospringe
Dunkirk
Boughton Street
Selling
Sheldwich
Doddington
Newnham
Eastling
Throwley
Badlesmere
Shottenden
Chilham
Old Wives Lees
Leaveland
Molash
Godmersham
Challock
Stalisfield Green
Charing
Westwell
Wye
Boughton Lees
Kennington
ASHFORD
Great Chart
Kingsnorth
Mersham
Sevington
Hinxhill
Brabourne
Brabourne Lees
Smeeth
Sellindge
Stanford
Shadoxhurst
Pluckley
Hothfield
Herne Bay
Reculver
Hillborough
Beltinge
Hampton
Tankerton
Swalecliffe
Chestfield
Seasalter
Yorkletts
Herne
Herne Common
Broomfield
Hersden
Westbere
Sturry
Blean
Tyler Hill
Rough Common
Harbledown
CANTERBURY
Fordwich
Wickhambreaux
Littlebourne
Ickham
Bekesbourne
Patrixbourne
Bridge
Chartham
Chartham Hatch
Shalmsford Street
Petham
Lower Hardres
Bishopsbourne
Kingston
Barham
Adisham
Aylesham
Nonington
Womenswold
Derringstone
Bossingham
Waltham
Stelling Minnis
Elham
Lyminge
Lyminge Forest
Densole
Hawkinge
Paddlesworth
Acrise Place
Swingfield Minnis
Denton
Wootton
Lydden
Ewell Minnis
Alkham
Capel le Ferne
West Hougham
Etchinghill
Postling
Stowting
Sixmile
Birchington
Westgate on Sea
Westbrook
MARGATE
Cliftonville
Kingsgate
Foreness Point
Long Nose Spit
White Ness
North Foreland
Broadstairs
Ramsgate
ISLE OF THANET
St Nicholas at Wade
Acol
KENT INTERNATIONAL
Manston
Minster
Monkton
Sarre
Upstreet
Boyden Gate
Chislet
Hoath
Preston
Grove
West Stourmouth
East Stourmouth
Stodmarsh
Elmstone
Cliffs End
Pegwell Bay
Sandwich Flats
Sandwich Bay
Sandwich
Ash
Wingham
Staple
Goodnestone
Chillenden
Knowlton
Eastry
Woodnesborough
Worth
Ham
Hacklinge
Finglesham
Betteshanger
Northbourne
Great Mongeham
Deal
Sholden
Walmer
Ripple
Tilmanstone
Elvington
Eythorne
East Studdal
Sutton
Ashley
Kingsdown
Ringwould
West Langdon
East Langdon
Shepherdswell
Coldred
Guston
St Margaret's at Cliffe
St Margaret's Bay
South Foreland
River
Whitfield
DOVER
Channel Tunnel
South Channel
Gunfleet Sand
hours
Boulogne..........¾
Calais..........1¼-1½
Dunkerque..........2

A
B
C
D
E
1
2
3
4
5
6
7
CEREDIGION
PEMBROKESHIRE
CARMARTHEN
SA
Cardigan (Aberteifi)
Aberaeron
New Quay (Ceinewydd)
Lampeter (Llanbedr Pont Steffan)
Newcastle Emlyn (Castell Newydd Emlyn)
Llandysul
Carmarthen (Caerfyrddin)
Whitland (Hendy-Gwyn)
St Clears (Sanclêr)
Kidwelly (Cydweli)
Cardigan Island
Cemaes Head
New Quay Head
Aberporth
Llanrhystud
Crymych
Laugharne (Lacharn)
0 2 4 6 miles
0 2 4 6 8 10 km

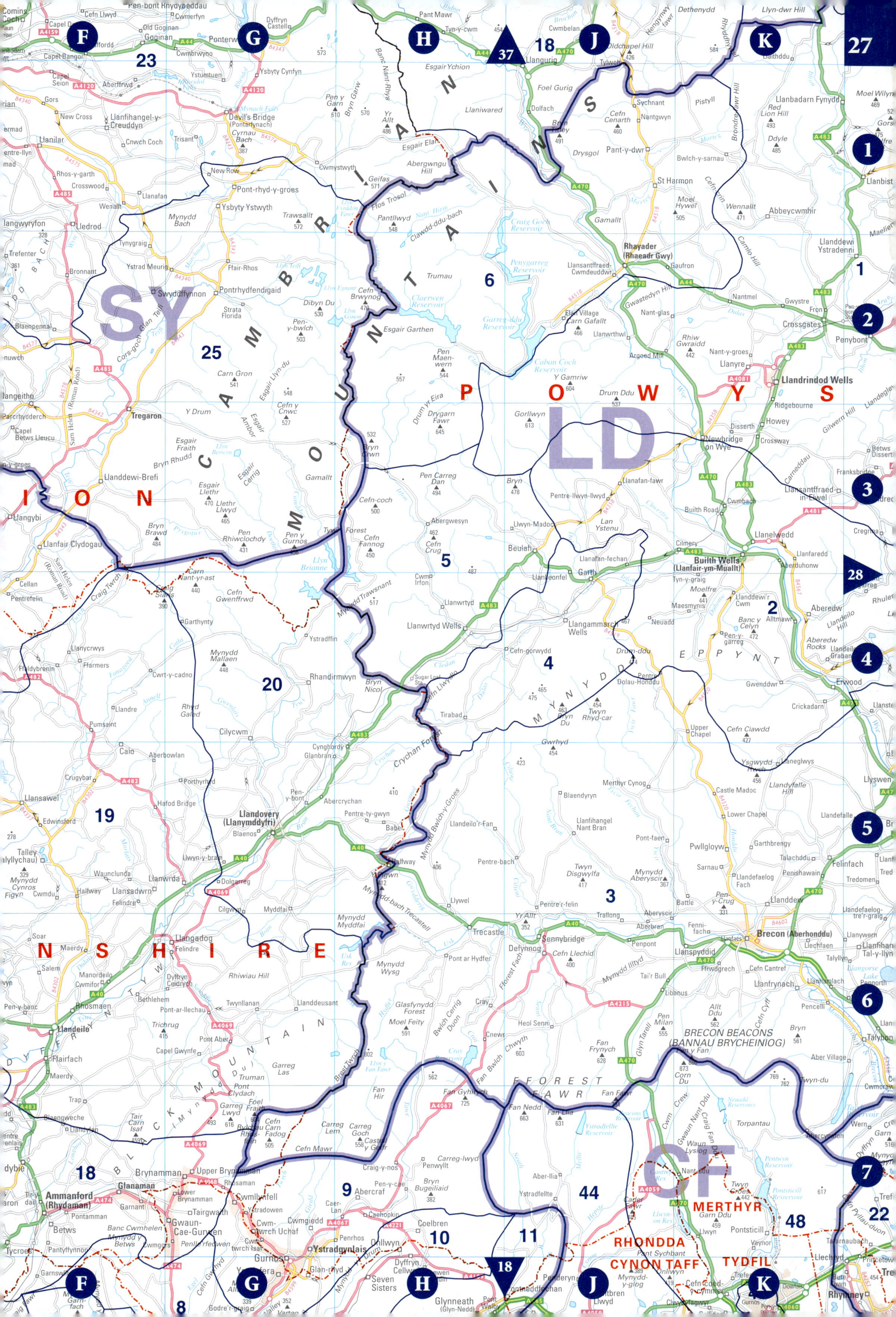
27
28
37
18
22
CAMBRIAN MOUNTAINS
POWYS
LD
SY
CF
CEREDIGION
CARMARTHENSHIRE
BLACK MOUNTAIN
MYNYDD EPPYNT
FFOREST FAWR
BRECON BEACONS (BANNAU BRYCHEINIOG)
MERTHYR TYDFIL
RHONDDA CYNON TAFF
Aberystwyth
Goginan
Ponterwyd
Capel Bangor
Devil's Bridge (Pontarfynach)
Ysbyty Cynfyn
Llangurig
Llanidloes
Pant Mawr
Esgair Ychion
Llaniwared
Dolfach
St Harmon
Rhayader (Rhaeadr Gwy)
Abbeycwmhir
Llanbadarn Fynydd
Llanbister
Llanddewi Ystradenni
Crossgates
Penybont
Llandrindod Wells
Howey
Newbridge on Wye
Llanafan-fawr
Builth Wells (Llanfair-ym-Muallt)
Llanelwedd
Cilmery
Beulah
Garth
Llangammarch Wells
Llanwrtyd Wells
Abergwesyn
Craig Goch Reservoir
Penygarreg Reservoir
Garreg-ddu Reservoir
Caban Coch Reservoir
Claerwen Reservoir
Elan Village
Pontrhydfendigaid
Ffair-Rhos
Ysbyty Ystwyth
Pont-rhyd-y-groes
Tregaron
Llanddewi-Brefi
Lledrod
Bronnant
Llangybi
Llanfair Clydogau
Llyn Brianne
Rhandirmwyn
Cilycwm
Cynghordy
Llandovery (Llanymddyfri)
Myddfai
Llangadog
Llandeilo
Ffairfach
Trecastle
Sennybridge
Defynnog
Brecon (Aberhonddu)
Llanspyddid
Libanus
Llanfrynach
Talybont
Upper Chapel
Merthyr Cynog
Erwood
Llyswen
Pwllgloyw
Felinfach
Llanddew
Brynamman
Ammanford (Rhydaman)
Glanaman
Gwaun-Cae-Gurwen
Ystradgynlais
Abercraf
Coelbren
Glynneath (Glyn-Nedd)
Ystradfellte
Pontsticill
Merthyr
Penderyn
Rhymney
Cefn-coed-y-cymmer
Seven Sisters
Usk Reservoir

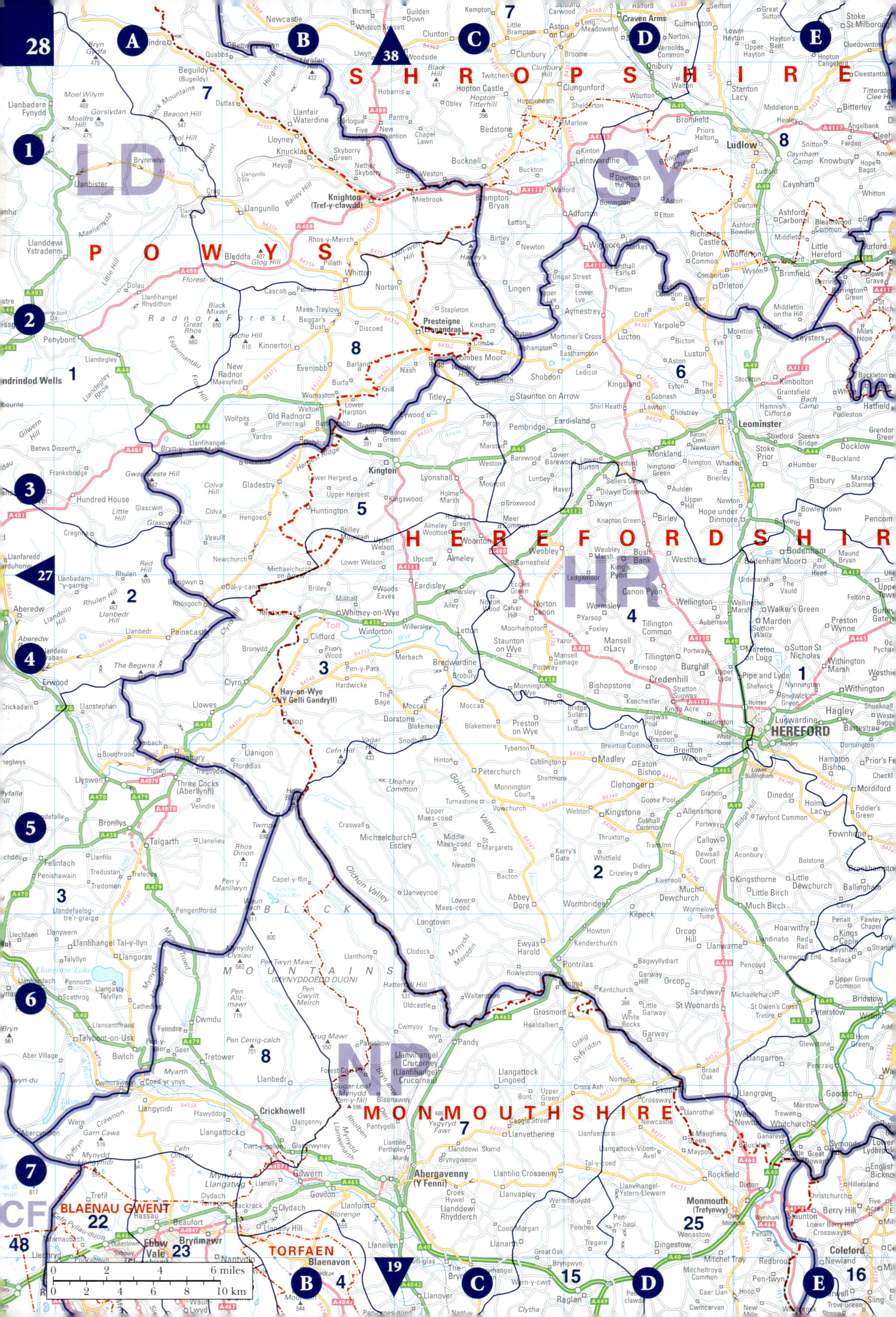
38
27
19
SHROPSHIRE
POWYS
HEREFORDSHIRE
MONMOUTHSHIRE
BLAENAU GWENT
TORFAEN
LD
SY
HR
NP
CF
Radnor Forest
BLACK MOUNTAINS (MYNYDDOEDD DUON)
Knighton (Tref-y-clawdd)
Presteigne (Llanandras)
Kington
Hay-on-Wye (Y Gelli Gandryll)
Ludlow
Leominster
HEREFORD
Abergavenny (Y Fenni)
Crickhowell
Monmouth (Trefynwy)
Llandrindod Wells
Talgarth
Brynmawr
Ebbw Vale
Blaenavon
Craven Arms
Clun
Clunbury
Bucknell
Brampton Bryan
Wigmore
Mortimer's Cross
Pembridge
Weobley
Eardisley
Whitney-on-Wye
Clifford
Peterchurch
Pontrilas
Grosmont
Skenfrith
Raglan
Kingstone
Madley
Credenhill
Bodenham
Much Dewchurch
Whitchurch
Symonds Yat
Coleford
Rhayader
New Radnor
Old Radnor
Painscastle
Glasbury
Llangorse
Bwlch
Llanthony
Usk
0 2 4 6 miles
0 2 4 6 8 10 km

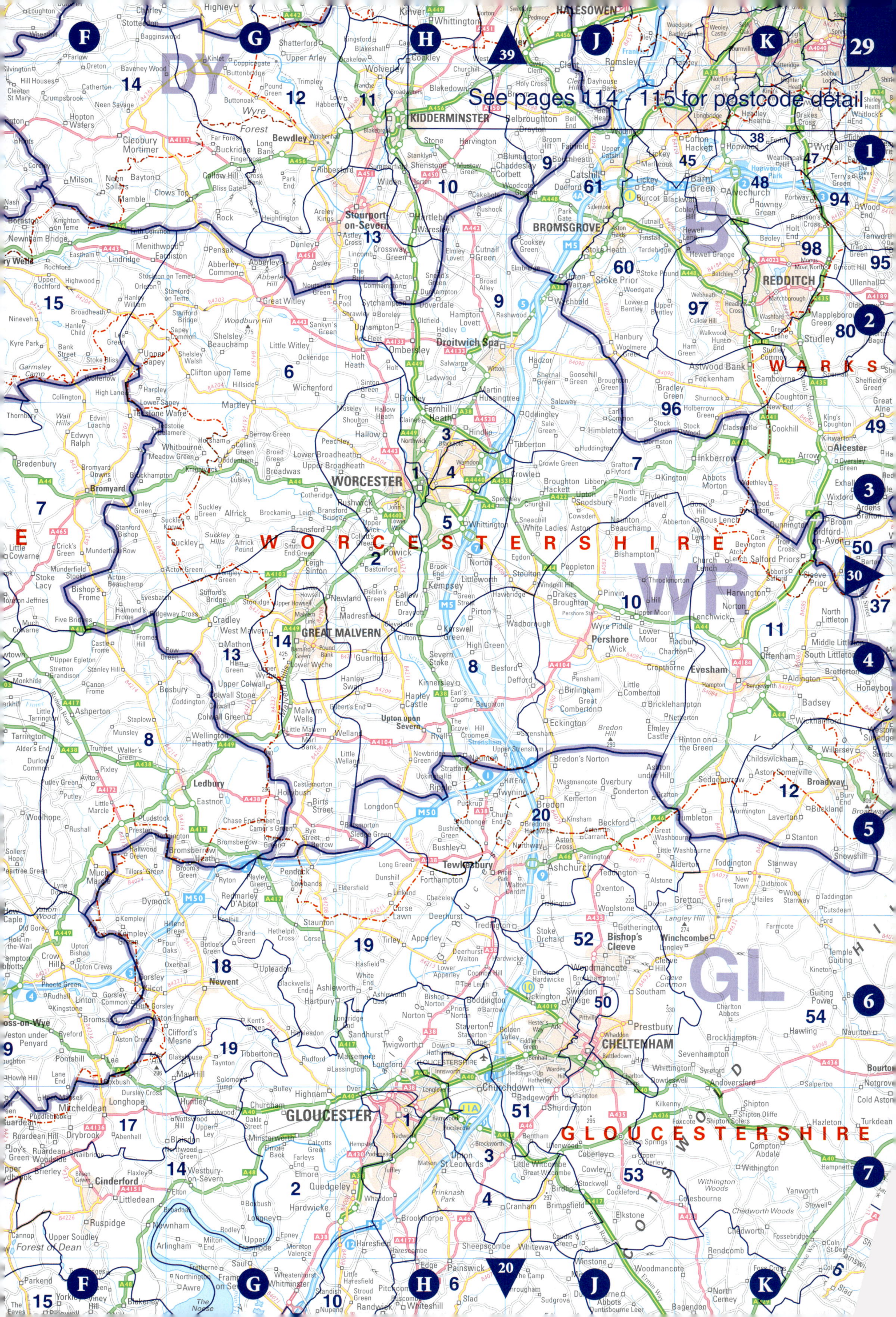

29
See pages 114 - 115 for postcode detail
39
30
20
F
G
H
J
K
1
2
3
4
5
6
7
DY
WR
GL
B
WORCESTERSHIRE
GLOUCESTERSHIRE
WARKS
KIDDERMINSTER
BROMSGROVE
REDDITCH
WORCESTER
GREAT MALVERN
CHELTENHAM
GLOUCESTER
HALESOWEN
Stourport-on-Severn
Droitwich Spa
Bewdley
Evesham
Pershore
Tewkesbury
Ledbury
Newent
Bromyard
Alcester
Cinderford
Winchcombe
Bishop's Cleeve
Upton upon Severn
Forest of Dean

See pages 114 - 115 for postcode detail

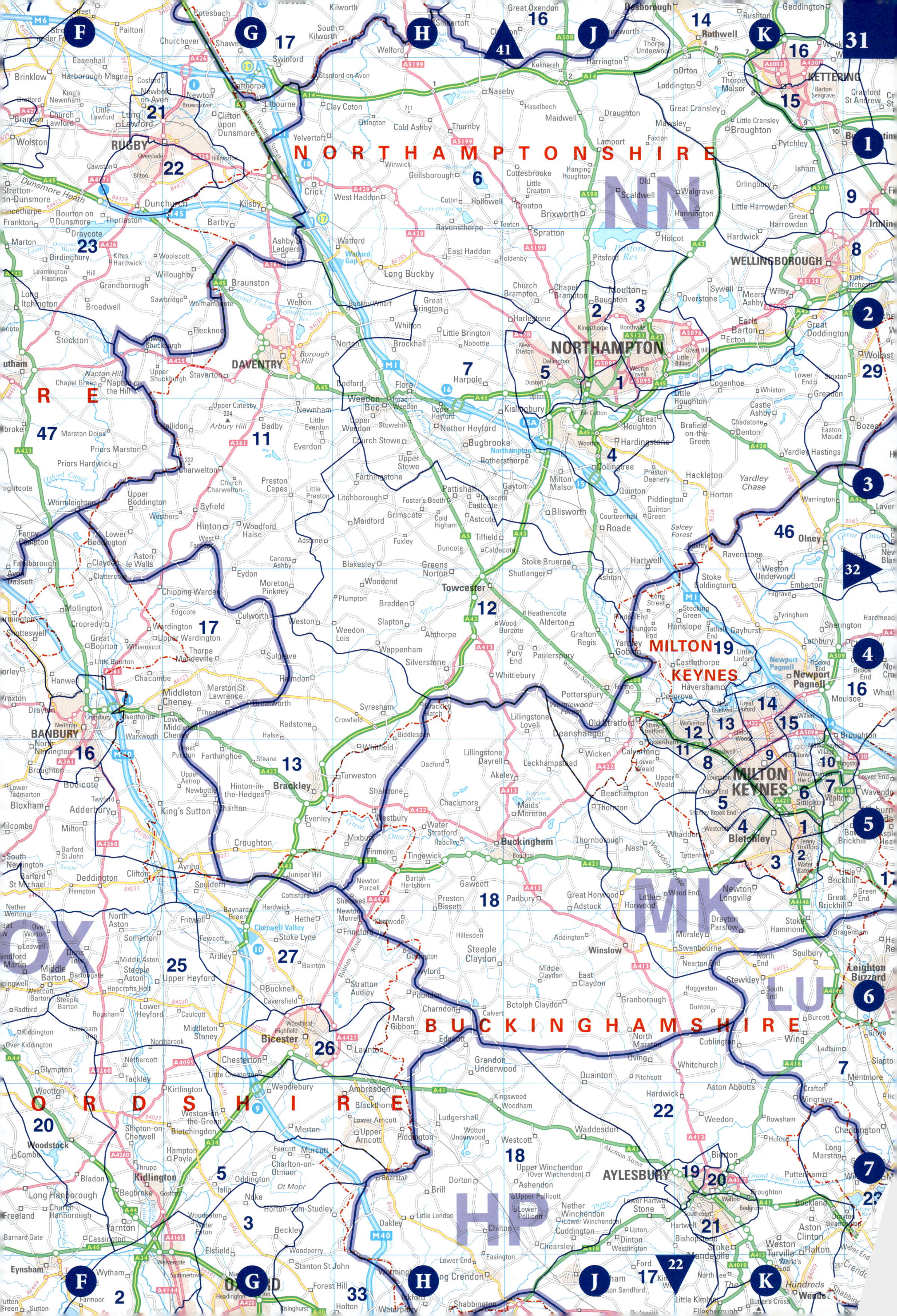
NORTHAMPTONSHIRE
NN
NORTHAMPTON
WELLINGBOROUGH
KETTERING
RUGBY
DAVENTRY
Towcester
Brackley
BANBURY
MILTON KEYNES
MK
Newport Pagnell
Buckingham
BUCKINGHAMSHIRE
Bicester
OXFORDSHIRE
OX
Kidlington
Woodstock
Winslow
AYLESBURY
HP
LU
Leighton Buzzard
Rothwell
Desborough
Olney
Bletchley
Crick
Long Buckby
Brixworth
Moulton
Harpole
Bugbrooke
Roade
Stony Stratford
Woburn
Hanslope
Silverstone
Deddington
Steeple Claydon
Waddesdon
Wing
Cherwell Valley
Watford Gap
Kilsby
Dunchurch
Southam
Cropredy
Middleton Cheney
Aynho
Brill
Long Crendon
Thame
Eynsham
Oakley
Islip
Chalgrove
Great Oxendon
Naseby
Clay Coton
Welford
Stanford on Avon
Kelmarsh
Harrington
Lamport
Maidwell
Walgrave
Hannington
Pitsford
Earls Barton
Ecton
Great Doddington
Wollaston
Grendon
Yardley Hastings
Hackleton
Piddington
Horton
Salcey Forest
Hartwell
Ashton
Stoke Bruerne
Blisworth
Gayton
Kislingbury
Nether Heyford
Weedon Bec
Flore
Brockhall
Norton
Whilton
Great Brington
Little Brington
Badby
Everdon
Newnham
Byfield
Woodford Halse
Eydon
Canons Ashby
Moreton Pinkney
Culworth
Sulgrave
Helmdon
Syresham
Whittlebury
Paulerspury
Potterspury
Deanshanger
Wicken
Akeley
Leckhampstead
Maids' Moreton
Thornborough
Padbury
Gawcott
Tingewick
Finmere
Mixbury
Evenley
Croughton
Souldern
Fritwell
Somerton
Ardley
Stoke Lyne
Hethe
Fringford
Stratton Audley
Launton
Marsh Gibbon
Charndon
Edgcott
Grendon Underwood
Calvert
Quainton
North Marston
Oving
Whitchurch
Cublington
Aston Abbotts
Hardwick
Weedon
Rowsham
Bierton
Stoke Mandeville
Wendover
Weston Turville
Aston Clinton
Halton
Stone
Dinton
Haddenham
Chearsley
Cuddington
Nether Winchendon
Upper Winchendon
Ashendon
Westcott
Wotton Underwood
Ludgershall
Piddington
Arncott
Ambrosden
Blackthorne
Merton
Murcott
Charlton-on-Otmoor
Oddington
Noke
Beckley
Horton-cum-Studley
Woodeaton
Elsfield
Stanton St John
Forest Hill
Wheatley
Holton
Waterperry
Worminghall
Ickford
Shabbington
Tiddington
Headington
OXFORD
Wytham
Cassington
Yarnton
Begbroke
Bladon
Long Hanborough
Church Hanborough
Freeland
Barnard Gate
Combe
Shipton-on-Cherwell
Hampton Poyle
Bletchingdon
Weston-on-the-Green
Kirtlington
Tackley
Wootton
Glympton
Kiddington
Rousham
Lower Heyford
Upper Heyford
Middleton Stoney
Caulcott
Bucknell
Caversfield
Chesterton
Wendlebury
North Aston
Middle Aston
Steeple Aston
Duns Tew
Barford St Michael
Bloxham
Adderbury
King's Sutton
Charlton
Hinton-in-the-Hedges
Farthinghoe
Thenford
Marston St Lawrence
Greatworth
Chacombe
Wardington
Chipping Warden
Edgcote
Aston le Walls
Fenny Compton
Wormleighton
Priors Marston
Priors Hardwick
Napton on the Hill
Stockton
Long Itchington
Marton
Birdingbury
Leamington Hastings
Grandborough
Willoughby
Braunston
Barby
Hillmorton
Clifton upon Dunsmore
Newton
Swinford
Lilbourne
Catthorpe
Yelvertoft
West Haddon
Guilsborough
Cottesbrooke
Creaton
Spratton
Holdenby
East Haddon
Ravensthorpe
Hollowell
Church Brampton
Chapel Brampton
Boughton
Overstone
Sywell
Mears Ashby
Wilby
Great Harrowden
Little Harrowden
Orlingbury
Isham
Pytchley
Broughton
Burton Latimer
Great Cransley
Loddington
Orton
Thorpe Malsor
Barton Seagrave
Cranford St Andrew
Rushton
Geddington
Weekley
Newton Longville
Drayton Parslow
Mursley
Swanbourne
Stewkley
Soulbury
Great Brickhill
Little Brickhill
Stoke Hammond
Great Horwood
Little Horwood
Addington
East Claydon
Middle Claydon
Botolph Claydon
Granborough
Hoggeston
Dunton
Mentmore
Cheddington
Long Marston
Puttenham
Buckland
Ledburn
Slapton
Crafton
Wingrave
Sherington
Emberton
Ravenstone
Weston Underwood
Stoke Goldington
Gayhurst
Tyringham
Filgrave
Lathbury
Moulsoe
Broughton
Castlethorpe
Haversham
Wolverton
Great Linford
Newport Pagnell
Simpson
Walton
Wavendon
Fenny Stratford
Water Eaton
Whaddon
Nash
Shenley Brook End
Beachampton
Thornton
Calverton
Old Stratford
Cosgrove
Yardley Gobion
Grafton Regis
Alderton
Pury End
Wood Burcote
Abthorpe
Slapton
Bradden
Wappenham
Weedon Lois
Weston
Plumpton
Woodend
Blakesley
Greens Norton
Tiffield
Pattishall
Litchborough
Maidford
Farthingstone
Preston Capes
Charwelton
Hellidon
Catesby
Staverton
Welton
Flecknoe
Cold Ashby
Thornby
Elkington
Winwick
Haselbech
Clipston
Sibbertoft
Kilworth
Lutterworth
Shawell
Churchover
Pailton
Brinklow
Easenhall
Harborough Magna
Newbold on Avon
Long Lawford
Church Lawford
Brandon
Wolston
Stretton-on-Dunsmore
Frankton
Draycote
Bourton on Dunsmore
Thurlaston
Cawston
Woolscott
Sawbridge
Kites Hardwick
Broadwell

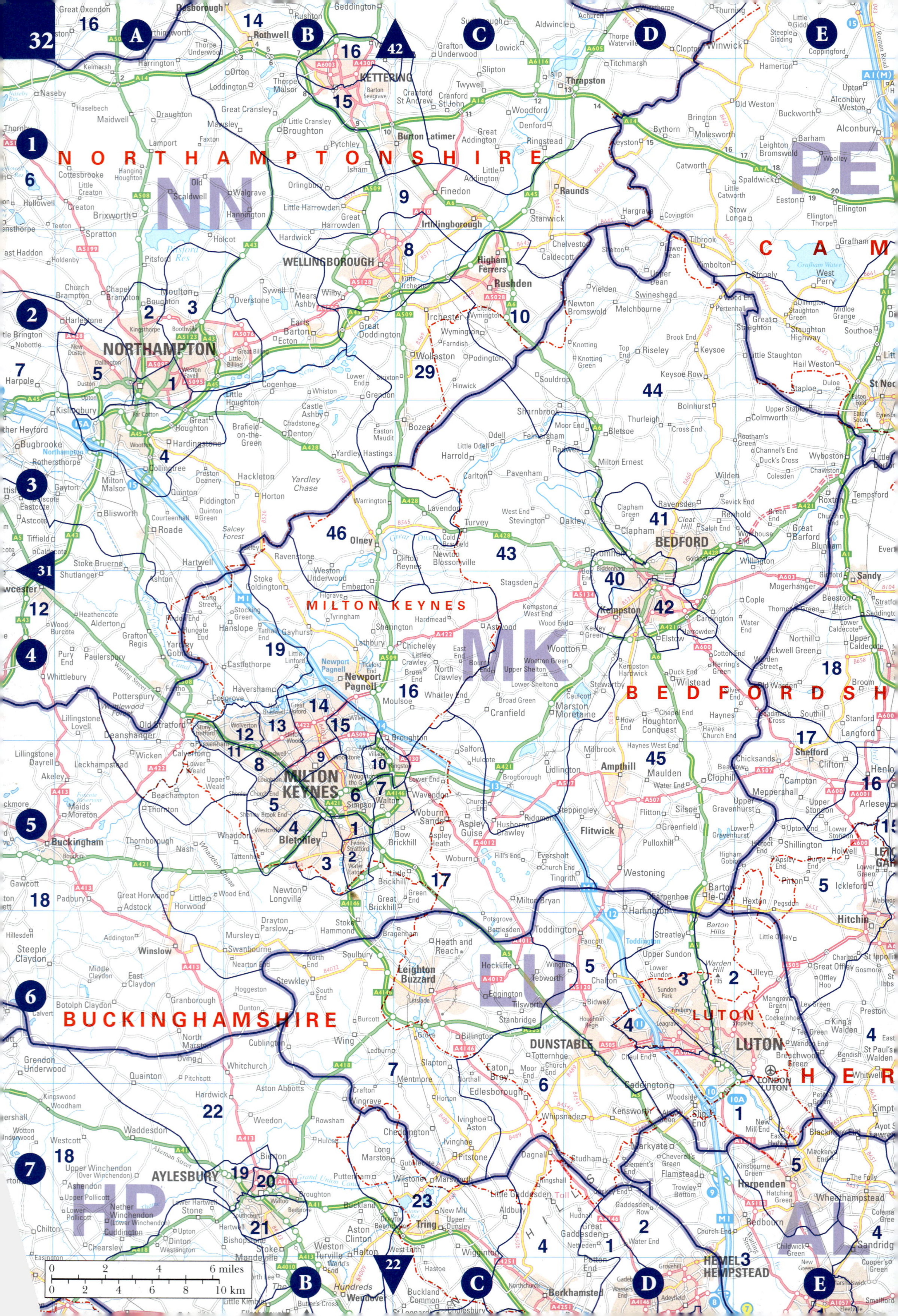

A
B
C
D
E
1
2
3
4
5
6
7
42
31
22
NORTHAMPTONSHIRE
MILTON KEYNES
BEDFORDSHIRE
BUCKINGHAMSHIRE
CAM
HER
NN
MK
LU
PE
HP
AL
KETTERING
Rothwell
Desborough
Burton Latimer
Thrapston
Raunds
Irthlingborough
Finedon
WELLINGBOROUGH
Higham Ferrers
Rushden
NORTHAMPTON
Olney
Newport Pagnell
MILTON KEYNES
Bletchley
BEDFORD
Kempston
Sandy
Ampthill
Flitwick
Shefford
Hitchin
Leighton Buzzard
DUNSTABLE
LUTON
Harpenden
HEMEL HEMPSTEAD
Berkhamsted
Tring
AYLESBURY
Wendover
Buckingham
Winslow
Stony Stratford
Woburn
Toddington
0 2 4 6 miles
0 2 4 6 8 10 km

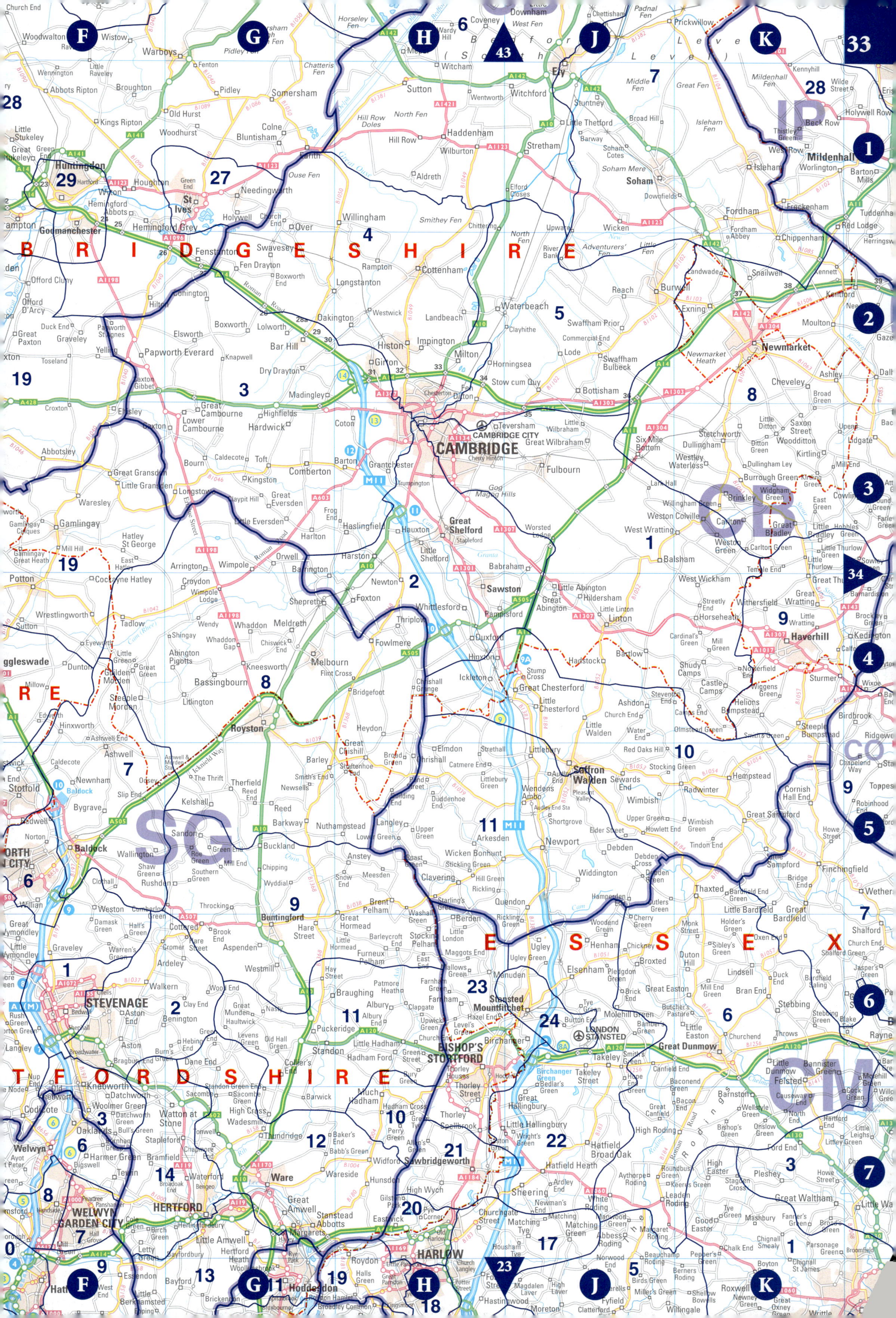

CAMBRIDGE
CAMBRIDGE CITY
Huntingdon
Godmanchester
St Ives
Ely
Soham
Mildenhall
Newmarket
Haverhill
Royston
Saffron Walden
Baldock
Stevenage
Hertford
Ware
Welwyn Garden City
Welwyn
Buntingford
Bishop's Stortford
Sawbridgeworth
Harlow
Hoddesdon
Great Dunmow
Thaxted
London Stansted
Stansted Mountfitchet
Linton
Sawston
Great Shelford
Histon
Cottenham
Waterbeach
Burwell
Fordham
Chippenham
Bottisham
Fulbourn
Great Chesterford
Duxford
Melbourn
Bassingbourn
Potton
Gamlingay
Papworth Everard
Bar Hill
Willingham
Haddenham
Sutton
Witcham
Somersham
Warboys
Great Cambourne
Lower Cambourne
Comberton
Harston
Foxton
Fowlmere
Ashwell
Stotfold
Letchworth
Ashdon
Steeple Bumpstead
Finchingfield
Great Bardfield
Felsted
High Easter
Great Waltham
Hatfield Broad Oak
Sheering
Matching Green
Much Hadham
Puckeridge
Standon
Braughing
Knebworth
Datchworth
Watton at Stone
Tewin
Codicote
Stanstead Abbotts
Great Amwell
Roydon
Little Hallingbury
Takeley
Elsenham
Henham
Newport
Clavering
Barkway
Reed
Therfield
Kelshall
Sandon
Wallington
Walkern
Benington
Aston
Ardeley
Cottered
Westmill
B R I D G E S H I R E
E S S E X
T F O R D S H I R E
SG
CB
CM
IP
F
G
H
J
K
43
23
34
M11
A14
A10
A11
A505
A120
A1307
A1303
A1198
A1123
A142
A602
A414

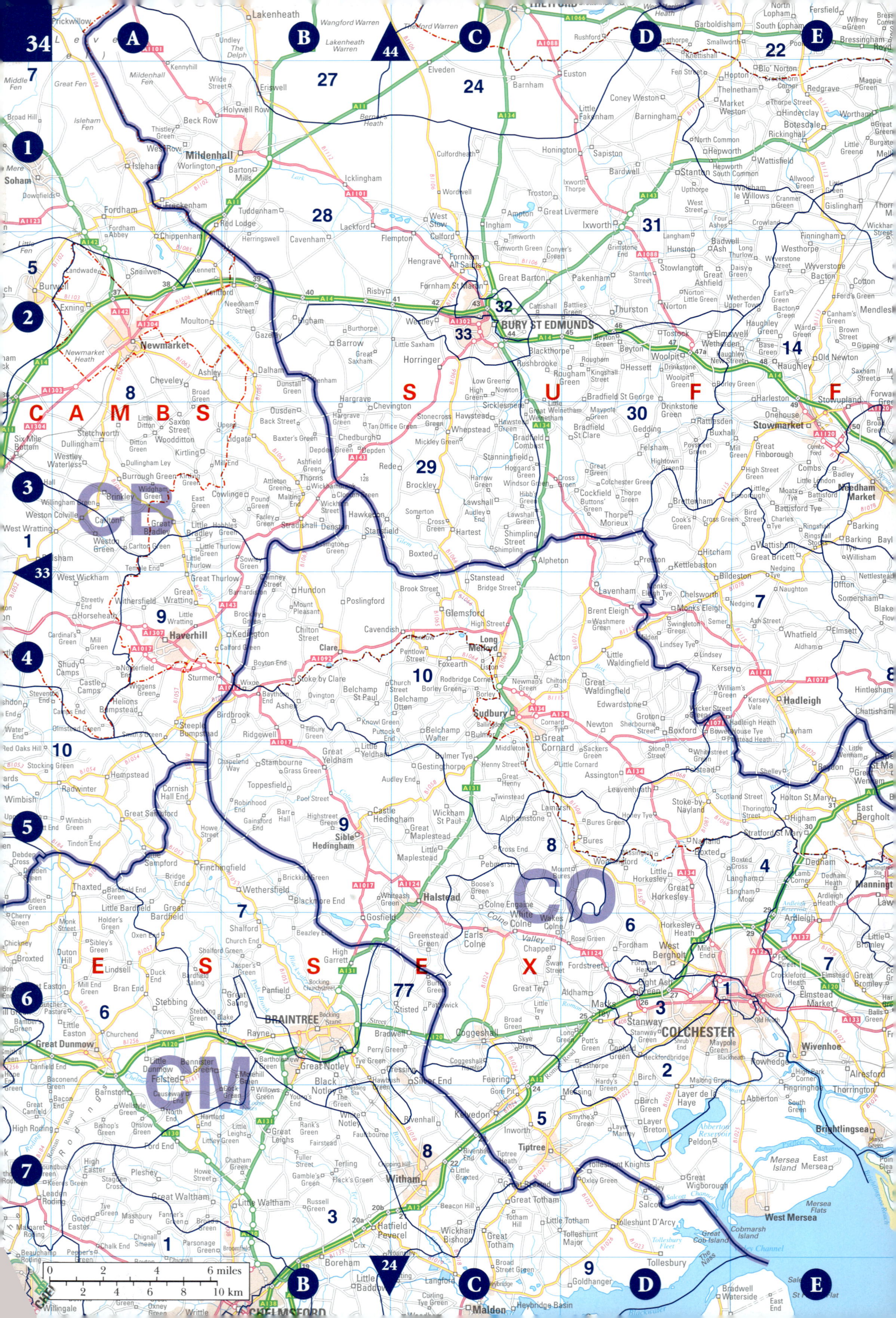
A
B
C
D
E
44
24
33
1
2
3
4
5
6
7
CB
CO
CM
CAMBS
SUFF
ESSEX
Lakenheath
Mildenhall
Newmarket
Haverhill
Clare
Long Melford
Sudbury
Hadleigh
Stowmarket
Needham Market
BURY ST EDMUNDS
Thetford
Elveden
Barnham
Euston
Ixworth
Soham
Fordham
Kentford
Glemsford
Cavendish
Lavenham
Halstead
Sible Hedingham
Castle Hedingham
BRAINTREE
Coggeshall
Kelvedon
Witham
Tiptree
COLCHESTER
Wivenhoe
Brightlingsea
West Mersea
Great Dunmow
Thaxted
Maldon
CHELMSFORD
Manningtree
Dedham
Boxford
Great Cornard
0
2
4
6 miles
8
10 km

IPSWICH
Woodbridge
Felixstowe
Harwich
Aldeburgh
Southwold
Halesworth
Saxmundham
Framlingham
Leiston
Walton on the Naze
Frinton-on-Sea
CLACTON-ON-SEA
Diss
Eye
Orford
Orford Ness
Hollesley Bay
Rendlesham Forest
Tunstall Forest
Thorpe Ness
Landguard Point
Stone Point
Sandy Point
Gunfleet Sand
hours
Esbjerg............................19
Hook of Holland......3¾-6¼
F
G
H
J
K
1
2
3
4
5
6
7

A
B
C
D
E
46
54
51
49
52
53
1
2
3
4
5
6
7
LLEYN PENINSULA
(PEN LLŶN)
TREMADOG BAY
CARDIGAN BAY
(BAE CEREDIGION)
Bardsey Island
(Ynys Enlli)
Aberdaron
Abersoch
Pwllheli
Nefyn
Criccieth
Porthmadog
Tremadog
Harlech
Tywyn
Aberystwyth
Llanbedrog
Morfa Nefyn
Tudweiliog
Sarn Meyllteyrn
Botwnnog
Llanaelhaearn
Llithfaen
Trefor
Chwilog
Y Ffôr
Abererch
Llanystumdwy
Garndolbenmaen
Penygroes
Llanllyfni
Talysarn
Nebo
Nasareth
Pontllyfni
Aberdesach
Efailnewydd
Mynytho
Rhiw
Llangian
Llanengan
Sarn Bach
Bwlchtocyn
St Tudwal's Islands
Trwyn Cilan
Trwyn yr Wylfa
Porth Neigwl (Hell's Mouth)
Ynys Gwylan-fawr
Pen y Cil
Uwchmynydd
Braich y Pwll
Mynydd Anelog
Carn Fadryn
Garn Boduan
Yr Eifl
Carreg Ddu
Porth Dinllaen
Black Rock Sands
Morfa Harlech
Barmouth Bay (Bae Bermo)
Aberdyfi Bar
Sarn Cynfelyn
The Bar
A499
A497
A487
A496
A493
B4417
B4413
B4354
B4415
0 2 4 6 miles
0 2 4 6 8 10 km

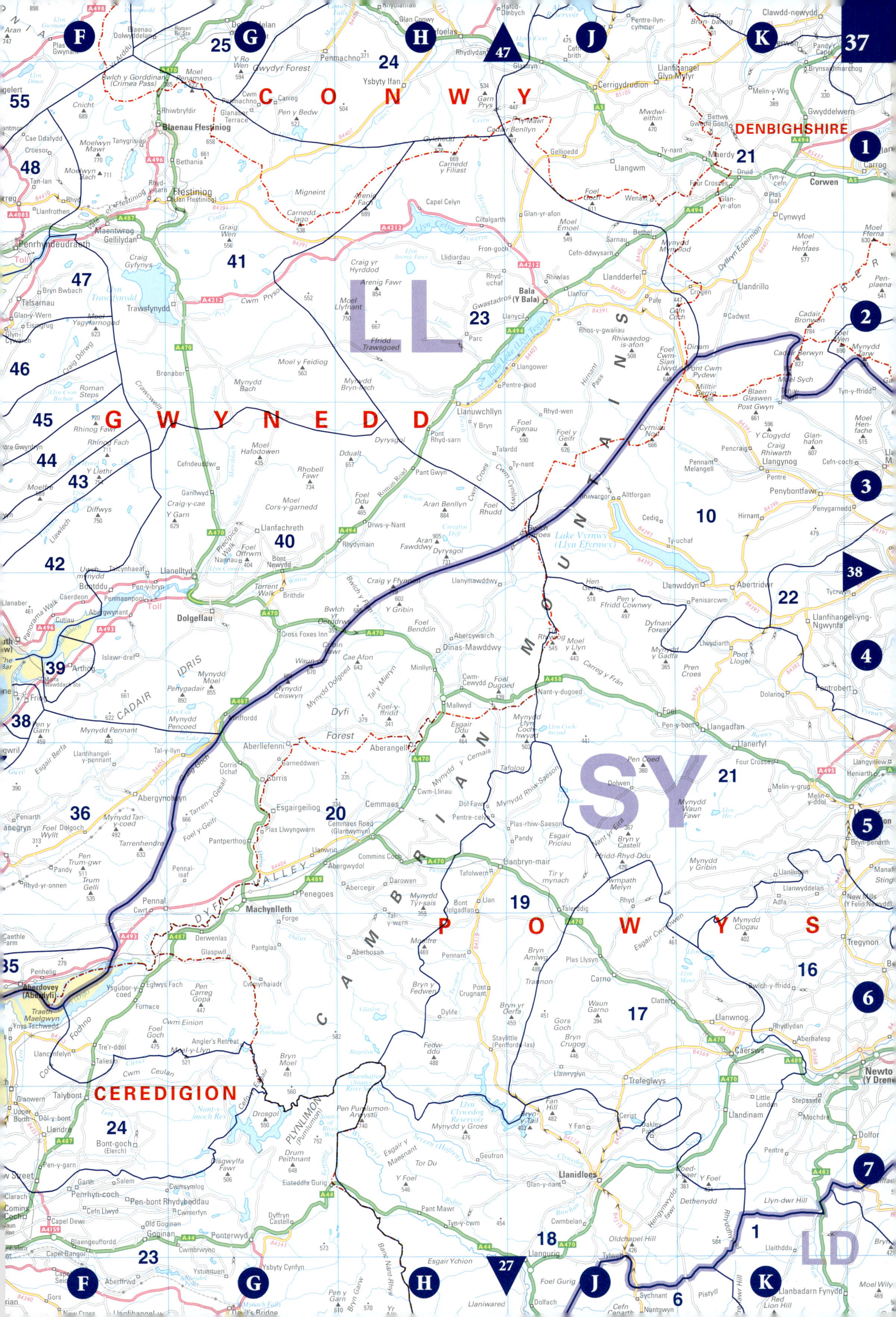

F
G
H
J
K
47
38
27
1
2
3
4
5
6
7
CONWY
DENBIGHSHIRE
GWYNEDD
POWYS
CEREDIGION
LL
SY
LD
BERWYN
ARENIG
MOUNTAINS
CAMBRIAN MOUNTAINS
CADAIR IDRIS
Gwydyr Forest
Dyfi Forest
Blaenau Ffestiniog
Ffestiniog
Maentwrog
Penrhyndeudraeth
Talsarnau
Trawsfynydd
Bala (Y Bala)
Bala Lake (Llyn Tegid)
Llyn Celyn
Lake Vyrnwy (Llyn Efyrnwy)
Corwen
Cerrigydrudion
Llandrillo
Llanuwchllyn
Dolgellau
Barmouth
Llanelltyd
Dinas-Mawddwy
Mallwyd
Llanwddyn
Llangadfan
Llanerfyl
Aberangell
Corris
Machynlleth
Aberdovey (Aberdyfi)
Pennal
Derwenlas
Cemmaes
Cemmaes Road (Glantwymyn)
Llanbrynmair
Carno
Caersws
Llanidloes
Llangurig
Trefeglwys
Llandinam
Newtown (Y Drenewydd)
Talybont
Ponterwyd
Goginan
Devil's Bridge
Plynlimon (Pumlumon)
Nant-y-moch Reservoir
Llyn Clywedog Reservoir
Lake Vyrnwy
Cader Berwyn
Aran Fawddwy
Arenig Fawr
Ysbyty Ifan
Penmachno
Pentrefoelas
Dolwyddelan
A470
A494
A487
A458
A489
A44
A5
A4212
A493
A483

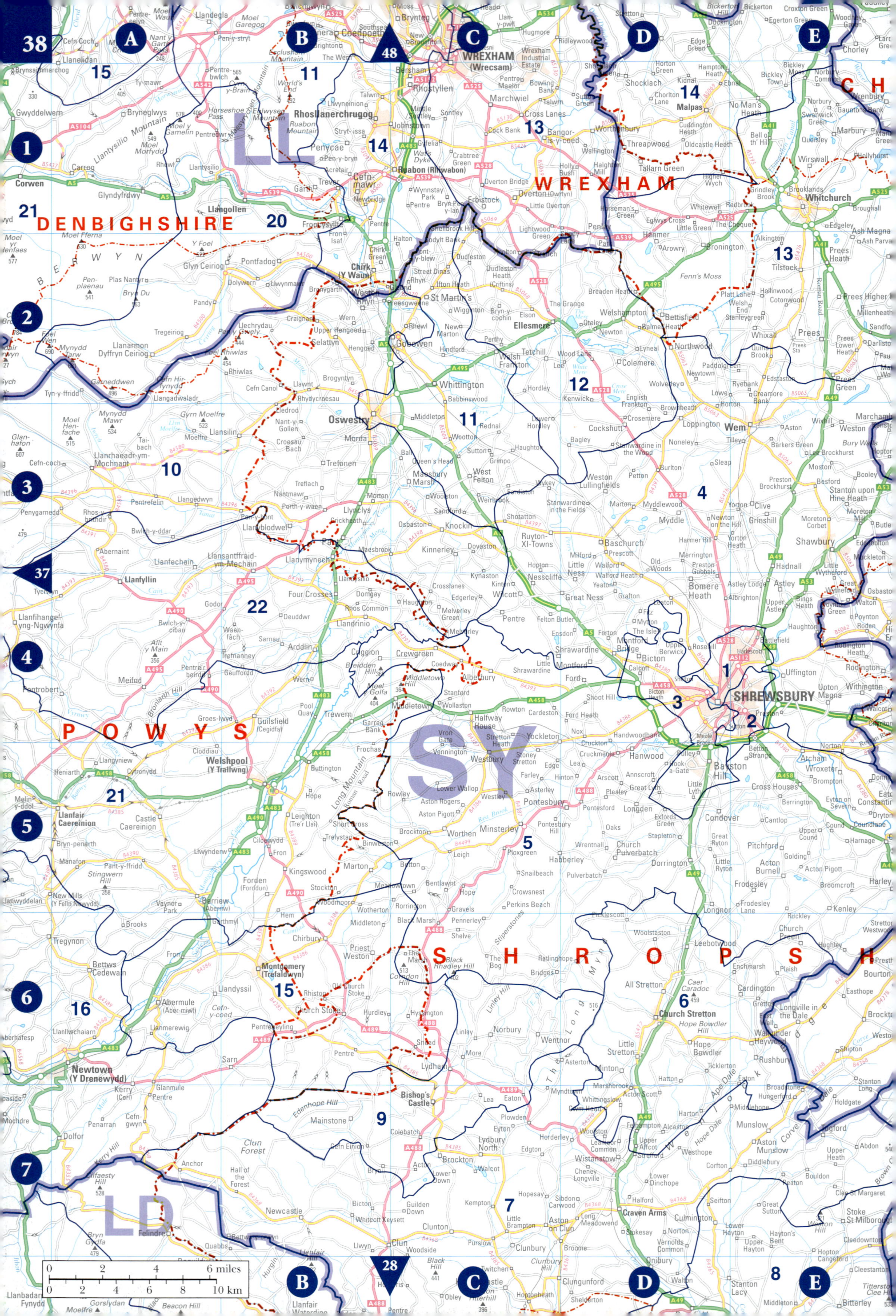
38
48
37
28
A
B
C
D
E
1
2
3
4
5
6
7
LL
SY
LD
DENBIGHSHIRE
WREXHAM
POWYS
SHROPSHIRE
WREXHAM (Wrecsam)
SHREWSBURY
Oswestry
Whitchurch
Wem
Ellesmere
Llangollen
Corwen
Chirk (Y Waun)
Ruabon (Rhiwabon)
Welshpool (Y Trallwng)
Newtown (Y Drenewydd)
Montgomery (Trefaldwyn)
Bishop's Castle
Church Stretton
Craven Arms
Clun
Malpas
Llanfyllin
Llanfair Caereinion
Minsterley
Pontesbury
Baschurch
Shawbury
Clun Forest
Long Mountain
Stiperstones
The Long Mynd
Wenlock Edge
0 2 4 6 miles
0 2 4 6 8 10 km

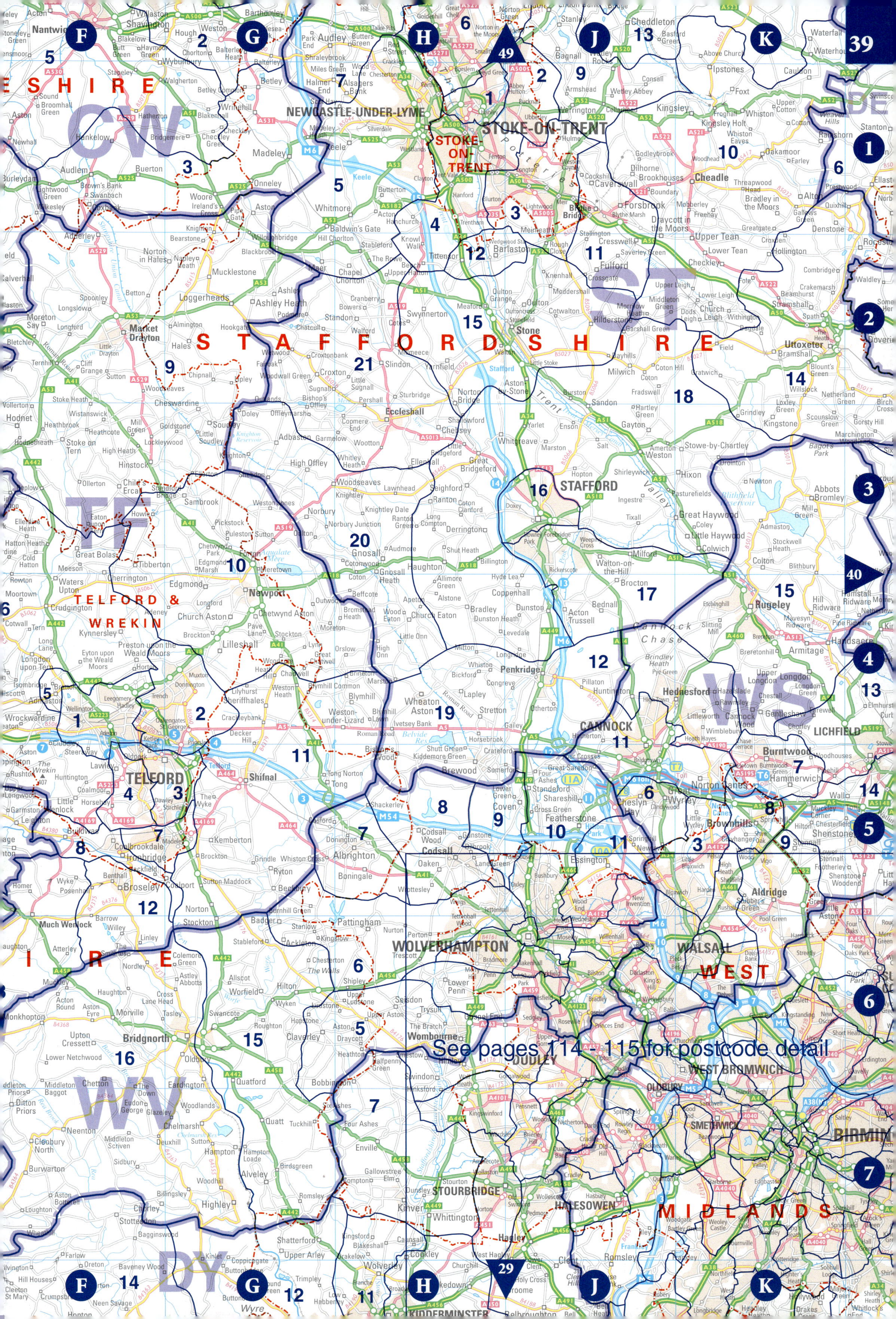
F
G
H
J
K
49
40
29
1
2
3
4
5
6
7
CW
ST
TF
WS
WV
DY
S T A F F O R D S H I R E
TELFORD & WREKIN
WEST MIDLANDS
NEWCASTLE-UNDER-LYME
STOKE-ON-TRENT
STAFFORD
Stone
Uttoxeter
Cheadle
Market Drayton
Newport
Eccleshall
Rugeley
Hednesford
CANNOCK
LICHFIELD
Penkridge
TELFORD
Shifnal
Bridgnorth
WOLVERHAMPTON
WALSALL
DUDLEY
WEST BROMWICH
STOURBRIDGE
HALESOWEN
KIDDERMINSTER
Much Wenlock
Madeley
Audley
Aldridge
Brownhills
Burntwood
Codsall
Wombourne
Oldbury
Smethwick
Kinver
Hagley
Cheslyn Hay
Great Wyrley
Broseley
Ironbridge
Kingswinford
See pages 114 - 115 for postcode detail

A
B
C
D
E
50
30
39
65
1
2
3
4
5
6
7
NEWCASTLE-UNDER-LYME
STOKE-ON-TRENT
STOKE-ON-TRENT
Cheadle
Ashbourne
DERB
DE
ST
STAFFORDSHIRE
Uttoxeter
Stone
STAFFORD
Rugeley
BURTON UPON TRENT
SWADLINCOTE
Penkridge
CANNOCK
Hednesford
WS
LICHFIELD
Burntwood
TAMWORTH
B
WY
WOLVERHAMPTON
WALSALL
Aldridge
WEST
SUTTON COLDFIELD
Wombourne
DUDLEY
WEST BROMWICH
OLDBURY
SMETHWICK
BIRMINGHAM
Coleshill
WARWIC
STOURBRIDGE
HALESOWEN
MIDLANDS
SOLIHULL
KIDDERMINSTER
BIRMINGHAM INT
M6 Toll
M42
M54
M5
M6
Cannock Chase
Albrighton
Codsall
Fazeley
Kingsbury
Tutbury
Abbots Bromley
Armitage
Shenstone
Eccleshall
Gnosall
Brewood
Kinver
Hagley
Bickenhill
Castle Bromwich
Sandon
Hixon
Alrewas
Barton-under-Needwood
Sudbury
See pages 114 - 115 for postcode detail
0 2 4 6 miles
0 2 4 6 8 10 km

F
G
H
J
K
51
42
31
1
2
3
4
5
6
7
NG
LE
CV
NN
NOTTINGHAMSHIRE
LEICESTERSHIRE
NORTHANTS
DERBY
NOTTINGHAM
LEICESTER
Hucknall
Arnold
Carlton
West Bridgford
Ilkeston
Eastwood
Beeston
Stapleford
Long Eaton
Ripley
Heanor
Belper
Loughborough
Shepshed
Coalville
Ashby de la Zouch
Melton Mowbray
Bingham
Oadby
Wigston
Hinckley
Nuneaton
Lutterworth
Market Harborough
Market Bosworth
Castle Donington
Nottingham East Midlands
Syston
Enderby
Narborough
Bedworth
Atherstone
Kegworth
Ruddington
Keyworth
Radcliffe on Trent
Desborough
Charnwood Forest

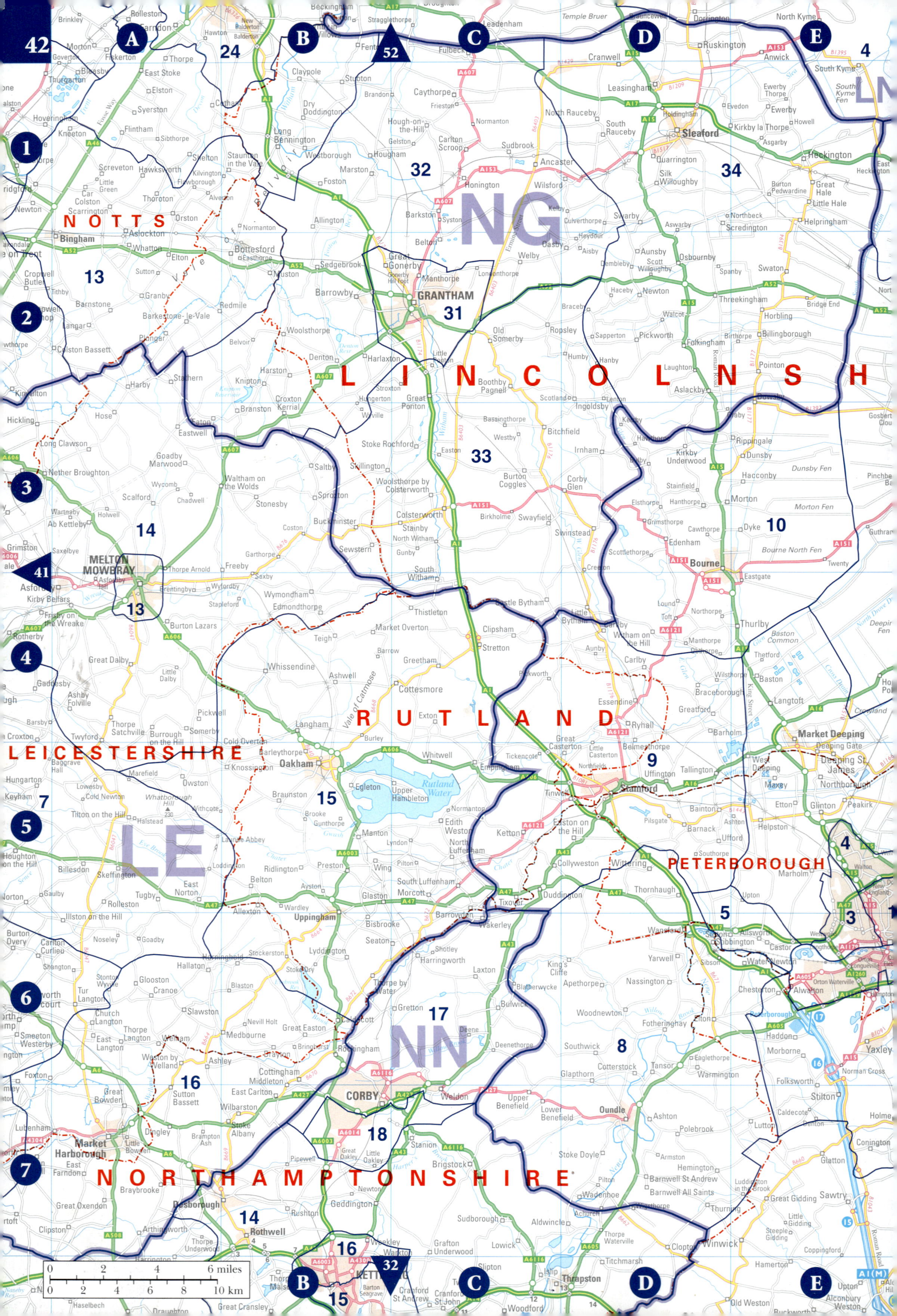
NOTTS
LINCOLNSHIRE
RUTLAND
LEICESTERSHIRE
NORTHAMPTONSHIRE
PETERBOROUGH
NG
LE
NN
GRANTHAM
MELTON MOWBRAY
Sleaford
Bourne
Stamford
Oakham
Uppingham
Market Deeping
Market Harborough
CORBY
Oundle
Desborough
Rothwell
Thrapston
Bingham
Bottesford
Rutland Water
Vale of Belvoir
Vale of Catmose
Cranwell
Leadenham
Caythorpe
Ancaster
Colsterworth
Corby Glen
Castle Bytham
Cottesmore
Empingham
Ketton
Wansford
Fotheringhay
Yaxley
Stilton
Sawtry
Kettering
Weldon
Rockingham
Caldecott
Medbourne
Hallaton
Billesdon
Waltham on the Wolds
Harby
Long Bennington
Claypole
Fulbeck
Heckington
Billingborough
Pointon
Dunsby Fen
Morton Fen
Bourne North Fen
Deeping St James
0 2 4 6 miles
0 2 4 6 8 10 km

BOSTON
THE WASH
Boston Deeps
Lynn Deeps
Long Sand
Roger Sand
Toft Sand
Gat Sand
Old South
Seal Sand
Peter Black Sand
Bulldog Sand
Black Buoy Sand
Hunstanton
Heacham
Dersingham
KING'S LYNN
SPALDING
Holbeach
Long Sutton
Sutton Bridge
Wisbech
Terrington St Clement
Downham Market
March
Chatteris
Whittlesey
PETERBOROUGH
Ramsey
Littleport
Ely
Crowland
Fishtoft
Wyberton
Kirton
Frampton
Sutterton
Pinchbeck
Whaplode
Moulton
Gedney
Emneth
Outwell
Upwell
Welney
Denver
Hilgay
Southery
Feltwell
Manea
Doddington
Benwick
Warboys
Somersham
Witchford
Sutton St James
Tydd St Mary
Walpole St Andrew
Walpole St Peter
Clenchwarton
Castle Rising
North Wootton
Snettisham
Sandringham
Wolferton
Stowbridge
Runcton Holme
Watlington
Tottenhill
Wormegay
Shouldham
Thorney
Eye
PE
CB
IP
NORFOLK
CAMBRIDGESHIRE
SUFFOLK
Marshland
Bedford Level
North Level
Middle Level
South Level
F
G
H
J
K
1
2
3
4
5
6
7
53
44
33

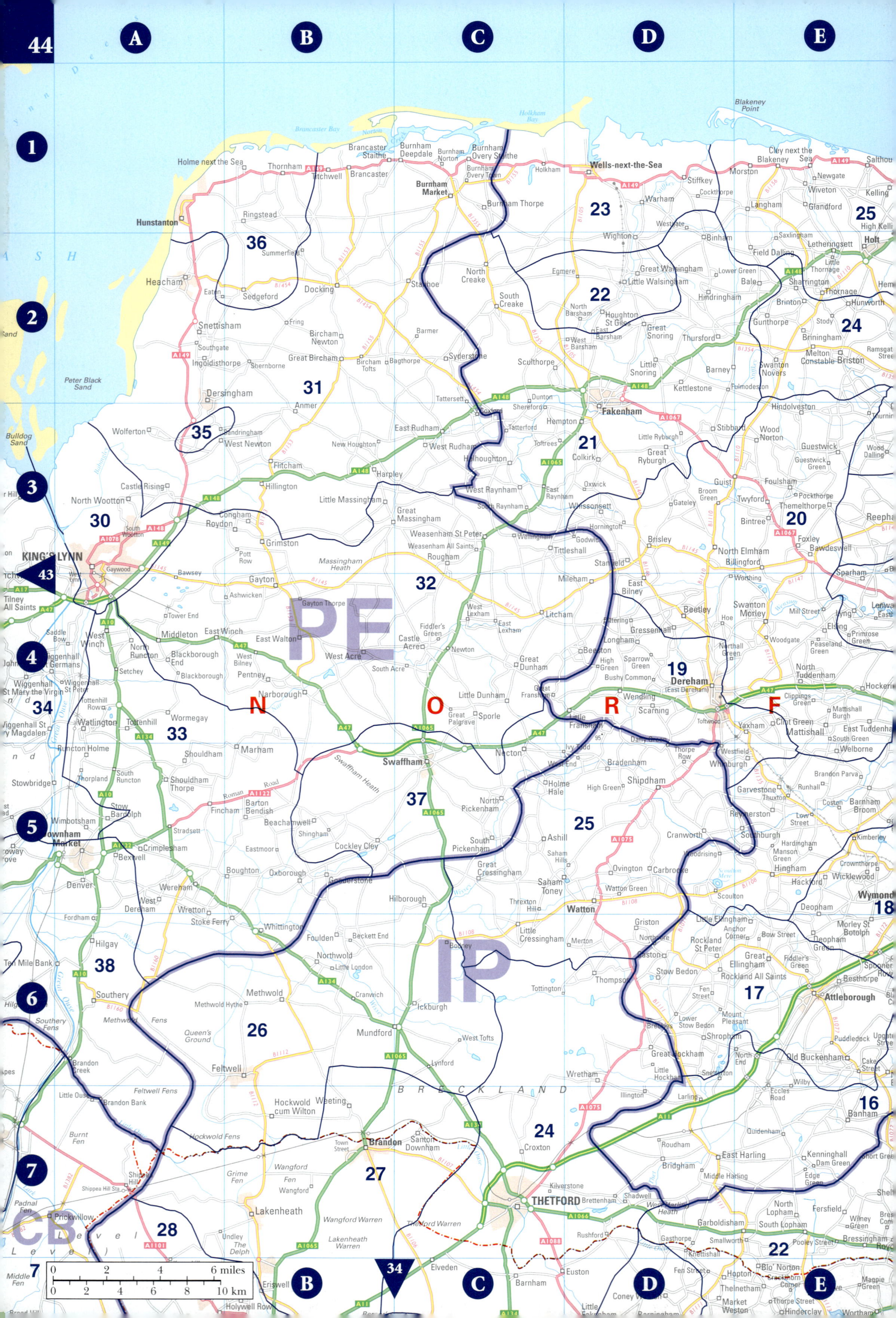
A
B
C
D
E
1
2
3
4
5
6
7
Brancaster Bay
Holkham Bay
Blakeney Point
Holme next the Sea
Thornham
Titchwell
Brancaster Staithe
Brancaster
Burnham Deepdale
Burnham Norton
Burnham Overy Staithe
Burnham Overy Town
Holkham
Wells-next-the-Sea
Stiffkey
Cley next the Sea
Blakeney
Morston
Salthouse
Burnham Market
Burnham Thorpe
Hunstanton
Ringstead
36
Summerfield
Heacham
Sedgeford
Docking
Stanhoe
North Creake
South Creake
Egmere
22
23
Warham
Wighton
Binham
Langham
Great Walsingham
Little Walsingham
Field Dalling
Letheringsett
Holt
25
High Kelling
Kelling
Glandford
Wiveton
Newgate
Snettisham
Fring
Bircham Newton
Barmer
North Barsham
Houghton St Giles
West Barsham
East Barsham
Great Snoring
Thursford
Hindringham
Sharrington
Thornage
Brinton
Hunworth
Gunthorpe
Stody
Briningham
24
Melton Constable
Briston
Swanton Novers
Southgate
Ingoldisthorpe
Shernborne
Great Bircham
Bircham Tofts
Bagthorpe
Syderstone
Sculthorpe
Little Snoring
Barney
Kettlestone
Fulmodeston
Peter Black Sand
Dersingham
31
Anmer
Tattersett
Coxford
Dunton
Shereford
Fakenham
Hindolveston
35
Sandringham
West Newton
Wolferton
East Rudham
West Rudham
New Houghton
Tatterford
Hempton
21
Toftrees
Colkirk
Little Ryburgh
Great Ryburgh
Stibbard
Wood Norton
Guestwick
Bulldog Sand
Flitcham
Harpley
Helhoughton
Castle Rising
Hillington
North Wootton
30
Little Massingham
West Raynham
South Raynham
East Raynham
Oxwick
Whissonsett
Guist
Foulsham
Twyford
Themelthorpe
20
Bintree
Congham
Roydon
Great Massingham
Weasenham St Peter
Weasenham All Saints
Wellingham
Horningtoft
Brisley
Foxley
Bawdeswell
KING'S LYNN
43
Gaywood
Bawsey
Grimston
Pott Row
Massingham Heath
Rougham
Tittleshall
Godwick
Stanfield
North Elmham
Billingford
Gayton
32
Mileham
East Bilney
Worthing
Sparham
Tilney All Saints
Ashwicken
Gayton Thorpe
PE
Tower End
West Lexham
East Lexham
Litcham
Beetley
Swanton Morley
Mill Street
Lyng
Saddle Bow
West Winch
Middleton
East Winch
East Walton
Fiddler's Green
Castle Acre
Newton
Kempstone
Gressenhall
Elsing
Longham
Beeston
Sparrow Green
High Green
Bushy Common
North Tuddenham
Wiggenhall St Germans
North Runcton
Blackborough End
Blackborough
West Bilney
West Acre
South Acre
Pentney
Great Dunham
19
Dereham
(East Dereham)
Narborough
Little Dunham
Fransham
Wendling
Scarning
34
Setchey
N
O
R
F
Watlington
Tottenhill
Wormegay
33
Great Palgrave
Sporle
Little Fransham
Toftwood
Yaxham
Clint Green
Mattishall
East Tuddenham
Runcton Holme
Marham
Swaffham
Necton
Dale Green
Thorpe Row
Westfield
Whinburgh
Welborne
Shouldham
Swaffham Heath
Ivy Todd
West End
Bradenham
Shipdham
Stowbridge
Thorpland
South Runcton
Shouldham Thorpe
37
Holme Hale
High Green
Garvestone
Runhall
Brandon Parva
Roman Road
Barton Bendish
Fincham
North Pickenham
Thuxton
Reymerston
Barnham Broom
Coston
Stow Bardolph
Wimbotsham
Downham Market
Beachamwell
Shingham
Stradsett
Crimplesham
Bexwell
Cockley Cley
South Pickenham
25
Ashill
Saham Hills
Cranworth
Woodrising
Southburgh
Kimberley
Hardingham
Hingham
Eastmoor
Boughton
Oxborough
Gooderstone
Great Cressingham
Ovington
Carbrooke
Saham Toney
Watton Green
Hackford
Wicklewood
Denver
Wereham
West Dereham
Hilborough
Threxton Hill
Watton
Scoulton
Deopham
Wymondham
18
Fordham
Wretton
Stoke Ferry
Whittington
Little Cressingham
Merton
Griston
Little Ellingham
Morley St Botolph
Hilgay
Foulden
Beckett End
Northwold
Little London
Bodney
IP
Thompson
Rockland St Peter
Great Ellingham
Rockland All Saints
Stow Bedon
Bow Street
Attleborough
Ten Mile Bank
38
Southery
Southery Fens
Methwold
Methwold Hythe
Methwold Fens
Cranwich
Ickburgh
Tottington
17
Queen's Ground
26
Mundford
West Tofts
Lower Stow Bedon
Mount Pleasant
Shropham
Puddledock
Brandon Creek
Feltwell
Lynford
Great Hockham
Little Hockham
Wretham
North End
Old Buckenham
Little Ouse
Brandon Bank
Feltwell Fens
Hockwold cum Wilton
Weeting
BRECKLAND
Illington
Larling
Eccles Road
Wilby
16
Banham
Burnt Fen
Hockwold Fens
Brandon
Town Street
Santon Downham
24
Croxton
Roudham
Quidenham
East Harling
Kenninghall
Bridgham
Middle Harling
Ship Hill
Shippea Hill Sta.
Grime Fen
Wangford
Wangford Fen
27
Kilverstone
THETFORD
Brettenham
Shadwell
West Harling Heath
North Lopham
South Lopham
Fersfield
Garboldisham
Padnal Fen
Prickwillow
CB
28
Lakenheath
Wangford Warren
Lakenheath Warren
Thetford Warren
Rushford
Gasthorpe
Smallworth
Bressingham
Undley
The Delph
Level
Middle Fen
7
Eriswell
34
Elveden
Barnham
Euston
Fen Street
Hopton
Thelnetham
Blo' Norton
Market Weston
Thorpe Street
Hinderclay
Coney Weston
Holywell Row
0 2 4 6 miles
0 2 4 6 8 10 km

F
G
H
J
K
1
2
3
4
5
6
7
Sheringham
Weybourne
Upper Sheringham
West Runton
East Runton
Cromer
Beeston Regis
Bodham
East Beckham
West Beckham
Aylmerton
Felbrigg
Overstrand
Sidestrand
Trimingham
Northrepps
Roughton
Gresham
Baconsthorpe
Plumstead
Matlaske
Hanworth
Aldborough
Thurgarton
Little Barningham
Southrepps
Gimingham
Mundesley
Thorpe Market
Lower Street
Trunch
Knapton
Paston
Bacton
Keswick
Walcott
Happisburgh
Whimpwell Green
Eccles-on-Sea
Antingham
Suffield
Bradfield
Swafield
Edingthorpe
Ridlington
Wickmere
Erpingham
Calthorpe
Itteringham
Saxthorpe
Colby
Ingworth
Banningham
North Walsham
Witton Bridge
Crostwight
Tungate
Felmingham
Skeyton
Meeting House Hill
Honing
Briggate
East Ruston
Happisburgh Common
Lessingham
Hempstead
Sea Palling
Waxham
Ingham Corner
Ingham
Stalham
Stalham Green
Hickling
Hickling Green
Hickling Heath
Sutton
Horsey Corner
Horsey
Hill Common
Oulton
Heydon
Oulton Street
Blickling
Aylsham
Silvergate
Brabblegate
Tuttington
Burgh next Aylsham
Westwick
Swanton Abbot
Worstead
Lyngate
Bengate
Dilham
Smallburgh
Barton Turf
Wood Street
Catfield
Cawston
Southgate
Eastgate
Marsham
Brampton
Oxnead
Lamas
Scottow
Buxton
Buxton Heath
Little Hautbois
Market Street
Beeston St Lawrence
Ashmanhaugh
Neatishead
Irstead
Sharp Street
Potter Heigham
West Somerton
Winterton-on-Sea
East Somerton
Martham
Mustard Hyrn
Hevingham
Brandiston
Stratton Strawless
Tunstead
Coltishall
Horstead
Hainford
Frettenham
Belaugh
Wroxham
Hoveton
Upper Street
Horning
Ludham
Bastwick
Repps
Hemsby
Newport
Scratby
California
Ormesby St Margaret
Ormesby St Michael
Rollesby
Swannington
Alderford
Morton
Attlebridge
Felthorpe
St Helena
Horsford
Newton St Faith
Horsham St Faith
Crostwick
Spixworth
Woodbastwick
Thurne
Clippesby
Fleggburgh
Burgh St Margaret
Billockby
Filby
Thrigby
Mautby
Caister-on-Sea
West Caister
Weston Longville
Weston Green
Ringland
Taverham
Drayton
NORWICH INTERNATIONAL
Costessey
Rackheath
New Rackheath
Salhouse
Little Plumstead
Panxworth
Ranworth
Pilson Green
Cargate Green
South Walsham
Upton
Fishley
Stokesby
Runham
Easton
Hellesdon
Sprowston
Thorpe End
Great Plumstead
Blofield Heath
Pedham
Town Green
North Burlingham
Acle
Damgate
Marlingford
Bawburgh
Bowthorpe
NORWICH
Colney
Earlham
Eaton
Thorpe St Andrew
Postwick
Witton
Blofield
Lingwood
Brundall
Strumpshaw
Beighton
Tunstall
Halvergate
Halvergate Marshes
Burgh Castle
Southtown
GREAT YARMOUTH
Gorleston-on-Sea
Little Melton
Hethersett
Cringleford
Keswick
Trowse Newton
Surlingham
Kirby Bedon
Buckenham
Hassingham
South Burlingham
Moulton St Mary
Freethorpe
Wickhampton
Freethorpe Common
High Green
Lynch Green
Arminghall
Caistor St Edmund
Bramerton
Rockland St Mary
Cantley
Limpenhoe
Claxton
Hellington
Framingham Pigot
Yelverton
Ashby St Mary
Carleton St Peter
Ketteringham
Swardeston
East Carleton
Mulbarton
Swainsthorpe
Upper Stoke
Dunston
Poringland
Framingham Earl
Stoke Holy Cross
Bergh Apton
Thurlton
Hardley Street
Langley Street
Reedham
Norton Marshes
Nogdam End
Belton
Bradwell
Browston Green
Hobland Hall
Fritton
Ashby Dell
Hopton
Silfield
Penny's Green
Wreningham
Bracon Ash
Shotesham
Howe
Hawe's Green
Brooke
Sisland
Chedgrave
Norton Subcourse
Lower Thurlton
Thorpe
Loddon
Lound
Blundeston
Corton
Ashwellthorpe
Toprow
Newton Flotman
Flordon
Saxlingham Nethergate
Saxlingham Green
Saxlingham Thorpe
Seething
Kirstead Green
Mundham
The Laurels
Stubbs Green
Hales
Heckingham
Herringfleet
Haddiscoe
Somerleyton
Fundenhall
Hapton
Tasburgh
Tacolneston
Forncett St Mary
Tharston
Hempnall
Thwaite St Mary
Kirby Green
Kirby Cane
Raveningham
Brundish
Maypole Green
Toft Monks
Waterheath
Wheatacre
Camps Heath
Oulton
Lowestoft Ness
LOWESTOFT
Bunwell Street
Forncett End
Forncett St Peter
Long Stratton
Stratton St Michael
Silver Green
Fritton
Road Green
Woodton
Hedenham
Bedingham Green
Ellingham
Stockton
Bull's Green
Aldeby
Burgh St Peter
Bunwell
Potter's Green
Morningthorpe
Wood Green
Hempnall Green
Topcroft
Topcroft Street
Upgate Street
Ditchingham
Kirby Row
Geldeston
Gillingham
Beccles
Oulton Broad
Kirkley
Carlton Colville
Pakefield
Hargate
Aslacton
Wacton
Great Moulton
Shelton
Hardwick
Harris Green
Great Green
Earsham
Broome
Bungay
Wainford
Shipmeadow
Barsham
Mettingham
North Cove
Barnby
Worlingham
Mutford
Gisleham
Tibenham
Pristow Green
Sneath Common
Cole's Common
Darrow Green
Denton
The City
Ringsfield
Ellough Moor
Beccles
Rushmere
Black Street
Kessingland
Kessingland Beach
Tivetshall St Margaret
Tivetshall St Mary
Colegate End
North Green
Bush Green
Alburgh
Flixton
Ilketshall St Andrew
Ringsfield Corner
Hulver Street
Henstead
Winfarthing
Gissing
Mill Green
Pulham Market
Pulham St Mary
Starston
Piccadilly Corner
Wortwell
Homersfield
Ilketshall St Margaret
Ilketshall St Lawrence
Beck's Green
Shadingfield
Sotterley
Benacre
Burston
Shimpling
Dickleburgh Moor
Dickleburgh
Rushall
Gaelic Street
Harleston
Redenhall
St Margaret South Elmham
St Michael South Elmham
St Cross South Elmham
Stone Street
Redisham
Brampton Sta
West End
Cuckold's Green
Frostenden
Wrentham
Covehithe
High Common
Walcot Green
Thelveton
Fuzze Green
Mendham
All Saints South Elmham
Alpheton Corner
Cox Common
Brampton
Stoven
South Cove
Diss
Upper Street
Thorpe Abbotts
Needham
Withersdale Street
Rumburgh
St James South Elmham
Spexhall
Westhall
Brampton Street
Clay Common
Cove Bottom
Scole
Billingford
Weybread
Weybread Street
Metfield
Uggeshall
Barnaby Green
Wangford
Reydon
Reydon Smear
Stuston
Great
Brome Street
Oakley
Hoxne
Cross
Wingfield Green
Wingfield
Fressingfield
Little Whittingham Green
North
Linstead Parva
Chediston
Halesworth
Holton
Blyford
NR
NORFOLK
BROADS
O
L
K
S U F F O L K
26
27
11
28
10
12
8
6
29
5
3
7
2
1
13
30
4
14
31
15
32
35
33
34
20
19
21
18
35
A149
A1082
A148
A140
A1151
A1062
A1067
A47
A1074
A11
A146
A143
A144
A145
A12
A1117
A1066
A1095
B1149
B1145
B1150
B1159
B1354
B1108
B1140
B1135
B1136
B1527
B1332
B1062
B1123
B1124
B1127
B1375
B1385
B1074

A
B
C
D
E
1
2
3
4
5
6
7
The Skerries
West Mouse
Middle Mouse
Carmel Head
Cemlyn Bay
Cemaes Bay
Porth Wen Bay
Bull Bay (Porth Llechog)
Point Lynas
Llanbadrig
Cemaes
67
Tregele
Neuadd
Burwen
Amlwch
Amlwch Port
Llaneilian
Pengorffwysfa
68
Llanfechell
Bodewryd
Mynydd-mechell
Rhos-goch
66
Parys Mountain
Pen-y-sarn
Nebo
Dulas
Ynys Dulas
Llanfairynghornwy
Llanrhyddlad
Carreglefn
Llanfflewyn
Rhos-y-bol
69
Dulas Bay
Lligwy Bay
HOLYHEAD BAY
Church Bay
Rhyd-wyn
ISLE OF
City Dulas
70
Llaneuddog
Brynrefail
Rhoslligwy
Moelfre
hours
Dublin.............$1^3/_4$-$3^1/_4$
Dún Laoghaire......$1^3/_4$
Llanfaethlu
Llanbabo
Gwredog
Capel Parc
Ceidio
72
73
North Stack
Llanddeusant
Elim
Llandyfrydog
Llanallgo
Marian-glas
Holyhead Mountain
220
Holyhead (Caergybi)
Llanfwrog
Stryd y Facsen
Llantrisant
Llannerch-y-medd
71
Bachau
Maenaddwyn
Llanfigael
Salt Island
South Stack
Llaingoch
Kingsland
Llanfachraeth
ANGLESEY
Bryn-teg
Benllech
Tyn-y-gongl
74
Carmel
Capel Coch
Red Wharf Bay
Puffin Island (Priestholm)
Penrhos
Llanynghenedl
Pen-llyn
Llechcynfarwy
Red Wharf Bay (Traeth Coch)
Mariandyrys
Glan-yr-afon
Caim
Penmon
Bodedern
Trefor
Llangwyllog
78
Llanbedrgoch
76
75
58
Llanddona
Llangoed
Penrhyn Mawr
Trearddur
Valley (Y Fali)
65
Caergeiliog
(YNYS MÔN)
Tregaian
Llanddyfnan
Mynydd Llwydiarth
Pentraeth
Dutchman Bank
Llan-faes
Holy Island
Four Mile Bridge
Bryngwran
Llynfaes
Rhosmeirch
LL
Llanfihangel yn-Nhywyn
Bodffordd
77
Talwrn
Bodior
Rhoscolyn
Llanfair-yn-neubwll
Capel Gwyn
Gwalchmai
Heneglwys
Llangefni
Llansadwrn
59
Beaumaris (Biwmares)
Lavan Sands
Llanfairfechan
Tywyn Trewan
Cymyran Bay
Rhostrehwfa
Ceint
Penmynydd
Llandegfan
Rhosneigr
64
Cerrigceinwen
Pencarnisiog
Llanfaelog
Ty Croes Sta
63
Llangristiolus
Capel Mawr
62
Pentre Berw
Gaerwen
Llanfairpwllgwyngyll
Bangor
Port Penrhyn
Menai Bridge (Porthaethwy)
Minffordd
Llandygai
Tal-y-bont
Abergwyngregyn
Crymlyn
Bethel
Trefdraeth
Llanddaniel Fab
Penrhos-garnedd
Llangadwaladr
60
Aberffraw
Malltraeth
Hermon
Llangaffo
Aberffraw Bay
Bodorgan
Malltraeth Sands
Y Felinheli
56
Capel-y-graig
Waen-wen
Glasinfryn
Llanllechid
Rachub
Moel Wnion
580
Aber Falls
Drosgl
758
Garnedd Uchaf
Rhyd-y-groes
Tal-y-Cae
Tregarth
Bethesda
Gerlan
Brynsiencyn
Pentir
Coed-y-parc
Dwyran
Newborough (Niwbwrch)
Saron
Bethel
Llanddeiniolen
Rhiwlas
Mynydd Llandygai
Braichmelyn
57
Foel Grach
Carnedd Llywelyn
Pen-lôn
61
Malltraeth Bay
Newborough Warren
Waterloo Port
Penisa'r Waun
Llandwyn Island
Llanddwyn Bay
Caernarfon
Pont-rug
Llanrug
Deiniolen
Bryn-refail
Clwt-y-bont
Mynydd Perfedd
812
Carnedd Dafydd
1044
Caeathro
Cwm-y-glo
Fachwen
Dinorwig
Elidyr Fawr
923
Llyn Padarn
Foel Goch
831
Abermenai Point
The Bar
Llanfaglan
Ceunant
Groeslon
Bontnewydd
Croesywaun
Llanberis
Y Garn
Pont Pen-y-benglog
Foryd Bay
Saron
Dinas
Waunfawr
Nant Peris
Glyder Fach
994
Glyder Fawr
999
Rhostryfan
Betws Garmon
Moel Eilio
726
Gwastadnant
55
Rhosgadfan
CAERNARFON BAY
Dinas Dinlle
Llanwnda
Penyffridd
Moel Tryfan
Salem
Pass of Llanberis
GWYNEDD
Pen-y-Pass
Pen-y-Gwryd Hotel
Llandwrog
Groeslon
Bwlchyllyn
Mynydd Mawr
698
Y Fron (Upper Llandwrog)
Llyn Cwellyn
SNOWDONIA (ERYRI)
Snowdon (Yr Wyddfa)
1085
Glaslyn
Llyn Llydaw
Carnedd y Cribau
Carmel
Penygroes
Talysarn
Nantlle
Rhyd-Ddu
Y Garn
634
Pontllyfni
Trwyn Maen Dylan
Aberdesach
Llyn Nantlle Uchaf
Trum y Ddysgl
709
Ffridd Uchaf
Yr Aran
747
Plas Gwynant
Llanllyfni
Nebo
54
Craig Cwm Silyn
734
Beddgelert Forest
Clynnog-fawr
Tai'n Lôn
Capeluchaf
Nasareth
700
605
Beddgelert
Llyn Dinas
Bwlch y Gorddinen (Crimea Pass)
41
36
Gyrn Goch
Bwlch Mawr
509
Bwlch-derwin
608 Garneddgoch
Pant Glas
Moel Hebog
Pass of Aberglaslyn
Cnicht
689
Rhiwbryfdir
Trefor
Gyrn Ddu
0 2 4 6 miles
0 2 4 6 8 10 km

F
G
H
J
K
1
2
3
4
5
6
7
Birkenhead to hours
Belfast............................8
Dublin.............................8
Liverpool to hours
Douglas...................2½-4
Dublin.............................8
LIVERPOOL BAY
48
West Hoyle Bank
Hilbre Island
West Kirby
Welsh Channel
Point of Ayr
Talacre
Mostyn Bank
Mostyn Quay
Dawpool Bank
Holywell Bank
Great Ormes Head
Little Ormes Head
Llandudno
Gogarth
Conwy Sands
Penrhyn Bay (Bae Penrhyn)
Rhos-on-Sea
Colwyn Bay (Bae Colwyn)
Abergele Roads
Llandulas
Abergele
Kinmel Bay (Bae Cinmel)
Towyn
Pensarn
Rhyl
Prestatyn
Gronant
Meliden (Gallt Melyd)
Dyserth
Rhuddlan
Bodelwyddan
St Asaph (Llanelwy)
Rhuallt
Tremeirchion
Trelogan
Mostyn
Whitford (Chwitffordd)
Glan-y-don
Greenfield (Maes-Glas)
Holywell
Gorsedd
Carmel
Pantasaph
Brynford
Halkyn
Halkyn Mountain
Rhes-y-cae
Nannerch
Rhosesmor
Rhydymwyn
Cilcain
Pantymwyn
Mold (Yr Wyddgrug)
Moel Famau
Cadole
Gwernymynydd
Tafarn-y-Gelyn
Llanferres
Maeshafn
Eryrys
Graianrhyd
Llanarmon-yn-Ial
Llandegla
Moel Garegog
Pen-y-stryt
Pentre-bwlch
Horseshoe Pass
FLINTSHIRE
CH
Conwy
Llandudno Junction
Deganwy
Glanwydden
Mochdre
Llansanffraid Glan Conwy
Dwygyfylchi
Capelulo
Foel Lus
Moelfre
Henryd
Pentrefelin
Rowen
Ty'n-y-groes
Tal-y-cafn
Eglwysbach
Llanbedr-y-cennin
Tal-y-bont
Dolgarrog
Pont Dolgarrog
Trefriw
Llanrwst
Vale of Conwy
Llanddoged
Pentre-tafarn-y-fedw
Melin-y-coed
Oerfa
Moel Seisiog
Nebo
Capel Garmon
Betws-y-coed
Oaklands
Capel Curig
Pont Cyfyng
Swallow Falls
Mynydd Cribau
Gwydyr Forest
Dolwyddelan
Pentre-bont
Penmachno
Rhydlanfair
Glan Conwy
Pentrefoelas
Ysbyty Ifan
Rhydlydan
Pont yr Alwen
Cefn-brith
Cerrigydrudion
Clocaenog Forest
Clocaenog
Cyffylliog
Bontuchel
Ruthin (Rhuthun)
Efenechtyd
Pwll-glas
Llanfair Dyffryn Clwyd
Graig-fechan
Pentre-celyn
Derwen
Llanelidan
Gwyddelwern
Bryneglwys
Llanbedr-Dyffryn-Clwyd
Rhewl
Llangynhafal
Gellifor
Hirwaen
Llandyrnog
Llanrhaeadr
Denbigh (Dinbych)
Henllan
Trefnant
Bodfari
Groes
Gwaenynog
Nantglyn
Cader
Pentre Saron
Llannefydd
Plas-yn-Cwm
Bont-newydd
Cefn Berain
Betws-yn-Rhos
Llanfair Talhaiarn
Llangernyw
Llansannan
Bylchau
Pen-cae-cwm
Gwytherin
Pandy Tudur
Mynydd Hiraethog
Sportsman's Arms
Gorsedd Bran
Alwen Res
Llyn Brenig
Old Colwyn
Llysfaen
Rhyd-y-foel
St George
Llanelian-yn-Rhos
Dolwen
Moelfre Isaf
Moelfre Uchaf
Mynydd Bodrochwyn
Bryn-y-maen
Trofarth
Mynydd Branar
Dawn
Gell
Mwdwl Eithin
Hafodunos
Rhos-y-mawn
Wenlli
Pentre Isaf
Tan-y-fron
Deunant
Rhydgaled
Llyn Aled
Aled Isaf Res
Moel Llyn
Hafod-Dinbych
Glasfryn
Llyn Alwen
CONWY
LL
DENBIGHSHIRE
VALE OF CLWYD
CLWYDIAN RANGE
Ffridd Fawr
Meifod
Cefn Du
Clawdd-newydd
Craig Bron-banog
Brynsaithmarchog
Pentre-llyn-cymmer
Nant y Garth Pass
Moel Wau
Mynydd Cricor
Cefn Coch
Moel y Gamelin
Glanaber Terrace
Pen y Bedw
Carrog
Garn Prys
Mwdwl-eithin
Llangwyfan
Moel Llys-y-coed
Ffordd-las
Brookhouse
Waen
Llanynys
Caerwys
Afon-wen
Ysceifiog
Lixwm
Walwen
Calcoed
Babell
Pen-y-cefn
Axton
Gwaenysgor
Gop Hill
Trelawnyd
Ochr-y-foel
Marian Cwm
Cwm
Llanasa
Pen-y-ffordd
Ffynnongroyw
Llanerch-y-Môr
Llannerch Hall
Graig
Groesffordd Marli
Pengwern
Morfa Rhuddlan
A55
A547
A548
A470
A5
A543
A544
A525
A541
A5026
A5151
A494
A5104
A546
B5113
B5381
B5382
B5384
B5106
B5427
B5428
B5429
B5105
37

A
B
C
D
E
55
1
2
3
4
5
6
7
47
38
SOUTHPORT
Formby
Formby Point
LIVERPOOL BAY
Birkenhead to hours
Belfast 8
Dublin 8
Liverpool to hours
Douglas 2½-4
Dublin 8
WALLASEY
BOOTLE
CROSBY
LIVERPOOL
BIRKENHEAD
See page 120 for postcode detail
MERSEYSIDE
HUYTON
ST HELENS
WIDNES
RUNCORN
HALTON
BEBINGTON
Hoylake
West Kirby
Heswall
Neston
ELLESMERE PORT
CHESTER
LIVERPOOL JOHN LENNON
ORMSKIRK
Skelmersdale
WIGAN
CHORLEY
LANCASHIRE
PR
WN
L
WA
CH
LL
SY
Frodsham
Helsby
Flint (Y Fflint)
Holywell (Treffynnon)
FLINTSHIRE
Mold (Yr Wyddgrug)
Buckley (Bwcle)
Connah's Quay
Queensferry
Hawarden (Penarlâg)
DENBIGHSHIRE
Ruthin (Rhuthun)
WREXHAM
WREXHAM (Wrecsam)
Point of Ayr
Hilbre Island
Talacre
Mostyn
Prestatyn
Tarporley
Kelsall
0 2 4 6 miles
0 2 4 6 8 10 km

49
56
50
39
See pages 116 - 117 for postcode detail
BLACKBURN WITH DARWEN
BL
OL
HX
HD
WEST YORKS
GREATER MANCHESTER
WA
SK
CW
ST
DE
DERBYSHIRE
CHESHIRE
STAFFS
WARRINGTON
BOLTON
BURY
ROCHDALE
OLDHAM
SALFORD
MANCHESTER
STOCKPORT
MACCLESFIELD
WINSFORD
HUDDERSFIELD
NEWCASTLE-UNDER-LYME
ASHTON-UNDER-LYNE
RAWTENSTALL
CREWE
Wilmslow
Knutsford
Altrincham
Sale
Stretford
Hyde
Glossop
Buxton
Congleton
Leek
Sandbach
Northwich
Middlewich
Alsager
Kidsgrove
Biddulph
Leigh
Atherton
Heywood
Middleton
Prestwich
Radcliffe
Whitefield
Swinton
Eccles
Irlam
Urmston
Stalybridge
Dukinfield
Denton
Marple
Hazel Grove
Poynton
Bramhall
Cheadle
Chapel-en-le-Frith
Whaley Bridge
New Mills
Hayfield
Holmfirth
Marsden
Meltham
Uppermill
Mossley
Littleborough
Milnrow
Ramsbottom
Tottington
Farnworth
Walkden
Westhoughton
Horwich
Tyldesley
Culcheth
Golborne
Lymm
Holmes Chapel
Bollington
Disley
F
G
H
J
K
1
2
3
4
5
6
7

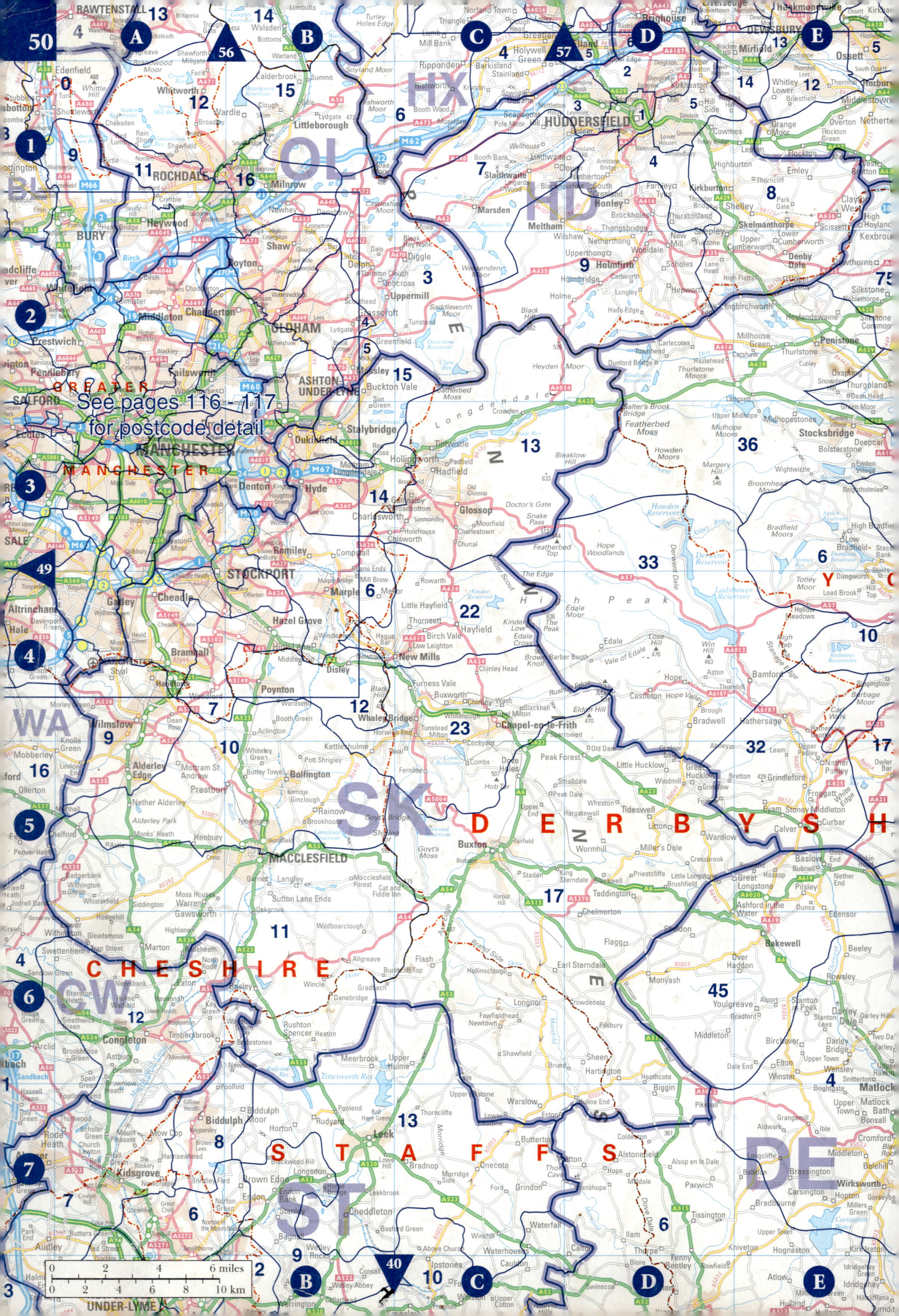
50
56
57
49
40
75
A
B
C
D
E
1
2
3
4
5
6
7
See pages 116 - 117
for postcode detail
GREATER
MANCHESTER
CHESHIRE
DERBYSHIRE
STAFFS
OL
HX
HD
SK
WA
CW
ST
DE
RAWTENSTALL
ROCHDALE
BURY
OLDHAM
HUDDERSFIELD
DEWSBURY
MANCHESTER
SALFORD
STOCKPORT
MACCLESFIELD
ASHTON-UNDER-LYNE
Heywood
Middleton
Whitefield
Prestwich
Milnrow
Littleborough
Whitworth
Royton
Shaw
Chadderton
Failsworth
Stalybridge
Dukinfield
Hyde
Denton
Romiley
Marple
Hazel Grove
Bramhall
Cheadle
Gatley
Altrincham
Hale
Wilmslow
Alderley Edge
Poynton
Disley
New Mills
Hayfield
Glossop
Hollingworth
Whaley Bridge
Chapel-en-le-Frith
Buxton
Bollington
Congleton
Biddulph
Leek
Kidsgrove
Bakewell
Matlock
Wirksworth
Holmfirth
Meltham
Marsden
Slaithwaite
Penistone
Stocksbridge
Honley
Kirkburton
Skelmanthorpe
Denby Dale
Uppermill
Mossley
Longdendale
High Peak
PEAK
Hathersage
Tideswell
Castleton
Grindleford
Edale
Kinder Scout
UNDER-LYME
0
2
4
6 miles
0
2
4
6
8
10 km

WEST YORKS
WF
NORTH YORKSHIRE
EAST RIDING OF YORKSHIRE
DN
NORTH LINCOLNSHIRE
SOUTH YORKSHIRE
S
DERBYSHIRE
NOTTINGHAMSHIRE
NG
F
G
H
J
K
58
52
41
1
2
3
4
5
6
7
DONCASTER
BARNSLEY
ROTHERHAM
SHEFFIELD
CHESTERFIELD
MANSFIELD
WORKSOP
Retford (East Retford)
NEWARK TRENT
KIRKBY IN ASHFIELD
Sutton in Ashfield
Goole
Thorne
Hatfield
Adwick le Street
Conisbrough
Mexborough
Wath upon Dearne
Hoyland
Dronfield
Staveley
Bolsover
Clowne
Alfreton
Ripley
Hucknall
Bawtry
Tickhill
Maltby
Dinnington
Eckington
Killamarsh
Ollerton
Edwinstowe
Warsop
Southwell
Bingham
ROBIN HOOD DONCASTER SHEFFIELD

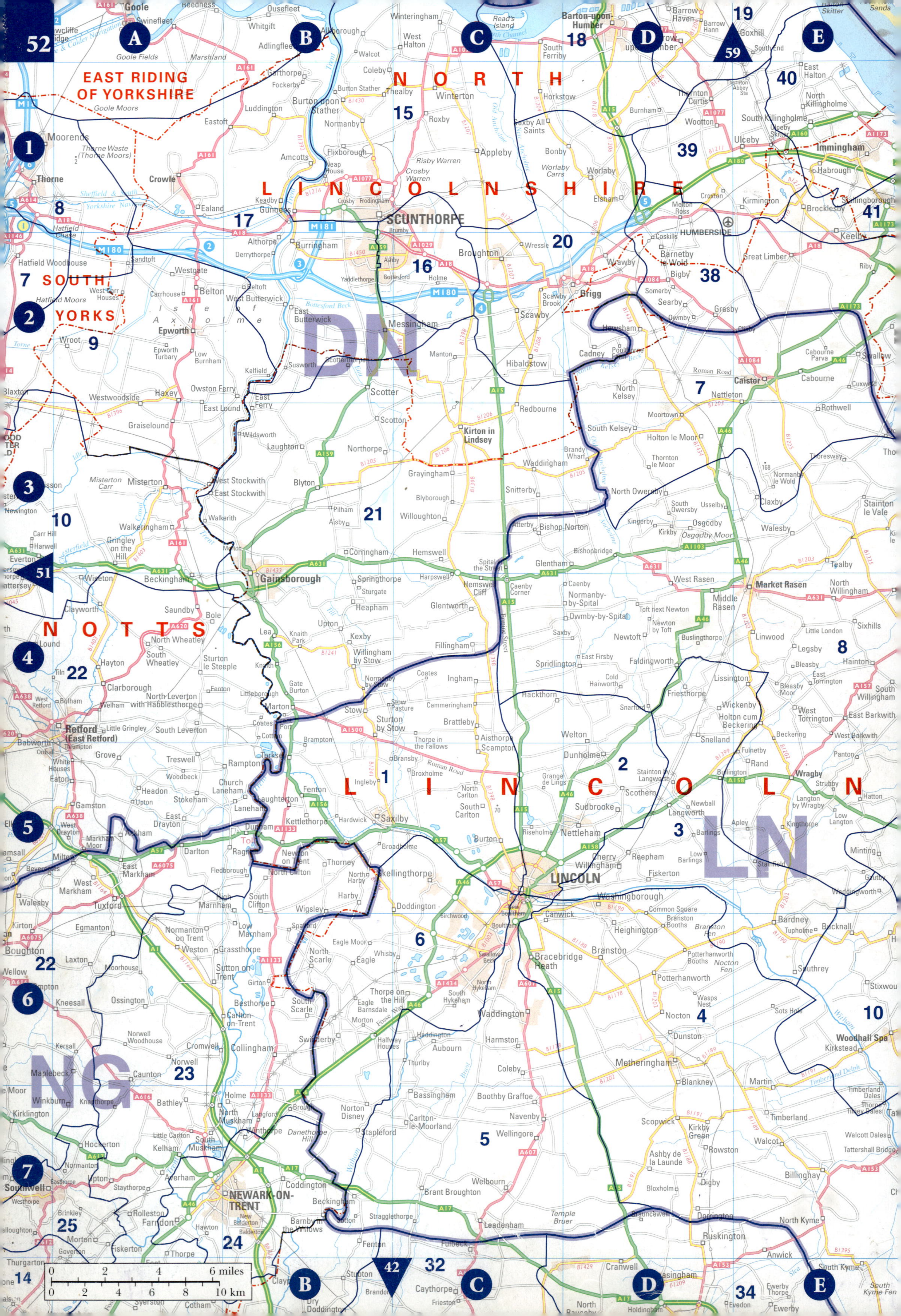

EAST RIDING OF YORKSHIRE
NORTH LINCOLNSHIRE
SOUTH YORKS
NOTTS
LINCOLN
DN
LN
NG
SCUNTHORPE
Gainsborough
LINCOLN
NEWARK-ON-TRENT
Retford (East Retford)
Market Rasen
Brigg
Goole
Barton-upon-Humber
Immingham
HUMBERSIDE
Caistor
Kirton in Lindsey
Epworth
Thorne
Crowle
Saxilby
Wragby
Metheringham
Woodhall Spa
Bracebridge Heath
Waddington
Welton
Nettleham
Tuxford
Collingham
Isle of Axholme
0 2 4 6 miles
0 2 4 6 8 10 km

F
G
H
J
K
1
2
3
4
5
6
7
HU
EAST RIDING OF YORKSHIRE
NORTH
EAST
LINCOLNSHIRE
S H I R E
THE WOLDS
PE
Patrington
Welwick
Weeton
Out Newton
Easington
Skeffling
Skeffling Clays
Sunk Island
Old Hall
Sunk Island Sands
Kilnsea
Kilnsea Clays
Spurn Head
Mouth of the Humber
Healing
GRIMSBY
Cleethorpes
Humberston
Aylesby
Bradley
Laceby
Scartho
Barnoldby le Beck
Waltham
New Waltham
Holton le Clay
Tetney Lock
Tetney
North Cotes
Brigsley
Ashby cum Fenby
Hatcliffe
East Ravendale
North Thoresby
Marshchapel
Grainthorpe
Donna Nook
North Somercotes
Fulstow
Covenham Res
Ludborough
Covenham St Bartholomew
Covenham St Mary
Conisholme
South Somercotes
Saltfleet
Utterby
Yarburgh
Binbrook
North Ormsby
Skidbrooke
Saltfleetby St Clements
Alvingham
North Cockerington
Fotherby
Little Grimsby
North Elkington
Kelstern
Saltfleetby All Saints
South Cockerington
Saltfleetby St Peter
Theddlethorpe St Helen
Theddlethorpe All Saints
Louth
Keddington
South Elkington
Welton le Wold
Burgh on Bain
Grimoldby
Manby
Little Carlton
Great Carlton
Legbourne
Gayton le Marsh
Mablethorpe
Trusthorpe
Sutton on Sea
Sandilands
Kingston upon Hull to
hours
Rotterdam 12
Zeebrugge 14
Gayton le Wold
Biscathorpe
Hallington
Raithby
Withcall
Donington on Bain
Little Cawthorpe
Tathwell
Haugham
Muckton
Authorpe
Strubby
Withern
Maltby le Marsh
Thorpe
Woodthorpe
Beesby
Hagnaby
Claythorpe
Belleau
Aby
Saleby
Markby
Hannah
Stenigot
Cawkwell
Asterby
Market Stainton
Goulceby
Scamblesby
Farforth
Ruckland
Burwell
Walmsgate
Worlaby
Oxcombe
Swaby
South Thoresby
Greenfield
Thoresthorpe
Alford
Bilsby
Asserby
Thurlby
Huttoft
Anderby Creek
Anderby
Mumby
Authorpe Row
Hogsthorpe
Chapel St Leonards
Flint Hill
Hemingby
Belchford
Tetford
Salmonby
Fulletby
South Ormsby
Ketsby
Calceby
Driby
Haugh
Rigsby
Bilsby Field
Farlesthorpe
Cumberworth
Mawthorpe
Well
Ulceby
Skendleby Psalter
Bonthorpe
Willoughby
Helsey
Sloothby
Ingoldmells
Ingoldmells Point
Addlethorpe
Wispington
Edlington
Farthorpe
Midthorpe
West Ashby
Low Toynton
Horncastle
High Toynton
Thimbleby
Langton
Ashby Puerorum
Somersby
Harrington
Bag Enderby
Brinkhill
Sutterby
Greetham
Claxby St Andrew
Langton
Sausthorpe
Skendleby
Welton le Marsh
Hasthorpe
Partney
Candlesby
Orby
Orby Marsh
Raithby
Scremby
Ashby by Partney
Gunby
Spilsby
Halton Holegate
Hundleby
Great Steeping
Bratoft
Irby in the Marsh
Burgh le Marsh
Winthorpe
Seathorne
Skegness
Thornton
Old Woodhall
Martin
Mareham on the Hill
Hameringham
Lusby
Asgarby
Dalderby
Claxby Pluckacre
Mavis Enderby
Old Bolingbroke
East Keal
West Keal
Toynton All Saints
Toynton St Peter
Toynton Fen Side
Little Steeping
Firsby
Thorpe Culvert
Thorpe St Peter
Croft
Croft Marsh
Seacroft
Roughton
Wood Enderby
Moorby
Miningsby
Haltham
Wilksby
East Kirkby
Hagnaby
Kirkby on Bain
Mareham le Fen
Revesby
Revesby Bridge
Keal Cotes
Stickford
Fendike Corner
Wainfleet Bank
Wainfleet All Saints
Havenhouse Sta
Gibraltar
Gibraltar Pt
Tumby
Coningsby
Moor Side
Tumby Woodside
New Bolingbroke
New Leake
Midville
Key's Toft
Wainfleet St. Mary
Stickney
East Fen
Friskney Eaudyke
Friskney
Wainfleet Sand
Hawthorn Hill
New York
Sandy Bank
Scrub Hill
Bunker's Hill
Carrington
Lade Bank
West Fen
Northlands
Wildmore Fen
Leake Commonside
Wrangle Lowgate
Wrangle
Friskney Flats
THE WASH
Boston Deeps
Lynn Deeps
Long Sand
Frithville
Sibsey
Old Leake
Gipsey Bridge
Holland Fen
Langrick
Langrick Bridge
Fishtoft Drove
High Ferry
Frith Bank
Leverton
Leake Hurn's End
Leverton Outgate
Leverton Lucasgate
Dyke
Amber Hill
Anton's Gowt
43
9
11
12
13
19
20
22
23
24
25
31
32
33
34
35
36
37

A
B
C
D
E
1
2
3
4
5
6
7
19
18
14
Stub Place
Corney
Whitfell
Bigert Mire
Ulpha Park
Prior Park
Stoneside Hill
Selker Bay
Hycemoor
Hyton
Bootle
Bootle Fell
Duddon Bridge
Annaside
Broadgate
White Combe
Black Combe
The Green
Lady Hall
Whitbeck
A595
Whicham
The Hill
Silecroft
A5093
Kirksanton
Millom
Haverigg
Steel Green
Haverigg Point
Duddon Sands
North Scale
Tummer Hill Scar
Isle of Walney
same scale as main map
ISLE OF MAN
IM
Point of Ayre
The Ayres
Rue Point
Cranstal
Glentruan
The Lhen
Bride
Andreas
Jurby East
Sartfield
Shellag Point
Jurby Head
Jurby West
Ballasalla
Sandygate
Regaby
St Judes
Crawyn
The Cronk
The Curraghs
Kella
Dhoor
Ramsey Bay
Ramsey
Sulby
Churchtown
Orrisdale
Ballaugh
Orrisdale Head
Glen Auldyn
Port e Vullen
Maughold Head
Maughold
Ravensdale
Dreemskerry
Slieau Managh
North Barrule
Kirk Michael
Slieau Curn
Ballajora
ISLE OF MAN
Slieau Dhoo
Corrany
Slieau Freoaghane
Clagh Ouyr
Glen Mona
Ballacarnane Beg
Sulby Reservoir
Snaefell
Slieau Lhean
Dhoon
Barregarrow
Gob y Deigan
Sartfell
Port Cornaa
Knocksharry
Little London
Beinn-y-Phott
Bulgham Bay
Peel
Ballagyr
Cronk-y-Voddy
St Patrick's Isle
Lambfell Moar
Injebreck
Colden
Laxey
Contrary Head
Ballig
Laxey Head
Ballacannell
Knockaloe Moar
Slieau Ruy
Greeba Mountain
Baldwin
Patrick
St John's
Baldrine
Garwick Bay
Clay Head
Glenmaye
Sulby
Hillberry
Dalby Point
Lower Foxdale
Crosby
Onchan
Dalby Mountain
Dalby
Glen Vine
Port Groudle
Foxdale
Eairy
Garth
Union Mills
Strang
Niarbyl Island
Niarbyl Bay
Onchan Head
South Barrule
Douglas Bay
DOUGLAS
Stuggadhoo
Braaid
Cooil
Close Clark
Stroin Vuigh
Quine's Hill
Douglas Head
Ballamodha
Ronague
St Mark's
Newtown
Lingague
Grenaby
Ballavoare
Little Ness
Fleshwick Bay
Ballakilpheric
Colby
Ballabeg
Bradda
Ballafesson
Ballasalla
Santon Head
Bradda Head
Port Erin
Croit e Caley
Balladoole
ISLE OF MAN
Port Grenaugh
Derbyhaven
Calf of Man
Cregneash
The Howe
Port St Mary
Bay ny Carrickey
Castletown
St Michael's Island
Perwick Bay
Spanish Head
Langness
Castletown Bay
Dreswick Point
Chicken Rock
hours
Belfast (summer only) 2¾
Dublin (summer only) 2¾-4¾
Heysham 2-3½
Liverpool 2½-4
0 2 4 6 miles
0 2 4 6 8 10 km

CUMBRIA
LANCASHIRE
LA
PR
BB
BLACKPOOL
BLACKBURN WITH DARWEN
MORECAMBE BAY
KENDAL
Sedbergh
Kirkby Lonsdale
Ulverston
BARROW-IN-FURNESS
Dalton-in-Furness
Grange-over-Sands
Arnside
Milnthorpe
Carnforth
Morecambe
Heysham
LANCASTER
Bolton-le-Sands
Galgate
Garstang
Fleetwood
Cleveleys
Thornton
Poulton-le-Fylde
Knott End-on-Sea
Preesall
Kirkham
LYTHAM ST ANNE'S
PRESTON
Longridge
Ribchester
BLACKBURN
Darwen
LEYLAND
CHORLEY
Bamber Bridge
Walton-le-Dale
Clitheroe
Ingleton
High Bentham
Slaidburn
Forest of Bowland
Douglas 2-3½ hrs
Larne 8 hrs
SOUTHPORT
Tarleton
Banks
Hesketh Bank
Freckleton
Warton
Broughton
Samlesbury
Whittle-le-Woods
Hoghton
Chipping
Dunsop Bridge
Newton
Hornby
Caton
Halton
Slyne
Silverdale
Yealand Conyers
Burton-in-Kendal
Cartmel
Newby Bridge
Levens
Sedgwick
Oxenholme
Killington Lake
Dent
Pilling
Cockerham
Glasson
Sunderland Point
Overton
Middleton
Great Eccleston
St Michael's on Wyre
Bilsborrow
Catterall
Goosnargh
Grimsargh
Wesham
Elswick
Singleton
Staining
Hambleton
Stalmine
BLACKPOOL INTERNATIONAL
Lytham
Longton
Hutton
Walmer Bridge
Much Hoole
Croston
Eccleston
Euxton
Whittle-le-Woods
Mellor
Wilpshire
Salesbury
Osbaldeston
F G H J K
1 2 3 4 5 6 7
60
23
56
48

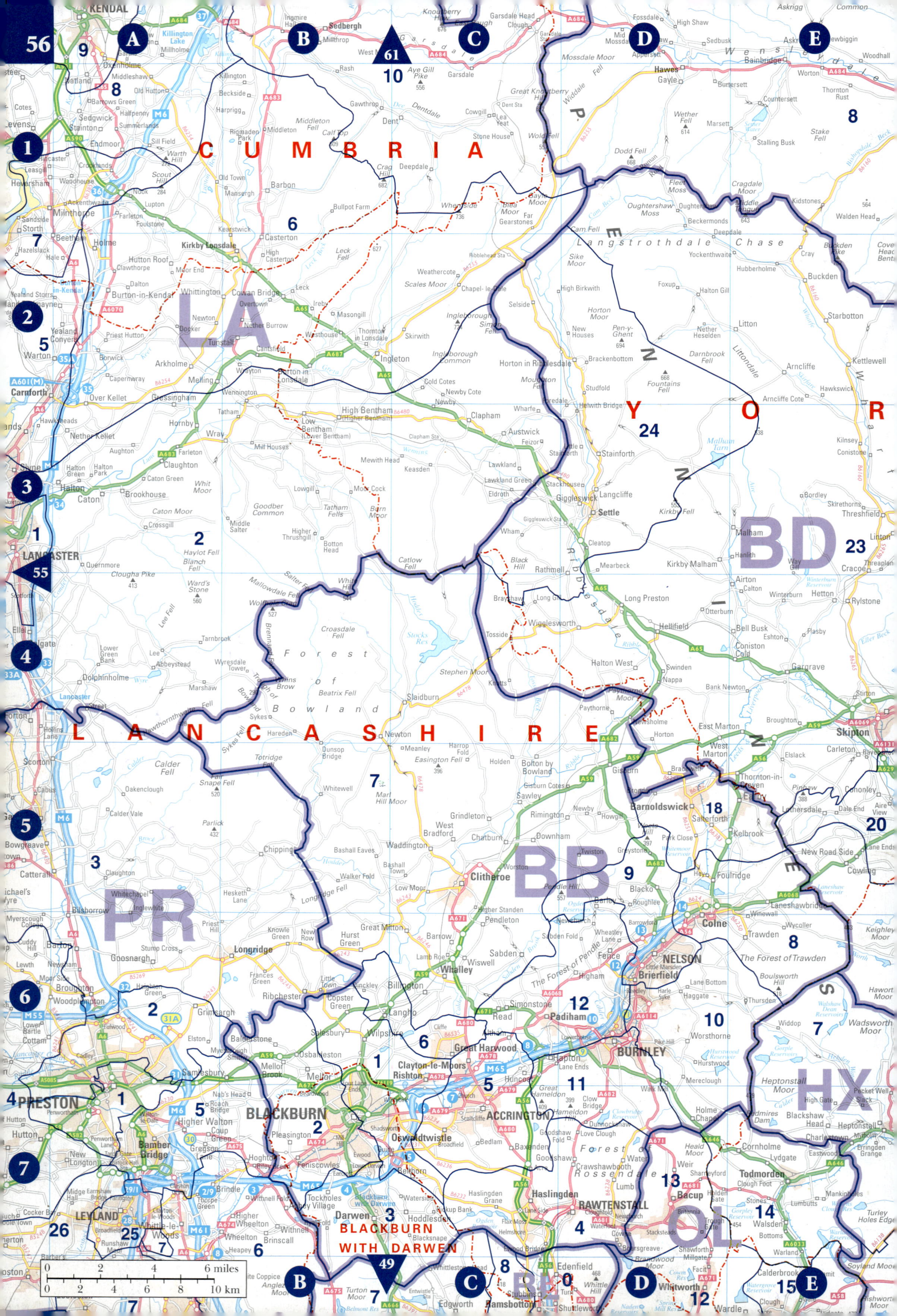
56
61
55
49
A
B
C
D
E
1
2
3
4
5
6
7
CUMBRIA
LANCASHIRE
YORKSHIRE
P. E N N I N E S
LA
BD
BB
PR
HX
OL
Kendal
Sedbergh
Hawes
Kirkby Lonsdale
Carnforth
Ingleton
High Bentham
Settle
Lancaster
Skipton
Clitheroe
Barnoldswick
Colne
Nelson
Burnley
Padiham
Accrington
Blackburn
Darwen
Preston
Leyland
Haslingden
Rawtenstall
Bacup
Todmorden
Longridge
Whalley
Forest of Bowland
Langstrothdale Chase
BLACKBURN WITH DARWEN
0 2 4 6 miles
0 2 4 6 8 10 km

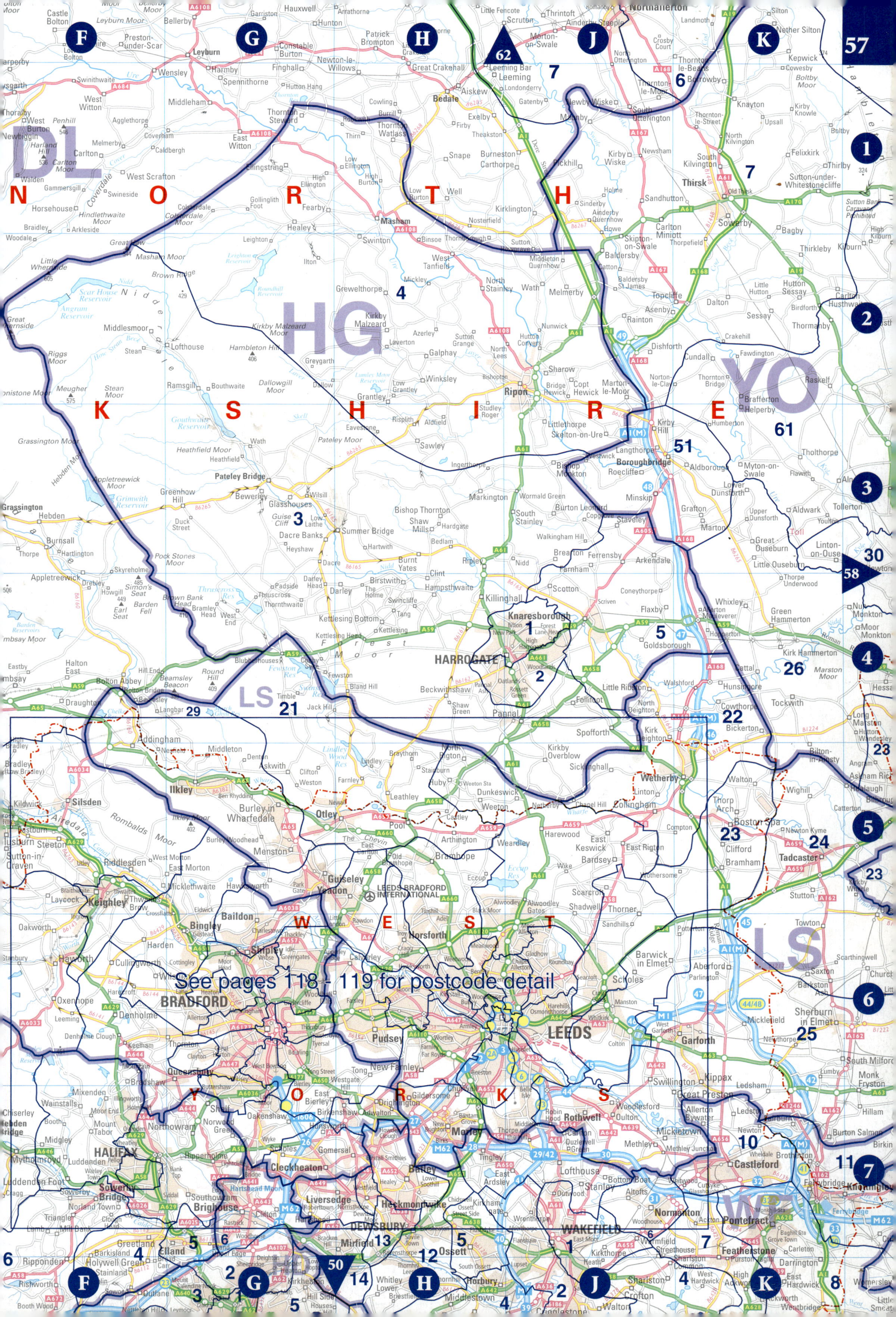
See pages 118 - 119 for postcode detail
DL
HG
YO
LS
WF
N O R T H
Y O R K S H I R E
W E S T
Y O R K S
62
58
50
Northallerton
Leyburn
Bedale
Thirsk
Masham
Ripon
Pateley Bridge
Boroughbridge
Knaresborough
HARROGATE
Wetherby
Ilkley
Otley
Keighley
Bingley
Shipley
BRADFORD
LEEDS
Pudsey
Morley
Tadcaster
Garforth
Castleford
Pontefract
Normanton
WAKEFIELD
HALIFAX
Brighouse
Cleckheaton
Dewsbury
Batley
Ossett
Elland
Heckmondwike
Horsforth
Guiseley
Yeadon
LEEDS BRADFORD INTERNATIONAL
Rothwell
Knottingley
Featherstone
Sherburn in Elmet

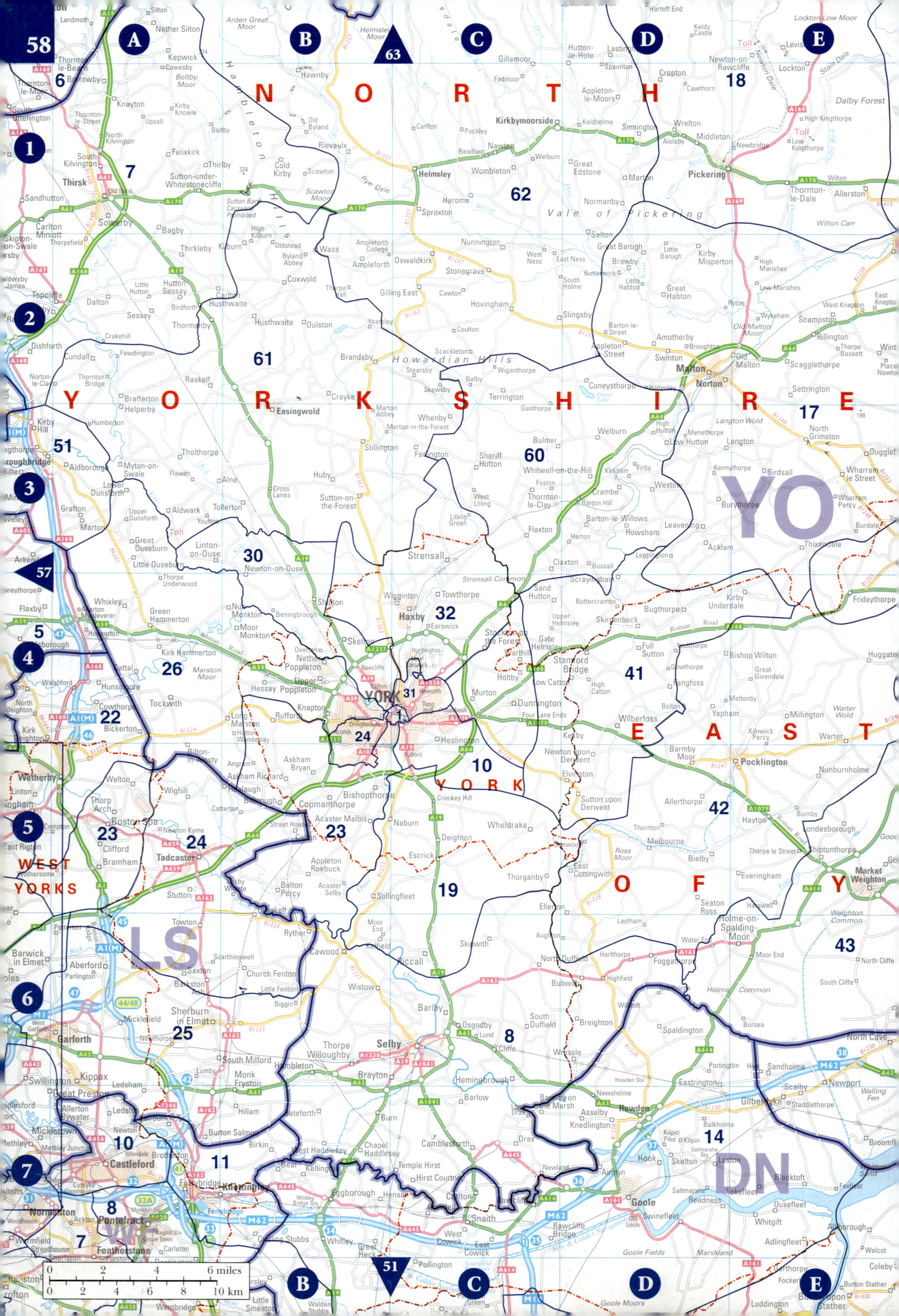

A
B
C
D
E
63
1
2
3
4
5
6
7
57
51
N O R T H
Y O R K S H I R E
E A S T
O F
Y
YO
LS
DN
WEST YORKS
YORK
Nether Silton
Arden Great Moor
Helmsley Moor
Hartoft End
Lockton Low Moor
Landmoth
Kepwick
Cowesby
Boltby Moor
Hawnby
Gillamoor
Fadmoor
Hutton-le-Hole
Lastingham
Spaunton
Keldy Castle
Levisham
Newton-on-Rawcliffe
Lockton
Cropton
Cawthorn
Appleton-le-Moors
Dalby Forest
Thornton-le-Beans
Borrowby
Thornton-le-Moor
South Otterington
Knayton
Thornton-le-Street
Upsall
Kirby Knowle
Boltby
Old Byland
Rievaulx
Carlton
Pockley
Kirkbymoorside
Keldholme
Sinnington
Wrelton
Aislaby
Middleton
Newbridge
High Kingthorpe
Low Kingthorpe
North Kilvington
South Kilvington
Felixkirk
Thirlby
Cold Kirby
Scawton
Scawton Moor
Thirsk
Old Thirsk
Sutton-under-Whitestonecliffe
Sutton Bank
Beadlam
Nawton
Welburn
Wombleton
Great Edstone
Marton
Pickering
Helmsley
Rye Dale
Harome
Sproxton
Vale of Pickering
Normanby
Thornton-le-Dale
Wilton
Allerston
Wilton Carr
Sandhutton
Sowerby
Carlton Miniott
Thorpefield
Skipton-on-Swale
Bagby
High Kilburn
Kilburn
Oldstead
Byland Abbey
Thirkleby
Wass
Ampleforth College
Ampleforth
Oswaldkirk
Nunnington
Stonegrave
West Ness
East Ness
Salton
Great Barugh
Little Barugh
Kirby Misperton
Brawby
Butterwick
Little Habton
Great Habton
High Marishes
Low Marishes
Coxwold
Thorpe Hall
Gilling East
Cawton
Hovingham
South Holme
Little Hutton
Hutton Sessay
Topcliffe
Dalton
Sessay
Birdforth
Carlton Husthwaite
Husthwaite
Thormanby
Oulston
Yearsley
Coulton
Slingsby
Barton-le-Street
Amotherby
Broughton
Ryton
Wykeham
Scampston
West Knapton
East Knapton
Old Malton Moor
Rillington
Thorpe Bassett
Scagglethorpe
Dishforth
Crakehill
Cundall
Fawdington
Norton-le-Clay
Thornton Bridge
Raskelf
Brandsby
Stearsby
Howardian Hills
Scackleton
Dalby
Wiganthorpe
Skewsby
Appleton-le-Street
Swinton
Malton
Old Malton
Norton
Settrington
Brafferton
Helperby
Easingwold
Crayke
Marton Abbey
Marton-in-the-Forest
Whenby
Terrington
Ganthorpe
Coneysthorpe
Great Lake
Langton Wold
North Grimston
Kirby Hill
Humberton
Boroughbridge
Aldborough
Myton-on-Swale
Tholthorpe
Flawith
Stillington
Farlington
Sheriff Hutton
Bulmer
Welburn
High Hutton
Menethorpe
Low Hutton
Langton
Duggleby
Whitwell-on-the-Hill
Kirkham
Firby
Westow
Kennythorpe
Birdsall
Wharram-le-Street
Wharram Percy
Grafton
Lower Dunsforth
Upper Dunsforth
Alne
Huby
Cross Lanes
Sutton-on-the-Forest
West Lilling
Lilling Green
Foston
Thornton-le-Clay
Crambe
Barton Hill
Barton-le-Willows
Howsham
Leavening
Burythorpe
Burdale
Marton
Aldwark
Youlton
Tollerton
Great Ouseburn
Little Ouseburn
Linton-on-Ouse
Newton-on-Ouse
Thorpe Underwood
Strensall
Strensall Common
Flaxton
Harton
Claxton
Bossall
Scrayingham
Leppington
Acklam
Thixendale
Arkendale
Whixley
Green Hammerton
Flaxby
Nun Monkton
Moor Monkton
Beningbrough
Shipton
Wigginton
Towthorpe
Haxby
Earswick
Sand Hutton
Buttercrambe
Upper Helmsley
Skirpenbeck
Bugthorpe
Kirby Underdale
Fridaythorpe
Kirk Hammerton
Marston Moor
Overton
Nether Poppleton
Upper Poppleton
Skelton
Huntington
Stockton on the Forest
Warthill
Gate Helmsley
Full Sutton
Stamford Bridge
Youlthorpe
Bishop Wilton
Great Givendale
Huggate
Walshford
Hunsingore
Cattal
Tockwith
Hessay
Rawcliffe
Clifton
Heworth
Holtby
Murton
Low Catton
High Catton
Gowthorpe
Fangfoss
Meltonby
Yapham
Bolton
Millington
Warter Wold
North Deighton
Kirk Deighton
Cowthorpe
Bickerton
Knapton
Rufforth
Long Marston
Hutton Wandesley
Dringhouses
Acomb
Heslington
Dunnington
Four Lane Ends
Kexby
Wilberfoss
Kilnwick Percy
Warter
Wetherby
Linton
Bilton-in-Ainsty
Angram
Askham Bryan
Askham Richard
Fulford
Newton upon Derwent
Elvington
Barmby Moor
Pocklington
Nunburnholme
Walton
Wighill
Healaugh
Thorp Arch
Boston Spa
Bilbrough
Catterton
Copmanthorpe
Bishopthorpe
Crockey Hill
Sutton upon Derwent
Allerthorpe
Hayton
Burnby
Londesborough
Newton Kyme
Street Houses
Acaster Malbis
Naburn
Wheldrake
Thornton
Melbourne
Shiptonthorpe
Market Weighton
East Rigton
Clifford
Bramham
Tadcaster
Colton
Deighton
Escrick
Storwood
Ross Moor
Bielby
Thorpe le Street
Appleton Roebuck
East Cottingwith
Thorganby
Everingham
Bolton Percy
Acaster Selby
Stillingfleet
Ellerton
Seaton Ross
Harswell
Stutton
Towton
Ryther
Moor End
Kelfield
Skipwith
Laytham
Aughton
Holme-on-Spalding-Moor
Weighton Common
Barwick in Elmet
Aberford
Parlington
Scarthingwell
Saxton
Church Fenton
Barkston Ash
Little Fenton
Cawood
Riccall
North Duffield
Harlthorpe
Highfield
Foggathorpe
Water End
Moor End
North Cliffe
South Cliffe
Holme Common
Bubwith
Biggin
Wistow
Barlby
Willitoft
Garforth
Micklefield
Sherburn in Elmet
Newthorpe
South Duffield
Osgodby
Lund
Cliffe
Breighton
Spaldington
Bursea
North Cave
Thorpe Willoughby
Selby
Hambleton
South Milford
Lumby
Monk Fryston
Brayton
Hemingbrough
Wressle
Portington
Sandholme
Newport
Walling Fen
Kippax
Swillington
Great Preston
Ledsham
Allerton Bywater
Ledston
Hillam
Burton Salmon
Gateforth
Barlow
Long Drax
Barmby on the Marsh
Howden
Newsholme
Asselby
Knedlington
Eastrington
Gilberdyke
Scalby
Staddlethorpe
Balkholme
Methley
Mickletown
Castleford
Whitwood
Normanton
Newton
Brotherton
Fairburn
Ferrybridge
Knottingley
Birkin
West Haddlesey
Chapel Haddlesey
Burn
Camblesforth
Drax
Newland
Airmyn
Hook
Kilpin
Kilpin Pike
Skelton
Saltmarshe
Laxton
Blacktoft
Faxfleet
Broomfleet
Beal
Kellington
Eggborough
Hensall
Temple Hirst
Hirst Courtney
Carlton
Snaith
Rawcliffe
Rawcliffe Bridge
Goole
Old Goole
Swinefleet
Reedness
Yokefleet
Ousefleet
Whitgift
Pontefract
Ackton
Featherstone
Purston Jaglin
Carleton
Darrington
Whitley
Cridling Stubbs
Great Heck
Pollington
West Cowick
East Cowick
Goole Fields
Marshland
Adlingfleet
Alkborough
Walcot
Coleby
Garthorpe
Fockerby
Burton upon Stather
Luddington
Goole Moors
Little Smeaton
Walden Stubbs
Wentbridge
Sharlston
Snydale
Wrenthorpe
Toll
0 2 4 6 miles
0 2 4 6 8 10 km

F
G
H
J
K
1
2
3
4
5
6
7
SCARBOROUGH
Cromer Point
Scalby
Hackness
Suffield
Silpho
Langdale End
Wrench Green
Everley
Irton Moor
Wykeham Forest
West Ayton
East Ayton
Hutton Buscel
Sawdon
Eastfield
Osgodby
Cayton Bay
Black Rocks
South Bay
Crossgates
Irton
Seamer
Cayton
Lebberston
Gristhorpe
The Wyke
Filey Brigg
Filey
Filey Bay
Ruston
Wykeham
Snainton
Brompton
Staxton
Flixton
Folkton
West Flotmanby
Muston
Willerby
Ganton
Potter Brompton
Sherburn
East Heslerton
West Heslerton
Sherburn Wold
Hunmanby
Reighton
Reighton Sands
Speeton
Crab Rocks
Buckton
Bempton
Flamborough Head
Flamborough
Marton
Sewerby
Fordon
Foxholes
Wold Newton
Burton Fleming
Grindale
Butterwick
Weaverthorpe
Helperthorpe
Octon
Thwing
Boynton
Bridlington
Hilderthorpe
Bessingby
Carnaby
Swaythorpe
Rudston
Gypsey Race
Roman Road
East Lutton
West Lutton
Kirby Grindalythe
Cowlam Manor
Sledmere
Langtoft
WOLDS
West End
Kilham
Haisthorpe
Thornholme
Burton Agnes
Ruston Parva
Wilsthorpe
Carnaby Moor
BRIDLINGTON BAY
Fraisthorpe
Harpham
Lowthorpe
Nafferton
Gransmoor
Barmston
Garton-on-the-Wolds
Wetwang
Elmswell
Driffield
Little Driffield
Kelleythorpe
Great Kelk
Lissett
Gembling
Ulrome
Tibthorpe Wold
Tibthorpe
Kirkburn
Eastburn
Southburn
Sunderlandwick
Skerne
Wansford
Foston on the Wolds
Beeford
Upton
Skipsea
Skipsea Brough
Brigham
Church End
North Frodingham
Dunnington
North End
Atwick
North Dalton
Bainton
Hutton Cranswick
Rotsea
Middleton-on-the-Wolds
Cawkeld
Watton
Watton Carrs
Hempholme
Bewholme
Hornsea
Hornsea Mere
RIDING
YORKSHIRE
Kilnwick
Lund
Beswick
Lockington
Thorpe
Burshill
Little Burton
Brandesburton
Seaton
Holme on the Wolds
South Dalton
Leven
Catwick
Little Catwick
Sigglesthorne
Goxhill
Rolston
Mappleton
Etton
Scorborough
New Arram
Arram
Leconfield
Little Hatfield
Great Hatfield
Great Cowden
Gardham
Cherry Burton
Arras
Routh
Tickton
Long Riston
Arnold
Rise
North End
Withernwick
Molescroft
BEVERLEY
Bishop Burton
Bishop Burton Wold
Weel
Skirlaugh
New Ellerby
Marton
Old Ellerby
West Newton
Aldbrough
East Newton
Etherdwick Grange
Newbald Wold
North Newbald
South Newbald
Walkington
Woodmansey
Wawne
Thearne
Swine
Coniston
Flinton
Garton
Grimston
Bentley
Risby
Dunswell
High Hunsley
Little Weighton
Skidby
Cottingham
Bransholme
Sutton-on-Hull
Ganstead
Thirtleby
Sproatley
Humbleton
Fitling
Hilston
Wyton
Bilton
Lelley
Danthorpe
Owstwick
Tunstall
Riplingham
Eppleworth
Haltemprice
Newland
Sutton Ings
Elstronwick
North End
South Cave
Willerby
Kirk Ella
West Ella
Anlaby
KINGSTON UPON HULL
Marfleet
Preston
East End
Burton Pidsea
Roos
HU
Dairy House
Wadworth Hill
Waxholme
Brantingham
Elloughton
Brough
Welton
Swanland
Melton
North Ferriby
Hessle
Hedon
Burstwick
Rimswell
Withernsea
Halsham
East End
Thorngumbald
Paull
Camerton
Ryehill
Keyingham
Hollym
Humber Bridge
Whitton Ness
Redcliff Channel
Read's Island
South Channel
Barton-upon-Humber
New Holland
Barrow Haven
Barrow Hann
Goxhill
Barrow upon Humber
East Halton Skitter
Paull Holme
Paull Holme Sands
Ottringham
Winestead
Patrington
Holmpton
Out Newton
Cherry Cobb Sands
Salthaugh Grange
Patrington Haven
Welwick
Weeton
Foulholme Sands
Sunk Island
Skeffling
Easington
Skeffling Clays
Old Hall
Whitton
West Halton
South Ferriby
Winteringham
NORTH LINCOLNSHIRE
South End
East Halton
Killingholme
Thornton Curtis
Horkstow
Winterton
Burnham
Rotterdam 12hrs
Zeebrugge 14hrs
Immingham
South Killingholme
52
40
A165
A171
A170
A64
A1039
A614
A166
A164
A1035
A1079
A1174
A1033
A1034
A15
A1077
A63
B1249
B1253
B1229
B1255
B1259
B1251
B1252
B1248
B1242
B1244
B1243
B1230
B1237
B1238
B1240
B1239
B1362
B1445
B1261
B1231
B1232
B1206
B1204
B1218
13
12
11
14
15
16
25
17
18
16
20
6
7
8
9
10
5
4
3
2
1
14
13
18
19
11
12
19
5

DUMFRIES & GALLOWAY
DG
SOLWAY FIRTH
Blackshaw Bank
Criffell
Carsethorn
Kirkbean
Southerness
Southerness Point
Borron Point
65
69
54
Bowness-on-Solway
Port Carlisle
Glasson
Burgh Marsh
Burgh by Sands
Rockcliffe Cross
CARLISLE
Grune Point
Skinburness
Silloth
Abbey Town
Kirkbride
Wigton
Dalston
Thursby
Aspatria
Allonby
Maryport
Cockermouth
WORKINGTON
WHITEHAVEN
Cleator Moor
Egremont
St Bees
St Bees Head
Seascale
Gosforth
Drigg
Ravenglass
Bootle
Keswick
Bassenthwaite
Bassenthwaite Lake
Derwent Water
Borrowdale
Buttermere
Crummock Water
Loweswater
Ennerdale Water
Wast Water
The Screes
Skiddaw
Skiddaw Forest
Blencathra (Saddleback)
Helvellyn
Thirlmere
Grasmere
Ambleside
Windermere
Bowness-on-Windermere
Coniston
Coniston Water
Hawkshead
Penruddock
Greystoke Forest
Hesket Newmarket
Sebergham
Caldbeck
Caldbeck Fells
Copeland Forest
CUMBRIAN MOUNTAINS
Furness Fells
CA
LA
CUM
DUMFRIES & GALLOWAY
6 miles
10 km

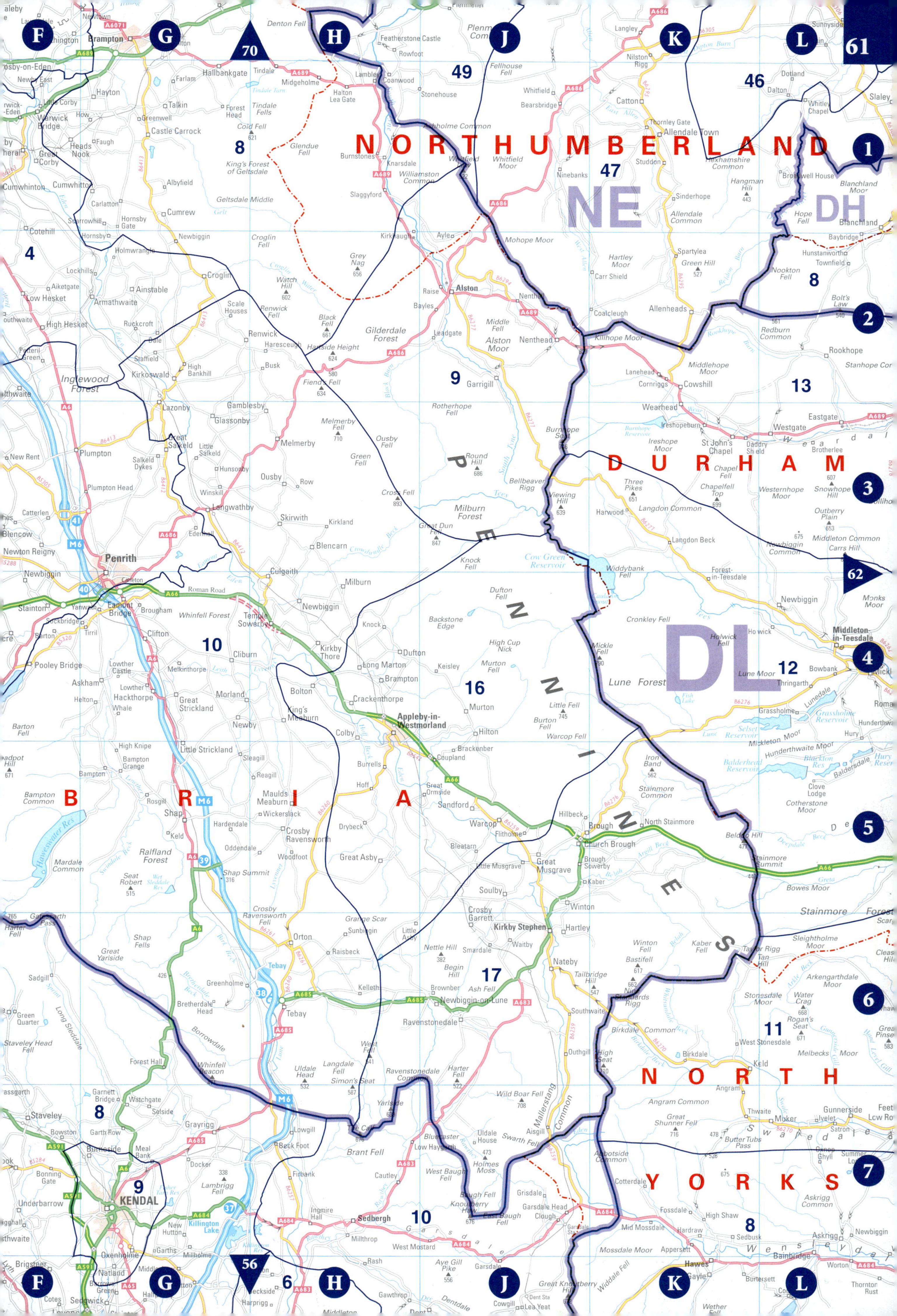
NORTHUMBERLAND
NE
DH
DURHAM
DL
CUMBRIA
NORTH YORKS
PENNINES
70
62
56
Brampton
Hallbankgate
Tindale
Featherstone Castle
Lambley
Stonehouse
Fellhouse Fell
Langley
Nilston Rigg
Catton
Allendale Town
Whitfield
Bearsbridge
Dalton
Slaley
Whitley Chapel
Hexhamshire Common
Blanchland
Sinderhope
Allenheads
Hayton
Talkin
Castle Carrock
King's Forest of Geltsdale
Geltsdale Middle
Glendue Fell
Knarsdale
Slaggyford
Williamston Common
Cumwhitton
Cumrew
Croglin
Kirkhaugh
Alston
Garrigill
Nenthead
Nenthall
Coalcleugh
Killhope Moor
Rookhope
Cowshill
Wearhead
Ireshopeburn
St John's Chapel
Westgate
Eastgate
Stanhope Common
Newbiggin
Kirkoswald
Lazonby
Great Salkeld
Plumpton
Melmerby
Ousby
Penrith
Eamont Bridge
Clifton
Brougham
Temple Sowerby
Kirkby Thore
Dufton
Knock
Milburn
Milburn Forest
Cross Fell
Great Dun Fell
Cow Green Reservoir
Widdybank Fell
Forest-in-Teesdale
Middleton-in-Teesdale
Lune Forest
Grassholme Reservoir
Selset Reservoir
Balderhead Reservoir
Blackton Res
Hury Res
Pooley Bridge
Askham
Helton
Bampton
Haweswater Res
Shap
Orton
Tebay
Crosby Ravensworth
Appleby-in-Westmorland
Brough
Church Brough
Kirkby Stephen
Warcop
Great Musgrave
Nateby
Newbiggin-on-Lune
Ravenstonedale
Sedbergh
Kendal
Staveley
Burneside
Killington Lake
Oxenholme
Natland
Mallerstang Common
Garsdale Head
Hawes
Gayle
Bainbridge
Askrigg
Keld
Thwaite
Muker
Swaledale
Wensleydale
Stainmore
Bowes Moor
Tan Hill
A6
A66
A686
A689
A683
A684
A685
A591
A69
M6

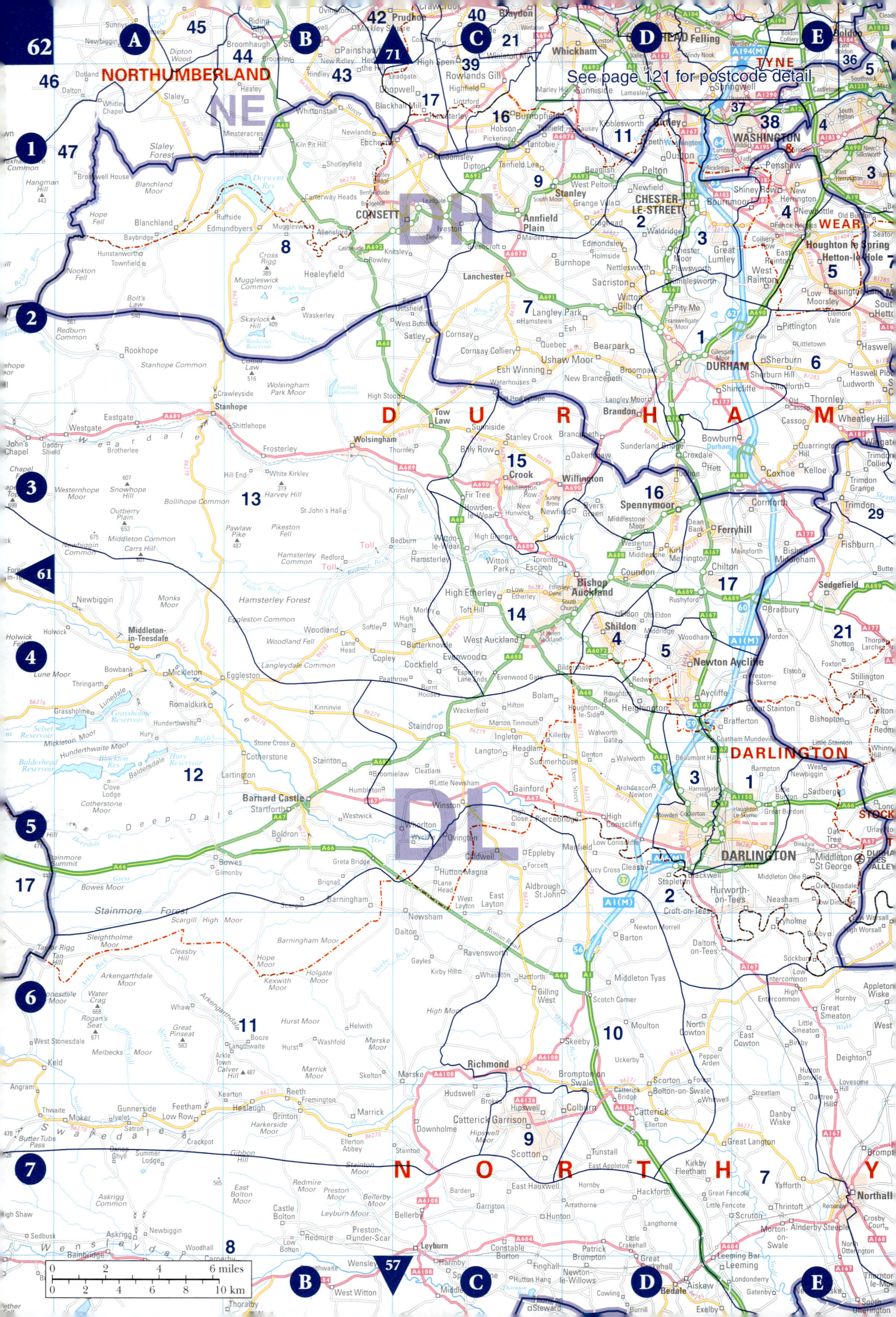
NORTHUMBERLAND
NE
DH
DL
See page 121 for postcode detail
TYNE
WEAR
DURHAM
DARLINGTON
NORTH YORKS
CONSETT
Stanhope
Wolsingham
Crook
Spennymoor
Ferryhill
Bishop Auckland
Shildon
Newton Aycliffe
Middleton-in-Teesdale
Barnard Castle
Staindrop
Richmond
Catterick Garrison
Leyburn
Bedale
Northallerton
Sedgefield
Chester-le-Street
Washington
Stanley
Lanchester
Annfield Plain
Houghton le Spring
Hetton-le-Hole
Hurworth-on-Tees
Croft-on-Tees
Gateshead
Felling
Whickham
Prudhoe
Blaydon
Derwent Res
Hamsterley Forest
Stainmore Forest
Swaledale
Wensleydale
Weardale
Teesdale
Deep Dale
Selset Reservoir
Grassholme Reservoir
Balderhead Reservoir
Blackton Res
Hury Reservoir
Tunstall Reservoir
Waskerley Reservoir
Smiddy Shaw Reservoir
A1(M)
A66
A68
A688
A689
A690
A691
A692
A693
A167
A177
A181
A6108
A684
71
61
57
0 2 4 6 miles
0 2 4 6 8 10 km

same scale as main map
F
G
H
J
K
1
2
3
4
5
6
7
SUNDERLAND
Whitburn
Seaham
Nose's Point
Dalton-le-Dale
Cold Hesledon
Hawthorn
Easington Colliery
Easington
Little Thorpe
Horden
Peterlee
Dene Mouth
Blackhall Colliery
Blackhall Rocks
Castle Eden
Hesleden
High Hesleden
Crimdon Park
Monk Hesleden
Hutton Henry
Sheraton
Hart
High Throston
The Headland
Hartlepool Bay
HARTLEPOOL
Elwick
Dalton Piercy
Rift House
Seaton Carew
Tees Bay
Embleton
Brierton
Claxton Grange
Greatham
Newton Bewley
Wolviston
Billingham
Cowpen Bewley
Seal Sands
Haverton Hill
Port Clarence
MIDDLESBROUGH
STOCKTON-ON-TEES
Thornaby-on-Tees
Acklam
Yarm
Maltby
Hilton
Stainton
Coulby Newham
Nunthorpe
Marton
Newby
Great Ayton
Seamer
Middleton-on-Leven
Crathorne
Hutton Rudby
Rudby
Enterpen
Potto
East Rounton
West Lees
Ingleby Arncliffe
Swainby
Faceby
Whorlton
Ingleby Cross
Cleveland Tontine Inn
Harlsey
Osmotherley
Whorlton Moor
Snilesworth Moor
Arnsgill Ridge
Ellerbeck
Thimbleby
Black Hambleton
Jeater Houses
Over Silton
Nether Silton
Arden Great Moor
Kepwick
Cowesby
Boltby Moor
Kirby Knowle
Thornton-le-Beans
Borrowby
Stokesley
Easby
Great Broughton
Ingleby Greenhow
Kirkby
Great Busby
Carlton-in-Cleveland
Urra
Round Hill
Seave Green
Chop Gate
Cockayne Ridge
Cockayne
Bilsdale West Moor
Bilsdale East Moor
Fangdale Beck
Helmsley Moor
Redcar
Warrenby
Coatham
Dormanstown
Marske-by-the-Sea
Saltburn-by-the-Sea
Kirkleatham
Lazenby
Eston
Grangetown
South Bank
Normanby
Yearby
Wilton
Dunsdale
New Marske
Upleatham
Skelton
Brotton
Skinningrove
Carlin How
Loftus
North Skelton
Kilton
Kilton Thorpe
Boosbeck
Margrove Park
Lingdale
Charltons
Stanghow
Guisborough
Pinchinthorpe
Newton under Roseberry
Roseberry Topping
Gisborough Moor
REDCAR
AND
CLEVELAND
Commondale Moor
Commondale
Freebrough Hill
Moorsholm
Moorsholm Moor
Liverton
Handale
Easington
Boulby
Staithes
Dalehouse
Roxby
Borrowby
Newton Mulgrave
Ellerby
Roxby Low Moor
Scaling
Scaling Reservoir
Roxby High Moor
Danby Low Moor
Danby Beacon
Lealholm Moor
Port Mulgrave
Hinderwell
Runswick Bay
Kettle Ness
Kettleness
Goldsborough
Lythe
Sandsend Ness
Sandsend
Whitby
Mickleby
West Barnby
East Barnby
East Row
Dunsley
Newholm
Ugthorpe
Hutton Mulgrave
Ruswarp
Briggswath
Aislaby
Egton Low Moor
Sneaton
Stainsacre
Ugglebarnby
Egton
Grosmont
Sleights
Littlebeck
Moor
Falling Foss
Egton Bridge
Glaisdale
Beck Hole
Goathland
Egton High Moor
Pike Hill Moss
Mallyan Spout
Hunt House
Flask Inn
Fylingdales Moor
Burn Howe Rigg
Lockton High Moor
Allerston High Moor
Saltergate
Lockton Low Moor
Levisham
Lockton
Newton-on-Rawcliffe
Newton Dale
Stain Dale
Dalby Forest
High Kingthorpe
Kildale
Kildale Moor
Baysdale
Baysdale Moor
Westerdale
Westerdale Moor
Castleton
Castleton Ridge
Danby
Ainthorpe
Houlsyke
Lealholm
Stonegate
Danby High Moor
Farndale Moor
Glaisdale Rigg
Glaisdale Moor
Rosedale Moor
Wheeldale Moor
Hill Cottages
Church Houses
Thorgill
Rosedale Abbey
Cropton Forest
Hartoft End
Spaunton Moor
Lastingham
Spaunton
Appleton-le-Moors
Gillamoor
Fadmoor
Kirkbymoorside
Keldy Castle
Cawthorn
Low Mill
Rudland Rigg
Blakey Ridge
Bransdale
CLEVELAND HILLS
YORKSHIRE
NORTH YORKS
Mulgrave
Thorpe
Egton Bridge
Robin Hood's Bay
Fylingthorpe
Ness Point (North Cheek)
High Hawsker
Low Hawsker
Sneatonthorpe
Raw
Low Moor
Old Peak (South Cheek)
Ravenscar
Staintondale
Cloughton Newlands
Cloughton Wyke
Cloughton
Burniston
Cromer Point
Harwood Dale
Broxa Forest
Silpho
Suffield
Broxa
Langdale End
Hackness
Scalby
Scalby Ness Rocks
Saltwick Bay
SR
TS
YO
Toll
58
62

A
B
C
D
E
1
2
3
4
5
6
7
67
66
19
6
26
8
9
SOUTH
AYRSHIRE
CARRICK
KA
DUMFRIES AND
Ailsa Craig
Dowhill
Dipple
Chapeldonan
Grangeston
Low Craighead
Dailly
Kilkerran
Craig
Maratz Hill
Craigengillan
Tairlaw
Water of Girvan
Old Dailly
Penkill
Hadyard Hill
324
Garleffin Fell
429
Girvan
Houdston
Saugh Hill
296
Penwhapple Reservoir
Glengennet
North Balloch
Loch Bradan Reservoir
Loch Finlas
Craiglee
523
Glendoune
Glendrissaig
Black Neuk
South Balloch
Waterhead
Shiel Hill
508
Pinminnoch
Barr
Changue Forest
Nick of the Balloch Pass
341
Kennedy's Pass
Ardwell
297
Grey Hill
Stinchar
Shalloch
Starr
Loch Riecawr
Loch Macaterick
Pinmore
565
Polmaddie Hill
479
Shalloch on Minnoch
Lendalfoot
Aldons
Carleton Fishery
Daljarrock
Carlin Cairn
Poundland
Pinwherry
Kirriereoch Hill
786
Bennane Head
Colmonell
Dalreoch
Glenduisk
Rhinns
Merrick
843
Knockdolian
265
Craigneil
Ballochmorrie
Black Clauchrie
Garwall Hill
349
Palgowan
Loch Enoch
Mains of Tig
Water of Tig
Duisk
Loch Neldricken
Craignaw
Ballantrae Bay
Ballantrae
Auchairne
Balkissock
Shiel Hill
230
Barrhill
Buchan Hill
493
Loch Valley
Glenapp Castle
Eldrick
Downan Point
Smyrton
Lochton
Corwar House
Glen Trool Lodge
Loch Trool
Loch Dee
Kilantringan Loch
Craigie Fell
Beneraird
439
Drumlamford Loch
557
Mulldonoch
Craigencallie
Milljoan Hill
403
Chirmorrie
Drumlamford House
Glentrool
Lamachan Hill
716
323
Carlock Hill
Altimeg Hill
Bargrennan
Larg Hill
675
Millfore
656
Glen App
Loch Maberry
Loch Ochiltree
Finnarts Point
Milleur Point
Markdhu
Clachaneasy
Larg
Garlick Hill
445
Miltonise
Polbae
Cordorcan
Barnhills
Glenwhilly
Knockville
Knowe
Dalnigap
Urrall Fell
184
Corsewall Point
LOCH RYAN
Penninghame
Garlies Castle
Dallash
Cairnryan
Kirkcolm
Corsewall
Loch Connell
Boreland
Airies
Ervie
Glenrazie
Carseriggan
Cumloden
Cairn Ryan Point
Artfield Fell
Challoch
Minnigaff
Bargaly
St Mary's Croft
Brad Fell
225
Newton Stewart
Creebridge
Blackcraig
Leswalt
Soleburn
New Luce
213
Culvennan Fell
Balminnoch
Tarf Bridge
Loch Ronald
Cairnsmore
Benfield
Innermessan
Auchmantle
Shennanton
Nether Barr
Palnure
Lochinch Castle
Galdenoch
Black Loch
Loch of Barhoise
Kirkcowan
THE RINNS OF GALLOWAY
164
Craig Fell
Barraer
Balteran
Stranraer
Carscreugh
Barlae
Craighlaw
Spittal
Portslogan
Castle Kennedy
Loch Magillie
Soulseat Loch
Dunragit Moor
Whitecairn
Causeway End
Barholm Mains
Carsegowan
Creetown
Cassencarie
Whiteleys
Dunragit
Glenluce
Spittal
Head
Cairn Pat
182
Lochans
Genoch
Piltanton Burn
Dernaglar Loch
Knock Moss
Wigtown Sands
Kildrochet House
Genoch Square
Whitecrook
Whitefield Loch
175
Knock Fell
Culquhirk
Dinvin
Colfin
Fell Loch
Bladnoch
Wigtown
Carsluith
Portpatrick
Awhirk
Milton
Sands of Luce
Crow's Nest
Castle Loch
Culmalzie
Baldoon Sands
Stoneykirk
Auchenmalg
Water of Malzie
Braehead
Port of Spittal Bay
Mochrum Loch
Barnbarroch
Auchenmalg Bay
Culshabbin
Kirkinner
Balgreggan
Sandhead
Alticry
Barrachan
Whauphill
Orchardton Bay
Stewarton
Elrig Loch
Loch Head
Innerwell Port
Cairngarroch Bay
Elrig
Money Head
Kirkland of Longcastle
Eggerness
LUCE BAY
Sorbie
Garlieston
Clachanmore
Airyhassen
Mochrum
Barr Point
THE MACHARS
Ardwell
Ardwell Bay
Chapel Rossan
Cruggleton Bay
Port William
Barwinnock
Cults
Drumbreddan Bay
Balgowan
Logan
White Loch
Castlewigg
New England Bay
Mull of Logan
Barsalloch Point
Monreith
Craigdhu
Whithorn
Port Allen
Port Logan
Monreith Bay
Terally
Glasserton
Cairndoon
Portyerrock
Clanyard Bay
Kilstay
Fell of Carleton
Laggantalluch Head
Drummore
Kirkmaiden
Cailiness Point
Kidsdale
Isle of Whithorn
Damnaglaur
St. Ninian's Cave
Port Castle Bay
Cutcloy
Maryport
Crammag Head
Dunman
160
Devil's Bridge
Burrow Head
Portankill
Nick of Kindram
East Tarbet
West Tarbet
Mull of Galloway
A77
A714
A747
A75
A751
A716
A718
A712
A746
B734
B7027
B7044
B7043
B738
B798
B7077
B7084
B733
B735
B7052
B7005
B7065
B7041
B7004
B7063
B7021
B7085
B741

F
G
H
J
K
65
68
69
60
11
14
1
2
3
4
5
6
7
GALLOWAY
DG
DUMFRIES
Castle Douglas
Kirkcudbright
Dalbeattie
Gatehouse of Fleet
New Galloway
St John's Town of Dalry
Moniaive
Thornhill
Carsphairn
Locharbriggs
Penpont
Closeburn
Auldgirth
Dunscore
Crocketford or Ninemile Bar
Springholm
Kirkpatrick Durham
Haugh of Urr
Crossmichael
Laurieston
Balmaclellan
Corsock
Mossdale
Parton
Twynholm
Tongland
Bridge of Dee
Rhonehouse (Kelton Hill)
Gelston
Palnackie
Kippford (Scaur)
Rockcliffe
Auchencairn
Dundrennan
Borgue
New Abbey
Kirkbean
Southerness
Carsethorn
Beeswing
Lochfoot
Cargenbridge
Shawhead
Amisfield Town
Holywood
Ae Village
Forest of Ae
Dalswinton Common
Keir Hills
Garcrogo Forest
Dalbeattie Forest
Loch Ken
Clatteringshaws Loch
Forest Drive (summer only)
Toll
Wigtown Bay
Solway Firth
Mersehead Sands
Barnhourie Sands
Preston Merse
Balcary Point
Abbey Head
Little Ross
Port Mary
Ringdoo Point
Murray's Isles
Islands of Fleet
Ardwall Island
Barlocco Island
St Mary's Isle
Kirkcudbright Bay
Fleet Bay
Rough Firth
Hestan Island
Almorness Point
Castlehill Point
Port o' Warren
Carse Bay
Borron Point
Criffell 569
Cairnsmore of Dee 493
Cairnsmore of Carsphairn 797
Black Shoulder 688
Craig of Knockgray 383
Dodd Hill 498
Colt Hill 598
Countam 500
Countam 475
Cairnkinna Hill 552
Windy Standard 698
Benbrack 448
Bail Hill 516
Torbraehead 400
Bogrie Hill 432
Blackcraig Hill 406
Largliear Hill 282
Marscalloch Hill 381
Bennan 381
Round Fell 402
Shaw Hill 385
Fell of Fleet 471
Auchencloy Hill 209
Airie Hill 291
White Top of Culreoch 344
Screel Hill 343
Bengairn 391
Lotus Hill 321
Crawston Hill 217
Great Hill 353
Rashy Height 380
Wee Queensberry 512
Queensberry 697
Workington
Seaton
A75
A76
A701
A702
A709
A710
A711
A712
A713
A745
A755
A756
A762
A780
A596
B729
B727
B794
B795
B796
B793
B736
B7000

ARGYLL AND BUTE
PA
KINTYRE
NORTH AYRSHIRE
KA
ARRAN
27
28
73
9
Bellochantuy
Killocraw
Lussa Loch
Corrylach
Saddell
Bunlarie
Saddell Bay
Sgreadan Hill
397
Ugadale Point
Tangy
Ballochgair
Westport
Skeroblingarry
Drumgarve
Glen Lussa
Low Ballevain
Calliburn
Kilchenzie
Peninver
Ardnacross Bay
Machrihanish Bay
East Darlochan
A83
CAMPBELTOWN
Kilmichael
Drumore
Campbeltown
Machrihanish
Dalivaddy
Witchburn
Davaar Island
Drumlemble
B843
Davaar
Kilkerran
Chiscan
Knocknaha
Glenramskill
Beinn Ghuilean
352
New Orleans
Oatfield
Kilchrist
The Slate
385
Cnoc Moy
446
Killellan
312
Arinarach Hill
Largybaan
273
Cnoc Reamhar
Cnoc Odhar
Conie Glen
Glen Kerran
Feochaig
Ru Stafnish
Sheanachie
Glen Breackerie
Brecklate
Kepriglan
Kildavie
Strone Glen
Carrine
Machariach
Polliwilline Bay
Beinn na Lice
428
Southend
Keil
Garveld
Feorlan
Carskey Bay
Mull of Kintyre
Borgadelmore Point
Sanda Sound
Sheep Island
Sanda Island
KILBRANNAN SOUND
Tormore
A841
Ballymichael
Torbeg
Shiskine
Blackwaterfoot
Drumadoon Bay
Kilpatrick
Brown Head
Cnoc a' Chapuill
417
Glenkiln
Benlister Glen
Lamlash
Clauchlands Point
Holy Island
458
Tighvein
Glen Scorrodale
Kingscross Point
Kingscross
Knockenkelly
Whiting Bay
Kiscadale
Ashdale
Largymore
Corriecravie
Sliddery
Largybeg
Largybeg Point
Dippen
Dippen Head
Kilmory
Levencorroch
Lagg
Shannochie
Kildonan
Bennan Head
Sound of Pladda
Pladda
Ailsa Craig
Bennane Head
Ballantrae Bay
Ballantrae
Glenapp Castle
Downan Point
Kilantringan Loch
323
Carlock Hill
Glen App
Finnarts Point
Milleur Point
A77
Corsewall Point
Larne 1-1¾ hrs
Barnhills
North Cairn
South Cairn
Kirkcolm
Corsewall
Cairnryan
Cairn Point
Dounan Bay
Airies
Ervie
Loch Connell
A718
LOCH RYAN
Portobello
St Mary's Croft
Belfast 1¾-3¼ hrs
Knocknain
Leswalt
Soleburn
Innermessan
B7043
B738
B798
THE RHINS
Stranraer
Broadsea Bay
Portslogan
Whiteleys
Lochans

67
74
68
65
64
F
G
H
J
K
1
2
3
4
5
6
7
EAST AYRSHIRE
SOUTH AYRSHIRE
DUMFRIES AND GALLOWAY
KA
DG
FIRTH OF CLYDE
Larne (summer only) 1¾ hrs
KYLE
CARRICK
Troon
Barassie
Loans
Prestwick
GLASGOW PRESTWICK
Lady Isle
Ayr Bay
AYR
Heads of Ayr
Tarbolton
Mauchline
Catrine
Sorn
Crosshands
Mossblown
Annbank
Stair
Ochiltree
Auchinleck
Cumnock
Netherthird
Skares
Drongan
Coylton
Joppa
Belston
Alloway
Dunure
Fisherton
Brown Carrick Hill
Dalrymple
Hollybush
Rankinston
Littlemill
Patna
Lethanhill
Waterside
Kilmein Hill
Stannery Knowe
Dalgig
New Cumnock
Connel Park
Bankglen
Culzean Bay
Knoweside
Maybole
Minishant
Kirkmichael
Crosshill
Maidens
Kirkoswald
Turnberry Bay
Turnberry
Straiton
Dalmellington
Bellsbank
Burnton
Pennyvenie
Benbeoch
Enoch Hill
Windy Standard
Craigdarroch
Dailly
Bargany Mains
Chapeldonan
Grangeston
Old Dailly
Penkill
Hadyard Hill
Garleffin Fell
Tairlaw
Loch Doon
Craiglee
Waterhead
Girvan
Glendoune
Black Neuk
Kennedy's Pass
Ardwell
Pinmore
Barr
North Balloch
South Balloch
Changue Forest
Nick of the Balloch Pass
Shalloch
Polmaddy Hill
Shalloch on Minnoch
Meaul
Carsphairn
Knockgray
Drumjohn
Brochloch
Garryhorn
Bardennoch
Marscalloch Hill
Cairnsmore of Carsphairn
Black Shoulder
Craig of Knockgray
Lendalfoot
Carleton Fishery
Aldons
Daljarrock
Pinwherry
Poundland
Colmonell
Dalreoch
Glenduick
Craigneil
Black Clauchrie
Kirriereoch Hill
Merrick
Corserine
Carlin's Cairn
Rhinns of Kells
Forrest Lodge
Burnhead
Millfire
Knocknalling
Meikle Millyea
Garwall Hill
Palgowan
Ballochmorrie
Mains of Tig
Balkissock
Shiel Hill
Barrhill
Eldrick
Lochton
Corwar House
Buchan Hill
Craignaw
Glen Trool Lodge
Darrou
Garroch
Glenlee
Bennan
Mulldonoch
Lamachan Hill
Larg Hill
Glentrool
Craigencallie
New Galloway
Clatteringshaws Loch
Cairnsmore of Dee
Darnaw
Millfore
Drumlamford House
Chirmorrie
Beneraird
Bargrennan
Markdhu
Miltonise
Glenwhilly
Clachaneasy
Larg
Polbae
Knockville
Cordorcan
Garlick Hill
Round Fell
Fell of Fleet
Shaw Hill
Forest Drive (summer only)
Airie Hill
Dalnigap
Knowe
Urrall Fell
Penninghame
Garlies Castle
Dallash
Craignelder
Boreland
Cumloden
Glenrazie
Carseriggan
Artfield Fell
Challoch
Minnigaff
Newton Stewart
Creebridge
Bargaly
Blackcraig
Cairnsmore of Fleet
Cairnsmore
Door of Cairnsmore
White Top of Culreoch
Balminnoch
Tarf Bridge
Culvennan Fell
New Luce
Shennanton
Benfield
Nether Barr
Palnure
Balteran
Auchenantle
Galdenoch
Craig Fell
Lochinch Castle
Barrae
Spittal
Castramont
Carscreugh
Barlae
Craighlaw
Kirkcowan
Castle Kennedy
Whitecairn
Glenluce
Glenquicken Moor
Rusko
Low Barlay
Cassencarie
Lauchentyre
Gatehouse
Wigtown
Knock Moss

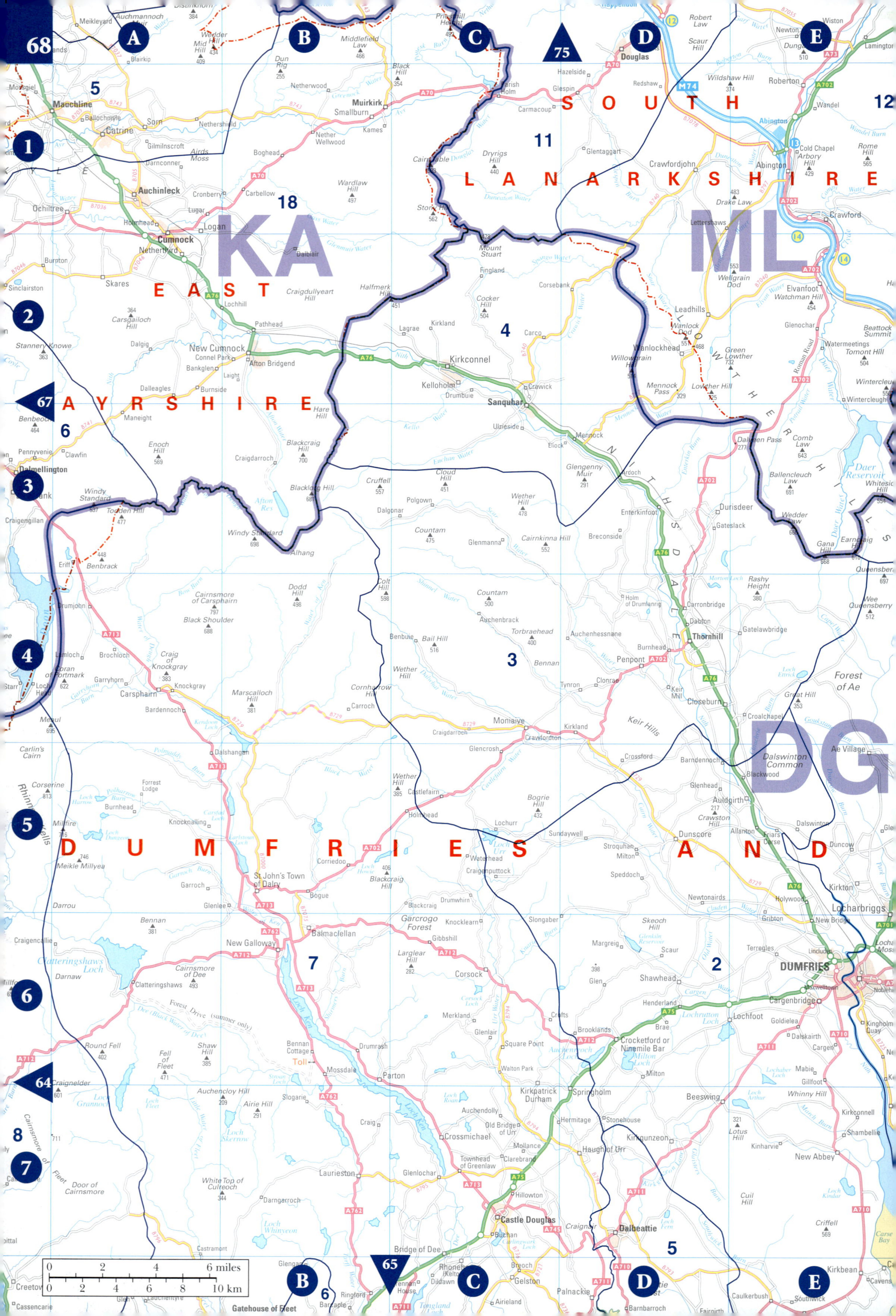
A
B
C
D
E
75
67
64
65
EAST
AYRSHIRE
KA
SOUTH
LANARKSHIRE
ML
DUMFRIES
AND
DG
LOWTHER HILLS
NITHSDALE
Mauchline
Catrine
Sorn
Auchinleck
Cumnock
Netherthird
Logan
Ochiltree
Muirkirk
Smallburn
Douglas
Glespin
Carmacoup
Glentaggart
Crawfordjohn
Abington
Roberton
Wandel
Crawford
Leadhills
Elvanfoot
Wanlockhead
Kirkconnel
Kelloholm
Sanquhar
New Cumnock
Afton Bridgend
Pathhead
Dalmellington
Maneight
Benbeoch
Enoch Hill
Blackcraig Hill
Windy Standard
Carsphairn
Knockgray
Dalshangan
Moniaive
Kirkland
Crawfordton
Penpont
Thornhill
Carronbridge
Closeburn
Auldgirth
Dunscore
Holywood
DUMFRIES
Locharbriggs
Cargenbridge
Lochfoot
Crocketford or Ninemile Bar
Springholm
Kirkpatrick Durham
Corsock
Balmaclellan
New Galloway
St John's Town of Dalry
Clatteringshaws Loch
Loch Ken
Mossdale
Parton
Laurieston
Crossmichael
Castle Douglas
Haugh of Urr
Dalbeattie
Kirkgunzeon
Beeswing
New Abbey
Kirkbean
Gelston
Bridge of Dee
Palnackie
Forest of Ae
Queensberry
Durisdeer
Enterkinfoot
Mennock
Afton Res
Dalswinton Common
Forest Drive (summer only)
Gatehouse of Fleet
Toll
0 2 4 6 miles
0 2 4 6 8 10 km

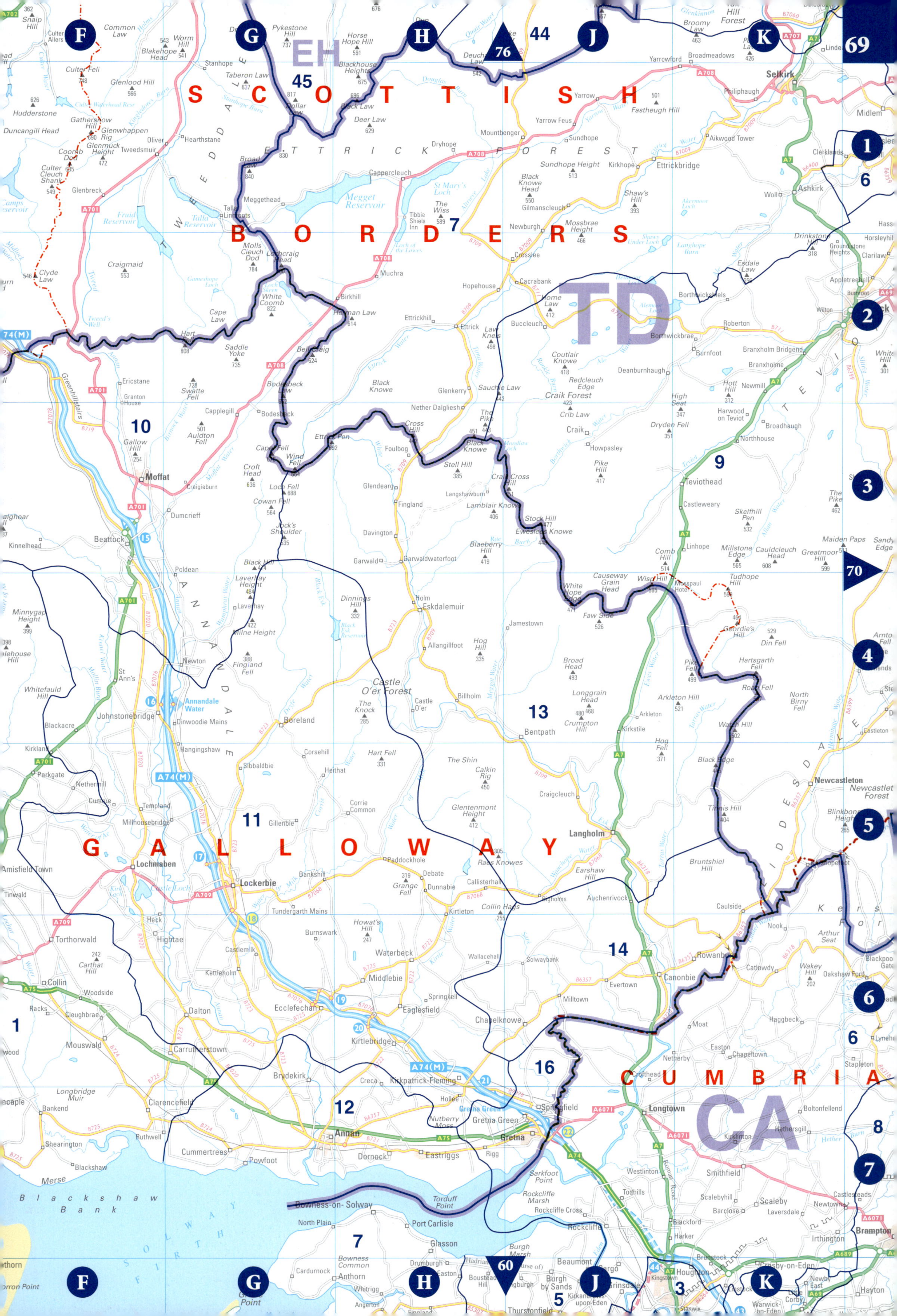

SCOTTISH BORDERS
EH
45
76
44
TD
DUMFRIES AND GALLOWAY
CUMBRIA
CA
ETTRICK FOREST
ANNANDALE
TEVIOTDALE
LIDDESDALE
Kershope Forest
Selkirk
Yarrow
Yarrowford
Broadmeadows
Philiphaugh
Midlem
Ettrickbridge
Ashkirk
Mountbenger
Yarrow Feus
Aikwood Tower
Dryhope
Cappercleuch
Megget Reservoir
St Mary's Loch
Tibbie Shiels Inn
Gilmanscleuch
Newburgh
Crosslee
Talla Reservoir
Tweedsmuir
Hearthstone
Stanhope
Fruid Reservoir
Glenbreck
Culter Allers
Hudderstone
Duncangill Head
Cacrabank
Hopehouse
Ettrickhill
Ettrick
Buccleuch
Borthwickbrae
Roberton
Burnfoot
Branxholm Bridgend
Branxholme
Deanburnhaugh
Newmill
Harwood on Teviot
Broadhaugh
Northhouse
Teviothead
Castleweary
Linhope
Mosspaul Hotel
Craik
Craik Forest
Howpasley
Nether Dalgliesh
Glenkerry
Ericstane
Granton House
Capplegill
Bodesbeck
Moffat
Craigieburn
Dumcrieff
Beattock
Kinnelhead
Poldean
Foulbog
Glendearg
Fingland
Langshawburn
Davington
Garwald
Garwaldwaterfoot
Holm
Eskdalemuir
Jamestown
Allangillfoot
Castle O'er Forest
Castle O'er
Billholm
Bentpath
Boreland
Newton
Lavernay
St Ann's
Annandale Water
Johnstonebridge
Dinwoodie Mains
Hangingshaw
Sibbaldbie
Corsehill
Heithat
Corrie Common
Gillenbie
Templand
Millhousebridge
Kirkland
Parkgate
Nethermill
Cumrue
Blackacre
Lochmaben
Lockerbie
Amisfield Town
Tinwald
Torthorwald
Collin
Woodside
Racks
Cleughbrae
Mouswald
Dalton
Carrutherstown
Heck
Hightae
Castlemilk
Kettleholm
Tundergarth Mains
Bankshill
Paddockhole
Debate
Dunnabie
Callisterhall
Kirkleton
Burnswark
Waterbeck
Middlebie
Wallacehall
Solwaybank
Springkell
Eaglesfield
Ecclefechan
Kirtlebridge
Chapelknowe
Milltown
Evertown
Canonbie
Rowanburn
Catlowdy
Langholm
Craigcleuch
Auchenrivock
Irvington
Arkleton
Kirkstile
Newcastleton
Newcastleton Forest
Caulside
Nook
Oakshaw Ford
Moat
Easton
Chapeltown
Netherby
Stapleton
Lyneholme
Longtown
Crofthead
Kirklinton
Hethersgill
Boltonfellend
Smithfield
Westlinton
Scaleby
Scalebyhill
Laversdale
Newtown
Castlesteads
Brampton
Irthington
Blackford
Harker
Rockcliffe
Rockcliffe Cross
Rockcliffe Marsh
Sarkfoot Point
Torduff Point
Springfield
Gretna Green
Gretna
Rigg
Eastriggs
Dornock
Annan
Nutberry Moss
Kirkpatrick-Fleming
Hollee
Creca
Brydekirk
Clarencefield
Cummertrees
Powfoot
Bankend
Buthwell
Shearington
Blackshaw
Longbridge Muir
Merse
Blackshaw Bank
SOLWAY FIRTH
Bowness-on-Solway
North Plain
Port Carlisle
Glasson
Bowness Common
Cardurnock
Anthorn
Whitrigg
Drumburgh
Easton
Burgh Marsh
Beaumont
Burgh by Sands
Kirkandrews-upon-Eden
Grinsdale
Houghton
Kingstown
Brunstock
Crosby-on-Eden
Thurstonfield
Newby East
Hayton
Warwick
Corby
Burnfoot
Appletreehall
Wilton
Hawick
Horsleyhill
Clarilaw
Groundistone Heights
Clerklands
Woll
A7
A68
A69
A74(M)
A75
A701
A708
A709
A6071
A689
60
70
69

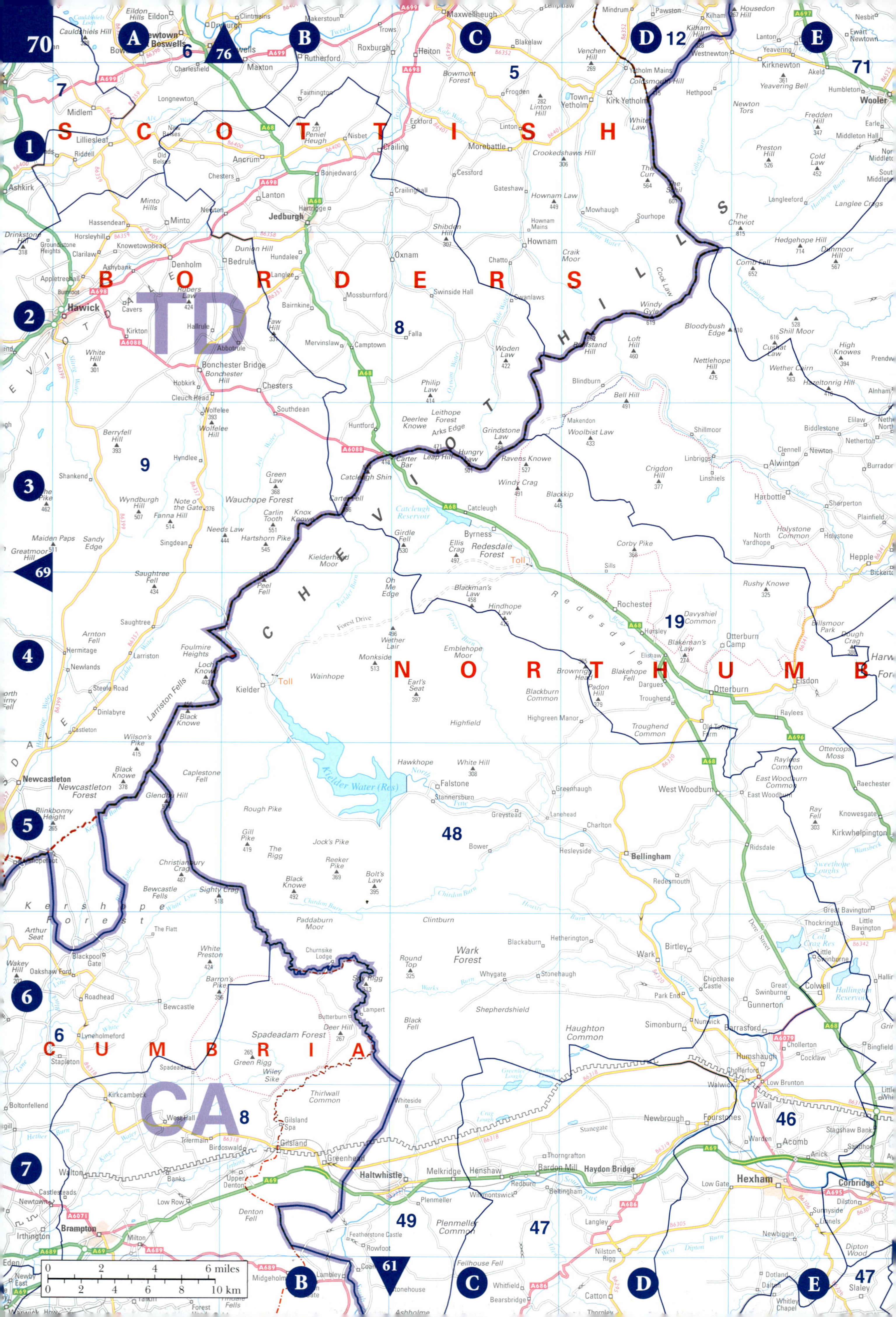

70
76
69
61
71
SCOTTISH
BORDERS
CHEVIOT HILLS
NORTHUMBERLAND
CUMBRIA
TD
CA
Kielder Water (Res)
Kielder
Wark Forest
Spadeadam Forest
Kershope Forest
Redesdale Forest
Wauchope Forest
Newcastleton
Hawick
Jedburgh
Denholm
Ancrum
Lilliesleaf
Midlem
Bowden
Newtown St Boswells
St Boswells
Dryburgh
Maxton
Rutherford
Roxburgh
Maxwellheugh
Heiton
Kelso
Eckford
Crailing
Nisbet
Morebattle
Linton
Town Yetholm
Kirk Yetholm
Yetholm Mains
Kilham
Kirknewton
Wooler
Akeld
Humbleton
Hethpool
The Cheviot 815
Hedgehope Hill 714
Windy Gyle 619
Carter Bar
Catcleugh
Catcleugh Reservoir
Byrness
Rochester
Otterburn
Otterburn Camp
Elsdon
Alwinton
Harbottle
Hepple
Falstone
Stannersburn
Greenhaugh
Bellingham
West Woodburn
East Woodburn
Ridsdale
Kirkwhelpington
Wark
Birtley
Simonburn
Chollerton
Humshaugh
Chollerford
Walwick
Wall
Acomb
Hexham
Corbridge
Dilston
Slaley
Haydon Bridge
Bardon Mill
Henshaw
Melkridge
Haltwhistle
Greenhead
Gilsland
Birdoswald
Banks
Walton
Brampton
Irthington
Milton
Lambley
Featherstone Castle
Plenmeller
Plenmeller Common
Whitfield
Catton
Langley
Newbrough
Fourstones
Low Brunton
Kirkcambeck
Bewcastle
Roadhead
Stapleton
Spadeadam
Saughtree
Steele Road
Riccarton
Chesters
Bonchester Bridge
Hobkirk
Camptown
Oxnam
Hownam
Chatto
Swinside Hall
Redesdale
Kielder Forest
Larriston Fells
Peel Fell
Deadwater Fell
Hindhope Law
Blakehope Fell
Troughend Common
Colt Crag Res
Hallington Reservoirs
Haughton Common
Shepherdshield
Thirlwall Common
Denton Fell
Hadrian's Wall
A68
A69
A698
A6088
A696
A697
A686
A689
A6079
A695
A699
0 2 4 6 miles
0 2 4 6 8 10 km

F
G
H
J
K
1
2
3
4
5
6
7
Seahouses
Beadnell
Beadnell Bay
High Newton-by-the-Sea
Snook Point
Newton Haven (St Mary's)
Low Newton-by-the-Sea
Embleton
Embleton Bay
Dunstan Steads
Craster
Cullernose Point
Howick
Howick Haven
Longhoughton
Longhoughton Steel
Boulmer
Boulmer Haven
Alnmouth
Alnmouth Bay
Warkworth
Amble
Coquet Island
Hauxley Haven
Hadston Carrs
Druridge Bay
Widdrington
Cresswell
The Scars
Ellington
Snab Point
Lynemouth
Beacon Point
Newbiggin-by-the-Sea
ASHINGTON
Morpeth
Bedlington
BLYTH
See page 121 for postcode detail
Seaton Sluice
St Mary's Island (Bait Island)
Whitley Bay
Tynemouth
North Shields
SOUTH SHIELDS
NEWCASTLE UPON TYNE
NEWCASTLE INTERNATIONAL
GATESHEAD
WALLSEND
Jarrow
Gosforth
Cramlington
Ponteland
Whitburn
SUNDERLAND
Alnwick
Rothbury
Chatton
Eglingham
Powburn
Whittingham
Longframlington
Felton
Ulgham
Pegswood
Prudhoe
Ryton
Blaydon
Whickham
Felling
Boldon
hours
Amsterdam........15
Kristiansand........17
then Gothenburg........25
Stavanger........19
then Haugesund......21½
then Bergen..........22-26
NE
TYNE AND WEAR

78
same scale as main map
continued in main map square A5
COLONSAY
Oronsay
ISLAY
JURA
ARGYLL AND
PA
Oban 2¼ hrs
1¼ hrs (summer only)
2 hrs
2¼ hrs
Scalasaig
Kiloran
Colonsay House
Port Askaig
Feolin Ferry
Craighouse
Bridgend
Bowmore
Port Charlotte
Bruichladdich
Port Ellen
Ardbeg
Lagavulin
Laphroaig
Portnahaven
Port Wemyss
Ballygrant
Keills
Gigha
Ardminish
Tayinloan
Muasdale
Bellochantuy
Paps of Jura
Sound of Islay
Loch Indaal
Laggan Bay
The Oa
Mull of Oa
Texa
Cara Island
Small Isles
Rinns of Islay

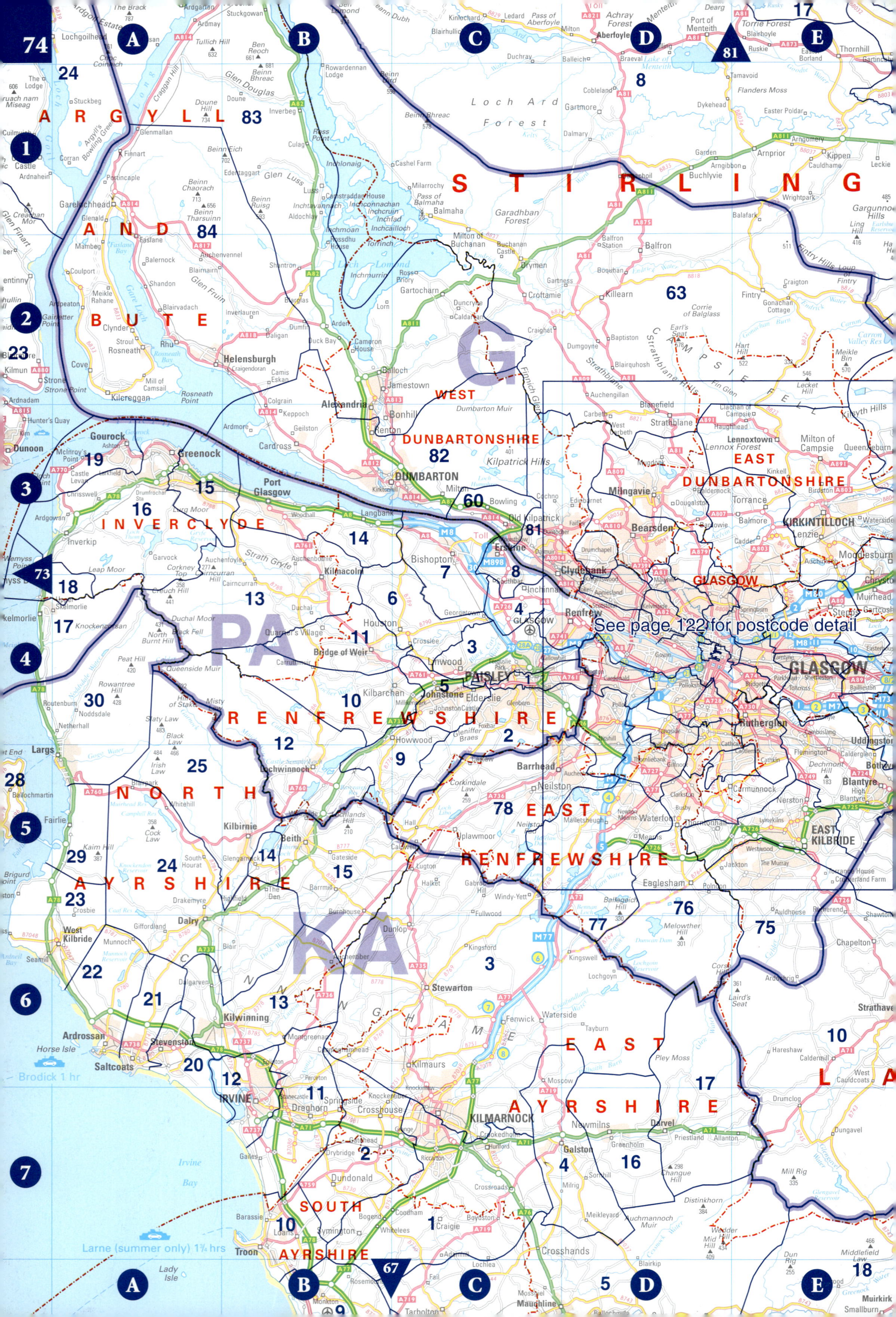
A
B
C
D
E
1
2
3
4
5
6
7
81
73
67
A R G Y L L
A N D
B U T E
S T I R L I N G
WEST DUNBARTONSHIRE
EAST DUNBARTONSHIRE
INVERCLYDE
RENFREWSHIRE
EAST RENFREWSHIRE
NORTH AYRSHIRE
EAST AYRSHIRE
SOUTH AYRSHIRE
GLASGOW
G
PA
KA
See page 122 for postcode detail
Lochgoilhead
Helensburgh
Gourock
Greenock
Port Glasgow
Dunoon
Alexandria
DUMBARTON
Clydebank
Milngavie
Bearsden
KIRKINTILLOCH
Lennoxtown
Milton of Campsie
Strathblane
Balfron
Aberfoyle
Drymen
Balloch
Renfrew
PAISLEY
Johnstone
Bridge of Weir
Kilmacolm
Barrhead
Neilston
Rutherglen
EAST KILBRIDE
Eaglesham
Largs
Fairlie
West Kilbride
Ardrossan
Saltcoats
Stevenston
Kilwinning
IRVINE
Dalry
Beith
Lochwinnoch
Kilbirnie
Stewarton
KILMARNOCK
Galston
Newmilns
Darvel
Troon
Dundonald
Crosshouse
Kilmaurs
Fenwick
Dunlop
Mauchline
Crosshands
Blantyre
Uddingston
Loch Lomond
Irvine Bay
Brodick 1 hr
Larne (summer only) 1¾ hrs
Lady Isle
Horse Isle

75
82
76
68
CLACKMANNANSHIRE
PERTH AND KINROSS
FIFE
FALKIRK
WEST LOTHIAN
NORTH LANARKSHIRE
SOUTH LANARKSHIRE
EDINBURGH
MIDLOTHIAN
SCOTTISH BORDERS
PENTLAND HILLS
FK
KY
EH
ML
Firth of Forth
STIRLING
Alloa
Dunfermline
Grangemouth
FALKIRK
Bo'ness
Linlithgow
LIVINGSTON
Bathgate
Cumbernauld
Airdrie
Coatbridge
MOTHERWELL
Wishaw
Lanark
Biggar
Kinross
Dunblane
Bridge of Allan
Tillicoultry
Dollar
Alva
Cowdenbeath
Inverkeithing
Rosyth
Queensferry
Kirkliston
Broxburn
Whitburn
West Calder
Shotts
Carluke
Larkhall
Lesmahagow
Douglas
West Linton
Carnwath

76
83
75
69
FIFE
KY
EH
EAST LOTHIAN
MIDLOTHIAN
SCOTTISH BORDERS
LAMMERMUIR HILLS
MOORFOOT HILLS
LAUDERDALE
FIRTH OF FORTH
EDINBURGH
Glenrothes
Markinch
Kennoway
Windygates
Leven
Methil
Buckhaven
Lundin Links
Upper Largo
Largo Bay
Earlsferry
Kilconquhar
St Monans
Pittenweem
Anstruther
Isle of May
Kinglassie
Lochore
Auchterderran
Cardenden
Thornton
East Wemyss
Coaltown of Wemyss
West Wemyss
Dysart
Kirkcaldy
Auchtertool
Kinghorn
Burntisland
Aberdour
Hawkcraig Point
Inchcolm
Inchkeith
Inchmickery
Fidra
Lamb
North Berwick
Craigleith
Bass Rock
Zeebrugge 17½ hrs
Dirleton
Gullane
Gullane Point
Aberlady
Aberlady Bay
Whitekirk
East Fortune
Athelstaneford
Drem
East Linton
Tyninghame
Dunbar
West Barns
Cockenzie and Port Seton
Prestonpans
Longniddry
Musselburgh
Tranent
Haddington
Macmerry
Gladsmuir
Pencaitland
East Saltoun
West Saltoun
Ormiston
Dalkeith
Gifford
Garvald
Stenton
Spott
Dunbar Common
Bonnyrigg
Loanhead
Lasswade
Roslin
Penicuik
Gorebridge
Newtongrange
Mayfield
Pathhead
North Middleton
Temple
Howgate
Humbie
Soutra Hill
Lauder
Oxton
Carfraemill
Stow
Galashiels
Melrose
Newstead
Earlston
Gattonside
Darnick
Newtown St Boswells
St Boswells
Dryburgh
Selkirk
Innerleithen
Walkerburn
Peebles
Eddleston
Traquair
Clovenfords
Westruther
Gordon
Smailholm
Lyne
Kirkton Manor
Maxton
Rutherford
Roxburgh
Fastheugh Hill
0 2 4 6 miles
0 2 4 6 8 10 km

F
G
H
J
K
1
2
3
4
5
6
Barns Ness
Skateraw
Thorntonloch
Reed Point
Cove
Cockburnspath
Oldhamstocks
Siccar Point
Wheat Stack
Telegraph Hill
St Abb's Head
St Abbs
Lumsdaine
Coldingham Moor
Northfield
Coldingham
Coldingham Bay
Eyemouth
Grantshouse
Houndwood
Cairncross
Reston
Auchencrow
Ayton
Burnmouth
Abbey St Bathans
Ellemford
Cockburn Law
Drakemire
Marygold
Preston
Lintlaw
Blanerne
Chirnside
Chirnsidebridge
Foulden
Lamberton
Lamberton Beach
Marshall Meadows
Mordington Holdings
Clappers
Halidon Hill
Needles Eye
Sharper's Head
Berwick-upon-Tweed
Highfields
Tweedmouth
Spittal
East Ord
Redshin Cove
Duns
Edrom
Allanton
Hutton
Paxton
Blackadder
Whitelaw
Gavinton
Choicelee
Polwarth
Sinclair's Hill
Whitsome
Fishwick
Horncliffe
Longridge Towers
Scremerston
Horndean
Thornton Park
Murton
Thornton
Fogo
Fogorig
Swinton
Swinton Quarter
Ladykirk
Upsettlington
Norham
Shoreswood
Shoresdean
West Allerdean
Cheswick
Cheswick Black Rocks
Goswick
Cheswick Buildings
Ancroft
Greenlaw
Swintonmill
Simprim
Purves Hall
Leitholm
Grindon
Felkington
Berrington
Haggerston
Holy Island (Lindisfarne)
Emmanuel Head
Orange Lane
Lambden
Eccles
Duddo
Bowsden
Beal
West Mains
Holy Island
Castle Point
Holy Island Sands
Castle Heaton
Lennel
Coldstream
Birgham
Barmoor Lane End
West Kyloe
Fenham
Guile Point
Fenham Flats
New Heaton
Etal
Lowick
East Kyloe
Kyloe Hills
Buckton
Stichill
Ednam
Carham
Wark
West Learmouth
Cornhill on Tweed
Pallinsburn House
Crookham Eastfield
Crookham
Branxton
Mardon
Ford
Detchant
Elwick
Ross
Budle Bay
Budle Point
Hendersyde Park
Hadden
Sprouston
East Learmouth
Pressen
Flodden
Kimmerston
Holburn
Middleton
Low Middleton
Easington
Warenmill
Kelso
Maxwellheugh
Lempitlaw
Mindrummill
Mindrum
Downham
Pawston
Howtel
Housedon Hill
Milfield
Fenton
Nesbit
North Hazelrigg
South Hazelrigg
Belford
Outchester
Bamburgh
Glororum
Spindlestone
Burton
Bradford
Ewart Newtown
Doddington
Kilham
Kilham Hill
Lanton
Coupland
Yeavering
West Horton
East Horton
Waren
Bellshill
Adderstone
Lucker
Elford
New Shoreston
North Sunderland
Heiton
Blakelaw
Venchen Hill
Westnewton
Yetholm Mains
Kirknewton
Akeld
Wooler
Wandon
Greendykes
Chatton
Newham Hall
East Fleetham
Newham
Swinhoe
West Fleetham
Frogden
Linton Hill
Town Yetholm
Kirk Yetholm
Hethpool
Yeavering Bell
Newton Tors
Fredden
Twizell House
Rosebrough
Newstead
Chathill
NORTHUMBERLAND
TD
NE
Longstone
Farne Islands
Staple Sound
Farne Island
Inner Sound
Monks House Rocks
Seahouses
Budle Bay
same scale as main map
A1
A1107
A6105
A6112
A698
A697
A1167
A699
71

SEA OF THE HEBRIDES
INNER HEBRIDES
COLL
78
TIREE
77
IONA
76
66
67
74
Lochboisdale 5-7 hrs
Castlebay 5¼ hrs
2¾ hrs
1 hr
3½-4¼ hrs
Arinagour
Scarinish
Balemartine
Fionnphort
Baile Mòr
Bunessan
Gometra
Staffa
Lunga
Treshnish Isles
Torran Rocks
Erraid
Ross of Mull
Dubh Artach

HIGHLAND
ARGYLL AND BUTE
MULL
ARDNAMURCHAN
MORVERN
SUNART
PH
PA
Tobermory
Salen
Oban
Craignure
Lochaline
Kilchoan
Strontian
Acharacle
Dervaig
Kilmelford
Lismore
Kerrera
Seil
Luing
Shuna
Scarba
Firth of Lorn
Sound of Mull
Loch Linnhe
Loch Sunart
Colonsay 2¼ hours
Garvellachs
Isles of the Sea
Ulva
Eorsa
Inch Kenneth
Ben More
Fiunary Forest
Lynn of Morven
Frank Lockwood's Island
Glen More
Loch Buie
Loch Scridain
Craignure ¾ hr
½ hr (summer only)

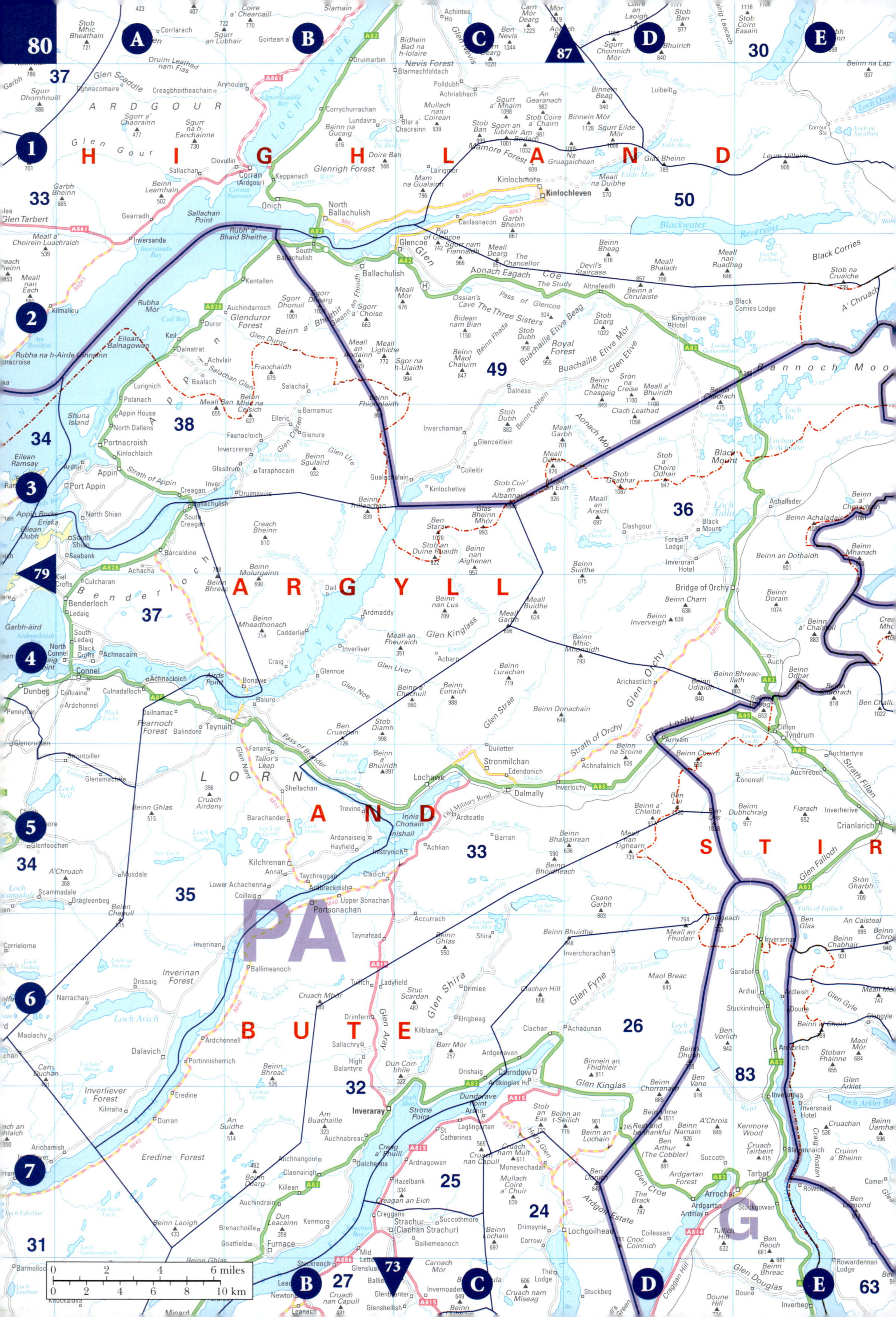
A
B
C
D
E
1
2
3
4
5
6
7
87
79
73
H I G H L A N D
A R G Y L L
A N D
B U T E
S T I R
PA
G
A R D G O U R
Glen Scaddle
Glen Gour
Glen Tarbert
Loch Linnhe
Corran
Onich
North Ballachulish
Kinlochleven
Kinlochmore
Mamore Forest
Nevis Forest
Ben Nevis 1344
Blackwater Reservoir
Glencoe
Glen Coe
Ballachulish
South Ballachulish
Kentallen
Duror
Glenduror Forest
Rubha Mòr
Appin
Strath of Appin
Port Appin
Portnacroish
Shuna Island
Creagan
Barcaldine
Benderloch
Connel
Dunbeg
Oban
Achnacloich
Taynuilt
Bonawe
Glen Etive
Royal Forest
Buachaille Etive Mòr
Buachaille Etive Beag
Kingshouse Hotel
Rannoch Moor
Black Mount
Bridge of Orchy
Inveroran Hotel
Forest Lodge
Loch Tulla
Glen Orchy
Strath of Orchy
Tyndrum
Clifton
Crianlarich
Strath Fillan
Glen Falloch
Falls of Falloch
Inverarnan
Ardlui
Glen Kinglass
Dalmally
Lochawe
Stronmilchan
Pass of Brander
Innis Chonain
Inishail
Kilchrenan
Portsonachan
Ardbrecknish
Cladich
Loch Awe
Inverinan Forest
Dalavich
Loch Avich
Inverliever Forest
Eredine Forest
Glen Aray
Glen Shira
Inveraray
Strone Point
Cairndow
Ardkinglas Ho
Glen Fyne
Clachan
Achadunan
St Catherines
Creggans
Strachur (Clachan Strachur)
Furnace
Glen Croe
Rest and be thankful
Ben Arthur (The Cobbler)
Arrochar
Ardgartan
Tarbet
Inveruglas
Glen Douglas
Lochgoilhead
Ardgoil Estate
Glen Kinglas
Loch Lomond
Ben Lomond 974
Lorn
33
37
38
34
35
36
49
50
30
26
32
25
24
27
83
31
63
0 2 4 6 miles
0 2 4 6 8 10 km

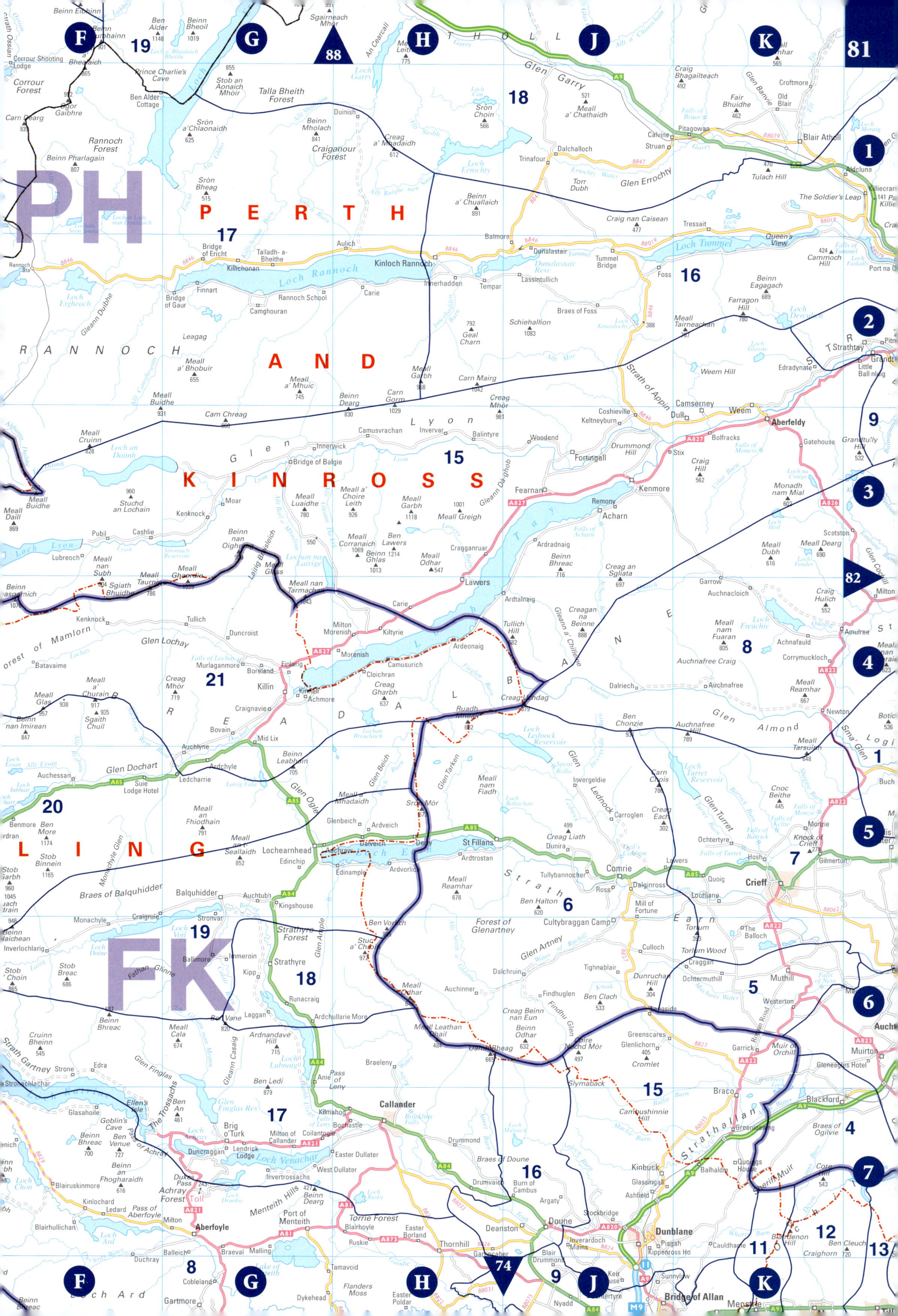
PERTH AND KINROSS
PH
FK
STIRLING
RANNOCH
ATHOLL
BREADALBANE
Loch Rannoch
Loch Tummel
Loch Tay
Loch Earn
Loch Lyon
Loch Ericht
Loch Venachar
Loch Lubnaig
Loch Voil
Loch Katrine
Glen Lyon
Glen Garry
Glen Errochty
Glen Lochay
Glen Dochart
Glen Almond
Glen Artney
Glen Turret
Strath of Appin
Strath Earn
Strathallan
Strath Gartney
Rannoch Forest
Craiganour Forest
Talla Bheith Forest
Corrour Forest
Strathyre Forest
Forest of Glenartney
Achray Forest
Torrie Forest
Menteith Hills
Schiehallion
Ben Lawers
Ben More
Ben Vorlich
Ben Ledi
Ben Chonzie
Blair Atholl
Pitlochry
Kinloch Rannoch
Tummel Bridge
Aberfeldy
Weem
Kenmore
Fortingall
Killin
Lochearnhead
St Fillans
Comrie
Crieff
Muthill
Callander
Doune
Dunblane
Bridge of Allan
Aberfoyle
Strathyre
Balquhidder
Braco
Blackford
Port of Menteith
Deanston
Thornhill
Auchterarder
Calvine
Struan
Trinafour
Rannoch Sta
Bridge of Gaur
Lawers
Ardeonaig
Amulree
Gleneagles Hotel
Gilmerton
Queen's View
The Soldier's Leap
Killiecrankie
A9
A85
A84
A827
A826
A822
A821
A81
A873
A823
A820
M9
B846
B847
B8019
B8079
B827
B8033
B8032
B8031
B826
88
82
74
F
G
H
J
K
1
2
3
4
5
6
7
9

A
B
C
D
E
89
75
81
1
2
3
4
5
6
7
PH
KY
FK
PERTH AND KINROSS
ANGUS
FIFE
DUNDEE
Pitlochry
Blairgowrie
Coupar Angus
Dunkeld
Perth
Kinross
Auchterarder
Alyth
Kirriemuir
Newburgh
Auchtermuchty
Glenrothes
Cupar
Leslie
Markinch
Kennoway
Methil
Buckhaven
Loch Leven
Firth of Tay
0 2 4 6 miles
0 2 4 6 8 10 km

F
G
H
J
K
90
76
1
2
3
4
5
6
7
ABERDEENSHIRE
AB
DD
ANGUS
30
9
10
11
5
4
7
6
16
E
Laurencekirk
Inverbervie
Gourdon
Johnshaven
St Cyrus
Milton Ness
Edzell
Marykirk
Logie Pert
Brechin
Little Brechin
Montrose
Montrose Basin
Ferryden
Scurdie Ness
Hillside
Kinnaber
Fishtown of Usan
Long Craig
Boddin Point
Lunan Bay
Lunan
Red Head
Lang Craig
Inverkeilor
Auchmithie
Meg's Craig
Carlingheugh Bay
The Deil's Heid
Arbroath
Friockheim
Colliston
St Vigeans
Letham
Guthrie
Forfar
Lunanhead
Aberlemno
Finavon
Tannadice
Memus
Oathlaw
Kirriemuir
Kingsmuir
Monikie
Muirdrum
Carnoustie
Barry
Monifieth
Broughty Ferry
Barry Links
Buddon Ness
Tay Road Bridge
Tayport
Newport-on-Tay
Tentsmuir Point
Tentsmuir Forest
Leuchars
Guardbridge
Eden Mouth
Out Head
St Andrews Bay
St Andrews
Kinkell Ness
Buddo Ness
Babbet Ness
Boarhills
Kingsbarns
Cambo Ness
North Carr
Tullybothy Craigs
Craighead
Fife Ness
Crail
West Ness
Anstruther
Pittenweem
St Monans
Elie
Earlsferry
Colinsburgh
Largoward
Kilconquhar
Chapel Ness
Saucher Point
Ruddons Point
Largo Bay
North Ness
Isle of May
Bell Rock (Inchcape)
Pitscottie
Strathkinness
Magus Muir
Kellie Law

92
WESTERN
ISLES
(NA H-EILEANAN AN IAR)
OUTER HEBRIDES
HS
8
SOUTH UIST
(UIBHIST A DEAS)
Tarbert
Loch Sgioport
Ornish Island
Geirinis
Drimore
Groigearraidh
Stilligarry
(Stadhlaigearraidh)
Drimsdale
(Dreumasdal)
Homore
(Tobha Mòr)
Peighinn nan Aoireann
Snishival (Soisealbhal)
Hecla
606
Ben Corodale
527
Rubha Rossel
Rubha Aird-mhicheil
Staoinebrig
Rubha Bhilidh
Ormacleit
Beinn Mhòr
620
Prince's Cave
Rubha Hellisdale
Rubha Ardvule
Bornais
Kildonan
(Cilldonnain)
Arinambane
Ben na Hoe
258
Rubha Bolum
Sheaval
223
Gearraidh Bhailteas
Minngearraidh
Arnaval
252
Rubha na Gibhte
Stulaval
374
Askernish
(Aisgernis)
Stuley
Triuirebheinn
357
Dalabrog
Rubha na Creige Mòire
Cille Pheadair
Lochboisdale
(Loch Baghasdail)
Beinn Ruigh Choinnich
275
Rubha na Cruibe
Baghasdal
Orosay
Calvay
Leth Meadhanach
Taobh a' Deas Loch Baghasdail
Rubha Meall na Hoe
Gearraidh na Monadh
Trosairidh
Easaval
Oitir na Cudaig
Smerclet
Ceann a' Gharaidh
Poll a' Charra
Cille Bhrighde
Ludag
Roneval
201
Rubha na h- Ordaig
Sound of Eriskay
Haunn
Bunmhullin
Ben Scrien
185
Balla
Lingay
Hartamul
Eriskay
(Eiriosgaigh)
Ben Stack
122
Rubha Liath
Sound of Barra
Fiaray
Scurrival Point
Hornish
Heinish
Eolaigearraidh
80
Fuday
102
Traigh Eais
Stack Islands
Orosay
Greanamul
BARRA
(TRAIGH MHÒR)
Greian Head
Cleat
Ben Cliad
207
Ardmhòr
Gighay
95
73
Hellisay
Ardveenish
Allathasdal
Cuidhir
Northbay
Borve Point
Bruernish
107
Flodday
9
BARRA
(BARRAIGH)
Borgh
Ruleos
Bùaile nam Bodach
Fuiay
A888
1¾ hrs
Bruernish Point
Doirlinn Head
Ben Tangaval
333
Heaval
383
Earsairidh
Aird a' Chaolais
Castlebay
(Bàgh a'Chaisteil)
Leideag
Brevig
Rubha Mòr
Caolas
Heishival Mòr
190
Uidh
Vatersay
(Bhatarsaigh)
Vatersay
(Bhatarsaigh)
100
Am Meall
Muldoanich
153
Flodday
Sound of Sandray
Cairn Galtair
207
Sandray
(Sanndraigh)
Lingay
Sound of Pabbay
Pabbay
(Pabaigh)
The Hoe
171
Sound of Mingulay
Guarsay Mòr
Macphee's Hill
224
Mingulay
(Miughalaigh)
273
Càrnan
Mingulay Bay
Sròn an Dùin
Sound of Berneray
Skate Point
191
Nisam Point
Berneray
(Bearnaraigh)
A865
B890
0 2 4 6 miles
0 2 4 6 8 10 km

F
G
H
J
K
93
55
56
51
1
2
3
4
5
6
7
48
49
47
41
44
43
42
36
86
78
INNER HEBRIDES
SEA OF THE HEBRIDES
SKYE
HIGHLAND
IV
PH
Minginish
Cuillin Hills
CUILLIN SOUND
SOUND OF RUM
Sound of Canna
Sound of Eigg
CANNA
Sanday
RUM (RHUM)
EIGG
Muck
Soay
Oban 5-7 hrs
Oban 5¼ hrs
Hoe Rape
The Hoe
Lorgill
Ben Connan
Beinn na Boineid
Ben Idrigill
MacLeod's Maidens
Idrigill Point
An Dubh Sgeir
Harlosh Point
Harlosh Island
Tarner Island
Wiay
Oronsay
Loch Bracadale
Ebost
Ullinish
Struan
Bracadale
Coillore
Ardtreck Point
Portnalong
Fernilea
Rubha nan Clach
Carbost
Arnaval
Gleann Oraid
Talisker
Stockval
Biod Mòr
Eynort
Glen Eynort
Glenbrittle
Beinn Bhreac
Merkadale
Drynoch
Glen Drynoch
Beinn Duagrich
Beinn Totaig
Roineval
Mugeary
Stroc-bheinn
Meall an Fhuarain
Broc-bheinn
Glen Varragill
Sligachan
Glen Sligachan
Glamaig
Beinn Dearg
Ben Lee
Peinchorran
Lower Ollach
Camastianavaig
Penifiler
Am Maol
Beinn na Cloiche
Glen Ose
Ose
Balmore
Harlosh
Glenmore
Beinn Bhreac
Beinn a' Bhraghad
Beinn Staic
An Cruachan
Bruach na Frìthe
Am Basteir
Sgurr nan Gillean
Sgurr Thuilm
Sgurr a' Mhadaidh
Sgurr a' Ghreadaidh
Harta Corrie
Sgurr na Banachdich
Sgurr Dearg (Inaccessible Pinnacle)
Sgurr Mhic Choinnich
Sgurr Alasdair
Sgurr Dubh Mòr
Sgurr nan Eag
Gars-bheinn
Sgurr na Stri
Druim Hain
Bualintur
Cuilnamean
Beinn an Eoin
Rubha Thearna Sgurr
Ceann na Beinne
Rubh' an Dùnain
Loch Brittle
Loch Eynort
Leac nam Faoileann
Beinn Bhreac
Molchlach
Loch Scavaig
Elgol
Prince Charles's Cave
Camas nan Gall
Carn a' Ghaill
Compass Hill
A'Chill
Canna Harbour
Camas Tharbernish
Garrisdale Point
Sròn Ruail
Humla
Rubha Shamhnan Insir
Kilmory
Sgaorishal
Mullach Mòr
Rubha na Roinne
Bloodstone Hill
A'Bhrideanach
Kinloch
Orval
Sgor Reidh
Barkeval
Hallival
Askival
An Dornabac
Harris
Ainshval
Ival
Sgurr nan Gillean
Rubha Sgor an t-Snidhe
Rubha nam Meirleach
Garbh Sgeir
Oigh-sgeir
Cleadale
An Cruachan
Bay of Laig
Rubha an Fhasaidh
Beinn Tighe
Laig
Kildonnan
An Sgurr
Galmisdale
Eilean nan Each
Gòdag
Beinn Airein
Port Mòr
Rubh' Leam na Làraich
Sanna Point
Sanna
Sanna Bay
Fascadale
Achateny
Achnaha
Meall nan Con
Beinn an Leathaid
Point of Ardnamurchan
Portuairk
Achosnich
Grigadale
A863
A87
B885
B8009

86
94
85
79
A
B
C
D
E
1
2
3
4
5
6
7
SKYE
IV
PH
RAASAY
Scalpay
Pabay
Longay
Crowlin Islands
Soay
Cuillin Hills
SLEAT
KNOYDART
NORTH MORAR
SOUTH MORAR
ARISAIG
MOIDART
Ardnish
EIGG
Muck
SOUND OF SLEAT
SOUND OF RUM
Sound of Eigg
SOUND OF ARISAIG
Loch Hourn
Loch Nevis
Loch Morar
Loch Shiel
Loch Eishort
Loch Slapin
Loch Scavaig
Loch Alsh
Loch Ailort
Portree
Sconser
Sligachan
Glen Drynoch
Glen Varragill
Glen Sligachan
Broadford
Harrapool
Skulamus
Kyleakin
Kyle of Lochalsh
Plockton
Balmacara
Dornie
Lochcarron
Strath Ascaig
Kylerhea
Glenelg
Bernera
Arnisdale
Corran
Luib
Dunan
Torrin
Kilbride
Strathaird
Camasunary
Kirkibost
Kilmarie
Elgol
Drinan
Prince Charles's Cave
Spar Cave
Glasnakille
Ord
Tokavaig
Tarskavaig
Achnacloich
Teangue
Knock
Isleornsay
Duisdealmor
Drumfearn
Heast
Kilmore
Kilbeg
Armadale
Ardvasar
Calligarry
Aird of Sleat
Point of Sleat
Inverie
Airor
Sandaig
Inverguseran
Mallaig
Mallaigvaig
Glasnacardoch
Morar
Beoraidbeg
Bracora
Bracorina
Tarbet
Swordland
Kinlochmorar
Arisaig
Back of Keppoch
Portnaluchaig
Morroch
Druimindarroch
Glen Beasdale
Arnipol
Lochailort
Inverailort
Ranochan
Glenfinnan
Roshven
Glenuig
Smirisary
Samalaman Island
Eilean Shona
Kinlochmoidart
Glen Forslan
Ardmolich
Glen Moidart
Acharacle
Shiel Bridge
Dalnabreck
Kentra
Gorteneorn
Ockle
Swordle
Kilmory
Fascadale
Achateny
Sanna Point
Ardnamurchan
Polloch
Kinlochan
Cleadale
Kildonnan
Galmisdale
Laig
Port Mòr
Kinloch
½ hr
0 2 4 6 miles
0 2 4 6 8 10 km
A87
A863
A851
A830
A861
A890
B8083

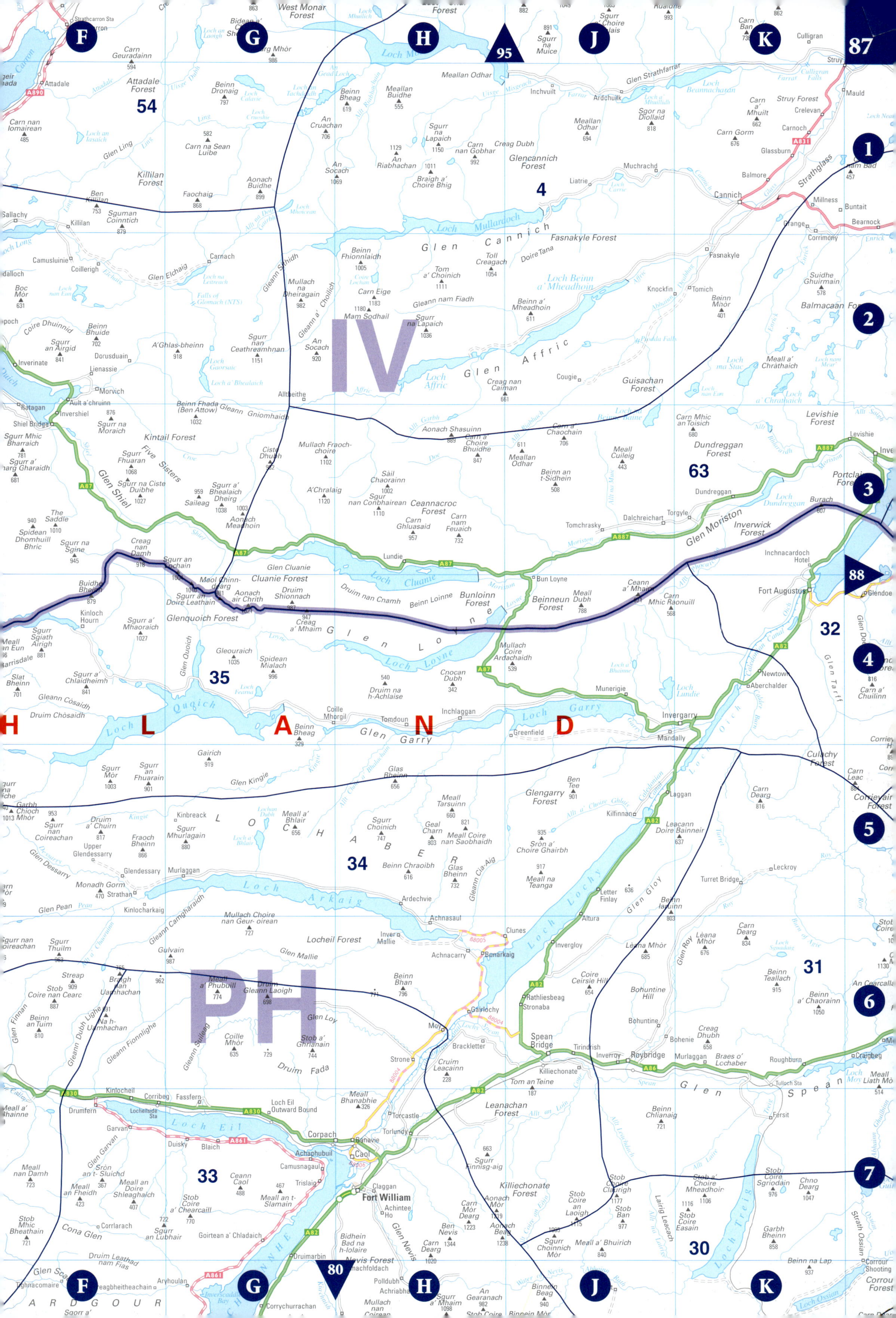
F
G
H
J
K
95
88
80
1
2
3
4
5
6
7
IV
PH
H L A N D
L O C H A B E R
54
4
63
35
32
34
31
33
30
West Monar Forest
Strathcarron Sta
Carn Geuradainn
Attadale Forest
Attadale
Carn nan Iomairean
Beinn Dronaig
Glen Ling
Carn na Sean Luibe
Killilan Forest
Killilan
Sallachy
Faochaig
Aonach Buidhe
Ben Killilan
Sguman Coinntich
Camusluinie
Coillerigh
Glen Elchaig
Carnach
Falls of Glomach (NTS)
Coire Dhuinnid
Beinn Bhuide
Sgurr an Airgid
Dorusduain
A'Ghlas-bheinn
Sgurr nan Ceathreamhnan
Inverinate
Lienassie
Morvich
Ratagan
Ault a'chruinn
Inversheil
Shiel Bridge
Sgurr na Moraich
Beinn Fhada (Ben Attow)
Gleann Gniomhaidh
Kintail Forest
Five Sisters
Glen Shiel
Sgurr Fhuaran
Sgurr na Ciste Duibhe
Saileag
Sgurr a' Bhealaich Dheirg
Aonach Meadhoin
Ciste Dhubh
The Saddle
Spidean Dhomhuill Bhric
Sgurr na Sgine
Creag nan Damh
Sgurr an Lochain
Maol Chinn-dearg
Sgurr an Doire Leathain
Aonach air Chrith
Druim Shionnach
Buidhe Bheinn
Kinloch Hourn
Sgurr a' Mhaoraich
Glenquoich Forest
Creag a' Mhaim
Glen Loyne
Loch Loyne
Gleouraich
Spidean Mialach
Glen Quoich
Sgurr a' Chlaidheimh
Gleann Cosaidh
Druim Chòsaidh
Slat Bheinn
Loch Quoich
Beinn Bheag
Coille Mhorgil
Tomdoun
Glen Garry
Inchlaggan
Loch Garry
Greenfield
Gairich
Sgurr Mòr
Sgurr an Fhuarain
Glen Kingie
Glas Bheinn
Garbh Chioch Mhòr
Sgurr nan Coireachan
Druim a' Chuirn
Kinbreack
Sgurr Mhurlagain
Meall a' Bhlair
Upper Glendessarry
Fraoch Bheinn
Glendessary
Glen Dessarry
Murlaggan
Monadh Gorm
Strathan
Kinlochargaig
Glen Pean
Loch Arkaig
Mullach Choire nan Geur-oirean
Gleann Camgharaidh
Sgurr Thuilm
Gulvain
Streap
Stob Coire nan Cearc
Beinn an Tuim
Glen Finnan
Gleann Dubh Lighe
Na h-Uamhachan
Braigh nan Uamhachan
Gleann Fionnlighe
Meall a' Phubuill
Druim Gleann Laoigh
Coille Mhòr
Gleann Suileag
Glen Loy
Stob a' Ghrianain
Druim Fada
Locheil Forest
Glen Mallie
Inver Mallie
Achnacarry
Bunarkaig
Clunes
Achnasaul
Ardechvie
Sgurr Choinich
Beinn Chraoibh
Geal Charn
Meall Coire nan Saobhaidh
Meall Tarsuinn
Glas Bheinn
Gleann Cia-aig
Loch Lochy
Glengarry Forest
Ben Tee
Sròn a' Choire Ghairbh
Meall na Teanga
Kilfinnan
Laggan
Leacann Doire Bainneir
Letter Finlay
Altura
Glen Gloy
Beinn Iaruinn
Turret Bridge
Leckroy
Invergloy
Coire Ceirsle Hill
Rathliesbeag
Stronaba
Gairlochy
Moy
Strone
Brackletter
Cruim Leacainn
Spean Bridge
Tirindrish
Inverroy
Roybridge
Murlaggan
Braes o' Lochaber
Roughburn
Killiechonate
Tom an Teine
Leanachan Forest
Glen Spean
Tulloch Sta
Craigbeg
Beinn Chlianaig
Fersit
Kinlocheil
Corribeg
Fassfern
Loch Eil Outward Bound
Drumfern
Lochailort Sta
Loch Eil
Garvan
Duisky
Blaich
Meall Bhanabhie
Torcastle
Torlundy
Corpach
Banavie
Caol
Achaphubuil
Camusnagaul
Trislaig
Claggan
Fort William
Achintee
Glen Gaorsaic
Sròn an t-Sluichd
Meall an Doire Shleaghaich
Ceann Caol
Meall an t-Slamain
Stob Coire a' Chearcaill
Cona Glen
Corrlarach
Sgurr an Lubhair
Goirtean a' Chladaich
Druim Leathad nam Fias
Glen Scaddle
Inverscaddle Bay
Aryhoulan
Druimarbin
Bidhein Bad na h-Iolaire
Glen Nevis
Ben Nevis
Carn Mòr Dearg
Aonach Mòr
Aonach Beag
Carn Dearg
Nevis Forest
Polldubh
Achriabhach
Sgurr a' Mhaim
Mullach nan Coirean
Corrychurrachan
An Gearanach
Binnein Beag
Sgurr Choinnich Mòr
Stob Coire an Laoigh
Stob Coire Claurigh
Stob Ban
Killiechonate Forest
Meall a' Bhuirich
Lairig Leacach
Loch Treig
Stob a' Choire Mheadhoin
Stob Coire Easain
Stob Coire Sgriodain
Chno Dearg
Garbh Bheinn
Beinn na Lap
Strath Ossian
Loch Ossian
Corrour Forest
Sgurr Finnisg-aig
Glen Roy
Lèana Mhòr
Carn Dearg
Beinn Teallach
Bohuntine Hill
Bohuntine
Bohenie
Creag Dhubh
Beinn a' Chaorainn
An Cearcallach
Culachy Forest
Carn Leac
Carn Dearg
Corrieyairack Forest
Loch Oich
Invergarry
Mandally
Munerigie
Loch Lundie
Aberchalder
Newtown
Glen Tarff
Carn a' Chuilinn
Fort Augustus
Glendoe
Inchnacardoch Hotel
Inverwick Forest
Glen Moriston
Burach
Torgyle
Dalchreichart
Tomchrasky
Dundreggan
Dundreggan Forest
Loch Dundreggan
Portclair Forest
Invermoriston
Levishie
Levishie Forest
Carn Mhic an Toisich
Meall Cuileig
Beinn an t-Sidhein
Carn a' Chaochain
Ceann a' Mhaim
Carn Mhic Raonuill
Beinneun Forest
Meall Dubh
Bun Loyne
Bunloinn Forest
Beinn Loinne
Druim nan Cnamh
Loch Cluanie
Cluanie Forest
Glen Cluanie
Lundie
Mullach Coire Ardachaidh
Cnocan Dubh
Druim na h-Achlaise
Ceannacroc Forest
Carn nam Feuaich
Carn Ghluasaid
Sgur nan Conbhairean
Sàil Chaorainn
A'Chralaig
Mullach Fraoch-choire
Aonach Shasuinn
Carn a' Choire Bhuidhe
Meallan Odhar
Alltbeithe
Glen Affric
Loch Affric
Creag nan Calman
Cougie
Guisachan Forest
Loch na Beinne Baine
Loch Beinn a' Mheadhoin
Beinn a' Mheadhoin
Sgurr na Lapaich
Gleann nam Fiadh
Mam Sodhail
Carn Eige
Mullach na Dheiragain
Gleann a' Choilich
An Socach
Beinn Fhionnlaidh
Tom a' Choinich
Toll Creagach
Glen Cannich
Loch Mullardoch
Fasnakyle Forest
Doire Tana
Fasnakyle
Knockfin
Tomich
Beinn Mhòr
Plodda Falls
Loch ma Stac
Meall a' Chràthaich
Balmacaan Forest
Suidhe Ghuirmain
Corrimony
Grange
Bearnock
Buntait
Millness
Cannich
Strathglass
Balmore
Glassburn
Carnoch
Carn Gorm
Crelevan
Struy Forest
Carn a' Mhuilt
Sgor na Diollaid
Mucherachd
Liatrie
Glencannich Forest
Creag Dubh
Carn nan Gobhar
Sgurr na Lapaich
Braigh a' Choire Bhig
An Riabhachan
An Socach
An Cruachan
Beinn Bheag
Meallan Buidhe
Meallan Odhar
Inchvuilt
Glen Strathfarrar
Ardchuilk
Loch Beannacharan
Meallan Odhar
Culligran
Struy
Mauld
Carn Ban
Sgurr na Muice
Sgurr a' Choire Ghlais
Loch Monar
Bidean a' Choire Sheasgaich
Lurg Mhòr
Loch Cluanie
Loch Lochy
Loch Eil
A87
A887
A82
A86
A830
A861
A831
B8004
B8005
B8006

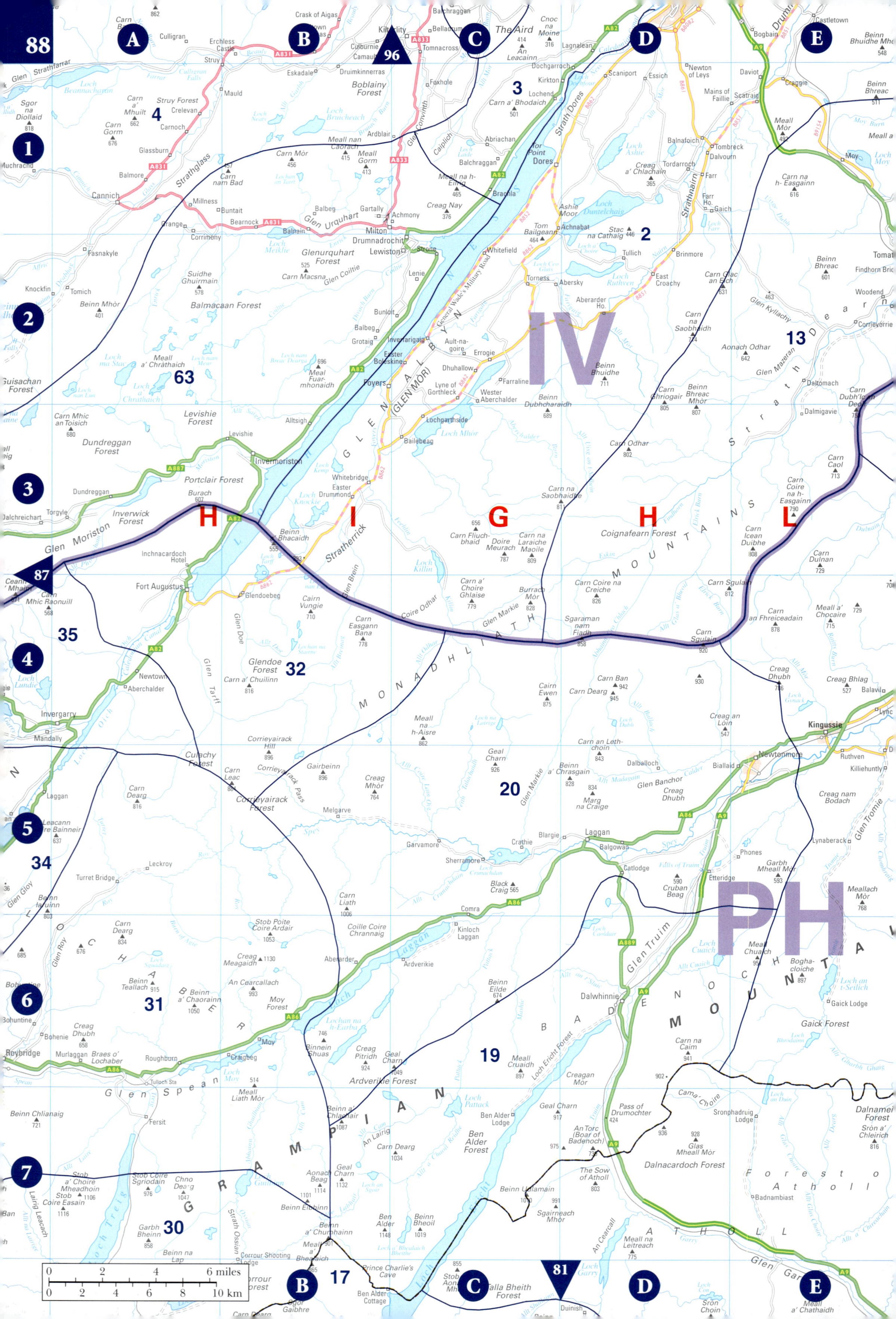

Cannich
Strathglass
Glen Urquhart
Drumnadrochit
Invermoriston
Fort Augustus
Foyers
Inverfarigaig
Dores
Strath Dores
Glenurquhart Forest
Balmacaan Forest
Portclair Forest
Glen Moriston
Inverwick Forest
Invergarry
Laggan
Newtonmore
Kingussie
Dalwhinnie
Glen Truim
Ardverikie Forest
Loch Ericht Forest
Dalnacardoch Forest
Gaick Forest
Coignafearn Forest
Glendoe Forest
Corrieyairack Forest
Corrieyairack Pass
Moy Forest
Roybridge
Glen Spean
Tulloch Sta
Monadhliath Mountains
Grampian Mountains
Strathdearn
Glen Mazeran
Highland
IV
PH
0 2 4 6 miles
0 2 4 6 8 10 km

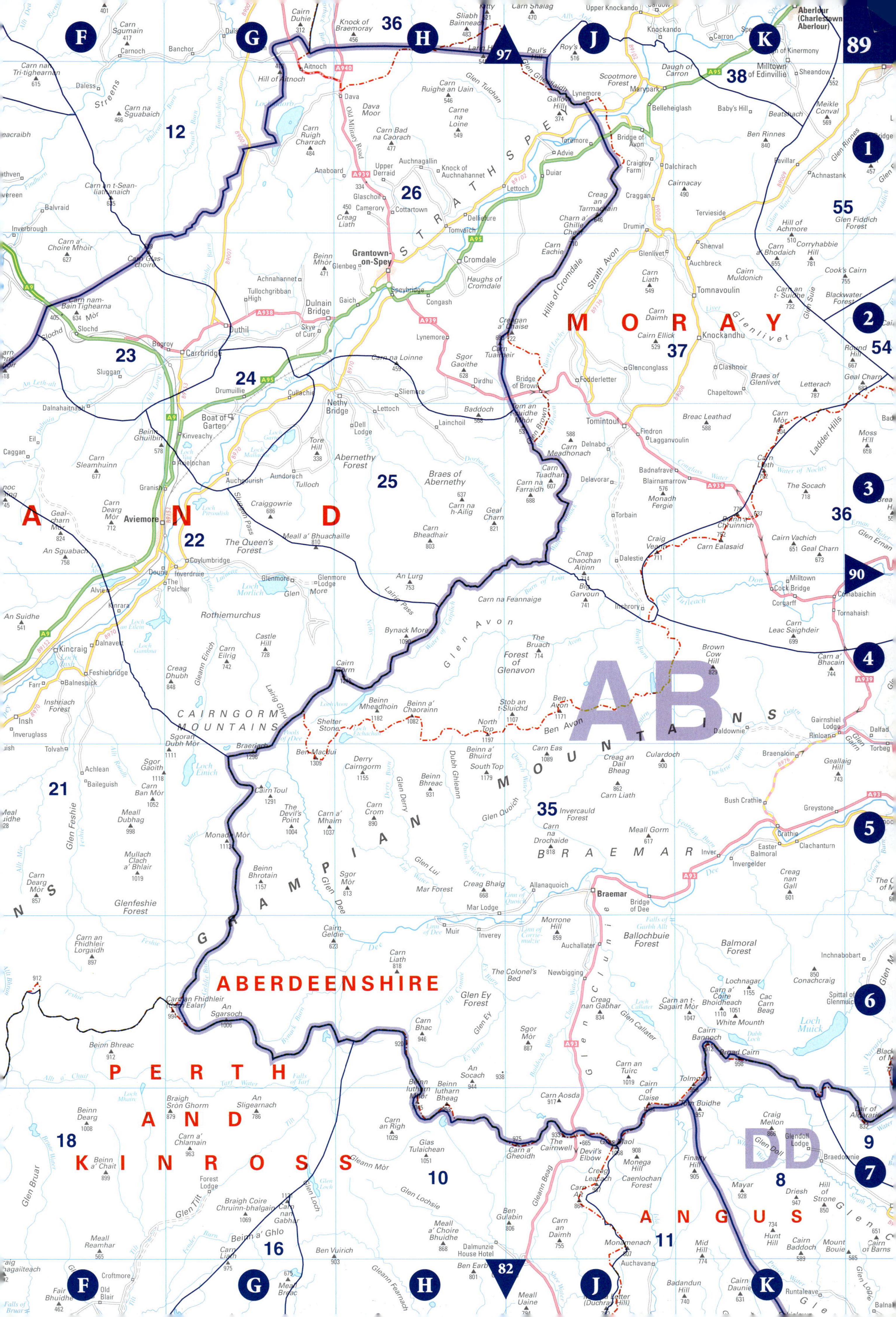

MORAY
ABERDEENSHIRE
PERTH AND KINROSS
ANGUS
CAIRNGORM MOUNTAINS
GRAMPIAN MOUNTAINS
STRATHSPEY
BRAEMAR
Grantown-on-Spey
Aviemore
Braemar
Tomintoul
Carrbridge
Nethy Bridge
Boat of Garten
Kincraig
Tomnavoulin
Knockandhu
Cairn Gorm
Ben Macdui
Lochnagar
Glen Avon
Abernethy Forest
Rothiemurchus
Glenfeshie Forest
Glen Tilt
Glen Shee
89
90
97
82

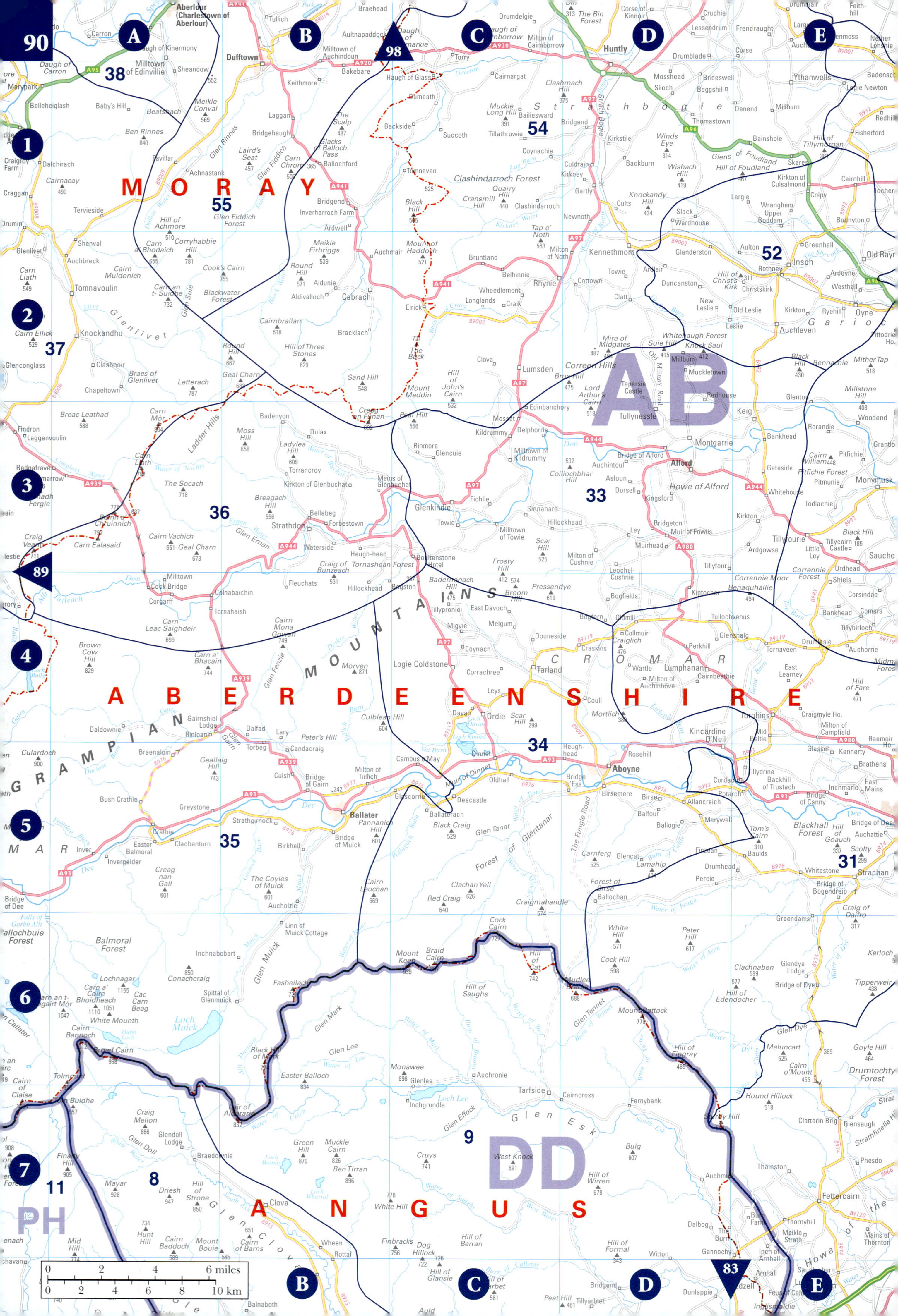

A
B
C
D
E
1
2
3
4
5
6
7
98
89
83
MORAY
ABERDEENSHIRE
ANGUS
AB
DD
PH
GRAMPIAN MOUNTAINS
Strathbogie
Garioch
CROMAR
MAR
Huntly
Dufftown
Aberlour (Charlestown of Aberlour)
Keith
Rhynie
Lumsden
Alford
Insch
Kennethmont
Tullynessle
Montgarrie
Keig
Strathdon
Glenkindie
Towie
Logie Coldstone
Tarland
Lumphanan
Torphins
Kincardine O'Neil
Aboyne
Dinnet
Ballater
Crathie
Braemar
Tomnavoulin
Knockandhu
Cabrach
Clashindarroch Forest
Glen Fiddich Forest
Blackwater Forest
Corrennie Forest
Pitfichie Forest
Forest of Birse
Forest of Glentanar
Balmoral Forest
Drumtochty Forest
Glen Esk
Glen Clova
Glen Muick
Loch Muick
Loch Lee
Glenlivet
Tarfside
Clova
Fettercairn
Strachan
Banchory
Mount Keen
Morven
Lochnagar
Tap o' Noth
Ben Rinnes
Bennachie
Ladder Hills
The Fungle Road
A941
A920
A97
A96
A95
A944
A939
A93
A980
37
38
55
54
52
36
33
34
35
31
9
8
11
0
2
4
6 miles
6
8
10 km

F
G
H
J
K
99
1
2
3
4
5
6
7
53
41
42
51
21
22
23
24
16
25
11
10
15
14
13
12
32
39
30
DD
Kirktown of Auchterless
Fyvie
Woodhead
Rothienorman
Methlick
Tarves
Ellon
Cruden Bay
Port Erroll
Bay of Cruden
The Skares
Whinnyfold
The Veshels
Hatton
Auchmacoy
Kirktown of Slains
Collieston
St Catherine's Dub
Forvie Ness (Hackley Head)
Sands of Forvie
Newburgh
Newburgh Bar
Foveran House
Blairythan Cottage
Drums
Menie House
Balmedie
Oldmeldrum
Pitmedden
Udny Green
Udny Station
Inverurie
Port Elphinstone
Kintore
Kemnay
Newmachar
Hatton of Fintray
Potterton
Skelly Rock
Blackdog
Blackdog Rock
North Tarbothill
Dyce
ABERDEEN
Bridge of Don
Old Aberdeen
Westhill
Kingswells
Hazlehead
Girdle Ness
Nigg Bay
Greg Ness
Altens
Souter Head
Cove Bay
Peterculter
Milltimber
Cults
Echt
Dunecht
Kirkton of Skene
Kirkton of Maryculter
Portlethen
Findon
Findon Ness
Portlethen Village
Downies
Newtonhill
Muchalls
Doonie Point
Castle Rock of Muchalls
Garron Point
Cowie
Stonehaven
Strathlethan Bay
Castle Haven
Thornyhive Bay
Trelung Ness
Crawton
Crawton Bay
Catterline
Braidon Bay
Todhead Point
Kinneff
Inverbervie
Bervie Bay
Gourdon
Johnshaven
Laurencekirk
Auchenblae
Fordoun
Drumlithie
Fetteresso Forest
Durris Forest
Banchory
Drumoak
Crathes
Murdoch Head
North Haven
hours
Kirkwall.................6-7¼
Lerwick.............12-12½
A90
A92
A93
A96
A947
A948
A952
A956
A957
A944
A920

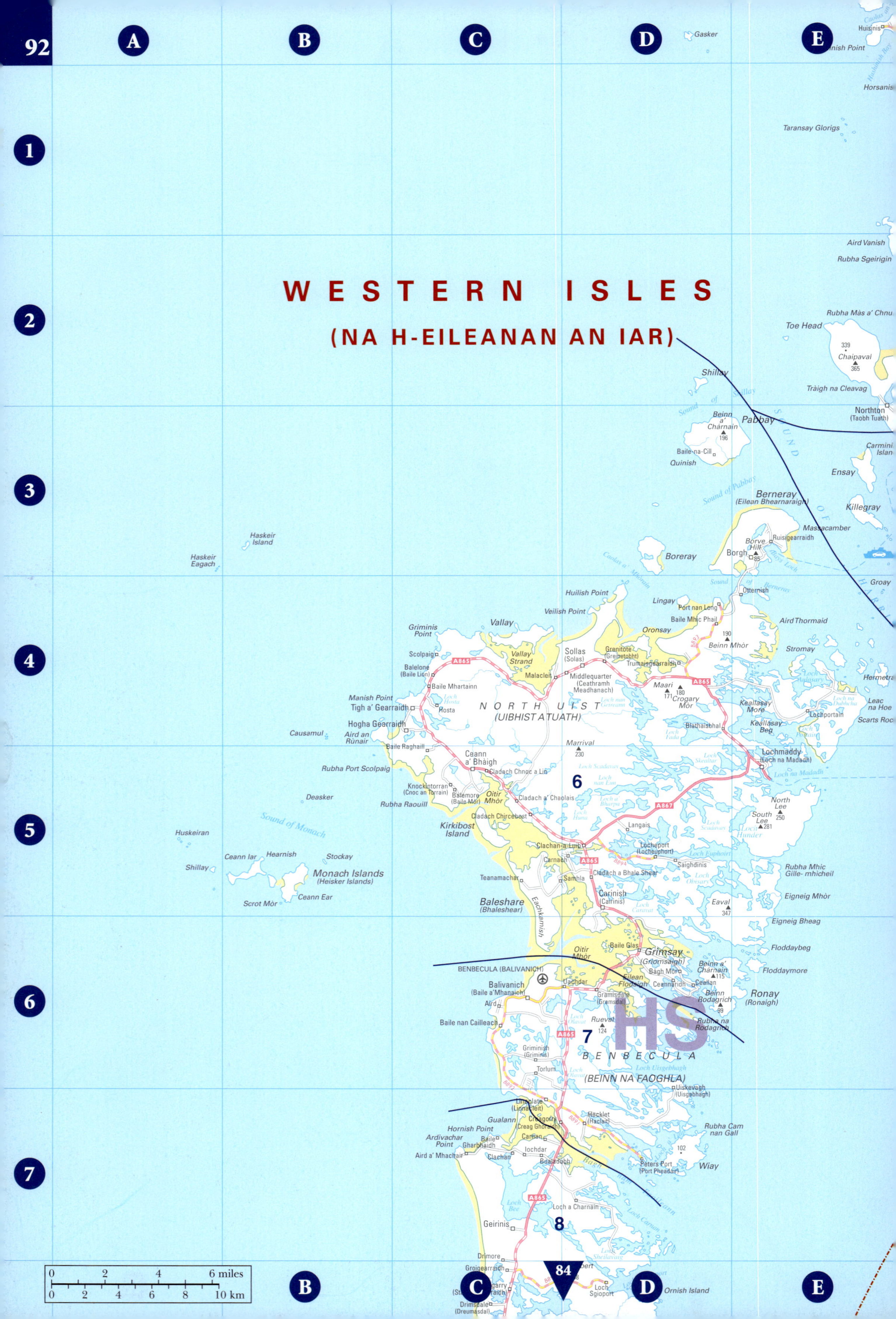
A
B
C
D
E
1
2
3
4
5
6
7
WESTERN ISLES
(NA H-EILEANAN AN IAR)
NORTH UIST
(UIBHIST A TUATH)
BENBECULA
(BEINN NA FAOGHLA)
HS
Gasker
Taransay Glorigs
Aird Vanish
Rubha Sgeirigin
Toe Head
Chaipaval
Shillay
Pabbay
Northton
(Taobh Tuath)
Ensay
Killegray
Berneray
(Eilean Bhearnaraigh)
Boreray
Haskeir Island
Haskeir Eagach
Vallay
Sollas
(Solas)
Lochmaddy
(Loch na Madadh)
Causamul
Deasker
Huskeiran
Monach Islands
(Heisker Islands)
Ceann Iar
Shillay
Stockay
Baleshare
(Bhaleshear)
Eaval
Grimsay
(Griomsaigh)
Ronay
(Ronaigh)
BENBECULA (BALIVANICH)
Balivanich
(Baile a'Mhanaich)
Wiay
Ornish Island
Marrival
Carinish
(Cairinis)
Clachan-a-Luib
Drimsdale
(Dreumasdal)
6
7
8
B
C
D
E
0 2 4 6 miles
0 2 4 6 8 10 km

84

F
G
H
J
K
1
2
3
4
5
6
7
100
94
85
NORTH HARRIS
(CEANN A TUATH NA HEARADH)
SOUTH HARRIS
(CEANN A DEAS NA HEARADH)
HS
IV
HIGHLAND
SKYE
Husival Mòr
489
Tirga Mòr
Ullaval
659
Oreval
662
Stulaval
579
Leosaval
412
Forest of Harris
Gobhaig
Cleiseval
511
Abhainnsuidhe
Uisgnaval Mòr
729
Mulla-fo-dheas
743
Clisham
799
Clett Ard
328
Soay Beg
Soay Mòr
Miabhag
Tolmachan
Bun Abhainn Eadarra
Sgaoth Aird
559
Straiaval
389
Toddun
528
Maraig (Maaruig)
Kenmore
Caiteshal
449
WEST LOCH TARBERT
Aird Asaig
Ben Raah
267
Beinn Dhubh
506
Beesdale
Taobh Siar
Tarbert (Tairbeart)
Urgha
Rhenigidale (Reinigeadal)
Beinn na h-Uamha
389
Beinn Mhòr
572
Beannan Mòr
242
Eisgean
Corlabhadh
298
Leumrabhagh
Gob na Milaid
Srianach
Eilean Iubhard
Uisenis
371
Mulhagery
Crionaig
470
Tathas Mhòr
Bhalamus
Mol Truisg
Gob Rubh' Uisenis
Rubha Bhrollum
Rubh' a' Bhaird
Sgeir na h-Eigheach
Eilean Mòr a' Bhàigh
SOUND OF SHIANT
Garbh Eilean
161
Eilean Mhuire
Eilean an Tighe
Shiant Islands
Paible
Losgaintir
Ceann Reamhar
467
South Harris Forest
287
Corran Seilebost
Sound of Taransay
Carragrich
Uieseval
334
Kyles Scalpay (Caolas Scalpaigh)
Sgeotasaigh
Scalpay
Scalpay (Eilean Scalpaigh)
Ben Scoravick
104
Kennavay
Meall Challibost
Rubha Romagi
Seilebost
158
Clett Nisabost
Na-Buirgh
Miabhag
A859
175
East Stockletts
East Loch Tarbert
Drinisiader
Kennacley
Plocropol
Bulabhall
354
Heileasbhal Mòr
384
An Coileach
386
Greosabhagh
Aird Mhige
Liceasto
Lacklee (Leac a' Li)
Scadabhagh
Sgarasta Mhòr
Bleaval
398
Geocrab
Cluer (Cluthar)
Beacravik
Stockinish (Stocinis)
Rubha Bocaig
Loch Langavat
Bràigh-nam-bàgh
Manish (Manais)
Aird Leimhe
Ard Manish
Rubha Cluer
Fleoideabhagh
Màs Garbh
Aird Mhighe
Finsbay
(Fionnsbhagh)
Quidinish (Cuidhtinis)
Rubha Quidnish
Roneval
459
Leverburgh (An t-Ob)
Strondeval
Cairminis
211
Borseam
Ceann a' Bhàigh
Lingarabay Island
Strannda
Rodel (Roghadal)
Rubha Vallarip
Renish Point
Gilsay
Lingay
Scaravay
1¾ hrs
Fladda-chuain
Gaeilavore Island
Gearran Island
Eilean Trodday
Rubha Hunish
Rubha na h-Aiseig
The Aird
Tulm Island
Kilmaluag
Balmaqueen
Duntulm
Galta Mòr
A855
Flodigarry
Sgeir Eirin
Eilean Flodigarry
Ru Bornaskitaig
Borniskitaig
Hunglader
Kilmuir
Quiraing
Meall na Suiramach
543
The Needle
Digg
Staffin Island
Kilvaxter
Suidh' a' Mhinn
350
Balgown
Staffin
Rubha Garbhaig
Stenscholl
Monkstadt
Kilbride Point
Linicro
Totscore
Bioda Buidhe
466
Stack of Skudiburgh
Ben Gorm
Maligar
Ellishadder
Idrigil
Rubha Idrigil
Uig
Ascrib Islands
South Ascrib
Balnaknock
Beinn Edra
611
Marishader
Garros
Culnaknock
Rubha Chorachan
Earlish
LITTLE MINCH
Vaternish Point
Sròn Ocrhulan
251
Ben Geary
284
Geary
Trumpan
Vaternish
Loch Snizort
Trotternish
Lealt
Ardmore Point
Halistra
Gillen
Stac a' Bhothain
Cuidrach
Peinlich
Glenuachdarach
Creag a' Lain
608
Baca Ruadh
637
Hallin
Isay
Mingay Island
Bod nan Laogh
Greshornish Point
Lyndale Point
A87
Dunvegan Head
Rubha Maol
Stein
Lusta
Beinn a' Sga
452
Hartaval
668
Rigg
Ben Skriaig
313
307
Boreraig
Galtrigill
Lampay Islands
Ben Diubaig
214
Lyndale Ho.
Kingsburgh
The Storr
719
Claigan
Beinn Bhreac
327
Beinn Chreagach
326
Greshornish
Flashader
Treaslane
Romesdal
51
Uig
Husabost
Totaig
Eyre
The Aird
Milovaig
Feriniquarrie
Edinbane
Kensaleyre
Ben Horneval
264
Bernisdale
Ben Dearg
552
Upper Milovaig
Lephin
Colbost
55
A850
Tote
Waterstein Head
296
Beinn na Creiche
264
Skinidin
Uiginish
Dunvegan
Ben Uigshader
246
Ben Sca
286
Borve
Neist Point
Kilmuir
Lonmore
Cruachan Beinn a' Chearcaill
271
Skeabost
Carbost
Sithean Bhealaich Chumhaing
392
Ben Corkeval
Healabhal Mhòr (Macleod's Table North)
468
Ben Aketil
265
Drumuie
Roskhill
Beinn a' Ghlinne Bhig
208
Uigshader
A863
Glengrasco
Torvaig
Ramasaig
Roag
Vatten
Orbost
Portree
Hoe Rape
Harlosh
Glen Ose
Beinn na Cloiche
232
Am Maol
212
The Hoe
233
Lorgill
488
Healabhal Bheag (Macleod's Table South)
Balmore
Ose
56
Penifiler
417
Beinn na Greine
Ben Tianavaig
413
Ben Connan
244
Beinn na Boineid
371
Harlosh Point
Glenmore
Camastianavaig
Ben Idrigil
340
Harlosh Island
Ebost
Ben Duagrich
304
Mugeary
400
Struan
Coillore
An Dubh Sgeir
Ullinish
Loch Bracadale
Lower Ollach

WESTERN ISLES
(NA H-EILEANAN AN IAR)
HS
Stornoway 2¾ hrs
Shiant Islands
Eilean Mhuire
Eilean an Tighe
Eilean Trodday
Rubha Hunish
Staffin Island
Eilean Flodigarry
Trotternish
SKYE
Portree
Uig
Staffin
RAASAY
RONA
SOUND OF RAASAY
INNER SOUND
Applecross
Applecross Forest
Shieldaig
Gairloch
Poolewe
Rubha Reidh
Longa Island
LOCH TORRIDON
LOCH EWE
Isle of Ewe
Aultbea
Upper Loch Torridon
Shieldaig Forest
Ben-damph Forest
Lochcarron
21
40
51
54
0 2 4 6 miles
0 2 4 6 8 10 km

93
86

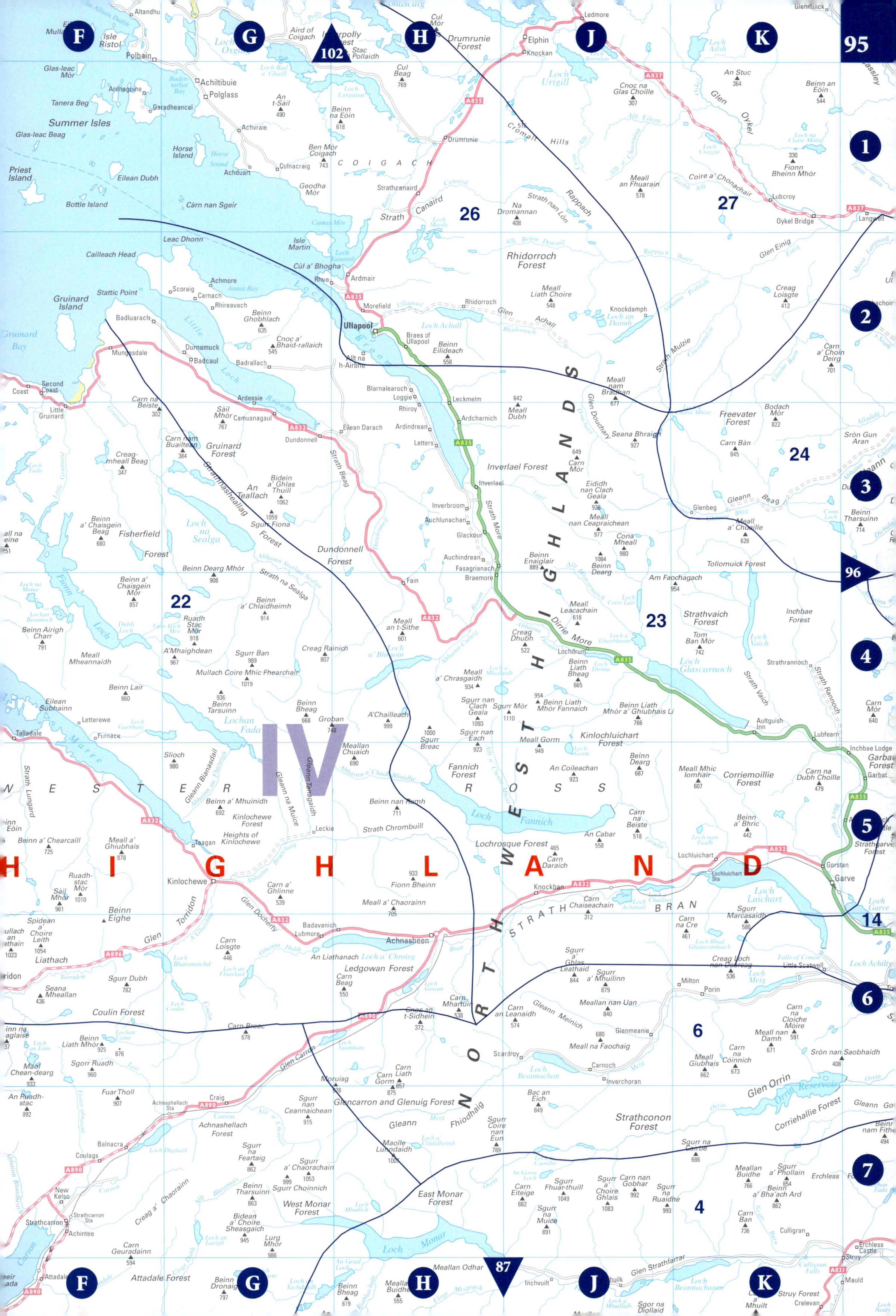
F
G
H
J
K
102
96
87
14
1
2
3
4
5
6
7
22
23
24
26
27
6
4
IV
HIGHLAND
WESTER ROSS
NORTH WEST HIGHLANDS
STRATH BRAN
COIGACH
Altandhu
Isle Ristol
Polbain
Aird of Coigach
Inverpolly Forest
Stac Pollaidh
Cul Mòr
Drumrunie Forest
Ledmore
Elphin
Knockan
Glenmuick
Loch Osgaig
Loch Lurgainn
Cul Beag 769
Loch Urigill
Cnoc na Glas Choille 307
An Stuc 364
Beinn an Eòin 544
Glas-leac Mòr
Achiltibuie
Polglass
Ardnagoine
Tanera Beg
Garadheancal
Summer Isles
Glas-leac Beag
An t-Sàil 490
Beinn na Eòin 618
Achvraie
Drumrunie
Cromalt Hills
Glen Oykel
Horse Island
Horse Sound
Culnacraig
Ben Mòr Coigach 743
Priest Island
Eilean Dubh
Achduart
Geodha Mòr
Strathcanaird
Meall an Fhuarain 578
Fionn Bheinn Mhòr 330
Coire a' Chonachair
Lubcroy
Bottle Island
Càrn nan Sgeir
Strath Canaird
Na Dromannan 408
Strath nan Lòn
Rappach
Oykel Bridge
Langwell
Leac Dhonn
Isle Martin
Rhidorroch Forest
Glen Einig
Cailleach Head
Cùl a' Bhogha
Rhue
Ardmair
Achmore
Annat Bay
Static Point
Scoraig
Carnach
Rhireavach
Morefield
Meall Liath Choire 548
Rhidorroch
Glen Achall
Knockdamph
Loch an Daimh
Creag Loisgte 412
Gruinard Island
Gruinard Bay
Badluarach
Little Loch Broom
Beinn Ghobhlach 635
Cnoc a' Bhaid-rallaich 545
Ullapool
Braes of Ullapool
Loch Achall
Beinn Eilideach 558
Strath Mulzie
Carn a' Choin Deirg 701
Mungasdale
Durnamuck
Badcaul
Badrallach
Allt na h-Airbhe
Loch Broom
Meall nam Bradhan 677
Coast
Second Coast
Little Gruinard
Carn na Beiste 302
Ardessie
Sàil Mhòr 767
Camusnagaul
Blarnalearoch
Loggie
Rhiroy
Leckmelm
642 Meall Dubh
Ardcharnich
Glen Douchary
Seana Bhraigh 927
Freevater Forest
Bodach Mòr 822
Carn Bàn 845
Sròn Gun Aran
Dundonnell
Eilean Darach
Ardindrean
Letters
Carn nam Buailtean 384
Gruinard Forest
Creag-mheall Beag 347
Strath Beag
Inverlael Forest
649 Carn Mòr
Bidein a' Ghlas Thuill 1062
An Teallach
Inverlael
Eididh nan Clach Geala 928
Glenbeg
Gleann Beag
Beinn Tharsuinn 714
Inverbroom
Auchlunachan
Glackour
Strath More
Meall nan Ceapraichean 977
Meall a' Chuaille 628
Beinn a' Chaisgein Beag 680
Fisherfield Forest
Loch na Sealga
Sgurr Fiona
1059
Dundonnell Forest
Cona' Mheall 980
Beinn Enaiglair 889
Auchindrean
Fasagrianach
Braemore
1084 Beinn Dearg
Tollomuick Forest
Beinn Dearg Mhòr 908
Strath na Sealga
Fain
Am Faochagach 954
Beinn a' Chaisgein Mòr 857
Beinn a' Chlaidheimh 914
Meall Leacachain 618
Strathvaich Forest
Inchbae Forest
Beinn Airigh Charr 791
Ruadh Stac Mòr 918
Meall an t-Sithe 601
Creag Dhubh 522
Dirrie More
Tom Ban Mòr 742
Loch Vaich
A'Mhaighdean 967
Sgurr Ban 989
Creag Rainich 807
Lochdrum
Loch Droma
Beinn Liath Bheag 665
Loch Glascarnoch
Strath Vaich
Strathrannoch
Strath Rannoch
Meall Mheannaidh
Mullach Coire Mhic Fhearchair 1019
Meall a' Chrasgaidh 934
954 Beinn Liath Mhòr Fannaich
Beinn Liath Mhòr a' Ghiubhais Li 766
Beinn Lair 860
936 Beinn Tarsuinn
Beinn Bheag 668
Groban 748
A'Chailleach 999
Sgurr nan Clach Geala 1093
Sgurr Mòr 1110
Aultguish Inn
Carn Mòr 640
Eilean Subhainn
Letterewe
Lochan Fada
1000 Sgurr Breac
Sgurr nan Each 923
Meall Gorm 949
Kinlochluichart Forest
Lubfearn
Talladale
Furnace
Loch Maree
Meallan Chuaich 690
Beinn Dearg 687
Inchbae Lodge
Garbat Forest
Garbat
Slioch 980
Gleann Bianasdail
Gleann Tanagaidh
Fannich Forest
An Coileachan 923
Meall Mhic Iomhair 607
Corriemoillie Forest
Carn na Dubh Choille 479
Strath Lungard
Beinn a' Mhuinidh 692
Gleann na Muice
Beinn nan Ramh 711
Loch Fannich
Carn na Beiste 518
Beinn a' Bhric 442
Kinlochewe Forest
Leckie
Strath Chrombuill
Lochrosque Forest
An Cabar 558
Strathgarve Forest
Beinn a' Chearcall 725
Meall a' Ghiubhais 878
Heights of Kinlochewe
Taagan
465 Carn Daraich
Lochluichart
Gorstan
Garve
Ruadh-stac Mòr 1010
Sàil Mhòr 981
Kinlochewe
Carn a' Ghlinne 539
933 Fionn Bheinn
Knockban
Carn Chaiseachain 312
Loch Luichart
Loch Garve
Spidean a' Choire Leith 1054
Beinn Eighe
Glen Docherty
Badavanich
Lubmore
Meall a' Chaorainn 705
Achnasheen
Carn na Cre 461
Sgurr Marcasaidh 580
Liathach
Glen Torridon
Carn Loisgte 446
An Liathanach
Loch a' Chroisg
Ledgowan Forest
Sgurr a' Ghlas Leathaid 844
Sgurr a' Mhuilinn 879
Creag Loch nan Dearcag 536
Little Scatwell
Loch Achilty
Torridon
Sgurr Dubh 782
Carn Beag 550
Carn Mhartuin 538
Milton
Porin
Seana Mheallan 436
Coulin Forest
Carn Breac 678
Cnoc an t-Sidhein 372
Carn an Leanaidh 574
Gleann Meinich
Meallan nan Uan 840
Glenmeanie
Carn na Cloiche Moire 591
Beinn Liath Mhòr 925
876
680 Meall na Faochaig
Meall nan Damh 671
Sròn nan Saobhaidh 408
Sgorr Ruadh 960
Maol Chean-dearg 933
Glen Carron
Scardroy
Carnoch
Loch Beannachan
Meall Giubhais 662
Carn na Coinnich 673
Fuar Tholl 907
Moruisg 928
Carn Gorm 875
Carn Liath 857
Invercoran
Glen Orrin
Orrin Reservoir
An Ruadh-stac 892
Craig
Achnashellach Sta
Achnashellach Forest
Sgurr nan Ceannaichean 915
Glencarron and Glenuig Forest
Bac an Eich 849
Fiodhaig
Gleann Fhiodhaig
Sgurr Coire nan Eun 789
Strathconon Forest
Corriehallie Forest
Balnacra
Sgurr na Feartaig 862
Sgurr a' Chaorachain 1053
Maoile Lunndaidh 1007
Sgurr na Coinnich 686
Beinn nam Fitheach 494
Coulags
999
Sgurr Choinnich
Mealian Buidhe 766
Sgurr a' Phollain 854
Erchless
New Kelso
Creag a' Chaorainn
Beinn Tharsuinn 863
West Monar Forest
East Monar Forest
Carn Eiteige 882
Sgurr Fhuar-thuill 1049
Sgurr a' Choire Ghlais 1083
Carn nan Gobhar 992
Sgurr na Ruaidhe 993
Beinn a' Bha'ach Ard 862
Strathcarron
Strathcarron Sta
Achintee
Bidean a' Choire Sheasgaich 945
Lurg Mhòr 986
Sgurr na Muice 891
Carn Ban 736
Culligran
Loch Monar
Carn Geuradainn 594
Erchless Castle
Struy
Attadale
Attadale Forest
Beinn Dronaig 797
Beinn Bheag 619
Meallan Odhar
Meallan Buidhe 555
Inchvuilt
Glen Strathfarrar
Loch Beannacharan
Sgor na Diollaid
Culligran Falls
Mauld
Struy Forest
Crelevan
A835
A837
A832
A890
A896
A831

A
B
C
D
E
103
95
88
1
2
3
4
5
6
7
IV
H I G H L A N D
NORTHWEST HIGHLANDS
Loch Ailsh
An Stuc
Beinn an Eòin
Glen Oykel
Cassley
Badintagairt
Carn nam Bo Maola
Colaboll
Dalchork
Achnairn
Dalmichy
Lairg
Saval
Sallachy
Savalbeg
Meall Dola
Balcharn
Rhaoine
Muie
Tomich
Torroble
Strath Fleet
Ardachu
Creagan Glas
Grumby Rock
West Langwell
East Langwell
Strath Brora
Tannachy
Rhilochan
Knockarthur
Farlary
Little Rogart
Blairmore
Rogart
Pittentrail
Morvich
Aberscross
Mound Rock
Cnoc na Glas Choille
Meall an Fhuarain
Coire a' Chonachair
Fionn Bheinn Mhòr
Lubcroy
Oykel Bridge
Langwell
Brae
Doune
Strath Oykel
Invercassley
Rosehall
Glenrossal
Oykel Forest
Cnoc a' Choire
Aucharrigill
Altass
Auchintoul
Cnoc Ceann nam Bad
Shin Forest
Achany
Gruids
Braemore
Achinduich
Linsidemore
Birchfield
Achnahanat
Inveran
Rhelonie
Strath Tollaidh
Dalnamain
Little Torboll
Ardshave
Sròn Ach' a' Bhacaidh
Beinn Domhnaill
Glen Einig
Creag Loisgte
Beinn Ulbhaidh
Lubachoinnich
Breac-Bheinn
Meall Dheirgidh
Strathcarron
Sgodachail
Croick
Wester Gruinards
The Craigs
Amat Forest
Culrain
Balblair
Invershin
Clashban
Clashcoig
Meall Mòrag
Achvaich
Achosnich
Rearquhar
Badninish
Skelbo
Creagan Asdale
Gablon
Birichen
Clashmore Wood
Clashmore
Evelix
Camore
Tulloch
Migdale
Loch Migdale
Kyloag
Soyal
Bonar Bridge
Ardgay
Dounie
Lower Gledfield
Oldtown
Kincardine
Spinningdale
Little Creich
Ardchronie
Whiteface
Pulrossie
Lonemore
Cuthill
Dornoch Sands
Strath Mulzie
Loch an Daimh
Carn a' Choin Deirg
Freevater Forest
Bodach Mòr
Seana Bhraigh
Carn Bàn
Sròn Gun Aran
Gleann Mòr
Glencalvie Forest
Glen Calvie
Carn Bhrain
Easter Fearn
Struie Hill
Struie
Balblair
Edderton
Ardmore
Ardjachie Point
Morangie
Tain
Dunan Liath
Gleann Beag
Diebidale Forest
Beinn Tharsuinn
Carn Chuinneag
Glen Diebidale
Creag Ruadh
Meall Bhenneit
Beinn Clach an Fheadain
Cnoc Muigh-bhlàraidh
Aultnamain Inn
Morangie Forest
Lairgs of Tain
Glengeg
Meall a' Chuaille
Cam Cas nan Gabhar
Tollomuick Forest
Aldie
Cnoc an t-Sabhail
Strath Rory
Lamington
Newfield
Logie Hill
Scotsburn
Torran
Balnagown Castle
Ballchraggan
Kildary
Milton
Inchindown
Cnoc Corr Guinie
Strathvaich Forest
Inchbae Forest
Kildermorie Forest
Kildermorie Lodge
Braeantra
Strath Rusdale
Beinn Tharsuinn
Loch Morie
Inchlumpie
Beinn nan Eun
Meall Mòr
Wyvis Lodge
Loch Glass
Meall an Tuirc
Boath
Ardross
Easter Ardross
Stittenham
Dalnavie
Achandunie
Wester Lealty
Contullich
Rhicullen
Tulloch Muir
Kilmuir
Tarbat Ho.
Barbaraville
Nigg Bay
Tom Ban Mòr
Loch Vaich
Loch Glascarnoch
Strathrannoch
Strath Vaich
Strath Rannoch
Beinn Liath Mhòr a' Ghiubhais Li
Carn Mòr
Queen's Cairn
Wyvis Forest
Meall na Drochaide
Kinloch
Bendcallt
Cnoc Ceislein
Wester Lonvine
Tomich
Delny
Balintraid
Saltburn
Balnabruaich
Balnapaling
Aultguish Inn
Lubfearn
Inchbae Lodge
Garbat Forest
Garbat
Ben Wyvis
Glas Leathad Mòr
An Cabar
Beinn Enaiglair
Glen Glass
Carn Mòr
Alness
Rosskeen
Achnagarron
Dalmore
Invergordon
Cromarty Firth
Beinn Dearg
Meall Mhic Iomhair
Corriemoillie Forest
Carn na Dubh Choille
Redburn
Swordale
Drummond
Evanton
Alness Bay
Balblair
Newhall Point
Cromarty Bay
Cromarty
Newton
Shoremill
Jemimaville
Udale Bay
Navity
Resolis
Cullicudden
Newmills
Poyntzfield
Beinn a' Bhric
Achnaclerach
Little Wyvis
Meall na Speireig
Balconie Point
The Den
Easter Brae
Munlochy
Upper Eathie
Glenurquhart
Craighead
Lochluichart
Strathgarve Forest
Carn Gorm
Cloch Mhòr
Strath Sgitheach
Mountgerald
Ardullie
Shoreton
Culbo
Millbuie
Millbuie Forest
Gorstan
Lochluichart Sta
Garve
Loch Luichart
Glensgaich
Bottacks
Heights of Brae
Auchterneed
Fodderty
Findon Mains
Mount Eagle
Balmungie
Janefield
Whiteness Head
Sgurr Marcasaidh
Carn na Cre
Loch Garve
Castle Leod
Strath Peffer
Dingwall
Urquhart
Culbokie
Black Isle
Killen
Rosemarkie
Fortrose
Fort George
Kirkton
Strathpeffer
Tarvie
Creag Loch nan Dearcag
Little Scatwell
Loch Meig
Jamestown
Contin
Lochussie
Maryburgh
Alcaig
Duncanston
Belmaduthy
Easter Suddie
Avoch
Avoch Bay
Chanonry Point
Ardersier
Milton
Porin
Torrachilty Wood
Conon Bridge
Cornton
Easter Kinkell
Bogbuie
Knockbain
Shantullich
Munlochy
Strathconon
Marybank
Urray
Leanaig
Tore
Glenmeanie
Carn na Cloiche Moire
Meall nan Damh
Carn na Coinnich
Sròn nan Saobhaidh
Meall Giubhais
Balvaird
Kilcoy
Newton
Drumderfit
Bogallan
Inverness
Fisherton
Castle Stuart
Tornagrain
Glen Orrin
Faebait
Muir of Ord
Redcastle
Milton
Kilmuir
Alturlie Point
Dalcross
Cantraywood
Gleann Goibhre
Orrin Reservoir
Corriehallie Forest
Beinn nam Fitheach
Cnoc Eille Mòr
Urchany and Farley Forest
Aultvaich
Windhill
Clashdorran
Rheindown
Ruilick
Beauly
Beauly Firth
Charlestown
North Kessock
South Kessock
Merkinch
Craigton
Craigton Point
Longman Point
Allanfearn
Balloch
Culloden
Culloden Forest
Culloden Muir
Clachnaharry
Smithton
Westhill
Leanach
Sgurr na Cairbe
Meallan Buidhe
Sgurr a' Phollain
Erchless Forest
Beinn a' Bha'ach Ard
Kirkhill
Rhindouie
Achnagairn
Drumchardine
Bunchrew
Leachkin
Culcabock
Kilmorack
Balchraggan
Easter Moniack
The Aird
Sgurr na Ruaidhe
Carn Ban
Culligran
Crask of Aigas
Oldtown of Aigas
Culburnie
Kiltarlity
Belladrum
Tomnacross
An Leacainn
Cnoc na Moine
Lagnalean
Drummossie
Castletown
Bogbain
Beinn Bhuidhe Mhor
Struy
Erchless Castle
Craigdhu
Camault Muir
Dochgarroch
Kirkton
Newton of Leys
Scaniport
Daviot
Craggie
Glen Strathfarrar
Eskadale
Druimkinnerras
Foxhole
Boblainy Forest
Carn a' Bhodaich
Lochend
Mains of Faillie
Scatraig
Beinn Bhreac
Sgor na Diollaid
Muhuil
Crelevan
Loch Bruicheach
0 2 4 6 miles
0 2 4 6 8 10 km
A838
A836
A837
A839
A949
A9
A835
A832
A834
A862
A833
A831
A82
A96

F
G
H
J
K
104
98
89
1
2
3
4
5
6
7
KW
IV
AB
PH
9
10
20
12
26
30
31
32
36
37
38
55
M O R A Y
MORAY FIRTH
DORNOCH FIRTH
Sletdale
Col-bheinn
538
Creag a' Chrionaich
Lothmore
Culgower
Kilmote
Lothbeg
Lothbeg Point
Kilbraur
Gordonbush
Loch Brora
Kilbraur Hill
323
Carrol Rock
208
Kintradwell
Killin
Killin Rock
215
Carrol
West Clyne
East Clyne
Greenhill
Dalchalm
Cagar Feosaig
378
Clynelish
East Brora
Brora
Doll
Backies
Dunrobin Castle Sta
Golspie
Littleferry
Embo
Embo Street
Dornoch Point
Whiteness Sands
Innis Mhòr
Innis Bheag
Tarbat Ness
Port Mòr
Wilkhaven
Hilton
Portmahomack
Bindal
Balcherry
Inver
Rockfield
Balnagall
Tarrel
Lochslin
Baldie
Rhynie
Geanies Ho.
Hill of Fearn
Fearn
Fearn Sta
Cadboll
Tullich
Hilton of Cadboll
Clay of Allan
Balintore
Shandwick
Chapelhill
Nigg
Hill of Nigg
Castlecraig
North Sutor
Sutor Stacks
Sutors of Cromarty
Blue Head
McFarquhar's Caves
Halliman Skerries
Covesea Skerries
Clashach Point
Covesea
Stotfield
Branderburgh
Lossiemouth
Hopeman
Burghead
Cummingstown
Duffus
Gordonstoun
Roseisle
Oakenhead
Boar's Head Rock
Lossie Forest
Innes Links
Salterhill
Roseisle Forest
Burghead Bay
Buthill
Findrassie
Lochhill
Findhorn
Hempriggs
Quarrywood
Bishopmill
Findhorn Bay
Muirhead
Coltfield
Miltonhill
Ardgye
Urquhart
ELGIN
Culbin Forest
Kinloss
Alves
New Elgin
Muir of Lochs
Wellhill
Kintessack
Inverene
Grange Hall
Toreduff
Clover
Palmerscross
Lhanbryde
Moss of Barmuckity
Moy House
Springfield
Hillside
Pittendreich
Mosstodloch
Muirtown
The Bar
Forres
Monaughty Forest
Miltonduff
Dyke
Mains of Burgie
Paddockhaugh
Blackhills
Longmorn
Clackmarras
Kingsteps
Macbeth's Hillock
Newton of Dalvey
Heldon Hill
234
Barnhill
Cloddach
Auchtertyre
Fogwatt
Altonside
Orbliston
Nairn
Hilton of Delnies
Tradespark
Househill
Blervie Castle
Califer
Rafford
Tulloch
Whitewreath
Thomshill
Teindland Forest
Auldearn
Boghole Fm
Loch of Blairs
Crofts of Buinach
Kellas
Dallas Forest
Blackcastle
Whitemire
Altyre Woods
Hill of the Wangie
319
Leanoch
Coleburn
Findlay's Seat
262
Muir of the Clans
Moss-side
Laiken Forest
Milton
Conicavel
Newtyle Forest
Branchill
Edinvale
Craigend
Glenlatterach
Glenlatterach Reservoir
Bardon
Brylach Hill
325
Wood of Dundurcas
Torrich
Regoul
Maths of Sluie
Old Military Road
Phorp
Dallas
Mill Buie
355
Pikey Hill
355
Auchinroath
Clephanton
Piperhill
Fornighty
Darnaway Forest
Presley
Romach Hill
313
Mill Buie
371
Ardoch
Meikle Hill
280
Cairn Uish
365
The Kettles
Rothes
Kirkhill
Cawdor
Culcharry
Littlemill
Lethen Bar
258
Logie
Drumine Forest
Tomnamoon
Craigroy
Knock More
Urchany
Hill of Tomechole
344
Cairn na Cailliche
404
Burn of Rothes
Ben Aigan
471
Dallaschyle
Easter Galcantray
Achindown
Relugas
Loch Dallas
Carnachie
359
Hill of Stob
308
Cairn Cattoch
369
Hunt Hill
365
Whiteacen
Dandaleith
Assich Forest
Kirkton of Barevan
Clunas
Redburn
Bruachmary
Findhorn
Mount
Carn Ghiubhais
430
Burn of Coulatt
Elchies Forest
Craigellachie
Balmore
Ferness
Tomdow
Archiestown
Robertstown
Ringorm
Carn a' Chrasgie
401
Daltra
Carn Kitty
521
Carn Shalag
470
Cardow
Upper Knockando
Aberlour (Charlestown of Aberlour)
Cairn Duhie
312
Knock of Braemoray
456
Sliabh Bainneach
483
Knockando
Speyview
Carron
Carn Sgumain
417
Dulsie
Roy's Hill
516
Kinermony
Milltown of Edinvillie
Carnoch
Banchor
Milltown
Lady Hill
545
Paul's Hill
Dufftown
Carn nan Tri-tighearnan
615
Hill of Aitnoch
413
Aitnoch
Carn Ruighe an Uain
546
Daugh of Carron
Sheandow
552
Streens
Carn na Sguabaich
Dava
Dava Moor
Glen Tulchan
Carne
Gallow Hill
Scootmore Forest
Marypark
Belleheiglash
Baby's Hill
Beatshach
Meikle Conval
A9
A96
A939
A940
A941
A95
B9165
B9166
B9175
B9090
B9091
B9092
B9101
B9007
B9010
B9011
B9012
B9013
B9089
B9040
B9135
B9015
B9102
B9009

A
B
C
D
E
1
2
3
4
5
6
7
Halliman Skerries
Covesea Skerries
Stotfield
Branderburgh
Lossiemouth
97
31
Lossie Forest
Innes Links
Boar's Head Rock
Spey Mouth
Kingston
Spey Bay
Garmouth
Nether Dallachy
Upper Dallachy
Portgordon
Portknockie
Findochty
Scar Nose
Logie Head
Redhythe Point
Portessie
Ianstown
Bauds of Cullen
Rathven
Buckie
Seatown
Cullen
Sandend
Portsoy
Knock Head
Whitehills
Banff
ELGIN
Bishopmill
New Elgin
Lhanbryde
Urquhart
Mosstodloch
Fochabers
Lochhill
Muir of Lochs
Newton
Bogmoor
Dipple
Orbliston
Ordiequish
Speymouth Forest
Wood of Ordiequish
Clochan
Arradoul
Slackhead
Drybridge
56
Hill of Maud
Bin of Cullen
Slate Haugh
Weston
Shiel Muir
Lintmill
Clune
Milton
Fordyce
Durn Hill
Fordyce Hill
Kirktown of Deskford
Berryhillock
Ardiecow
Boyndie
Blairshinnoch
Wester Culbeuchly
Hill of Culbirnie
45
Kirktown of Alvah
Pittendreich
Paddockhaugh
Longmorn
Blackhills
Clackmarras
Altonside
Fogwatt
Whitewreath
Thomshill
30
32
IV
M
O
R
A
Y
Teindland Forest
Coleburn
Bardon
Glenlatterach
Findlay's Seat
Brylach Hill
Pikey Hill
Glen of Rothes
The Kettles
Cairn Uish
Wood of Dundurcas
Auchinroath
Rothes
Boat o' Brig
Mulben
Knock More
Keith
Newmill
Fife Keith
Aultmore
Millstone Hill
Addie Hill
Aultmore
Black Hill
Deerhill
Broadrashes
Garralburn
Grange Crossroads
Cranloch
Bracobrae
Sillyearn
Floors
Farmtown
Davoch of Grange
Knock
Knock Hill
Lurg Hill
Backies
Gordonstown
Glen Barry
Cornhill
Park
Canterbury
Wether Hill
Culvie
Knabbygates
Drumnagorrach
Old Crombie
Milltown of Rothiemay
Mayen
Marnoch
Aberchirder
Bogton
Clunie
Carnousie
Laithers
Forgie
North Bogbain
Hill of Mulderie
Thief's Hill
Tauchers
Auchlunkart
Rosarie
Rosarie Forest
Ben Aigan
Hill of Towie
Towiemore
Blackhillock
Meikle Balloch Hill
Balloch Wood
Glen of Coachford
Edintore
Coachford
Haughs
Ruthven
Redhill
Fourman Hill
Yonder Bognie
Bogniebrae
Inverkeithny
Auchininna
Fortrie
Hill of Carlincraig
Carn na Cailliche
Hill of Stob
Cairn Catoch
Hunt Hill
38
Whiteacen
Dandaleith
Maggieknockater
Knockan
Craigellachie
Archiestown
Robertstown
Ringorm
Aberlour (Charlestown of Aberlour)
Drummuir Castle
Drummuir
55
Hillend
Newton
Cairnie
The Bin
The Bin Forest
A
B
E
R
D
E
Huntly
Corse of Kinnoir
Lessendrum
Cobairdy
Conland
Drumblair
Largue
Denmoss
Frendraught
Auchernie
Cardow
Knockando
Carron
Speyview
Daugh of Kinermony
Milltown of Edinvillie
Dufftown
Parkmore
Tullich
Braehead
Aultnapaddock
Daugh of Invermarkie
Daugh of Cairnborrow
Milton of Cairnborrow
Drumdelgie
Torry
54
Drumblade
Mosshead
Brideswell
Beggshill
Ythanwells
Daugh of Carron
Marypark
Belleheiglash
37
Baby's Hill
Sheandow
Meikle Conval
Ben Rinnes
Beatshach
Bakebare
Keithmore
Haugh of Glass
Dumeath
Cairnargat
Clashmach Hill
Muckle Long Hill
Bailiesward
S t r a t h b o g i e
Thomastown
Millburn
Denend
Sliach
Laggan
Bridgehaugh
The Scalp
Backside
Succoth
Tillathrowie
Bridgend
Kirkstile
Winds Eye
Bainshole
Tillymorgan
Fisherford
Glens of Foudland
Hill of Foudland
Dalchirach
Achnastank
Favillar
Laird's Seat
Carn Chrom
Glacks of Balloch Pass
Ballochford
Tomnaven
Coynachie
Clashindarroch Forest
Quarry Hill
Cransmill Hill
Clashindarroch
Gartly
Kirkney
Culdrain
Backburn
Wishach Hill
Kirkton of Culsalmond
Cairnhill
Craggan
Cairnacay
Tervieside
Hill of Achmore
Glen Fiddich Forest
Bridgend
Inverharroch Farm
Ardwell
Black Hill
Knockandy Hill
Cults
Slack
Wardhouse
Largie
Wrangham
Colpy
Upper Boddam
Newnoth
Tap o' Noth
Drumin
Glenlivet
Carn Liath
Muldonich
Meikle Firbriggs
90
Mount of Haddoch
Belhinnie
Milton of Noth
Kennethmont
Glanderston
Aulton
52
Rothney
Insch
Hill of Christ's Kirk
Ardoyne
Old Rayne
Rhynie
Cottown
Towie
Aldunie
0 2 4 6 miles
0 2 4 6 8 10 km

F
G
H
J
K
1
2
3
4
5
6
7
Kinnairds Head
Fraserburgh
Fraserburgh Bay
Cairnbulg Point
Cairnbulg
Inverallochy
Whitelinks Bay
Charlestown
St Combs
Inzie Head
South Inch
Strathbeg Bay
Rosehearty
Pittulie
Sandhaven
Broadsea
Quarry Head
Peathill
Percyhorner
Pitblae
Cardno
Memsie
Troup Head
Crovie Head
Crovie
Northfield
Pennan Head
Pennan
Aberdour Bay
Head of Garness
Gamrie Bay
Gardenstown
Macduff
44
Melrose
Protstonhill
Dubford
Gamrie
Cushnie
Towie
New Aberdour
Coburty
Upper Boyndie
Mid Ardlaw
Tyrie
Broomhead
Longmanhill
Wester Greenskares
Lenihas
Windyheads Hill
231
225
Woodhead
Ladysford
Whitewell
43
Whitebog
Rathen
Cairness
Craigellie
Coralhill
Gowanhill
Foulzie
Minnonie
Netherbrae
Overbrae
Bracklamore Hill
220
Hill of Fishrie
227
Bracklamore
Nether Glasslaw
Craigmaud
Bogfold
Turclossie
Hillhead of Auchentumb
Newburgh
Waughton Hill
234
Mormond Hill
230
Waughtonhill
Whitestripe
Lonmay
Crimonmogate
Old Rattray
Seatown
Rattray Head
Loch of Strathbeg
Dartfield
Crimond
Keilhill
Balgreen
Gorrachie
Castleton
Milltown of Craigston
Plaidy
AB
Finlry
Brackens
New Byth
Garmond
Wester Badentyre
Muiryfold
Balthangie
Cairnywhing
New Pitsligo
Knowhead
Strichen
New Leeds
Upper Bidinghill
Blackhill
North Essie
Rattray Bay
Gas Terminal
St Fergus Moss
St Fergus
Scotstown Head
Kirkton Head
Bonnykelly
Craigculter
Whitehill
Ironside
Adziel
Carnichal
Denhead
Longhill
Leys
Backfolds
Hythie
Rora Moss
Kirktown
Rora
Cuttyhill
Fetterangus
Forest of Deer
Toux
Mains of Pitfour
Oldwhat
Hill of Corsegight
188
Corsegight
Turriff
Delgaty Forest
Cuminestown
B U C H A N
Middlehill
Mains of Fedderate
Lunderton
Craig Ewen
Bridgend
Mill of Colp
Darra
Gask
53
Hatton Castle
Howe of Teuchar
West Cairncake
Waggle Hill
178
Northumbhill
North Commonty
Mains of Culsh
Maud
Mintlaw
Millbank
Torterston
Inverugie
Grainhow
New Deer
Waterhill of Bruxie
Old Deer
Longside
Flushing
Thunderton
Buchanhaven
Peterhead
Braefoot
Birkenhills
Muirtack
Drymuir
Backhill of Clackriach
Inverquhomery
Keith Inch
Peterhead Bay
Kingsford
South Redbriggs
Deer's Hill
178
Maryhill
Clockhill
Bulwark
Stuartfield
Millbreck
42
Hillhead of Cocklaw
Burnhaven
Sandford Bay
Invernettie
Tillyfar
North Millbrex
Dykeside
Moss of Belnagoak
Nethermuir
Crichie
Clola
Little Dens
Newmill
Knaven
Kinnadie
Nether Kinmundy
Blackhill
Stirling
Boddam
Buchan Ness
E N S H I R E
Steinmanhill
Mackerry
Skelmuir
Newton
Inverythan
Gourdas
Darnabo
Lethenty
Monkshill
Burnend
Cairnorrie
South Upper Barrack
Auchnagatt
Skelmuir Hill
149
Kinknockie
Carse of Balloch
Smallburn
Moss of Cruden
Sandfordhill
Kirktown of Auchterless
Tifty
Backhill
Cottown
Brownhill
Monteach
Hill of Skilmafilly
176
Mill of Elrick
Aldie
Gask
Coldwells
Murdoch Head
Gordonstown
Woodhead
Ardo
Skelmonae
Inkhorn
Upper Hawkhillock
Ardallie
Greenheads
Teuchan
North Haven
Rothiebrisbane
Fyvie
Crofts of Haddo
Quilquox
Loanhead
Milton of Coldwells
Hill of Dudwick
174
Muirtack
Auchiries
Petty
Greenmyre
Methlick
Mains of Dudwick
Hatton
Errollston
Cruden Bay
Rothienorman
Collynie
Drumwhindle
Arthrath
Chapel Hill
Port Erroll
Tanglandford
41
Blindburn
Waterloo
Cromlet
St Katherines
Barthol Chapel
Hillbrae
Craigie Brae
Bearnie
Toll of Birness
Bogbrae
Bay of Cruden
Springlove
Folla Rule
South Flobbets
Eastford
Inverebrie
Hilton Croft
Kiplaw Croft
The Skares
Whinnyfold
Core Hill
245
The Banking
Silvermoss
Thornroan
Cookston
Newseat
51
Cross of Jackston
South Blackbog
Balgove
Wedderlairs
Raxton
Broomfield
Leask
Meikle Wartle
Jackstown
Tulloch
Tarves
Artrochie
The Veshels
Pitinnan
Craigdam
Kinharrachie
Ellon
Auchmacoy
Meikle Loch
Clochtow
Rayne
F o r m a r t i n e
Yrthsie
Esslemont
Mounie Castle
Auquhorthies
Kirkton
Logie Buchan
91
Slains
Mains of Glack
Whitefield
Cairnhill
Meikle Tarty
Waterside
Fingask
Oldmeldrum
Pitmedden
St Catherine's Dub
A90
A98
A947
A950
A981
A952
A948
A920
A975
A982
B9031
B9032
B9033
B9093
B9105
B9170
B9029
B9030
B9106
B9005
B9001
B9000
B9107
B9170
B9121
B9008
B992
Idoch Water
North Ugie Water
South Ugie Water
Ythan

WESTERN ISLES
(NA H-EILEANAN AN IAR)
A
B
C
D
E
1
2
3
4
5
6
7
Gallan Head
Aird Uig
Geodha Nasavig
Bhaltos
Forsnaval
Miavaig (Miabhaig)
Timsgearraidh
Cairisiadar
Great Bernera
Breacleit
Barraglom
Callanish (Calanais)
Carloway (Carlabhagh)
Shawbost (Siabost)
Tolastadh a' Chaolais
Breascleit
Garrynahine (Gearraidh na h-Aibhne)
Mangurstadh
Aird Mhòr Mangurstadh
Aird Fenish
Islibhig
Breanais
Aird Breanais
Mealasta
Mealasta Island
Griomaval
Liongam
Kearstay
Scarp
Huisinis
Hushinish Point
Horsanish
Taransay Glorigs
Taransay (Tarasaigh)
Morsgail Forest
Kintarvie
Aird an Troim
Ath Linne
Seaforth Island
NORTH HARRIS
(CEANN A TUATH NA HEARADH)
Forest of Harris
Clisham
Tarbert (Tairbeart)
WEST LOCH TARBERT
Maraig (Maaruig)
Kenmore
Kyles Scalpay (Caolas Scalpaigh)
Balallan (Baile Ailein)
HS
2
3
A858
A859
B887
B8011
B8059
0 2 4 6 miles
0 2 4 6 8 10 km

93

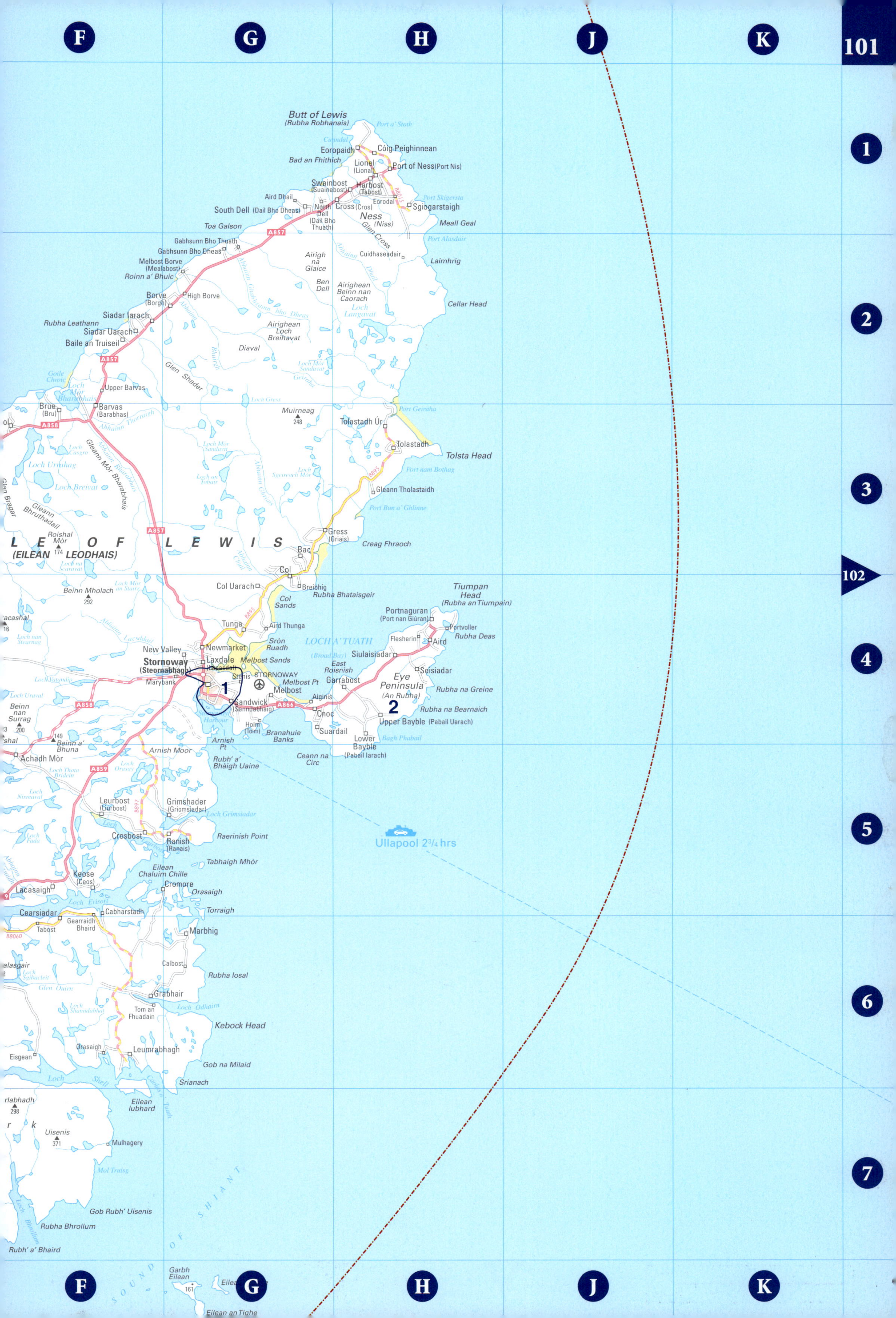
F
G
H
J
K
1
2
3
4
5
6
7
102
Butt of Lewis
(Rubha Robhanais)
Port a' Stoth
Eoropaidh
Còig Peighinnean
Bad an Fhithich
Lionel
(Lional)
Port of Ness (Port Nis)
Swainbost
(Suainebost)
Habost
(Tabost)
Eorodal
Port Skigersta
Sgiogarstaigh
Aird Dhail
South Dell (Dail Bho Dheas)
North Dell
(Dail Bho Thuath)
Cross (Cros)
Ness
(Niss)
Meall Geal
Toa Galson
Glen Cross
Port Alasdair
Gabhsunn Bho Thuath
Gabhsunn Bho Dheas
Airigh na Glaice
Cuidhaseadair
Laimhrig
Melbost Borve
(Mealabost)
Roinn a' Bhuic
Ben Dell
Airighean Beinn nan Caorach
Borve
(Borgh)
High Borve
Loch Langavat
Cellar Head
Siadar Iarach
Rubha Leathann
Siadar Uarach
Airighean Loch Breihavat
Baile an Truiseil
Diaval
A857
Glen Shader
Loch Mòr Sandavat
Upper Barvas
Brue
(Bru)
Barvas
(Barabhas)
A858
Muirneag
248
Port Geiraha
Tolestadh Ùr
Tolastadh
Tolsta Head
Port nam Bothag
Gleann Mòr Bharabhais
Loch Urrahag
Loch Breivat
Gleann Tholastaidh
B895
Port Ban a' Ghlinne
Glen Bragar
Gleann Bhruthadail
Roishal Mòr
174
Gress
(Griais)
Creag Fhraoch
L E O F L E W I S
(EILEAN LEODHAIS)
Bac
Col
Col Uarach
Breibhig
Rubha Bhataisgeir
Col Sands
Beinn Mholach
292
Tiumpan Head
(Rubha an Tiumpain)
Portnaguran
(Port nan Giùran)
Portvoller
Rubha Deas
Tunga
Aird Thunga
Flesherin
Aird
New Valley
Newmarket
Sròn Ruadh
LOCH A' TUATH
(Broad Bay)
Stornoway
(Steornabhagh)
Laxdale
(Lacasdal)
Melbost Sands
Siulaisiadar
East Roisnish
Seisiadar
STORNOWAY
Melbost Pt
Garrabost
Eye Peninsula
(An Rubha)
Rubha na Greine
Marybank
Melbost
1
Aiginis
2
Sandwick
(Sanndabhaig)
A866
Cnoc
Rubha na Bearnaich
Upper Bayble (Pabail Uarach)
Beinn nan Surrag
200
Holm
(Tolm)
Branahuie Banks
Suardail
Lower Bayble
(Pabail Iarach)
Bagh Phabail
149
Beinn a' Bhuna
Arnish Pt
Ceann na Circ
Achadh Mòr
Arnish Moor
Rubh' a' Bhàigh Uaine
A859
Leurbost
(Liurbost)
Grimshader
(Griomsiadar)
Loch Grimsiadar
Crosbost
Raerinish Point
Ranish
(Ranais)
Ullapool 2¾ hrs
Tabhaigh Mhòr
Eilean Chaluim Chille
Keose
(Ceos)
Cromore
Lacasaigh
Orasaigh
Cearsiadar
Cabharstadh
Torraigh
Tabost
Gearraidh Bhaird
B8060
Marbhig
Calbost
Rubha Iosal
Glen Ouirn
Grabhair
Tom an Fhuadain
Loch Odhairn
Kebock Head
Orasaigh
Leumrabhagh
Eisgean
Gob na Milaid
Loch Shell
Srianach
Eilean Iubhard
298
Uisenis
371
Mulhagery
Mol Truisg
Gob Rubh' Uisenis
Rubha Bhrollum
Rubh' a' Bhaird
SOUND OF SHIANT
Garbh Eilean
161
Eilean an Tighe

A
B
C
D
E
1
2
3
4
5
6
7
101
95
26
Cape Wrath
Duslic
Kearvaig
Geodha Ruadh na Fola
Cnoc a' Ghiubhais
297
Bay of Keisgaig
Am Balg
Sandwood Bay
Am Buachaille
Beinn Dearg
423
Creag Riabhach
485
Sandwood Loch
An Grianan
467
Meall na Moine
464
Rubh' an Fhir Leithe
Strath Shinary
Sheigra
Balchrick
Blairmore
Oldshore Beg
Beinn a' Chraisg
257
Oldshoremore
Eilean an Ròin Mòr
An Socach
358
Loch Clash
Kinlochbervie
Rubha na Leacaig
Badcall
Achriesgill
Achlyness
Ardmore Point
Ceathramh Garbh
Rhiconich
Rubha Ruadh
Fanagmore
Tarbet
Foindle
A838
Handa Island
Laxford Bridge
Badnabay
A894
Scourie More
Scourie
Rubh' Aird an t- Sionnaich
Ben Stack
721
Badcall
Ben Auskaird
386
Strath Stack
Achfary
Eilean a' Bhreitheimh
Reay Forest
Rubh' a' Mhucard
Meall Mòr
Meall Beag
Calbha Beag
Ben Strome
426
Loch an Leathaid Bhuain
Point of Stoer
Sgeir nan Gall
Oldany Island
Calbha Mòr
Eddrachillis Bay
Kylestrome
Glendhu Forest
Cirean Geardail
161
Rubha nan Còsan
Ardvar
Kylesku
Unapool
Culkein
Eilean Chrona
Drumbeg
Cluas Deas
Raffin
Achnacarnin
Nedd
Newton
Ben Aird da Loch
530
Clashmore
Sàil Gorm
776
Balchladich
Clashnessie
Gleann Leireag
Rubh' a' Mhill Dheirg
Stoer
Quinag
808
Bay of Stoer
Clachtoll
Spidean Coinich
764
A894
Rubha Leumair
A837
Glas Bheinn
776
Achmelvich Bay
Rhicarn
Little Assynt
Beinn Uidhe
740
Achmelvich
Loch Assynt
Ardroe
Rubha Rodha
Baddidarach
Lochinver
Beinn Gharbh
540
Inchnadamph
Soyea Island
Loch Inver
Kirkaig Point
Badnaban
Strathan
A'Chleit
Inverkirkaig
Glencanisp Forest
Rubha na Brèige
Stronechrubie
Canisp
846
Rubha Coigeach
Suilven
731
Eilean Mòr
Rhegreanoch
Enard Bay
Breabag
814
Rubh' a' Choin
Rubha Mòr
Reiff
Loch Sionascaig
Brae of Achnahaird
Ledbeg
Altandhu
Ledmore
Eilean Mullagrach
Aird of Coigach
Inverpolly Forest
Cul Mòr
849
Drumrunie Forest
Elphin
Knockan
Ullapool - Stornoway 2¾ hrs
Isle Ristol
Loch Osgaig
Polbain
Stac Pollaidh
613
Achiltibuie
Polglass
Ardnagoine
Tanera Beg
Glas-leac
Garadheancal
An t-Sàil
490
A835
Loch Urigill
Cnoc na Glas Choille
307
THE MINCH
0 2 4 6 miles
0 2 4 6 8 10 km

Durness
Tongue
Bettyhill
Altnaharra
Loch Shin
Loch Naver
Loch Loyal
Loch Hope
Loch Eriboll
Kyle of Tongue
Strathnaver
Ben Hope
Ben Loyal
Ben Klibreck
NORTH WEST HIGHLANDS
HIGHLAND
IV
KW
27
28
14
11
104
96

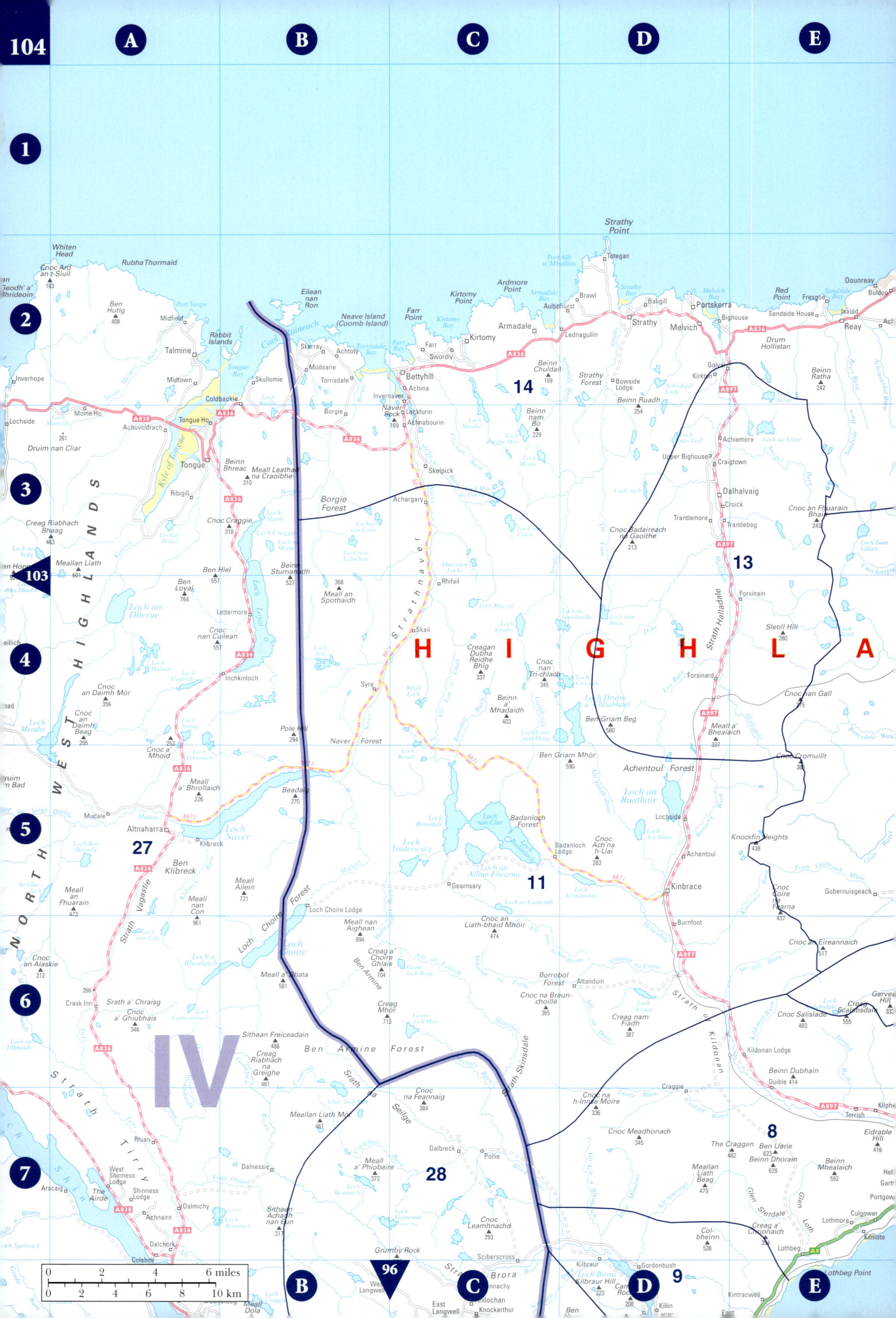
A
B
C
D
E
1
2
3
4
5
6
7
HIGHLA
NORTH WEST HIGHLANDS
IV
103
96
27
28
14
13
11
8
9
Whiten Head
Cnoc Ard an t-Siuil
183
Rubha Thormaid
Ben Hutig
408
Midfield
Talmine
Rabbit Islands
Eilean nan Ron
Caol Raineach
Port Vasgo
Tongue Bay
Midtown
Skullomie
Coldbackie
Inverhope
Lochside
Moine Ho.
Achuvoldrach
Tongue Ho.
Druim nan Cliar
Kyle of Tongue
Tongue
Ribigill
Beinn Bhreac
Meall Leathad na Craoibhe
310
Creag Riabhach Bheag
463
Cnoc Craggie
318
Meallan Liath
601
Ben Hiel
557
Ben Loyal
764
Loch an Dherue
Lettermore
Loch Loyal
Beinn Stumanadh
527
Cnoc nan Cuilean
557
Inchkinloch
Cnoc an Daimh Mòr
356
Cnoc an Daimh Beag
295
Loch Meadie
Cnoc a' Mhoid
253
Pole Hill
294
Meall a' Bhrollaich
226
Mudale
Altnaharra
Klibreck
Loch Naver
Ben Klibreck
Beadaig
270
Strath Vagastie
Meall an Fhuarain
473
Meall Ailein
721
Meall nan Con
961
Cnoc an Alaskie
312
Crask Inn
266
Strath a' Chraisg
Cnoc a' Ghiubhais
346
Sithean Freiceadain
486
Creag Riabhach na Greighe
461
Strath Tirry
Rhian
West Shinness Lodge
Shinness Lodge
The Airde
Loch Shin
Arscaig
Dalnessie
Dalmichy
Achnairn
Dalchork
Colaboll
Sithean Achadh nan Eun
317
Meall Dola
Loch Choire Forest
Loch Choire Lodge
Loch Choire
Meall a' Bhata
581
Ben Armine Forest
Strath na Seilge
Meallan Liath Mòr
461
Cnoc na Feannaig
384
Meall a' Phiobaire
372
Dalbreck
Pollie
Cnoc Leamhnachd
293
Grumby Rock
Sciberscross
Strath Brora
West Langwell
East Langwell
Killochan
Knockarthur
Neave Island (Coomb Island)
Skerray
Achtoty
Torrisdale Bay
Modsarie
Torrisdale
Borgie
Farr Point
Farr Bay
Farr
Swordly
Bettyhill
Achina
Invernaver
Naver Rock
169
Leckfurin
Achnabourin
Skelpick
Borgie Forest
Achargary
Strathnaver
Rhifail
Meall an Spothaidh
368
Skail
Syre
Naver Forest
Kirtomy Point
Kirtomy Bay
Kirtomy
Armadale
Ardmore Point
Armadale Bay
Beinn Chuldail
169
Beinn nam Bo
229
Creagan Dubha Reidhe Bhig
337
Cnoc nan Tri-chlach
345
Beinn a' Mhadaidh
403
Ben Griam Beg
580
Ben Griam Mhòr
590
Badanloch Forest
Loch nan Clar
Badanloch Lodge
Loch Badanloch
Loch an Alltan Fhearna
Gearnsary
Cnoc Ach'na h-Uai
283
Meall nan Aighean
694
Creag a' Choire Ghlais
704
Ben Armine
Creag Mhor
713
Cnoc an Liath-bhaid Mhòir
474
Borrobol Forest
Altanduin
Cnoc na Breun-choille
365
Creag nam Fiadh
387
Strathy Point
Totegan
Port Allt a' Mhuilinn
Brawl
Aultiphurst
Strathy Bay
Strathy
Baligill
Lednagullin
Strathy Forest
Bowside Lodge
Beinn Ruadh
254
Melvich Bay
Melvich
Portskerra
Bighouse
Golval
Kirkton
Achiemore
Upper Bighouse
Craigtown
Dalhalvaig
Croick
Trantlemore
Trantlebeg
Cnoc Badaireach na Gaoithe
213
Strath Halladale
Forsinain
Forsinard
Loch Druim a' Chliabhain
Meall a' Bhealaich
337
Achentoul Forest
Loch an Ruathair
Lochside
Achentoul
Kinbrace
Burnfoot
Strath Kildonan
Kildonan Lodge
Craggie
Cnoc na h-Innse Mòire
336
Cnoc Meadhonach
345
The Craggan
482
Meallan Liath Beag
479
Glen Sletdale
Col-bheinn
538
Kilbraur
Loch Brora
Kilbraur Hill
323
Gordonbush
Carrol Rock
208
Killin
Red Point
Fresgoe
Sandside Bay
Sandside House
Dounreay
Buldoo
Isauld
Reay
Drum Hollistan
Beinn Ratha
242
Cnoc an Fhuarain Bhain
243
Sletill Hill
280
Cnoc nan Gall
275
Cnoc Cromuillt
385
Knockfin Heights
438
Gobernuisgeach
Cnoc Coire na Fearna
437
Cnoc an Eireannaich
517
Cnoc Salislade
483
Creag Scalabsdale
555
Garvel Hill
Beinn Dubhain
Duible
414
Ben Uarie
623
Beinn Dhorain
628
Beinn Mhealaich
592
Glen Loth
Creag a' Chrionaich
394
Lothbeg
Lothmore
Culgower
Kilmote
Lothbeg Point
Torrish
Kilphedir
Eldrable Hill
416
Portgower
A836
A838
A897
A9
B871
B873
0 2 4 6 miles
0 2 4 6 8 10 km

F
G
H
J
K
1
2
3
4
5
6
7
106
17
PENTLAND FIRTH
Stromness 1¾ hrs
St. Margaret's Hope 1hr
Liddel
Old Head
Brough Ness
Muckle Skerry
Pentland Skerries
Langaton Point
Island of Stroma
Nethertown
Red Head
Uppertown
Mell Head
Inner Sound
Boars of Duncansby
Men of Mey
St John's Point
Head of Crees
Ness of Duncansby
Duncansby Head
Stacks of Duncansby
Dunnet Head
Easter Head
Dunnet Hill
121
Brough
Ham
Scarfskerry
Skarfskerry Point
Tang Head
Harrow
East Mey
Mey
Rigifa
Gills
Gills Bay
Huna
Kirkstyle
Canisbay
John o' Groats
Upper Gills
The Thirl
Hunspow
St John's Loch
Rattar
Whitebridge
Barrock
West Dunnet
Dunnet
Dwarwick Head
The Spur
Dunnet Bay
Inkstack
Brims Ness
Ness of Litter
Clett
Holborn Head
Clardon Head
Crosskirk Bay
Crosskirk
Scrabster
Thurso Bay
Murkle Bay
Links of Dunnet
Warth Hill
124
Wife Geo
Brabster
Lybster
A836
Thurso
Murkle
Bridge of Forss
Viewfield
Ormlie
Clardon
Castletown
Greenland
Loch Heilen
Lochend
Everley
Tofts
Skirza
Skirza Head
Freswick Bay
Freswick
A99
Ness Head
Achreamie
Lythmore
Janetstown
Haimer
Orrig House
Hayfield
Thurdistoft
Tain
Slickly
Newlands of Geise
Glengolly
Shalmstry
Lochside
Reaster
Alterwall
Auckengill
Westfield
Weydale
Hilliclay
Durran
Hoy
Bowermadden
Lyth
Sortat
Ruthers of Howe
Nybster
Shebster
14
Forsie
Lieurary
Buckies
Carsgoe
Aimster
Achingills
Brough Head
Loch Calder
Sordale
Stemster
Tister
Bowertower
Howe
Skinnet
Knockdee
Stemster House
Halcro
Hastigrow
Mireland
Keiss
Tang Head
Broubster
Braal Castle
Roadside
Corsback
Calder Mains
Clayock
Gillock
Stain
Gerston
Halkirk
Georgemas Junc. Sta
Loch Scarmclate
North Watten
Kirk
Shurrery
A882
Loch of Wester
Westerloch
Brawlbin
Sinclair's Bay
Loch Olginey
Bloody Moss
Lyngear
Killimster
Quoys of Reiss
Shurrery Lodge
Scotscalder Sta
Harpsdale
Spittal Hill
Loch Watten
Mains of Watten
B874
Loch Scye
Ben Dorrery
244
Olgrinmore
Dunn
Oldhall
Houstry of Dunn
Loch of Winless
Loch Shurrery
Dorrery
Achies
Newton
Watten
Winless
Reiss
Noss Head
Beinn Nam Bad Mor
290
Spital
Backlass
Whitefield
Bilbster
Sibster
Ackergill
WICK
Staxigoe
KW
Mybster
Strath
Thuster
Broadhaven
Loch Calium
Westerdale
Loch of Toftingall
Haster
Milton
North Head
Tormsdale
Stirkoe House
Janetstown
Wick
Newton
South Head
Lochan Dubh nan Geodh
Loch Meadie
Badlipster
Whiterow
Northfield
Pulddagon
Tannach
Loch Eileanach
Hempriggs House
Loch Hempriggs
Tacher
Toftcarl
Altnabreac Sta
N
D
Lower Camster
Ires Geo
Lochdhu Hotel
Stemster
Ballharn Hill
145
Thrumster
Loch More
Corbiegoe
Sarclet
Hill of Yarrows
213
Whiteleen
Sarclet Head
12
Loch of Yarrows
Loch Rangag
Achavanich
Loch Stemster
Stemster Hill
248
Cnoc an Earrannaiche
211
Upper Camster
Stack of Ulbster
Loch a' Mhuilinn
Loch Sand
Lochan Thulachan
Ulbster
Whaligoe
Coire na Beinne
226
Sheppardstown
Dalganachan
Roster
East Clyth
Bruan
Crofts of Benachielt
Ben-a-chielt
287
Rumster Forest
Upper Lybster
Mid Clyth
Blackness
Ben Alisky
349
Cnocan Conachreag
269
Reisgill
Occumster
Cnoc na Saobhaidhe
290
Nottingham
Swiney
Lybster
Inver shore
Houstry
Gillivoan
Achnaclyth
Landhallow
Forse
Smerral
Latheron
Latheronwheel
Badnagie
Berriedale
Braemore
Achorn
Dunbeath
Toremore
Maiden Pap
484
Knockally
Inver
Dunbeath Bay
Meall na Caorach
356
Ramscraigs
Scaraben
626
Borgue
Wag
Langwell Forest
Newport
Aultibea
Ceann Leathad nam Bo
Mid Hill
312
Langwell House
Berriedale
Braigh na h-Eaglaise
422
Ousdale
Creag Thoraraidh
404
Badbea
Caen
Navidale
East Helmsdale
Helmsdale
A9
B870
B874
B876
B855

A
B
C
D
E
F
G
H
1
2
3
4
5
6
7
8
9
10
11
ORKNEY ISLANDS
Mull Head
17 Papa Westray
PAPA WESTRAY
Holland
Bow Head
WESTRAY
Noup Head
Rackwick
Pierowall
WESTRAY 17
Midbea
Skelwick
Stanger Head
Rapness
Berst Ness
THE NORTH SOUND
North Ronaldsay
Point of Sinsoss
NORTH RONALDSAY
17
Hollandstoun
Strom Ness
North Ronaldsay Firth
3 hrs
Tofts Ness
Burness
Otters Wick
Sandquoy
Linklet Bay
Start Point
Newark
Roadside
SANDAY
Broughtown
17
SANDAY
Kettletoft
Quoy Ness
Tres Ness
Calf of Eday
Calfsound
Faray
Braeswick
WESTRAY FIRTH
1½ hrs
Guith
Millbounds
SANDAY SOUND
Sacquoy Head
ROUSAY
Wasbister
EDAY
Loth
EDAY
Eday Sound
Spur Ness
Sourin
17
Backaland
Costa Head
Westness
17
Egilsay
STRONSAY
Papa Stronsay
Brough Head
A966
Birsay
Costa
Brinian
Whitehall
Linga Holm
STRONSAY
A967
Evie
Wyre
Marwick Head
Marwick
Kirbuster
Redland
Woodwick
Gairsay Sound
Aith
Everbay
Twatt
KW
B9057
Rothiesholm
Grobister
Isbister
Tingwall
Gairsay
STRONSAY FIRTH
17
Burgh Head
Lerwick 7¾ hours
Quoyloo
Dounby 17
Edmonstone
Lamb Head
Skaill
MAINLAND
Settiscarth
SHAPINSAY
A967
A986
17
Auskerry
Yesnaby
Loch of Harray
Bimbister
A966
Wide Firth
Balfour
Sandgarth
Voy
Bay of Firth
Finstown
Shapinsay Sound
Loch of Stenness
A965
Rerwick Head
A965
Kirkwall
15
16
Stromness
Mull Head
Loch of Kirbister
Scapa
KIRKWALL
Ward Hill
268
A964
Hoy Sound
Clestrain
Kirbister
Greenigo
A964
Orphir
Gyre
Hobbister
A961
Toab
Skaill
17
A960
17
Graemsay
Linksness
Gritley
Houton
ORKNEY
Point of Ayre
Upper Sanday
Ward Hill
479
½ hr
Bring Deeps
St Mary's
Cornquoy
Copinsay
Rackwick
SCAPA FLOW
Rora Head
Cava
Rose Ness
Knap of Trowieglen
399
Rysa Little
Rack Wick
HOY
Hunda
Burray
16
Southtown
Sneuk Head
Fara
Oil Terminal
Flotta
Lyness
Bow
St Margaret's Hope
Grim Ness
Heldale Water
B9044
Herston
Widewall
B9047
Longhope
Cantick Head
Lythes
Melsetter
SOUTH RONALDSAY
17
Tor Ness
South Walls
118
Ward Hill
1¾ hrs
A961
Swona
Cleat
Aberdeen 6-7¼ hrs
Burwick
Brough Ness
Old Head
PENTLAND FIRTH
1hr
Island of Stroma
Muckle Skerry
1
Dunnet Head
Mell Head
Pentland Skerries
Ness of Duncansby
Duncansby Head
Brough
Scarfskerry
Huna
Hunspow
Ham
Rattar
Gills
Mey
Kirkstyle
John o' Groats
Clett
Barrock
Canisbay
Holborn Head
Scrabster
Dunnet Bay
Dunnet
St John's Loch
Inkstack
A99
Thurso Bay
Warth Hill
Thurso
Murkle
Loch Heilen
Tofts
Skirza
Forss
A836
Castletown
Lochend
Freswick
Freswick Bay
Olrig House
KW
Slickly
1
Ness Head
14
Alterwall
A9
Auckengill
Bowermadden
HIGHLAND
Lyth
Sortat
Lieurary
12
Bowertower
Sordale
Howe
Keiss
Knockdee
Hastigrow
Braal Castle
Roadside
Halcro
Mireland
Gillock
Halkirk
Kirk
North Watten
Westerloch
Killimster
Watten
Reiss
Noss Head
0 2 4 6 miles
0 2 4 6 8 10 km
105
B
C
D
E
F
G
H

J
K
L
M
N
P
Q
R
1
2
3
4
5
6
7
8
9
10
11
FAIR ISLE
ZE
FAIR ISLE
Bu Ness
Stonybreck
FOULA
ZE
Strem Ness
Ham
418 The Sneug
FOULA
South Ness
same scale as main map
SHETLAND ISLANDS
Out Stack
Muckle Flugga
Herma Ness
Saxa Vord 285
Lamba Ness
Norwick
Burrafirth
Valsgarth
Haroldswick
UNST
Baliasta
Baltasound
Balta
UNST
Westing
Gloup
Cullivoe
Uyeasound
Belmont
Mu Ness
Uyea
Gutcher
Sellafirth
North Sandwick
½ hr
Nev of Stuis
Colvister
Ramna Stacks
Gruney
Point of Fethaland
Uyea
Grimister
Camb
Mid Yell
Hascosay
Oddsta
Vord Hill 158
FETLAR
Strandburgh Ness
Brough Lodge
Tresta
Houbie
Aith
Funzie
The Snap
West Sandwick
YELL
Yell Sound
Colgrave Sound
North Roe
Isbister
The Faither
Ronas Hill 450
Housetter
North Collafirth
Aywick
Otterswick
Gossabrough
West Yell
Ulsta
Hamnavoe
Burravoe
Copister
Ollaberry
Esha Ness
Stenness
Hillswick
Urafirth
Bardister
¼ hr
Samphrey
Sullom Voe Oil Terminal
Toft
Mossbank
Firth
Gunnister
Sullom
Sullom Voe
Graven
Frora Ness
Muckle Skerry
Out Skerries
OUT SKERRIES
Hamnavoe
Haggrister
Trondavoe
ST MAGNUS BAY
Brae
Burravoe
Lunna
1½ hrs
¾ hr
Collafirth
Lunning
West Linga
Skaw Taing
WHALSAY
Busta
Roesound
Wethersta
Muckle Roe
Vidlin
Brough
Marrister
Isbister
WHALSAY
Ve Skerries
Papa Stour
PAPA STOUR
Hillside
Voe
Laxo
Skelberry
Symbister
½ hr
Dury Voe
Swarbacks Minn
Vementry
Gonfirth
Melby
Sandness
West Burrafirth
Unifirth
East Burrafirth
Clousta
Aith
Scalla Field 281
Brettabister
South Nesting Bay
ZE
SHETLAND
MAINLAND
Sandness Hill 249
Twatt
Skellister
Benston
Mu Ness
Dale of Walls
Bridge of Walls
Effirth
Bixter
Weisdale
Loch of Girlsta
Freester
Tresta
Girlsta
Gletness
2½ hrs
Wats Ness
Walls
Gruting
Semblister
Wadbister
Sandsound
Haggersta
Loch of Strom
Garderhouse
Vaila
Gossa Water
Whiteness
TINGWALL (LERWICK)
Score Head
Culswick
Reawick
Veensgarth
Bressay
Wester Skeld
Westerwick
Skeld (Easter Skeld)
Heogan
Maryfield
The Deeps
Lerwick
Isle of Noss
Scalloway
Sound
Trebister
Grindiscol
226
Kirkabister
Ward of Bressay
Gulberwick
Brindister
Bard Head
Hamnavoe
Wester Quarff
Quarff
Bridge End
East Burra
Fladdabister
hours
Burra
Bergen (summer only)............12½
Cliff Sound
Royl Field 293
Cunningsburgh
Helli Ness
South Havra
Mail
Maywick
Leebotten
Mousa
Hoswick
Sandwick
Ireland
St Ninian's Isle
Bigton
Levenwick
Scousburgh
Boddam
hours
Aberdeen............................12-12½
Kirkwall................................5½-7¼
Seydisfjordur (summer only)....31
Torshaven (summer only)..........13
Quendale 283
Fitful Head
Exnaboe
Toab
SUMBURGH
Grutness
Sumburgh
Sumburgh Head
Sumburgh Roost
A968
A970
A971
B9081
B9082
B9088
B9071
B9074
B9075
B9076
B9078
B9122

A
B
C
D
E
1
2
3
4
5
6
7
8
Tory Island
An Baile Thiar
(West Town)
Tory Sound
Malin Head
Ballygorman
Glengad Head
Portaleen
Malin
Culdaff
Earra Thíre na Binne
(Arryheernabin)
Fanad Head
Dunaff Head
Dunaff
Ballyliffin
Clonmany
Ballymagaraghy
Melmore Head
Horn Head
Dumhaigh Bhig
(Doagh Beg)
Carndonagh
Gleneely
Inishowen
Inishowen Head
Rosguill
Sheep Haven
Fanad
Portsalon
Drumfree
Slieve Snaght
615
Greencastle
Inishbofin
Dunfanaghy
Na Dúnaibh
(Downies)
Tawny
Gleann Bhairr
(Glenvar)
Moville
(Bun an Phobail)
Downhill
Magilligan
Carraig Airt
(Carrickart)
Redcastle
Bloody Foreland
Cranford
Buncrana
(Bun Cranncha)
Bun na Leaca
(Brinlack)
An Fál Carrach
(Falcarragh)
Gort an Choirce
(Gortahork)
Creeslough
Carrowkeel
Carrowkeel
Lough Foyle
49
Gola Island
Gweedore
Lough Salt Mountain
471
Milford
Rathmullan
Fahan
Aghanloo
Bolea
Doirí Beaga
(Derrybeg)
Cloghaneely
An Bun Beag
(Bunbeg)
Gaoth Dobhair
(Gweedore)
Termon
(An Tearmann)
Tooban
Muff
Owey I.
Cionn Caslach
(Kincaslough)
Errigal
752
Kilmacrenan
Ramelton
(Rath Mealtain)
Burnfoot
City of Derry
Ballykelly
Limavady
Eglinton
Greysteel
Anagaire
(Annagry)
The Rosses
Croithlí
(Crolly)
Dún Lúiche
(Dunlewy)
Slieve Snaght
683
Derryveagh Mts
Glendowan Mts
Bridge End
Culmore
Coolkeeragh
48
LONDONDERRY
(DERRY)
Glenhead
Drumsurn
Loch an Iúir
(Loughanure)
Church Hill
Newtowncunningham
Lackagh
Burtonport
Gleann Doimhin
(Glendowan)
Letterkenny
(Leitir Ceanainn)
Prehen
Drumahoe
Lettershendony
LIMAVADY
Gortnahey
DONEGAL
Clochán Liath
(Dungloe)
Old Town
Manorcunningham
Carrigans
New Buildings
LONDONDERRY
(DERRY)
Ervey Cross Roads
Benbradagh
468
Rashedoge
Pluck
St Johnstown
Magheramason
Foreglen
Dungiven
47
Claudy
Craigdarragh
Boviel
An Dúchoraidh
(Doochary)
Knockbrack
Bready
Mín na Croise
(Meenacross)
Raphoe
(Ráth Bhoth)
Cloghcor
Liscloon
Feeny
Baile na Finne
(Fintown)
Béal an Átha Móir
(Bellanamore)
Ballymagorry
Donemana
Ballyneaner
Park
Gweebarra Bay
Dunmore Head
Drumnacross
Convoy
Artigarvan
Portnoo
Clooney
Leitir Mhic an Bhaird
(Lettermacaward)
Cloghfin
Ballindrait
Ballynamallaght
Mullaghmore
556
Narin
Maas
An Clochán
(Cloghan)
Stranorlar
(Srath an Urláir)
Kilross
Lifford (Leifear)
Strabane
82
Craig
Sawel Mt.
683
Moneyneany
An Coimín
(Commeen)
Liscooly
Castlefinn
Mullaghclogo
Sperrin Mountains
Glenties
Clady
Butterlope
Mount Hamilton
Draperstown
Kilrean
Ballybofey
(Bealach Féich)
Killygordon
Sion Mills
STRABANE
Cranagh
The Six Towns
Glebe
Victoria Bridge
Plumbridge
Ardara
(Ard an Rátha)
Blue Stack
676
Croaghnageer
546
Blue Stack Mts
Ardstraw
Gortin
Rousky
Glenhull
Spamount
Newtownstewart
BT
Greencastle
Letterbarra
Castlederg
Croagh
Frosses
Donegal
(Dún na nGall)
Killeter
Killen
Drumlegagh
Mullaghcarn
542
Dunnamore
Lissan
Croaghnameal
440
81
Creggan
80
Inver
Mountfield
79
Mountjoy
Killybegs
(Na Cealla Beaga)
Mountcharles
Laghey
Lough Derg
Killyclogher
Loughmacrory
Drumquin
Omagh
Drumnakilly
Carrickmore
Pomeroy
Bridgetown
Ballintra
78
Clanabogan
OMAGH
Ballynahatty
Sixmilecross
St John's Point
Rossnowlagh
Coolmore
Keeran
Beragh
Cappagh
70
Donegal Bay
Pettigo
Clonelly
Lack
Gortaclare
Donaghmore
Letter
Kesh
Ederny
Dromore
The Diamond
Mullaghmassa
Castlecaulfield
Ballyshannon
(Béal Átha Seanaidh)
Assaroe Lake
Leggs
FERMANAGH
Drumduff
Fintona
Seskinore
Dungannon
Bundoran
(Bun Dobhráin)
Belleek
Lisnarrick
Garvaghy
Eskragh
Granville
Mullaghmore Head
Mullaghmore
Tullaghan
Single Street
Lower Lough Erne
Irvinestown
Ballymackilroy
Ballygawley
Moygashel
Rosscor
93
Church Hill
Trillick
77
DUNGANNON
Eglish
Kinlough
Killadeas
Carnteel
Cliffoney
Buckode
Garrison
Blaney
Kilskeery
69
Aughnacloy
Ballaghnatrillack
Derrygonnelly
Ballinamallard
Augher
Clogher
Crilly
Moneylahan
Lough Melvin
Tully
Ballycassidy
Murley
Clabby
76
68
Truskmore
Glenade
Rossinver
Tullybrack
376
Monea
Trory
Tempo
Creagh
Fivemiletown
Benbulben
525
Dartry Mountains
Scribbagh
Springfield
Boho
74
Garvary
Enniskillen
94
75
Carrickroe
Drumcliff
Glencar
Kiltyclogher
Dough Mt.
461
Lough Macnean Upper
Lisbellaw
Cooneen
Slieve Beagh
Emyvale
Letterbreen
Cullkey
Brookeborough
Glaslough
Rathbraghan
Sligo (Sligeach)
Manorhamilton
Holywell
Blacklion
Belcoo
Bellanaleck
Lough Macnean Lower
Tamlaght
Knockatallan
Tedavnet
LEITRIM
Glenfarne
Arney
Maguiresbridge
Eshnadarragh
Scotstown
Bellanode
Drummacabranagher
Lisnaskea
Monaghan
(Muineachán)
Gubaveeny
Mackan
Rosslea
Tydavnet
Castleshane
Drumcard
Killarga
Dromahair
Upper Lough Erne
Tully
Smithborough
Three Mile House
Ballygawley
Ballintogher
Mullan
Donagh
Magheraveely
Cavanagarven
Swanlinbar
Derrylin
92
Clones
(Cluain Eois)
MONAGHAN
Scotch Corner
Dowra
Glengavlen
Killeevan
Anlore
Toberscanavan
Drumkeeran
Corry
Derrynacreeve
Newtownbutler
Newbliss
Swan's Cross Roads
Ballybay
(Béal Átha Beithe)
Iron Mountains
Teemore
Drummacool
Lough Allen
Riverstown
Geevagh
Corraleehan
Bawnboy
Ballyconnell
Scotshouse
Rockcorry
Castleblayney
(Baile na Lorgan)
Slieve Anierin
586
Belturbet
Redhills
Drum
Ballymote
Arigna
Castlebaldwin
Ballyfarnon
Milltown
Cloverhill
Cootehill
Latton
Kesh
Keadew
Drumshanbo
Newtown Gore
Ardlougher
Ballyhaise
Drung
Tullyvin
Ballinafad
Ballinamore
Butlers Bridge
Culfadda
Drumcong
Killeshandra
CAVAN
Shantonagh
Gurteen
Knockvicar
Fenagh
Drumlea
Tullcoe
Cavan (An Cabhán)
Shercock
Carrickmacross
(Carraig Mhachaire Rois)
Mullaghroe
Cootehall
Leitrim
Greagh
Carrigallen
Poles
Stradone
Canningstown
Northlands
Derrylane
Lavey
Arghavas
Crossdoney
Drumanespick
Edmondstown
Jamestown
Drumsna
Mohill
Corriga
Arvagh
Cornafean
Ballinagh
Crosserlough
Crosskeys
Bailieborough
Moyer
0 5 10 15 20 miles
0 5 10 20 30 km

NORTH CHANNEL
Mull of Kintyre
Southend
Machrioch
Feochaig
Sanda Island
Ailsa Craig
Rathlin Island
Bull Point
Giants Causeway
Fair Head
Torr Head
MOYLE
Ballycastle
Ballintoy
Bushmills
Portballintrae
Portrush
Armoy
Cushendun
Cushendall
Red Bay
Garron Point
Ballymoney
BALLYMONEY
COLERAINE
Glens of Antrim
Antrim Hills
Carnlough
Glenarm
BALLYMENA
LARNE
Larne
Island Magee
Ballygalley
Cairnryan
Troon (summer only)
The Maidens or Hulin Rocks
Fleetwood 8 hrs
Stranraer 1¾-3¼ hrs
Douglas (summer only)
Birkenhead
hours
Ballantrae
Cairnryan
Kirkcolm
Leswalt
Stranraer
Lochans
Portpatrick
Sandhead
Rinns of Galloway
Colmon
CARRICKFERGUS
Whitehead
Black Head
NEWTOWNABBEY
ANTRIM
Antrim
BELFAST INTERNATIONAL
COOKSTOWN
MAGHERAFELT
Lough Neagh
CRAIGAVON
BELFAST
BELFAST CITY
See inset for postcode detail
CASTLEREAGH
NORTH DOWN
BANGOR
Mew Island
Copeland Island
Donaghadee
NEWTOWNARDS
ARDS
Ards Peninsula
Strangford Lough
LISBURN
Lisburn
Hillsborough
DOWN
Downpatrick
Ballynahinch
BANBRIDGE
Banbridge
ARMAGH
Armagh
Portadown
Newry
NEWRY & MOURNE
Mourne Mountains
Slieve Donard
Newcastle
Dundrum Bay
Ardglass
Killough
Kilkeel
Annalong
Warrenpoint
Carlingford
LOUTH
DUNDALK (DUN DEALGAN)
Dundalk Bay
Crossmaglen
IRISH SEA
A2
A26
A6
M2
M1
M22
A1
A24
A55
F
G
H
J
K
1
2
3
4
5
6
7
8

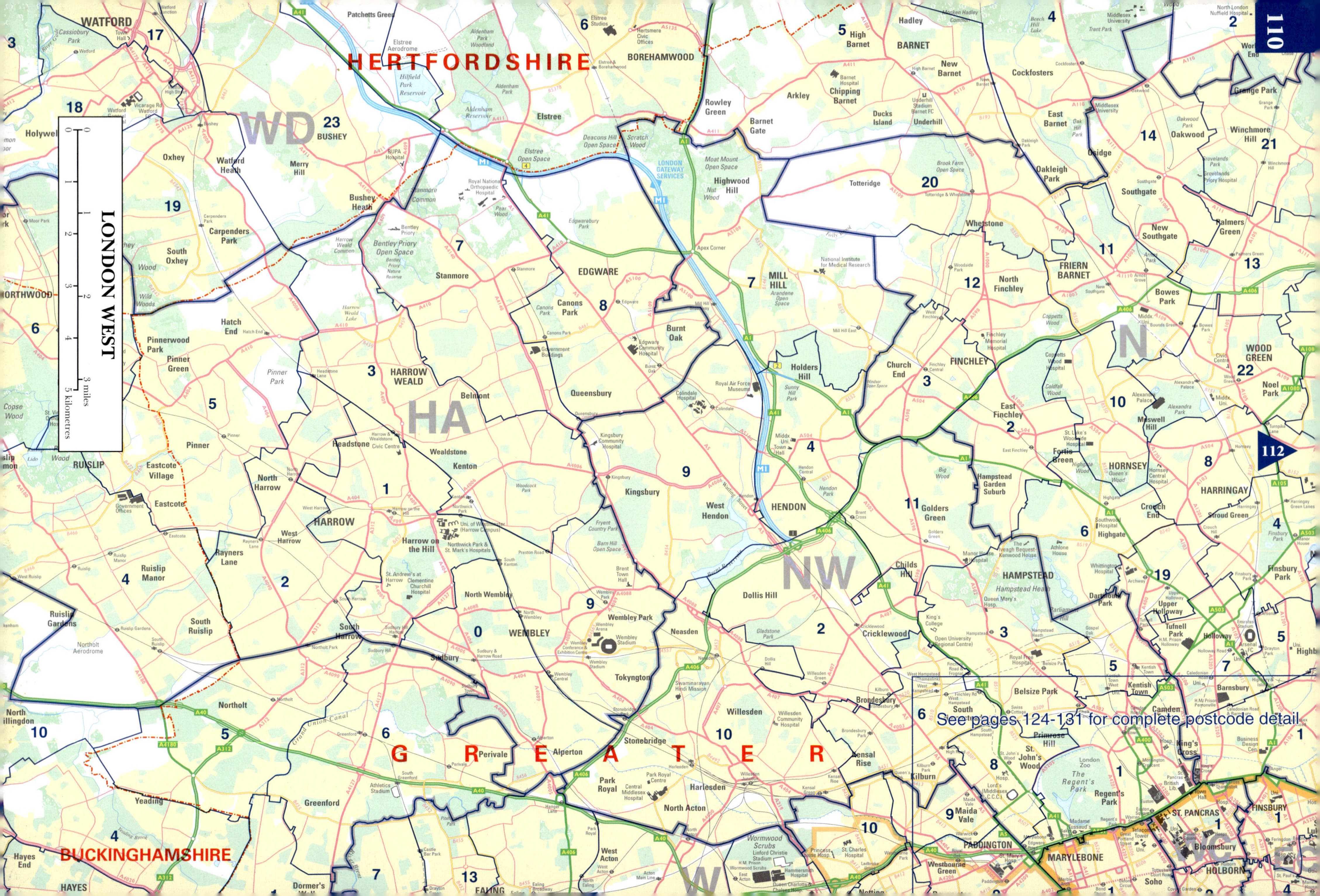
LONDON WEST
0 1 2 3 miles
0 1 2 3 4 5 kilometres
See pages 124-131 for complete postcode detail
112
HERTFORDSHIRE
BUCKINGHAMSHIRE
G R E A T E R
WD
HA
NW
N
W
WATFORD
BOREHAMWOOD
BUSHEY
Elstree
Oxhey
Watford Heath
Merry Hill
Carpenders Park
South Oxhey
Bushey Heath
Stanmore
EDGWARE
Canons Park
Burnt Oak
MILL HILL
Highwood Hill
Totteridge
Whetstone
High Barnet
BARNET
Hadley
New Barnet
Cockfosters
Arkley
Chipping Barnet
Rowley Green
Barnet Gate
Ducks Island
Underhill
East Barnet
Oakleigh Park
Southgate
Oakwood
Winchmore Hill
Grange Park
Palmers Green
New Southgate
FRIERN BARNET
North Finchley
FINCHLEY
East Finchley
Church End
Holders Hill
Bowes Park
WOOD GREEN
Noel Park
Muswell Hill
HORNSEY
HARRINGAY
Crouch End
Highgate
Stroud Green
Finsbury Park
Upper Holloway
Tufnell Park
Holloway
Highbury
Barnsbury
Kentish Town
Camden Town
King's Cross
ST. PANCRAS
FINSBURY
Bloomsbury
HOLBORN
Soho
MARYLEBONE
Regent's Park
St. John's Wood
Primrose Hill
Belsize Park
HAMPSTEAD
Hampstead Garden Suburb
Golders Green
Childs Hill
Cricklewood
Dollis Hill
HENDON
West Hendon
Kingsbury
Queensbury
HARROW WEALD
Belmont
Wealdstone
Kenton
Headstone
HARROW
Harrow on the Hill
North Harrow
West Harrow
Pinner
Hatch End
Pinnerwood Park
Pinner Green
Eastcote
Eastcote Village
RUISLIP
Ruislip Manor
Ruislip Gardens
South Ruislip
Rayners Lane
South Harrow
North Wembley
WEMBLEY
Wembley Park
Sudbury
Neasden
Tokyngton
Stonebridge
Alperton
Perivale
Willesden
Harlesden
Brondesbury
Kensal Rise
Kilburn
Maida Vale
PADDINGTON
Westbourne Green
Park Royal
North Acton
West Acton
Northolt
Greenford
Yeading
HAYES
Hayes End
Dormer's Wells
EALING
Holywell
NORTHWOOD
Patchetts Green
South Hampstead
Dartmouth Park
Whitestone
Fortis Green
Osidge

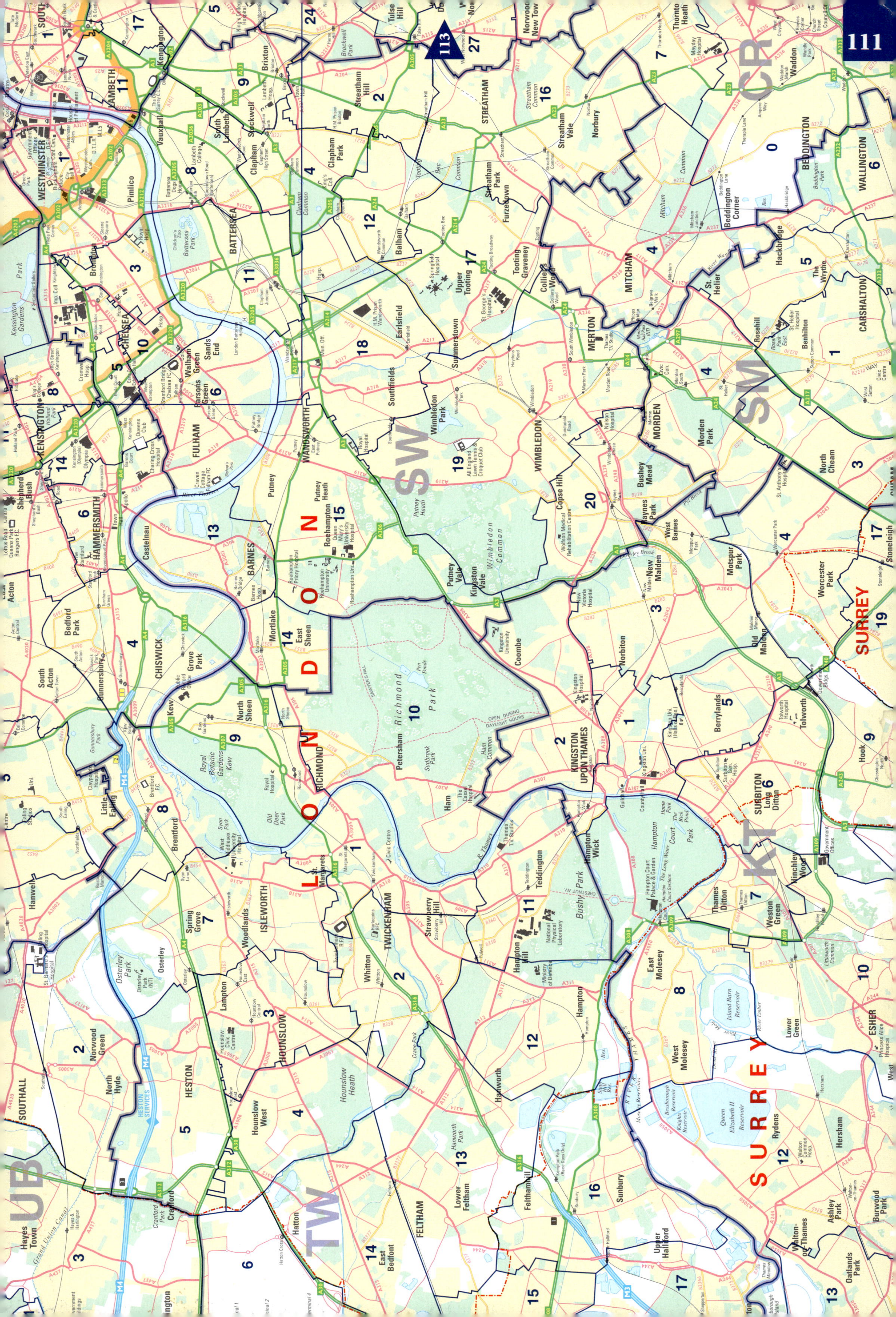
113
LONDON
SW
TW
KT
SM
CR
UB
SURREY
WESTMINSTER
LAMBETH
Kennington
Vauxhall
Pimlico
Brixton
Stockwell
Clapham
Clapham Park
Streatham Hill
STREATHAM
Streatham Vale
Norbury
Thornton Heath
Waddon
BEDDINGTON
Beddington Corner
WALLINGTON
Hackbridge
CARSHALTON
The Wrythe
St. Helier
MITCHAM
Mitcham Common
Colliers Wood
MERTON
Rosehill
Benhilton
MORDEN
Morden Park
North Cheam
Worcester Park
Stoneleigh
Motspur Park
West Barnes
Raynes Park
Bushey Mead
WIMBLEDON
Wimbledon Park
Southfields
Earlsfield
Summerstown
Tooting Graveney
Upper Tooting
Balham
Tooting Bec Common
Furzedown
Streatham Park
Streatham Common
BATTERSEA
Battersea Park
CHELSEA
Brompton
KENSINGTON
Kensington Gardens
Walham Green
Sands End
Parsons Green
FULHAM
WANDSWORTH
Putney
Putney Heath
Roehampton
Wimbledon Common
Putney Vale
Kingston Vale
Coombe
Copse Hill
New Malden
Norbiton
Old Malden
Berrylands
Tolworth
Hook
SURBITON
Long Ditton
Hinchley Wood
Thames Ditton
Weston Green
East Molesey
West Molesey
Lower Green
ESHER
Hersham
Rydens
Walton-on-Thames
Ashley Park
Burwood Park
Oatlands Park
Upper Halliford
Sunbury
Feltham Hill
Lower Feltham
Hanworth Park
Hanworth
FELTHAM
East Bedfont
Hatton
Cranford Park
Cranford
Hayes Town
SOUTHALL
North Hyde
Norwood Green
HESTON
Hounslow West
Hounslow Heath
HOUNSLOW
Lampton
Osterley Park
Osterley
Spring Grove
Woodlands
ISLEWORTH
Whitton
TWICKENHAM
Strawberry Hill
Teddington
Hampton Hill
Hampton
Hampton Wick
Bushy Park
Hampton Court Park
KINGSTON UPON THAMES
Ham
Petersham
Richmond Park
RICHMOND
St. Margarets
Old Deer Park
Royal Botanic Gardens Kew
Kew
North Sheen
East Sheen
Mortlake
BARNES
Castelnau
HAMMERSMITH
Shepherds Bush
CHISWICK
Grove Park
Gunnersbury
South Acton
Acton
Bedford Park
Brentford
Little Ealing
Hanwell
Gunnersbury Park
Heston Services
Grand Union Canal
Princess Alice Hospice
Island Barn Reservoir
Queen Elizabeth II Reservoir
Knight Reservoir
Bessborough Reservoir
Longford Hill

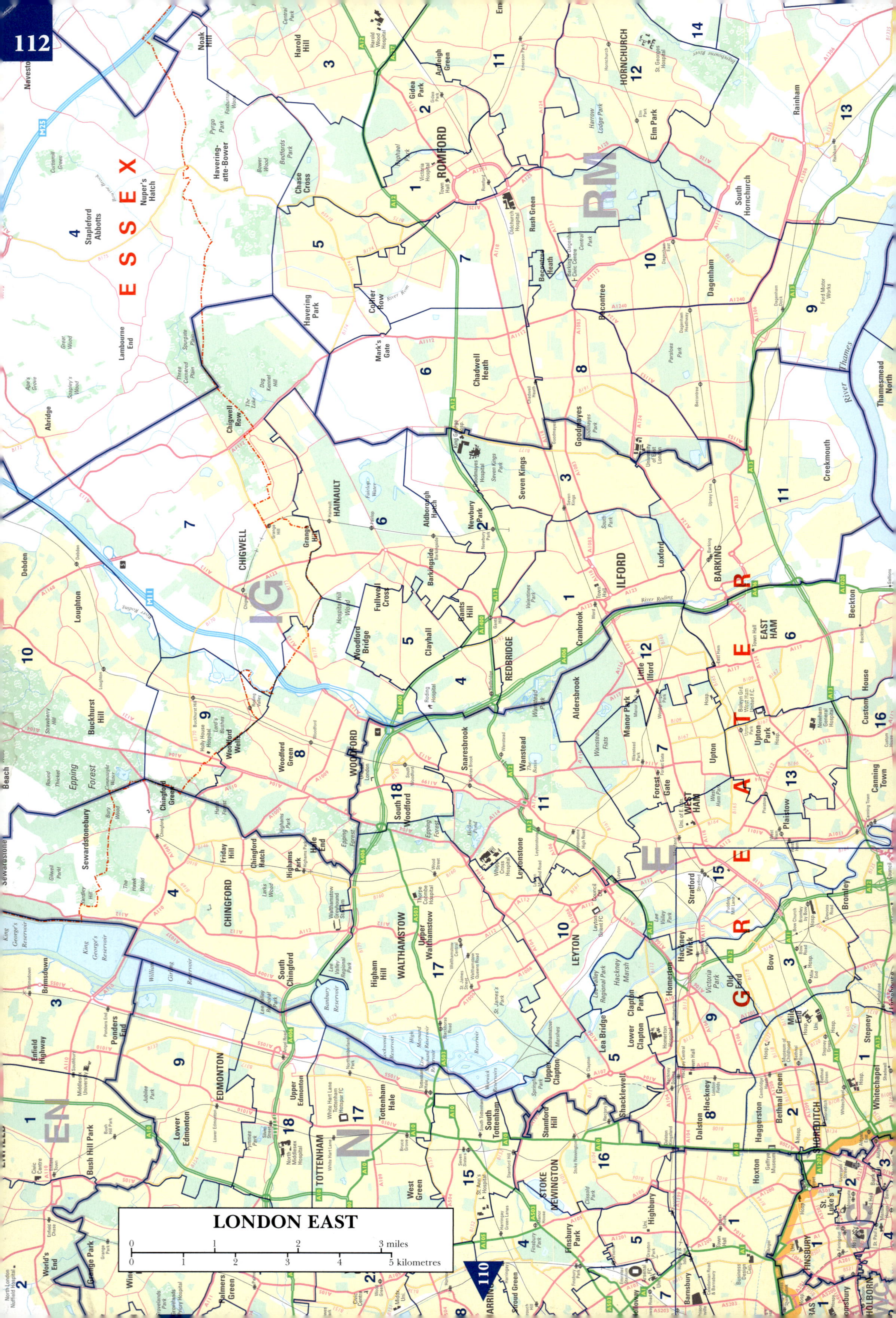
LONDON EAST
0 1 2 3 miles
0 1 2 3 4 5 kilometres
ESSEX
RM
IG
E
N
EN
GREATER
110
Stapleford Abbotts
Nuper's Hatch
Havering-atte-Bower
Harold Hill
Noak Hill
Gidea Park
Ardleigh Green
ROMFORD
HORNCHURCH
Elm Park
South Hornchurch
Rainham
Chase Cross
Collier Row
Havering Park
Rush Green
Becontree Heath
Becontree
Dagenham
Chadwell Heath
Mark's Gate
Lambourne End
Abridge
Chigwell Row
CHIGWELL
HAINAULT
Aldborough Hatch
Newbury Park
Seven Kings
Goodmayes
Barkingside
Fullwell Cross
Gants Hill
Clayhall
Woodford Bridge
REDBRIDGE
ILFORD
Cranbrook
Loxford
BARKING
Creekmouth
Thamesmead North
Beckton
EAST HAM
Debden
Loughton
Buckhurst Hill
Woodford Wells
Woodford Green
WOODFORD
South Woodford
Snaresbrook
Wanstead
Aldersbrook
Little Ilford
Manor Park
Forest Gate
Upton
Upton Park
Plaistow
Custom House
Canning Town
WEST HAM
Epping Forest
Sewardstonebury
Chingford Green
Chingford Hatch
Friday Hill
CHINGFORD
Highams Park
Hale End
Leytonstone
LEYTON
Stratford
WALTHAMSTOW
Upper Walthamstow
Higham Hill
South Chingford
Brimsdown
Enfield Highway
Ponders End
EDMONTON
Lower Edmonton
Upper Edmonton
Bush Hill Park
TOTTENHAM
Tottenham Hale
West Green
South Tottenham
Stamford Hill
STOKE NEWINGTON
Upper Clapton
Lower Clapton
Clapton Park
Lea Bridge
Hackney Marsh
Hackney Wick
Homerton
Victoria Park
Old Ford
Bow
Bromley
Shacklewell
Dalston
Hackney
Haggerston
Bethnal Green
Mile End
Stepney
Whitechapel
Hoxton
SHOREDITCH
FINSBURY
Highbury
Finsbury Park
Stroud Green
World's End
Grange Park
River Thames
River Roding
Ford Motor Works
Parsloes Park
Valentines Park
Wanstead Flats
William Girling Reservoir
King George's Reservoir
Banbury Reservoir
Lockwood Reservoir

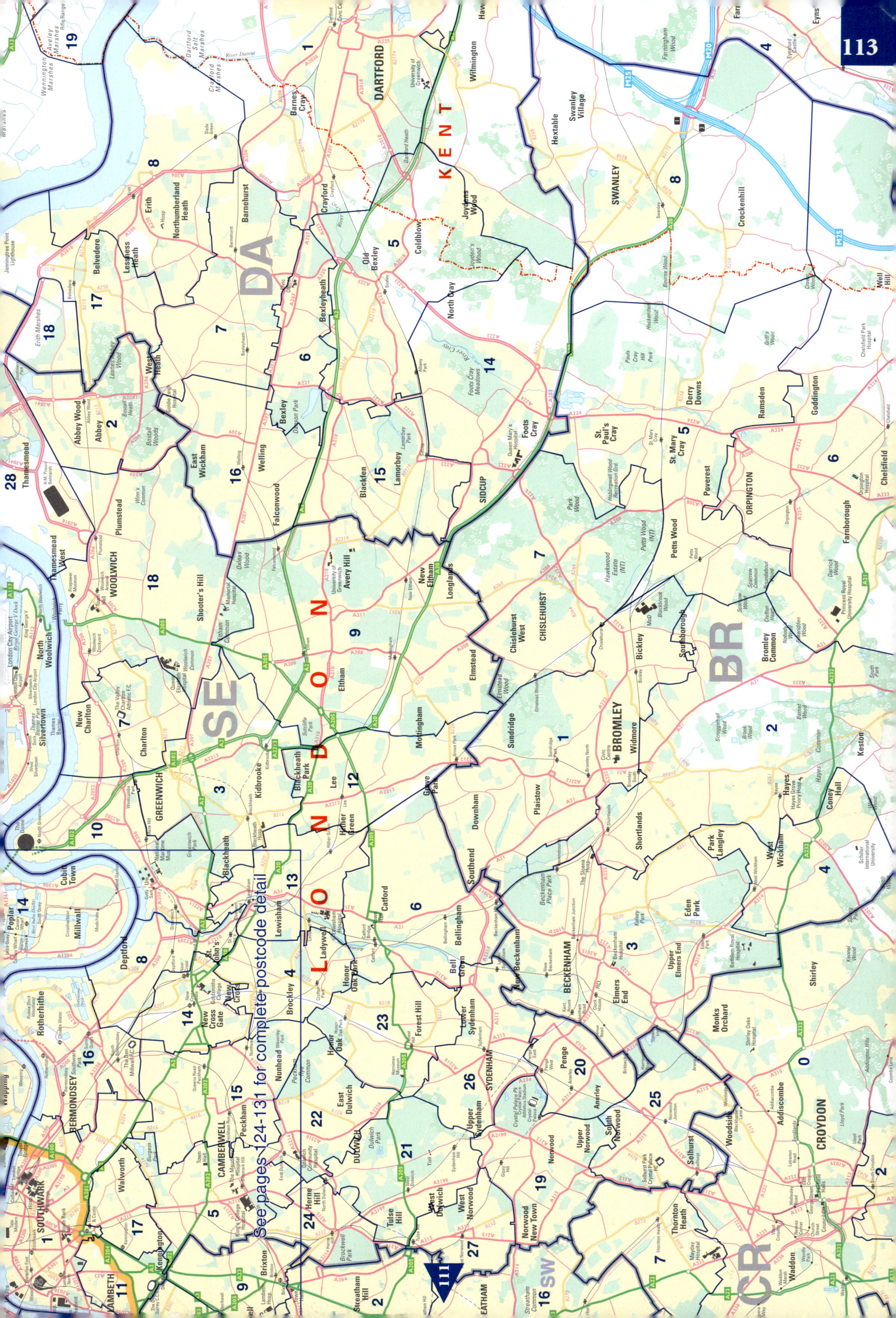

See pages 124-131 for complete postcode detail

WEST MIDLANDS
0 1 2 3 4 miles
0 1 2 3 4 5 6 kilometres
WV
DY
STAFFORDSHIRE
WORCESTERSHIRE
WOLVERHAMPTON
DUDLEY
WEST BROMWICH
SANDWELL
WALSALL
KIDDERMINSTER
STOURBRIDGE
HALESOWEN
Codsall
Bilbrook
Oaken
Lane Green
Moseley
Bushbury
Fordhouses
Essington
Pelsall Wood
Pelsall
Wallington Heath
Little Bloxwich
Heath End
Wrottesley
Oxley
Wood Hayes
Ashmore Park
Bloxwich
Blakenall Heath
Harden
Claregate
Old Fallings
Wood End
Wednesfield
New Invention
Perton
Tettenhall
Dunstall Hill
Park Village
Leamore
Coal Pool
Tettenhall Wood
Heath Town
Ashmore Lake
Lane Head
Nurton
Springfield
Compton
Bentley
Birchills
Old Purton
Willenhall
Monmore Green
Moseley
Portobello
The Chuckery
Castlecroft
Bradmore
Merry Hill
Stow Lawn
Darlaston Green
Pleck
Caldmore
Palfrey
Trescott
Blakenhall
Priestfield
Darlaston
Fallings Heath
Bescot
Goldthorn Park
Parkfield
Kings Hill
Wood Green
Lower Penn
Penn
Colton Hills
Ettingshall
Bilston
Woods Bank
Wednesbury
The Delves
Spring Hill
Lanesfield
Ettingshall Park
Spring Vale
Moxley
The Woods
Yew Tree
Orton
Cinder Hill
Bradley
Lower Bradley
Church Hill
Mesty Croft
Seisdon
Coseley
Wednesbury Oak
Friar Park
Stone Cross
Trysull
Gospel End
Sedgley
Hurst Hill
Princes End
Ocker Hill
Balls Hill
Hateley Heath
The Batch
Roseville
Wallbrook
Summer Hill
Golds Green
Hill Top
Charlemont
Dunsdale
Wombourne
Bramford
Bloomfield
Toll End
Black Lake
Giggetty
Blakeley
Upper Gornal
Tipton Green
Tipton
Horseley Heath
Harvills Hawthorn
Churchfield
Smestow
Himley
Ruiton
Woodsetton
Swan Village
Guns Village
Lyndon
Lower Gornal
New Town
Redhall
Gornalwood
Dudley Port
Swindon
London Fields
Eve Hill
Burnt Tree
Tividale
Wall Heath
Russell's Hall
Kate's Hill
Brades Village
Rounds Green
Hinksford
Dixon's Green
Oakham
Darby's Hill
Pensnett
Waterfront
Oldbury
Langley
Rood End
Ashwood
Summer Hill
Kingswinford
Baptist End
Netherton
Portway
Smethwick
Bromley
Brockmoor
Darby End
The Knowle
Langley Green
Mount Pleasant
Rowley Regis
Causeway Green
Wordsley
Buckpool
Brierley Hill
Primrose Hill
Bowling Green
Ross
Bristnall Fields
Prestwood
Hawbush
Dudley Wood
Bearwood
Audnam
Withymoor Village
Quarry Bank
Old Hill
Blackheath
Amblecote
Amblecote Bank
Cradley Heath
Cockshot
Warley
Stourton
Dunn's Bank
Netherton
Haden Cross
Hurst Green
Gallowstree Elm
Wollaston
Holloway End
Lye
Overend
Coombeswood
Harborne
High Park
Stambermill
The Hayes
Cradley
Hawne
Quinton
Ridgacre
Kinver
Potters Cross
Dunsley
Wollescote
Belle Vale
Gigmill
Norton
Swindford
Pedmore
Hasbury
Spring Hill
Lapal
Moor Street
California
Whittington
Woodgate
Bartley Green
Lodge
Weoley Castle
Blakeshall
Caunsall
Hunnington
Illey
Shenley Fields
Hagley
Cookley
Lower Clent
Churchill
West Hagley
Clent
Romsley
Frankley
Northfield
Wolverley
Romsley Hill
Broadwaters
Blakedown
Broome
Holy Cross
Dayhouse Bank
Turves Green
Greenhill
Bell Heath
Rubery
Rednal
Longbridge
Bell End
Fairfield
Cofton Hackett
Stone
Frankley Services

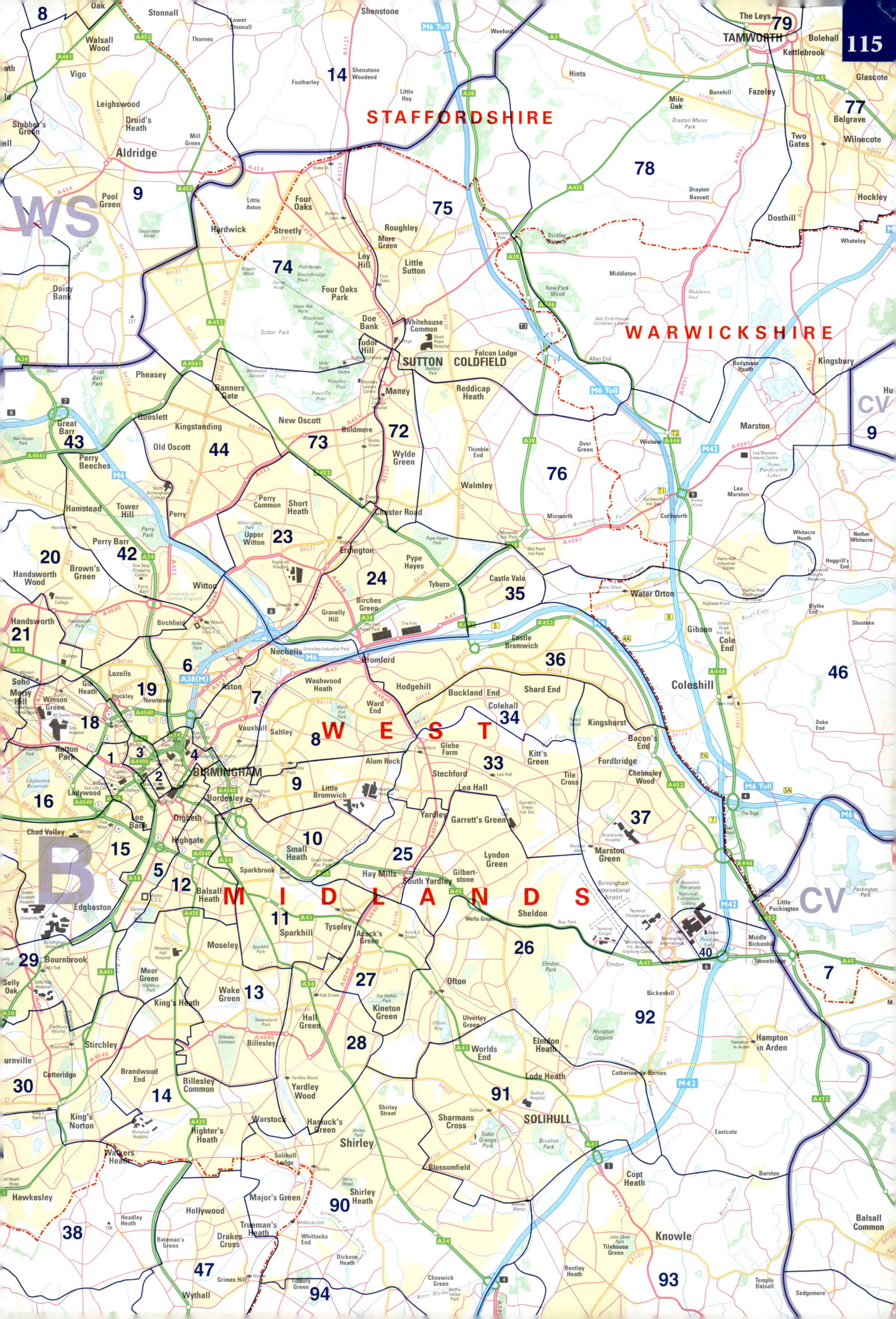
STAFFORDSHIRE
WARWICKSHIRE
WEST MIDLANDS
WS
B
CV
Stonnall
Shenstone
Weeford
The Leys
TAMWORTH
Bolehall
Kettlebrook
Walsall Wood
Thornes
Shenstone Woodend
Hints
Glascote
Vigo
Footherley
Little Hay
Bonehill
Fazeley
Mile Oak
Belgrave
Leighswood
Druid's Heath
Stubber's Green
Mill Green
Two Gates
Wilnecote
Aldridge
Drayton Bassett
Hockley
Pool Green
Little Aston
Four Oaks
Roughley
Dosthill
Hardwick
Streetly
Mere Green
Whateley
Daisy Bank
Ley Hill
Little Sutton
Middleton
Four Oaks Park
Sutton Park
Doe Bank
Whitehouse Common
Tudor Hill
SUTTON COLDFIELD
Falcon Lodge
Kingsbury
Pheasey
Banners Gate
Reddicap Heath
Queslett
Maney
Marston
Great Barr
Kingstanding
New Oscott
Boldmere
Old Oscott
Wylde Green
Thimble End
Over Green
Perry Beeches
Walmley
Lea Marston
Hamstead
Tower Hill
Perry Common
Short Heath
Chester Road
Perry
Minworth
Curdworth
Whitacre Heath
Nether Whitacre
Perry Barr
Upper Witton
Erdington
Handsworth Wood
Brown's Green
Pype Hayes
Hoggrill's End
Witton
Tyburn
Castle Vale
Water Orton
Handsworth
Birchfield
Birches Green
Gravelly Hill
Gibson
Cole End
Shustoke
Castle Bromwich
Nechells
Bromford
Lozells
Aston
Washwood Heath
Hodgehill
Shard End
Coleshill
Soho
Gib Heath
Hockley
Newtown
Buckland End
Colehall
Ward End
Winson Green
Vauxhall
Saltley
Kingshurst
Duke End
Rotton Park
Glebe Farm
Kitt's Green
Bacon's End
Alum Rock
BIRMINGHAM
Stechford
Fordbridge
Tile Cross
Chelmsley Wood
Lea Hall
Ladywood
Bordesley
Little Bromwich
Edgbaston Reservoir
Digbeth
Yardley
Garrett's Green
Chad Valley
Lee Bank
Highgate
Small Heath
Marston Green
Lyndon Green
Sparkbrook
Hay Mills
South Yardley
Gilbertstone
Birmingham International Airport
Balsall Heath
Edgbaston
Sheldon
Little Packington
Wells Green
Middle Bickenhill
Sparkhill
Tyseley
Acock's Green
Stonebridge
Bournbrook
Moseley
Selly Oak
Olton
Elmdon
Bickenhill
Moor Green
Wake Green
King's Heath
Kineton Green
Hall Green
Ulverley Green
Hampton in Arden
Stirchley
Billesley
Worlds End
Elmdon Heath
Catherine-de-Barnes
Brandwood End
Billesley Common
Cotteridge
Yardley Wood
Lode Heath
King's Norton
Warstock
Hasluck's Green
Sharmans Cross
SOLIHULL
Shirley Street
Eastcote
Highter's Heath
Shirley
Walkers Heath
Solihull Lodge
Blossomfield
Copt Heath
Barston
Hawkesley
Major's Green
Shirley Heath
Hollywood
Headley Heath
Trueman's Heath
Knowle
Whitlocks End
Balsall Common
Drakes Cross
Bateman's Green
Dickens Heath
Grimes Hill
Tilehouse Green
Bentley Heath
Temple Balsall
Wythall
Tidbury Green
Cheswick Green
Sedgemere
M6 Toll
M6
M42
A38(M)
ASTON EXPRESSWAY
8
79
77
14
9
78
75
74
72
43
44
73
76
42
23
20
24
35
21
6
36
46
19
7
18
34
8
33
1
3
4
2
9
16
37
10
15
25
5
12
11
26
40
7
29
27
13
92
28
30
14
91
38
90
47
94
93

MANCHESTER
0 1 2 3 4 miles
0 1 2 3 4 5 6 kilometres
WN
BL
M
WA
WARRINGTON
CHESHIRE
Horwich
Wallsuches
Bottom o th' Moor
Barrow Bridge
Delph Hill
Halliwell
Doffcocker
Markland Hill
Heaton Cemetery
Astley Br.
Walshaw
Harwood
Ainsworth
Breightmet
Tonge Fold
BOLTON
Darcy Lever
Burnden
Little Lever
Radcliffe
Furnhill
Deane
Daubhill
Great Lever
Lever Edge
Moses Gate
Harper Green
Edge Fold
Hollins
Highfield
Farnworth
New Bury
Nob End
Prestolee
Stoneclough
Kearsley
Cinder Hill
Ringley
Kearsley Moss
Clifton
Hill Top
Linnyshaw
Walkden
Little Hulton
Greenheys
Shakerley
Tyldesley
Atherton
Hag Fold
Howe Bridge
Hindsford
Parr Brow
Mosley Common
Astley
Ellenbrook
Roe Green
Worsley
Hazelhurst
Swinton
Moorside
Wardley
Dales Brow
Alder Forest
Ellesmere
Boothstown
Higher Green
Astley Green
Gin Pit
Higher Folds
Blackmoor
Lark Hill
Town Lane
Moss Side
Botany Bay Wood
Worsley Moss
Astley Moss
Chat Moss
Winton
Monton
Patricroft
Peel Green
Barton upon Irwell
Dumplington
Barton Moss
Barton Airport
Crofts Bank
Davyhulme
URMSTON
Flixton
Higher Irlam
Irlam
Larkhill
Irlam Moss
Cadishead Moss
Lower Irlam
Cadishead
Carrington
Carrington Moss
Chemical Works
Partington
Woodhouses
Sinderland Green
Broadheath
Oldfield Brow
Dunham Woodhouses
Dunham Town
Carr Green
Mossbrow
Warburton
Heatley
Little Bollington
Bowdon
Rosehill
Bowgreen
Ashley Heath
Arthill
Booth Bank
Ashley
Rostherne
Bucklow Hill
Hulseheath
High Legh
Broomedge
Big Wood
Lymm
Rushgreen
Statham
Westy
Howley
Victoria Park
Latchford
Stockton Heath
Lower Walton
Hillcliffe
Cobbs
Higher Walton
Appleton Park
Appleton Reservoir
Moore
Daresbury
Hatton
Stretton
Great Sankey
Sankey Bridges
Old Hall
Bewsey
Callands
Dallam
Longford
Orford
Padgate
Cinnamon Brow
Houghton Green
Hulme
Winwick
Birchwood
Risley
Risley Moss
Woolston Moss
Rixton Moss
Hollins Green
Glazebrook
Holcroft Moss
Croft
Little Town
Culcheth
Twiss Green
Fowley Common
Kenyon
New Lane End
Glazebury
Little Woolden Moss
Newton-le-Willows
Wargrave
Vulcan Village
Town of Lowton
Lane Head
Lowton
Lowton St Mary's
Golborne
Haydock Park
Ashton in Makerfield
Abram
Platt Bridge
Hawkley
Plank Lane
Westleigh
Tamer Lane End
Bickershaw
Hindley Green
Hindley
Daisy Hill
Dangerous Corner
LEIGH
Bedford
Pennington
Firs Lane
The Flash
Aspull Common
Pocket Nook
Dirty Common
Wingates
Westhoughton
Water's Nook
Chew Moor
Hunger Hill
Over Hulton
Chequerbent
Blackrod
Haigh
Scot Lane End
Aspull
New Springs
Marylebone
Wigan
Ince-in-Makerfield
Manchester Ship Canal
Bridgewater Canal
Leeds & Liverpool Canal
River Mersey

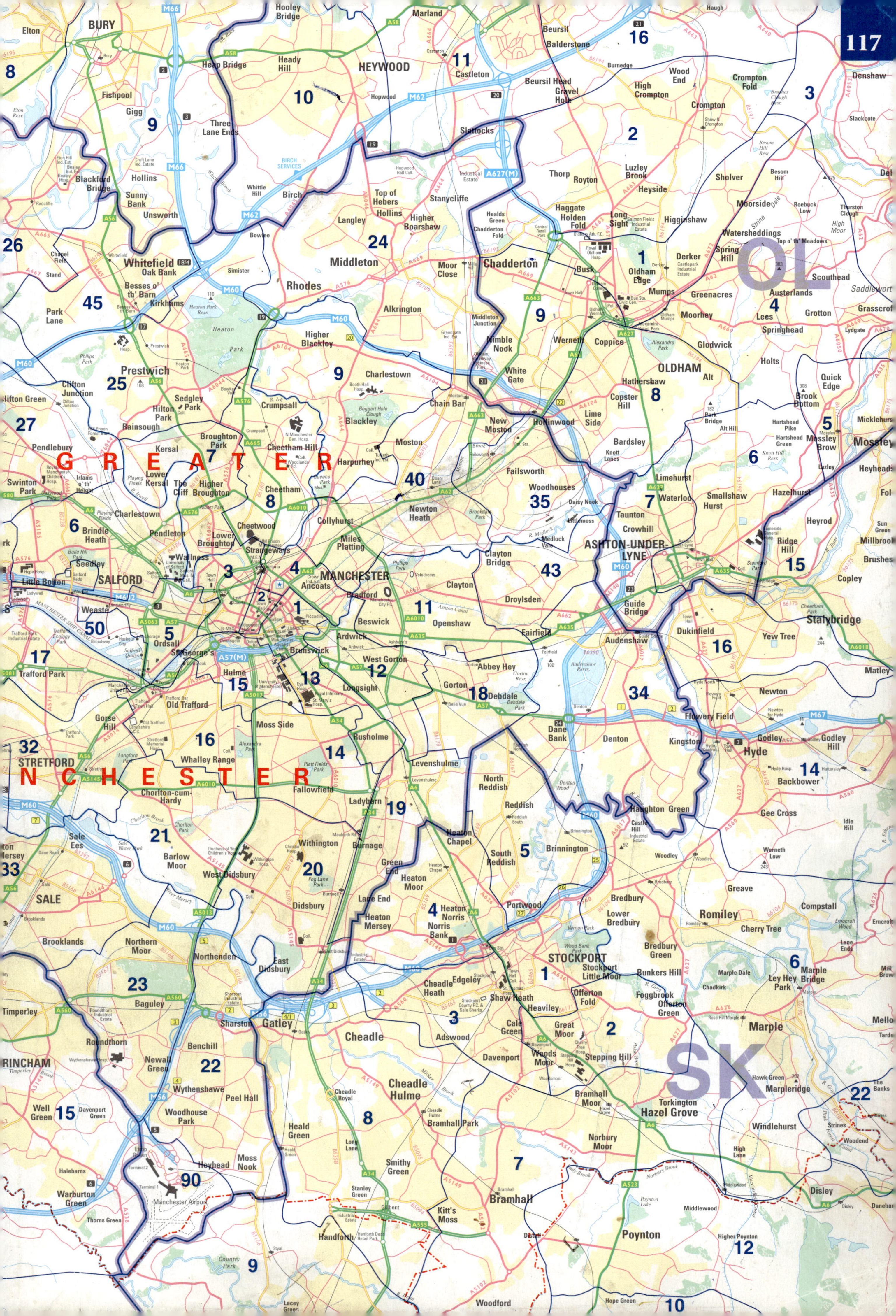
GREATER MANCHESTER
OL
SK
BURY
HEYWOOD
Middleton
Whitefield
Prestwich
Chadderton
OLDHAM
SALFORD
MANCHESTER
ASHTON-UNDER-LYNE
Stalybridge
Dukinfield
Hyde
Denton
Droylsden
Failsworth
STRETFORD
SALE
Gatley
Cheadle
Cheadle Hulme
STOCKPORT
Hazel Grove
Bramhall
Poynton
Romiley
Marple
Mossley
Manchester Airport
Elton
Fishpool
Gigg
Hollins
Sunny Bank
Unsworth
Heap Bridge
Heady Hill
Three Lane Ends
Birch
Langley
Rhodes
Alkrington
Higher Blackley
Charlestown
Blackley
Moston
Harpurhey
Crumpsall
Cheetham Hill
Cheetham
Broughton Park
Kersal
Pendlebury
Swinton Park
Pendleton
Ordsall
Weaste
Trafford Park
Old Trafford
Hulme
Moss Side
Whalley Range
Chorlton-cum-Hardy
Fallowfield
Levenshulme
Withington
Didsbury
West Didsbury
Northenden
Baguley
Wythenshawe
Benchill
Sharston
Heald Green
Handforth
Woodford
Ardwick
Longsight
Gorton
Openshaw
Clayton
Newton Heath
Miles Platting
Collyhurst
Ancoats
Beswick
Abbey Hey
Audenshaw
Guide Bridge
Heaton Chapel
Heaton Moor
Heaton Mersey
Heaton Norris
Reddish
North Reddish
South Reddish
Brinnington
Bredbury
Woodley
Offerton
Edgeley
Cheadle Heath
Adswood
Davenport
Norbury Moor
Disley
Shaw Heath
Royton
Crompton
High Crompton
Shaw
Lees
Springhead
Grotton
Scouthead
Austerlands
Werneth
Hollinwood
Woodhouses
Lime Side
Bardsley
Crowhill
Waterloo
Smallshaw
Hurst
Heyrod
Ridge Hill
Copley
Newton
Godley
Gee Cross
Backbower
Brookland
Brooklands
Timperley
Roundthorn
Peel Hall
Woodhouse Park
Moss Nook
Heyhead
Halebarns
Warburton Green
Well Green
Davenport Green

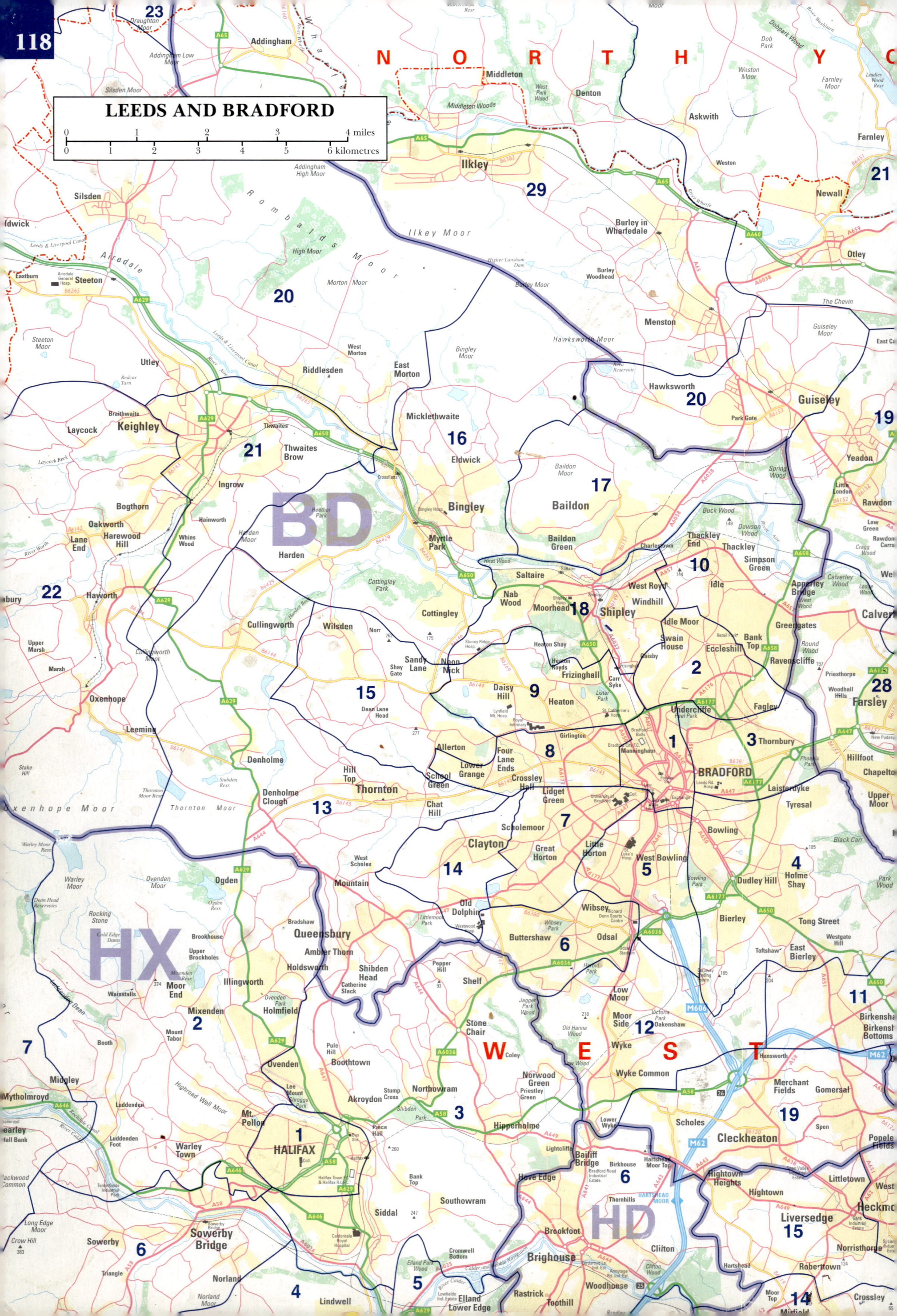

LEEDS AND BRADFORD
0 1 2 3 4 miles
0 1 2 3 4 5 6 kilometres
N O R T H Y
W E S T
BD
HX
HD
Addingham
Middleton
Denton
Askwith
Ilkley
Silsden
Rombalds Moor
Ilkey Moor
Burley in Wharfedale
Otley
Newall
Steeton
Menston
Utley
Riddlesden
East Morton
Hawksworth
Guiseley
Keighley
Laycock
Micklethwaite
Eldwick
Bingley
Baildon
Ingrow
Thwaites Brow
Yeadon
Bogthorn
Oakworth
Harewood Hill
Lane End
Harden
Myrtle Park
Baildon Green
Thackley
Idle
Haworth
Cullingworth
Wilsden
Cottingley
Saltaire
Nab Wood
Shipley
Windhill
Moorhead
Eccleshill
Apperley Bridge
Greengates
Ravenscliffe
Oxenhope
Sandy Lane
Daisy Hill
Heaton
Frizinghall
Undercliffe
Fagley
Farsley
Leeming
Allerton
Four Lane Ends
Manningham
Thornbury
Denholme
Thornton
Lower Grange
BRADFORD
Laisterdyke
Denholme Clough
Chat Hill
Crossley Hall
Lidget Green
Tyresal
Clayton
Scholemoor
Great Horton
Little Horton
Bowling
West Bowling
Holme Shay
Ogden
Mountain
Dudley Hill
Old Dolphin
Wibsey
Bierley
Queensbury
Buttershaw
Odsal
Tong Street
Ambler Thorn
Holdsworth
Shibden Head
East Bierley
Illingworth
Moor End
Shelf
Mixenden
Holmfield
Stone Chair
Low Moor
Moor Side
Wyke
Ovenden
Boothtown
Wyke Common
Norwood Green
Northowram
Akroydon
Mytholmroyd
Midgley
Mt. Pellon
Hipperholme
Scholes
Cleckheaton
HALIFAX
Warley Town
Bailiff Bridge
Hove Edge
Hightown Heights
Hightown
Littletown
Sowerby Bridge
Siddal
Southowram
Brookfoot
Clifton
Liversedge
Brighouse
Norland
Lindwell
Elland
Lower Edge
Rastrick
Woodhouse
Toothill
Robertown

YORKSHIRE
HG
3
LS
WF
Staniston Hill
Springs Moor
North Rigton
Braythorn
Stainburn
Huby
Leathley
Weeton
Riffa Wood
Farnley Lake
Pool
Arthington Pastures
Arthington
Swindon Wood
Dunkeswick
Kirkby Overblow
Spofforth Park
Sicklinghall
Clap Gate
Kirk Deighton
Stockeld Park
Spring Wood
Devonshire Wood
Wetherby
22
Linton
Carthick Wood
Wharfedale
Collingham
Compton
Harewood
Weardley
Bog Plantation
Fish Pond
Harewood Park
17
East Keswick
Rigton Hill
Thornhurst
Keswick Beck
Bardsey
East Rigton
Lady Wood
West Woods
Wothersome
23
Old Bramhope
Bramhope
Spring Wood
Eccup
Eccup Reservoir
Wike
Norwood Bottoms
Bramham Park
Yeadon Moor
Leeds and Bradford International Airport
16
Cookridge
Holt Park
Adel
Alwoodley Park
Alwoodley Gates
Alwoodley
Scarcroft
Shadwell
Thorner
Sandhills
Saw Wood
Kiddal Lane End
Potterton
24
14
Tinshill
Lawnswood
Moor Allerton
Moortown
Lane Ends
18
Horsforth
Horsforth Woodside
Cookridge & Ida Hosps
Claydon Wood
West Park
Meanwood Park
Meanwood
Weetwood
Roundhay Park
Roundhay
8
Monkswood
Wellington Hill
Whinmoor
Barwick in Elmet
Scholes
Newlay Wood
Hawksworth
Leeds Metropolitan University
Beckett Park
Chapel Allerton
Gledhow
Oakwood
Beechwood
Seacroft
Whinmoor
Swarcliffe
Rodley
Bagley
Whitecote
Moorside
Kirkstall
5
Headingley
6
7
Potternewton
Brooklands
Parklands
13
Stanningley
Bramley
4
Burley
Woodhouse
2
Gipton
Harehills
Manston
Cross Gates
15
Swinnow Moor
Hill Top
Upper Armley
3
LEEDS
Burmantofts
Halton
Whitkirk
25
Garforth
West Garforth
Pudsey
Gamble Hill
Armley
1
Osmondthorpe
East End Park
9
Halton Moor
Colton
Wortley
Farnley
12
Holbeck
Cross Green Industrial Estate
Avenue Wood
Far Royds
Hunslet
Beeston Hill
Beeston
11
New Farnley
Mill Shaw
Stourton
Swillington
Upper Moor Side
Power Station
Newsam Green
Kippax
Cockersdale
Beeston Park Side
10
Moor Head
Gildersome
Churwell
Middleton Park
Belle Isle
John O' Gaunts
Woodlesford
Great Preston
Drighlington
Adwalton
27
Daisy Hill
Rothwell
Gildersome Street
Bantam Grove
26
Oulton
Allerton Bywater
Moorside
New Brighton
Middleton
Robin Hood
Bruntcliffe
Morley
Carlton
Royds Green
Topcliffe
Thorpe on the Hill
Mickletown
Copley Hill
Birstall
Tingley
Lofthouse
Oulzelwell Green
Methley
Methley Junction
Wilton Park
Upper Green
East Ardsley
Lee Moor
Carlinghow
Woodkirk
Ardsley Rese
Lofthouse Gate
Bottom Boat
Batley
17
Healey
Beggarington Hill
Haigh Moor
Carr Gate
Stanley Lane Ends
Whitwood
Clerk Green
Mount Pleasant
Staincliffe
Hanging Heaton
12
Stanley
Outwood
Altofts
6
Hopetown
Batley Carr
Chidswell
Dogloitch Wood
Jaw Hill
Stanley Marsh Nature Reserve
1
Newton Hill
Stanley Ferry
DEWSBURY
Kirkhamgate
2
Wrenthorpe
Snow Hill
Normanton
7
Dewsbury Moor
Boothroyd
5
Gawthorpe
WAKEFIELD
Woodhouse
Ackton
Chickenley
Alverthorpe
River Aire
River Calder
River Wharfe
Leeds & Liverpool Canal
Aire and Calder Navigation

LIVERPOOL
0 1 2 3 4 miles
0 1 2 3 4 5 6 kilometres
MERSEYSIDE
LANCS
CHESHIRE
WN
WA
L
CH
LIVERPOOL BAY
Crosby Channel
River Mersey
Birkenhead to hours
Belfast 8
Dublin 8
Liverpool to hours
Douglas 2½-4
Dublin 8
LIVERPOOL
BIRKENHEAD
BOOTLE
WALLASEY
CROSBY
BEBINGTON
ELLESMERE PORT
SKELMERSDALE
Prescot
Knowsley
Kirkby
Maghull
Aintree
Lydiate
Aughton
Town Green
Ince Blundell
Hightown
Little Crosby
Thornton
Blundellsands
Great Crosby
Waterloo
Seaforth
Litherland
Orrell
Walton
Fazakerley
Anfield
Everton
Kirkdale
Clubmoor
Tuebrook
Stoneycroft
West Derby
Old Swan
Knotty Ash
Dovecot
Swanside
Fairfield
Wavertree
Edge Hill
Princes Park
Toxteth
Dingle
St Michael's Hamlet
Mossley Hill
Calderstones
Aigburth
Otterspool
Grassendale
Garston
Speke
Allerton
Woolton
Gateacre
Belle Vale
Childwall
Netherley
Halewood
Hunts Cross
Huyton
Huyton with Roby
Page Moss
Roby
Court Hey
Bowring Park
Whiston
Rainhill
Croxteth
Gillmoss
Norris Green
Dog and Gun
Northwood
Westvale
Southdene
Buckley Hill
New Brighton
Liscard
Egremont
Poulton
Seacombe
Bidston
Claughton
Noctorum
Oxton
Prenton
Tranmere
Rock Ferry
Upton
Woodchurch
Landican
Thingwall
Barnston
Heswall
Gayton
Higher Bebington
Lower Bebington
Port Sunlight
New Ferry
Bromborough Pool
Bromborough
Eastham
Brookhurst
Raby
Parkgate
Neston
Willaston
Hooton
Childer Thornton
Overpool
Little Neston
Woodhey
Storeton
Brimstage
Thornton Hough
Liverpool John Lennon Airport
Manchester Ship Canal
M53
M57
M58
M62
A59
A580
A5036
A565
A41
A561
A562
A506
A5300
A570
120

NEWCASTLE UPON TYNE
0 1 2 3 4 miles
0 1 2 3 4 5 6 kilometres
NORTHUMBERLAND
TYNE & WEAR
NE
SR
Morpeth
High Church
Shadfen
Stakeford
Sheepwash
Guide Post
Scotland Gate
East Sleekburn
Cambois
The Rockers
Clifton
Cowpen
Bedlington
Nedderton
Bedside
Blyth
Pier
Seaton Sea Rocks
Saltwick
Stannington
East Hartford
New Delaval
Newsham
Shankhouse
Shotton
Nelson Village
Cramlington
East Cramlington
New Hartley
Seaton Sluice
Seaton
Hartley
Seaton Delaval
Holywell
Berwick Hill
Horton Grange
Brenkley
Moor Farm Roundabout
Seghill
Seaton Burn
Annitsford
Dudley
Prestwick Carr
Mason
Dinnington
Prestwick
Brunswick Village
Wide Open
Burradon
Backworth
Earsdon
Monkseaton
Whitley Bay
Brown's Point
Camperdown
Killingworth
Shiremoor
Murton
Marden
Cullercoats
Saddle Rocks
Hazlerigg
Newcastle International Airport
East Brunton
Gosforth Lake
Gosforth Wood
West Moor
Palmersville
Holystone
Benton Square
New York
Preston Grange
Preston
Long Sands
Black Callerton
Woolsington Park
Woolsington
Forest Hall
Benton
Billy Mill
North Shields
The Narrows
Callerton
Kenton Bankfoot
Fawdon
Kingston Park
Coxlodge
Longbenton
Battle Hill
West Chirton
Chirton
Newbiggin Hall Estate
North Walbottle
Gosforth
Kenton Bar
Kenton
South Gosforth
High Heaton
Holy Cross
Willington
Howdon
Percy Main
Royal Quays
Albert Edward Dock
Westerhope
Nuns Moor
Rosehill
Willington Quay
Blakelaw
NEWCASTLE UPON TYNE
Heaton
Wallsend
Howdon Pans
West Denton
East Denton
Town Moor
Jesmond
Walbottle
Cowgate
Jarrow
West Park
Fenham
Spital Tongues
Sandyford
Denton Burn
Lemington
Old Benwell
Arthur's Hill
Shieldfield
Byker
Walker
Brough Park
Riverside Park
Hebburn
West Harton
Bell's Close
Scotswood
Benwell
Walker Park
Hebburn Park
Simonside
Stella
Elswick
St. Peter's
Monkton
Primrose
Path Head
Blaydon
Gateshead
St. Anthony's
Hedworth
Whiteleas
Bill Quay
Felling
Pelaw
Winlaton
Dunston
Teams
Mount Pleasant
Bensham
Fellgate
Boldon Colliery
Boldon
East Boldon
Swalwell
Dunston Hill
Deckham
Heworth
Wardley
West Boldon
Winlaton Mill
Whickham
Lobley Hill
High Felling
Carr Hill
Windy Nook
Oliver Henderson Park
Team Valley
Low Fell
Wrekenton
Downhill
Town End Farm
Hylton Red House
Sunniside
Street Gate
Harlow Green
Chowdene
Eighton Banks
Springwell
Stephenson
Hylton Castle
Southwick
Castletown
Marley Hill
Donwell
Usworth
Sulgrave
Concord
Washington
Lamesley
Kibblesworth
Blackfell
Washington Village
North Hylton
South Hylton
SUNDERLAND
River Tyne
River Derwent
River Don
R. Team
R. Blyth
A1
A19
A189
A167(M)
A194(M)
A184
A1058
A692
A696
A695
A1231
63
62
22
61
24
23
26
25
20
13
27
12
3
30
5
7
28
29
33
2
15
6
1
4
32
31
34
21
8
35
10
36
11
39
16
9
37
38
4
5

GLASGOW
0 1 2 3 4 miles
0 1 2 3 4 5 6 kilometres
STIRLING
EAST DUNBARTONSHIRE
GLASGOW
NORTH LANARKSHIRE
SOUTH LANARKSHIRE
EAST RENFREWSHIRE
G
PA
ML
CAMPSIE FELLS
Lennox Forest
Strathblane
Blanefield
Carbeth
Lennoxtown
Milton of Campsie
Kirkintilloch
Lenzie
Milngavie
Bearsden
Bishopbriggs
Torrance
Balmore
Cadder
Kenmure
Harestanes
Twechar
Moodiesburn
Chryston
Muirhead
Gartcosh
Stepps
Drumchapel
Knightswood
Yoker
Scotstounhill
Scotstoun
Anniesland
Kelvindale
Kelvinside
Maryhill
Gilshochill
Lambhill
Summerston
Springburn
Possilpark
Balornock
Barmulloch
Provanmill
Riddrie
Royston
Dowanhill
Partick
Whiteinch
Shieldhall
Finnieston
Dennistoun
Carntyne
Easterhouse
Garthamlock
Ruchazie
Springboig
Barlanark
Baillieston
Swinton
Shettleston
Parkhead
Bridgeton
GLASGOW
Govan
Ibrox
Cardonald
Craigton
Hillington
Crookston
Mosspark
Pollok
Pollokshields
Dumbreck
Crossmyloof
Govanhill
Polmadie
Rutherglen
Oatlands
Shawlands
Langside
Mount Florida
Battlefield
Cathcart
King's Park
Croftfoot
Pollokshaws
Priesthill
Nitshill
Hurlet
Mansewood
Newlands
Merrylee
Muirend
Arden
Carnwardric
Darnley
Barrhead
Thornliebank
Giffnock
Netherlee
Castlemilk
Carmunnock
Stamperland
Williamwood
Clarkston
Sheddens
Busby
Whitecraigs
Crookfur
Broom
Newton Mearns
Mearns
Eaglesham
Waterfoot
Thorntonhall
Braehead
Jackton
Lawmuir
High Crosshill
Burnside
Eastfield
Cambuslang
Flemington
Hallside
Newton
Carmyle
Braidfauld
Mount Vernon
Broomhouse
Uddingston
Kylepark
Birkenshaw
Bothwell
Low Blantyre
Blantyre
High Blantyre
Hamilton
East Kilbride
Calderwood
East Mains
West Mains
The Murray
Westwood
St. Leonards
Birniehill
Stewartfield
Rogerton
Nerston
Greenhills
63
65
66
68
81
62
61
64
15
23
13
12
20
22
21
33
69
4
14
11
3
2
1
5
31
34
51
52
41
40
32
42
73
43
53
44
46
45
72
71
78
76
74
75
77
10

London key to map pages

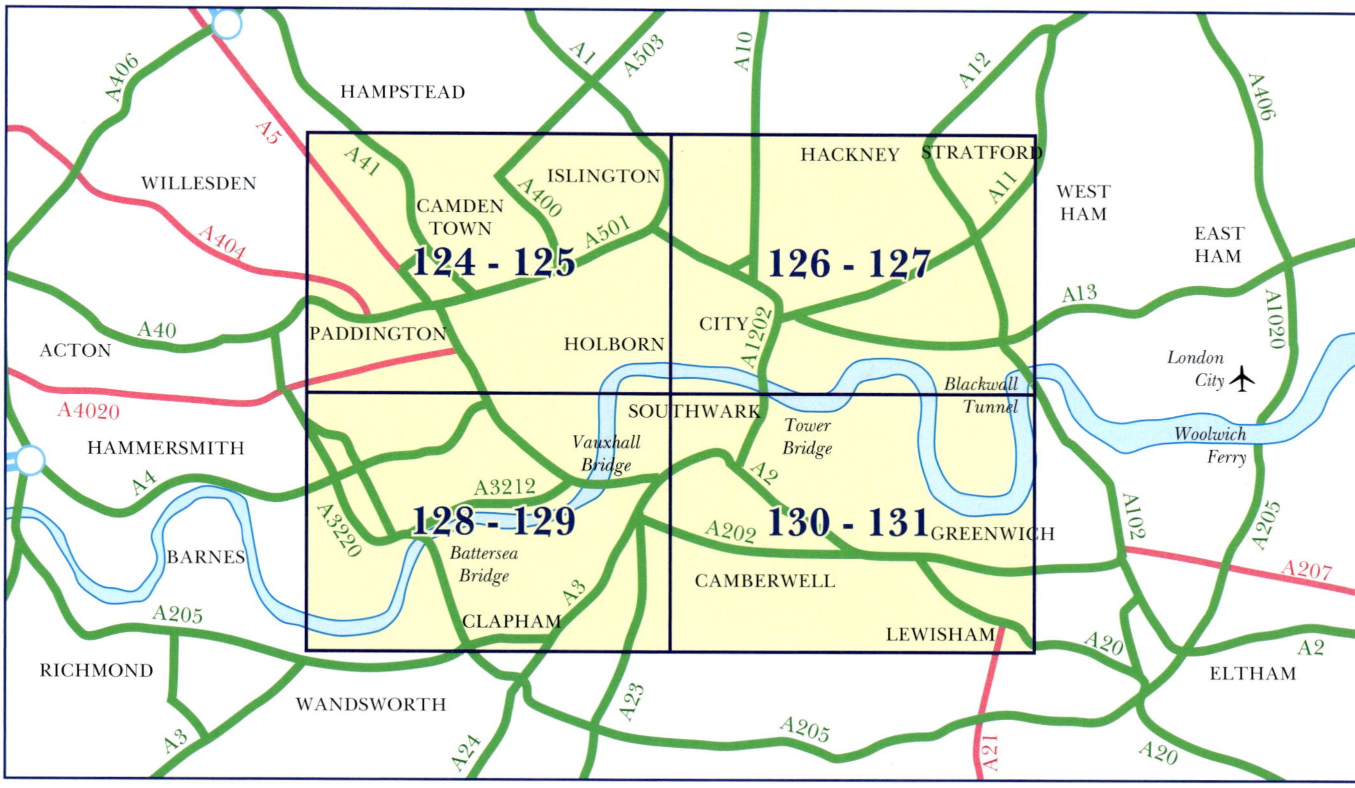

London key to symbols

Symbol	Description	Symbol	Description	Symbol	Description
	Postcode area boundary		Cycle path		Youth hostel
E	Postcode area		Track/Footpath		Historic site
	Postcode district boundary		Long distance footpath	+	Church
4	Postcode district	P	Pedestrian ferry		Mosque
3N	Postcode sub-district		Borough boundary		Synagogue
	Postcode sector boundary		Main National Rail station		Windmill
5	Postcode sector		Other National Rail station		Leisure & tourism
	Extent of congestion charging zone		London Underground station		Shopping
	Extended congestion charging zone (effective from February 2007)		Docklands Light Railway station		Administration & law
M4	Motorway		Pedestrian ferry landing stage		Health & welfare
Dual A4	Primary route	P	Car park		Education
Dual A40	'A' road		Bus/Coach station		Industry & commerce
B504	'B' road	H	Heliport		Cemetery
	Other road/ One way street	USA	Embassy		Golf course
	Toll	Pol	Police station		Public open space/ Allotments
	Street market	Fire Sta	Fire station		Park/Garden/Sports ground
	Restricted access road	PO	Post Office		Wood/Forest
	Pedestrian street	Lib	Library		Orchard
		i	Information centre for visitors		Built-up area

SCALE

0 — 1/4 — 1/2 — 3/4 — 1 mile

0 — 0.25 — 0.5 — 0.75 — 1 — 1.25 — 1.5 kilometres

1:20,000 3.2 inches to 1 mile / 5 cm to 1 km

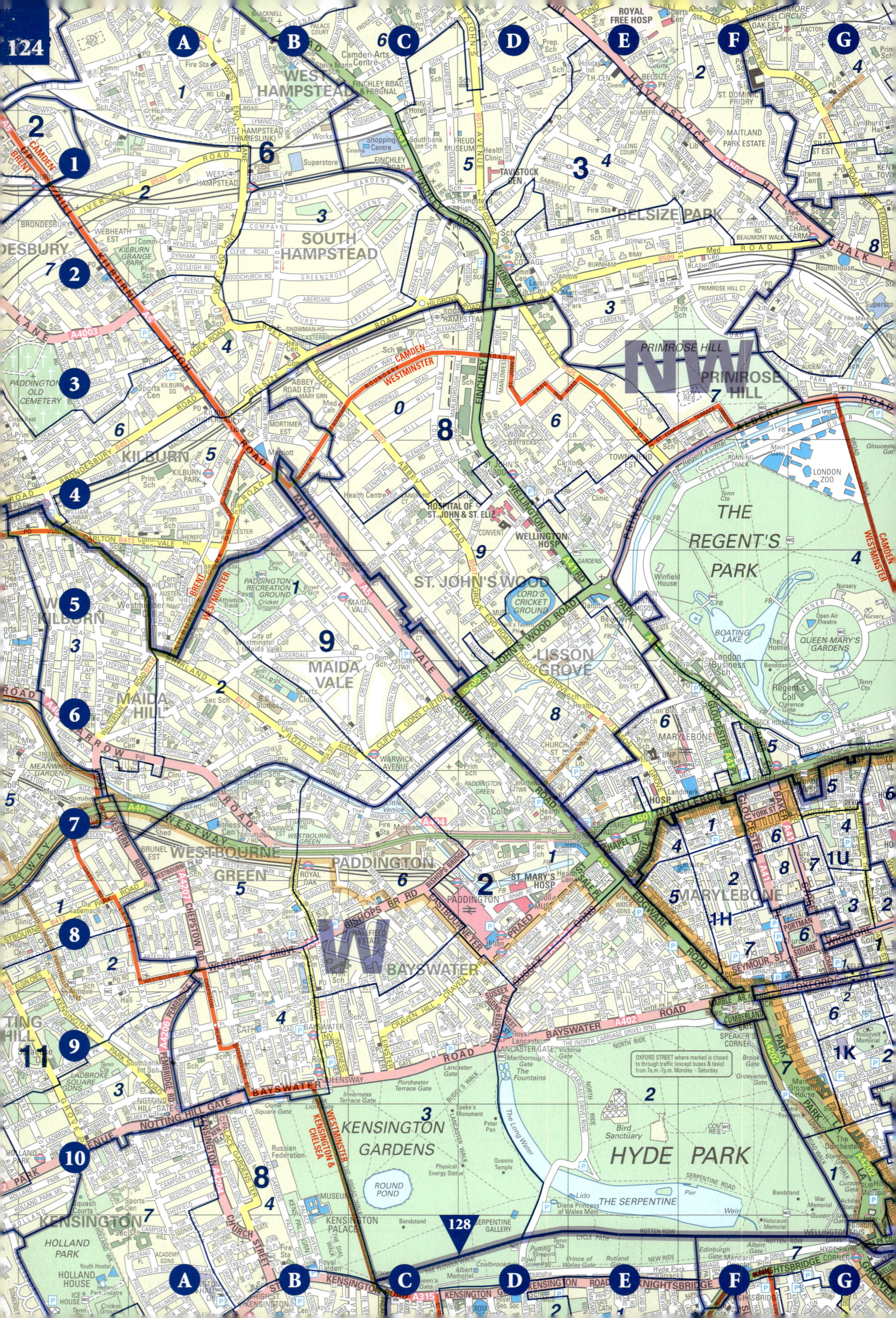

NW
W
WEST HAMPSTEAD
SOUTH HAMPSTEAD
BELSIZE PARK
PRIMROSE HILL
KILBURN
WEST KILBURN
MAIDA HILL
MAIDA VALE
ST. JOHN'S WOOD
LISSON GROVE
MARYLEBONE
PADDINGTON
WESTBOURNE GREEN
BAYSWATER
NOTTING HILL GATE
KENSINGTON
KENSINGTON GARDENS
HYDE PARK
THE REGENT'S PARK
THE SERPENTINE
ROUND POND
LONDON ZOO
LORD'S CRICKET GROUND
QUEEN MARY'S GARDENS
PADDINGTON OLD CEMETERY
PADDINGTON RECREATION GROUND
HOLLAND PARK
ROYAL FREE HOSP
HOSPITAL OF ST. JOHN & ST. ELIZ
WELLINGTON HOSP
ST. MARY'S HOSP
CAMDEN
WESTMINSTER
BRENT
KENSINGTON & CHELSEA
OXFORD STREET where marked is closed to through traffic (except buses & taxis) from 7a.m.-7p.m. Monday - Saturday
128

H
J
K
L
M
N
P
HOLLOWAY
HIGHBURY
KENTISH TOWN
CALEDONIAN PARK
PENTONVILLE PRISON
BARNSBURY
CANONBURY
KING'S CROSS
CAMDEN TOWN
ISLINGTON
N
SOMERS TOWN
BRITISH LIB
EUSTON
REGENT'S PARK
ST. PANCRAS
FINSBURY
EC
WC
CLERKENWELL
BLOOMSBURY
BRITISH MUSEUM
HOLBORN
BART'S HOSP
ST. PAUL'S CATH
SOHO
MAYFAIR
STRAND
CHARING CROSS
EMBANKMENT
RIVER
SHAKESPEARE GLOBE THEATRE
TATE MODERN
ROYAL FESTIVAL HALL
WATERLOO
SOUTHWARK
SE
SW
ST. JAMES'S
THE GREEN PARK
ST. JAMES'S PARK
BUCKINGHAM PALACE
THE BOROUGH
126
129

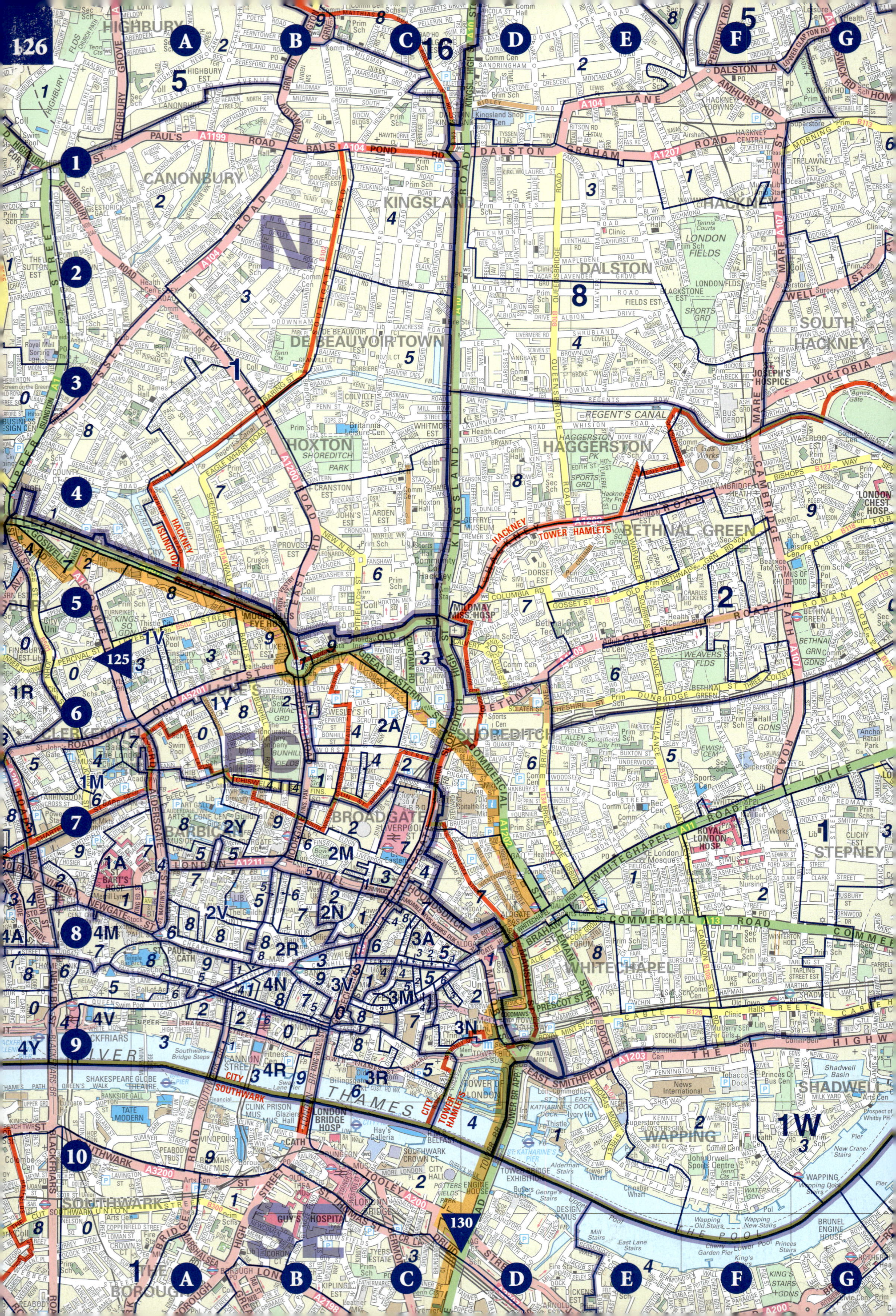
HIGHBURY
CANONBURY
KINGSLAND
DALSTON
HACKNEY
LONDON FIELDS
SOUTH HACKNEY
DE BEAUVOIR TOWN
HOXTON
HAGGERSTON
REGENT'S CANAL
BETHNAL GREEN
SHOREDITCH
CLERKENWELL
BROADGATE
BARBICAN
STEPNEY
WHITECHAPEL
SHADWELL
WAPPING
SOUTHWARK
THE BOROUGH
RIVER THAMES
TOWER OF LONDON
TATE MODERN
GUY'S HOSPITAL
N
EC
SE
1W
125
130
A
B
C
D
E
F
G
1
2
3
4
5
6
7
8
9
10

HOMERTON
HACKNEY WICK
STRATFORD
STRATFORD INTERNATIONAL (under construction)
VICTORIA PARK
OLD FORD
WELL STREET COMMON
BOW
MILE END
BROMLEY
LIMEHOUSE
POPLAR
RIVER THAMES
TOWER HAMLETS
NEWHAM
SOUTHWARK
GREENWICH
HACKNEY
WALTHAM FOREST
WICK COMMUNITY WOODLAND
LEE VALLEY CYCLE CIRCUIT
GROVE HALL PARK
THREE MILLS GREEN
LEE VALLEY PARK
TOWER HAMLETS CEMETERY PARK
MILE END PARK
MILE END STADIUM
ROYAL LOND. HOSP (ST. CLEMENTS)
MILE END HOSP
Queen Mary University of London
EAST INDIA DOCK BASIN NATURE RES
EAST INDIA
WEST INDIA QUAY
WEST INDIA DOCKS
CANARY WHARF
ISLE
Blackwall Basin
The Dome Redevelopment (Open 2007)
NORTH GREENWICH
MEMORIAL GDNS
CODY ROAD BUSINESS CENTRE
ELECTRA BUSINESS PARK
BLACKWALL TRADING EST
PENINSULA ECOLOGICAL PARK
Channel Tunnel Rail Link (under construction)
BOW INDUSTRIAL PARK
PUDDING MILL LANE
BOW CHURCH
BROMLEY BY BOW
DEVONS ROAD
ALL SAINTS
WEST HAM
CANNING TOWN
EAST INDIA DOCK RD
COMMERCIAL ROAD
ROMAN ROAD
BOW ROAD
MILE END ROAD
GROVE ROAD
BURDETT ROAD
WHITE POST LA
CARPENTERS RD
HIGH STREET
ASPEN WAY
LOWER LEA CROSSING
BLACKWALL TUNNEL
NORTHERN APPROACH
EAST CROSS ROUTE
HERTFORD UNION CANAL
River Lee or Lea
RATCLIFFE
SURREY WATER
H J K L M N P
1 2 3 4 5 6 7 8 9 10
131

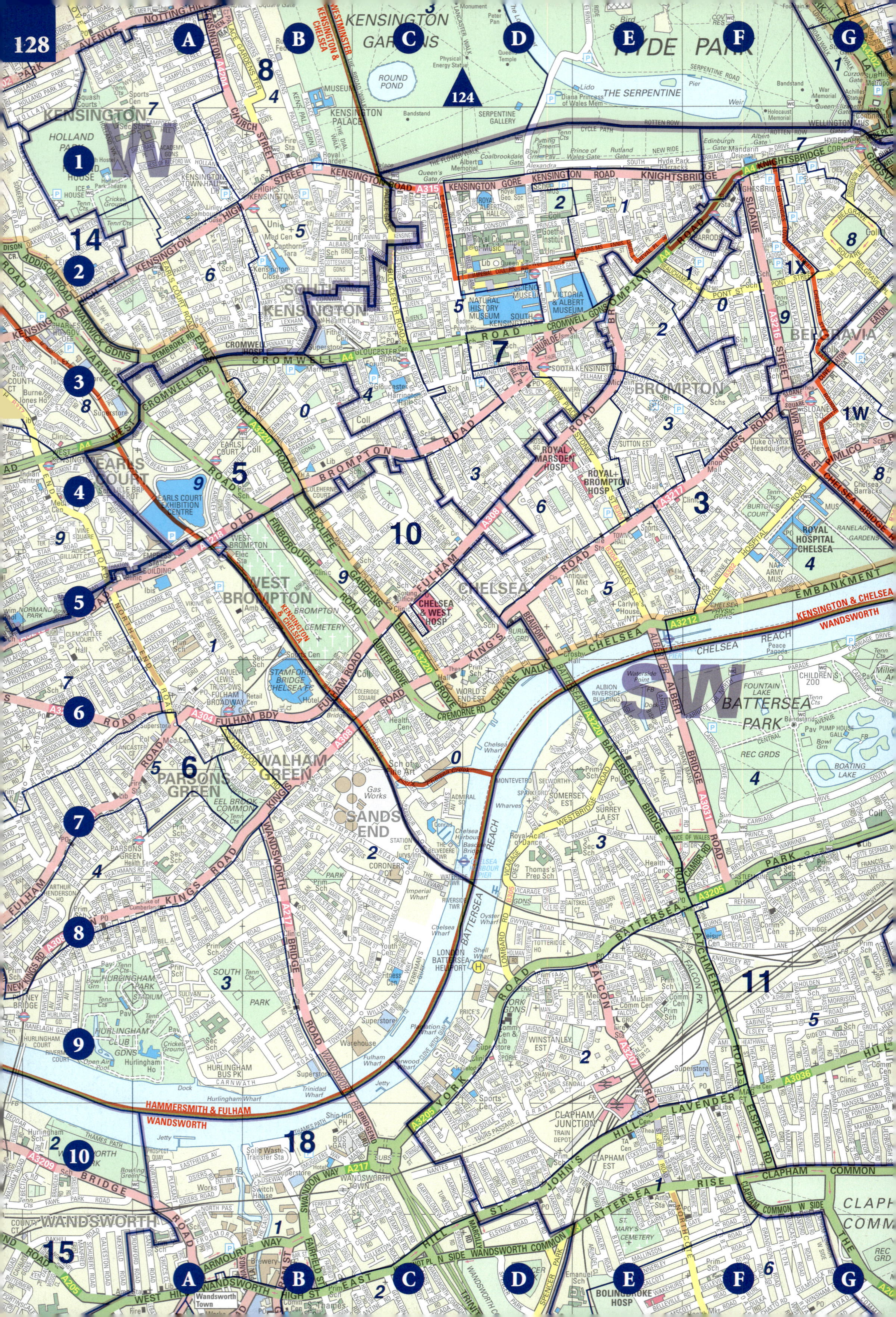
A
B
C
D
E
F
G
KENSINGTON GARDENS
HYDE PARK
ROUND POND
THE SERPENTINE
124
NOTTING HILL
KENSINGTON
HOLLAND PARK
W
KENSINGTON PALACE
KENSINGTON ROAD
KENSINGTON GORE
KNIGHTSBRIDGE
SOUTH KENSINGTON
ROYAL ALBERT HALL
NATURAL HISTORY MUSEUM
VICTORIA & ALBERT MUSEUM
BROMPTON
BELGRAVIA
CROMWELL ROAD
A4
EARLS COURT
EARLS COURT EXHIBITION CENTRE
WEST BROMPTON
BROMPTON CEMETERY
CHELSEA
ROYAL MARSDEN HOSP
ROYAL BROMPTON HOSP
CHELSEA & WEST. HOSP
ROYAL HOSPITAL CHELSEA
KING'S ROAD
FULHAM ROAD
STAMFORD BRIDGE CHELSEA FC
FULHAM BDY
WALHAM GREEN
PARSONS GREEN
SANDS END
CHELSEA EMBANKMENT
KENSINGTON & CHELSEA
WANDSWORTH
HAMMERSMITH & FULHAM
SW
BATTERSEA PARK
BATTERSEA BRIDGE
ALBERT BRIDGE
CHELSEA BRIDGE
HURLINGHAM PARK
HURLINGHAM CLUB
NEW KINGS ROAD
WANDSWORTH BRIDGE
CLAPHAM JUNCTION
LAVENDER HILL
ST. JOHN'S HILL
CLAPHAM COMMON
WANDSWORTH
WANDSWORTH COMMON
BOLINGBROKE HOSP
1
2
3
4
5
6
7
8
9
10
11
14
15
18
1W
1X

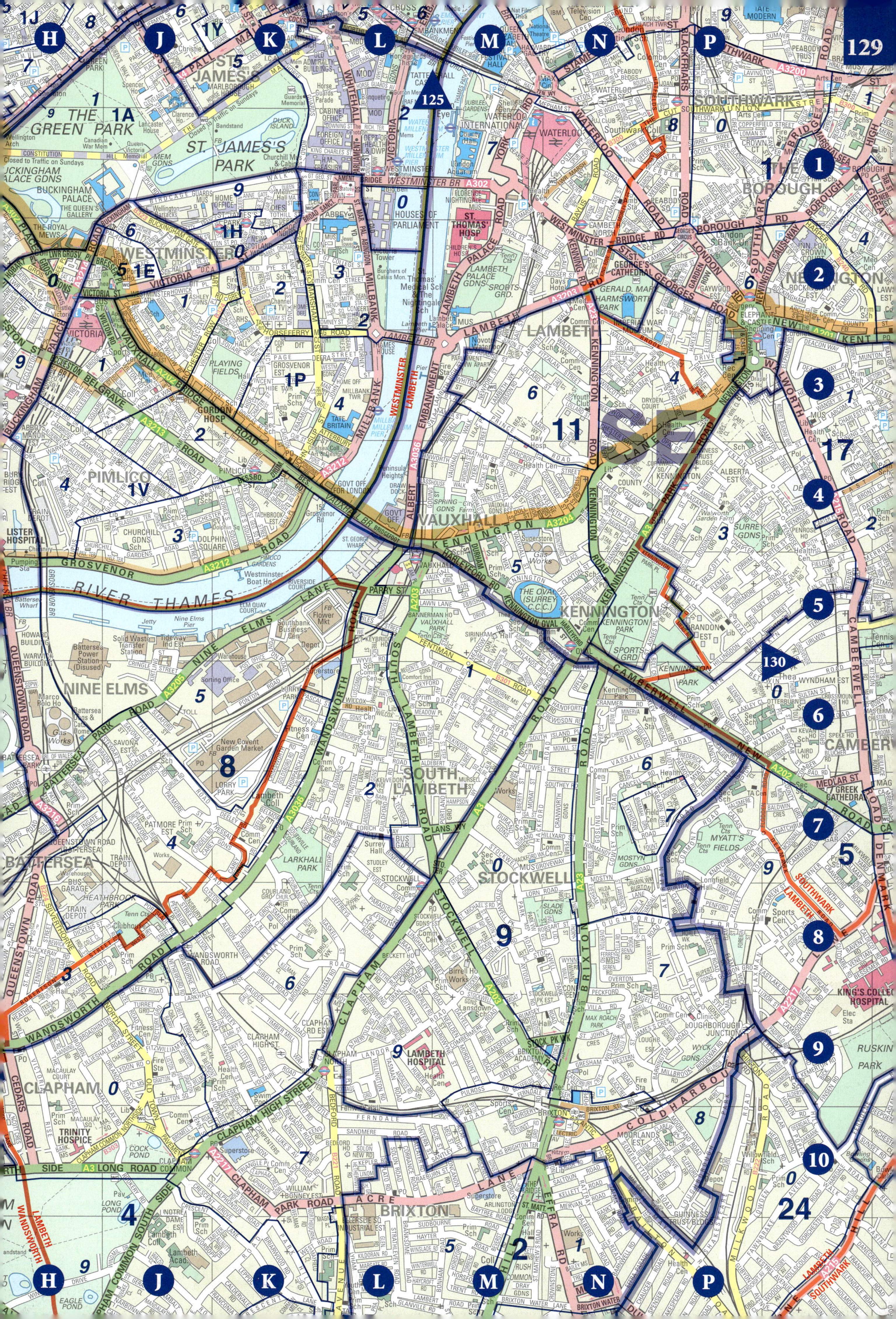
H
J
K
L
M
N
P
125
130
THE GREEN PARK
ST. JAMES'S PARK
BUCKINGHAM PALACE
WESTMINSTER
HOUSES OF PARLIAMENT
ST. THOMAS' HOSP
WATERLOO
SOUTHWARK
THE BOROUGH
NEWINGTON
LAMBETH
VICTORIA
PIMLICO
VAUXHALL
KENNINGTON
SE 11
17
RIVER THAMES
NINE ELMS
BATTERSEA
SOUTH LAMBETH
STOCKWELL
CLAPHAM
BRIXTON
CAMBERWELL
KING'S COLLEGE HOSPITAL
LAMBETH HOSPITAL
TRINITY HOSPICE
RUSKIN PARK
MYATT'S FIELDS
THE OVAL (SURREY C.C.C.)
KENNINGTON PARK
LARKHALL PARK
NEW COVENT GARDEN MARKET
WESTMINSTER BR
LAMBETH BR
VAUXHALL BR
GROSVENOR
WANDSWORTH ROAD
CLAPHAM ROAD
BRIXTON ROAD
CAMBERWELL NEW ROAD
COLDHARBOUR LANE
ACRE LANE
CLAPHAM HIGH STREET
KENNINGTON ROAD
KENNINGTON LANE
QUEENSTOWN ROAD
CEDARS ROAD
24

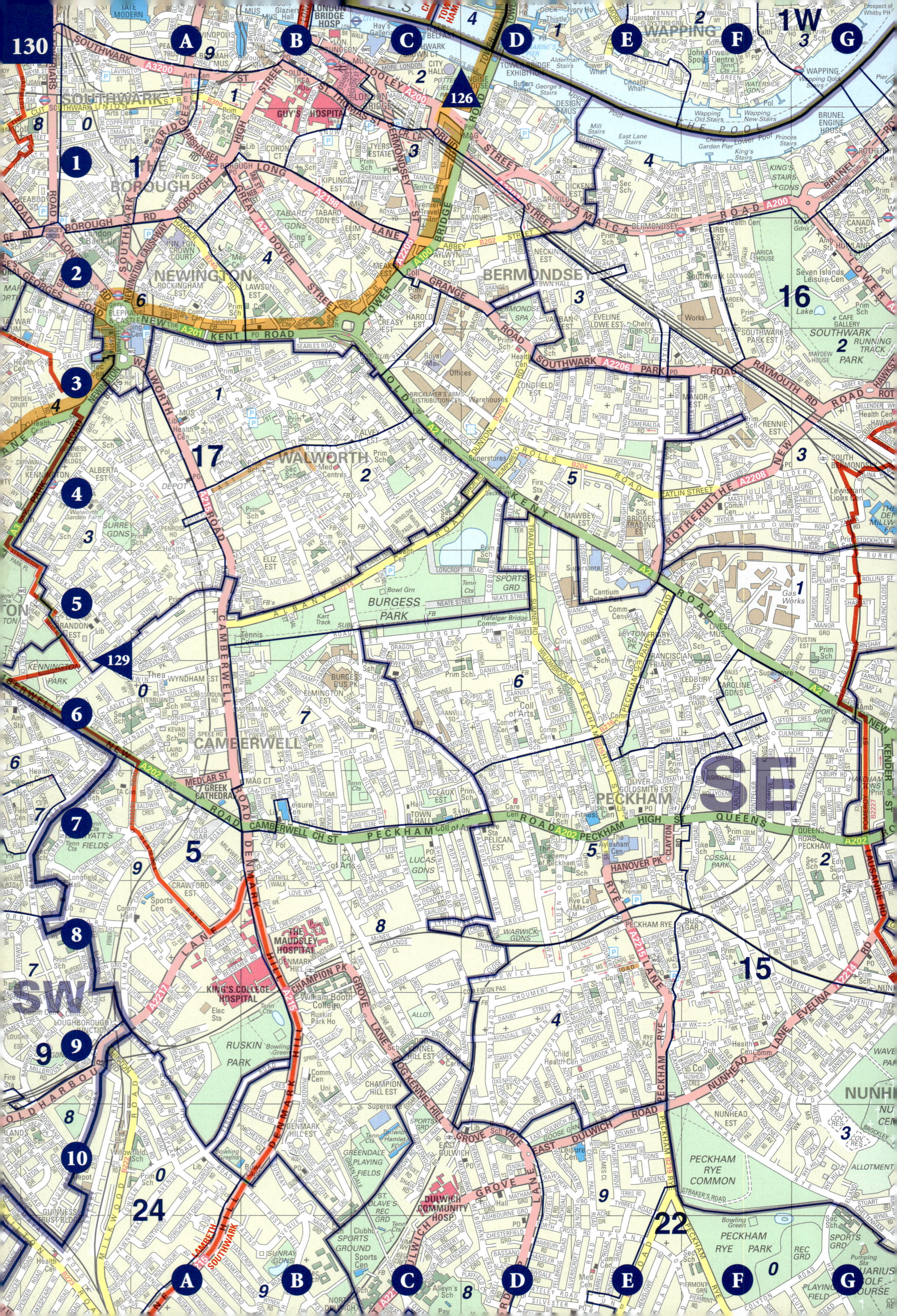
SOUTHWARK
THE BOROUGH
NEWINGTON
BERMONDSEY
WALWORTH
CAMBERWELL
PECKHAM
WAPPING
SE
SW
1W
BURGESS PARK
SOUTHWARK PARK
RUSKIN PARK
PECKHAM RYE COMMON
PECKHAM RYE PARK
GUY'S HOSPITAL
KING'S COLLEGE HOSPITAL
THE MAUDSLEY HOSPITAL
DULWICH COMMUNITY HOSP
OLD KENT ROAD
JAMAICA ROAD
SOUTHWARK PARK ROAD
CAMBERWELL NEW ROAD
PECKHAM HIGH ST
QUEENS ROAD
EAST DULWICH ROAD
DENMARK HILL
TOWER BRIDGE
LONDON BRIDGE
126
129

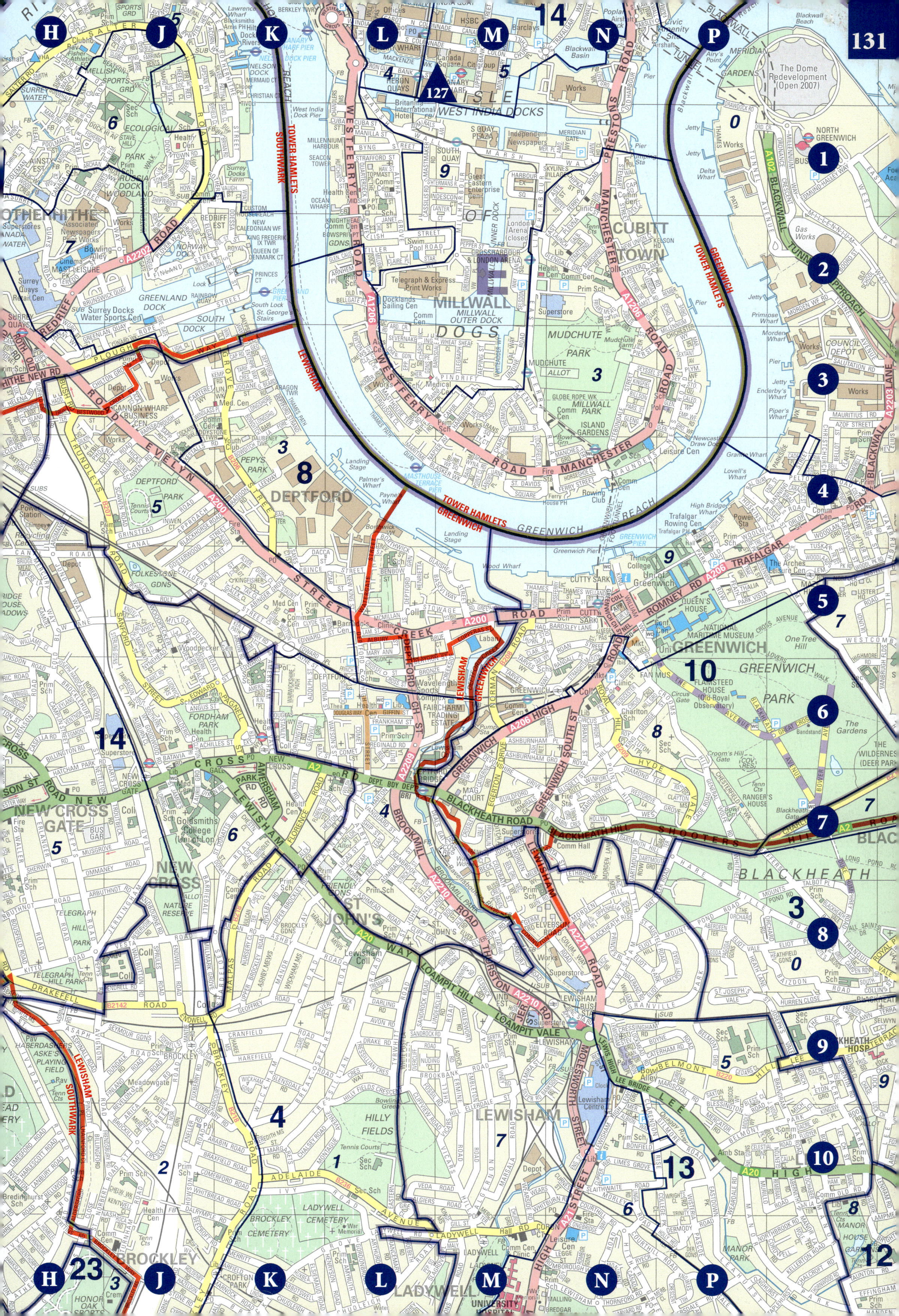
H
J
K
L
M
N
P
14
127
ISLE OF DOGS
WEST INDIA DOCKS
MILLWALL
MILLWALL INNER DOCK
MILLWALL OUTER DOCK
MUDCHUTE PARK
CUBITT TOWN
The Dome Redevelopment (Open 2007)
NORTH GREENWICH
ROTHERHITHE
GREENLAND DOCK
SOUTH DOCK
Surrey Docks Water Sports Cen
DEPTFORD
DEPTFORD PARK
PEPYS PARK
GREENWICH
GREENWICH PARK
NATIONAL MARITIME MUSEUM
QUEEN'S HOUSE
FLAMSTEED HOUSE (Old Royal Observatory)
Blackheath
BLACKHEATH
NEW CROSS
NEW CROSS GATE
ST JOHN'S
LEWISHAM
HILLY FIELDS
BROCKLEY
BROCKLEY CEMETERY
LADYWELL CEMETERY
LADYWELL
TOWER HAMLETS
SOUTHWARK
LEWISHAM
GREENWICH
GREENWICH REACH
LIMEHOUSE REACH
EVELYN STREET
CREEK ROAD
ROMNEY RD
TRAFALGAR RD
BLACKHEATH ROAD
SHOOTERS HILL
LEWISHAM WAY
LOAMPIT HILL
LOAMPIT VALE
BROCKLEY ROAD
MANCHESTER ROAD
WESTFERRY ROAD
BLACKWALL TUNNEL APPROACH
A2
A20
A200
A206
A2209
A2210
A2211
A102
A1206
1
2
3
4
5
6
7
8
9
10
12
13
23

Administrative areas

Notes: Listed below are the administrative areas for Great Britain, Northern Ireland and Isle of Man used in this Postcode Atlas. Where an area is dual language, the English form is given first, followed by the alternative in parenthesis. Each entry includes its standard abbreviation in *italics* which will appear in the index. Population figures are derived from 2001 Census information. A brief description of the area then follows, which includes: adjoining administrative areas; main centres (based on descending order of population); historical, physical and economic characteristics. For English counties or former Metropolitan counties, each district, city or borough authority is listed under the heading, **Districts.**

Aberdeen *Aberdeen* Population: 212,125.
Unitary authority surrounding Aberdeen, Scotland's third largest city, on the NE coast and neighbouring Aberdeenshire. Aberdeen is the major commercial and administrative centre for N Scotland. It is the second largest fishing port in Scotland, with docks at the mouth of the River Dee, and is the oil and gas capital of Europe.

Aberdeenshire *Aber.* Population: 226,871.
Unitary authority on the NE coast of Scotland neighbouring Aberdeen, Angus, Highland, Moray and Perth & Kinross. Main centres are Peterhead, Fraserburgh, Inverurie, Stonehaven, Ellon, Banchory, Portlethan and Huntly. Aberdeenshire is split geographically into two main areas. The W is dominated by the Grampian Mountains and is largely unpopulated. The undulating lowlands of the E are mainly rural and are populated by farming and fishing communities. The major rivers are the Dee, which flows through Royal Deeside, and the Don.

Angus *Angus* Population: 108,400.
Unitary authority on the E coast of Scotland neighbouring Aberdeenshire, Dundee and Perth & Kinross. The chief centres are Arbroath, Forfar, Montrose, Carnoustie, the ancient cathedral city of Brechin, Kirriemuir and Monifieth. Angus occupies an area of 2200 square km and is an important agricultural area. It combines ancient relics and castles with highland terrain and market towns. Rivers include the North Esk, Isla and Prosen Water.

Antrim *Antrim* Population: 48,366
Covering around 4% of the total area of Northern Ireland, Antrim borders the eastern and northern shores of Lough Neagh, the largest freshwater lake in the United Kingdom. Major towns include Antrim, Crumlin, Templepatrick, Toombridge, internationally famous for its eel industry and Randalstown. Chief industries are heavy engineering, construction, transport and distribution, plus agriculture and tourism.

Ards *Ards* Population: 73,244
Designated as an Area of Outstanding Natural Beauty (AONB). Over half the area is a peninsula created by Strangford Lough. Newtownards is the largest town, with smaller ones being Donaghdee, Portaferry, where the ferry can be caught to the other side of the lough, Kircubbin, Ballygowan, Comber, Millisle and Portavogie. The Copeland Islands lie about a mile offshore and there are several small islands in Strangford Lough itself. Main industries are agriculture and tourism.

Argyll & Bute *Arg. & B.* Population: 91,306.
Unitary authority on the W coast of Scotland combining mainland and island life and neighbouring Highland, Inverclyde, North Ayrshire, Perth & Kinross, Stirling and West Dunbartonshire. The main towns are Helensburgh, Dunoon, Oban, Campbeltown, Rothesay and Lochgilphead. It includes the former districts of Argyll and Bute as well as the islands of Islay, Jura, Colonsay and Mull. The main industries are fishing, agriculture, whisky production and tourism.

Armagh *Armagh* Population: 54,263.
The southern border of Armagh abuts the Republic of Ireland and the city of Armagh is home to the Archbishops of both the Church of Ireland and the Roman Catholic Church. Other towns include Keady, Tandragee, Richill, Loughgall and Markethill. Chief industries are agriculture (particularly orchard fruits), food processing, small scale manufacturing and tourism, with IT as an emerging sector.

Bath & North East Somerset *B. & N.E.Som.* Population: 169,040.
Unitary authority in SW England neighbouring Bristol, North Somerset, Somerset, South Gloucestershire and Wiltshire. It surrounds the city of Bath, and includes the towns of Keynsham, Radstock and Midsomer Norton. The Georgian spa of Bath is considered to be one of the most beautiful cities in Britain, and is an important commercial and ecclesiastical centre popular with tourists. The River Avon flows through the area.

Ballymena *Ballymena* Population: 58,610.
The river Bann, which forms the western border, affords some of the best coarse fishing in Europe. To the east are the Antrim Hills. The main town is Ballymena, where around half the population live. Other towns include Broughshane, Cullybackey and Ahogill. Main industries are agriculture, textiles, manufacturing and tourism.

Ballymoney *Ballymoney* Population: 26,894.
This predominantly rural district contains much of the Antrim Coast & Glens AONB, in the north-east corner of Northern Ireland. Ballymoney is the principle town, lying on the main A26 road. Many small villages dot the area, with agriculture being the main industry. There are a high proportion of self-employed and small businesses, along with textiles and pharmaceuticals.

Banbridge *Banbr.* Population: 41,392.
Crossed by the river Bann and dotted with glacial drumlins, Banbridge is a peaceful, unspoilt district, with the rugged Slieve Croob mountain in the east. Banbridge is the main town, while the historic cathedral town of Dromore on the river Lagan is the other major settlement. Other villages include Scarva, Loughbrickland and Gilford. Main industries are textiles (linen), construction, light engineering and agriculture.

Bedfordshire *Beds.* Population: 381,572.
S midland county of England bounded by Buckinghamshire, Cambridgeshire, Hertfordshire, Luton, Milton Keynes and Northamptonshire. Main centres are the county town of Bedford, Dunstable, Leighton Buzzard, Kempston and Biggleswade. The N end of the Chiltern Hills runs through the S and SE of the county, which is otherwise mostly flat. Most of Bedfordshire is rural, and includes many stately homes. Industries include light engineering, brick manufacture, mineral extraction and vegetable growing. Chief river is the Great Ouse.
Districts: Bedford; Mid Bedfordshire; South Bedfordshire.

Belfast *Belfast.* Population: 277,391.
Belfast has the highest population and population density of all the Northern Ireland Districts. The city of Belfast sits on the river Lagan at the mouth of Belfast Lough and is a lively, vibrant city. There are no other settlements of significance within the area. A busy port, shipbuilding is still a major industry, the Titanic was built here, along with aircraft manufacturing, textiles, construction, oil refining, brewing, retail and tourism. Belfast city airport handles tourist and business flights.

Blackburn with Darwen *B'burn.* Population: 137,470.
Unitary authority in NW England surrounding Blackburn and Darwen and neighbouring Greater Manchester and Lancashire. Blackburn is a market and retail centre with a wide spread of industry including textiles, brewing and electronic engineering.

Blackpool *B'pool* Population: 142,283.
Unitary authority on the NW coast of England surrounding Blackpool and neighbouring Lancashire. Blackpool receives around 7.2 million visitors each year, making it the most popular seaside resort in Europe. Attractions including the Tower, Pleasure Beach, Winter Gardens and Illuminations.

Blaenau Gwent *B.Gwent* Population: 70,064.
Unitary authority in S Wales bounded by Caerphilly, Monmouthshire, Powys and Torfaen. The chief towns are Ebbw Vale, Tredegar, Bryn-mawr and Abertillery. The area was

previously dependent upon coal, iron and steel industries but has since developed a broader industrial base. Part of the Brecon Beacons are in the N of the area.

Bournemouth *Bourne.* Population: 163,444.
Unitary authority on the S coast of England surrounding Bournemouth and neighbouring Dorset and Poole. Bournemouth is a major resort, conference and commercial centre.

Bracknell Forest *Brack.F.* Population: 109,617.
Unitary authority to the W of Greater London and bounded by Hampshire, Surrey, Windsor & Maidenhead and Wokingham. Bracknell is the chief town, while to the N of the area there are the villages of Winkfield and Binfield. To the S lies forest and heathland, and the towns of Crowthorne and Sandhurst. Bracknell has many hi-tech industries, and is a shopping and leisure centre.

Bridgend (Pen-y-Bont ar Ogwr). *Bridgend* Population: 128,645.
Unitary authority in S Wales bounded by Neath Port Talbot, Rhondda Cynon Taff, Vale of Glamorgan and the sea. Main centres are Bridgend, Maesteg and Porthcawl. The area is mountainous to the N, having ribbon development along river valleys; there is greater urbanisation in the S.

Brighton & Hove *B. & H.* Population: 247,817.
Unitary authority on the S coast of England neighbouring East Sussex and West Sussex. It encompasses the seaside resort of Brighton, which is a major commercial and conference centre, and the surrounding area which includes Hove, Portslade-by-Sea, Portslade, Rottingdean, Saltdean and part of the South Downs.

Bristol *Bristol* Population: 380,615.
Unitary authority in SW England neighbouring Bath & North East Somerset, North Somerset, South Gloucestershire and the Bristol Channel. The area includes the city of Bristol and surrounding urban area, including Avonmouth. Bristol is an important industrial and commercial centre of W England. A former major port, its character varies from docks and a busy city centre, to parks and gardens and Georgian terracing. The city hosts the Balloon Fiesta and Harbour Regatta. River Avon forms part of the W border of the area.

Buckinghamshire *Bucks.* Population: 479,026.
S midland county of England bounded by Bedfordshire, Greater London, Hertfordshire, Northamptonshire, Oxfordshire, Surrey, Windsor & Maidenhead and Wokingham. Chief towns are High Wycombe, the county town of Aylesbury, Amersham, Chesham, Marlow and Beaconsfield, around which, and other smaller towns, is a variety of light industry, as well as extensive residential areas. The chalk downs of the Chiltern Hills traverse the S part of the county, which is otherwise mostly flat. The River Thames flows along its S border.
Districts: Aylesbury Vale; Chiltern; South Bucks; Wycombe.

Caerphilly (Caerffili). *Caerp.* Population: 169,519.
Unitary authority in S Wales bordered by Blaenau Gwent, Cardiff, Merthyr Tydfil, Rhondda Cynon Taff and Torfaen. The chief centres are Caerphilly, Gelligaer, Risca, Bargoed, Blackwood and Bedwas. The geography of the area varies from open moorland to busy market towns. The former mining industry has been replaced by electronics and automotive companies, with tourism also being important to the local economy. Rivers include the Rhymney and Sirhowy.

Cambridgeshire *Cambs.* Population: 552,658.
County of E England bounded by Bedfordshire, Essex, Hertfordshire, Lincolnshire, Norfolk, Northamptonshire, Peterborough and Suffolk. Cambridgeshire is mostly flat, with fenland to N and E, although there are low chalk hills in the S and SE. Chief centres are the city and county town of Cambridge, Wisbech, St. Ives, March, Huntingdon, St. Neots and the cathedral city of Ely. Agriculture is a major industry with sugar beet, potatoes and corn all important crops; soft fruit and vegetable cultivation and canning are also significant rural industries. There has been recent growth of medical, pharmaceutical and hi-tech industries around Cambridge. Rivers include the Cam, Nene, and Great Ouse.
Districts: Cambridge; East Cambridgeshire; Fenland; Huntingdonshire; South Cambridgeshire.

Cardiff (Caerdydd). *Cardiff* Population: 305,353.
Unitary authority in S Wales surrounding the city of Cardiff and bordered by Caerphilly, Newport, Rhondda Cynon Taff, Vale of Glamorgan and the Bristol Channel. Cardiff, the capital of Wales, is a major administrative, commercial, cultural and tourism centre. It contains the Welsh Office, Welsh National Stadium, remains of medieval castle, cathedral at Llandarff and university. Cardiff docks, which were formerly used to export Welsh coal, are part of an ongoing major redevelopment. The city has excellent shopping facilities, notably at the St. David's Centre. The birthplace of Roald Dahl.

Carmarthenshire (Sir Gaerfyrddin). *Carmar.* Population: 172,842.
Unitary authority in S Wales bounded by Ceredigion, Neath Port Talbot, Pembrokeshire, Powys, Swansea and the sea. The chief towns are Llanelli, Carmarthen and Ammanford. The geography varies from the Brecon Beacons in the E, to the river valleys in the N, and the fishing villages, beaches and coastal towns in the S. The 50m coastline runs along the S of the area. Rivers include the Tywi, Cothi, Gwendaeth Fach and Gwendaeth Fawr.

Carrickfergus *Carrick.* Population: 37,659.
A small district, with Belfast Lough at its eastern boundary. The main town of Carrickfergus is an ancient harbour with the impressive Carrickfergus Norman Castle built on a volcanic dyke. Smaller towns include Greenisland and Whitehead. Main industries are construction, manufacturing, retailing and tourism.

Castlereagh *Castle.* Population: 66,488.
To the south-east of Belfast, the main town of the district is Castlereagh, with other towns being Carryduff and Dundonald, which still has a Norman motte. Agriculture is the main industry but many people work in the shipbuilding and aircraft industries in Belfast.

Ceredigion *Cere.* Population: 74,941.
Unitary authority in W Wales bounded by Carmarthenshire, Gwynedd, Pembrokeshire, Powys and the sea at Cardigan Bay. The main towns are Aberystwyth, Cardigan, Aberaeron, Lampeter, Tregaron and Llandysul. Part of the Cambrian Mountains lie in the E of the area and the 50m coast has many sandy beaches. Tourism and agriculture are the most important industries. The main river is the Teifi.

Cheshire *Ches.* Population: 673,788.
County of NW England bounded by Derbyshire, Greater Manchester, Halton, Merseyside, Staffordshire, Shropshire, Warrington and the Welsh authorities of Flintshire and Wrexham. Chief centres are the cathedral city of Chester and the towns of Ellesmere Port, Crewe, Macclesfield, Northwich, Wilmslow, Winsford and Congleton. The country is mainly flat, except in the NE, where the foothills of The Pennines enter the county. The rural areas, which are mostly in the S and W, are noted for dairy products. Much of the county is industrialised; there are large salt mines with an associated chemicals industry in the N, silk and cotton mills, and engineering. Chief rivers are the Dane, Dee, and Weaver. In the NW the county reaches the estuaries of the River Dee and River Mersey.
Districts: Chester; Congleton; Crewe & Nantwich; Ellesmere Port & Neston; Macclesfield; Vale Royal.

Clackmannanshire *Clack.* Population: 48,077.
Unitary authority in central Scotland neighbouring Fife, Perth & Kinross and Stirling. The N includes the Ochil Hills, while the lowland surrounding the Forth estuary contains the chief towns which are Alloa, Tullibody, Tillicoultry and Alva. Clackmannanshire has over 50 sites of nature conservation and five historic castles and towers. The main rivers are the Devon and the Forth.

Coleraine *Coleraine* Population: 56,315.
This beautiful district borders the coast on its northern edge, with the ports of Portrush, Portstewart and Portballintrae. The resorts of Downhill and Castlerock are popular with tourists, the latter at the outlet of the River Bann. Coleraine is the main town, an ancient but busy shopping centre. Smaller towns include Garvagh and Kilrea. Industries centre on agriculture and tourism.

Conwy *Conwy* Population: 109,596.
Unitary authority in N Wales bordered by Denbighshire, Gwynedd and the sea. The chief towns are Colwyn Bay, Llandudno, Abergele, Rhôs-on-Sea and Conwy. Around 40 per cent of Conwy is within Snowdonia National Park and there are 29m of coastline. The coastal resorts attract tourism which is a key industry, but agriculture and light manufacturing are also important to the local economy. The main river is the Conwy.

Cookstown *Cookstown* Population: 32,581.
With Lough Neagh at its eastern border and the foothills of the Sperrin Mountains to the west, Cookstown has been designated an AONB. The main town of Cookstown has the longest main street in Northern Ireland, with one mile of shops. Another town of significance is Moneymore, with other settlements being scattered, smaller villages. Industries are based around small businesses, agriculture and tourism.

Cornwall *Cornw.* Population: 499,114.
South-westernmost county of England bounded by Devon and the sea. Chief centres are St. Austell, Falmouth, Penzance, the cathedral city and administrative centre of Truro, Redruth, Camborne and Newquay. The coastline is wild and rocky; headlands and cliffs are interspersed with large sandy beaches in the N, and deeply indented with river estuaries in the S. The interior is dominated by areas of moorland, notably the granite mass of Bodmin Moor in the NE. There are also farmlands providing rich cattle-grazing, and deep river valleys. The climate is mild, and flower cultivation is carried on extensively. The many derelict tin mines are witness to the former importance of this industry; there has recently been a partial revival. The chief industry is tourism. China clay is produced in large quantities in the St. Austell area, and there is some fishing. Rivers include the Tamar, forming the boundary with Devon; Fowey, East and West Looe, Fal, Camel, and Lynher.
Districts: Caradon; Carrick; Kerrier; North Cornwall; Penwith; Restormel.

Craigavon *Craigavon* Population: 80,671.
Craigavon's northern boundary is the southern shore of Lough Neagh. The M1 motorway crosses east-west, providing a link to Lisburn, Belfast and Antrim. Its principle towns are Craigavon itself, Lurgan, home to the Carnegie library and Portadown. Main industries include manufacturing, retail, public service and construction.

Cumbria *Cumb.* Population: 487,607.
County of NW England bounded by Durham, Lancashire, Northumberland and North Yorkshire; the Scottish authorities of Dumfries & Galloway and Scottish Borders; and the Solway Firth and Irish Sea. Chief centres are the city of Carlisle and the towns of Barrow-in-Furness, Whitehaven, Workington, Kendal, Penrith and Ulverston. A narrow strip of flat country along the coast widens to a plain in the N and around Carlisle. Otherwise the county is composed of mountains, moorland and lakes, and includes the scenically famous Lake District. Cumbria is mostly rural and uncultivated, with industry centred on Carlisle and the urban centres. Whitehaven, Workington, and Maryport all once relied on coal, while Barrow-in-Furness developed due to shipbuilding and heavy industry. There are links with nuclear technology: Calder Hall, N of Seascale, was Britain's first atomic power station, Sellafield is the site of a nuclear reprocessing plant and Trident submarines were built at Barrow-in-Furness. Tourism in the Lake District and sheep farming are also important industries. The area is noted for its radial drainage, with Windermere and Ullswater being the largest of the lakes and the River Eden being the chief of many rivers.
Districts: Allerdale; Barrow-in-Furness; Carlisle; Copeland; Eden; South Lakeland.

Darlington *Darl.* Population: 97,838.
Unitary authority in NE England surrounding Darlington and neighbouring Durham, North Yorkshire and Stockton-on-Tees. Darlington has a variety of industries, including iron, steel and textiles. The River Tees forms the S border.

Denbighshire (Sir Ddinbych). *Denb.* Population: 93,065.
Unitary authority in N Wales neighbouring Conwy, Flintshire, Gwynedd, Powys, Wrexham and the sea. The chief towns are Rhyl, Prestatyn, Denbigh, Ruthin, the ancient city of St. Asaph, and Llangollen. Main industries are tourism, centred on the coastal resorts of Rhyl and Prestatyn, and agriculture. Rivers include the Morwynion.

Derby *Derby* Population: 221,708.
Unitary authority in central England surrounding the city of Derby and bordered by Derbyshire. Derby has a history dating back to Roman times and is now important in the rail industry; other key industries are manufacturing and aerospace engineering. The River Derwent passes through the area.

Derbyshire *Derbys.* Population: 734,585.
Midland county of England bounded by Cheshire, Derby, Greater Manchester, Leicestershire, Nottinghamshire, South Yorkshire, Staffordshire and West Yorkshire. Chief towns are Chesterfield, Long Eaton, Swadlincote, Ilkeston, Staveley, Dronfield, Alfreton, Heanor and Buxton. The high steep hills in the N, which include the dramatic scenery of The Peak, are the S extremity of The Pennines, and provide grazing for sheep and cattle. There is some textile industry in the towns of the N and W, while the S of the county is dominated by heavy industry, mining, and quarrying. Tourism is based on the scenic Peak District National Park, most of which falls in the county. Principal rivers are the Dove, forming much of the boundary with Staffordshire and noted for its scenery and fishing, and the Derwent; the Trent flows through the S corner of the county.
Districts: Amber Valley; Bolsover; Chesterfield; Derbyshire Dales; Erewash; High Peak; North East Derbyshire; South Derbyshire.

Devon *Devon* Population: 704,493.
Large county in SW peninsula of England bounded by Cornwall, Dorset, Plymouth, Somerset, Torbay and the Bristol and English Channels. The chief centres are the city of Exeter, Exmouth, Barnstaple, Newton Abbot, Tiverton, Bideford and Teignmouth. The county includes the W end of Exmoor and the whole of the granite mass of Dartmoor, whose summit, High Willhays, is the highest point in S England. Moorland areas apart, the county is largely given over to agriculture, and on the coast, to fishing and tourism. On Dartmoor there are quarries and a military training area; there are china clay workings in the S. Daffodils are grown commercially in River Tamar valley. Chief rivers are Exe, Teign, Dart, Avon, Erme, Tamar and Tavy in the S; and Taw and Torridge in the N. The granite island of Lundy is included in the county for administrative purposes.
Districts: East Devon; Exeter; Mid Devon; North Devon; South Hams; Teignbridge; Torridge; West Devon.

Dorset *Dorset* Population: 390,980.
County in SW England bounded by Bournemouth, Devon, Hampshire, Poole, Somerset, Wiltshire and the English Channel. The chief towns are Weymouth, Christchurch, Wimborne Minster, the county town of Dorchester, Bridport, Swanage and Blandford Forum. The county is hilly, with chalk downs and impressive geological formations along the coastline. Sand, gravel, stone and oil extraction takes place around the Isle of Portland and the Isle of Purbeck. Dorset is also noted for its agricultural and dairy produce. Tourism is an important industry due to the beautiful scenery, the proliferation of prehistoric and Roman remains, and the connection with Thomas Hardy's Wessex. Among numerous minor rivers are the Stour, Frome, and Piddle or Trent.
Districts: Christchurch; East Dorset; North Dorset; Purbeck; West Dorset; Weymouth & Portland.

Down *Down* Population: 63,828.
The southern tip of Down includes part of the beautiful Mourne Mountains, and the eastern edge consists of a long coastline, with the long sandy beach of Dundrum Bay and the shores of Strangford Lough. The main town is Downpatrick, others being Ballynahinch, Crossgar and Saintfield along with the coastal towns of Killyleagh, Newcastle and Ardglass. Industries include engineering and agriculture.

Dumfries & Galloway *D. & G.* Population: 147,765.
Unitary authority in SW Scotland neighbouring East Ayrshire, Scottish Borders, South Ayrshire, South Lanarkshire, the English county of Cumbria and the sea. It comprises the former counties of Dumfries, Kirkcudbright and Wigtown. Chief towns are Dumfries, Stranraer, Annan, Dalbeattie, Lockerbie, Castle Douglas, Newton Stewart and Kirkcudbright. The hilly area to the N is largely given over to sheep-grazing and afforestation, while farther S there is some good-quality arable farmland. At

the extreme W of the area is the peninsula known as the Rinns of Galloway, and the port of Stranraer, which provides passenger and car ferry services to Larne in Northern Ireland. Main rivers are the Esk, Annan, Nith, Dee and Cree which descend S to the Solway Firth from the Tweedsmuir Hills, Lowther Hills and the Rhinns of Kells in the N.

Dundee *Dundee* Population: 145,663.
Unitary authority on the E coast of Scotland surrounding the city of Dundee and neighbouring Angus and Perth & Kinross. Dundee is Scotland's fourth largest city and is a centre of excellence in a variety of areas from telecommunications to medical research. The Firth of Tay borders Dundee to the S.

Dungannon *Dungannon* Population: 47,735.
Dungannon includes the scenic Clogher valley, and the Republic of Ireland forms its southern boundary. The north-east corner meets Lough Neagh and the main A4 road bisects it east-west. Dungannon town has almost a quarter of the whole population, with the rest of the area being basically rural. Coalisland still has a linen industry and Tyrone Crystal is famous worldwide. Industries include agriculture, construction, retail and manufacturing.

Durham *Dur.* Population: 493,470.
County in NE England bounded by Cumbria, Darlington, Hartlepool, Northumberland, North Yorkshire, Stockton-on-Tees, Tyne & Wear and the North Sea. Chief centres are the cathedral city and county town of Durham; and the towns of Chester-le-Street, Peterlee, Newton Aycliffe, Bishop Auckland, Seaham and Consett. The W part of the county includes The Peninnes and consists mostly of open moorlands which provide rough sheep-grazing and water for the urban areas from a number of large reservoirs. Economic activity is concentrated on the lowland in the E which is more heavily populated, and was formerly a centre for coal-mining and heavy industry. Diversification has since provided a broad industrial base. The principal rivers are the Tees and the Wear.
Districts: Chester-le-Street; Derwentside; Durham; Easington; Sedgefield; Teesdale; Wear Valley.

East Ayrshire *E.Ayr.* Population: 120,235.
Unitary authority in SW Scotland bounded by Dumfries & Galloway, East Renfrewshire, North Ayrshire, South Ayrshire and South Lanarkshire. The principal towns are Kilmarnock, Cumnock, Stewarton, Galston and Auchinleck. Traditional industries centred on textiles and lace in the Irvine valley, coal mining and engineering. Dairy farming is also an important industry, particularly beef and sheep production. The area is a popular tourist destination, with several castles, battle sites and associations with Robert Burns and Keir Hardie. Rivers include the Irvine, Annick and Cessnock.

East Dunbartonshire *E.Dun.* Population: 108,243.
Unitary authority in central Scotland bounded by Glasgow, North Lanarkshire, Stirling and West Dunbartonshire. The chief centres are Bearsden, Bishopbriggs, Kirkintilloch and Milngavie. Much of the urban and industrial development occurs on the N periphery of Greater Glasgow. The Campsie Fells lie in the N of the area.

East Lothian *E.Loth.* Population: 90,088.
Unitary authority in central Scotland neighbouring Edinburgh, Midlothian, Scottish Borders and the North Sea. The main towns are Musselburgh, Haddington, Tranent, Prestonpans, Dunbar, North Berwick and Cockenzie and Port Seton. There are 43m of varied coastline and the topography includes the Lammermuir Hills in the S, and the ancient volcanoes at North Berwick and Traprain. Much of the urban and industrial development is in the NW and N of the area. Rivers include Whitehead Water, the Tyne, Peffer Burn and Gifford Water.

East Renfrewshire *E.Renf.* Population: 89,311.
Unitary authority in SW Scotland bounded by East Ayrshire, Glasgow, Inverclyde, North Ayrshire, Renfrewshire and South Lanarkshire. The principal centres are Newton Mearns, Clarkston, Barrhead and Giffnock, which lie on the S periphery of Greater Glasgow. Over two-thirds of East Renfrewshire is farmland; the rest being mostly residential, with some light industry.

East Riding of Yorkshire *E.Riding* Population: 314,113.
Unitary authority on the E coast of England neighbouring Kingston upon Hull, North Lincolnshire, North Yorkshire, South Yorkshire and York. The chief centres are Bridlington, Beverley, Goole, Great Driffield, Hornsea, Brough, Hedon and Withernsea. The area is mostly low-lying, except for the central ridge which forms part of The Wolds. The coastline is subject to much erosion, with material being moved from Flamborough Head to the large spit of Spurn Head, at the mouth of the River Humber. Key industries in the area include agriculture, aerospace, gas and oil industries.

East Sussex *E.Suss.* Population: 492,324.
County of SE England bounded by Brighton & Hove, Kent, Surrey, West Sussex and the English Channel. Main towns are Eastbourne, Hastings, Bexhill, Seaford, Crowborough, Hailsham, Peacehaven and the county town of Lewes; Rye is a small historic town in the E of the county. In the W, the coast is backed by the chalk ridge of the South Downs, ending with the white cliffs of the Seven Sisters and Beachy Head, just W of Eastbourne. E of this point, there are extensive areas of reclaimed marshland, which provide good sheep-grazing. Inland is the heavily wooded Weald, a former centre of the iron industry, interspersed with hill ridges, the largest being the open heathland of Ashdown Forest. Rivers, none large, include the Cuckmere, Ouse, Rother, and upper reaches of the Medway.
Districts: Eastbourne; Hastings; Lewes; Rother; Wealden.

Edinburgh *Edin.* Population: 448,624.
Unitary authority on the E coast of central Scotland surrounding the city of Edinburgh and neighbouring East Lothian, Midlothian, West Lothian and the sea at the Firth of Forth. Edinburgh as the capital of Scotland, is a major administrative, cultural, commercial and tourist centre. It contains most of Scotland's national and cultural institutions. Its historic core is centred around Edinburgh Castle and the Royal Mile, attracting much tourism. The city is also a centre for education and scientific research; other important industries are electronics and food and drink production. The river Water of Leith runs through the city to the docks at Leith.

Essex *Essex* Population: 1,310,835.
County of SE England bounded by Cambridgeshire, Greater London, Hertfordshire, Southend, Suffolk, Thurrock and the sea at the Thames estuary and North Sea. Chief towns are Basildon, the county town of Chelmsford, Colchester, Harlow, Brentwood, Clacton-on-Sea, Loughton, Canvey Island, Billericay and Braintree. The landscape is mostly flat or gently undulating, and the low-lying coast is deeply indented with river estuaries. Along the county's S and W sides, there is a concentration of urban development, with a mixture of light engineering and service industries. In the N and central parts are farmlands, orchards, market and nursery gardens. The NE coast has the busy passenger and container port of Harwich, and the popular seaside resort of Clacton-on-Sea. Rivers include the Stour, forming part of the boundary with Suffolk, the Lea, forming part of the boundary with Hertfordshire, and the Blackwater.
Districts: Basildon; Braintree; Brentwood; Castle Point; Chelmsford; Colchester; Epping Forest; Harlow; Maldon; Rochford; Tendring; Uttlesford.

Falkirk *Falk.* Population: 145,191.
Unitary authority in central Scotland surrounding Falkirk and neighbouring Clackmannanshire, Fife, North Lanarkshire, Stirling and West Lothian. Main towns are Falkirk, Grangemouth, Polmont, Stenhousemuir and Bo'ness. Petrochemical and chemical industries are important to the local economy, as well as bus manufacturing, toffees and paper-making. The Firth of Forth borders Falkirk to the N. Other rivers include the Carron and Pow Burn.

Fermanagh *Ferm.* Population: 57,527.
One third of this district is water, mainly taken up by Upper and Lower Lough Erne. Consequently, there are around 150 inland islands, and the population density is one of the lowest in Northern Ireland. Large areas have been planted with conifers for timber. The north-west and south-west boundaries border the Republic of Ireland. The main town of Enniskillen lies on the River Erne at the junction of the two major loughs and other towns include Irvinestown, Rosslea and Lisnaskea. Main industries are agriculture and tourism, engineering and timber milling.

Fife *Fife* Population: 349,429.
Unitary authority in E Scotland neighbouring Clackmannanshire and Perth & Kinross, and lying between the Firth of Tay and Firth of Forth. Main towns are Dunfermline, Kirkcaldy, Glenrothes, Buckhaven, Cowdenbeath and St. Andrews. Fife comprises the former county of the same name, known since ancient times as the Kingdom of Fife, and is noted for its fine coastline with many distinctive small towns and fishing ports. The historic town of St. Andrews, on the coast between the two firths, is a university town, and the home of the world's premier golf club. Inland, the area is outstandingly fertile, with agriculture being an important industry. The SW of the area is a former coal-mining area.

Flintshire (Sir y Fflint). *Flints.* Population: 148,594.
Unitary authority in N Wales neighbouring Conwy, Denbighshire, Wrexham, the English county of Cheshire and the mouth of the River Dee. Main towns are Buckley, Connah's Quay, Flint, Hawarden, Shotton, Queensferry, Mold and Holywell. Known as the Gateway to N Wales, the landscape varies from the mountains which form the Clwydian Range, to small villages and woodlands.

Glasgow *Glas.* Population: 577,869.
Unitary authority in SW Scotland surrounding Glasgow and bounded by East Dunbartonshire, East Renfrewshire, North Lanarkshire, Renfrewshire, South Lanarkshire and West Dunbartonshire. Glasgow is Scotland's largest city and its principal industrial and shopping centre. The city developed significantly due to heavy industry, notably shipbuilding, being centred on the Clyde. While such industry has declined, Glasgow has emerged as a major cultural centre of Europe, due to its impressive arts and cultural scene. The River Clyde runs through the city.

Gloucestershire *Glos.* Population: 564,559.
County of W England bounded by Herefordshire, Oxfordshire, South Gloucestershire, Swindon, Warwickshire, Wiltshire, Worcestershire and the Welsh authority of Monmouthshire. Main centres are the cathedral city and county town of Gloucester and the towns of Cheltenham, Stroud, Cirencester and Dursley. The limestone mass of the Cotswold Hills dominates the centre of the county, and provides the characteristic pale golden stone of many of its buildings. The River Severn forms a wide valley to the W, ending in a long tidal estuary, beyond which are the hills of the Forest of Dean. Industry is centred on the fertile Severn Vale, with aerospace, light engineering, food production, and service industries in and around the towns; in rural areas market gardening and orchards dominate. The River Thames rises in the county, and forms part of its S boundary in the vicinity of Lechlade. Apart from the Severn and the Thames, there is the River Wye, which forms part of the boundary with Monmouthshire, and many smaller rivers, among them the Chelt, Coln, Evenlode, Leach, Leadon, and Windrush.
Districts: Cheltenham; Cotswold; Forest of Dean; Gloucester; Stroud; Tewkesbury.

Greater London *Gt.Lon.* Population: 7,172,091.
Former metropolitan county of 32 boroughs and the City of London which together form the conurbation of London, the capital of the UK. Greater London is the largest financial, commercial, cultural, distribution and communications centre in the country, including all but primary industrial sectors. London developed from the City of London, a walled Roman settlement on the Thames, and Westminster, which was a Saxon religious settlement and later a Norman seat of government. The Great Fire of 1666 destroyed most of the medieval city, and was followed by a period of rebuilding and rapid, unplanned expansion. Industrialisation and improved public transport over the last two centuries have caused major suburban growth, and the absorption of most of the surrounding settlements and countryside. Tourism is a major industry, with most attractions situated in and around the historic core, and along the Thames bankside. Other notable tourist areas include Greenwich, Hampstead, Kew and Richmond. Industrial activity is widespread, with major concentrations in the E along the Thames. Leisure facilities include national and major sports stadiums, and many big parks and gardens. Airports at Heathrow and docklands. The main river is the Thames.
Districts: Barking & Dagenham; Barnet; Bexley; Brent; Bromley; Camden; City of London; City of Westminster; Croydon; Ealing; Enfield; Greenwich; Hackney; Hammersmith & Fulham; Haringey; Harrow; Havering; Hillingdon; Hounslow; Islington; Kensington & Chelsea; Kingston upon Thames; Lambeth; Lewisham; Merton; Newham; Redbridge; Richmond upon Thames; Southwark; Sutton; Tower Hamlets; Waltham Forest; Wandsworth.

Greater Manchester *Gt.Man.* Population: 2,482,328.
Former metropolitan county of NW England neighbouring Blackburn with Darwen, Cheshire, Derbyshire, Lancashire, Merseyside, Warrington and West Yorkshire. It comprises the near-continuous urban complex which includes the adjoining cities of Manchester and Salford; and towns including Bolton, Stockport, Oldham, Rochdale, Wigan, Bury and Sale. The conurbation is framed by the wild moorland of The Pennines to the N and the Peak District and Cheshire Plain to the S. Development occurred during the 18c and 19c, creating a series of cotton producing textile towns, while Manchester established itself as the commercial and trading hub, later becoming an inland port linked to Liverpool via the canal network. As textile production declined, the industrial base of the area broadened to include brewing, food production, electronics, plastics, printing, light engineering, financial, leisure and service sectors. Retail is based on town shopping centres and malls such as the Arndale and Trafford Centres. There are many major sporting venues in the area, and cultural facilities include the G-MEX centre, numerous universities, museums and galleries and a diverse nightlife. The area is served by Manchester Airport. Main rivers are Irwell and Mersey.
Districts: Bolton; Bury; Manchester; Oldham; Rochdale; Salford; Stockport; Tameside; Trafford; Wigan.

Gwynedd *Gwyn.* Population: 116,843.
Unitary authority in NW Wales bounded by Ceredigion, Conwy, Denbighshire, Isle of Anglesey, Powys and the sea. Main centres are the cathedral city of Bangor, Caernarfon, Ffestiniog, Blaenau Ffestiniog, Llanddeiniolen, Pwllheli, Llanllynfi, Bethesda and Porthmadog. The whole mainland area, except the Lleyn Peninsula in the NW, is extremely mountainous and contains the scenically famous Snowdonia National Park. There is slate-quarrying in the Ffestiniog valley, otherwise sheep-farming and tourism are the principal occupations; the coastline has been much developed for the holiday trade. The area contains many lakes and reservoirs, among them are Llyn Trawsfynedd, Llyn Celyn and Llyn Tegid. Of the many rivers, the Wnion and the Dyfi, which flows through part of the area, are most significant.

Halton *Halton* Population: 118,208.
Unitary authority in NW England neighbouring Cheshire, Merseyside and Warrington. The principal towns are Runcorn and Widnes, separated by the River Mersey. The area is industrialised, being dominated by petro-chemicals and chemicals industries due to the nearby salt mines and port facilities.

Hampshire *Hants.* Population: 1,240,103.
County of S England bounded by Bracknell Forest, Dorset, Portsmouth, Southampton, Surrey, West Berkshire, West Sussex, Wiltshire, Wokingham and the English Channel. Main towns are Basingstoke, Gosport, Waterlooville, Farnborough, Aldershot, Eastleigh, Havant, the ancient city and county town of Winchester, Andover and Fleet. The centre of the county consists largely of chalk downs interspersed with fertile valleys. In the SW is the New Forest, while in the NE is the military area centred on Aldershot. The much indented coastline borders The Solent and looks across to the Isle of Wight. Main industries are in the service sector, with chemicals and pharmaceuticals also important. The chief rivers are the Itchen and Test, both chalk streams flowing into Southampton Water, and the Meon flowing into The Solent.
Districts: Basingstoke & Deane; East Hampshire; Eastleigh; Fareham; Gosport; Hart; Havant; New Forest; Rushmoor; Test Valley; Winchester.

Hartlepool *Hart.* Population: 88,611.
Unitary authority on the NE coast of England surrounding Hartlepool and bordering Darlington, Durham, Stockton-on-Tees and the North Sea. Fishing is a major industry and a marina has been created from part of the old docks. The mouth of the River Tees forms part of the E border.

Herefordshire *Here.* Population: 174,871.
Unitary authority in W England bounded by Gloucestershire, Shropshire, Worcestershire and the Welsh authorities of

Monmouthshire and Powys. Main centres are the cathedral city of Hereford and the towns of Ross-on-Wye, Leominster and Ledbury. Herefordshire lies between the Malvern Hills to the E and the Black Mountains to the W. It is mainly rural, with dairy farming, orchards and market gardening in evidence. The main river is the Wye, which provides excellent fishing.

Hertfordshire *Herts.* Population: 1,033,977.
S midland county of England bounded by Bedfordshire, Buckinghamshire, Cambridgeshire, Essex, Greater London and Luton. Chief centres are Watford, the cathedral city of St. Albans, Hemel Hempstead, Stevenage, Cheshunt, Welwyn Garden City, Hoddesdon, Hitchin, Letchworth and Hatfield; the county town is Hertford. The Chilterns rise along the W border, and there are chalk hills in the N around Royston; otherwise the landscape is mostly flat or gently undulating. There is a mixture of rural and urban life, with agricultural and hi-tech industries represented. While the urban centres in the S lie on the N periphery of the Greater London conurbation, there are many villages with the traditional large green or common. The more urban S part of the county includes a dense network of major roads bypassing, and leading N from London. Rivers include the Colne, Ivel, and Lee.
Districts: Broxbourne; Dacorum; East Herts; Hertsmere; North Hertfordshire; St. Albans; Stevenage; Three Rivers; Watford; Welwyn Hatfield.

Highland *High.* Population: 208,914.
Unitary authority covering a large part of N Scotland and neighbouring Aberdeenshire, Argyll & Bute, Moray and Perth & Kinross. It contains a mixture of mainland and island life, comprising the former districts of Badenoch and Strathspey, Caithness, Inverness, Lochaber, Nairn, Ross and Cromarty, Skye and Lochalsh and Sutherland. Main towns are Inverness, Fort William, Thurso, Nairn, Wick, Alness and Dingwall. Overall, Highland is very sparsely inhabited, being wild and remote in character. It is scenically outstanding, containing as it does part of the Cairngorm Mountains, Ben Nevis, and the North West Highlands. Many of the finest sea and inland lochs in Scotland are also here, such as Loch Ness, Loch Linnhe, Loch Torridon and Loch Broom. The discovery of North Sea oil has made an impact on the towns and villages around the Moray Firth. Elsewhere, tourism, crofting, fishing and skiing are important locally.

Inverclyde *Inclyde* Population: 84,203.
Unitary authority on the W coast of central Scotland, on the S bank of the River Clyde. It is bordered by North Ayrshire, Renfrewshire and the Firth of Clyde. The chief towns are Greenock, Port Glasgow, Gourock and Kilmacolm.

Isle of Anglesey (Sir Ynys Môn). *I.o.A.* Population: 66,829.
Unitary authority island of NW Wales divided from Gwynedd and the mainland by the Menai Strait, and with Holy Island lying to the W. Main towns are Holyhead, Llangefni, Amlwch and Menai Bridge. Anglesey has 125m of coastline and 16 beaches. Agriculture is an important industry to the island, with other industries including aluminium smelting and food processing. Holyhead is an important port terminus for the Republic of Ireland. Rivers include the Braint and Cefni.

Isle of Man *I.o.M.* Population: 76,315.
Self-governing island in the Irish Sea, situated in the centre of the British Isles. The chief towns are Douglas, Ramsey, Peel, Castletown, Port St. Mary, Port Erin and Laxey. Apart from the N tip, the topography is generally mountainous, rising to a peak at Snaefell. The main industries are agriculture, fishing and tourism as well as financial services and manufacturing. The island is synonymous with motorsport, being the home of the internationally renowned Tourist Trophy Circuit. Rivers include the Glen Auldyn and Neb.

Isle of Wight *I.o.W.* Population: 132,731.
County and island with an area of 147 square miles or 381 square km, separated from the S coast of England by The Solent. Chief towns are the capital, Newport, Ryde, Cowes, Shanklin, Sandown, Ventnor and Yarmouth. The island is geologically diverse, composed of sedimentary rocks and contains many important fossil remains. Tourism flourishes owing to the mild climate and the natural beauty of the island. There are Royal associations as Queen Victoria lived and died at Osborne House in the N of the island. There is a strong naval tradition, with the island historically acting as a defence for Portsmouth. Cowes is internationally famous for yachting. There are ferry and hovercraft connections at Cowes, Ryde, and Yarmouth (ferry to Lymington). Chief river is the Medina.

Isles of Scilly *I.o.S.* Population: 2153.
Group of some 140 islands 48m/45km SW of Land's End, Cornwall, of which five are inhabited: Bryher, St. Agnes, St. Martin's, St. Mary's and Tresco. Chief industries are fishing, and the growing of early flowers and vegetables due to the exceptionally mild climate.

Kent *Kent* Population: 1,329,718.
South-easternmost county of England bounded by East Sussex, Greater London, Medway, Surrey and the sea at the Thames estuary and the Strait of Dover. Chief centres are the county town of Maidstone, Royal Tunbridge Wells, Dartford, Margate, Ashford, Gravesend, Folkestone, Sittingbourne, Ramsgate, the cathedral city of Canterbury, Tonbridge and Dover. The chalk ridge of the North Downs runs along the N side, then SE to Folkestone and Dover. The River Medway cuts through the chalk in the vicinity of Maidstone, and there are low lying areas to the E of Canterbury and of Tonbridge, on Romney Marsh in the S, and bordering the Thames estuary in the N. Chief industrial areas are around Maidstone, Ashford and Tonbridge; Dover and Folkestone are major ports, with the Channel Tunnel terminus to the N of Folkestone; Sheerness is a port of growing importance. Industrial activity includes mineral extraction, cement manufacture and papermaking. On the highly productive agricultural land, Kent's reputation as the Garden of England is earned, with market gardening, fruit and hop production. Romney Marsh is used for extensive sheep-grazing. Rivers include the Medway, Stour, and Beult.
Districts: Ashford; Canterbury; Dartford; Dover; Gravesham; Maidstone; Sevenoaks; Shepway; Swale; Thanet; Tonbridge & Malling; Tunbridge Wells.

Kingston upon Hull *Hull* Population: 243,589.
Unitary authority on the E coast of England surrounding the city of Kingston upon Hull and bounded by East Riding of Yorkshire and the mouth of the River Humber. Kingston upon Hull is a major sea port and a great industrial city, with key industries including chemicals, food processing, pharmaceuticals and engineering. The River Hull passes through the area, and the River Humber forms the S border.

Lancashire *Lancs.* Population: 1,134,974.
County of NW England bounded by Blackburn with Darwen, Cumbria, Greater Manchester, Merseyside, North Yorkshire, West Yorkshire and the Irish Sea. Chief centres are the administrative city of Preston, Burnley, Morecambe, the historic county town of Lancaster, Skelmersdale, Lytham St. Anne's, Leyland, Accrington and Chorley; Fleetwood and Heysham are ports. The inland side of the county is hilly and includes the wild and impressive Forest of Bowland. The W side contains the coastal plain, where vegetables are extensively cultivated. The S is largely urban; industries include cotton spinning and weaving, chemicals, glass, rubber, electrical goods, and motor vehicles. The principal rivers are the Lune and the Ribble.
Districts: Burnley; Chorley; Fylde; Hyndburn; Lancaster; Pendle; Preston; Ribble Valley; Rossendale; South Ribble; West Lancashire; Wyre.

Larne *Larne* Population: 30,832.
On the east coast of Northern Ireland, Larne port is one of the main points of entry to Northern Ireland and is also an important centre for freight. The northern part of the district contains the southern tip of the Antrim Hills and the coastline has an amazing range of geological features, from the most ancient rocks, to remains from the last glaciation. Other towns include Carnlough, Ballygalley and Portmuck on the coast, and Kilwaughter, Ballynure and Ballycarry inland. Industries are based around freight, agriculture and tourism.

Leicester *Leic.* Population: 279,921.
Unitary authority in central England surrounding Leicester and bounded by Leicestershire. It is one of the leading shopping regions in the Midlands. Traditional industries such as hosiery and footwear, as well as hi-tech industries, are important to the local economy. Leicester is aiming to be one of the most

environmentally-friendly cities in Europe. It is involved in pioneering electronic toll road schemes in order to encourage the use of public transport. The Rivers Sence and Soar run through the area.

Leicestershire *Leics.* Population: 609,578.
Midland county of England bounded by Derbyshire, Leicester, Lincolnshire, Northamptonshire, Nottinghamshire, Rutland, Staffordshire and Warwickshire. Chief towns are Loughborough, Hinckley, Wigston, Coalville, Melton Mowbray, Oadby, Market Harborough, Shepshed and Ashby de la Zouch. The landscape is mostly of low, rolling hills. E and W of Leicester are areas of higher ground, notably Charnwood Forest. The W is largely industrial; industries include light engineering, hosiery, and footwear. The E is rural, with large fields and scattered woods, and is noted for field sports and food production. Part of the legacy left by the Roman occupation of Leicestershire are the Great North Road, Watling Street and Fosse Way which dissect the county. River Soar traverses the county from S to N, while River Welland forms part of the boundary with Northamptonshire to the S.
Districts: Blaby; Charnwood; Harborough; Hinckley & Bosworth; Melton; North West Leicestershire; Oadby & Wigston.

Limavady *Limavady* Population: 32,422.
There are two AONBs in this district, which contains the Sperrin mountains to the south and the wide, fertile valley of the river Roe in the centre. To the north is Lough Foyle and the long, sandy beach of Magilligan Strand. Main towns are Limavady, Dungiven and Ballykelly and a car ferry runs across Lough Foyle from Magilligan Point to the Inishowen Peninsula in the Republic of Ireland. Industries include agriculture, services, small-scale manufacturing, construction and tourism.

Lincolnshire *Lincs.* Population: 646,645.
County of E England bounded by Cambridgeshire, Leicestershire, Norfolk, Northamptonshire, North East Lincolnshire, North Lincolnshire, Nottinghamshire, Peterborough, Rutland and the North Sea. Main towns are the cathedral city and county town of Lincoln and the towns of Boston, Grantham, Gainsborough, Spalding, Stamford, Skegness and Louth. Much of the county is flat and includes a large area of The Fens in the S. This reclaimed marshland is richly fertile, producing large crops of peas (for canning), sugar beet, potatoes, corn, and around Spalding, flower bulbs. Two ranges of hills traverse the county N and S: the narrow limestone ridge, a continuation of the Cotswold Hills, running from Grantham to Scunthorpe, and the chalk Wolds, about 12m/20km wide, running N from Spilsby and Horncastle. Apart from agriculture, industries include manufacture of agricultural machinery and tourism, which is centred on historic Lincoln, and the coastal resorts of Skegness and Mablethorpe. The rivers, of which the chief are the Witham and Welland, are largely incorporated into the extensive land-drainage system, and scarcely distinguishable from man-made channels.
Districts: Boston; East Lindsey; Lincoln; North Kesteven; South Holland; South Kesteven; West Lindsey.

Lisburn *Lisburn* Population: 108,694.
This district borders Belfast in the east and touches Lough Neagh in the west. Lisburn city itself sits in the valley of the River Lagan, with other towns being Dunmurry, Hillsborough, Magheraberry and Derriaghy. The Giants' Ring is a massive 656 feet (200m) diameter earthwork near the village of Drumbo. Industries include textiles (linen) and light engineering.

Londonderry/Derry *London.* Population: 105,066.
The city of Londonderry (Derry) is an important seaport and the second city of Northern Ireland, sitting astride the wide estuary of the river Foyle. The city walls, erected in 1619, are complete and some of the finest in Europe. Other towns include New Buildings and Eglinton, with several small villages scattered in the rural areas. In the south, are the forested glens of the Sperrin Mountains. Agriculture is the main industry, along with textiles (linen), distilling and chemicals.

Luton *Luton* Population: 184,371.
Unitary authority in SE England surrounding Luton and bounded by Bedfordshire and Hertfordshire. Luton is one of the major centres of employment and manufacturing in SE England, with automotive, electrical and retail industries among the most important. The production and export of high fashion and straw hats remains a feature of the local economy. London Luton Airport is situated in the SE of the area, and the River Lea rises nearby.

Magherafelt *Magh.* Population: 39,780.
The Sperrin Mountains form the western boundary and the River Bann, the eastern. The main town of Magherafelt is the administrative and marketing centre of the district and is also well known for its arts festival. Other small towns include Maghera and Draperstown. Agriculture is the main industry, along with some manufacturing and construction.

Medway *Med.* Population: 249,488.
Unitary authority on SE coast of England S of the River Thames estuary and neighbouring Kent. The chief centres are Gillingham, the naval base of Chatham, Strood and the cathedral city of Rochester. The S part of the area, surrounding the River Medway, is largely urban and industrialised. The marshland to the N includes Kingsnorth Power Station and the Isle of Grain, but is mostly rural, and contains Northward Hill Nature Reserve which is a haven for birds.

Merseyside *Mersey.* Population: 1,362,026.
Former metropolitan county of NW England. It neighbours Cheshire, Greater Manchester, Halton, Lancashire, Warrington and the sea. It comprises the near-continuous urban complex which includes the city of Liverpool and the towns of St. Helens, Birkenhead, Southport, Bootle, Wallasey, Bebington, Huyton and Crosby. The county straddles the long, wide estuary of the River Mersey, which accounts for the development of the area. During the 18c, growing Imperial trade of goods and slaves, led to the explosion of urban development surrounding the docks at Liverpool, Birkenhead and Bootle. Liverpool went on to become Britain's premier transatlantic port and a significant terminus during the migration flows of the 19c, leading to an ethnically diverse city culture. Over the last century the docks have declined, leaving behind an impressive waterfront and cityscape as testament to a mercantile and maritime heritage. Inland, the urban spread has reached the industrial town of St. Helens which is famed for glass production. To the N are the residential areas of Crosby, Formby and the coastal resort of Southport. The area includes race courses at Aintree and Haydock, and an airport at Speke.
Districts: Knowsley; Liverpool; St. Helens; Sefton; Wirral.

Merthyr Tydfil *M.Tyd.* Population: 55,981.
Unitary authority in S Wales bounded by Caerphilly, Powys and Rhondda Cynon Taff. Main centres are the town of Merthyr Tydfil and the villages of Treharris, Abercanaid and Troedyrhiw. The area stretches from the Brecon Beacons, along the Taff Valley, to the centre of the former Welsh coal mining district. The local economy has diversified from primary industry, with Merthyr Tydfil being an important centre for public administration, shopping and employment for the region. The River Taff flows through the area.

Middlesbrough *Middbro.* Population: 134,855.
Unitary authority in NE England surrounding Middlesbrough and bounded by North Yorkshire, Redcar & Cleveland and Stockton-on-Tees. Middlesbrough is an industrial town, with chemical and petro-chemical industries in evidence. It is also an important sub-regional shopping and entertainment centre between Leeds and Newcastle upon Tyne.

Midlothian *Midloth.* Population: 80,941.
Unitary authority in central Scotland neighbouring East Lothian, Edinburgh and Scottish Borders. Main towns are Penicuik, Bonnyrigg, Dalkeith, Gorebridge and Loanhead. The area is mostly rural, including the rolling moorland of the Pentland Hills and Moorfoot Hills in the S. To the N, the urban area is comprised of satellite towns to the SE of Edinburgh. Rivers include Tyne Water and South Esk.

Milton Keynes *M.K.* Population: 207,057.
S midland unitary authority of England bounded by Bedfordshire, Buckinghamshire and Northamptonshire. The area includes the city of Milton Keynes, Bletchley, Newport Pagnell, Great Linford, Stony Stratford and Wolverton. Over the past 30 years, the area has undergone the fastest rate of growth in the country, attracting numerous industries. The Great Ouse and Ouzel rivers pass through the area.

Monmouthshire (Sir Fynwy). *Mon.* Population: 84,885.
Unitary authority in SE Wales bounded by Blaenau Gwent, Newport, Powys, Torfaen, the English areas of Gloucestershire, Herefordshire and the Bristol Channel. The main towns are Abergavenny, Caldicot, Chepstow and Monmouth. Part of the Brecon Beacons are found in NW Monmouthshire, whereas the SW area is mainly flat. Agriculture, mineral extraction and the service sector are important to the local economy. Rivers include the Wye, which forms part of E border, and the Usk, Trothy and Monnow.

Moray *Moray* Population: 86,940.
Unitary authority in N Scotland neighboured by Aberdeenshire, Highland and the sea. Main towns are Elgin, Forres, Buckie, Lossiemouth and Keith. The area is mainly mountainous, including part of the Cairngorm Mountains in the S. It is dissected by many deep river valleys, most notably that of the River Spey. Along with the local grain and peat, the abundant waters provide the raw materials for half of Scotland's malt whisky distilleries, leading to the Whisky Trail and much tourism through Speyside.

Moyle *Moyle* Population: 15,933.
This is Northern Ireland's smallest district by population but it is famous for the amazing basalt columns of the Giant's Causeway on the north coast, a UNESCO World Heritage Site. The entire Causeway Coast has been designated as an AONB. Ballycastle is the largest town, others being Cushendun, Cushendall and Bushmills, which has the world's oldest licensed distillery. Off the north coast is Rathlin Island where Northern Ireland's largest seabird colony breeds under the management of the RSPB. The main industry is agriculture, with some light industry and tourism.

Neath Port Talbot (Castell-nedd Port Talbot). *N.P.T.* Population: 134,468.
Unitary authority in S Wales neighbouring Bridgend, Powys, Rhondda Cynon Taff, Swansea and the sea. The chief centres are Neath, Port Talbot, Pontardawe, Baglan, Glyncorrwg and Briton Ferry. The area is mostly mountainous, divided up by the river valleys of the Tawe, Neath, Afan and Dulais, which all flow out to sea at Swansea Bay. The lower valley of the River Neath is heavily industrialised.

Newport (Casnewydd). *Newport* Population: 137,011.
Unitary authority on the S coast of Wales, N of the mouth of the River Severn, and bounded by Caerphilly, Cardiff, Monmouthshire and Torfaen. Main centres are Newport, Liswerry, Malpas and Caerleon. Steel manufacturing and hi-tech industries are important to the local economy. The rivers Ebbw and Usk run through the area.

Newry & Mourne *N. & M.* Population: 87,058.
Bordering the Republic of Ireland on its southern edge, the district contains the beautiful Mourne mountains in the east and has two areas designated as AONBs. Newry is the main town and has been an important centre for cross-border trade development. Warrenpoint is a modern port. Other towns include Killkeel, with its important fishing industry, Rostrevor, Bessbrook and Annalong. Besides fishing, industries are mainly agriculture and tourism.

Newtownabbey *Newtown.* Population: 79,995.
Bordering the north-western shore of Belfast Lough, this small district is a mix of the urban and rural. It has a high population density compared to the rest of Northern Ireland. The main town is Newtownabbey, others being Ballyclare, which hosts one of the oldest horse fairs in Ireland, Mossley and Mallusk which is a busy commercial centre. There are many small businesses in the area as well as agriculture.

Norfolk *Norf.* Population: 796,728.
County of E England bounded by Cambridgeshire, Lincolnshire, Suffolk and the North Sea. Chief centres are the cathedral city and county town of Norwich, Great Yarmouth on the E coast, the expanding port of King's Lynn near the mouth of the Great Ouse and The Wash, Thetford, which is known as the Breckland 'capital', East Dereham and Wymondham. Norfolk is mainly flat or gently undulating, with fenland in the W characterised by large drainage channels emptying into The Wash. In the SW is Breckland, an expanse of heath and conifer forest used for military training; other afforested areas are near King's Lynn and North Walsham. NE of Norwich are The Broads, an area of meres and rivers popular for boating; reeds for thatching are grown here. The N Norfolk coastline is an Area of Outstanding Natural Beauty and Heritage Coast, and includes the popular resorts of Cromer and Sheringham. Otherwise the county is almost entirely agricultural, with farming an important activity; service and manufacturing industries are also significant. Rivers include the Great Ouse, Bure, Nar, Wensum, Wissey, and Yare; the Little Ouse and Waveney both enter the county briefly, but mainly form the boundary with Suffolk.
Districts: Breckland; Broadland; Great Yarmouth; King's Lynn & West Norfolk; North Norfolk; Norwich; South Norfolk.

North Ayrshire *N.Ayr.* Population: 135,817.
Unitary authority in central Scotland including the islands of Arran, Great Cumbrae and Little Cumbrae. It is bounded by East Ayrshire, East Renfrewshire, Inverclyde, Renfrewshire, South Ayrshire and the sea. The principal towns are Irvine, Kilwinning, Saltcoats, Largs, Ardrossan, Stevenston and Kirbirnie. The area includes mountains and part of Clyde Muirshiel Regional Park in the N, and the lower lands of Cunninghame in the S. There is a maritime heritage to the area; ferry routes operate from Largs and Ardrossan. Rivers include the Garnock, Dusk Water and Noddsdale Water.

North Down *N.Down* Population: 76,323.
On the southern shore of Belfast Lough, this is another high population density district. The main town of Bangor is an important maritime resort with a large, modern marina and shopping centre. Other towns are Helen's Bay and Holywood. Main industries include light engineering, food processing, retail and tourism.

North East Lincolnshire *N.E.Lincs.* Population: 157,979.
Unitary authority in NE England, S of the mouth of the River Humber and bounded by Lincolnshire, North Lincolnshire and the North Sea. Chief towns are Grimsby, Cleethorpes and Immingham. Grimsby and Cleethorpes together are the shopping and commercial centres of the area. Fishing, food, tourism, chemical and port industries are all important to the local economy. The main rivers are the Humber and Freshney.

North Lanarkshire *N.Lan.* Population: 321,067.
Unitary authority in central Scotland neighbouring East Dunbartonshire, Falkirk, Glasgow, South Lanarkshire, Stirling and West Lothian. The chief centres are Cumbernauld, Coatbridge, Airdrie, Motherwell, Wishaw and Bellshill. North Lanarkshsire contains a mixture of urban and rural areas, and formerly depended heavily upon the coal, engineering and steel industries. Regeneration and diversification have occurred in recent years.

North Lincolnshire *N.Lincs.* Population: 152,849.
Unitary authority in NE England neighbouring East Riding of Yorkshire, Leicestershire, Norfolk, North East Lincolnshire, Nottinghamshire, Peterborough, Rutland, South Yorkshire and the River Humber. The main centres are Scunthorpe, Bottesford, Barton-upon-Humber and Brigg. The area is mainly rural, but does include oil refineries, steel and manufacturing industries; the River Humber provides pool and wharf facilities. Rivers include the Humber, Trent and the Old Ancholme.

North Somerset *N.Som.* Population: 188,564.
Unitary authority in W England, S of the mouth of the River Severn, and neighbouring Bath & North East Somerset, Bristol, Somerset and the Bristol Channel. Chief towns are Weston-super-Mare, Clevedon, Nailsea and Portishead. The area is largely rural with tourism, centred on the coastal resort of Weston-super-Mare, being a major industry. Bristol International Airport is located in the E of the area.

North Yorkshire *N.Yorks.* Population: 569,660.
Large county of N England bounded by Cumbria, Darlington, Durham, East Riding of Yorkshire, Lancashire, Middlesbrough, Redcar & Cleveland, South Yorkshire, Stockton-on-Tees, West Yorkshire, York and the North Sea. Main centres are Harrogate, Scarborough, Hetton, Selby, the cathedral city of Ripon, the county town of Northallerton, Whitby, Skipton and Knaresborough. Apart from the wide plain around York, through which flow River Ouse and its tributaries, and the

smaller Vale of Pickering, watered by the Derwent and its tributary the Rye, the county is dominated by two ranges of hills; The Pennines in the W and the Cleveland Hills in the NE. The plains are pastoral and agricultural, while the hills provide rough sheep-grazing. The county includes the popular resorts of Scarborough and Whitby, and the majority of the North York Moors and Yorkshire Dales National Parks which promote tourism. Other economic activities include light engineering, service and hi-tech industries. Principal rivers are the Ouse, fed by the Derwent, Swale, Ure, Nidd and Wharfe, and draining into the Humber; the Esk, flowing into the North Sea at Whitby; and in the W, the Ribble, passing out into Lancashire and the Irish Sea.

Districts: Craven; Hambleton; Harrogate; Richmondshire; Ryedale; Scarborough; Selby.

Northamptonshire *Northants.* Population: 629,676.
Midland county of England bounded by Bedfordshire, Buckinghamshire, Cambridgeshire, Leicestershire, Lincolnshire, Milton Keynes, Oxfordshire, Peterborough, Rutland and Warwickshire. Chief towns are Northampton, Corby, Kettering, Wellingborough, Rushden and Daventry. The county consists largely of undulating agricultural country rising locally to low hills, especially along the W border. Large fields and scattered woods provide terrain for field sports. Northamptonshire still retains its rural and agricultural charm, despite undergoing rapid population growth recently. There are many villages of architectural, scenic and historic interest. Industrial development is modest, concentrating on the traditional footwear manufacture. Corby is undergoing regeneration following the decline of its steel industry. Tourism is set to increase due to the county's natural Middle England ambience, and the seasonal opening of the Althorp Estate, the family home and resting place of Diana, Princess of Wales. The principal rivers are the Nene and Welland.

Districts: Corby; Daventry; East Northamptonshire; Kettering; Northampton; South Northamptonshire; Wellingborough.

Northumberland *Northumb.* Population: 307,190.
Northernmost county of England bounded by Cumbria, Durham and Tyne & Wear, the Scottish authority of Scottish Borders and the North Sea. The principal towns are Blyth, Ashington, Cramlington, Bedlington, Morpeth, Berwick-upon-Tweed, Prudhoe and Hexham. There is some industry in the SE coastal area, otherwise the county is almost entirely rural, the greater part being high moorland, culminating in the Cheviot Hills along the Scottish border. The most spectacular stretches of Hadrian's Wall traverse the county to the N of Haltwhistle and Hexham. There is extensive afforestation, including Kielder Forest Park and part of the Northumberland National Park in the NW; parts of these forests are used for military training. The large reservoir, Kielder Water, also occurs in the NW of the area. Rivers include the Aln, Blyth, Breamish, Coquet, East and West Allen, North and South Tyne, Till, and Wansbeck. The Tweed forms part of the Scottish border and flows out to sea at Berwick-upon-Tweed.

Districts: Alnwick; Berwick-upon-Tweed; Blyth Valley; Castle Morpeth; Tynedale; Wansbeck.

Nottingham *Nott.* Population: 266,988.
Unitary authority in central England surrounding the city of Nottingham and bounded by Nottinghamshire. The city of Nottingham has a long history, having been granted many Royal Charters; Nottingham Castle and Wollaton Hall are among its many historical buildings. It is also an industrial and engineering centre, and a university city. Its main industries include the manufacture of chemicals, tobacco, cycles, lace and hosiery. The River Trent flows through the city.

Nottinghamshire *Notts.* Population: 748,510.
Midland county of England bounded by Derbyshire, Leicestershire, Lincolnshire, North Lincolnshire, Nottingham and South Yorkshire. Principal towns are Mansfield, Carlton, Sutton in Ashfield, Arnold, Worksop, Newark-on-Trent, West Bridgford, Beeston, Stapleford, Hucknall and Kirkby in Ashfield. Much of the county is rural, with extensive woodlands in the central area of The Dukeries, part of the larger Sherwood Forest. Cattle-grazing is the chief farming activity. Around the large towns there is much industry, including iron and steel, engineering, knitwear, pharmaceuticals, and coal-mining. The county has associations with Robin Hood, at Sherwood Forest, and D.H. Lawrence, at Eastwood. The most important river is the Trent.

Districts: Ashfield; Bassetlaw; Broxtowe; Gedling; Mansfield; Newark & Sherwood; Rushcliffe.

Omagh *Omagh.* Population: 47,952.
One of the largest districts by area of Northern Ireland, the borders are mainly hills, with the town of Omagh in a central valley, at the confluence of several rivers where almost one third of the total population live. The area is primarily rural, with small towns and villages scattered throughout the landscape. These include Fintona, Dromore and Carrickmore. Agriculture is the main industry.

Orkney *Ork.* Population: 19,245.
Group of some fifteen main islands and numerous smaller islands, islets and rocks. Designated an Islands Area for administrative purposes, and lying N of the NE end of the Scottish mainland across the Pentland Firth. Kirkwall is the capital, situated on the island Mainland, 24m/38km N of Duncansby Head. Stromness is the only other town. About twenty of the islands are inhabited. In general the islands are low-lying but have steep, high cliffs on W side. The climate is generally mild for the latitude but storms are frequent. Fishing and farming (mainly cattle-rearing) are the chief industries. The oil industry is also represented, with an oil terminal on the island of Flotta, and oil service bases at Car Ness and Stromness, Mainland and at Lyness, Hoy. Lesser industries include whisky distilling, knitwear and tourism. The islands are noted for their unique prehistoric and archaeological remains. The main airport is at Grimsetter, near Kirkwall, with most of the populated islands being served by airstrips. Ferries also operate from the Scottish mainland, and between islands in the group.

Oxfordshire *Oxon.* Population: 605,488.
S midland county of England bounded by Buckinghamshire, Gloucestershire, Northamptonshire, Reading, Swindon, Warwickshire, West Berkshire, Wiltshire and Wokingham. Chief centres are the county town, cathedral and university city of Oxford and towns of Banbury, Abingdon, Bicester, Witney, Didcot, Thame and Henley-on-Thames. Burford and Chipping Norton are small Cotswold towns in the W and NW respectively. The landscape is predominantly flat or gently undulating, forming part of the Thames Valley. High ground occurs where the Chiltern Hills enter the county in the SE and the Cotswold Hills in the NW. The county is largely agricultural, with industries centred on the towns. Scientific, medical and research establishments are attracted by the proximity of Oxford's universities. Printing and publishing industries have their greatest concentration outside London. The motor industry is well represented with car manufacture at Cowley, Oxford, and the county has the world's largest concentration of performance car development and manufacturing. Tourism, attracted to stately homes, notably Blenheim Palace, and Oxford city centre, is also important. Chief rivers are the Thames (or Isis), Cherwell, Ock, Thame, and Windrush.

Districts: Cherwell; Oxford; South Oxfordshire; Vale of White Horse; West Oxfordshire.

Pembrokeshire (Sir Benfro). *Pembs.* Population: 114,131.
Unitary authority in the SW corner of Wales neighbouring Carmarthenshire, Ceredigion and the sea. The chief centres are Haverfordwest, Pembroke Dock, Pembroke, Tenby, Saundersfoot, Neyland, Fishguard and the ancient cathedral city of St. David's. Key industries are tourism, agriculture and oil refining. The deep estuarial waters of Milford Haven provide a berth for oil tankers. A large part of Pembrokeshire's coastline forms Britain's only coastal National Park. Ferries sail from Fishguard and Pembroke Dock to Rosslare in the Republic of Ireland.

Perth & Kinross *P. & K.* Population: 134,949.
Unitary authority in Scotland bounded by Aberdeenshire, Angus, Argyll & Bute, Clackmannanshire, Fife, Highland and Stirling. Chief centres are the city of Perth, Blairgowrie, Crieff, Kinross, Auchterader and Pitlochry. The area is mountainous, containing large areas of remote open moorland, especially in the N and W; the vast upland expanses of Breadalbane, Rannoch and Atholl, form the S edge of the Grampian Mountains. The lower land of the S and E is more heavily populated and is dominated by the ancient city of Perth. The area is rich in history as it links the Highlands to the N with the central belt and lowlands to the S via important mountain passes, most notably the Pass of Dromochter.

The area has many castles, and Scottish Kings were traditionally enthroned at Scone Abbey, to the N of Perth. There are many lochs, including Loch Rannoch and Loch Tay. Main industries are tourism and whisky production. The world famous Gleneagles golf course is in the S of the area. Rivers include the Tay, Almond and Earn.

Peterborough *Peter.* Population: 156,061.
Unitary authority in E England neighbouring Cambridgeshire, Lincolnshire, Northamptonshire and Rutland. The area includes the city of Peterborough, which lies at the heart of an important agricultural area. Developing as a railway hub, it has become a major industrial, distribution and shopping centre. The River Nene passes through Peterborough.

Plymouth *Plym.* Population: 240,720.
Unitary authority on the SW coast of England surrounding the city of Plymouth and neighbouring Cornwall and Devon. Plymouth stands at the mouth of the River Tamar and is the largest city on the S coast of England. It has strong mercantile and naval traditions; it is closely linked with Sir Francis Drake, and has maintained a Royal Naval Dockyard for 300 years. Plymouth is a regional shopping centre and a popular resort.

Poole *Poole* Population: 138,288.
Unitary authority on S coast of England surrounding Poole and bordered by Bournemouth and Dorset. Poole Harbour is the second largest natural harbour in the world, which enabled Poole to prosper through trading, especially with Newfoundland. Poole has now attracted a variety of industries including boat-building, fishing, pottery, engineering and electronics. Ferries run to the Channel Islands and France.

Portsmouth *Ports.* Population: 186,701.
Unitary authority on the S coast of England surrounding the city of Portsmouth and bordered by Hampshire. Portsmouth developed as a strategic port around Portsmouth Harbour, and it is still the home of the Royal Navy. It has become a culturally diverse centre, attracting a wide range of industries which include leisure, tourism, financial services, distribution, manufacturing and hi-tech industries.

Powys *Powys* Population: 126,354.
Large unitary authority in central Wales bordering Blaenau Gwent, Caerphilly, Carmarthenshire, Ceredigion, Denbighshire, Gwynedd, Merthyr Tydfil, Monmouthshire, Neath Port Talbot, Rhondda Cynon Taff, Wrexham and the English areas of Herefordshire and Shropshire. Main centres are Newtown, Gurnos, Brecon, Welshpool, Ystradgynlais, Llanllwchaiarn, Llandrindod Wells, Knighton, Llanidloes, Builth Wells and Machynlleth. Powys is almost entirely rural, with mountainous terrain; most of the Brecon Beacons National Park falls within the S part of the area, while the Cambrian Mountains are in the W. There is considerable afforestation, and a number of large reservoirs, including Lake Vyrnwy. To the N of Brecon, on Mynydd Eppynt, is an extensive military training area. Main economic activities are agriculture, which is predominantly based around hill farming. Tourism is significant, owing to the natural beauty of the area, and innovative attractions such as the Centre for Alternative Technology. Industrial development is gradually increasing. Among the many rivers, the largest are the Severn, Usk, and Wye.

Reading *Read.* Population: 143,096.
Unitary authority in S England to W of Greater London, surrounding Reading and bordered by Oxfordshire, West Berkshire, Windsor & Maidenhead and Wokingham. Reading developed as a crossing point of the River Thames and River Kennet. Traditional industries include brewing and food production, notably biscuits. These are accompanied by an increasing sector of hi-tech and computer-based companies, attracted by Reading's location in the M4 corridor. Reading has also established itself as a major entertainments centre.

Redcar & Cleveland *R. & C.* Population: 139,132.
Unitary authority on the NE coast of England neighbouring Hartlepool, Middlesbrough and North Yorkshire. The main centres are Redcar, South Bank, Eston, Guisborough, Marske-by-the-Sea, Saltburn-by-the-Sea, Loftus and Skelton. The area is one of great contrasts. It combines rural villages, market towns and coastal resorts, along with heavily populated urban areas and industrialised port facilities. Industries include steel-making, due to the local ironstone, and chemicals, based around the River Tees to the NW of the area. The coastal towns attract some tourism. The River Tees forms part of the border to the W.

Renfrewshire *Renf.* Population: 172,867.
Unitary authority in central Scotland bordering East Renfrewshire, Glasgow, Inverclyde, North Ayrshire, West Dunbartonshire and the Firth of Clyde. Main centres are Paisley, Renfrew, Johnstone, Erskine and Linwood. The area emerges W from the Greater Glasgow periphery into a contrasting countryside of highlands, lochs and glens. Industry is centred on the urban area and includes electronics, engineering, food and drink production and service sectors; in rural areas to the W, agriculture is still important. The W part of the area includes some of Clyde Muirshiels Regional Park; Glasgow Airport is in the E.

Rhondda Cynon Taff (Rhondda Cynon Taf). *R.C.T.* Population: 231,946.
Unitary authority in S Wales bounded by Bridgend, Caerphilly, Cardiff, Merthyr Tydfil, Neath Port Talbot, Powys and Vale of Glamorgan. The principal towns are Treorchy, Aberdare, Pontypridd, Ferndale and Mountain Ash. Rhondda Cynon Taff is a mountainous area, dissected by deep narrow valleys, with urbanisation typified by ribbon development. The area was the former heart of the Welsh coal mining industry, and has experienced a sharp economic decline as pits closed. Diversification into light engineering and service sectors are gradually improving the industrial base. Main rivers are the Rhondda and Cynon.

Rutland *Rut.* Population: 34,563.
Unitary authority in E England neighbouring Leicestershire, Lincolnshire, Northamptonshire and Peterborough. The main town is Oakham. Agriculture is the main industry; other important industries are engineering, cement-making, plastics, clothing and tourism. The area includes the large reservoir, Rutland Water, which is an important feature for leisure, tourism and wildlife.

Scottish Borders *Sc.Bord.* Population: 106,764.
Administrative region of SE Scotland bordering Dumfries & Galloway, East Lothian, Midlothian, South Lanarkshire, West Lothian, the English counties of Cumbria and Northumberland and the North Sea. It comprises the former counties of Berwick, Peebles, Roxburgh and Selkirk. Main towns are Hawick, Galashiels, Peebles, Kelso, Selkirk and Jedburgh. It extends from the Tweedsmuir Hills in the W to the North Sea on either side of St. Abb's Head in the E, and from the Pentland, Moorfoot and Lammermuir Hills in the N to the Cheviot Hills and the English border in the S. The fertile area of rich farmland between the hills to N and S is known as The Merse. The area around Peebles and Galashiels is noted for woollen manufacture. Elsewhere, the electronics industry is of growing importance. The River Tweed rises in the extreme W and flows between Kelso and Coldstream, finally passing into England, 4m/6km W of Berwick-upon-Tweed.

Shetland *Shet.* Population: 21,988.
Group of over 100 islands, lying beyond Orkney to the NE of the Scottish mainland; Sumburgh Head being about 100m/160km from Duncansby Head. Designated an Islands Area for administrative purposes, the chief islands are Mainland, on which the capital and chief port of Lerwick is situated, Unst and Yell. Some twenty of the islands are inhabited. The islands are mainly low-lying, the highest point being Ronas Hill, on Mainland. The oil industry has made an impact on Shetland, with oil service bases at Lerwick and Sandwick, and a large terminal at Sullom Voe. Other industries include cattle and sheep-rearing, knitwear and fishing. The climate is mild, considering the latitude, but severe storms are frequent. The islands are famous for the small Shetland breed of pony, which is renowned for its strength and hardiness. There is an airport at Sumburgh, on S part of Mainland.

Shropshire *Shrop.* Population: 283,173.
W midland county of England bounded by Cheshire, Herefordshire, Staffordshire, Telford & Wrekin, Worcestershire and the Welsh authorities of Powys and Wrexham. Main towns are the county town of Shrewsbury, Oswestry, Bridgnorth, Market Drayton, Ludlow and Whitchurch. The S and W borders

are hilly, with large areas of open moorland, including The Long Mynd and Wenlock Edge, which provide good sheep-grazing. Elsewhere the county undulates towards the Severn Valley, which provides fertile agricultural land served by prosperous market towns. Agricultural output includes dairy, poultry and pig farming, along with corn crops. As the former heart of the Marches of Wales, Shropshire contains the remains of numerous border defences. There are also the remains of several monasteries, for instance, at Much Wenlock and Buildwas. The most important river is the Severn, which flows across the county from W to SE; others include the Clun, Corve, Perry, Rea Brook, and Teme.
Districts: Bridgnorth; North Shropshire; Oswestry; Shrewsbury & Atcham; South Shropshire.

Slough *Slo.* Population: 119,067.
Unitary authority in SE England to the W of London, surrounding Slough and bordering Buckinghamshire, Greater London, Surrey and Windsor & Maidenhead. Slough has grown significantly over the past 30 years, and is a major regional shopping centre. Industry is centred on the large Slough Trading Estate, which was planned after World War I. Numerous sectors are represented in Slough, among them is confectionery.

Somerset *Som.* Population: 498,093.
County in SW England bounded by Bath & North East Somerset, Devon, Dorset, North Somerset, Wiltshire and the Bristol Channel. The chief centres are the county town of Taunton, Yeovil, Bridgwater, Frome, Chard, Street, Burnham-on-Sea, Highbridge, the small cathedral city of Wells, Wellington and Minehead. Somerset consists of several hill ranges, including the Mendip, Polden, Quantock, Brendon Hills, along with most of Exmoor. These uplands are separated by valleys, or, on either side of the River Parrett, by the extensive marshy flats of Sedgemoor. Economic activity is mainly based on agriculture in the fertile vales, with manufacturing, distribution and service industries centred on the urban areas. Tourism is important with attractions including Exmoor National Park, a holiday complex at Minehead and the county's natural rural charm. Somerset also holds one of Europe's largest music festivals at Glastonbury. The chief rivers are Axe, Brue, Parrett, and Tone, draining into the Bristol Channel; and Barle and Exe, rising on Exmoor and flowing into Devon and the English Channel.
Districts: Mendip; Sedgemoor; South Somerset; Taunton Deane; West Somerset.

South Ayrshire *S.Ayr.* Population: 112,097.
Unitary authority in SW Scotland bounded by Dumfries & Galloway, East Ayrshire, North Ayrshire and the sea. The chief towns are Ayr, Troon, Prestwick, Girvan and Maybole. The area consists of a long coastline, with lowlands surrounding Ayr Bay and higher ground to the S. Agriculture is a major economic activity on the uplands. To the N, aerospace and hi-tech industries are located near Prestwick International Airport and Ayr, the main retail centre. Notable sporting venues include a race course at Ayr and open championship golf courses at Troon and Turnberry. Tourism is a major feature of the local economy. The area was the birthplace of Robert the Bruce and Robert Burns; it contains Scotland's first country park at Culzean Castle; and it has a holiday camp on the coast near Ayr. Rivers include the Ayr, Water of Girvan and Stinchar.

South Gloucestershire *S.Glos.* Population: 245,641.
Unitary authority in SW England neighbouring Bath & North East Somerset, Bristol, Gloucestershire and Wiltshire. The chief centres are Kingswood, Chipping Sodbury, Mangotsfield, Frampton Cotterell, Yate, Thornbury, Patchway and Filton. The S part of the area lies on the N and E fringes of Bristol. The Cotswold hills are in the E, and the Severn Vale in the W. Main industries are in the S, and include aerospace engineering; the N is mainly agricultural. South Gloucestershire includes the English side of both Severn road bridges. Badminton Park in the E of the area, is the location for the Badminton Horse Trials. The River Severn borders the area to the NW.

South Lanarkshire *S.Lan.* Population: 302,216.
Unitary authority in central Scotland bordering Dumfries & Galloway, East Ayrshire, East Renfrewshire, Glasgow, North Lanarkshire, Scottish Borders and West Lothian. The main towns are East Kilbride, Hamilton, Blantyre, Larkhall, Carluke, Lanark and Bothwell. Urban development is mainly in the N, merging with the SE periphery of Greater Glasgow. The S part is mostly farmland and not highly populated. Tourism is mainly centred on the picturesque valley of the upper Clyde; there is a race course at Hamilton. The area has associations with the industrial philanthropist, Robert Owen, who built a model village at New Lanark. Rivers include the Clyde, Avon and Dippool Water.

South Yorkshire *S.Yorks.* Population: 1,266,338.
Former metropolitan county of N England bordered by Derbyshire, East Riding of Yorkshire, North Lincolnshire, North Yorkshire, Nottinghamshire and West Yorkshire. It comprises the industrial and urban area around the city of Sheffield and the towns of Rotherham, Barnsley and Doncaster. Located at the heart of a major coalfield, South Yorkshire prospered through the development of heavy industry. Barnsley and Rotherham were coal mining towns, with steel and fine cutlery centred on Sheffield. The decline of these industries has led to the area redefining itself. Sheffield has become a centre of learning, tourism and conferences, aided by its environmental improvements. Barnsley, Rotherham and Doncaster have increased their industrial base, especially via light industries. Leisure and recreation are an important feature of the area, with venues including Barnsley's Metrodome, Doncaster's race course and Dome, and Sheffield's Arena and Don Valley Stadium. Retail has increased with city and town centre redevelopment, and the Meadowhall complex. The surrounding countryside includes country parks at Rother Valley and Thrybergh, with part of the Peak District National Park W and NW of Sheffield. The chief river is the Don.
Districts: Barnsley; Doncaster; Rotherham; Sheffield.

Southampton *S'ham.* Population: 217,445.
Unitary authority on the S coast of England surrounding the city of Southampton, and bordered by Hampshire. Southampton owes much to the deep waters of Southampton Water, which have enabled the development of Europe's busiest cruise port. Water and the waterfront remain very important to the local economy, with marine technology, oceanography, boat shows and yacht races all prominent. The city is also a leading media, recreational, entertainment and retail centre. The chief river is the Itchen.

Southend *S'end* Population: 160,257.
Unitary authority in SE England, N of the mouth of the River Thames, surrounding Southend-on-Sea and bordering Essex. Southend is a commerical, residential, shopping and holiday centre, with tourism among its main industries. It includes a 7m shoreline from Leigh-on-Sea to Shoeburyness, a famous pier and a sea life centre.

Staffordshire *Staffs.* Population: 806,744.
Midland county of England bounded by Cheshire, Derbyshire, Leicestershire, Shropshire, Stoke-on-Trent, Telford & Wrekin, Warwickshire, West Midlands and Worcestershire. Chief centres are Newcastle-under-Lyme, Tamworth, the county town of Stafford, Burton upon Trent, Cannock, Burntwood, the cathedral city of Lichfield, Kidsgrove, Rugeley and Leek. The urban development occurs around the West Midlands conurbation in the S, where main industries include engineering, iron and steel, rubber goods and leather production, while to the N, there is an urban concentration around Stoke-on-Trent. Burton upon Trent is noted for brewing. The ancient hunting forest and former mining district of Cannock Chase is in the centre of the county and contains preserved tracts of moorland. In the NE lies part of the Peak District National Park. The rest of the county is predominantly agricultural, with milk, wheat and sugar beet produced. To the E of Leek, moorland broken up by limestone walls extends across the Manifold valley to the Derbyshire border. In additon to the Trent, which dominates much of the county, rivers include the Blithe, Manifold, Sow and Tame. River Dove forms the boundary with Derbyshire.
Districts: Cannock Chase; East Staffordshire; Lichfield; Newcastle-under-Lyme; South Staffordshire; Stafford; Staffordshire Moorlands; Tamworth.

Stirling *Stir.* Population: 86,212.
Unitary authority in central Scotland neighbouring Argyll & Bute, Clackmannanshire, East Dunbartonshire, Falkirk, North Lanarkshire, Perth & Kinross and West Dunbartonshire. The chief centres are Stirling, the ancient cathedral city of Dunblane, Bannockburn, Bridge of Allan and Callander. The fertile

agricultural lands of the Forth valley are in the centre of the area, bounded by mountains: The Trossachs and the mountain peaks of Ben Lomond, Ben More and Ben Lui in the N, while in the S are the Campsie Fells. Tourism is an important industry with Stirling including many sites of historical significance to Scotland, particularly during the struggle to retain independence. There are associations with Rob Roy, and the battle site of Bannockburn. Other features include The Trossachs, part of the Loch Lomond Regional Park and the Queen Elizabeth Forest Park. There are several lochs, including Loch Lomond, which forms part of the W border, and Loch Katrine. Scotland's only lake named as such, Lake of Menteith, is also in Stirling. The main river is the Forth.

Stockton-on-Tees *Stock.* Population: 178,408.
Unitary authority in NE England neighbouring Darlington, Durham, Hartlepool, Middlesbrough, North Yorkshire and Redcar & Cleveland. The main centres are Stockton-on-Tees, Billingham, Thornaby-on-Tees, Eaglescliffe, Egglescliffe and Yarm. The area has a diverse mix of picturesque villages, large-scale urbanisation and heavy industry. The area has recently undergone major renewal and regeneration, with industries now including electronics, food technology and chemical production. Stockton is the main shopping centre for the area, and includes the Teesside Retail Park. The main river is the Tees, which is controlled by the Tees Barrage. This has created Britain's largest purpose-built whitewater canoeing course.

Stoke-on-Trent *Stoke* Population: 240,636.
Unitary authority in England surrounding the city of Stoke-on-Trent and neighbouring Staffordshire. The city has six town centres: Burslem, Fenton, Hanley, Longton, Stoke-upon-Trent and Tunstall. Hanley is where most current city centre activities are located. The area forms The Potteries, and is the largest claywear producer in the world, although now it is largely a finishing centre for imported pottery. There are a wide variety of other industries, including steel, engineering, paper, glass and furniture. Stoke-on-Trent is a centre of employment, leisure and shopping for the surrounding areas. It is noted for its environmental approach, particularly with land reclamation which accounts for around 10 per cent of the city area; sites include Festival Park, Central Forest Park and Westport Lake. The River Trent flows through the area.

Strabane *Strabane* Population: 38,248.
To the east lie the Sperrin Mountains (an AONB) with the Republic of Ireland border and the River Mourne to the west. The main town of the district is Strabane, an historic market town. Other towns include Castlederg in the Derg valley, Newtonstewart, with Baronscourt Forest nearby, Sion Mills, with its model linen village, Plumbridge and Mount Hamilton. Main industries are agriculture, manufacturing and tourism.

Suffolk *Suff.* Population: 668,553.
Easternmost county of England bounded by Cambridgeshire, Essex, Norfolk and the North Sea. Main towns are the county town of Ipswich, Lowestoft, Bury St. Edmunds, Felixstowe, Sudbury, Haverhill, Newmarket, Stowmarket and Woodbridge. The county is low-lying and gently undulating. It is almost entirely agricultural, with cereal crops and oil seed rape in abundance. The low coastline, behind which are areas of heath and marsh, afforested in places, is subject to much erosion; it is deeply indented with long river estuaries which provide good sailing. The NW corner of the county forms part of Breckland. The central region includes many notable historic Wool Towns, for instance, Lavenham. Apart from agriculture, industries include electronics, telecommunications, printing and port facilities. Lowestoft is a prominent fishing port and Felixstowe is a container port of growing importance. River Stour forms the S boundary with Essex, and the Little Ouse and Waveney form most of the N boundary with Norfolk. The many other small rivers include the Alde with its estuary the Ore, Deben, and Gipping with its estuary the Orwell, in the E and Lark in the W.
Districts: Babergh; Forest Heath; Ipswich; Mid Suffolk; St. Edmundsbury; Suffolk Coastal; Waveney.

Surrey *Surr.* Population: 1,059,015.
County of SE England bounded by Bracknell Forest, East Sussex, Greater London, Hampshire, Kent, Slough, West Sussex and Windsor & Maidenhead. The principal towns are Woking, the cathedral and university town of Guildford, Staines, Leatherhead, Farnham, Epsom, Ewell, Sunbury, Walton-on-Thames, Weybridge, Egham, Redhill, Reigate, Esher, Camberley, Frimley and Godalming. The chalk ridge of the North Downs, gently sloping on the N side but forming a steep escarpment on the S, traverses the county from E to W. Extensive sandy heaths in the W are much used for military training. The county is heavily wooded, and contains many traces of the former iron industry in the predominantly rural S. Much of the urbanised E and N areas include commuter or dormitory towns which form the residential outskirts of the Greater London conurbation. Industries include the agricultural activites of dairy farming and horticulture. Tourism and recreation are also important, with Surrey including numerous stately homes, Wentworth golf course, four race courses, and a theme park at Thorpe Park. The chief river is the Thames, into which flow the Wey and the Mole.
Districts: Elmbridge; Epsom & Ewell; Guildford; Mole Valley; Reigate & Banstead; Runnymede; Spelthorne; Surrey Heath; Tandridge; Waverley; Woking.

Swansea (Abertawe). *Swan.* Population: 223,301.
Unitary authority in S Wales bordering Carmarthenshire, Neath Port Talbot and the sea. Main centres are the city of Swansea, Gorseinon, The Mumbles, Sketty, Cockett and Clydach. The area includes mountains in the N, the urban centre surrounding Swansea, and the Gower peninsula in the S. Swansea originally developed as a port serving the W coalfield of S Wales. The area gained an international reputation for tin-plating and copper and nickel production. Swansea is now a regional shopping and commercial centre, including a university and marina development. The Gower peninsula attracts many tourists with its fine beaches and cliff scenery; hang-gliding is popular at Rhossili Down, and there are associations with Dylan Thomas. The Mumbles is a popular resort, formerly connected to Swansea via a tramway. The chief river is the Tawe.

Swindon *Swin.* Population: 180,051.
Unitary authority in SW England neighbouring Gloucestershire, Oxfordshire and Wiltshire. Main centres are Swindon, Stratton St. Margaret, Highworth and Wroughton. The area is located between the Cotswold Hills and Wiltshire Downs, on the fringes of the Thames Valley. Originally a railway town, Swindon has experienced rapid recent growth and is now a centre for car manufacture and central commercial operations. The town is a regional shopping centre with a redeveloped town centre and the Designer Outlet Village. The River Thames borders the area to the N and the River Cole to the E.

Telford & Wrekin *Tel. & W.* Population: 158,325.
Unitary authority in W England bordered by Shropshire and Staffordshire. Main centres are Telford, Wellington, Madeley, Donnington, Oakengates, Hadley and Newport. The area was the cradle of the Industrial Revolution, with notable firsts including Darby's discovery of the iron smelting process at Coalbrookdale, the casting and construction of the first cold blast iron bridge at Ironbridge, and the construction of the first iron ship. The new town of Telford, named after the famous engineer, surveyor and road builder, Thomas Telford, is the major commercial centre. The River Severn runs S through the area.

Thurrock *Thur.* Population: 143,128.
Unitary authority in SE England, N of the mouth of the River Thames. It is bounded by Essex and Greater London. The main centres are Grays, South Ockendon, Stanford-le-Hope, Corringham and Tilbury. The area is a mix of old and modern, rural and urban. In the N there are historic villages set in agricultural land, while in the S, there are the modern urban developments, and industrial activities surrounding oil refining and the container port of Tilbury. Grays is the commercial centre of Thurrock, with the major retail centre being Thurrock Lakeside. The area includes the N stretch of the Dartford Tunnel and Queen Elizabeth II Bridge, both of which cross the River Thames.

Torbay *Torbay* Population: 129,706.
Unitary authority located on the SW coast of England neighbouring Devon. The major towns are Torquay, Paignton and Brixham. The area, situated on Tor Bay, is among Britain's main holiday resorts, and is widely regarded as the English Riviera. Tourism is the main industry, with Torbay receiving

over 1.5 million visitors per year. Excellent leisure, recreation and conference facilities are added attractions.

Torfaen (Tor-faen). *Torfaen* Population: 90,949.
Unitary authority in S Wales bounded by Blaenau Gwent, Caerphilly, Monmouthshire and Newport. The principal towns are Cwmbran, Pontypool and Blaenavon. Torfaen contains rugged mountains with a 12-mile-long valley running N to S from Blaenavon to Cwmbran. The area is a manufacturing centre which includes electronics, engineering and automotive companies. The industrial past of the area has led to the growth of tourist attractions, with notable sites including The Valley Inheritance at Pontypool, and Big Pit National Mining Museum of Wales and 19c ironworks at Blaenavon. The river Afon Llwyd runs through the area.

Tyne & Wear *T. & W.* Population: 1,075,938.
Maritime county of NE England bordered by Durham and Northumberland. It comprises the urban complex around the cities of Newcastle upon Tyne and Sunderland, South Shields, Gateshead, Washington and Wallsend. Named after its two important rivers, the area developed largely through the coal mining and ship-building industries. As these industries declined, the area has undergone urban and industrial regeneration. Newcastle upon Tyne is now a commercial, university and cultural centre, with a historic heart including a cathedral, 12c castle and the Tyne Bridge; the historic Quayside has recently been developed. Sunderland gained city status in 1992, and is now a centre for car manufacture, with recreational facilities including the Crowtree Leisure Complex and the National Glass Centre. Elsewhere, Wallsend has hi-tech and off-shore industries; South Tyneside has electronics industries, and tourism, via its Catherine Cookson links. Gateshead has an international athletics stadium, Europe's largest undercover shopping centre, the Metrocentre, and the modern symbol of renewal, the Angel of the North. The area is served by the Port of Tyne and Newcastle International Airport.
Districts: Gateshead; Newcastle upon Tyne; North Tyneside; South Tyneside; Sunderland.

Vale of Glamorgan (Bro Morgannwg). *V. of Glam.*
Population: 119,292.
Unitary authority on the S coast of Wales neighbouring Bridgend, Cardiff and Rhondda Cynon Taff. The chief towns are Barry, Penarth and Llantwit Major. Vale of Glamorgan is a lowland area between Cardiff and Bridgend, with some agricultural activities, and tourism at the resorts of Barry and Penarth. Cardiff International Airport is situated in the SE near Rhoose. Main river is the Ely, which passes through the area.

Warrington *Warr.* Population: 191,080.
Unitary authority in NW England surrounding Warrington and bounded by Cheshire, Greater Manchester, Halton and Merseyside. The area developed as a main crossing point of the River Mersey and latterly the Manchester Ship Canal. During industrialisation it became an important strategic trading centre for the NW region. In 1968, Warrington was granted New Town status, leading to traditional industries such as chemicals, brewing and food processing being joined by hi-tech industries and research and development facilities. Warrington retains its importance as a regional shopping, leisure and commercial centre. The River Mersey flows through the area.

Warwickshire *Warks.* Population: 505,860.
Midland county of England bounded by Gloucestershire, Leicestershire, Northamptonshire, Oxfordshire, Staffordshire, West Midlands and Worcestershire. Chief towns are Nuneaton, Rugby, Royal Leamington Spa, Bedworth, the county town of Warwick, Stratford-upon-Avon and Kenilworth. Warwickshire consists of mostly flat or undulating farmland, although the foothills of the Cotswold Hills spill over the SW border. Main manufacturing activites occur in an industrial belt extending NW from Rugby to the boundary with Staffordshire. They include motor and component industries, service sectors, electrical and general engineering. Tourism is centred on the historic town of Warwick with its medieval castle, and Stratford-upon-Avon with its Shakespeare associations. The principal river is the Avon.
Districts: North Warwickshire; Nuneaton & Bedworth; Rugby; Stratford-on-Avon; Warwick.

West Berkshire *W.Berks.* Population: 144,483.
Unitary authority in S England bordered by Hampshire, Oxfordshire, Reading, Wiltshire and Wokingham. The chief centres are Newbury, Thatcham and Hungerford. West Berkshire is a mixture of old market towns, historic buildings and waterways, and includes the famous Newbury racecourse. Rivers include the Kennet and the Pang.

West Dunbartonshire *W.Dun.* Population: 93,378.
Unitary authority in central Scotland bordered by Argyll & Bute, East Dunbartonshire, Glasgow, Inverclyde, Renfrewshire and Stirling. The chief towns are Clydebank, Dumbarton, Alexandria and Bonhill. The area is mountainous, containing the Kilpatrick Hills, and is bounded by Loch Lomond in the N and the Firth of Clyde in the S. The urban SE area of West Dunbartonshire forms part of the NW periphery of Greater Glasgow. There is a broad base of light manufacturing and service sector industries. Tourism and leisure are a feature, with the SE tip of Loch Lomond Regional Park and the whole of Balloch Castle Country Park falling within the area. West Dunbartonshire includes the Erskine Bridge which spans the River Clyde, other rivers include the Leven.

West Lothian *W.Loth.* Population: 158,714.
Unitary authority in central Scotland neighbouring Edinburgh, Falkirk, Midlothian, North Lanarkshire, Scottish Borders and South Lanarkshire. The chief towns are Livingston, Bathgate, Linlithgow, Broxburn, Whitburn and Armadale. The area undulates to the S of the Firth of Forth, and rises to moorland at the foot of the Pentland Hills in the S. The main urban areas are situated along commuter corridors between Glasgow, Edinburgh and Falkirk; elsewhere the area is mostly rural. Hi-tech and computing industries are in evidence.

West Midlands *W.Mid.* Population: 2,555,592.
Former metropolitan county of central England bordered by Staffordshire, Warwickshire and Worcestershire. It comprises the urban complex around the cities of Birmingham and Coventry, and the towns of Wolverhampton, Dudley, Walsall, West Bromwich, Sutton Coldfield and Solihull. The West Midlands developed as a manufacturing and engineering centre which specialised in the metalworking and motor trades. The area around Dudley, Walsall and Wolverhampton became known as the Black Country, with heavy industry centred on the local deposits of coal, iron ore and limestone. Other local trades included glassware, saddlery and lock-making. Birmingham became Britain's second city by specialising in 1001 trades from confectionery to cars, and has developed into the major business, industrial, commercial and cultural centre for the area. As the traditional industries have declined, there has been a shift towards service, leisure and recreation sectors of the economy; several significant corporate service centres and venues, such as the National Exhibition Centre and the Indoor Arena, are in the West Midlands. The area is served by Birmingham International Airport. Rivers include the Tame and the Cole.
Districts: Birmingham; Coventry; Dudley; Sandwell; Solihull; Walsall; Wolverhampton.

West Sussex *W.Suss.* Population: 753,614.
County of S England bounded by Brighton & Hove, East Sussex, Hampshire, Surrey and the English Channel. Main towns are Worthing, Crawley, Bognor Regis, Littlehampton, Horsham, Haywards Heath, East Grinstead, the cathedral city and county town of Chichester, Burgess Hill and Shoreham-by-Sea. N of a level coastal strip run the South Downs, a steep-sided chalk ridge which is thickly wooded in parts. The remaining inland area, The Weald, is largely well-wooded farmland, although there is industrial development around Crawley, Gatwick (London) Airport, Horsham, and Haywards Heath, as well as among the predominantly residential towns on the coast. Tourism is a major activity throughout the county. There are many castles and stately homes, such as Arundel Castle and Goodwood House, the popular seaside resorts of Bognor Regis and Worthing, race courses at Goodwood and Fontwell, Chichester Harbour, which is a centre for yachtsmen and wildfowl, historic Chichester itself, and numerous picturesque villages. The N of the county includes Gatwick (London) Airport. The rivers, none large, include the Adur and Arun, with its tributary the Rother; the Medway rises in the E of the county.
Districts: Adur; Arun; Chichester; Crawley; Horsham; Mid Sussex; Worthing.

West Yorkshire *W.Yorks.* Population: 2,079,211.
Former metropolitan county of N England bordering Derbyshire, Greater Manchester, Lancashire, North Yorkshire and South Yorkshire. It comprises the area around the cities of Leeds, Bradford and Wakefield, and the towns of Huddersfield, Halifax, Dewsbury, Keighley, Batley, Morley, Castleford, Brighouse, Pudsey, Pontefract and Shipley. West Yorkshire developed as a centre for wool and textiles, manufacturing and engineering, creating an industrial urban landscape set against rural moorland. As the traditional industries have declined, the area has undergone regeneration and diversification, moving towards tertiary economic sectors. Leeds is the industrial, administrative, commercial and cultural centre of the area, containing regional government offices and many corporate service centres and head offices. Emerging economic activities across West Yorkshire have included printing, distribution, chemicals, food and drink production, hi-tech industries and financial services. Haworth with its Brontë associations, Holmfirth and the moorlands are the centres of tourism. The area includes Leeds Bradford International Airport. The chief rivers are the Aire and the Calder, while the Wharfe forms its N boundary below Addingham.
Districts: Bradford; Calderdale; Kirklees; Leeds; Wakefield.

Western Isles (Na h-Eileanan an Iar. Also known as Outer Hebrides.) *W.Isles* Population: 26,502.
String of islands off the W coast of Scotland and separated from Skye and the mainland by The Minch. They extend for some 130m/209km from Butt of Lewis in the N, to Barra Head in the S. Stornoway, situated on the Isle of Lewis, is the main town; elsewhere, there are mainly scattered coastal villages and settlements. The chief islands are Isle of Lewis, North Uist, Benbecula, South Uist and Barra. North Harris and South Harris form significant areas in the S part of the Isle of Lewis. The topography of the islands consists of undulating moorland, mountains and lochs. The main industries are fishing, grazing and, on the Isle of Lewis, tweed manufacture. There are airfields with scheduled passenger flights on the Isle of Lewis, Benbecula and Barra.

Wiltshire *Wilts.* Population: 432,973.
County of S England bounded by Bath & North East Somerset, Dorset, Gloucestershire, Hampshire, Oxfordshire, Somerset, South Gloucestershire, Swindon and West Berkshire. Main centres are the cathedral city of Salisbury, the county town of Trowbridge, Chippenham, Warminster, Devizes and Melksham. Wiltshire consists of extensive chalk uplands scattered with prehistoric remains, notably at Avebury and Stonehenge, and interspersed with wide, well-watered valleys. The N of the county is dominated by the Marlborough Downs which are much used for racehorse training, while in the S, the chalk plateau of Salisbury Plain is an important military training area. Between these two upland areas lies the fertile Vale of Pewsey where dairy production and bacon-curing are important agricultural activities. Other industries include electronics, computing, pharmaceuticals, plastics, telecommunications and service sector activities. Wiltshire attracts tourism with its prehistoric remains, stately houses and picturesque market towns and villages. Rivers include the so-called Bristol and Wiltshire Avons, Ebble, Kennet, Nadder, Wylye, and the upper reaches of the Thames.
Districts: Kennet; North Wiltshire; Salisbury; West Wiltshire.

Windsor & Maidenhead *W. & M.* Population: 133,626.
Unitary authority in SE England to the W of Greater London, and bounded by Bracknell Forest, Buckinghamshire, Slough, Surrey and Wokingham. The towns of Maidenhead and Windsor are the main centres for industry, leisure and recreation. The area is particularly noted for its strong Royal connections as it includes Windsor Castle and the former Royal hunting estate of Windsor Great Park. Other popular tourist attractions include Ascot race course, Windsor Legoland and Eton College. The River Thames forms the N boundary.

Wokingham *W'ham* Population: 150,229.
Unitary authority in SE England, to the W of Greater London. The area encompasses Wokingham and is bordered by Bracknell Forest, Buckinghamshire, Hampshire, Oxfordshire, Reading, West Berkshire and Windsor & Maidenhead. The area includes riverside villages in the N, with undulating ridges covered by woodlands and commons in the S. Wokingham is a growing centre for hi-tech and computer industries. The River Thames forms the N border, and the River Blackwater forms the border to the S.

Worcestershire *Worcs.* Population: 542,107.
S midland county of England neighbouring Gloucestershire, Herefordshire, Shropshire, Warwickshire and West Midlands. Main centres are the cathedral city and the county town of Worcester, and the towns of Redditch, Kidderminster, Great Malvern, Bromsgrove, Droitwich Spa, Stourport-on-Severn and Evesham. The urban areas in the N of the county form part of the periphery and commuter belt of the West Midlands conurbation, and attract much of the industrial development. The central and S sections of the county are largely rural, containing the fertile Severn Valley and Vale of Evesham, with market gardening and orchard-growing being the main agricultural activities. Tourism is an important industry, much of it being centred on historic Worcester, with its cathedral, the triennial Three Choirs Festival, Worcester Sauce and china factories. Other popular attractions include boating on the River Severn and visiting the Vale of Evesham whilst the flowers are in full bloom. The main river is the Severn.
Districts: Bromsgrove; Malvern Hills; Redditch; Worcester; Wychavon; Wyre Forest.

Wrexham (Wrecsam). *Wrex.* Population: 128,476.
Unitary authority in NE Wales bordering Denbighshire, Flintshire, Powys and the English counties of Cheshire and Shropshire. Main centres are Wrexham, Rhosllanerchrugog, Gwersyllt, Cefn-mawr and Coedpoeth. The area is mountainous in the SW, containing part of the Berwyn range; the Dee valley lies in the NE. The area was formerly dominated by the iron, coal and limestone industries. Food manufacture, brewing, plastics and hi-tech industries are now important to the local economy. Wrexham is the largest commercial and shopping centre in N Wales. The River Dee flows through the area.

York *York* Population: 181,094.
Unitary authority in N England surrounding the historic cathedral city of York and bordered by East Riding of Yorkshire and North Yorkshire. York is a major archaeological, episcopal, industrial, commercial and cultural centre, situated at the confluence of the River Foss and the River Ouse. The city has a unique history dating from the original Roman military camp, which has led to it becoming one of the main museum and tourist centres in the country. The historic core, situated around the centrepiece of the medieval Minster, is well preserved. Other major attractions include the Jorvik Viking Centre, the medieval city walls and the National Railway Museum. Economic sectors include the confectionery industry, company head offices, Government departmental offices, and research and development establishments. The main river is the Ouse.

WALES Counties
BLAENAU GWENT
BRIDGEND
CAERPHILLY
CARDIFF
CARMARTHENSHIRE
CEREDIGION
CONWY
DENBIGHSHIRE
FLINTSHIRE
GWYNEDD
ISLE OF ANGLESEY
MERTHYR TYDFIL
MONMOUTHSHIRE
NEATH PORT TALBOT
NEWPORT
PEMBROKESHIRE
POWYS
RHONDDA CYNON TAFF
SWANSEA
TORFAEN
VALE OF GLAMORGAN
WREXHAM
ISLE OF ANGLESEY
CONWY
DENBIGHSHIRE
FLINTSHIRE
WREXHAM
GWYNEDD
POWYS
CEREDIGION
WALES
CARMARTHENSHIRE
PEMBROKESHIRE
SWANSEA
NEATH PORT TALBOT
BRIDGEND
RHONDDA CYNON TAFF
MERTHYR TYDFIL
CAERPHILLY
MONMOUTHSHIRE
NEWPORT
CARDIFF
VALE OF GLAMORGAN
CHESHIRE
SHROPSHIRE
HEREFORDSHIRE
SOMERSET
DEVON
CORNWALL
DORSET
Caernarfon Bay
Cardigan Bay
Bristol Channel
ISLES OF SCILLY
ENGLAND
Counties & Districts
BATH AND NORTH EAST SOMERSET
BEDFORDSHIRE
1 North Bedfordshire
2 Mid Bedfordshire
3 South Bedfordshire
BOURNEMOUTH
BRACKNELL FOREST
BRIGHTON & HOVE
BRISTOL
BUCKINGHAMSHIRE
1 Aylesbury Vale
2 Wycombe
3 Chiltern
4 South Buckinghamshire
CAMBRIDGESHIRE
1 Fenland
2 Huntingdonshire
3 East Cambridgeshire
4 South Cambridgeshire
5 Cambridge
CHESHIRE
1 Ellesmere Port & Neston
2 Vale Royal
3 Macclesfield
4 Chester
5 Crewe & Nantwich
6 Congleton
CORNWALL
1 North Cornwall
2 Caradon
3 Restormel
4 Carrick
5 Kerrier
6 Penwith
DERBY
DERBYSHIRE
1 High Peak
2 Derbyshire Dales
3 North East Derbyshire
4 Chesterfield
5 Bolsover
6 Amber Valley
7 Erewash
8 South Derbyshire
DEVON
1 North Devon
2 Torridge
3 Mid Devon
4 East Devon
5 Exeter
6 Teignbridge
7 West Devon
8 South Hams
DORSET
1 North Dorset
2 East Dorset
3 Christchurch
4 Purbeck
5 West Dorset
6 Weymouth & Portland
0 10 20 30 40 kilometres
0 10 20 30 miles
1:1,250,000 20 miles to 1 inch/12.5 km to 1 cm

EAST SUSSEX
1 Lewes
2 Wealden
3 Eastbourne
4 Rother
5 Hastings

ESSEX
1 Uttlesford
2 Braintree
3 Colchester
4 Tendring
5 Maldon
6 Chelmsford
7 Epping Forest
8 Harlow
9 Brentwood
10 Basildon
11 Rochford
12 Castle Point

GLOUCESTERSHIRE
1 Forest of Dean
2 Gloucester
3 Tewkesbury
4 Cheltenham
5 Cotswold
6 Stroud

GREATER LONDON
See pages 152-153 for map of boroughs

HAMPSHIRE
1 Basingstoke & Deane
2 Hart
3 Rushmoor
4 Test Valley
5 Winchester
6 East Hampshire
7 New Forest
8 Eastleigh
9 Fareham
10 Gosport
11 Havant

HEREFORDSHIRE

HERTFORDSHIRE
1 North Hertfordshire
2 Stevenage
3 East Hertfordshire
4 Broxbourne
5 Welwyn Hatfield
6 St Albans
7 Dacorum
8 Three Rivers
9 Watford
10 Hertsmere

ISLE OF WIGHT

ISLES OF SCILLY

KENT
1 Dartford
2 Gravesham
3 Swale
4 Canterbury
5 Thanet
6 Dover
7 Shepway
8 Ashford
9 Maidstone
10 Tonbridge & Malling
11 Sevenoaks
12 Tunbridge Wells

LEICESTER

LEICESTERSHIRE
1 North West Leicestershire
2 Charnwood
3 Melton
4 Harborough
5 Oadby & Wigston
6 Blaby
7 Hinckley & Bosworth

LINCOLNSHIRE
1 West Lindsey
2 Lincoln
3 East Lindsey
4 North Kesteven
5 Boston
6 South Kesteven
7 South Holland

LUTON

MEDWAY

MILTON KEYNES

NORFOLK
1 Kings Lynn & West Norfolk
2 North Norfolk
3 Great Yarmouth
4 Broadland
5 Norwich
6 South Norfolk
7 Breckland

NORTH SOMERSET

NORTHAMPTONSHIRE
1 East Northamptonshire
2 Corby
3 Kettering
4 Daventry
5 Wellingborough
6 Northampton
7 South Northamptonshire

NOTTINGHAMSHIRE
1 Bassetlaw
2 Mansfield
3 Newark & Sherwood
4 Ashfield
5 Gedling
6 Broxtowe
7 Rushcliffe

OXFORDSHIRE
1 Cherwell
2 West Oxfordshire
3 Oxford
4 Vale of White Horse
5 South Oxfordshire

PETERBOROUGH

PLYMOUTH

POOLE

PORTSMOUTH

READING

RUTLAND

SHROPSHIRE
1 Oswestry
2 North Shropshire
3 Shrewsbury & Atcham
4 South Shropshire
5 Bridgnorth

SLOUGH

SOMERSET
1 West Somerset
2 Taunton Deane
3 Sedgemoor
4 Mendip
5 South Somerset

SOUTH GLOUCESTERSHIRE

SOUTHAMPTON

SOUTHEND

STAFFORDSHIRE
1 Newcastle-under-Lyme
2 Staffordshire Moorlands
3 Stafford
4 East Staffordshire
5 South Staffordshire
6 Cannock Chase
7 Lichfield
8 Tamworth

STOKE-ON-TRENT

SUFFOLK
1 Forest Heath
2 St Edmundsbury
3 Mid Suffolk
4 Waveney
5 Suffolk Coastal
6 Ipswich
7 Babergh

SURREY
1 Spelthorne
2 Runnymede
3 Surrey Heath
4 Woking
5 Elmbridge
6 Epsom & Ewell
7 Reigate & Banstead
8 Tandridge
9 Mole Valley
10 Guildford
11 Waverley

SWINDON

TELFORD AND WREKIN

THURROCK

TORBAY

WARWICKSHIRE
1 North Warwickshire
2 Nuneaton & Bedworth
3 Rugby
4 Warwick
5 Stratford-on-Avon

WEST BERKSHIRE

WEST MIDLANDS
(Former Metropolitan County)
1 Walsall
2 Wolverhampton
3 Dudley
4 Sandwell
5 Birmingham
6 Solihull
7 Coventry

WEST SUSSEX
1 Chichester
2 Horsham
3 Crawley
4 Mid Sussex
5 Adur
6 Worthing
7 Arun

WILTSHIRE
1 North Wiltshire
2 Kennet
3 West Wiltshire
4 Salisbury

WINDSOR AND MAIDENHEAD

WOKINGHAM

WORCESTERSHIRE
1 Wyre Forest
2 Bromsgrove
3 Redditch
4 Wychavon
5 Worcester
6 Malvern Hills

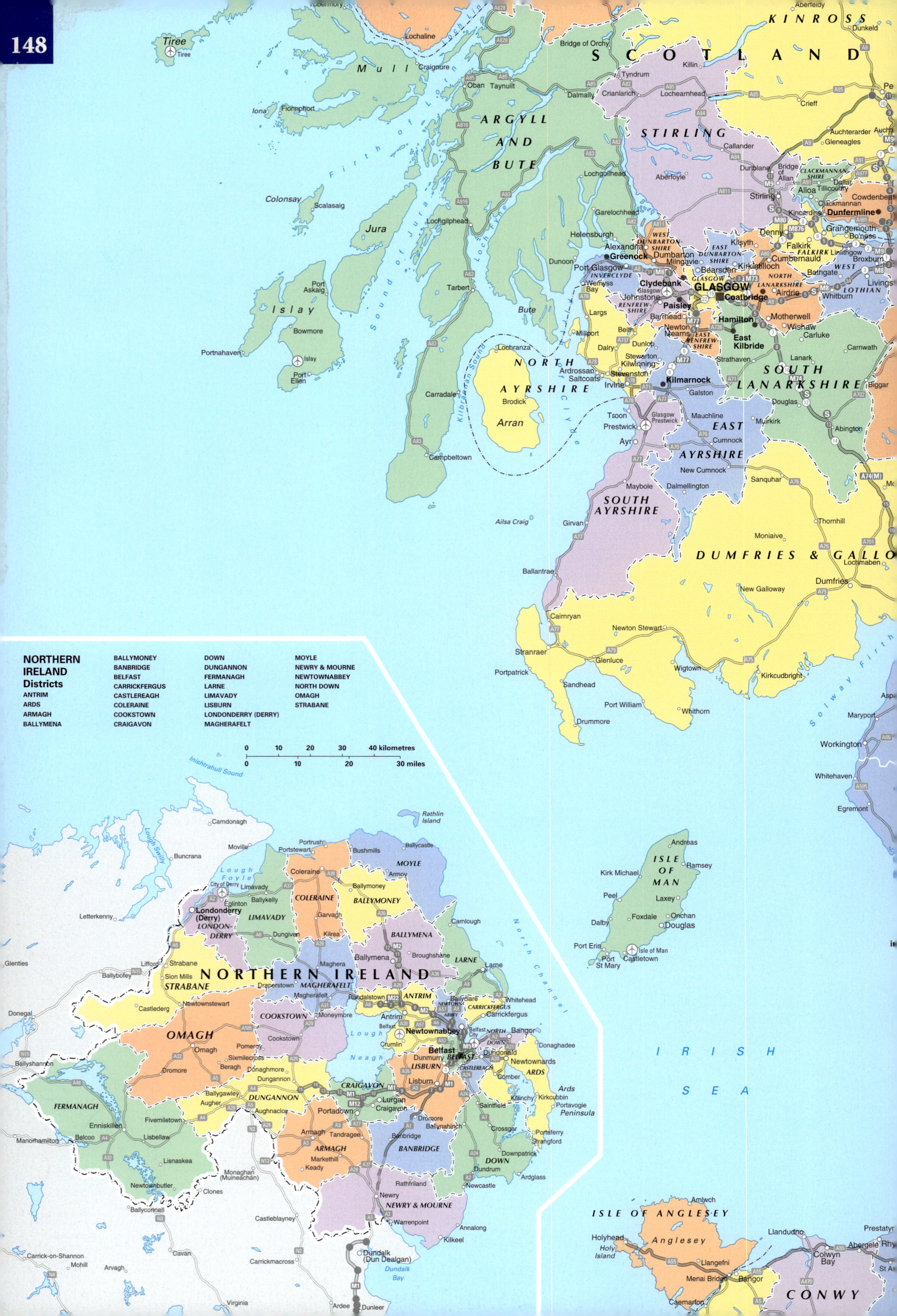
SCOTLAND
KINROSS
ARGYLL AND BUTE
STIRLING
CLACKMANNAN-SHIRE
WEST DUNBARTON-SHIRE
EAST DUNBARTON-SHIRE
FALKIRK
WEST LOTHIAN
INVERCLYDE
RENFREW-SHIRE
GLASGOW
NORTH LANARKSHIRE
EAST RENFREW-SHIRE
NORTH AYRSHIRE
SOUTH LANARKSHIRE
EAST AYRSHIRE
SOUTH AYRSHIRE
DUMFRIES & GALLO
Mull
Iona
Colonsay
Jura
Islay
Tiree
Arran
Bute
Firth of Lorn
Sound of Jura
Loch Fyne
Kilbrannan Sound
Firth of Clyde
Ailsa Craig
Solway Firth
Glasgow
Edinburgh
Dunfermline
Greenock
Clydebank
Paisley
Coatbridge
Hamilton
East Kilbride
Kilmarnock
Stirling
Oban
Campbeltown
Ayr
Dumfries
Stranraer
NORTHERN IRELAND
Districts
ANTRIM
ARDS
ARMAGH
BALLYMENA
BALLYMONEY
BANBRIDGE
BELFAST
CARRICKFERGUS
CASTLEREAGH
COLERAINE
COOKSTOWN
CRAIGAVON
DOWN
DUNGANNON
FERMANAGH
LARNE
LIMAVADY
LISBURN
LONDONDERRY (DERRY)
MAGHERAFELT
MOYLE
NEWRY & MOURNE
NEWTOWNABBEY
NORTH DOWN
OMAGH
STRABANE
0 10 20 30 40 kilometres
0 10 20 30 miles
NORTHERN IRELAND
Londonderry (Derry)
Belfast
Lough Neagh
Lough Foyle
Rathlin Island
Inishtrahull Sound
North Channel
ISLE OF MAN
Douglas
IRISH SEA
ISLE OF ANGLESEY
Anglesey
Holy Island
CONWY
Dundalk (Dun Dealgan)
Dundalk Bay

ENGLAND Counties & Districts

BLACKBURN WITH DARWEN

BLACKPOOL

CHESHIRE
1 Ellesmere Port & Neston
2 Vale Royal
3 Macclesfield
4 Chester
6 Congleton

CUMBRIA
1 Carlisle
2 Allerdale
3 Eden
4 Copeland
5 South Lakeland
6 Barrow-in-Furness

DARLINGTON

DERBYSHIRE
1 High Peak
2 Derbyshire Dales
3 North East Derbyshire
4 Chesterfield
5 Bolsover

DURHAM
1 Chester-le-Street
2 Derwentside
3 Durham
4 Easington
5 Sedgefield
6 Wear Valley
7 Teesdale

EAST RIDING OF YORKSHIRE

GREATER MANCHESTER
(Former Metropolitan County)
1 Wigan
2 Bolton
3 Bury
4 Rochdale
5 Oldham
6 Tameside
7 Stockport
8 Manchester
9 Salford
10 Trafford

HALTON

HARTLEPOOL

ISLE OF MAN

KINGSTON UPON HULL

LANCASHIRE
1 Lancaster
2 Wyre
3 Fylde
4 Preston
5 Ribble Valley
6 Pendle
7 Burnley
8 Rossendale
9 Hyndburn
10 Chorley
11 South Ribble
12 West Lancashire

LINCOLNSHIRE
1 West Lindsey
2 Lincoln
3 East Lindsey
4 North Kesteven

MERSEYSIDE
(Former Metropolitan County)
1 Wirral
2 Sefton
3 Liverpool
4 Knowsley
5 St Helens

MIDDLESBROUGH

NORTH EAST LINCOLNSHIRE

NORTH LINCOLNSHIRE

NORTH YORKSHIRE
1 Scarborough
2 Ryedale
3 Hambleton
4 Richmondshire
5 Craven
6 Harrogate
7 Selby

NORTHUMBERLAND
1 Berwick-upon-Tweed
2 Alnwick
3 Castle Morpeth
4 Wansbeck
5 Blyth Valley
6 Tynedale

NOTTINGHAM

NOTTINGHAMSHIRE
1 Bassetlaw
2 Mansfield
3 Newark & Sherwood
4 Ashfield

REDCAR AND CLEVELAND

SOUTH YORKSHIRE
(Former Metropolitan County)
1 Barnsley
2 Doncaster
3 Rotherham
4 Sheffield

STOCKTON-ON-TEES

TYNE AND WEAR
(Former Metropolitan County)
1 Newcastle upon Tyne
2 North Tyneside
3 South Tyneside
4 Gateshead
5 Sunderland

WARRINGTON

WEST YORKSHIRE
(Former Metropolitan County)
1 Calderdale
2 Bradford
3 Leeds
4 Wakefield
5 Kirklees

YORK

0 10 20 30 40 kilometres
0 10 20 30 miles
1:1,250,000 20 miles to 1 inch/12.5 km to 1 cm

WESTERN ISLES
(NA H-EILEANAN AN IAR)
Port of Ness
Portnaguran
Stornoway
Garrynahine
Lewis
North Harris
Tarbert
South Harris
Rodel
North Uist
Lochmaddy
Benbecula
South Uist
Lochboisdale
Barra
Castlebay
Vatersay
Little Minch
The Minch
Summer Isles
Canna
Rum (Rhum)
Eigg
Coll
Tiree
Skye
Uig
Dunvegan
Portree
Raasay
Inner Sound
Sligachan
Broadford
Kyle of Lochalsh
Kyleakin
Elgol
Ardvasar
Sound of Sleat
Mallaig
Arisaig
Glenfinnan
Fort William
Salen
Tobermory
Lochaline
Mull
Craignure
Iona
Fionnphort
Firth of Lorn
Loch Linnhe
Colonsay
Scalasaig
Jura
Sound of Jura
Islay
Port Askaig
Bowmore
Portnahaven
Port Ellen
Inishtrahull Sound
Carndonagh
Rathlin Island
Durness
Tongue
Bettyhill
Scrabster
Thurso
Halkirk
Rhiconich
Laxford Bridge
Scourie
Sutherland
Kinbrace
Lochinver
Ledmore
Helmsdale
Brora
Golspie
Ullapool
Bonar Bridge
Dornoch Firth
Portmahomack
Aultbea
Poolewe
Gairloch
Easter Ross
HIGHLAND
Wester Ross
Kinlochewe
Achnasheen
Garve
Strathpeffer
Dingwall
Invergordon
Cromarty
Cromarty Firth
Moray Firth
Burghead
Nairn
Fortrose
Inverness
Muir of Ord
Beauly
Shieldaig
Lochcarron
Stromeferry
Drumnadrochit
Grantown-on-Spey
Carrbridge
Aviemore
Invermoriston
Fort Augustus
Invergarry
Kingussie
Newtonmore
Dalwhinnie
Spean Bridge
Kinlochleven
Ballachulish
Rannoch Sta
Kinloch Rannoch
Blair Atholl
Pitlochry
Aberfeldy
PERTH AND KINROSS
SCOTLAND
Bridge of Orchy
Tyndrum
Killin
Crianlarich
Lochearnhead
Crieff
Oban
Taynuilt
Dalmally
ARGYLL AND BUTE
STIRLING
Callander
Auchterarder
Gleneagles
Aberfoyle
Dunblane
Bridge of Allan
CLACKMANNANSHIRE
Alloa
Tillicoultry
Dollar
Stirling
Kincardine
Dunfermline
Grangemouth
Falkirk
FALKIRK
Linlithgow
Denny
Kilsyth
Cumbernauld
Bathgate
WEST LOTHIAN
Whitburn
Lochgoilhead
Lochgilphead
Garelochhead
Helensburgh
WEST DUNBARTONSHIRE
EAST DUNBARTONSHIRE
Alexandria
Dumbarton
Milngavie
Kirkintilloch
Bearsden
Greenock
INVERCLYDE
Port Glasgow
Clydebank
GLASGOW
Coatbridge
Airdrie
NORTH LANARKSHIRE
Dunoon
Wemyss Bay
Johnstone
RENFREWSHIRE
Paisley
Barrhead
Newton Mearns
EAST RENFREWSHIRE
Hamilton
East Kilbride
Motherwell
Wishaw
Carluke
Largs
Millport
Beith
Dunlop
Tarbert
Bute
Lochranza
NORTH AYRSHIRE
Arran
Brodick
Kilbrannan Sound
Firth of Clyde
Dalry
Stewarton
Kilwinning
Ardrossan
Saltcoats
Stevenston
Irvine
Kilmarnock
Galston
Strathaven
Lanark
SOUTH LANARKSHIRE
Douglas
Abington
Carradale
Campbeltown
Troon
Prestwick
Ayr
Mauchline
Muirkirk
EAST AYRSHIRE
Cumnock
New Cumnock
Sanquhar
Maybole
Dalmellington
SOUTH AYRSHIRE
DUMFRIES & G

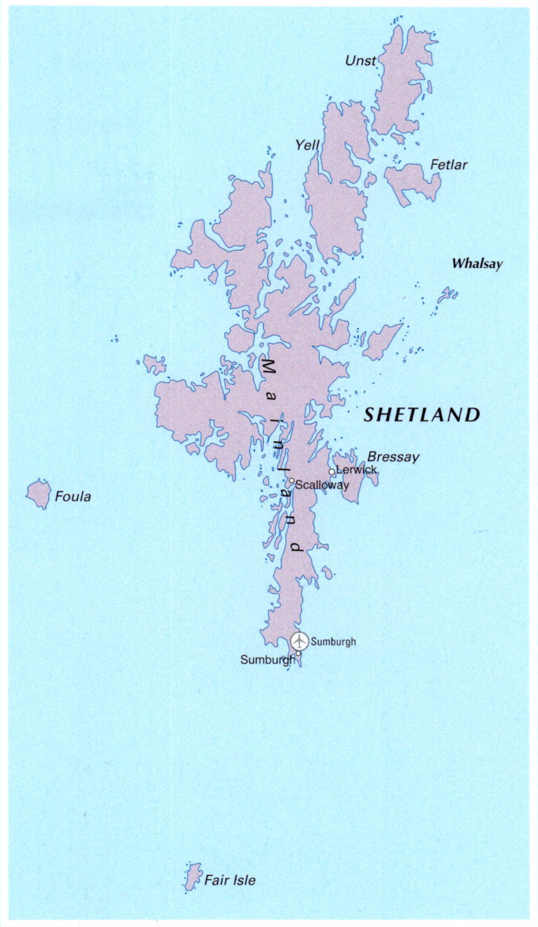

SCOTLAND Councils

ABERDEEN
ABERDEENSHIRE
ANGUS
ARGYLL AND BUTE
CLACKMANNANSHIRE
DUMFRIES AND GALLOWAY
DUNDEE
EAST AYRSHIRE
EAST DUNBARTONSHIRE
EAST LOTHIAN
EAST RENFREWSHIRE
EDINBURGH
FALKIRK
FIFE
GLASGOW
HIGHLAND
INVERCLYDE
MIDLOTHIAN
MORAY
NORTH AYRSHIRE
NORTH LANARKSHIRE
ORKNEY
PERTH AND KINROSS
RENFREWSHIRE
SCOTTISH BORDERS
SHETLAND
SOUTH AYRSHIRE
SOUTH LANARKSHIRE
STIRLING
WEST DUNBARTONSHIRE
WEST LOTHIAN
WESTERN ISLES (NA H-EILEANAN AN IAR)

0 10 20 30 40 kilometres
0 10 20 30 miles
1:1,250,000 20 miles to 1 inch/12.5 km to 1 cm

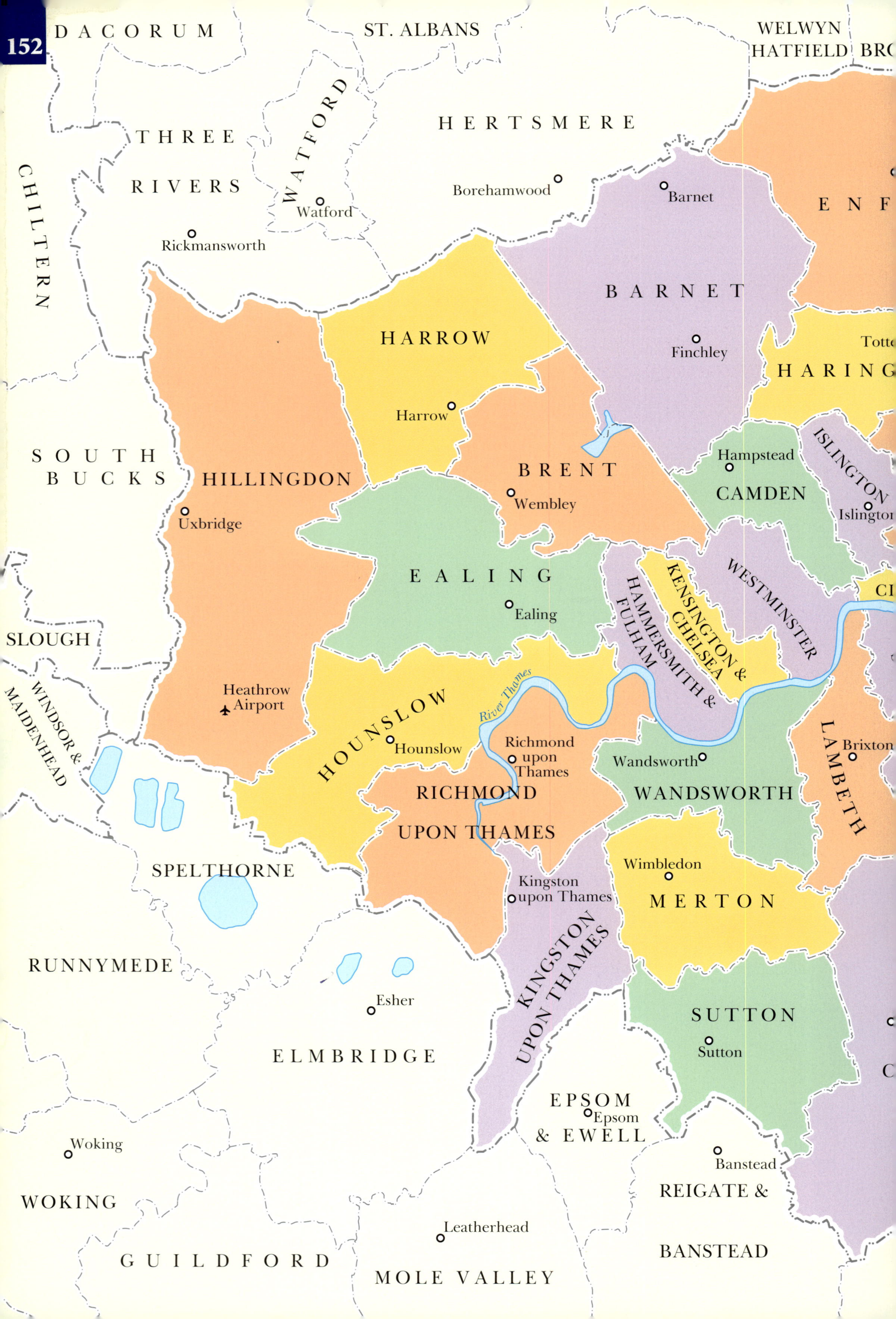
DACORUM
ST. ALBANS
WELWYN HATFIELD
THREE RIVERS
WATFORD
Watford
HERTSMERE
Borehamwood
CHILTERN
Rickmansworth
Barnet
BARNET
HARROW
Harrow
Finchley
HARING
SOUTH BUCKS
HILLINGDON
Uxbridge
BRENT
Wembley
Hampstead
CAMDEN
ISLINGTON
Islington
EALING
Ealing
HAMMERSMITH & FULHAM
KENSINGTON & CHELSEA
WESTMINSTER
SLOUGH
WINDSOR & MAIDENHEAD
Heathrow Airport
HOUNSLOW
Hounslow
River Thames
Richmond upon Thames
RICHMOND UPON THAMES
Wandsworth
WANDSWORTH
LAMBETH
Brixton
SPELTHORNE
Wimbledon
Kingston upon Thames
MERTON
KINGSTON UPON THAMES
RUNNYMEDE
Esher
ELMBRIDGE
SUTTON
Sutton
EPSOM & EWELL
Epsom
Woking
Banstead
WOKING
REIGATE & BANSTEAD
Leatherhead
GUILDFORD
MOLE VALLEY

Waltham Abbey
EPPING FOREST
BRENTWOOD
Brentwood
Edmonton
WALTHAM FOREST
Woodford
REDBRIDGE
Walthamstow
Romford
HAVERING
Ilford
Upminster
Hackney
Dagenham
Barking
West Ham
BARKING & DAGENHAM
TOWER HAMLETS
NEWHAM
Stepney
Beckton
River Thames
THURROCK
London City Airport
Southwark
GREENWICH
Greenwich
Lewisham
BEXLEY
Tilbury
Dartford
DARTFORD
Bexley
LEWISHAM
GRAVESHAM
GREATER LONDON BOROUGHS
BARKING & DAGENHAM
BARNET
BEXLEY
BRENT
BROMLEY
CAMDEN
CORPORATION OF LONDON (CITY)
CROYDON
EALING
ENFIELD
GREENWICH
HACKNEY
HAMMERSMITH & FULHAM
HARINGEY
HARROW
HAVERING
HILLINGDON
HOUNSLOW
ISLINGTON
ROYAL BOROUGH OF KENSINGTON & CHELSEA
ROYAL BOROUGH OF KINGSTON UPON THAMES
LAMBETH
LEWISHAM
MERTON
NEWHAM
REDBRIDGE
RICHMOND UPON THAMES
SOUTHWARK
SUTTON
TOWER HAMLETS
WALTHAM FOREST
WANDSWORTH
WESTMINSTER
Bromley
BROMLEY
SEVENOAKS
TONBRIDGE & MALLING
Sevenoaks

INDEX TO CENTRAL LONDON

General Abbreviations

All	Alley
Allot	Allotments
Amb	Ambulance
App	Approach
Apts	Apartments
Arc	Arcade
Av/Ave	Avenue
Bdy	Broadway
Bk	Bank
Bldgs	Buildings
Boul	Boulevard
Bowl	Bowling
Br/Bri	Bridge
Bus	Business
C of E	Church of England
Cath	Cathedral
Cem	Cemetery
Cen	Central, Centre
Cft	Croft
Cfts	Crofts
Ch	Church
Chyd	Churchyard
Cin	Cinema
Circ	Circus
Cl/Clo	Close
Co	County
Coll	College
Comm	Community
Conv	Convent
Cor	Corner
Coron	Coroners
Cors	Corners
Cotts	Cottages
Cov	Covered
Crem	Crematorium
Cres	Crescent
Ct	Court
Cts	Courts
Ctyd	Courtyard
Dep	Depot
Dev	Development
Dr	Drive
Dws	Dwellings
E	East
Ed	Education
Elec	Electricity
Embk	Embankment
Est	Estate
Ex	Exchange
Exhib	Exhibition
FB	Footbridge
FC	Football Club
Fld	Field
Flds	Fields
Fm	Farm
Gall	Gallery
Gar	Garage
Gdn	Garden
Gdns	Gardens
Govt	Government
Gra	Grange
Grd	Ground
Grds	Grounds
Grn	Green
Grns	Greens
Gro	Grove
Gros	Groves
Gt	Great
Ho	House
Hos	Houses
Hosp	Hospital
Hts	Heights
Ind	Industrial
Int	International
Junct	Junction
La	Lane
Las	Lanes
Lib	Library
Lo	Lodge
Lwr	Lower
Mag	Magistrates
Mans	Mansions
Mem	Memorial
Mkt	Market
Mkts	Markets
Ms	Mews
Mt	Mount
Mus	Museum
N	North
NT	National Trust
Nat	National
PH	Public House
PO	Post Office
Par	Parade
Pas	Passage
Pav	Pavilion
Pk	Park
Pl	Place
Pol	Police
Prec	Precinct
Prim	Primary
Prom	Promenade
Pt	Point
Quad	Quadrant
Rbt	Roundabout
RC	Roman Catholic
Rd	Road
Rds	Roads
Rec	Recreation
Res	Reservoir
Ri	Rise
S	South
Sch	School
Sec	Secondary
Shop	Shopping
Sq	Square
St.	Saint
St	Street
Sta	Station
Sts	Streets
Sub	Subway
Swim	Swimming
TA	Territorial Army
TH	Town Hall
Tenn	Tennis
Ter	Terrace
Thea	Theatre
Trd	Trading
Twr	Tower
Twrs	Towers
Uni	University
Vil	Villa, Villas
Vw	View
W	West
Wd	Wood
Wds	Woods
Wf	Wharf
Wk	Walk
Wks	Works
Yd	Yard

1 Canada Sq **E14** **127** M10

A

Abbey Cl **SW8** **129** K7
Abbey Gdns **NW8** **124** C4
Abbey La **E15** **127** N4
Abbey Orchard St **SW1** **129** K2
Abbey Rd **NW6** **124** B2
Abbey Rd **NW8** **124** C4
Abbey Rd Est **NW8** **124** B3
Abbey St **SE1** **130** C2
Abbeyfield Rd **SE16** **130** G3
Abbot St **E8** **126** D1
Abbots Manor Est **SW1** **129** H3
Abbot's Pl **NW6** **124** B3
Abbotsbury Cl **E15** **127** N4
Abbotsbury Ms **SE15** **130** G9
Abbotshade Rd **SE16** **127** H10
Abbotswood Rd **SE22** **130** C10
Abbott Rd **E14** **127** N7
Abchurch La **EC4** **126** B9
Aberavon Rd **E3** **127** J5
Abercorn Cl **NW8** **124** C5
Abercorn Pl **NW8** **124** C5
Abercorn Way **SE1** **130** E4
Abercrombie St **SW11** **128** E8
Aberdare Gdns **NW6** **124** B2
Aberdeen Pl **NW8** **124** D6
Aberdeen Ter **SE3** **131** P8
Aberdour St **SE1** **130** C3
Aberfeldy St **E14** **127** N8
Abingdon Rd **W8** **128** A2
Abingdon St **SW1** **129** L2
Abingdon Vil **W8** **128** A2
Abinger Gro **SE8** **131** K5
Ablett St **SE16** **130** G4
Acacia Cl **SE8** **131** J3
Acacia Pl **NW8** **124** D4
Acacia Rd **NW8** **124** D4
Academy Gdns **W8** **128** A1
Acanthus Dr **SE1** **130** E4
Acanthus Rd **SW11** **128** G9
Acfold Rd **SW6** **128** B7
Achilles Cl **SE1** **130** E4
Achilles St **SE14** **131** J6
Ackmar Rd **SW6** **128** A7
Ackroyd Dr **E3** **127** K7
Acland Cres **SE5** **130** B10
Acol Rd **NW6** **124** A2
Acorn Wk **SE16** **127** J10
Acre Dr **SE22** **130** E10
Acre La **SW2** **129** L10
Acton Ms **E8** **126** D3
Acton St **WC1** **125** M5
Ada Gdns **E14** **127** P8
Ada Pl **E2** **126** E3
Ada Rd **SE5** **130** C6
Ada St **E8** **126** F3
Adam & Eve Ms **W8** **128** A2
Adam St **WC2** **125** L9
Adams Row **W1** **124** G9
Adamson Rd **NW3** **124** D2
Adderley St **E14** **127** N8
Addington Rd **E3** **127** L5
Addington Sq **SE5** **130** A6
Adelaide Av **SE4** **131** K10
Adelaide Rd **NW3** **124** D2
Adelina Gro **E1** **126** G7
Adeline Pl **WC1** **125** K7
Adler St **E1** **126** E8
Admiral Pl **SE16** **127** J10
Admiral Sq **SW10** **128** D7
Admiral St **SE8** **131** L8
Admiral Wk **W9** **124** A7
Admirals Gate **SE10** **131** M7
Admirals Way **E14** **131** L1
Adolphus St **SE8** **131** K6
Adpar St **W2** **124** D6
Adrian Ms **SW10** **128** B5
Adys Rd **SE15** **130** D9
Afghan Rd **SW11** **128** E8
Agar Gro **NW1** **125** J2
Agar Gro Est **NW1** **125** K2
Agar Pl **NW1** **125** J2
Agar St **WC2** **125** L9
Agdon St **EC1** **125** P6
Agnes St **E14** **127** K8
Ailsa St **E14** **127** N7
Ainger Rd **NW3** **124** F2
Ainsdale Dr **SE1** **130** E4
Ainsley St **E2** **126** F5
Ainsty Est **SE16** **131** H1
Ainsworth Rd **E9** **126** G2
Ainsworth Way **NW8** **124** C3
Air St **W1** **125** J9
Airdrie Cl **N1** **125** M2
Akerman Rd **SW9** **129** P8
Albany Mans **SW11** **128** E6
Albany Rd **SE5** **130** B5
Albany Rd **SE17** **130** B5
Albany St **NW1** **125** H4
Albatross Way **SE16** **131** H1
Albemarle St **W1** **125** H9
Albert Av **SW8** **129** M6
Albert Br **SW3** **128** E5
Albert Br **SW11** **128** E5
Albert Br Rd **SW11** **128** E6
Albert Embk **SE1** **129** L4
Albert Gdns **E1** **127** H8
Albert Gate **SW1** **128** F1
Albert Pl **W8** **128** B1
Albert Sq **SW8** **129** M6
Albert St **NW1** **125** H3
Albert Ter **NW1** **124** G3
Albert Way **SE15** **130** F6
Alberta Est **SE17** **129** P4
Alberta St **SE17** **129** P4
Albion Av **SW8** **129** K8
Albion Dr **E8** **126** D2
Albion Est **SE16** **130** G1
Albion Ms **N1** **125** N3
Albion Ms **W2** **124** E8
Albion Pl **EC1** **125** P7
Albion Riverside Bldg **SW11** **128** E6
Albion Sq **E8** **126** D2
Albion St **SE16** **130** G1
Albion St **W2** **124** E8
Albion Ter **E8** **126** D2
Albion Way **SE13** **131** N10
Albrighton Rd **SE22** **130** C9
Albury St **SE8** **131** L5
Albyn Rd **SE8** **131** L7
Aldbridge St **SE17** **130** C4
Aldebert Ter **SW8** **129** L6
Aldenham St **NW1** **125** K4
Alder Cl **SE15** **130** D5
Aldermanbury **EC2** **126** A8
Alderney Ms **SE1** **130** B2
Alderney Rd **E1** **127** H6
Alderney St **SW1** **129** H3
Aldersgate St **EC1** **126** A7
Alderton Rd **SE24** **130** A9
Aldford St **W1** **124** G10
Aldgate **EC3** **126** C8
Aldgate High St **EC3** **126** D8
Aldsworth Cl **W9** **124** B6
Aldwych **WC2** **125** M9
Alexander Pl **SW7** **128** E3
Alexander Sq **SW3** **128** E3
Alexander St **W2** **124** A8
Alexandra Av **SW11** **128** G7
Alexandra Cl **SE8** **131** K5
Alexandra Cotts **SE14** **131** K7
Alexandra Pl **NW8** **124** C3
Alexandra Rd **NW8** **124** C2
Alexandra St **SE14** **131** J6
Alexis St **SE16** **130** E3
Alfred Ms **W1** **125** K7
Alfred Pl **WC1** **125** K7
Alfred Rd **W2** **124** A7
Alfred St **E3** **127** K5
Alfreda St **SW11** **129** H7
Algernon Rd **NW6** **124** A3
Algernon Rd **SE13** **131** M10
Algiers Rd **SE13** **131** L10
Alice La **E3** **127** K3
Alice St **SE1** **130** C2
Alie St **E1** **126** D8
Aliwal Rd **SW11** **128** E10
All Saints St **N1** **125** M4
Allardyce St **SW4** **129** M10
Allen Edwards Dr **SW8** **129** L7
Allen Rd **E3** **127** K4
Allen St **W8** **128** A2
Allensbury Pl **NW1** **125** K2
Allingham St **N1** **126** A4
Allington St **SW1** **129** H2
Allitsen Rd **NW8** **124** E4
Alloa Rd **SE8** **131** H4
Alloway Rd **E3** **127** J5
Allsop Pl **NW1** **124** F6
Alma Gro **SE1** **130** D3
Alma Sq **NW8** **124** C5
Alma St **E15** **127** P1
Alma St **NW5** **125** H1
Almeida St **N1** **125** P2
Almeric Rd **SW11** **128** F10
Almond Cl **SE15** **130** E8
Almond Rd **SE16** **130** F3
Almorah Rd **N1** **126** B2
Alpha Gro **E14** **131** L1
Alpha Pl **NW6** **124** A4
Alpha Pl **SW3** **128** E5
Alpha Rd **SE14** **131** K7
Alpha St **SE15** **130** E8
Alpine Gro **E9** **126** G2
Alpine Rd **SE16** **131** H4
Alsace Rd **SE17** **130** C4
Alscot Rd **SE1** **130** D3
Alscot Way **SE1** **130** D3
Altenburg Gdns **SW11** **128** F10
Althea St **SW6** **128** B8
Alton St **E14** **127** M7
Alverton St **SE8** **131** K4
Alvey Est **SE17** **130** C3
Alvey St **SE17** **130** C4
Alwyne Pl **N1** **126** A1
Alwyne Rd **N1** **126** A2
Alwyne Sq **N1** **126** A1
Alwyne Vil **N1** **125** P2
Alzette Ho **E2** **127** H5
Ambergate St **SE17** **129** P4
Amberley Rd **W9** **124** A7
Ambrosden Av **SW1** **129** J2
Ambrose Ms **SW11** **128** E8
Ambrose St **SE16** **130** F3
Amelia St **SE17** **129** P4
Amersham Gro **SE14** **131** K6
Amersham Rd **SE14** **131** K6
Amersham Vale **SE14** **131** K6
Amiel St **E1** **126** G6
Amies St **SW11** **128** F9
Amott Rd **SE15** **130** E9
Amoy Pl **E14** **127** L8
Ampton St **WC1** **125** M5
Amsterdam Rd **E14** **131** N2
Amwell St **EC1** **125** N5
Anchor Retail Pk **E1** **126** G6
Anchor St **SE16** **130** F3
Andalus Rd **SW9** **129** L9
Anderson Rd **E9** **127** H1
Anderson St **SW3** **128** F4
Anderton Cl **SE5** **130** B9
Andover Pl **NW6** **124** B4
Andrew St **E14** **127** N8
Andrew's Rd **E8** **126** F3
Anerley St **SW11** **128** F8
Angel Ct **EC2** **126** B8
Angel La **E15** **127** P1
Angel Ms **N1** **125** N4
Angel St **EC1** **126** A8
Angell Pk Gdns **SW9** **129** N9
Angell Rd **SW9** **129** N9
Angler's La **NW5** **125** H1
Anglia Ho **E14** **127** J8
Anglo Rd **E3** **127** K4
Angrave Ct **E8** **126** D3
Angus St **SE14** **131** J6
Anhalt Rd **SW11** **128** E6
Ann La **SW10** **128** D6
Ann Moss Way **SE16** **130** G2
Anna Cl **E8** **126** D3
Annabel Cl **E14** **127** M8
Annie Besant Cl **E3** **127** K3
Annis Rd **E9** **127** J1
Ansdell Rd **SE15** **130** G8
Ansdell St **W8** **128** B2
Anselm Rd **SW6** **128** A5
Anstey Rd **SE15** **130** E9
Antill Rd **E3** **127** J5
Antill Ter **E1** **127** H8
Antrim Gro **NW3** **124** F1
Antrim Mans **NW3** **124** E1
Antrim Rd **NW3** **124** F1
Apollo Pl **SW10** **128** D6
Appleby Rd **E8** **126** E2
Appleby St **E2** **126** D4
Appold St **EC2** **126** C7
Approach Rd **E2** **126** G4
Aquila St **NW8** **124** D4
Arabin Rd **SE4** **131** J10
Aragon Twr **SE8** **131** K3
Arbery Rd **E3** **127** J5
Arbour Sq **E1** **127** H8
Arbuthnot Rd **SE14** **131** H8
Arbutus St **E8** **126** C3
Arcadia St **E14** **127** L8
Arch St **SE1** **130** A2
Archangel St **SE16** **131** H1
Archery Cl **W2** **124** E8
Archibald Ms **W1** **124** G9
Archibald St **E3** **127** L5
Arden Cres **E14** **131** L3
Arden Est **N1** **126** C4
Ardleigh Rd **N1** **126** B1
Argon Ms **SW6** **128** A6
Argyle Rd **E1** **127** H6
Argyle Sq **WC1** **125** L5
Argyle St **WC1** **125** L5
Argyle Way **SE16** **130** E4
Argyll Rd **W8** **128** A1
Argyll St **W1** **125** J8
Arica Ho **SE16** **130** F2
Arica Rd **SE4** **131** J10
Ariel Rd **NW6** **124** A1
Aristotle Rd **SW4** **129** K9
Arklow Rd **SE14** **131** K5
Arlesford Rd **SW9** **129** L9
Arlington Av **N1** **126** A4
Arlington Lo **SW2** **129** M10
Arlington Rd **NW1** **125** H3
Arlington Sq **N1** **126** A3
Arlington St **SW1** **125** J10
Arlington Way **EC1** **125** N5
Armadale Rd **SW6** **128** A6
Armagh Rd **E3** **127** K3
Armoury Rd **SE8** **131** M8
Armstrong Rd **SW7** **128** D2
Arne St **WC2** **125** L8
Arnhem Pl **E14** **131** L2
Arnold Circ **E2** **126** D5
Arnold Est **SE1** **130** D1
Arnold Rd **E3** **127** L5
Arnould Av **SE5** **130** B10
Arnside St **SE17** **130** A5
Arran Wk **N1** **126** A2
Arrow Rd **E3** **127** M5
Artesian Rd **W2** **124** A8
Artillery La **E1** **126** C7
Artillery Row **SW1** **129** K2
Arundel Pl **N1** **125** N1
Arundel Sq **N7** **125** N1
Arundel St **WC2** **125** M9
Ascalon St **SW8** **129** J6
Ash Gro **E8** **126** F3
Ashbridge St **NW8** **124** E6
Ashburn Gdns **SW7** **128** C3
Ashburn Pl **SW7** **128** C3
Ashburnham Gro **SE10** **131** M6
Ashburnham Pl **SE10** **131** M6
Ashburnham Retreat **SE10** **131** M6
Ashburnham Rd **SW10** **128** C6
Ashbury Rd **SW11** **128** F9
Ashby Gro **N1** **126** A2
Ashby Ms **SE4** **131** K8
Ashby Rd **SE4** **131** K8
Ashcombe St **SW6** **128** B8
Ashcroft Rd **E3** **127** J5
Ashdene **SE15** **130** F7
Ashdown Wk **E14** **131** L3
Asher Way **E1** **126** E10
Ashfield St **E1** **126** F7
Ashland Pl **W1** **124** G7
Ashley Cres **SW11** **128** G9
Ashley Gdns **SW1** **129** J2
Ashley Pl **SW1** **129** J2
Ashmead Rd **SE8** **131** L8
Ashmere Gro **SW2** **129** L10
Ashmill St **NW1** **124** E7
Ashmole Pl **SW8** **129** M5
Ashmole St **SW8** **129** M5
Ashmore Cl **SE15** **130** D6
Ashton St **E14** **127** N9
Ashwin St **E8** **126** D1
Ashworth Rd **W9** **124** B5
Aspen Way **E14** **127** L9
Aspinall Rd **SE4** **131** H9
Aspinden Rd **SE16** **130** F3
Assembly Pas **E1** **126** G7
Astbury Rd **SE15** **130** G7
Aste St **E14** **131** N1
Astell St **SW3** **128** E4
Astle St **SW11** **128** G8
Aston St **E14** **127** J8
Astoria Wk **SW9** **129** N9
Astwood Ms **SW7** **128** B3
Asylum Rd **SE15** **130** F6
Athelstane Gro **E3** **127** K4
Atherfold Rd **SW9** **129** L9
Atherstone Ms **SW7** **128** C3
Atherton St **SW11** **128** E8
Athlone St **NW5** **124** G1
Athol Sq **E14** **127** N8
Atlantic Rd **SW9** **129** N10
Atlas Ms **N7** **125** M1
Atley Rd **E3** **127** L3
Atterbury St **SW1** **129** K3
Auburn Cl **SE14** **131** J6
Auckland Rd **SW11** **128** E10
Auden Pl **NW1** **124** G3
Audley Cl **SW11** **128** G9
Audrey St **E2** **126** E4
Augusta St **E14** **127** M8
Augustus St **NW1** **125** H4
Aulton Pl **SE11** **129** N4
Austen Ho **NW6** **124** A5
Austin Friars **EC2** **126** B8
Austin Rd **SW11** **128** G7
Austin St **E2** **126** D5
Austral St **SE11** **129** P3
Autumn St **E3** **127** L3
Avalon Rd **SW6** **128** B7
Ave Maria La **EC4** **125** P8
Aveline St **SE11** **129** N4
Avenue, The **SE10** **131** P6
Avenue Cl **NW8** **124** E3
Avenue Rd **NW3** **124** D2
Avenue Rd **NW8** **124** D2
Avery Row **W1** **125** H9
Avignon Rd **SE4** **131** H9
Avis Sq **E1** **127** H8
Avon Rd **SE4** **131** L9
Avondale Ri **SE15** **130** D9
Avondale Sq **SE1** **130** E4
Avonley Rd **SE14** **130** G6
Avonmouth St **SE1** **130** A2
Aybrook St **W1** **124** G7
Aylesbury Rd **SE17** **130** B4
Aylesbury St **EC1** **125** P6
Aylesford St **SW1** **129** K4
Aylesham Cen, The **SE15** **130** E7
Aylward St **E1** **126** G8
Aylwyn Est **SE1** **130** C2
Ayres St **SE1** **130** A1
Aytoun Pl **SW9** **129** M8
Aytoun Rd **SW9** **129** M8
Azenby Rd **SE15** **130** D8

B

Baches St **N1** **126** B5
Back Ch La **E1** **126** E9
Back Hill **EC1** **125** N6
Bacon Gro **SE1** **130** D2
Bacon St **E1** **126** D6
Bacon St **E2** **126** D6
Baddow Wk **N1** **126** A3
Badsworth Rd **SE5** **130** A6
Bagley's La **SW6** **128** B7
Bagshot St **SE17** **130** C4
Baildon St **SE8** **131** K6
Bainbridge St **WC1** **125** K8
Baker St **NW1** **124** F6
Baker St **W1** **124** F7
Baker's Row **EC1** **125** N6
Bakery Cl **SW9** **129** M7
Balaclava Rd **SE1** **130** D3

Balcombe St **NW1** 124 F6
Balcorne St **E9** 126 G2
Balderton St **W1** 124 G8
Baldock St **E3** 127 M4
Baldwin Cres **SE5** 130 A7
Baldwin Ter **N1** 126 A4
Baldwin's Gdns **EC1** 125 N7
Bale Rd **E1** 127 J7
Balfe St **N1** 125 L4
Balfern St **SW11** 128 E7
Balfour St **SE17** 130 B3
Balladier Wk **E14** 127 M7
Ballance Rd **E9** 127 H1
Ballantine St **SW18** 128 C10
Ballast Quay **SE10** 131 P4
Ballater Rd **SW2** 129 L10
Balls Pond Rd **N1** 126 B1
Balmer Rd **E3** 127 K4
Balmes Rd **N1** 126 B3
Balmoral Gro **N7** 125 M1
Balmore Cl **E14** 127 N8
Balniel Gate **SW1** 129 K4
Baltic St E **EC1** 126 A6
Baltic St W **EC1** 126 A6
Balvaird Pl **SW1** 129 K4
Banbury Rd **E9** 127 H2
Banbury St **SW11** 128 E8
Bancroft Rd **E1** 126 G5
Banfield Rd **SE15** 130 F9
Bank End **SE1** 126 A10
Bank St **E14** 127 L10
Bankside Av **SE13** 131 M9
Bankton Rd **SW2** 129 N10
Banner St **EC1** 126 A6
Bannerman Ho **SW8** 129 M5
Banstead St **SE15** 130 G9
Bantry St **SE5** 130 B6
Barbers Rd **E15** 127 M4
Barbican, The **EC2** 126 A7
Barchester St **E14** 127 M7
Barclay Cl **SW6** 128 A6
Barclay Rd **SW6** 128 A6
Bardsley La **SE10** 131 N5
Barfleur La **SE8** 131 K3
Barford St **N1** 125 N3
Barforth Rd **SE15** 130 F9
Baring St **N1** 126 B3
Bark Pl **W2** 124 B9
Barker Dr **NW1** 125 J2
Barker Ms **SW4** 129 H10
Barker St **SW10** 128 C5
Barkston Gdns **SW5** 128 B3
Barkworth Rd **SE16** 130 F4
Barlborough St **SE14** 130 G6
Barleycorn Way **E14** 127 K9
Barnaby Pl **SW7** 128 D3
Barnard Ms **SW11** 128 E10
Barnard Rd **SW11** 128 E10
Barnby St **NW1** 125 J4
Barnes St **E14** 127 J8
Barnes Ter **SE8** 131 K4
Barnet Gro **E2** 126 E5
Barnfield Pl **E14** 131 L3
Barnham St **SE1** 130 C1
Barnsbury Gro **N7** 125 M2
Barnsbury Pk **N1** 125 N2
Barnsbury Rd **N1** 125 N4
Barnsbury Sq **N1** 125 N2
Barnsbury St **N1** 125 N2
Barnsbury Ter **N1** 125 M2
Barnsdale Av **E14** 131 L3
Barnsley St **E1** 126 F6
Barnwood Cl **W9** 124 B6
Baron St **N1** 125 N4
Barons Pl **SE1** 129 N1
Barrett St **W1** 124 G8
Barriedale **SE14** 131 J7
Barrington Rd **SW9** 129 P9
Barrow Hill Rd **NW8** 124 E4
Barset Rd **SE15** 130 G9
Barter St **WC1** 125 L7
Bartholomew Cl **EC1** 126 A7
Bartholomew Cl **SW18** 128 C10
Bartholomew Rd **NW5** 125 J1
Bartholomew Sq **EC1** 126 A6
Bartholomew St **SE1** 130 B2
Bartholomew Vil **NW5** 125 J1
Bartlett Cl **E14** 127 L8
Basevi Way **SE8** 131 M5
Basil St **SW3** 128 F2
Basing Ct **SE15** 130 D7
Basingdon Way **SE5** 130 B10
Basinghall Av **EC2** 126 B7
Basinghall St **EC2** 126 A7
Basire St **N1** 126 A3
Basnett Rd **SW11** 128 G9
Bassett St **NW5** 124 G1
Bastwick St **EC1** 125 P6
Basuto Rd **SW6** 128 A7
Batavia Rd **SE14** 131 J6
Batchelor St **N1** 125 N4
Bateman's Row **EC2** 126 C6
Bath St **EC1** 126 B5
Bath Ter **SE1** 130 A2
Bathurst St **W2** 124 D9
Batten St **SW11** 128 E9
Battersea Br **SW3** 128 D6
Battersea Br **SW11** 128 D6
Battersea Br Rd **SW11** 128 E6
Battersea Ch Rd **SW11** 128 D7
Battersea High St **SW11** 128 D7
Battersea Pk **SW11** 128 F6
Battersea Pk Rd **SW8** 129 H7
Battersea Pk Rd **SW11** 128 E8
Battle Br La **SE1** 126 C10
Battle Br Rd **NW1** 125 L4
Batty St **E1** 126 E8
Bavent Rd **SE5** 130 A8
Bawtree Rd **SE14** 131 J6
Baxendale St **E2** 126 E5
Baxter Rd **N1** 126 B1
Bayford St **E8** 126 F2
Bayham Pl **NW1** 125 J3
Bayham St **NW1** 125 J3
Bayley St **WC1** 125 K7
Baylis Rd **SE1** 129 N1
Baynes St **NW1** 125 J2
Bayswater Rd **W2** 124 D9
Baythorne St **E3** 127 K7
Baytree Rd **SW2** 129 M10
Bazely St **E14** 127 N9
Beachy Rd **E3** 127 L2
Beacon Gate **SE14** 131 H9
Beaconsfield Rd **SE17** 130 B4
Beak St **W1** 125 J9
Beale Pl **E3** 127 K4
Beale Rd **E3** 127 K3
Beanacre Cl **E9** 127 K1
Bear Gdns **SE1** 126 A10
Bear La **SE1** 125 P10
Beaton Cl **SE15** 130 D7
Beatrice Pl **W8** 128 B2
Beatrice Rd **SE1** 130 E3
Beatson Wk **SE16** 127 H10
Beatty St **NW1** 125 J4
Beauchamp Pl **SW3** 128 E2
Beauchamp Rd **SW11** 128 E10
Beaufort Gdns **SW3** 128 E2
Beaufort St **SW3** 128 D5
Beaufoy Wk **SE11** 129 M3
Beaulieu Cl **SE5** 130 B9
Beaumont Gro **E1** 127 H6
Beaumont Pl **W1** 125 J6
Beaumont Sq **E1** 127 H6
Beaumont St **W1** 124 G7
Beaumont Wk **NW3** 124 F2
Beccles St **E14** 127 K9
Beck Cl **SE13** 131 M7
Beck Rd **E8** 126 F3
Beckett Ho **SW9** 129 L8
Beckway St **SE17** 130 B3
Bedale St **SE1** 126 B10
Bedford Av **WC1** 125 K7
Bedford Gdns **W8** 124 A10
Bedford Ho **SW4** 129 L10
Bedford Pl **WC1** 125 L7
Bedford Rd **SW4** 129 L9
Bedford Row **WC1** 125 M7
Bedford Sq **WC1** 125 K7
Bedford St **WC2** 125 L9
Bedford Way **WC1** 125 K6
Beech St **EC2** 126 A7
Beechmore Rd **SW11** 128 F7
Beechwood Rd **E8** 126 D1
Beehive Cl **E8** 126 D2
Beehive Pl **SW9** 129 N9
Beeston Pl **SW1** 129 H2
Belfort Rd **SE15** 130 G8
Belgrave Gdns **NW8** 124 B3
Belgrave Ms N **SW1** 128 G2
Belgrave Ms S **SW1** 128 G2
Belgrave Ms W **SW1** 128 G2
Belgrave Pl **SW1** 128 G2
Belgrave Rd **SW1** 129 H3
Belgrave Sq **SW1** 128 G2
Belgrave St **E1** 127 H8
Belgrove St **WC1** 125 L5
Belinda Rd **SW9** 129 P9
Belitha Vil **N1** 125 M2
Bell La **E1** 126 D7
Bell St **NW1** 124 E7
Bell Wf La **EC4** 126 A9
Bell Yd **WC2** 125 N8
Bellefields Rd **SW9** 129 M9
Bellenden Rd **SE15** 130 D8
Bellevue Pl **E1** 126 G6
Bells All **SW6** 128 A8
Bellwood Rd **SE15** 131 H10
Belmont Cl **SW4** 129 J9
Belmont Gro **SE13** 131 P9
Belmont Hill **SE13** 131 P9
Belmont Pk **SE13** 131 P10
Belmont Pk Cl **SE13** 131 P10
Belmont Rd **SW4** 129 J9
Belmont St **NW1** 124 G2
Belmore St **SW8** 129 K7
Belsham St **E9** 126 G1
Belsize Av **NW3** 124 D1
Belsize Gro **NW3** 124 E1
Belsize La **NW3** 124 D1
Belsize Pk **NW3** 124 D1
Belsize Pk Gdns **NW3** 124 E1
Belsize Rd **NW6** 124 B3
Belsize Sq **NW3** 124 D1
Belsize Ter **NW3** 124 D1
Belton Way **E3** 127 L7
Beltran Rd **SW6** 128 B8
Belvedere Ms **SE15** 130 G9
Belvedere Pl **SE1** 129 P1
Belvedere Rd **SE1** 125 M10
Belvedere Twr, The **SW10** 128 C7
Bemerton Est **N1** 125 M2
Bemerton St **N1** 125 M3
Ben Jonson Rd **E1** 127 J7
Benbow St **SE8** 131 L5
Benedict Rd **SW9** 129 M9
Bengeworth Rd **SE5** 130 A9
Benham Cl **SW11** 128 D9
Benhill Rd **SE5** 130 B6
Benjamin Cl **E8** 126 E3
Benjamin St **EC1** 125 P7
Benledi St **E14** 127 P8
Benn St **E9** 127 J1
Bennett Gro **SE13** 131 M7
Bennett Rd **SW9** 129 N8
Bentham Rd **E9** 127 H1
Bentinck St **W1** 124 G8
Benworth St **E3** 127 K5
Berger Rd **E9** 127 H1
Berkeley Ho **E3** 127 L6
Berkeley Sq **W1** 125 H9
Berkeley St **W1** 125 H9
Berkley Rd **NW1** 124 F2
Berkshire Rd **E9** 127 K1
Bermondsey St **SE1** 130 C1
Bermondsey Wall E **SE16** 130 E1
Bermondsey Wall W **SE16** 130 E1
Bernard St **WC1** 125 L6
Bernays Gro **SW9** 129 M10
Berners Ms **W1** 125 J7
Berners Pl **W1** 125 J8
Berners Rd **N1** 125 N4
Berners St **W1** 125 J7
Bernhardt Cres **NW8** 124 E6
Berry St **EC1** 125 P6
Berryfield Rd **SE17** 129 P4
Berthon St **SE8** 131 L6
Bertrand St **SE13** 131 M9
Berwick St **W1** 125 J8
Bessborough Gdns **SW1** 129 K4
Bessborough Pl **SW1** 129 K4
Bessborough St **SW1** 129 K4
Bessemer Rd **SE5** 130 A8
Besson St **SE14** 130 G7
Bestwood St **SE8** 131 H3
Bethnal Grn Est **E2** 126 G5
Bethnal Grn Rd **E1** 126 D6
Bethnal Grn Rd **E2** 126 D6
Bethwin Rd **SE5** 129 P6
Betterton St **WC2** 125 L8
Bevan St **N1** 126 A3
Bevenden St **N1** 126 B5
Beverley Ct **SE4** 131 K9
Bevington St **SE16** 130 E1
Bevis Marks **EC3** 126 C8
Bewdley St **N1** 125 N2
Bewick Ms **SE15** 130 F6
Bewick St **SW8** 129 H8
Bianca Rd **SE15** 130 D5
Bickenhall St **W1** 124 F7
Bicknell Rd **SE5** 130 A9
Bidborough St **WC1** 125 K5
Bidbury Cl **SE15** 130 C5
Biddulph Rd **W9** 124 B5
Bidwell St **SE15** 130 F7
Biggerstaff Rd **E15** 127 N3
Bigland St **E1** 126 F8
Billing Pl **SW10** 128 B6
Billing Rd **SW10** 128 B6
Billing St **SW10** 128 B6
Billingford Cl **SE4** 131 H10
Billington Rd **SE14** 131 H6
Billiter St **EC3** 126 C8
Billson St **E14** 131 N3
Bina Gdns **SW5** 128 C3
Binfield Rd **SW4** 129 L7
Bingfield St **N1** 125 L3
Bingham St **N1** 126 B1
Binney St **W1** 124 G8
Birchfield St **E14** 127 L9
Birchin La **EC3** 126 B8
Birchington Rd **NW6** 124 A3
Bird in Bush Rd **SE15** 130 E6
Birdcage Wk **SW1** 129 J1
Birdhurst Rd **SW18** 128 C10
Birdsfield La **E3** 127 K3
Birkbeck St **E2** 126 F5
Birkenhead St **WC1** 125 L5
Birley St **SW11** 128 G8
Biscoe Way **SE13** 131 P9
Bishop St **N1** 126 A3
Bishops Br **W2** 124 C8
Bishops Br Rd **W2** 124 B8
Bishop's Rd **SW11** 128 E6
Bishops Ter **SE11** 129 N3
Bishops Way **E2** 126 F4
Bishopsgate **EC2** 126 C8
Bisson Rd **E15** 127 N4
Black Friars La **EC4** 125 P9
Black Prince Rd **SE1** 129 M3
Black Prince Rd **SE11** 129 M3
Blackburn Rd **NW6** 124 B1
Blackburne's Ms **W1** 124 G9
Blackfriars Br **EC4** 125 P9
Blackfriars Br **SE1** 125 P9
Blackfriars Rd **SE1** 125 P10
Blackheath Av **SE10** 131 P6
Blackheath Hill **SE10** 131 N7
Blackheath Ri **SE13** 131 N8
Blackheath Rd **SE10** 131 M7
Blackhorse Rd **SE8** 131 J4
Blacklands Ter **SW3** 128 F3
Blackpool Rd **SE15** 130 F8
Blackstone Est **E8** 126 F2
Blackthorn St **E3** 127 L6
Blacktree Ms **SW9** 129 N9
Blackwall Trd Est **E14** 127 P7
Blackwall Tunnel **E14** 127 P10
Blackwall Tunnel Northern App **E3** 127 L4
Blackwall Tunnel Northern App **E14** 127 L4
Blackwall Way **E14** 127 N9
Blackwood St **SE17** 130 B4
Blair Cl **N1** 126 A1
Blair St **E14** 127 N8
Blake Gdns **SW6** 128 B7
Blaker Rd **E15** 127 N3
Blakes Rd **SE15** 130 C6
Blanchard Way **E8** 126 E1
Blanchedowne **SE5** 130 B10
Blandford Sq **NW1** 124 E6
Blandford St **W1** 124 G7
Blantyre St **SW10** 128 D6
Blashford **NW3** 124 F2
Blasker Wk **E14** 131 L4
Blenheim Gro **SE15** 130 E8
Blenheim Rd **NW8** 124 C4
Blenheim Ter **NW8** 124 C4
Blessington Cl **SE13** 131 P9
Blessington Rd **SE13** 131 P9
Bletchley Ct **N1** 126 B4
Bletchley St **N1** 126 A4
Bliss Cres **SE13** 131 M8
Blissett St **SE10** 131 N7
Blithfield St **W8** 128 B2
Blomfield Rd **W9** 124 C7
Blomfield St **EC2** 126 B7
Blomfield Vil **W2** 124 B7
Blondel St **SW11** 128 G8
Blondin St **E3** 127 L4
Bloomfield Pl **W1** 125 H9
Bloomfield Ter **SW1** 128 G4
Bloomsbury Pl **WC1** 125 L7
Bloomsbury Sq **WC1** 125 L7
Bloomsbury St **WC1** 125 K7
Bloomsbury Way **WC1** 125 L8
Blossom St **E1** 126 C7
Blount St **E14** 127 J8
Blucher Rd **SE5** 130 A6
Blue Anchor La **SE16** 130 E3
Blue Anchor Yd **E1** 126 E9
Blundell St **N7** 125 L2
Blythe St **E2** 126 F5
Boardwalk Pl **E14** 127 N10
Boathouse Wk **SE15** 130 D6
Bobbin Cl **SW4** 129 J9
Bocking St **E8** 126 F3
Bohemia Pl **E8** 126 F1
Bohn Rd **E1** 127 J7
Bolden St **SE8** 131 M8
Bolina Rd **SE16** 130 G4
Bolingbroke Gro **SW11** 128 E10
Bolingbroke Wk **SW11** 128 D6
Bolney St **SW8** 129 M6
Bolsover St **W1** 125 H6
Bolton Cres **SE5** 129 P5
Bolton Gdns **SW5** 128 B4
Bolton Gdns Ms **SW10** 128 B4
Bolton Rd **NW8** 124 B3
Bolton St **W1** 125 H10
Boltons, The **SW10** 128 C4
Boltons Pl **SW5** 128 C4
Bombay St **SE16** 130 F3
Bonar Rd **SE15** 130 E6
Bond Ct **EC4** 126 B8
Bondway **SW8** 129 L5
Bonfield Rd **SE13** 131 N10
Bonhill St **EC2** 126 B6
Bonita Ms **SE4** 131 H9
Bonner Rd **E2** 126 G4
Bonner St **E2** 126 G4
Bonnington Sq **SW8** 129 M5
Bonny St **NW1** 125 J2
Bonsor St **SE5** 130 C6
Boot St **N1** 126 C5
Borland Rd **SE15** 130 G10
Borough High St **SE1** 130 A1
Borough Rd **SE1** 129 P2
Borthwick St **SE8** 131 L4
Boscobel Pl **SW1** 128 G3
Boscobel St **NW8** 124 D6
Boston Pl **NW1** 124 F6
Boswell St **WC1** 125 L7
Boulcott St **E1** 127 H8
Boulevard, The **SW6** 128 C7
Boundary La **SE17** 130 A5
Boundary Rd **NW8** 124 B3
Boundary St **E2** 126 D6
Bourdon St **W1** 125 H9
Bourne Est **EC1** 125 N7
Bourne St **SW1** 128 G3
Bourne Ter **W2** 124 B7
Bournemouth Cl **SE15** 130 E8
Bournemouth Rd **SE15** 130 E8
Bousfield Rd **SE14** 131 H8
Boutflower Rd **SW11** 128 E10
Bouverie Pl **W2** 124 D8
Bouverie St **EC4** 125 N8
Bovingdon Rd **SW6** 128 B7
Bow Back Rivers Wk **E15** 127 M2
Bow Br Est **E3** 127 M5
Bow Common La **E3** 127 K6
Bow Ind Pk **E15** 127 L2
Bow La **EC4** 126 A8
Bow Rd **E3** 127 K5
Bow St **WC2** 125 L8
Bowden St **SE11** 129 N4
Bowditch **SE8** 131 K4
Bowen St **E14** 127 M8
Bower St **E1** 127 H8
Bowerdean St **SW6** 128 B7
Bowerman Av **SE14** 131 J5
Bowhill Cl **SW9** 129 N6
Bowl Ct **EC2** 126 C6
Bowland Rd **SW4** 129 K10
Bowling Grn La **EC1** 125 N6
Bowling Grn Pl **SE1** 130 B1
Bowling Grn St **SE11** 129 N5
Bowood Rd **SW11** 128 G10
Bowsprit Pt **E14** 131 L2
Bowyer Pl **SE5** 130 B6
Bowyer St **SE5** 130 A6
Boyd St **E1** 126 E8
Boyfield St **SE1** 129 P1
Boyne Rd **SE13** 131 N9
Boyson Rd **SE17** 130 B5
Brabazon St **E14** 127 M8
Brabourn Gro **SE15** 130 G8
Brackley Av **SE15** 130 F9
Bracklyn St **N1** 126 B4
Bradbourne St **SW6** 128 A8
Bradenham Cl **SE17** 130 B5
Bradmead **SW8** 129 H6
Bradstock Rd **E9** 127 H1
Bradwell St **E1** 127 H5
Brady St **E1** 126 F6
Braes St **N1** 125 P2
Braganza St **SE17** 129 P4
Braham St **E1** 126 D8
Braintree St **E2** 126 G5
Braithwaite Twr **W2** 124 D7
Bramah Grn **SW9** 129 N7
Bramcote Gro **SE16** 130 G4
Bramerton St **SW3** 128 E5
Bramford Rd **SW18** 128 C10
Bramham Gdns **SW5** 128 B4
Bramlands Cl **SW11** 128 E9
Bramshaw Rd **E9** 127 H1
Bramwell Ms **N1** 125 M3
Branch Pl **N1** 126 B3
Branch Rd **E14** 127 J9
Branch St **SE15** 130 C6
Brand St **SE10** 131 N6
Brandon Est **SE17** 129 P5
Brandon Rd **N7** 125 L2
Brandon St **SE17** 130 A3
Brangton Rd **SE11** 129 M4
Branscombe St **SE13** 131 M9
Brassey Sq **SW11** 128 G9
Braxfield Rd **SE4** 131 J10
Bray **NW3** 124 E2
Bray Pl **SW3** 128 F3
Brayards Rd **SE15** 130 F8
Brayburne Av **SW4** 129 J8
Bread St **EC4** 126 A9
Breakspears Rd **SE4** 131 K9
Bream St **E3** 127 L2
Bream's Bldgs **EC4** 125 N8
Breer St **SW6** 128 B9
Bremner Rd **SW7** 128 C1
Brendon St **W1** 124 E8
Brenthouse Rd **E9** 126 F2
Brenton St **E14** 127 J8
Bressenden Pl **SW1** 129 H2
Brewer St **W1** 125 J9
Brewery Rd **N7** 125 L2
Brewhouse La **E1** 126 F10
Brewhouse Wk **SE16** 127 J10
Brewster Ho **E14** 127 K9
Briant St **SE14** 131 H7
Brick La **E1** 126 D7
Brick La **E2** 126 D5
Brick St **W1** 125 H10
Bricklayer's Arms Distribution Cen **SE1** 130 C3
Bride St **N7** 125 M1
Bridewain St **SE1** 130 D2
Bridge App **NW1** 124 G2
Bridge La **SW11** 128 E7
Bridge Meadows **SE14** 131 H5
Bridge Pl **SW1** 129 H3
Bridge Rd **E15** 127 P2
Bridge St **SW1** 129 L1
Bridgefoot **SE1** 129 L4
Bridgeman Rd **N1** 125 M2
Bridgeman St **NW8** 124 E4
Bridgend Rd **SW18** 128 C10
Bridges Ct **SW11** 128 D9
Bridgeway St **NW1** 125 J4
Bridgwater Rd **E15** 127 N3
Bridport Pl **N1** 126 B4
Brief St **SE5** 129 P7
Bright St **E14** 127 M8
Brightlingsea Pl **E14** 127 K9
Brighton Ter **SW9** 129 M10
Brill Pl **NW1** 125 K4
Brindley St **SE14** 131 K7
Brinklow Ho **W2** 124 B7
Brinkworth Way **E9** 127 K1
Brion Pl **E14** 127 N7
Brisbane St **SE5** 130 B6
Bristol Gdns **W9** 124 B6
Britannia Rd **E14** 131 L3
Britannia Rd **SW6** 128 B6
Britannia Row **N1** 125 P3
Britannia St **WC1** 125 M5
Britannia Wk **N1** 126 B5
British St **E3** 127 K5
Britten St **SW3** 128 E4
Britton St **EC1** 125 P6
Brixton Oval **SW2** 129 N10
Brixton Rd **SW9** 129 N8
Brixton Sta Rd **SW9** 129 N10
Broad La **EC2** 126 C7
Broad Sanctuary **SW1** 129 K1
Broad Wk **NW1** 125 H5
Broad Wk **W1** 124 G10
Broad Wk, The **W8** 124 B10
Broadfield La **NW1** 125 L2
Broadhinton Rd **SW4** 129 H9
Broadhurst Gdns **NW6** 124 B1
Broadley St **NW8** 124 E7
Broadley Ter **NW1** 124 E6
Broadwalk Ct **W8** 124 A10
Broadwall **SE1** 125 N10
Broadway **E15** 127 P2
Broadway **SW1** 129 K2
Broadway Mkt **E8** 126 F3
Broadwick St **W1** 125 J8
Brock Pl **E3** 127 M6
Brockham St **SE1** 130 A2
Brockill Cres **SE4** 131 J10
Brocklehurst St **SE14** 131 H6
Brockley Footpath **SE15** 130 G10
Brockley Gdns **SE4** 131 K8
Brockley Rd **SE4** 131 K9
Brodlove La **E1** 127 H9
Broke Wk **E8** 126 E3
Brokesley St **E3** 127 K6
Bromar Rd **SE5** 130 C9
Bromell's Rd **SW4** 129 J10
Bromfelde Rd **SW4** 129 K8
Bromfelde Wk **SW4** 129 K8
Bromfield St **N1** 125 N4
Bromley Hall Rd **E14** 127 N7
Bromley High St **E3** 127 M5
Bromley St **E1** 127 H7
Brompton Pk Cres **SW6** 128 B5
Brompton Pl **SW3** 128 E2
Brompton Rd **SW1** 128 E2
Brompton Rd **SW3** 128 E2
Brompton Rd **SW7** 128 E2
Brompton Sq **SW3** 128 E2
Bromyard Ho **SE15** 130 F6
Bronte Ho **NW6** 124 A5
Bronti Cl **SE17** 130 A4
Bronze St **SE8** 131 L6
Brook Dr **SE11** 129 N3
Brook Gate **W1** 124 F9
Brook St **W1** 125 H8
Brook St **W2** 124 D9
Brookbank Rd **SE13** 131 L9
Brooke St **EC1** 125 N7
Brookfield Rd **E9** 127 J1
Brookmill Rd **SE8** 131 L7
Brook's Ms **W1** 125 H9
Brooksbank St **E9** 126 G1
Brooksby St **N1** 125 N2
Broome Way **SE5** 130 B6
Broomfield St **E14** 127 L7
Broomgrove Rd **SW9** 129 M8
Broomhouse La **SW6** 128 A8
Broomhouse Rd **SW6** 128 A8
Brougham Rd **E8** 126 E3
Brougham St **SW11** 128 F8
Broughton Dr **SW9** 129 N10
Broughton Rd **SW6** 128 B8

Broughton St SW8 128 G8
Brown Hart Gdns W1 124 G9
Brown St W1 124 F8
Brownfield St E14 127 M8
Browning St SE17 130 A4
Brownlow Ms WC1 125 M6
Brownlow Rd E8 126 D3
Brown's Bldgs EC3 126 C8
Broxwood Way NW8 124 E3
Bruce Rd E3 127 M5
Bruford Ct SE8 131 L5
Brune St E1 126 D7
Brunel Est W2 124 A7
Brunel Rd SE16 130 G1
Brunswick Ct SE1 130 C1
Brunswick Gdns W8 124 A10
Brunswick Pk SE5 130 B7
Brunswick Pl N1 126 B5
Brunswick Pl NW1 124 G6
Brunswick Quay SE16 131 H2
Brunswick Sq WC1 125 L6
Brunswick Vil SE5 130 C7
Brunton Pl E14 127 J8
Brushfield St E1 126 C7
Brussels Rd SW11 128 D10
Bruton La W1 125 H9
Bruton Pl W1 125 H9
Bruton St W1 125 H9
Bryan Rd SE16 131 K1
Bryanston Pl W1 124 F7
Bryanston Sq W1 124 F7
Bryanston St W1 124 F8
Bryant Ct E2 126 D4
Bryant St E15 127 P2
Brymay Cl E3 127 L4
Brynmaer Rd SW11 128 F7
Buchan Rd SE15 130 G9
Buck St NW1 125 H2
Buckfast St E2 126 E5
Buckhurst St E1 126 F6
Buckingham Gate SW1 129 J2
Buckingham Palace Rd SW1 129 H3
Buckingham Rd N1 126 C1
Buckland Cres NW3 124 D2
Buckland St N1 126 B4
Bucklersbury EC4 126 B8
Buckmaster Rd SW11 128 E10
Bucknall St WC2 125 K8
Bucknell Cl SW2 129 M10
Buckner Rd SW2 129 M10
Buckters Rents SE16 127 J10
Budge's Wk W2 124 C9
Bulinga St SW1 129 K3
Bullace Row SE5 130 B6
Bullards Pl E2 127 H5
Bullen St SW11 128 E8
Buller Cl SE15 130 E6
Bullivant St E14 127 N9
Bulmer Pl W11 124 A10
Bulstrode St W1 124 G8
Bunhill Row EC1 126 B6
Bunhouse Pl SW1 128 G4
Bunning Way N7 125 L2
Burbage Cl SE1 130 B2
Burcham St E14 127 M8
Burchell Rd SE15 130 F7
Burder Cl N1 126 C1
Burdett Rd E3 127 K6
Burdett Rd E14 127 K6
Burford Rd E15 127 P2
Burge St SE1 130 B3
Burgess Business Pk SE5 130 B6
Burgess St E14 127 L7
Burgh St N1 125 P4
Burgos Gro SE10 131 M7
Burgoyne Rd SW9 129 M9
Burlington Arc W1 125 J9
Burlington Gdns W1 125 J9
Burnaby St SW10 128 C6
Burne St NW1 124 E7
Burney St SE10 131 N6
Burnham NW3 124 E2
Burnham St E2 126 G5
Burnley Rd SW9 129 M8
Burns Rd SW11 128 F8
Burnsall St SW3 128 E4
Burnside Cl SE16 127 H10
Burnthwaite Rd SW6 128 A6
Burr Cl E1 126 E10
Burrell St SE1 125 P10
Burrells Wf Sq E14 131 M4
Burrow Rd SE22 130 C10
Burslem St E1 126 E8
Burton La SW9 129 N8
Burton Rd SW9 129 P8
Burton St WC1 125 K5
Burwell Wk E3 127 L6
Burwood Pl W2 124 E8
Bury Pl WC1 125 L7
Bury St EC3 126 C8
Bury St SW1 125 J10
Bury Wk SW3 128 E4
Busby Pl NW5 125 K1
Bush Rd E8 126 F3
Bush Rd SE8 131 H3
Bushberry Rd E9 127 J1
Bushey Hill Rd SE5 130 C7
Bushwood Dr SE1 130 D3
Butcher Row E1 127 H9
Butcher Row E14 127 H9
Bute St SW7 128 D3
Butlers Wf SE1 126 D10
Buttermere Wk E8 126 D1
Buttesland St N1 126 B5
Buxhall Cres E9 127 K1
Buxted Rd E8 126 D2
Buxted Rd SE22 130 C10
Buxton Ms SW4 129 K8
Buxton St E1 126 D6
Byam St SW6 128 C8
Byfield Cl SE16 131 J1
Bygrove St E14 127 M8
Byng Pl WC1 125 K6
Byng St E14 131 L1
Byron Cl E8 126 E3
Bythorn St SW9 129 M9
Byward St EC3 126 C9
Bywater Pl SE16 127 J10
Bywater St SW3 128 F4

C

Cabbell St NW1 124 E7
Cable St E1 126 E9
Cabot Pl E14 127 L10
Cabot Sq E14 127 L10
Cabul Rd SW11 128 E8
Cade Rd SE10 131 P7
Cadet Dr SE1 130 E3
Cadiz St SE17 130 A4
Cadogan Gdns SW3 128 F3
Cadogan Gate SW1 128 F3
Cadogan La SW1 128 G2
Cadogan Pl SW1 128 F2
Cadogan Sq SW1 128 F2
Cadogan St SW3 128 F3
Cadogan Ter E9 127 K1
Cahir St E14 131 M3
Calabria Rd N5 125 P1
Calais St SE5 129 P7
Caldecot Rd SE5 130 A8
Caldwell St SW9 129 M6
Cale St SW3 128 E4
Caledonia St N1 125 L4
Caledonian Rd N1 125 M4
Caledonian Wf E14 131 P3
Callendar Rd SW7 128 D2
Callow St SW3 128 D5
Calshot St N1 125 M4
Calthorpe St WC1 125 M6
Calvert Av E2 126 C5
Calverton SE5 130 C5
Calvin St E1 126 D6
Calypso Cres SE15 130 D6
Calypso Way SE16 131 K2
Cam Rd E15 127 P3
Camberwell Ch St SE5 130 B7
Camberwell Glebe SE5 130 B7
Camberwell Grn SE5 130 B7
Camberwell Gro SE5 130 B7
Camberwell New Rd SE5 129 N6
Camberwell Rd SE5 130 A5
Camberwell Sta Rd SE5 130 A7
Cambria Rd SE5 130 A9
Cambria St SW6 128 B6
Cambridge Av NW6 124 A4
Cambridge Circ WC2 125 K8
Cambridge Cres E2 126 F4
Cambridge Gdns NW6 124 A4
Cambridge Heath Rd E1 126 F4
Cambridge Heath Rd E2 126 F4
Cambridge Pl W8 128 B1
Cambridge Rd NW6 124 A5
Cambridge Rd SW11 128 F7
Cambridge Sq W2 124 E8
Cambridge St SW1 129 H4
Camden High St NW1 125 H3
Camden Ms NW1 125 K1
Camden Pk Rd NW1 125 K1
Camden Pas N1 125 P3
Camden Rd NW1 125 J3
Camden Sq NW1 125 K1
Camden St NW1 125 H2
Camden Wk N1 125 P3
Camdenhurst St E14 127 J8
Camera Pl SW10 128 D5
Camilla Rd SE16 130 F3
Camlet St E2 126 D6
Camley St NW1 125 K2
Camomile St EC3 126 C8
Campana Rd SW6 128 A7
Campbell Rd E3 127 L5
Campden Gro W8 128 A1
Campden Hill W8 128 A1
Campden Hill Gdns W8 124 A10
Campden Hill Rd W8 124 A10
Campden St W8 124 A10
Camplin St SE14 131 H6
Canada Est SE16 130 G2
Canada Sq E14 127 M10
Canada St SE16 131 H1
Canal App SE8 131 J5
Canal Boul NW1 125 K1
Canal Cl E1 127 J6
Canal Gro SE15 130 E5
Canal Path E2 126 D3
Canal St SE5 130 B5
Canal Wk N1 126 B3
Cancell Rd SW9 129 N7
Candahar Rd SW11 128 E8
Candle Gro SE15 130 F9
Candy St E3 127 K3
Canfield Gdns NW6 124 C2
Canning Cross SE5 130 C8
Canning Pas W8 128 C2
Canning Pl W8 128 C2
Cannon Dr E14 127 L9
Cannon St EC4 126 A8
Cannon St Rd E1 126 F8
Cannon Wf Business Cen SE8 131 J3
Canon Beck Rd SE16 130 G1
Canon Row SW1 129 L1
Canon St N1 126 A3
Canonbury Cres N1 126 A2
Canonbury Gro N1 126 A2
Canonbury La N1 125 P2
Canonbury Pk N N1 126 A1
Canonbury Pk S N1 126 A1
Canonbury Pl N1 125 P1
Canonbury Rd N1 125 P1
Canonbury Sq N1 125 P2
Canonbury St N1 126 A2
Canonbury Vil N1 125 P2
Canrobert St E2 126 F5
Cantelowes Rd NW1 125 K1
Canterbury Cres SW9 129 N9
Canterbury Pl SE17 129 P3
Canterbury Rd NW6 124 A4
Canterbury Ter NW6 124 A4
Cantium Retail Pk SE1 130 E5
Canton St E14 127 L8
Cantrell Rd E3 127 K6
Canute Gdns SE16 131 H3
Capland St NW8 124 D6
Capper St WC1 125 J6
Capstan Rd SE8 131 K3
Capstan Sq E14 131 N1
Capstan Way SE16 127 J10
Caradoc Cl W2 124 A8
Carbis Rd E14 127 K8
Carburton St W1 125 H7
Carden Rd SE15 130 F9
Cardigan Rd E3 127 K4
Cardigan St SE11 129 N4
Cardinal Bourne St SE1 130 B2
Cardine Ms SE15 130 F6
Cardington St NW1 125 J5
Carew St SE5 130 A8
Carey Gdns SW8 129 J7
Carey St WC2 125 M8
Carlile Cl E3 127 K4
Carlisle La SE1 129 M2
Carlisle Ms NW8 124 D7
Carlisle Pl SW1 129 J2
Carlos Pl W1 124 G9
Carlton Ct SW9 129 P7
Carlton Gdns SW1 125 K10
Carlton Gro SE15 130 F7
Carlton Hill NW8 124 B4
Carlton Ho Ter SW1 125 K10
Carlton Twr Pl SW1 128 F2
Carlton Vale NW6 124 B4
Carlyle Sq SW3 128 D4
Carmelite St EC4 125 N9
Carmen St E14 127 M8
Carnaby St W1 125 J8
Carnegie St N1 125 M3
Carnoustie Dr N1 125 M2
Carnwath Rd SW6 128 A9
Carol St NW1 125 J3
Caroline Gdns SE15 130 F6
Caroline Pl SW11 128 G8
Caroline Pl W2 124 B9
Caroline St E1 127 H8
Caroline Ter SW1 128 G3
Carpenters Pl SW4 129 K10
Carpenters Rd E15 127 M1
Carr St E14 127 J7
Carriage Dr E SW11 128 G6
Carriage Dr N SW11 128 G5
Carriage Dr S SW11 128 F7
Carriage Dr W SW11 128 F6
Carron Cl E14 127 M8
Carroun Rd SW8 129 M6
Carter La EC4 125 P8
Carter Pl SE17 130 A4
Carter St SE17 130 A5
Carteret St SW1 129 K1
Carteret Way SE8 131 J3
Cartier Circle E14 127 M10
Carting La WC2 125 L9
Cartwright Gdns WC1 125 L5
Cartwright St E1 126 D9
Casella Rd SE14 131 H6
Casey Cl NW8 124 E5
Caspian St SE5 130 B6
Cassidy Rd SW6 128 A6
Cassilis Rd E14 131 L1
Cassland Rd E9 126 G2
Casson St E1 126 E7
Castellain Rd W9 124 B6
Casterbridge NW6 124 B3
Castle La SW1 129 J2
Castle Pl NW1 125 H1
Castle Rd NW1 125 H1
Castlebrook Cl SE11 129 P3
Castlehaven Rd NW1 125 H2
Castlemain St E1 126 F7
Castlemaine Twr SW11 128 F7
Castor La E14 127 M9
Caterham Rd SE13 131 N9
Catesby St SE17 130 B3
Cathay St SE16 130 F1
Cathcart Rd SW10 128 C5
Cathcart St NW5 125 H1
Cathedral St SE1 126 B10
Catherine Gro SE10 131 M7
Catherine Pl SW1 129 J2
Catherine St WC2 125 M9
Catlin St SE16 130 E4
Cato Rd SW4 129 K9
Cato St W1 124 E7
Cator St SE15 130 D5
Catton St WC1 125 M7
Caulfield Rd SE15 130 F8
Causeway, The SW18 128 B10
Causton St SW1 129 K3
Cavell St E1 126 F7
Cavendish Av NW8 124 D4
Cavendish Cl NW8 124 D5
Cavendish Pl W1 125 H8
Cavendish Sq W1 125 H8
Cavendish St N1 126 B4
Caversham Rd NW5 125 J1
Caversham St SW3 128 F5
Caxton Gro E3 127 L5
Caxton St SW1 129 J2
Cedar Cl E3 127 K3
Cedar Way NW1 125 K2
Cedarne Rd SW6 128 B6
Cedars Cl SE13 131 P9
Cedars Rd SW4 129 H9
Celandine Cl E14 127 L7
Celandine Dr E8 126 D2
Celestial Gdns SE13 131 P10
Celtic St E14 127 M7
Centaur St SE1 129 M2
Central Av SW11 128 F6
Central Mkts EC1 125 P7
Central St EC1 126 A5
Centre St E2 126 F4
Centrepoint WC1 125 K8
Centurion Cl N7 125 M2
Cephas Av E1 126 G6
Cephas St E1 126 G6
Cerise Rd SE15 130 E7
Chabot Dr SE15 130 F9
Chadbourn St E14 127 M7
Chadwell St EC1 125 N5
Chadwick Rd SE15 130 D8
Chadwick St SW1 129 K2
Chagford St NW1 124 F6
Chalbury Wk N1 125 M4
Chalcot Cres NW1 124 F3
Chalcot Gdns NW3 124 F1
Chalcot Rd NW1 124 G2
Chalcot Sq NW1 124 G2
Chalk Fm Rd NW1 124 G2
Chalsey Rd SE4 131 K10
Chalton St NW1 125 K4
Chamber St E1 126 D9
Chambers St SE16 130 E1
Chambord St E2 126 D5
Champion Gro SE5 130 B9
Champion Hill SE5 130 B9
Champion Hill Est SE5 130 C9
Champion Pk SE5 130 B8
Chance St E1 126 D6
Chance St E2 126 D6
Chancel St SE1 125 P10
Chancery La WC2 125 N7
Chandler Way SE15 130 D6
Chandlers Ms E14 131 L1
Chandos Pl WC2 125 L9
Chandos St W1 125 H7
Channelsea Rd E15 127 P3
Chant Sq E15 127 P2
Chant St E15 127 P2
Chantrey Rd SW9 129 M9
Chantry St N1 125 P3
Chapel Ho St E14 131 M4
Chapel Mkt N1 125 N4
Chapel Pl W1 125 H8
Chapel Side W2 124 B9
Chapel St NW1 124 E7
Chapel St SW1 128 G2
Chaplin Cl SE1 129 N1
Chapman Rd E9 127 K1
Chapman St E1 126 F9
Chapter Rd SE17 129 P4
Chapter St SW1 129 K3
Charing Cross Rd WC2 125 K8
Charlbert St NW8 124 E4
Charles Barry Cl SW4 129 J9
Charles Coveney Rd SE15 130 D7
Charles Dickens Ho E2 126 F5
Charles II St SW1 125 K10
Charles Sq N1 126 B5
Charles St W1 125 H10
Charleston St SE17 130 A3
Charlotte Despard Av SW11 128 G7
Charlotte Rd EC2 126 C6
Charlotte Row SW4 129 J9
Charlotte St W1 125 J7
Charlotte Ter N1 125 M3
Charlton Pl N1 125 P4
Charlwood Pl SW1 129 J3
Charlwood St SW1 129 J4
Charnwood Gdns E14 131 L3
Charrington St NW1 125 K4
Chart St N1 126 B5
Charterhouse Sq EC1 125 P7
Charterhouse St EC1 125 P7
Chase, The SW4 129 H9
Chaseley St E14 127 J8
Chatfield Rd SW11 128 C9
Chatham Pl E9 126 G1
Chatham St SE17 130 B3
Chatsworth Ct W8 128 A3
Chaucer Dr SE1 130 D3
Cheapside EC2 126 A8
Chelsea Br SW1 129 H5
Chelsea Br SW8 129 H5
Chelsea Br Rd SW1 128 G4
Chelsea Embk SW3 128 E5
Chelsea Harbour SW10 128 C7
Chelsea Harbour Dr SW10 128 C7
Chelsea Manor Gdns SW3 128 E5
Chelsea Manor St SW3 128 E4
Chelsea Pk Gdns SW3 128 D5
Chelsea Sq SW3 128 D4
Chelsea Wf SW10 128 D6
Chelsham Rd SW4 129 K9
Cheltenham Rd SE15 130 G10
Cheltenham Ter SW3 128 F4
Chelwood Wk SE4 131 J10
Chenies Pl NW1 125 K4
Chenies St WC1 125 K7
Cheniston Gdns W8 128 B2
Chepstow Cres W11 124 A9
Chepstow Pl W2 124 A8
Chepstow Rd W2 124 A8
Cherbury St N1 126 B4
Cherry Gdn St SE16 130 F1
Cherrywood Cl E3 127 J5
Cheryls Cl SW6 128 B7
Chesham Ms SW1 128 G2
Chesham Pl SW1 128 G2
Chesham St SW1 128 G2
Cheshire Cl SE4 131 K8
Cheshire St E2 126 D6
Chesil Ct E2 126 G4
Chesney St SW11 128 G7
Chester Cl SW1 128 G1
Chester Ct SE5 130 B6
Chester Gate NW1 125 H5
Chester Ms SW1 129 H2
Chester Rd NW1 124 G5
Chester Row SW1 128 G3
Chester Sq SW1 129 H2
Chester St E2 126 E6
Chester St SW1 128 G2
Chester Way SE11 129 N3
Chesterfield Gdns W1 125 H10
Chesterfield Hill W1 125 H9
Chesterfield St W1 125 H10
Chesterfield Wk SE10 131 P7
Chesterfield Way SE15 130 G6
Chestnut Cl SE14 131 K7
Cheval Pl SW7 128 E2
Cheval St E14 131 L2
Cheyne Gdns SW3 128 E5
Cheyne Ms SW3 128 E5
Cheyne Pl SW3 128 F5
Cheyne Row SW3 128 E5
Cheyne Wk SW3 128 E5
Cheyne Wk SW10 128 D6
Chicheley St SE1 129 M1
Chichester Rd NW6 124 A4
Chichester Rd W2 124 B7
Chichester St SW1 129 J4
Chichester Way E14 131 P3
Chicksand St E1 126 D7
Chiddingstone St SW6 128 A8
Childeric Rd SE14 131 J6
Childers St SE8 131 J5
Child's Pl SW5 128 A3
Child's St SW5 128 A3
Chillington Dr SW11 128 C10
Chiltern Rd E3 127 L6
Chiltern St W1 124 G7
Chilton Gro SE8 131 H3
Chilton St E2 126 D6
Chilworth Ms W2 124 C8
Chilworth St W2 124 C8
Chip St SW4 129 K9
Chipka St E14 131 N1
Chipley St SE14 131 J5
Chippenham Gdns NW6 124 A5
Chippenham Ms W9 124 A6
Chippenham Rd W9 124 A6
Chipstead St SW6 128 A7
Chisenhale Rd E3 127 J4
Chiswell St EC1 126 A7
Chitty St W1 125 J7
Choumert Gro SE15 130 E8
Choumert Ms SE15 130 E8
Choumert Rd SE15 130 D9
Choumert Sq SE15 130 E8
Chrisp St E14 127 M7
Christchurch St SW3 128 F5
Christian Ct SE16 127 K10
Christian St E1 126 E8
Christie Rd E9 127 J1
Christopher Cl SE16 131 H1
Christopher St EC2 126 B6
Chryssell Rd SW9 129 N6
Chubworthy St SE14 131 J5
Chudleigh St E1 127 H8
Chumleigh St SE5 130 C5
Church Cres E9 127 H2
Church Gro SE13 131 M10
Church Rd N1 126 A1
Church St NW8 124 D7
Church St W2 124 D7
Church St Est NW8 124 D6
Church Ter SW8 129 K8
Churchill Gdns SW1 129 J4
Churchill Gdns Rd SW1 129 H4
Churchill Pl E14 127 M10
Churchway NW1 125 K5
Churton Pl SW1 129 J3
Churton St SW1 129 J3
Cicely Rd SE15 130 E7
Cinnabar Wf E1 126 E10
Cinnamon Row SW11 128 C9
Cinnamon St E1 126 F10
Circus Rd NW8 124 D5
Circus St SE10 131 N6
Cirencester St W2 124 B7
City Gdn Row N1 125 P4
City Mill River Towpath E15 127 M2
City Rd EC1 125 P4
Clabon Ms SW1 128 F2
Clack St SE16 130 G1
Claire Pl E14 131 L2
Clancarty Rd SW6 128 A8
Clandon St SE8 131 L8
Clanricarde Gdns W2 124 A9
Clapham Common N Side SW4 129 H10
Clapham Common W Side SW4 128 G10
Clapham Cres SW4 129 K10
Clapham Est SW11 128 E10
Clapham High St SW4 129 K10
Clapham Junct Sta SW11 128 D10
Clapham Manor St SW4 129 J9
Clapham Pk Rd SW4 129 K10
Clapham Rd SW9 129 L9
Clapham Rd Est SW4 129 K9
Clare Ho E3 127 K3
Clare La N1 126 A2
Clare Rd SE14 131 K7
Clare St E2 126 F4
Claredale St E2 126 E4
Claremont Cl N1 125 N4
Claremont Sq N1 125 N4
Claremont St SE10 131 M5
Clarence Gdns NW1 125 H5
Clarence Ms SE16 127 H10
Clarence Rd SE8 131 M5
Clarence Wk SW4 129 L8
Clarence Way NW1 125 H2
Clarence Way Est NW1 125 H2
Clarendon Cl E9 126 G2
Clarendon Gdns W9 124 C6
Clarendon Pl W2 124 E9
Clarendon Ri SE13 131 N9
Clarendon St SW1 129 H4
Clareville Gro SW7 128 C3
Clareville St SW7 128 C3
Clarewood Wk SW9 129 P10
Clarges Ms W1 125 H10
Clarges St W1 125 H10
Claribel Rd SW9 129 P8
Clarissa St E8 126 D3
Clark St E1 126 F7
Clarkson Row NW1 125 J4
Clarkson St E2 126 F5
Claude Rd SE15 130 F8
Claude St E14 131 L3
Clavell St SE10 131 N5

Claverton St SW1 129 J4
Claylands Pl SW8 129 N6
Claylands Rd SW8 129 M5
Claypole Rd E15 127 N4
Clayton Cres N1 125 L3
Clayton Ms SE10 131 P7
Clayton Rd SE15 130 E7
Clayton St SE11 129 N5
Clearwell Dr W9 124 B6
Cleaver Sq SE11 129 N4
Cleaver St SE11 129 N4
Clemence St E14 127 K7
Clement Av SW4 129 K10
Clement's Inn WC2 125 M8
Clements La EC4 126 B9
Clements Rd SE16 130 E2
Clephane Rd N1 126 A1
Clerkenwell Cl EC1 125 N6
Clerkenwell Grn EC1 125 P6
Clerkenwell Rd EC1 125 N7
Clermont Rd E9 126 G3
Cleve Rd NW6 124 A2
Cleveland Gdns W2 124 C8
Cleveland Rd N1 126 B2
Cleveland Row SW1 125 J10
Cleveland Sq W2 124 C8
Cleveland St W1 125 H6
Cleveland Ter W2 124 C8
Cleveland Way E1 126 G6
Clichy Est E1 126 G7
Cliff Rd NW1 125 K1
Cliff Ter SE8 131 L8
Cliff Vil NW1 125 K1
Clifford Dr SW9 129 P10
Clifford St W1 125 J9
Cliffview Rd SE13 131 L9
Clifton Cres SE15 130 F6
Clifton Gdns W9 124 C6
Clifton Gro E8 126 E1
Clifton Hill NW8 124 B4
Clifton Pl W2 124 D9
Clifton Ri SE14 131 J6
Clifton Rd N1 126 A1
Clifton Rd W9 124 C6
Clifton St EC2 126 C7
Clifton Vil W9 124 B7
Clifton Way SE15 130 F6
Clink St SE1 126 A10
Clinton Rd E3 127 J5
Clipper Way SE13 131 N10
Clipstone Ms W1 125 J6
Clipstone St W1 125 J7
Clitheroe Rd SW9 129 L8
Cliveden Pl SW1 128 G3
Cloak La EC4 126 A9
Clock Twr Pl N7 125 L1
Cloth Fair EC1 125 P7
Cloudesley Pl N1 125 N3
Cloudesley Rd N1 125 N3
Cloudesley Sq N1 125 N3
Cloudesley St N1 125 N3
Clove Cres E14 127 P9
Clove Hitch Quay SW11 128 C9
Cloysters Grn E1 126 E10
Club Row E1 126 D6
Club Row E2 126 D6
Cluny Ms SW5 128 A3
Clutton St E14 127 M7
Clyde St SE8 131 K5
Clyston St SW8 129 J8
Coate St E2 126 E4
Cobb St E1 126 D7
Cobbett St SW8 129 M6
Coborn Rd E3 127 K5
Coborn St E3 127 K5
Cobourg Rd SE5 130 D5
Cobourg St NW1 125 J5
Cochrane St NW8 124 D4
Cock La EC1 125 P7
Cockayne Way SE8 131 J4
Cockspur St SW1 125 K10
Code St E1 126 D6
Cody Rd E16 127 P6
Cody Rd Business Cen E16 127 P6
Coin St SE1 125 N10
Coity Rd NW5 124 G1
Coke St E1 126 E8
Colbeck Ms SW7 128 B3
Cold Blow La SE14 131 H6
Cold Harbour E14 131 N1
Coldbath St SE13 131 M7
Coldharbour La SE5 129 N10
Coldharbour La SW9 129 N10
Cole St SE1 130 A1
Colebeck Ms N1 125 P1
Colebert Av E1 126 G6
Colebrooke Row N1 125 P4
Colegrove Rd SE15 130 D6
Coleherne Ct SW5 128 B4
Coleherne Ms SW10 128 B4
Coleherne Rd SW10 128 B4
Coleman Flds N1 126 A3
Coleman Rd SE5 130 C6
Coleman St EC2 126 B8
Coleridge Cl SW8 129 H8
Coleridge Gdns SW10 128 B6
Coleridge Sq SW10 128 C6
Colestown St SW11 128 E8
Coley St WC1 125 M6
College App SE10 131 N5
College Cres NW3 124 D1
College Cross N1 125 N2
College Pk Cl SE13 131 P10
College Pl NW1 125 J3
College Ter E3 127 K5
Collent St E9 126 G1
Collett Rd SE16 130 E2
Collier St N1 125 M4
Collingham Gdns SW5 128 B3
Collingham Pl SW5 128 B3
Collingham Rd SW5 128 B3
Collingwood St E1 126 F6
Colls Rd SE15 130 G7
Colmore Ms SE15 130 F7
Colnbrook St SE1 129 P2
Cologne Rd SW11 128 D10
Colombo St SE1 125 P10
Colonnade WC1 125 L6
Colonnade Wk SW1 129 H3
Colonnades, The W2 124 B8
Columbia Rd E2 126 D5
Columbine Way SE13 131 N8
Colville Est N1 126 B3
Colyer Cl N1 125 M4
Comber Gro SE5 130 A7
Combermere Rd SW9 129 M9
Comerford Rd SE4 131 J10
Comet Pl SE8 131 L6
Comet St SE8 131 L6
Comfort St SE15 130 C5
Commercial Rd E1 126 E8
Commercial Rd E14 126 G8
Commercial St E1 126 D6
Commercial Way SE15 130 D6
Commodore St E1 127 J6
Compayne Gdns NW6 124 B2
Compton Av N1 125 P1
Compton Cl E3 127 L7
Compton Rd N1 125 P1
Compton St EC1 125 P6
Compton Ter N1 125 P1
Comus Pl SE17 130 C3
Comyn Rd SW11 128 E10
Concanon Rd SW2 129 M10
Concert Hall App SE1 125 M10
Concorde Way SE16 131 H3
Condell Rd SW8 129 J7
Condray Pl SW11 128 E6
Conduit Ms W2 124 D8
Conduit Pl W2 124 D8
Conduit St W1 125 H9
Coney Way SW8 129 M5
Congreve St SE17 130 C3
Coniger Rd SW6 128 A8
Conington Rd SE13 131 M8
Coniston Ho SE5 130 A6
Conistone Way N7 125 L2
Connaught Pl W2 124 F9
Connaught Sq W2 124 F8
Connaught St W2 124 E8
Consort Rd SE15 130 F7
Constitution Hill SW1 129 H1
Content St SE17 130 B3
Conway St W1 125 J6
Conyer St E3 127 J4
Cook's Rd E15 127 M4
Cooks Rd SE17 129 P5
Coombs St N1 125 P4
Coopers Cl E1 126 G6
Coopers La NW1 125 K4
Coopers Rd SE1 130 D4
Cope Pl W8 128 A2
Cope St SE16 131 H3
Copeland Dr E14 131 L3
Copeland Rd SE15 130 E8
Copenhagen Pl E14 127 K8
Copenhagen St N1 125 L3
Copleston Pas SE15 130 D9
Copleston Rd SE15 130 D9
Copley St E1 127 H7
Copper Row SE1 126 D10
Copperas St SE8 131 M5
Copperfield Rd E3 127 J6
Copperfield St SE1 129 P1
Coppock Cl SW11 128 E8
Copthall Av EC2 126 B8
Copthall Ct EC2 126 B8
Coptic St WC1 125 L7
Coral St SE1 129 N1
Coram St WC1 125 L6
Corbden Cl SE15 130 D7
Corbiere Ho N1 126 C3
Corbridge Cres E2 126 F4
Cordelia Cl SE24 129 P10
Cordelia St E14 127 M8
Corfield St E2 126 F5
Coriander Av E14 127 P8
Cork St W1 125 J9
Corlett St NW1 124 E7
Cormont Rd SE5 129 P7
Cornelia St N7 125 M1
Cornhill EC3 126 B8
Cornmill La SE13 131 M9
Cornwall Av E2 126 G5
Cornwall Gdns SW7 128 B2
Cornwall Ms S SW7 128 C2
Cornwall Rd SE1 125 N10
Cornwall Sq SE11 129 P4
Cornwood Dr E1 126 G8
Coronet St N1 126 C5
Corporation Row EC1 125 N6
Corrance Rd SW2 129 L10
Corry Dr SW9 129 P10
Corsham St N1 126 B5
Corsica St N5 125 P1
Corunna Rd SW8 129 J7
Corunna Ter SW8 129 J7
Cossall Wk SE15 130 F7
Cosser St SE1 129 N2
Costa St SE15 130 E8
Cosway St NW1 124 E7
Cotall St E14 127 L8
Cotleigh Rd NW6 124 A2
Cottage Grn SE5 130 B6
Cottage Gro SW9 129 L9
Cottage Pl SW3 128 E2
Cottage St E14 127 M9
Cottesmore Gdns W8 128 B2
Cottingham Rd SW8 129 M6
Cotton Row SW11 128 C9
Cotton St E14 127 N9
Coulgate St SE4 131 J9
Coulson St SW3 128 F3
Councillor St SE5 130 A6
County Gro SE5 130 A7
County St SE1 130 A2
Courland Gro SW8 129 K7
Courland Gro Hall SW8 129 K8
Courland St SW8 129 K7
Court Gdns N7 125 N1
Courtenay St SE11 129 N4
Courtfield Gdns SW5 128 B3
Courtfield Rd SW7 128 B3
Courthill Rd SE13 131 N10
Courtnell St W2 124 A8
Courtyard, The N1 125 M2
Covent Gdn WC2 125 L9
Coventry Rd E1 126 F6
Coventry Rd E2 126 F6
Coventry St W1 125 K9
Coverley Cl E1 126 E7
Cowcross St EC1 125 P7
Cowdenbeath Path N1 125 M3
Cowley Rd SW9 129 N7
Cowper St EC2 126 B6
Cowthorpe Rd SW8 129 K7
Crabtree Cl E2 126 D4
Crampton St SE17 129 P3
Cranbourn St WC2 125 K9
Cranbrook Rd SE8 131 L7
Cranbury Rd SW6 128 B8
Crane Gro N7 125 N1
Crane St SE10 131 P4
Crane St SE15 130 D7
Cranfield Rd SE4 131 K9
Cranford St E1 127 H9
Cranleigh Ms SW11 128 E8
Cranleigh St NW1 125 J4
Cranley Gdns SW7 128 C4
Cranley Ms SW7 128 C4
Cranley Pl SW7 128 D3
Cranmer Ct SW4 129 K9
Cranmer Rd SW9 129 N6
Cranston Est N1 126 B4
Cranswick Rd SE16 130 F4
Cranwell Cl E3 127 M6
Cranwood St EC1 126 B5
Cranworth Gdns SW9 129 N7
Craven Hill W2 124 C9
Craven Hill Gdns W2 124 C9
Craven Hill Ms W2 124 C9
Craven Pas WC2 125 L10
Craven Rd W2 124 C9
Craven St WC2 125 L10
Craven Ter W2 124 C9
Crawford Est SE5 130 A8
Crawford Pl W1 124 E8
Crawford Rd SE5 130 A7
Crawford St W1 124 F7
Crawthew Gro SE22 130 D10
Creasy Est SE1 130 C2
Credon Rd SE16 130 F4
Creechurch La EC3 126 C8
Creek Rd SE8 131 L5
Creek Rd SE10 131 L5
Creekside SE8 131 M6
Cremer St E2 126 D4
Cremorne Rd SW10 128 C6
Crescent Gro SW4 129 J10
Crescent Pl SW3 128 E3
Crescent St N1 125 M2
Crescent Way SE4 131 L9
Cresford Rd SW6 128 B7
Cresset Rd E9 126 G1
Cresset St SW4 129 K9
Cressingham Rd SE13 131 N9
Cresswell Gdns SW5 128 C4
Cresswell Pl SW10 128 C4
Cressy Pl E1 126 G7
Crestfield St WC1 125 L5
Crewdson Rd SW9 129 N6
Crews St E14 131 L3
Crewys Rd SE15 130 F8
Cricketers Ct SE11 129 P3
Crimscott St SE1 130 C2
Crimsworth Rd SW8 129 K7
Crinan St N1 125 L4
Cringle St SW8 129 J6
Crispin St E1 126 D7
Croft St SE8 131 J3
Crofters Way NW1 125 K3
Crofton Rd SE5 130 C7
Crofts St E1 126 E9
Crogsland Rd NW1 124 G2
Cromer St WC1 125 L5
Crompton St W2 124 D6
Cromwell Cres SW5 128 A3
Cromwell Gdns SW7 128 D2
Cromwell Ms SW7 128 D3
Cromwell Pl SW7 128 D3
Cromwell Rd SW5 128 B3
Cromwell Rd SW7 128 B3
Cromwell Rd SW9 129 P7
Cromwell Twr EC2 126 A7
Crondace Rd SW6 128 A7
Crondall St N1 126 B4
Cronin St SE15 130 D6
Crooke Rd SE8 131 J4
Crooms Hill SE10 131 P6
Crooms Hill Gro SE10 131 N6
Cropley St N1 126 B4
Cropthorne Ct W9 124 C5
Crosby Row SE1 130 B1
Cross Av SE10 131 P5
Cross Rd SE5 130 C8
Cross St N1 125 P3
Crossfield Rd NW3 124 D2
Crossfield St SE8 131 L6
Crossford St SW9 129 M8
Crosslet Vale SE10 131 M7
Crossley St N7 125 N1
Crossmount Ho SE5 130 A6
Crossthwaite Av SE5 130 B10
Crosswall EC3 126 D9
Croston St E8 126 E3
Crowder St E1 126 F9
Crowhurst Cl SW9 129 N8
Crowland Ter N1 126 B2
Crown Cl E3 127 L3
Crown Cl NW6 124 B1
Crown Pas SW1 125 J10
Crown Pl EC2 126 C7
Crown St SE5 130 A6
Crowndale Rd NW1 125 J4
Crows Rd E15 127 P5
Crucifix La SE1 130 C1
Cruden St N1 125 P3
Cruikshank St WC1 125 N5
Crutched Friars EC3 126 C9
Crystal Palace Rd SE22 130 E10
Cuba St E14 131 L1
Cubitt St WC1 125 M5
Cubitt Ter SW4 129 J9
Cudworth St E1 126 F6
Cuff Pt E2 126 D5
Culford Gdns SW3 128 F3
Culford Gro N1 126 C1
Culford Rd N1 126 C2
Culloden Cl SE16 130 E4
Culloden St E14 127 N8
Culmore Rd SE15 130 F6
Culross St W1 124 G9
Culvert Pl SW11 128 G8
Culvert Rd SW11 128 F8
Cumberland Cl E8 126 D1
Cumberland Gate W1 124 F9
Cumberland Mkt NW1 125 H5
Cumberland St SW1 129 H4
Cumming St N1 125 M4
Cunard Wk SE16 131 J3
Cundy St SW1 128 G3
Cunningham Pl NW8 124 D6
Cupar Rd SW11 128 G7
Cureton St SW1 129 K3
Curlew St SE1 130 D1
Curness St SE13 131 N10
Cursitor St EC4 125 N8
Curtain Rd EC2 126 C6
Curtis St SE1 130 D3
Curtis Way SE1 130 D3
Curzon Gate W1 124 G10
Curzon St W1 124 G10
Custom Ho Reach SE16 131 K1
Custom Ho Wk EC3 126 C9
Cut, The SE1 129 N1
Cutcombe Rd SE5 130 A8
Cuthbert St W2 124 D6
Cuthill Wk SE5 130 B7
Cutler St E1 126 C8
Cyclops Ms E14 131 L3
Cynthia St N1 125 M4
Cyntra Pl E8 126 F2
Cyprus Pl E2 126 G4
Cyprus St E2 126 G4
Cyril Mans SW11 128 F7
Cyrus St EC1 125 P6
Czar St SE8 131 L5

D

Dabin Cres SE10 131 N7
Dacca St SE8 131 K5
Dace Rd E3 127 L2
Dacre St SW1 129 K2
Dagmar Rd SE5 130 C7
Dagmar Ter N1 125 P3
Dagnall St SW11 128 F8
Dairy Ms SW9 129 L9
Daisy La SW6 128 A9
Dalberg Rd SW2 129 N10
Dalby Rd SW18 128 C10
Dalby St NW5 125 H1
Dale Rd SE17 129 P5
Daleham Ms NW3 124 D1
Dalehead NW1 125 J4
Daley St E9 127 H1
Daley Thompson Way SW8 129 H8
Dalgleish St E14 127 J8
Daling Way E3 127 J3
Dallington St EC1 125 P6
Dalrymple Rd SE4 131 J10
Dalston La E8 126 D1
Dalwood St SE5 130 C7
Dalyell Rd SW9 129 M9
Dame St N1 126 A4
Damien St E1 126 F8
Danbury St N1 125 P4
Danby St SE15 130 D9
Danesdale Rd E9 127 J1
Danesfield SE5 130 C5
Daneville Rd SE5 130 B7
Daniel Gdns SE15 130 D6
Daniels Rd SE15 130 G9
Dante Rd SE11 129 P3
Danvers St SW3 128 D5
D'Arblay St W1 125 J8
Darien Rd SW11 128 D9
Darling Rd SE4 131 L9
Darling Row E1 126 F6
Darnley Ho E14 127 J8
Darnley Rd E9 126 F1
Darsley Dr SW8 129 K7
Dartford St SE17 130 A5
Dartmouth Gro SE10 131 N7
Dartmouth Hill SE10 131 N7
Dartmouth Row SE10 131 N8
Dartmouth St SW1 129 K1
Dartmouth Ter SE10 131 P7
Darwin St SE17 130 B3
Datchelor Pl SE5 130 B7
Date St SE17 130 A4
Daubeney Twr SE8 131 K4
Davenant St E1 126 E7
Daventry St NW1 124 E7
Davey Cl N7 125 M1
Davey Rd E9 127 L2
Davey St SE15 130 D5
David St E15 127 P1
Davidge St SE1 129 P1
Davidson Gdns SW8 129 L6
Davies St W1 125 H9
Dawes St SE17 130 B4
Dawson Pl W2 124 A9
Dawson St E2 126 D4
Dayton Gro SE15 130 G7
De Beauvoir Cres N1 126 C3
De Beauvoir Est N1 126 B3
De Beauvoir Rd N1 126 C3
De Beauvoir Sq N1 126 C2
De Crespigny Pk SE5 130 B8
De Laune St SE17 129 P4
De Morgan Rd SW6 128 B9
De Vere Gdns W8 128 C1
Deacon Ms N1 126 B2
Deacon Way SE17 130 A3
Deal Porters Way SE16 130 G2
Deal St E1 126 E7
Deals Gateway SE13 131 L7
Dean Bradley St SW1 129 L2
Dean Farrar St SW1 129 K2
Dean Ryle St SW1 129 L3
Dean Stanley St SW1 129 L2
Dean St W1 125 K8
Dean Trench St SW1 129 L2
Deancross St E1 126 G8
Deanery St W1 124 G10
Deans Bldgs SE17 130 B3
Decima St SE1 130 C2
Dee St E14 127 N8
Deeley Rd SW8 129 K7
Deepdene Rd SE5 130 B10
Deerdale Rd SE24 130 A10
Delaford Rd SE16 130 F4
Delamere Ter W2 124 B7
Delancey St NW1 125 H3
Delaware Rd W9 124 B6
Delhi St N1 125 L3
Delius Gro E15 127 P4
Dell Cl E15 127 P3
Dellow St E1 126 F9
Deloraine St SE8 131 L7
Delverton Rd SE17 129 P4
Delvino Rd SW6 128 A7
Denbigh Pl SW1 129 J4
Denbigh St SW1 129 J3
Dene Cl SE4 131 J9
Denman Rd SE15 130 D7
Denmark Gro N1 125 N4
Denmark Hill SE5 130 B7
Denmark Hill Est SE5 130 B10
Denmark Rd SE5 130 A7
Denmark St WC2 125 K8
Denne Ter E8 126 D3
Dennetts Rd SE14 130 G7
Denning Cl NW8 124 C5
Dennington Pk Rd NW6 124 A1
Dennison Pt E15 127 N2
Denny St SE11 129 N4
Denyer St SW3 128 E3
Deptford Br SE8 131 L7
Deptford Bdy SE8 131 L7
Deptford Ch St SE8 131 L5
Deptford Ferry Rd E14 131 L3
Deptford Grn SE8 131 L5
Deptford High St SE8 131 L5
Deptford Strand SE8 131 K3
Deptford Wf SE8 131 K3
Derby Rd E9 127 H3
Derbyshire St E2 126 E5
Dericote St E8 126 E3
Dering St W1 125 H8
Derry St W8 128 B1
Derwent Gro SE22 130 D10
Desborough Cl W2 124 B7
Desmond St SE14 131 J5
Devas St E3 127 M6
Deverell St SE1 130 B2
Devon St SE15 130 F5
Devonia Rd N1 125 P4
Devonport St E1 126 G8
Devons Est E3 127 M5
Devons Rd E3 127 L7
Devonshire Cl W1 125 H7
Devonshire Dr SE10 131 M6
Devonshire Gro SE15 130 F5
Devonshire Ms S W1 125 H7
Devonshire Ms W W1 125 H7
Devonshire Pl W1 124 G6
Devonshire St W1 125 H7
Devonshire Ter W2 124 C8
Dewar St SE15 130 E9
Dewberry St E14 127 N7
Dewey Rd N1 125 N4
D'Eynsford Rd SE5 130 B7
Dial Wk, The W8 128 B1
Diamond St SE15 130 C6
Diamond Ter SE10 131 N7
Dibden St N1 125 P3
Dickens Est SE1 130 D1
Dickens Est SE16 130 D1
Dickens Ho NW6 124 A5
Dickens Sq SE1 130 A2
Dickens St SW8 129 H8
Digby Rd E9 127 H1
Digby St E2 126 G5
Dighton Ct SE5 130 A5
Dilke St SW3 128 F5
Dimson Cres E3 127 L6
Dingle Gdns E14 127 L9
Dingley Pl EC1 126 A5
Dingley Rd EC1 126 A5
Discovery Wk E1 126 F10
Diss St E2 126 D5
Distaff La EC4 126 A9
Distin St SE11 129 N3
Ditch All SE10 131 M7
Ditchburn St E14 127 N9
Dixon Rd SE14 131 J7
Dixon's All SE16 130 F1
Dobson Cl NW6 124 D2
Dock Hill Av SE16 131 H1
Dock St E1 126 E9
Dockers Tanner Rd E14 131 L2
Dockhead SE1 130 D1
Dockley Rd SE16 130 E2
Docwra's Bldgs N1 126 C1
Dod St E14 127 K8
Doddington Gro SE17 129 P5
Doddington Pl SE17 129 P5
Dodson St SE1 129 N1
Dog Kennel Hill SE22 130 C9
Dog Kennel Hill Est SE22 130 C9
Dolben St SE1 125 P10
Dolland St SE11 129 M4
Dolman St SW4 129 M10
Dolphin La E14 127 M9
Dolphin Sq SW1 129 J4
Dombey St WC1 125 M7

Domett Cl **SE5** 130 B10
Don Phelan Cl **SE5** 130 B7
Donegal St **N1** 125 M4
Dongola Rd **E1** 127 J7
Donne Pl **SW3** 128 E3
Dora St **E14** 127 K8
Dora Way **SW9** 129 N8
Doran Wk **E15** 127 N2
Doric Way **NW1** 125 K5
Dorking Cl **SE8** 131 K5
Dorman Way **NW8** 124 D3
Dorney **NW3** 124 E2
Dorothy Rd **SW11** 128 F9
Dorrington St **EC1** 125 N7
Dorset Est **E2** 126 D5
Dorset Pl **E15** 127 P1
Dorset Ri **EC4** 125 P8
Dorset Rd **SW8** 129 M6
Dorset Sq **NW1** 124 F6
Dorset St **W1** 124 G7
Doughty Ms **WC1** 125 M6
Doughty St **WC1** 125 M6
Douglas Rd **N1** 126 A2
Douglas St **SW1** 129 K3
Douglas Way **SE8** 131 K6
Douro Pl **W8** 128 B2
Douro St **E3** 127 L4
Dove Ms **SW5** 128 C3
Dove Rd **N1** 126 B1
Dove Row **E2** 126 E3
Dovehouse St **SW3** 128 D4
Dover St **W1** 125 H9
Dovercourt Est **N1** 126 B1
Doves Yd **N1** 125 N3
Dowgate Hill **EC4** 126 B9
Dowlas St **SE5** 130 C6
Down St **W1** 125 H10
Downfield Cl **W9** 124 B6
Downham Rd **N1** 126 B2
Downing St **SW1** 129 L1
Downtown Rd **SE16** 131 J1
Dowson Cl **SE5** 130 B10
D'Oyley St **SW1** 128 G3
Draco St **SE17** 130 A5
Dragon Rd **SE15** 130 C5
Dragoon Rd **SE8** 131 K4
Drake Rd **SE4** 131 L9
Drakefell Rd **SE4** 131 H8
Drakefell Rd **SE14** 131 H8
Draper Ho **SE1** 129 P3
Drawdock Rd **SE10** 127 P10
Draycott Av **SW3** 128 E3
Draycott Pl **SW3** 128 F3
Draycott Ter **SW3** 128 F3
Drayson Ms **W8** 128 A1
Drayton Gdns **SW10** 128 C4
Dresden Cl **NW6** 124 B1
Driffield Rd **E3** 127 J4
Drovers Pl **SE15** 130 F6
Druid St **SE1** 130 C1
Drummond Cres **NW1** 125 K5
Drummond Gate **SW1** 129 K4
Drummond Rd **SE16** 130 F2
Drummond St **NW1** 125 J6
Drury La **WC2** 125 L8
Dryden Ct **SE11** 129 N3
Drysdale St **N1** 126 C5
Dublin Av **E8** 126 E3
Duchess of Bedford's Wk **W8** 128 A1
Duchess St **W1** 125 H7
Duchy St **SE1** 125 N10
Ducie St **SW4** 129 M10
Duckett St **E1** 127 H6
Dudley St **W2** 124 D7
Duff St **E14** 127 M8
Dufferin St **EC1** 126 A6
Dugard Way **SE11** 129 P3
Duke of Wellington Pl **SW1** 128 G1
Duke of York Sq **SW3** 128 F3
Duke of York St **SW1** 125 J10
Duke St **SW1** 125 J10
Duke St **W1** 124 G8
Dukes La **W8** 128 A1
Dukes Pl **EC3** 126 C8
Duke's Rd **WC1** 125 K5
Dunbridge St **E2** 126 E6
Duncan Rd **E8** 126 F3
Duncan St **N1** 125 P4
Duncan Ter **N1** 125 P4
Duncannon St **WC2** 125 L9
Dundalk Rd **SE4** 131 J9
Dundas Rd **SE15** 130 G8
Dundee St **E1** 126 F10
Dunelm St **E1** 127 H8
Dunloe St **E2** 126 D4
Dunston Rd **E8** 126 D3
Dunston Rd **SW11** 128 G8
Dunston St **E8** 126 D3
Dunton Rd **SE1** 130 D4
Durand Gdns **SW9** 129 M7
Durands Wk **SE16** 131 K1
Durant St **E2** 126 E4
Durham Row **E1** 127 J7
Durham St **SE11** 129 M4
Durham Ter **W2** 124 B8
Durward St **E1** 126 F7
Durweston St **W1** 124 F7
Dutton St **SE10** 131 N7
Dye Ho La **E3** 127 L3
Dylan Rd **SE24** 129 P10
Dylways **SE5** 130 B10
Dymock St **SW6** 128 B9
Dynham Rd **NW6** 124 A2
Dyott St **WC1** 125 K8

E

Eagle Ct **EC1** 125 P7
Eagle St **WC1** 125 M7
Eagle Wf Rd **N1** 126 A4
Eamont St **NW8** 124 E4
Eardley Cres **SW5** 128 A4
Earl St **EC2** 126 B7
Earlham St **WC2** 125 K8
Earls Ct Gdns **SW5** 128 B3
Earls Ct Rd **SW5** 128 A3
Earls Ct Rd **W8** 128 A3
Earls Ct Sq **SW5** 128 B4
Earls Wk **W8** 128 A2
Earlsferry Way **N1** 125 M2
Earlston Gro **E9** 126 F3
Earnshaw St **WC2** 125 K8
East Arbour St **E1** 127 H8
East Cross Cen **E15** 127 L1
East Cross Route **E3** 127 K2
East Cross Route **E9** 127 K2
East Dulwich Rd **SE15** 130 D10
East Dulwich Rd **SE22** 130 D10
East Ferry Rd **E14** 131 M2
East India Dock Rd **E14** 127 L8
East La **SE16** 130 E1
East Mt St **E1** 126 F7
East Rd **N1** 126 B5
East Smithfield **E1** 126 D9
East St **SE17** 130 A4
East Surrey Gro **SE15** 130 D6
East Tenter St **E1** 126 D8
Eastbourne Ms **W2** 124 C8
Eastbourne Ter **W2** 124 C8
Eastbury Ter **E1** 127 H6
Eastcastle St **W1** 125 J8
Eastcheap **EC3** 126 B9
Eastcote St **SW9** 129 M8
Eastdown Pk **SE13** 131 P10
Eastern Rd **SE4** 131 L10
Eastfield St **E14** 127 J7
Eastfields Av **SW18** 128 A10
Eastlake Rd **SE5** 129 P8
Eastney St **SE10** 131 P4
Eastway **E9** 127 K1
Eaton Cl **SW1** 128 G3
Eaton Dr **SW9** 129 P10
Eaton Gate **SW1** 128 G3
Eaton La **SW1** 129 H2
Eaton Ms N **SW1** 128 G2
Eaton Ms S **SW1** 129 H2
Eaton Ms W **SW1** 128 G3
Eaton Pl **SW1** 128 G2
Eaton Row **SW1** 129 H2
Eaton Sq **SW1** 128 G3
Eaton Ter **SW1** 128 G3
Ebbisham Dr **SW8** 129 M5
Ebenezer St **N1** 126 B5
Ebley Cl **SE15** 130 D5
Ebor St **E1** 126 D6
Ebury Br **SW1** 129 H4
Ebury Br Est **SW1** 129 H4
Ebury Br Rd **SW1** 128 G4
Ebury Ms **SW1** 129 H3
Ebury Sq **SW1** 128 G3
Ebury St **SW1** 128 G3
Eccles Rd **SW11** 128 F10
Ecclesbourne Rd **N1** 126 A2
Eccleston Br **SW1** 129 H3
Eccleston Ms **SW1** 128 G2
Eccleston Pl **SW1** 129 H3
Eccleston Sq **SW1** 129 H3
Eccleston Sq Ms **SW1** 129 H3
Eccleston St **SW1** 128 G2
Eckford St **N1** 125 N4
Eckstein Rd **SW11** 128 E10
Edbrooke Rd **W9** 124 A6
Eddystone Twr **SE8** 131 J3
Edenbridge Rd **E9** 127 H2
Edenvale St **SW6** 128 B8
Edgar Kail Way **SE22** 130 C10
Edgar Rd **E3** 127 M5
Edgeley Rd **SW4** 129 K9
Edgware Rd **W2** 124 E8
Edinburgh Gate **SW1** 128 F1
Edinburgh Ho **W9** 124 C5
Edis St **NW1** 124 G3
Edith Gro **SW10** 128 C5
Edith Row **SW6** 128 B7
Edith St **E2** 126 E4
Edith Ter **SW10** 128 C6
Edithna St **SW9** 129 L9
Edmeston Cl **E9** 127 J1
Edmund St **SE5** 130 B6
Edna St **SW11** 128 E7
Edric Rd **SE14** 131 H6
Edrich Ho **SW4** 129 L7
Edward Pl **SE8** 131 K5
Edward St **SE8** 131 K5
Edward St **SE14** 131 J6
Edwardes Sq **W8** 128 A2
Edwards Ms **N1** 125 N2
Edwards Ms **W1** 124 G8
Edwin St **E1** 126 G6
Effie Pl **SW6** 128 A6
Effie Rd **SW6** 128 A6
Effra Rd **SW2** 129 N10
Egbert St **NW1** 124 G3
Egremont Rd **SE13** 131 M8
Egerton Cres **SW3** 128 E3
Egerton Dr **SE10** 131 M7
Egerton Gdns **SW3** 128 E2
Egerton Gdns Ms **SW3** 128 E2
Egerton Pl **SW3** 128 E2
Egerton Ter **SW3** 128 E2
Egmont St **SE14** 131 H6
Elam Cl **SE5** 129 P8
Elam St **SE5** 129 P8
Eland Rd **SW11** 128 F9
Elbe St **SW6** 128 C8
Elcho St **SW11** 128 E6
Elcot Av **SE15** 130 F6
Elder St **E1** 126 D7
Eldon Rd **W8** 128 B2
Eldon St **EC2** 126 B7
Eleanor Cl **SE16** 131 H1
Eleanor Rd **E8** 126 F2
Eleanor St **E3** 127 L5
Electra Business Pk **E16** 127 P7
Electric Av **SW9** 129 N10
Electric La **SW9** 129 N10
Elephant & Castle **SE1** 129 P3
Elephant La **SE16** 130 G1
Elephant Rd **SE17** 130 A3
Elf Row **E1** 126 G9
Elgar St **SE16** 131 J2
Elgin Av **W9** 124 B5
Elia Ms **N1** 125 P4
Elia St **N1** 125 P4
Elias Pl **SW8** 129 N5
Elim Est **SE1** 130 B2
Eliot Hill **SE13** 131 N8
Eliot Ms **NW8** 124 C4
Eliot Pk **SE13** 131 N9
Eliot Vale **SE3** 131 P8
Elizabeth Av **N1** 126 A2
Elizabeth Br **SW1** 129 H3
Elizabeth Est **SE17** 130 B5
Elizabeth Ms **NW3** 124 E1
Elizabeth St **SW1** 128 G3
Elland Rd **SE15** 130 G10
Ellen St **E1** 126 E8
Ellerdale St **SE13** 131 M10
Ellery St **SE15** 130 F8
Ellesmere Rd **E3** 127 J4
Ellesmere St **E14** 127 M8
Ellingfort Rd **E8** 126 F2
Ellington St **N7** 125 N1
Elliott Rd **SW9** 129 P6
Elliott Sq **NW3** 124 E2
Elliotts Row **SE11** 129 P3
Ellis St **SW1** 128 F3
Ellsworth St **E2** 126 F5
Elm Friars Wk **NW1** 125 K2
Elm Gro **SE15** 130 D8
Elm Pk Gdns **SW10** 128 D4
Elm Pk La **SW3** 128 D4
Elm Pk Rd **SW3** 128 D5
Elm Pl **SW7** 128 D4
Elm Quay Ct **SW8** 129 K5
Elm St **WC1** 125 M6
Elm Tree Cl **NW8** 124 D5
Elm Tree Rd **NW8** 124 D5
Elmfield Way **W9** 124 A7
Elmhurst St **SW4** 129 K9
Elmington Est **SE5** 130 B6
Elmington Rd **SE5** 130 B7
Elmira St **SE13** 131 M9
Elmore St **N1** 126 A2
Elms Ms **W2** 124 D9
Elmslie Pt **E3** 127 K7
Elmstone Rd **SW6** 128 A7
Elmwood Ct **SW11** 129 H7
Elrington Rd **E8** 126 E1
Elsa St **E1** 127 J7
Elsdale St **E9** 126 G1
Elsie Rd **SE22** 130 D10
Elsley Rd **SW11** 128 F9
Elspeth Rd **SW11** 128 F10
Elsted St **SE17** 130 B3
Elswick Rd **SE13** 131 M8
Elswick St **SW6** 128 C8
Elsworthy Ri **NW3** 124 E2
Elsworthy Rd **NW3** 124 E3
Elsworthy Ter **NW3** 124 E2
Elthiron Rd **SW6** 128 A7
Elton Ho **E3** 127 K3
Eltringham St **SW18** 128 C10
Elvaston Ms **SW7** 128 C2
Elvaston Pl **SW7** 128 C2
Elverson Ms **SE8** 131 M8
Elverson Rd **SE8** 131 M8
Elverton St **SW1** 129 K3
Elwin St **E2** 126 E5
Elystan Pl **SW3** 128 E4
Elystan St **SW3** 128 E3
Emba St **SE16** 130 E1
Embankment Gdns **SW3** 128 F5
Embankment Pl **WC2** 125 L10
Emberton **SE5** 130 C5
Embleton Rd **SE13** 131 M9
Emden St **SW6** 128 B7
Emerald St **WC1** 125 M7
Emerson St **SE1** 126 A10
Emery Hill St **SW1** 129 J2
Emma St **E2** 126 F4
Emmott Cl **E1** 127 J6
Emperor's Gate **SW7** 128 B2
Empire Wf Rd **E14** 131 P3
Empress Ms **SE5** 130 A8
Empress Pl **SW6** 128 A4
Empress St **SE17** 130 A5
Empson St **E3** 127 M6
Emu Rd **SW8** 129 H8
Endell St **WC2** 125 L8
Endsleigh Gdns **WC1** 125 K6
Endsleigh Pl **WC1** 125 K6
Endsleigh St **WC1** 125 K6
Endwell Rd **SE4** 131 J8
Enfield Rd **N1** 126 C2
Enford St **W1** 124 F7
Engate St **SE13** 131 N10
Englands La **NW3** 124 F1
Englefield Rd **N1** 126 B1
English St **E3** 127 K6
Enid St **SE16** 130 D2
Ennerdale Ho **E3** 127 K6
Ennismore Gdns **SW7** 128 E1
Ennismore Gdns Ms **SW7** 128 E2
Ennismore Ms **SW7** 128 E1
Ennismore St **SW7** 128 E2
Ensign St **E1** 126 E9
Enterprise Way **SW18** 128 A10
Enterprize Way **SE8** 131 K3
Epirus Ms **SW6** 128 A6
Epping Cl **E14** 131 L3
Epworth St **EC2** 126 B6
Erasmus St **SW1** 129 K3
Eresby Pl **NW6** 124 A2
Eric St **E3** 127 K6
Erlanger Rd **SE14** 131 H7
Ermine Rd **SE13** 131 M9
Ernest St **E1** 127 H6
Errol St **EC1** 126 A6
Erskine Rd **NW3** 124 F2
Esmeralda Rd **SE1** 130 E3
Essendine Rd **W9** 124 A6
Essex Rd **N1** 125 P3
Essex Vil **W8** 128 A1
Essian St **E1** 127 J7
Este Rd **SW11** 128 E9
Esterbrooke St **SW1** 129 K3
Ethelburga St **SW11** 128 E7
Ethnard Rd **SE15** 130 F5
Eton Av **NW3** 124 D2
Eton Coll Rd **NW3** 124 F1
Eton Rd **NW3** 124 F2
Eton Vil **NW3** 124 F1
Etta St **SE8** 131 J5
Ettrick St **E14** 127 N8
Eugenia Rd **SE16** 130 G3
Eustace Rd **SW6** 128 A6
Euston Gro **NW1** 125 K5
Euston Rd **N1** 125 K6
Euston Rd **NW1** 125 H6
Euston Sq **NW1** 125 K5
Euston Sta **NW1** 125 J5
Euston St **NW1** 125 J5
Euston Twr **NW1** 125 J6
Evandale Rd **SW9** 129 N8
Evelina Rd **SE15** 130 G9
Eveline Lowe Est **SE16** 130 E2
Evelyn Gdns **SW7** 128 D4
Evelyn St **SE8** 131 J4
Evelyn Wk **N1** 126 B4
Everest Pl **E14** 127 N7
Evergreen Sq **E8** 126 D2
Everilda St **N1** 125 M3
Eversholt St **NW1** 125 J4
Eversleigh Rd **SW11** 128 F9
Everthorpe Rd **SE15** 130 D9
Evesham Wk **SW9** 129 N8
Evesham Way **SW11** 128 G9
Ewe Cl **N7** 125 L1
Ewer St **SE1** 126 A10
Ewhurst Cl **E1** 126 G7
Excelsior Gdns **SE13** 131 N8
Exchange Sq **EC2** 126 C7
Exeter St **WC2** 125 L9
Exeter Way **SE14** 131 K6
Exhibition Rd **SW7** 128 D2
Exmouth Mkt **EC1** 125 N6
Exmouth Pl **E8** 126 F2
Exon St **SE17** 130 C4
Exton St **SE1** 125 N10
Eythorne Rd **SW9** 129 N7
Ezra St **E2** 126 D5

F

Fairbairn Grn **SW9** 129 N7
Faircharm Trd Est **SE8** 131 M6
Fairclough St **E1** 126 E8
Fairfax Pl **NW6** 124 C2
Fairfax Rd **NW6** 124 C2
Fairfield Rd **E3** 127 L4
Fairfoot Rd **E3** 127 L6
Fairhazel Gdns **NW6** 124 B1
Fairmont Av **E14** 127 P10
Fakruddin St **E1** 126 E6
Falcon Ct **EC4** 125 N8
Falcon Gro **SW11** 128 E9
Falcon La **SW11** 128 E9
Falcon Rd **SW11** 128 E8
Falcon Ter **SW11** 128 E9
Falcon Way **E14** 131 M3
Falkirk Ho **W9** 124 B5
Falkirk St **N1** 126 C4
Falmouth Rd **SE1** 130 A2
Fann St **EC1** 126 A6
Fann St **EC2** 126 A6
Fanshaw St **N1** 126 C5
Farm La **SW6** 128 A5
Farm St **W1** 125 H9
Farmers Rd **SE5** 129 P6
Farncombe St **SE16** 130 E1
Farrance St **E14** 127 K8
Farrell Ho **E1** 126 G8
Farrier St **NW1** 125 H2
Farrier Wk **SW10** 128 C5
Farringdon La **EC1** 125 N6
Farringdon Rd **EC1** 125 N6
Farringdon St **EC4** 125 P7
Farrins Rents **SE16** 127 J10
Farrow La **SE14** 130 G6
Farthingale Wk **E15** 127 P2
Fashion St **E1** 126 D7
Fassett Rd **E8** 126 E1
Fassett Sq **E8** 126 E1
Faulkner St **SE14** 130 G7
Favart Rd **SW6** 128 A7
Fawcett Cl **SW11** 128 D8
Fawcett St **SW10** 128 C5
Fawe St **E14** 127 M7
Feathers Pl **SE10** 131 P5
Featherstone St **EC1** 126 B6
Featley Rd **SW9** 129 P9
Fellows Ct **E2** 126 D4
Fellows Rd **NW3** 124 D2
Felstead St **E9** 127 K1
Felton St **N1** 126 B3
Fenchurch Av **EC3** 126 C8
Fenchurch St **EC3** 126 C9
Fendall St **SE1** 130 C2
Fenham Rd **SE15** 130 E6
Fentiman Rd **SW8** 129 L5
Fenton Cl **SW9** 129 M8
Fenwick Gro **SE15** 130 E9
Fenwick Pl **SW9** 129 L9
Fenwick Rd **SE15** 130 E9
Ferdinand St **NW1** 124 G1
Ferguson Cl **E14** 131 L3
Fern St **E3** 127 L6
Ferndale Rd **SW4** 129 L10
Ferndale Rd **SW9** 129 M9
Ferndene Rd **SE24** 130 A10
Fernshaw Rd **SW10** 128 C5
Ferrey Ms **SW9** 129 N8
Ferrier St **SW18** 128 B10
Ferris Rd **SE22** 130 E10
Ferry St **E14** 131 N4
Ferryman's Quay **SW6** 128 C8
Fetter La **EC4** 125 N8
Ffinch St **SE8** 131 L6
Field St **WC1** 125 M5
Fieldgate St **E1** 126 E7
Fielding Ho **NW6** 124 A5
Fielding St **SE17** 130 A5
Fields Est **E8** 126 E2
Fife Ter **N1** 125 M4
Finborough Rd **SW10** 128 B4
Finch Ms **SE15** 130 D6
Finchley Pl **NW8** 124 D4
Finchley Rd **NW3** 124 C1
Finchley Rd **NW8** 124 D3
Findhorn St **E14** 127 N8
Finland Rd **SE4** 131 J9
Finland St **SE16** 131 J2
Finnis St **E2** 126 F5
Finsbury Circ **EC2** 126 B7
Finsbury Est **EC1** 125 N5
Finsbury Mkt **EC2** 126 C6
Finsbury Pavement **EC2** 126 B7
Finsbury Sq **EC2** 126 B7
Finsbury St **EC2** 126 B7
Finsen Rd **SE5** 130 A9
Fir Trees Cl **SE16** 127 J10
Firbank Rd **SE15** 130 F8
First St **SW3** 128 E3
Fish St Hill **EC3** 126 B9
Fisher St **WC1** 125 M7
Fishermans Dr **SE16** 131 H1
Fisherman's Wk **E14** 127 L10
Fisherton St **NW8** 124 D6
Fitzalan St **SE11** 129 M3
Fitzgerald Ho **E14** 127 M8
Fitzhardinge St **W1** 124 G8
Fitzmaurice Pl **W1** 125 H9
Fitzroy Rd **NW1** 124 G3
Fitzroy Sq **W1** 125 J6
Fitzroy St **W1** 125 J6
Fitzwilliam Rd **SW4** 129 J9
Fiveways Rd **SW9** 129 N8
Flamborough St **E14** 127 J8
Flanders Way **E9** 127 H1
Flaxman Rd **SE5** 129 P8
Flaxman Ter **WC1** 125 K5
Fleet St **EC4** 125 N8
Fleming Rd **SE17** 129 P5
Fleur de Lis St **E1** 126 C6
Flint St **SE17** 130 B3
Flinton St **SE17** 130 C4
Flodden Rd **SE5** 130 A7
Flood St **SW3** 128 E4
Flood Wk **SW3** 128 E5
Flora Cl **E14** 127 M8
Floral St **WC2** 125 L9
Florence Rd **SE14** 131 K7
Florence St **N1** 125 P2
Florence Ter **SE14** 131 K7
Florida St **E2** 126 E5
Flower Wk, The **SW7** 128 C1
Foley St **W1** 125 J7
Folgate St **E1** 126 C7
Follett St **E14** 127 N8
Folly Wall **E14** 131 N1
Fontarabia Rd **SW11** 128 G10
Ford Rd **E3** 127 J3
Ford Sq **E1** 126 F7
Ford St **E3** 127 J3
Fordham St **E1** 126 E8
Fore St **EC2** 126 A7
Foreign St **SE5** 129 P8
Foreshore **SE8** 131 K3
Forest Gro **E8** 126 D1
Forest Rd **E8** 126 D1
Forester Rd **SE15** 130 F10
Forfar Rd **SW11** 128 G7
Formosa St **W9** 124 B7
Forset St **W1** 124 E8
Forsyth Gdns **SE17** 129 P5
Fort Rd **SE1** 130 D3
Forthbridge Rd **SW11** 128 G10
Fortune St **EC1** 126 A6
Fossil Rd **SE13** 131 L9
Foster La **EC2** 126 A8
Foubert's Pl **W1** 125 J8
Foulis Ter **SW7** 128 D4
Foundry Cl **SE16** 127 J10
Fount St **SW8** 129 K6
Fountain Ms **NW3** 124 F1
Fountain Pl **SW9** 129 N7
Fountain Sq **SW1** 129 H3
Four Seasons Cl **E3** 127 L4
Fournier St **E1** 126 D7
Fowler Cl **SW11** 128 D9
Fownes St **SW11** 128 E9
Fox Cl **E1** 126 G6
Foxberry Rd **SE4** 131 J9
Foxcote **SE5** 130 C4
Foxley Rd **SW9** 129 N6
Foxmore St **SW11** 128 F7
Foxwell St **SE4** 131 J9
Frampton Pk Rd **E9** 126 G1
Frampton St **NW8** 124 D6
Francis Chichester Way **SW11** 128 G7
Francis St **SW1** 129 J3
Frankham St **SE8** 131 L6
Frankland Cl **SE16** 130 F2
Franklin Cl **SE13** 131 M7
Franklin Pl **SE13** 131 M7
Franklin St **E3** 127 M5
Franklin's Row **SW3** 128 F4
Frazier St **SE1** 129 N1
Frean St **SE16** 130 E2
Frederick Cl **W2** 124 E9
Frederick Cres **SW9** 129 P6
Frederick St **WC1** 125 M5
Freedom St **SW11** 128 F8
Freemantle St **SE17** 130 C4
Freke Rd **SW11** 128 G9
Fremont St **E9** 126 G3
Frendsbury Rd **SE4** 131 J10
Frensham St **SE15** 130 E5
Frere St **SW11** 128 E8
Freshfield Av **E8** 126 D2
Friars Mead **E14** 131 N2
Friary Est **SE15** 130 E5
Friary Rd **SE15** 130 E6
Friday St **EC4** 126 A8
Friend St **EC1** 125 P5

Friendly St **SE8** 131 L7
Frimley Way **E1** 127 H6
Friston St **SW6** 128 B8
Frith St **W1** 125 K8
Frogley Rd **SE22** 130 D10
Frognal Ct **NW3** 124 C1
Frome St **N1** 126 A4
Frostic Wk **E1** 126 D7
Froude St **SW8** 129 H8
Fulford St **SE16** 130 F1
Fulham Bdy **SW6** 128 A6
Fulham Rd **SW3** 128 C5
Fulham Rd **SW10** 128 B6
Fulmead St **SW6** 128 B7
Fulwood Pl **WC1** 125 M7
Furley Rd **SE15** 130 E6
Furlong Rd **N7** 125 N1
Furness Rd **SW6** 128 B8
Furnival St **EC4** 125 N8
Furze St **E3** 127 L7
Fyfield Rd **SW9** 129 N9
Fynes St **SW1** 129 K3

G

Gables Cl **SE5** 130 C7
Gabrielle Ct **NW3** 124 D1
Gainsford St **SE1** 130 D1
Gairloch Rd **SE5** 130 C8
Gaisford St **NW5** 125 J1
Gaitskell Ct **SW11** 128 E8
Galbraith St **E14** 131 N2
Gale St **E3** 127 L7
Gales Gdns **E2** 126 F5
Galleywall Rd **SE16** 130 F3
Galsworthy Av **E14** 127 J7
Galway St **EC1** 126 A5
Gambetta St **SW8** 129 H8
Garden Rd **NW8** 124 C5
Garden Row **SE1** 129 P2
Garden St **E1** 127 H7
Gardens, The **SE22** 130 E10
Garfield Rd **SW11** 128 G9
Garford St **E14** 127 L9
Garlick Hill **EC4** 126 A9
Garnet St **E1** 126 G9
Garnies Cl **SE15** 130 D6
Garrick Cl **SW18** 128 C10
Garrick St **WC2** 125 L9
Garsington Ms **SE4** 131 K9
Gartons Way **SW11** 128 C9
Garway Rd **W2** 124 B8
Gascoigne Pl **E2** 126 D5
Gascony Av **NW6** 124 A2
Gascoyne Rd **E9** 127 H2
Gaselee St **E14** 127 N9
Gaskell St **SW4** 129 L8
Gaskin St **N1** 125 P3
Gataker St **SE16** 130 F2
Gate Ms **SW7** 128 E1
Gateforth St **NW8** 124 E6
Gateley Rd **SW9** 129 M9
Gateway **SE17** 130 A5
Gateways, The **SW3** 128 F3
Gatliff Rd **SW1** 128 G4
Gatonby St **SE15** 130 D7
Gauden Cl **SW4** 129 K9
Gauden Rd **SW4** 129 K8
Gautrey Rd **SE15** 130 G8
Gawber St **E2** 126 G5
Gay Rd **E15** 127 P4
Gaydon Ho **W2** 124 B7
Gayfere St **SW1** 129 L2
Gayhurst Rd **E8** 126 E2
Gayton Ho **E3** 127 L6
Gaywood Est **SE1** 129 P2
Gedling Pl **SE1** 130 D1
Gee St **EC1** 126 A6
Geffrye St **E2** 126 D4
Geldart Rd **SE15** 130 F6
Gellatly Rd **SE14** 130 G8
General Wolfe Rd **SE10** 131 P7
Geneva Dr **SW9** 129 N10
Geoffrey Cl **SE5** 130 A8
Geoffrey Rd **SE4** 131 K9
George Beard Rd **SE8** 131 K3
George Mathers Rd **SE11** 129 P3
George Row **SE16** 130 E1
George St **W1** 124 G8
George Yd **W1** 124 G9
Georgiana St **NW1** 125 J3
Gerald Rd **SW1** 128 G3
Geraldine St **SE11** 129 P2
Gerards Cl **SE16** 130 G4
Gernon Rd **E3** 127 J4
Gerrard Rd **N1** 125 P4
Gerrard St **W1** 125 K9
Gerridge St **SE1** 129 N2
Gertrude St **SW10** 128 C5
Gervase St **SE15** 130 F6
Gibbins Rd **E15** 127 N2
Gibbon Rd **SE15** 130 G8
Gibraltar Wk **E2** 126 D5
Gibson Rd **SE11** 129 M3
Gibson Sq **N1** 125 N3
Gideon Rd **SW11** 128 G9
Giffin St **SE8** 131 L6
Gifford St **N1** 125 L2
Gilbert Rd **SE11** 129 N3
Gilbert St **W1** 124 G8
Gilbeys Yd **NW1** 124 G2
Gill St **E14** 127 K8
Gillender St **E3** 127 N6
Gillender St **E14** 127 N6
Gillfoot **NW1** 125 J4
Gilling Ct **NW3** 124 E1
Gillingham St **SW1** 129 H3
Gilmore Rd **SE13** 131 P10
Gilstead Rd **SW6** 128 B8
Gilston Rd **SW10** 128 C4
Giltspur St **EC1** 125 P8
Giraud St **E14** 127 M8
Gladstone St **SE1** 129 P2
Gladys Rd **NW6** 124 A2
Glaisher St **SE8** 131 L5
Glamis Pl **E1** 126 G9
Glamis Rd **E1** 126 G9
Glasgow Ho **W9** 124 B4
Glasgow Ter **SW1** 129 J4
Glasshill St **SE1** 129 P1
Glasshouse Flds **E1** 127 H9
Glasshouse St **W1** 125 J9
Glasshouse Wk **SE11** 129 L4
Glaucus St **E3** 127 M7
Glebe Pl **SW3** 128 E5
Gledhow Gdns **SW5** 128 C3
Glenaffric Av **E14** 131 P3
Glendall St **SW9** 129 M10
Glendower Pl **SW7** 128 D3
Glenfinlas Way **SE5** 129 P6
Glengall Causeway **E14** 131 L2
Glengall Gro **E14** 131 M2
Glengall Rd **SE15** 130 D5
Glengall Ter **SE15** 130 D5
Glengarnock Av **E14** 131 N3
Glenilla Rd **NW3** 124 E1
Glenloch Rd **NW3** 124 E1
Glenmore Rd **NW3** 124 E1
Glenrosa St **SW6** 128 C8
Glensdale Rd **SE4** 131 K9
Glentworth St **NW1** 124 F6
Glenville Gro **SE8** 131 K6
Glenworth Av **E14** 131 P3
Globe Pond Rd **SE16** 127 J10
Globe Rd **E1** 126 G5
Globe Rd **E2** 126 G5
Globe Rope Wk **E14** 131 N3
Globe St **SE1** 130 A2
Gloucester Av **NW1** 124 G2
Gloucester Circ **SE10** 131 N6
Gloucester Cres **NW1** 125 H3
Gloucester Gate **NW1** 125 H4
Gloucester Ho **NW6** 124 A4
Gloucester Ms **W2** 124 C8
Gloucester Pl **NW1** 124 F6
Gloucester Pl **W1** 124 F7
Gloucester Rd **SW7** 128 C2
Gloucester Sq **W2** 124 D8
Gloucester St **SW1** 129 J4
Gloucester Ter **W2** 124 D9
Gloucester Wk **W8** 128 A1
Gloucester Way **EC1** 125 N5
Glycena Rd **SW11** 128 F9
Godalming Rd **E14** 127 M7
Godfrey St **E15** 127 N4
Godfrey St **SW3** 128 E4
Goding St **SE11** 129 L4
Godliman St **EC4** 126 A8
Godman Rd **SE15** 130 F8
Godson St **N1** 125 N4
Goffers Rd **SE3** 131 P7
Golden Jubilee Br **SE1** 125 L10
Golden Jubilee Br **WC2** 125 L10
Golden La **EC1** 126 A6
Golden Sq **W1** 125 J9
Goldhurst Ter **NW6** 124 B2
Golding St **E1** 126 E8
Goldington Cres **NW1** 125 K4
Goldington St **NW1** 125 K4
Goldman Cl **E2** 126 E6
Goldney Rd **W9** 124 A6
Goldsboro Rd **SW8** 129 K7
Goldsmith Rd **SE15** 130 E7
Goldsmith's Row **E2** 126 E4
Goldsmith's Sq **E2** 126 E4
Goldsworthy Gdns **SE16** 130 G3
Goldwin Cl **SE14** 130 G7
Gomm Rd **SE16** 130 G2
Gonson St **SE8** 131 M5
Goodge St **W1** 125 J7
Goodhart Pl **E14** 127 J9
Goodinge Cl **N7** 125 L1
Goodman's Stile **E1** 126 E8
Goodmans Yd **E1** 126 D9
Goods Way **NW1** 125 L4
Goodway Gdns **E14** 127 P8
Goodwin Cl **SE16** 130 E2
Goodwood Rd **SE14** 131 J6
Gopsall St **N1** 126 B3
Gordon Gro **SE5** 129 P8
Gordon Pl **W8** 128 A1
Gordon Rd **SE15** 130 F8
Gordon Sq **WC1** 125 K6
Gordon St **WC1** 125 K6
Gore Rd **E9** 126 G3
Gore St **SW7** 128 C2
Gorefield Pl **NW6** 124 A4
Goring St **EC3** 126 C8
Gorsuch St **E2** 126 D5
Gosfield St **W1** 125 J7
Gosling Way **SW9** 129 N7
Gosset St **E2** 126 D5
Gosterwood St **SE8** 131 J5
Goswell Rd **EC1** 125 P5
Gough Sq **EC4** 125 N8
Gough St **WC1** 125 M6
Goulden Ho App **SW11** 128 E8
Goulston St **E1** 126 D8
Gower Ms **WC1** 125 K7
Gower Pl **WC1** 125 J6
Gower St **WC1** 125 J6
Gower's Wk **E1** 126 E8
Gowlett Rd **SE15** 130 E9
Gowrie Rd **SW11** 128 G9
Grace St **E3** 127 M5
Gracechurch St **EC3** 126 B9
Grace's All **E1** 126 E9
Graces Ms **SE5** 130 C8
Graces Rd **SE5** 130 C8
Grafton Cres **NW1** 125 H1
Grafton Ho **E3** 127 L5
Grafton Pl **NW1** 125 K5
Grafton Sq **SW4** 129 J9
Grafton St **W1** 125 H9
Grafton Way **W1** 125 J6
Grafton Way **WC1** 125 J6
Graham Rd **E8** 126 D1
Graham St **N1** 125 P4
Graham Ter **SW1** 128 G3
Granary Rd **E1** 126 F6
Granary St **NW1** 125 K3
Granby St **E2** 126 D6
Granby Ter **NW1** 125 J4
Grand Junct Wf **N1** 126 A4
Grand Union Cres **E8** 126 E2
Grand Union Wk **NW1** 125 H2
Granfield St **SW11** 128 D7
Grange, The **SE1** 130 D2
Grange Gro **N1** 125 P1
Grange Pl **NW6** 124 A2
Grange Rd **SE1** 130 C2
Grange St **N1** 126 B3
Grange Wk **SE1** 130 C2
Grange Yd **SE1** 130 D2
Gransden Av **E8** 126 F2
Grant Rd **SW11** 128 D10
Grantbridge St **N1** 125 P4
Grantham Rd **SW9** 129 L8
Grantley St **E1** 127 H5
Grantully Rd **W9** 124 B5
Granville Ct **N1** 126 B3
Granville Gro **SE13** 131 N9
Granville Pk **SE13** 131 N9
Granville Pl **W1** 124 G8
Granville Rd **NW6** 124 A4
Granville Sq **SE15** 130 C6
Granville Sq **WC1** 125 M5
Grayling Sq **E2** 126 E5
Gray's Inn **WC1** 125 M7
Gray's Inn Rd **WC1** 125 M5
Grayshott Rd **SW11** 128 G8
Great Castle St **W1** 125 J8
Great Cen St **NW1** 124 F7
Great Chapel St **W1** 125 K8
Great Chart St **SW11** 128 D10
Great Coll St **SW1** 129 L2
Great Cumberland Pl **W1** 124 F8
Great Dover St **SE1** 130 A1
Great Eastern Enterprise Cen **E14** 131 M1
Great Eastern Rd **E15** 127 P2
Great Eastern St **EC2** 126 C5
Great George St **SW1** 129 K1
Great Guildford St **SE1** 126 A10
Great James St **WC1** 125 M7
Great Marlborough St **W1** 125 J8
Great Maze Pond **SE1** 130 B1
Great Ormond St **WC1** 125 L7
Great Percy St **WC1** 125 M5
Great Peter St **SW1** 129 K2
Great Portland St **W1** 125 H6
Great Pulteney St **W1** 125 J9
Great Queen St **WC2** 125 L8
Great Russell St **WC1** 125 L7
Great St. Helens **EC3** 126 C8
Great Scotland Yd **SW1** 125 L10
Great Smith St **SW1** 129 K2
Great Suffolk St **SE1** 125 P10
Great Sutton St **EC1** 125 P6
Great Titchfield St **W1** 125 J8
Great Twr St **EC3** 126 C9
Great Winchester St **EC2** 126 B8
Great Windmill St **W1** 125 K9
Greatfield Cl **SE4** 131 L10
Greatorex St **E1** 126 E7
Greek St **W1** 125 K8
Green Bk **E1** 126 F10
Green Dale **SE5** 130 B10
Green Hundred Rd **SE15** 130 E5
Green St **W1** 124 G9
Greenberry St **NW8** 124 E4
Greencoat Pl **SW1** 129 J3
Greencroft Gdns **NW6** 124 B2
Greenfield Rd **E1** 126 E7
Greenham Cl **SE1** 129 N1
Greenland Quay **SE16** 131 H3
Greenland Rd **NW1** 125 J3
Greenman St **N1** 126 A2
Greenwell St **W1** 125 H6
Greenwich Ch St **SE10** 131 N5
Greenwich Foot Tunnel **E14** 131 N4
Greenwich Foot Tunnel **SE10** 131 N4
Greenwich High Rd **SE10** 131 M7
Greenwich Pk St **SE10** 131 P4
Greenwich Quay **SE8** 131 M5
Greenwich S St **SE10** 131 M7
Greenwich Vw Pl **E14** 131 M2
Greenwood Ct **SW1** 129 J4
Greenwood Rd **E8** 126 E1
Greet St **SE1** 125 N10
Gregory Pl **W8** 128 B1
Grenade St **E14** 127 K9
Grenard Cl **SE15** 130 E6
Grendon St **NW8** 124 E6
Grenville Ms **SW7** 128 C3
Grenville Pl **SW7** 128 C2
Grenville St **WC1** 125 L6
Gresham Rd **SW9** 129 N9
Gresham St **EC2** 126 A8
Gresse St **W1** 125 K7
Greville Pl **NW6** 124 B4
Greville Rd **NW6** 124 B3
Greville St **EC1** 125 N7
Grey Eagle St **E1** 126 D7
Greycoat Pl **SW1** 129 K2
Greycoat St **SW1** 129 K2
Grimwade Cl **SE15** 130 G9
Grinling Pl **SE8** 131 L5
Grinstead Rd **SE8** 131 J4
Grittleton Rd **W9** 124 A6
Groom Pl **SW1** 128 G2
Groombridge Rd **E9** 127 H2
Grosvenor Cres **SW1** 128 G1
Grosvenor Cres Ms **SW1** 128 G1
Grosvenor Est **SW1** 129 K3
Grosvenor Gdns **SW1** 129 H2
Grosvenor Gate **W1** 124 F9
Grosvenor Hill **W1** 125 H9
Grosvenor Pk **SE5** 130 A5
Grosvenor Pl **SW1** 128 G1
Grosvenor Rd **SW1** 129 H5
Grosvenor Sq **W1** 124 G9
Grosvenor St **W1** 125 H9
Grosvenor Ter **SE5** 129 P6
Grosvenor Wf Rd **E14** 131 P3
Grove Cotts **SW3** 128 E5
Grove Cres Rd **E15** 127 P1
Grove End Rd **NW8** 124 D5
Grove Hill Rd **SE5** 130 C9
Grove La **SE5** 130 B7
Grove Pk **SE5** 130 C8
Grove Pas **E2** 126 F4
Grove Rd **E3** 127 H3
Grove St **SE8** 131 K3
Grove Vale **SE22** 130 C10
Grove Vil **E14** 127 M9
Grovelands Cl **SE5** 130 C8
Groveway **SW9** 129 M7
Grummant Rd **SE15** 130 D7
Grundy St **E14** 127 M8
Guerin Sq **E3** 127 K5
Guildford Gro **SE10** 131 M7
Guildford Rd **SW8** 129 L7
Guildhouse St **SW1** 129 J3
Guilford Pl **WC1** 125 M6
Guilford St **WC1** 125 L6
Guinness Cl **E9** 127 J2
Guinness Trust Bldgs **SE11** 129 P4
Guinness Trust Bldgs **SW9** 129 P10
Gulliver St **SE16** 131 K2
Gun St **E1** 126 D7
Gunmakers La **E3** 127 J3
Gunter Gro **SW10** 128 C5
Gunthorpe St **E1** 126 D7
Gunwhale Cl **SE16** 127 H10
Gurney Rd **SW6** 128 C9
Gutter La **EC2** 126 A8
Guy St **SE1** 130 B1
Gwyn Cl **SW6** 128 C6
Gwynne Rd **SW11** 128 D8
Gylcote Cl **SE5** 130 B10

H

Haberdasher St **N1** 126 B5
Hackford Rd **SW9** 129 M7
Hackford Wk **SW9** 129 M7
Hackney Rd **E2** 126 D5
Haddo St **SE10** 131 M5
Haddonfield **SE8** 131 H3
Hadleigh St **E2** 126 G6
Hadley St **NW1** 125 H1
Hadrian Est **E2** 126 E4
Hafer Rd **SW11** 128 F10
Haggerston Rd **E8** 126 D2
Hainford Cl **SE4** 131 H10
Hainton Cl **E1** 126 F8
Halcomb St **N1** 126 C3
Hale St **E14** 127 M9
Halesworth Rd **SE13** 131 M9
Half Moon Cres **N1** 125 M4
Half Moon St **W1** 125 H10
Halford Rd **SW6** 128 A5
Halkin Arc **SW1** 128 F2
Halkin Pl **SW1** 128 G2
Halkin St **SW1** 128 G1
Hall Pl **W2** 124 D6
Hall Rd **NW8** 124 C5
Hall St **EC1** 125 P5
Hall Twr **W2** 124 D7
Hallam St **W1** 125 H7
Halley Gdns **SE13** 131 P10
Halley St **E14** 127 J7
Hallfield Est **W2** 124 C8
Halliford St **N1** 126 A2
Halsey St **SW3** 128 F3
Halsmere Rd **SE5** 129 P7
Halton Cross St **N1** 125 P3
Halton Rd **N1** 125 P2
Hamble St **SW6** 128 B9
Hamilton Cl **NW8** 124 D5
Hamilton Gdns **NW8** 124 C5
Hamilton Pl **W1** 124 G10
Hamilton Ter **NW8** 124 B4
Hamlet, The **SE5** 130 B9
Hamlets Way **E3** 127 K6
Hammond St **NW5** 125 J1
Hampson Way **SW8** 129 M7
Hampstead Rd **NW1** 125 J4
Hampton Cl **NW6** 124 A5
Hampton St **SE1** 129 P3
Hampton St **SE17** 129 P3
Hanbury St **E1** 126 D7
Hancock Rd **E3** 127 N5
Hand Ct **WC1** 125 M7
Handel St **WC1** 125 L6
Handforth Rd **SW9** 129 N6
Handley Rd **E9** 126 G2
Hankey Pl **SE1** 130 B1
Hannibal Rd **E1** 126 G7
Hannington Rd **SW4** 129 H9
Hanover Gdns **SE11** 129 N5
Hanover Gate **NW1** 124 E5
Hanover Pk **SE15** 130 E7
Hanover Sq **W1** 125 H8
Hanover St **W1** 125 H8
Hanover Ter **NW1** 124 E5
Hans Cres **SW1** 128 F2
Hans Pl **SW1** 128 F2
Hans Rd **SW3** 128 F2
Hanson St **W1** 125 J7
Hanway St **W1** 125 K8
Harben Rd **NW6** 124 C2
Harbet Rd **W2** 124 D7
Harbinger Rd **E14** 131 M3
Harbledown Rd **SW6** 128 A7
Harbour Av **SW10** 128 C7
Harbour Ex Sq **E14** 131 M1
Harbour Rd **SE5** 130 A9
Harbut Rd **SW11** 128 D10
Harcourt Rd **SE4** 131 J10
Harcourt St **W1** 124 E7
Harcourt Ter **SW10** 128 B4
Harders Rd **SE15** 130 F8
Hardinge St **E1** 126 G8
Hardwick St **EC1** 125 N5
Hare & Billet Rd **SE3** 131 P7
Hare Row **E2** 126 F4
Hare Wk **N1** 126 C4
Harecourt Rd **N1** 126 A1
Haredale Rd **SE24** 130 A10
Harefield Ms **SE4** 131 K9
Harefield Rd **SE4** 131 K9
Harewood Av **NW1** 124 E6
Harfield Gdns **SE5** 130 C9
Harford St **E1** 127 J6
Hargwyne St **SW9** 129 M9
Harlescott Rd **SE15** 131 H10
Harley Gdns **SW10** 128 C4
Harley Gro **E3** 127 K5
Harley Pl **W1** 125 H7
Harley Rd **NW3** 124 D2
Harley St **W1** 125 H6
Harleyford Rd **SE11** 129 M5
Harleyford St **SE11** 129 N5
Harmood St **NW1** 125 H2
Harmsworth St **SE17** 129 P4
Harold Est **SE1** 130 C2
Harold Pl **SE11** 129 N4
Harper Rd **SE1** 130 A2
Harpley Sq **E1** 126 G5
Harpsden St **SW11** 128 G7
Harpur St **WC1** 125 M7
Harrap St **E14** 127 N9
Harriet Cl **E8** 126 E3
Harriet Wk **SW1** 128 F1
Harrington Gdns **SW7** 128 B3
Harrington Rd **SW7** 128 D3
Harrington Sq **NW1** 125 J4
Harrington St **NW1** 125 J5
Harris St **SE5** 130 B6
Harrison St **WC1** 125 L5
Harrow La **E14** 127 N9
Harrow Pl **E1** 126 C8
Harroway Rd **SW11** 128 D8
Harrowby St **W1** 124 E8
Harrowgate Rd **E9** 127 J1
Hartfield Ter **E3** 127 L4
Hartington Rd **SW8** 129 L7
Hartlake Rd **E9** 127 H1
Hartland Rd **NW1** 125 H2
Hartley St **E2** 126 G5
Harton St **SE8** 131 L7
Harts La **SE14** 131 J6
Harvey Rd **SE5** 130 B7
Harvey St **N1** 126 B3
Harwood Rd **SW6** 128 A6
Harwood Ter **SW6** 128 B7
Haselrigge Rd **SW4** 129 K10
Hasker St **SW3** 128 E3
Haslam Cl **N1** 125 N2
Haslam St **SE15** 130 D6
Hassett Rd **E9** 127 H1
Hastings Cl **SE15** 130 E6
Hastings St **WC1** 125 L5
Hatcham Pk Rd **SE14** 131 H7
Hatcham Rd **SE15** 130 G5
Hatfields **SE1** 125 P10
Hatherley Gro **W2** 124 B8
Hathorne Cl **SE15** 130 F8
Hatton Gdn **EC1** 125 N7
Hatton Pl **EC1** 125 N6
Hatton Wall **EC1** 125 N7
Haul Rd **NW1** 125 L4
Havannah St **E14** 131 L1
Havelock St **N1** 125 L3
Havelock Ter **SW8** 129 H6
Haverfield Rd **E3** 127 J5
Haverstock St **N1** 125 P4
Havil St **SE5** 130 C6
Hawes St **N1** 125 P2
Hawgood St **E3** 127 L7
Hawkstone Est **SE16** 130 G3
Hawkstone Rd **SE16** 130 G3
Hawley Cres **NW1** 125 H2
Hawley Rd **NW1** 125 H2
Hawley St **NW1** 125 H2
Hawthorn Av **E3** 127 K3
Hawthorne Cl **N1** 126 C1
Hawtrey Rd **NW3** 124 E2
Hay Currie St **E14** 127 M8
Hay Hill **W1** 125 H9
Hay St **E2** 126 E3
Haydon Way **SW11** 128 D10
Hayes Gro **SE22** 130 D10
Hayles St **SE11** 129 P3
Haymarket **SW1** 125 K9
Haymerle Rd **SE15** 130 E5
Hay's Galleria **SE1** 126 C10
Hay's Ms **W1** 125 H9
Hazel Cl **SE15** 130 E8
Hazelmere Rd **NW6** 124 A3
Hazlebury Rd **SW6** 128 B8
Head St **E1** 127 H8
Headfort Pl **SW1** 128 G1
Headlam St **E1** 126 F6
Heald St **SE14** 131 K7
Healey St **NW1** 125 H1
Hearn St **EC2** 126 C6
Heath La **SE3** 131 P8
Heath Rd **SW8** 129 H8
Heathcote St **WC1** 125 M6
Heather Cl **SW8** 129 H9
Heathwall St **SW11** 128 F9
Heaton Rd **SE15** 130 E9
Heddon St **W1** 125 J9
Hedgers Gro **E9** 127 J1
Heiron St **SE17** 129 P5
Helmet Row **EC1** 126 A6
Helmsley Pl **E8** 126 F2
Helsinki Sq **SE16** 131 J2
Hemans St **SW8** 129 K6
Hemberton Rd **SW9** 129 L9
Hemingford Rd **N1** 125 M3
Hemming St **E1** 126 E6
Hemp Wk **SE17** 130 B3
Hemstal Rd **NW6** 124 A2
Hemsworth St **N1** 126 C4
Heneage St **E1** 126 D7
Henley Dr **SE1** 130 D3
Henley St **SW11** 128 G8
Henning St **SW11** 128 E7
Henrietta Cl **SE8** 131 L5
Henrietta Pl **W1** 125 H8

Henrietta St WC2 125 L9
Henriques St E1 126 E8
Henry Dent Cl SE5 130 B9
Henshall St N1 126 B1
Henshaw St SE17 130 B3
Henstridge Pl NW8 124 E4
Henty Cl SW11 128 E6
Hepscott Rd E9 127 L2
Herbal Hill EC1 125 N6
Herbert St NW5 124 G1
Herbrand St WC1 125 L6
Hercules Rd SE1 129 M2
Hereford Ho NW6 124 A4
Hereford Rd W2 124 A8
Hereford Sq SW7 128 C3
Hereford St E2 126 E6
Heritage Cl SW9 129 P9
Hermit St EC1 125 P5
Hermitage St W2 124 D7
Hermitage Wall E1 126 E10
Herne Hill Rd SE24 130 A9
Heron Pl SE16 127 J10
Heron Quay E14 127 L10
Heron Rd SE24 130 A10
Herrick St SW1 129 K3
Hertford Rd N1 126 C3
Hertford St W1 125 H10
Hertsmere Rd E14 127 L9
Hesper Ms SW5 128 B4
Hesperus Cres E14 131 M3
Hessel St E1 126 F8
Hester Rd SW11 128 E6
Heston St SE14 131 K7
Hetherington Rd SW4 129 L10
Hewison St E3 127 K4
Hewlett Rd E3 127 J4
Heyford Av SW8 129 L6
Heygate St SE17 130 A3
Hibbert St SW11 128 C9
Hickmore Wk SW4 129 J9
Hicks Cl SW11 128 E9
Hicks St SE8 131 J4
Hide Pl SW1 129 K3
Hide Twr SW1 129 K3
High Br SE10 131 P4
High Br Wf SE10 131 P4
High Holborn WC1 125 L8
High St E15 127 N4
High Timber St EC4 126 A9
Highbury Cor N5 125 N1
Highbury Gro N5 125 P1
Highbury Pl N5 125 P1
Highbury Sta Rd N1 125 N1
Highshore Rd SE15 130 D8
Highway, The E1 126 F9
Highway, The E14 126 F9
Hilary Cl SW6 128 B6
Hilda Ter SW9 129 N8
Hildyard Rd SW6 128 A5
Hilgrove Rd NW6 124 C2
Hill Rd NW8 124 C4
Hill St W1 125 H10
Hillbeck Cl SE15 130 G6
Hillgate Pl W8 124 A10
Hillgate St W8 124 A10
Hillingdon St SE17 129 P6
Hillman St E8 126 F1
Hillmead Dr SW9 129 P10
Hillside Cl NW8 124 B4
Hilltop Rd NW6 124 A2
Hilly Flds Cres SE4 131 L9
Hillyard St SW9 129 N7
Hinckley Rd SE15 130 E10
Hind Gro E14 127 L8
Hinde St W1 124 G8
Hinton Rd SE24 129 P9
Hitchin Sq E3 127 J4
Hobart Pl SW1 129 H2
Hobday St E14 127 M7
Hobury St SW10 128 C5
Hodnet Gro SE16 131 H3
Hogarth Rd SW5 128 B3
Holbeck Row SE15 130 E6
Holbein Ms SW1 128 G4
Holbein Pl SW1 128 G3
Holborn EC1 125 N7
Holborn Viaduct EC1 125 N7
Holcroft Rd E9 126 G2
Holden St SW11 128 G8
Holford St WC1 125 N5
Holgate Av SW11 128 D9
Holland Gro SW9 129 N6
Holland St SE1 125 P10
Holland St W8 128 A1
Hollen St W1 125 J8
Holles St W1 125 H8
Holly Gro SE15 130 D8
Holly St E8 126 D1
Hollybush Gdns E2 126 F5
Hollydale Rd SE15 130 G7
Hollydene SE15 130 F7
Hollymount Cl SE10 131 N7
Hollywood Rd SW10 128 C5
Holman Rd SW11 128 D8
Holmead Rd SW6 128 B6
Holmefield Ct NW3 124 E1
Holmes Cl SE22 130 E10
Holmes Ter SE1 129 N1
Holms St E2 126 E4
Holton St E1 127 H6
Holwood Pl SW4 129 K10
Holyhead Cl E3 127 L5
Holywell La EC2 126 C6
Holywell Row EC2 126 C6
Home Rd SW11 128 E8
Homefield St N1 126 C4
Homer Dr E14 131 L3
Homer Rd E9 127 J1
Homer Row W1 124 E7
Homer St W1 124 E7
Hooper St E1 126 E8
Hope St SW11 128 D9
Hopewell St SE5 130 B6
Hopton Gdns SE1 125 P10
Hopton St SE1 125 P10
Hopwood Rd SE17 130 B5
Horatio St E2 126 D4
Horbury Cres W11 124 A9
Horle Wk SE5 129 P8
Hornby Cl NW3 124 D2
Hornshay St SE15 130 G5
Hornton Pl W8 128 A1
Hornton St W8 124 A10
Horse Guards Av SW1 125 L10
Horse Guards Rd SW1 125 K10
Horse Ride SW1 125 J10
Horseferry Pl SE10 131 N5
Horseferry Rd E14 127 J9
Horseferry Rd SW1 129 K3
Horselydown La SE1 130 D1
Horseshoe Cl E14 131 N4
Horsley St SE17 130 B5
Hortensia Rd SW10 128 C6
Horton Rd E8 126 F1
Horton St SE13 131 M9
Hosier La EC1 125 P7
Hoskins St SE10 131 P4
Hotspur St SE11 129 N4
Houndsditch EC3 126 C8
Howard Bldg SW8 129 H5
Howbury Rd SE15 130 G9
Howden St SE15 130 E9
Howick Pl SW1 129 J2
Howie St SW11 128 E6
Howitt Rd NW3 124 E1
Howland Est SE16 130 G2
Howland St W1 125 J7
Howland Way SE16 131 J1
Howley Pl W2 124 C7
Hows St E2 126 D4
Howson Rd SE4 131 J10
Hoxton Sq N1 126 C5
Hoxton St N1 126 C3
Hubert Gro SW9 129 L9
Huddart St E3 127 K7
Huddleston Cl E2 126 G4
Hugh St SW1 129 H3
Hugon Rd SW6 128 B9
Huguenot Pl E1 126 D7
Hull Cl SE16 131 H1
Humphrey St SE1 130 D4
Hungerford Br SE1 125 L10
Hungerford Br WC2 125 L10
Hunsdon Rd SE14 131 H5
Hunter St WC1 125 L6
Huntingdon St N1 125 M2
Huntley St WC1 125 J6
Hunton St E1 126 E6
Hunts La E15 127 N4
Huntsman St SE17 130 B3
Hurlingham Business Pk SW6 128 A9
Hurlingham Sq SW6 128 A9
Huson Cl NW3 124 E2
Hutchings St E14 131 L1
Hyde Pk SW7 124 E10
Hyde Pk W1 124 E10
Hyde Pk W2 124 E10
Hyde Pk Cor W1 128 G1
Hyde Pk Cres W2 124 E8
Hyde Pk Gdns W2 124 D9
Hyde Pk Gate SW7 128 C1
Hyde Pk Pl W2 124 E9
Hyde Pk Sq W2 124 E8
Hyde Pk St W2 124 E8
Hyde Rd N1 126 B3
Hyde Vale SE10 131 N6
Hyndman St SE15 130 F5

I

Iceland Rd E3 127 L3
Ida St E14 127 N8
Idonia St SE8 131 K6
Ifield Rd SW10 128 B5
Ilchester Gdns W2 124 B9
Ilderton Rd SE15 130 G6
Ilderton Rd SE16 130 F4
Iliffe St SE17 129 P4
Ilminster Gdns SW11 128 E10
Imber St N1 126 B3
Imperial Coll SW7 128 D2
Imperial Coll Rd SW7 128 D2
Imperial Cres SW6 128 C8
Imperial Rd SW6 128 B7
Imperial Sq SW6 128 B7
Imperial St E3 127 N5
Imperial Wf SW6 128 C8
Indescon Ct E14 131 L1
Ingate Pl SW8 129 H7
Ingelow Rd SW8 129 H8
Ingleborough St SW9 129 N8
Inglesham Wk E9 127 K1
Ingleton St SW9 129 N8
Inglewood Cl E14 131 L3
Inglis St SE5 129 P7
Ingrave St SW11 128 D9
Inkerman Rd NW5 125 H1
Inner Circle NW1 124 G5
Innes St SE15 130 C6
Inverness Pl W2 124 B9
Inverness St NW1 125 H3
Inverness Ter W2 124 B9
Inverton Rd SE15 131 H10
Inville Rd SE17 130 B4
Inwen Ct SE8 131 J4
Inworth St SW11 128 E8
Ireland Yd EC4 125 P8
Irene Rd SW6 128 A7
Ironmonger Row EC1 126 A5
Irving Gro SW9 129 M8
Irving St WC2 125 K9
Isabel St SW9 129 M7
Isabella St SE1 125 P10
Isambard Ms E14 131 N2
Island Rd SE16 131 H3
Island Row E14 127 K8
Islington Grn N1 125 P3
Islington High St N1 125 P4
Islington Pk St N1 125 N2
Ivanhoe Rd SE5 130 D9
Iveagh Cl E9 127 H3
Iveley Rd SW4 129 J8
Iverna Ct W8 128 A2
Iverna Gdns W8 128 A2
Ives St SW3 128 E3
Ivimey St E2 126 E5
Ivor Pl NW1 124 F6
Ivor St NW1 125 J2
Ivy Rd SE4 131 K10
Ivy St N1 126 C4
Ivydale Rd SE15 131 H9
Ixworth Pl SW3 128 E4

J

Jacaranda Gro E8 126 D2
Jackman St E8 126 F3
Jackson Cl E9 126 G2
Jacob St SE1 130 D1
Jago Wk SE5 130 B6
Jamaica Rd SE1 130 D1
Jamaica Rd SE16 130 D1
Jamaica St E1 126 G8
James St W1 124 G8
Jameson Ct E2 126 G4
Jameson St W8 124 A10
Jamestown Rd NW1 125 H3
Jamestown Way E14 127 P9
Jamuna Cl E14 127 J7
Janet St E14 131 L2
Janeway St SE16 130 E1
Jardine Rd E1 127 H9
Jarrow Rd SE16 130 G3
Jay Ms SW7 128 C1
Jebb St E3 127 L4
Jedburgh St SW11 128 G10
Jeffreys Rd SW4 129 L8
Jeffreys St NW1 125 H2
Jeffreys Wk SW4 129 L8
Jeger Av E2 126 D3
Jerdan Pl SW6 128 A6
Jeremiah St E14 127 M8
Jermyn St SW1 125 K9
Jerningham Rd SE14 131 J8
Jerome Cres NW8 124 E6
Jerrard St SE13 131 M9
Jewry St EC3 126 D8
Jew's Row SW18 128 B10
Joan St SE1 125 P10
Jocelyn St SE15 130 E7
Jockey's Flds WC1 125 M7
Jodane St SE8 131 K3
Jodrell Rd E3 127 K3
John Adam St WC2 125 L9
John Aird Ct W2 124 C7
John Carpenter St EC4 125 P9
John Felton Rd SE16 130 E1
John Fisher St E1 126 E9
John Islip St SW1 129 L3
John Maurice Cl SE17 130 B3
John Penn St SE13 131 M7
John Princes St W1 125 H8
John Roll Way SE16 130 E2
John Ruskin St SE5 129 P6
John Silkin La SE8 131 H4
John Spencer Sq N1 125 P1
John St WC1 125 M6
John Williams Cl SE14 131 H5
John's Ms WC1 125 M6
Johnson Cl E8 126 E3
Johnson's Pl SW1 129 J4
Jonathan St SE11 129 M4
Joseph Hardcastle Cl SE14 131 H6
Joseph St E3 127 K6
Joubert St SW11 128 F8
Jowett St SE15 130 D6
Jubilee Cres E14 131 N2
Jubilee Pl SW3 128 E4
Jubilee St E1 126 G8
Judd St WC1 125 L5
Juer St SW11 128 E6
Julian Pl E14 131 M4
Junction App SE13 131 N9
Junction App SW11 128 E9
Juniper Cres NW1 124 G2
Juniper St E1 126 G9
Juno Way SE14 131 H5
Jupiter Way N7 125 M1
Jupp Rd E15 127 P2
Jupp Rd W E15 127 N3
Juxon St SE11 129 M3

K

Kambala Rd SW11 128 D8
Kassala Rd SW11 128 F7
Kathleen Rd SW11 128 F9
Kay Rd SW9 129 L8
Kay St E2 126 E4
Kean St WC2 125 M8
Keel Cl SE16 127 H10
Keeley St WC2 125 M8
Keetons Rd SE16 130 F2
Keildon Rd SW11 128 F10
Kellett Rd SW2 129 N10
Kelly Av SE15 130 D6
Kelly St NW1 125 H1
Kelman Cl SW4 129 K8
Kelmore Gro SE22 130 E10
Kelsey St E2 126 F6
Kelso Pl W8 128 B2
Kelson Ho E14 131 N2
Kelvedon Ho SW8 129 L7
Kemble St WC2 125 M8
Kemerton Rd SE5 130 A9
Kempsford Gdns SW5 128 A4
Kempsford Rd SE11 129 N3
Kempson Rd SW6 128 A7
Kempthorne Rd SE8 131 J3
Kenbury St SE5 130 A8
Kenchester Cl SW8 129 L6
Kendal Cl SW9 129 P6
Kendal St W2 124 E8
Kender St SE14 130 G6
Kendoa Rd SW4 129 K10
Kendrick Pl SW7 128 D3
Kenilworth Rd E3 127 J4
Kennard Rd E15 127 P2
Kennard St SW11 128 G8
Kennet St E1 126 E10
Kenning Ter N1 126 C3
Kennings Way SE11 129 N4
Kennington La SE11 129 M4
Kennington Oval SE11 129 M5
Kennington Pk SW9 129 N6
Kennington Pk Gdns SE11 129 P5
Kennington Pk Pl SE11 129 N5
Kennington Pk Rd SE11 129 N5
Kennington Rd SE1 129 N2
Kennington Rd SE11 129 N3
Kensington Ch Ct W8 128 B1
Kensington Ch St W8 124 A10
Kensington Ch Wk W8 128 B1
Kensington Ct W8 128 B1
Kensington Ct Pl W8 128 B2
Kensington Gdns W2 124 C10
Kensington Gdns Sq W2 124 B8
Kensington Gate W8 128 C2
Kensington Gore SW7 128 D1
Kensington High St W8 128 A2
Kensington Mall W8 124 A10
Kensington Palace Gdns W8 124 B10
Kensington Pl W8 124 A10
Kensington Rd SW7 128 D1
Kensington Rd W8 128 B1
Kensington Sq W8 128 B1
Kent Pas NW1 124 F5
Kent St E2 126 D4
Kent Ter NW1 124 E5
Kentish Town Rd NW1 125 H2
Kentish Town Rd NW5 125 H2
Kenton Rd E9 127 H1
Kenton St WC1 125 L6
Kentwell Cl SE4 131 J10
Kenway Rd SW5 128 B3
Kenwyn Rd SW4 129 K10
Kepler Rd SW4 129 L10
Keppel St WC1 125 K7
Kerbey St E14 127 M8
Kerfield Cres SE5 130 B7
Kerfield Pl SE5 130 B7
Kerridge Ct N1 126 C1
Kerrison Rd E15 127 P3
Kerrison Rd SW11 128 E9
Kerry Path SE14 131 K5
Kerry Rd SE14 131 K5
Kersley Ms SW11 128 F8
Kersley St SW11 128 F8
Keston Rd SE15 130 E9
Kestrel Ho EC1 125 P5
Kevan Ho SE5 130 A6
Key Cl E1 126 F6
Keybridge Ho SW8 129 L5
Keyworth St SE1 129 P2
Khyber Rd SW11 128 E8
Kibworth St SW8 129 M6
Kilburn Pk Rd NW6 124 A5
Kilburn Pl NW6 124 A3
Kilburn Priory NW6 124 B3
Kilburn Sq NW6 124 A3
Kildare Gdns W2 124 A8
Kildare Ter W2 124 A8
Kilkie St SW6 128 C8
Killick St N1 125 M4
Killowen Rd E9 127 H1
Killyon Rd SW8 129 J8
Killyon Ter SW8 129 J8
Kilner St E14 127 L7
Kimberley Av SE15 130 F8
Kimberley Rd SW9 129 L8
Kimpton Rd SE5 130 B7
Kinburn St SE16 131 H1
Kincaid Rd SE15 130 F6
King & Queen St SE17 130 A4
King Arthur Cl SE15 130 G6
King Charles St SW1 129 K1
King David La E1 126 G9
King Edward St EC1 126 A8
King Edward Wk SE1 129 N2
King Edwards Rd E9 126 F3
King Frederik IX Twr SE16 131 K2
King George St SE10 131 N6
King Henry's Rd NW3 124 E2
King Henry's Wk N1 126 C1
King James St SE1 129 P1
King John St E1 127 H7
King St EC2 126 A8
King St SW1 125 J10
King St WC2 125 L9
King William St EC4 126 B9
King William Wk SE10 131 N5
Kingdon Rd NW6 124 A1
Kingfield St E14 131 N3
Kingfisher Ms SE13 131 M10
Kingfisher Sq SE8 131 K5
Kinglake St SE17 130 C4
Kingly St W1 125 J8
Kings Coll Rd NW3 124 E2
King's Cross Rd WC1 125 M5
King's Cross Sta N1 125 L4
Kings Gro SE15 130 F6
King's Ms WC1 125 M7
King's Reach Twr SE1 125 N10
King's Rd SW1 128 F4
King's Rd SW3 128 F4
King's Rd SW6 128 B7
King's Rd SW10 128 B7
Kingsbury Rd N1 126 C1
Kingsbury Ter N1 126 C1
Kingsgate Pl NW6 124 A2
Kingsgate Rd NW6 124 A2
Kingshold Rd E9 126 G2
Kingsland Grn E8 126 C1
Kingsland Rd E2 126 C4
Kingsland Rd E8 126 C4
Kingsland Shop Cen E8 126 D1
Kingsley St SW11 128 F9
Kingsmill Ter NW8 124 D4
Kingstown St NW1 124 G3
Kingsway WC2 125 M8
Kingswood Cl SW8 129 L6
Kinnerton St SW1 128 G1
Kinsale Rd SE15 130 E9
Kipling Est SE1 130 B1
Kipling St SE1 130 B1
Kirby Est SE16 130 F2
Kirby Gro SE1 130 C1
Kirkland Wk E8 126 D1
Kirkwall Pl E2 126 G5
Kirkwood Rd SE15 130 F8
Kirtling St SW8 129 J6
Kirwyn Way SE5 129 P6
Kitcat Ter E3 127 L5
Kitson Rd SE5 130 A6
Kitto Rd SE14 131 H8
Knapp Rd E3 127 L6
Knaresborough Pl SW5 128 B3
Knatchbull Rd SE5 130 A7
Kneller Rd SE4 131 J10
Knighten St E1 126 E10
Knighthead Pt E14 131 L2
Knightsbridge SW1 128 F1
Knightsbridge SW7 128 E1
Knivet Rd SW6 128 A5
Knobs Hill Rd E15 127 M3
Knottisford St E2 126 G5
Knowle Cl SW9 129 N9
Knowles Wk SW4 129 J9
Knowsley Rd SW11 128 F8
Knox St W1 124 F7
Knoyle St SE14 131 J5
Kylemore Rd NW6 124 A2
Kynance Ms SW7 128 B2
Kynance Pl SW7 128 C2

L

Laburnum St E2 126 D3
Lacey Wk E3 127 L4
Lackington St EC2 126 B7
Lacon Rd SE22 130 E10
Ladycroft Rd SE13 131 M9
Lafone St SE1 130 D1
Lagado Ms SE16 127 H10
Laird Ho SE5 130 A6
Lamb La E8 126 F2
Lamb St E1 126 D7
Lambert St N1 125 N2
Lambeth Br SE1 129 L3
Lambeth Br SW1 129 L3
Lambeth High St SE1 129 M3
Lambeth Hill EC4 126 A9
Lambeth Palace Rd SE1 129 M2
Lambeth Rd SE1 129 M3
Lambeth Rd SE11 129 M3
Lambeth Wk SE1 129 M3
Lambeth Wk SE11 129 M3
Lambolle Pl NW3 124 E1
Lambolle Rd NW3 124 E1
Lambourn Rd SW4 129 H9
Lambourne Gro SE16 131 H3
Lamb's Conduit St WC1 125 M6
Lamb's Pas EC1 126 B7
Lamerton St SE8 131 L5
Lammas Rd E9 127 H2
Lamont Rd SW10 128 C5
Lanark Pl W9 124 C6
Lanark Rd W9 124 B4
Lanark Sq E14 131 M2
Lanbury Rd SE15 131 H10
Lancaster Dr NW3 124 E1
Lancaster Gate W2 124 C9
Lancaster Gro NW3 124 D1
Lancaster Ms W2 124 C9
Lancaster Pl WC2 125 M9
Lancaster St SE1 129 P1
Lancaster Ter W2 124 D9
Lancaster Wk W2 124 C10
Lancelot Pl SW7 128 F1
Lanchester Way SE14 130 G7
Lancresse Ct N1 126 C3
Landmann Way SE14 131 H5
Landon Pl SW1 128 F2
Landons Cl E14 127 N10
Landor Rd SW9 129 L9
Lanfranc Rd E3 127 J4
Lang St E1 126 G6
Langbourne Pl E14 131 M4
Langdale Cl SE17 130 A5
Langdale Rd SE10 131 N6
Langford Ct NW8 124 C4
Langford Grn SE5 130 C9
Langford Pl NW8 124 C4
Langford Rd SW6 128 B8
Langham Pl W1 125 H7
Langham St W1 125 H7
Langley La SW8 129 M5
Langley St WC2 125 L8
Langton Rd SW9 129 P6
Langton St SW10 128 C5
Langtry Rd NW8 124 B3
Lanhill Rd W9 124 A6
Lanrick Rd E14 127 P8
Lansbury Est E14 127 M8
Lansbury Gdns E14 127 P8
Lanscombe Wk SW8 129 L7
Lansdowne Dr E8 126 E1
Lansdowne Gdns SW8 129 L7
Lansdowne Ter WC1 125 L6
Lansdowne Way SW8 129 K7
Lant St SE1 130 A1
Lanterns Ct E14 131 L1
Lanvanor Rd SE15 130 G8
Larcom St SE17 130 A3
Lark Row E2 126 G3
Larkhall La SW4 129 K8
Larkhall Ri SW4 129 J9
Lassell St SE10 131 P4
Latchmere Rd SW11 128 F8
Latchmere St SW11 128 F8
Latham Ho E1 127 H8
Latona Rd SE15 130 E5
Lauderdale Rd W9 124 B5
Lauderdale Twr EC2 126 A7
Launceston Pl W8 128 C2

Launch St **E14** 131 N2
Laurel St **E8** 126 D1
Laurie Gro **SE14** 131 J7
Lauriston Rd **E9** 127 H3
Lausanne Rd **SE15** 130 G7
Lavender Gdns **SW11** 128 F10
Lavender Gro **E8** 126 D2
Lavender Hill **SW11** 128 E10
Lavender Rd **SE16** 127 J10
Lavender Rd **SW11** 128 D9
Lavender Sweep **SW11** 128 F10
Lavender Wk **SW11** 128 F10
Laverton Pl **SW5** 128 B3
Lavington St **SE1** 125 P10
Law St **SE1** 130 B2
Lawford Rd **N1** 126 C2
Lawford Rd **NW5** 125 J1
Lawless St **E14** 127 M9
Lawn Ho Cl **E14** 131 N1
Lawn La **SW8** 129 L5
Lawrence Cl **E3** 127 L4
Lawrence St **SW3** 128 E5
Lawson Est **SE1** 130 B2
Lawton Rd **E3** 127 J5
Laxley Cl **SE5** 129 P6
Layard Rd **SE16** 130 F3
Layard Sq **SE16** 130 F3
Laycock St **N1** 125 N1
Laystall St **EC1** 125 N6
Lea Valley Wk **E3** 127 N6
Lea Valley Wk **E14** 127 M7
Lea Valley Wk **E15** 127 N5
Leabank Sq **E9** 127 L1
Leadenhall St **EC3** 126 C8
Leake St **SE1** 129 M1
Leamouth Rd **E14** 127 P8
Leander Ct **SE8** 131 L7
Leather La **EC1** 125 N7
Leather Rd **SE16** 131 H3
Leathermarket Ct **SE1** 130 C1
Leathermarket St **SE1** 130 C1
Leathwaite Rd **SW11** 128 F10
Leathwell Rd **SE8** 131 M8
Lecky St **SW7** 128 D4
Ledbury Est **SE15** 130 F6
Ledbury St **SE15** 130 E6
Lee Br **SE13** 131 N9
Lee High Rd **SE12** 131 P9
Lee High Rd **SE13** 131 P9
Lee St **E8** 126 D3
Leeke St **WC1** 125 M5
Leerdam Dr **E14** 131 N2
Lees Pl **W1** 124 G9
Leeson Rd **SE24** 129 N10
Leeway **SE8** 131 K4
Lefevre Wk **E3** 127 K3
Leggatt Rd **E15** 127 N4
Legion Cl **N1** 125 N1
Leicester Sq **WC2** 125 K9
Leigh St **WC1** 125 L6
Leinster Gdns **W2** 124 C8
Leinster Ms **W2** 124 C9
Leinster Pl **W2** 124 C8
Leinster Sq **W2** 124 A8
Leinster Ter **W2** 124 C9
Leman St **E1** 126 D8
Lendal Ter **SW4** 129 K9
Lennox Gdns **SW1** 128 F2
Lennox Gdns Ms **SW1** 128 F2
Lenthall Rd **E8** 126 E2
Leo St **SE15** 130 F6
Leonard St **EC2** 126 B6
Leontine Cl **SE15** 130 E6
Leopold St **E3** 127 K7
Leroy St **SE1** 130 C3
Lethbridge Cl **SE13** 131 N7
Lett Rd **E15** 127 P2
Lettsom St **SE5** 130 C8
Levehurst Way **SW4** 129 L8
Leven Rd **E14** 127 N7
Lever St **EC1** 125 P5
Lewey Ho **E3** 127 K6
Lewis Gro **SE13** 131 N9
Lewis St **NW1** 125 H1
Lewisham Cen **SE13** 131 N9
Lewisham High St **SE13** 131 N9
Lewisham Hill **SE13** 131 N8
Lewisham Rd **SE13** 131 M7
Lewisham Way **SE4** 131 K7
Lewisham Way **SE14** 131 K7
Lexham Gdns **W8** 128 B2
Lexham Gdns Ms **W8** 128 B2
Lexham Ms **W8** 128 A3
Lexington St **W1** 125 J8
Leybourne Rd **NW1** 125 H2
Leylang Rd **SE14** 131 H6
Liardet St **SE14** 131 J5
Liberia Rd **N5** 125 P1
Liberty St **SW9** 129 M7
Libra Rd **E3** 127 K3
Library St **SE1** 129 P1
Lichfield Rd **E3** 127 J5
Lidcote Gdns **SW9** 129 N8
Liddell Rd **NW6** 124 A1
Lidlington Pl **NW1** 125 J4
Lighter Cl **SE16** 131 J3
Lighterman Ms **E1** 127 H8
Lightermans Rd **E14** 131 L1
Lilac Pl **SE11** 129 M3
Lilestone St **NW8** 124 E6
Lilford Rd **SE5** 129 P8
Lillie Yd **SW6** 128 A5
Lillieshall Rd **SW4** 129 H9
Lily Pl **EC1** 125 N7
Limburg Rd **SW11** 128 F10
Lime Cl **E1** 126 E10
Lime St **EC3** 126 C9
Limeburner La **EC4** 125 P8
Limeharbour **E14** 131 M2
Limehouse Causeway **E14** 127 K9
Limehouse Flds Est **E14** 127 J7
Limehouse Link **E14** 127 J9
Limerston St **SW10** 128 C5
Limes Gro **SE13** 131 N10
Limes Wk **SE15** 130 F10
Limesford Rd **SE15** 131 H10
Linacre Cl **SE15** 130 F9
Linberry Wk **SE8** 131 K3
Lincoln St **SW3** 128 F3
Lincoln's Inn **WC2** 125 N8
Lincoln's Inn Flds **WC2** 125 M8
Lind St **SE8** 131 M8
Linden Gdns **W2** 124 A9
Linden Gro **SE15** 130 F9
Lindfield St **E14** 127 L8
Lindley St **E1** 126 G7
Lindore Rd **SW11** 128 F10
Lindrop St **SW6** 128 C8
Lindsay Sq **SW1** 129 K4
Lindsell St **SE10** 131 N7
Lindsey Ms **N1** 126 A2
Lindsey St **EC1** 125 P7
Linford St **SW8** 129 J7
Lingards Rd **SE13** 131 N10
Lingham St **SW9** 129 L8
Linhope St **NW1** 124 F6
Link St **E9** 126 G1
Linnell Rd **SE5** 130 C8
Linom Rd **SW4** 129 L10
Linsey St **SE16** 130 E3
Linstead St **NW6** 124 A2
Linton St **N1** 126 A3
Linver Rd **SW6** 128 A8
Linwood Cl **SE5** 130 D8
Lisford St **SE15** 130 D7
Lisle St **WC2** 125 K9
Lisson Grn Est **NW8** 124 E6
Lisson Gro **NW1** 124 E6
Lisson Gro **NW8** 124 D5
Lisson St **NW1** 124 E7
Liston Rd **SW4** 129 J9
Litchfield St **WC2** 125 K9
Lithos Rd **NW3** 124 B1
Little Boltons, The **SW5** 128 B4
Little Boltons, The **SW10** 128 B4
Little Britain **EC1** 125 P7
Little Chester St **SW1** 129 H2
Little Dorrit Ct **SE1** 130 A1
Little Newport St **WC2** 125 K9
Little Portland St **W1** 125 H8
Little Russell St **WC1** 125 L7
Little St. James's St **SW1** 125 J10
Littlebury Rd **SW4** 129 K9
Livermere Rd **E8** 126 D3
Liverpool Gro **SE17** 130 B4
Liverpool Rd **N1** 125 N4
Liverpool St **EC2** 126 C7
Livingstone Rd **E15** 127 N3
Livingstone Wk **SW11** 128 D9
Lizard St **EC1** 126 A5
Lloyd Baker St **WC1** 125 M5
Lloyd Sq **WC1** 125 N5
Lloyd St **WC1** 125 N5
Lloyd's Av **EC3** 126 C8
Loampit Hill **SE13** 131 L8
Loampit Vale **SE13** 131 M9
Lochnagar St **E14** 127 N7
Lockesfield Pl **E14** 131 M4
Lockhart Cl **N7** 125 M1
Lockhart St **E3** 127 K6
Lockington Rd **SW8** 129 H7
Lockmead Rd **SE13** 131 N9
Locksley Est **E14** 127 K8
Locksley St **E14** 127 K7
Lockwood Sq **SE16** 130 F2
Loddiges Rd **E9** 126 G2
Loder St **SE15** 130 G7
Lodge Rd **NW8** 124 D5
Lodore St **E14** 127 N8
Loftie St **SE16** 130 E1
Lofting Rd **N1** 125 M2
Logan Ms **W8** 128 A3
Logan Pl **W8** 128 A3
Lollard St **SE11** 129 M3
Loman St **SE1** 129 P1
Lomas Dr **E8** 126 D2
Lomas St **E1** 126 E7
Lombard Rd **SW11** 128 D8
Lombard St **EC3** 126 B8
Lomond Gro **SE5** 130 B6
Loncroft Rd **SE5** 130 C5
London Br **EC4** 126 B10
London Br **SE1** 126 B10
London Br St **SE1** 126 B10
London Br Wk **SE1** 126 B10
London Flds **E8** 126 F2
London Flds E Side **E8** 126 F2
London Flds W Side **E8** 126 E2
London La **E8** 126 F2
London Rd **SE1** 129 P2
London Silver Vaults **WC2** 125 N7
London St **W2** 124 D8
London Trocadero, The **W1** 125 K9
London Wall **EC2** 126 A7
Long Acre **WC2** 125 L9
Long La **EC1** 125 P7
Long La **SE1** 130 B1
Long Rd **SW4** 129 H10
Long St **E2** 126 D5
Long Yd **WC1** 125 M6
Longbeach Rd **SW11** 128 F9
Longfield Est **SE1** 130 D3
Longford St **NW1** 125 H6
Longhedge St **SW11** 128 G8
Longhope Cl **SE15** 130 C5
Longley St **SE1** 130 E3
Longmoore St **SW1** 129 J3
Longnor Rd **E1** 127 H5
Longridge Rd **SW5** 128 A3
Long's Ct **WC2** 125 K9
Longshore **SE8** 131 K3
Lonsdale Sq **N1** 125 N2
Lord Amory Way **E14** 131 N1
Lord Hills Rd **W2** 124 B7
Lord N St **SW1** 129 L2
Lorden Wk **E2** 126 E5
Lorenzo St **WC1** 125 M5
Loring Rd **SE14** 131 J7
Lorn Ct **SW9** 129 N8
Lorn Rd **SW9** 129 M8
Lorrimore Rd **SE17** 129 P5
Lorrimore Sq **SE17** 129 P5
Lothbury **EC2** 126 B8
Lothian Rd **SW9** 129 P7
Lots Rd **SW10** 128 C6
Loudoun Rd **NW8** 124 C3
Lough Rd **N7** 125 M1
Loughborough Pk **SW9** 129 P10
Loughborough Rd **SW9** 129 N8
Loughborough St **SE11** 129 M4
Louisa St **E1** 127 H6
Louvaine Rd **SW11** 128 D10
Love La **EC2** 126 A8
Love Wk **SE5** 130 B8
Lovegrove St **SE1** 130 E4
Lovegrove Wk **E14** 127 N10
Lovelinch Cl **SE15** 130 G5
Lovell Ho **E8** 126 E3
Lover's Wk **W1** 124 G10
Lowden Rd **SE24** 129 P10
Lowell St **E14** 127 J8
Lower Belgrave St **SW1** 129 H2
Lower Grosvenor Pl **SW1** 129 H2
Lower Marsh **SE1** 129 N1
Lower Merton Ri **NW3** 124 E2
Lower Rd **SE8** 130 G2
Lower Rd **SE16** 130 G2
Lower Sloane St **SW1** 128 G3
Lower Thames St **EC3** 126 B9
Lowfield Rd **NW6** 124 A2
Lowndes Cl **SW1** 128 G2
Lowndes Pl **SW1** 128 G2
Lowndes Sq **SW1** 128 F1
Lowndes St **SW1** 128 F2
Lowth Rd **SE5** 130 A8
Lowther Gdns **SW7** 128 D1
Lubbock St **SE14** 130 G6
Lucan Pl **SW3** 128 E3
Lucas St **SE8** 131 L7
Lucey Rd **SE16** 130 E2
Lucey Way **SE16** 130 E2
Ludgate Hill **EC4** 125 P8
Ludgate Sq **EC4** 125 P8
Ludwick Ms **SE14** 131 J6
Lugard Rd **SE15** 130 F8
Luke Ho **E1** 126 F8
Luke St **EC2** 126 C6
Lukin St **E1** 126 G8
Lulworth Rd **SE15** 130 F8
Lupus St **SW1** 129 H5
Lurline Gdns **SW11** 128 G7
Luscombe Way **SW8** 129 L6
Luton Pl **SE10** 131 N6
Luton St **NW8** 124 D6
Luxborough St **W1** 124 G6
Luxford St **SE16** 131 H3
Luxmore St **SE4** 131 K7
Luxor St **SE5** 129 P8
Lyal Rd **E3** 127 J4
Lyall Ms **SW1** 128 G2
Lyall St **SW1** 128 G2
Lydon Rd **SW4** 129 J9
Lyme St **NW1** 125 J2
Lymington Rd **NW6** 124 B1
Lympstone Gdns **SE15** 130 E6
Lynbrook Gro **SE15** 130 C6
Lyncott Cres **SW4** 129 H10
Lyndhurst Gro **SE15** 130 C8
Lyndhurst Sq **SE15** 130 D7
Lyndhurst Way **SE15** 130 D7
Lynton Rd **SE1** 130 D3
Lyons Pl **NW8** 124 D6
Lytham St **SE17** 130 B4
Lyttelton Cl **NW3** 124 E2

M

Mabledon Pl **WC1** 125 K5
Mabley St **E9** 127 J1
Macaulay Ct **SW4** 129 H9
Macaulay Rd **SW4** 129 H9
Macaulay Sq **SW4** 129 H10
Macauley Ms **SE13** 131 N8
Macclesfield Br **NW1** 124 E4
Macclesfield Rd **EC1** 126 A5
Macclesfield St **W1** 125 K9
Macduff Rd **SW11** 128 G7
Mace St **E2** 127 H4
Macfarland Gro **SE15** 130 C6
Machell Rd **SE15** 130 G9
Mackay Rd **SW4** 129 H9
Mackennal St **NW8** 124 E4
Mackenzie Rd **N7** 125 M1
Mackenzie Wk **E14** 127 L10
Macklin St **WC2** 125 L8
Macks Rd **SE16** 130 E3
Mackworth St **NW1** 125 J5
Macleod St **SE17** 130 A4
Maconochies Rd **E14** 131 M4
Macquarie Way **E14** 131 M3
Maddams St **E3** 127 M6
Maddock Way **SE17** 129 P5
Maddox St **W1** 125 H9
Madinah Rd **E8** 126 E1
Madras Pl **N7** 125 N1
Madrigal La **SE5** 129 P6
Madron St **SE17** 130 C4
Magdalen St **SE1** 126 C10
Magee St **SE11** 129 N5
Maguire St **SE1** 130 D1
Mahogany Cl **SE16** 127 J10
Maida Av **W2** 124 C7
Maida Vale **W9** 124 B4
Maiden La **NW1** 125 K2
Maiden La **WC2** 125 L9
Maidenstone Hill **SE10** 131 N7
Maitland Pk Est **NW3** 124 F1
Maitland Pk Rd **NW3** 124 F1
Maitland Pk Vil **NW3** 124 F1
Major Cl **SW9** 129 P9
Makins St **SW3** 128 E3
Malabar St **E14** 131 L1
Malcolm Pl **E2** 126 G6
Malcolm Rd **E1** 126 G6
Malden Cres **NW1** 124 G1
Maldon Cl **SE5** 130 C9
Malet Pl **WC1** 125 K6
Malet St **WC1** 125 K6
Malfort Rd **SE5** 130 C9
Mall, The **SW1** 129 J1
Mallard Cl **NW6** 124 A4
Mallord St **SW3** 128 D5
Mallory Cl **SE4** 131 J10
Mallory St **NW8** 124 E6
Malmesbury Rd **E3** 127 K5
Malpas Rd **E8** 126 F1
Malpas Rd **SE4** 131 K8
Malt St **SE1** 130 E5
Maltby St **SE1** 130 D1
Malting Ho **E14** 127 K9
Maltings Pl **SW6** 128 B7
Malvern Ct **SW7** 128 D3
Malvern Rd **E8** 126 E2
Malvern Rd **NW6** 124 A5
Malvern Ter **N1** 125 N3
Manaton Cl **SE15** 130 F9
Manchester Gro **E14** 131 N4
Manchester Rd **E14** 131 N4
Manchester Sq **W1** 124 G8
Manchester St **W1** 124 G7
Manciple St **SE1** 130 B2
Mandela St **NW1** 125 J3
Mandela St **SW9** 129 N6
Mandela Way **SE1** 130 C3
Mandeville Pl **W1** 124 G8
Manette St **W1** 125 K8
Manger Rd **N7** 125 L1
Manilla St **E14** 131 L1
Manley St **NW1** 124 G3
Manor Av **SE4** 131 K8
Manor Est **SE16** 130 F3
Manor Gro **SE15** 130 G5
Manor Ms **SE4** 131 K8
Manor Pk **SE13** 131 P10
Manor Pl **SE17** 129 P4
Manresa Rd **SW3** 128 E4
Mansell St **E1** 126 D8
Mansfield St **W1** 125 H7
Mansford St **E2** 126 E4
Mansion Ho **EC4** 126 B8
Manson Ms **SW7** 128 C3
Manson Pl **SW7** 128 D3
Mantle Rd **SE4** 131 J9
Mantua St **SW11** 128 D9
Mantus Rd **E1** 126 G6
Mape St **E2** 126 F6
Maple St **E2** 126 E4
Maple St **W1** 125 J7
Mapledene Rd **E8** 126 D2
Maplin St **E3** 127 K5
Marble Arch **W1** 124 F9
Marble Quay **E1** 126 E10
Marcella Rd **SW9** 129 N8
Marchant St **SE14** 131 J5
Marchmont St **WC1** 125 L6
Marchwood Cl **SE5** 130 C6
Marcia Rd **SE1** 130 C3
Marcon Pl **E8** 126 F1
Marcus Garvey Way **SE24** 129 N10
Marden Sq **SE16** 130 F2
Mare St **E8** 126 F3
Margaret St **W1** 125 H8
Margaretta Ter **SW3** 128 E5
Margery St **WC1** 125 N5
Maria Ter **E1** 127 H7
Marian Pl **E2** 126 F4
Marigold St **SE16** 130 F1
Marinefield Rd **SW6** 128 B8
Mariners Ms **E14** 131 P3
Marischal Rd **SE13** 131 P9
Maritime Quay **E14** 131 L4
Maritime St **E3** 127 K6
Marjorie Gro **SW11** 128 F10
Mark La **EC3** 126 C9
Market Est **N7** 125 L1
Market Ms **W1** 125 H10
Market Pl **W1** 125 J8
Market Rd **N7** 125 L1
Markham Sq **SW3** 128 F4
Markham St **SW3** 128 E4
Marl Rd **SW18** 128 B10
Marlborough Av **E8** 126 E3
Marlborough Ct **W8** 128 A3
Marlborough Gro **SE1** 130 E4
Marlborough Hill **NW8** 124 C3
Marlborough Pl **NW8** 124 C4
Marlborough Rd **SW1** 125 J10
Marlborough St **SW3** 128 E3
Marloes Rd **W8** 128 B2
Marlow Way **SE16** 131 H1
Marlowes, The **NW8** 124 D3
Marmion Rd **SW11** 128 G10
Marmont Rd **SE15** 130 E7
Marney Rd **SW11** 128 G10
Maroon St **E14** 127 J7
Marquess Rd **N1** 126 B1
Marquis Rd **NW1** 125 K1
Marsala Rd **SE13** 131 M10
Marsden Rd **SE15** 130 D9
Marsden St **NW5** 124 G1
Marsh Wall **E14** 127 L10
Marshall St **W1** 125 J8
Marshalsea Rd **SE1** 130 A1
Marsham St **SW1** 129 K2
Marshfield St **E14** 131 N2
Marshgate La **E15** 127 M3
Marshgate Sidings **E15** 127 M3
Marsland Cl **SE17** 129 P4
Marston Cl **NW6** 124 C2
Martello St **E8** 126 F2
Martello Ter **E8** 126 F2
Martha Ct **E2** 126 F4
Martha St **E1** 126 F8
Martineau St **E1** 126 G9
Mary Ann Gdns **SE8** 131 L5
Mary Datchelor Cl **SE5** 130 B7
Mary Grn **NW8** 124 B3
Mary St **N1** 126 A3
Mary Ter **NW1** 125 H3
Marylands Rd **W9** 124 A6
Marylebone High St **W1** 124 G7
Marylebone La **W1** 124 G8
Marylebone Ms **W1** 125 H7
Marylebone Rd **NW1** 124 E7
Marylebone St **W1** 124 G7
Marylee Way **SE11** 129 M3
Maskelyne Cl **SW11** 128 E7
Mason St **SE17** 130 B3
Mason's Pl **EC1** 125 P5
Massingham St **E1** 127 H6
Mast Leisure Pk **SE16** 131 H2
Masterman Ho **SE5** 130 A6
Masters Dr **SE16** 130 F4
Masters St **E1** 127 H7
Masthouse Ter **E14** 131 L3
Mastmaker Rd **E14** 131 L1
Matham Gro **SE22** 130 D10
Matilda St **N1** 125 M3
Matlock Cl **SE24** 130 A10
Matlock St **E14** 127 J8
Matrimony Pl **SW8** 129 J8
Matthew Parker St **SW1** 129 K1
Matthews St **SW11** 128 F8
Maude Rd **SE5** 130 C7
Maunsel St **SW1** 129 K3
Maverton Rd **E3** 127 L3
Mawbey Est **SE1** 130 D4
Mawbey Pl **SE1** 130 D4
Mawbey St **SW8** 129 L6
Maxted Rd **SE15** 130 D9
Maxwell Rd **SW6** 128 B6
Maya Cl **SE15** 130 F8
Maydew Ho **SE16** 130 G3
Mayfair Pl **W1** 125 H10
Mayfield Rd **E8** 126 D2
Mayflower Rd **SW9** 129 L9
Mayflower St **SE16** 130 G1
Maygood St **N1** 125 M4
Maysoule Rd **SW11** 128 D10
Mazenod Av **NW6** 124 A2
McAuley Cl **SE1** 129 N2
McCullum Rd **E3** 127 K3
McDermott Cl **SW11** 128 E9
McDermott Rd **SE15** 130 E9
McDowall Rd **SE5** 130 A7
McEwen Way **E15** 127 P3
McKerrell Rd **SE15** 130 E7
McMillan St **SE8** 131 L5
McNeil Rd **SE5** 130 C8
Mead Pl **E9** 126 G1
Meadcroft Rd **SE11** 129 P5
Meadow Ms **SW8** 129 M5
Meadow Pl **SW8** 129 L6
Meadow Rd **SW8** 129 M5
Meadow Row **SE1** 130 A2
Meadowbank **NW3** 124 F2
Meakin Est **SE1** 130 C2
Meard St **W1** 125 K8
Meath St **SW11** 129 H7
Mecklenburgh Pl **WC1** 125 M6
Mecklenburgh Sq **WC1** 125 M6
Medburn St **NW1** 125 K4
Medlar St **SE5** 130 A7
Medley Rd **NW6** 124 A1
Medway Rd **E3** 127 J4
Medway St **SW1** 129 K2
Medwin St **SW4** 129 M10
Meeting Ho La **SE15** 130 F7
Mehetabel Rd **E9** 126 G1
Melba Way **SE13** 131 M7
Melbourne Gro **SE22** 130 C10
Melbourne Ms **SW9** 129 N7
Melbourne Pl **WC2** 125 M9
Melcombe Pl **NW1** 124 F7
Melcombe St **NW1** 124 F6
Melina Pl **NW8** 124 D5
Melior St **SE1** 130 B1
Mellish St **E14** 131 L2
Melon Rd **SE15** 130 E7
Melton St **NW1** 125 K5
Mendip Rd **SW11** 128 C9
Mentmore Ter **E8** 126 F2
Mepham St **SE1** 125 M10
Mercator Rd **SE13** 131 P10
Mercer St **WC2** 125 L8
Merceron St **E1** 126 F6
Merchant St **E3** 127 K5
Mercia Gro **SE13** 131 N10
Mercury Way **SE14** 131 H5
Mercy Ter **SE13** 131 M10
Meredith Ms **SE4** 131 K10
Meretone Cl **SE4** 131 J10
Meridian Gate **E14** 131 N1
Meridian Pl **E14** 131 M1
Meridian Sq **E15** 127 P2
Mermaid Ct **SE1** 130 B1
Mermaid Ct **SE16** 127 K10
Merriam Av **E9** 127 K1
Merrick Sq **SE1** 130 A2
Merrington Rd **SW6** 128 A5
Merrow St **SE17** 130 A5
Merton Ri **NW3** 124 E2
Mervan Rd **SW2** 129 N10
Messina Av **NW6** 124 A2
Meteor St **SW11** 128 G10
Methley St **SE11** 129 N4
Mews St **E1** 126 E10
Meymott St **SE1** 125 P10
Meynell Cres **E9** 127 H2
Meynell Gdns **E9** 127 H2
Meynell Rd **E9** 127 H2
Meyrick Rd **SW11** 128 D9
Micawber St **N1** 126 A5
Michael Rd **SW6** 128 B7
Micklethwaite Rd **SW6** 128 A5
Middle Fld **NW8** 124 D3
Middle Temple La **EC4** 125 N8
Middlesex St **E1** 126 C7
Middleton Dr **SE16** 131 H1
Middleton Rd **E8** 126 D2
Middleton St **E2** 126 F5
Middleton Way **SE13** 131 P10
Midland Rd **NW1** 125 K4
Midship Pt **E14** 131 L1
Milborne Gro **SW10** 128 C4
Milborne St **E9** 126 G1

Milcote St **SE1** 129 P1
Mildmay Av **N1** 126 B1
Mildmay St **N1** 126 B1
Mile End Pl **E1** 127 H6
Mile End Rd **E1** 126 G7
Mile End Rd **E3** 126 G7
Miles St **SW8** 129 L5
Milford La **WC2** 125 M9
Milk Yd **E1** 126 G9
Milkwell Yd **SE5** 130 A7
Mill Row **N1** 126 C3
Mill St **SE1** 130 D1
Mill St **W1** 125 J9
Millbank **SW1** 129 L2
Millbank Twr **SW1** 129 L3
Millbrook Rd **SW9** 129 P9
Millender Wk **SE16** 130 G3
Millennium Br **EC4** 126 A9
Millennium Br **SE1** 126 A9
Millennium Dr **E14** 131 P3
Millennium Harbour **E14** 131 K1
Millennium Pl **E2** 126 F4
Miller St **NW1** 125 J4
Miller Wk **SE1** 125 N10
Millgrove St **SW11** 128 G8
Millharbour **E14** 131 M2
Milligan St **E14** 127 K9
Millman Ms **WC1** 125 M6
Millman St **WC1** 125 M6
Millmark Gro **SE14** 131 J8
Millstream Rd **SE1** 130 D1
Millwall Dock Rd **E14** 131 L2
Milman's St **SW10** 128 D5
Milner Pl **N1** 125 N3
Milner Sq **N1** 125 P2
Milner St **SW3** 128 F3
Milton Cl **SE1** 130 D3
Milton Ct Rd **SE14** 131 J5
Milton St **EC2** 126 B7
Milverton St **SE11** 129 N4
Mina Rd **SE17** 130 C4
Mincing La **EC3** 126 C9
Minera Ms **SW1** 128 G3
Minerva Cl **SW9** 129 N6
Minerva St **E2** 126 F4
Minet Rd **SW9** 129 P8
Ming St **E14** 127 L9
Minories **EC3** 126 D8
Minson Rd **E9** 127 H3
Mintern St **N1** 126 B4
Mission Pl **SE15** 130 E7
Mitchell St **EC1** 126 A6
Mitchison Rd **N1** 126 B1
Mitre Rd **SE1** 129 N1
Mitre St **EC3** 126 C8
Moat Pl **SW9** 129 M9
Modling Ho **E2** 126 G4
Molesford Rd **SW6** 128 A7
Molesworth St **SE13** 131 N9
Molyneux St **W1** 124 E7
Mona Rd **SE15** 130 G8
Monck St **SW1** 129 K2
Monclar Rd **SE5** 130 B10
Moncrieff St **SE15** 130 E8
Monier Rd **E3** 127 L2
Monkton St **SE11** 129 N3
Monmouth Rd **W2** 124 B8
Monmouth St **WC2** 125 L9
Monnow Rd **SE1** 130 E3
Monson Rd **SE14** 131 H6
Montagu Ms N **W1** 124 F7
Montagu Pl **W1** 124 F7
Montagu Sq **W1** 124 F7
Montagu St **W1** 124 F8
Montague Av **SE4** 131 K10
Montague Cl **SE1** 126 B10
Montague Pl **WC1** 125 K7
Montague Sq **SE15** 126 A8
Montague St **WC1** 125 L7
Monteagle Way **SE15** 130 F9
Montefiore St **SW8** 129 H8
Montevetro **SW11** 128 D7
Montford Pl **SE11** 129 N4
Montgomery St **E14** 127 M10
Montpelier Pl **E1** 126 G8
Montpelier Pl **SW7** 128 E2
Montpelier Rd **SE15** 130 F7
Montpelier Sq **SW7** 128 E1
Montpelier St **SW7** 128 E1
Montpelier Wk **SW7** 128 E2
Montrose Ct **SW7** 128 D1
Montrose Pl **SW1** 128 G1
Monument St **EC3** 126 B9
Monza St **E1** 126 G9
Moodkee St **SE16** 130 G2
Moody Rd **SE15** 130 D6
Moody St **E1** 127 H5
Moon St **N1** 125 P3
Moor La **EC2** 126 B7
Moore Pk Rd **SW6** 128 B6
Moore St **SW3** 128 F3
Moorfields **EC2** 126 B7
Moorgate **EC2** 126 B8
Moorhouse Rd **W2** 124 A8
Moorland Rd **SW9** 129 P10
Moorlands Est **SW9** 129 N10
Mora St **EC1** 126 A5
Morant St **E14** 127 L9
Morat St **SW9** 129 M7
Moravian St **E2** 126 G5
Mordaunt St **SW9** 129 M9
Morden Hill **SE13** 131 N8
Morden La **SE13** 131 N7
Morden St **SE13** 131 M7
More London Pl **SE1** 126 C10
Morecambe Cl **E1** 127 H7
Morecambe St **SE17** 130 A3
Moreland St **EC1** 125 P5
Moresby Wk **SW8** 129 H8
Moreton Pl **SW1** 129 J4
Moreton St **SW1** 129 K4
Moreton Ter **SW1** 129 J4
Morgan St **E3** 127 J5
Morgans La **SE1** 126 C10
Morley Rd **SE13** 131 N10
Morley St **SE1** 129 N1
Morna Rd **SE5** 130 A8
Morning La **E9** 126 G1
Mornington Cres **NW1** 125 J4
Mornington Gro **E3** 127 L5
Mornington Ms **SE5** 130 A7
Mornington Rd **SE8** 131 K6
Mornington St **NW1** 125 H4
Mornington Ter **NW1** 125 H3
Morocco St **SE1** 130 C1
Morpeth Gro **E9** 127 H3
Morpeth Rd **E9** 126 G3
Morpeth St **E2** 127 H5
Morpeth Ter **SW1** 129 J2
Morris Rd **E14** 127 M7
Morris St **E1** 126 F8
Morrison St **SW11** 128 G9
Morshead Rd **W9** 124 A5
Mortham St **E15** 127 P3
Mortimer Cres **NW6** 124 B3
Mortimer Est **NW6** 124 B3
Mortimer Pl **NW6** 124 B3
Mortimer Rd **N1** 126 C2
Mortimer St **W1** 125 H8
Morton Rd **N1** 126 A2
Morville St **E3** 127 L4
Moscow Rd **W2** 124 A9
Mossbury Rd **SW11** 128 E9
Mossford St **E3** 127 K6
Mossop St **SW3** 128 E3
Mostyn Gro **E3** 127 K4
Mostyn Rd **SW9** 129 N7
Motcomb St **SW1** 128 G2
Moulins Rd **E9** 126 G3
Mount Pleasant **WC1** 125 N6
Mount Row **W1** 125 H9
Mount St **W1** 124 G9
Mountague Pl **E14** 127 N9
Mounts Pond Rd **SE3** 131 P8
Mowlem St **E2** 126 F4
Mowll St **SW9** 129 N6
Moxon St **W1** 124 G7
Mozart Ter **SW1** 128 G3
Mulberry Rd **E8** 126 D2
Mulberry Wk **SW3** 128 D5
Mulvaney Way **SE1** 130 B1
Mundy St **N1** 126 C5
Munro Ter **SW10** 128 D6
Munster Sq **NW1** 125 H5
Munton Rd **SE17** 130 A3
Murdock St **SE15** 130 F5
Muriel St **N1** 125 M4
Murillo Rd **SE13** 131 P10
Murphy St **SE1** 129 N1
Murray Gro **N1** 126 A4
Murray Ms **NW1** 125 K2
Murray St **NW1** 125 K2
Mursell Est **SW8** 129 M7
Musbury St **E1** 126 G8
Muschamp Rd **SE15** 130 D9
Museum St **WC1** 125 L8
Musgrave Cres **SW6** 128 A7
Musgrove Rd **SE14** 131 H7
Mutrix Rd **NW6** 124 A3
Myatt Rd **SW9** 129 P7
Myddelton Sq **EC1** 125 N5
Myddelton St **EC1** 125 N5
Myers La **SE14** 131 H5
Mylne St **EC1** 125 N5
Myrdle St **E1** 126 E7
Myron Pl **SE13** 131 N9
Myrtle Wk **N1** 126 C4
Mysore Rd **SW11** 128 F9

N

N1 Shop Cen **N1** 125 N4
Nairn St **E14** 127 N7
Nankin St **E14** 127 L8
Nansen Rd **SW11** 128 G10
Nantes Cl **SW18** 128 C10
Napier Av **E14** 131 L4
Napier Gro **N1** 126 A4
Napier Ter **N1** 125 P2
Narborough St **SW6** 128 B8
Narrow St **E14** 127 J9
Naseby Cl **NW6** 124 C2
Nash Rd **SE4** 131 H10
Nassau St **W1** 125 J7
Naval Row **E14** 127 N9
Navarino Gro **E8** 126 E1
Navarino Rd **E8** 126 E1
Navarre St **E2** 126 D6
Navy St **SW4** 129 K9
Naylor Rd **SE15** 130 F6
Nazareth Gdns **SE15** 130 F8
Nazrul St **E2** 126 D5
Neal St **WC2** 125 L8
Nealden St **SW9** 129 M9
Neate St **SE5** 130 D5
Nebraska St **SE1** 130 B1
Neckinger **SE16** 130 D2
Neckinger Est **SE16** 130 D2
Neckinger St **SE1** 130 D1
Nectarine Way **SE13** 131 M8
Needleman St **SE16** 131 H1
Nelldale Rd **SE16** 130 G3
Nelson Cl **NW6** 124 A5
Nelson Gdns **E2** 126 E5
Nelson Pl **N1** 125 P4
Nelson Rd **SE10** 131 N5
Nelson Sq **SE1** 129 P1
Nelson St **E1** 126 F8
Nelson Ter **N1** 125 P4
Nelson's Row **SW4** 129 K10
Nepaul Rd **SW11** 128 E8
Neptune St **SE16** 130 G2
Nesham St **E1** 126 E10
Netherford Rd **SW4** 129 J8
Netherhall Gdns **NW3** 124 C1
Netherton Gro **SW10** 128 C5
Nettleton Rd **SE14** 131 H7
Nevada St **SE10** 131 N5
Nevern Pl **SW5** 128 A3
Nevern Rd **SW5** 128 A3
Nevern Sq **SW5** 128 A3
Neville Cl **SE15** 130 E6
Neville St **SW7** 128 D4
Neville Ter **SW7** 128 D4
New Bond St **W1** 125 H9
New Br St **EC4** 125 P8
New Broad St **EC2** 126 C7
New Burlington St **W1** 125 J9
New Butt La **SE8** 131 L6
New Caledonian Wf **SE16** 131 K2
New Cavendish St **W1** 124 G7
New Change **EC4** 126 A8
New Ch Rd **SE5** 130 A6
New Compton St **WC2** 125 K8
New Covent Gdn Mkt **SW8** 129 K6
New Cross Rd **SE14** 130 G6
New Fetter La **EC4** 125 N8
New Globe Wk **SE1** 126 A10
New Inn Yd **EC2** 126 C6
New Kent Rd **SE1** 130 A2
New King St **SE8** 131 L5
New Mt St **E15** 127 P2
New N Rd **N1** 126 B4
New N St **WC1** 125 M7
New Oxford St **WC1** 125 K8
New Pl Sq **SE16** 130 F2
New Quebec St **W1** 124 F8
New Ride **SW7** 128 E1
New River Wk **N1** 126 A1
New Rd **E1** 126 F7
New Row **WC2** 125 L9
New Sq **WC2** 125 M8
New St **EC2** 126 C7
New Union Cl **E14** 131 N2
New Union St **EC2** 126 B7
New Wf Rd **N1** 125 L4
Newark St **E1** 126 F7
Newburgh St **W1** 125 J8
Newburn St **SE11** 129 M4
Newby Pl **E14** 127 N9
Newby St **SW8** 129 H9
Newcastle Pl **W2** 124 D7
Newcomen Rd **SW11** 128 D9
Newcomen St **SE1** 130 B1
Newcourt St **NW8** 124 E4
Newell St **E14** 127 K8
Newent Cl **SE15** 130 C6
Newgate St **EC1** 125 P8
Newington Butts **SE1** 129 P3
Newington Butts **SE11** 129 P3
Newington Causeway **SE1** 129 P2
Newington Grn Rd **N1** 126 B1
Newlands Quay **E1** 126 G9
Newman St **W1** 125 J7
Newport Av **E14** 127 P9
Newport Pl **WC2** 125 K9
Newport St **SE11** 129 M3
Newton Pl **E14** 131 L3
Newton Rd **W2** 124 A8
Newton St **WC2** 125 L8
Nicholas Rd **E1** 126 G6
Nicholl St **E2** 126 E3
Nicholson St **SE1** 125 P10
Nigel Rd **SE15** 130 E9
Nightingale Rd **N1** 126 A1
Nile St **N1** 126 B5
Nile Ter **SE15** 130 D4
Nine Elms La **SW8** 129 J6
Noble St **EC2** 126 A8
Noel Rd **N1** 125 P4
Noel St **W1** 125 J8
Norbiton Rd **E14** 127 K8
Norfolk Cres **W2** 124 E8
Norfolk Pl **W2** 124 D8
Norfolk Rd **NW8** 124 D3
Norfolk Sq **W2** 124 D8
Norman Gro **E3** 127 J4
Norman Rd **SE10** 131 M6
Normandy Rd **SW9** 129 N7
North Audley St **W1** 124 G8
North Bk **NW8** 124 E5
North Carriage Dr **W2** 124 E9
North Colonnade **E14** 127 L10
North Cres **E16** 127 P6
North Cres **WC1** 125 K7
North Gower St **NW1** 125 J5
North Ms **WC1** 125 M6
North Pas **SW18** 128 A10
North Ride **W2** 124 E9
North Rd **N7** 125 L1
North Row **W1** 124 F9
North St **SW4** 129 J9
North Tenter St **E1** 126 D8
North Ter **SW3** 128 E2
North Vil **NW1** 125 K1
North Wf Rd **W2** 124 D7
Northampton Pk **N1** 126 A1
Northampton Rd **EC1** 125 N6
Northampton Sq **EC1** 125 P5
Northampton St **N1** 126 A2
Northbourne Rd **SW4** 129 K10
Northburgh St **EC1** 125 P6
Northchurch Rd **N1** 126 B2
Northchurch Ter **N1** 126 C2
Northcote Rd **SW11** 128 E10
Northdown St **N1** 125 M4
Northey St **E14** 127 J9
Northfields **SW18** 128 A10
Northiam St **E9** 126 F3
Northington St **WC1** 125 M6
Northlands St **SE5** 130 A8
Northpoint Sq **NW1** 125 K1
Northport St **N1** 126 B3
Northumberland All **EC3** 126 C8
Northumberland Av **WC2** 125 L10
Northumberland Pl **W2** 124 A8
Northumberland St **WC2** 125 L10
Northumbria St **E14** 127 L8
Northway Rd **SE5** 130 A9
Northwick Ter **NW8** 124 D6
Norton Folgate **E1** 126 C7
Norway Gate **SE16** 131 J2
Norway St **SE10** 131 M5
Norwich St **EC4** 125 N8
Notley St **SE5** 130 B6
Notre Dame Est **SW4** 129 J10
Notting Hill Gate **W11** 124 A10
Nottingham Pl **W1** 124 G6
Nottingham St **W1** 124 G7
Novello St **SW6** 128 A7
Nuding Cl **SE13** 131 L9
Nugent Ter **NW8** 124 C4
Nunhead Cres **SE15** 130 F9
Nunhead Est **SE15** 130 F10
Nunhead Grn **SE15** 130 F9
Nunhead Gro **SE15** 130 F9
Nunhead La **SE15** 130 F9
Nursery Cl **SE4** 131 K8
Nursery La **E2** 126 D3
Nursery Rd **SW9** 129 M10
Nutbrook St **SE15** 130 E9
Nutcroft Rd **SE15** 130 F6
Nutford Pl **W1** 124 F8
Nutley Ter **NW3** 124 C1
Nutmeg La **E14** 127 P8
Nutt St **SE15** 130 D6
Nuttall St **N1** 126 C4
Nynehead St **SE14** 131 J6

O

Oak La **E14** 127 K9
Oak Tree Rd **NW8** 124 E5
Oakbank Gro **SE24** 130 A10
Oakbury Rd **SW6** 128 B8
Oakcroft Rd **SE13** 131 P8
Oakdale Rd **SE15** 130 G9
Oakden St **SE11** 129 N3
Oakey La **SE1** 129 N2
Oakfield St **SW10** 128 C5
Oakhurst Gro **SE22** 130 E10
Oakington Rd **W9** 124 A6
Oakley Gdns **SW3** 128 E5
Oakley Pl **SE1** 130 D4
Oakley Rd **N1** 126 B2
Oakley Sq **NW1** 125 J4
Oakley St **SW3** 128 E5
Oat La **EC2** 126 A8
Oban St **E14** 127 P8
Oberstein Rd **SW11** 128 D10
Observatory Gdns **W8** 128 A1
Occupation Rd **SE17** 130 A4
Ocean Est **E1** 127 H7
Ocean St **E1** 127 H7
Ocean Wf **E14** 131 K1
Ockendon Rd **N1** 126 B1
Octavia St **SW11** 128 E7
Octavius St **SE8** 131 L6
Odessa St **SE16** 131 K1
Odger St **SW11** 128 F8
Offenbach Ho **E2** 127 H4
Offerton Rd **SW4** 129 J9
Offley Rd **SW9** 129 N6
Offord Rd **N1** 125 M2
Offord St **N1** 125 M2
Oglander Rd **SE15** 130 D10
Ogle St **W1** 125 J7
Old Bailey **EC4** 125 P8
Old Bellgate Pl **E14** 131 L2
Old Bethnal Grn Rd **E2** 126 E5
Old Bond St **W1** 125 J9
Old Broad St **EC2** 126 B8
Old Brompton Rd **SW5** 128 A4
Old Brompton Rd **SW7** 128 A4
Old Burlington St **W1** 125 J9
Old Castle St **E1** 126 D7
Old Cavendish St **W1** 125 H8
Old Ch Rd **E1** 127 H8
Old Ch St **SW3** 128 D4
Old Compton St **W1** 125 K9
Old Ct Pl **W8** 128 B1
Old Ford Rd **E2** 126 G4
Old Ford Rd **E3** 127 J4
Old Gloucester St **WC1** 125 L7
Old Jamaica Rd **SE16** 130 E2
Old James St **SE15** 130 F9
Old Jewry **EC2** 126 B8
Old Kent Rd **SE1** 130 C3
Old Kent Rd **SE15** 130 C3
Old Marylebone Rd **NW1** 124 E7
Old Montague St **E1** 126 E7
Old Nichol St **E2** 126 D6
Old Palace Yd **SW1** 129 L2
Old Paradise St **SE11** 129 M3
Old Pk La **W1** 124 G10
Old Pye St **SW1** 129 K2
Old Quebec St **W1** 124 F8
Old Queen St **SW1** 129 K1
Old Royal Free Sq **N1** 125 N3
Old S Lambeth Rd **SW8** 129 L6
Old Spitalfields Mkt **E1** 126 D7
Old Sq **WC2** 125 N8
Old St **EC1** 126 A6
Old Town **SW4** 129 J9
Old Woolwich Rd **SE10** 131 P5
Oldbury Pl **W1** 124 G6
Oldfield Gro **SE16** 131 H3
O'Leary Sq **E1** 126 G7
Olga St **E3** 127 J4
Oliver Ms **SE15** 130 E8
Oliver-Goldsmith Est **SE15** 130 E7
Ollerton Grn **E3** 127 K3
Olliffe St **E14** 131 N2
Olmar St **SE1** 130 E5
Olney Rd **SE17** 129 P5
O'Meara St **SE1** 126 A10
Omega St **SE14** 131 L7
Ommaney Rd **SE14** 131 H7
Ondine Rd **SE15** 130 D10
Onega Gate **SE16** 131 J2
Ongar Rd **SW6** 128 A5
Onslow Cres **SW7** 128 D3
Onslow Gdns **SW7** 128 D4
Onslow Sq **SW7** 128 D3
Ontario St **SE1** 129 P2
Ontario Way **E14** 127 L9
Opal St **SE11** 129 P3
Ophir Ter **SE15** 130 E7
Oppenheim Rd **SE13** 131 N8
Oppidans Rd **NW3** 124 F2
Orange St **WC2** 125 K9
Oransay Rd **N1** 126 A1
Orb St **SE17** 130 B3
Orbel St **SW11** 128 E7
Orchard, The **SE3** 131 P8
Orchard Cl **N1** 126 A2
Orchard St **W1** 124 G8
Orchardson St **NW8** 124 D6
Orde Hall St **WC1** 125 M6
Ordell Rd **E3** 127 K4
Ordnance Cres **SE10** 131 P1
Ordnance Hill **NW8** 124 D3
Oregano Dr **E14** 127 P8
Oriel Rd **E9** 127 H1
Orkney St **SW11** 128 G8
Orlando Rd **SW4** 129 J9
Orleston Ms **N7** 125 N1
Orleston Rd **N7** 125 N1
Orme Ct **W2** 124 B9
Orme La **W2** 124 B9
Ormonde Gate **SW3** 128 F4
Ormonde Ter **NW8** 124 F3
Ormsby St **E2** 126 D4
Ormside St **SE15** 130 G5
Orpheus St **SE5** 130 B7
Orsett St **SE11** 129 M4
Orsett Ter **W2** 124 C8
Orsman Rd **N1** 126 C3
Orville Rd **SW11** 128 D8
Osborn Cl **E8** 126 E3
Osborn St **E1** 126 D7
Osborne Rd **E9** 127 K1
Oscar St **SE8** 131 L7
Oseney Cres **NW5** 125 J1
Osier St **E1** 126 G6
Osiers Rd **SW18** 128 A10
Oslo Sq **SE16** 131 J2
Osnaburgh St **NW1** 125 H6
Osnaburgh St (north section) **NW1** 125 H5
Osric Path **N1** 126 C4
Ossington St **W2** 124 A9
Ossory Rd **SE1** 130 E4
Ossulston St **NW1** 125 K5
Oswell Ho **E1** 126 F10
Oswin St **SE11** 129 P3
Oswyth Rd **SE5** 130 C8
Otis St **E3** 127 N5
Otter Cl **E15** 127 N3
Otterburn Ho **SE5** 130 A6
Otto St **SE17** 129 P5
Outer Circle **NW1** 125 H4
Outram Pl **N1** 125 L3
Oval, The **E2** 126 F4
Oval Pl **SW8** 129 M6
Oval Rd **NW1** 125 H3
Oval Way **SE11** 129 M4
Overcliff Rd **SE13** 131 L9
Oversley Ho **W2** 124 A7
Overton Rd **SW9** 129 N8
Ovex Cl **E14** 131 N1
Ovington Gdns **SW3** 128 E2
Ovington Ms **SW3** 128 E2
Ovington Sq **SW3** 128 E2
Ovington St **SW3** 128 E2
Oxendon St **SW1** 125 K9
Oxenford St **SE15** 130 D9
Oxenholme **NW1** 125 J4
Oxestalls Rd **SE8** 131 J4
Oxford Rd **E15** 127 P1
Oxford Rd **NW6** 124 A4
Oxford Sq **W2** 124 E8
Oxford St **W1** 125 H8
Oxley Cl **SE1** 130 D4
Oxo Twr Wf **SE1** 125 N9
Oxonian St **SE22** 130 D10
Oyster Wf **SW11** 128 D8

P

Packington Sq **N1** 126 A3
Packington St **N1** 125 P3
Padbury **SE17** 130 C4
Padbury Ct **E2** 126 D5
Paddington Grn **W2** 124 D7
Paddington Sta **W2** 124 C8
Paddington St **W1** 124 G7
Paddington Underground Sta **W2** 124 C8
Padfield Rd **SE5** 130 A9
Padfield Rd **SW9** 130 A9
Pagden St **SW8** 129 H7
Page St **SW1** 129 K3
Pages Wk **SE1** 130 C3
Pagnell St **SE14** 131 K6
Pagoda Gdns **SE3** 131 P8
Pakenham St **WC1** 125 M5
Palace Av **W8** 124 B10
Palace Ct **W2** 124 B9
Palace Gdns Ms **W8** 124 A10
Palace Gdns Ter **W8** 124 A10
Palace Gate **W8** 128 C1
Palace Grn **W8** 128 B1
Palace St **SW1** 129 J2
Palfrey Pl **SW8** 129 M6
Palgrave Gdns **NW1** 124 E6
Pall Mall **SW1** 125 J10
Pall Mall E **SW1** 125 K10
Palmer St **SW1** 129 K2
Palmers Rd **E2** 127 H4
Palmerston Rd **NW6** 124 A2
Pancras Rd **NW1** 125 K4
Pandora Rd **NW6** 124 A1
Parade, The **SW11** 128 F6
Paradise Rd **SW4** 129 L8
Paradise St **SE16** 130 F1
Paradise Wk **SW3** 128 F5
Paragon Rd **E9** 126 G1
Pardoner St **SE1** 130 B2
Parfett St **E1** 126 E7
Paris Gdn **SE1** 125 P10
Park Cl **E9** 126 G3
Park Cl **SW1** 128 F1
Park Cres **W1** 125 H6
Park La **W1** 124 G9
Park Pl **E14** 127 L10

Park Pl **N1** 126 B3
Park Pl **SW1** 125 J10
Park Pl Vil **W2** 124 C7
Park Rd **NW1** 124 E5
Park Rd **NW8** 124 E5
Park Row **SE10** 131 P5
Park Sq E **NW1** 125 H6
Park Sq Ms **NW1** 125 H6
Park Sq W **NW1** 125 H6
Park St **SE1** 126 A10
Park St **W1** 124 G9
Park Vw Est **E2** 127 H4
Park Vw Ms **SW9** 129 M8
Park Village E **NW1** 125 H4
Park Village W **NW1** 125 H4
Park Vista **SE10** 131 P5
Park Wk **SW10** 128 C5
Parker St **WC2** 125 L8
Parkfield Rd **SE14** 131 K7
Parkgate Rd **SW11** 128 E6
Parkham St **SW11** 128 E7
Parkholme Rd **E8** 126 D1
Parkhouse St **SE5** 130 B6
Parkside Rd **SW11** 128 G7
Parkway **NW1** 125 H3
Parliament Sq **SW1** 129 L1
Parliament St **SW1** 129 L1
Parliament Vw Apts **SE1** 129 M3
Parma Cres **SW11** 128 F10
Parmiter St **E2** 126 F4
Parnell Rd **E3** 127 K3
Parr St **N1** 126 B4
Parry St **SW8** 129 L5
Parsonage St **E14** 131 N3
Parsons Grn **SW6** 128 A7
Parsons Grn La **SW6** 128 A7
Parson's Ho **W2** 124 D6
Parthenia Rd **SW6** 128 A7
Parvin St **SW8** 129 K7
Pascal St **SW8** 129 K6
Passmore St **SW1** 128 G3
Pastor St **SE11** 129 P3
Patcham Ter **SW8** 129 H7
Pater St **W8** 128 A2
Patience Rd **SW11** 128 E8
Patmore Est **SW8** 129 J7
Patmore St **SW8** 129 J7
Patmos Rd **SW9** 129 P6
Paton Cl **E3** 127 L5
Patriot Sq **E2** 126 F4
Patshull Rd **NW5** 125 J1
Patterdale Rd **SE15** 130 G6
Pattina Wk **SE16** 127 K10
Paul Julius Cl **E14** 127 P9
Paul St **E15** 127 P3
Paul St **EC2** 126 B6
Paulet Rd **SE5** 129 P8
Paul's Wk **EC4** 126 A9
Paultons Sq **SW3** 128 D5
Paultons St **SW3** 128 D5
Paveley Dr **SW11** 128 E6
Paveley St **NW8** 124 E6
Pavement, The **SW4** 129 J10
Pavilion Rd **SW1** 128 F1
Paxton Ter **SW1** 129 H5
Payne Rd **E3** 127 M4
Payne St **SE8** 131 K5
Peabody Est **SW1** 129 J3
Peabody Sq **SE1** 129 P1
Peabody Trust **SE1** 126 A10
Pear Tree Cl **E2** 126 D3
Pear Tree Ct **EC1** 125 N6
Pear Tree St **EC1** 125 P6
Peardon St **SW8** 129 H8
Pearman St **SE1** 129 N1
Pearscroft Ct **SW6** 128 B7
Pearscroft Rd **SW6** 128 B7
Pearson St **E2** 126 C4
Peckford Pl **SW9** 129 N8
Peckham Gro **SE15** 130 C6
Peckham High St **SE15** 130 E7
Peckham Hill St **SE15** 130 E6
Peckham Pk Rd **SE15** 130 E6
Peckham Rd **SE5** 130 C7
Peckham Rd **SE15** 130 C7
Peckham Rye **SE15** 130 E9
Peckham Rye **SE22** 130 E10
Pedlars Wk **N7** 125 L1
Pedley St **E1** 126 D6
Peel Gro **E2** 126 G4
Peel Prec **NW6** 124 A4
Peel St **W8** 124 A10
Peerless St **EC1** 126 B5
Pekin St **E14** 127 L8
Pelham Cl **SE5** 130 C8
Pelham Cres **SW7** 128 E3
Pelham Pl **SW7** 128 E3
Pelham St **SW7** 128 E3
Pelican Est **SE15** 130 D7
Pelling St **E14** 127 L8
Pelter St **E2** 126 D5
Pembridge Cres **W11** 124 A9
Pembridge Gdns **W2** 124 A9
Pembridge Ms **W11** 124 A9
Pembridge Pl **W2** 124 A9
Pembridge Rd **W11** 124 A9
Pembridge Sq **W2** 124 A9
Pembridge Vil **W2** 124 A9
Pembridge Vil **W11** 124 A9
Pembroke Av **N1** 125 L3
Pembroke Cl **SW1** 128 G1
Pembroke Gdns Cl **W8** 128 A2
Pembroke Pl **W8** 128 A2
Pembroke Rd **W8** 128 A3
Pembroke Sq **W8** 128 A2
Pembroke St **N1** 125 L2
Pembroke Vil **W8** 128 A3
Pembroke Wk **W8** 128 A3
Pembry Cl **SW9** 129 N7
Penang St **E1** 126 F10
Penarth St **SE15** 130 G5
Pencraig Way **SE15** 130 F5
Pendrell Rd **SE4** 131 J8
Penfold Pl **NW1** 124 E7
Penfold St **NW1** 124 D6
Penfold St **NW8** 124 D6
Penford St **SE5** 129 P8
Penn St **N1** 126 B3
Pennack Rd **SE15** 130 D5
Pennant Ms **W8** 128 B3
Pennethorne Rd **SE15** 130 F6
Pennington St **E1** 126 E9
Pennyfields **E14** 127 L9
Penpoll Rd **E8** 126 F1
Penrose Gro **SE17** 130 A4
Penrose Ho **SE17** 130 A4
Penrose St **SE17** 130 A4
Penryn St **NW1** 125 K4
Pensbury Pl **SW8** 129 J8
Pensbury St **SW8** 129 J8
Penshurst Rd **E9** 127 H2
Pentland Rd **NW6** 124 A5
Penton Pl **SE17** 129 P4
Penton Ri **WC1** 125 M5
Penton St **N1** 125 N4
Pentonville Rd **N1** 125 M4
Pentridge St **SE15** 130 D6
Penywern Rd **SW5** 128 A4
Pepper St **E14** 131 M2
Pepys Rd **SE14** 131 H7
Pepys St **EC3** 126 C9
Percival St **EC1** 125 P6
Percy Circ **WC1** 125 M5
Percy St **W1** 125 K7
Peregrine Ho **EC1** 125 P5
Perkin's Rents **SW1** 129 K2
Perrymead St **SW6** 128 A7
Perseverance Pl **SW9** 129 N6
Peter St **W1** 125 K9
Peterborough Ms **SW6** 128 A8
Peterborough Rd **SW6** 128 A8
Peterborough Vil **SW6** 128 B7
Petergate **SW11** 128 C10
Petersham La **SW7** 128 C2
Petersham Ms **SW7** 128 C2
Petersham Pl **SW7** 128 C2
Peto Pl **NW1** 125 H6
Petticoat La **E1** 126 C7
Petticoat Sq **E1** 126 D8
Petty France **SW1** 129 J2
Petty Wales **EC3** 126 C9
Petworth St **SW11** 128 E7
Petyward **SW3** 128 E3
Peyton Pl **SE10** 131 N6
Phelp St **SE17** 130 B5
Phene St **SW3** 128 E5
Philbeach Gdns **SW5** 128 A4
Philip Wk **SE15** 130 E9
Phillimore Gdns **W8** 128 A1
Phillimore Pl **W8** 128 A1
Phillimore Wk **W8** 128 A2
Phillipp St **N1** 126 C3
Philpot St **E1** 126 F8
Phipp St **EC2** 126 C6
Phoenix Pl **WC1** 125 M6
Phoenix Rd **NW1** 125 K5
Piccadilly **W1** 125 H10
Piccadilly Circ **W1** 125 K9
Pickfords Wf **N1** 126 A4
Picton St **SE5** 130 B6
Pier St **E14** 131 N3
Pigott St **E14** 127 L8
Pilgrimage St **SE1** 130 B1
Pilkington Rd **SE15** 130 F8
Pilot Cl **SE8** 131 K5
Pilton Pl **SE17** 130 A4
Pimlico Rd **SW1** 128 G4
Pinchin St **E1** 126 E9
Pincott Pl **SE4** 131 H10
Pindar St **EC2** 126 C7
Pine St **EC1** 125 N6
Pinefield Cl **E14** 127 L9
Pioneer St **SE15** 130 E7
Piper Cl **N7** 125 M1
Pitchford St **E15** 127 P2
Pitfield Est **N1** 126 B5
Pitfield St **N1** 126 C5
Pitman St **SE5** 130 A6
Pitsea St **E1** 127 H8
Pitt St **W8** 128 A1
Pitt's Head Ms **W1** 124 G10
Pixley St **E14** 127 K8
Plantation Wf **SW11** 128 C9
Plato Rd **SW2** 129 L10
Platt St **NW1** 125 K4
Plaza Shop Cen, The **W1** 125 J8
Pleasant Pl **N1** 125 P2
Pleasant Row **NW1** 125 H3
Plender St **NW1** 125 J3
Plevna St **E14** 131 N2
Plough Rd **SW11** 128 D9
Plough Ter **SW11** 128 D10
Plough Way **SE16** 131 H3
Plough Yd **EC2** 126 C6
Plover Way **SE16** 131 J2
Plumbers Row **E1** 126 E7
Plymouth Wf **E14** 131 P3
Plympton St **NW8** 124 E6
Pocock St **SE1** 129 P1
Podmore Rd **SW18** 128 C10
Point Hill **SE10** 131 N6
Point Pleasant **SW18** 128 A10
Pointers Cl **E14** 131 M4
Poland Ho **E15** 127 P3
Poland St **W1** 125 J8
Polesworth Ho **W2** 124 A7
Pollard Row **E2** 126 E5
Pollard St **E2** 126 E5
Polygon Rd **NW1** 125 K4
Pomeroy St **SE14** 130 G7
Pond Pl **SW3** 128 E3
Ponler St **E1** 126 F8
Ponsford St **E9** 126 G1
Ponsonby Pl **SW1** 129 K4
Ponsonby Ter **SW1** 129 K4
Pont St **SW1** 128 F2
Pont St Ms **SW1** 128 F2
Ponton Rd **SW8** 129 K5
Poole Rd **E9** 127 H1
Poole St **N1** 126 B3
Poolmans St **SE16** 131 H1
Pope St **SE1** 130 C1
Popes Rd **SW9** 129 N9
Popham Rd **N1** 126 A3
Popham St **N1** 125 P3
Poplar Business Pk **E14** 127 N9
Poplar High St **E14** 127 L9
Poplar Pl **W2** 124 B9
Poplar Rd **SE24** 130 A10
Poplar Wk **SE24** 130 A10
Porchester Cl **SE5** 130 A10
Porchester Gdns **W2** 124 B9
Porchester Ms **W2** 124 B8
Porchester Pl **W2** 124 E8
Porchester Rd **W2** 124 B7
Porchester Sq **W2** 124 B8
Porchester Ter **W2** 124 C9
Porchester Ter N **W2** 124 B8
Porden Rd **SW2** 129 M10
Porlock St **SE1** 130 B1
Portelet Rd **E1** 127 H5
Porteus Rd **W2** 124 C7
Portia Way **E3** 127 K6
Portland Gro **SW8** 129 M7
Portland Pl **W1** 125 H7
Portland St **SE17** 130 B4
Portman Cl **W1** 124 F8
Portman Ms S **W1** 124 G8
Portman Pl **E2** 126 G5
Portman Sq **W1** 124 F8
Portman St **W1** 124 G8
Portpool La **EC1** 125 N7
Portree St **E14** 127 P8
Portslade Rd **SW8** 129 J8
Portsoken St **E1** 126 D9
Portugal St **WC2** 125 M8
Post Office Way **SW8** 129 K6
Potier St **SE1** 130 B2
Pott St **E2** 126 F5
Potters Rd **SW6** 128 C8
Pottery St **SE16** 130 F1
Poultry **EC2** 126 B8
Pountney Rd **SW11** 128 G9
Powis Pl **WC1** 125 L6
Powis Rd **E3** 127 M5
Pownall Rd **E8** 126 D3
Poyntz Rd **SW11** 128 F8
Poyser St **E2** 126 F4
Praed St **W2** 124 D8
Prairie St **SW8** 128 G8
Pratt St **NW1** 125 J3
Pratt Wk **SE11** 129 M3
Prebend St **N1** 126 A3
Prescot St **E1** 126 D9
Prescott Pl **SW4** 129 K9
Prestage Way **E14** 127 N9
Prestons Rd **E14** 131 N1
Price's Ct **SW11** 128 D9
Prices Ms **N1** 125 M3
Price's St **SE1** 125 P10
Prideaux Pl **WC1** 125 M5
Prideaux Rd **SW9** 129 L9
Prima Rd **SW9** 129 N6
Primrose Cl **E3** 127 L4
Primrose Gdns **NW3** 124 E1
Primrose Hill Ct **NW3** 124 F2
Primrose Hill Rd **NW3** 124 E2
Primrose Sq **E9** 126 G2
Primrose St **EC2** 126 C7
Prince Albert Rd **NW1** 124 E4
Prince Albert Rd **NW8** 124 E4
Prince Consort Rd **SW7** 128 C2
Prince Edwards Rd **E9** 127 K1
Prince of Wales Dr **SW8** 129 H6
Prince of Wales Dr **SW11** 128 F7
Prince of Wales Gate **SW7** 128 E1
Prince of Wales Rd **NW5** 124 G1
Prince St **SE8** 131 K5
Princelet St **E1** 126 D7
Princes Ct **SE16** 131 K2
Princes Ct Business Cen **E1** 126 F9
Princes Gdns **SW7** 128 D2
Princes Gate **SW7** 128 E1
Princes Gate Ms **SW7** 128 D2
Princes Ri **SE13** 131 N8
Princes Riverside Rd **SE16** 127 H10
Princes Sq **W2** 124 B9
Princes St **EC2** 126 B8
Princes St **W1** 125 H8
Princess Rd **NW1** 124 G3
Princess Rd **NW6** 124 A4
Princess St **SE1** 129 P2
Princethorpe Ho **W2** 124 A7
Princeton St **WC1** 125 M7
Printers Ms **E3** 127 J3
Prior Bolton St **N1** 125 P1
Prior St **SE10** 131 N6
Prioress St **SE1** 130 B2
Priory Ct **SW8** 129 K7
Priory Grn Est **N1** 125 M4
Priory Gro **SW8** 129 L7
Priory Ms **SW8** 129 K7
Priory Rd **NW6** 124 B3
Priory St **E3** 127 M5
Priory Ter **NW6** 124 B3
Priory Wk **SW10** 128 C4
Pritchard's Rd **E2** 126 E3
Priter Rd **SE16** 130 E2
Procter St **WC1** 125 M7
Prospect Pl **E1** 126 G10
Prospect Quay **SW18** 128 A10
Providence Ct **W1** 124 G9
Provost Est **N1** 126 B4
Provost Rd **NW3** 124 F2
Provost St **N1** 126 B5
Prusom St **E1** 126 F10
Pudding La **EC3** 126 B9
Pudding Mill La **E15** 127 M3
Pulross Rd **SW9** 129 M9
Pulteney Cl **E3** 127 K3
Pulteney Ter **N1** 125 M3
Pulton Pl **SW6** 128 A6
Pump La **SE14** 130 G6
Pundersons Gdns **E2** 126 F5
Purbrook St **SE1** 130 C2
Purcell St **N1** 126 C4
Purchese St **NW1** 125 K4
Purdy St **E3** 127 M6
Purelake Ms **SE13** 131 P9
Puteaux Ho **E2** 127 H4
Pytchley Rd **SE22** 130 C9

Q

Quaker St **E1** 126 D6
Quality Ct **WC2** 125 N8
Quarrendon St **SW6** 128 A8
Quarterdeck, The **E14** 131 L1
Quebec Way **SE16** 131 H1
Queen Anne Rd **E9** 127 H1
Queen Anne St **W1** 125 H8
Queen Anne's Gate **SW1** 129 K1
Queen Elizabeth St **SE1** 130 D1
Queen of Denmark Ct **SE16** 131 K2
Queen Sq **WC1** 125 L6
Queen St **EC4** 126 A9
Queen St **W1** 125 H10
Queen Victoria St **EC4** 125 P9
Queenhithe **EC4** 126 A9
Queen's Cres **NW5** 124 G1
Queens Gdns **W2** 124 C9
Queen's Gate **SW7** 128 D3
Queen's Gate Gdns **SW7** 128 C2
Queen's Gate Ms **SW7** 128 C1
Queen's Gate Pl **SW7** 128 C2
Queen's Gate Pl Ms **SW7** 128 C2
Queen's Gate Ter **SW7** 128 C2
Queen's Gro **NW8** 124 D3
Queen's Gro Ms **NW8** 124 D3
Queen's Head St **N1** 125 P3
Queens Ms **W2** 124 B9
Queens Rd **SE14** 130 F7
Queens Rd **SE15** 130 F7
Queen's Row **SE17** 130 B5
Queen's Ter **NW8** 124 D4
Queen's Wk **SE1** 126 C10
Queen's Wk **SW1** 125 J10
Queensberry Pl **SW7** 128 D3
Queensborough Ter **W2** 124 B9
Queensbridge Rd **E2** 126 D3
Queensbridge Rd **E8** 126 D2
Queensbury St **N1** 126 A2
Queensgate Pl **NW6** 124 A2
Queensmead **NW8** 124 D3
Queenstown Rd **SW8** 129 H5
Queensway **W2** 124 B8
Querrin St **SW6** 128 C8
Quex Rd **NW6** 124 A3
Quick St **N1** 125 P4
Quilter St **E2** 126 E5
Quince Rd **SE13** 131 M8
Quixley St **E14** 127 P9
Quorn Rd **SE22** 130 C10

R

Racton Rd **SW6** 128 A5
Radcot St **SE11** 129 N4
Radlett Pl **NW8** 124 E3
Radley Ms **W8** 128 A2
Radnor Pl **W2** 124 E8
Radnor Rd **SE15** 130 E6
Radnor St **EC1** 126 A5
Radnor Wk **SW3** 128 E4
Radstock St **SW11** 128 E6
Raeburn St **SW2** 129 L10
Raglan St **NW5** 125 H1
Railton Rd **SE24** 129 N10
Railway App **SE1** 126 B10
Railway Av **SE16** 130 G1
Railway St **N1** 125 L4
Rainbow Av **E14** 131 M4
Rainbow Quay **SE16** 131 J2
Rainbow St **SE5** 130 C6
Raine St **E1** 126 F10
Rainhill Way **E3** 127 L5
Rainsborough Av **SE8** 131 J3
Raleana Rd **E14** 127 N10
Raleigh St **N1** 125 P3
Ramillies Pl **W1** 125 J8
Rampayne St **SW1** 129 K4
Ramsey St **E2** 126 E6
Ramsey Wk **N1** 126 B1
Randall Cl **SW11** 128 E7
Randall Pl **SE10** 131 N6
Randall Rd **SE11** 129 M3
Randell's Rd **N1** 125 L3
Randolph Av **W9** 124 C6
Randolph Cres **W9** 124 C6
Randolph Gdns **NW6** 124 B4
Randolph Ms **W9** 124 C6
Randolph Rd **W9** 124 C6
Randolph St **NW1** 125 J2
Ranelagh Gdns **SW3** 128 G4
Ranelagh Gro **SW1** 128 G4
Rangers Sq **SE10** 131 P7
Ranwell St **E3** 127 K3
Raphael St **SW7** 128 F1
Ratcliffe Cross St **E1** 127 H8
Ratcliffe La **E14** 127 J8
Ratcliffe Orchard **E1** 127 H9
Rathbone Pl **W1** 125 K8
Rathbone St **W1** 125 J7
Rattray Rd **SW2** 129 N10
Raul Rd **SE15** 130 E7
Raven Row **E1** 126 F7
Ravensbourne Pl **SE13** 131 M8
Ravenscroft St **E2** 126 D4
Ravensdon St **SE11** 129 N4
Ravenstone **SE17** 130 C4
Rawlings St **SW3** 128 F3
Rawstorne St **EC1** 125 P5
Ray St **EC1** 125 N6
Raymouth Rd **SE16** 130 F3
Reading La **E8** 126 F1
Reardon Path **E1** 126 F10
Reardon St **E1** 126 F10
Reaston St **SE14** 130 G6
Record St **SE15** 130 G5
Rector St **N1** 126 A3
Rectory Gro **SW4** 129 J9
Rectory Sq **E1** 127 H7
Reculver Rd **SE16** 131 H4
Red Lion Row **SE17** 130 A5
Red Lion Sq **WC1** 125 M7
Red Lion St **WC1** 125 M7
Red Path **E9** 127 K1
Red Post Hill **SE24** 130 B10
Redan Pl **W2** 124 B8
Redbridge Gdns **SE5** 130 C6
Redburn St **SW3** 128 F5
Redcar St **SE5** 130 A6
Redcastle Cl **E1** 126 G9
Redchurch St **E2** 126 D6
Redcliffe Gdns **SW5** 128 B4
Redcliffe Gdns **SW10** 128 B4
Redcliffe Ms **SW10** 128 B4
Redcliffe Pl **SW10** 128 C5
Redcliffe Rd **SW10** 128 C4
Redcliffe Sq **SW10** 128 B4
Redcliffe St **SW10** 128 B5
Redcross Way **SE1** 130 A1
Reddins Rd **SE15** 130 E5
Redesdale St **SW3** 128 F5
Redfield La **SW5** 128 A3
Redhill St **NW1** 125 H4
Redman's Rd **E1** 126 G7
Redriff Est **SE16** 131 K2
Redriff Rd **SE16** 131 H3
Redruth Rd **E9** 127 H3
Redwood Cl **E3** 127 L4
Redwood Cl **SE16** 127 J10
Reece Ms **SW7** 128 D3
Reed Pl **SW4** 129 K10
Reedham St **SE15** 130 E8
Reedworth St **SE11** 129 N3
Rees St **N1** 126 A3
Reeves Ms **W1** 124 G9
Reeves Rd **E3** 127 M6
Reform St **SW11** 128 F8
Regan Way **N1** 126 C4
Regency St **SW1** 129 K3
Regeneration Rd **SE16** 131 H3
Regent Sq **E3** 127 M5
Regent Sq **WC1** 125 L5
Regent St **SW1** 125 K9
Regent St **W1** 125 H8
Regents Br Gdns **SW8** 129 L6
Regent's Pk, The **NW1** 124 G4
Regents Pk Rd **NW1** 124 F3
Regents Row **E8** 126 E3
Reginald Rd **SE8** 131 L6
Reginald Sq **SE8** 131 L6
Regis Pl **SW2** 129 M10
Relf Rd **SE15** 130 E9
Rembrandt Cl **E14** 131 P2
Remington St **N1** 125 P4
Renforth St **SE16** 130 G1
Renfrew Rd **SE11** 129 P3
Rennell St **SE13** 131 N9
Rennie Est **SE16** 130 F3
Rennie St **SE1** 125 P10
Repton St **E14** 127 J8
Reservoir Rd **SE4** 131 J8
Retreat Pl **E9** 126 G1
Revelon Rd **SE4** 131 J10
Reverdy Rd **SE1** 130 E3
Rheidol Ter **N1** 125 P4
Rhodesia Rd **SW9** 129 L8
Rhodeswell Rd **E14** 127 J7
Rhondda Gro **E3** 127 J5
Rhyl St **NW5** 124 G1
Ricardo St **E14** 127 M8
Rich St **E14** 127 K9
Richborne Ter **SW8** 129 M6
Richmond Av **N1** 125 M3
Richmond Cres **N1** 125 M3
Richmond Gro **N1** 125 P2
Richmond Rd **E8** 126 D2
Richmond Ter **SW1** 129 L1
Rick Roberts Way **E15** 127 N3
Rickett St **SW6** 128 A5
Ridgdale St **E3** 127 M4
Ridgeway Rd **SW9** 129 P9
Riding Ho St **W1** 125 H7
Rifle Ct **SE11** 129 N5
Rifle St **E14** 127 M7
Rigden St **E14** 127 M8
Rigge Pl **SW4** 129 K10
Riley Rd **SE1** 130 D2
Riley St **SW10** 128 D5
Ring, The **W2** 124 D9
Ripplevale Gro **N1** 125 M2
Risdon St **SE16** 130 G1
Risinghill St **N1** 125 M4
Rita Rd **SW8** 129 M6
Ritchie St **N1** 125 N4
Ritson Rd **E8** 126 E1
Rivaz Pl **E9** 126 G1
River Pl **N1** 126 A2
River St **EC1** 125 N5
Riverside Ct **SW8** 129 K5
Riverside Rd **E15** 127 N4
Riverside Twr **SW6** 128 C8
Rivington St **EC2** 126 C5
Roach Rd **E3** 127 L2
Roan St **SE10** 131 N5
Robert Adam St **W1** 124 G8
Robert Dashwood Way **SE17** 130 A3
Robert Lowe Cl **SE14** 131 H6
Robert St **NW1** 125 H5
Roberta St **E2** 126 E5
Roberts Cl **SE16** 131 H1
Robertson Rd **E15** 127 N3
Robertson St **SW8** 129 H9
Robin Ct **SE16** 130 E3
Robin Hood La **E14** 127 N9
Robinson Rd **E2** 126 G4
Robsart St **SW9** 129 M8
Rochelle Cl **SW11** 128 D10
Rochester Ms **NW1** 125 J2
Rochester Pl **NW1** 125 J1
Rochester Rd **NW1** 125 J1
Rochester Row **SW1** 129 J3
Rochester Sq **NW1** 125 J2

Rochester St SW1 129 K2
Rochester Ter NW1 125 J1
Rockingham Est SE1 130 A2
Rockingham St SE1 130 A2
Rodmarton St W1 124 F7
Rodney Pl SE17 130 A3
Rodney Rd SE17 130 A3
Rodney St N1 125 M4
Roffey St E14 131 N1
Roger Dowley Ct E2 126 G4
Roger St WC1 125 M6
Rokeby Rd SE4 131 K8
Roland Gdns SW7 128 C4
Roland Way SE17 130 B4
Rollins St SE15 130 G5
Rolls Rd SE1 130 D4
Rolt St SE8 131 J5
Roman Rd E2 126 G5
Roman Rd E3 127 J4
Roman Way N7 125 M1
Romford St E1 126 E7
Romilly St W1 125 K9
Romney Rd SE10 131 N5
Romney St SW1 129 K2
Rood La EC3 126 C9
Rookery Rd SW4 129 J10
Rope St SE16 131 J3
Ropemaker Rd SE16 131 J2
Ropemaker St EC2 126 B7
Ropery St E3 127 K6
Ropley St E2 126 E4
Rosary Gdns SW7 128 C3
Rose All SE1 126 A10
Rose Sq SW3 128 D4
Rosebank Gdns E3 127 K4
Roseberry Pl E8 126 D1
Roseberry St SE16 130 F3
Rosebery Av EC1 125 N6
Rosebury Rd SW6 128 B8
Rosefield Gdns E14 127 L9
Rosemary Dr E14 127 P8
Rosemary Rd SE15 130 D6
Rosemont Rd NW3 124 C1
Rosemoor St SW3 128 F3
Rosenau Cres SW11 128 E7
Rosenau Rd SW11 128 E7
Roserton St E14 131 N1
Rosetta Cl SW8 129 L6
Rosher Cl E15 127 P2
Rosoman St EC1 125 N5
Rossendale Way NW1 125 J2
Rossetti Rd SE16 130 F4
Rossmore Rd NW1 124 E6
Rothbury Rd E9 127 K2
Rotherfield St N1 126 A2
Rotherhithe New Rd SE16 130 E4
Rotherhithe Old Rd SE16 131 H3
Rotherhithe St SE16 130 G1
Rotherhithe Tunnel E1 126 G10
Rotherhithe Tunnel App E14 127 J9
Rotherhithe Tunnel App SE16 130 G1
Rothery Ter SW9 129 P6
Rothsay St SE1 130 C2
Rothwell St NW1 124 F3
Rotten Row SW1 128 F1
Rotten Row SW7 128 E1
Rotterdam Dr E14 131 N2
Rouel Rd SE16 130 E2
Rounton Rd E3 127 L6
Roupell St SE1 125 N10
Rousden St NW1 125 J2
Rowcross St SE1 130 D4
Rowditch La SW11 128 G8
Rowena Cres SW11 128 E8
Rowington Cl W2 124 B7
Rowley Way NW8 124 B3
Rowse Cl E15 127 N3
Roxby Pl SW6 128 A5
Royal Av SW3 128 F4
Royal Cl SE8 131 K5
Royal Coll St NW1 125 J2
Royal Ct SE16 131 K2
Royal Ex EC3 126 B8
Royal Hill SE10 131 N6
Royal Hosp Rd SW3 128 F5
Royal Ms, The SW1 129 H2
Royal Mint Ct EC3 126 D9
Royal Mint St E1 126 D9
Royal Naval Pl SE14 131 K6
Royal Oak Rd E8 126 F1
Royal Oak Yd SE1 130 C1
Royal Opera Arc SW1 125 K10
Royal Pl SE10 131 N6
Royal Rd SE17 129 P5
Royal St SE1 129 M2
Royal Victor Pl E3 127 H4
Royston St E2 126 G4
Rozel Ct N1 126 C3
Rozel Rd SW4 129 J8
Ruby St SE15 130 F5
Rudolph Rd NW6 124 A4
Rufford St N1 125 L3
Rugby St WC1 125 M6
Rugg St E14 127 L9
Rum Cl E1 126 G9
Rumbold Rd SW6 128 B6
Rumsey Rd SW9 129 M9
Rupert Gdns SW9 129 P8
Rupert St W1 125 K9
Rush Hill Rd SW11 128 G9
Rushcroft Rd SW2 129 N10
Rushton St N1 126 B4
Rushworth St SE1 129 P1
Ruskin Pk Ho SE5 130 B9
Russell Gro SW9 129 N6
Russell Sq WC1 125 L7
Russell St WC2 125 M8
Russia Dock Rd SE16 127 J10
Russia La E2 126 G4
Russia Wk SE16 131 J1
Rust Sq SE5 130 B6
Ruston St E3 127 K3
Rutherford St SW1 129 K3
Rutland Gdns SW7 128 E1
Rutland Gate SW7 128 E1
Rutland Rd E9 126 G3
Rutland St SW7 128 E2
Rutts Ter SE14 131 H7
Ryder Dr SE16 130 F4
Ryder St SW1 125 J10
Rye Hill Pk SE15 130 G10
Rye La SE15 130 E7
Rye Pas SE15 130 E9
Rye Rd SE15 131 H10
Ryecroft St SW6 128 B7
Ryland Rd NW5 125 H1
Rysbrack St SW3 128 F2

S

Sabella Ct E3 127 K4
Sabine Rd SW11 128 F9
Sable St N1 125 P2
Sackville St W1 125 J9
Saffron Av E14 127 P9
Saffron Hill EC1 125 N6
Sail St SE11 129 M3
St. Agnes Pl SE11 129 N5
St. Albans Gro W8 128 B2
St. Alban's Pl N1 125 P3
St. Alfege Pas SE10 131 N5
St. Alphonsus Rd SW4 129 J10
St. Andrew St EC4 125 N7
St. Andrew's Hill EC4 125 P9
St. Andrews Pl NW1 125 H6
St. Andrews Way E3 127 M6
St. Ann's St SW1 129 K2
St. Ann's Ter NW8 124 D4
St. Anthonys Cl E1 126 E10
St. Asaph Rd SE4 131 H9
St. Augustines Rd NW1 125 K2
St. Austell Rd SE13 131 N8
St. Barnabas St SW1 128 G4
St. Barnabas Vil SW8 129 L7
St. Botolph St EC3 126 D8
St. Bride St EC4 125 P8
St. Chad's Pl WC1 125 L5
St. Chad's St WC1 125 L5
St. Clements St N7 125 N1
St. Cross St EC1 125 N7
St. Davids Sq E14 131 M4
St. Donatts Rd SE14 131 K7
St. Dunstan's Hill EC3 126 C9
St. Edmunds Ter NW8 124 E3
St. Elmos Rd SE16 131 H1
St. Francis Rd SE22 130 C10
St. George St W1 125 H8
St. George Wf SW8 129 L4
St. Georges Circ SE1 129 P2
St. George's Dr SW1 129 H3
St. Georges Flds W2 124 E8
St. Georges Rd SE1 129 N2
St. Georges Sq SE8 131 K3
St. George's Sq SW1 129 K4
St. George's Sq Ms SW1 129 K4
St. Georges Way SE15 130 C5
St. Giles High St WC2 125 K8
St. Giles Rd SE5 130 C6
St. Gilles Ho E2 127 H4
St. Helena Rd SE16 131 H3
St. James Ms E14 131 N2
St. James's SE14 131 J7
St. James's Av E2 126 G4
St. James's Ct SW1 129 J2
St. James's Cres SW9 129 N9
St. James's Palace SW1 125 J10
St. James's Pk SW1 129 K1
St. James's Pl SW1 125 J10
St. James's Rd SE1 130 E4
St. James's Rd SE16 130 E2
St. James's Sq SW1 125 J10
St. James's St SW1 125 J10
St. James's Ter Ms NW8 124 F3
St. James's Wk EC1 125 P6
St. John St EC1 125 P6
St. John's Cres SW9 129 N9
St. John's Est N1 126 B4
St. John's Hill SW11 128 D10
St. John's Hill Gro SW11 128 D10
St. John's La EC1 125 P6
St. John's Rd SW11 128 E10
St. Johns Vale SE8 131 L8
St. John's Wd High St NW8 124 D4
St. John's Wd Pk NW8 124 D3
St. John's Wd Rd NW8 124 D6
St. John's Wd Ter NW8 124 D4
St. Joseph's Vale SE3 131 P8
St. Jude's Rd E2 126 F4
St. Katharine's Way E1 126 D10
St. Lawrence St E14 127 N10
St. Lawrence Way SW9 129 N7
St. Leonards Ct N1 126 B5
St. Leonards Rd E14 127 M7
St. Leonards Sq NW5 124 G1
St. Leonards St E3 127 M5
St. Leonard's Ter SW3 128 F4
St. Loo Av SW3 128 E5
St. Luke's Av SW4 129 K10
St. Luke's Cl EC1 126 A6
St. Luke's Est EC1 126 B5
St. Luke's St SW3 128 E4
St. Margarets La W8 128 B2
St. Margarets Rd SE4 131 K10
St. Margaret's St SW1 129 L1
St. Mark St E1 126 D8
St. Marks Cres NW1 124 G3
St. Mark's Gro SW10 128 B5
St. Marks Sq NW1 124 G3
St. Martins Cl NW1 125 J3
St. Martin's La WC2 125 L9
St. Martin's Pl WC2 125 L9
St. Martin's Rd SW9 129 M8
St. Martin's-le-Grand EC1 126 A8
St. Mary at Hill EC3 126 C9
St. Mary Axe EC3 126 C8
St. Marychurch St SE16 130 G1
St. Mary's Gdns SE11 129 N3
St. Mary's Gate W8 128 B2
St. Mary's Gro N1 125 P1
St. Marys Mans W2 124 C7
St. Marys Path N1 125 P3
St. Mary's Pl W8 128 B2
St. Mary's Rd SE15 130 G7
St. Marys Sq W2 124 D7
St. Marys Ter W2 124 D7
St. Mary's Wk SE11 129 N3
St. Matthew's Rd SW2 129 M10
St. Matthew's Row E2 126 E5
St. Michael's Rd SW9 129 M8
St. Michaels St W2 124 D8
St. Norbert Grn SE4 131 J10
St. Norbert Rd SE4 131 J10
St. Olav's Sq SE16 130 G2
St. Oswald's Pl SE11 129 M4
St. Pancras Way NW1 125 J2
St. Paul St N1 126 A3
St. Paul's Av SE16 127 H10
St. Paul's Chyd EC4 125 P8
St. Paul's Cres NW1 125 K2
St. Paul's Ms NW1 125 K2
St. Paul's Pl N1 126 B1
St. Paul's Rd N1 125 P1
St. Paul's Shrubbery N1 126 B1
St. Pauls Way E3 127 K7
St. Pauls Way E14 127 K7
St. Peter's Cl E2 126 E4
St. Peters St N1 125 P3
St. Peter's Way N1 126 C2
St. Petersburgh Ms W2 124 B9
St. Petersburgh Pl W2 124 B9
St. Philip Sq SW8 129 H8
St. Philip St SW8 129 H8
St. Philip's Rd E8 126 E1
St. Rule St SW8 129 J8
St. Saviour's Est SE1 130 D2
St. Silas Pl NW5 124 G1
St. Silas St Est NW5 124 G1
St. Stephens Cres W2 124 A8
St. Stephens Gdns W2 124 A8
St. Stephens Gro SE13 131 N9
St. Stephen's Rd E3 127 K4
St. Stephens Ter SW8 129 M6
St. Stephen's Wk SW7 128 C3
St. Swithin's La EC4 126 B9
St. Thomas St SE1 126 B10
St. Thomas's Pl E9 126 G2
St. Thomas's Sq E9 126 F2
Salamanca St SE1 129 L3
Sale Pl W2 124 E7
Salem Rd W2 124 B9
Salisbury Ct EC4 125 P8
Salisbury Pl SW9 129 P6
Salisbury Pl W1 124 F7
Salisbury St NW8 124 E6
Salisbury Ter SE15 130 G9
Salmon La E14 127 J8
Salter Rd SE16 127 H10
Salter St E14 127 L9
Saltoun Rd SW2 129 N10
Saltwell St E14 127 L9
Samford St NW8 124 E6
Sampson St E1 126 E10
Samuel Cl SE14 131 H5
Samuel Lewis Trust Dws SW6 128 A6
Samuel St SE15 130 D6
Sancroft St SE11 129 M4
Sandall Rd NW5 125 J1
Sandbourne Rd SE4 131 J8
Sandgate St SE15 130 F5
Sandilands Rd SW6 128 B7
Sandison St SE15 130 D9
Sandland St WC1 125 M7
Sandmere Rd SW4 129 L10
Sandpiper Cl SE16 131 K1
Sandrock Rd SE13 131 L9
Sand's End La SW6 128 B7
Sandwell Cres NW6 124 A1
Sandwich St WC1 125 L5
Sandy's Row E1 126 C7
Sanford St SE14 131 J5
Sangora Rd SW11 128 D10
Sans Wk EC1 125 N6
Sansom St SE5 130 B6
Santley St SW4 129 M10
Saperton Wk SE11 129 M3
Sapphire Rd SE8 131 J3
Saracen St E14 127 L8
Sartor Rd SE15 131 H10
Satchwell Rd E2 126 E5
Saunders Ness Rd E14 131 N4
Saunders St SE11 129 N3
Savile Row W1 125 J9
Savona Est SW8 129 J6
Savona St SW8 129 J6
Savoy Ms SW9 129 L9
Savoy Pl WC2 125 L9
Savoy St WC2 125 M9
Sawmill Yd E3 127 J3
Sawyer St SE1 130 A1
Saxon Rd E3 127 K4
Saxton Cl SE13 131 P9
Sayes Ct St SE8 131 K5
Scala St W1 125 J7
Scandrett St E1 126 F10
Scarsdale Vil W8 128 A2
Scawen Rd SE8 131 J4
Scawfell St E2 126 D4
Sceaux Est SE5 130 C7
Sceptre Rd E2 126 G5
Schoolhouse La E1 127 H9
Schooner Cl E14 131 P2
Sclater St E1 126 D6
Scoresby St SE1 125 P10
Scott Ellis Gdns NW8 124 D5
Scott Lidgett Cres SE16 130 E1
Scott St E1 126 F6
Scriven St E8 126 D3
Scrutton St EC2 126 C6
Scylla Rd SE15 130 F9
Seacon Twr E14 131 K1
Seaford St WC1 125 M5
Seagrave Rd SW6 128 A5
Searles Cl SW11 128 E6
Searles Rd SE1 130 B3
Sears St SE5 130 B6
Sebastian St EC1 125 P5
Sebbon St N1 125 P2
Sedding St SW1 128 G3
Sedgmoor Pl SE5 130 C6
Seething La EC3 126 C9
Sekforde St EC1 125 P6
Selby St E1 126 E6
Selden Rd SE15 130 G8
Selsdon Way E14 131 M2
Selsey St E14 127 L7
Selwood Pl SW7 128 D4
Selworthy Ho SW11 128 D7
Selwyn Rd E3 127 K4
Semley Pl SW1 128 G3
Senate St SE15 130 G8
Sendall Ct SW11 128 D9
Senior St W2 124 B7
Senrab St E1 127 H8
Serenaders Rd SW9 129 N8
Serle St WC2 125 M8
Serpentine Rd W2 124 F10
Settles St E1 126 E7
Settrington Rd SW6 128 B8
Severnake Cl E14 131 L3
Severus Rd SW11 128 E10
Seville Ms N1 126 C2
Seville St SW1 128 F1
Sevington St W9 124 B6
Seward St EC1 126 A5
Sewardstone Rd E2 126 G4
Sextant Av E14 131 P3
Seymour Gdns SE4 131 J9
Seymour Ms W1 124 G8
Seymour Pl W1 124 E7
Seymour St W1 124 F8
Seymour St W2 124 F8
Seymour Wk SW10 128 C5
Seyssel St E14 131 N3
Shacklewell St E2 126 D6
Shad Thames SE1 126 D10
Shaftesbury Av W1 125 K9
Shaftesbury Av WC2 125 K9
Shaftesbury St N1 126 A4
Shafton Rd E9 127 H3
Shalbourne Sq E9 127 K1
Shalcomb St SW10 128 C5
Shamrock St SW4 129 K9
Shand St SE1 130 C1
Shandy St E1 127 H7
Shannon Gro SW9 129 M10
Shardeloes Rd SE4 131 K9
Shardeloes Rd SE14 131 K9
Sharon Gdns E9 126 G3
Sharpleshall St NW1 124 F2
Sharratt St SE15 130 G5
Sharsted St SE17 129 P4
Shaw Ct SW11 128 D9
Shaw Rd SE22 130 C10
Shawfield St SW3 128 E4
Shearling Way N7 125 L1
Sheep La E8 126 F3
Sheepcote La SW11 128 F8
Sheffield Ter W8 124 A10
Sheldon Pl E2 126 E4
Sheldon Sq W2 124 C7
Shell Rd SE13 131 M9
Shelley Cl SE15 130 F8
Shellwood Rd SW11 128 F8
Shelmerdine Cl E3 127 L7
Shelton St WC2 125 L8
Shenfield St N1 126 C4
Shenley Rd SE5 130 C7
Shepherdess Wk N1 126 A4
Sheppard Dr SE16 130 F4
Shepperton Rd N1 126 A3
Sherborne St N1 126 B3
Sheringham Rd N7 125 M1
Sherriff Rd NW6 124 A1
Sherwin Rd SE14 131 H7
Sherwood Gdns E14 131 L3
Sherwood Gdns SE16 130 E4
Shetland Rd E3 127 K4
Ship St SE8 131 L7
Shipton St E2 126 D5
Shipwright Rd SE16 131 J1
Shirbutt St E14 127 M9
Shirland Rd W9 124 A5
Shirley Gro SW11 128 G9
Shoe La EC4 125 N8
Shooters Hill Rd SE10 131 P7
Shore Pl E9 126 G2
Shore Rd E9 126 G2
Shoreditch High St E1 126 C6
Shorncliffe Rd SE1 130 D4
Short Wall E15 127 N5
Shorter St E1 126 D9
Shorts Gdns WC2 125 L8
Shottendane Rd SW6 128 A7
Shouldham St W1 124 E7
Shrewsbury Rd W2 124 A8
Shroton St NW1 124 E7
Shrubland Rd E8 126 E3
Shuttleworth Rd SW11 128 E8
Sibella Rd SW4 129 K8
Sidmouth St WC1 125 L5
Sidney Rd SW9 129 M8
Sidney Sq E1 126 G8
Sidney St E1 126 F7
Sidworth St E8 126 F2
Silex St SE1 129 P1
Silk Mills Sq E9 127 K1
Silk St EC2 126 A7
Silver Rd SE13 131 M9
Silver Wk SE16 127 K10
Silverthorne Rd SW8 129 H8
Silvocea Way E14 127 P8
Silwood St SE16 130 G3
Simms Rd SE1 130 E3
Simpson St SW11 128 E8
Simpsons Rd E14 127 M9
Sirinham Pt SW8 129 M5
Sisters Av SW11 128 F10
Sisulu Pl SW9 129 N9
Sivill Ho E2 126 D5
Six Bridges Trd Est SE1 130 E4
Sketchley Gdns SE16 131 H4
Skinner St EC1 125 N5
Skipworth Rd E9 126 G3
Skylines Village E14 131 N1
Slaidburn St SW10 128 C5
Slaithwaite Rd SE13 131 N10
Sleaford Ho E3 127 L6
Sleaford St SW8 129 J6
Slippers Pl SE16 130 F2
Sloane Av SW3 128 E3
Sloane Ct W SW3 128 G4
Sloane Gdns SW1 128 G3
Sloane Sq SW1 128 F3
Sloane St SW1 128 F1
Sloane Ter SW1 128 F3
Smart St E2 127 H5
Smeaton St E1 126 F10
Smedley St SW4 129 K8
Smedley St SW8 129 K8
Smeed Rd E3 127 L2
Smiles Pl SE13 131 N8
Smith Cl SE16 127 H10
Smith Sq SW1 129 L2
Smith St SW3 128 F4
Smith Ter SW3 128 F4
Smithy St E1 126 G7
Smokehouse Yd EC1 125 P7
Smugglers Way SW18 128 B10
Smyrks Rd SE17 130 C4
Smyrna Rd NW6 124 A2
Smythe St E14 127 M9
Snow Hill EC1 125 P7
Snowbury Rd SW6 128 B8
Snowden St EC2 126 C6
Snowman Ho NW6 124 B3
Snowsfields SE1 130 B1
Soames St SE15 130 D9
Soho Sq W1 125 K8
Solebay St E1 127 J6
Solomon's Pas SE15 130 F10
Solon New Rd SW4 129 L10
Solon Rd SW2 129 L10
Solway Rd SE22 130 E10
Somerfield St SE16 131 H4
Somerford St E1 126 F6
Somerford Way SE16 131 J1
Somerleyton Pas SW9 129 P10
Somerleyton Rd SW9 129 N10
Somers Cres W2 124 E8
Somerset Est SW11 128 D7
Somerset Gdns SE13 131 M8
Somerton Rd SE15 130 F10
Sondes St SE17 130 B5
Sopwith Way SW8 129 H6
Sorrel La E14 127 P8
Sotheran Cl E8 126 E3
Sotheron Rd SW6 128 B6
Soudan Rd SW11 128 F7
South Audley St W1 124 G9
South Bolton Gdns SW5 128 B4
South Carriage Dr SW1 128 E1
South Carriage Dr SW7 128 E1
South Colonnade E14 127 L10
South Cres E16 127 P6
South Cres WC1 125 K7
South Eaton Pl SW1 128 G3
South End Row W8 128 B2
South Island Pl SW9 129 M6
South Kensington Underground Sta SW7 128 D3
South Lambeth Pl SW8 129 L5
South Lambeth Rd SW8 129 L5
South Molton La W1 125 H8
South Molton St W1 125 H8
South Par SW3 128 D4
South Pk SW6 128 A8
South Pk Ms SW6 128 B9
South Pl EC2 126 B7
South Quay Plaza E14 131 M1
South Sea St SE16 131 K2
South St W1 124 G10
South Tenter St E1 126 D9
South Ter SW7 128 E3
South Vil NW1 125 K1
South Wf Rd W2 124 D8
Southall Pl SE1 130 B1
Southampton Pl WC1 125 L7
Southampton Row WC1 125 L7
Southampton St WC2 125 L9
Southampton Way SE5 130 B6
Southbank Business Cen SW8 129 K5
Southborough Rd E9 126 G3
Southern Gro E3 127 K5
Southern St N1 125 M4
Southerngate Way SE14 131 J6
Southey Rd SW9 129 N7
Southgate Gro N1 126 B2
Southgate Rd N1 126 B3
Southmoor Way E9 127 K1
Southolm St SW11 129 H7
Southville SW8 129 K7
Southwark Br EC4 126 A10
Southwark Br SE1 126 A10
Southwark Br Rd SE1 129 P2
Southwark Pk SE16 130 G3
Southwark Pk Est SE16 130 F3
Southwark Pk Rd SE16 130 D3
Southwark St SE1 125 P10
Southwater Cl E14 127 K8
Southwell Gdns SW7 128 C3
Southwell Rd SE5 130 A9
Southwick Pl W2 124 E8
Southwick St W2 124 E8
Sovereign Cl E1 126 F9
Spa Grn Est EC1 125 N5
Spa Rd SE16 130 D2
Spanby Rd E3 127 L6
Spanish Pl W1 124 G8
Sparkford Ho SW11 128 D7
Sparta St SE10 131 M7
Spear Ms SW5 128 A3
Speke Ho SE5 130 A6
Speldhurst Rd E9 127 H2

Spelman St **E1** 126 E7
Spencer Rd **SW18** 128 D10
Spencer St **EC1** 125 P5
Spenser St **SW1** 129 J2
Spert St **E14** 127 J9
Spey St **E14** 127 N7
Spicer Cl **SW9** 129 P8
Spindrift Av **E14** 131 M3
Spital Sq **E1** 126 C7
Spital St **E1** 126 E6
Sporle Ct **SW11** 128 D9
Sprimont Pl **SW3** 128 F4
Spring St **W2** 124 D8
Springall St **SE15** 130 F6
Springfield La **NW6** 124 B3
Springfield Rd **NW8** 124 C3
Springfield Wk **NW6** 124 B3
Springhill Cl **SE5** 130 B9
Springwood Cl **E3** 127 L4
Sprules Rd **SE4** 131 J8
Spur Rd **SE1** 129 N1
Spur Rd **SW1** 129 J1
Spurgeon St **SE1** 130 B2
Spurling Rd **SE22** 130 D10
Squirries St **E2** 126 E5
Stable Yd Rd **SW1** 125 J10
Stables Way **SE11** 129 N4
Stacey St **WC2** 125 K8
Stadium St **SW10** 128 C6
Stafford Cl **NW6** 124 A5
Stafford Ct **W8** 128 A2
Stafford Pl **SW1** 129 J2
Stafford Rd **E3** 127 K4
Stafford Rd **NW6** 124 A5
Stafford St **W1** 125 J10
Stafford Ter **W8** 128 A2
Staffordshire St **SE15** 130 E7
Stag Pl **SW1** 129 J2
Stainer St **SE1** 126 B10
Staining La **EC2** 126 A8
Stainsby Rd **E14** 127 L8
Stalham St **SE16** 130 F2
Stamford Rd **N1** 126 C2
Stamford St **SE1** 125 N10
Stamp Pl **E2** 126 D5
Stanbury Rd **SE15** 130 F7
Stanfield Rd **E3** 127 J4
Stanford Rd **W8** 128 B2
Stanhope Gdns **SW7** 128 C3
Stanhope Gate **W1** 124 G10
Stanhope Ms E **SW7** 128 C3
Stanhope Ms W **SW7** 128 C3
Stanhope Pl **W2** 124 F8
Stanhope St **NW1** 125 J5
Stanhope Ter **W2** 124 D9
Stanley Cl **SW8** 129 M5
Stanley Gro **SW8** 128 G8
Stanley Rd **E15** 127 P3
Stanley St **SE8** 131 K6
Stanmer St **SW11** 128 E7
Stannard Ms **E8** 126 E1
Stannard Rd **E8** 126 E1
Stannary Pl **SE11** 129 N4
Stannary St **SE11** 129 N5
Stansfield Rd **SW9** 129 M9
Stanswood Gdns **SE5** 130 C6
Stanway St **N1** 126 C4
Stanworth St **SE1** 130 D1
Staple Inn Bldgs **WC1** 125 N7
Staple St **SE1** 130 B1
Staples Cl **SE16** 127 J10
Star St **W2** 124 E7
Starboard Way **E14** 131 L2
Starcross St **NW1** 125 J5
Station App **SE1** 129 N1
Station Ct **SW6** 128 C7
Station Pas **SE15** 130 G7
Station Rd **SE13** 131 N9
Station St **E15** 127 P2
Station Ter **SE5** 130 A7
Staunton St **SE8** 131 K5
Stave Yd Rd **SE16** 127 J10
Stayner's Rd **E1** 127 H6
Stead St **SE17** 130 B3
Stean St **E8** 126 D3
Stebondale St **E14** 131 N4
Steeles Rd **NW3** 124 F1
Steers Way **SE16** 131 J1
Stephan Cl **E8** 126 E3
Stephen St **W1** 125 K7
Stephendale Rd **SW6** 128 B8
Stephenson Way **NW1** 125 J6
Stepney Causeway **E1** 127 H8
Stepney Grn **E1** 126 G7
Stepney High St **E1** 127 H7
Stepney Way **E1** 126 F7
Sterling Gdns **SE14** 131 J5
Sternhall La **SE15** 130 E9
Sterry St **SE1** 130 B1
Stevens Av **E9** 126 G1
Stevenson Cres **SE16** 130 E4
Steward St **E1** 126 C7
Stewart St **E14** 131 N1
Stewart's Gro **SW3** 128 D3
Stewart's Rd **SW8** 129 J6
Stillington St **SW1** 129 J3
Stirling Rd **SW9** 129 L8
Stockholm Ho **E1** 126 E9
Stockholm Rd **SE16** 130 G4
Stockholm Way **E1** 126 E10
Stockwell Av **SW9** 129 M9
Stockwell Gdns **SW9** 129 M8
Stockwell Gdns Est **SW9** 129 L8
Stockwell Grn **SW9** 129 M8
Stockwell La **SW9** 129 M8
Stockwell Pk Cres **SW9** 129 M8
Stockwell Pk Est **SW9** 129 M8
Stockwell Pk Rd **SW9** 129 M7
Stockwell Pk Wk **SW9** 129 M9
Stockwell Rd **SW9** 129 M8
Stockwell St **SE10** 131 N5
Stockwell Ter **SW9** 129 M7
Stokenchurch St **SW6** 128 B7
Stone Bldgs **WC2** 125 M7
Stonecutter St **EC4** 125 P8
Stonefield St **N1** 125 N3
Stones End St **SE1** 130 A1
Stoney St **SE1** 126 B10
Stonhouse St **SW4** 129 K9
Stopes St **SE15** 130 D6
Stopford Rd **SE17** 129 P4
Store St **WC1** 125 K7
Storers Quay **E14** 131 P3
Storey's Gate **SW1** 129 K1
Stories Ms **SE5** 130 C8
Stories Rd **SE5** 130 C9
Storks Rd **SE16** 130 E2
Stormont Rd **SW11** 128 G9
Stour Rd **E3** 127 L2
Stourcliffe St **W1** 124 F8
Stowage **SE8** 131 L5
Strafford St **E14** 131 L1
Strahan Rd **E3** 127 J5
Straightsmouth **SE10** 131 N6
Straker's Rd **SE15** 130 F10
Strand **WC2** 125 L9
Stranraer Way **N1** 125 L2
Strasburg Rd **SW11** 129 H7
Stratford Cen, The **E15** 127 P2
Stratford Pl **W1** 125 H8
Stratford Rd **W8** 128 A2
Stratford Vil **NW1** 125 J2
Strath Ter **SW11** 128 E10
Strathblaine Rd **SW11** 128 D10
Strathearn Pl **W2** 124 E9
Strathnairn St **SE1** 130 E3
Strathray Gdns **NW3** 124 E1
Stratton St **W1** 125 H10
Strattondale St **E14** 131 N2
Streatham St **WC1** 125 K8
Streimer Rd **E15** 127 N4
Strickland St **SE8** 131 L8
Stroudley Wk **E3** 127 M5
Strutton Grd **SW1** 129 K2
Stuart Rd **NW6** 124 A5
Stuart Rd **SE15** 130 G10
Stuart Twr **W9** 124 C6
Stubbs Dr **SE16** 130 F4
Studd St **N1** 125 P3
Studdridge St **SW6** 128 A8
Studholme St **SE15** 130 F6
Studley Est **SW4** 129 L7
Studley Rd **SW4** 129 L7
Stukeley St **WC1** 125 L8
Stukeley St **WC2** 125 L8
Sturdy Rd **SE15** 130 F8
Sturgeon Rd **SE17** 130 A4
Sturry St **E14** 127 M8
Sturt St **N1** 126 A4
Stutfield St **E1** 126 E8
Styles Gdns **SW9** 129 P9
Sudeley St **N1** 125 P4
Sudlow Rd **SW18** 128 A10
Sugar Ho La **E15** 127 N4
Sugar Quay Wk **EC3** 126 C9
Sugden Rd **SW11** 128 G9
Sulivan Ct **SW6** 128 A9
Sulivan Rd **SW6** 128 A9
Sullivan Cl **SW11** 128 E9
Sullivan Rd **SE11** 129 N3
Sultan St **SE5** 130 A6
Summercourt Rd **E1** 126 G8
Sumner Pl **SW7** 128 D3
Sumner Rd **SE15** 130 D6
Sumner St **SE1** 126 A10
Sumpter Cl **NW3** 124 C1
Sun St **EC2** 126 B7
Sunbury La **SW11** 128 D7
Sunderland Ter **W2** 124 B8
Sunlight Sq **E2** 126 F5
Sunninghill Rd **SE13** 131 M8
Sunray Av **SE24** 130 B10
Sunset Rd **SE5** 130 A10
Surma Cl **E1** 126 F6
Surrendale Pl **W9** 124 A6
Surrey Canal Rd **SE14** 130 G5
Surrey Canal Rd **SE15** 130 G5
Surrey La **SW11** 128 E7
Surrey La Est **SW11** 128 E7
Surrey Quays Retail Cen **SE16** 131 H2
Surrey Quays Rd **SE16** 130 G2
Surrey Row **SE1** 129 P1
Surrey Sq **SE17** 130 C4
Surrey St **WC2** 125 M9
Surrey Ter **SE17** 130 C4
Surrey Water Rd **SE16** 127 H10
Susannah St **E14** 127 M8
Sussex Gdns **W2** 124 D8
Sussex Pl **NW1** 124 F5
Sussex Pl **W2** 124 D8
Sussex Sq **W2** 124 D9
Sussex St **SW1** 129 H4
Sutherland Av **W9** 124 C5
Sutherland Pl **W2** 124 A8
Sutherland Row **SW1** 129 H4
Sutherland Sq **SE17** 130 A4
Sutherland St **SW1** 129 H4
Sutherland Wk **SE17** 130 A4
Sutterton St **N7** 125 M1
Sutton Est **SW3** 128 E4
Sutton Est, The **N1** 125 P2
Sutton Row **W1** 125 K8
Sutton St **E1** 126 G8
Swain St **NW8** 124 E6
Swallow Cl **SE14** 130 G7
Swan Mead **SE1** 130 C2
Swan Rd **SE16** 130 G1
Swan St **SE1** 130 A2
Swan Wk **SW3** 128 F5
Swandon Way **SW18** 128 B10
Swanfield St **E2** 126 D5
Swaton Rd **E3** 127 L6
Sweden Gate **SE16** 131 J2
Swedenborg Gdns **E1** 126 E9
Sweeney Cres **SE1** 130 D1
Swinford Gdns **SW9** 129 P9
Swinton Pl **WC1** 125 M5
Swinton St **WC1** 125 M5
Swiss Ter **NW6** 124 D2
Sybil Phoenix Cl **SE8** 131 H4
Sycamore Av **E3** 127 K3
Sycamore Ms **SW4** 129 J9
Sydney Cl **SW3** 128 D3
Sydney Ms **SW3** 128 D3
Sydney Pl **SW7** 128 D3
Sydney St **SW3** 128 E3
Sylvan Gro **SE15** 130 F6
Sylvester Rd **E8** 126 F1
Symons St **SW3** 128 F3

T

Tabard Gdn Est **SE1** 130 B1
Tabard St **SE1** 130 B1
Tabernacle St **EC2** 126 B6
Tachbrook Est **SW1** 129 K4
Tachbrook St **SW1** 129 J3
Tack Ms **SE4** 131 L9
Tadema Rd **SW10** 128 C6
Taeping St **E14** 131 M3
Talacre Rd **NW5** 124 G1
Talbot Rd **SE22** 130 C10
Talbot Rd **W2** 124 A8
Talbot Sq **W2** 124 D8
Talfourd Pl **SE15** 130 D7
Talfourd Rd **SE15** 130 D7
Tallis St **EC4** 125 N9
Talma Rd **SW2** 129 N10
Talwin St **E3** 127 M5
Tamworth St **SW6** 128 A5
Tanner St **SE1** 130 C1
Tanners Hill **SE8** 131 K7
Taplow **NW3** 124 D2
Taplow St **N1** 126 A4
Tapp St **E1** 126 F6
Tappesfield Rd **SE15** 130 G9
Tariff Cres **SE8** 131 K3
Tarling St **E1** 126 F8
Tarling St Est **E1** 126 G8
Tarragon Cl **SE14** 131 J6
Tarrant Pl **W1** 124 F7
Tarver Rd **SE17** 129 P4
Tarves Way **SE10** 131 M6
Tasman Rd **SW9** 129 L9
Tatham Pl **NW8** 124 D4
Tatum St **SE17** 130 B3
Taunton Pl **NW1** 124 F6
Tavern La **SW9** 129 N8
Tavistock Pl **WC1** 125 L6
Tavistock Sq **WC1** 125 K6
Tavistock St **WC2** 125 L9
Taviton St **WC1** 125 K6
Tavy Cl **SE11** 129 N4
Tawny Way **SE16** 131 H3
Taybridge Rd **SW11** 128 G9
Tayburn Cl **E14** 127 N8
Taylor Cl **SE8** 131 K5
Tayport Cl **N1** 125 L2
Teak Cl **SE16** 127 J10
Teale St **E2** 126 E4
Tedworth Sq **SW3** 128 F4
Teesdale Cl **E2** 126 F4
Teesdale St **E2** 126 F4
Teignmouth Cl **SW4** 129 K10
Telegraph Pl **E14** 131 M3
Telford Ter **SW1** 129 J5
Tell Gro **SE22** 130 D10
Templar St **SE5** 129 P8
Temple, The **EC4** 125 N9
Temple Av **EC4** 125 N9
Temple Pl **WC2** 125 M9
Temple St **E2** 126 F4
Temple W Ms **SE11** 129 P2
Templecombe Rd **E9** 126 G3
Templeton Pl **SW5** 128 A3
Tench St **E1** 126 F10
Tenison Way **SE1** 125 M10
Tennis St **SE1** 130 B1
Tennyson St **SW8** 129 H8
Tent St **E1** 126 F6
Tenterden St **W1** 125 H8
Teredo St **SE16** 131 H2
Terminus Pl **SW1** 129 H2
Terrace, The **NW6** 124 A3
Terrace Rd **E9** 126 G2
Tessa Sanderson Pl **SW8** 129 H9
Tetcott Rd **SW10** 128 C6
Teversham La **SW8** 129 L7
Teviot St **E14** 127 N7
Thackeray Rd **SW8** 129 H8
Thackeray St **W8** 128 B1
Thalia Cl **SE10** 131 P5
Thame Rd **SE16** 131 H1
Thames Av **SW10** 128 C7
Thames St **SE10** 131 M5
Thanet St **WC1** 125 L5
Thayer St **W1** 124 G7
Theatre St **SW11** 128 F9
Theberton St **N1** 125 N3
Theed St **SE1** 125 N10
Theobald's Rd **WC1** 125 M7
Thermopylae Gate **E14** 131 M3
Thessaly Rd **SW8** 129 J6
Thirleby Rd **SW1** 129 J2
Thirsk Rd **SW11** 128 G9
Thistle Gro **SW10** 128 C4
Thomas Baines Rd **SW11** 128 D9
Thomas Doyle St **SE1** 129 P2
Thomas More St **E1** 126 E9
Thomas Rd **E14** 127 K8
Thompson's Av **SE5** 130 A6
Thorburn Sq **SE1** 130 E3
Thoresby St **N1** 126 A5
Thorncroft St **SW8** 129 L6
Thorndike Cl **SW10** 128 C6
Thorndike Rd **N1** 126 A1
Thorndike St **SW1** 129 J3
Thorne Rd **SW8** 129 L6
Thorney Cres **SW11** 128 D6
Thorney St **SW1** 129 L3
Thorngate Rd **W9** 124 A6
Thornham St **SE10** 131 M5
Thornhaugh St **WC1** 125 K6
Thornhill Cres **N1** 125 M2
Thornhill Rd **N1** 125 N2
Thornhill Sq **N1** 125 M2
Thornton Pl **W1** 124 F7
Thornton St **SW9** 129 N8
Thornville St **SE8** 131 L7
Thorparch Rd **SW8** 129 K7
Thoydon Rd **E3** 127 J4
Thrale St **SE1** 126 A10
Thrawl St **E1** 126 D7
Threadneedle St **EC2** 126 B8
Three Colt St **E14** 127 K9
Three Colts La **E2** 126 F6
Three Kings Yd **W1** 125 H9
Three Mill La **E3** 127 N5
Three Quays Wk **EC3** 126 C9
Throgmorton Av **EC2** 126 B8
Throgmorton St **EC2** 126 B8
Thurland Rd **SE16** 130 E2
Thurloe Cl **SW7** 128 E2
Thurloe Pl **SW7** 128 D3
Thurloe Sq **SW7** 128 E3
Thurloe St **SW7** 128 D3
Thurlow St **SE17** 130 B4
Thurston Rd **SE13** 131 M8
Thurtle Rd **E2** 126 D3
Tibbatts Rd **E3** 127 M6
Tideway Ind Est **SW8** 129 J5
Tidey St **E3** 127 L7
Tidworth Rd **E3** 127 L6
Tileyard Rd **N7** 125 L2
Tiller Rd **E14** 131 L2
Tilney Gdns **N1** 126 B1
Tilney St **W1** 124 G10
Timber Mill Way **SW4** 129 K9
Timber Pond Rd **SE16** 131 H1
Timberland Rd **E1** 126 F8
Timothy Rd **E3** 127 K7
Tindal St **SW9** 129 P7
Tinsley Rd **E1** 126 G7
Tintagel Cres **SE22** 130 D10
Tintern St **SW4** 129 L10
Tinworth St **SE11** 129 M4
Tipthorpe Rd **SW11** 128 G9
Tisdall Pl **SE17** 130 B3
Titchfield Rd **NW8** 124 F3
Tite St **SW3** 128 F4
Tiverton St **SE1** 130 A2
Tivoli Ct **SE16** 131 K1
Tobacco Dock **E1** 126 F9
Tobin Cl **NW3** 124 E2
Toby La **E1** 127 J6
Tollet St **E1** 127 H6
Tollgate Gdns **NW6** 124 B4
Tolpuddle St **N1** 125 N4
Tomlins Gro **E3** 127 L5
Tomlinson Cl **E2** 126 D5
Tonbridge St **WC1** 125 L5
Tooley St **SE1** 126 B10
Topmast Pt **E14** 131 L1
Tor Gdns **W8** 128 A1
Torrens St **EC1** 125 N4
Torridge Gdns **SE15** 130 G10
Torrington Pl **E1** 126 E10
Torrington Pl **WC1** 125 K7
Torrington Sq **WC1** 125 K6
Tothill St **SW1** 129 K1
Tottan Ter **E1** 127 H8
Tottenham Ct Rd **W1** 125 J6
Tottenham Rd **N1** 126 C1
Tottenham St **W1** 125 J7
Totteridge Ho **SW11** 128 D8
Toulmin St **SE1** 130 A1
Toulon St **SE5** 130 A6
Tours Pas **SW11** 128 D10
Towcester Rd **E3** 127 M6
Tower 42 **EC2** 126 C8
Tower Br **E1** 126 D10
Tower Br **SE1** 126 D10
Tower Br App **E1** 126 D10
Tower Br Rd **SE1** 130 C2
Tower Br Wf **E1** 126 E10
Tower Mill Rd **SE15** 130 C6
Tower Millennium Pier **EC3** 126 C10
Tower St **WC2** 125 K8
Town Hall Rd **SW11** 128 F9
Townmead Rd **SW6** 128 C8
Townsend St **SE17** 130 B3
Townshend Est **NW8** 124 E4
Townshend Rd **NW8** 124 E3
Toynbee St **E1** 126 D7
Tradescant Rd **SW8** 129 L6
Trafalgar Av **SE15** 130 D4
Trafalgar Gdns **E1** 127 H7
Trafalgar Gro **SE10** 131 P5
Trafalgar Ms **E9** 127 K1
Trafalgar Rd **SE10** 131 P5
Trafalgar Sq **SW1** 125 K10
Trafalgar Sq **WC2** 125 K10
Trafalgar St **SE17** 130 B4
Trafalgar Way **E14** 127 N10
Trahorn Cl **E1** 126 E6
Transept St **NW1** 124 E7
Transom Sq **E14** 131 M3
Tranton Rd **SE16** 130 E2
Treadway St **E2** 126 F4
Treaty St **N1** 125 M3
Trebovir Rd **SW5** 128 A4
Treby St **E3** 127 K6
Tredegar Rd **E3** 127 K4
Tredegar Sq **E3** 127 K5
Tredegar Ter **E3** 127 K5
Trederwen Rd **E8** 126 E3
Tregarvon Rd **SW11** 128 G10
Trego Rd **E9** 127 L2
Tregothnan Rd **SW9** 129 L9
Tregunter Rd **SW10** 128 C5
Trelawney Est **E9** 126 G1
Tremadoc Rd **SW4** 129 K10
Tremaine Cl **SE4** 131 L8
Trenchard St **SE10** 131 P4
Trenchold St **SW8** 129 L5
Tresco Rd **SE15** 130 F10
Tresham Cres **NW8** 124 E6
Tressillian Cres **SE4** 131 L9
Tressillian Rd **SE4** 131 K10
Trevithick St **SE8** 131 L4
Trevor Pl **SW7** 128 E1
Trevor Sq **SW7** 128 F1
Trevor St **SW7** 128 E1
Triangle Pl **SW4** 129 K10
Triangle Rd **E8** 126 F3
Trident St **SE16** 131 H3
Trigon Rd **SW8** 129 M6
Trim St **SE14** 131 K5
Trinidad St **E14** 127 K9
Trinity Ch Sq **SE1** 130 A2
Trinity Cl **E8** 126 D1
Trinity Cl **SE13** 131 P10
Trinity Gdns **SW9** 129 M10
Trinity Gro **SE10** 131 N7
Trinity Sq **EC3** 126 C9
Trinity St **SE1** 130 A1
Trinity Wk **NW3** 124 C1
Triton Sq **NW1** 125 J6
Trott St **SW11** 128 E7
Troutbeck Rd **SE14** 131 J7
Trowbridge Rd **E9** 127 K1
Troy Town **SE15** 130 E9
Trundleys Rd **SE8** 131 H4
Trundleys Ter **SE8** 131 H3
Truro St **NW5** 124 G1
Tryon Cres **E9** 126 G3
Tryon St **SW3** 128 F4
Tudor Gro **E9** 126 G2
Tudor Rd **E9** 126 F3
Tudor St **EC4** 125 N9
Tufton St **SW1** 129 K2
Tuilerie St **E2** 126 E4
Tunnel Av **SE10** 131 P1
Tunstall Rd **SW9** 129 M10
Turenne Cl **SW18** 128 C10
Turin St **E2** 126 E5
Turks Row **SW3** 128 F4
Turner Cl **SW9** 129 P7
Turner St **E1** 126 F7
Turners Rd **E3** 127 K7
Turnmill St **EC1** 125 N6
Turnpike Ho **EC1** 125 P5
Turnpin La **SE10** 131 N5
Turret Gro **SW4** 129 J9
Tustin Est **SE15** 130 G5
Twelvetrees Cres **E3** 127 N6
Twine Ct **E1** 126 G9
Twyford St **N1** 125 M3
Tyburn Way **W1** 124 F9
Tyers Est **SE1** 130 C1
Tyers St **SE11** 129 M4
Tyers Ter **SE11** 129 M4
Tyler Cl **E2** 126 D4
Tyndale Ct **E14** 131 M4
Tyneham Rd **SW11** 128 G8
Tynemouth St **SW6** 128 C8
Type St **E2** 127 H4
Tyrawley Rd **SW6** 128 B7
Tyrrell Rd **SE22** 130 E10
Tyrwhitt Rd **SE4** 131 L9
Tyssen Pas **E8** 126 D1
Tyssen St **E8** 126 D1

U

Uamvar St **E14** 127 M7
Ufford St **SE1** 129 N1
Ufton Gro **N1** 126 B2
Ufton Rd **N1** 126 B2
Undercliff Rd **SE13** 131 L9
Undershaft **EC3** 126 C8
Underwood Rd **E1** 126 E6
Underwood Row **N1** 126 A5
Underwood St **N1** 126 A5
Undine Rd **E14** 131 M3
Union Gro **SW8** 129 K8
Union Rd **SW4** 129 K8
Union Rd **SW8** 129 K8
Union Sq **N1** 126 A3
Union St **E15** 127 N3
Union St **SE1** 125 P10
University St **WC1** 125 J6
Unwin Cl **SE15** 130 E5
Upcerne Rd **SW10** 128 C6
Upper Bk St **E14** 127 M10
Upper Belgrave St **SW1** 128 G2
Upper Berkeley St **W1** 124 F8
Upper Brockley Rd **SE4** 131 K8
Upper Brook St **W1** 124 G9
Upper Cheyne Row **SW3** 128 E5
Upper Grosvenor St **W1** 124 G9
Upper Grd **SE1** 125 N10
Upper Marsh **SE1** 129 M2
Upper Montagu St **W1** 124 F7
Upper N St **E14** 127 L7
Upper Phillimore Gdns **W8** 128 A1
Upper St **N1** 125 N4
Upper Tachbrook St **SW1** 129 J3
Upper Thames St **EC4** 126 A9
Upper Wimpole St **W1** 124 G7
Upper Woburn Pl **WC1** 125 K5
Upstall St **SE5** 129 P7
Urlwin St **SE5** 130 A5
Urlwin Wk **SW9** 129 N8
Ursula St **SW11** 128 E7
Usborne Ms **SW8** 129 M6
Usher Rd **E3** 127 K4
Usk Rd **SW11** 128 C10
Usk St **E2** 127 H5
Uverdale Rd **SW10** 128 C6
Uxbridge St **W8** 124 A10

V

Vale, The **SW3** 128 D5
Vale Ct **W9** 124 C5
Vale Royal **N7** 125 L2
Valentine Pl **SE1** 129 P1
Valentine Rd **E9** 127 H1
Valentine Row **SE1** 129 P1
Valette St **E9** 126 F1
Vallance Rd **E1** 126 E6
Vallance Rd **E2** 126 E5
Valmar Rd **SE5** 130 A7
Vandon St **SW1** 129 J2
Vanguard St **SE8** 131 L7
Vansittart St **SE14** 131 J6

Vanston Pl **SW6** 128 A6
Varcoe Rd **SE16** 130 F4
Varden St **E1** 126 F8
Vardens Rd **SW11** 128 D10
Varndell St **NW1** 125 J5
Vassall Rd **SW9** 129 N6
Vauban Est **SE16** 130 D2
Vauban St **SE16** 130 D2
Vaughan Rd **SE5** 130 A8
Vaughan St **SE16** 131 K1
Vaughan Way **E1** 126 E9
Vauxhall Br **SE1** 129 L4
Vauxhall Br **SW1** 129 L4
Vauxhall Br Rd **SW1** 129 J3
Vauxhall Gdns Est **SE11** 129 M4
Vauxhall Gro **SW8** 129 L5
Vauxhall St **SE11** 129 M4
Vauxhall Wk **SE11** 129 M4
Vawdrey Cl **E1** 126 G6
Veda Rd **SE13** 131 L10
Velletri Ho **E2** 127 H4
Venables St **NW8** 124 D6
Venetian Rd **SE5** 130 A8
Venn St **SW4** 129 J10
Ventnor Rd **SE14** 131 H6
Venue St **E14** 127 N7
Vere St **W1** 125 H8
Verney Rd **SE16** 130 E5
Verney Way **SE16** 130 F4
Vernon Pl **WC1** 125 L7
Vernon Ri **WC1** 125 M5
Vernon Rd **E3** 127 K4
Vesta Rd **SE4** 131 J8
Vestry Ms **SE5** 130 C7
Vestry Rd **SE5** 130 C7
Vestry St **N1** 126 B5
Viaduct St **E2** 126 F5
Vian St **SE13** 131 M9
Vicarage Cres **SW11** 128 D7
Vicarage Gdns **W8** 124 A10
Vicarage Gate **W8** 128 B1
Vicarage Gro **SE5** 130 B7
Vicars Hill **SE13** 131 M10
Viceroy Rd **SW8** 129 L7
Victoria Embk **EC4** 125 M9
Victoria Embk **SW1** 129 L1
Victoria Embk **WC2** 129 L1
Victoria Gdns **W11** 124 A10
Victoria Gro **W8** 128 C2
Victoria Ms **NW6** 124 A3
Victoria Pk **E9** 127 J2
Victoria Pk Rd **E9** 126 G3
Victoria Pk Sq **E2** 126 G5
Victoria Pl **SW1** 129 H3
Victoria Ri **SW4** 129 H9
Victoria Rd **W8** 128 C2
Victoria Sta **SW1** 129 H3
Victoria St **SW1** 129 J2
Victoria Wf **E14** 127 J9
Victory Pl **SE17** 130 A3
Victory Way **SE16** 131 J1
Vigo St **W1** 125 J9
Viking Ct **SW6** 128 A5
Villa Rd **SW9** 129 N9
Villa St **SE17** 130 B4
Villiers St **WC2** 125 L9
Vince St **EC1** 126 B5
Vincent Cl **SE16** 131 J1
Vincent Sq **SW1** 129 J3
Vincent St **SW1** 129 K3
Vincent Ter **N1** 125 P4
Vine St Br **EC1** 125 N6
Viney Rd **SE13** 131 M9
Vineyard Wk **EC1** 125 N6
Vining St **SW9** 129 N10
Violet Hill **NW8** 124 C4
Violet Rd **E3** 127 M6
Virgil St **SE1** 129 M2
Virginia Rd **E2** 126 D5
Virginia St **E1** 126 E9
Vivian Rd **E3** 127 J4
Voltaire Rd **SW4** 129 K9
Voss St **E2** 126 E5
Vulcan Rd **SE4** 131 K8
Vulcan Ter **SE4** 131 K8
Vulcan Way **N7** 125 M1
Vyner St **E2** 126 F3

W

Wadding St **SE17** 130 B3
Waddington St **E15** 127 P1
Wades Pl **E14** 127 M9
Wadeson St **E2** 126 F4
Wadham Gdns **NW3** 124 E3
Wadhurst Rd **SW8** 129 J7
Wager St **E3** 127 K6
Waghorn St **SE15** 130 E9
Wagner St **SE15** 130 G6
Waite St **SE15** 130 D5
Wakefield St **WC1** 125 L5
Wakeham St **N1** 126 B1
Wakeling St **E14** 127 J8
Wakley St **EC1** 125 P5
Walberswick St **SW8** 129 L6
Walbrook **EC4** 126 B9
Walcot Sq **SE11** 129 N3
Walden St **E1** 126 F8
Walerand Rd **SE13** 131 N8
Wales Cl **SE15** 130 F6
Waley St **E1** 127 H7
Walham Gro **SW6** 128 A6
Wall St **N1** 126 B1
Wallace Rd **N1** 126 A1
Wallbutton Rd **SE4** 131 J8
Waller Rd **SE14** 131 H7
Wallgrave Rd **SW5** 128 B3
Wallis Cl **SW11** 128 D9
Wallis Rd **E9** 127 K1
Wallwood St **E14** 127 K7
Walnut Tree Wk **SE11** 129 N3
Walpole St **SW3** 128 F4
Walsham Rd **SE14** 131 H8
Walter St **E2** 127 H5
Walter Ter **E1** 127 H8
Walton Cl **SW8** 129 L6
Walton Pl **SW3** 128 F2
Walton St **SW3** 128 E3
Walworth Pl **SE17** 130 A4
Walworth Rd **SE1** 130 A3
Walworth Rd **SE17** 130 A3
Wandon Rd **SW6** 128 B6
Wandsworth Br **SW6** 128 B9
Wandsworth Br **SW18** 128 B9
Wandsworth Br Rd **SW6** 128 B7
Wandsworth Rd **SW8** 129 K6
Wanless Rd **SE24** 130 A9
Wanley Rd **SE5** 130 B10
Wansbeck Rd **E3** 127 K2
Wansbeck Rd **E9** 127 K2
Wansey St **SE17** 130 A3
Wapping High St **E1** 126 E10
Wapping La **E1** 126 F9
Wapping Wall **E1** 126 G10
Warburton Rd **E8** 126 F2
Ward Rd **E15** 127 P3
Wardalls Gro **SE14** 130 G6
Warden Rd **NW5** 124 G1
Wardour St **W1** 125 K9
Warham St **SE5** 129 P6
Warley St **E2** 127 H5
Warlock Rd **W9** 124 A6
Warndon St **SE16** 131 H3
Warneford St **E9** 126 F3
Warner Pl **E2** 126 E4
Warner Rd **SE5** 130 A7
Warner St **EC1** 125 N6
Warren St **W1** 125 J6
Warriner Gdns **SW11** 128 F7
Warrington Cres **W9** 124 C6
Warton Rd **E15** 127 N2
Warwick Av **W2** 124 C6
Warwick Av **W9** 124 C6
Warwick Bldg **SW8** 129 H5
Warwick Ct **SE15** 130 E8
Warwick Cres **W2** 124 C7
Warwick Est **W2** 124 B7
Warwick Ho St **SW1** 125 K10
Warwick La **EC4** 125 P8
Warwick Pl **W9** 124 C7
Warwick Pl N **SW1** 129 J3
Warwick Row **SW1** 129 H2
Warwick Sq **SW1** 129 J4
Warwick Sq Ms **SW1** 129 J3
Warwick St **W1** 125 J9
Warwick Way **SW1** 129 J3
Warwickshire Path **SE8** 131 K6
Washington Cl **E3** 127 M5
Wat Tyler Rd **SE3** 131 N8
Wat Tyler Rd **SE10** 131 N8
Water Gdns, The **W2** 124 E8
Water La **SE14** 130 G6
Water Ms **SE15** 130 G10
Waterford Rd **SW6** 128 B7
Watergate St **SE8** 131 L5
Waterloo Br **SE1** 125 M9
Waterloo Br **WC2** 125 M9
Waterloo Est **E2** 126 G4
Waterloo Gdns **E2** 126 G4
Waterloo Pl **SW1** 125 K10
Waterloo Rd **SE1** 129 N1
Waterloo Sta **SE1** 129 N1
Waterloo Ter **N1** 125 P2
Waterman Way **E1** 126 F10
Watermans Wk **SE16** 131 J2
Watermeadow La **SW6** 128 C8
Waterside Cl **E3** 127 K3
Waterside Pt **SW11** 128 E6
Waterside Twr **SW6** 128 C7
Waterson St **E2** 126 C5
Waterview Ho **E14** 127 J7
Watkinson Rd **N7** 125 M1
Watling St **EC4** 126 A8
Watney St **E1** 126 F8
Watson's St **SE8** 131 L6
Watts Gro **E3** 127 M7
Watts St **E1** 126 F10
Watts St **SE15** 130 D7
Waveney Av **SE15** 130 F10
Waverley Pl **NW8** 124 D4
Waverley Wk **W2** 124 A7
Waverton Ho **E3** 127 K3
Waverton St **W1** 124 G10
Wayford St **SW11** 128 E8
Wayman Ct **E8** 126 F1
Wear Pl **E2** 126 F5
Weardale Rd **SE13** 131 P10
Wearside Rd **SE13** 131 M10
Weatherley Cl **E3** 127 K7
Weaver St **E1** 126 E6
Weavers Ter **SW6** 128 A5
Weavers Way **NW1** 125 K3
Webb St **SE1** 130 C2
Webber Row **SE1** 129 P1
Webber St **SE1** 129 N1
Webster Rd **SE16** 130 E2
Weighhouse St **W1** 124 G8
Weir's Pas **NW1** 125 K5
Welbeck St **W1** 124 G7
Welbeck Way **W1** 125 H8
Welby St **SE5** 129 P7
Well St **E9** 126 F2
Welland St **SE10** 131 N5
Wellclose Sq **E1** 126 E9
Wellesley Ct **W9** 124 C5
Wellesley St **E1** 127 H7
Wellesley Ter **N1** 126 A5
Wellington Pl **NW8** 124 E4
Wellington Rd **NW8** 124 D4
Wellington Row **E2** 126 D5
Wellington Sq **SW3** 128 F4
Wellington St **WC2** 125 L9
Wellington Ter **E1** 126 F10
Wellington Way **E3** 127 L5
Wells Ri **NW8** 124 F3
Wells St **W1** 125 J8
Wells Way **SE5** 130 B5
Wells Way **SW7** 128 D2
Welmar Ms **SW4** 129 K10
Welsford St **SE1** 130 E4
Wendle Ct **SW8** 129 L5
Wendon St **E3** 127 K3
Wendover **SE17** 130 C4
Wenlock Rd **N1** 126 A4
Wenlock St **N1** 126 A4
Wennington Rd **E3** 127 H4
Wentworth Cres **SE15** 130 E6
Wentworth St **E1** 126 D8
Werrington St **NW1** 125 J4
Wesley Cl **SE17** 129 P3
Wessex St **E2** 126 G5
West Arbour St **E1** 127 H8
West Carriage Dr **W2** 124 D9
West Eaton Pl **SW1** 128 G3
West End La **NW6** 124 A2
West Gdns **E1** 126 F9
West Gro **SE10** 131 N7
West Halkin St **SW1** 128 G2
West Hampstead Ms **NW6** 124 B1
West India Av **E14** 127 L10
West India Dock Rd **E14** 127 K8
West La **SE16** 130 F1
West One Shop Cen **W1** 125 H8
West Rd **SW3** 128 F5
West Smithfield **EC1** 125 P7
West Sq **SE11** 129 P2
West St **E2** 126 F4
West Tenter St **E1** 126 D8
Westbourne Br **W2** 124 C7
Westbourne Cres **W2** 124 D9
Westbourne Gdns **W2** 124 B8
Westbourne Gro **W2** 124 A8
Westbourne Gro **W11** 124 A8
Westbourne Gro Ter **W2** 124 B8
Westbourne Pk Rd **W2** 124 A7
Westbourne Pk Vil **W2** 124 A7
Westbourne Rd **N7** 125 N1
Westbourne St **W2** 124 D9
Westbourne Ter **W2** 124 D8
Westbourne Ter Ms **W2** 124 C8
Westbourne Ter Rd **W2** 124 C7
Westbridge Rd **SW11** 128 D7
Westbury St **SW8** 129 J8
Westcott Rd **SE17** 129 P5
Western Rd **SW9** 129 N9
Westferry Circ **E14** 127 K10
Westferry Rd **E14** 127 L10
Westfield Cl **SW10** 128 C6
Westfield Way **E1** 127 J5
Westgate St **E8** 126 F3
Westgate Ter **SW10** 128 B4
Westgrove La **SE10** 131 N7
Westminster Br **SE1** 129 L1
Westminster Br **SW1** 129 L1
Westminster Br Rd **SE1** 129 N2
Westminster Gdns **SW1** 129 K3
Westmoreland Pl **SW1** 129 H4
Westmoreland Rd **SE17** 130 A5
Westmoreland St **W1** 124 G7
Westmoreland Ter **SW1** 129 H4
Westmoreland Wk **SE17** 130 B5
Weston Ri **WC1** 125 M4
Weston St **SE1** 130 B2
Westport St **E1** 127 H8
Westway **W2** 124 A7
Westway **W9** 124 A7
Wetherby Gdns **SW5** 128 C3
Wetherby Pl **SW7** 128 C3
Wetherell Rd **E9** 127 H3
Weybridge Pt **SW11** 128 G8
Weymouth Ms **W1** 125 H7
Weymouth St **W1** 125 H7
Weymouth Ter **E2** 126 D4
Wharf Pl **E2** 126 E3
Wharf Rd **N1** 126 A4
Wharf Rd (King's Cross) **N1** 125 L4
Wharfdale Rd **N1** 125 L4
Wharfedale St **SW10** 128 B4
Wharton St **WC1** 125 M5
Wheat Sheaf Cl **E14** 131 M3
Wheatsheaf La **SW8** 129 L6
Wheelwright St **N7** 125 M2
Wheler St **E1** 126 D6
Whidborne St **WC1** 125 L5
Whiskin St **EC1** 125 P5
Whistlers Av **SW11** 128 D6
Whiston Rd **E2** 126 D4
Whitbread Rd **SE4** 131 J10
Whitburn Rd **SE13** 131 M10
Whitcher Cl **SE14** 131 J5
Whitcomb St **WC2** 125 K9
White Ch La **E1** 126 E8
White Hart St **SE11** 129 N4
White Horse La **E1** 127 H6
White Horse Rd **E1** 127 J8
White Horse St **W1** 125 H10
White Lion Hill **EC4** 125 P9
White Lion St **N1** 125 N4
White Post La **E9** 127 K2
White Post La **SE13** 131 L9
White Post St **SE15** 130 G6
Whiteadder Way **E14** 131 M3
Whitear Wk **E15** 127 P1
Whitechapel High St **E1** 126 D8
Whitechapel Rd **E1** 126 E8
Whitecross St **EC1** 126 A6
Whitefriars St **EC4** 125 N8
Whitehall **SW1** 125 L10
Whitehall Ct **SW1** 125 L10
Whitehall Pl **SW1** 125 L10
Whitehead's Gro **SW3** 128 E4
Whiteleys Shop Cen **W2** 124 B8
Whites Grds **SE1** 130 C1
White's Row **E1** 126 D7
Whitethorn St **E3** 127 L6
Whitfield Rd **SE3** 131 P7
Whitfield St **W1** 125 K7
Whitgift St **SE11** 129 M3
Whitmore Est **N1** 126 C3
Whitmore Rd **N1** 126 C3
Whittaker St **SW1** 128 G3
Whitton Wk **E3** 127 L4
Whorlton Rd **SE15** 130 F9
Wick La **E3** 127 L4
Wick Rd **E9** 127 H1
Wickersley Rd **SW11** 128 G8
Wickford St **E1** 126 G6
Wickham Cl **E1** 126 G7
Wickham Gdns **SE4** 131 K9
Wickham Ms **SE4** 131 K8
Wickham Rd **SE4** 131 K10
Wickham St **SE11** 129 M4
Wicklow St **WC1** 125 M5
Wickwood St **SE5** 129 P8
Widdin St **E15** 127 P2
Widley Rd **W9** 124 A5
Wigmore Pl **W1** 125 H8
Wigmore St **W1** 124 G8
Wilbraham Pl **SW1** 128 F3
Wilcox Cl **SW8** 129 L6
Wilcox Rd **SW8** 129 L6
Wild Ct **WC2** 125 M8
Wild Goose Dr **SE14** 130 G7
Wild St **WC2** 125 L8
Wilde Cl **E8** 126 E3
Wild's Rents **SE1** 130 C2
Wilfred St **SW1** 129 J2
Wilkes St **E1** 126 D7
Wilkin St **NW5** 125 H1
Wilkinson St **SW8** 129 M6
Willard St **SW8** 129 H9
Willes Rd **NW5** 125 H1
William Bonney Est **SW4** 129 K10
William Cl **SE13** 131 N8
William IV St **WC2** 125 L9
William Morris Way **SW6** 128 C9
William Rd **NW1** 125 H5
William St **SW1** 128 F1
Williams Bldgs **E2** 126 G6
Willington Rd **SW9** 129 L9
Willis St **E14** 127 M8
Willoughby Pas **E14** 127 L10
Willow Br Rd **N1** 126 A1
Willow Pl **SW1** 129 J3
Willow St **EC2** 126 C6
Willow Wk **SE1** 130 C3
Willowbrook Rd **SE15** 130 D5
Wilman Gro **E8** 126 E2
Wilmcote Ho **W2** 124 A7
Wilmer Gdns **N1** 126 C3
Wilmer Lea Cl **E15** 127 N2
Wilmington Sq **WC1** 125 N5
Wilmington St **WC1** 125 N5
Wilmot Cl **SE15** 130 E6
Wilmot Pl **NW1** 125 J2
Wilmot St **E2** 126 F6
Wilshaw St **SE14** 131 L7
Wilson Gro **SE16** 130 F1
Wilson Rd **SE5** 130 C7
Wilson St **EC2** 126 B7
Wilton Cres **SW1** 128 G1
Wilton Ms **SW1** 128 G2
Wilton Pl **SW1** 128 G1
Wilton Rd **SW1** 129 H2
Wilton Row **SW1** 128 G1
Wilton Sq **N1** 126 B3
Wilton St **SW1** 129 H2
Wilton Ter **SW1** 128 G2
Wilton Vil **N1** 126 B3
Wilton Way **E8** 126 E1
Wiltshire Rd **SW9** 129 N9
Wiltshire Row **N1** 126 B3
Wimbolt St **E2** 126 E5
Wimbourne St **N1** 126 B4
Wimpole Ms **W1** 125 H7
Wimpole St **W1** 125 H8
Winans Wk **SW9** 129 N8
Winchester Cl **SE17** 129 P3
Winchester Rd **NW3** 124 D2
Winchester Sq **SE1** 126 B10
Winchester St **SW1** 129 H4
Winchester Wk **SE1** 126 B10
Wincott St **SE11** 129 N3
Winders Rd **SW11** 128 E8
Windlass Pl **SE8** 131 J3
Windmill Cl **SE13** 131 N8
Windmill La **E15** 127 P1
Windmill Row **SE11** 129 N4
Windmill St **W1** 125 K7
Windmill Wk **SE1** 125 N10
Windrose Cl **SE16** 131 H1
Windsock Cl **SE16** 131 K3
Windsor Gdns **W9** 124 A7
Windsor St **N1** 125 P3
Windsor Ter **N1** 126 A5
Windsor Wk **SE5** 130 B8
Wine Cl **E1** 126 G9
Winford Ho **E3** 127 K2
Winforton St **SE10** 131 N7
Wingfield St **SE15** 130 E9
Wingmore Rd **SE24** 130 A9
Winifred Gro **SW11** 128 F10
Winkley St **E2** 126 F4
Winsland St **W2** 124 D8
Winsley St **W1** 125 J8
Winslow **SE17** 130 C4
Winstanley Est **SW11** 128 D9
Winstanley Rd **SW11** 128 D9
Winterton Ho **E1** 126 F8
Winthrop St **E1** 126 F7
Wise Rd **E15** 127 P3
Wisteria Rd **SE13** 131 P10
Witan St **E2** 126 F5
Wivenhoe Cl **SE15** 130 F9
Wixs La **SW4** 129 H10
Woburn Pl **WC1** 125 K6
Woburn Sq **WC1** 125 K6
Woburn Wk **WC1** 125 K5
Wodeham Gdns **E1** 126 E7
Wodehouse Av **SE5** 130 D7
Wolfe Cres **SE16** 131 H1
Wolftencroft Cl **SW11** 128 D9
Wolseley St **SE1** 130 D1
Wolsey Ms **NW5** 125 J1
Wood Cl **E2** 126 E6
Wood St **EC2** 126 A8
Wood Wf **SE10** 131 M5
Woodbridge St **EC1** 125 P6
Woodchester Sq **W2** 124 B7
Woodchurch Rd **NW6** 124 A2
Woodfall St **SW3** 128 F4
Woodfarrs **SE5** 130 B10
Woodhouse Cl **SE22** 130 E10
Woodland Cres **SE16** 131 H1
Woodpecker Rd **SE14** 131 J5
Woods Ms **W1** 124 F9
Woods Rd **SE15** 130 F7
Woodseer St **E1** 126 D7
Woodstock Ter **E14** 127 M9
Wooler St **SE17** 130 B4
Woolmore St **E14** 127 N9
Woolneigh St **SW6** 128 B9
Woolstaplers Way **SE16** 130 E3
Wooster Gdns **E14** 127 P8
Wootton St **SE1** 125 N10
Worfield St **SW11** 128 E6
Worgan St **SE11** 129 M4
Worgan St **SE16** 131 H2
World's End Est **SW10** 128 C6
Worlingham Rd **SE22** 130 D10
Wormwood St **EC2** 126 C8
Woronzow Rd **NW8** 124 D3
Worship St **EC2** 126 B6
Wotton Rd **SE8** 131 K5
Wren Rd **SE5** 130 B7
Wren St **WC1** 125 M6
Wrexham Rd **E3** 127 L4
Wrigglesworth St **SE14** 131 H6
Wrights Cl **SE13** 131 P10
Wrights La **W8** 128 B1
Wrights Rd **E3** 127 K4
Wroxton Rd **SE15** 130 F8
Wyatt Cl **SE16** 131 K1
Wycliffe Rd **SW11** 128 G8
Wye St **SW11** 128 D8
Wyke Rd **E3** 127 L2
Wyllen Cl **E1** 126 G6
Wymering Rd **W9** 124 A5
Wynan Rd **E14** 131 M4
Wyndham Est **SE5** 130 A6
Wyndham Pl **W1** 124 F7
Wyndham Rd **SE5** 129 P6
Wyndham St **W1** 124 F7
Wynford Rd **N1** 125 M4
Wynne Rd **SW9** 129 N8
Wynnstay Gdns **W8** 128 A2
Wynter St **SW11** 128 C10
Wynyard Ter **SE11** 129 M4
Wyvil Rd **SW8** 129 L5
Wyvis St **E14** 127 M7

Y

Yabsley St **E14** 127 N10
Yalding Rd **SE16** 130 E2
Yardley St **WC1** 125 N5
Yeate St **N1** 126 B2
Yelverton Rd **SW11** 128 D8
Yeo St **E3** 127 M7
Yeoman St **SE8** 131 J3
Yeoman's Row **SW3** 128 E2
York Br **NW1** 124 G6
York Gate **NW1** 124 G6
York Gro **SE15** 130 G7
York Ho Pl **W8** 128 B1
York Pl **SW11** 128 D9
York Rd **SE1** 129 M1
York Rd **SW11** 128 C10
York Rd **SW18** 128 C10
York Sq **E14** 127 J8
York St **W1** 124 F7
York Ter E **NW1** 124 G6
York Ter W **NW1** 124 G6
York Way **N1** 125 L3
York Way **N7** 125 K1
York Way Ct **N1** 125 L3
Yorkshire Rd **E14** 127 J8
Yorkton St **E2** 126 E4
Young St **W8** 128 B1

Z

Zampa Rd **SE16** 130 G4
Zealand Rd **E3** 127 J4
Zenoria St **SE22** 130 D10
Zetland St **E14** 127 M7

INDEX TO GREAT BRITAIN

Administrative area abbreviations

Aber.	Aberdeenshire	*Dur.*	Durham	*Inclyde*	Inverclyde	*P. & K.*	Perth & Kinross	*Surr.*	Surrey
Arg. & B.	Argyll & Bute	*E.Ayr.*	East Ayrshire	*Lancs.*	Lancashire	*Pembs.*	Pembrokeshire	*Swan.*	Swansea
B'burn.	Blackburn with Darwen	*E.Dun.*	East Dunbartonshire	*Leic.*	Leicester	*Peter.*	Peterborough	*Swin.*	Swindon
B'pool	Blackpool	*E.Loth.*	East Lothian	*Leics.*	Leicestershire	*Plym.*	Plymouth	*T. & W.*	Tyne & Wear
B. & H.	Brighton & Hove	*E.Renf.*	East Renfrewshire	*Lincs.*	Lincolnshire	*Ports.*	Portsmouth	*Tel. & W.*	Telford & Wrekin
B. & N.E.Som.	Bath & North East Somerset	*E.Riding*	East Riding of Yorkshire	*M.K.*	Milton Keynes	*R. & C.*	Redcar & Cleveland	*Thur.*	Thurrock
B.Gwent	Blaenau Gwent	*E.Suss.*	East Sussex	*M.Tyd.*	Merthyr Tydfil	*R.C.T.*	Rhondda Cynon Taff	*V. of Glam.*	Vale of Glamorgan
Beds.	Bedfordshire	*Edin.*	Edinburgh	*Med.*	Medway	*Read.*	Reading	*W'ham*	Wokingham
Bourne.	Bournemouth	*Falk.*	Falkirk	*Mersey.*	Merseyside	*Renf.*	Renfrewshire	*W. & M.*	Windsor & Maidenhead
Brack.F.	Bracknell Forest	*Flints.*	Flintshire	*Middbro.*	Middlesbrough	*Rut.*	Rutland	*W.Berks.*	West Berkshire
Bucks.	Buckinghamshire	*Glas.*	Glasgow	*Midloth.*	Midlothian	*S'end*	Southend	*W.Dun.*	West Dunbartonshire
Caerp.	Caerphilly	*Glos.*	Gloucestershire	*Mon.*	Monmouthshire	*S'ham.*	Southampton	*W.Isles*	Western Isles (Na h-Eileanan an Iar)
Cambs.	Cambridgeshire	*Gt.Lon.*	Greater London	*N.Ayr.*	North Ayrshire	*S.Ayr.*	South Ayrshire	*W.Loth.*	West Lothian
Carmar.	Carmarthenshire	*Gt.Man.*	Greater Manchester	*N.E.Lincs.*	North East Lincolnshire	*S.Glos.*	South Gloucestershire	*W.Mid.*	West Midlands
Cere.	Ceredigion	*Gwyn.*	Gwynedd	*N.Lan.*	North Lanarkshire	*S.Lan.*	South Lanarkshire	*W.Suss.*	West Sussex
Chan.I.	Channel Islands	*Hants.*	Hampshire	*N.Lincs.*	North Lincolnshire	*S.Yorks.*	South Yorkshire	*W.Yorks.*	West Yorkshire
Ches.	Cheshire	*Hart.*	Hartlepool	*N.P.T.*	Neath Port Talbot	*Sc.Bord.*	Scottish Borders	*Warks.*	Warwickshire
Cornw.	Cornwall	*Here.*	Herefordshire	*N.Som.*	North Somerset	*Shet.*	Shetland	*Warr.*	Warrington
Cumb.	Cumbria	*Herts.*	Hertfordshire	*N.Yorks.*	North Yorkshire	*Shrop.*	Shropshire	*Wilts.*	Wiltshire
D. & G.	Dumfries & Galloway	*High.*	Highland	*Norf.*	Norfolk	*Slo.*	Slough	*Worcs.*	Worcestershire
Darl.	Darlington	*Hull*	Kingston upon Hull	*Northants.*	Northamptonshire	*Som.*	Somerset	*Wrex.*	Wrexham
Denb.	Denbighshire	*I.o.A.*	Isle of Anglesey	*Northumb.*	Northumberland	*Staffs.*	Staffordshire		
Derbys.	Derbyshire	*I.o.M.*	Isle of Man	*Nott.*	Nottingham	*Stir.*	Stirling		
		I.o.S.	Isles of Scilly	*Notts.*	Nottinghamshire	*Stock.*	Stockton-on-Tees		
		I.o.W.	Isle of Wight	*Ork.*	Orkney	*Stoke*	Stoke-on-Trent		
				Oxon.	Oxfordshire	*Suff.*	Suffolk		

Notes

This index reads in the sequence: Place Name / Postal District / Map Page Number / Grid Reference.

Example: Bishop's Cleeve **GL52** **29** J6

Where there is more than one place with the same name, the index reads in the sequence:
Place Name / Administrative Area / Postal District / Map Page Number / Grid Reference.

Example: Prestbury, *Ches.* **SK10** **49** H5
Prestbury, *Glos.* **GL52** **29** J6

Entries in the index shown in **BOLD CAPITALS** indicate the principal post town within a postcode area.
Entries in the index shown in **bold** indicate other post towns.

Example: **GLOUCESTER GL 29 H7**
Example: **Cheltenham GL50 29 J6**

A

Ab Kettleby **LE14** **42** A3
Ab Lench **WR10** **30** B3
Abbas Combe **BA8** **9** G2
Abberley **WR6** **29** G2
Abberley Common **WR6** **29** G2
Abberton *Essex* **CO5** **34** E7
Abberton *Worcs.* **WR10** **29** J3
Abberwick **NE66** **71** G2
Abbess Roding **CM5** **33** J7
Abbey Dore **HR2** **28** C5
Abbey Hulton **ST2** **40** B1
Abbey St. Bathans **TD11** **77** F4
Abbey Town **CA7** **60** C1
Abbey Village **PR6** **56** B7
Abbey Wood **SE2** **23** H4
Abbeycwmhir **LD1** **27** K1
Abbeydale **S7** **51** F4
Abbeystead **LA2** **55** J4
Abbotrule **TD9** **70** B2
Abbots Bickington **EX22** **6** B4
Abbots Bromley **WS15** **40** C3
Abbots Langley WD5 22 D1
Abbots Leigh **BS8** **19** J4
Abbots Morton **WR7** **30** B3
Abbots Ripton **PE28** **33** F1
Abbot's Salford **WR11** **30** B3
Abbots Worthy **SO21** **11** F1
Abbotsbury **DT3** **8** E6
Abbotsfield Farm **WA9** **48** E3
Abbotsham **EX39** **6** C3
Abbotskerswell **TQ12** **5** J4
Abbotsley **PE19** **33** F3
Abbotstone **SO24** **11** G1
Abbotts Ann **SP11** **21** G7
Abbott's Barton **SO23** **11** F1
Abbottswood **SO51** **10** E2
Abdon **SY7** **38** E7
Abdy **S62** **51** G3
Abenhall **GL17** **29** F7
Aber **SA40** **17** H1
Aber Village **LD3** **28** A6
Aberaeron SA46 26 D2
Aberaman **CF44** **18** D1
Aberangell **SY20** **37** H5
Aber-Arad **SA38** **17** G1
Aberarder **PH20** **88** B6
Aberarder House **IV2** **88** D2
Aberargie **PH2** **82** C6
Aberarth **SA46** **26** D2
Aberavon **SA12** **18** A3
Aber-banc **SA44** **17** G1
Aberbargoed **CF81** **18** E1
Aberbeeg **NP13** **19** F1
Aberbowlan **SA19** **17** K2
Aberbran **LD3** **27** J6
Abercanaid **CF48** **18** D1
Abercarn **NP11** **19** F2
Abercastle **SA62** **16** B2
Abercegir **SY20** **37** H5
Aberchalder **PH35** **87** K4
Aberchirder **AB54** **98** E5
Abercorn **EH30** **75** J3
Abercraf **SA9** **27** H7
Abercregan **SA13** **18** B2
Abercrombie **KY10** **83** G7
Abercrychan **SA20** **27** G5
Abercwmboi **CF44** **18** D1
Abercych **SA37** **17** F1
Abercynafon **LD3** **27** K7
Abercynon **CF45** **18** D2
Abercywarch **SY20** **37** H4
Aberdalgie **PH2** **82** B5
Aberdare CF44 18 C1
Aberdaron **LL53** **36** A3
Aberdaugleddau (Milford Haven) SA73 16 B5
ABERDEEN AB 91 H4
Aberdeen Airport **AB21** **91** G3
Aberdesach **LL54** **46** C7
Aberdour **KY3** **75** K2
Aberdovey (Aberdyfi) LL35 37 F6
Aberduhonw **LD2** **27** K3
Aberdulais **SA10** **18** A2
Aberdyfi (Aberdovey) LL35 37 F6
Aberedw **LD2** **27** K4
Abereiddy **SA62** **16** A2
Abererch **LL53** **36** C2
Aberfan **CF48** **18** D1
Aberfeldy PH15 81 K3
Aberffraw **LL63** **46** B6
Aberffrwd **SY23** **27** F1
Aberford **LS25** **57** K6
Aberfoyle **FK8** **81** G7
Abergavenny (Y Fenni) NP7 28 B7
Abergele LL22 47 H5
Aber-Giâr **SA40** **17** J1
Abergorlech **SA32** **17** J2
Abergwaun (Fishguard) SA65 16 C2
Abergwesyn **LD5** **27** H3
Abergwili **SA31** **17** H3
Abergwydol **SY20** **37** G5
Abergwynant **LL40** **37** F4
Abergwynfi **SA13** **18** B2
Abergwyngregyn **LL33** **46** E5
Abergynolwyn **LL36** **37** F5
Aberhafesp **SY16** **37** K6
Aberhonddu (Brecon) LD3 27 K6
Aberhosan **SY20** **37** H6
Aberkenfig **CF32** **18** B3
Aberlady **EH32** **76** C2
Aberlemno **DD8** **83** G2
Aberllefenni **SY20** **37** G5
Aber-Ilia **CF44** **27** J7
Aberllynfi (Three Cocks) **LD3** **28** A5
Aberlour (Charlestown of Aberlour) AB38 97 K7
Abermad **SY23** **26** E1
Abermaw (Barmouth) LL42 37 F4
Abermeurig **SA48** **26** E3
Aber-miwl (Abermule) **SY15** **38** A6
Abermule (Aber-miwl) **SY15** **38** A6
Abernaint **SY22** **38** A3
Abernant *Carmar.* **SA33** **17** G3
Aber-nant *R.C.T.* **CF44** **18** D1
Abernethy **PH2** **82** C6
Abernyte **PH14** **82** D4
Aberpennar (Mountain Ash) CF45 18 D2
Aberporth **SA43** **26** B3
Aberriw (Berriew) **SY21** **38** A5
Aberscross **KW10** **96** E2
Abersky **IV2** **88** C2
Abersoch **LL53** **36** C3
Abersychan **NP4** **19** F1
ABERTAWE (SWANSEA) SA 17 K6
Aberteifi (Cardigan) SA43 16 E1
Aberthin **CF71** **18** D4
Abertillery NP13 19 F1
Abertridwr *Caerp.* **CF83** **18** E3
Abertridwr *Powys* **SY10** **37** K4
Abertysswg **NP22** **18** E1
Aberuthven **PH3** **82** A6
Aberyscir **LD3** **27** J6
Aberystwyth SY23 36 E7
Abhainnsuidhe **HS3** **100** C7
Abingdon OX14 21 H2
Abinger Common **RH5** **22** E7
Abinger Hammer **RH5** **22** D7
Abington **ML12** **68** E1
Abington Pigotts **SG8** **33** G4
Abingworth **RH20** **12** E5
Ablington *Glos.* **GL7** **20** E1
Ablington *Wilts.* **SP4** **20** E7
Abney **S32** **50** D5
Above Church **ST10** **50** C7
Aboyne AB34 90 D5
Abram **WN2** **49** F2
Abriachan **IV3** **88** C1
Abridge **RM4** **23** H2
Abronhill **G67** **75** F3
Abson **BS30** **20** A4
Abthorpe **NN12** **31** H4
Abune-the-Hill **KW17** **106** B5
Aby **LN13** **53** H5
Acaster Malbis **YO23** **58** B5
Acaster Selby **YO23** **58** B5
Accrington BB5 56 C7
Accurrach **PA33** **80** C5
Acha **PA78** **78** C2
Achacha **PA37** **80** A3
Achadacaie **PA29** **73** G4
Achadh Mòr **HS2** **101** F5
Achadh-chaorrunn **PA29** **73** F5
Achadunan **PA26** **80** D6
Achagavel **PH33** **79** J2
Achaglass **PA29** **73** F6
Achahoish **PA31** **73** F3
Achalader **PH10** **82** C3
Achallader **PA36** **80** E3
Achamore **PA60** **72** D3
Achandunie **IV17** **96** D4
Achany **IV27** **96** C1
Achaphubuil **PH33** **87** G7
Acharacle PH36 79 H1
Achargary **KW11** **104** C3
Acharn *Arg. & B.* **PA35** **80** C4
Acharn *P. & K.* **PH15** **81** J3
Acharonich **PA73** **79** F4
Acharosson **PA21** **73** H3
Achateny **PH36** **86** B7
Achath **AB32** **91** F3
Achavanich **KW5** **105** G4
Achddu **SA16** **17** H5
Achduart **IV26** **95** G1
Achentoul **KW11** **104** D5
Achfary **IV27** **102** E5
Achgarve **IV22** **94** E2
Achiemore *High.* **IV27** **103** F2
Achiemore *High.* **KW13** **104** D3
Achies **KW12** **105** G3
A'Chill **PH44** **85** H4
Achiltibuie **IV26** **95** G1
Achina **KW14** **104** C2
Achindown **IV12** **97** F7
Achinduich **IV27** **96** C2
Achingills **KW12** **105** G2
Achintee **IV54** **95** F7
Achintee House **PH33** **87** H7
Achintraid **IV54** **86** E1
Achlean **PH21** **89** F5
Achleanan **PA34** **79** G2
Achleek **PH33** **79** J2
Achlian **PA33** **80** C5
Achlyness **IV27** **102** E3
Achmelvich **IV27** **102** C6
Achmony **IV63** **88** C1
Achmore *High.* **IV53** **86** E1
Achmore *High.* **IV23** **95** G2
Achmore *Stir.* **FK21** **81** G4
Achnaba **PA31** **73** H2
Achnabat **IV2** **88** C1
Achnabourin **KW14** **104** C3
Achnacairn **PA37** **80** A4
Achnacarnin **IV27** **102** C5
Achnacarry **PH34** **87** H6
Achnaclerach **IV23** **96** B5
Achnacloich *Arg. & B.* **PA37** **80** A4
Achnacloich *High.* **IV46** **86** B4
Achnaclyth **KW6** **105** F5
Achnacraig **PA73** **79** F3
Achnacroish **PA34** **79** K3
Achnadrish **PA75** **79** F2
Achnafalnich **PA33** **80** D5
Achnafauld **PH8** **81** K4
Achnagairn **IV5** **96** C7
Achnagarron **IV18** **96** D4
Achnaha *High.* **PA34** **79** H3
Achnaha *High.* **PH36** **79** F1
Achnahanat **IV24** **96** C2
Achnahannet **PH26** **89** G2
Achnairn **IV27** **103** H7
Achnalea **PH33** **79** K1
Achnamara **PA31** **73** F2
Achnanellan **PH37** **79** J1
Achnasaul **PH34** **87** H6
Achnasheen IV22 95 H6
Achnashelloch **PA31** **73** G1
Achnastank **AB55** **89** K1
Achorn **KW6** **105** G5
Achosnich *High.* **IV25** **96** E2
Achosnich *High.* **PH36** **79** F1
Achreamie **KW14** **105** F2
Achriabhach **PH33** **80** C1
Achriesgill **IV27** **102** E3
Achtoty **KW14** **103** J2
Achurch **PE8** **42** D7
Achuvoldrach **IV27** **103** H3
Achvaich **IV25** **96** E2
Achvarasdal **KW14** **104** E2
Achvlair **PA38** **80** A2
Achvraie **IV26** **95** G1
Ackenthwaite **LA7** **55** J1
Ackergill **KW1** **105** J3
Acklam *Middbro.* **TS5** **63** F5
Acklam *N.Yorks.* **YO17** **58** D3
Ackleton **WV6** **39** G6
Acklington **NE65** **71** H3
Ackton **WF7** **57** K7
Ackworth Moor Top **WF7** **51** G1
Acle **NR13** **45** J4
Acock's Green **B27** **40** D7
Acol **CT7** **25** K5
Acomb *Northumb.* **NE46** **70** E7
Acomb *York* **YO24** **58** B4
Aconbury **HR2** **28** E5
Acre **BB5** **56** C7
Acrefair **LL14** **38** B1
Acrise Place **CT18** **15** G3
Acton *Ches.* **CW5** **49** F7
Acton *Dorset* **BH19** **9** J7
Acton *Gt.Lon.* **W3** **22** E3
Acton *Shrop.* **SY9** **38** C7
Acton *Staffs.* **ST5** **40** A1
Acton *Suff.* **CO10** **34** C4
Acton *Worcs.* **DY13** **29** H2
Acton *Wrex.* **LL12** **48** C7
Acton Beauchamp **WR6** **29** F3
Acton Bridge **CW8** **48** E5
Acton Burnell **SY5** **38** E5
Acton Green **WR6** **29** F3
Acton Pigott **SY5** **38** E5
Acton Round **WV16** **39** F6
Acton Scott **SY6** **38** D7
Acton Trussell **ST17** **40** B4
Acton Turville **GL9** **20** B3
Adamhill **KA1** **74** C7
Adbaston **ST20** **39** G3
Adber **DT9** **8** E2
Adderbury **OX17** **31** F5
Adderley **TF9** **39** F2
Adderstone **NE70** **77** K7
Addiewell **EH55** **75** H4
Addingham **LS29** **57** F5
Addington *Bucks.* **MK18** **31** J6
Addington *Gt.Lon.* **CR0** **23** G5
Addington *Kent* **ME19** **23** K6
Addiscombe **CR0** **23** G5
Addlestone KT15 22 D5
Addlethorpe **PE24** **53** J6
Adel **LS16** **57** H6
Adeney **TF10** **39** G4
Adeyfield **HP2** **22** D1
Adfa **SY16** **37** K5
Adforton **SY7** **28** D1
Adisham **CT3** **15** H2
Adlestrop **GL56** **30** D6
Adlingfleet **DN14** **58** E7
Adlington *Ches.* **SK10** **49** J4
Adlington *Lancs.* **PR7** **48** E1
Admaston *Staffs.* **WS15** **40** C3
Admaston *Tel. & W.* **TF5** **39** F4
Admington **CV36** **30** D4
Adsborough **TA2** **8** B2
Adscombe **TA5** **7** K2
Adstock **MK18** **31** J5
Adstone **NN12** **31** G3
Adversane **RH14** **12** D4
Advie **PH26** **89** J1
Adwalton **BD11** **57** H7
Adwell **OX9** **21** K2

Adwick le Street **DN6** 51 H2
Adwick upon Dearne **S64** 51 G2
Adziel **AB43** 99 H5
Ae Village **DG1** 68 E5
Affetside **BL8** 49 G1
Affleck **AB21** 91 G2
Affpuddle **DT2** 9 H5
Afon Wen **LL53** 36 D2
Afon-wen **CH7** 47 K5
Afton **PO40** 10 E6
Afton Bridgend **KA18** 68 B2
Agglethorpe **DL8** 57 F1
Aigburth **L17** 48 C4
Aiginis **HS2** 101 G4
Aike **YO25** 59 G5
Aikerness **KW17** 106 D2
Aikers **KW17** 106 D8
Aiketgate **CA4** 61 F2
Aikshaw **CA7** 60 C2
Aikton **CA7** 60 D1
Aikwood Tower **TD7** 69 K1
Ailby **LN13** 53 H5
Ailey **HR3** 28 C4
Ailsworth **PE5** 42 E6
Aimes Green **EN9** 23 H1
Aimster **KW14** 105 G2
Ainderby Quernhow **YO7** 57 J1
Ainderby Steeple **DL7** 62 E7
Aingers Green **CO7** 35 F6
Ainsdale **PR8** 48 C1
Ainsdale-on-Sea **PR8** 48 C1
Ainstable **CA4** 61 G2
Ainsworth **BL2** 49 G1
Ainthorpe **YO21** 63 J6
Aintree **L10** 48 C3
Aird *W.Isles* **HS7** 92 C6
Aird *W.Isles* **HS2** 101 H4
Aird a' Mhachair **HS8** 92 C7
Aird a' Mhulaidh **HS3** 100 D6
Aird Asaig **HS3** 100 D7
Aird Dhail **HS2** 101 G1
Aird Leimhe **HS3** 93 G3
Aird Mhige **HS3** 93 G2
Aird Mhighe **HS3** 93 F3
Aird of Sleat **IV45** 86 B4
Aird Thunga **HS2** 101 G4
Aird Uig **HS2** 100 C4
Airdrie *Fife* **KY10** 83 G7
Airdrie *N.Lan.* ML6 75 F4
Aire View **BD20** 56 E5
Airidh a' Bhruaich **HS2** 100 E6
Airieland **DG7** 65 H5
Airies **DG9** 66 D7
Airigh-drishaig **IV54** 86 D1
Airmyn **DN14** 58 D7
Airntully **PH1** 82 B4
Airor **PH41** 86 D4
Airth **FK2** 75 G2
Airton **BD23** 56 E4
Airyhassen **DG8** 64 D6
Aisby *Lincs.* **DN21** 52 B3
Aisby *Lincs.* **NG32** 42 D2
Aisgernis (Askernish) **HS8** 84 C2
Aisgill **CA17** 61 J7
Aish *Devon* **TQ10** 5 G4
Aish *Devon* **TQ9** 5 J5
Aisholt **TA5** 7 K2
Aiskew **DL8** 57 H1
Aislaby *N.Yorks.* **YO21** 63 K6
Aislaby *N.Yorks.* **YO18** 58 D1
Aislaby *Stock.* **TS16** 63 F5
Aisthorpe **LN1** 52 C4
Aith *Ork.* **KW16** 106 B6
Aith *Ork.* **KW17** 106 F5
Aith *Shet.* **ZE2** 107 M7
Aith *Shet.* **ZE2** 107 Q3
Aithsetter **ZE2** 107 N9
Aitnoch **PH26** 89 G1
Akeld **NE71** 70 E1
Akeley **MK18** 31 J5
Akenham **IP1** 35 F4
Albaston **PL18** 4 E3
Albecq **GY5** 3 H5
Alberbury **SY5** 38 C4
Albert Town **SA61** 16 C4
Albourne **BN6** 13 F5
Albourne Green **BN6** 13 F5
Albrighton *Shrop.* **WV7** 40 A5
Albrighton *Shrop.* **SY4** 38 D4
Alburgh **IP20** 45 G7
Albury *Herts.* **SG11** 33 H6
Albury *Oxon.* **OX9** 21 K1
Albury *Surr.* **GU5** 22 D7
Albury End **SG11** 33 H6
Albury Heath **GU5** 22 D7
Albyfield **CA8** 61 G1
Alcaig **IV7** 96 C6
Alcaston **SY6** 38 D7
Alcester B49 30 B3
Alciston **BN26** 13 J6
Alcombe **TA24** 7 H1
Alconbury **PE28** 32 E1
Alconbury Hill **PE28** 32 E1
Alconbury Weston **PE28** 32 E1
Aldborough *N.Yorks.* **YO51** 57 K3
Aldborough *Norf.* **NR11** 45 F2
Aldbourne **SN8** 21 F4
Aldbrough **HU11** 59 J6
Aldbrough St. John **DL11** 62 D5
Aldbury **HP23** 32 C7
Aldclune **PH16** 82 A1
Aldeburgh IP15 35 J3
Aldeby **NR34** 45 J6
Aldenham **WD25** 22 E2
Alderbury **SP5** 10 C2
Alderford **NR9** 45 F4
Alderholt **SP6** 10 C3
Alderley **GL12** 20 A2
Alderley Edge SK9 49 H5
Aldermaston **RG7** 21 J5
Aldermaston Wharf **RG7** 21 K5
Alderminster **CV37** 30 D4
Alderney **GY9** 3 K4
Alderney Airport **GY9** 3 J4
Alder's End **HR1** 29 F5
Aldersey Green **CH3** 48 D7
Aldershot GU11 22 B6
Alderton *Glos.* **GL20** 29 J5
Alderton *Northants.* **NN12** 31 J4
Alderton *Suff.* **IP12** 35 H4
Alderton *Wilts.* **SN14** 20 B3
Alderwasley **DE56** 51 F7
Aldfield **HG4** 57 H3
Aldford **CH3** 48 D7
Aldham *Essex* **CO6** 34 D6
Aldham *Suff.* **IP7** 34 E4
Aldie *Aber.* **AB42** 99 J6
Aldie *High.* **IV19** 96 E3
Aldingbourne **PO20** 12 C6
Aldingham **LA12** 55 F2
Aldington *Kent* **TN25** 15 F4
Aldington *Worcs.* **WR11** 30 B4
Aldivalloch **AB54** 90 B2
Aldochlay **G83** 74 B1
Aldons **KA26** 67 F5
Aldous's Corner **IP19** 45 H7
Aldreth **CB6** 33 H1
Aldridge **WS9** 40 C5
Aldringham **IP16** 35 J2
Aldsworth *Glos.* **GL54** 20 E1
Aldsworth *W.Suss.* **PO10** 11 J4
Aldunie **AB54** 90 B2
Aldville **PH8** 82 A4
Aldwark *Derbys.* **DE4** 50 E7
Aldwark *N.Yorks.* **YO61** 57 K3
Aldwick **PO21** 12 C7
Aldwincle **NN14** 42 D7
Aldworth **RG8** 21 J4
Alexandria G83 74 B3
Aley **TA5** 7 K2
Aley Green **LU1** 32 D7
Alfardisworthy **EX22** 6 A4
Alfington **EX11** 7 K6
Alfold **GU6** 12 D3
Alfold Crossways **GU6** 12 D3
Alford *Aber.* AB33 90 D3
Alford *Lincs.* LN13 53 H5
Alford *Som.* **BA7** 9 F1
Alfreton DE55 51 G7
Alfrick **WR6** 29 G3
Alfrick Pound **WR6** 29 G3
Alfriston **BN26** 13 J6
Algarkirk **PE20** 43 F2
Alhampton **BA4** 9 F1
Alkborough **DN15** 58 E7
Alkerton **OX15** 30 E4
Alkham **CT15** 15 H3
Alkington **SY13** 38 E2
Alkmonton **DE6** 40 D2
All Cannings **SN10** 20 D5
All Saints South Elmham **IP19** 45 H7
All Stretton **SY6** 38 D6
Allaleigh **TQ9** 5 J5
Allanaquoich **AB35** 89 J5
Allancreich **AB34** 90 D5
Allanfearn **IV2** 96 E7
Allangillfoot **DG13** 69 H4
Allanton *D. & G.* **DG2** 68 E5
Allanton *E.Ayr.* **KA17** 74 E7
Allanton *N.Lan.* **ML7** 75 G5
Allanton *S.Lan.* **ML3** 75 F5
Allanton *Sc.Bord.* **TD11** 77 G5
Allardice **DD10** 91 G7
Allathasdal **HS9** 84 B4
Allbrook **SO50** 11 F2
Allendale Town **NE47** 61 K1
Allenheads **NE47** 61 K2
Allen's Green **CM21** 33 H7
Allensford **DH8** 62 B1
Allensmore **HR2** 28 D5
Allenton **DE24** 41 F2
Aller **TA10** 8 D2
Allerby **CA7** 60 B3
Allercombe **EX5** 7 J6
Allerford *Devon* **EX20** 6 C7
Allerford *Som.* **TA24** 7 H1
Allerston **YO18** 58 E1
Allerthorpe **YO42** 58 D5
Allerton *Mersey.* **L18** 48 D4
Allerton *W.Yorks.* **BD15** 57 G6
Allerton Bywater **WF10** 57 K7
Allerton Mauleverer **HG5** 57 K4
Allesley **CV5** 40 E7
Allestree **DE22** 41 F2
Allet Common **TR4** 2 E4
Allexton **LE15** 42 B5
Allgreave **SK11** 49 J6
Allhallows **ME3** 24 E4
Allhallows-on-Sea **ME3** 24 E4
Alligin Shuas **IV22** 94 E6
Allimore Green **ST18** 40 A4
Allington *Dorset* **DT6** 8 D5
Allington *Lincs.* **NG32** 42 B1
Allington *Wilts.* **SP4** 10 D1
Allington *Wilts.* **SN10** 20 D5
Allington *Wilts.* **SN14** 20 B4
Allithwaite **LA11** 55 G2
Allnabad **IV27** 103 G4
Alloa FK10 75 G1
Allonby **CA15** 60 B2
Allostock **WA16** 49 G5
Alloway **KA7** 67 H2
Allowenshay **TA17** 8 C3
Allscot **WV15** 39 G6
Allscott **TF6** 39 F4
Allt na h-Airbhe **IV26** 95 H2
Alltachonaich **PA34** 79 J2
Alltbeithe **IV4** 87 G2
Alltforgan **SY10** 37 J3
Alltmawr **LD2** 27 K4
Alltnacaillich **IV27** 103 G4
Allt-na-subh **IV40** 87 F1
Alltsigh **IV63** 88 B3
Alltwalis **SA32** 17 H2
Alltwen **SA8** 18 A1
Alltyblaca **SA40** 17 J1
Allwood Green **IP22** 34 E1
Almeley **HR3** 28 C3
Almeley Wootton **HR3** 28 C3
Almer **DT11** 9 J5
Almington **TF9** 39 G2
Almiston Cross **EX39** 6 B3
Almondbank **PH1** 82 B5
Almondbury **HD4** 50 D1
Almondsbury **BS32** 19 K3
Alne **YO61** 57 K3
Alness IV17 96 D5
Alnham **NE66** 70 E2
Alnmouth **NE66** 71 H2
Alnwick NE66 71 G2
Alperton **HA0** 22 E3
Alphamstone **CO8** 34 C5
Alpheton **CO10** 34 C3
Alphington **EX2** 7 H6
Alport **DE45** 50 E6
Alpraham **CW6** 48 E7
Alresford **CO7** 34 E6
Alrewas **DE13** 40 D4
Alrick **PH11** 82 C1
Alsager **ST7** 49 G7
Alsagers Bank **ST7** 40 A1
Alsop en le Dale **DE6** 50 D7
Alston *Cumb.* CA9 61 J2
Alston *Devon* **EX13** 8 C4
Alston Sutton **BS26** 19 H6
Alstone *Glos.* **GL20** 29 J5
Alstone *Som.* **TA9** 19 G7
Alstone *Staffs.* **ST18** 40 A4
Alstonefield **DE6** 50 D7
Alswear **EX36** 7 F3
Alt **OL8** 49 J2
Altandhu **IV26** 102 B7
Altanduin **KW11** 104 D6
Altarnun **PL15** 4 C2
Altass **IV27** 96 C1
Altens **AB12** 91 H4
Alterwall **KW1** 105 H2
Altham **BB5** 56 C6
Althorne **CM3** 25 F2
Althorpe **DN17** 52 B2
Alticry **DG8** 64 C5
Altnafeadh **PH49** 80 D2
Altnaharra **IV27** 103 H5
Altofts **WF6** 57 J7
Alton *Derbys.* **S42** 51 F6
Alton *Hants.* GU34 11 J1
Alton *Staffs.* **ST10** 40 C1
Alton Barnes **SN8** 20 E5
Alton Pancras **DT2** 9 G4
Alton Priors **SN8** 20 E5
Altonside **IV30** 97 K6
Altrincham WA14 49 G4
Altura **PH34** 87 J5
Alva FK12 75 G1
Alvanley **WA6** 48 D5
Alvaston **DE24** 41 F2
Alvechurch **B48** 30 B1
Alvecote **B79** 40 E5
Alvediston **SP5** 9 J2
Alveley **WV15** 39 G7
Alverdiscott **EX31** 6 D3
Alverstoke **PO12** 11 H5
Alverstone **PO36** 11 G6
Alverthorpe **WF2** 57 J7
Alverton **NG13** 42 A1
Alves **IV30** 97 J5
Alvescot **OX18** 21 F1
Alveston *S.Glos.* **BS35** 19 K3
Alveston *Warks.* **CV37** 30 D3
Alvie **PH21** 89 F4
Alvingham **LN11** 53 G3
Alvington **GL15** 19 K1
Alwalton **PE2** 42 E6
Alweston **DT9** 9 F3
Alwington **EX39** 6 C3
Alwinton **NE65** 70 E3
Alwoodley **LS17** 57 J5
Alwoodley Gates **LS17** 57 J5
Alyth **PH11** 82 D3
Amalebra **TR20** 2 B5
Ambaston **DE72** 41 G2
Amber Hill **PE20** 43 F1
Ambergate **DE56** 51 F7
Amberley *Glos.* **GL5** 20 B1
Amberley *W.Suss.* **BN18** 12 D5
Amble **NE65** 71 H3
Amblecote **DY8** 40 A7
Ambleside LA22 60 E6
Ambleston **SA62** 16 D3
Ambrismore **PA20** 73 J5
Ambrosden **OX25** 31 H7
Amcotts **DN17** 52 B1
Amersham HP6 22 C2
Amerton **ST18** 40 B3
Amesbury **SP4** 20 E7
Ameysford **BH22** 10 B4
Amington **B77** 40 E5
Amisfield Town **DG1** 69 F5
Amlwch LL68 46 C3
Amlwch Port **LL68** 46 C3
Ammanford (Rhydaman) SA18 17 K4
Amotherby **YO17** 58 D2
Ampfield **SO51** 10 E2
Ampleforth **YO62** 58 B2
Ampleforth College **YO62** 58 B2
Ampney Crucis **GL7** 20 D1
Ampney St. Mary **GL7** 20 D1
Ampney St. Peter **GL7** 20 D1
Amport **SP11** 21 G7
Ampthill **MK45** 32 D5
Ampton **IP31** 34 C1
Amroth **SA67** 16 E5
Amulree **PH8** 81 K4
An T-Òb (Leverburgh) **HS5** 93 F3
Anaboard **PH26** 89 H1
Anaheilt **PH36** 79 K1
Ancaster **NG32** 42 C1
Anchor **SY7** 38 A7
Anchor Corner **NR17** 44 E6
Ancroft **TD15** 77 H6
Ancrum **TD8** 70 B1
Ancton **PO22** 12 C6
Anderby **PE24** 53 J5
Anderby Creek **PE24** 53 J5
Andersea **TA7** 8 C1
Andersfield **TA5** 8 B1
Anderson **DT11** 9 H5
Anderton **CW9** 49 F5
Andover SP10 21 G7
Andover Down **SP11** 21 G7
Andoversford **GL54** 30 B7
Andreas **IM7** 54 D4
Anelog **LL53** 36 A3
Anfield **L4** 48 C3
Angarrack **TR27** 2 C5
Angarrick **TR3** 2 E5
Angelbank **SY8** 28 E1
Angerton **CA7** 60 D1
Angle **SA71** 16 B5
Angler's Retreat **SY20** 37 G6
Anglesey (Ynys Môn) **LL** 46 B4
Angmering **BN16** 12 D6
Angmering-on-Sea **BN16** 12 D6
Angram *N.Yorks.* **YO23** 58 B5
Angram *N.Yorks.* **DL11** 61 K7
Anick **NE46** 70 E7
Anie **FK17** 81 G6
Ankerville **IV19** 97 F4
Anlaby **HU10** 59 G7
Anmer **PE31** 44 B3
Anmore **PO7** 11 H3
Anna Valley **SP11** 21 G7
Annan DG12 69 G7
Annaside **LA19** 54 D1
Annat *Arg. & B.* **PA35** 80 B5
Annat *High.* **IV22** 94 E6
Annbank **KA6** 67 J1
Annesley **NG15** 51 H7
Annesley Woodhouse **NG17** 51 G7
Annfield Plain **DH9** 62 C1
Anniesland **G13** 74 D4
Annscroft **SY5** 38 D5
Ansdell **FY8** 55 G7
Ansford **BA7** 9 F1
Ansley **CV10** 40 E6
Anslow **DE13** 40 E3
Anslow Gate **DE13** 40 D3
Ansteadbrook **GU27** 12 C3
Anstey *Herts.* **SG9** 33 H5
Anstey *Leics.* **LE7** 41 H5
Anstruther KY10 83 G7
Ansty *W.Suss.* **RH17** 13 F4
Ansty *Warks.* **CV7** 41 F7
Ansty *Wilts.* **SP3** 9 J2
Ansty Coombe **SP3** 9 J2
Ansty Cross **DT2** 9 G4
Anthill Common **PO7** 11 H3
Anthorn **CA7** 60 C1
Antingham **NR28** 45 G2
Anton's Gowt **PE22** 43 F1
Antony **PL11** 4 D5
Antrobus **CW9** 49 F5
Anvil Corner **EX22** 6 B5
Anvil Green **CT4** 15 G3
Anwick **NG34** 52 E7
Anwoth **DG7** 65 F5
Aoradh **PA44** 72 A4
Apethorpe **PE8** 42 D6
Apeton **ST20** 40 A4
Apley **LN8** 52 E5
Apperknowle **S18** 51 F5
Apperley **GL19** 29 H6
Apperley Bridge **BD10** 57 G6
Appersett **DL8** 61 K7
Appin PA38 80 A3
Appin House **PA38** 80 A3
Appleby **DN15** 52 C1
Appleby Magna **DE12** 41 F4
Appleby Parva **DE12** 41 F5
Appleby-in-Westmorland CA16 61 H4
Applecross **IV54** 94 D7
Appledore *Devon* **EX39** 6 C2
Appledore *Devon* **EX16** 7 J4
Appledore *Kent* **TN26** 14 E5
Appledore Heath **TN26** 14 E4
Appleford **OX14** 21 J2
Appleshaw **SP11** 21 G7
Applethwaite **CA12** 60 D4
Appleton *Halton* **WA8** 48 E4
Appleton *Oxon.* **OX13** 21 H1
Appleton Roebuck **YO23** 58 B5
Appleton Thorn **WA4** 49 F4
Appleton Wiske **DL6** 62 E6
Appleton-le-Moors **YO62** 58 D1
Appleton-le-Street **YO17** 58 D2
Appletreehall **TD9** 70 A2
Appletreewick **BD23** 57 F3
Appley **TA21** 7 J3
Appley Bridge **WN6** 48 E2
Apse Heath **PO36** 11 G6
Apsey Green **IP13** 35 G2
Apsley **HP3** 22 D1
Apsley End **SG5** 32 E5
Apuldram **PO20** 12 B6
Arberth (Narberth) SA67 16 E4
Arbirlot **DD11** 83 G3
Arborfield **RG2** 22 A5
Arborfield Cross **RG2** 22 A5
Arborfield Garrison **RG2** 22 A5
Arbourthorne **S2** 51 F4
Arbroath DD11 83 H3
Arbuthnott **AB30** 91 F7
Archdeacon Newton **DL2** 62 D5
Archiestown **AB38** 97 K7
Arclid **CW11** 49 G6
Ard a' Chapuill **PA22** 73 J2
Ardachearanbeg **PA22** 73 J2
Ardacheranmor **PA22** 73 J2
Ardachoil **PA65** 79 J4
Ardachu **IV28** 96 D1
Ardailly **PA41** 72 E5
Ardalanish **PA67** 78 E6
Ardallie **AB42** 91 J1
Ardanaiseig **PA35** 80 B5
Ardaneaskan **IV54** 86 E1
Ardanstur **PA34** 79 K6
Ardantiobairt **PA34** 79 H2
Ardantrive **PA34** 79 K5
Ardarroch **IV54** 94 E7
Ardbeg *Arg. & B.* **PA20** 73 J4
Ardbeg *Arg. & B.* **PA42** 72 C6
Ardbeg *Arg. & B.* **PA23** 73 K2
Ardblair **IV4** 88 C1
Ardbrecknish **PA33** 80 B5
Ardcharnich **IV23** 95 H3
Ardchiavaig **PA67** 78 E6
Ardchonnel **PA37** 80 A4
Ardchonnell **PA33** 80 A6
Ardchrishnish **PA70** 79 F5
Ardchronie **IV24** 96 D3
Ardchuilk **IV4** 87 J1
Ardchullarie More **FK18** 81 G6
Ardchyle **FK21** 81 G5
Arddlin **SY22** 38 B4
Ardechvie **PH34** 87 H5
Ardeley **SG2** 33 G6
Ardelve **IV40** 86 E2
Arden **G83** 74 B2
Ardencaple House **PA34** 79 J6
Ardens Grafton **B49** 30 C3
Ardentallan **PA34** 79 K5
Ardentinny **PA23** 73 K2
Ardeonaig **FK21** 81 H4
Ardersier **IV2** 96 E6
Ardery **PH36** 79 J1
Ardessie **IV23** 95 G3
Ardfad **PA34** 79 J6
Ardfern **PA31** 79 K7
Ardfin **PA60** 72 C4
Ardgartan **G83** 80 D7
Ardgay IV24 96 D2
Ardgenavan **PA26** 80 C6
Ardgour (Corran) **PH33** 80 B1
Ardgowan **PA16** 74 A3
Ardgowse **AB33** 90 E3
Ardgye **IV30** 97 J5
Ardhallow **PA23** 73 K3
Ardheslaig **IV54** 94 D6
Ardiecow **AB45** 98 D4
Ardinamar **PA34** 79 J6
Ardindrean **IV23** 95 H3
Ardingly **RH17** 13 G4
Ardington **OX12** 21 H3
Ardington Wick **OX12** 21 H3
Ardintoul **IV40** 86 E2
Ardkinglas House **PA26** 80 C6
Ardlair **AB52** 90 D2
Ardlamont **PA21** 73 H4
Ardleigh **CO7** 34 E6
Ardleigh Green **RM2** 23 J3
Ardleigh Heath **CO7** 34 E5
Ardleish **G83** 80 E6
Ardler **PH12** 82 D3
Ardley **OX27** 31 G6
Ardley End **CM22** 33 J7
Ardlui **G83** 80 E6
Ardlussa **PA60** 72 E2
Ardmaddy **PA35** 80 B4
Ardmair **IV26** 95 H2
Ardmaleish **PA20** 73 J4
Ardmay **G83** 80 D7
Ardmenish **PA60** 72 D3
Ardmhòr **HS9** 84 C4
Ardminish **PA41** 72 E6
Ardmolich **PH36** 86 D7
Ardmore *Arg. & B.* **PA42** 72 C5
Ardmore *Arg. & B.* **PA34** 79 J5
Ardmore *Arg. & B.* **G82** 74 B3
Ardmore *High.* **IV19** 96 E3
Ardnackaig **PA31** 73 F1
Ardnacross **PA72** 79 G3
Ardnadam **PA23** 73 K2
Ardnadrochit **PA64** 79 J4
Ardnagoine **IV26** 95 F1
Ardnagowan **PA25** 80 C7
Ardnahein **PA24** 73 K1
Ardnahoe **PA46** 72 C3
Ardnarff **IV53** 86 E1
Ardnastang **PH36** 79 K1
Ardnave **PA44** 72 A3
Ardno **PA26** 80 C7
Ardo **AB41** 91 G1
Ardoch *D. & G.* **DG3** 68 D3
Ardoch *Moray* **IV36** 97 J6
Ardoch *P. & K.* **PH1** 82 B4
Ardochrig **G75** 74 E6
Ardoyne **AB52** 90 E2
Ardpatrick **PA29** 73 F4
Ardpeaton **G84** 74 A2
Ardradnaig **PH15** 81 J3
Ardrishaig **PA30** 73 G2
Ardroe **IV27** 102 C6
Ardross **IV17** 96 D4
Ardrossan KA22 74 A6
Ardscalpsie **PA20** 73 J5

Ardshave **IV25** 96 E2
Ardshealach **PH36** 79 H1
Ardshellach **PA34** 79 J6
Ardsley **S71** 51 F2
Ardslignish **PH36** 79 G1
Ardtalla **PA42** 72 C5
Ardtalnaig **PH15** 81 J4
Ardtaraig **PA23** 73 J2
Ardteatle **PA33** 80 C5
Ardtoe **PH36** 86 C7
Ardtornish **PA34** 79 J3
Ardtrostan **PH6** 81 H5
Ardtur **PA38** 80 A3
Arduaine **PA34** 79 K6
Ardullie **IV15** 96 C5
Ardura **PA65** 79 H4
Ardvar **IV27** 102 D5
Ardvasar **IV45** 86 C4
Ardveenish **HS9** 84 C4
Ardveich **FK19** 81 H5
Ardverikie **PH20** 88 C6
Ardvorlich *Arg. & B.* **G83** 80 E6
Ardvorlich *P. & K.* **FK19** 81 H5
Ardwall **DG7** 65 F5
Ardwell *D. & G.* **DG9** 64 B6
Ardwell *Moray* **AB54** 90 B1
Ardwell *S.Ayr.* **KA26** 67 F4
Ardwick **M12** 49 H3
Areley Kings **DY13** 29 H1
Arford **GU35** 12 B3
Argaty **FK16** 81 J7
Argoed **NP12** 18 E2
Argoed Mill **LD1** 27 J2
Argos Hill **TN20** 13 J4
Argrennan House **DG7** 65 H5
Arichamish **PA31** 80 A7
Arichastlich **PA33** 80 D4
Arichonan **PA31** 73 F1
Aridhglas **PA66** 78 E5
Arienskill **PH38** 86 D6
Arileod **PA78** 78 C2
Arinacrinachd **IV54** 94 D6
Arinafad Beg **PA31** 73 F2
Arinagour **PA78** 78 D2
Arinambane **HS8** 84 C2
Arisaig PH39 **86** **C6**
Arivegaig **PH36** 79 H1
Arkendale **HG5** 57 J3
Arkesden **CB11** 33 H5
Arkholme **LA6** 55 J2
Arkle Town **DL11** 62 B6
Arkleby **CA7** 60 C3
Arkleside **DL8** 57 F1
Arkleton **DG13** 69 J4
Arkley **EN5** 23 F2
Arksey **DN5** 51 H2
Arkwright Town **S44** 51 G5
Arlary **KY13** 82 C7
Arle **GL51** 29 J6
Arlecdon **CA26** 60 B5
Arlesey SG15 **32** **E5**
Arleston **TF1** 39 F4
Arley **CW9** 49 F4
Arlingham **GL2** 29 G7
Arlington *Devon* **EX31** 6 E1
Arlington *E.Suss.* **BN26** 13 J6
Arlington *Glos.* **GL7** 20 E1
Arlington Beccott **EX31** 6 E1
Armadale *High.* **KW14** 104 C2
Armadale *High.* **IV45** 86 C4
Armadale *W.Loth.* **EH48** 75 H4
Armathwaite **CA4** 61 G2
Arminghall **NR14** 45 G5
Armitage **WS15** 40 C4
Armitage Bridge **HD4** 50 D1
Armley **LS12** 57 H6
Armscote **CV37** 30 D4
Armshead **ST9** 40 B1
Armston **PE8** 42 D7
Armthorpe **DN3** 51 J2
Arnabost **PA78** 78 D1
Arnaby **LA18** 54 E1
Arncliffe **BD23** 56 E2
Arncliffe Cote **BD23** 56 E2
Arncroach **KY10** 83 G7
Arne **BH20** 9 J6
Arnesby **LE8** 41 J6
Arngask **PH2** 82 C6
Arngibbon **FK8** 74 E1
Arngomery **FK8** 74 E1
Arnhall **DD9** 83 H1
Arnicle **PA29** 73 F7
Arnipol **PH38** 86 D6
Arnisdale **IV40** 86 E3
Arnish **IV40** 94 B7
Arniston Engine **EH23** 76 B4
Arnol **HS2** 101 F3
Arnold *E.Riding* **HU11** 59 H5
Arnold *Notts.* **NG5** 41 H1
Arnprior **FK8** 74 E1
Arnside **LA5** 55 H2
Arowry **SY13** 38 D2
Arrad Foot **LA12** 55 G1
Arradoul **AB56** 98 C4
Arram **HU17** 59 G5
Arran KA27 **73** **H7**
Arras **YO43** 59 F5
Arrat **DD9** 83 H2
Arrathorne **DL8** 62 D7
Arreton **PO30** 11 G6
Arrington **SG8** 33 G3
Arrivain **FK20** 80 D4
Arrochar G83 **80** **E7**
Arrow **B49** 30 B3
Arscaig **IV27** 103 H7
Arscott **SY5** 38 D5
Arthington **LS21** 57 H5
Arthingworth **LE16** 42 A7
Arthog LL39 **37** **F4**
Arthrath **AB41** 91 H1
Arthurstone **PH12** 82 D3
Artrochie **AB41** 91 J1
Aruadh **PA49** 72 A4
Arundel BN18 **12** **D6**
Aryhoulan **PH33** 80 B1
Asby **CA14** 60 B4
Ascog **PA20** 73 K4
Ascot SL5 **22** **C5**
Ascott **CV36** 30 E5
Ascott d'Oyley **OX7** 30 E7
Ascott Earl **OX7** 30 D7
Ascott-under-Wychwood **OX7** 30 E7
Ascreavie **DD8** 82 E2
Asenby **YO7** 57 K2
Asfordby **LE14** 42 A4
Asfordby Hill **LE14** 42 A4
Asgarby *Lincs.* **PE23** 53 G6
Asgarby *Lincs.* **NG34** 42 E1
Ash *Dorset* **DT11** 9 H3
Ash *Kent* **CT3** 15 H2
Ash *Kent* **TN15** 24 C5
Ash *Som.* **TA12** 8 D2
Ash *Surr.* **GU12** 22 B6
Ash Barton **EX20** 6 D5
Ash Bullayne **EX17** 7 F5
Ash Green *Surr.* **GU12** 22 C7
Ash Green *Warks.* **CV7** 41 F7
Ash Magna **SY13** 38 E2
Ash Mill **EX36** 7 F3
Ash Parva **SY13** 38 E2
Ash Priors **TA4** 7 K3
Ash Street **IP7** 34 E4
Ash Thomas **EX16** 7 J4
Ash Vale **GU12** 22 B6
Ashampstead **RG8** 21 J4
Ashbocking **IP6** 35 F3
Ashbourne DE6 **40** **D1**
Ashbrittle **TA21** 7 J3
Ashburnham Place **TN33** 13 K5
Ashburton **TQ13** 5 H4
Ashbury *Devon* **EX20** 6 D6
Ashbury *Oxon.* **SN6** 21 F3
Ashby **DN16** 52 B2
Ashby by Partney **PE23** 53 H6
Ashby cum Fenby **DN37** 53 F2
Ashby de la Launde **LN4** 52 D7
Ashby de la Zouch LE65 **41** **F4**
Ashby Dell **NR32** 45 J6
Ashby Folville **LE14** 42 A4
Ashby Hill **DN37** 53 F2
Ashby Magna **LE17** 41 H6
Ashby Parva **LE17** 41 H7
Ashby Puerorum **LN9** 53 G5
Ashby St. Ledgers **CV23** 31 G2
Ashby St. Mary **NR14** 45 H5
Ashchurch **GL20** 29 J5
Ashcombe *Devon* **EX7** 5 K3
Ashcombe *N.Som.* **BS22** 19 G5
Ashcott **TA7** 8 D1
Ashdon **CB10** 33 J4
Ashe **RG25** 21 J7
Asheldham **CM0** 25 F1
Ashen **CO10** 34 B4
Ashenden **TN30** 14 D4
Ashendon **HP18** 31 J7
Ashens **PA29** 73 G3
Ashfield *Arg. & B.* **PA31** 73 F2
Ashfield *Here.* **HR9** 28 E6
Ashfield *Stir.* **FK15** 81 J7
Ashfield *Suff.* **IP14** 35 G2
Ashfield Green *Suff.* **IP21** 35 G1
Ashfield Green *Suff.* **CB8** 34 B3
Ashfold Crossways **RH13** 13 F4
Ashford *Devon* **TQ7** 5 G6
Ashford *Devon* **EX31** 6 D2
Ashford *Hants.* **SP6** 10 C3
Ashford *Kent* TN23 **15** **F3**
Ashford *Surr.* TW15 **22** **D4**
Ashford Bowdler **SY8** 28 E1
Ashford Carbonel **SY8** 28 E1
Ashford Hill **RG19** 21 J5
Ashford in the Water **DE45** 50 D5
Ashgill **ML9** 75 F5
Ashiestiel **TD1** 76 C7
Ashill *Devon* **EX15** 7 J4
Ashill *Norf.* **IP25** 44 C5
Ashill *Som.* **TA19** 8 C3
Ashingdon **SS4** 24 E2
Ashington *Northumb.* NE63 **71** **H5**
Ashington *Som.* **BA22** 8 E2
Ashington *W.Suss.* **RH20** 12 E5
Ashkirk **TD7** 69 K1
Ashlett **SO45** 11 F4
Ashleworth **GL19** 29 H6
Ashleworth Quay **GL19** 29 H6
Ashley *Cambs.* **CB8** 33 K2
Ashley *Ches.* **WA15** 49 G4
Ashley *Devon* **EX18** 6 E4
Ashley *Glos.* **GL8** 20 C2
Ashley *Hants.* **SO20** 10 E1
Ashley *Hants.* **BH25** 10 D5
Ashley *Kent* **CT15** 15 J3
Ashley *Northants.* **LE16** 42 A6
Ashley *Staffs.* **TF9** 39 G2
Ashley *Wilts.* **SN13** 20 B5
Ashley Down **BS7** 19 J4
Ashley Green **HP5** 22 C1
Ashley Heath *Dorset* **BH24** 10 C4
Ashley Heath *Staffs.* **TF9** 39 G2
Ashmanhaugh **NR12** 45 H3
Ashmansworth **RG20** 21 H6
Ashmansworthy **EX39** 6 B4
Ashmore *Dorset* **SP5** 9 J3
Ashmore *P. & K.* **PH10** 82 C2
Ashmore Green **RG18** 21 J5
Ashorne **CV35** 30 E3
Ashover **S45** 51 F6
Ashover Hay **S45** 51 F6
Ashow **CV8** 30 E1
Ashperton **HR8** 29 F4
Ashprington **TQ9** 5 J5
Ashreigney **EX18** 6 E4
Ashtead KT21 **22** **E6**
Ashton *Ches.* **CH3** 48 E6
Ashton *Cornw.* **TR13** 2 D6
Ashton *Cornw.* **PL17** 4 D4
Ashton *Hants.* **SO32** 11 G3
Ashton *Here.* **HR6** 28 E2
Ashton *Inclyde* **PA19** 74 A3
Ashton *Northants.* **PE8** 42 D7
Ashton *Northants.* **NN7** 31 J4
Ashton *Peter.* **PE9** 42 E5
Ashton Common **BA14** 20 B6
Ashton Keynes **SN6** 20 D2
Ashton under Hill **WR11** 29 J5
Ashton upon Mersey **M33** 49 G3
Ashton-in-Makerfield **WN4** 48 E3
Ashton-under-Lyne OL7 **49** **J3**
Ashurst *Hants.* **SO40** 10 E3
Ashurst *Kent* **TN3** 13 J3
Ashurst *W.Suss.* **BN44** 12 E5
Ashurst Bridge **SO40** 10 E3
Ashurstwood **RH18** 13 H3
Ashwater **EX21** 6 B6
Ashwell *Herts.* **SG7** 33 F5
Ashwell *Rut.* **LE15** 42 B4
Ashwell End **SG7** 33 F4
Ashwellthorpe **NR16** 45 F6
Ashwick **BA3** 19 K7
Ashwicken **PE32** 44 B4
Ashybank **TD9** 70 A2
Askam in Furness LA16 **55** **F2**
Askern **DN6** 51 H1
Askernish (Aisgernis) **HS8** 84 C2
Askerswell **DT2** 8 E5
Askett **HP27** 22 B1
Askham *Cumb.* **CA10** 61 G4
Askham *Notts.* **NG22** 51 K5
Askham Bryan **YO23** 58 B5
Askham Richard **YO23** 58 B5
Asknish **PA31** 73 H1
Askrigg **DL8** 62 A7
Askwith **LS21** 57 G5
Aslackby **NG34** 42 D2
Aslacton **NR15** 45 F6
Aslockton **NG13** 42 A1
Asloun **AB33** 90 D3
Aspall **IP14** 35 F2
Aspatria **CA7** 60 C2
Aspenden **SG9** 33 G6
Asperton **PE20** 43 F2
Aspley Guise **MK17** 32 C5
Aspley Heath **MK17** 32 C5
Aspull **WN2** 49 F2
Asselby **DN14** 58 D7
Asserby **LN13** 53 H5
Assington **CO10** 34 D5
Assington Green **CO10** 34 B3
Astbury **CW12** 49 H6
Astcote **NN12** 31 H3
Asterby **LN11** 53 F5
Asterley **SY5** 38 C5
Asterton **SY7** 38 D6
Asthall **OX18** 30 D7
Asthall Leigh **OX29** 30 E7
Astle **SK10** 49 H5
Astley *Gt.Man.* **M29** 49 G2
Astley *Shrop.* **SY4** 38 E4
Astley *Warks.* **CV10** 41 F7
Astley *Worcs.* **DY13** 29 G2
Astley Abbotts **WV16** 39 G6
Astley Bridge **BL1** 49 G1
Astley Cross **DY13** 29 H2
Astley Green **M29** 49 G3
Astley Lodge **SY4** 38 E4
Aston *Ches.* **CW5** 39 F1
Aston *Ches.* **WA7** 48 E5
Aston *Derbys.* **S33** 50 D4
Aston *Derbys.* **DE6** 40 D2
Aston *Flints.* **CH5** 48 C6
Aston *Here.* **SY8** 28 D1
Aston *Here.* **HR6** 28 D2
Aston *Herts.* **SG2** 33 F6
Aston *Oxon.* **OX18** 21 G1
Aston *S.Yorks.* **S26** 51 G4
Aston *Shrop.* **SY4** 38 E3
Aston *Shrop.* **WV5** 40 A6
Aston *Staffs.* **TF9** 39 G1
Aston *Tel. & W.* **TF6** 39 F5
Aston *W'ham* **RG9** 22 A3
Aston *W.Mid.* **B6** 40 C7
Aston Abbotts **HP22** 32 B6
Aston Botterell **WV16** 39 F7
Aston Cantlow **B95** 30 C3
Aston Clinton **HP22** 32 B7
Aston Crews **HR9** 29 F6
Aston Cross **GL20** 29 J5
Aston End **SG2** 33 F6
Aston Eyre **WV16** 39 F6
Aston Fields **B60** 29 J2
Aston Flamville **LE10** 41 G6
Aston Heath **WA7** 48 E5
Aston Ingham **HR9** 29 F6
Aston juxta Mondrum **CW5** 49 F7
Aston le Walls **NN11** 31 F3
Aston Magna **GL56** 30 C5
Aston Munslow **SY7** 38 E7
Aston on Carrant **GL20** 29 J5
Aston on Clun **SY7** 38 C7
Aston Pigott **SY5** 38 C5
Aston Rogers **SY5** 38 C5
Aston Rowant **OX49** 22 A2
Aston Sandford **HP17** 22 A1
Aston Somerville **WR12** 30 B5
Aston Subedge **GL55** 30 C4
Aston Tirrold **OX11** 21 J3
Aston Upthorpe **OX11** 21 J3
Aston-by-Stone **ST15** 40 B2
Aston-on-Trent **DE72** 41 G3
Astwick **SG5** 33 F5
Astwood **MK16** 32 C4
Astwood Bank **B96** 30 B2
Aswarby **NG34** 42 D1
Aswardby **PE23** 53 G5
Aswick Grange **PE12** 43 G4
Atch Lench **WR11** 30 B3
Atcham **SY5** 38 E5
Ath Linne **HS2** 100 D6
Athelhampton **DT2** 9 G5
Athelington **IP21** 35 G1
Athelney **TA7** 8 C2
Athelstaneford **EH39** 76 D3
Atherington *Devon* **EX37** 6 D3
Atherington *W.Suss.* **BN17** 12 D6
Athersley North **S71** 51 F2
Atherstone CV9 **41** **F6**
Atherstone on Stour **CV37** 30 D3
Atherton **M46** 49 F2
Atlow **DE6** 40 E1
Attadale **IV54** 87 F1
Attenborough **NG9** 41 H2
Atterby **LN8** 52 C3
Attercliffe **S9** 51 F4
Atterley **TF13** 39 F6
Atterton **CV13** 41 F6
Attleborough *Norf.* NR17 **44** **E6**
Attleborough *Warks.* **CV11** 41 F6
Attlebridge **NR9** 45 F4
Attleton Green **CB8** 34 B3
Atwick **YO25** 59 H4
Atworth **SN12** 20 B5
Auberrow **HR4** 28 D4
Aubourn **LN5** 52 C6
Auch **PA36** 80 E4
Auchairne **KA26** 67 F5
Auchallater **AB35** 89 J6
Auchameanach **PA29** 73 G5
Auchamore **KA27** 73 G6
Aucharnie **AB54** 98 E6
Aucharrigill **IV27** 96 B1
Auchattie **AB31** 90 E5
Auchavan **PH11** 82 C1
Auchbraad **PA30** 73 G2
Auchbreck **AB37** 89 K2
Auchenback **G78** 74 D5
Auchenblae **AB30** 91 F7
Auchenbothie **PA13** 74 B3
Auchenbrack **DG3** 68 C4
Auchenbreck **PA22** 73 J2
Auchencairn **DG7** 65 H5
Auchencrow **TD14** 77 G4
Auchendinny **EH26** 76 A4
Auchendolly **DG7** 65 H4
Auchenfoyle **PA13** 74 B3
Auchengillan **G63** 74 D2
Auchengray **ML11** 75 H5
Auchenhalrig **IV32** 98 B4
Auchenheath **ML11** 75 G6
Auchenhessnane **DG3** 68 D4
Auchenlochan **PA21** 73 H3
Auchenmalg **DG8** 64 C5
Auchenrivock **DG14** 69 J5
Auchentiber **KA13** 74 B6
Auchenvennel **G84** 74 A2
Auchessan **FK20** 81 F5
Auchgourish **PH24** 89 G3
Auchinafaud **PA29** 73 F5
Auchincruive **KA6** 67 H1
Auchindarrach **PA31** 73 G2
Auchindarroch **PA38** 80 B2
Auchindrain **PA32** 80 B7
Auchindrean **IV23** 95 H3
Auchininna **AB53** 98 E6
Auchinleck **KA18** 67 K1
Auchinloch **G66** 74 E3
Auchinner **PH6** 81 H6
Auchinroath **AB38** 97 K6
Auchintoul *Aber.* **AB33** 90 D3
Auchintoul *Aber.* **AB54** 98 E5
Auchintoul *High.* **IV27** 96 C2
Auchiries **AB42** 91 J1
Auchleven **AB52** 90 E2
Auchlochan **ML11** 75 G7
Auchlunachan **IV23** 95 H3
Auchlunies **AB12** 91 G5
Auchlunkart **AB55** 98 B6
Auchlyne **FK21** 81 G5
Auchmacoy **AB41** 91 H1
Auchmair **AB54** 90 B2
Auchmantle **DG8** 64 B4
Auchmithie **DD11** 83 H3
Auchmuirbridge **KY6** 82 D7
Auchmull **DD9** 90 D7
Auchnabony **DG6** 65 H6
Auchnabreac **PA32** 80 B7
Auchnacloich **PH8** 81 K4
Auchnacraig **PA64** 79 J4
Auchnacree **DD8** 83 F1
Auchnafree **PH8** 81 K4
Auchnagallin **PH26** 89 H1
Auchnagatt **AB41** 99 H6
Auchnaha **PA21** 73 H2
Auchnangoul **PA32** 80 B7
Aucholzie **AB35** 90 B5
Auchorrie **AB51** 90 E4
Auchrannie **PH11** 82 D2
Auchraw **FK19** 81 G5
Auchreoch **FK20** 80 E5
Auchronie **DD9** 90 C6
Auchterarder PH3 **82** **A6**
Auchtercairn **IV21** 94 E4
Auchterderran **KY5** 76 A1
Auchterhouse **DD3** 82 E4
Auchtermuchty **KY14** 82 D6
Auchterneed **IV14** 96 B6
Auchtertool **KY2** 76 A1
Auchtertyre *Angus* **PH12** 82 D3
Auchtertyre *High.* **IV40** 86 E2
Auchtertyre *Moray* **IV30** 97 J6
Auchtertyre *Stir.* **FK20** 80 E5
Auchtubh **FK19** 81 G5
Auckengill **KW1** 105 J2
Auckley **DN9** 51 J2
Audenshaw **M34** 49 J3
Audlem **CW3** 39 F1
Audley **ST7** 49 G7
Audley End *Essex* **CB11** 33 J5
Audley End *Essex* **CO9** 34 C5
Audley End *Suff.* **IP29** 34 C3
Audmore **ST20** 40 A3
Auds **AB45** 98 E4
Aughton *E.Riding* **YO42** 58 D6
Aughton *Lancs.* **L39** 48 C2
Aughton *Lancs.* **LA2** 55 J3
Aughton *S.Yorks.* **S26** 51 G4
Aughton *Wilts.* **SN8** 21 F6
Aughton Park **L39** 48 D2
Auldearn **IV12** 97 G6
Aulden **HR6** 28 D3
Auldgirth **DG2** 68 E5
Auldhame **EH39** 76 D2
Auldhouse **G75** 74 E5
Aulich **PH17** 81 H2
Ault a'chruinn **IV40** 87 F2
Ault Hucknall **S44** 51 G6
Aultanrynie **IV27** 103 F5
Aultbea **IV22** 94 E3
Aultgrishan **IV21** 94 D3
Aultguish Inn **IV23** 95 K4
Aultibea **KW7** 105 F6
Aultiphurst **KW14** 104 D2
Aultmore **AB55** 98 C5
Ault-na-goire **IV2** 88 C2
Aultnamain Inn **IV19** 96 D3
Aultnapaddock **AB55** 98 B6
Aulton **AB52** 90 E2
Aultvaich **IV4** 96 C7
Aultvoulin **PH41** 86 D4
Aunby **PE9** 42 D4
Aundorach **PH25** 89 G3
Aunk **EX15** 7 J5
Aunsby **NG34** 42 D2
Auquhorthies **AB51** 91 G2
Aust **BS35** 19 J3
Austerfield **DN10** 51 J3
Austrey **CV9** 40 E5
Austwick **LA2** 56 C3
Authorpe **LN11** 53 H4
Authorpe Row **PE24** 53 J5
Avebury **SN8** 20 E4
Avebury Trusloe **SN8** 20 D5
Aveley **RM15** 23 J3
Avening **GL8** 20 B2
Averham **NG23** 51 K7
Avery Hill **SE9** 23 H4
Aveton Gifford **TQ7** 5 G6
Avielochan **PH22** 89 G3
Aviemore PH22 **89** **F3**
Avington *Hants.* **SO21** 11 G1
Avington *W.Berks.* **RG17** 21 G5
Avoch IV9 **96** **D6**
Avon **BH23** 10 C5
Avon Dassett **CV47** 31 F3
Avonbridge **FK1** 75 H3
Avoncliff **BA15** 20 B6
Avonmouth **BS11** 19 J4
Avonwick **TQ10** 5 H5
Awbridge **SO51** 10 E2
Awhirk **DG9** 64 A5
Awkley **BS35** 19 J3
Awliscombe **EX14** 7 K5
Awre **GL14** 20 A1
Awsworth **NG16** 41 G1
Axbridge BS26 **19** **H6**
Axford *Hants.* **RG25** 21 K7
Axford *Wilts.* **SN8** 21 F4
Axminster EX13 **8** **B5**
Axmouth **EX12** 8 B5
Axton **CH8** 47 K4
Axtown **PL20** 5 F4
Aycliffe **DL5** 62 D4
Aydon **NE45** 71 F7
Aylburton **GL15** 19 K1
Ayle **CA9** 61 J2
Aylesbeare **EX5** 7 J6
Aylesbury HP20 **32** **B7**
Aylesby **DN37** 53 F2
Aylesford ME20 **14** **C2**
Aylesham **CT3** 15 H2
Aylestone **LE2** 41 H5
Aylmerton **NR11** 45 F2
Aylsham **NR11** 45 F3
Aylton **HR8** 29 F5
Aymestrey **HR6** 28 D2
Aynho **OX17** 31 G5
Ayot Green **AL6** 33 F7
Ayot St. Lawrence **AL6** 32 E7
Ayot St. Peter **AL6** 33 F7
Ayr KA7 **67** **H1**
Aysgarth **DL8** 57 F1
Ayshford **EX16** 7 J4
Ayside **LA11** 55 G1
Ayston **LE15** 42 B5
Aythorpe Roding **CM6** 33 J7
Ayton *P. & K.* **PH2** 82 C6
Ayton *Sc.Bord.* **TD14** 77 H4
Aywick **ZE2** 107 P4
Azerley **HG4** 57 H2

B

Babbacombe **TQ1** 5 K4
Babbinswood **SY11** 38 C2
Babb's Green **SG12** 33 G7
Babcary **TA11** 8 E2

Babel SA20 27 H5
Babell CH8 47 K5
Babeny TQ13 5 G3
Bablock Hythe OX29 21 H1
Babraham CB2 33 J3
Babworth DN22 51 J4
Baby's Hill AB37 89 K1
Bac HS2 101 G3
Bachau LL71 46 C4
Back of Keppoch PH39 86 C6
Back Street CB8 34 B3
Backaland KW17 106 E4
Backaskaill KW17 106 D2
Backbarrow LA12 55 G1
Backburn AB54 90 D1
Backe SA33 17 F4
Backfolds AB42 99 J5
Backford CH2 48 D5
Backhill AB53 91 F1
Backhill of Clackriach AB42 99 H6
Backhill of Trustach AB31 90 E5
Backies High. KW10 97 F1
Backies Moray AB56 98 D5
Backlass KW1 105 H3
Backside AB54 90 C1
Backwell BS48 19 H5
Backworth NE23 71 H6
Bacon End CM6 33 J7
Baconend Green CM6 33 J7
Baconsthorpe NR25 45 F2
Bacton Here. HR2 28 C5
Bacton Norf. NR12 45 H2
Bacton Suff. IP14 34 E2
Bacton Green IP14 34 E2
Bacup OL13 56 D7
Badachro IV21 94 D4
Badanloch Lodge KW11 104 C5
Badavanich IV22 95 H6
Badbea KW7 105 F7
Badbury SN4 20 E3
Badbury Wick SN4 20 E3
Badby NN11 31 G3
Badcall High. IV27 102 D4
Badcall High. IV27 102 E3
Badcaul IV23 95 G2
Baddeley Green ST2 49 J7
Badden PA31 73 G2
Baddesley Clinton B93 30 C1
Baddesley Ensor CV9 40 E6
Baddidarach IV27 102 C6
Badenscoth AB51 91 F1
Badenyon AB36 90 B3
Badgall PL15 4 C2
Badger WV6 39 G6
Badgerbank SK11 49 H5
Badgers Mount TN14 23 H5
Badgeworth GL51 29 J7
Badgworth BS26 19 G6
Badicaul IV40 86 D2
Badingham IP13 35 H2
Badintagairt IV27 103 G7
Badlesmere ME13 15 F2
Badley IP6 34 E3
Badlipster KW1 105 H4
Badluarach IV23 95 F2
Badminton GL9 20 B3
Badnaban IV27 102 C6
Badnabay IV27 102 E4
Badnafrave AB37 89 K3
Badnagie KW6 105 G5
Badnambiast PH18 88 E7
Badninish IV25 96 E2
Badrallach IV23 95 G2
Badsey WR11 30 B4
Badshot Lea GU9 22 B7
Badsworth WF9 51 G1
Badwell Ash IP31 34 D2
Badworthy TQ10 5 G4
Badyo PH16 82 A1
Bae Cinmel (Kinmel Bay) LL18 47 H4
Bae Colwyn (Colwyn Bay) LL29 47 G5
Bae Penrhyn (Penrhyn Bay) LL30 47 G4
Bag Enderby PE23 53 G5
Bagber DT10 9 G3
Bagby YO7 57 K1
Bagendon GL7 20 D1
Bagginswood DY14 39 F7
Baggrave Hall LE7 41 J5
Baggrow CA7 60 C2
Bàgh a'Chaisteil (Castlebay) HS9 84 B5
Bàgh Mòr HS6 92 D6
Baghasdal HS8 84 C3
Bagillt CH6 48 B5
Baginton CV8 30 E1
Baglan SA12 18 A2
Bagley Shrop. SY12 38 D3
Bagley Som. BS28 19 H7
Bagmore RG25 21 K7
Bagnall ST9 49 J7
Bagnor RG20 21 H5
Bagpath GL8 20 B2
Bagshot Surr. GU19 22 C5
Bagshot Wilts. RG17 21 G5
Bagstone GL12 19 K3
Bagthorpe Norf. PE31 44 B2
Bagthorpe Notts. NG16 51 G7
Baguley M23 49 H4
Bagworth LE67 41 G5
Bagwyllydiart HR2 28 D6
Baildon BD17 57 G6
Baile Ailein (Balallan) HS2 100 E5
Baile a'Mhanaich (Balivanich) HS7 92 C6
Baile an Truiseil HS2 101 F2
Baile Boidheach PA31 73 F3
Baile Gharbhaidh HS8 92 C7
Baile Glas HS6 92 D6
Baile Lion (Balelone) HS6 92 C4
Baile Mhartainn HS6 92 C4
Baile Mhic Phail HS6 92 D4
Baile Mòr Arg. & B. PA76 78 D5
Baile Mòr (Balemore) W.Isles HS6 92 C5
Baile nan Cailleach HS7 92 C6
Baile Raghaill HS6 92 C5
Bailebeag IV2 88 C3
Baileguish PH21 89 F5
Baile-na-Cille HS6 92 D3
Bailetonach PH36 86 C7
Bailiesward AB54 90 C1
Bailiff Bridge HD6 57 G7
Baillieston G69 74 E4
Bainbridge DL8 62 A7
Bainsford FK2 75 G2
Bainshole AB54 90 E1
Bainton E.Riding YO25 59 F4
Bainton Oxon. OX27 31 G6
Bainton Peter. PE9 42 D5
Bairnkine TD8 70 B2
Bakebare AB55 90 B1
Baker Street RM16 24 C3
Baker's End SG12 33 G7
Bakewell DE45 50 E6
Bala (Y Bala) LL23 37 J2
Balachuirn IV40 94 B7
Balado KY13 82 B7
Balafark G63 74 E1
Balaldie IV20 97 F4
Balallan (Baile Ailein) HS2 100 E5
Balavil PH21 88 E4
Balbeg High. IV63 88 B1
Balbeg High. IV63 88 B2
Balbeggie PH2 82 C5
Balbirnie KY7 82 D7
Balbithan AB51 91 F3
Balblair High. IV7 96 E5
Balblair High. IV24 96 C2
Balblair High. IV19 96 E3
Balby DN4 51 H2
Balcharn IV27 96 C1
Balcherry IV19 97 F3
Balchers AB45 99 F5
Balchladich IV27 102 C5
Balchraggan High. IV5 96 C7
Balchraggan High. IV3 88 C1
Balchrick IV27 102 D3
Balcombe RH17 13 G3
Balcurvie KY8 82 E7
Baldernock G62 74 D3
Baldersby YO7 57 J2
Baldersby St. James YO7 57 J2
Balderstone Gt.Man. OL16 49 J1
Balderstone Lancs. BB2 56 B6
Balderton Ches. CH4 48 C6
Balderton Notts. NG24 52 B7
Baldhu TR3 2 E4
Baldinnie KY15 83 F6
Baldock SG7 33 F5
Baldon Row OX44 21 J1
Baldovan DD3 82 E4
Baldovie Angus DD8 82 E2
Baldovie Dundee DD5 83 F4
Baldrine IM4 54 D5
Baldslow TN37 14 C6
Baldwin IM4 54 C5
Baldwinholme CA5 60 E1
Baldwin's Gate ST5 39 G1
Baldwins Hill RH19 13 G3
Bale NR21 44 E2
Balelone (Baile Lion) HS6 92 C4
Balemartine PA77 78 A3
Balemore (Baile Mòr) HS6 92 C5
Balendoch PH12 82 D3
Balephuil PA77 78 A3
Balerno EH14 75 K4
Balernock G84 74 A2
Baleromindubh PA61 72 B1
Balerominmore PA61 72 B1
Baleshare (Bhaleshear) HS6 92 C5
Balevulin PA69 79 F5
Balfield DD9 83 G1
Balfour Aber. AB34 90 D5
Balfour Ork. KW17 106 D6
Balfron G63 74 D2
Balfron Station G63 74 D2
Balgonar KY12 75 J1
Balgove AB51 91 G1
Balgowan D. & G. DG9 64 B6
Balgowan High. PH20 88 D5
Balgown IV51 93 J5
Balgreen AB45 99 F5
Balgreggan DG9 64 A5
Balgy IV54 94 E6
Balhaldie FK15 81 K7
Balhalgardy AB51 91 F2
Balham SW12 23 F4
Balhary PH11 82 D3
Balhelvie KY14 82 E5
Balhousie KY8 83 F7
Baliasta ZE2 107 Q2
Baligill KW14 104 D2
Baligrundle PA34 79 K3
Balindore PA35 80 A4
Balintore Angus DD8 82 D2
Balintore High. IV20 97 F4
Balintraid IV18 96 E4
Balintyre PH15 81 H3
Balivanich (Baile a'Mhanaich) HS7 92 C6
Balkeerie DD8 82 E3
Balkholme DN14 58 D7
Balkissock KA26 67 F5
Ball SY10 38 C3
Ball Haye Green ST13 49 J7
Ball Hill RG20 21 H5
Balla HS8 84 C3
Ballabeg IM9 54 B6
Ballacannell IM4 54 D5
Ballacarnane Beg IM6 54 B5
Ballachulish PH49 80 B2
Balladoole IM9 54 B7
Ballafesson IM9 54 B6
Ballagyr IM5 54 B5
Ballajora IM7 54 D4
Ballakilpheric IM9 54 B6
Ballamodha IM9 54 B6
Ballantrae KA26 66 E5
Ballards Gore SS4 25 F2
Ballasalla I.o.M. IM9 54 B6
Ballasalla I.o.M. IM7 54 C4
Ballater AB35 90 B5
Ballaterach AB34 90 C5
Ballaugh IM7 54 C4
Ballaveare IM4 54 C6
Ballchraggan IV18 96 E4
Ballechin PH9 82 A2
Balleich FK8 81 G7
Ballencrieff EH32 76 C3
Ballidon DE6 50 E7
Balliekine KA27 73 G6
Balliemeanoch PA27 80 C7
Balliemore Arg. & B. PA27 73 K1
Balliemore Arg. & B. PA34 79 K5
Ballig IM4 54 B5
Ballimeanoch PA33 80 B6
Ballimore Arg. & B. PA21 73 H2
Ballimore Stir. FK19 81 G6
Ballinaby PA44 72 A4
Ballindean PH14 82 D5
Ballingdon CO10 34 C4
Ballinger Common HP16 22 C1
Ballingham HR2 28 E5
Ballingry KY5 75 K1
Ballinlick PH8 82 A3
Ballinluig P. & K. PH9 82 A2
Ballinluig P. & K. PH10 82 B2
Ballintuim PH10 82 C2
Balloch Angus DD8 82 E2
Balloch High. IV2 96 E7
Balloch N.Lan. G68 75 F3
Balloch W.Dun. G83 74 B2
Ballochan AB31 90 D5
Ballochandrain PA22 73 H2
Ballochford AB54 90 B1
Ballochgair PA28 66 B1
Ballochmartin KA28 73 K5
Ballochmorrie KA26 67 G5
Ballochmyle KA5 67 K1
Ballochroy PA29 73 F5
Ballogie AB34 90 D5
Balls Cross GU28 12 C4
Balls Green Essex CO7 34 E6
Ball's Green Glos. GL6 20 B2
Balls Hill B71 40 B6
Ballyaurgan PA31 73 F3
Ballygown PA73 79 F3
Ballygrant PA45 72 B4
Ballyhaugh PA78 78 C2
Ballymeanoch PA31 73 G1
Ballymichael KA27 73 H7
Balmacara IV40 86 E2
Balmaclellan DG7 65 G3
Balmacneil PH8 82 A2
Balmadies DD8 83 G3
Balmae DG6 65 G6
Balmaha G63 74 C1
Balmalcolm KY15 82 E7
Balmaqueen IV51 93 K4
Balmeanach Arg. & B. PA65 79 H3
Balmeanach Arg. & B. PA68 79 F4
Balmedie AB23 91 H3
Balmer Heath SY12 38 D2
Balmerino DD6 82 E5
Balmerlawn SO42 10 E4
Balminnoch DG8 64 C4
Balmore E.Dun. G64 74 E3
Balmore High. IV12 97 F7
Balmore High. IV4 87 K1
Balmore High. IV55 93 H7
Balmore P. & K. PH16 81 J2
Balmullo KY16 83 F5
Balmungie IV10 96 E6
Balmyle PH10 82 B2
Balnaboth DD8 82 E1
Balnabruaich IV19 96 E4
Balnacra IV54 95 F7
Balnafoich IV2 88 D1
Balnagall IV20 97 F3
Balnagown Castle IV18 96 E4
Balnaguard PH9 82 A2
Balnaguisich IV18 96 D4
Balnahard Arg. & B. PA61 72 C1
Balnahard Arg. & B. PA68 79 F4
Balnain IV63 88 B1
Balnakeil IV27 103 F2
Balnaknock IV51 93 K5
Balnamoon DD9 83 G1
Balnapaling IV19 96 E5
Balnespick PH21 89 F4
Balquhidder FK19 81 G5
Balsall CV7 30 D1
Balsall Common CV7 30 D1
Balsall Heath B12 40 C7
Balscote OX15 30 E4
Balsham CB1 33 J3
Baltasound ZE2 107 Q2
Balterley CW2 49 G7
Balterley Heath CW2 49 G7
Baltersan DG8 64 E4
Balthangie AB53 99 G5
Balthayock PH2 82 C5
Baltonsborough BA6 8 E1
Baluachraig PA31 73 G1
Balulive PA45 72 C4
Balure Arg. & B. PA35 80 B4
Balure Arg. & B. PA37 79 K4
Balvaird IV6 96 C6
Balvarran PH10 82 B1
Balvicar PA34 79 J6
Balvraid High. IV40 86 E3
Balvraid High. IV13 89 F1
Bamber Bridge PR5 55 J7
Bamber's Green CM22 33 J6
Bamburgh NE69 77 K7
Bamff PH11 82 D2
Bamford Derbys. S33 50 E4
Bamford Gt.Man. OL11 49 H1
Bampton Cumb. CA10 61 G5
Bampton Devon EX16 7 H3
Bampton Oxon. OX18 21 G1
Bampton Grange CA10 61 G5
Banavie PH33 87 H7
Banbury OX16 31 F4
Bancffosfelen SA15 17 H4
Banchor IV12 97 G7
Banchory AB31 91 F5
Banchory-Devenick AB12 91 H4
Bancycapel SA32 17 H4
Bancyfelin SA33 17 G4
Bancyffordd SA44 17 H2
Bandon KY7 82 D7
Bandrake Head LA12 55 G1
Banff AB45 98 E4
Bangor LL57 46 D5
Bangor-is-y-coed LL13 38 C1
Bangor's Green L39 48 C2
Banham NR16 44 E7
Bank SO43 10 D4
Bank End LA20 54 E1
Bank Newton BD23 56 E4
Bank Street WR15 29 F2
Bank Top Lancs. WN8 48 E2
Bank Top W.Yorks. HX3 57 G7
Bankend DG1 69 F7
Bankfoot PH1 82 B4
Bankglen KA18 67 K2
Bankhead Aber. AB33 90 E3
Bankhead Aber. AB51 90 E4
Bankhead Aberdeen AB21 91 G3
Bankhead D. & G. DG6 65 H6
Bankland TA7 8 C2
Banknock FK4 75 F3
Banks Cumb. CA8 70 A7
Banks Lancs. PR9 55 G7
Bankshill DG11 69 G5
Banningham NR11 45 G3
Bannister Green CM6 33 K6
Bannockburn FK7 75 G1
Banstead SM7 23 F6
Bantam Grove LS27 57 H7
Bantham TQ7 5 G6
Banton G65 75 F3
Banwell BS29 19 G6
Banwen Pyrddin SA10 18 B1
Banyard's Green IP13 35 H1
Bapchild ME9 25 F5
Baptiston G63 74 D2
Bapton BA12 9 J1
Bar End SO23 11 F2
Bar Hill CB3 33 G2
Barabhas (Barvas) HS2 101 F3
Barachander PA35 80 B5
Barassie KA10 74 B7
Barbaraville IV18 96 E4
Barber Booth S33 50 D4
Barber Green LA11 55 G1
Barber's Moor PR26 48 D1
Barbon LA6 56 B1
Barbridge CW5 49 F7
Barbrook EX35 7 F1
Barby CV23 31 G1
Barcaldine PA37 80 A3
Barcaple DG7 65 G5
Barcheston CV36 30 D5
Barclose CA6 69 K7
Barcombe BN8 13 H5
Barcombe Cross BN8 13 H5
Barden DL8 62 C7
Barden Park TN9 23 J7
Bardennoch DG7 67 K4
Bardfield End Green CM6 33 K5
Bardfield Saling CM7 33 K6
Bardister ZE2 107 M5
Bardney LN3 52 E6
Bardon Leics. LE67 41 G4
Bardon Moray IV30 97 K6
Bardon Mill NE47 70 C7
Bardowie G62 74 D3
Bardsea LA12 55 F2
Bardsey LS17 57 J5
Bardsey Island (Ynys Enlli) LL53 36 A3
Bardwell IP31 34 D1
Bare LA4 55 H3
Barewood HR6 28 C3
Barfad PA29 73 G4
Barford Norf. NR9 45 F5
Barford Warks. CV35 30 D2
Barford St. John OX15 31 F5
Barford St. Martin SP3 10 B1
Barford St. Michael OX15 31 F5
Barfrestone CT15 15 H2
Bargaly DG8 64 E4
Bargany Mains KA26 67 G3
Bargeddie G69 74 E4
Bargoed CF81 18 E2
Bargrennan DG8 64 D3
Barham Cambs. PE28 32 E1
Barham Kent CT4 15 H2
Barham Suff. IP6 35 F3
Barharrow DG7 65 G5
Barholm PE9 42 D4
Barholm Mains DG8 64 E5
Barkby LE7 41 J5
Barkby Thorpe LE7 41 J5
Barkers Green SY4 38 E3
Barkestone-le-Vale NG13 42 A2
Barkham RG41 22 A5
Barking Gt.Lon. IG11 23 H3
Barking Suff. IP6 34 E3
Barking Tye IP6 34 E3
Barkisland HX4 57 F7
Barkston NG32 42 C1
Barkston Ash LS24 57 K6
Barkway SG8 33 G5
Barlae DG8 64 C4
Barland LD8 28 B2
Barlaston ST12 40 A2
Barlavington GU28 12 C5
Barlborough S43 51 G5
Barlby YO8 58 C6
Barlestone CV13 41 G5
Barley Herts. SG8 33 G5
Barley Lancs. BB12 56 D5
Barley Green IP21 35 G1
Barleycroft End SG9 33 H6
Barleyhill NE44 62 B1
Barleythorpe LE15 42 B5
Barling SS3 25 F3
Barlings LN3 52 D5
Barlow Derbys. S18 51 F5
Barlow N.Yorks. YO8 58 C7
Barlow T. & W. NE21 71 G7
Barmby Moor YO42 58 D5
Barmby on the Marsh DN14 58 C7
Barmer PE31 44 C2
Barmolloch PA31 73 G1
Barmoor Lane End TD15 77 J7
Barmouth (Abermaw) LL42 37 F4
Barmpton DL1 62 E5
Barmston YO25 59 H4
Barnaby Green NR34 35 J1
Barnacabber PA23 73 K2
Barnacarry PA27 73 H1
Barnack PE9 42 D5
Barnacle CV7 41 F7
Barnamuc PA38 80 B3
Barnard Castle DL12 62 B5
Barnard Gate OX29 31 F7
Barnardiston CB9 34 B4
Barnard's Green WR14 29 G4
Barnbarroch D. & G. DG8 64 D5
Barnbarroch D. & G. DG5 65 J5
Barnburgh DN5 51 G2
Barnby NR34 45 J7
Barnby Dun DN3 51 J2
Barnby in the Willows NG24 52 B7
Barnby Moor DN22 51 J4
Barndennoch DG2 68 D5
Barne Barton PL5 4 E5
Barnehurst DA7 23 J4
Barnes SW13 23 F4
Barnes Street TN11 23 K7
Barnet EN5 23 F2
Barnet Gate EN5 23 F2
Barnetby le Wold DN38 52 D2
Barney NR21 44 D2
Barnham Suff. IP24 34 C1
Barnham W.Suss. PO22 12 C6
Barnham Broom NR9 44 E5
Barnhead DD10 83 H2
Barnhill Ches. CH3 48 D7
Barnhill Dundee DD5 83 F4
Barnhill Moray IV30 97 J6
Barnhills DG9 66 D6
Barningham Dur. DL11 62 B5
Barningham Suff. IP31 34 D1
Barningham Green NR11 45 F2
Barnoldby le Beck DN37 53 F2
Barnoldswick BB18 56 D5
Barns Green RH13 12 E4
Barnsdale Bar WF8 51 H1
Barnsley Glos. GL7 20 D1
Barnsley S.Yorks. S70 51 F2
Barnsole CT3 15 H2
Barnstaple EX31 6 D2
Barnston Essex CM6 33 K7
Barnston Mersey. CH61 48 B4
Barnstone NG13 42 A2
Barnt Green B45 30 B1
Barnton Ches. CW8 49 F5
Barnton Edin. EH4 75 K3
Barnwell All Saints PE8 42 D7
Barnwell St. Andrew PE8 42 D7
Barnwood GL4 29 H7
Barons' Cross HR6 28 D3
Barr Arg. & B. PA44 72 B4
Barr High. PA34 79 H2
Barr S.Ayr. KA26 67 G4
Barr Som. TA4 7 K3
Barr Hall CO9 34 B5
Barra (Barraigh) HS9 84 B4
Barra (Tràigh Mhòr) Airport HS9 84 B4
Barrachan DG8 64 D6
Barrackan PA31 79 J7
Barraer DG8 64 D4
Barraglom HS2 100 D4
Barrahormid PA31 73 F2
Barraigh (Barra) HS9 84 B4
Barran PA33 80 C5
Barrapoll PA77 78 A3
Barrasford NE48 70 E6
Barravullin PA31 79 K7
Barregarrow IM6 54 C5
Barrets Green CW6 48 E7
Barrhead G78 74 C5

Barrhill KA26 67 G5
Barrington *Cambs.* CB2 33 G4
Barrington *Som.* TA19 8 C3
Barripper TR14 2 D5
Barrisdale PH35 86 E4
Barrmill KA15 74 B5
Barrnacarry PA34 79 K5
Barrock KW14 105 H1
Barrow *Glos.* GL51 29 H6
Barrow *Lancs.* BB7 56 C6
Barrow *Rut.* LE15 42 B4
Barrow *Shrop.* TF12 39 F5
Barrow *Som.* BA9 9 G1
Barrow *Som.* BA4 19 J7
Barrow *Suff.* IP29 34 B2
Barrow Gurney BS48 19 J5
Barrow Hann DN19 59 G7
Barrow Haven DN19 59 G7
Barrow Hill S43 51 G5
Barrow Nook L39 48 D2
Barrow Street BA12 9 H1
Barrow upon Humber DN19 59 G7
Barrow upon Soar LE12 41 H4
Barrow upon Trent DE73 41 F3
Barroway Drove PE38 43 J5
Barrowby NG32 42 B2
Barrowcliff YO12 59 G1
Barrowden LE15 42 C5
Barrowford BB9 56 D6
Barrow-in-Furness LA14 55 F3
Barrows Green LA8 55 J1
Barry *Angus* DD7 83 G4
Barry *V. of Glam.* CF62 18 E5
Barsby LE7 41 J4
Barsham NR34 45 H7
Barskimming KA5 67 J1
Barsloisnoch PA31 73 G1
Barston B92 30 D1
Bartestree HR1 28 E4
Barthol Chapel AB51 91 G1
Bartholomew Green CM77 34 B6
Barthomley CW2 49 G7
Bartley SO40 10 E3
Bartley Green B32 40 C7
Bartlow CB1 33 J4
Barton *Cambs.* CB3 33 H3
Barton *Ches.* SY14 48 D7
Barton *Cumb.* CA10 61 F4
Barton *Glos.* GL54 30 B6
Barton *Lancs.* PR3 55 J6
Barton *Lancs.* L39 48 C2
Barton *N.Yorks.* DL10 62 D6
Barton *Oxon.* OX3 21 J1
Barton *Torbay* TQ2 5 K4
Barton *Warks.* B50 30 C3
Barton Bendish PE33 44 B5
Barton End GL6 20 B2
Barton Green DE13 40 D4
Barton Hartshorn MK18 31 H5
Barton Hill YO60 58 D3
Barton in Fabis NG11 41 H2
Barton in the Beans CV13 41 F5
Barton Mills IP28 34 B1
Barton on Sea BH25 10 D5
Barton St. David TA11 8 E1
Barton Seagrave NN15 32 B1
Barton Stacey SO21 21 H7
Barton Town EX31 6 E1
Barton Turf NR12 45 H3
Bartongate OX7 31 F6
Barton-le-Clay MK45 32 D5
Barton-le-Street YO17 58 D2
Barton-le-Willows YO60 58 D3
Barton-on-the-Heath GL56 30 D5
Barton-under-Needwood DE13 40 D4
Barton-upon-Humber DN18 59 G7
Barvas (Barabhas) HS2 101 F3
Barway CB7 33 J1
Barwell LE9 41 G6
Barwhinnock DG6 65 G5
Barwick *Herts.* SG11 33 G7
Barwick *Som.* BA22 8 E3
Barwick in Elmet LS15 57 J6
Barwinnock DG8 64 D6
Baschurch SY4 38 D3
Bascote CV47 31 F2
Base Green IP14 34 E2
Basford Green ST13 49 J7
Bashall Eaves BB7 56 B5
Bashall Town BB7 56 C5
Bashley BH25 10 D5
Basildon *Essex* SS14 24 D3
Basildon *W.Berks.* RG8 21 K4
Basingstoke RG21 21 K6
Baslow DE45 50 E5
Bason Bridge TA9 19 G7
Bassaleg NP10 19 F3
Bassenthwaite CA12 60 D3
Basset's Cross EX20 6 D5
Bassett SO16 11 F3
Bassingbourn SG8 33 G4
Bassingfield NG12 41 J2
Bassingham LN5 52 C7
Bassingthorpe NG33 42 C3
Basta ZE2 107 P3
Baston PE6 42 E4
Bastonford WR2 29 H3
Bastwick NR29 45 J4
Batavaime FK21 81 F4
Batch BS24 19 G6
Batchley B97 30 B2
Batchworth WD3 22 D2
Batchworth Heath WD3 22 D2
Batcombe *Dorset* DT2 9 F4
Batcombe *Som.* BA4 9 F1
Bate Heath CW9 49 F5
BATH BA 20 A5
Bathampton BA2 20 A5
Bathealton TA4 7 J3
Batheaston BA1 20 A5
Bathford BA1 20 A5
Bathgate EH48 75 H4
Bathley NG23 51 K7
Bathpool *Cornw.* PL15 4 C3
Bathpool *Som.* TA2 8 B2
Bathway BA3 19 J6
Batley WF17 57 H7
Batsford GL56 30 C5
Batson TQ8 5 H7
Battersby TS9 63 G6
Battersea SW11 23 F4
Battisborough Cross PL8 5 G6
Battisford IP14 34 E3
Battisford Tye IP14 34 E3
Battle *E.Suss.* TN33 14 C6
Battle *Powys* LD3 27 K5
Battledown GL52 29 J6
Battlefield SY1 38 E4
Battlesbridge SS11 24 D2
Battlesden MK17 32 C6
Battlesea Green IP21 35 G1
Battleton TA22 7 H3
Battlies Green IP30 34 D2
Battramsley SO41 10 E5
Batt's Corner GU10 22 B7
Bauds of Cullen AB56 98 C4
Baugh PA77 78 B3
Baughton WR8 29 H4
Baughurst RG26 21 J5
Baulds AB31 90 E5
Baulking SN7 21 G2
Baumber LN9 53 F5
Baunton GL7 20 D1
Baveney Wood DY14 29 F1
Baverstock SP3 10 B1
Bawburgh NR9 45 F5
Bawdeswell NR20 44 E3
Bawdrip TA7 8 C1
Bawdsey IP12 35 H4
Bawdsey Manor IP12 35 H5
Bawsey PE32 44 A4
Bawtry DN10 51 J3
Baxenden BB5 56 C7
Baxterley CV9 40 E6
Baxter's Green CB8 34 B3
Bay SP8 9 H2
Baybridge DH8 62 A2
Baycliff LA12 55 F2
Baydon SN8 21 F4
Bayford *Herts.* SG13 23 G1
Bayford *Som.* BA9 9 G2
Bayfordbury SG13 33 G7
Bayham Abbey TN3 13 K3
Bayles CA9 61 J2
Baylham IP6 35 F3
Baynards Green OX27 31 G6
Baysham HR9 28 E6
Bayston Hill SY3 38 D5
Bayswater W2 23 F3
Baythorn End CO9 34 B4
Bayton DY14 29 F1
Bayworth OX13 21 J1
Beach *High.* PA34 79 J2
Beach *S.Glos.* BS30 20 A4
Beachampton MK19 31 J5
Beachamwell PE37 44 B5
Beacharr PA29 72 E6
Beachley NP16 19 J2
Beacon *Devon* EX14 7 K5
Beacon *Devon* EX14 8 B4
Beacon Hill *Dorset* BH16 9 J5
Beacon Hill *Essex* CM8 34 C7
Beacon Hill *Surr.* GU26 12 B3
Beacon's Bottom HP14 22 A2
Beaconsfield HP9 22 C2
Beacravik HS3 93 G2
Beadlam YO62 58 C1
Beadlow SG17 32 E5
Beadnell NE67 71 H1
Beaford EX19 6 D4
Beal *N.Yorks.* DN14 58 B7
Beal *Northumb.* TD15 77 J6
Bealach PA38 80 A2
Bealsmill PL17 4 D3
Beambridge CW5 49 F7
Beamhurst ST14 40 C2
Beaminster DT8 8 D4
Beamish DH9 62 D1
Beamsley BD23 57 F4
Bean DA2 23 J4
Beanacre SN12 20 C5
Beanley NE66 71 F2
Beaquoy KW17 106 C5
Beardon EX20 6 D7
Beardwood BB2 56 B7
Beare EX5 7 H5
Beare Green RH5 22 E7
Bearley CV37 30 C2
Bearnie AB41 91 H1
Bearnock IV63 88 B1
Bearnus PA73 78 E3
Bearpark DH7 62 D2
Bearsbridge NE47 61 J1
Bearsden G61 74 D3
Bearsted ME14 14 C2
Bearstone TF9 39 G2
Bearwood *Poole* BH11 10 B5
Bearwood *W.Mid.* B66 40 C7
Beattock DG10 69 F3
Beauchamp Roding CM5 33 J7
Beauchief S8 51 F4
Beaudesert B95 30 C2
Beaufort NP23 28 A7
Beaulieu SO42 10 E4
Beauly IV4 96 C7
Beaumaris (Biwmares) LL58 46 E5
Beaumont *Chan.I.* JE3 3 J7
Beaumont *Cumb.* CA5 60 E1
Beaumont *Essex* CO16 35 F6
Beaumont Hill DL1 62 D5
Beaumont Leys LE4 41 H5
Beausale CV35 30 D1
Beauvale NG16 41 G1
Beauworth SO24 11 G2
Beaver Green TN23 14 E3
Beaworthy EX21 6 C6
Beazley End CM7 34 B6
Bebington CH63 48 C4
Bebside NE24 71 H5
Beccles NR34 45 J6
Beccles Heliport NR34 45 J7
Becconsall PR4 55 H7
Beck Foot LA8 61 H7
Beck Hole YO22 63 K6
Beck Row IP28 33 K1
Beck Side *Cumb.* LA17 55 F1
Beck Side *Cumb.* LA11 55 G1
Beckbury TF11 39 G5
Beckenham BR3 23 G5
Beckering LN8 52 E4
Beckermet CA21 60 B6
Beckermonds BD23 56 D1
Beckett End IP26 44 B6
Beckfoot *Cumb.* CA19 60 C6
Beckfoot *Cumb.* CA7 60 B2
Beckford GL20 29 J5
Beckhampton SN8 20 D5
Beckingham *Lincs.* LN5 52 B7
Beckingham *Notts.* DN10 51 K4
Beckington BA11 20 B6
Beckley *E.Suss.* TN31 14 D5
Beckley *Oxon.* OX3 31 G7
Beck's Green NR34 45 H7
Beckside LA6 56 B1
Beckton E6 23 H3
Beckwithshaw HG3 57 H4
Becontree RM8 23 H3
Bedale DL8 57 H1
Bedburn DL13 62 B3
Bedchester SP7 9 H3
Beddau CF38 18 D3
Beddgelert LL55 36 E1
Beddingham BN8 13 H6
Beddington SM6 23 F5
Beddington Corner CR4 23 F5
Bedfield IP13 35 G2
Bedfield Little Green IP13 35 G2
Bedford MK40 32 D4
Bedgebury Cross TN17 14 C4
Bedgrove HP21 32 B7
Bedham RH20 12 D4
Bedhampton PO9 11 J4
Bedingfield IP23 35 F2
Bedingfield Green IP23 35 F2
Bedingfield Street IP23 35 F2
Bedingham Green NR35 45 G6
Bedlam *Lancs.* BB5 56 C7
Bedlam *N.Yorks.* HG3 57 H3
Bedlar's Green CM22 33 J6
Bedlington NE22 71 H5
Bedlinog CF46 18 D1
Bedminster BS3 19 J4
Bedmond WD5 22 D1
Bednall ST17 40 B4
Bedol CH6 48 B5
Bedrule TD9 70 B2
Bedstone SY7 28 C1
Bedwas CF83 18 E3
Bedwell SG1 33 F6
Bedwellty NP12 18 E1
Bedworth CV12 41 F7
Bedworth Woodlands CV12 41 F7
Beeby LE7 41 J5
Beech *Hants.* GU34 11 H1
Beech *Staffs.* ST4 40 A2
Beech Hill RG7 21 K5
Beechingstoke SN9 20 D6
Beechwood WA7 48 E4
Beedon RG20 21 H4
Beeford YO25 59 H4
Beeley DE4 50 E6
Beelsby DN37 53 F2
Beenham RG7 21 J5
Beeny PL35 4 B1
Beer EX12 8 B6
Beer Hackett DT9 9 F3
Beercrocombe TA3 8 C2
Beesands TQ7 5 J6
Beesby *Lincs.* LN13 53 H4
Beesby *N.E.Lincs.* DN36 53 F3
Beeson TQ7 5 J6
Beeston *Beds.* SG19 32 E4
Beeston *Ches.* CW6 48 E7
Beeston *Norf.* PE32 44 D4
Beeston *Notts.* NG9 41 H2
Beeston *W.Yorks.* LS11 57 H6
Beeston Regis NR26 45 F1
Beeston St. Lawrence NR12 45 H3
Beeswing DG2 65 J4
Beetham *Cumb.* LA7 55 H2
Beetham *Som.* TA20 8 B3
Beetley NR20 44 D4
Beffcote ST20 40 A4
Began CF3 19 F3
Begbroke OX5 31 F7
Begdale PE14 43 H5
Begelly SA68 16 E5
Beggar's Bush LD8 28 B2
Beggearn Huish TA23 7 J2
Beggshill AB54 90 D1
Beguildy (Bugeildy) LD7 28 A1
Beighton *Norf.* NR13 45 H5
Beighton *S.Yorks.* S20 51 G4
Beili-glas NP7 19 G1
Beinn na Faoghla (Benbecula) HS7 92 D6
Beith KA15 74 B5
Bekesbourne CT4 15 G2
Belaugh NR12 45 G4
Belbroughton DY9 29 J1
Belchalwell DT11 9 G4
Belchalwell Street DT11 9 G4
Belchamp Otten CO10 34 C4
Belchamp St. Paul CO10 34 B4
Belchamp Walter CO10 34 C4
Belchford LN9 53 F5
Belfield OL16 49 J1
Belford NE70 77 K7
Belgrave LE4 41 H5
Belhaven EH42 76 E3
Belhelvie AB23 91 H3
Belhinnie AB54 90 C2
Bell Bar AL9 23 F1
Bell Busk BD23 56 E4
Bell End DY9 29 J1
Bell Heath DY9 29 J1
Bell Hill GU32 11 J2
Bell o' th' Hill SY13 38 E1
Bellabeg AB36 90 B3
Belladrum IV4 96 C7
Bellanoch PA31 73 G1
Bellaty PH11 82 D2
Belle Isle LS10 57 J7
Belle Vue CA2 60 E1
Belleau LN13 53 H5
Belleheiglash AB37 89 J1
Bellerby DL8 62 C7
Bellever PL20 5 G3
Bellfields GU1 22 C6
Belliehill DD9 83 G1
Bellingdon HP5 22 C1
Bellingham *Gt.Lon.* SE6 23 G4
Bellingham *Northumb.* NE48 70 D5
Belloch PA29 72 E7
Bellochantuy PA28 72 E7
Bell's Cross IP6 35 F3
Bells Yew Green TN3 13 K3
Bellsbank KA6 67 J3
Bellshill *N.Lan.* ML4 75 F4
Bellshill *Northumb.* NE70 77 K7
Bellside ML1 75 G5
Bellsmyre G82 74 C3
Bellsquarry EH54 75 J4
Belluton BS39 19 K5
Belmaduthy IV8 96 D6
Belmesthorpe PE9 42 D4
Belmont *B'burn.* BL7 49 F1
Belmont *Gt.Lon.* SM2 23 F5
Belmont *Gt.Lon.* HA7 22 E2
Belmont *Shet.* ZE2 107 P2
Belnie PE11 43 F2
Belowda PL26 3 G2
Belper DE56 41 F1
Belper Lane End DE56 41 F1
Belsay NE20 71 G6
Belsford TQ9 5 H5
Belsize WD3 22 D1
Belstead IP8 35 F4
Belston KA6 67 H1
Belstone EX20 6 E6
Belstone Corner EX20 6 E6
Belsyde EH49 75 H3
Belthorn BB1 56 C7
Beltinge CT6 25 H5
Beltingham NE47 70 C7
Beltoft DN9 52 B2
Belton *Leics.* LE12 41 G3
Belton *Lincs.* NG32 42 C2
Belton *N.Lincs.* DN9 51 K2
Belton *Norf.* NR31 45 J5
Belton *Rut.* LE15 42 B5
Beltring TN12 23 K7
Belvedere DA17 23 H4
Belvoir NG32 42 B2
Bembridge PO35 11 H6
Bemersyde TD6 76 D7
Bemerton SP2 10 C1
Bempton YO15 59 H2
Ben Alder Cottage PH17 81 F1
Ben Alder Lodge PH19 88 C7
Ben Rhydding LS29 57 G5
Benacre NR34 45 K7
Benbecula (Beinn na Faoghla) HS7 92 D6
Benbecula (Balivanich) Airport HS7 92 C6
Benbuie DG3 68 C4
Benderloch PA37 80 A4
Bendish SG4 32 E6
Benenden TN17 14 D4
Benfield DG8 64 D4
Benfieldside DH8 62 B1
Bengate NR28 45 H3
Bengeo SG14 33 G7
Bengeworth WR11 30 B4
Benhall GL51 29 J6
Benhall Green IP17 35 H2
Benhall Street IP17 35 H2
Benholm DD10 83 K1
Beningbrough YO30 58 B4
Benington *Herts.* SG2 33 F6
Benington *Lincs.* PE22 43 G1
Benington Sea End PE22 43 H1
Benllech LL74 46 D4
Benmore *Arg. & B.* PA23 73 K2
Benmore *Stir.* FK20 81 F5
Bennacott PL15 4 C1
Bennan Cottage DG7 65 G3
Bennett End HP14 22 A2
Bennetts End HP3 22 D1
Benniworth LN8 53 F4
Benover ME18 14 C3
Benson OX10 21 K2
Benston ZE2 107 N7
Benthall *Northumb.* NE67 71 H1
Benthall *Shrop.* TF12 39 F5
Bentham GL51 29 J7
Benthoul AB14 91 G4
Bentlawnt SY5 38 C5
Bentley *E.Riding* HU17 59 G6
Bentley *Essex* CM15 23 J2
Bentley *Hants.* GU10 22 A7
Bentley *S.Yorks.* DN5 51 H2
Bentley *Suff.* IP9 35 F5
Bentley *W.Mid.* WS2 40 B6
Bentley *W.Yorks.* LS6 57 H6
Bentley *Warks.* CV9 40 E6
Bentley Heath *Herts.* EN5 23 F2
Bentley Heath *W.Mid.* B93 30 C1
Bentley Rise DN5 51 H2
Benton EX32 6 E2
Benton Square NE12 71 J6
Bentpath DG13 69 J4
Bentworth GU34 21 K7
Benvie DD2 82 E4
Benville Lane DT2 8 E4
Benwell NE15 71 H7
Benwick PE15 43 G6
Beoley B98 30 B2
Beoraidbeg PH40 86 C5
Bepton GU29 12 B5
Berden CM23 33 H6
Bere Alston PL20 4 E4
Bere Ferrers PL20 4 E4
Bere Regis BH20 9 H5
Berea SA62 16 A2
Berepper TR12 2 D6
Bergh Apton NR15 45 H5
Berinsfield OX10 21 J2
Berkeley GL13 19 K2
Berkhamsted HP4 22 C1
Berkley BA11 20 B7
Berkswell CV7 30 D1
Bermondsey SE16 23 G4
Bernera IV40 86 E2
Berneray (Eilean Bhearnaraigh) HS6 92 E3
Berners Roding CM5 24 C1
Bernice PA23 73 K1
Bernisdale IV51 93 K6
Berrick Prior OX10 21 K2
Berrick Salome OX10 21 K2
Berriedale KW7 105 G6
Berriew (Aberriw) SY21 38 A5
Berrington *Northumb.* TD15 77 J6
Berrington *Shrop.* SY5 38 E5
Berrington *Worcs.* WR15 28 E2
Berrington Green WR15 28 E2
Berriowbridge PL15 4 C3
Berrow *Som.* TA8 19 F6
Berrow *Worcs.* WR13 29 G5
Berrow Green WR6 29 G3
Berry Cross EX38 6 C4
Berry Down Cross EX34 6 D1
Berry Hill *Glos.* GL16 28 E7
Berry Hill *Pembs.* SA42 16 D1
Berry Pomeroy TQ9 5 J4
Berryhillock AB56 98 D4
Berrynarbor EX34 6 D1
Berry's Green TN16 23 H6
Bersham LL14 38 C1
Berstane KW15 106 D6
Berthlŵyd SA4 17 J6
Berwick BN26 13 J6
Berwick Bassett SN4 20 E4
Berwick Hill NE20 71 G6
Berwick St. James SP3 10 B1
Berwick St. John SP7 9 J2
Berwick St. Leonard SP3 9 J1
Berwick-upon-Tweed TD15 77 H5
Bescar L40 48 C1
Bescot WS2 40 C6
Besford *Shrop.* SY4 38 E3
Besford *Worcs.* WR8 29 J4
Bessacarr DN4 51 J2
Bessels Leigh OX13 21 H1
Besses o' th' Barn M45 49 H2
Bessingby YO16 59 H3
Bessingham NR11 45 F2
Best Beech Hill TN5 13 K3
Besthorpe *Norf.* NR17 44 E6
Besthorpe *Notts.* NG23 52 B6
Bestwood Village NG5 41 H1
Beswick *E.Riding* YO25 59 G5
Beswick *Gt.Man.* M11 49 H3
Betchworth RH3 23 F6
Bethania *Cere.* SY23 26 E2
Bethania *Gwyn.* LL41 37 G1
Bethel *Gwyn.* LL55 46 D6
Bethel *Gwyn.* LL23 37 J2
Bethel *I.o.A.* LL62 46 B5
Bethersden TN26 14 E4
Bethesda *Gwyn.* LL57 46 E6
Bethesda *Pembs.* SA67 16 D4
Bethlehem SA19 17 K3
Bethnal Green E2 23 G3
Betley CW3 39 G1
Betley Common CW3 39 G1
Betsham DA13 24 C4
Betteshanger CT14 15 J2
Bettiscombe DT6 8 C5
Bettisfield SY13 38 D2
Betton *Shrop.* SY5 38 C5
Betton *Shrop.* TF9 39 F2
Betton Strange SY5 38 E5
Bettws *Bridgend* CF32 18 C3
Bettws *Newport* NP20 19 F2
Bettws Bledrws SA48 26 E3
Bettws Cedewain SY16 38 A6
Bettws Gwerfil Goch LL21 37 K1
Bettws Newydd NP15 19 G1

Bettws-y-crwyn SY7 38 B7
Bettyhill KW14 104 C2
Betws SA18 17 K4
Betws Disserth LD1 28 A3
Betws Garmon LL54 46 D7
Betws Ifan SA38 17 G1
Betws-y-coed LL24 47 F7
Betws-yn-Rhos LL22 47 H5
Beulah Cere. SA38 17 F1
Beulah Powys LD5 27 J3
Bevendean BN2 13 G6
Bevercotes NG22 51 J5
Beverley HU17 59 G6
Beverstone GL8 20 B2
Bevington GL13 19 K2
Bewaldeth CA13 60 D3
Bewcastle CA6 70 A6
Bewdley DY12 29 G1
Bewerley HG3 57 G3
Bewholme YO25 59 H4
Bewley Common SN15 20 C5
Bexhill TN40 14 C7
Bexley DA5 23 H4
Bexleyheath DA6 23 H4
Bexwell PE38 44 A5
Beyton IP30 34 D2
Beyton Green IP30 34 D2
Bhalamus HS2 100 E7
Bhaleshear (Baleshare) HS6 92 C5
Bhaltos HS2 100 C4
Bhatarsaigh (Vatersay) HS9 84 B5
Biallaid PH20 88 E5
Bibury GL7 20 E1
Bicester OX26 31 G6
Bickenhall TA3 8 B3
Bickenhill B92 40 D7
Bicker PE20 43 F2
Bickershaw WN2 49 F2
Bickerstaffe L39 48 D2
Bickerton Ches. SY14 48 E7
Bickerton Devon TQ7 5 J7
Bickerton N.Yorks. LS22 57 K4
Bickerton Northumb. NE65 70 E3
Bickford ST19 40 A4
Bickham TA24 7 H1
Bickham Bridge TQ9 5 H5
Bickham House EX6 7 H7
Bickington Devon EX31 6 D2
Bickington Devon TQ12 5 H3
Bickleigh Devon PL6 5 F4
Bickleigh Devon EX16 7 H5
Bickleton EX31 6 D2
Bickley BR1 23 H5
Bickley Moss SY13 38 E1
Bickley Town SY14 38 E1
Bicknacre CM3 24 D1
Bicknoller TA4 7 K2
Bicknor ME9 14 D2
Bickton SP6 10 C3
Bicton Here. HR6 28 D2
Bicton Shrop. SY3 38 D4
Bicton Shrop. SY7 38 B7
Bicton Heath SY3 38 D4
Bidborough TN4 23 J7
Biddenden TN27 14 D4
Biddenden Green TN27 14 D3
Biddenham MK40 32 D4
Biddestone SN14 20 B4
Biddick NE38 62 E1
Biddisham BS26 19 G6
Biddlesden NN13 31 H4
Biddlestone NE65 70 E3
Biddulph ST8 49 H7
Biddulph Moor ST8 49 J7
Bideford EX39 6 C3
Bidford-on-Avon B50 30 C3
Bidham Dock ME9 25 F5
Bidlake EX20 6 C7
Bidston CH43 48 B3
Bidwell LU5 32 D6
Bielby YO42 58 D5
Bieldside AB15 91 G4
Bierley I.o.W. PO38 11 G7
Bierley W.Yorks. BD4 57 G6
Bierton HP22 32 B7
Big Sand IV21 94 D4
Bigbury TQ7 5 G6
Bigbury-on-Sea TQ7 5 G6
Bigby DN38 52 D2
Bigert Mire LA20 60 C7
Biggar Cumb. LA14 54 E3
Biggar S.Lan. ML12 75 J7
Biggin Derbys. DE6 40 E1
Biggin Derbys. SK17 50 D7
Biggin N.Yorks. LS25 58 B6
Biggin Hill TN16 23 H6
Biggings ZE2 107 K6
Biggleswade SG18 32 E4
Bigholms DG13 69 J5
Bighouse KW14 104 D2
Bighton SO24 11 H1
Biglands CA7 60 D1
Bignor RH20 12 C5
Bigrigg CA24 60 B5
Bigton ZE2 107 M10
Bilberry PL26 4 A5
Bilborough NG8 41 H1
Bilbrook Som. TA24 7 J1
Bilbrook Staffs. WV8 40 A5
Bilbrough YO23 58 B5
Bilbster KW1 105 H3
Bilby DN22 51 J4
Bildershaw DL14 62 C4
Bildeston IP7 34 D4
Billericay CM12 24 C2
Billesdon LE7 42 A5
Billesley B49 30 C3
Billholm DG13 69 H4
Billingborough NG34 42 E2
Billinge WN5 48 E3
Billingford Norf. IP21 35 F1
Billingford Norf. NR20 44 E3
Billingham TS23 63 F4
Billinghay LN4 52 E7
Billingley S72 51 G2
Billingshurst RH14 12 D4
Billingsley WV16 39 G7
Billington Beds. LU7 32 C6
Billington Lancs. BB7 56 C6
Billington Staffs. ST18 40 A3
Billister ZE2 107 N6
Billockby NR29 45 J4
Billy Row DL15 62 C3
Bilsborrow PR3 55 J6
Bilsby LN13 53 H5
Bilsby Field LN13 53 H5
Bilsdean TD13 77 F3
Bilsham BN18 12 C6
Bilsington TN25 15 F4
Bilson Green GL14 29 F7
Bilsthorpe NG22 51 J6
Bilsthorpe Moor NG22 51 J7
Bilston Midloth. EH25 76 A4
Bilston W.Mid. WV14 40 B6
Bilstone CV13 41 F5
Bilting TN25 15 F3
Bilton E.Riding HU11 59 H6
Bilton N.Yorks. HG1 57 J4
Bilton Northumb. NE66 71 H2
Bilton Warks. CV22 31 F1
Bilton-in-Ainsty YO26 57 K5
Bimbister KW17 106 C6
Binbrook LN8 53 F3
Bincombe DT3 9 F6
Bindal IV20 97 G3
Bindon TA21 7 K3
Binegar BA3 19 K7
Bines Green RH13 12 E5
Binfield RG42 22 B4
Binfield Heath RG9 22 A4
Bingfield NE19 70 E6
Bingham NG13 42 A2
Bingham's Melcombe DT2 9 G4
Bingley BD16 57 G6
Bings Heath SY4 38 E4
Binham NR21 44 D2
Binley Hants. SP11 21 H6
Binley W.Mid. CV3 30 E1
Binniehill FK1 75 G3
Binsoe HG4 57 H2
Binstead PO33 11 G5
Binsted Hants. GU34 22 A7
Binsted W.Suss. BN18 12 C6
Binton CV37 30 C3
Bintree NR20 44 E3
Binweston SY5 38 C5
Birch Essex CO2 34 D6
Birch Gt.Man. M24 49 H2
Birch Cross ST14 40 D2
Birch Green Essex CO2 34 D7
Birch Green Herts. SG14 33 F7
Birch Grove RH17 13 H4
Birch Heath CW6 48 E6
Birch Vale SK22 50 C4
Birch Wood TA20 8 B3
Bircham Newton PE31 44 B2
Bircham Tofts PE31 44 B2
Birchanger CM23 33 J6
Bircher HR6 28 D2
Bircher Common HR6 28 D2
Birchfield IV24 96 B2
Birchgrove Cardiff CF14 18 E3
Birchgrove Swan. SA7 18 A2
Birchington CT7 25 K5
Birchmoor B78 40 E5
Birchover DE4 50 E6
Birchwood Lincs. LN6 52 C6
Birchwood Warr. WA3 49 F3
Bircotes DN11 51 J3
Bird Street IP7 34 E3
Birdbrook CO9 34 B4
Birdbush SP7 9 J2
Birdfield PA32 73 H1
Birdforth YO7 57 K2
Birdham PO20 12 B6
Birdingbury CV23 31 F2
Birdlip GL4 29 J7
Birdoswald CA8 70 B7
Birds Green CM5 23 J1
Birdsall YO17 58 E3
Birdsgreen WV15 39 G7
Birdsmoor Gate DT6 8 C4
Birdston G66 74 E3
Birdwell S70 51 F2
Birdwood GL19 29 G7
Birgham TD12 77 F7
Birichen IV25 96 E2
Birkby Cumb. CA15 60 B3
Birkby N.Yorks. DL7 62 E6
Birkdale Mersey. PR8 48 C1
Birkdale N.Yorks. DL11 61 K6
Birkenhead CH41 48 C4
Birkenhills AB53 99 F6
Birkenshaw BD11 57 H7
Birkhall AB35 90 B5
Birkhill Angus DD2 82 E4
Birkhill Sc.Bord. TD4 76 D6
Birkhill Sc.Bord. TD7 69 H2
Birkholme NG33 42 C3
Birkin WF11 58 B7
Birks LS27 57 H7
Birkwood ML11 75 G7
Birley HR4 28 D3
Birley Carr S6 51 F3
Birling Kent ME19 24 C5
Birling Northumb. NE65 71 H3
Birling Gap BN20 13 J7
Birlingham WR10 29 J4
BIRMINGHAM B 40 C7
Birmingham International Airport B26 40 D7
Birnam PH8 82 B3
Birsay KW17 106 B5
Birse AB34 90 D5
Birsemore AB34 90 D5
Birstall LE4 41 H5
Birstall Smithies WF17 57 H7
Birstwith HG3 57 H4
Birthorpe NG34 42 E2
Birtle OL11 49 H1
Birtley Here. SY7 28 C2
Birtley Northumb. NE48 70 D6
Birtley T.& W. DH3 62 D1
Birts Street WR13 29 G5
Birtsmorton WR13 29 H5
Bisbrooke LE15 42 B6
Biscathorpe LN11 53 F4
Bish Mill EX36 7 F3
Bisham SL7 22 B3
Bishampton WR10 29 J3
Bishop Auckland DL14 62 D4
Bishop Burton HU17 59 F5
Bishop Middleham DL17 62 E3
Bishop Monkton HG3 57 J3
Bishop Norton LN8 52 C3
Bishop Sutton BS39 19 J6
Bishop Thornton HG3 57 H3
Bishop Wilton YO42 58 D4
Bishopbridge LN8 52 D3
Bishopbriggs G64 74 E3
Bishopmill IV30 97 K5
Bishops Cannings SN10 20 D5
Bishop's Castle SY9 38 C7
Bishop's Caundle DT9 9 F3
Bishop's Cleeve GL52 29 J6
Bishop's Frome WR6 29 F4
Bishops Gate TW20 22 C4
Bishop's Green Essex CM6 33 K7
Bishop's Green Hants. RG19 21 J5
Bishop's Hull TA1 8 B2
Bishop's Itchington CV47 30 E3
Bishop's Lydeard TA4 7 K3
Bishop's Norton GL2 29 H6
Bishops Nympton EX36 7 F3
Bishop's Offley ST21 39 G3
Bishop's Stortford CM23 33 H6
Bishop's Sutton SO24 11 H1
Bishop's Tachbrook CV33 30 E2
Bishop's Tawton EX32 6 D2
Bishop's Waltham SO32 11 G3
Bishop's Wood ST19 40 A5
Bishopsbourne CT4 15 G2
Bishopsteignton TQ14 5 K3
Bishopstoke SO50 11 F3
Bishopston Bristol BS6 19 J4
Bishopston Swan. SA3 17 J7
Bishopstone Bucks. HP17 32 B7
Bishopstone E.Suss. BN25 13 H6
Bishopstone Here. HR4 28 D4
Bishopstone Swin. SN6 21 F3
Bishopstone Wilts. SP5 10 B2
Bishopstrow BA12 20 B7
Bishopswood TA20 8 B3
Bishopsworth BS13 19 J5
Bishopthorpe YO23 58 B5
Bishopton Darl. TS21 62 E4
Bishopton N.Yorks. HG4 57 H2
Bishopton Renf. PA7 74 C3
Bishopton Warks. CV37 30 C3
Bishton NP18 19 G3
Bisley Glos. GL6 20 C1
Bisley Surr. GU24 22 C6
Bispham FY2 55 G6
Bispham Green L40 48 D1
Bissoe TR4 2 E4
Bisterne BH24 10 C4
Bisterne Close BH24 10 D4
Bitchet Green TN15 23 J6
Bitchfield NG33 42 C3
Bittadon EX31 6 D1
Bittaford PL21 5 G5
Bittering NR19 44 D4
Bitterley SY8 28 E1
Bitterne SO18 11 F3
Bitteswell LE17 41 H7
Bitton BS30 19 K5
Biwmares (Beaumaris) LL58 46 E5
Bix RG9 22 A3
Bixter ZE2 107 M7
Blaby LE8 41 H6
Black Bourton OX18 21 F1
Black Bridge SA73 16 C5
Black Callerton NE5 71 G7
Black Carr NR17 44 E6
Black Clauchrie KA26 67 G5
Black Corries Lodge PH49 80 D2
Black Crofts PA37 80 A4
Black Cross TR8 3 G2
Black Dog EX17 7 G5
Black Heddon NE20 71 F6
Black Hill CV37 30 D3
Black Marsh SY5 38 C6
Black Moor LS17 57 H5
Black Mount PA36 80 D3
Black Notley CM77 34 B6
Black Pill SA3 17 K6
Black Street NR33 45 K7
Black Torrington EX21 6 C5
Blackaburn NE48 70 C6
Blackacre DG11 69 F4
Blackadder TD11 77 G5
Blackawton TQ9 5 J5
Blackborough Devon EX15 7 J5
Blackborough Norf. PE32 44 A4
Blackborough End PE32 44 A4
Blackboys TN22 13 J4
Blackbraes Aber. AB21 91 G3
Blackbraes Falk. FK1 75 H3
Blackbrook Derbys. DE56 41 F1
Blackbrook Leics. LE12 41 G4
Blackbrook Mersey. WA11 48 E3
Blackbrook Staffs. ST5 39 G2
Blackburn Aber. AB21 91 G3
BLACKBURN B'burn. BB 56 B7
Blackburn W.Loth. EH47 75 H4
Blackbushe GU17 22 A6
Blackcastle IV2 97 F6
Blackchambers AB32 91 F3
Blackcraig D.& G. DG8 64 E4
Blackcraig D.& G. DG7 68 C5
Blackden Heath CW4 49 G5
Blackdog AB23 91 H3
Blackdown Devon PL19 5 F3
Blackdown Dorset DT8 8 C4
Blackdown Warks. CV32 30 E2
Blacker Hill S74 51 F2
Blackfen DA15 23 H4
Blackfield SO45 11 F4
Blackford Aber. AB51 91 F1
Blackford Cumb. CA6 69 J7
Blackford P.& K. PH4 81 K7
Blackford Som. BA22 9 F2
Blackford Som. BS28 19 H7
Blackford Bridge BL9 49 H2
Blackfordby DE11 41 F4
Blackgang PO38 11 F7
Blackhall Edin. EH4 76 A3
Blackhall Renf. PA1 74 C4
Blackhall Colliery TS27 63 F3
Blackhall Mill NE17 62 C1
Blackhall Rocks TS27 63 F3
Blackham TN3 13 J3
Blackhaugh TD1 76 C7
Blackheath Essex CO2 34 E6
Blackheath Gt.Lon. SE3 23 G4
Blackheath Suff. IP19 35 J1
Blackheath Surr. GU4 22 D7
Blackheath W.Mid. B65 40 B7
Blackhill Aber. AB42 99 J5
Blackhill Aber. AB42 99 J6
Blackhillock AB55 98 C6
Blackhills IV30 97 K6
Blackland SN11 20 D5
Blacklands TA24 7 G2
Blackleach PR4 55 H6
Blackley M9 49 H2
Blacklunans PH10 82 C1
Blackmill CF35 18 C3
Blackmoor Hants. GU33 11 J1
Blackmoor Som. TA21 7 K4
Blackmoor Gate EX31 6 E1
Blackmoorfoot HD7 50 C1
Blackmore CM4 24 C1
Blackmore End Essex CM7 34 B5
Blackmore End Herts. AL4 32 E7
Blackness Aber. AB31 90 E5
Blackness Falk. EH49 75 J3
Blackness High. KW3 105 H5
Blacknest GU34 22 A7
Blackney DT6 8 D5
Blacko BB9 56 D5
Blackpole WR3 29 H3
BLACKPOOL B'pool FY 55 G6
Blackpool Devon TQ6 5 J6
Blackpool Bridge SA67 16 D4
Blackpool Gate CA6 70 A6
Blackpool International Airport FY4 55 G6
Blackridge EH48 75 G4
Blackrock Arg.& B. PA44 72 B4
Blackrock Mon. NP7 28 B7
Blackrod BL6 49 F1
Blackshaw DG1 69 F7
Blackshaw Head HX7 56 E7
Blacksmith's Green IP14 35 F2
Blacksnape BB3 56 C7
Blackstone BN5 13 F5
Blackthorn OX25 31 H7
Blackthorpe IP30 34 D2
Blacktoft DN14 58 E7
Blacktop AB15 91 G4
Blacktown CF3 19 F3
Blackwater Cornw. TR4 2 E4
Blackwater Hants. GU17 22 B6
Blackwater I.o.W. PO30 11 G6
Blackwater Norf. NR9 44 E3
Blackwater Som. TA20 8 B3
Blackwaterfoot KA27 66 D1
Blackwell Darl. DL3 62 D5
Blackwell Derbys. SK17 50 D5
Blackwell Derbys. DE55 51 G7
Blackwell W.Suss. RH19 13 G3
Blackwell Warks. CV36 30 D4
Blackwell Worcs. B60 29 J1
Blackwells End GL19 29 G6
Blackwood (Coed-duon) Caerp. NP12 18 E2
Blackwood D.& G. DG2 68 E5
Blackwood S.Lan. ML11 75 F6
Blackwood Hill ST9 49 J7
Blacon CH1 48 C6
Bladbean CT4 15 G3
Bladnoch DG8 64 E5
Bladon OX20 31 F7
Blaen Clydach CF40 18 C2
Blaenannerch SA43 17 F1
Blaenau Dolwyddelan LL25 46 E7
Blaenau Ffestiniog LL41 37 F1
Blaenavon NP4 19 F1
Blaenawey NP7 28 B7
Blaencelyn SA44 26 C3
Blaencwm CF42 18 C1
Blaendyryn LD3 27 J5
Blaenffos SA37 16 E2
Blaengarw CF32 18 C2
Blaengeuffordd SY23 37 F7
Blaengweche SA18 17 K4
Blaengwrach SA11 18 B1
Blaengwynfi SA13 18 B2
Blaenllechau CF43 18 D2
Blaenos SA20 27 G5
Blaenpennal SY23 27 F2
Blaenplwyf SY23 26 E1
Blaenporth SA43 17 F1
Blaenrhondda CF42 18 C1
Blaenwaun SA34 17 F3
Blaen-y-coed SA33 17 G3
Blagdon N.Som. BS40 19 H6
Blagdon Torbay TQ3 5 J4
Blagdon Hill TA3 8 B3
Blaguegate WN8 48 D2
Blaich PH33 87 G7
Blaina NP13 18 E1
Blair KA24 74 B6
Blair Atholl PH18 81 K1
Blair Drummond FK9 75 F1
Blairannaich G83 80 E7
Blairbuie PA23 73 K3
Blairgowrie PH10 82 C3
Blairhall KY12 75 J2
Blairhoyle FK8 81 H7
Blairhullichan FK8 81 F7
Blairingone FK14 75 H1
Blairkip KA5 74 D7
Blairlogie FK9 75 G1
Blairmore Arg.& B. PA23 73 K2
Blairmore High. IV28 96 E1
Blairmore High. IV27 102 D3
Blairnairn G84 74 A2
Blairnamarrow AB37 89 K3
Blairpark KA24 74 A5
Blairquhan KA19 67 H3
Blairquhosh G63 74 D2
Blair's Ferry PA21 73 H4
Blairshinnoch AB45 98 E4
Blairuskinmore FK8 81 F7
Blairvadach G84 74 A2
Blairydryne AB31 91 F5
Blairythan Cottage AB41 91 H2
Blaisdon GL17 29 G7
Blake End CM77 34 B6
Blakebrook DY11 29 H1
Blakedown DY10 29 H1
Blakelaw Sc.Bord. TD5 77 F7
Blakelaw T.& W. NE5 71 H7
Blakeley WV5 40 A6
Blakelow CW5 49 F7
Blakemere HR2 28 C4
Blakeney Glos. GL15 19 K1
Blakeney Norf. NR25 44 E1
Blakenhall Ches. CW5 39 G1
Blakenhall W.Mid. WV2 40 B6
Blakeshall DY11 40 A7
Blakesley NN12 31 H3
Blanchland DH8 62 A1
Bland Hill HG3 57 H4
Blandford Camp DT11 9 J4
Blandford Forum DT11 9 H4
Blandford St. Mary DT11 9 H4
Blanefield G63 74 D3
Blanerne TD11 77 G5
Blankney LN4 52 D6
Blantyre G72 74 E5
Blar a' Chaorainn PH33 80 C1
Blargie PH20 88 D5
Blarglas G83 74 B2
Blarmachfoldach PH33 80 B1
Blarnalearoch IV23 95 H2
Blashford BH24 10 C4
Blaston LE16 42 B6
Blathaisbhal HS6 92 D4
Blatherwycke PE8 42 C6
Blawith LA12 55 F1
Blaxhall IP12 35 H3
Blaxton DN9 51 J2
Blaydon NE21 71 G7
Bleadney BA5 19 H7
Bleadon BS24 19 G6
Bleak Hey Nook OL3 50 C2
Blean CT2 25 H5
Bleasby Lincs. LN8 52 E4
Bleasby Notts. NG14 42 A1
Bleasby Moor LN8 52 E4
Bleatarn CA16 61 J5
Bleathwood Common SY8 28 E2
Blebocraigs KY15 83 F6
Bleddfa LD7 28 B2
Bledington OX7 30 D6
Bledlow HP27 22 A1
Bledlow Ridge HP14 22 A2
Blencarn CA10 61 H3
Blencogo CA7 60 C2
Blencow CA11 61 F3
Blendworth PO8 11 J3
Blennerhasset CA7 60 C2
Blervie Castle IV36 97 H6
Bletchingdon OX5 31 G7
Bletchingley RH1 23 G6
Bletchley M.K. MK3 32 B5
Bletchley Shrop. TF9 39 F2
Bletherston SA63 16 D3
Bletsoe MK44 32 D3
Blewbury OX11 21 J3
Blickling NR11 45 F3
Blidworth NG21 51 H7
Blidworth Bottoms NG21 51 H7
Blindburn Aber. AB41 91 H1
Blindburn Northumb. NE65 70 D2
Blindcrake CA13 60 C3
Blindley Heath RH7 23 G7

Blisland **PL30** 4 A3
Bliss Gate **DY14** 29 G1
Blissford **SP6** 10 C3
Blisworth **NN7** 31 J3
Blithbury **WS15** 40 C3
Blitterlees **CA7** 60 C1
Blo' Norton **IP22** 34 E1
Blockley **GL56** 30 C5
Blofield **NR13** 45 H5
Blofield Heath **NR13** 45 H4
Blore **DE6** 40 D1
Blossomfield **B91** 30 C1
Blount's Green **ST14** 40 C2
Blowick **PR9** 48 C1
Bloxham **OX15** 31 F5
Bloxholm **LN4** 52 D7
Bloxwich **WS3** 40 B5
Bloxworth **BH20** 9 H5
Blubberhouses **LS21** 57 G4
Blue Anchor *Cornw.* **TR9** 3 G3
Blue Anchor *Som.* **TA24** 7 J1
Blue Bell Hill **ME5** 24 D5
Bluewater **DA9** 23 J4
Blundellsands **L23** 48 C3
Blundeston **NR32** 45 K6
Blunham **MK44** 32 E3
Blunsdon St. Andrew **SN26** 20 E3
Bluntington **DY10** 29 H1
Bluntisham **PE28** 33 G1
Blunts **PL12** 4 D4
Blurton **ST3** 40 A1
Blyborough **DN21** 52 C3
Blyford **IP19** 35 J1
Blymhill **TF11** 40 A4
Blymhill Common **TF11** 39 G4
Blymhill Lawn **TF11** 40 A4
Blyth *Northumb.* NE24 71 J5
Blyth *Notts.* **S81** 51 J4
Blyth Bridge **EH46** 75 K6
Blyth End **B46** 40 E6
Blythburgh **IP19** 35 J1
Blythe Bridge **ST11** 40 B1
Blythe Marsh **ST11** 40 B1
Blyton **DN21** 52 B3
Boarhills **KY16** 83 G6
Boarhunt **PO17** 11 H4
Boars Hill **OX1** 21 H1
Boarsgreave **BB4** 56 D7
Boarshead **TN6** 13 J3
Boarstall **HP18** 31 H7
Boarzell **TN19** 14 C5
Boasley Cross **EX20** 6 D6
Boat o' Brig **IV32** 98 B5
Boat of Garten PH24 89 G3
Boath **IV17** 96 C4
Bobbing **ME9** 24 E5
Bobbington **DY7** 40 A6
Bobbingworth **CM5** 23 J1
Bocaddon **PL13** 4 B5
Bochastle **FK17** 81 H7
Bockhampton **RG17** 21 G4
Bocking **CM7** 34 B6
Bocking Churchstreet **CM7** 34 B6
Bockleton **WR15** 28 E2
Boconnoc **PL22** 4 B4
Boddam *Aber.* **AB42** 99 K6
Boddam *Shet.* **ZE2** 107 M11
Bodden **BA4** 19 K7
Boddington **GL51** 29 H6
Bodedern **LL65** 46 B4
Bodelwyddan **LL18** 47 J5
Bodenham *Here.* **HR1** 28 E3
Bodenham *Wilts.* **SP5** 10 C2
Bodenham Moor **HR1** 28 E3
Bodesbeck **DG10** 69 G3
Bodewryd **LL66** 46 B3
Bodfari **LL16** 47 J5
Bodffordd **LL77** 46 C5
Bodfuan **LL53** 36 C2
Bodham **NR25** 45 F1
Bodiam **TN32** 14 C5
Bodicote **OX15** 31 F5
Bodieve **PL27** 3 G1
Bodinnick **PL23** 4 B5
Bodior **LL65** 46 A5
Bodle Street Green **BN27** 13 K5
Bodmin PL31 4 A4
Bodney **IP26** 44 C6
Bodorgan LL62 46 B6
Bodrane **PL14** 4 C4
Bodsham Green **TN25** 15 G3
Bodwen **PL26** 4 A4
Bodymoor Heath **B76** 40 D6
Bogallan **IV1** 96 D6
Bogbain **IV2** 96 E7
Bogbrae **AB42** 91 J1
Bogbuie **IV7** 96 C6
Bogend **KA1** 74 B7
Bogfern **AB33** 90 D4
Bogfields **AB33** 90 D4
Bogfold **AB43** 99 G5
Boghead *Aber.* **AB45** 98 E5
Boghead *E.Ayr.* **KA18** 68 B1
Boghead *S.Lan.* **ML11** 75 F6
Boghole Farm **IV12** 97 G6
Bogmoor **IV32** 98 B4
Bogniebrae **AB54** 98 D6
Bognor Regis PO21 12 C7
Bograxie **AB51** 91 F3
Bogroy **PH23** 89 G2
Bogside **FK10** 75 H1
Bogston **AB36** 90 B4
Bogton **AB53** 98 E5
Bogue **DG7** 68 B5
Bohemia **SP5** 10 D3
Bohenie **PH31** 87 J6
Bohetherick **PL12** 4 E4
Bohortha **TR2** 3 F5
Bohuntine **PH31** 87 J6
Boirseam **HS3** 93 F3
Bojewyan **TR19** 2 A5
Bokiddick **PL30** 4 A4
Bolam *Dur.* **DL2** 62 C4
Bolam *Northumb.* **NE61** 71 F5
Bolberry **TQ7** 5 G7
Bold Heath **WA8** 48 E4
Bolderwood **SO43** 10 D4
Boldon **NE36** 71 J7
Boldon Colliery NE35 71 J7
Boldre **SO41** 10 E5
Boldron **DL12** 62 B5
Bole **DN22** 51 K4
Bolehill **DE4** 50 E7
Boleigh **TR19** 2 B6
Bolenowe **TR14** 2 D5
Boleside **TD1** 76 C7
Bolfracks **PH15** 81 K3
Bolgoed **SA4** 17 K5
Bolham *Devon* **EX16** 7 H4
Bolham *Notts.* **DN22** 51 K4
Bolham Water **EX15** 7 K4
Bolingey **TR6** 2 E3
Bollington **SK10** 49 J5
Bolney **RH17** 13 F4
Bolnhurst **MK44** 32 D3
Bolshan **DD11** 83 H2
Bolsover **S44** 51 G5
Bolsterstone **S36** 50 E3
Bolstone **HR2** 28 E5
Boltby **YO7** 57 K1
Bolter End **HP14** 22 A2
Bolton *Cumb.* **CA16** 61 H4
Bolton *E.Loth.* **EH41** 76 D3
Bolton *E.Riding* **YO42** 58 D4
BOLTON *Gt.Man.* BL 49 G2
Bolton *Northumb.* **NE66** 71 G2
Bolton Abbey **BD23** 57 F4
Bolton Bridge **BD23** 57 F4
Bolton by Bowland **BB7** 56 C5
Bolton Houses **PR4** 55 H6
Bolton Low Houses **CA7** 60 D2
Bolton Percy **YO23** 58 B5
Bolton upon Dearne **S63** 51 G2
Bolton Wood Lane **CA7** 60 D2
Boltonfellend **CA6** 69 K7
Boltongate **CA7** 60 D2
Bolton-le-Sands **LA5** 55 H3
Bolton-on-Swale **DL10** 62 D7
Bolventor **PL15** 4 B3
Bombie **DG6** 65 H6
Bomere Heath **SY4** 38 D4
Bonar Bridge **IV24** 96 D2
Bonawe **PA37** 80 B4
Bonby **DN20** 52 D1
Boncath SA37 17 F2
Bonchester Bridge **TD9** 70 A2
Bonchurch **PO38** 11 G7
Bondleigh **EX20** 6 E5
Bonds **PR3** 55 H5
Bonehill **B78** 40 D5
Bo'ness EH51 75 H2
Bonhill **G83** 74 B3
Boningale **WV7** 40 A5
Bonjedward **TD8** 70 B1
Bonkle **ML2** 75 G5
Bonning Gate **LA8** 61 F7
Bonnington *Edin.* **EH27** 75 K4
Bonnington *Kent* **TN25** 15 F4
Bonnybank **KY8** 82 E7
Bonnybridge FK4 75 G2
Bonnykelly **AB53** 99 G5
Bonnyrigg EH19 76 B4
Bonnyton *Aber.* **AB52** 90 E1
Bonnyton *Angus* **DD11** 83 G4
Bonnyton *Angus* **DD10** 83 H2
Bonnyton *Angus* **DD3** 82 E4
Bonsall **DE4** 50 E7
Bont **NP7** 28 C7
Bont Dolgadfan **SY19** 37 H5
Bont Newydd **LL40** 37 G3
Bontddu **LL40** 37 F4
Bont-goch (Elerch) **SY24** 37 F7
Bonthorpe **LN13** 53 H5
Bont-newydd *Conwy* **LL17** 47 J5
Bontnewydd *Gwyn.* **LL55** 46 C6
Bontuchel **LL15** 47 J7
Bonvilston **CF5** 18 D4
Bon-y-maen **SA1** 17 K6
Boode **EX33** 6 D2
Boohay **TQ6** 5 K5
Booker **HP12** 22 B2
Booley **SY4** 38 E3
Boor **IV22** 94 E3
Boorley Green **SO32** 11 G3
Boosbeck **TS12** 63 H5
Boose's Green **CO6** 34 C5
Boot **CA19** 60 C6
Boot Street **IP6** 35 G4
Booth **HX2** 57 F7
Booth Bank **HD7** 50 C1
Booth Green **SK10** 49 J4
Booth Wood **HX6** 50 C1
Boothby Graffoe **LN5** 52 C7
Boothby Pagnell **NG33** 42 C2
Boothstown **M28** 49 G2
Boothville **NN3** 31 J2
Bootle *Cumb.* **LA19** 54 E1
Bootle *Mersey.* L20 48 C3
Booton **NR10** 45 F3
Boots Green **WA16** 49 G5
Booze **DL11** 62 B6
Boquhan **G63** 74 D2
Boraston **WR15** 29 F1
Bordeaux **GY3** 3 J5
Borden *Kent* **ME9** 24 E5
Borden *W.Suss.* **GU30** 12 B4
Bordley **BD23** 56 E3
Bordon GU35 11 J1
Boreham *Essex* **CM3** 24 D1
Boreham *Wilts.* **BA12** 20 B7
Boreham Street **BN27** 13 K5
Borehamwood WD6 22 E2
Boreland *D. & G.* **DG11** 69 G4
Boreland *D. & G.* **DG8** 64 D4
Boreland *Stir.* **FK21** 81 G4
Boreley **WR9** 29 H2
Boreraig **IV55** 93 G6
Borgh *W.Isles* **HS6** 92 E3
Borgh *W.Isles* **HS9** 84 B4
Borgh (Borve) *W.Isles* **HS2** 101 G2
Borghastan **HS2** 100 D3
Borgie **KW14** 103 J3
Borgue *D. & G.* **DG6** 65 G6
Borgue *High.* **KW7** 105 G6
Borley **CO10** 34 C4
Borley Green *Essex* **CO10** 34 C4
Borley Green *Suff.* **IP30** 34 D2
Bornais **HS8** 84 C2
Borness **DG6** 65 G6
Bornisketaig **IV51** 93 J4
Borough Green **TN15** 23 K6
Boroughbridge **YO51** 57 J3
Borras Head **LL13** 48 C7
Borrowash **DE72** 41 G2
Borrowby *N.Yorks.* **TS13** 63 J5
Borrowby *N.Yorks.* **YO7** 57 K1
Borrowdale **CA12** 60 D5
Borrowfield **AB39** 91 G5
Borstal **ME1** 24 D5
Borth SY24 37 F7
Borthwick **EH23** 76 B5
Borthwickbrae **TD9** 69 K2
Borthwickshiels **TD9** 69 K2
Borth-y-Gest **LL49** 36 E2
Borve *High.* **IV51** 93 K7
Borve (Borgh) *W.Isles* **HS2** 101 G2
Borwick **LA6** 55 J2
Borwick Rails **LA18** 54 E2
Bosavern **TR19** 2 A5
Bosbury **HR8** 29 F4
Boscarne **PL30** 4 A4
Boscastle PL35 4 A1
Boscombe *Bourne.* **BH5** 10 C5
Boscombe *Wilts.* **SP4** 10 D1
Bosham **PO18** 12 B6
Bosham Hoe **PO18** 12 B6
Bosherston **SA71** 16 C6
Bosley **SK11** 49 J6
Bossall **YO60** 58 D3
Bossiney **PL34** 4 A2
Bossingham **CT4** 15 G3
Bossington *Hants.* **SO20** 10 E1
Bossington *Som.* **TA24** 7 G1
Bostadh **HS2** 100 D4
Bostock Green **CW10** 49 F6
Boston PE21 43 G1
Boston Spa **LS23** 57 K5
Boswarthan **TR20** 2 B5
Boswinger **PL26** 3 G4
Botallack **TR19** 2 A5
Botany Bay **EN2** 23 G2
Botcheston **LE9** 41 G5
Botesdale **IP22** 34 E1
Bothal **NE61** 71 H5
Bothamsall **DN22** 51 J5
Bothel **CA7** 60 C3
Bothenhampton **DT6** 8 D5
Bothwell **G71** 75 F5
Botley *Bucks.* **HP5** 22 C1
Botley *Hants.* **SO30** 11 G3
Botley *Oxon.* **OX2** 21 H1
Botloe's Green **GL18** 29 G6
Botolph Claydon **MK18** 31 J6
Botolphs **BN44** 12 E6
Botolph's Bridge **CT21** 15 G4
Bottacks **IV14** 96 B5
Bottesford *Leics.* **NG13** 42 B2
Bottesford *N.Lincs.* **DN16** 52 B2
Bottisham **CB5** 33 J2
Bottlesford **SN9** 20 E6
Bottom Boat **WF3** 57 J7
Bottom of Hutton **PR4** 55 H7
Bottom o'th'Moor **BL6** 49 F1
Bottomcraig **DD6** 82 E5
Bottoms **OL14** 56 E7
Botton Head **LA2** 56 B3
Botusfleming **PL12** 4 E4
Botwnnog **LL53** 36 B2
Bough Beech **TN8** 23 H7
Boughrood **LD3** 28 A5
Boughspring **NP16** 19 J2
Boughton *Norf.* **PE33** 44 B5
Boughton *Northants.* **NN2** 31 J2
Boughton *Notts.* **NG22** 51 J6
Boughton Aluph **TN25** 15 F3
Boughton Green **ME17** 14 C2
Boughton Lees **TN25** 15 F3
Boughton Malherbe **ME17** 14 D3
Boughton Street **ME13** 15 F2
Boulby **TS13** 63 J5
Bouldnor **PO41** 10 E6
Bouldon **SY7** 38 E7
Boulge **IP13** 35 G3
Boulmer **NE66** 71 H2
Boulston **SA62** 16 C4
Boultenstone Hotel **AB36** 90 C3
Boultham **LN6** 52 C6
Boundary *Derbys.* **DE11** 41 F4
Boundary *Staffs.* **ST10** 40 B1
Bourn **CB3** 33 G3
Bourne PE10 42 D3
Bourne End *Beds.* **MK43** 32 C4
Bourne End *Bucks.* SL8 22 B3
Bourne End *Herts.* **HP1** 22 D1
Bournebridge **RM4** 23 J2
BOURNEMOUTH BH 10 B5
Bournemouth Airport **BH23** 10 C5
Bournheath **B61** 29 J1
Bournmoor **DH4** 62 E1
Bournville **B30** 40 C7
Bourton *Bucks.* **MK18** 31 J5
Bourton *Dorset* **SP8** 9 G1
Bourton *N.Som.* **BS22** 19 G5
Bourton *Oxon.* **SN6** 21 F3
Bourton *Shrop.* **TF13** 38 E6
Bourton *Wilts.* **SN10** 20 D5
Bourton on Dunsmore **CV23** 31 F1
Bourton-on-the-Hill **GL56** 30 C5
Bourton-on-the-Water **GL54** 30 C6
Bousd **PA78** 78 D1
Boustead Hill **CA5** 60 D1
Bouth **LA12** 55 G1
Bouthwaite **HG3** 57 G2
Bovain **FK21** 81 G4
Boveney **SL4** 22 C4
Boveridge **BH21** 10 B3
Boverton **CF61** 18 C5
Bovey Tracey **TQ13** 5 J3
Bovingdon **HP3** 22 D1
Bovinger **CM5** 23 J1
Bovington Camp **BH20** 9 H6
Bow *Cumb.* **CA5** 60 E1
Bow *Devon* **EX17** 7 F5
Bow *Devon* **TQ9** 5 J5
Bow *Ork.* **KW16** 106 C8
Bow Brickhill **MK17** 32 C5
Bow of Fife **KY15** 82 E6
Bow Street *Cere.* SY24 37 F7
Bow Street *Norf.* **NR17** 44 E6
Bowbank **DL12** 62 A4
Bowburn **DH6** 62 E3
Bowcombe **PO30** 11 F6
Bowd **EX10** 7 K6
Bowden *Devon* **TQ6** 5 J6
Bowden *Sc.Bord.* **TD6** 76 D7
Bowden Hill **SN15** 20 C5
Bowdon **WA14** 49 G4
Bower **NE48** 70 C5
Bower Hinton **TA12** 8 D3
Bower House Tye **CO6** 34 D4
Bowerchalke **SP5** 10 B2
Bowerhill **SN12** 20 C5
Bowermadden **KW1** 105 H2
Bowers **ST21** 40 A2
Bowers Gifford **SS13** 24 D3
Bowershall **KY12** 75 J1
Bowertower **KW1** 105 H2
Bowes **DL12** 62 A5
Bowgreave **PR3** 55 H5
Bowhousebog **ML7** 75 G5
Bowithick **PL15** 4 B2
Bowker's Green **L39** 48 D2
Bowland Bridge **LA11** 55 H1
Bowley **HR1** 28 E3
Bowley Town **HR1** 28 E3
Bowlhead Green **GU8** 12 C3
Bowling *W.Dun.* **G60** 74 C3
Bowling *W.Yorks.* **BD4** 57 G6
Bowling Bank **LL13** 38 C1
Bowlish **BA4** 19 K7
Bowmanstead **LA21** 60 E7
Bowmore **PA43** 72 B4
Bowness-on-Solway **CA7** 69 H7
Bowness-on-Windermere **LA23** 60 F7
Bowscale **CA11** 60 E3
Bowsden **TD15** 77 H6
Bowside Lodge **KW14** 104 D2
Bowston **LA8** 61 F7
Bowthorpe **NR5** 45 F5
Bowtrees **FK2** 75 H2
Box *Glos.* **GL6** 20 B1
Box *Wilts.* **SN13** 20 B5
Box End **MK43** 32 D4
Boxbush *Glos.* **GL14** 29 G7
Boxbush *Glos.* **GL17** 29 F6
Boxford *Suff.* **CO10** 34 D4
Boxford *W.Berks.* **RG20** 21 H4
Boxgrove **PO18** 12 C6
Boxley **ME14** 14 C2
Boxmoor **HP1** 22 D1
Box's Shop **EX23** 6 A5
Boxted *Essex* **CO4** 34 D5
Boxted *Suff.* **IP29** 34 C3
Boxted Cross **CO4** 34 D5
Boxwell **GL8** 20 B2
Boxworth **CB3** 33 G2
Boxworth End **CB4** 33 G2
Boyden Gate **CT3** 25 J5
Boydston **KA1** 74 C7
Boylestone **DE6** 40 D2
Boyndie **AB45** 98 E4
Boynton **YO16** 59 H3
Boys Hill **DT9** 9 F4
Boysack **DD11** 83 H3
Boyton *Cornw.* **PL15** 6 B6
Boyton *Suff.* **IP12** 35 H4
Boyton *Wilts.* **BA12** 9 J1
Boyton Cross **CM1** 24 C1
Boyton End **CO10** 34 B4
Bozeat **NN29** 32 C3
Braaid **IM4** 54 C6
Braal Castle **KW12** 105 G2
Brabling Green **IP13** 35 G2
Brabourne **TN25** 15 F3
Brabourne Lees **TN25** 15 F3
Brabster **KW1** 105 J2
Bracadale **IV56** 85 J1
Braceborough **PE9** 42 D4
Bracebridge Heath **LN4** 52 C6
Braceby **NG34** 42 D2
Bracewell **BD23** 56 D5
Brachla **IV3** 88 C1
Bracken Hill **WF14** 57 G7
Brackenber **CA16** 61 J5
Brackenbottom **BD24** 56 D2
Brackenfield **DE55** 51 F7
Brackens **AB53** 99 F5
Bracklach **AB54** 90 B2
Bracklamore **AB43** 99 G5
Bracklesham **PO20** 12 B7
Brackletter **PH34** 87 H6
Brackley *Arg. & B.* **PA31** 73 G2
Brackley *High.* **IV2** 97 F6
Brackley *Northants.* NN13 31 G5
Brackley Gate **DE7** 41 F1
Brackley Hatch **NN13** 31 H4
Bracknell RG12 22 B5
Braco **FK15** 81 K7
Bracobrae **AB55** 98 D5
Bracon Ash **NR14** 45 F6
Bracora **PH40** 86 D5
Bracorina **PH40** 86 D5
Bradbourne **DE6** 50 E7
Bradbury **TS21** 62 E4
Bradda **IM9** 54 A6
Bradden **NN12** 31 H4
Braddock **PL22** 4 B4
Bradenham *Bucks.* **HP14** 22 B2
Bradenham *Norf.* **IP25** 44 D5
Bradenstoke **SN15** 20 D4
Bradfield *Devon* **EX15** 7 J5
Bradfield *Essex* **CO11** 35 F5
Bradfield *Norf.* **NR28** 45 G2
Bradfield *W.Berks.* **RG7** 21 K4
Bradfield Combust **IP30** 34 C3
Bradfield Green **CW1** 49 F7
Bradfield Heath **CO11** 35 F6
Bradfield St. Clare **IP30** 34 D3
Bradfield St. George **IP30** 34 D2
Bradford *Cornw.* **PL30** 4 B3
Bradford *Derbys.* **DE45** 50 E6
Bradford *Devon* **EX22** 6 C5
Bradford *Northumb.* **NE70** 77 K7
Bradford *Northumb.* **NE20** 71 F6
BRADFORD *W.Yorks.* BD 57 G6
Bradford Abbas **DT9** 8 E3
Bradford Leigh **BA15** 20 B5
Bradford Peverell **DT2** 9 F5
Bradford-on-Avon BA15 20 B5
Bradford-on-Tone **TA4** 7 K3
Bradiford **EX31** 6 D2
Brading **PO36** 11 H6
Bradley *Ches.* **WA6** 48 E5
Bradley *Derbys.* **DE6** 40 E1
Bradley *Hants.* **SO24** 21 K7
Bradley *N.E.Lincs.* **DN37** 53 F2
Bradley (Low Bradley) *N.Yorks.* **BD20** 57 F5
Bradley *Staffs.* **ST18** 40 A4
Bradley *W.Mid.* **WV14** 40 B6
Bradley Fold **BL2** 49 G2
Bradley Green *Warks.* **CV9** 40 E5
Bradley Green *Worcs.* **B96** 29 J2
Bradley in the Moors **ST10** 40 C1
Bradley Mills **HD5** 50 D1
Bradley Stoke **BS32** 19 K3
Bradmore *Notts.* **NG11** 41 H2
Bradmore *W.Mid.* **WV3** 40 A6
Bradney **TA7** 8 C1
Bradninch **EX5** 7 J5
Bradnop **ST13** 50 C7
Bradnor Green **HR5** 28 B3
Bradpole **DT6** 8 D5
Bradshaw *Gt.Man.* **BL2** 49 G1
Bradshaw *W.Yorks.* **HX2** 57 F6
Bradstone **PL19** 6 B7
Bradwall Green **CW11** 49 G6
Bradwell *Derbys.* **S33** 50 D4
Bradwell *Devon* **EX34** 6 C1
Bradwell *Essex* **CM77** 34 C6
Bradwell *M.K.* **MK13** 32 B5
Bradwell *Norf.* **NR31** 45 K5
Bradwell Grove **OX18** 21 F1
Bradwell Waterside **CM0** 25 F1
Bradwell-on-Sea **CM0** 25 G1
Bradworthy **EX22** 6 B4
Brae *D. & G.* **DG2** 65 J3
Brae *High.* **IV24** 96 B1
Brae *Shet.* **ZE2** 107 M6
Brae of Achnahaird **IV26** 102 C7
Braeantra **IV17** 96 C4
Braedownie **DD8** 89 K7
Braefoot **AB53** 99 F6
Braegrum **PH1** 82 B5
Braehead *D. & G.* **DG8** 64 E5
Braehead *Glas.* **G51** 74 D4
Braehead *Moray* **AB55** 98 B6
Braehead *Ork.* **KW17** 106 E7
Braehead *Ork.* **KW17** 106 D3
Braehead *S.Lan.* **ML11** 75 G7
Braehead *S.Lan.* **ML11** 75 H5
Braehead of Lunan **DD10** 83 H2
Braehoulland **ZE2** 107 L5
Braeleny **FK17** 81 H6
Braemar **AB35** 89 J5
Braemore *High.* **IV27** 96 C1
Braemore *High.* **KW6** 105 F5
Braemore *High.* **IV23** 95 H4
Braenaloin **AB35** 89 K5
Braes of Enzie **AB56** 98 B5
Braes of Foss **PH16** 81 J2
Braes of Ullapool **IV26** 95 H2
Braeswick **KW17** 106 F4
Braeval **FK8** 81 G7
Braewick **ZE2** 107 M7
Brafferton *Darl.* **DL1** 62 D4
Brafferton *N.Yorks.* **YO61** 57 K2
Brafield-on-the-Green **NN7** 32 B3
Bragar **HS2** 100 E3

Bragbury End SG2 33 F6
Bragenham LU7 32 C6
Bragleenbeg PA34 80 A5
Braichmelyn LL57 46 E6
Braides LA2 55 H4
Braidley DL8 57 F1
Braidwood ML8 75 G6
Braigo PA44 72 A4
Brailsford DE6 40 E1
Brain's Green GL15 19 K1
Braintree CM7 34 B6
Braiseworth IP23 35 F1
Braishfield SO51 10 E2
Braithwaite *Cumb.* CA12 60 D4
Braithwaite *S.Yorks.* DN7 51 J1
Braithwaite *W.Yorks.* BD22 57 F5
Braithwell S66 51 H3
Bramber BN44 12 E5
Brambletye RH18 13 H3
Brambridge SO50 11 F2
Bramcote *Notts.* NG9 41 H2
Bramcote *Warks.* CV11 41 G7
Bramdean SO24 11 H2
Bramerton NR14 45 G5
Bramfield *Herts.* SG14 33 F7
Bramfield *Suff.* IP19 35 H1
Bramford IP8 35 F4
Bramhall SK7 49 H4
Bramham LS23 57 K5
Bramhope LS16 57 H5
Bramley *Hants.* RG26 21 K6
Bramley *S.Yorks.* S66 51 G3
Bramley *Surr.* GU5 22 D7
Bramley Corner RG26 21 K6
Bramley Head HG3 57 G4
Bramley Vale S44 51 G6
Bramling CT3 15 H2
Brampford Speke EX5 7 H6
Brampton *Cambs.* PE28 33 F1
Brampton *Cumb.* CA8 70 A7
Brampton *Cumb.* CA16 61 H4
Brampton *Derbys.* S40 51 F5
Brampton *Lincs.* LN1 52 B5
Brampton *Norf.* NR10 45 G3
Brampton *S.Yorks.* S73 51 G2
Brampton *Suff.* NR34 45 J7
Brampton Abbotts HR9 29 F6
Brampton Ash LE16 42 A7
Brampton Bryan SY7 28 C1
Brampton en le Morthen S66 51 G4
Brampton Street NR34 45 J7
Bramshall ST14 40 C2
Bramshaw SO43 10 D3
Bramshill RG27 22 A5
Bramshott GU30 12 B3
Bramwell TA10 8 D2
Bran End CM6 33 K6
Branault PH36 79 G1
Brancaster PE31 44 B1
Brancaster Staithe PE31 44 B1
Brancepeth DH7 62 D3
Branchill IV36 97 H6
Brand Green GL19 29 G6
Brandelhow CA12 60 D4
Branderburgh IV31 97 K4
Brandesburton YO25 59 H5
Brandeston IP13 35 G2
Brandis Corner EX22 6 C5
Brandiston NR10 45 F3
Brandon *Dur.* DH7 62 D3
Brandon *Lincs.* NG32 42 C1
Brandon *Northumb.* NE66 71 F2
Brandon *Suff.* IP27 44 B7
Brandon *Warks.* CV8 31 F1
Brandon Bank PE38 44 A7
Brandon Creek PE38 44 A6
Brandon Parva NR9 44 E5
Brandsby YO61 58 B2
Brandy Wharf DN21 52 D3
Brane TR20 2 B6
Branksome BH12 10 B5
Branksome Park BH13 10 B5
Bransbury SO21 21 H7
Bransby LN1 52 B5
Branscombe EX12 7 K7
Bransford WR6 29 G3
Bransford Bridge WR6 29 H3
Bransgore BH23 10 C5
Bransholme HU7 59 H6
Branson's Cross B98 30 B1
Branston *Leics.* NG32 42 B3
Branston *Lincs.* LN4 52 D6
Branston *Staffs.* DE14 40 E3
Branston Booths LN4 52 D6
Brant Broughton LN5 52 C7
Brantham CO11 35 F5
Branthwaite *Cumb.* CA7 60 D3
Branthwaite *Cumb.* CA14 60 B4
Brantingham HU15 59 F7
Branton *Northumb.* NE66 71 F2
Branton *S.Yorks.* DN3 51 J2
Brantwood LA21 60 E7
Branxholm Bridgend TD9 69 K2
Branxholme TD9 69 K2
Branxton TD12 77 G7
Brassey Green CW6 48 E6
Brassington DE4 50 E7
Brasted TN16 23 H6
Brasted Chart TN16 23 H6
Brathens AB31 90 E5
Bratoft PE24 53 H6
Brattleby LN1 52 C4
Bratton *Som.* TA24 7 H1
Bratton *Tel. & W.* TF5 39 F4
Bratton *Wilts.* BA13 20 C6
Bratton Clovelly EX20 6 C6
Bratton Fleming EX31 6 E2
Bratton Seymour BA9 9 F2
Braughing SG11 33 G6
Brauncewell NG34 52 D7
Braunston *Northants.* NN11 31 G2
Braunston *Rut.* LE15 42 B5
Braunstone LE3 41 H5
Braunton EX33 6 C2
Brawby YO17 58 D2
Brawdy SA62 16 B3
Brawith TS9 63 G6
Brawl KW14 104 D2
Brawlbin KW12 105 F3
Bray SL6 22 C4
Bray Shop PL17 4 D3
Bray Wick SL6 22 B4
Braybrooke LE16 42 A7
Braydon Side SN15 20 D3
Brayford EX32 6 E2
Brayshaw BD23 56 C4
Braythorn LS21 57 H5
Brayton YO8 58 C6
Braywoodside SL6 22 B4
Brazacott PL15 4 C1
Brea TR15 2 D4
Breach *Kent* CT4 15 G3
Breach *Kent* ME9 24 E5
Breachwood Green SG4 32 E6
Breacleit HS2 100 D4
Breaden Heath SY13 38 D2
Breadsall DE21 41 F2
Breadstone GL13 20 A1
Breage TR13 2 D6
Breakon ZE2 107 P2
Bream GL15 19 K1
Breamore SP6 10 C3
Brean TA8 19 F6
Breanais HS2 100 B5
Brearton HG3 57 J3
Breascleit HS2 100 E4
Breaston DE72 41 G2
Brechfa SA32 17 J2
Brechin DD9 83 H1
Brecklate PA28 66 A2
Breckles NR17 44 D6
Brecon (Aberhonddu) LD3 27 K6
Breconside DG3 68 D3
Bredbury SK6 49 J3
Brede TN31 14 D6
Bredenbury HR7 29 F3
Bredfield IP13 35 G3
Bredgar ME9 24 E5
Bredhurst ME7 24 D5
Bredon GL20 29 J5
Bredon's Hardwick GL20 29 J5
Bredon's Norton GL20 29 J5
Bredwardine HR3 28 C4
Breedon on the Hill DE73 41 G3
Breibhig HS2 101 G4
Breich EH55 75 H4
Breightmet BL2 49 G2
Breighton YO8 58 D6
Breinton HR4 28 D5
Breinton Common HR4 28 D5
Bremhill SN11 20 C4
Bremhill Wick SN11 20 C4
Brenachoille PA32 80 B7
Brenchley TN12 23 K7
Brendon *Devon* EX35 7 F1
Brendon *Devon* EX22 6 B4
Brendon *Devon* EX22 6 B5
Brenkley NE13 71 H6
Brent Eleigh CO10 34 D4
Brent Knoll TA9 19 G6
Brent Pelham SG9 33 H5
Brentford TW8 22 E4
Brentingby LE14 42 A4
Brentwood CM14 23 J2
Brenzett TN29 15 F5
Brenzett Green TN29 15 F5
Breoch DG7 65 H5
Brereton WS15 40 C4
Brereton Green CW11 49 G6
Brereton Heath CW12 49 H6
Breretonhill WS15 40 C4
Bressay ZE2 107 P8
Bressingham IP22 44 E7
Bressingham Common IP22 44 E7
Bretby DE15 40 E3
Bretford CV23 31 F1
Bretforton WR11 30 B4
Bretherdale Head CA10 61 G6
Bretherton PR26 55 H7
Brettabister ZE2 107 N7
Brettenham *Norf.* IP24 44 D7
Brettenham *Suff.* IP7 34 D3
Bretton *Derbys.* S32 50 D5
Bretton *Flints.* CH4 48 C6
Brevig HS9 84 B5
Brewood ST19 40 A5
Briach IV36 97 H6
Briantspuddle DT2 9 H5
Brick End CM6 33 J6
Brickendon SG13 23 G1
Bricket Wood AL2 22 E1
Brickkiln Green CM7 34 B5
Bricklehampton WR10 29 J4
Bride IM7 54 D3
Bridekirk CA13 60 C3
Bridell SA43 16 E1
Bridestones CW12 49 J6
Bridestowe EX20 6 D7
Brideswell AB54 90 D1
Bridford EX6 7 G7
Bridge *Cornw.* TR16 2 D4
Bridge *Kent* CT4 15 G2
Bridge End *Cumb.* LA20 55 F1
Bridge End *Devon* TQ7 5 G6
Bridge End *Essex* CM7 33 K5
Bridge End *Lincs.* NG34 42 E2
Bridge End *Shet.* ZE2 107 M9
Bridge Hewick HG4 57 J2
Bridge o'Ess AB34 90 D5
Bridge of Alford AB33 90 D3
Bridge of Allan FK9 75 F1
Bridge of Avon AB37 89 J1
Bridge of Balgie PH15 81 G3
Bridge of Bogendreip AB31 90 E5
Bridge of Brewlands PH11 82 C1
Bridge of Brown AB37 89 J2
Bridge of Cally PH10 82 C2
Bridge of Canny AB31 90 E5
Bridge of Craigisla PH11 82 D2
Bridge of Dee *Aber.* AB35 89 J5
Bridge of Dee *Aber.* AB31 90 E5
Bridge of Dee *D. & G.* DG7 65 H4
Bridge of Don AB23 91 H4
Bridge of Dun DD10 83 H2
Bridge of Dye AB31 90 E6
Bridge of Earn PH2 82 C6
Bridge of Ericht PH17 81 G2
Bridge of Feugh AB31 90 E5
Bridge of Forss KW14 105 F2
Bridge of Gairn AB35 90 B5
Bridge of Gaur PH17 81 G2
Bridge of Muchalls AB39 91 G5
Bridge of Muick AB35 90 B5
Bridge of Orchy PA36 80 D4
Bridge of Tynet AB56 98 B4
Bridge of Walls ZE2 107 L7
Bridge of Weir PA11 74 B4
Bridge Reeve EX18 6 E4
Bridge Sollers HR4 28 D4
Bridge Street CO10 34 C4
Bridge Trafford CH2 48 D5
Bridgefoot *Angus* DD3 82 E4
Bridgefoot *Cambs.* SG8 33 H4
Bridgefoot *Cumb.* CA14 60 B4
Bridgehampton BA22 8 E2
Bridgehaugh AB55 90 B1
Bridgehill DH8 62 B1
Bridgemary PO13 11 G4
Bridgemere CW5 39 G1
Bridgend *Aber.* AB54 90 D1
Bridgend *Aber.* AB53 99 F6
Bridgend *Angus* DD9 83 G1
Bridgend *Arg. & B.* PA44 72 B4
Bridgend *Arg. & B.* PA31 73 G1
Bridgend (Pen-y-bont ar Ogwr) *Bridgend* CF31 18 C4
Bridgend *Cornw.* PL22 4 B5
Bridgend *Cumb.* CA11 60 F5
Bridgend *Fife* KY15 82 E6
Bridgend *Moray* AB54 90 B1
Bridgend *P. & K.* PH2 82 C5
Bridgend *W.Loth.* EH49 75 J3
Bridgend of Lintrathen DD8 82 D2
Bridgerule EX22 6 A5
Bridges SY5 38 C6
Bridgeton *Aber.* AB33 90 D3
Bridgeton *Glas.* G40 74 E4
Bridgetown *Cornw.* PL15 6 B7
Bridgetown *Som.* TA22 7 H2
Bridgeyate BS30 19 K4
Bridgham NR16 44 D7
Bridgnorth WV16 39 G6
Bridgtown WS11 40 B5
Bridgwater TA6 8 B1
Bridlington YO16 59 H3
Bridport DT6 8 D5
Bridstow HR9 28 E6
Brierfield BB9 56 D6
Brierley *Glos.* GL17 29 F7
Brierley *Here.* HR6 28 D3
Brierley *S.Yorks.* S72 51 G1
Brierley Hill DY5 40 B7
Brierton TS22 63 F4
Briestfield WF12 50 E1
Brig o'Turk FK17 81 G7
Brigg DN20 52 D2
Briggate NR28 45 H3
Briggswath YO21 63 K6
Brigham *Cumb.* CA13 60 B3
Brigham *E.Riding* YO25 59 G4
Brighouse HD6 57 G7
Brighstone PO30 11 F6
Brightgate DE4 50 E7
Brighthampton OX29 21 G1
Brightholmlee S35 50 E3
Brightling TN32 13 K4
Brightlingsea CO7 34 E7
BRIGHTON *B. & H.* BN 13 G6
Brighton *Cornw.* TR2 3 G3
Brightons FK2 75 H3
Brightwalton RG20 21 H4
Brightwalton Green RG20 21 H4
Brightwell IP10 35 G4
Brightwell Baldwin OX49 21 K2
Brightwell Upperton OX49 21 K2
Brightwell-cum-Sotwell OX10 21 J2
Brignall DL12 62 B5
Brigsley DN37 53 F2
Brigsteer LA8 55 H1
Brigstock NN14 42 C7
Brill *Bucks.* HP18 31 H7
Brill *Cornw.* TR11 2 E6
Brilley HR3 28 B4
Brilley Mountain HR3 28 B3
Brimaston SA62 16 C3
Brimfield SY8 28 E2
Brimington S43 51 G5
Brimington Common S43 51 G5
Brimley TQ13 5 J3
Brimpsfield GL4 29 J7
Brimpton RG7 21 J5
Brims KW16 106 B9
Brimscombe GL5 20 B1
Brimstage CH63 48 C4
Brinacory PH41 86 D5
Brindham BA6 19 J7
Brindister *Shet.* ZE2 107 N9
Brindister *Shet.* ZE2 107 L7
Brindle PR6 55 J7
Brindley Ford ST8 49 H7
Brineton TF11 40 A4
Bringhurst LE16 42 B6
Brington PE28 32 D1
Brinian KW17 106 D5
Briningham NR24 44 E2
Brinkhill LN11 53 G5
Brinkley *Cambs.* CB8 33 K3
Brinkley *Notts.* NG25 51 K7
Brinklow CV23 31 F1
Brinkworth SN15 20 D3
Brinmore IV2 88 D2
Brinscall PR6 56 B7
Brinsea BS49 19 H5
Brinsley NG16 41 G1
Brinsop HR4 28 D4
Brinsworth S60 51 G3
Brinton NR24 44 E2
Brisco CA4 60 F1
Brisley NR20 44 D3
Brislington BS4 19 K4
Brissenden Green TN26 14 E4
BRISTOL BS 19 J4
Bristol Filton Airport BS10 19 J3
Bristol International Airport BS48 19 J5
Briston NR24 44 E2
Britannia OL13 56 D7
Britford SP5 10 C2
Brithdir *Caerp.* NP24 18 E1
Brithdir *Gwyn.* LL40 37 G4
Brithem Bottom EX15 7 J4
Briton Ferry (Llansawel) SA11 18 A2
Britwell SL2 22 C3
Britwell Salome OX49 21 K2
Brixham TQ5 5 K5
Brixton *Devon* PL8 5 F5
Brixton *Gt.Lon.* SW2 23 G4
Brixton Deverill BA12 9 H1
Brixworth NN6 31 J1
Brize Norton OX18 21 F1
Broad Alley WR9 29 H2
Broad Blunsdon SN26 20 E2
Broad Campden GL55 30 C5
Broad Carr HX4 50 C1
Broad Chalke SP5 10 B2
Broad Ford TN12 14 C4
Broad Green *Beds.* MK43 32 C4
Broad Green *Cambs.* CB8 33 K3
Broad Green *Essex* CO6 34 C6
Broad Green *Essex* SG8 33 H5
Broad Green *Mersey.* L14 48 D3
Broad Green *Suff.* IP6 34 E3
Broad Green *Worcs.* WR6 29 G3
Broad Haven SA62 16 B4
Broad Hill CB7 33 J1
Broad Hinton SN4 20 E4
Broad Laying RG20 21 H5
Broad Marston CV37 30 C4
Broad Oak *Carmar.* SA32 17 J3
Broad Oak *Cumb.* CA18 60 C7
Broad Oak *E.Suss.* TN31 14 D6
Broad Oak *E.Suss.* TN21 13 K4
Broad Oak *Here.* HR2 28 D6
Broad Road IP21 35 G1
Broad Street *E.Suss.* TN36 14 D6
Broad Street *Kent* ME17 14 D2
Broad Street *Kent* TN25 15 G4
Broad Street *Wilts.* SN9 20 E6
Broad Street Green CM9 24 E1
Broad Town SN4 20 D4
Broadbottom SK14 49 J3
Broadbridge PO18 12 B6
Broadbridge Heath RH12 12 E3
Broadclyst EX5 7 H6
Broadfield *Lancs.* BB5 56 C7
Broadfield *Lancs.* PR25 55 J7
Broadford IV49 86 C2
Broadford Bridge RH14 12 D4
Broadgate LA18 54 E1
Broadhaugh TD9 69 K3
Broadhaven KW1 105 J3
Broadheath *Gt.Man.* WA14 49 G4
Broadheath *Worcs.* WR15 29 F2
Broadhembury EX14 7 K5
Broadhempston TQ9 5 J4
Broadholme LN1 52 B5
Broadland Row TN31 14 D6
Broadlay SA17 17 G5
Broadley *Lancs.* OL12 49 H1
Broadley *Moray* AB56 98 B4
Broadley Common EN9 23 H1
Broadmayne DT2 9 G6
Broadmeadows TD7 76 C7
Broadmere RG25 21 K7
Broadmoor SA68 16 D5
Broadnymett EX17 7 F5
Broadoak *Dorset* DT6 8 D5
Broadoak *Glos.* GL14 29 F7
Broadoak *Kent* CT2 25 H5
Broadoak End SG14 33 G7
Broadrashes AB55 98 C5
Broad's Green CM3 33 K7
Broadsea AB43 99 H4
Broadstairs CT10 25 K5
Broadstone *Poole* BH18 10 B5
Broadstone *Shrop.* SY7 38 E7
Broadstreet Common NP18 19 G3
Broadwas WR6 29 G3
Broadwater *Herts.* SG2 33 F6
Broadwater *W.Suss.* BN14 12 E6
Broadwater Down TN2 13 J3
Broadwaters DY10 29 H1
Broadway *Carmar.* SA17 17 G5
Broadway *Carmar.* SA33 17 F4
Broadway *Pembs.* SA62 16 B4
Broadway *Som.* TA19 8 C3
Broadway *Suff.* IP19 35 H1
Broadway *Worcs.* WR12 30 C5
Broadwell *Glos.* GL56 30 D6
Broadwell *Oxon.* GL7 21 F1
Broadwell *Warks.* CV23 31 F2
Broadwell House NE47 62 A1
Broadwey DT3 9 F6
Broadwindsor DT8 8 D4
Broadwood Kelly EX19 6 E5
Broadwoodwidger PL16 6 C7
Brobury HR3 28 C4
Brocastle CF35 18 C4
Brochel IV40 94 B7
Brochloch DG7 67 K4
Brock PA77 78 B3
Brockamin WR6 29 G3
Brockbridge SO32 11 H3
Brockdish IP21 35 G1
Brockenhurst SO42 10 D4
Brockford Green IP14 35 F2
Brockford Street IP14 35 F2
Brockhall NN7 31 H2
Brockham RH3 22 E7
Brockhampton *Glos.* GL54 30 B6
Brockhampton *Glos.* GL51 29 J6
Brockhampton *Here.* HR1 28 E5
Brockhampton *Here.* WR6 29 F3
Brockhampton Green DT2 9 G4
Brockholes HD9 50 D1
Brockhurst *Hants.* PO12 11 G4
Brockhurst *W.Suss.* RH19 13 H3
Brocklebank CA7 60 E2
Brocklesby DN41 52 E1
Brockley *N.Som.* BS48 19 H5
Brockley *Suff.* IP29 34 C3
Brockley Green CO10 34 B4
Brock's Green RG20 21 H5
Brockton *Shrop.* TF13 38 E6
Brockton *Shrop.* TF11 39 G5
Brockton *Shrop.* SY5 38 C5
Brockton *Shrop.* SY7 38 C7
Brockton *Tel. & W.* TF10 39 G4
Brockweir NP16 19 J1
Brockwood Park SO24 11 H2
Brockworth GL3 29 H7
Brocton ST17 40 B4
Brodick KA27 73 J7
Brodsworth DN5 51 H2
Brogborough MK43 32 C5
Brogden BB18 56 D5
Brogyntyn SY10 38 B2
Broken Cross *Ches.* SK11 49 H5
Broken Cross *Ches.* CW9 49 F5
Brokenborough SN16 20 C3
Brokes DL11 62 C7
Bromborough CH62 48 C4
Brome IP23 35 F1
Brome Street IP23 35 F1
Bromeswell IP12 35 H3
Bromfield *Cumb.* CA7 60 C2
Bromfield *Shrop.* SY8 28 D1
Bromham *Beds.* MK43 32 D3
Bromham *Wilts.* SN15 20 C5
BROMLEY *Gt.Lon.* BR 23 H5
Bromley *S.Yorks.* S35 51 F3
Bromley Cross BL7 49 G1
Bromley Green TN26 14 E4
Brompton *Med.* ME7 24 D5
Brompton *N.Yorks.* DL6 62 E7
Brompton *N.Yorks.* YO13 59 F1
Brompton *Shrop.* SY5 38 E5
Brompton on Swale DL10 62 D7
Brompton Ralph TA4 7 J2
Brompton Regis TA22 7 H2
Bromsash HR9 29 F6
Bromsberrow HR8 29 G5
Bromsberrow Heath HR8 29 G5
Bromsgrove B61 29 J1
Bromstead Heath TF10 40 A4
Bromyard HR7 29 F3
Bromyard Downs HR7 29 F3
Bronaber LL41 37 G2
Brondesbury NW6 23 F3
Brongest SA38 17 G1
Bronington SY13 38 D2
Bronllys LD3 28 A5
Bronnant SY23 27 F2
Bronwydd Arms SA33 17 H3
Bronydd HR3 28 B4
Bron-y-gaer SA33 17 G4
Bronygarth SY10 38 B2
Brook *Carmar.* SA33 17 F5
Brook *Hants.* SO43 10 D3
Brook *Hants.* SO20 10 E2
Brook *I.o.W.* PO30 10 E6
Brook *Kent* TN25 15 F3
Brook *Surr.* GU8 12 C3
Brook *Surr.* GU5 22 D7
Brook Bottom OL5 49 J2
Brook End *Beds.* MK44 32 D2
Brook End *Herts.* SG9 33 G6
Brook End *M.K.* MK16 32 C4
Brook End *Worcs.* WR5 29 H4
Brook Hill SO43 10 D3
Brook Street *Essex* CM14 23 J2
Brook Street *Kent* TN26 14 E4
Brook Street *Suff.* CO10 34 C4
Brook Street *W.Suss.* RH17 13 G4
Brooke *Norf.* NR15 45 G6
Brooke *Rut.* LE15 42 B5
Brookend *Glos.* GL15 19 J2

Brookend Glos. GL13 19 K1
Brookfield SK14 50 C3
Brookhampton OX44 21 K2
Brookhouse Ches. SK10 49 J5
Brookhouse Denb. LL16 47 J6
Brookhouse Lancs. LA2 55 J3
Brookhouse S.Yorks. S25 51 H4
Brookhouse Green CW11 49 H6
Brookhouses ST10 40 B1
Brookland TN29 14 E5
Brooklands D. & G. DG2 65 J3
Brooklands Shrop. SY13 38 E1
Brookmans Park AL9 23 F1
Brooks SY21 38 A6
Brooks Green RH13 12 E4
Brooksby LE14 41 J4
Brookthorpe GL4 29 H7
Brookwood GU24 22 C6
Broom Beds. SG18 32 E4
Broom Fife KY8 82 E7
Broom Warks. B50 30 B3
Broom Green NR20 44 D3
Broom Hill Dorset BH21 10 B4
Broom Hill Worcs. DY9 29 J1
Broom of Dalreach PH3 82 B6
Broomcroft SY5 38 E5
Broome Norf. NR35 45 H6
Broome Shrop. SY7 38 D7
Broome Worcs. DY9 29 J1
Broome Wood NE66 71 G2
Broomedge WA13 49 G4
Broomer's Corner RH13 12 E4
Broomfield Aber. AB41 91 H1
Broomfield Essex CM1 34 B7
Broomfield Kent CT6 25 H5
Broomfield Kent ME17 14 D2
Broomfield Som. TA5 8 B1
Broomfleet HU15 58 E7
Broomhall Green CW5 39 F1
Broomhaugh NE44 71 F7
Broomhead AB43 99 H4
Broomhill Bristol BS16 19 K4
Broomhill Northumb. NE65 71 H3
Broomielaw DL12 62 B5
Broomley NE43 71 F7
Broompark DH7 62 D2
Broom's Green GL18 29 G5
Brora KW9 97 G1
Broseley TF12 39 F5
Brotherlee DL13 62 A3
Brothertoft PE20 43 F1
Brotherton WF11 57 K7
Brotton TS12 63 H5
Broubster KW14 105 F2
Brough Cumb. CA17 61 J5
Brough Derbys. S33 50 D4
Brough E.Riding HU15 59 F7
Brough High. KW14 105 H1
Brough Notts. NG23 52 B7
Brough Ork. KW17 106 C6
Brough Shet. ZE2 107 P8
Brough Shet. ZE2 107 N5
Brough Shet. ZE2 107 P6
Brough Shet. ZE2 107 P5
Brough Lodge ZE2 107 P3
Brough Sowerby CA17 61 J5
Broughall SY13 38 E1
Brougham CA10 61 G4
Broughton Bucks. HP20 32 B7
Broughton Cambs. PE28 33 F1
Broughton Flints. CH4 48 C6
Broughton Hants. SO20 10 E1
Broughton Lancs. PR3 55 J6
Broughton M.K. MK16 32 B4
Broughton N.Lincs. DN20 52 C2
Broughton N.Yorks. YO17 58 D2
Broughton N.Yorks. BD23 56 E4
Broughton Northants. NN14 32 B1
Broughton Ork. KW17 106 D3
Broughton Oxon. OX15 31 F5
Broughton Sc.Bord. ML12 75 K7
Broughton V. of Glam. CF71 18 C4
Broughton Astley LE9 41 H6
Broughton Beck LA12 55 F1
Broughton Gifford SN12 20 B5
Broughton Green WR9 29 J2
Broughton Hackett WR7 29 J3
Broughton in Furness LA20 55 F1
Broughton Mills LA20 60 D7
Broughton Moor CA15 60 B3
Broughton Poggs GL7 21 F1
Broughtown KW17 106 F3
Broughty Ferry DD5 83 F4
Browland ZE2 107 L7
Brown Candover SO24 11 G1
Brown Edge Lancs. PR8 48 C1
Brown Edge Staffs. ST6 49 J7
Brown Heath CH3 48 D6
Brown Lees ST8 49 H7
Brown Street IP14 34 E2
Brownber CA17 61 J6
Browndown PO13 11 G5
Brownheath SY12 38 D3
Brownhill AB41 99 G6
Brownhills Fife KY16 83 G6
Brownhills W.Mid. WS8 40 C5
Brownieside NE67 71 G1
Brownlow CW12 49 H6
Brownlow Heath CW12 49 H6
Brown's Bank CW3 39 F1
Brownsea Island BH15 10 B6
Brownshill GL6 20 B1
Brownshill Green CV5 41 F7
Brownsover CV21 31 G1
Brownston PL21 5 G5
Browston Green NR31 45 J5
Broxa YO13 63 J3
Broxbourne EN10 23 G1
Broxburn E.Loth. EH42 76 E3
Broxburn W.Loth. EH52 75 J3
Broxholme LN1 52 C5
Broxted CM6 33 J6
Broxton CH3 48 D7
Broxwood HR6 28 C3
Broyle Side BN8 13 H5
Bru (Brue) HS2 101 F3
Bruachmary IV12 97 F7
Bruan KW2 105 J5
Brue (Bru) HS2 101 F3
Bruera CH3 48 D6
Bruern OX7 30 D6
Bruernish HS9 84 C4
Bruichladdich PA49 72 A4
Bruisyard IP17 35 H2
Bruisyard Street IP17 35 H2
Brumby DN16 52 C1
Brund SK17 50 D6
Brundall NR13 45 H5
Brundish Norf. NR14 45 H6
Brundish Suff. IP13 35 G2
Brundish Street IP13 35 G1
Brunstock CA6 60 F1
Brunswick Village NE13 71 H6
Bruntingthorpe LE17 41 J6
Bruntland AB54 90 C2
Brunton Fife KY15 82 E5
Brunton Northumb. NE66 71 H1
Brunton Wilts. SN8 21 F6
Brushfield SK17 50 D5
Brushford Devon EX18 6 E5
Brushford Som. TA22 7 H3
Bruton BA10 9 F1
Bryanston DT11 9 H4
Bryant's Bottom HP16 22 B2
Brydekirk DG12 69 G6
Brymbo LL11 48 B7
Brympton BA22 8 E3
Bryn Caerp. NP12 18 E2
Bryn Carmar. SA14 17 J5
Bryn Ches. CW8 49 F5
Bryn Gt.Man. WN4 48 E2
Bryn N.P.T. SA13 18 B2
Bryn Shrop. SY9 38 B7
Bryn Bwbach LL47 37 F2
Bryn Gates WN2 48 E2
Bryn Pen-y-lan LL14 38 C1
Brynamman SA18 27 G7
Brynberian SA41 16 E2
Brynbuga (Usk) NP15 19 G1
Bryncae CF72 18 C3
Bryncethin CF32 18 C3
Bryncir LL51 36 D1
Bryncoch Bridgend CF32 18 C3
Bryn-côch N.P.T. SA10 18 A2
Bryncroes LL53 36 B2
Bryncrug LL36 37 F5
Bryneglwys LL21 38 A1
Brynford CH8 47 K5
Bryngwran LL65 46 B5
Bryngwyn Mon. NP15 19 G1
Bryngwyn Powys HR5 28 A4
Bryn-henllan SA42 16 D2
Brynhoffnant SA44 26 C3
Bryning PR4 55 H6
Brynithel NP13 19 F1
Brynmawr B.Gwent NP23 28 A7
Bryn-mawr Gwyn. LL53 36 B2
Brynmelyn LD1 28 A1
Brynmenyn CF32 18 C3
Brynna CF72 18 C3
Brynnau Gwynion CF72 18 C3
Brynog SA48 26 E3
Bryn-penarth SY21 38 A5
Brynrefail Gwyn. LL55 46 D6
Brynrefail I.o.A. LL70 46 C4
Brynsadler CF72 18 D3
Brynsaithmarchog LL21 47 J7
Brynsiencyn LL61 46 C6
Bryn-teg I.o.A. LL78 46 C4
Brynteg Wrex. LL11 48 C7
Bryn-y-cochin SY12 38 C2
Brynygwenin NP7 28 C7
Bryn-y-maen LL28 47 G5
Buaile nam Bodach HS9 84 C4
Bualadubh HS8 92 C7
Bualintur IV47 85 K2
Bualnaluib IV22 94 E2
Bubbenhall CV8 30 E1
Bubnell DE45 50 E5
Bubwith YO8 58 D6
Buccleuch TD9 69 J2
Buchan DG7 65 H4
Buchanan Castle G63 74 C2
Buchanhaven AB42 99 K6
Buchanty PH1 82 A5
Buchlyvie FK8 74 D1
Buckabank CA5 60 E2
Buckby Wharf NN11 31 H2
Buckden Cambs. PE19 32 E2
Buckden N.Yorks. BD23 56 E2
Buckenham NR13 45 H5
Buckerell EX14 7 K5
Buckfast TQ11 5 H4
Buckfastleigh TQ11 5 H4
Buckhaven KY8 76 B1
Buckholm TD1 76 C7
Buckholt NP25 28 E7
Buckhorn Weston SP8 9 G2
Buckhurst Hill IG9 23 H2
Buckie AB56 98 C4
Buckies KW14 105 G2
Buckingham MK18 31 H5
Buckland Bucks. HP22 32 B7
Buckland Devon TQ7 5 G6
Buckland Glos. WR12 30 B5
Buckland Hants. SO41 10 E5
Buckland Here. HR6 28 E3
Buckland Herts. SG9 33 G5
Buckland Kent CT16 15 J3
Buckland Oxon. SN7 21 G2
Buckland Surr. RH3 23 F6
Buckland Brewer EX39 6 C3
Buckland Common HP23 22 C1
Buckland Dinham BA11 20 A6
Buckland Filleigh EX21 6 C5
Buckland in the Moor TQ13 5 H3
Buckland Monachorum PL20 4 E4
Buckland Newton DT2 9 F4
Buckland Ripers DT3 9 F6
Buckland St. Mary TA20 8 B3
Buckland-tout-Saints TQ7 5 H6
Bucklebury RG7 21 J4
Bucklerheads DD5 83 F4
Bucklers Hard SO42 11 F5
Bucklesham IP10 35 G4
Buckley (Bwcle) CH7 48 B6
Buckley Green B95 30 C2
Bucklow Hill WA16 49 G4
Buckman Corner RH14 12 E4
Buckminster NG33 42 B3
Bucknall Lincs. LN10 52 E6
Bucknall Stoke ST2 40 B1
Bucknell Oxon. OX27 31 G6
Bucknell Shrop. SY7 28 C1
Buckridge DY14 29 G1
Buck's Cross EX39 6 B3
Bucks Green RH12 12 D3
Bucks Hill WD4 22 D1
Bucks Horn Oak GU10 22 B7
Buck's Mills EX39 6 B3
Bucksburn AB21 91 G4
Buckspool SA71 16 C6
Buckton E.Riding YO15 59 H2
Buckton Here. SY7 28 C1
Buckton Northumb. NE70 77 J7
Buckton Vale SK15 49 J2
Buckworth PE28 32 E1
Budbrooke CV35 30 D2
Budby NG22 51 J5
Buddon DD7 83 G4
Bude EX23 6 A5
Budge's Shop PL12 4 D5
Budlake EX5 7 H5
Budle NE69 77 K7
Budleigh Salterton EX9 7 J7
Budock Water TR11 2 E5
Budworth Heath CW9 49 F5
Buerton CW3 39 F1
Bugbrooke NN7 31 H3
Bugeildy (Beguildy) LD7 28 A1
Buglawton CW12 49 H6
Bugle PL26 4 A5
Bugthorpe YO41 58 D4
Building End SG8 33 H5
Buildwas TF8 39 F5
Builth Road LD2 27 K3
Builth Wells (Llanfair-ym-Muallt) LD2 27 K3
Bulby PE10 42 D3
Bulcote NG14 41 J1
Buldoo KW14 104 E2
Bulford SP4 20 E7
Bulford Camp SP4 20 E7
Bulkeley SY14 48 E7
Bulkington Warks. CV12 41 F7
Bulkington Wilts. SN10 20 C6
Bulkworthy EX22 6 B4
Bull Bay (Porth Llechog) LL68 46 C3
Bull Green TN26 14 E4
Bullbridge DE56 51 F7
Bullbrook RG12 22 B5
Bullen's Green AL4 23 F1
Bulley GL2 29 G7
Bullington LN3 52 D5
Bullpot Farm LA6 56 B1
Bulls Cross EN2 23 G2
Bull's Green Herts. SG3 33 F7
Bull's Green Norf. NR34 45 J6
Bullwood PA23 73 K3
Bulmer Essex CO10 34 C4
Bulmer N.Yorks. YO60 58 C3
Bulmer Tye CO10 34 C5
Bulphan RM14 24 C3
Bulstone EX12 7 K7
Bulverhythe TN38 14 C7
Bulwark AB42 99 H6
Bulwell NG6 41 H1
Bulwick NN17 42 C6
Bumble's Green EN9 23 H1
Bun Abhainn Eadarra HS3 100 D7
Bun Loyne IV63 87 J4
Bunarkaig PH34 87 H6
Bunbury CW6 48 E7
Bunbury Heath CW6 48 E7
Bunchrew IV3 96 D7
Bundalloch IV40 86 E2
Buness ZE2 107 Q2
Bunessan PA67 78 E5
Bungay NR35 45 H7
Bunker's Hill LN4 53 F7
Bunlarie PA28 73 F7
Bunloit IV63 88 C2
Bunmhullin HS8 84 C3
Bunnahabhain PA46 72 C3
Bunny NG11 41 H3
Buntait IV63 87 K1
Buntingford SG9 33 G6
Bunwell NR16 45 F6
Bunwell Street NR16 45 F6
Burbage Derbys. SK17 50 C5
Burbage Leics. LE10 41 G6
Burbage Wilts. SN8 21 F5
Burchett's Green SL6 22 B3
Burcombe SP2 10 B1
Burcot Oxon. OX14 21 J2
Burcot Worcs. B60 29 J1
Burcott LU7 32 B6
Burdale YO17 58 E3
Burdocks RH14 12 D4
Burdon SR3 62 E1
Burdrop OX15 30 E5
Bures CO8 34 D5
Bures Green CO8 34 D5
Burfa LD8 28 B2
Burford Oxon. OX18 30 D7
Burford Shrop. WR15 28 E2
Burg PA74 78 E3
Burgate IP22 34 E1
Burgates GU33 11 J2
Burge End SG5 32 E5
Burgess Hill RH15 13 G5
Burgh IP13 35 G3
Burgh by Sands CA5 60 E1
Burgh Castle NR31 45 J5
Burgh Heath KT20 23 F6
Burgh le Marsh PE24 53 H6
Burgh next Aylsham NR11 45 G3
Burgh on Bain LN8 53 F4
Burgh St. Margaret (Fleggburgh) NR29 45 J4
Burgh St. Peter NR34 45 J6
Burghclere RG20 21 H5
Burghead IV30 97 J5
Burghfield RG30 21 K5
Burghfield Common RG7 21 K5
Burghfield Hill RG7 21 K5
Burghill HR4 28 D4
Burghwallis DN6 51 H1
Burham ME1 24 D5
Buriton GU31 11 J2
Burland CW5 49 F7
Burlawn PL27 3 G2
Burleigh SL5 22 C5
Burlescombe EX16 7 J4
Burleston DT2 9 G5
Burley Hants. BH24 10 D4
Burley Rut. LE15 42 B4
Burley W.Yorks. LS6 57 H6
Burley Gate HR1 28 E4
Burley in Wharfedale LS29 57 G5
Burley Street BH24 10 D4
Burley Woodhead LS29 57 G5
Burleydam SY13 39 F1
Burlingjobb LD8 28 B3
Burlow TN21 13 J5
Burlton SY4 38 D3
Burmarsh TN29 15 G4
Burmington CV36 30 D5
Burn YO8 58 B7
Burn Farm DD9 90 E7
Burn Naze FY5 55 G5
Burn of Cambus FK16 81 J7
Burnage M19 49 H3
Burnaston DE65 40 E2
Burnby YO42 58 E5
Burncross S35 51 F3
Burndell BN18 12 C6
Burnden BL3 49 G2
Burnedge OL2 49 J1
Burnend AB41 99 G6
Burneside LA9 61 G7
Burness KW17 106 F3
Burneston DL8 57 J1
Burnett BS31 19 K5
Burnfoot High. KW11 104 D6
Burnfoot P. & K. FK14 82 A7
Burnfoot Sc.Bord. TD9 70 A2
Burnfoot Sc.Bord. TD9 69 K2
Burnham Bucks. SL1 22 C3
Burnham N.Lincs. DN18 52 D1
Burnham Deepdale PE31 44 C1
Burnham Green AL6 33 F7
Burnham Market PE31 44 C1
Burnham Norton PE31 44 C1
Burnham Overy Staithe PE31 44 C1
Burnham Overy Town PE31 44 C1
Burnham Thorpe PE31 44 C1
Burnham-on-Crouch CM0 25 F2
Burnham-on-Sea TA8 19 G7
Burnhaven AB42 99 K6
Burnhead D. & G. DG7 67 K5
Burnhead D. & G. DG3 68 D4
Burnhervie AB51 91 F3
Burnhill Green WV6 39 G5
Burnhope DH7 62 C2
Burnhouse KA15 74 B5
Burniston YO13 63 K3
Burnley BB11 56 D6
Burnmouth TD14 77 H4
Burnopfield NE16 62 C1
Burn's Green SG2 33 G6
Burnsall BD23 57 F3
Burnside Aber. AB32 91 F3
Burnside Angus DD8 83 G2
Burnside E.Ayr. KA18 67 K2
Burnside Fife KY13 82 C7
Burnside Shet. ZE2 107 L5
Burnside W.Loth. EH52 75 J3
Burnside of Duntrune DD4 83 F4
Burnstones CA8 61 H1
Burnswark DG11 69 G6
Burnt Hill RG18 21 J4
Burnt Houses DL13 62 C4
Burnt Oak HA8 23 F2
Burnt Yates HG3 57 H3
Burntcliff Top SK11 49 J6
Burntisland KY3 76 A2
Burnton E.Ayr. KA18 67 J3
Burnton E.Ayr. KA6 67 J3
Burntwood WS7 40 C5
Burntwood Green WS7 40 C5
Burnworthy TA3 7 K4
Burpham Surr. GU1 22 D6
Burpham W.Suss. BN18 12 D6
Burra ZE2 107 M9
Burradon Northumb. NE65 70 E3
Burradon T. & W. NE23 71 H6
Burrafirth ZE2 107 Q1
Burraland ZE2 107 M5
Burras TR13 2 D5
Burraton Cornw. PL12 4 E4
Burraton Cornw. PL12 4 E5
Burravoe Shet. ZE2 107 P5
Burravoe Shet. ZE2 107 M6
Burray KW17 106 D8
Burrells CA16 61 H5
Burrelton PH13 82 D4
Burridge Devon EX13 8 C4
Burridge Hants. SO31 11 G3
Burrill DL8 57 H1
Burringham DN17 52 B2
Burrington Devon EX37 6 E4
Burrington Here. SY8 28 D1
Burrington N.Som. BS40 19 H6
Burrough Green CB8 33 K3
Burrough on the Hill LE14 42 A4
Burrow Som. TA24 7 H1
Burrow Som. TA12 8 D3
Burrow Bridge TA7 8 C1
Burrowhill GU24 22 C5
Burrows Cross GU5 22 D7
Burry SA3 17 H6
Burry Green SA3 17 H6
Burry Port SA16 17 H5
Burscough L40 48 D1
Burscough Bridge L40 48 D1
Bursea YO43 58 E6
Burshill YO25 59 G5
Bursledon SO31 11 F4
Burslem ST6 40 A1
Burstall IP8 35 F4
Burstock DT8 8 D4
Burston Norf. IP22 45 F7
Burston Staffs. ST18 40 B2
Burstow RH6 23 G7
Burstwick HU12 59 J7
Burtersett DL8 56 D1
Burthorpe IP29 34 B2
Burthwaite CA4 60 F2
Burtle TA7 19 H7
Burtle Hill TA7 19 G7
Burton Ches. CH64 48 C5
Burton Ches. CW6 48 E6
Burton Dorset BH23 10 C5
Burton Lincs. LN1 52 C5
Burton Northumb. NE69 77 K7
Burton Pembs. SA73 16 C5
Burton Som. TA5 7 K1
Burton Wilts. SN14 20 B4
Burton Wilts. BA12 9 H1
Burton Agnes YO25 59 H3
Burton Bradstock DT6 8 D6
Burton Coggles NG33 42 C3
Burton End CM24 33 J6
Burton Ferry SA73 16 C5
Burton Fleming YO25 59 G2
Burton Green Warks. CV8 30 D1
Burton Green Wrex. LL12 48 C7
Burton Hastings CV11 41 G7
Burton in Lonsdale LA6 56 B2
Burton Joyce NG14 41 J1
Burton Latimer NN15 32 C1
Burton Lazars LE14 42 A4
Burton Leonard HG3 57 J3
Burton on the Wolds LE12 41 H3
Burton Overy LE8 41 J6
Burton Pedwardine NG34 42 E1
Burton Pidsea HU12 59 J6
Burton Salmon LS25 57 K7
Burton Stather DN15 52 B1
Burton upon Stather DN15 52 B1
Burton upon Trent DE14 40 E3
Burton-in-Kendal LA6 55 J2
Burton's Green CM77 34 C6
Burtonwood WA5 48 E3
Burwardsley CH3 48 E7
Burwarton WV16 39 F7
Burwash TN19 13 K4
Burwash Common TN19 13 K4
Burwash Weald TN19 13 K4
Burwell Cambs. CB5 33 J2
Burwell Lincs. LN11 53 G5
Burwen LL68 46 C3
Burwick Ork. KW17 106 D9
Burwick Shet. ZE1 107 M8
Bury Cambs. PE26 43 F7
Bury Gt.Man. BL9 49 H1
Bury Som. TA22 7 H3
Bury W.Suss. RH20 12 D5
Bury End WR12 30 B5
Bury Green SG11 33 H6
Bury St. Edmunds IP33 34 C2
Buryas Bridge TR19 2 B6
Burythorpe YO17 58 D3
Busbridge GU7 22 C7
Busby E.Renf. G76 74 D5
Busby P. & K. PH1 82 B5
Buscot SN7 21 F2
Bush EX23 6 A5
Bush Bank HR4 28 D3
Bush Crathie AB35 89 K5
Bush Green IP21 45 G7
Bushbury WV10 40 B5
Bushby LE7 41 J5
Bushey WD23 22 E2
Bushey Heath WD23 22 E2
Bushley GL20 29 H5
Bushley Green GL20 29 H5
Bushton SN4 20 D4
Bushy Common NR19 44 D4

Busk CA10 61 H2
Buslingthorpe LN8 52 D4
Bussage GL6 20 B1
Busta ZE2 107 M6
Butcher's Common NR12 45 H3
Butcher's Cross TN20 13 J4
Butcher's Pasture CM6 33 K6
Butcombe BS40 19 J5
Bute PA20 73 J4
Bute Town NP22 18 E1
Buthill IV30 97 J5
Butleigh BA6 8 E1
Butleigh Wootton BA6 8 E1
Butler's Cross HP17 22 B1
Butler's Hill NG15 41 H1
Butlers Marston CV35 30 E4
Butlersbank SY4 38 E3
Butley IP12 35 H3
Butley Abbey IP12 35 H4
Butley Low Corner IP12 35 H4
Butley Mills IP12 35 H3
Butley Town SK10 49 J5
Butt Green CW5 49 F7
Butt Lane ST7 49 H7
Butterburn CA8 70 B6
Buttercrambe YO41 58 D4
Butterknowle DL13 62 C4
Butterleigh EX15 7 H5
Butterley DE5 51 G7
Buttermere *Cumb.* CA13 60 C5
Buttermere *Wilts.* SN8 21 G5
Butters Green ST7 49 H7
Buttershaw BD6 57 G6
Butterstone PH8 82 B3
Butterton *Staffs.* ST13 50 C7
Butterton *Staffs.* ST5 40 A1
Butterwick *Dur.* TS21 62 E4
Butterwick *Lincs.* PE22 43 G1
Butterwick *N.Yorks.* YO17 59 F2
Butterwick *N.Yorks.* YO17 58 D2
Buttington SY21 38 B5
Buttonbridge DY12 29 G1
Buttonoak DY12 29 G1
Buttons' Green IP30 34 D3
Butts EX6 7 G7
Butt's Green *Essex* CM2 24 D1
Butt's Green *Hants.* SO51 10 D2
Buttsash SO45 11 F4
Buxhall IP14 34 E3
Buxted TN22 13 H4
Buxton *Derbys.* SK17 50 C5
Buxton *Norf.* NR10 45 G3
Buxton Heath NR10 45 F3
Buxworth SK23 50 C4
Bwcle (Buckley) CH7 48 B6
Bwlch LD3 28 A6
Bwlch-clawdd SA44 17 G2
Bwlch-derwin LL51 36 D1
Bwlchgwyn LL11 48 B7
Bwlch-llan SA48 26 E3
Bwlchnewydd SA33 17 G3
Bwlchtocyn LL53 36 C3
Bwlch-y-cibau SY22 38 A4
Bwlch-y-ddar SY10 38 A3
Bwlchyfadfa SA44 17 H1
Bwlch-y-ffridd SY16 37 K6
Bwlch-y-groes SA35 17 F2
Bwlchyllyn LL54 46 D7
Bwlchymynydd SA4 17 J6
Bwlch-y-sarnau LD6 27 K1
Byers Green DL16 62 D3
Byfield NN11 31 G3
Byfleet KT14 22 D5
Byford HR4 28 C4
Bygrave SG7 33 F5
Byker NE6 71 H7
Byland Abbey YO61 58 B2
Bylane End PL14 4 C5
Bylchau LL16 47 H6
Byley CW10 49 G6
Bynea SA14 17 J6
Byrness NE19 70 C3
Bystock EX8 7 J7
Bythorn PE28 32 D1
Byton LD8 28 C2
Bywell NE43 71 F7
Byworth GU28 12 C4

C

Cabharstadh HS2 101 F5
Cabourne LN7 52 E2
Cabourne Parva LN7 52 E2
Cabrach *Arg. & B.* PA60 72 C4
Cabrach *Moray* AB54 90 B2
Cabus PR3 55 H5
Cackle Street *E.Suss.* TN31 14 D6
Cackle Street *E.Suss.* TN22 13 H4
Cacrabank TD7 69 J2
Cadboll IV20 97 F4
Cadbury EX5 7 H5
Cadbury Barton EX18 6 E4
Cadbury Heath BS30 19 K4
Cadder G64 74 E3
Cadderlie PA35 80 B4
Caddington LU1 32 D7
Caddleton PA34 79 J6
Caddonfoot TD1 76 C7
Cade Street TN21 13 K4
Cadeby *Leics.* CV13 41 G5
Cadeby *S.Yorks.* DN5 51 H2
Cadeleigh EX16 7 H5
Cader LL16 47 J6
Cadgwith TR12 2 E7
Cadham KY7 82 D7
Cadishead M44 49 G3
Cadle SA5 17 K6
Cadley *Lancs.* PR2 55 J6
Cadley *Wilts.* SN8 21 F5
Cadmore End HP14 22 A2
Cadnam SO40 10 D3
Cadney DN20 52 D2
Cadole CH7 48 B6
Cadover Bridge PL7 5 F4
Cadoxton CF63 18 E5
Cadoxton-Juxta-Neath SA10 18 A2
Cadwell SG5 32 E5
Cadwst LL21 37 K2
Cadzow ML3 75 F5
Cae Ddafydd LL48 37 F1
Caeathro LL55 46 D6
Caehopkin SA9 27 H7
Caen KW8 105 F7
Caenby LN8 52 D4
Caenby Corner LN8 52 C4
Caer Llan NP25 19 H1
Caerau *Bridgend* CF34 18 B2
Caerau *Cardiff* CF5 18 E4
Caerdeon LL42 37 F4
CAERDYDD (CARDIFF) CF 18 E4
Caerfarchell SA62 16 A3
Caerfyrddin (Carmarthen) SA31 17 H3
Caergeiliog LL65 46 B5
Caergwrle LL12 48 C7
Caergybi (Holyhead) LL65 46 A4
Caerhun LL32 47 F5
Caer-Lan SA9 27 H7
Caerleon NP18 19 G2
Caernarfon LL55 46 C6
Caerphilly CF83 18 E3
Caersws SY17 37 K6
Caerwedros SA44 26 C3
Caerwent NP26 19 H2
Caerwys CH7 47 K5
Caethle Farm LL36 37 F6
Caggan PH22 89 F3
Caggle Street NP7 28 C7
Caim *High.* PH36 79 G1
Caim *I.o.A.* LL58 46 E4
Caio SA19 17 K2
Cairinis (Carinish) HS6 92 D5
Cairisiadar HS2 100 C4
Cairminis HS5 93 F3
Cairnargat AB54 90 C1
Cairnbaan PA31 73 G1
Cairnbeathie AB31 90 D4
Cairnbrogie AB51 91 G2
Cairnbulg AB43 99 J4
Cairncross *Angus* DD9 90 D7
Cairncross *Sc.Bord.* TD14 77 G4
Cairncurran PA13 74 B4
Cairndoon DG8 64 D7
Cairndow PA26 80 C6
Cairness AB43 99 J4
Cairney Lodge KY15 82 E6
Cairneyhill KY12 75 J2
Cairnhill *Aber.* AB41 91 H2
Cairnhill *Aber.* AB52 90 E1
Cairnie *Aber.* AB32 91 G4
Cairnie *Aber.* AB54 98 C6
Cairnorrie AB41 99 G6
Cairnryan DG9 64 A4
Cairnsmore DG8 64 E4
Caister-on-Sea NR30 45 K4
Caistor LN7 52 E2
Caistor St. Edmund NR14 45 G5
Caistron NE65 70 E3
Cake Street NR17 44 E6
Cakebole DY10 29 H1
Calanais (Callanish) HS2 100 E4
Calbost HS2 101 G6
Calbourne PO30 11 F6
Calceby LN13 53 G5
Calcoed CH8 47 K5
Calcot RG31 21 K4
Calcott *Kent* CT3 25 H5
Calcott *Shrop.* SY3 38 D4
Calcotts Green GL2 29 G7
Calcutt SN6 20 E2
Caldarvan G83 74 C2
Caldback ZE2 107 Q2
Caldbeck CA7 60 E3
Caldbergh DL8 57 F1
Caldecote *Cambs.* CB3 33 G3
Caldecote *Cambs.* PE7 42 E7
Caldecote *Herts.* SG7 33 F5
Caldecote *Northants.* NN12 31 H3
Caldecote *Warks.* CV10 41 F6
Caldecott *Northants.* NN9 32 C2
Caldecott *Oxon.* OX14 21 H2
Caldecott *Rut.* LE16 42 B6
Calder Bridge CA20 60 B6
Calder Grove WF4 51 F1
Calder Mains KW12 105 F3
Calder Vale PR3 55 J5
Calderbank ML6 75 F4
Calderbrook OL15 49 J1
Caldercruix ML6 75 G4
Calderglen G72 74 E5
Caldermill ML10 74 E6
Caldey Island SA70 16 E6
Caldhame DD8 83 F3
Caldicot NP26 19 H3
Caldwell *Derbys.* DE12 40 E4
Caldwell *E.Renf.* G78 74 C5
Caldwell *N.Yorks.* DL11 62 C5
Caldy CH48 48 B4
Calebreck CA7 60 E3
Caledrhydiau SA48 26 D3
Calford Green CB9 33 K4
Calfsound KW17 106 E4
Calgary PA75 78 E2
Califer IV36 97 H6
California *Falk.* FK1 75 H3
California *Norf.* NR29 45 K4
California *Suff.* IP4 35 G4
Calke DE73 41 F3
Callakille IV54 94 C6
Callaly NE66 71 F3
Callander FK17 81 H7
Callanish (Calanais) HS2 100 E4
Callaughton TF13 39 F6
Callerton Lane End NE5 71 G7
Calliburn PA28 66 B1
Calligarry IV45 86 C4
Callington PL17 4 D4
Callingwood DE13 40 D3
Callisterhall DG11 69 H5
Callow HR2 28 D5
Callow End WR2 29 H4
Callow Hill *Wilts.* SN15 20 D3
Callow Hill *Worcs.* DY14 29 G1
Callow Hill *Worcs.* B97 30 B2
Callows Grave WR15 28 E2
Calmore SO40 10 E3
Calmsden GL7 20 D1
Calne SN11 20 C4
Calow S44 51 G5
Calrossie IV19 96 E4
Calshot SO45 11 F4
Calstock PL18 4 E4
Calstone Wellington SN11 20 D5
Calthorpe NR11 45 F2
Calthwaite CA11 61 F2
Calton *N.Yorks.* BD23 56 E4
Calton *Staffs.* ST10 50 D7
Calveley CW6 48 E7
Calver S32 50 E5
Calver Hill HR4 28 C4
Calverhall SY13 39 F2
Calverleigh EX16 7 H4
Calverley LS28 57 H6
Calvert MK18 31 H6
Calverton *M.K.* MK19 31 J5
Calverton *Notts.* NG14 41 J1
Calvine PH18 81 J1
Calvo CA7 60 C1
Cam GL11 20 A2
Camasnacroise PH33 79 K2
Camastianavaig IV51 86 B1
Camasunary IV49 86 B3
Camault Muir IV4 96 C7
Camb ZE2 107 P3
Camber TN31 14 E6
Camberley GU15 22 B5
Camberwell SE15 23 G4
Camblesforth YO8 58 C7
Cambo NE61 71 F5
Cambois NE24 71 J5
Camborne TR14 2 D5
CAMBRIDGE *Cambs.* CB 33 H3
Cambridge *Glos.* GL2 20 A1
Cambridge City Airport CB5 33 H3
Cambus FK10 75 G1
Cambus o'May AB35 90 C5
Cambusbarron FK7 75 F1
Cambuskenneth FK9 75 G1
Cambuslang G72 74 E4
Cambusnethan ML2 75 G5
Camden Town NW1 23 F3
Camel Hill BA22 8 E2
Cameley BS39 19 K6
Camelford PL32 4 B2
Camelon FK1 75 G2
Camelsdale GU27 12 B3
Camer DA13 24 C5
Cameron House G83 74 B2
Camerory PH26 89 H1
Camer's Green WR13 29 G5
Camerton *B. & N.E.Som.* BA2 19 K6
Camerton *Cumb.* CA14 60 B3
Camerton *E.Riding* HU12 59 J7
Camghouran PH17 81 G2
Camis Eskan G84 74 B2
Cammachmore AB39 91 H5
Cammeringham LN1 52 C4
Camore IV25 96 E2
Camp Hill *Pembs.* SA67 16 E4
Camp Hill *Warks.* CV10 41 F6
Campbeltown PA28 66 B1
Campbeltown Airport PA28 66 A1
Camperdown NE12 71 H6
Campmuir PH13 82 D4
Camps EH27 75 K4
Camps End CB1 33 K4
Camps Heath NR32 45 K6
Campsall DN6 51 H1
Campsea Ashe IP13 35 H3
Campton SG17 32 E5
Camptown TD8 70 B2
Camquhart PA22 73 H2
Camrose SA62 16 C3
Camserney PH15 81 K3
Camstraddan House G83 74 B1
Camus Croise IV43 86 C3
Camus-luinie IV40 87 F2
Camusnagaul *High.* PH33 87 G7
Camusnagaul *High.* IV23 95 G3
Camusrory PH41 86 E5
Camusteel IV54 94 D7
Camusterrach IV54 94 D7
Camusurich FK21 81 H4
Camusvrachan PH15 81 H3
Canada SO51 10 D3
Canaston Bridge SA67 16 D4
Candacraig AB35 90 B5
Candlesby PE23 53 H6
Candy Mill ML12 75 J6
Cane End RG4 21 K4
Canewdon SS4 24 E2
Canfield End CM6 33 J6
Canford Bottom BH21 10 B4
Canford Cliffs BH13 10 B6
Canford Magna BH21 10 B5
Canham's Green IP14 34 E2
Canisbay KW1 105 J1
Canley CV4 30 E1
Cann SP7 9 H2
Cann Common SP7 9 H2
Canna PH44 85 H4
Cannard's Grave BA4 19 K7
Cannich IV4 87 K1
Canning Town E16 23 H3
Cannington TA5 8 B1
Cannock WS11 40 B5
Cannock Wood WS15 40 C4
Cannop GL16 29 F7
Canon Bridge HR2 28 D4
Canon Frome HR8 29 F4
Canon Pyon HR4 28 D4
Canonbie DG14 69 J6
Canons Ashby NN11 31 G3
Canon's Town TR27 2 C5
Canterbury *Aber.* AB45 98 D5
CANTERBURY *Kent* CT 15 G2
Cantley *Norf.* NR13 45 H5
Cantley *S.Yorks.* DN3 51 J2
Cantlop SY5 38 E5
Canton CF11 18 E4
Cantray IV2 96 E7
Cantraydoune IV12 96 E7
Cantraywood IV2 96 E7
Cantsfield LA6 56 B2
Canvey Island SS8 24 D3
Canwell Hall B75 40 D5
Canwick LN4 52 C6
Canworthy Water PL15 4 C1
Caol PH33 87 H7
Caolas *Arg. & B.* PA77 78 B3
Caolas *W.Isles* HS9 84 B5
Caolas Scalpaigh (Kyles Scalpay) HS3 93 H2
Caolasnacon PH50 80 C1
Capel *Kent* TN12 23 K7
Capel *Surr.* RH5 22 E7
Capel Bangor SY23 37 F7
Capel Betws Lleucu SY25 27 F3
Capel Carmel LL53 36 A3
Capel Celyn LL23 37 H1
Capel Coch LL77 46 C4
Capel Curig LL24 47 F7
Capel Cynon SA44 17 G1
Capel Dewi *Carmar.* SA32 17 H3
Capel Dewi *Cere.* SY23 37 F7
Capel Dewi *Cere.* SA44 17 H1
Capel Garmon LL26 47 G7
Capel Gwyn *Carmar.* SA32 17 H3
Capel Gwyn *I.o.A.* LL65 46 B5
Capel Gwynfe SA19 27 G6
Capel Hendre SA18 17 J4
Capel Isaac SA19 17 J3
Capel Iwan SA38 17 F2
Capel le Ferne CT18 15 H4
Capel Llanilltern CF5 18 D3
Capel Mawr LL62 46 C5
Capel Parc LL71 46 C4
Capel St. Andrew IP12 35 H4
Capel St. Mary IP9 34 E5
Capel St. Silin SA48 26 E3
Capel Seion SY23 27 F1
Capel Tygwydd SA38 17 F1
Capeluchaf LL54 36 D1
Capelulo LL34 47 F5
Capel-y-ffin NP7 28 B5
Capel-y-graig LL57 46 D6
Capenhurst CH1 48 C5
Capernwray LA6 55 J2
Capheaton NE19 71 F5
Caplaw G78 74 C5
Capon's Green IP13 35 G2
Cappercleuch TD7 69 H1
Capplegill DG10 69 G3
Capstone ME7 24 D5
Capton *Devon* TQ6 5 J5
Capton *Som.* TA4 7 J2
Caputh PH1 82 B3
Car Colston NG13 42 A1
Caradon Town PL14 4 C3
Carbellow KA18 68 B1
Carbeth G63 74 D3
Carbis Bay TR26 2 C5
Carbost *High.* IV51 93 K7
Carbost *High.* IV47 85 J1
Carbrain G67 75 F3
Carbrooke IP25 44 D5
Carburton S80 51 J5
Carcary DD9 83 H2
Carco DG4 68 C2
Carcroft DN6 51 H1
Cardenden KY5 76 A1
Cardeston SY5 38 C4
Cardew CA5 60 E2
CARDIFF (CAERDYDD) CF 18 E4
Cardiff International Airport CF62 18 D5
Cardigan (Aberteifi) SA43 16 E1
Cardinal's Green CB1 33 K4
Cardington *Beds.* MK44 32 D4
Cardington *Shrop.* SY6 38 E6
Cardinham PL30 4 B4
Cardno AB43 99 H4
Cardonald G52 74 D4
Cardoness DG7 65 F5
Cardow AB38 97 J7
Cardrona EH45 76 A7
Cardross G82 74 B3
Cardurnock CA7 60 C1
Careby PE9 42 D4
Careston DD9 83 G2
Carew SA70 16 D5
Carew Cheriton SA70 16 D5
Carew Newton SA68 16 D5
Carey HR2 28 E5
Carfin ML1 75 F5
Carfrae EH41 76 D4
Carfraemill TD2 76 D5
Cargate Green NR13 45 H4
Cargen DG2 65 K3
Cargenbridge DG2 65 K3
Cargill PH2 82 C4
Cargo CA6 60 E1
Cargreen PL12 4 E4
Carham TD12 77 F7
Carhampton TA24 7 J1
Carharrack TR16 2 E4
Carie *P. & K.* PH17 81 H2
Carie *P. & K.* PH15 81 H4
Carines TR8 2 E3
Carinish (Cairinis) HS6 92 D5
Carisbrooke PO30 11 F6
Cark LA11 55 G2
Carkeel PL12 4 E4
Carlabhagh (Carloway) HS2 100 E3
Carland Cross TR8 3 F3
Carlatton CA8 61 G1
Carlby PE9 42 D4
Carlecotes S36 50 D2
Carleen TR13 2 D6
Carleton *Cumb.* CA1 60 F1
Carleton *Cumb.* CA11 61 G4
Carleton *Lancs.* FY6 55 G5
Carleton *N.Yorks.* BD23 56 E5
Carleton *W.Yorks.* WF8 57 K7
Carleton Fishery KA26 67 F5
Carleton Forehoe NR9 44 E5
Carleton Rode NR16 45 F6
Carleton St. Peter NR14 45 H5
Carlin How TS13 63 J5
CARLISLE CA 60 F1
Carloggas TR8 3 F2
Carlops EH26 75 K5
Carloway (Carlabhagh) HS2 100 E3
Carlton *Beds.* MK43 32 C3
Carlton *Cambs.* CB8 33 K3
Carlton *Leics.* CV13 41 F5
Carlton *N.Yorks.* DN14 58 C7
Carlton *N.Yorks.* DL8 57 F1
Carlton *N.Yorks.* YO62 58 C1
Carlton *Notts.* NG4 41 J1
Carlton *S.Yorks.* S71 51 F1
Carlton *Stock.* TS21 62 E4
Carlton *Suff.* IP17 35 H2
Carlton *W.Yorks.* WF3 57 J7
Carlton Colville NR33 45 K6
Carlton Curlieu LE8 41 J6
Carlton Green CB8 33 K3
Carlton Husthwaite YO7 57 K2
Carlton in Lindrick S81 51 H4
Carlton Miniott YO7 57 J1
Carlton Scroop NG32 42 C1
Carlton-in-Cleveland TS9 63 G6
Carlton-le-Moorland LN5 52 C7
Carlton-on-Trent NG23 52 B6
Carluke ML8 75 G5
Carlyon Bay PL25 4 A5
Carmacoup ML11 68 C1
Carmarthen (Caerfyrddin) SA31 17 H3
Carmel *Carmar.* SA14 17 J4
Carmel *Flints.* CH8 47 K5
Carmel *Gwyn.* LL54 46 C7
Carmel *I.o.A.* LL71 46 B4
Carmichael ML12 75 H7
Carmont AB39 91 G6
Carmunnock G76 74 D5
Carmyle G32 74 E4
Carmyllie DD11 83 G3
Carn PA48 72 A5
Carn Brea Village TR15 2 D4
Carn Dearg IV21 94 D4
Carnaby YO16 59 H3
Carnach *High.* IV40 87 G2
Carnach *High.* IV23 95 G2
Carnach *W.Isles* HS6 92 D5
Carnan HS8 92 C7
Carnassarie PA31 79 K7
Carnbee KY10 83 G7
Carnbo KY13 82 B7
Carndu IV40 86 E2
Carnduncan PA44 72 A4
Carnforth LA5 55 H2
Carnhedryn SA62 16 B3
Carnhell Green TR14 2 D5
Carnichal AB42 99 H5
Carnkie *Cornw.* TR16 2 D5
Carnkie *Cornw.* TR13 2 E5
Carnmore PA42 72 B6
Carno SY17 37 J6
Carnoch *High.* IV4 87 K1
Carnoch *High.* IV6 95 J6
Carnoch *High.* IV12 97 F7
Carnock KY12 75 J2
Carnon Downs TR3 3 F4
Carnousie AB53 98 E5
Carnoustie DD7 83 G4
Carntyne G32 74 E4
Carnwath ML11 75 H6
Carnyorth TR19 2 A5
Carol Green CV7 30 D1
Carperby DL8 57 F1
Carr S66 51 H3
Carr Hill DN10 51 J3
Carr Houses L38 48 C2
Carr Shield NE47 61 K2
Carr Vale S44 51 G5
Carradale PA28 73 F7
Carradale East PA28 73 G7
Carragrich HS3 93 G2
Carrbridge PH23 89 G2
Carrefour Selous JE3 3 J7
Carreg-lefn LL68 46 B4
Carreg-wen SA37 17 F1

Carrhouse DN9 51 K2
Carrick PA31 73 H2
Carrick Castle PA24 73 K1
Carriden EH51 75 J2
Carrine PA28 66 A3
Carrington Gt.Man. M31 49 G3
Carrington Lincs. PE22 53 G7
Carrington Midloth. EH23 76 B4
Carroch DG7 68 B4
Carrog Conwy LL24 37 G1
Carrog Denb. LL21 38 A1
Carroglen PH6 81 J5
Carrol KW9 97 F1
Carron Arg. & B. PA31 73 H1
Carron Falk. FK2 75 G2
Carron Moray AB38 97 K7
Carron Bridge FK6 75 F2
Carronbridge DG3 68 D4
Carronshore FK2 75 G2
Carrot DD8 83 F3
Carrow Hill NP26 19 H2
Carrutherstown DG1 69 G6
Carruthmuir PA10 74 B4
Carrville DH1 62 E2
Carry PA21 73 H4
Carsaig PA70 79 G5
Carscreugh DG8 64 C4
Carse PA29 73 F4
Carse of Ardersier IV2 97 F6
Carsegowan DG8 64 E5
Carseriggan DG8 64 D4
Carsethorn DG2 65 K5
Carsgoe KW12 105 G2
Carshalton SM5 23 F5
Carshalton Beeches SM5 23 F5
Carsie PH10 82 C3
Carsington DE4 50 E7
Carsluith DG8 64 E5
Carsphairn DG7 67 K4
Carstairs ML11 75 H6
Carstairs Junction ML11 75 H6
Carswell Marsh SN7 21 G2
Carter's Clay SO51 10 E2
Carterton OX18 21 F1
Carterway Heads DH8 62 B1
Carthew PL26 4 A5
Carthorpe DL8 57 J1
Cartington NE65 71 F3
Cartland ML11 75 G6
Cartmel LA11 55 G2
Cartmel Fell LA11 55 H1
Cartworth HD9 50 D2
Carway SA17 17 H5
Cascob LD8 28 B2
Cas-gwent (Chepstow) NP16 19 J2
Cashel Farm G63 74 C1
Cashes Green GL5 20 B1
Cashlie PH15 81 F3
Cashmoor DT11 9 J3
Caskieberran KY6 82 D7
CASNEWYDD (NEWPORT) NP 19 G3
Cassencarie DG8 64 E5
Cassington OX29 31 F7
Cassop DH6 62 E3
Castell LL32 47 F6
Castell Gorfod SA33 17 F3
Castell Howell SA44 17 H1
Castell Newydd Emlyn (Newcastle Emlyn) SA38 17 G1
Castellau CF38 18 D3
Castell-nedd (Neath) SA11 18 A2
Castell-y-bwch NP44 19 F2
Casterton LA6 56 B2
Castle Acre PE32 44 C4
Castle Ashby NN7 32 B3
Castle Bolton DL8 62 B7
Castle Bromwich B36 40 D7
Castle Bytham NG33 42 C4
Castle Caereinion SY21 38 A5
Castle Camps CB1 33 K4
Castle Carrock CA8 61 G1
Castle Cary BA7 9 F1
Castle Combe SN14 20 B4
Castle Donington DE74 41 G3
Castle Douglas DG7 65 H4
Castle Eaton SN6 20 E2
Castle Eden TS27 63 F3
Castle End CV8 30 D1
Castle Frome HR8 29 F4
Castle Gate TR20 2 B5
Castle Goring BN13 12 E6
Castle Green GU24 22 C5
Castle Gresley DE11 40 E4
Castle Heaton TD12 77 H6
Castle Hedingham CO9 34 B5
Castle Hill Kent TN12 23 K7
Castle Hill Suff. IP1 35 F4
Castle Kennedy DG9 64 B5
Castle Leod IV14 96 B6
Castle Levan PA19 74 A3
Castle Madoc LD3 27 K5
Castle Morris SA62 16 C2
Castle O'er DG13 69 H4
Castle Rising PE31 44 A3
Castle Stuart IV2 96 E7
Castlebay (Bàgh a'Chaisteil) HS9 84 B5
Castlebythe SA62 16 D3
Castlecary G68 75 F3
Castlecraig High. IV19 97 F4
Castlecraig Sc.Bord. EH46 75 K6
Castlefairn DG3 68 C5
Castleford WF10 57 K7
Castlemartin SA71 16 C6
Castlemilk D. & G. DG11 69 G6
Castlemilk Glas. G45 74 E5
Castlemorton WR13 29 G5
Castlerigg CA12 60 D4
Castleside DH8 62 B2
Castlesteads CA8 70 A7
Castlethorpe MK19 31 J4
Castleton Aber. AB45 99 F5
Castleton Angus DD8 82 E3
Castleton Arg. & B. PA31 73 G2
Castleton Derbys. S33 50 D4
Castleton Gt.Man. OL11 49 H1
Castleton N.Yorks. YO21 63 H6
Castleton Newport CF3 19 F3
Castleton Sc.Bord. TD9 70 A4
Castletown Dorset DT5 9 F7
Castletown High. KW14 105 G2
Castletown High. IV2 96 E7
Castletown I.o.M. IM9 54 B7
Castletown T. & W. SR5 62 E1
Castleweary TD9 69 K3
Castlewigg DG8 64 E6
Castley LS21 57 H5
Caston NR17 44 D6
Castor PE5 42 E6
Castramont DG7 65 F4
Caswell SA3 17 J7
Cat and Fiddle Inn SK11 50 C5
Catacol KA27 73 H6
Catbrain BS10 19 J3
Catbrook NP16 19 J1
Catchall TR19 2 B6
Catcleugh NE19 70 C3
Catcliffe S60 51 G4
Catcott TA7 8 C1
Caterham CR3 23 G6
Catfield NR29 45 H3
Catfirth ZE2 107 N7
Catford SE6 23 G4
Catforth PR4 55 H6
Cathays CF24 18 E4
Cathcart G44 74 D4
Cathedine LD3 28 A6
Catherine-de-Barnes B91 40 D7
Catherington PO8 11 H3
Catherston Leweston DT6 8 C5
Catherton DY14 29 F1
Cathkin G73 74 E5
Catisfield PO15 11 G4
Catlodge PH20 88 D5
Catlowdy CA6 69 K6
Catmere End CB11 33 H5
Catmore RG20 21 H3
Caton Devon TQ13 5 H3
Caton Lancs. LA2 55 J3
Caton Green LA2 55 J3
Cator Court TQ13 5 G3
Catrine KA5 67 K1
Catsfield TN33 14 C6
Catsfield Stream TN33 14 C6
Catshaw S36 50 E2
Catshill B61 29 J1
Cattadale PA44 72 B4
Cattal YO26 57 K4
Cattawade CO11 34 E5
Catterall PR3 55 J5
Catterick DL10 62 D7
Catterick Bridge DL10 62 D7
Catterick Garrison DL9 62 C7
Catterlen CA11 61 F3
Catterline AB39 91 G7
Catterton LS24 58 B5
Catteshall GU7 22 C7
Catthorpe LE17 31 G1
Cattishall IP31 34 C2
Cattistock DT2 8 E4
Catton N.Yorks. YO7 57 J2
Catton Norf. NR6 45 G4
Catton Northumb. NE47 61 K1
Catton Hall DE12 40 E4
Catwick HU17 59 H5
Catworth PE28 32 D1
Caudle Green GL53 29 J7
Caulcott Beds. MK43 32 D4
Caulcott Oxon. OX25 31 G6
Cauldcots DD11 83 H3
Cauldhame Stir. FK8 74 E1
Cauldhame Stir. FK15 81 K7
Cauldon ST10 40 C1
Caulkerbush DG2 65 K5
Caulside DG14 69 K5
Caundle Marsh DT9 9 F3
Caunsall DY11 40 A7
Caunton NG23 51 K6
Causeway End D. & G. DG8 64 E4
Causeway End Essex CM6 33 K7
Causeway End Lancs. L40 48 D1
Causewayhead Cumb. CA7 60 C1
Causewayhead Stir. FK9 75 G1
Causey DH9 62 D1
Causey Park NE61 71 G4
Causeyend AB23 91 H3
Cautley LA10 61 H7
Cavendish CO10 34 C4
Cavendish Bridge DE72 41 G3
Cavenham IP28 34 B2
Cavens DG2 65 K5
Cavers TD9 70 A2
Caversfield OX27 31 G6
Caversham RG4 22 A4
Caverswall ST11 40 B1
Cawdor IV12 97 F6
Cawkeld YO25 59 F4
Cawkwell LN11 53 F4
Cawood YO8 58 B6
Cawsand PL10 4 E6
Cawston Norf. NR10 45 F3
Cawston Warks. CV22 31 F1
Cawthorn YO18 58 D1
Cawthorne S75 50 E2
Cawthorpe PE10 42 D3
Cawton YO62 58 C2
Caxton CB3 33 G3
Caxton Gibbet CB3 33 F2
Caynham SY8 28 E1
Caythorpe Lincs. NG32 42 C1
Caythorpe Notts. NG14 41 J1
Cayton YO11 59 G1
Ceallan HS6 92 D6
Ceann a' Bhàigh W.Isles HS6 92 C5
Ceann a' Bhàigh W.Isles HS3 93 F3
Ceann Loch Shiphoirt HS2 100 E6
Ceann Lochroag (Kinlochroag) HS2 100 D5
Ceannaridh HS6 92 D6
Cearsiadar HS2 101 F6
Ceathramh Meadhanach (Middlequarter) HS6 92 D4
Cedig SY10 37 J3
Cefn Berain LL16 47 H6
Cefn Bychan (Newbridge) NP11 19 F2
Cefn Canol SY10 38 B2
Cefn Cantref LD3 27 K6
Cefn Coch LL15 47 K7
Cefn Cribwr CF32 18 B3
Cefn Cross CF32 18 B3
Cefn Einion SY9 38 B7
Cefn Hengoed CF82 18 E2
Cefn Llwyd SY23 37 F7
Cefn Rhigos CF44 18 C1
Cefn-brith LL21 47 H7
Cefn-caer-Ferch LL53 36 D1
Cefn-coch SY10 38 A3
Cefn-coed-y-cymmer CF48 18 D1
Cefn-ddwysarn LL23 37 J2
Cefndeuddwr LL40 37 G3
Cefneithin SA14 17 J4
Cefn-gorwydd LD4 27 J4
Cefn-gwyn SY16 38 A7
Cefn-mawr LL14 38 B1
Cefnpennar CF45 18 D1
Cefn-y-bedd LL12 48 C7
Cefn-y-pant SA34 16 E3
Cegidfa (Guilsfield) SY21 38 B4
Ceidio LL71 46 C4
Ceidio Fawr LL53 36 B2
Ceinewydd (New Quay) SA45 26 C2
Ceint LL77 46 C5
Cellan SA48 17 K1
Cellardyke KY10 83 G7
Cellarhead ST9 40 B1
Cemaes LL67 46 B3
Cemmaes SY20 37 H5
Cemmaes Road (Glantwymyn) SY20 37 H5
Cenarth SA38 17 F1
Cennin LL51 36 D1
Ceos (Keose) HS2 101 F5
Ceres KY15 83 F6
Ceri (Kerry) SY16 38 A6
Cerist SY17 37 J7
Cerne Abbas DT2 9 F4
Cerney Wick GL7 20 D2
Cerrigceinwen LL62 46 C5
Cerrigydrudion LL21 37 J1
Cessford TD5 70 C1
Ceunant LL55 46 D6
Chaceley GL19 29 H5
Chacewater TR4 2 E4
Chackmore MK18 31 H5
Chacombe OX17 31 F4
Chad Valley B15 40 C7
Chadderton OL9 49 J2
Chadderton Fold OL9 49 H2
Chaddesden DE21 41 F2
Chaddesley Corbett DY10 29 H1
Chaddleworth RG20 21 H4
Chadlington OX7 30 E6
Chadshunt CV35 30 E3
Chadstone NN7 32 B3
Chadwell Leics. LE14 42 A3
Chadwell Shrop. TF10 39 G4
Chadwell St. Mary RM16 24 C4
Chadwick End B93 30 D1
Chaffcombe TA20 8 C3
Chafford Hundred RM16 24 C4
Chagford TQ13 7 F7
Chailey BN8 13 G5
Chainhurst TN12 14 C3
Chalbury BH21 10 B4
Chalbury Common BH21 10 B4
Chaldon CR3 23 G6
Chaldon Herring (East Chaldon) DT2 9 G6
Chale PO38 11 F7
Chale Green PO38 11 F6
Chalfont Common SL9 22 D2
Chalfont St. Giles HP8 22 C2
Chalfont St. Peter SL9 22 D2
Chalford Glos. GL6 20 B1
Chalford Wilts. BA13 20 B7
Chalgrove OX44 21 K2
Chalk DA12 24 C4
Chalk End CM1 33 K7
Challacombe EX31 6 E1
Challister ZE2 107 P6
Challoch DG8 64 D4
Challock TN25 15 F2
Chalmington DT2 8 E4
Chalton Beds. LU4 32 D6
Chalton Hants. PO8 11 J3
Chalvey SL1 22 C4
Chalvington BN27 13 J6
Champany EH49 75 J3
Chancery SY23 26 E1
Chandler's Cross WD3 22 D2
Chandler's Ford SO53 11 F2
Channel Islands GYJE 3 G7
Channel's End MK44 32 E3
Channerwick ZE2 107 N10
Chantry Som. BA11 20 A7
Chantry Suff. IP2 35 F4
Chapel KY2 76 A1
Chapel Allerton Som. BS26 19 H6
Chapel Allerton W.Yorks. LS7 57 J6
Chapel Amble PL27 3 G1
Chapel Brampton NN6 31 J2
Chapel Chorlton ST5 40 A2
Chapel Cleeve TA24 7 J1
Chapel Cross TN21 13 K4
Chapel End MK45 32 D4
Chapel Green Warks. CV7 40 E7
Chapel Green Warks. CV47 31 F2
Chapel Haddlesey YO8 58 B7
Chapel Hill Aber. AB42 91 J1
Chapel Hill Lincs. LN4 53 F7
Chapel Hill Mon. NP16 19 J1
Chapel Hill N.Yorks. LS22 57 J5
Chapel Knapp SN13 20 B5
Chapel Lawn SY7 28 C1
Chapel Leigh TA4 7 K3
Chapel Milton SK23 50 C4
Chapel of Garioch AB51 91 F2
Chapel Rossan DG9 64 B6
Chapel Row Essex CM3 24 D1
Chapel Row W.Berks. RG7 21 J5
Chapel St. Leonards PE24 53 J5
Chapel Stile LA22 60 E6
Chapel Town TR8 3 F3
Chapelbank PH3 82 B6
Chapeldonan KA26 67 F3
Chapelend Way CO9 34 B5
Chapel-en-le-Frith SK23 50 C4
Chapelgate PE12 43 H3
Chapelhall ML6 75 F4
Chapelhill High. IV20 97 F4
Chapelhill P. & K. PH2 82 D5
Chapelhill P. & K. PH1 82 B4
Chapelknowe DG14 69 J6
Chapel-le-Dale LA6 56 C2
Chapelthorpe WF2 51 F1
Chapelton Aber. AB39 91 G6
Chapelton Angus DD11 83 H3
Chapelton Devon EX37 6 D3
Chapelton S.Lan. ML10 74 E6
Chapeltown B'burn. BL7 49 G1
Chapeltown Cumb. CA6 69 K6
Chapeltown Moray AB37 89 K2
Chapeltown S.Yorks. S35 51 F3
Chapmans Well PL15 6 B6
Chapmanslade BA13 20 B7
Chapmore End SG12 33 G7
Chappel CO6 34 C6
Charaton PL14 4 D4
Chard TA20 8 C4
Chard Junction TA20 8 C4
Chardleigh Green TA20 8 C3
Chardstock EX13 8 C4
Charfield GL12 20 A2
Charing TN27 14 E3
Charing Cross SP6 10 C3
Charing Heath TN27 14 E3
Charingworth GL55 30 C5
Charlbury OX7 30 E7
Charlcombe BA1 20 A5
Charlecote CV35 30 D3
Charles EX32 6 E2
Charles Tye IP14 34 E3
Charlesfield TD6 70 A1
Charleshill GU10 22 B7
Charleston DD8 82 E3
Charlestown Aber. AB43 99 J4
Charlestown Aberdeen AB12 91 H4
Charlestown Cornw. PL25 4 A5
Charlestown Derbys. SK13 50 C3
Charlestown Dorset DT3 9 F7
Charlestown Fife KY11 75 J2
Charlestown Gt.Man. M7 49 H2
Charlestown High. IV21 94 E4
Charlestown High. IV1 96 D7
Charlestown W.Yorks. BD17 57 G6
Charlestown W.Yorks. HX7 56 E7
Charlestown of Aberlour (Aberlour) AB38 97 K7
Charlesworth SK13 50 C3
Charleton KY9 83 F7
Charlinch TA5 8 B1
Charlotteville GU1 22 D7
Charlton Gt.Lon. SE7 23 H4
Charlton Hants. SP10 21 G7
Charlton Herts. SG5 32 E6
Charlton Northants. OX17 31 G5
Charlton Northumb. NE48 70 D5
Charlton Oxon. OX12 21 H3
Charlton Som. BA3 19 K6
Charlton Som. BA4 19 K7
Charlton Som. TA3 8 B2
Charlton Tel. & W. TF6 38 E4
Charlton W.Suss. PO18 12 B5
Charlton Wilts. SP7 9 J2
Charlton Wilts. SN16 20 C3
Charlton Wilts. SN9 20 E6
Charlton Worcs. WR10 30 B4
Charlton Abbots GL54 30 B6
Charlton Adam TA11 8 E2
Charlton Down DT2 9 F5
Charlton Horethorne DT9 9 F2
Charlton Kings GL52 29 J6
Charlton Mackrell TA11 8 E2
Charlton Marshall DT11 9 H4
Charlton Musgrove BA9 9 G2
Charlton on the Hill DT11 9 H4
Charlton-All-Saints SP5 10 C2
Charlton-on-Otmoor OX5 31 G7
Charltons TS12 63 H5
Charlwood RH6 23 F7
Charminster DT2 9 F5
Charmouth DT6 8 C5
Charndon OX27 31 H6
Charney Bassett OX12 21 G2
Charnock Richard PR7 48 E1
Charsfield IP13 35 G3
Chart Corner ME17 14 C3
Chart Sutton ME17 14 D3
Charter Alley RG26 21 J6
Charterhouse BS40 19 H6
Charterville Allotments OX29 21 G1
Chartham CT4 15 G2
Chartham Hatch CT4 15 G2
Chartridge HP5 22 C1
Charvil RG10 22 A4
Charwelton NN11 31 G3
Chase End Street HR8 29 G5
Chase Terrace WS7 40 C5
Chasetown WS7 40 C5
Chastleton GL56 30 D6
Chasty EX22 6 B5
Chatburn BB7 56 C5
Chatcull ST21 39 G2
Chatham ME4 24 D5
Chatham Green CM3 34 B7
Chathill NE67 71 G1
Chattenden ME3 24 D4
Chatteris PE16 43 G7
Chattisham IP8 34 E4
Chatto TD5 70 C2
Chatton NE66 71 F1
Chaul End LU1 32 D6
Chavey Down SL5 22 B5
Chawleigh EX18 7 F4
Chawley OX2 21 H1
Chawston MK44 32 E3
Chawton GU34 11 J1
Chazey Heath RG4 21 K4
Cheadle Gt.Man. SK8 49 H4
Cheadle Staffs. ST10 40 C1
Cheadle Heath SK3 49 H4
Cheadle Hulme SK8 49 H4
Cheam SM3 23 F5
Cheapside SL5 22 C5
Chearsley HP18 31 J7
Chebsey ST21 40 A3
Checkendon RG8 21 K3
Checkley Ches. CW5 39 G1
Checkley Here. HR1 28 E5
Checkley Staffs. ST10 40 C2
Checkley Green CW5 39 G1
Chedburgh IP29 34 B3
Cheddar BS27 19 H6
Cheddington LU7 32 C7
Cheddleton ST13 49 J7
Cheddon Fitzpaine TA2 8 B2
Chedglow SN16 20 C2
Chedgrave NR14 45 H6
Chedington DT8 8 D4
Chediston IP19 35 H1
Chediston Green IP19 35 H1
Chedworth GL54 30 B7
Chedzoy TA7 8 C1
Cheesden OL12 49 H1
Cheeseman's Green TN24 15 F4
Cheetham Hill M8 49 H2
Cheglinch EX34 6 D1
Cheldon EX18 7 F4
Chelford SK11 49 H5
Chellaston DE73 41 F2
Chells SG2 33 F6
Chelmarsh WV16 39 G7
Chelmondiston IP9 35 G5
Chelmorton SK17 50 D6
CHELMSFORD CM 24 D1
Chelmsley Wood B37 40 D7
Chelsea SW3 23 F4
Chelsfield BR6 23 H5
Chelsham CR6 23 G6
Chelston Heath TA21 7 K3
Chelsworth IP7 34 D4
Cheltenham GL50 29 J6
Chelveston NN9 32 C2
Chelvey BS48 19 H5
Chelwood BS39 19 K5
Chelwood Common RH17 13 H4
Chelwood Gate RH17 13 H4
Chelworth SN16 20 C2
Cheney Longville SY7 38 D7
Chenies WD3 22 D2
Chepstow (Cas-gwent) NP16 19 J2
Cherhill SN11 20 D4
Cherington Glos. GL8 20 C2
Cherington Warks. CV36 30 D5
Cheriton Devon EX35 7 F1
Cheriton Hants. SO24 11 G2
Cheriton Kent CT19 15 G4
Cheriton Pembs. SA71 16 C6
Cheriton Swan. SA3 17 H6
Cheriton Bishop EX6 7 F6
Cheriton Cross EX6 7 F6
Cheriton Fitzpaine EX17 7 G5
Cherrington TF6 39 F3
Cherry Burton HU17 59 F5
Cherry Green CM6 33 J6
Cherry Hinton CB1 33 H3
Cherry Willingham LN3 52 D5
Chertsey KT16 22 D5
Cheselbourne DT2 9 G5
Chesham HP5 22 C1
Chesham Bois HP6 22 C1
Cheshunt EN8 23 G1
Cheslyn Hay WS6 40 B5

Chessington KT9 22 E5
Chestall WS15 40 C4
CHESTER CH 48 D6
Chester Moor DH2 62 D2
Chesterblade BA4 19 K7
Chesterfield *Derbys.* S40 51 F5
Chesterfield *Staffs.* WS14 40 D5
Chester-le-Street DH3 62 D1
Chesters *Sc.Bord.* TD9 70 B2
Chesters *Sc.Bord.* TD8 70 B1
Chesterton *Cambs.* CB4 33 H2
Chesterton *Cambs.* PE7 42 E6
Chesterton *Oxon.* OX26 31 G6
Chesterton *Shrop.* WV15 39 G6
Chesterton *Staffs.* ST5 40 A1
Chesterton *Warks.* CV33 30 E3
Chesterton Green CV33 30 E3
Chestfield CT5 25 H5
Cheston TQ10 5 G5
Cheswardine TF9 39 G3
Cheswick TD15 77 J6
Cheswick Buildings TD15 77 J6
Cheswick Green B90 30 C1
Chetnole DT9 9 F4
Chettiscombe EX16 7 H4
Chettisham CB6 43 J7
Chettle DT11 9 J3
Chetton WV16 39 F6
Chetwode MK18 31 H6
Chetwynd Aston TF10 39 G4
Chetwynd Park TF10 39 G3
Cheveley CB8 33 K2
Chevening TN14 23 H6
Cheverell's Green AL3 32 D7
Chevington IP29 34 B3
Chevington Drift NE61 71 H4
Chevithorne EX16 7 H4
Chew Magna BS40 19 J5
Chew Moor BL6 49 F2
Chew Stoke BS40 19 J5
Chewton Keynsham BS31 19 K5
Chewton Mendip BA3 19 J6
Chichacott EX20 6 E6
Chicheley MK16 32 C4
Chichester PO19 12 B6
Chickerell DT3 9 F6
Chickering IP21 35 G1
Chicklade SP3 9 J1
Chickney CM6 33 J6
Chicksands SG17 32 E5
Chidden PO7 11 H3
Chidden Holt PO7 11 H3
Chiddingfold GU8 12 C3
Chiddingly BN8 13 J5
Chiddingstone TN8 23 H7
Chiddingstone Causeway TN11 23 J7
Chiddingstone Hoath TN8 23 H7
Chideock DT6 8 D5
Chidham PO18 11 J4
Chidswell WF12 57 H7
Chieveley RG20 21 H4
Chignall St. James CM1 24 C1
Chignall Smealy CM1 33 K7
Chigwell IG7 23 H2
Chigwell Row IG7 23 H2
Chilbolton SO20 21 G7
Chilcomb SO21 11 G2
Chilcombe DT6 8 E5
Chilcompton BA3 19 K6
Chilcote DE12 40 E4
Child Okeford DT11 9 H3
Childer Thornton CH66 48 C5
Childerditch CM13 24 C3
Childrey OX12 21 G3
Child's Ercall TF9 39 F3
Childs Hill NW3 23 F3
Childswickham WR12 30 B5
Childwall L16 48 D4
Childwick Green AL3 32 E7
Chilfrome DT2 8 E5
Chilgrove PO18 12 B5
Chilham CT4 15 F2
Chilhampton SP2 10 B1
Chilla EX21 6 C5
Chillaton PL16 6 C7
Chillenden CT3 15 H2
Chillerton PO30 11 F6
Chillesford IP12 35 H3
Chilley TQ9 5 H5
Chillingham NE66 71 F1
Chillington *Devon* TQ7 5 H6
Chillington *Som.* TA19 8 C3
Chilmark SP3 9 J1
Chilson *Oxon.* OX7 30 E7
Chilson *Som.* TA20 8 C4
Chilsworthy *Cornw.* PL18 4 E3
Chilsworthy *Devon* EX22 6 B5
Chilthorne Domer BA22 8 E3
Chilton *Bucks.* HP18 31 H7
Chilton *Devon* EX17 7 G5
Chilton *Dur.* DL17 62 D4
Chilton *Oxon.* OX11 21 H3
Chilton *Suff.* CO10 34 C4
Chilton Candover SO24 11 G1
Chilton Cantelo BA22 8 E2
Chilton Foliat RG17 21 G4
Chilton Polden TA7 8 C1
Chilton Street CO10 34 B4
Chilton Trinity TA5 8 B1
Chilvers Coton CV10 41 F6
Chilwell NG9 41 H2
Chilworth *Hants.* SO16 11 F3
Chilworth *Surr.* GU4 22 D7
Chimney OX18 21 G1
Chimney Street CO10 34 B4
Chineham RG24 21 K6
Chingford E4 23 G2
Chinley SK23 50 C4
Chinley Head SK23 50 C4
Chinnor OX39 22 A1
Chipchase Castle NE48 70 D6
Chipley TA21 7 K3
Chipnall TF9 39 G2
Chippenham *Cambs.* CB7 33 K2
Chippenham *Wilts.* SN15 20 C4
Chipperfield WD4 22 D1
Chipping *Herts.* SG9 33 G5
Chipping *Lancs.* PR3 56 B5
Chipping Campden GL55 30 C5
Chipping Hill CM8 34 C7
Chipping Norton OX7 30 E6
Chipping Ongar CM5 23 J1
Chipping Sodbury BS37 20 A3
Chipping Warden OX17 31 F4
Chipstable TA4 7 J3
Chipstead *Kent* TN13 23 H6
Chipstead *Surr.* CR5 23 F6
Chirbury SY15 38 B6
Chirk (Y Waun) LL14 38 B2
Chirk Green LL14 38 B2
Chirmorrie KA26 64 C3
Chirnside TD11 77 G5
Chirnsidebridge TD11 77 G5
Chirton *T. & W.* NE29 71 J7
Chirton *Wilts.* SN10 20 D6
Chisbury SN8 21 F5
Chiscan PA28 66 A2
Chiselborough TA14 8 D3
Chiseldon SN4 20 E4
Chiserley HX7 57 F7
Chislehampton OX44 21 J2
Chislehurst BR7 23 H4
Chislet CT3 25 J5
Chiswell Green AL2 22 E1
Chiswick W4 23 F4
Chiswick End SG8 33 G4
Chisworth SK13 49 J3
Chithurst GU31 12 B4
Chittering CB5 33 H1
Chitterne BA12 20 C7
Chittlehamholt EX37 6 E3
Chittlehampton EX37 6 E3
Chittoe SN15 20 C5
Chivelstone TQ7 5 H7
Chivenor EX31 6 D2
Chobham GU24 22 C5
Choicelee TD11 77 F5
Cholderton SP4 21 F7
Cholesbury HP23 22 C1
Chollerford NE46 70 E6
Chollerton NE46 70 E6
Cholsey OX10 21 J3
Cholstrey HR6 28 D3
Cholwell *B. & N.E.Som.* BS39 19 K6
Cholwell *Devon* PL19 4 E3
Chop Gate TS9 63 G7
Choppington NE62 71 H5
Chopwell NE17 62 C1
Chorley *Ches.* CW5 48 E7
Chorley *Lancs.* PR7 48 E1
Chorley *Shrop.* WV16 39 F7
Chorley *Staffs.* WS13 40 C4
Chorleywood WD3 22 D2
Chorlton CW2 49 G7
Chorlton Lane SY14 38 D1
Chorlton-cum-Hardy M21 49 H3
Chowley CH3 48 D7
Chrishall SG8 33 H5
Chrishall Grange SG8 33 H4
Chrisswell PA16 74 A3
Christchurch *Cambs.* PE14 43 H6
Christchurch *Dorset* BH23 10 C5
Christchurch *Glos.* GL16 28 E7
Christchurch *Newport* NP18 19 G3
Christian Malford SN15 20 C4
Christleton CH3 48 D6
Christmas Common OX49 22 A2
Christon BS26 19 G6
Christon Bank NE66 71 H1
Christow EX6 7 G7
Christskirk AB52 90 E2
Chryston G69 74 E3
Chudleigh TQ13 5 J3
Chudleigh Knighton TQ13 5 J3
Chulmleigh EX18 6 E4
Chunal SK13 50 C3
Church BB5 56 C7
Church Aston TF10 39 G4
Church Brampton NN6 31 J2
Church Brough CA17 61 J5
Church Broughton DE65 40 E2
Church Charwelton NN11 31 G3
Church Common IP17 35 H3
Church Crookham GU52 22 B6
Church Eaton ST20 40 A4
Church End *Beds.* SG15 32 E5
Church End *Beds.* LU6 32 C6
Church End *Beds.* SG19 32 E3
Church End *Beds.* MK43 32 C5
Church End *Beds.* MK17 32 C5
Church End *Cambs.* PE13 43 G5
Church End *Cambs.* CB4 33 G1
Church End *Cambs.* PE28 43 F7
Church End *E.Riding* YO25 59 G4
Church End *Essex* CB10 33 J4
Church End *Essex* CM7 34 B6
Church End *Glos.* GL20 29 H5
Church End *Hants.* RG27 21 K6
Church End *Herts.* AL3 32 E7
Church End *Herts.* SG11 33 H6
Church End *Lincs.* PE11 43 F2
Church End *Lincs.* LN11 53 H3
Church End *Warks.* CV10 40 E6
Church End *Wilts.* SN15 20 D4
Church Enstone OX7 30 E6
Church Fenton LS24 58 B6
Church Green EX24 7 K6
Church Gresley DE11 40 E4
Church Hanborough OX29 31 F7
Church Hill *Ches.* CW7 49 F6
Church Hill *Derbys.* S42 51 G6
Church Houses YO62 63 H7
Church Knowle BH20 9 J6
Church Laneham DN22 52 B5
Church Langley CM17 23 H1
Church Langton LE16 42 A6
Church Lawford CV23 31 F1
Church Lawton ST7 49 H7
Church Leigh ST10 40 C2
Church Lench WR11 30 B3
Church Mayfield DE6 40 D1
Church Minshull CW5 49 F6
Church Norton PO20 12 B7
Church Preen SY6 38 E6
Church Pulverbatch SY5 38 D5
Church Stoke SY15 38 B6
Church Stowe NN7 31 H3
Church Street *Essex* CO10 34 B4
Church Street *Kent* ME3 24 D4
Church Stretton SY6 38 D6
Church Town *Leics.* LE67 41 F4
Church Town *Surr.* RH9 23 G6
Church Village CF38 18 D3
Church Warsop NG20 51 H6
Church Westcote OX7 30 D6
Church Wilne DE72 41 G2
Churcham GL2 29 G7
Churchdown GL3 29 H7
Churchend *Essex* SS3 25 G2
Churchend *Essex* CM6 33 K6
Churchend *S.Glos.* GL12 20 A2
Churchfield B71 40 C6
Churchgate EN7 23 G1
Churchgate Street CM17 33 H7
Churchill *Devon* EX31 6 D1
Churchill *Devon* EX13 8 B4
Churchill *N.Som.* BS25 19 H6
Churchill *Oxon.* OX7 30 D6
Churchill *Worcs.* WR7 29 J3
Churchill *Worcs.* DY10 29 H1
Churchingford TA3 8 B3
Churchover CV23 41 H7
Churchstanton TA3 7 K4
Churchstow TQ7 5 H6
Churchtown *Devon* EX31 6 E1
Churchtown *I.o.M.* IM7 54 D4
Churchtown *Lancs.* PR3 55 H5
Churchtown *Mersey.* PR9 48 C1
Churnsike Lodge NE48 70 B6
Churston Ferrers TQ5 5 K5
Churt GU10 12 B3
Churton CH3 48 D7
Churwell LS27 57 H7
Chute Cadley SP11 21 G6
Chute Standen SP11 21 G6
Chwilog LL53 36 D2
Chwitffordd (Whitford) CH8 47 K5
Chyandour TR18 2 B5
Chysauster TR20 2 B5
Cilan Uchaf LL53 36 B3
Cilcain CH7 47 K6
Cilcennin SA48 26 E2
Cilcewydd SY21 38 B5
Cilfrew SA10 18 A1
Cilfynydd CF37 18 D2
Cilgerran SA43 16 E1
Cilgwyn *Carmar.* SA20 27 G5
Cilgwyn *Pembs.* SA42 16 D2
Ciliau Aeron SA48 26 E3
Cilldonnain (Kildonan) HS8 84 C2
Cille Bhrighde HS8 84 C3
Cille Pheadair HS8 84 C3
Cilmaengwyn SA8 18 A1
Cilmery LD2 27 K3
Cilrhedyn SA35 17 F2
Cilrhedyn Bridge SA65 16 D2
Cilsan SA19 17 J3
Ciltalgarth LL23 37 H1
Cilwendeg SA37 17 F2
Cilybebyll SA8 18 A1
Cilycwm SA20 27 G4
Cimla SA11 18 A2
Cinderford GL14 29 F7
Cippenham SL1 22 C3
Cippyn SA43 16 E1
Cirbhig HS2 100 D3
Circebost (Kirkibost) HS2 100 D4
Cirencester GL7 20 D1
City *Gt.Lon.* EC3M 23 G3
City *V. of Glam.* CF71 18 C4
City Airport E16 23 H3
City Dulas LL70 46 C4
Clabhach PA78 78 C2
Clachaig PA23 73 K2
Clachan *Arg. & B.* PA26 80 C6
Clachan *Arg. & B.* PA34 79 K3
Clachan *Arg. & B.* PA29 73 F5
Clachan *High.* IV40 86 B1
Clachan *W.Isles* HS8 92 C7
Clachan Mòr PA77 78 A3
Clachan of Campsie G66 74 E3
Clachan of Glendaruel PA22 73 H2
Clachan Strachur (Strachur) PA27 80 B7
Clachan-a-Luib HS6 92 D5
Clachandhu PA68 79 F4
Clachaneasy DG8 64 D3
Clachanmore DG9 64 A6
Clachan-Seil PA34 79 J6
Clachanturn AB35 89 K5
Clachbreck PA31 73 F3
Clachnabrain DD8 82 E1
Clachnaharry IV3 96 D7
Clachtoll IV27 102 C6
Clackmannan FK10 75 H1
Clackmarras IV30 97 K6
Clacton-on-Sea CO15 35 F7
Cladach a Bhale Shear HS6 92 D5
Cladach a' Chaolais HS6 92 C5
Cladach Chircebost HS6 92 C5
Cladach Chnoc a Lin HS6 92 C5
Cladich PA33 80 B5
Cladswell B49 30 B3
Claggan *High.* PH33 87 H7
Claggan *High.* PA34 79 J3
Claigan IV55 93 H6
Claines WR3 29 H3
Clandown BA3 19 K6
Clanfield *Hants.* PO8 11 J3
Clanfield *Oxon.* OX18 21 F1
Clannaborough Barton EX17 7 F5
Clanville SP11 21 G7
Claonaig PA29 73 G5
Claonairigh PA32 80 B7
Claonel IV27 96 C1
Clapgate SG11 33 H6
Clapham *Beds.* MK41 32 D3
Clapham *Devon* EX2 7 G7
Clapham *Gt.Lon.* SW4 23 F4
Clapham *N.Yorks.* LA2 56 C3
Clapham *W.Suss.* BN13 12 D6
Clapham Green MK41 32 D3
Clapham Hill CT5 25 H5
Clappers TD15 77 H5
Clappersgate LA22 60 E6
Clapton *Som.* TA18 8 D4
Clapton *Som.* BA3 19 K6
Clapton-in-Gordano BS20 19 H4
Clapton-on-the-Hill GL54 30 C7
Clapworthy EX36 6 E3
Clara Vale NE40 71 G7
Clarach SY23 37 F7
Clarbeston SA63 16 D3
Clarbeston Road SA63 16 D3
Clarborough DN22 51 K4
Clardon KW14 105 G2
Clare CO10 34 B4
Clarebrand DG7 65 H4
Clarencefield DG1 69 F7
Clarilaw TD9 70 A2
Clark's Green RH5 12 E3
Clarkston G76 74 D5
Clashban IV24 96 D2
Clashcoig IV24 96 D2
Clashdorran IV4 96 C7
Clashgour PA36 80 D3
Clashindarroch AB54 90 C1
Clashmore *High.* IV25 96 E3
Clashmore *High.* IV27 102 C5
Clashnessie IV27 102 C5
Clashnoir AB37 89 K2
Clatford SN8 20 E5
Clathy PH7 82 A5
Clatt AB54 90 D2
Clatter SY17 37 J6
Clattercote OX17 31 F4
Clatterford PO30 11 F6
Clatterford End CM5 23 J1
Clatterin Brig AB30 90 E7
Clatteringshaws DG7 65 F3
Clatworthy TA4 7 J2
Claughton *Lancs.* LA2 55 J3
Claughton *Lancs.* PR3 55 J5
Clavelshay TA6 8 B1
Claverdon CV35 30 C2
Claverham BS49 19 H5
Clavering CB11 33 H5
Claverley WV5 39 G6
Claverton BA2 20 A5
Claverton Down BA2 20 A5
Clawdd-côch CF71 18 D4
Clawdd-newydd LL15 47 J7
Clawfin KA6 67 K3
Clawthorpe LA6 55 J2
Clawton EX22 6 B6
Claxby LN8 52 E3
Claxby Pluckacre LN9 53 G6
Claxby St. Andrew LN13 53 H5
Claxton *N.Yorks.* YO60 58 C3
Claxton *Norf.* NR14 45 H5
Claxton Grange TS22 63 F4
Clay Common NR34 45 J7
Clay Coton NN6 31 G1
Clay Cross S45 51 F6
Clay End SG2 33 G6
Clay Hill BS16 19 K4
Clay of Allan IV20 97 F4
Claybrooke Magna LE17 41 G7
Claybrooke Parva LE17 41 G7
Claydene TN8 23 H7
Claydon *Oxon.* OX17 31 F3
Claydon *Suff.* IP6 35 F4
Claygate *Kent* TN12 14 C3
Claygate *Surr.* KT10 22 E5
Claygate Cross TN15 23 K6
Clayhanger *Devon* EX16 7 J3
Clayhanger *W.Mid.* WS8 40 C5
Clayhidon EX15 7 K4
Clayhill *E.Suss.* TN31 14 D5
Clayhill *Hants.* SO43 10 E4
Clayhithe CB5 33 J2
Clayock KW12 105 G3
Claypit Hill CB3 33 G3
Claypits GL10 20 A1
Claypole NG23 42 B1
Claythorpe LN13 53 H5
Clayton *S.Yorks.* DN5 51 G2
Clayton *Staffs.* ST5 40 A1
Clayton *W.Suss.* BN6 13 F5
Clayton *W.Yorks.* BD14 57 G6
Clayton Green PR6 55 J7
Clayton West HD8 50 E1
Clayton-le-Moors BB5 56 C6
Clayton-le-Woods PR25 55 J7
Clayworth DN22 51 K4
Cleadale PH42 85 K6
Cleadon SR6 71 J7
Clearbrook PL20 5 F4
Clearwell GL16 19 J1
Cleasby DL2 62 D5
Cleat *Ork.* KW17 106 D9
Cleat *W.Isles* HS9 84 B4
Cleatlam DL2 62 C5
Cleatop BD24 56 D3
Cleator CA23 60 B5
Cleator Moor CA25 60 B5
Cleckheaton BD19 57 G7
Clee St. Margaret SY7 38 E7
Cleedownton SY8 38 E7
Cleehill SY8 28 E1
Cleestanton SY8 28 E1
Cleethorpes DN35 53 G2
Cleeton St. Mary DY14 29 F1
Cleeve *N.Som.* BS49 19 H5
Cleeve *Oxon.* RG8 21 K3
Cleeve Hill GL52 29 J6
Cleeve Prior WR11 30 B4
Cleghorn ML11 75 G6
Clehonger HR2 28 D5
Cleigh PA34 79 K5
Cleish KY13 75 J1
Cleland ML1 75 F5
Clement's End LU6 32 D7
Clench Common SN8 20 E5
Clenchwarton PE34 43 J3
Clennell NE65 70 E3
Clent DY9 29 J1
Cleobury Mortimer DY14 29 F1
Cleobury North WV16 39 F7
Clephanton IV2 97 F6
Clerklands TD6 70 A1
Clermiston EH4 75 K3
Clestrain KW17 106 C7
Cleuch Head TD9 70 A2
Cleughbrae DG1 69 F6
Clevancy SN11 20 D4
Clevedon BS21 19 H4
Cleveland Tontine Inn DL6 63 F7
Cleveley OX7 30 E6
Cleveleys FY5 55 G5
Clevelode WR13 29 H4
Cleverton SN15 20 C3
Clewer BS28 19 H6
Clewer Green SL4 22 C4
Clewer Village SL4 22 C4
Cley next the Sea NR25 44 E1
Cliburn CA10 61 G4
Cliddesden RG25 21 K7
Cliff *Carmar.* SA17 17 G5
Cliff *High.* PH36 79 H1
Cliff End TN35 14 D6
Cliff Grange TF9 39 F2
Cliffe *Lancs.* BB6 56 C6
Cliffe *Med.* ME3 24 D4
Cliffe *N.Yorks.* YO8 58 C6
Cliffe Woods ME3 24 D4
Clifford *Here.* HR3 28 B4
Clifford *W.Yorks.* LS23 57 K5
Clifford Chambers CV37 30 C3
Clifford's Mesne GL18 29 F6
Cliffs End CT12 25 K5
Clifton *Beds.* SG17 32 E5
Clifton *Bristol* BS8 19 J4
Clifton *Cumb.* CA10 61 G4
Clifton *Derbys.* DE6 40 D1
Clifton *Devon* EX31 6 D1
Clifton *Lancs.* PR4 55 H6
Clifton *N.Yorks.* LS21 57 G5
Clifton *Northumb.* NE61 71 H5
Clifton *Nott.* NG11 41 H2
Clifton *Oxon.* OX15 31 F5
Clifton *S.Yorks.* S66 51 H3
Clifton *Stir.* FK20 80 E4
Clifton *W.Yorks.* HD6 57 G7
Clifton *Worcs.* WR8 29 H4
Clifton *York* YO30 58 B4
Clifton Campville B79 40 E4
Clifton Hampden OX14 21 J2
Clifton Maybank BA22 8 E3
Clifton Reynes MK46 32 C3
Clifton upon Dunsmore CV23 31 G1
Clifton upon Teme WR6 29 G2
Cliftonville CT9 25 K4
Climping BN17 12 D6
Climpy ML11 75 H5
Clink BA11 20 A7
Clint HG3 57 H4
Clint Green NR19 44 E4
Clinterty AB21 91 G3
Clintmains TD6 76 E7
Clippesby NR29 45 J4
Clippings Green NR20 44 E4
Clipsham LE15 42 C4
Clipston *Northants.* LE16 42 A7
Clipston *Notts.* NG12 41 J2
Clipstone NG21 51 H6
Clitheroe BB7 56 C5
Cliuthar (Cluer) HS3 93 G2
Clive SY4 38 E3
Clivocast ZE2 107 Q2
Clixby DN38 52 E2
Clocaenog LL15 47 J7
Clochan AB56 98 C4
Clochtow AB41 91 J1
Clock Face WA9 48 E3
Clockhill AB42 99 G6
Cloddach IV30 97 J6
Cloddiau SY21 38 A5
Clodock HR2 28 C6
Cloford BA11 20 A7
Cloichran FK21 81 H4
Clola AB42 99 J6
Clonrae DG3 68 D4
Clophill MK45 32 D5

Clopton **NN14** 42 D7
Clopton Corner **IP13** 35 G3
Clopton Green *Suff.* **CB8** 34 B3
Clopton Green *Suff.* **IP13** 35 G3
Close Clark **IM9** 54 B6
Closeburn **DG3** 68 D4
Closworth **BA22** 8 E3
Clothall **SG7** 33 F5
Clothan **ZE2** 107 N4
Clotton **CW6** 48 E6
Clough *Cumb.* **LA10** 61 J7
Clough *Gt.Man.* **OL15** 49 J1
Clough *Gt.Man.* **OL2** 49 J2
Clough *W.Yorks.* **HD7** 50 C1
Clough Foot **OL14** 56 E7
Clough Head **HX6** 57 F7
Cloughfold **BB4** 56 D7
Cloughton **YO13** 63 K3
Cloughton Newlands **YO13** 63 K3
Clounlaid **PA34** 79 J2
Clousta **ZE2** 107 M7
Clouston **KW16** 106 C6
Clova *Aber.* **AB54** 90 C2
Clova *Angus* **DD8** 90 B7
Clove Lodge **DL12** 62 A5
Clovelly **EX39** 6 B3
Clovelly Cross **EX39** 6 B3
Clovenfords **TD1** 76 C7
Clovenstone **AB51** 91 F3
Cloverhill **AB23** 91 H3
Cloves **IV36** 97 J5
Clovullin **PH33** 80 B1
Clow Bridge **BB11** 56 D7
Clowne **S43** 51 G5
Clows Top **DY14** 29 G1
Cloyntie **KA19** 67 H3
Cluanach **PA43** 72 B5
Clubworthy **PL15** 4 C1
Cluddley **TF6** 39 F4
Cluer (Cliuthar) **HS3** 93 G2
Clun **SY7** 38 B7
Clunas **IV12** 97 F7
Clunbury **SY7** 38 C7
Clune *High.* **IV13** 88 E2
Clune *Moray* **AB56** 98 D4
Clunes **PH34** 87 J6
Clungunford **SY7** 28 C1
Clunie *Aber.* **AB53** 98 E5
Clunie *P. & K.* **PH10** 82 C3
Clunton **SY7** 38 C7
Cluny **KY2** 76 A1
Clutton *B. & N.E.Som.* **BS39** 19 K6
Clutton *Ches.* **CH3** 48 D7
Clwt-y-bont **LL55** 46 D6
Clwydyfagwyr **CF48** 18 D1
Clydach *Mon.* **NP7** 28 B7
Clydach *Swan.* **SA6** 17 K5
Clydach Terrace **NP23** 28 A7
Clydach Vale **CF40** 18 C2
Clydebank G81 74 C3
Clydey **SA35** 17 F2
Clyffe Pypard **SN4** 20 D4
Clynder **G84** 74 A2
Clynderwen SA66 16 E4
Clyne **SA11** 18 B1
Clynelish **KW9** 97 F1
Clynfyw **SA37** 17 F2
Clynnog-fawr **LL54** 36 D1
Clyro **HR3** 28 B4
Clyst Honiton **EX5** 7 H6
Clyst Hydon **EX15** 7 J5
Clyst St. George **EX3** 7 H7
Clyst St. Lawrence **EX15** 7 J5
Clyst St. Mary **EX5** 7 H6
Clyst William **EX15** 7 J5
Cnewr **LD3** 27 H6
Cnoc **HS2** 101 G4
Cnoc an Torrain (Knockintorran) **HS6** 92 C5
Cnwch Coch **SY23** 27 F1
Coachford **AB54** 98 C6
Coad's Green **PL15** 4 C3
Coal Aston **S18** 51 F5
Coalbrookdale **TF8** 39 F5
Coalbrookvale **NP13** 18 E1
Coalburn **ML11** 75 G7
Coalburns **NE40** 71 G7
Coalcleugh **NE47** 61 K2
Coaley **GL11** 20 A1
Coalmoor **TF6** 39 F5
Coalpit Heath **BS36** 19 K3
Coalpit Hill **ST7** 49 H7
Coalport **TF8** 39 G5
Coalsnaughton **FK13** 75 H1
Coaltown of Balgonie **KY7** 76 B1
Coaltown of Wemyss **KY1** 76 B1
Coalville LE67 41 G4
Coalway **GL16** 28 E7
Coanwood **NE49** 61 H1
Coast **IV22** 95 F2
Coat **TA12** 8 D2
Coatbridge ML5 75 F4
Coate *Swin.* **SN3** 20 E3
Coate *Wilts.* **SN10** 20 D5
Coates *Cambs.* **PE7** 43 G6
Coates *Glos.* **GL7** 20 C1
Coates *Lincs.* **LN1** 52 C4
Coates *Notts.* **DN22** 52 B4
Coates *W.Suss.* **RH20** 12 C5
Coatham **TS10** 63 G4
Coatham Mundeville **DL3** 62 D4
Cobairdy **AB54** 98 D6
Cobbaton **EX37** 6 E3
Cobbler's Plain **NP16** 19 H1
Cobby Syke **HG3** 57 G4
Cobden **EX5** 7 J6
Coberley **GL53** 29 J7
Cobhall Common **HR2** 28 D5
Cobham *Kent* **DA12** 24 C5
Cobham *Surr.* KT11 22 E5
Cobleland **FK8** 74 D1
Cobley Hill **B60** 30 B1
Cobnash **HR6** 28 D2
Coburty **AB43** 99 H4
Cochno **G81** 74 C3
Cock Alley **S44** 51 G6
Cock Bank **LL13** 38 C1
Cock Bevington **WR11** 30 B3
Cock Bridge **AB36** 89 K4
Cock Clarks **CM3** 24 E1
Cock Green **CM6** 34 B7
Cock Marling **TN31** 14 D6
Cockayne **YO62** 63 H7
Cockayne Hatley **SG19** 33 F4
Cockburnspath TD13 77 F3
Cockenzie and Port Seton **EH32** 76 C3
Cocker Bar **PR26** 55 J7
Cockerham **LA2** 55 H4
Cockermouth CA13 60 C3
Cockernhoe **LU2** 32 E6
Cockerton **DL3** 62 D5
Cockett **SA2** 17 K6
Cockfield *Dur.* **DL13** 62 C4
Cockfield *Suff.* **IP30** 34 D3
Cockfosters **EN4** 23 F2
Cocking **GU29** 12 B5
Cockington **TQ2** 5 J4
Cocklake **BS28** 19 H7
Cocklaw **NE46** 70 E6
Cockle Park **NE61** 71 H4
Cockleford **GL53** 29 J7
Cockley Beck **LA20** 60 D6
Cockley Cley **PE37** 44 B5
Cockpen **EH19** 76 B4
Cockpole Green **RG10** 22 A3
Cockshutt **SY12** 38 D3
Cockthorpe **NR23** 44 D1
Cockwood *Devon* **EX6** 7 H7
Cockwood *Som.* **TA5** 19 F7
Cockyard **SK23** 50 C4
Codda **PL15** 4 B3
Coddenham **IP6** 35 F3
Coddington *Ches.* **CH3** 48 D7
Coddington *Here.* **HR8** 29 G4
Coddington *Notts.* **NG24** 52 B7
Codford St. Mary **BA12** 9 J1
Codford St. Peter **BA12** 9 J1
Codicote **SG4** 33 F7
Codmore Hill **RH20** 12 D5
Codnor **DE5** 41 G1
Codnor Park **NG16** 51 G7
Codrington **BS37** 20 A4
Codsall **WV8** 40 A5
Codsall Wood **WV8** 40 A5
Coed Morgan **NP7** 28 C7
Coed Ystumgwern **LL44** 36 E3
Coedcae **NP4** 19 F1
Coed-duon (Blackwood) NP12 18 E2
Coedely **CF39** 18 D3
Coedkernew **NP10** 19 F3
Coedpoeth **LL11** 48 B7
Coedway **SY5** 38 C4
Coed-y-bryn **SA44** 17 G1
Coed-y-caerau **NP18** 19 G2
Coed-y-paen **NP4** 19 G2
Coed-y-parc **LL57** 46 E6
Coed-yr-ynys **NP8** 28 A6
Coelbren **SA10** 27 H7
Coffinswell **TQ12** 5 J4
Cofton **EX6** 7 H7
Cofton Hackett **B45** 30 B1
Cogan **CF64** 18 E4
Cogenhoe **NN7** 32 B2
Cogges **OX28** 21 G1
Coggeshall **CO6** 34 C6
Coggeshall Hamlet **CO6** 34 C6
Coggins Mill **TN20** 13 J4
Cóig Peighinnean **HS2** 101 H1
Coilantogle **FK17** 81 G7
Coileitir **PH49** 80 C3
Coilessan **G83** 80 D7
Coillaig **PA35** 80 B5
Coille Mhorgil **PH35** 87 G4
Coille-righ **IV40** 87 F2
Coillore **IV56** 85 J1
Coity **CF35** 18 C3
Col **HS2** 101 G4
Col Uarach **HS2** 101 G4
Colaboll **IV27** 103 H7
Colan **TR8** 3 F2
Colaton Raleigh **EX10** 7 J7
Colbost **IV55** 93 H7
Colburn **DL9** 62 D7
Colbury **SO40** 10 E3
Colby *Cumb.* **CA16** 61 H4
Colby *I.o.M.* **IM9** 54 B6
Colby *Norf.* **NR11** 45 G2
COLCHESTER CO 34 D6
Colchester Green **IP30** 34 D3
Colcot **CF62** 18 E5
Cold Ash **RG18** 21 J5
Cold Ashby **NN6** 31 H1
Cold Ashton **SN14** 20 A4
Cold Aston **GL54** 30 C7
Cold Blow **SA67** 16 E4
Cold Brayfield **MK46** 32 C3
Cold Chapel **ML12** 68 E1
Cold Cotes **LA2** 56 C2
Cold Hanworth **LN8** 52 D4
Cold Harbour **RG8** 21 K3
Cold Hatton **TF6** 39 F3
Cold Hatton Heath **TF6** 39 F3
Cold Hesledon **SR7** 63 F2
Cold Higham **NN12** 31 H3
Cold Inn **SA68** 16 E5
Cold Kirby **YO7** 58 B1
Cold Newton **LE7** 42 A5
Cold Northcott **PL15** 4 C2
Cold Norton **CM3** 24 E1
Cold Overton **LE15** 42 B5
Cold Row **FY6** 55 G5
Coldbackie **IV27** 103 J2
Coldblow **DA5** 23 J4
Coldean **BN1** 13 G6
Coldeast **TQ12** 5 J3
Coldeaton **DE6** 50 D7
Colden Common **SO21** 11 F2
Coldfair Green **IP17** 35 J2
Coldham **PE14** 43 H5
Coldharbour *Glos.* **GL15** 19 J1
Coldharbour *Surr.* **RH5** 22 E7
Coldingham **TD14** 77 H4
Coldrain **KY13** 82 B7
Coldred **CT15** 15 H3
Coldrey **GU34** 22 A7
Coldridge **EX17** 6 E5
Coldrife **NE61** 71 F4
Coldstream TD12 77 G7
Coldvreath **PL26** 3 G3
Coldwaltham **RH20** 12 D5
Coldwells **AB42** 99 K6
Cole **BA10** 9 F1
Cole End **B46** 40 D7
Cole Green **SG14** 33 F7
Cole Henley **RG28** 21 H6
Colebatch **SY9** 38 C7
Colebrook **EX15** 7 J5
Colebrooke **EX17** 7 F5
Coleburn **IV30** 97 K6
Coleby *Lincs.* **LN5** 52 C6
Coleby *N.Lincs.* **DN15** 52 B1
Coleford *Devon* **EX17** 7 F5
Coleford *Glos.* GL16 28 E7
Coleford *Som.* **BA3** 19 K7
Colegate End **IP21** 45 F7
Colehill **BH21** 10 B4
Coleman Green **AL4** 32 E7
Coleman's Hatch **TN7** 13 H3
Colemere **SY12** 38 D2
Colemore **GU34** 11 J1
Colemore Green **WV16** 39 G6
Colenden **PH2** 82 C5
Coleorton **LE67** 41 G4
Colerne **SN14** 20 B4
Cole's Common **IP21** 45 G7
Cole's Cross **TQ9** 5 H6
Cole's Green **IP13** 35 G2
Colesbourne **GL53** 30 B7
Colesden **MK44** 32 E3
Coleshill *Bucks.* **HP7** 22 C2
Coleshill *Oxon.* **SN6** 21 F2
Coleshill *Warks.* **B46** 40 E7
Colestocks **EX14** 7 J5
Coley *B. & N.E.Som.* **BS40** 19 J6
Coley *Staffs.* **ST18** 40 C3
Colfin **DG9** 64 A5
Colgate **RH12** 13 F3
Colgrain **G82** 74 B3
Colindale **NW9** 23 F3
Colinsburgh **KY9** 83 F7
Colinton **EH13** 76 A4
Colintraive PA22 73 J3
Colkirk **NR21** 44 D3
Coll PA78 78 C2
Collace **PH2** 82 D4
Collafirth **ZE2** 107 N6
Collamoor Head **PL32** 4 B1
Collaton St. Mary **TQ3** 5 J4
Collessie **KY15** 82 D6
Colleton Mills **EX37** 6 E4
Collett's Green **WR2** 29 H3
Collier Row **RM5** 23 J2
Collier Street **TN12** 14 C3
Collier's End **SG11** 33 G6
Collier's Wood **SW19** 23 F4
Colliery Row **DH4** 62 E2
Collieston **AB41** 91 J2
Collin **DG1** 69 F6
Collingbourne Ducis **SN8** 21 F6
Collingbourne Kingston **SN8** 21 F6
Collingham *Notts.* **NG23** 52 B6
Collingham *W.Yorks.* **LS22** 57 J5
Collington **HR7** 29 F2
Collingtree **NN4** 31 J3
Collins End **RG8** 21 K4
Collins Green *Warr.* **WA5** 48 E3
Collins Green *Worcs.* **WR6** 29 G3
Colliston **DD11** 83 H3
Colliton **EX14** 7 J5
Collmuir **AB31** 90 D4
Collycroft **CV12** 41 F7
Collyhurst **M8** 49 H2
Collynie **AB41** 91 G1
Collyweston **PE9** 42 C5
Colmonell **KA26** 67 F5
Colmworth **MK44** 32 E3
Coln Rogers **GL54** 20 D1
Coln St. Aldwyns **GL7** 20 E1
Coln St. Dennis **GL54** 30 B7
Colnabaichin **AB36** 89 K4
Colnbrook **SL3** 22 D4
Colne *Cambs.* **PE28** 33 G1
Colne *Lancs.* BB8 56 D6
Colne Engaine **CO6** 34 C5
Colney **NR4** 45 F5
Colney Heath **AL4** 23 F1
Colney Street **AL2** 22 E1
Colonsay PA61 72 B1
Colonsay House **PA61** 72 B1
Colpy **AB52** 90 E1
Colquhar **EH44** 76 B6
Colsterdale **HG4** 57 G1
Colsterworth **NG33** 42 C3
Colston Bassett **NG12** 42 A2
Coltfield **IV36** 97 J5
Colthouse **LA22** 60 E7
Coltishall **NR12** 45 G4
Coltness **ML2** 75 G5
Colton *Cumb.* **LA12** 55 G1
Colton *N.Yorks.* **LS24** 58 B5
Colton *Norf.* **NR9** 45 F5
Colton *Staffs.* **WS15** 40 C3
Colton *W.Yorks.* **LS15** 57 J6
Colva **HR5** 28 B3
Colvend **DG5** 65 J5
Colvister **ZE2** 107 P3
Colwall WR13 29 G4
Colwall Green **WR13** 29 G4
Colwall Stone **WR13** 29 G4
Colwell **NE46** 70 E6
Colwich **ST18** 40 C3
Colwick **NG4** 41 J2
Colwinston **CF71** 18 C4
Colworth **PO20** 12 C6
Colwyn Bay (Bae Colwyn) LL29 47 G5
Colyford **EX24** 8 B5
Colyton EX24 8 B5
Combe *Here.* **LD8** 28 C2
Combe *Oxon.* **OX29** 31 F7
Combe *Som.* **TA10** 8 D2
Combe *W.Berks.* **RG17** 21 G5
Combe Common **GU8** 12 C3
Combe Cross **TQ13** 5 H3
Combe Down **BA2** 20 A5
Combe Florey **TA4** 7 K2
Combe Hay **BA2** 20 A6
Combe Martin **EX34** 6 D1
Combe Pafford **TQ1** 5 K4
Combe Raleigh **EX14** 7 K5
Combe St. Nicholas **TA20** 8 C3
Combeinteignhead **TQ12** 5 J3
Comberbach **CW9** 49 F5
Comberford **B79** 40 D5
Comberton *Cambs.* **CB3** 33 G3
Comberton *Here.* **SY8** 28 D2
Combpyne **EX13** 8 B5
Combridge **ST14** 40 C2
Combrook **CV35** 30 E3
Combs *Derbys.* **SK23** 50 C5
Combs *Suff.* **IP14** 34 E3
Combs Ford **IP14** 34 E3
Combwich **TA5** 19 F7
Comer **FK8** 80 E7
Comers **AB51** 90 E4
Comhampton **DY13** 29 H2
Comins Coch **SY23** 37 F7
Commercial End **CB5** 33 J2
Commins Coch **SY20** 37 H5
Common Edge **FY4** 55 G6
Common Moor **PL14** 4 C3
Common Platt **SN5** 20 E3
Common Side **S18** 51 F5
Common Square **LN4** 52 D5
Commondale **YO21** 63 H5
Commonside **DE6** 40 E1
Compstall **SK6** 49 J3
Compton *Devon* **TQ3** 5 J4
Compton *Hants.* **SO21** 11 F2
Compton *Plym.* **PL3** 4 E5
Compton *Staffs.* **DY7** 40 A7
Compton *Surr.* **GU3** 22 C7
Compton *W.Berks.* **RG20** 21 J4
Compton *W.Suss.* **PO18** 11 J3
Compton *W.Yorks.* **LS22** 57 K5
Compton *Wilts.* **SN9** 20 E6
Compton Abbas **SP7** 9 H3
Compton Abdale **GL54** 30 B7
Compton Bassett **SN11** 20 D4
Compton Beauchamp **SN6** 21 F3
Compton Bishop **BS26** 19 G6
Compton Chamberlayne **SP3** 10 B2
Compton Dando **BS39** 19 K5
Compton Dundon **TA11** 8 D1
Compton Martin **BS40** 19 J6
Compton Pauncefoot **BA22** 9 F2
Compton Valence **DT2** 8 E5
Compton Verney **CV35** 30 E3
Compton Wynyates **CV35** 30 E4
Comra **PH20** 88 C5
Comrie *Fife* **KY12** 75 J2
Comrie *P. & K.* **PH6** 81 J5
Conchra *Arg. & B.* **PA22** 73 J2
Conchra *High.* **IV40** 86 E2
Concraigie **PH10** 82 C3
Conder Green **LA2** 55 H4
Conderton **GL20** 29 J5
Condicote **GL54** 30 C6
Condorrat **G67** 75 F3
Condover **SY5** 38 D5
Coney Weston **IP31** 34 D1
Coneyhurst **RH14** 12 E4
Coneysthorpe **YO60** 58 D2
Coneythorpe **HG5** 57 J4
Conford **GU30** 12 B3
Congash **PH26** 89 H2
Congdon's Shop **PL15** 4 C3
Congerstone **CV13** 41 F5
Congham **PE32** 44 B3
Congleton CW12 49 H6
Congresbury **BS49** 19 H5
Congreve **ST19** 40 B4
Conicavel **IV36** 97 G6
Coningsby **LN4** 53 F7
Conington *Cambs.* **PE7** 42 E7
Conington *Cambs.* **CB3** 33 G2
Conisbrough **DN12** 51 H3
Conisby **PA49** 72 A4
Conisholme **LN11** 53 H3
Coniston *Cumb.* LA21 60 E7
Coniston *E.Riding* **HU11** 59 H6
Coniston Cold **BD23** 56 E4
Conistone **BD23** 56 E3
Conland **AB54** 98 E6
Connah's Quay **CH5** 48 B6
Connel **PA37** 80 A4
Connel Park **KA18** 68 B2
Connor Downs **TR27** 2 C5
Conock **SN10** 20 D6
Conon Bridge **IV7** 96 C6
Cononish **FK20** 80 E5
Cononley **BD20** 56 E5
Cononsyth **DD11** 83 G3
Consall **ST9** 40 B1
Consett DH8 62 C1
Constable Burton **DL8** 62 C7
Constantine **TR11** 2 E6
Constantine Bay **PL28** 3 F1
Contin **IV14** 96 B6
Contlaw **AB13** 91 G4
Contullich **IV17** 96 D4
Conwy LL32 47 F5
Conyer **ME9** 25 F5
Conyer's Green **IP31** 34 C2
Cooden **TN39** 14 C7
Coodham **KA1** 74 C7
Cooil **IM4** 54 C6
Cookbury **EX22** 6 C5
Cookbury Wick **EX22** 6 B5
Cookham **SL6** 22 B3
Cookham Dean **SL6** 22 B3
Cookham Rise **SL6** 22 B3
Cookhill **B49** 30 B3
Cookley *Suff.* **IP19** 35 H1
Cookley *Worcs.* **DY10** 40 A7
Cookley Green *Oxon.* **RG9** 21 K2
Cookley Green *Suff.* **IP19** 35 H1
Cookney **AB39** 91 G5
Cook's Green **IP7** 34 D3
Cooksbridge **BN7** 13 G5
Cooksey Green **B61** 29 J2
Cookshill **ST11** 40 B1
Cooksmill Green **CM1** 24 C1
Cookston **AB41** 91 H1
Coolham **RH13** 12 E4
Cooling **ME3** 24 D4
Cooling Street **ME3** 24 D4
Coombe *Cornw.* **PL26** 3 G3
Coombe *Cornw.* **EX23** 6 A4
Coombe *Cornw.* **TR14** 2 D4
Coombe *Cornw.* **TR3** 3 F4
Coombe *Devon* **TQ9** 5 H6
Coombe *Devon* **EX6** 7 G7
Coombe *Devon* **EX10** 7 K6
Coombe *Som.* **TA2** 8 B2
Coombe *Som.* **TA18** 8 D4
Coombe *Wilts.* **SN9** 20 E6
Coombe Bissett **SP5** 10 C2
Coombe End **TA4** 7 J3
Coombe Hill **GL19** 29 H6
Coombe Keynes **BH20** 9 H6
Coombes **BN15** 12 E6
Coombes Moor **LD8** 28 C2
Cooper's Corner *E.Suss.* **TN19** 14 C5
Cooper's Corner *Kent* **TN14** 23 H7
Cooper's Green **AL4** 22 E1
Coopersale **CM16** 23 H1
Coopersale Street **CM16** 23 H1
Cootham **RH20** 12 D5
Cop Street **CT3** 15 H2
Copdock **IP8** 35 F4
Copford Green **CO6** 34 D6
Copgrove **HG3** 57 J3
Copister **ZE2** 107 N5
Cople **MK44** 32 E4
Copley *Dur.* **DL13** 62 B4
Copley *W.Yorks.* **HX4** 57 F7
Coplow Dale **SK17** 50 D5
Copmanthorpe **YO23** 58 B5
Copmere End **ST21** 40 A3
Copp **PR3** 55 H6
Coppathorne **EX23** 6 A5
Coppenhall **ST18** 40 B4
Coppenhall Moss **CW1** 49 G7
Copperhouse **TR27** 2 C5
Coppicegate **DY12** 39 G7
Coppingford **PE28** 42 E7
Coppleridge **SP7** 9 H2
Copplestone **EX17** 7 F5
Coppull **PR7** 48 E1
Coppull Moor **PR7** 48 E1
Copsale **RH13** 12 E4
Copse Hill **SW20** 23 F5
Copster Green **BB1** 56 B6
Copston Magna **LE10** 41 G7
Copt Heath **B93** 30 C1
Copt Hewick **HG4** 57 J2
Copt Oak **LE67** 41 G4
Copthall Green **EN9** 23 H1
Copthorne **RH10** 13 G3
Copy Lake **EX18** 6 E4
Copythorne **SO40** 10 E3
Coralhill **AB43** 99 J4
Corbets Tey **RM14** 23 J3
Corbiegoe **KW1** 105 J4
Corbridge NE45 70 E7
Corby NN17 42 B7
Corby Glen **NG33** 42 D3
Cordach **AB34** 90 E5
Cordorcan **DG8** 64 D3
Coreley **SY8** 29 F1
Corfcott Green **EX22** 6 B6
Corfe **TA3** 8 B3
Corfe Castle **BH20** 9 J6
Corfe Mullen **BH21** 9 J5
Corfton **SY7** 38 D7
Corgarff **AB36** 89 K4
Corhampton **SO32** 11 H2
Corley **CV7** 40 E7
Corley Ash **CV7** 40 E7
Corley Moor **CV7** 40 E7
Cornabus **PA42** 72 B6

Cornard Tye CO10 34 D4
Corndon TQ13 6 E7
Corney LA19 60 C7
Cornforth DL17 62 E3
Cornhill AB45 98 D5
Cornhill on Tweed TD12 77 G7
Cornholme OL14 56 E7
Cornish Hall End CM7 33 K5
Cornquoy KW17 106 E7
Cornriggs DL13 61 K2
Cornsay DH7 62 C2
Cornsay Colliery DH7 62 C2
Corntown High. IV7 96 C6
Corntown V. of Glam. CF35 18 C4
Cornwell OX7 30 D6
Cornwood PL21 5 G5
Cornworthy TQ9 5 J5
Corpach PH33 87 H7
Corpusty NR11 45 F3
Corrachree AB34 90 C4
Corran Arg. & B. PA24 74 A1
Corran High. IV40 86 E4
Corran (Ardgour) High. PH33 80 B1
Corranbuie PA29 73 G4
Corranmore PA31 79 J7
Corrany IM7 54 D5
Corribeg PH33 87 F7
Corrie KA27 73 J6
Corrie Common DG11 69 H5
Corriechrevie PA29 73 F5
Corriecravie KA27 66 D1
Corriedoo DG7 68 B5
Corriekinloch IV27 103 F6
Corrielorne PA34 79 K6
Corrievorrie IV13 88 E2
Corrimony IV63 87 K1
Corringham Lincs. DN21 52 B3
Corringham Thur. SS17 24 D3
Corris SY20 37 G5
Corris Uchaf SY20 37 G5
Corrlarach PH33 87 F7
Corrour Shooting Lodge PH30 81 F1
Corrow PA24 80 C7
Corry IV49 86 C2
Corrychurrachan PH33 80 B1
Corrylach PA28 73 F7
Corrymuckloch PH8 81 K4
Corsback KW1 105 H2
Corscombe DT2 8 E4
Corse Aber. AB54 98 E6
Corse Glos. GL19 29 G6
Corse Lawn GL19 29 H5
Corse of Kinnoir AB54 98 D6
Corsebank DG4 68 D2
Corsegight AB53 99 G5
Corsehill DG11 69 G5
Corsewall DG9 64 A4
Corsham SN13 20 B4
Corsindae AB51 90 E4
Corsley BA12 20 B7
Corsley Heath BA12 20 B7
Corsock DG7 65 H3
Corston B. & N.E.Som. BA2 19 K5
Corston Wilts. SN16 20 C3
Corstorphine EH12 75 K3
Cortachy DD8 82 E2
Corton Suff. NR32 45 K6
Corton Wilts. BA12 20 C7
Corton Denham DT9 9 F2
Corwar House KA26 67 G5
Corwen LL21 37 K1
Coryton Devon EX20 6 C7
Coryton Thur. SS17 24 D3
Cosby LE9 41 H6
Coscote OX11 21 J3
Coseley WV14 40 B6
Cosford Shrop. WV7 39 G5
Cosford Warks. CV21 31 G1
Cosgrove MK19 31 J4
Cosham PO6 11 H4
Cosheston SA72 16 D5
Coshieville PH15 81 J3
Coskills DN38 52 D2
Cosmeston CF64 18 E5
Cossall NG16 41 G1
Cossington Leics. LE7 41 J4
Cossington Som. TA7 19 G7
Costa KW17 106 C5
Costessey NR8 45 F4
Costock LE12 41 H3
Coston Leics. LE14 42 B3
Coston Norf. NR9 44 E5
Cote Oxon. OX18 21 G1
Cote Som. TA9 19 G7
Cotebrook CW6 48 E6
Cotehill CA4 61 F1
Cotes Cumb. LA8 55 H1
Cotes Leics. LE12 41 H3
Cotes Staffs. ST15 40 A2
Cotesbach LE17 41 H7
Cotgrave NG12 41 J2
Cothall AB21 91 G3
Cotham NG23 42 A1
Cothelstone TA4 7 K2
Cotheridge WR6 29 G3
Cotherstone DL12 62 B5
Cothill OX13 21 H2
Cotleigh EX14 8 B4
Cotmanhay DE7 41 G1
Coton Cambs. CB3 33 H3
Coton Northants. NN6 31 H1
Coton Staffs. ST18 40 B2
Coton Staffs. B79 40 D5
Coton Staffs. ST20 40 A3
Coton Clanford ST18 40 A3
Coton Hill ST18 40 B2
Coton in the Clay DE6 40 D3
Coton in the Elms DE12 40 E4
Cotonwood Shrop. SY13 38 E2
Cotonwood Staffs. ST20 40 A3
Cott TQ9 5 H4
Cottam Lancs. PR4 55 H6
Cottam Notts. DN22 52 B4
Cottartown PH26 89 H1
Cottenham CB4 33 H2
Cotterdale DL8 61 K7
Cottered SG9 33 G6
Cotteridge B30 30 B1
Cotterstock PE8 42 D6
Cottesbrooke NN6 31 J1
Cottesmore LE15 42 C4
Cottingham E.Riding HU16 59 G6
Cottingham Northants. LE16 42 B6
Cottingley BD16 57 G6
Cottisford NN13 31 G5
Cotton Staffs. ST10 40 C1
Cotton Suff. IP14 34 E2
Cotton End MK45 32 D4
Cottonworth SP11 10 E1
Cottown Aber. AB54 90 D2
Cottown Aber. AB53 99 G6
Cottown Aber. AB51 91 F3
Cotts PL20 4 E4
Cottwood EX18 6 E4
Cotwall TF6 39 F4
Cotwalton ST15 40 B2
Couch's Mill PL22 4 B5
Coughton Here. HR9 28 E6
Coughton Warks. B49 30 B2
Cougie IV4 87 J2
Coulaghailtro PA29 73 F4
Coulags IV54 95 F7
Coulby Newham TS8 63 G5
Coulderton CA22 60 A6
Coull AB34 90 D4
Coulport G84 74 A2
Coulsdon CR5 23 F6
Coulston BA13 20 C6
Coulter ML12 75 J7
Coultershaw Bridge GU28 12 C5
Coultings TA5 19 F7
Coulton YO62 58 C2
Coultra KY15 82 E5
Cound SY5 38 E5
Coundlane SY5 38 E5
Coundon Dur. DL14 62 D4
Coundon W.Mid. CV6 41 F7
Countersett DL8 56 E1
Countess Wear EX2 7 H6
Countesthorpe LE8 41 H6
Countisbury EX35 7 F1
Coup Green PR5 55 J7
Coupar Angus PH13 82 D3
Coupland Cumb. CA16 61 J5
Coupland Northumb. NE71 77 H7
Cour PA28 73 G6
Court Colman CF32 18 B3
Court Henry SA32 17 J3
Court House Green CV6 41 F7
Court-at-Street CT21 15 F4
Courteenhall NN7 31 J3
Courtsend SS3 25 G2
Courtway TA5 8 B1
Cousland EH22 76 B4
Cousley Wood TN5 13 K3
Coustonn PA22 73 J3
Cove Arg. & B. G84 74 A2
Cove Devon EX16 7 H4
Cove Hants. GU14 22 B6
Cove High. IV22 94 E2
Cove Sc.Bord. TD13 77 F3
Cove Bay AB12 91 H4
Cove Bottom NR34 45 J7
Covehithe NR34 45 K7
Coven WV9 40 B5
Coveney CB6 43 H7
Covenham St. Bartholomew LN11 53 G3
Covenham St. Mary LN11 53 G3
COVENTRY CV 30 E1
Coventry Airport CV3 30 E1
Coverack TR12 2 E7
Coverham DL8 57 G1
Covesea IV30 97 J4
Covingham SN3 20 E3
Covington Cambs. PE28 32 D1
Covington S.Lan. ML12 75 H7
Cowan Bridge LA6 56 B2
Cowbeech BN27 13 K5
Cowbit PE12 43 F4
Cowbridge Som. TA24 7 H1
Cowbridge V. of Glam. CF71 18 C4
Cowden TN8 23 H7
Cowden Pound TN8 23 H7
Cowdenbeath KY4 75 K1
Cowdenburn EH46 76 A5
Cowers Lane DE56 41 F1
Cowes PO31 11 F5
Cowesby YO7 57 K1
Cowesfield Green SP5 10 D2
Cowey Green CO7 34 E6
Cowfold RH13 13 F4
Cowgill LA10 56 C1
Cowie Aber. AB39 91 G6
Cowie Stir. FK7 75 G2
Cowlam Manor YO25 59 F3
Cowley Devon EX4 7 H6
Cowley Glos. GL53 29 J7
Cowley Gt.Lon. UB8 22 D3
Cowley Oxon. OX4 21 J1
Cowling Lancs. PR7 48 E1
Cowling N.Yorks. BD22 56 E5
Cowling N.Yorks. DL8 57 H1
Cowlinge CB8 34 B3
Cowmes HD8 50 D1
Cowpe BB4 56 D7
Cowpen NE24 71 H5
Cowpen Bewley TS23 63 F4
Cowplain PO8 11 H3
Cowsden WR7 29 J3
Cowshill DL13 61 K2
Cowthorpe LS22 57 K4
Cox Common IP19 45 H7
Coxbank CW3 39 F1
Coxbench DE21 41 F1
Coxbridge BA6 8 E1
Coxford PE31 44 C3
Coxheath ME17 14 C2
Coxhoe DH6 62 E3
Coxley BA5 19 J7
Coxley Wick BA5 19 J7
Coxpark PL18 4 E3
Coxtie Green CM14 23 J2
Coxwold YO61 58 B2
Coychurch CF35 18 C4
Coylet PA23 73 K2
Coylton KA6 67 J2
Coylumbridge PH22 89 G3
Coynach AB34 90 C4
Coynachie AB54 90 C1
Coytrahen CF32 18 B3
Crabbet Park RH10 13 G3
Crabgate NR11 44 E3
Crabtree Plym. PL3 5 F5
Crabtree S.Yorks. S4 51 F4
Crabtree W.Suss. RH13 13 F4
Crabtree Green LL13 38 C1
Crackaig PA60 72 D4
Crackenthorpe CA16 61 H4
Crackington EX23 4 B1
Crackington Haven EX23 4 B1
Crackley ST5 40 A1
Crackleybank TF11 39 G4
Crackpot DL11 62 A7
Crackthorn Corner IP22 34 E1
Cracoe BD23 56 E3
Craddock EX15 7 J4
Cradhlastadh HS2 100 C4
Cradley Here. WR13 29 G4
Cradley W.Mid. B63 40 B7
Cradley Heath B64 40 B7
Crafthole PL11 4 D5
Crafton LU7 32 B7
Cragg HX7 57 F7
Cragg Hill LS18 57 H6
Craggan Moray AB37 89 J1
Craggan P. & K. PH5 81 K6
Cragganruar PH15 81 H3
Craggie High. IV2 88 E1
Craggie High. KW8 104 D7
Craghead DH9 62 D1
Craibstone Aberdeen AB21 91 G3
Craibstone Moray AB56 98 C5
Craichie DD8 83 G3
Craig Arg. & B. PA35 80 B4
Craig Arg. & B. PA70 79 G4
Craig D. & G. DG7 65 G4
Craig High. IV22 94 D5
Craig High. IV54 95 G7
Craig S.Ayr. KA19 67 H3
Craig Berthlŵyd CF46 18 D2
Craigans PA31 73 G1
Craigbeg PH31 88 B6
Craig-cefn-parc SA6 17 K5
Craigcleuch DG13 69 J5
Craigculter AB43 99 H5
Craigdallie PH14 82 D5
Craigdam AB41 91 G1
Craigdarroch D. & G. DG3 68 C4
Craigdarroch E.Ayr. KA18 68 B3
Craigdhu D. & G. DG8 64 D6
Craigdhu High. IV4 96 B7
Craigearn AB51 91 F3
Craigellachie AB38 97 K7
Craigellie AB43 99 J4
Craigencallie DG7 65 F3
Craigend Moray IV36 97 J6
Craigend P. & K. PH2 82 C5
Craigendive PA23 73 J2
Craigendoran G84 74 B2
Craigengillan KA6 67 J3
Craigenputtock DG2 68 C5
Craigens PA44 72 A4
Craigglas PA31 73 G1
Craighall KY15 83 F6
Craighat G63 74 C2
Craighead Fife KY10 83 H6
Craighead High. IV11 96 E5
Craighlaw DG8 64 D4
Craighouse PA60 72 D4
Craigie Aber. AB23 91 H3
Craigie Dundee DD4 83 F4
Craigie P. & K. PH10 82 C3
Craigie S.Ayr. KA1 74 C7
Craigie Brae AB41 91 G1
Craigieburn DG10 69 G3
Craigieholm PH13 82 C4
Craigielaw EH32 76 C3
Craiglockhart EH14 76 A3
Craiglug AB31 91 G5
Craigmaud AB43 99 G5
Craigmillar EH16 76 A3
Craigmore PA20 73 K4
Craigmyle House AB31 90 E4
Craignafeoch PA21 73 H3
Craignant SY10 38 B2
Craignavie FK21 81 G4
Craigneil KA26 67 F5
Craigneuk ML1 75 F5
Craignure PA65 79 J4
Craigo DD10 83 H1
Craigoch KA19 67 G3
Craigow KY13 82 B7
Craigrothie KY15 82 E6
Craigroy IV36 97 J6
Craigroy Farm AB37 89 J1
Craigruie FK19 81 F5
Craigsanquhar KY15 82 E6
Craigton Aberdeen AB14 91 G4
Craigton Angus DD5 83 G4
Craigton Angus DD8 82 E2
Craigton High. IV1 96 D7
Craigton Stir. G63 74 E2
Craigtown KW13 104 D3
Craig-y-nos SA9 27 H7
Craik Aber. AB54 90 C2
Craik Sc.Bord. TD9 69 J3
Crail KY10 83 H7
Crailing TD8 70 B1
Crailinghall TD8 70 B1
Crakehill YO7 57 K2
Crakemarsh ST14 40 C2
Crambe YO60 58 D3
Cramlington NE23 71 H6
Cramond EH4 75 K3
Cranage CW4 49 G6
Cranberry ST21 40 A2
Cranborne BH21 10 B3
Cranbourne SL4 22 C4
Cranbrook Gt.Lon. IG1 23 H3
Cranbrook Kent TN17 14 C4
Cranbrook Common TN17 14 C4
Crane Moor S35 51 F2
Cranfield MK43 32 C4
Cranford Devon EX39 6 B3
Cranford Gt.Lon. TW5 22 E4
Cranford St. Andrew NN14 32 C1
Cranford St. John NN14 32 C1
Cranham Glos. GL4 29 H7
Cranham Gt.Lon. RM14 23 J3
Crank WA11 48 E3
Cranleigh GU6 12 D3
Cranmer Green IP31 34 E1
Cranmore I.o.W. PO41 10 E6
Cranmore Som. BA4 19 K7
Cranna AB54 98 E5
Crannoch AB55 98 C5
Cranoe LE16 42 A6
Cransford IP13 35 H2
Cranshaws TD11 76 E4
Cranstal IM7 54 D3
Crantock TR8 2 E2
Cranwell NG34 42 D1
Cranwich IP26 44 B6
Cranworth IP25 44 D5
Craobh Haven PA31 79 J7
Crapstone PL20 5 F4
Crarae PA32 73 H1
Crask Inn IV27 103 H6
Crask of Aigas IV4 96 B7
Craskins AB34 90 D4
Craster NE66 71 H2
Craswall HR2 28 B5
Crateford ST19 40 B5
Cratfield IP19 35 H1
Crathes AB31 91 F5
Crathie Aber. AB35 89 K5
Crathie High. PH20 88 C5
Crathorne TS15 63 F6
Craven Arms SY7 38 D7
Craw KA27 73 G6
Crawcrook NE40 71 G7
Crawford Lancs. WN8 48 D2
Crawford S.Lan. ML12 68 E1
Crawfordjohn ML12 68 D1
Crawfordton DG3 68 C4
Crawick DG4 68 C2
Crawley Devon EX14 8 B4
Crawley Hants. SO21 11 F1
Crawley Oxon. OX29 30 E7
Crawley W.Suss. RH11 13 F3
Crawley Down RH10 13 G3
Crawleyside DL13 62 A2
Crawshawbooth BB4 56 D7
Crawton AB39 91 G7
Crawyn IM7 54 C4
Cray N.Yorks. BD23 56 E2
Cray P. & K. PH10 82 C1
Cray Powys LD3 27 H6
Crayford DA1 23 J4
Crayke YO61 58 B2
Crays Hill CM11 24 D2
Cray's Pond RG8 21 K3
Crazies Hill RG10 22 A3
Creacombe EX16 7 G4
Creag Ghoraidh (Creagorry) HS7 92 C7
Creagan PA38 80 A3
Creagbheitheachain PH33 80 A1
Creagorry (Creag Ghoraidh) HS7 92 C7
Creamore Bank SY4 38 E2
Creaton NN6 31 J1
Creca DG12 69 H6
Credenhill HR4 28 D4
Crediton EX17 7 G5
Creebridge DG8 64 E4
Creech Heathfield TA3 8 B2
Creech St. Michael TA3 8 B2
Creed TR2 3 G4
Creedy Park EX17 7 G5
Creekmouth IG11 23 H3
Creeting St. Mary IP6 34 E3
Creeton NG33 42 D3
Creetown DG8 64 E5
Creggans PA27 80 B7
Cregneash IM9 54 A7
Cregrina LD1 28 A3
Creich KY15 82 E5
Creigau NP16 19 H2
Creigiau CF15 18 D3
Crelevan IV4 87 K1
Crelly TR13 2 D5
Cremyll PL10 4 E5
Crendell SP6 10 B3
Cressage SY5 38 E5
Cressbrook SK17 50 D5
Cresselly SA68 16 D5
Cressing CM77 34 B6
Cresswell Northumb. NE61 71 H4
Cresswell Staffs. ST11 40 B2
Cresswell Quay SA68 16 D5
Creswell S80 51 H5
Cretingham IP13 35 G3
Cretshengan PA29 73 F4
CREWE Ches. CW 49 G7
Crewe Ches. CH3 48 D7
Crewe Green CW1 49 G7
Crewgreen SY5 38 C4
Crewkerne TA18 8 D4
Crew's Hole BS5 19 K4
Crewton DE24 41 F2
Crianlarich FK20 80 E5
Cribbs Causeway BS34 19 J3
Cribyn SA48 26 E3
Criccieth LL52 36 D2
Crich DE4 51 F7
Crich Carr DE4 51 F7
Crich Common DE4 51 F7
Crichie AB42 99 H6
Crichton EH37 76 B4
Crick Mon. NP26 19 H2
Crick Northants. NN6 31 G1
Crickadarn LD2 27 K4
Cricket Hill GU46 22 B5
Cricket St. Thomas TA20 8 C4
Crickham BS28 19 H7
Crickheath SY10 38 B3
Crickhowell NP8 28 B7
Cricklade SN6 20 E2
Cricklewood NW2 23 F3
Crick's Green HR7 29 F3
Criddlestyle SP6 10 C3
Cridling Stubbs WF11 58 B7
Crieff PH7 81 K5
Criftins (Dudleston Heath) SY12 38 C2
Criggan PL26 4 A4
Criggion SY5 38 B4
Crigglestone WF4 51 F1
Crimble OL11 49 H1
Crimchard TA20 8 C4
Crimdon Park TS27 63 F3
Crimond AB43 99 J5
Crimonmogate AB43 99 J5
Crimplesham PE33 44 A5
Crinan PA31 73 F1
Crinan Ferry PA31 73 F1
Cringleford NR4 45 F5
Cringletie EH45 76 A6
Crinow SA67 16 E4
Cripplestyle SP6 10 B3
Cripp's Corner TN32 14 C5
Crix CM3 34 B7
Crizeley HR2 28 D5
Croalchapel DG3 68 E4
Croasdale CA23 60 B5
Crock Street TA19 8 C3
Crockenhill BR8 23 J5
Crocker End RG9 22 A3
Crockerhill PO17 11 G4
Crockernwell EX6 7 F6
Crockerton BA12 20 B7
Crockerton Green BA12 20 B7
Crocketford (Ninemile Bar) DG2 65 J3
Crockey Hill YO19 58 C5
Crockham Hill TN8 23 H6
Crockhurst Street TN11 23 K7
Crockleford Heath CO7 34 E6
Croes Hywel NP7 28 C7
Croes y pant NP4 19 G1
Croesau Bach SY10 38 B3
Croeserw SA13 18 B2
Croesgoch SA62 16 B2
Croes-lan SA44 17 G1
Croesor LL48 37 F1
Croespenmaen NP11 18 E2
Croesyceiliog Carmar. SA32 17 H4
Croesyceiliog Torfaen NP44 19 G2
Croes-y-mwyalch NP44 19 G2
Croesywaun LL55 46 D7
Croford TA4 7 K3
Croft Here. HR6 28 D2
Croft Leics. LE9 41 H6
Croft Lincs. PE24 53 J6
Croft Warr. WA3 49 F3
Croftamie G63 74 C2
Crofthead CA6 69 J6
Croftmore PH18 81 K1
Crofton W.Yorks. WF4 51 F1
Crofton Wilts. SN8 21 F5
Croft-on-Tees DL2 62 D6
Crofts DG7 65 H3
Crofts of Benachielt KW5 105 G5
Crofts of Buinach IV30 97 J6
Crofts of Haddo AB41 91 G1
Crofty SA4 17 J6
Crogen LL21 37 K2
Croggan PA63 79 J5
Croglin CA4 61 G2
Croick High. IV24 96 B2
Croick High. KW13 104 D3
Croig PA75 79 F2
Crois Dughaill HS8 84 C3
Croit e Caley IM9 54 B7
Cromarty IV11 96 E5
Crombie KY12 75 J2

Crombie Mill DD7 83 G4
Cromblet AB51 91 F1
Cromdale PH26 89 H2
Cromer *Herts.* SG2 33 F6
Cromer *Norf.* NR27 45 G1
Cromford DE4 50 E7
Cromhall GL12 19 K2
Cromhall Common GL12 19 K3
Cromore HS2 101 G5
Crompton Fold OL2 49 J1
Cromwell NG23 51 K6
Cronberry KA18 68 B1
Crondall GU10 22 A7
Cronk-y-Voddy IM6 54 C5
Cronton WA8 48 D4
Crook *Cumb.* LA8 61 F7
Crook *Dur.* DL15 62 C3
Crook of Devon KY13 82 B7
Crooked Soley RG17 21 G4
Crookedholm KA3 74 C7
Crookham *Northumb.* TD12 77 H7
Crookham *W.Berks.* RG19 21 J5
Crookham Eastfield TD12 77 H7
Crookham Village GU51 22 A6
Crooklands LA7 55 J1
Cropredy OX17 31 F4
Cropston LE7 41 H4
Cropthorne WR10 29 J4
Cropton YO18 58 D1
Cropwell Bishop NG12 41 J2
Cropwell Butler NG12 41 J2
Cros (Cross) HS2 101 H1
Crosbie KA23 74 A6
Crosbost HS2 101 F5
Crosby *Cumb.* CA15 60 B3
Crosby *I.o.M.* IM4 54 C6
Crosby *Mersey.* L23 48 C3
Crosby *N.Lincs.* DN15 52 B1
Crosby Court DL6 62 E7
Crosby Garrett CA17 61 J6
Crosby Ravensworth CA10 61 H5
Crosby Villa CA15 60 B3
Crosby-on-Eden CA6 60 F1
Croscombe BA5 19 J7
Crosemere SY12 38 D3
Crosland Hill HD4 50 D1
Cross *Som.* BS26 19 H6
Cross (Cros) *W.Isles* HS2 101 H1
Cross Ash NP7 28 D7
Cross Bank DY12 29 G1
Cross End *Beds.* MK44 32 D3
Cross End *Essex* CO9 34 C5
Cross Foxes Inn LL40 37 G4
Cross Gates LS15 57 J6
Cross Green *Devon* PL15 6 B7
Cross Green *Staffs.* WV10 40 B5
Cross Green *Suff.* IP7 34 D3
Cross Green *Suff.* IP30 34 C3
Cross Green *Suff.* IP29 34 C3
Cross Hands *Carmar.* SA14 17 J4
Cross Hands *Pembs.* SA67 16 D4
Cross Hill DE5 41 G1
Cross Hills BD20 57 F5
Cross Houses SY5 38 E5
Cross in Hand TN21 13 J4
Cross Inn *Cere.* SA44 26 C3
Cross Inn *Cere.* SY23 26 E2
Cross Inn *R.C.T.* CF72 18 D3
Cross Keys SN13 20 B4
Cross Lane PO30 11 G6
Cross Lane Head WV16 39 G6
Cross Lanes *Cornw.* TR4 2 E4
Cross Lanes *Cornw.* TR12 2 D6
Cross Lanes *N.Yorks.* YO61 58 B3
Cross Lanes *Wrex.* LL13 38 C1
Cross of Jackston AB51 91 F1
Cross o'th'hands DE56 40 E1
Cross Street IP21 35 F1
Crossaig PA29 73 G5
Crossapol PA78 78 C2
Crossapoll PA77 78 A3
Cross-at-Hand TN12 14 C3
Crossbush BN18 12 D6
Crosscanonby CA15 60 B3
Crossdale Street NR27 45 G2
Crossens PR9 48 C1
Crossflatts BD16 57 G5
Crossford *D. & G.* DG3 68 D5
Crossford *Fife* KY12 75 J2
Crossford *S.Lan.* ML8 75 G6
Crossgate *Lincs.* PE11 43 F3
Crossgate *Staffs.* ST11 40 B2
Crossgatehall EH22 76 B4
Crossgates *Fife* KY4 75 K2
Crossgates *N.Yorks.* YO12 59 G1
Crossgates *P. & K.* PH2 82 B5
Crossgates *Powys* LD1 27 K2
Crossgill LA2 55 J3
Crosshands KA5 74 C7
Crosshill *Fife* KY5 75 K1
Crosshill *S.Ayr.* KA19 67 H3
Crosshouse KA2 74 B7
Crosskeys NP11 19 F2
Crosskirk KW14 105 F1
Crosslanes SY10 38 C4
Crosslee *Renf.* PA6 74 C4
Crosslee *Sc.Bord.* TD7 69 J2
Crossmichael DG7 65 H4
Crossmoor PR4 55 H6
Crossroads *Aber.* AB31 91 F5
Crossroads *E.Ayr.* KA1 74 C7
Crossway *Mon.* NP25 28 D7
Crossway *Powys* LD1 27 K3
Crossway Green *Mon.* NP16 19 J2
Crossway Green *Worcs.* DY13 29 H2
Crossways *Dorset* DT2 9 G6
Crossways *Glos.* GL16 28 E7
Crosswell SA41 16 E2
Crosswood SY23 27 F1
Crosthwaite LA8 60 F7
Croston PR26 48 D1
Crostwick NR12 45 G4
Crostwight NR28 45 H3
Crothair HS2 100 D4
Crouch TN15 23 K6
Crouch End N8 23 F3
Crouch Hill DT9 9 G3
Croucheston SP5 10 B2
Croughton NN13 31 G5
Crovie AB45 99 G4
Crow BH24 10 C4
Crow Edge S36 50 D2
Crow Green CM15 23 J2
Crow Hill HR9 29 F6
Crowan TR14 2 D5
Crowborough TN6 13 J3
Crowborough Warren TN6 13 J3
Crowcombe TA4 7 K2
Crowdecote SK17 50 D6
Crowden SK13 50 C3
Crowdhill SO50 11 F2
Crowell OX39 22 A2
Crowfield *Northants.* NN13 31 H4
Crowfield *Suff.* IP6 35 F3
Crowhurst *E.Suss.* TN33 14 C6
Crowhurst *Surr.* RH7 23 G7
Crowhurst Lane End RH7 23 G7
Crowland *Lincs.* PE6 43 F4
Crowland *Suff.* IP31 34 E1
Crowlas TR20 2 C5
Crowle *N.Lincs.* DN17 51 K1
Crowle *Worcs.* WR7 29 J3
Crowle Green WR7 29 J3
Crowmarsh Gifford OX10 21 K3
Crown Corner IP13 35 G1
Crownhill PL6 4 E5
Crownthorpe NR18 44 E5
Crowntown TR13 2 D5
Crow's Nest PL14 4 C4
Crows-an-wra TR19 2 A6
Crowsnest SY5 38 C5
Crowthorne RG45 22 B5
Crowton CW8 48 E5
Croxall WS13 40 E4
Croxby LN7 52 E3
Croxdale DH6 62 D3
Croxden ST14 40 C2
Croxley Green WD3 22 D2
Croxton *Cambs.* PE19 33 F3
Croxton *N.Lincs.* DN39 52 D1
Croxton *Norf.* IP24 44 C7
Croxton *Staffs.* ST21 39 G2
Croxton Green SY14 48 E7
Croxton Kerrial NG32 42 B3
Croxtonbank ST21 39 G2
Croy *High.* IV2 96 E7
Croy *N.Lan.* G65 75 F3
Croyde EX33 6 C2
Croyde Bay EX33 6 C2
Croydon *Cambs.* SG8 33 G4
CROYDON *Gt.Lon.* CR 23 G5
Cruach PA43 72 B5
Cruchie AB54 98 D6
Cruckmeole SY5 38 D5
Cruckton SY5 38 D4
Cruden Bay AB42 91 J1
Crudgington TF6 39 F4
Crudwell SN16 20 C2
Crug LD1 28 A1
Crugmeer PL28 3 G1
Crugybar SA19 17 K2
Crùlabhig HS2 100 D4
Crumlin NP11 19 F2
Crumpsall M8 49 H2
Crumpsbrook DY14 29 F1
Crundale *Kent* CT4 15 F3
Crundale *Pembs.* SA62 16 C4
Crunwere Farm SA67 16 E4
Crutherland Farm G75 74 E5
Cruwys Morchard EX16 7 G4
Crux Easton RG20 21 H6
Crwbin SA17 17 H4
Cryers Hill HP15 22 B2
Crymlyn LL33 46 E5
Crymych SA41 16 E2
Crynant SA10 18 A1
Crystal Palace SE26 23 G4
Cuaig IV54 94 D6
Cubbington CV32 30 E2
Cubert TR8 2 E3
Cubley S36 50 E2
Cublington *Bucks.* LU7 32 B6
Cublington *Here.* HR2 28 D5
Cuckfield RH17 13 G4
Cucklington BA9 9 G2
Cuckney NG20 51 H5
Cuckold's Green NR34 45 J7
Cuckoo Bridge PE11 43 F3
Cuckoo's Corner GU34 22 A7
Cuckoo's Nest CH4 48 C6
Cuddesdon OX44 21 J1
Cuddington *Bucks.* HP18 31 J7
Cuddington *Ches.* CW8 48 E5
Cuddington Heath SY14 38 D1
Cuddy Hill PR4 55 H6
Cudham TN14 23 H6
Cudlipptown PL19 5 F3
Cudworth *S.Yorks.* S72 51 F2
Cudworth *Som.* TA19 8 C3
Cuerdley Cross WA5 48 E4
Cuffley EN6 23 G1
Cuidhaseadair HS2 101 H2
Cuidhir HS9 84 B4
Cuidhtinis (Quidinish) HS3 93 F3
Cuidrach IV51 93 J6
Cuilmuich PA24 73 K1
Cuil-uaine PA37 80 A4
Culag G83 74 B1
Culbo IV7 96 D5
Culbokie IV7 96 D6
Culbone TA24 7 G1
Culburnie IV4 96 B7
Culcabock IV2 96 D7
Culcharan PA37 80 A4
Culcharry IV12 97 F6
Culcheth WA3 49 F3
Culdrain AB54 90 D1
Culduie IV54 94 D7
Culford IP28 34 C2
Culfordheath IP31 34 C1
Culgaith CA10 61 H4
Culgower KW8 104 E7
Culham OX14 21 J2
Culindrach PA29 73 H5
Culkein IV27 102 C5
Culkerton GL8 20 C2
Cullachie PH24 89 G2
Cullen AB56 98 D4
Cullercoats NE30 71 J6
Cullicudden IV7 96 D5
Culligran IV4 95 K7
Cullingworth BD13 57 F6
Cullipool PA34 79 J6
Cullivoe ZE2 107 P2
Culloch PH6 81 J6
Culloden IV2 96 E7
Cullompton EX15 7 J5
Culmaily KW10 97 F2
Culmalzie DG8 64 D5
Culmington SY8 38 D7
Culmstock EX15 7 K4
Culnacraig IV26 95 G1
Culnadalloch PA37 80 A4
Culnaknock IV51 94 B5
Culnamean IV47 85 K2
Culpho IP6 35 G4
Culquhirk DG8 64 E5
Culrain IV24 96 C2
Culross KY12 75 H2
Culroy KA19 67 H2
Culsh AB35 90 B5
Culshabbin DG8 64 D5
Culswick ZE2 107 L8
Culter Allers Farm ML12 75 J7
Cultercullen AB41 91 H2
Cults *Aber.* AB54 90 D1
Cults *Aberdeen* AB15 91 G4
Cults *D. & G.* DG8 64 E6
Cultybraggan Camp PH6 81 J6
Culverhouse Cross CF5 18 E4
Culverstone Green DA13 24 C5
Culverthorpe NG32 42 D1
Culvie AB54 98 D5
Culworth OX17 31 G4
Cumberhead ML11 75 F7
Cumberlow Green SG9 33 G5
Cumbernauld G67 75 F3
Cumberworth LN13 53 J5
Cuminestown AB53 99 G6
Cumloden DG8 64 E4
Cummersdale CA2 60 E1
Cummertrees DG12 69 G7
Cummingstown IV30 97 J5
Cumnock KA18 67 K1
Cumnor OX2 21 H1
Cumrew CA8 61 G1
Cumrue DG11 69 F5
Cumstoun DG6 65 G5
Cumwhinton CA4 61 F1
Cumwhitton CA8 61 G1
Cundall YO61 57 K2
Cunninghamhead KA3 74 B6
Cunningsburgh ZE2 107 N10
Cunnister ZE2 107 P3
Cunnoquhie KY15 82 E6
Cupar KY15 82 E6
Cupar Muir KY15 82 E6
Curbar S32 50 E5
Curborough WS13 40 D4
Curbridge *Hants.* SO30 11 G3
Curbridge *Oxon.* OX29 21 G1
Curdridge SO32 11 G3
Curdworth B76 40 D6
Curland TA3 8 B3
Curlew Green IP17 35 H2
Curling Tye Green CM9 24 E1
Curload TA3 8 C2
Curridge RG18 21 H4
Currie EH14 75 K4
Curry Mallet TA3 8 C2
Curry Rivel TA10 8 C2
Curteis' Corner TN27 14 D4
Curtisden Green TN17 14 C3
Curtisknowle TQ9 5 H5
Cury TR12 2 D6
Cusgarne TR4 2 E4
Cushnie AB45 99 F4
Cushuish TA2 7 K2
Cusop HR3 28 B4
Cusworth DN5 51 H2
Cutcloy DG8 64 E7
Cutcombe TA24 7 H2
Cutgate OL11 49 H1
Cuthill IV25 96 E3
Cutiau LL42 37 F4
Cutlers Green CM6 33 J5
Cutnall Green WR9 29 H2
Cutsdean GL54 30 B5
Cutsyke WF10 57 K7
Cutthorpe S42 51 F5
Cutts ZE1 107 N9
Cuttyhill AB42 99 J5
Cuxham OX49 21 K2
Cuxton ME2 24 D5
Cuxwold LN7 52 E2
Cwm *B.Gwent* NP23 18 E1
Cwm *Denb.* LL18 47 J5
Cwm Ffrwd-oer NP4 19 F1
Cwm Gwaun SA65 16 D2
Cwm Head SY6 38 D7
Cwm Irfon LD5 27 H4
Cwm Penmachno LL24 37 G1
Cwm Plysgog SA43 16 E1
Cwmafan SA12 18 A2
Cwmaman CF44 18 D2
Cwmann SA48 17 J1
Cwmbach *Carmar.* SA34 17 F3
Cwmbach *Carmar.* SA15 17 H5
Cwmbach *Powys* HR3 28 A5
Cwmbach *Powys* LD2 27 K3
Cwmbach *R.C.T.* CF44 18 D1
Cwmbelan SY18 37 J7
Cwmbrân NP44 19 F2
Cwmbrwyno SY23 37 G7
Cwmcarn NP11 19 F2
Cwmcarvan NP25 19 H1
Cwm-Cewydd SY20 37 H4
Cwm-cou SA38 17 F1
Cwmcrawnon LD3 28 A7
Cwmdare CF44 18 C1
Cwmdu *Carmar.* SA19 17 K2
Cwmdu *Powys* NP8 28 A6
Cwmduad SA33 17 G2
Cwmerfyn SY23 37 G7
Cwmfelin CF46 18 D1
Cwmfelin Boeth SA34 16 E4
Cwmfelin Mynach SA34 17 F3
Cwmfelinfach NP11 18 E2
Cwmffrwd SA31 17 H4
Cwmgiedd SA9 27 G7
Cwmgors SA18 27 G7
Cwmgwili SA14 17 J4
Cwmgwrach SA11 18 B1
Cwmgwyn SA2 17 K6
Cwmhiraeth SA44 17 G2
Cwmifor SA19 17 K3
Cwmisfael SA32 17 H4
Cwm-Llinau SY20 37 H5
Cwmllyfri SA33 17 G4
Cwmllynfell SA9 27 G7
Cwm-mawr SA14 17 J4
Cwm-miles SA34 16 E3
Cwm-Morgan SA38 17 F2
Cwm-parc CF42 18 C2
Cwmpengraig SA44 17 G2
Cwmpennar CF45 18 D1
Cwmsychbant SA40 17 H1
Cwmsymlog SY23 37 F7
Cwmtillery NP13 19 F1
Cwm-twrch Isaf SA9 27 G7
Cwm-twrch Uchaf SA9 27 G7
Cwm-y-glo LL55 46 D6
Cwmyoy NP7 28 C6
Cwm-yr-Eglwys SA42 16 D1
Cwmyrhaiadr SY20 37 G6
Cwmystwyth SY23 27 G1
Cwrt SY20 37 F5
Cwrt-newydd SA40 17 H1
Cwrt-y-cadno SA19 17 K1
Cwrt-y-gollen NP8 28 B7
Cydweli (Kidwelly) SA17 17 H5
Cyffylliog LL15 47 J7
Cyfronydd SY21 38 A5
Cymau LL11 48 B7
Cymmer *N.P.T.* SA13 18 B2
Cymmer *R.C.T.* CF39 18 D2
Cyncoed CF23 18 E3
Cynghordy SA20 27 H5
Cynheidre SA15 17 H5
Cynwyd LL21 37 K1
Cynwyl Elfed SA33 17 G3

D

Dabton DG3 68 D4
Daccombe TQ12 5 K4
Dacre *Cumb.* CA11 61 F4
Dacre *N.Yorks.* HG3 57 G3
Dacre Banks HG3 57 G3
Daddry Shield DL13 61 K3
Dadford MK18 31 H5
Dadlington CV13 41 G6
Dafen SA14 17 J5
Daffy Green IP25 44 D5
Dagdale ST14 40 C2
Dagenham RM10 23 H3
Daggons SP6 10 C3
Daglingworth GL7 20 C1
Dagnall HP4 32 C7
Dail PA35 80 B4
Dail Beag HS2 100 E3
Dail Bho Dheas (South Dell) HS2 101 G1
Dail Bho Thuath (North Dell) HS2 101 G1
Dail Mòr HS2 100 E3
Dailly KA26 67 G3
Dailnamac PA35 80 A4
Dainton TQ12 5 J4
Dairsie (Osnaburgh) KY15 83 F6
Dairy House HU12 59 J7
Daisy Bank WS5 40 C6
Daisy Green IP31 34 E2
Dalabrog HS8 84 C2
Dalavich PA35 80 A6
Dalballoch PH20 88 D5
Dalbeattie DG5 65 J4
Dalblair KA18 68 B2
Dalbog DD9 90 D7
Dalbreck IV28 104 C7
Dalbury DE6 40 E2
Dalby *I.o.M.* IM5 54 B6
Dalby *Lincs.* PE23 53 H6
Dalby *N.Yorks.* YO60 58 C2
Dalcairnie KA6 67 J3
Dalchalloch PH18 81 J1
Dalchalm KW9 97 G1
Dalchenna PA32 80 B7
Dalchirach AB37 89 J1
Dalchork IV27 103 H7
Dalchreichart IV63 87 J3
Dalchruin PH6 81 J6
Dalcross IV2 96 E7
Dalderby LN9 53 F6
Dalditch EX9 7 J7
Daldownie AB35 89 K4
Dale *Cumb.* CA4 61 G2
Dale *Gt.Man.* OL3 49 J2
Dale *Pembs.* SA62 16 B5
Dale Abbey DE7 41 G2
Dale End *Derbys.* DE45 50 E6
Dale End *N.Yorks.* BD20 56 E5
Dale Head CA10 60 F5
Dale of Walls ZE2 107 K7
Dale Park BN18 12 C5
Dalehouse TS13 63 J5
Dalelia PH36 79 J1
Daless IV12 89 F1
Dalestie AB37 89 J3
Dalfad AB35 90 B4
Dalganachan KW12 105 F4
Dalgarven KA13 74 A6
Dalgety Bay KY11 75 K2
Dalgig KA18 67 K2
Dalginross PH6 81 J5
Dalgonar DG3 68 C3
Dalguise PH8 82 A3
Dalhalvaig KW13 104 D3
Dalham CB8 34 B2
Daligan G84 74 B2
Dalinlongart PA23 73 K2
Dalivaddy PA28 66 A1
Daljarrock KA26 67 F5
Dalkeith EH22 76 B4
Dallachulish PA37 80 A3
Dallas IV36 97 J6
Dallaschyle IV12 97 F7
Dallash DG8 64 E4
Dalleagles KA18 67 K2
Dallinghoo IP13 35 G3
Dallington *E.Suss.* TN21 13 K5
Dallington *Northants.* NN5 31 J2
Dallow HG4 57 G2
Dalmadilly AB51 91 F3
Dalmally PA33 80 C5
Dalmarnock PH8 82 B3
Dalmary FK8 74 D1
Dalmellington KA6 67 J3
Dalmeny EH30 75 K3
Dalmichy IV27 103 H7
Dalmigavie IV13 88 E3
Dalmore IV17 96 D5
Dalmuir G81 74 C3
Dalmunzie House Hotel PH10 89 H7
Dalnabreck PH36 79 J1
Dalnacarn PH10 82 B1
Dalnaglar Castle PH10 82 C1
Dalnaha PA63 79 H5
Dalnahaitnach PH23 89 F3
Dalnamain IV25 96 E2
Dalnatrat PA38 80 A2
Dalnavert PH21 89 F4
Dalnavie IV17 96 D4
Dalness PH49 80 C2
Dalnessie IV27 103 J7
Dalnigap DG8 64 B3
Dalqueich KY13 82 B7
Dalreoch KA26 67 F5
Dalriech PH8 81 J4
Dalroy IV2 96 E7
Dalrulzian PH10 82 C2
Dalry KA24 74 A6
Dalrymple KA6 67 H2
Dalscote NN12 31 H3
Dalserf ML9 75 F5
Dalsetter ZE2 107 P3
Dalshangan DG7 67 K5
Dalskairth DG2 65 K3
Dalston CA5 60 E1
Dalswinton DG2 68 E5
Daltomach IV13 88 E2
Dalton *Cumb.* LA6 55 J2
Dalton *D. & G.* DG11 69 G6
Dalton *Lancs.* WN8 48 D2
Dalton *N.Yorks.* YO7 57 K2
Dalton *N.Yorks.* DL11 62 C6
Dalton *Northumb.* NE18 71 G6
Dalton *Northumb.* NE46 62 A1
Dalton *S.Yorks.* S65 51 G3
Dalton Magna S65 51 G3
Dalton Piercy TS27 63 F3
Dalton-in-Furness LA15 55 F2
Dalton-le-Dale SR7 63 F2
Dalton-on-Tees DL2 62 D6
Daltote PA31 73 F2
Daltra IV12 97 G7
Dalveich FK19 81 H5
Dalvennan KA19 67 H2
Dalvourn IV2 88 D1
Dalwhinnie PH19 88 D6
Dalwood EX13 8 B4
Dam Green NR16 44 E7
Damask Green SG4 33 F6
Damerham SP6 10 C3
Damgate NR13 45 J5
Damnaglaur DG9 64 B7
Damside PH3 82 A6
Danaway ME9 24 E5
Danbury CM3 24 D1
Danby YO21 63 J6
Danby Wiske DL7 62 E7

Dancers Hill EN5 23 F2
Dandaleith AB38 97 K7
Danderhall EH22 76 B4
Dane Bank M34 49 J3
Dane End SG12 33 G6
Dane Hills LE3 41 H5
Danebridge SK11 49 J6
Danehill RH17 13 H4
Danesmoor S45 51 G6
Danestone AB22 91 H3
Daniel's Water TN26 14 E3
Danskine EH41 76 D4
Danthorpe HU12 59 J6
Danzey Green B94 30 C2
Darby End B64 40 B7
Darby Green GU46 22 B5
Darenth DA2 23 J4
Daresbury WA4 48 E4
Darfield S73 51 G2
Dargate ME13 25 G5
Dargues NE19 70 D4
Darite PL14 4 C4
Darland ME7 24 D5
Darlaston WS10 40 B6
Darley HG3 57 H4
Darley Bridge DE4 50 E6
Darley Dale DE4 50 E6
Darley Head HG3 57 G4
Darley Hillside DE4 50 E6
Darlingscott CV36 30 D4
DARLINGTON DL 62 D5
Darliston SY13 38 E2
Darlton NG22 51 K5
Darnabo AB53 99 F6
Darnall S9 51 F4
Darnconner KA18 67 K1
Darnford AB31 91 F5
Darngarroch DG7 65 G4
Darnick TD6 76 D7
Darowen SY20 37 H5
Darra AB53 99 F6
Darracott EX39 6 A4
Darras Hall NE20 71 G6
Darrington WF8 51 G1
Darrow Green IP20 45 G7
Darsham IP17 35 J2
Dartfield AB43 99 J5
DARTFORD DA 23 J4
Dartington TQ9 5 H4
Dartmeet TQ13 5 G3
Dartmouth TQ6 5 J5
Darton S75 51 F1
Darvel KA17 74 D7
Darvell TN32 14 C5
Darwell Hole TN33 13 K5
Darwen BB3 56 B7
Datchet SL3 22 C4
Datchworth SG3 33 F7
Datchworth Green SG3 33 F7
Daubhill BL3 49 F2
Daugh of Kinermony AB38 97 K7
Dauntsey SN15 20 C3
Dauntsey Green SN15 20 C3
Dauntsey Lock SN15 20 C3
Dava PH26 89 H1
Davaar PA28 66 B2
Davan AB34 90 C4
Davenham CW9 49 F5
Davenport Green WA15 49 H4
Daventry NN11 31 G2
Davidstow PL32 4 B2
Davington DG13 69 H3
Daviot Aber. AB51 91 F2
Daviot High. IV2 88 E1
Davoch of Grange AB55 98 C5
Davyhulme M41 49 G3
Dawley TF4 39 F5
Dawlish EX7 5 K3
Dawn LL22 47 G5
Daws Heath SS7 24 E3
Daw's House PL15 6 B7
Dawsmere PE12 43 H2
Day Green CW11 49 G7
Dayhills ST15 40 B2
Dayhouse Bank B62 29 J1
Daylesford GL56 30 D6
Ddôl CH7 47 K5
Deadman's Cross MK45 32 E4
Deadwaters ML11 75 F6
Deal CT14 15 J2
Deal Hall CM0 25 G2
Dean Cumb. CA14 60 B4
Dean Devon TQ11 5 H4
Dean Dorset SP5 9 J3
Dean Hants. SO32 11 G3
Dean Oxon. OX7 30 E6
Dean Som. BA4 19 K7
Dean Bank DL17 62 D3
Dean Cross EX34 6 D1
Dean Head S35 50 E2
Dean Prior TQ11 5 H4
Dean Row SK9 49 H4
Dean Street ME15 14 C2
Deanburnhaugh TD9 69 J2
Deane Gt.Man. BL3 49 F2
Deane Hants. RG25 21 J6
Deanland SP5 9 J3
Deanlane End PO9 11 J3
Deans Bottom ME9 24 E5
Deanscales CA13 60 B4
Deansgreen WA13 49 F4
Deanshanger MK19 31 J5
Deanston FK16 81 J7
Dearham CA15 60 B3
Debach IP13 35 G3
Debate DG11 69 H5
Debden CB11 33 J5
Debden Cross CB11 33 J5
Debden Green Essex CB11 33 J5
Debden Green Essex IG10 23 H2
Debenham IP14 35 F2
Deblin's Green WR2 29 H4
Dechmont EH52 75 J3
Decker Hill TF11 39 G4
Deddington OX15 31 F5
Dedham CO7 34 E5
Dedham Heath CO7 34 E5
Dedworth SL4 22 C4
Deecastle AB34 90 C5
Deene NN17 42 C6
Deenethorpe NN17 42 C6
Deepcar S36 50 E3
Deepcut GU16 22 C6
Deepdale Cumb. LA10 56 C1
Deepdale N.Yorks. BD23 56 D2
Deeping Gate PE6 42 E5
Deeping St. James PE6 42 E5
Deeping St. Nicholas PE11 43 F4
Deepweir NP26 19 H3
Deerhill AB55 98 C5
Deerhurst GL19 29 H6
Deerhurst Walton GL19 29 H6
Deerton Street ME9 25 F5
Defford WR8 29 J4
Defynnog LD3 27 J6
Deganwy LL31 47 F5
Degnish PA34 79 J6
Deighton N.Yorks. DL6 62 E6
Deighton W.Yorks. HD2 50 D1
Deighton York YO19 58 C5
Deiniolen LL55 46 D6
Delabole PL33 4 A2
Delamere CW8 48 E6
Delavorar AB37 89 J3
Delfrigs AB23 91 H2
Dell Lodge PH25 89 H3
Dell Quay PO20 12 B6
Delliefure PH26 89 H1
Delly End OX29 30 E7
Delnabo AB37 89 J3
Delny IV18 96 E4
Delph OL3 49 J2
Delphorrie AB33 90 C3
Delves DH8 62 C2
Delvine PH1 82 C3
Dembleby NG34 42 D2
Denaby DN12 51 G3
Denaby Main DN12 51 G3
Denbigh (Dinbych) LL16 47 J6
Denbury TQ12 5 J4
Denby DE5 41 F1
Denby Dale HD8 50 E2
Denchworth OX12 21 G2
Dendron LA12 55 F2
Denend AB54 90 E1
Denford NN14 32 C1
Dengie CM0 25 F1
Denham Bucks. UB9 22 D3
Denham Suff. IP21 35 F1
Denham Suff. IP29 34 B2
Denham Green UB9 22 D3
Denham Street IP23 35 F1
Denhead Aber. AB51 91 F3
Denhead Aber. AB42 99 J5
Denhead Fife KY16 83 F6
Denhead of Arbirlot DD11 83 G3
Denhead of Gray DD2 82 E4
Denholm TD9 70 A2
Denholme BD13 57 F6
Denholme Clough BD13 57 F6
Denio LL53 36 C2
Denmead PO7 11 H3
Denmill AB51 91 G3
Denmoss AB54 98 E6
Dennington IP13 35 G2
Denny FK6 75 G2
Dennyloanhead FK4 75 G2
Denshaw OL3 49 J1
Denside AB31 91 G5
Densole CT18 15 H3
Denston CB8 34 B3
Denstone ST14 40 C1
Dent LA10 56 C1
Denton Cambs. PE7 42 E7
Denton Darl. DL2 62 D5
Denton E.Suss. BN9 13 H6
Denton Gt.Man. M34 49 J3
Denton Kent CT4 15 H3
Denton Kent DA12 24 C4
Denton Lincs. NG32 42 B2
Denton N.Yorks. LS29 57 G5
Denton Norf. IP20 45 G7
Denton Northants. NN7 32 B3
Denton Oxon. OX44 21 J1
Denton's Green WA10 48 D3
Denver PE38 44 A5
Denvilles PO9 11 J4
Denwick NE66 71 H2
Deopham NR18 44 E5
Deopham Green NR18 44 E6
Depden IP29 34 B3
Depden Green IP29 34 B3
Deptford Gt.Lon. SE8 23 G4
Deptford Wilts. BA12 10 B1
DERBY DE 41 F2
Derbyhaven IM9 54 B7
Dereham (East Dereham) NR19 44 D4
Dererach PA70 79 G5
Deri CF81 18 E1
Derril EX22 6 B5
Derringstone CT4 15 H3
Derrington ST18 40 A3
Derriton EX22 6 B5
Derry FK19 81 H5
Derry Hill SN11 20 C4
Derrythorpe DN17 52 B2
Dersingham PE31 44 A2
Dervaig PA75 79 F2
Derwen LL21 47 J7
Derwenlas SY20 37 G6
Derwydd SA18 17 K4
Derybruich PA21 73 H3
Desborough NN14 42 B7
Desford LE9 41 G5
Detchant NE70 77 J7
Dethick DE4 51 F7
Detling ME14 14 C2
Deuddwr SY22 38 B4
Deunant LL16 47 H6
Deuxhill WV16 39 F7
Devauden NP16 19 H2
Devil's Bridge (Pontarfynach) SY23 27 G1
Devitts Green CV7 40 E6
Devizes SN10 20 D5
Devonport PL1 4 E5
Devonside FK13 75 H1
Devoran TR3 2 E5
Dewar EH38 76 B6
Dewlish DT2 9 G5
Dewsall Court HR2 28 D5
Dewsbury WF12 57 H7
Dewsbury Moor WF15 57 H7
Dhiseig PA68 79 F4
Dhoon IM7 54 D5
Dhoor IM7 54 D4
Dhowin IM7 54 D3
Dhuhallow IV2 88 C2
Dial Green GU28 12 C4
Dial Post RH13 12 E5
Dibden SO45 11 F4
Dibden Hill HP8 22 C2
Dibden Purlieu SO45 11 F4
Dickleburgh IP21 45 F7
Dickleburgh Moor IP21 45 F7
Didbrook GL54 30 B5
Didcot OX11 21 J2
Diddington PE19 32 E2
Diddlebury SY7 38 E7
Didley HR2 28 D5
Didling GU29 12 B5
Didmarton GL9 20 B3
Didsbury M20 49 H3
Didworthy TQ10 5 G4
Digby LN4 52 D7
Digg IV51 93 K5
Diggle OL3 50 C2
Digmoor WN8 48 D2
Digswell AL6 33 F7
Dihewyd SA48 26 D3
Dildawn DG7 65 H5
Dilham NR28 45 H3
Dilhorne ST10 40 B1
Dillington PE19 32 E2
Dilston NE45 70 E7
Dilton Marsh BA13 20 B7
Dilwyn HR4 28 D3
Dilwyn Common HR4 28 D3
Dimple BL7 49 G1
Dinas Carmar. SA33 17 F2
Dinas Gwyn. LL54 46 C7
Dinas Gwyn. LL53 36 B2
Dinas Cross SA42 16 D2
Dinas Dinlle LL54 46 C7
Dinas Powys CF64 18 E4
Dinas-Mawddwy SY20 37 H4
Dinbych (Denbigh) LL16 47 J6
Dinbych-y-pysgod (Tenby) SA70 16 E5
Dinckley BB6 56 B6
Dinder BA5 19 J7
Dinedor HR2 28 E5
Dingestow NP25 28 D7
Dingley LE16 42 A7
Dingwall IV15 96 C6
Dinlabyre TD9 70 A4
Dinnet AB34 90 C5
Dinnington S.Yorks. S25 51 H4
Dinnington Som. TA17 8 D3
Dinnington T.& W. NE13 71 H6
Dinorwig LL55 46 D6
Dinton Bucks. HP17 31 J7
Dinton Wilts. SP3 10 B1
Dinvin DG9 64 A5
Dinwoodie Mains DG11 69 G4
Dinworthy EX22 6 B4
Dipford TA3 8 B2
Dippen Arg. & B. PA28 73 F7
Dippen N.Ayr. KA27 66 E1
Dippenhall GU10 22 B7
Dipple Moray IV32 98 B5
Dipple S.Ayr. KA26 67 G3
Diptford TQ9 5 H5
Dipton DH9 62 C1
Dirdhu PH26 89 H2
Dirleton EH39 76 D2
Discoed LD8 28 B2
Diseworth DE74 41 G3
Dishes KW17 106 F5
Dishforth YO7 57 J2
Dishley LE11 41 H3
Disley SK12 49 J4
Diss IP22 45 F7
Disserth LD1 27 K3
Distington CA14 60 B4
Ditcheat BA4 9 F1
Ditchingham NR35 45 H6
Ditchley OX29 30 E6
Ditchling BN6 13 G5
Ditteridge SN13 20 B5
Dittisham TQ6 5 J5
Ditton Halton WA8 48 D4
Ditton Kent ME20 14 C2
Ditton Green CB8 33 K3
Ditton Priors WV16 39 F7
Dixton Glos. GL20 29 J5
Dixton Mon. NP25 28 E7
Dobcross OL3 49 J2
Dobwalls PL14 4 C4
Doc Penfro (Pembroke Dock) SA72 16 C5
Doccombe TQ13 7 F7
Dochgarroch IV3 88 D1
Dockenfield GU10 22 B7
Docker Cumb. LA8 61 G7
Docker Lancs. LA6 55 J2
Docking PE31 44 B2
Docklow HR6 28 E3
Dockray Cumb. CA11 60 E4
Dockray Cumb. CA7 60 D1
Dodbrooke TQ7 5 H6
Doddenham WR6 29 G3
Doddinghurst CM15 23 J2
Doddington Cambs. PE15 43 H6
Doddington Kent ME9 14 E2
Doddington Lincs. LN6 52 C5
Doddington Northumb. NE71 77 H7
Doddington Shrop. DY14 29 F1
Doddiscombsleigh EX6 7 G7
Doddycross PL14 4 D4
Dodford Northants. NN7 31 H2
Dodford Worcs. B61 29 J1
Dodington S.Glos. BS37 20 A3
Dodington Som. TA5 7 K1
Dodington Ash BS37 20 A4
Dodleston CH4 48 C6
Dods Leigh ST10 40 C2
Dodscott EX38 6 D4
Dodworth S75 51 F2
Doehole DE55 51 F7
Doffcocker BL1 49 F1
Dog Village EX5 7 H6
Dogdyke LN4 53 F7
Dogmersfield RG27 22 A6
Dogsthorpe PE1 43 F5
Dol Fawr SY19 37 H5
Dolanog SY21 37 K4
Dolau Powys LD1 28 A2
Dolau R.C.T. CF72 18 D3
Dolbenmaen LL51 36 E1
Doley ST20 39 G3
Dolfach SY18 27 J1
Dolfor SY16 38 A7
Dolgarreg SA20 27 G5
Dolgarrog LL32 47 F6
Dolgellau LL40 37 G4
Dolgoch LL36 37 F5
Dolgran SA39 17 H2
Doll KW9 97 F1
Dollar FK14 75 H1
Dollarbeg FK14 75 H1
Dolphin CH8 47 K5
Dolphinholme LA2 55 J4
Dolphinton EH46 75 K6
Dolton EX19 6 D4
Dolwen Conwy LL22 47 G5
Dolwen Powys SY21 37 J5
Dolwyddelan LL25 47 F7
Dôl-y-bont SY24 37 F7
Dol-y-cannau HR5 28 A4
Dolyhir LD8 28 B3
Dolywern LL20 38 B2
Domgay SY22 38 B4
DONCASTER DN 51 H2
Donhead St. Andrew SP7 9 J2
Donhead St. Mary SP7 9 J2
Donibristle KY4 75 K2
Doniford TA23 7 J1
Donington Lincs. PE11 43 F2
Donington Shrop. WV7 40 A5
Donington le Heath LE67 41 G4
Donington on Bain LN11 53 F4
Donisthorpe DE12 41 F4
Donna Nook LN11 53 H3
Donnington Glos. GL56 30 C6
Donnington Here. HR8 29 G5
Donnington Shrop. SY5 38 E5
Donnington Tel. & W. TF2 39 G4
Donnington W.Berks. RG14 21 H5
Donnington W.Suss. PO20 12 B6
Donyatt TA19 8 C3
DORCHESTER Dorset DT 9 F5
Dorchester Oxon. OX10 21 J2
Dordon B78 40 E5
Dore S17 51 F4
Dores IV2 88 C1
Dorket Head NG5 41 H1
Dorking RH4 22 E7
Dorley's Corner IP17 35 H2
Dormans Park RH19 23 G7
Dormansland RH7 23 H7
Dormanstown TS10 63 G4
Dormer's Wells UB1 22 E3
Dormington HR1 28 E4
Dormston WR7 29 J3
Dorn GL56 30 D5
Dorney SL4 22 C4
Dorney Reach SL6 22 C4
Dornie IV40 86 E2
Dornoch IV25 96 E3
Dornock DG12 69 H7
Dorrery KW12 105 F3
Dorridge B93 30 C1
Dorrington Lincs. LN4 52 D7
Dorrington Shrop. SY5 38 D5
Dorsell AB33 90 D3
Dorsington CV37 30 C4
Dorstone HR3 28 C4
Dorton HP18 31 H7
Dorusduain IV40 87 F2
Dosthill B77 40 E6
Dotland NE46 62 A1
Dottery DT6 8 D5
Doublebois PL14 4 B4
Dougalston G62 74 D3
Dougarie KA27 73 G7
Doughton GL8 20 B2
Douglas I.o.M. IM1 54 C6
Douglas S.Lan. ML11 75 G7
Douglas and Angus DD5 83 F4
Douglas Water ML11 75 G7
Douglastown DD8 83 F3
Doulting BA4 19 K7
Dounby KW17 106 B5
Doune Arg. & B. G83 74 B1
Doune Arg. & B. FK17 80 E6
Doune High. PH22 89 F3
Doune High. IV24 96 B1
Doune Stir. FK16 81 J7
Dounepark AB45 99 F4
Douneside AB34 90 C4
Dounie High. IV19 96 D3
Dounie High. IV24 96 C2
Dounreay KW14 104 E2
Dousland PL20 5 F4
Dovaston SY10 38 C3
Dove Holes SK17 50 C5
Dovenby CA13 60 B3
Dovendale LN11 53 G4
Dover CT16 15 J3
Dovercourt CO12 35 G5
Doverdale WR9 29 H2
Doveridge DE6 40 D2
Doversgreen RH2 23 F7
Dowally PH9 82 B3
Dowdeswell GL54 30 B6
Dowhill KA26 67 G3
Dowlais CF48 18 D1
Dowland EX19 6 D4
Dowlands DT7 8 B5
Dowlish Ford TA19 8 C3
Dowlish Wake TA19 8 C3
Down Ampney GL7 20 E2
Down End TA6 19 G7
Down Hatherley GL2 29 H6
Down St. Mary EX17 7 F5
Down Thomas PL9 5 F6
Downderry PL11 4 D5
Downe BR6 23 H5
Downend I.o.W. PO30 11 G6
Downend S.Glos. BS16 19 K4
Downend W.Berks. RG20 21 H4
Downfield DD3 82 E4
Downfields CB7 33 K1
Downgate PL17 4 D3
Downham Essex CM11 24 D2
Downham Lancs. BB7 56 C5
Downham Northumb. TD12 77 G7
Downham Market PE38 44 A5
Downhead Cornw. PL15 4 C2
Downhead Som. BA4 19 K7
Downhead Som. BA22 8 E2
Downholland Cross L39 48 C2
Downholme DL11 62 C7
Downies AB12 91 H5
Downley HP13 22 B2
Downs CF5 18 E4
Downside N.Som. BS48 19 H5
Downside Som. BA4 19 K7
Downside Som. BA3 19 K6
Downside Surr. KT11 22 E6
Downton Devon EX20 6 D7
Downton Devon TQ6 5 J5
Downton Hants. SO41 10 D5
Downton Wilts. SP5 10 C2
Downton on the Rock SY8 28 D1
Dowsby PE10 42 E3
Dowthwaitehead CA11 60 E4
Doxey ST16 40 B3
Doynton BS30 20 A4
Drabblegate NR11 45 G3
Draethen NP10 19 F3
Draffan ML11 75 F6
Dragley Beck LA12 55 F2
Drakeland Corner PL7 5 F5
Drakelow DY11 40 A7
Drakemyre KA24 74 A5
Drakes Broughton WR10 29 J4
Drakes Cross B47 30 B1
Draughton N.Yorks. BD23 57 F4
Draughton Northants. NN6 31 J1
Drax YO8 58 C7
Draycot Foliat SN4 20 E4
Draycote CV23 31 F2
Draycott Derbys. DE72 41 G2
Draycott Glos. GL56 30 C5
Draycott Shrop. WV5 40 A6
Draycott Som. BS27 19 H6
Draycott Worcs. WR5 29 H4
Draycott in the Clay DE6 40 D3
Draycott in the Moors ST10 40 B2
Drayford EX17 7 F4
Draynes PL14 4 C4
Drayton Leics. LE16 42 B6
Drayton Lincs. PE20 43 F2
Drayton Norf. NR8 45 F4
Drayton Oxon. OX15 31 F4
Drayton Oxon. OX14 21 H2
Drayton Ports. PO6 11 H4
Drayton Som. TA10 8 D2
Drayton Warks. CV37 30 C3
Drayton Worcs. DY9 29 J1
Drayton Bassett B78 40 D5
Drayton Beauchamp HP22 32 C7
Drayton Parslow MK17 32 B6
Drayton St. Leonard OX10 21 J2
Drebley BD23 57 F4
Dreemskerry IM7 54 D4
Dreenhill SA62 16 C4
Drefach Carmar. SA44 17 G2
Drefach Carmar. SA14 17 J4
Dre-fach Cere. SA40 17 J1
Drefelin SA44 17 G2

Dreghorn KA11 74 B7
Drem EH39 76 D3
Dreumasdal (Drimsdale) HS8 84 C1
Drewsteignton EX6 7 F6
Driby LN13 53 G5
Driffield *E.Riding* **YO25 59 G4**
Driffield *Glos.* GL7 20 D2
Drigg CA19 60 B7
Drighlington BD11 57 H7
Drimfern PA32 80 B6
Drimlee PA32 80 C6
Drimnin PA34 79 G2
Drimore HS8 92 C7
Drimpton DT8 8 D4
Drimsdale (Dreumasdal) HS8 84 C1
Drimsynie PA24 80 C7
Drimvore PA31 73 G1
Drinan IV49 86 B3
Dringhouses YO24 58 B4
Drinisiader HS3 93 G2
Drinkstone IP30 34 D2
Drinkstone Green IP30 34 D2
Drishaig PA32 80 C6
Drissaig PA35 80 A6
Drointon ST18 40 C3
Droitwich Spa WR9 29 H2
Dron PH2 82 C6
Dronfield S18 51 F5
Dronfield Woodhouse S18 51 F5
Drongan KA6 67 J2
Dronley DD3 82 E4
Droop DT10 9 G4
Dropmore SL1 22 C3
Droxford SO32 11 H3
Droylsden M43 49 J3
Druid LL21 37 K1
Druidston SA62 16 B4
Druimarbin PH33 87 G7
Druimavuic PA38 80 B3
Druimdrishaig PA31 73 F3
Druimindarroch PH39 86 C6
Druimkinnerras IV4 88 B1
Drum *Arg. & B.* PA21 73 H3
Drum *P. & K.* KY13 82 B7
Drumachloy PA20 73 J4
Drumbeg IV27 102 D5
Drumblade AB54 98 D6
Drumblair AB54 98 E6
Drumbuie *D. & G.* DG4 68 C2
Drumbuie *High.* IV40 86 D1
Drumburgh CA7 60 D1
Drumchapel G15 74 D3
Drumchardine IV5 96 C7
Drumchork IV22 94 E3
Drumclog ML10 74 E7
Drumdelgie AB54 98 C6
Drumderfit IV1 96 D6
Drumeldrie KY8 83 F7
Drumelzier ML12 75 K7
Drumfearn IV43 86 C3
Drumfern PH33 87 F7
Drumgarve PA28 66 B1
Drumgley DD8 83 F2
Drumguish PH21 88 E5
Drumhead AB31 90 E5
Drumin AB37 89 J1
Drumine IV2 96 E6
Drumjohn DG7 67 K4
Drumlamford House KA26 64 C3
Drumlasie AB31 90 E4
Drumlemble PA28 66 A2
Drumlithie AB39 91 F6
Drummond *High.* IV16 96 D5
Drummond *Stir.* FK17 81 H7
Drummore DG9 64 B7
Drummuir Castle AB55 98 B6
Drumnadrochit IV63 88 C2
Drumnagorrach AB54 98 D5
Drumnatorran PH36 79 K1
Drumoak AB31 91 F5
Drumore PA28 66 B1
Drumour PH8 82 A4
Drumrash DG7 65 G3
Drumrunie IV26 95 H1
Drums AB41 91 H2
Drumsturdy DD5 83 F4
Drumuie IV51 93 K7
Drumuillie PH24 89 G2
Drumvaich FK17 81 H7
Drumwhindle AB41 91 H1
Drumwhirn DG7 68 C5
Drunkendub DD11 83 H3
Druridge NE61 71 H4
Drury CH7 48 B6
Drws-y-nant LL40 37 H3
Dry Doddington NG23 42 B1
Dry Drayton CB3 33 G2
Dry Harbour IV40 94 C6
Dry Sandford OX13 21 H1
Dry Street SS16 24 C3
Drybeck CA16 61 H5
Drybridge *Moray* AB56 98 C4
Drybridge *N.Ayr.* KA11 74 B7
Drybrook GL17 29 F7
Dryburgh TD6 76 D7
Drygrange TD6 76 D7
Dryhope TD7 69 H1
Drymen G63 74 C2
Drymuir AB42 99 H6
Drynoch IV47 85 K1
Dryslwyn SA32 17 J3
Dryton SY5 38 E5
Duachy PA34 79 K5
Dubford AB45 99 F4
Dubhchladach PA29 73 G4
Dubheads PH7 82 A5
Dublin IP23 35 F2
Dubton DD8 83 G2
Duchal PA13 74 B4
Duchally IV27 103 F7
Duchray FK8 81 F7
Duck Bay G83 74 B2
Duck End *Beds.* MK45 32 D4
Duck End *Cambs.* PE19 33 F2
Duck End *Essex* CM6 33 K6
Duck Street HG3 57 G3
Duckington SY14 48 D7
Ducklington OX29 21 G1
Duckmanton S44 51 G5
Duck's Cross MK44 32 E3
Ducks Island EN5 23 F2
Duddenhoe End CB11 33 H5
Duddingston EH15 76 A3
Duddington PE9 42 C5
Duddlestone TA3 8 B2
Duddleswell TN22 13 H4
Duddo TD15 77 H6
Duddon CW6 48 E6
Duddon Bridge LA18 54 E1
Dudleston SY12 38 C2
Dudleston Heath (Criftins) SY12 38 C2
Dudley *T. & W.* NE23 71 H6
DUDLEY ***W.Mid.*** **DY 40 B6**
Dudley Port DY4 40 B6
Dudlow's Green WA4 49 F4
Dudsbury BH22 10 B5
Duffield DE56 41 F1
Duffryn SA13 18 B2
Dufftown AB55 90 B1
Duffus IV30 97 J5
Dufton CA16 61 H4
Duggleby YO17 58 E3
Duiar PH26 89 J1
Duible KW8 104 E6
Duiletter PA33 80 C5
Duinish PH17 81 H1
Duirinish IV40 86 D1
Duisdealmor IV43 86 D3
Duisky PH33 87 G7
Duke End B46 40 E7
Dukestown NP22 28 A7
Dukinfield SK16 49 J3
Dulas LL70 46 C4
Dulax AB36 90 B3
Dulcote BA5 19 J7
Dulford EX15 7 J5
Dull PH15 81 K3
Dullatur G68 75 F3
Dullingham CB8 33 K3
Dullingham Ley CB8 33 K3
Dulnain Bridge PH26 89 G2
Duloe *Beds.* PE19 32 E2
Duloe *Cornw.* PL14 4 C5
Dulsie IV12 97 G7
Dulverton TA22 7 H3
Dulwich SE21 23 G4
Dumbarton G82 74 B3
Dumbleton WR11 30 B5
Dumcrieff DG10 69 G3
Dumeath AB54 90 C1
Dumfin G84 74 B2
DUMFRIES DG 65 K3
Dumgoyne G63 74 D2
Dummer RG25 21 J7
Dun DD10 83 H2
Dunach PA34 79 K5
Dunalastair PH16 81 J2
Dunan *Arg. & B.* PA23 73 K3
Dunan *High.* IV49 86 B2
Dunans PA22 73 J1
Dunball TA6 19 G7
Dunbar EH42 76 E3
Dunbeath KW6 105 G5
Dunbeg PA37 79 K4
Dunblane FK15 81 J7
Dunbog KY14 82 D6
Dunbridge SO51 10 E2
Duncanston *Aber.* AB52 90 D2
Duncanston *High.* IV7 96 C6
Dunchideock EX2 7 G7
Dunchurch CV22 31 F1
Duncote NN12 31 H3
Duncow DG1 68 E5
Duncraggan FK17 81 G7
Duncrievie PH2 82 C7
Duncroist FK21 81 G4
Duncrub PH2 82 B6
Duncryne G83 74 C2
Duncton GU28 12 C5
DUNDEE DD 83 F4
Dundee Airport DD2 82 E5
Dundon TA11 8 D1
Dundon Hayes TA11 8 D1
Dundonald KA2 74 B7
Dundonnell IV23 95 G3
Dundraw CA7 60 D2
Dundreggan IV63 87 K3
Dundrennan DG6 65 H6
Dundridge SO32 11 G3
Dundry BS41 19 J5
Dunearn KY3 76 A2
Dunecht AB32 91 F4
Dunfermline KY12 75 J2
Dunfield GL7 20 E2
Dunford Bridge S36 50 D2
Dungate ME9 14 E2
Dungavel ML10 74 E7
Dungworth S6 50 E3
Dunham NG22 52 B5
Dunham Town WA14 49 G4
Dunham Woodhouses WA14 49 G4
Dunham-on-the-Hill WA6 48 D5
Dunhampton DY13 29 H2
Dunholme LN2 52 D5
Dunino KY16 83 G6
Dunipace FK6 75 G2
Dunira PH6 81 J5
Dunkeld PH8 82 B3
Dunkerton BA2 20 A6
Dunkeswell EX14 7 K5
Dunkeswick LS17 57 J5
Dunkirk *Ches.* CH1 48 C5
Dunkirk *Kent* ME13 15 F2
Dunk's Green TN11 23 K6
Dunlappie DD9 83 G1
Dunley *Hants.* RG28 21 H6
Dunley *Worcs.* DY13 29 G2
Dunlop KA3 74 C6
Dunloskin PA23 73 K3
Dunmere PL31 4 A4
Dunmore *Arg. & B.* PA29 73 F4
Dunmore *Falk.* FK2 75 G2
Dunn KW1 105 G3
Dunn Street ME7 24 D5
Dunnabie DG11 69 H5
Dunnet KW14 105 H1
Dunnichen DD8 83 G3
Dunning PH2 82 B6
Dunnington *E.Riding* YO25 59 H4
Dunnington *Warks.* B49 30 B3
Dunnington *York* YO19 58 C4
Dunnockshaw BB11 56 D7
Dunoon PA23 73 K3
Dunragit DG9 64 B5
Dunrostan PA31 73 F2
Duns TD11 77 F5
Duns Tew OX25 31 F6
Dunsa DE45 50 E5
Dunsby PE10 42 E3
Dunscore DG2 68 D5
Dunscroft DN7 51 J2
Dunsdale TS14 63 H5
Dunsden Green RG4 22 A4
Dunsfold GU8 12 D3
Dunsford EX6 7 G7
Dunshalt KY14 82 D6
Dunshill GL19 29 H5
Dunsinnan PH2 82 C4
Dunsland Cross EX22 6 C5
Dunsley *N.Yorks.* YO21 63 K5
Dunsley *Staffs.* DY7 40 A7
Dunsmore HP22 22 B1
Dunsop Bridge BB7 56 B4
Dunstable LU6 32 D6
Dunstall DE13 40 D3
Dunstall Green CB8 34 B2
Dunstan NE66 71 H2
Dunstan Steads NE66 71 H1
Dunster TA24 7 H1
Dunston *Lincs.* LN4 52 D6
Dunston *Norf.* NR14 45 G5
Dunston *Staffs.* ST18 40 B4
Dunston Heath ST18 40 B4
Dunston Hill NE11 71 H7
Dunstone *Devon* TQ13 5 H3
Dunstone *Devon* PL8 5 F5
Dunsville DN7 51 J2
Dunswell HU6 59 G6
Dunsyre ML11 75 J6
Dunterton PL19 4 D3
Duntisbourne Abbots GL7 20 C1
Duntisbourne Leer GL7 20 C1
Duntisbourne Rouse GL7 20 C1
Duntish DT2 9 F4
Duntocher G81 74 C3
Dunton *Beds.* SG18 33 F4
Dunton *Bucks.* MK18 32 B6
Dunton *Norf.* NR21 44 C2
Dunton Bassett LE17 41 H6
Dunton Green TN13 23 J6
Dunton Wayletts CM13 24 C2
Duntulm IV51 93 K4
Dunure KA7 67 G2
Dunure Mains KA7 67 G2
Dunvant SA2 17 J6
Dunvegan IV55 93 H7
Dunwich IP17 35 J1
Dura KY15 83 F6
Durdar CA2 60 F1
Durgan TR11 2 E6
Durgates TN5 13 K3
DURHAM DH 62 D2
Durham Tees Valley Airport DL2 62 E5
Durinemast PA34 79 H2
Durisdeer DG3 68 D3
Durleigh TA5 8 B1
Durley *Hants.* SO32 11 G3
Durley *Wilts.* SN8 21 F5
Durley Street SO32 11 G3
Durlow Common HR8 29 F5
Durnamuck IV23 95 G2
Durness IV27 103 G2
Durno AB51 91 F2
Duror PA38 80 A2
Durran *Arg. & B.* PA33 80 A7
Durran *High.* KW14 105 G2
Durrants PO9 11 J4
Durrington *W.Suss.* BN13 12 E6
Durrington *Wilts.* SP4 20 E7
Dursley GL11 20 A2
Dursley Cross GL17 29 F7
Durston TA3 8 B2
Durweston DT11 9 H4
Dury ZE2 107 N6
Duston NN5 31 J2
Duthil PH23 89 G2
Dutlas LD7 28 B1
Duton Hill CM6 33 K6
Dutson PL15 6 B7
Dutton WA4 48 E5
Duxford CB2 33 H4
Dwygyfylchi LL34 47 F5
Dwyran LL61 46 C6
Dyce AB21 91 G3
Dyfatty SA16 17 H5
Dyffryn *Bridgend* CF34 18 B2
Dyffryn *Pembs.* SA64 16 C2
Dyffryn *V. of Glam.* CF5 18 D4
Dyffryn Ardudwy LL44 36 E3
Dyffryn Castell SY23 37 G7
Dyffryn Ceidrych SA19 27 G6
Dyffryn Cellwen SA10 27 H7
Dyke *Devon* EX39 6 B3
Dyke *Lincs.* PE10 42 E3
Dyke *Moray* IV36 97 G6
Dykehead *Angus* DD8 82 E1
Dykehead *N.Lan.* ML7 75 G5
Dykehead *Stir.* FK8 74 D1
Dykelands AB30 83 J1
Dykends PH11 82 D2
Dykeside AB53 99 F6
Dylife SY19 37 H6
Dymchurch TN29 15 G5
Dymock GL18 29 G5
Dyrham SN14 20 A4
Dysart KY1 76 B1
Dyserth LL18 47 J5

E

Eachwick NE18 71 G6
Eadar dha Fhadhail HS2 100 C4
Eagland Hill PR3 55 H5
Eagle LN6 52 B6
Eagle Barnsdale LN6 52 B6
Eagle Moor LN6 52 B6
Eaglescliffe TS16 63 F5
Eaglesfield *Cumb.* CA13 60 B4
Eaglesfield *D. & G.* DG11 69 H6
Eaglesham G76 74 D5
Eaglethorpe PE8 42 D6
Eagley BL1 49 G1
Eairy IM4 54 B6
Eakley MK16 32 B3
Eakring NG22 51 J6
Ealand DN17 51 K1
Ealing W5 22 E3
Eamont Bridge CA10 61 G4
Earby BB18 56 E5
Earcroft BB2 56 B7
Eardington WV16 39 G6
Eardisland HR6 28 D3
Eardisley HR3 28 C4
Eardiston *Shrop.* SY11 38 C3
Eardiston *Worcs.* WR15 29 F2
Earith PE28 33 G1
Earl Shilton LE9 41 G6
Earl Soham IP13 35 G2
Earl Sterndale SK17 50 C6
Earl Stonham IP14 35 F3
Earle NE71 70 E1
Earlestown WA12 48 E3
Earley RG6 22 A4
Earlham NR4 45 F5
Earlish IV51 93 J5
Earls Barton NN6 32 B2
Earls Colne CO6 34 C6
Earl's Common WR9 29 J3
Earl's Court SW5 23 F4
Earl's Croome WR8 29 H4
Earl's Green IP14 34 E2
Earlsdon CV5 30 E1
Earlsferry KY9 83 F7
Earlsford AB51 91 G1
Earlsheaton WF12 57 H7
Earlston TD4 76 D7
Earlswood *Mon.* NP16 19 H2
Earlswood *Surr.* RH1 23 F7
Earlswood *Warks.* B94 30 C1
Earnley PO20 12 B7
Earnshaw Bridge PR26 55 J7
Earsairidh HS9 84 C5
Earsdon NE25 71 J6
Earsdon Moor NE61 71 G4
Earsham NR35 45 H7
Earsham Street IP21 35 G1
Earswick YO32 58 C4
Eartham PO18 12 C6
Earthcott Green BS35 19 K3
Easby TS9 63 G6
Easdale PA34 79 J6
Easebourne GU29 12 B4
Easenhall CV23 31 F1
Eashing GU7 22 C7
Easington *Bucks.* HP18 31 H7
Easington *Dur.* SR8 63 F2
Easington *E.Riding* HU12 53 G1
Easington *Northumb.* NE70 77 K7
Easington *Oxon.* OX49 21 K2
Easington *R. & C.* TS13 63 J5
Easington Colliery SR8 63 F2
Easington Lane DH5 62 E2
Easingwold YO61 58 B3
Easole Street CT15 15 H2
Eassie DD8 82 E3
East Aberthaw CF62 18 D5
East Acton W3 23 F3
East Allington TQ9 5 H6
East Anstey EX16 7 G3
East Anton SP11 21 G7
East Appleton DL10 62 D7
East Ardsley WF3 57 J7
East Ashey PO33 11 G6
East Ashling PO18 12 B6
East Auchronie AB32 91 G4
East Ayton YO12 59 F1
East Barkwith LN8 52 E4
East Barming ME16 14 C2
East Barnby YO21 63 K5
East Barnet EN4 23 F2
East Barsham NR22 44 D2
East Beckham NR11 45 F2
East Bedfont TW14 22 D4
East Bergholt CO7 34 E5
East Bierley BD4 57 G7
East Bilney NR20 44 D4
East Blatchington BN25 13 H7
East Boldon NE36 71 J7
East Boldre SO42 10 E4
East Bolton NE66 71 G2
East Bower TA6 8 C1
East Brent TA9 19 G6
East Bridge IP16 35 J2
East Bridgford NG13 41 J1
East Brora KW9 97 G1
East Buckland EX32 6 E2
East Budleigh EX9 7 J7
East Burnham SL2 22 C3
East Burra ZE2 107 M9
East Burrafirth ZE2 107 M7
East Burton BH20 9 H6
East Butsfield DL13 62 C2
East Butterleigh EX15 7 H5
East Butterwick DN17 52 B2
East Cairnbeg AB30 91 F7
East Calder EH53 75 J4
East Carleton NR14 45 F5
East Carlton *Northants.* LE16 42 B7
East Carlton *W.Yorks.* LS19 57 H5
East Chaldon (Chaldon Herring) DT2 9 G6
East Challow OX12 21 G3
East Charleton TQ7 5 H6
East Chelborough DT2 8 E4
East Chiltington BN7 13 G5
East Chinnock BA22 8 D3
East Chisenbury SN9 20 E6
East Clandon GU4 22 D6
East Claydon MK18 31 J6
East Clyne KW9 97 G1
East Clyth KW3 105 H5
East Coker BA22 8 E3
East Compton *Dorset* SP7 9 H3
East Compton *Som.* BA4 19 K7
East Coombe EX17 7 G5
East Cornworthy TQ9 5 J5
East Cottingwith YO42 58 D5
East Cowes PO32 11 G5
East Cowick DN14 58 C7
East Cowton DL7 62 E6
East Cramlington NE23 71 H6
East Cranmore BA4 19 K7
East Creech BH20 9 J6
East Croachy IV2 88 D2
East Darlochan PA28 66 A1
East Davoch AB34 90 C4
East Dean *E.Suss.* BN20 13 J7
East Dean *Hants.* SP5 10 D2
East Dean *W.Suss.* PO18 12 C5
East Dereham (Dereham) NR19 44 D4
East Down EX31 6 D1
East Drayton DN22 51 K5
East Dundry BS41 19 J5
East Ella HU5 59 G7
East End *E.Riding* HU12 59 H6
East End *E.Riding* HU12 59 J7
East End *Essex* CM0 25 G1
East End *Hants.* RG20 21 H5
East End *Hants.* SO41 10 E5
East End *Herts.* SG9 33 H6
East End *Kent* TN17 14 D4
East End *Kent* ME12 25 F4
East End *M.K.* MK16 32 C4
East End *N.Som.* BS48 19 H4
East End *Oxon.* OX29 30 E7
East End *Poole* BH21 9 J5
East End *Som.* BA3 19 J6
East End *Suff.* CO7 35 F5
East End *Suff.* IP14 35 F3
East Farleigh ME15 14 C2
East Farndon LE16 42 A7
East Ferry DN21 52 B3
East Firsby LN8 52 D4
East Fleetham NE68 71 H1
East Fortune EH39 76 D3
East Garston RG17 21 G4
East Ginge OX12 21 H3
East Goscote LE7 41 J4
East Grafton SN8 21 F5
East Green *Suff.* IP17 35 J2
East Green *Suff.* CB8 33 K3
East Grimstead SP5 10 D2
East Grinstead RH19 13 G3
East Guldeford TN31 14 E5
East Haddon NN6 31 H2
East Hagbourne OX11 21 J3
East Halton DN40 52 E1
East Ham E6 23 H3
East Hanney OX12 21 H2
East Hanningfield CM3 24 D1
East Hardwick WF8 51 G1
East Harling NR16 44 D7
East Harlsey DL6 63 F7
East Harnham SP2 10 C2
East Harptree BS40 19 J6
East Hartford NE23 71 H6
East Harting GU31 11 J3
East Hatch SP3 9 J2
East Hatley SG19 33 F3
East Hauxwell DL8 62 C7
East Haven DD7 83 G4
East Heckington PE20 42 E1
East Hedleyhope DL13 62 C2
East Helmsdale KW8 105 F7
East Hendred OX12 21 H3
East Herrington SR3 62 E1
East Heslerton YO17 59 F2
East Hewish BS24 19 H5
East Hoathly BN8 13 J5
East Holme BH20 9 H6
East Horndon CM13 24 C3

East Horrington BA5 19 J7
East Horsley KT24 22 D6
East Horton NE71 77 J7
East Howe BH10 10 B5
East Huntspill TA9 19 G7
East Hyde LU2 32 E7
East Ilsley RG20 21 H3
East Keal PE23 53 G6
East Kennett SN8 20 E5
East Keswick LS17 57 J5
East Kilbride G74 74 E5
East Kimber EX20 6 C6
East Kirkby PE23 53 G6
East Knapton YO17 58 E2
East Knighton DT2 9 H6
East Knowstone EX36 7 G3
East Knoyle SP3 9 H1
East Kyloe NE70 77 J7
East Lambrook TA13 8 D3
East Langdon CT15 15 J3
East Langton LE16 42 A6
East Langwell IV28 96 E1
East Lavant PO18 12 B6
East Lavington GU28 12 C5
East Layton DL11 62 C5
East Leake LE12 41 H3
East Learmouth TD12 77 G7
East Learney AB31 90 E4
East Leigh *Devon* EX17 7 F5
East Leigh *Devon* EX18 7 F4
East Leigh *Devon* TQ9 5 H5
East Leigh *Devon* PL21 5 G5
East Lexham PE32 44 C4
East Lilburn NE66 71 F1
East Linton EH40 76 D3
East Liss GU33 11 J2
East Lockinge OX12 21 H3
East Looe PL13 4 C5
East Lound DN9 51 K2
East Lulworth BH20 9 H6
East Lutton YO17 59 F3
East Lydford TA11 8 E1
East Lyn EX35 7 F1
East Lyng TA3 8 C2
East Mains AB31 90 E5
East Malling ME19 14 C2
East Malling Heath ME19 23 K6
East March DD4 83 F4
East Marden PO18 12 B5
East Markham NG22 51 K5
East Martin SP6 10 B3
East Marton BD23 56 E4
East Meon GU32 11 H2
East Mere EX16 7 H4
East Mersea CO5 34 E7
East Mey KW14 105 J1
East Molesey KT8 22 E5
East Moor WF1 57 J7
East Morden BH20 9 J5
East Morriston TD4 76 E6
East Morton BD20 57 G5
East Ness YO62 58 C2
East Newton HU11 59 J6
East Norton LE7 42 A5
East Oakley RG23 21 J6
East Ogwell TQ12 5 J3
East Orchard SP7 9 H3
East Ord TD15 77 H5
East Panson PL15 6 B6
East Parley BH23 10 C5
East Peckham TN12 23 K7
East Pennard BA4 8 E1
East Portlemouth TQ8 5 H7
East Prawle TQ7 5 H7
East Preston BN16 12 D6
East Pulham DT2 9 G4
East Putford EX22 6 B4
East Quantoxhead TA5 7 K1
East Rainton DH5 62 E2
East Ravendale DN37 53 F3
East Raynham NR21 44 C3
East Retford (Retford) DN22 51 K4
East Rigton LS17 57 J5
East Rolstone BS24 19 G5
East Rounton DL6 63 F6
East Row YO21 63 K5
East Rudham PE31 44 C3
East Runton NR27 45 G1
East Ruston NR12 45 H3
East Saltoun EH34 76 C4
East Shefford RG17 21 G4
East Sleekburn NE22 71 H5
East Somerton NR29 45 J4
East Stockwith DN21 51 K3
East Stoke *Dorset* BH20 9 H6
East Stoke *Notts.* NG23 42 A1
East Stour SP8 9 H2
East Stourmouth CT3 25 J5
East Stratton SO21 21 J7
East Street BA6 8 E1
East Studdal CT15 15 J3
East Suisnish IV40 86 B1
East Taphouse PL14 4 B4
East Thirston NE65 71 G4
East Tilbury RM18 24 C4
East Tisted GU34 11 J1
East Torrington LN8 52 E4
East Town BA4 19 K7
East Tuddenham NR20 44 E4
East Tytherley SP5 10 D2
East Tytherton SN15 20 C4
East Village EX17 7 G5
East Wall TF13 38 E6
East Walton PE32 44 B4
East Wellow SO51 10 E2
East Wemyss KY1 76 B1
East Whitburn EH47 75 H4
East Wickham DA16 23 H4
East Williamston SA70 16 D5
East Winch PE32 44 A4
East Winterslow SP5 10 D1
East Wittering PO20 11 J5
East Witton DL8 57 G1
East Woodburn NE48 70 E5
East Woodhay RG20 21 H5
East Woodlands BA11 20 A7
East Worldham GU34 11 J1
East Worlington EX17 7 F4
East Youlstone EX23 6 A4
Eastacott EX37 6 E3
Eastbourne BN21 13 K7
Eastbrook CF64 18 E4
Eastburn *E.Riding* YO25 59 F4
Eastburn *W.Yorks.* BD20 57 F5
Eastbury *Herts.* HA6 22 E2
Eastbury *W.Berks.* RG17 21 G4
Eastby BD23 57 F4
Eastchurch ME12 25 F4
Eastcombe *Glos.* GL6 20 B1
Eastcombe *Som.* TA4 7 K2
Eastcote *Gt.Lon.* HA5 22 E3
Eastcote *Northants.* NN12 31 H3
Eastcote *W.Mid.* B92 30 C1
Eastcott *Cornw.* EX23 6 A4
Eastcott *Wilts.* SN10 20 D6
Eastcourt SN16 20 C2
Eastdown TQ6 5 J6
Eastend OX7 30 E6
Easter Ardross IV17 96 D4
Easter Balgedie KY13 82 C7
Easter Balmoral AB35 89 K5
Easter Boleskine IV2 88 C2
Easter Borland FK8 81 H7
Easter Brae IV7 96 D5
Easter Buckieburn FK6 75 F2
Easter Compton BS35 19 J3
Easter Drummond IV2 88 B3
Easter Dullater FK17 81 H7
Easter Ellister PA48 72 A5
Easter Fearn IV24 96 D3
Easter Galcantray IV12 97 F7
Easter Howlaws TD10 77 F6
Easter Kinkell IV7 96 C6
Easter Knox DD11 83 G3
Easter Lednathie DD8 82 E1
Easter Moniack IV5 96 C7
Easter Ord AB32 91 G4
Easter Poldar FK8 74 E1
Easter Skeld (Skeld) ZE2 107 M8
Easter Suddie IV8 96 D6
Easter Tulloch AB30 91 F7
Easter Whyntie AB45 98 E4
Eastergate PO20 12 C6
Easterhouse G34 74 E4
Easterton SN10 20 D6
Easterton Sands SN10 20 D6
Eastertown BS24 19 G6
Eastfield *Bristol* BS9 19 J4
Eastfield *N.Lan.* ML7 75 G4
Eastfield *N.Yorks.* YO11 59 G1
Eastfield Hall NE65 71 H3
Eastgate *Dur.* DL13 62 A3
Eastgate *Lincs.* PE10 42 E4
Eastgate *Norf.* NR10 45 F3
Easthall SG4 33 F6
Eastham *Mersey.* CH62 48 C4
Eastham *Worcs.* WR15 29 F2
Easthampstead RG12 22 B5
Easthampton HR6 28 D2
Easthaugh NR9 44 E4
Eastheath RG41 22 B5
Easthope TF13 38 E6
Easthorpe *Essex* CO6 34 D6
Easthorpe *Leics.* NG13 42 B2
Easthorpe *Notts.* NG25 51 K7
Easthouses EH22 76 B4
Eastington *Devon* EX17 7 F5
Eastington *Glos.* GL54 30 C7
Eastington *Glos.* GL10 20 A1
Eastleach Martin GL7 21 F1
Eastleach Turville GL7 21 F1
Eastleigh *Devon* EX39 6 C3
Eastleigh *Hants.* SO50 11 F3
Eastling ME13 14 E2
Eastmoor *Derbys.* S42 51 F5
Eastmoor *Norf.* PE33 44 B5
Eastnor HR8 29 G5
Eastoft DN17 52 B1
Eastoke PO11 11 J5
Easton *Cambs.* PE28 32 E1
Easton *Cumb.* CA6 69 K6
Easton *Cumb.* CA7 60 D1
Easton *Devon* TQ13 7 F7
Easton *Dorset* DT5 9 F7
Easton *Hants.* SO21 11 G1
Easton *I.o.W.* PO40 10 E6
Easton *Lincs.* NG33 42 C3
Easton *Norf.* NR9 45 F4
Easton *Som.* BA5 19 J7
Easton *Suff.* IP13 35 G3
Easton *Wilts.* SN13 20 B4
Easton Grey SN16 20 B3
Easton Maudit NN29 32 B3
Easton on the Hill PE9 42 D5
Easton Royal SN9 21 F5
Easton-in-Gordano BS20 19 J4
Eastrea PE7 43 F6
Eastriggs DG12 69 H7
Eastrington DN14 58 D6
Eastry CT13 15 J2
Eastside KW17 106 D8
East-the-Water EX39 6 C3
Eastville BS16 19 K4
Eastwell LE14 42 A3
Eastwick CM20 33 H7
Eastwood *Notts.* NG16 41 G1
Eastwood *S'end* SS9 24 E3
Eastwood *S.Yorks.* S65 51 G3
Eastwood *W.Yorks.* OL14 56 E7
Eastwood End PE15 43 H6
Eathorpe CV33 30 E2
Eaton *Ches.* CW12 49 H6
Eaton *Ches.* CW6 48 E6
Eaton *Leics.* NG32 42 A3
Eaton *Norf.* NR2 45 G5
Eaton *Norf.* PE36 44 A2
Eaton *Notts.* DN22 51 K5
Eaton *Oxon.* OX13 21 H1
Eaton *Shrop.* SY6 38 E6
Eaton *Shrop.* SY9 38 C7
Eaton Bishop HR2 28 D5
Eaton Bray LU6 32 C6
Eaton Constantine SY5 39 F5
Eaton Ford PE19 32 E3
Eaton Hall CH4 48 D6
Eaton Hastings SN7 21 F2
Eaton Socon PE19 32 E3
Eaton upon Tern TF9 39 F3
Eaves Green CV7 40 E7
Eavestone HG4 57 H3
Ebberston YO13 58 E1
Ebbesborne Wake SP5 9 J2
Ebbw Vale (Glynebwy) NP23 18 E1
Ebchester DH8 62 C1
Ebdon BS22 19 G5
Ebford EX3 7 H7
Ebley GL5 20 B1
Ebnal SY14 38 D1
Ebost IV56 85 J1
Ebrington GL55 30 C4
Ebsworthy Town EX20 6 D6
Ecchinswell RG20 21 H6
Ecclaw TD13 77 F4
Ecclefechan DG11 69 G6
Eccles *Gt.Man.* M30 49 G3
Eccles *Kent* ME20 24 D5
Eccles *Sc.Bord.* TD5 77 F6
Eccles Green HR4 28 C4
Eccles Road NR16 44 E6
Ecclesfield S35 51 F3
Ecclesgreig DD10 83 J1
Eccleshall ST21 40 A3
Eccleshill BD10 57 G6
Ecclesmachan EH52 75 J3
Eccles-on-Sea NR12 45 J3
Eccleston *Ches.* CH4 48 D6
Eccleston *Lancs.* PR7 48 E1
Eccleston *Mersey.* WA10 48 D3
Eccup LS16 57 H5
Echt AB32 91 F4
Eckford TD5 70 C1
Eckington *Derbys.* S21 51 G5
Eckington *Worcs.* WR10 29 J4
Ecton *Northants.* NN6 32 B2
Ecton *Staffs.* SK17 50 C7
Edale S33 50 D4
Eday KW17 106 E4
Eday Airfield KW17 106 E4
Edburton BN5 13 F5
Edderside CA15 60 C2
Edderton IV19 96 E3
Eddington RG17 21 G5
Eddleston EH45 76 A6
Eden Park BR3 23 G5
Eden Vale TS27 63 F3
Edenbridge TN8 23 H7
Edendonich PA33 80 C5
Edenfield BL0 49 G1
Edenhall CA11 61 G3
Edenham PE10 42 D3
Edensor DE45 50 E5
Edentaggart G83 74 B1
Edenthorpe DN3 51 J2
Edern LL53 36 B2
Edgarley BA6 8 E1
Edgbaston B15 40 C7
Edgcote OX17 31 G4
Edgcott *Bucks.* HP18 31 H6
Edgcott *Som.* TA24 7 G2
Edgcumbe TR10 2 E5
Edge *Glos.* GL6 20 B1
Edge *Shrop.* SY5 38 C5
Edge End GL16 28 E7
Edge Green *Ches.* SY14 48 D7
Edge Green *Gt.Man.* WA3 48 E3
Edge Green *Norf.* NR16 44 E7
Edgebolton SY4 38 E3
Edgefield NR24 44 E2
Edgehead EH37 76 B4
Edgeley SY13 38 E1
Edgerley SY10 38 C4
Edgerton HD2 50 D1
Edgeworth GL6 20 C1
Edginswell TQ2 5 J4
Edgmond TF10 39 G4
Edgmond Marsh TF10 39 G3
Edgton SY7 38 C7
Edgware HA8 23 F2
Edgworth BL7 49 G1
Edinample FK19 81 H5
Edinbanchory AB33 90 C3
Edinbane IV51 93 J6
Edinbarnet G81 74 D3
EDINBURGH EH 76 A3
Edinburgh Airport EH12 75 K3
Edinchip FK19 81 G5
Edingale B79 40 E4
Edingley NG22 51 J7
Edingthorpe NR28 45 H2
Edingthorpe Green NR28 45 H2
Edington *Som.* TA7 8 C1
Edington *Wilts.* BA13 20 C6
Edintore AB55 98 C6
Edinvale IV36 97 J6
Edistone EX39 6 A3
Edith Weston LE15 42 C5
Edithmead TA9 19 G7
Edlaston DE6 40 D1
Edlesborough LU6 32 C7
Edlingham NE66 71 G3
Edlington LN9 53 F5
Edmondsham BH21 10 B3
Edmondsley DH7 62 D2
Edmondstown CF40 18 D2
Edmondthorpe LE14 42 B4
Edmonstone KW17 106 E5
Edmonton *Cornw.* PL27 3 G1
Edmonton *Gt.Lon.* N18 23 G2
Edmundbyers DH8 62 B1
Ednam TD5 77 F7
Ednaston DE6 40 E1
Edney Common CM1 24 C1
Edra FK17 81 F6
Edradynate PH15 81 K2
Edrom TD11 77 G5
Edstaston SY4 38 E2
Edstone B95 30 C2
Edvin Loach HR7 29 F3
Edwalton NG12 41 H2
Edwardstone CO10 34 D4
Edwardsville CF46 18 D2
Edwinsford SA19 17 K2
Edwinstowe NG21 51 J6
Edworth SG18 33 F4
Edwyn Ralph HR7 29 F3
Edzell DD9 83 H1
Efail Isaf CF38 18 D3
Efail-fâch SA12 18 A2
Efailnewydd LL53 36 C2
Efailwen SA66 16 E3
Efenechtyd LL15 47 K7
Effingham KT24 22 E6
Effirth ZE2 107 M7
Efflinch DE13 40 D4
Efford EX17 7 G5
Egbury SP11 21 H6
Egdean RH20 12 C4
Egdon WR7 29 J3
Egerton *Gt.Man.* BL7 49 G1
Egerton *Kent* TN27 14 E3
Egerton Forstal TN27 14 D3
Egerton Green SY14 48 E7
Egg Buckland PL6 4 E5
Eggborough DN14 58 B7
Eggerness DG8 64 E6
Eggesford Barton EX18 6 E4
Eggington LU7 32 C6
Egginton DE65 40 E3
Egglescliffe TS16 63 F5
Eggleston DL12 62 A4
Egham TW20 22 D4
Egham Wick TW20 22 C4
Egilsay KW17 106 D5
Egleton LE15 42 B5
Eglingham NE66 71 G2
Eglinton KA12 74 B6
Egloshayle PL27 4 A3
Egloskerry PL15 4 C2
Eglwys Cross SY13 38 D1
Eglwys Fach SY20 37 F6
Eglwys Nunydd SA13 18 A3
Eglwysbach LL28 47 G5
Eglwys-Brewis CF62 18 D5
Eglwyswrw SA41 16 E2
Egmanton NG22 51 K6
Egmere NR22 44 D2
Egremont CA22 60 B5
Egton YO21 63 K6
Egton Bridge YO21 63 K6
Egypt SO21 21 H7
Eigg PH42 85 K6
Eight Ash Green CO6 34 D6
Eignaig PA34 79 J3
Eil PH22 89 F3
Eilanreach IV40 86 E3
Eildon TD6 76 D7
Eilean Bhearnaraigh (Berneray) HS6 92 E3
Eilean Darach IV23 95 H3
Eilean Iarmain (Isleornsay) IV43 86 C3
Eilean Leodhais (Isle of Lewis) HS 101 F3
Eilean Scalpaigh (Scalpay) HS4 93 H2
Eilean Shona PH36 86 C7
Einacleit HS2 100 D5
Eiriosgaigh (Eriskay) HS8 84 C3
Eisgean HS2 101 F6
Eisingrug LL47 37 F2
Eisteddfa Gurig SY23 37 G7
Elan Village LD6 27 J2
Elberton BS35 19 K3
Elborough BS24 19 G6
Elburton PL9 5 F5
Elcho PH2 82 C5
Elcombe SN4 20 E3
Elder Street CB10 33 J5
Eldernell PE7 43 G6
Eldersfield GL19 29 G5
Elderslie PA5 74 C4
Eldon DL14 62 D4
Eldrick KA26 67 G5
Eldroth LA2 56 C3
Eldwick BD16 57 G5
Elemore Vale DH5 62 E2
Elerch (Bont-goch) SY24 37 F7
Elford *Northumb.* NE68 77 K7
Elford *Staffs.* B79 40 D4
Elford Closes CB6 33 J1
Elgin IV30 97 K5
Elgol IV49 86 B3
Elham CT4 15 G3
Elie KY9 83 F7
Elilaw NE65 70 E3
Elim LL65 46 B4
Eling *Hants.* SO40 10 E3
Eling *W.Berks.* RG18 21 J4
Eliock DG4 68 D3
Elishader IV51 93 K5
Elishaw NE19 70 D4
Elkesley DN22 51 J5
Elkington NN6 31 H1
Elkstone GL53 29 J7
Elland HX5 57 G7
Elland Upper Edge HX5 57 G7
Ellary PA31 73 F3
Ellastone DE6 40 D1
Ellbridge PL12 4 E4
Ellel LA2 55 H4
Ellemford TD11 77 F4
Ellenborough CA15 60 B3
Ellenhall ST21 40 A3
Ellen's Green RH12 12 D3
Ellerbeck DL6 63 F7
Ellerby TS13 63 J5
Ellerdine TF6 39 F3
Ellerdine Heath TF6 39 F3
Elleric PA38 80 B3
Ellerker HU15 59 F7
Ellerton *E.Riding* YO42 58 D5
Ellerton *N.Yorks.* DL10 62 D7
Ellerton *Shrop.* TF9 39 G3
Ellerton Abbey DL11 62 B7
Ellesborough HP17 22 B1
Ellesmere SY12 38 C2
Ellesmere Park M30 49 G3
Ellesmere Port CH65 48 D5
Ellingham *Hants.* BH24 10 C4
Ellingham *Norf.* NR35 45 H6
Ellingham *Northumb.* NE67 71 G1
Ellingstring HG4 57 G1
Ellington *Cambs.* PE28 32 E1
Ellington *Northumb.* NE61 71 H4
Ellington Thorpe PE28 32 E1
Elliot's Green BA11 20 A7
Ellisfield RG25 21 K7
Ellistown LE67 41 G4
Ellon AB41 91 H1
Ellonby CA11 60 F3
Ellough NR34 45 J7
Ellough Moor NR34 45 J7
Elloughton HU15 59 F7
Ellwood GL16 19 J1
Elm PE14 43 H5
Elm Park RM12 23 J3
Elmbridge WR9 29 J2
Elmdon *Essex* CB11 33 H5
Elmdon *W.Mid.* B26 40 D7
Elmdon Heath B92 40 D7
Elmers End BR3 23 G5
Elmer's Green WN8 48 D2
Elmesthorpe LE9 41 G6
Elmhurst WS13 40 D4
Elmley Castle WR10 29 J4
Elmley Lovett WR9 29 H2
Elmore GL2 29 G7
Elmore Back GL2 29 G7
Elmscott EX39 6 A3
Elmsett IP7 34 E4
Elmstead *Essex* CO7 34 E6
Elmstead *Gt.Lon.* BR7 23 H4
Elmstead Market CO7 34 E6
Elmstone CT3 25 J5
Elmstone Hardwicke GL51 29 J6
Elmswell *E.Riding* YO25 59 F4
Elmswell *Suff.* IP30 34 D2
Elmton S80 51 H5
Elphin IV27 102 E7
Elphinstone EH33 76 B3
Elrick *Aber.* AB32 91 G4
Elrick *Moray* AB54 90 C2
Elrig DG8 64 D6
Elrigbeag PA32 80 C6
Elsdon NE19 70 E4
Elsecar S74 51 F2
Elsenham CM22 33 J6
Elsfield OX3 31 G7
Elsham DN20 52 D1
Elsing NR20 44 E4
Elslack BD23 56 E5
Elson *Hants.* PO12 11 H4
Elson *Shrop.* SY12 38 C2
Elsrickle ML12 75 J6
Elstead GU8 22 C7
Elsted GU29 12 B5
Elsthorpe PE10 42 D3
Elstob TS21 62 E4
Elston *Lancs.* PR2 55 J6
Elston *Notts.* NG23 42 A1
Elstone EX18 6 E4
Elstow MK42 32 D4
Elstree WD6 22 E2
Elstronwick HU12 59 J6
Elswick PR4 55 H6
Elsworth CB3 33 G2
Elterwater LA22 60 E6
Eltham SE9 23 H4
Eltisley PE19 33 F3
Elton *Cambs.* PE8 42 D6
Elton *Ches.* CH2 48 D5
Elton *Derbys.* DE4 50 E6
Elton *Glos.* GL14 29 G7
Elton *Gt.Man.* BL8 49 G1
Elton *Here.* SY8 28 D1
Elton *Notts.* NG13 42 A2
Elton *Stock.* TS21 63 F5
Elton Green CH2 48 D5
Elvanfoot ML12 68 E2
Elvaston DE72 41 G2
Elveden IP24 34 C1
Elvingston EH33 76 C3
Elvington *Kent* CT15 15 H2
Elvington *York* YO41 58 D5
Elwick *Hart.* TS27 63 F3
Elwick *Northumb.* NE70 77 K7

Elworth CW11 49 G6
Elworthy TA4 7 J2
Ely Cambs. CB7 33 J1
Ely Cardiff CF5 18 E4
Emberton MK46 32 B4
Embleton Cumb. CA13 60 C3
Embleton Hart. TS22 63 F4
Embleton Northumb. NE66 71 H1
Embo IV25 97 F2
Embo Street IV25 97 F2
Emborough BA3 19 K6
Embsay BD23 57 F4
Emerson Park RM11 23 J3
Emery Down SO43 10 D4
Emley HD8 50 E1
Emmington OX39 22 A1
Emneth PE14 43 H5
Emneth Hungate PE14 43 J5
Empingham LE15 42 C5
Empshott GU33 11 J1
Empshott Green GU33 11 J1
Emsworth PO10 11 J4
Enborne RG20 21 H5
Enborne Row RG20 21 H5
Enchmarsh SY6 38 E6
Enderby LE19 41 H6
Endmoor LA8 55 J1
Endon ST9 49 J7
Endon Bank ST9 49 J7
ENFIELD EN 23 G2
Enfield Wash EN3 23 G2
Enford SN9 20 E6
Engine Common BS37 19 K3
Englefield RG7 21 K4
Englefield Green TW20 22 C4
Englesea-brook CW2 49 G7
English Bicknor GL16 28 E7
English Frankton SY12 38 D3
Englishcombe BA2 20 A5
Enham Alamein SP11 21 G7
Enmore TA5 8 B1
Ennerdale Bridge CA23 60 B5
Enniscaven PL26 3 G3
Ennochdhu PH10 82 B1
Ensay PA75 78 E3
Ensdon SY4 38 D4
Ensis EX31 6 D3
Enson ST18 40 B3
Enstone OX7 30 E6
Enterkinfoot DG3 68 D3
Enterpen TS15 63 F6
Enton Green GU8 22 C7
Enville DY7 40 A7
Eolaigearraidh HS9 84 C4
Eorabus PA67 78 E5
Eorodal HS2 101 H1
Eoropaidh HS2 101 H1
Epney GL2 29 G7
Epperstone NG14 41 J1
Epping CM16 23 H1
Epping Green Essex CM16 23 H1
Epping Green Herts. SG13 23 F1
Epping Upland CM16 23 H1
Eppleby DL11 62 C5
Eppleworth HU16 59 G6
Epsom KT17 23 F5
Epwell OX15 30 E4
Epworth DN9 51 K2
Epworth Turbary DN9 51 K2
Erbistock LL13 38 C1
Erbusaig IV40 86 D2
Erchless Castle IV4 96 B7
Erdington B24 40 D6
Eredine PA33 80 A7
Eriboll IV27 103 G3
Ericstane DG10 69 F2
Eridge Green TN3 13 J3
Eriff DG7 67 K3
Erines PA29 73 G3
Erisey Barton TR12 2 E7
Eriskay (Eiriosgaigh) HS8 84 C3
Eriswell IP28 34 B1
Erith DA8 23 J4
Erlestoke SN10 20 C6
Ermington PL21 5 G5
Ernesettle PL5 4 E4
Erpingham NR11 45 F2
Erringden Grange HX7 56 E7
Errogie IV2 88 C2
Errol PH2 82 D5
Errollston AB42 91 J1
Erskine PA8 74 C3
Ervie DG9 66 D7
Erwarton IP9 35 G5
Erwood LD2 27 K4
Eryholme DL2 62 E6
Eryrys CH7 48 B7
Escart PA29 73 G4
Escart Farm PA29 73 G5
Escomb DL14 62 C4
Escrick YO19 58 C5
Esgair SA33 17 G3
Esgairgeiliog SY20 37 G5
Esgyryn LL31 47 G5
Esh DH7 62 C2
Esh Winning DH7 62 C2
Esher KT10 22 E5
Eshott NE65 71 H4
Eshton BD23 56 E4
Eskadale IV4 88 B1
Eskbank EH22 76 B4
Eskdale Green CA19 60 C6
Eskdalemuir DG13 69 H4
Eskham DN36 53 G3
Esknish PA44 72 B4
Esperley Lane Ends DL13 62 C4
Espley Hall NE61 71 G4
Esprick PR4 55 H6
Essendine PE9 42 D4
Essendon AL9 23 F1
Essich IV2 88 D1
Essington WV11 40 B5
Esslemont AB41 91 H2
Eston TS6 63 G5
Eswick ZE2 107 N7
Etal TD12 77 H7
Etchilhampton SN10 20 D5
Etchingham TN19 14 C5
Etchinghill Kent CT18 15 G4
Etchinghill Staffs. WS15 40 C4
Etherdwick Grange HU11 59 J6
Etherley Dene DL14 62 C4
Ethie Mains DD11 83 H3
Eton SL4 22 C4
Eton Wick SL4 22 C4
Etteridge PH20 88 D5
Ettiley Heath CW11 49 G6
Ettington CV37 30 D4
Etton E.Riding HU17 59 F5
Etton Peter. PE6 42 E5
Ettrick TD7 69 H2
Ettrickbridge TD7 69 J1
Ettrickhill TD7 69 H2
Etwall DE65 40 E2
Eudon George WV16 39 F7
Eurach PA31 79 K7
Euston IP24 34 C1
Euxton PR7 48 E1
Evanstown CF39 18 C3
Evanton IV16 96 D5
Evedon NG34 42 D1
Evelix IV25 96 E2
Evenjobb LD8 28 B2
Evenley NN13 31 G5
Evenlode GL56 30 D6
Evenwood DL14 62 C4
Evenwood Gate DL14 62 C4
Everbay KW17 106 F5
Evercreech BA4 9 F1
Everdon NN11 31 G3
Everingham YO42 58 E5
Everleigh SN8 21 F6
Everley High. KW1 105 J2
Everley N.Yorks. YO13 59 F1
Eversholt MK17 32 C5
Evershot DT2 8 E4
Eversley RG27 22 A5
Eversley Cross RG27 22 A5
Everthorpe HU15 59 F6
Everton Beds. SG19 33 F3
Everton Hants. SO41 10 D5
Everton Mersey. L5 48 C3
Everton Notts. DN10 51 J3
Evertown DG14 69 J6
Eves Corner CM0 25 F2
Evesbatch WR6 29 F4
Evesham WR11 30 B4
Evie KW17 106 C5
Evington LE5 41 J5
Ewart Newtown NE71 77 H7
Ewden Village S36 50 E3
Ewell KT17 23 F5
Ewell Minnis CT15 15 H3
Ewelme OX10 21 K2
Ewen GL7 20 D2
Ewenny CF35 18 C4
Ewerby NG34 42 E1
Ewerby Thorpe NG34 42 E1
Ewhurst GU6 22 D7
Ewhurst Green E.Suss. TN32 14 C5
Ewhurst Green Surr. GU6 12 D3
Ewloe CH5 48 C6
Ewloe Green CH5 48 B6
Ewood BB2 56 B7
Ewood Bridge BB4 56 C7
Eworthy EX21 6 C6
Ewshot GU10 22 B7
Ewyas Harold HR2 28 C6
Exbourne EX20 6 E5
Exbury SO45 11 F4
Exceat BN25 13 J7
Exebridge TA22 7 H3
Exelby DL8 57 H1
EXETER EX 7 H6
Exeter International Airport EX5 7 H6
Exford TA24 7 G2
Exfords Green SY5 38 D5
Exhall Warks. B49 30 C3
Exhall Warks. CV7 41 F7
Exlade Street RG8 21 K3
Exminster EX6 7 H7
Exmouth EX8 7 J7
Exnaboe ZE3 107 M11
Exning CB8 33 K2
Exton Devon EX3 7 H7
Exton Hants. SO32 11 H2
Exton Rut. LE15 42 C4
Exton Som. TA22 7 H2
Exwick EX4 7 H6
Eyam S32 50 E5
Eydon NN11 31 G4
Eye Here. HR6 28 D2
Eye Peter. PE6 43 F5
Eye Suff. IP23 35 F1
Eye Green PE6 43 F5
Eyemouth TD14 77 H4
Eyeworth SG19 33 F4
Eyhorne Street ME17 14 D2
Eyke IP12 35 H3
Eynesbury PE19 32 E3
Eynort IV47 85 J2
Eynsford DA4 23 J5
Eynsham OX29 21 H1
Eype DT6 8 D5
Eyre IV51 93 K6
Eythorne CT15 15 H3
Eyton Here. HR6 28 D2
Eyton Shrop. SY7 38 C7
Eyton on Severn SY5 38 E5
Eyton upon the Weald Moors TF6 39 F4
Eywood HR5 28 C3

F

Faccombe SP11 21 G6
Faceby TS9 63 F6
Fachwen LL55 46 D6
Facit OL12 49 H1
Faddiley CW5 48 E7
Fadmoor YO62 58 C1
Faebait IV6 96 B6
Faifley G81 74 D3
Fail KA5 67 J1
Failand BS8 19 J4
Failford KA5 67 J1
Failsworth M35 49 H2
Fain IV23 95 H4
Fair Isle ZE2 107 K2
Fair Isle Airstrip ZE2 107 K2
Fair Oak Devon EX16 7 J4
Fair Oak Hants. SO50 11 F3
Fair Oak Hants. RG19 21 J5
Fair Oak Green RG7 21 K5
Fairbourne LL38 37 F4
Fairburn WF11 57 K7
Fairfield Derbys. SK17 50 C5
Fairfield Gt.Man. M43 49 J3
Fairfield Kent TN29 14 E5
Fairfield Mersey. CH63 48 B4
Fairfield Stock. TS19 63 F5
Fairfield Worcs. B61 29 J1
Fairford GL7 20 E1
Fairgirth DG5 65 J5
Fairhaven FY8 55 G7
Fairhill ML3 75 F5
Fairholm ML9 75 F5
Fairley AB15 91 G4
Fairlie KA29 74 A5
Fairlight TN35 14 D6
Fairlight Cove TN35 14 D6
Fairmile Devon EX11 7 J6
Fairmile Surr. KT11 22 E5
Fairmilehead EH10 76 A4
Fairnington TD5 70 B1
Fairoak ST21 39 G2
Fairseat TN15 24 C5
Fairstead CM3 34 B7
Fairwarp TN22 13 H4
Fairwater CF5 18 E4
Fairy Cross EX39 6 C3
Fairyhill SA3 17 H6
Fakenham NR21 44 D3
Fala EH37 76 C4
Fala Dam EH37 76 C4
Falahill EH38 76 B5
Faldingworth LN8 52 D4
Falfield Fife KY15 83 F7
Falfield S.Glos. GL12 19 K2
Falin-Wnda SA44 17 G1
Falkenham IP10 35 G5
FALKIRK FK 75 G3
Falkland KY15 82 D7
Falla TD8 70 C2
Fallgate S45 51 F6
Fallin FK7 75 G1
Falmer BN1 13 G6
Falmouth TR11 3 F5
Falsgrave YO12 59 G1
Falstone NE48 70 C5
Fanagmore IV27 102 D4
Fanans PA35 80 B5
Fancott LU5 32 D6
Fangdale Beck TS9 63 G7
Fangfoss YO41 58 D4
Fankerton FK6 75 F2
Fanmore PA73 79 F3
Fanner's Green CM3 33 K7
Fans TD4 76 E6
Far Cotton NN4 31 J3
Far Forest DY14 29 G1
Far Gearstones LA6 56 C1
Far Green GL11 20 A1
Far Moor WN5 48 E2
Far Oakridge GL6 20 C1
Far Royds LS12 57 H6
Far Sawrey LA22 60 E7
Farcet PE7 43 F6
Farden SY8 28 E1
Fareham PO16 11 G4
Farewell WS13 40 C4
Farforth LN11 53 G5
Faringdon SN7 21 F2
Farington PR25 55 J7
Farlam CA8 61 G1
Farlary IV28 96 E1
Farleigh N.Som. BS48 19 J5
Farleigh Surr. CR6 23 G5
Farleigh Hungerford BA2 20 B6
Farleigh Wallop RG25 21 K7
Farlesthorpe LN13 53 H5
Farleton Cumb. LA6 55 J1
Farleton Lancs. LA2 55 J3
Farley Derbys. DE4 50 E6
Farley Shrop. SY5 38 C5
Farley Staffs. ST10 40 C1
Farley Wilts. SP5 10 D2
Farley Green Suff. CB8 34 B3
Farley Green Surr. GU5 22 D7
Farley Hill RG7 22 A5
Farleys End GL2 29 G7
Farlington YO61 58 C3
Farlow DY14 39 F7
Farm Town LE67 41 F4
Farmborough BA2 19 K5
Farmcote GL54 30 B6
Farmington GL54 30 C7
Farmoor OX2 21 H1
Farmtown AB55 98 D5
Farnborough Gt.Lon. BR6 23 H5
Farnborough Hants. GU14 22 B6
Farnborough W.Berks. OX12 21 H3
Farnborough Warks. OX17 31 F4
Farnborough Street GU14 22 B6
Farncombe GU7 22 C7
Farndish NN29 32 C2
Farndon Ches. CH3 48 D7
Farndon Notts. NG24 51 K7
Farnell DD9 83 H2
Farnham Dorset DT11 9 J3
Farnham Essex CM23 33 H6
Farnham N.Yorks. HG5 57 J3
Farnham Suff. IP17 35 H2
Farnham Surr. GU9 22 B7
Farnham Common SL2 22 C3
Farnham Green CM23 33 H6
Farnham Royal SL2 22 C3
Farningham DA4 23 J5
Farnley N.Yorks. LS21 57 H5
Farnley W.Yorks. LS12 57 H6
Farnley Tyas HD4 50 D1
Farnsfield NG22 51 J7
Farnworth Gt.Man. BL4 49 G2
Farnworth Halton WA8 48 E4
Farr High. KW14 104 C2
Farr High. IV2 88 D1
Farr High. PH21 89 F4
Farr House IV2 88 D1
Farraline IV2 88 C2
Farringdon EX5 7 J6
Farrington Gurney BS39 19 K6
Farsley LS28 57 H6
Farthing Corner ME8 24 E5
Farthing Green TN12 14 D3
Farthinghoe NN13 31 G5
Farthingstone NN12 31 H3
Farthorpe LN9 53 F5
Fartown HD2 50 D1
Farway EX24 7 K6
Fasag IV22 94 E6
Fasagrianach IV23 95 H3
Fascadale PH36 86 B7
Faslane G84 74 A2
Fasnacloich PA38 80 B3
Fasnakyle IV4 87 K2
Fassfern PH33 87 G7
Fatfield NE38 62 E1
Fattahead AB45 98 E5
Faugh CA8 61 G1
Fauldhouse EH47 75 H4
Faulkbourne CM8 34 B7
Faulkland BA3 20 A6
Fauls SY13 38 E2
Faulston SP5 10 B2
Faversham ME13 25 G5
Favillar AB55 89 K1
Fawdington YO61 57 K2
Fawdon NE3 71 H7
Fawfieldhead SK17 50 C6
Fawkham Green DA3 23 J5
Fawler OX7 30 E7
Fawley Bucks. RG9 22 A3
Fawley Hants. SO45 11 F4
Fawley W.Berks. OX12 21 G3
Fawley Chapel HR1 28 E6
Fawsyde DD10 91 G7
Faxfleet DN14 58 E7
Faxton NN6 31 J1
Faygate RH12 13 F3
Fazakerley L9 48 C3
Fazeley B78 40 E5
Fearby HG4 57 G1
Fearn IV20 97 F4
Fearnan PH15 81 J3
Fearnbeg IV54 94 D6
Fearnhead WA2 49 F3
Fearnmore IV54 94 D5
Fearnoch Arg. & B. PA22 73 J3
Fearnoch Arg. & B. PA21 73 H3
Featherstone Staffs. WV10 40 B5
Featherstone W.Yorks. WF7 57 K7
Featherstone Castle NE49 70 B7
Feckenham B96 30 B2
Feering CO5 34 C6
Feetham DL11 62 A7
Feith-hill AB53 98 E6
Feizor LA2 56 C3
Felbridge RH19 13 G3
Felbrigg NR11 45 G2
Felcourt RH19 23 G7
Felden HP3 22 D1
Felhampton SY6 38 D7
Felindre Carmar. SA19 27 G6
Felindre Carmar. SA32 17 J3
Felindre Carmar. SA44 17 G2
Felindre Carmar. SA19 17 K2
Felindre Cere. SA48 26 E3
Felindre Powys LD7 38 A7
Felindre Powys NP8 28 A6
Felindre Swan. SA5 17 K5
Felinfach Cere. SA48 26 E3
Felinfach Powys LD3 27 K5
Felinfoel SA14 17 J5
Felingwmisaf SA32 17 J3
Felingwmuchaf SA32 17 J3
Felixkirk YO7 57 K1
Felixstowe IP11 35 H5
Felixstowe Ferry IP11 35 H5
Felkington TD15 77 H6
Felldownhead PL19 6 B7
Felling NE10 71 H7
Fellonmore PA65 79 H5
Felmersham MK43 32 C3
Felmingham NR28 45 G3
Felpham PO22 12 C7
Felsham IP30 34 D3
Felsted CM6 33 K6
Feltham TW13 22 E4
Felthamhill TW16 22 E4
Felthorpe NR10 45 F4
Felton Here. HR1 28 E4
Felton N.Som. BS40 19 J5
Felton Northumb. NE65 71 G3
Felton Butler SY4 38 C4
Feltwell IP26 44 B6
Fen Ditton CB5 33 H2
Fen Drayton CB4 33 G2
Fen End CV8 30 D1
Fen Street Norf. NR17 44 D6
Fen Street Norf. IP22 34 E1
Fen Street Suff. IP22 34 D1
Fen Street Suff. IP14 35 F2
Fenay Bridge HD8 50 D1
Fence BB12 56 D6
Fence Houses DH4 62 E1
Fencott OX5 31 G7
Fendike Corner PE24 53 H6
Fenham TD15 77 J6
Fenhouses PE20 43 F1
Feniscowles BB2 56 B7
Feniton EX14 7 K6
Fenn Street ME3 24 D4
Fenni-fach LD3 27 K6
Fenny Bentley DE6 50 D7
Fenny Bridges EX14 7 K6
Fenny Compton CV47 31 F3
Fenny Drayton CV13 41 F6
Fenny Stratford MK2 32 B5
Fenrother NE61 71 G4
Fenstanton PE28 33 G2
Fenton Cambs. PE28 33 G1
Fenton Lincs. LN1 52 B5
Fenton Lincs. NG23 52 B7
Fenton Northumb. NE71 77 H7
Fenton Notts. DN22 51 K4
Fenton Stoke ST4 40 A1
Fenton Barns EH39 76 D2
Fenwick E.Ayr. KA3 74 C6
Fenwick Northumb. NE18 71 F6
Fenwick Northumb. TD15 77 J6
Fenwick S.Yorks. DN6 51 H1
Feochaig PA28 66 B2
Feock TR3 3 F5
Feolin PA60 72 D4
Feolin Ferry PA60 72 C4
Feorlan PA28 66 A3
Feorlin PA32 73 H1
Ferguslie Park PA3 74 C4
Feriniquarrie IV55 93 G6
Fern DD8 83 F1
Ferndale CF43 18 C2
Ferndown BH22 10 B4
Ferness IV12 97 G7
Fernham SN7 21 F2
Fernhill Heath WR3 29 H3
Fernhurst GU27 12 B4
Fernie KY15 82 E6
Fernilea IV47 85 J1
Fernilee SK23 50 C5
Fernybank DD9 90 D7
Ferrensby HG5 57 J3
Ferrindonald IV44 86 C4
Ferring BN12 12 D6
Ferry Hill PE16 43 G7
Ferrybridge WF11 57 K7
Ferryden DD10 83 J2
Ferryhill DL17 62 D3
Ferryside (Glanyferi) SA17 17 G4
Fersfield IP22 44 E7
Fersit PH31 87 K7
Ferwig SA43 16 E1
Feshiebridge PH21 89 F4
Fetcham KT22 22 E6
Fetlar ZE2 107 Q3
Fetterangus AB42 99 H5
Fettercairn AB30 90 E7
Fetternear House AB51 91 F3
Feus of Caldhame AB30 83 H1
Fewcott OX27 31 G6
Fewston HG3 57 G4
Ffairfach SA19 17 K3
Ffair-Rhos SY25 27 G2
Ffaldybrenin SA19 17 K1
Ffarmers SA19 17 K1
Ffawyddog NP8 28 B7
Ffestiniog (Llan Ffestiniog) LL41 37 G1
Ffordd-las Denb. LL16 47 K6
Fforddlas Powys HR3 28 B5
Fforest SA4 17 J5
Fforest-fach SA5 17 K6
Ffostrasol SA44 17 G1
Ffos-y-ffin SA46 26 D2
Ffridd Uchaf LL54 46 D7
Ffrith Denb. LL19 47 J4
Ffrith Flints. LL11 48 B7
Ffrwdgrech LD3 27 K6
Ffynnon SA33 17 G4
Ffynnon Taf (Taff's Well) CF15 18 E3
Ffynnongroyw CH8 47 K4
Fibhig HS2 100 E3
Fichlie AB33 90 C3
Fidden PA66 78 E5
Fiddington Glos. GL20 29 J5
Fiddington Som. TA5 19 F7
Fiddleford DT10 9 H3
Fiddler's Green Glos. GL51 29 J6
Fiddler's Green Here. HR1 28 E5
Fiddler's Green Norf. PE32 44 C4
Fiddler's Green Norf. NR17 44 E6

Fiddlers Hamlet **CM16** 23 H1
Field **ST14** 40 C2
Field Broughton **LA11** 55 G1
Field Dalling **NR25** 44 E2
Field Head **LE67** 41 G5
Fife Keith **AB55** 98 C5
Fifehead Magdalen **SP8** 9 G2
Fifehead Neville **DT10** 9 G3
Fifehead St. Quintin **DT10** 9 G3
Fifield *Oxon.* **OX7** 30 D7
Fifield *W. & M.* **SL6** 22 C4
Fifield Bavant **SP5** 10 B2
Figheldean **SP4** 20 E7
Filby **NR29** 45 J4
Filey YO14 59 H1
Filgrave **MK16** 32 B4
Filham **PL21** 5 G5
Filkins **GL7** 21 F1
Filleigh *Devon* **EX32** 6 E3
Filleigh *Devon* **EX17** 7 F4
Fillingham **DN21** 52 C4
Fillongley **CV7** 40 E7
Filmore Hill **GU34** 11 H2
Filton **BS34** 19 K4
Fimber **YO25** 58 E3
Finavon **DD8** 83 F2
Fincham **PE33** 44 A5
Finchampstead **RG40** 22 A5
Finchdean **PO8** 11 J3
Finchingfield **CM7** 33 K5
Finchley **N3** 23 F2
Findern **DE65** 41 F2
Findhorn **IV36** 97 H5
Findhorn Bridge **IV13** 89 F2
Findhuglen **PH6** 81 J6
Findo Gask **PH1** 82 B5
Findochty **AB56** 98 C4
Findon *Aber.* **AB12** 91 H5
Findon *W.Suss.* **BN14** 12 E6
Findon Mains **IV7** 96 D5
Findon Valley **BN14** 12 E6
Findrassie **IV30** 97 J5
Findron **AB37** 89 J3
Finedon **NN9** 32 C1
Finegand **PH10** 82 C1
Fingal Street **IP13** 35 G1
Fingask **AB51** 91 F2
Fingerpost **DY14** 29 G1
Fingest **RG9** 22 A2
Finghall **DL8** 57 G1
Fingland *Cumb.* **CA7** 60 D1
Fingland *D. & G.* **DG13** 69 H3
Fingland *D. & G.* **DG4** 68 C2
Finglesham **CT14** 15 J2
Fingringhoe **CO5** 34 E6
Finkle Street **S35** 51 F3
Finlarig **FK21** 81 G4
Finmere **MK18** 31 H5
Finnart *Arg. & B.* **G84** 74 A1
Finnart *P. & K.* **PH17** 81 G2
Finney Hill **LE12** 41 G4
Finningham **IP14** 34 E2
Finningley **DN9** 51 J3
Finnygaud **AB54** 98 E5
Finsbay (Fionnsbhagh) **HS3** 93 F3
Finsbury **EC1R** 23 G3
Finstall **B60** 29 J1
Finsthwaite **LA12** 55 G1
Finstock **OX7** 30 E7
Finstown **KW17** 106 C6
Fintry *Aber.* **AB53** 99 F5
Fintry *Stir.* **G63** 74 E2
Finwood **CV35** 30 C2
Finzean **AB31** 90 D5
Fionnphort **PA66** 78 D5
Fionnsbhagh (Finsbay) **HS3** 93 F3
Fir Tree **DL15** 62 C3
Firbank **LA10** 61 H7
Firbeck **S81** 51 H4
Firby *N.Yorks.* **DL8** 57 H1
Firby *N.Yorks.* **YO60** 58 D3
Firgrove **OL16** 49 J1
Firs Lane **WN7** 49 F2
Firsby **PE23** 53 H6
Firsdown **SP5** 10 D1
Firth **ZE2** 107 N5
Fishbourne *I.o.W.* **PO33** 11 G5
Fishbourne *W.Suss.* **PO18** 12 B6
Fishburn **TS21** 62 E3
Fishcross **FK10** 75 H1
Fisherford **AB51** 90 E1
Fisher's Pond **SO50** 11 F2
Fisher's Row **PR3** 55 H5
Fishersgate **BN41** 13 F6
Fisherstreet **GU8** 12 C3
Fisherton *High.* **IV2** 96 E6
Fisherton *S.Ayr.* **KA7** 67 G2
Fisherton de la Mere **BA12** 9 J1
Fishguard (Abergwaun) SA65 16 C2
Fishlake **DN7** 51 J1
Fishleigh Barton **EX37** 6 D3
Fishley **NR13** 45 J4
Fishnish **PA65** 79 H3
Fishpond Bottom **DT6** 8 C5
Fishponds **BS16** 19 K4
Fishpool **BL9** 49 H2
Fishtoft **PE21** 43 G1
Fishtoft Drove **PE22** 43 G1
Fishtown of Usan **DD10** 83 J2
Fishwick **TD15** 77 H5
Fiskerton *Lincs.* **LN3** 52 D5
Fiskerton *Notts.* **NG25** 51 K7
Fitling **HU11** 59 J6
Fittleton **SP4** 20 E7
Fittleworth **RH20** 12 D5
Fitton End **PE13** 43 H4
Fitz **SY4** 38 D4
Fitzhead **TA4** 7 K3
Fitzroy **TA2** 7 K3
Fitzwilliam **WF9** 51 G1
Fiunary **PA34** 79 H3
Five Acres **GL16** 28 E7
Five Ash Down **TN22** 13 H4
Five Ashes **TN20** 13 J4
Five Bridges **WR6** 29 F4
Five Houses **PO30** 11 F6
Five Lanes **NP26** 19 H2
Five Oak Green **TN12** 23 K7
Five Oaks *Chan.I.* **JE2** 3 K7
Five Oaks *W.Suss.* **RH14** 12 D4
Five Roads **SA15** 17 H5
Five Turnings **LD7** 28 B1
Five Wents **ME17** 14 D2
Fivehead **TA3** 8 C2
Fivelanes **PL15** 4 C2
Flack's Green **CM3** 34 B7
Flackwell Heath **HP10** 22 B3
Fladbury **WR10** 29 J4
Fladdabister **ZE2** 107 N9
Flagg **SK17** 50 D6
Flamborough **YO15** 59 J2
Flamstead **AL3** 32 D7
Flamstead End **EN7** 23 G1
Flansham **PO22** 12 C6
Flanshaw **WF2** 57 J7
Flasby **BD23** 56 E4
Flash **SK17** 50 C6
Flashader **IV51** 93 J6
Flask Inn **YO22** 63 J2
Flaunden **HP3** 22 D1
Flawborough **NG13** 42 A1
Flawith **YO61** 57 K3
Flax Bourton **BS48** 19 J5
Flax Moss **BB4** 56 C7
Flaxby **HG5** 57 J4
Flaxholme **DE56** 41 F1
Flaxlands **NR16** 45 F6
Flaxley **GL14** 29 F7
Flaxpool **TA4** 7 K2
Flaxton **YO60** 58 C3
Fleckney **LE8** 41 J6
Flecknoe **CV23** 31 G2
Fledborough **NG22** 52 B5
Fleet *Hants.* GU51 22 B6
Fleet *Hants.* **PO11** 11 J4
Fleet *Lincs.* **PE12** 43 G3
Fleet Hargate **PE12** 43 G3
Fleetville **AL1** 22 E1
Fleetwood FY7 55 G5
Fleggburgh (Burgh St. Margaret) **NR29** 45 J4
Flemingston **CF62** 18 D4
Flemington **G72** 74 E5
Flempton **IP28** 34 C2
Fleoideabhagh **HS3** 93 F3
Flesherin **HS2** 101 H4
Fletchersbridge **PL30** 4 B4
Fletchertown **CA7** 60 D2
Fletching **TN22** 13 H4
Fleuchats **AB36** 90 B4
Fleur-de-lis **NP12** 18 E2
Flexbury **EX23** 6 A5
Flexford **GU3** 22 C6
Flimby **CA15** 60 B3
Flimwell **TN5** 14 C4
Flint (Y Fflint) CH6 48 B5
Flint Cross **SG8** 33 H4
Flint Mountain **CH6** 48 B5
Flintham **NG23** 42 A1
Flinton **HU11** 59 J6
Flint's Green **CV7** 30 D1
Flishinghurst **TN17** 14 C4
Flitcham **PE31** 44 B3
Flitholme **CA16** 61 J5
Flitton **MK45** 32 D5
Flitwick **MK45** 32 D5
Flixborough **DN15** 52 B1
Flixton *Gt.Man.* **M41** 49 G3
Flixton *N.Yorks.* **YO11** 59 G2
Flixton *Suff.* **NR35** 45 H7
Flockton **WF4** 50 E1
Flockton Green **WF4** 50 E1
Flodden **NE71** 77 H7
Flodigarry **IV51** 93 K4
Flood's Ferry **PE15** 43 G6
Flookburgh **LA11** 55 G2
Floors **AB55** 98 C5
Flordon **NR15** 45 F6
Flore **NN7** 31 H2
Flotta **KW16** 106 C8
Flotterton **NE65** 71 F3
Flowton **IP8** 34 E4
Flushdyke **WF5** 57 H7
Flushing *Aber.* **AB42** 99 J6
Flushing *Cornw.* **TR11** 3 F5
Flushing *Cornw.* **TR12** 2 E6
Fluxton **EX11** 7 J6
Flyford Flavell **WR7** 29 J3
Foals Green **IP21** 35 G1
Fobbing **SS17** 24 D3
Fochabers IV32 98 B5
Fochriw **CF81** 18 E1
Fockerby **DN17** 52 B1
Fodderletter **AB37** 89 J2
Fodderty **IV15** 96 C6
Foddington **TA11** 8 E2
Foel **SY21** 37 J4
Foelgastell **SA14** 17 J4
Foggathorpe **YO8** 58 D6
Fogo **TD11** 77 F6
Fogorig **TD11** 77 F6
Fogwatt **IV30** 97 K6
Foindle **IV27** 102 D4
Folda **PH11** 82 C1
Fole **ST14** 40 C2
Foleshill **CV6** 41 F7
Folke **DT9** 9 F3
Folkestone CT20 15 H4
Folkingham **NG34** 42 D2
Folkington **BN26** 13 J6
Folksworth **PE7** 42 E7
Folkton **YO11** 59 G2
Folla Rule **AB51** 91 F1
Follifoot **HG3** 57 J4
Folly *Dorset* **DT2** 9 G4
Folly *Pembs.* **SA62** 16 C3
Folly Gate **EX20** 6 D6
Fonmon **CF62** 18 D5
Fonthill Bishop **SP3** 9 J1
Fonthill Gifford **SP3** 9 J1
Fontmell Magna **SP7** 9 H3
Fontmell Parva **DT11** 9 H3
Fontwell **BN18** 12 C6
Font-y-gary **CF62** 18 D5
Foolow **S32** 50 D5
Footherley **WS14** 40 D5
Foots Cray **DA14** 23 H4
Forbestown **AB36** 90 B3
Force Forge **LA12** 60 E7
Force Green **TN16** 23 H6
Forcett **DL11** 62 C5
Forches Cross **EX17** 7 F5
Ford *Arg. & B.* **PA31** 79 K7
Ford *Bucks.* **HP17** 22 A1
Ford *Devon* **PL8** 5 G5
Ford *Devon* **EX39** 6 C3
Ford *Devon* **TQ7** 5 H6
Ford *Glos.* **GL54** 30 B6
Ford *Mersey.* **L30** 48 C3
Ford *Midloth.* **EH37** 76 B4
Ford *Northumb.* **TD15** 77 H7
Ford *Pembs.* **SA62** 16 C3
Ford *Plym.* **PL2** 4 E5
Ford *Shrop.* **SY5** 38 D4
Ford *Som.* **TA4** 7 J3
Ford *Staffs.* **ST13** 50 C7
Ford *W.Suss.* **BN18** 12 C6
Ford *Wilts.* **SN14** 20 B4
Ford End **CM3** 33 K7
Ford Green **PR3** 55 H5
Ford Heath **SY5** 38 D4
Ford Street **TA21** 7 K4
Forda **EX20** 6 D6
Fordbridge **B37** 40 D7
Fordcombe **TN3** 23 J7
Forddun (Forden) **SY21** 38 B5
Fordell **KY4** 75 K2
Forden (Forddun) **SY21** 38 B5
Forder Green **TQ13** 5 H4
Fordgate **TA7** 8 C1
Fordham *Cambs.* **CB7** 33 K1
Fordham *Essex* **CO6** 34 D6
Fordham *Norf.* **PE38** 44 A6
Fordham Abbey **CB7** 33 K2
Fordham Heath **CO3** 34 D6
Fordhouses **WV10** 40 B5
Fordingbridge SP6 10 C3
Fordon **YO25** 59 G2
Fordoun **AB30** 91 F7
Ford's Green **IP14** 34 E2
Fordstreet **CO6** 34 D6
Fordwells **OX29** 30 E7
Fordwich **CT2** 15 G2
Fordyce **AB45** 98 D4
Forebrae **PH1** 82 A5
Forebridge **ST17** 40 B3
Foredale **BD24** 56 D3
Foreland **PA49** 72 A4
Foremark **DE65** 41 F3
Forest **DL10** 62 D6
Forest Coal Pit **NP7** 28 B6
Forest Gate **E7** 23 H3
Forest Green **RH5** 22 E7
Forest Hall *Cumb.* **LA8** 61 G6
Forest Hall *T. & W.* **NE12** 71 H7
Forest Head **CA8** 61 G1
Forest Hill *Gt.Lon.* **SE23** 23 G4
Forest Hill *Oxon.* **OX33** 21 J1
Forest Lane Head **HG2** 57 J4
Forest Lodge *Arg. & B.* **PA36** 80 D3
Forest Lodge *P. & K.* **PH18** 89 G7
Forest Row RH18 13 H3
Forest Side **PO30** 11 F6
Forest Town **NG19** 51 H6
Forestburn Gate **NE61** 71 F4
Forest-in-Teesdale **DL12** 61 K4
Forestmill **FK10** 75 H1
Forestside **PO9** 11 J3
Forfar DD8 83 F2
Forgandenny **PH2** 82 B6
Forge **SY20** 37 G6
Forgie **AB55** 98 B5
Forhill **B38** 30 B1
Formby **L37** 48 B2
Forncett End **NR16** 45 F6
Forncett St. Mary **NR16** 45 F6
Forncett St. Peter **NR16** 45 F6
Forneth **PH10** 82 B3
Fornham All Saints **IP28** 34 C2
Fornham St. Martin **IP31** 34 C2
Fornighty **IV12** 97 G6
Forres IV36 97 H6
Forrest **ML6** 75 G4
Forrest Lodge **DG7** 67 K5
Forsbrook **ST11** 40 B1
Forse **KW5** 105 H5
Forsie **KW14** 105 F2
Forsinain **KW13** 104 E4
Forsinard **KW13** 104 D4
Forston **DT2** 9 F5
Fort Augustus PH32 87 K4
Fort George **IV2** 96 E6
Fort William PH33 87 H7
Forter **PH11** 82 C1
Forteviot **PH2** 82 B6
Forth **ML11** 75 H5
Forthampton **GL19** 29 H5
Fortingall **PH15** 81 J3
Fortis Green **N2** 23 F3
Forton *Hants.* **SP11** 21 H7
Forton *Lancs.* **PR3** 55 H4
Forton *Shrop.* **SY4** 38 D4
Forton *Som.* **TA20** 8 C4
Forton *Staffs.* **TF10** 39 G3
Fortrie **AB53** 98 E6
Fortrose IV10 96 E6
Fortuneswell **DT5** 9 F7
Forty Green **HP9** 22 C2
Forty Hill **EN2** 23 G2
Forward Green **IP14** 34 E3
Fosbury **SN8** 21 G6
Foscot **OX7** 30 D6
Fosdyke **PE20** 43 G2
Foss **PH16** 81 J2
Foss Cross **GL54** 20 D1
Fossdale **DL8** 61 K7
Fossebridge **GL54** 30 B7
Foster Street **CM17** 23 H1
Fosterhouses **DN14** 51 J1
Foster's Booth **NN12** 31 H3
Foston *Derbys.* **DE65** 40 D2
Foston *Leics.* **LE8** 41 J6
Foston *Lincs.* **NG32** 42 B1
Foston *N.Yorks.* **YO60** 58 C3
Foston on the Wolds **YO25** 59 H4
Fotherby **LN11** 53 G3
Fotheringhay **PE8** 42 D6
Foubister **KW17** 106 E7
Foul Mile **BN27** 13 K5
Foula **ZE2** 107 L2
Foula Airstrip **ZE2** 107 L2
Foulbog **DG13** 69 H3
Foulden *Norf.* **IP26** 44 B6
Foulden *Sc.Bord.* **TD15** 77 H5
Foulness Island **SS3** 25 G2
Foulridge **BB8** 56 D5
Foulsham **NR20** 44 E3
Foulstone **LA6** 55 J1
Foulzie **AB45** 99 F4
Fountainhall **TD1** 76 C6
Four Ashes *Staffs.* **WV10** 40 B5
Four Ashes *Staffs.* **DY7** 40 A7
Four Ashes *Suff.* **IP31** 34 D1
Four Crosses *Denb.* **LL21** 37 K1
Four Crosses *Powys* **SY22** 38 B4
Four Crosses *Powys* **SY21** 37 K5
Four Crosses *Staffs.* **WS11** 40 B5
Four Elms **TN8** 23 H7
Four Forks **TA5** 8 B1
Four Gotes **PE13** 43 H4
Four Lane Ends *B'burn.* **BB1** 56 B7
Four Lane Ends *Ches.* **CW6** 48 E6
Four Lane Ends *York* **YO19** 58 C4
Four Lanes **TR16** 2 D5
Four Marks **GU34** 11 H1
Four Mile Bridge **LL65** 46 A5
Four Oaks *E.Suss.* **TN31** 14 D5
Four Oaks *Glos.* **GL18** 29 F6
Four Oaks *W.Mid.* **CV7** 40 E7
Four Oaks *W.Mid.* **B74** 40 D6
Four Oaks Park **B74** 40 D6
Four Roads **SA17** 17 H5
Four Throws **TN18** 14 C5
Fourlane Ends **DE55** 51 F7
Fourlanes End **CW11** 49 H7
Fourpenny **IV25** 97 F2
Fourstones **NE47** 70 D7
Fovant **SP3** 10 B2
Foveran House **AB41** 91 H2
Fowey PL23 4 B5
Fowlis **DD2** 82 E4
Fowlis Wester **PH7** 82 A5
Fowlmere **SG8** 33 H4
Fownhope **HR1** 28 E5
Fox Hatch **CM15** 23 J2
Fox Lane **GU14** 22 B6
Fox Street **CO7** 34 E6
Foxbar **PA2** 74 C4
Foxcombe Hill **OX1** 21 H1
Foxcote *Glos.* **GL54** 30 B7
Foxcote *Som.* **BA3** 20 A6
Foxdale **IM4** 54 B6
Foxearth **CO10** 34 C4
Foxfield **LA20** 55 F1
Foxham **SN15** 20 C4
Foxhole *Cornw.* **PL26** 3 G3
Foxhole *High.* **IV4** 88 C1
Foxholes **YO25** 59 G2
Foxhunt Green **TN21** 13 J5
Foxley *Here.* **HR4** 28 D4
Foxley *Norf.* **NR20** 44 E3
Foxley *Northants.* **NN12** 31 H3
Foxley *Wilts.* **SN16** 20 B3
Foxt **ST10** 40 C1
Foxton *Cambs.* **CB2** 33 H4
Foxton *Dur.* **TS21** 62 E4
Foxton *Leics.* **LE16** 41 J6
Foxup **BD23** 56 D2
Foxwist Green **CW8** 49 F6
Foy **HR9** 28 E6
Foyers **IV2** 88 B2
Frachadil **PA75** 78 E2
Fraddam **TR27** 2 C5
Fraddon **TR9** 3 G3
Fradley **WS13** 40 D4
Fradswell **ST18** 40 B2
Fraisthorpe **YO15** 59 H3
Framfield **TN22** 13 H4
Framingham Earl **NR14** 45 G5
Framingham Pigot **NR14** 45 G5
Framlingham **IP13** 35 G2
Frampton *Dorset* **DT2** 9 F5
Frampton *Lincs.* **PE20** 43 G2
Frampton Cotterell **BS36** 19 K3
Frampton Mansell **GL6** 20 C1
Frampton on Severn **GL2** 20 A1
Frampton West End **PE20** 43 F1
Framsden **IP14** 35 G3
Framwellgate Moor **DH1** 62 D2
Frances Green **PR3** 56 B6
Franche **DY11** 29 H1
Frandley **CW9** 49 F5
Frankby **CH48** 48 B4
Frankfort **NR12** 45 H3
Frankley **B32** 40 B7
Franksbridge **LD1** 28 A3
Frankton **CV23** 31 F1
Frant **TN3** 13 J3
Fraserburgh AB43 99 H4
Frating **CO7** 34 E6
Fratton **PO1** 11 H4
Freasley **B78** 40 E6
Freathy **PL10** 4 D5
Freckenham **IP28** 33 K1
Freckleton **PR4** 55 H7
Freeby **LE14** 42 B3
Freefolk **RG28** 21 H7
Freehay **ST10** 40 C1
Freeland **OX29** 31 F7
Freester **ZE2** 107 N7
Freethorpe **NR13** 45 J5
Freethorpe Common **NR13** 45 J5
Freiston **PE22** 43 G1
Freiston Shore **PE22** 43 G1
Fremington *Devon* **EX31** 6 D2
Fremington *N.Yorks.* **DL11** 62 B7
Frenchay **BS16** 19 K4
Frenchbeer **TQ13** 6 E7
Frendraught **AB54** 98 E6
Frenich **FK8** 81 F7
Frensham **GU10** 22 B7
Fresgoe **KW14** 104 E2
Freshbrook **SN5** 20 E3
Freshfield **L37** 48 B2
Freshford **BA2** 20 A6
Freshwater PO40 10 E6
Freshwater Bay **PO40** 10 E6
Freshwater East **SA71** 16 D6
Fressingfield **IP21** 35 G1
Freston **IP9** 35 F5
Freswick **KW1** 105 J2
Fretherne **GL2** 20 A1
Frettenham **NR12** 45 G4
Freuchie **KY15** 82 D7
Freystrop Cross **SA62** 16 C4
Friars Carse **DG2** 68 E5
Friar's Gate **TN6** 13 H3
Friarton **PH2** 82 C5
Friday Bridge **PE14** 43 H5
Friday Street *E.Suss.* **BN23** 13 K6
Friday Street *Suff.* **IP13** 35 G3
Friday Street *Suff.* **IP12** 35 H3
Friday Street *Surr.* **RH5** 22 E7
Fridaythorpe **YO25** 58 E4
Friern Barnet **N11** 23 F2
Friesthorpe **LN3** 52 D4
Frieston **NG32** 42 C1
Frieth **RG9** 22 A2
Frilford **OX13** 21 H2
Frilsham **RG18** 21 J4
Frimley **GU16** 22 B6
Frimley Green **GU16** 22 B6
Frindsbury **ME2** 24 D5
Fring **PE31** 44 B2
Fringford **OX27** 31 H6
Friningham **ME14** 14 D2
Frinsted **ME9** 14 D2
Frinton-on-Sea CO13 35 G7
Friockheim **DD11** 83 G3
Friog **LL38** 37 F4
Frisby on the Wreake **LE14** 41 J4
Friskney **PE22** 53 H7
Friskney Eaudyke **PE22** 53 H7
Friston *E.Suss.* **BN20** 13 J7
Friston *Suff.* **IP17** 35 J2
Fritchley **DE56** 51 F7
Frith **ME13** 14 E2
Frith Bank **PE22** 43 G1
Frith Common **WR15** 29 F2
Fritham **SO43** 10 D3
Frithelstock **EX38** 6 C4
Frithelstock Stone **EX38** 6 C4
Frithville **PE22** 53 G7
Frittenden **TN17** 14 D3
Frittiscombe **TQ7** 5 J6
Fritton *Norf.* **NR15** 45 G6
Fritton *Norf.* **NR31** 45 J5
Fritwell **OX27** 31 G6
Frizinghall **BD9** 57 G6
Frizington CA26 60 B5
Frocester **GL10** 20 A1
Frochas **SY21** 38 B5
Frodesley **SY5** 38 E5
Frodesley Lane **SY5** 38 E5
Frodingham **DN15** 52 B1
Frodsham WA6 48 E5
Frog End **CB3** 33 H3
Frog Pool **WR6** 29 G2
Frogden **TD5** 70 C1
Froggatt **S32** 50 E5
Froghall **ST10** 40 C1
Frogham **SP6** 10 C3
Frogland Cross **BS36** 19 K3
Frogmore *Devon* **TQ7** 5 H6
Frogmore *Hants.* **GU17** 22 B6
Frogmore *Herts.* **AL2** 22 E1
Frogwell **PL17** 4 D4
Frolesworth **LE17** 41 H6
Frome BA11 20 A7
Frome Market **BA11** 20 B6
Frome St. Quintin **DT2** 8 E4
Frome Whitfield **DT2** 9 F5

Fromes Hill **HR8** 29 F4
Fron *Gwyn.* **LL53** 36 C2
Fron *Powys* **SY21** 38 B5
Fron *Powys* **LD1** 27 K2
Fron *Powys* **SY15** 38 A6
Fron Isaf **LL14** 38 B2
Froncysyllte **LL20** 38 B1
Fron-goch **LL23** 37 J2
Frostenden **NR34** 45 J7
Frosterley **DL13** 62 B3
Froxfield **SN8** 21 G5
Froxfield Green **GU32** 11 J2
Fryerning **CM4** 24 C1
Fugglestone St. Peter **SP2** 10 C1
Fulbeck **NG32** 52 C7
Fulbourn **CB1** 33 J3
Fulbrook **OX18** 30 D7
Fulflood **SO22** 11 F2
Fulford *Som.* **TA2** 8 B2
Fulford *Staffs.* **ST11** 40 B2
Fulford *York* **YO10** 58 C5
Fulham **SW6** 23 F4
Fulking **BN5** 13 F5
Full Sutton **YO41** 58 D4
Fullaford **EX31** 6 E2
Fuller Street **CM3** 34 B7
Fuller's Moor **CH3** 48 D7
Fullerton **SP11** 10 E1
Fulletby **LN9** 53 F5
Fullwood **KA3** 74 C5
Fulmer **SL3** 22 D3
Fulmodeston **NR21** 44 D2
Fulnetby **LN8** 52 E5
Fulready **CV37** 30 D4
Fulstone **HD9** 50 D2
Fulstow **LN11** 53 G3
Fulwell *Oxon.* **OX7** 30 E6
Fulwell *T. & W.* **SR5** 62 E1
Fulwood *Lancs.* **PR2** 55 J6
Fulwood *S.Yorks.* **S10** 51 F4
Fundenhall **NR16** 45 F6
Fundenhall Street **NR16** 45 F6
Funtington **PO18** 12 B6
Funtley **PO16** 11 G4
Funzie **ZE2** 107 Q3
Furley **EX13** 8 B4
Furnace *Arg. & B.* **PA32** 80 B7
Furnace *Carmar.* **SA15** 17 J5
Furnace *Cere.* **SY20** 37 F6
Furnace *High.* **IV22** 95 F4
Furnace End **B46** 40 E6
Furner's Green **TN22** 13 H4
Furness Vale **SK23** 50 C4
Furneux Pelham **SG9** 33 H6
Furnham **TA20** 8 C4
Further Quarter **TN26** 14 D4
Furtho **MK19** 31 J4
Furze Green **IP21** 45 G7
Furze Platt **SL6** 22 B3
Furzehill *Devon* **EX35** 7 F1
Furzehill *Dorset* **BH21** 10 B4
Furzeley Corner **PO7** 11 H3
Furzey Lodge **SO42** 10 E4
Furzley **SO43** 10 D3
Fyfett **TA20** 8 B3
Fyfield *Essex* **CM5** 23 J1
Fyfield *Glos.* **GL7** 21 F1
Fyfield *Hants.* **SP11** 21 F7
Fyfield *Oxon.* **OX13** 21 H2
Fyfield *Wilts.* **SN8** 20 E5
Fyfield *Wilts.* **SN9** 20 E5
Fylingthorpe **YO22** 63 J2
Fyning **GU31** 12 B4
Fyvie **AB53** 91 F1

G

Gabalfa **CF14** 18 E4
Gabhsunn Bho Dheas **HS2** 101 G2
Gabhsunn Bho Thuath **HS2** 101 G2
Gablon **IV25** 96 E2
Gabroc Hill **KA3** 74 C5
Gaddesby **LE7** 41 J4
Gaddesden Row **HP2** 32 D7
Gadebridge **HP1** 22 D1
Gadshill **ME3** 24 D4
Gaer *Newport* **NP20** 19 F3
Gaer *Powys* **NP8** 28 A6
Gaer-fawr **NP15** 19 H2
Gaerllwyd **NP16** 19 H2
Gaerwen LL60 **46** **C5**
Gagingwell **OX7** 31 F6
Gaich *High.* **PH26** 89 H2
Gaich *High.* **IV2** 88 D1
Gaick Lodge **PH21** 88 E6
Gailes **KA11** 74 B7
Gailey **ST19** 40 B4
Gainford **DL2** 62 C5
Gainsborough DN21 **52** **B3**
Gainsford End **CO9** 34 B5
Gairloch IV21 **94** **D4**
Gairlochy **PH34** 87 H6
Gairney Bank **KY13** 75 K1
Gairnshiel Lodge **AB35** 89 K4
Gaitsgill **CA5** 60 E2
Galabank **TD1** 76 C6
GALASHIELS TD **76** **C7**
Galdenoch **DG8** 64 B4
Gale **OL15** 49 J1
Galgate **LA2** 55 H4
Galhampton **BA22** 9 F2
Gallanach **PA34** 79 K5
Gallantry Bank **SY14** 48 E7
Gallatown **KY1** 76 A1
Gallchoille **PA31** 73 F1
Gallery **AB30** 83 H1
Galley Common **CV10** 41 F6
Galleyend **CM2** 24 D1
Galleywood **CM2** 24 D1
Gallowfauld **DD8** 83 F3
Gallowhill **PA3** 74 C4
Gallows Green **ST10** 40 C1
Gallowstree Common **RG4** 21 K3
Gallowstree Elm **DY7** 40 A7
Gallt Melyd (Meliden) **LL19** 47 J4
Galltair **IV40** 86 E2
Gallt-y-foel **LL55** 46 D6
Gallypot Street **TN7** 13 H3
Galmington **TA1** 8 B2
Galmisdale **PH42** 85 K6
Galmpton *Devon* **TQ7** 5 G6
Galmpton *Torbay* **TQ5** 5 J5
Galmpton Warborough **TQ4** 5 J5
Galphay **HG4** 57 H2
Galston KA4 **74** **C7**
Galtrigill **IV55** 93 G6
Gamble's Green **CM3** 34 B7
Gamblesby **CA10** 61 H3
Gamelsby **CA7** 60 D1
Gamesley **SK13** 50 C3
Gamlingay **SG19** 33 F3
Gamlingay Cinques **SG19** 33 F3
Gamlingay Great Heath **SG19** 33 F3
Gammaton **EX39** 6 C3
Gammaton Moor **EX39** 6 C3
Gammersgill **DL8** 57 F1
Gamrie **AB45** 99 F4
Gamston *Notts.* **DN22** 51 K5
Gamston *Notts.* **NG2** 41 J2
Ganarew **NP25** 28 E7
Gang **PL14** 4 D4
Ganllwyd **LL40** 37 G3
Gannochy **DD9** 90 E7
Ganstead **HU11** 59 H6
Ganthorpe **YO60** 58 C2
Ganton **YO12** 59 F2
Ganwick Corner **EN5** 23 F2
Gaodhail **PA72** 79 H4
Gappah **TQ13** 5 J3
Gara Bridge **TQ9** 5 H5
Garabal **G83** 80 E6
Garadheancal **IV26** 95 F1
Garbat **IV23** 96 B5
Garbhallt **PA27** 73 J1
Garboldisham **IP22** 44 E7
Garden **FK8** 74 D1
Garden City **CH5** 48 C6
Garden Village **S36** 50 E3
Gardeners Green **RG40** 22 B5
Gardenstown **AB45** 99 F4
Garderhouse **ZE2** 107 M8
Gardham **HU17** 59 F5
Gare Hill **BA11** 20 A7
Garelochhead **G84** 74 A1
Garford **OX13** 21 H2
Garforth **LS25** 57 K6
Gargrave **BD23** 56 E4
Gargunnock **FK8** 75 F1
Gariob **PA31** 73 F2
Garlic Street **IP20** 45 G7
Garlies Castle **DG8** 64 E4
Garlieston **DG8** 64 E6
Garlinge Green **CT4** 15 G2
Garlogie **AB32** 91 F4
Garmelow **ST21** 40 A3
Garmond **AB53** 99 G5
Garmony **PA65** 79 H3
Garmouth **IV32** 98 B4
Garmston **SY5** 39 F5
Garnant **SA18** 17 K4
Garndolbenmaen LL51 **36** **D1**
Garneddwen **SY20** 37 G5
Garnett Bridge **LA8** 61 G7
Garnfadryn **LL53** 36 B2
Garnswllt **SA18** 17 K5
Garrabost **HS2** 101 H4
Garrachra **PA23** 73 J2
Garralburn **AB55** 98 C5
Garras **TR12** 2 E6
Garreg **LL48** 37 F1
Garreg Bank **SY21** 38 B4
Garrett's Green **B33** 40 D7
Garrick **FK15** 81 K6
Garrigill **CA9** 61 J2
Garriston **DL8** 62 C7
Garroch **DG7** 67 K5
Garrochty **PA20** 73 J5
Garros **IV51** 93 K5
Garrow **PH8** 81 K4
Garryhorn **DG7** 67 K4
Garrynahine (Gearraidh na h-Aibhne) **HS2** 100 E4
Garsdale **LA10** 56 C1
Garsdale Head **LA10** 61 J7
Garsdon **SN16** 20 C3
Garshall Green **ST18** 40 B2
Garsington **OX44** 21 J1
Garstang **PR3** 55 H5
Garston **L19** 48 D4
Garswood **WN4** 48 E3
Gartachoil **G63** 74 D1
Gartally **IV63** 88 B1
Gartavaich **PA29** 73 G5
Gartbreck **PA43** 72 A5
Gartcosh **G69** 74 E4
Garth *Bridgend* **CF34** 18 B2
Garth *Cere.* **SY23** 37 F7
Garth *Gwyn.* **LL57** 46 D5
Garth *I.o.M.* **IM4** 54 C6
Garth *Powys* **LD4** 27 J4
Garth *Shet.* **ZE2** 107 L7
Garth *Wrex.* **LL20** 38 B1
Garth Row **LA8** 61 G7
Garthbrengy **LD3** 27 K5
Garthdee **AB15** 91 H4
Gartheli **SA48** 26 E3
Garthmyl **SY21** 38 A6
Garthorpe *Leics.* **LE14** 42 B3
Garthorpe *N.Lincs.* **DN17** 52 B1
Garths **LA8** 61 G7
Garthynty **SA20** 27 G4
Gartincaber **FK16** 81 H7
Gartly **AB54** 90 D1
Gartmore **FK8** 74 D1
Gartnagrenach **PA29** 73 F5
Gartnatra **PA43** 72 B4
Gartness **G63** 74 D2
Gartocharn **G83** 74 C2
Garton **HU11** 59 J6
Garton-on-the-Wolds **YO25** 59 F3
Gartymore **KW8** 105 F7
Garvald **EH41** 76 D3
Garvamore **PH20** 88 C5
Garvan **PH33** 87 F7
Garvard **PA61** 72 B1
Garve IV23 **95** **K5**
Garveld **PA28** 66 A3
Garvestone **NR9** 44 E5
Garvie **PA22** 73 J2
Garvock *Aber.* **AB30** 91 F7
Garvock *Inclyde* **PA16** 74 A3
Garvock *P. & K.* **PH2** 82 B6
Garwald **DG13** 69 H3
Garwaldwaterfoot **DG13** 69 H3
Garway **HR2** 28 D6
Garway Hill **HR2** 28 D6
Gask *Aber.* **AB42** 99 J6
Gask *Aber.* **AB53** 99 F6
Gask *P. & K.* **PH3** 82 A6
Gaskan **PH37** 86 E7
Gass **KA19** 67 J3
Gastard **SN13** 20 B5
Gasthorpe **IP22** 44 D7
Gaston Green **CM22** 33 J7
Gatcombe **PO30** 11 F6
Gate Burton **DN21** 52 B4
Gate Helmsley **YO41** 58 C4
Gate House **PA60** 72 D3
Gateacre **L25** 48 D4
Gateford **S81** 51 H4
Gateforth **YO8** 58 B7
Gatehead **KA2** 74 B7
Gatehouse **PH15** 81 K3
Gatehouse of Fleet **DG7** 65 G5
Gatelawbridge **DG3** 68 E4
Gateley **NR20** 44 D3
Gatenby **DL7** 57 J1
Gatesgarth **CA13** 60 C5
Gateshaw **TD5** 70 C1
Gateshead NE8 **71** **H7**
Gatesheath **CH3** 48 D6
Gateside *Aber.* **AB33** 90 E3
Gateside *Angus* **DD8** 83 F3
Gateside *Fife* **KY14** 82 C7
Gateside *N.Ayr.* **KA15** 74 B5
Gateslack **DG3** 68 D3
Gathurst **WN5** 48 E2
Gatley **SK8** 49 H4
Gattonside **TD6** 76 D7
Gatwick Airport (London Gatwick Airport) **RH6** 23 F7
Gaufron **LD6** 27 J2
Gaulby **LE7** 41 J5
Gauldry **DD6** 82 E5
Gauntons Bank **SY13** 38 E1
Gaunt's Common **BH21** 10 B4
Gaunt's Earthcott **BS32** 19 K3
Gautby **LN8** 52 E5
Gavinton **TD11** 77 F5
Gawber **S75** 51 F2
Gawcott **MK18** 31 H5
Gawsworth **SK11** 49 H5
Gawthrop **LA10** 56 B1
Gawthwaite **LA12** 55 F1
Gay Bowers **CM3** 24 D1
Gay Street **RH20** 12 D4
Gaydon **CV35** 30 E3
Gayhurst **MK16** 32 B4
Gayle **DL8** 56 D1
Gayles **DL11** 62 C6
Gayton *Mersey.* **CH60** 48 B4
Gayton *Norf.* **PE32** 44 B4
Gayton *Northants.* **NN7** 31 J3
Gayton *Staffs.* **ST18** 40 B3
Gayton le Marsh **LN13** 53 H4
Gayton le Wold **LN11** 53 F4
Gayton Thorpe **PE32** 44 B4
Gaywood **PE30** 44 A3
Gazeley **CB8** 34 B2
Geanies House **IV20** 97 F4
Gearach **PA48** 72 A5
Gearnsary **KW11** 104 C5
Gearradh **PH33** 80 A1
Gearraidh Bhailteas **HS8** 84 C2
Gearraidh Bhaird **HS2** 101 F5
Gearraidh na h-Aibhne (Garrynahine) **HS2** 100 E4
Gearraidh na Monadh **HS8** 84 C3
Gearrannan **HS2** 100 D3
Geary **IV55** 93 H5
Gedding **IP30** 34 D3
Geddington **NN14** 42 B7
Gedgrave Hall **IP12** 35 J4
Gedintailor **IV51** 86 B1
Gedling **NG4** 41 J1
Gedney **PE12** 43 H3
Gedney Broadgate **PE12** 43 H3
Gedney Drove End **PE12** 43 H3
Gedney Dyke **PE12** 43 H3
Gedney Hill **PE12** 43 G4
Gee Cross **SK14** 49 J3
Geilston **G82** 74 B3
Geirinis **HS8** 92 C7
Geisiadar **HS2** 100 D4
Geldeston **NR34** 45 H6
Gell *Conwy* **LL22** 47 G6
Gell *Gwyn.* **LL52** 36 D2
Gelli **CF41** 18 C2
Gelli Gynan **CH7** 47 K7
Gellideg **CF48** 18 D1
Gellifor **LL15** 47 K6
Gelligaer **CF82** 18 E2
Gellilydan **LL41** 37 F2
Gellioedd **LL21** 37 J1
Gelly **SA66** 16 D4
Gellyburn **PH1** 82 B4
Gellywen **SA33** 17 F3
Gelston *D. & G.* **DG7** 65 H5
Gelston *Lincs.* **NG32** 42 C1
Gembling **YO25** 59 H4
Gemmil **PA31** 79 J7
Genoch **DG9** 64 B5
Genoch Square **DG9** 64 B5
Gentleshaw **WS15** 40 C4
Geocrab **HS3** 93 G2
George Green **SL3** 22 D3
George Nympton **EX36** 7 F3
Georgeham **EX33** 6 C2
Georgetown **PA6** 74 C4
Gerlan **LL57** 46 E6
Germansweek **EX21** 6 C6
Germoe **TR20** 2 C6
Gerrans **TR2** 3 F5
Gerrards Cross SL9 **22** **D3**
Gerston **KW12** 105 G3
Gestingthorpe **CO9** 34 C5
Geuffordd **SY22** 38 B4
Geufron **SY18** 37 H7
Gibbet Hill **BA11** 20 A7
Gibbshill **DG7** 65 H3
Gibraltar *Lincs.* **PE24** 53 J7
Gibraltar *Suff.* **IP6** 35 F3
Giddeahall **SN14** 20 B4
Giddy Green **BH20** 9 H6
Gidea Park **RM2** 23 J3
Gidleigh **TQ13** 6 E7
Giffnock **G46** 74 D5
Gifford **EH41** 76 D4
Giffordland **KA24** 74 A6
Giffordtown **KY15** 82 D6
Giggleswick **BD24** 56 D3
Gigha PA41 **72** **E6**
Gilberdyke **HU15** 58 E7
Gilbert's End **WR8** 29 H4
Gilchriston **EH36** 76 C4
Gilcrux **CA7** 60 C3
Gildersome **LS27** 57 H7
Gildingwells **S81** 51 H4
Gilesgate Moor **DH1** 62 D2
Gileston **CF62** 18 D5
Gilfach **CF81** 18 E2
Gilfach Goch **CF39** 18 C3
Gilfachrheda **SA45** 26 D3
Gilgarran **CA14** 60 B4
Gill **CA11** 60 F4
Gillamoor **YO62** 58 C1
Gillen **IV55** 93 H5
Gillenbie **DG11** 69 G5
Gillfoot **DG2** 65 K3
Gilling East **YO62** 58 C2
Gilling West **DL10** 62 C6
Gillingham *Dorset* SP8 **9** **H2**
Gillingham *Med.* ME7 **24** **D5**
Gillingham *Norf.* **NR34** 45 J6
Gillivoan **KW5** 105 G5
Gillock **KW1** 105 H3
Gillow Heath **ST8** 49 H7
Gills **KW1** 105 J1
Gill's Green **TN18** 14 C4
Gilmanscleuch **TD7** 69 J1
Gilmerton *Edin.* **EH17** 76 A4
Gilmerton *P. & K.* **PH7** 81 K5
Gilmilnscroft **KA5** 67 K1
Gilmonby **DL12** 62 A5
Gilmorton **LE17** 41 H7
Gilsland **CA8** 70 B7
Gilsland Spa **CA8** 70 B7
Gilson **B46** 40 D7
Gilstead **BD16** 57 G6
Gilston **EH38** 76 C5
Gilston Park **CM20** 33 H7
Giltbrook **NG16** 41 G1
Gilwern **NP7** 28 B7
Gimingham **NR11** 45 G2
Gin Pit **M29** 49 F2
Ginclough **SK10** 49 J5
Ginger's Green **BN27** 13 K5
Giosla **HS2** 100 D5
Gipping **IP14** 34 E2
Gipsey Bridge **PE22** 43 F1
Girlsta **ZE2** 107 N7
Girsby **DL2** 62 E6
Girtford **SG19** 32 E4
Girthon **DG7** 65 G5
Girton *Cambs.* **CB3** 33 H2
Girton *Notts.* **NG23** 52 B6
Girvan KA26 **67** **F4**
Gisburn **BB7** 56 D5
Gisburn Cotes **BB7** 56 D5
Gisleham **NR33** 45 K7
Gislingham **IP23** 34 E1
Gissing **IP22** 45 F7
Gittisham **EX14** 7 K6
Givons Grove **KT22** 22 E6
Glackour **IV23** 95 H3
Gladestry **HR5** 28 B3
Gladsmuir **EH33** 76 C3
Glaic **PA22** 73 J3
Glais **SA7** 18 A1
Glaisdale **YO21** 63 J6
Glaister **KA27** 73 H7
Glame **IV40** 94 B7
Glamis **DD8** 82 E3
Glan Conwy **LL24** 47 G7
Glanaber Terrace **LL24** 37 G1
Glanaman **SA18** 17 K4
Glanbran **SA20** 27 H5
Glan-Denys **SA48** 26 E3
Glanderston **AB52** 90 D2
Glandford **NR25** 44 E1
Glan-Duar **SA40** 17 J1
Glandwr **SA34** 16 E3
Glan-Dwyfach **LL51** 36 D1
Glangrwyney **NP8** 28 B7
Glanllynfi **CF34** 18 B2
Glanmule **SY16** 38 A6
Glan-rhyd *N.P.T.* **SA9** 18 A1
Glanrhyd *Pembs.* **SA43** 16 E1
Glanton **NE66** 71 F2
Glanton Pyke **NE66** 71 F2
Glantwymyn (Cemmaes Road) **SY20** 37 H5
Glanvilles Wootton **DT9** 9 F4
Glanwern **SY24** 37 F7
Glanwydden **LL31** 47 G4
Glan-y-don **CH8** 47 K5
Glanyferi (Ferryside) SA17 **17** **G4**
Glan-y-llyn **CF15** 18 E3
Glan-y-nant **SY18** 37 J7
Glan-yr-afon *Gwyn.* **LL23** 37 J1
Glan-yr-afon *Gwyn.* **LL21** 37 K1
Glan-yr-afon *I.o.A.* **LL58** 46 E4
Glan-y-Wern **LL47** 37 F2
Glapthorn **PE8** 42 D6
Glapwell **S44** 51 G6
Glasahoile **FK8** 81 F7
Glasbury **HR3** 28 A5
Glaschoil **PH26** 89 H1
Glascoed *Mon.* **NP4** 19 G1
Glascoed *Wrex.* **LL11** 48 B7
Glascorrie **AB35** 90 C5
Glascote **B77** 40 E5
Glascwm **LD1** 28 A3
Glasdrum **PA38** 80 B3
Glasfryn **LL21** 47 H7
GLASGOW G **74** **D4**
Glasgow Airport **PA3** 74 C4
Glasgow Prestwick Airport **KA9** 67 H1
Glashmore **AB31** 91 F4
Glasinfryn **LL57** 46 D6
Glasnacardoch **PH41** 86 C5
Glasnakille **IV49** 86 B3
Glaspant **SA38** 17 F2
Glaspwll **SY20** 37 G6
Glassburn **IV4** 87 K1
Glassel **AB31** 90 E5
Glassenbury **TN17** 14 C4
Glasserton **DG8** 64 E7
Glassford **ML10** 75 F6
Glasshouse **GL17** 29 G6
Glasshouses **HG3** 57 G3
Glassingall **FK15** 81 J7
Glasslie **KY6** 82 D7
Glasson *Cumb.* **CA7** 69 H7
Glasson *Lancs.* **LA2** 55 H4
Glassonby **CA10** 61 G3
Glasterlaw **DD11** 83 G2
Glaston **LE15** 42 B5
Glastonbury BA6 **8** **D1**
Glatton **PE28** 42 E7
Glazebrook **WA3** 49 F3
Glazebury **WA3** 49 F3
Glazeley **WV16** 39 G7
Gleadless **S12** 51 F4
Gleadsmoss **SK11** 49 H6
Gleann Tholastaidh **HS2** 101 H3
Gleaston **LA12** 55 F2
Glecknabae **PA20** 73 J4
Gledhow **LS8** 57 J6
Gledrid **LL14** 38 B2
Glemsford **CO10** 34 C4
Glen *D. & G.* **DG2** 65 J3
Glen *D. & G.* **DG7** 65 F5
Glen Auldyn **IM7** 54 D4
Glen Mona **IM7** 54 D5
Glen Parva **LE2** 41 H6
Glen Trool Lodge **DG8** 67 J5
Glen Village **FK1** 75 G3
Glen Vine **IM4** 54 C6
Glenae **DG1** 68 E5
Glenaladale **PH37** 86 E7
Glenald **G84** 74 A1
Glenamachrie **PA34** 80 A5
Glenapp Castle **KA26** 66 E5
Glenarm **DD8** 82 E1
Glenbarr **PA29** 72 E7
Glenbatrick **PA60** 72 D3
Glenbeg *High.* **IV24** 95 K3
Glenbeg *High.* **PH26** 89 H2
Glenbeg *High.* **PH36** 79 G1
Glenbeich **FK19** 81 H5
Glenbervie *Aber.* **AB39** 91 F6
Glenbervie *Falk.* **FK5** 75 G2
Glenboig **ML5** 75 F4
Glenborrodale **PH36** 79 H1
Glenbranter **PA27** 73 K1
Glenbreck **ML12** 69 F1
Glenbrittle **IV47** 85 K2
Glenburn **PA2** 74 C4
Glenbyre **PA62** 79 G5
Glencaple **DG1** 65 K4
Glencarse **PH2** 82 C5
Glencat **AB34** 90 D5
Glenceitlein **PH49** 80 C3
Glencloy **KA27** 73 J7
Glencoe **PH49** 80 C2
Glenconglass **AB37** 89 J2
Glencraig **KY5** 75 K1
Glencripesdale **PH36** 79 H2
Glencrosh **DG3** 68 C5
Glencruitten **PA34** 79 K5
Glencuie **AB33** 90 C3
Glendearg *D. & G.* **DG13** 69 H3
Glendearg *Sc.Bord.* **TD1** 76 D7
Glendessary **PH34** 87 F5
Glendevon **FK14** 82 A7

Glendoebeg PH32 88 B4
Glendoick PH2 82 D5
Glendoll Lodge DD8 89 K7
Glendoune KA26 67 F4
Glendrissaig KA26 67 F4
Glenduckie KY14 82 D6
Glenduisk KA26 67 G5
Glendye Lodge AB31 90 E6
Gleneagles Hotel PH3 82 A6
Gleneagles House PH3 82 A7
Glenearn PH2 82 C6
Glenegedale PA42 72 B5
Glenelg IV40 86 E3
Glenfarg PH2 82 C6
Glenfeochan PA34 79 K5
Glenfield LE3 41 H5
Glenfinnan PH37 87 F6
Glenfoot PH2 82 C6
Glengalmadale PH33 79 K2
Glengap DG6 65 G5
Glengarnock KA14 74 B5
Glengarrisdale PA60 72 E1
Glengennet KA26 67 G4
Glengolly KW14 105 G2
Glengrasco IV51 93 K7
Glengyle FK8 80 E6
Glenhead DG2 68 D5
Glenhead Farm PH11 82 D1
Glenhurich PH37 79 K1
Glenkerry TD7 69 H2
Glenkiln KA27 73 J7
Glenkin PA23 73 K2
Glenkindie AB33 90 C3
Glenlair DG7 65 H3
Glenlatterach IV30 97 K6
Glenlean PA23 73 J2
Glenlee *Angus* DD9 90 C7
Glenlee *D. & G.* DG7 68 B5
Glenlichorn FK15 81 J6
Glenlivet AB37 89 J2
Glenlochar DG7 65 H4
Glenluce DG8 64 B5
Glenmallan G84 74 A1
Glenmanna DG3 68 C3
Glenmavis ML6 75 F4
Glenmaye IM5 54 B6
Glenmeanie IV6 95 J6
Glenmore *Arg. & B.* PA20 73 J4
Glenmore *High.* IV51 93 K7
Glenmore *High.* PH22 89 G4
Glenmore Lodge PH22 89 G4
Glenmoy DD8 83 F1
Glenmuick IV27 103 F7
Glennoe PA35 80 B4
Glenochar ML12 68 E2
Glenogil DD8 83 F1
Glenprosen Village DD8 82 E1
Glenquiech DD8 83 F1
Glenramskill PA28 66 B2
Glenrazie DG8 64 D4
Glenridding CA11 60 E5
Glenrisdell PA29 73 G5
Glenrossal IV27 96 B1
Glenrothes KY7 82 D7
Glensanda PA34 79 K3
Glensaugh AB30 90 E7
Glensgaich IV14 96 B5
Glenshalg AB31 90 D4
Glenshellish PA27 73 K1
Glensluain PA27 73 J1
Glentaggart ML11 68 D1
Glentham LN8 52 D3
Glenton AB51 90 E2
Glentress EH45 76 A7
Glentrool DG8 64 D3
Glentruan IM7 54 D3
Glentworth DN21 52 C4
Glenuachdarach IV51 93 K6
Glenuig PH38 86 C7
Glenure PA38 80 B3
Glenurquhart IV11 96 E5
Glenwhilly DG8 64 B3
Glespin ML11 68 D1
Gletness ZE2 107 N7
Glewstone HR9 28 E6
Glinton PE6 42 E5
Glooston LE16 42 A6
Glororum NE69 77 K7
Glossop SK13 50 C3
Gloster Hill NE65 71 H3
GLOUCESTER GL 29 H7
Gloup ZE2 107 P2
Gloweth TR1 2 E4
Glusburn BD20 57 F5
Gluss ZE2 107 M5
Glympton OX20 31 F6
Glyn LL24 47 F7
Glyn Ceiriog LL20 38 B2
Glynarthen SA44 17 G1
Glyncoch CF37 18 D2
Glyncorrwg SA13 18 B2
Glyn-Cywarch LL47 37 F2
Glynde BN8 13 H6
Glyndebourne BN8 13 H5
Glyndyfrdwy LL21 38 A1
Glynebwy (Ebbw Vale) NP23 18 E1
Glynneath (Glyn-Nedd) SA11 18 B1
Glyn-Nedd (Glynneath) SA11 18 B1
Glynogwr CF35 18 C3
Glyntaff CF37 18 D3
Gnosall ST20 40 A3
Gnosall Heath ST20 40 A3
Goadby LE7 42 A6
Goadby Marwood LE14 42 A3
Goatacre SN11 20 D4
Goatfield PA32 80 B7
Goathill DT9 9 F3
Goathland YO22 63 K6
Goathurst TA5 8 B1
Gobernuisgeach KW12 104 E5
Gobhaig HS3 100 C7
Gobowen SY11 38 C2
Godalming GU7 22 C7
Goddard's Corner IP13 35 G2
Goddards Green BN6 13 F4
Godden Green TN15 23 J6
Goddington BR6 23 H5
Godford Cross EX14 7 K5
Godington OX27 31 H6
Godleybrook ST10 40 B1
Godmanchester PE29 33 F1
Godmanstone DT2 9 F5
Godmersham CT4 15 F2
Godney BA5 19 H7
Godolphin Cross TR13 2 D5
Godor SY22 38 B4
Godre'r-graig SA9 18 A1
Godshill *Hants.* SP6 10 C3
Godshill *I.o.W.* PO38 11 G6
Godstone RH9 23 G6
Godwick PE32 44 D3
Goetre NP4 19 G1
Goff's Oak EN7 23 G1
Gogar EH12 75 K3
Gogarth LL30 47 F4
Goginan SY23 37 F7
Goirtean a' Chladaich PH33 87 G7
Goirtein PA27 73 H2
Golan LL51 36 E1
Golant PL23 4 B5
Golberdon PL17 4 D3
Golborne WA3 49 F3
Golcar HD7 50 D1
Gold Hill *Cambs.* PE14 43 J6
Gold Hill *Dorset* DT11 9 H3
Goldcliff NP18 19 G3
Golden Cross BN27 13 J5
Golden Green TN11 23 K7
Golden Grove SA32 17 J4
Golden Pot GU34 22 A7
Golden Valley *Derbys.* DE55 51 G7
Golden Valley *Glos.* GL51 29 J6
Goldenhill ST6 49 H7
Golders Green NW11 23 F3
Goldhanger CM9 25 F1
Goldielea DG2 65 K3
Golding SY5 38 E5
Goldington MK41 32 D3
Goldsborough *N.Yorks.* YO21 63 K5
Goldsborough *N.Yorks.* HG5 57 J4
Goldsithney TR20 2 C5
Goldstone TF9 39 G3
Goldthorn Park WV2 40 B6
Goldthorpe S63 51 G2
Goldworthy EX39 6 B3
Golford TN17 14 C4
Gollanfield IV2 97 F6
Gollinglith Foot HG4 57 G1
Golspie KW10 97 F2
Golval KW13 104 D2
Gomeldon SP4 10 C1
Gomersal BD19 57 H7
Gometra PA73 78 E3
Gometra House PA73 78 E3
Gomshall GU5 22 D7
Gonachan Cottage G63 74 E2
Gonalston NG14 41 J1
Gonerby Hill Foot NG31 42 C2
Gonfirth ZE2 107 M6
Good Easter CM1 33 K7
Gooderstone PE33 44 B5
Goodleigh EX32 6 E2
Goodmanham YO43 58 E5
Goodmayes IG3 23 H3
Goodnestone *Kent* CT3 15 H2
Goodnestone *Kent* ME13 25 G5
Goodrich HR9 28 E7
Goodrington TQ4 5 J5
Goodshaw BB4 56 D7
Goodshaw Fold BB4 56 D7
Goodwick (Wdig) SA64 16 C2
Goodworth Clatford SP11 21 G7
Goodyers End CV12 41 F7
Goole DN14 58 D7
Goom's Hill WR7 30 B3
Goonbell TR5 2 E4
Goonhavern TR4 2 E3
Goonvrea TR5 2 E4
Goose Green *Essex* CO11 35 F6
Goose Green *Essex* CO16 35 F6
Goose Green *Gt.Man.* WN3 48 E2
Goose Green *Kent* TN11 23 K6
Goose Green *S.Glos.* BS30 19 K4
Goose Pool HR2 28 D5
Gooseham EX23 6 A4
Goosehill Green WR9 29 J2
Goosewell PL9 5 F5
Goosey SN7 21 G2
Goosnargh PR3 55 J6
Goostrey CW4 49 G5
Gorcott Hill B98 30 B2
Gorddinog LL33 46 E5
Gordon TD3 76 E6
Gordonbush KW9 97 F1
Gordonstoun IV30 97 J5
Gordonstown *Aber.* AB45 98 D5
Gordonstown *Aber.* AB51 91 F1
Gore Cross SN10 20 D6
Gore End RG20 21 H5
Gore Pit CO5 34 C7
Gore Street CT12 25 J5
Gorebridge EH23 76 B4
Gorefield PE13 43 H4
Gorey JE3 3 K7
Gorgie EH11 76 A3
Goring RG8 21 K3
Goring Heath RG8 21 K4
Goring-by-Sea BN12 12 E6
Gorleston-on-Sea NR31 45 K5
Gorllwyn SA33 17 G2
Gornalwood DY3 40 B6
Gorrachie AB45 99 F5
Gorran Churchtown PL26 3 G4
Gorran Haven PL26 4 A6
Gors SY23 27 F1
Gorsedd CH8 47 K5
Gorseinon SA4 17 J6
Gorseness KW17 106 D6
Gorseybank DE4 50 E7
Gorsgoch SA40 26 D3
Gorslas SA14 17 J4
Gorsley HR9 29 F6
Gorsley Common HR9 29 F6
Gorstage CW8 49 F5
Gorstan IV23 95 K5
Gorstanvorran PH37 86 E7
Gorsty Hill ST14 40 D3
Gorten PA64 79 J4
Gortenbuie PA70 79 G4
Gorteneorn PH36 79 H1
Gorton *Arg. & B.* PA78 78 C2
Gorton *Gt.Man.* M18 49 H3
Gosbeck IP6 35 F3
Gosberton PE11 43 F2
Gosberton Clough PE11 42 E3
Goseley Dale DE11 41 F3
Gosfield CO9 34 B6
Gosford *Here.* SY8 28 E2
Gosford *Oxon.* OX5 31 G7
Gosforth *Cumb.* CA20 60 B6
Gosforth *T. & W.* NE3 71 H7
Gosland Green CW6 48 E7
Gosmore SG4 32 E6
Gospel End DY3 40 B6
Gosport PO12 11 H5
Gossabrough ZE2 107 P4
Gossington GL2 20 A1
Gossops Green RH11 13 F3
Goswick TD15 77 J6
Gotham NG11 41 H2
Gotherington GL52 29 J6
Gothers PL26 3 G3
Gott ZE2 107 N8
Gotton TA2 8 B2
Goudhurst TN17 14 C4
Goulceby LN11 53 F5
Gourdas AB53 99 F6
Gourdon DD10 91 G7
Gourock PA19 74 A3
Govan G51 74 D4
Goverton NG14 51 K7
Goveton TQ7 5 H6
Govilon NP7 28 B7
Gowanhill AB43 99 J4
Gowdall DN14 58 C7
Gowerton SA4 17 J6
Gowkhall KY12 75 J2
Gowkthrapple ML2 75 F5
Gowthorpe YO41 58 D4
Goxhill *E.Riding* HU11 59 H5
Goxhill *N.Lincs.* DN19 59 H7
Goytre SA13 18 A3
Gozzard's Ford OX13 21 H2
Grabhair HS2 101 F6
Graby NG34 42 D3
Gradbach SK17 49 J6
Grade TR12 2 E7
Gradeley Green CW5 48 E7
Graffham GU28 12 C5
Grafham *Cambs.* PE28 32 E2
Grafham *Surr.* GU5 22 D7
Grafton *Here.* HR2 28 D5
Grafton *N.Yorks.* YO51 57 K3
Grafton *Oxon.* OX18 21 F1
Grafton *Shrop.* SY4 38 D4
Grafton *Worcs.* HR6 28 E2
Grafton *Worcs.* GL20 29 J5
Grafton Flyford WR7 29 J3
Grafton Regis NN12 31 J4
Grafton Underwood NN14 42 C7
Grafty Green ME17 14 D3
Graianrhyd CH7 48 B7
Graig *Carmar.* SA16 17 H5
Graig *Conwy* LL28 47 G5
Graig *Denb.* LL17 47 J5
Graig-fechan LL15 47 K7
Grain ME3 24 E4
Grainel PA44 72 A4
Grainhow AB53 99 G6
Grains Bar OL4 49 J2
Grainsby DN36 53 F3
Grainthorpe LN11 53 G3
Graiselound DN9 51 K3
Gramisdale (Gramsdal) HS7 92 D6
Grampound TR2 3 G4
Grampound Road TR2 3 G3
Gramsdal (Gramisdale) HS7 92 D6
Granborough MK18 31 J6
Granby NG13 42 A2
Grandborough CV23 31 F2
Grandes Rocques GY5 3 J5
Grandtully PH9 82 A2
Grange *Cumb.* CA12 60 D5
Grange *E.Ayr.* KA1 74 C7
Grange *High.* IV63 87 K1
Grange *Med.* ME7 24 D5
Grange *Mersey.* CH48 48 B4
Grange *P. & K.* PH2 82 D5
Grange Crossroads AB55 98 C5
Grange de Lings LN2 52 C5
Grange Hall IV36 97 H5
Grange Hill IG7 23 H2
Grange Moor WF4 50 E1
Grange of Lindores KY14 82 D6
Grange Villa DH2 62 D1
Grangemill DE4 50 E7
Grangemouth FK3 75 H2
Grangemuir KY10 83 G7
Grange-over-Sands LA11 55 H2
Grangeston KA26 67 G4
Grangetown *Cardiff* CF11 18 E4
Grangetown *R. & C.* TS6 63 G4
Granish PH22 89 G3
Gransmoor YO25 59 H4
Granston SA62 16 B2
Grantchester CB3 33 H3
Grantham NG31 42 C2
Grantley HG4 57 H2
Grantlodge AB51 91 F3
Granton EH5 76 A3
Granton House DG10 69 F3
Grantown-on-Spey PH26 89 H2
Grantsfield HR6 28 E2
Grantshouse TD11 77 G4
Grappenhall WA4 49 F4
Grasby DN38 52 D2
Grasmere LA22 60 E6
Grass Green CO9 34 B5
Grasscroft OL4 49 J2
Grassendale L19 48 C4
Grassgarth LA8 60 F7
Grassholme DL12 62 A4
Grassington BD23 57 F3
Grassmoor S42 51 G6
Grassthorpe NG23 51 K6
Grateley SP11 21 F7
Gratwich ST14 40 C2
Gravel Hill SL9 22 D2
Graveley *Cambs.* PE19 33 F2
Graveley *Herts.* SG4 33 F6
Gravelly Hill B23 40 D6
Gravels SY5 38 C5
Graven ZE2 107 N5
Graveney ME13 25 G5
Gravesend DA11 24 C4
Grayingham DN21 52 C3
Grayrigg LA8 61 G7
Grays RM17 24 C4
Grayshott GU26 12 B3
Grayswood GU27 12 C3
Grazeley RG7 21 K5
Greasbrough S61 51 G3
Greasby CH49 48 B4
Great Abington CB1 33 J4
Great Addington NN14 32 C1
Great Alne B49 30 C3
Great Altcar L37 48 C2
Great Amwell SG12 33 G7
Great Asby CA16 61 H5
Great Ashfield IP31 34 D2
Great Ayton TS9 63 G5
Great Baddow CM2 24 D1
Great Bardfield CM7 33 K5
Great Barford MK44 32 E3
Great Barr B43 40 C6
Great Barrington OX18 30 D7
Great Barrow CH3 48 D6
Great Barton IP31 34 C2
Great Barugh YO17 58 D2
Great Bavington NE19 70 E5
Great Bealings IP13 35 G4
Great Bedwyn SN8 21 F5
Great Bentley CO7 35 F6
Great Bernera HS2 100 D4
Great Billing NN3 32 B2
Great Bircham PE31 44 B2
Great Blakenham IP6 35 F3
Great Bolas TF6 39 F3
Great Bookham KT23 22 E6
Great Bourton OX17 31 F4
Great Bowden LE16 42 A7
Great Bradley CB8 33 K3
Great Braxted CM8 34 C7
Great Bricett IP7 34 E3
Great Brickhill MK17 32 C5
Great Bridgeford ST18 40 A3
Great Brington NN7 31 H2
Great Bromley CO7 34 E6
Great Broughton *Cumb.* CA13 60 B3
Great Broughton *N.Yorks.* TS9 63 G6
Great Buckland DA13 24 C5
Great Budworth CW9 49 F5
Great Burdon DL1 62 E5
Great Burstead CM12 24 C2
Great Busby TS9 63 G6
Great Cambourne CB3 33 G3
Great Canfield CM6 33 J7
Great Canney CM3 24 E1
Great Carlton LN11 53 H4
Great Casterton PE9 42 D5
Great Chalfield SN12 20 B5
Great Chart TN23 14 E3
Great Chatwell TF10 39 G4
Great Chell ST6 49 H7
Great Chesterford CB10 33 J4
Great Cheverell SN10 20 C6
Great Chishill SG8 33 H5
Great Clacton CO15 35 F7
Great Clifton CA14 60 B4
Great Coates DN37 53 F2
Great Comberton WR10 29 J4
Great Corby CA4 61 F1
Great Cornard CO10 34 C4
Great Cowden HU11 59 J5
Great Coxwell SN7 21 F2
Great Crakehall DL8 57 H1
Great Cransley NN14 32 B1
Great Cressingham IP25 44 C5
Great Crosby L23 48 C2
Great Crosthwaite CA12 60 D4
Great Cubley DE6 40 D2
Great Cumbrae KA28 73 K5
Great Dalby LE14 42 A4
Great Doddington NN29 32 B2
Great Doward HR9 28 E7
Great Dunham PE32 44 C4
Great Dunmow CM6 33 K6
Great Durnford SP4 10 C1
Great Easton *Essex* CM6 33 K6
Great Easton *Leics.* LE16 42 B6
Great Eccleston PR3 55 H5
Great Edstone YO62 58 D1
Great Ellingham NR17 44 E6
Great Elm BA11 20 A7
Great Eversden CB3 33 G3
Great Fencote DL7 62 D7
Great Finborough IP14 34 E3
Great Fransham NR19 44 C4
Great Gaddesden HP1 32 D7
Great Gidding PE28 42 E7
Great Givendale YO42 58 E4
Great Glemham IP17 35 H2
Great Glen LE8 41 J6
Great Gonerby NG31 42 B2
Great Gransden SG19 33 F3
Great Green *Cambs.* SG8 33 F4
Great Green *Norf.* IP20 45 G7
Great Green *Suff.* IP30 34 D3
Great Green *Suff.* IP21 35 F1
Great Green *Suff.* IP22 34 E1
Great Habton YO17 58 D2
Great Hale NG34 42 E1
Great Hallingbury CM22 33 J7
Great Hampden HP16 22 B1
Great Harrowden NN9 32 B1
Great Harwood BB6 56 C6
Great Haseley OX44 21 K1
Great Hatfield HU11 59 H5
Great Haywood ST18 40 C3
Great Heath CV6 41 F7
Great Heck DN14 58 B7
Great Henny CO10 34 C5
Great Hinton BA14 20 C6
Great Hockham IP24 44 D6
Great Holland CO13 35 G7
Great Horkesley CO6 34 D5
Great Hormead SG9 33 H5
Great Horton BD7 57 G6
Great Horwood MK17 31 J5
Great Houghton *Northants.* NN4 31 J3
Great Houghton *S.Yorks.* S72 51 G2
Great Hucklow SK17 50 D5
Great Kelk YO25 59 H4
Great Kimble HP17 22 B1
Great Kingshill HP15 22 B2
Great Langton DL7 62 D7
Great Leighs CM3 34 B7
Great Limber DN37 52 E2
Great Linford MK14 32 B4
Great Livermere IP31 34 C1
Great Longstone DE45 50 E5
Great Lumley DH3 62 D2
Great Lyth SY3 38 D5
Great Malvern WR14 29 G4
Great Maplestead CO9 34 C5
Great Marton FY4 55 G6
Great Massingham PE32 44 B3
Great Melton NR9 45 F5
Great Milton OX44 21 K1
Great Missenden HP16 22 B1
Great Mitton BB7 56 C6
Great Mongeham CT14 15 J2
Great Moulton NR15 45 F6
Great Munden SG11 33 G6
Great Musgrave CA17 61 J5
Great Ness SY4 38 D4
Great Notley CM77 34 B6
Great Nurcot TA24 7 H2
Great Oak NP15 19 G1
Great Oakley *Essex* CO12 35 F6
Great Oakley *Northants.* NN18 42 B7
Great Offley SG5 32 E6
Great Ormside CA16 61 J5
Great Orton CA5 60 E1
Great Ouseburn YO26 57 K3
Great Oxendon LE16 42 A7
Great Oxney Green CM1 24 C1
Great Palgrave PE32 44 C4
Great Parndon CM19 23 H1
Great Paxton PE19 33 F2
Great Plumpton PR4 55 G6
Great Plumstead NR13 45 H5
Great Ponton NG33 42 C2
Great Potheridge EX20 6 D4
Great Preston LS26 57 J7
Great Purston NN13 31 G5
Great Raveley PE28 43 F7
Great Rissington GL54 30 C7
Great Rollright OX7 30 E5
Great Ryburgh NR21 44 D3
Great Ryle NE66 71 F2
Great Ryton SY5 38 D5
Great Saling CM7 34 B6
Great Salkeld CA11 61 G3
Great Sampford CB10 33 K5
Great Sankey WA5 48 E4
Great Saredon WV10 40 B5
Great Saxham IP29 34 B2
Great Shefford RG17 21 G4
Great Shelford CB2 33 H3
Great Smeaton DL6 62 E6
Great Snoring NR21 44 D2
Great Somerford SN15 20 C3
Great Stainton TS21 62 E4
Great Stambridge SS4 25 F2
Great Staughton PE19 32 E2

Great Steeping **PE23** 53 H6
Great Stonar **CT13** 15 J2
Great Strickland **CA10** 61 G4
Great Stukeley **PE28** 33 F1
Great Sturton **LN9** 53 F5
Great Sutton *Ches.* **CH66** 48 C5
Great Sutton *Shrop.* **SY8** 38 E7
Great Swinburne **NE48** 70 E6
Great Tew **OX7** 30 E6
Great Tey **CO6** 34 C6
Great Thorness **PO31** 11 F5
Great Thurlow **CB9** 33 K4
Great Torr **TQ7** 5 G6
Great Torrington EX38 6 **C4**
Great Tosson **NE65** 71 F3
Great Totham *Essex* **CM9** 34 C7
Great Totham *Essex* **CM9** 34 C7
Great Tows **LN8** 53 F3
Great Urswick **LA12** 55 F2
Great Wakering **SS3** 25 F3
Great Waldingfield **CO10** 34 D4
Great Walsingham NR22 44 **D2**
Great Waltham **CM3** 33 K7
Great Warley **CM13** 23 J2
Great Washbourne **GL20** 29 J5
Great Weeke **TQ13** 7 F7
Great Welnetham **IP30** 34 C3
Great Wenham **CO7** 34 E5
Great Whittington **NE19** 71 F6
Great Wigborough **CO5** 34 D7
Great Wigsell **TN32** 14 C5
Great Wilbraham **CB1** 33 J3
Great Wilne **DE72** 41 G2
Great Wishford **SP2** 10 B1
Great Witcombe **GL3** 29 J7
Great Witley **WR6** 29 G2
Great Wolford **CV36** 30 D5
Great Wratting **CB9** 33 K4
Great Wymondley **SG4** 33 F6
Great Wyrley **WS6** 40 B5
Great Wytheford **SY4** 38 E4
Great Yarmouth NR30 45 **K5**
Great Yeldham **CO9** 34 B5
Greatford **PE9** 42 D4
Greatgate **ST10** 40 C1
Greatham *Hants.* **GU33** 11 J1
Greatham *Hart.* **TS25** 63 F4
Greatham *W.Suss.* **RH20** 12 D5
Greatness **TN14** 23 J6
Greatstone-on-Sea **TN28** 15 F5
Greatworth **OX17** 31 G4
Green **LL16** 47 J6
Green Cross **GU10** 12 B3
Green End *Beds.* **MK44** 32 E3
Green End *Bucks.* **MK17** 32 C5
Green End *Cambs.* **PE29** 33 F1
Green End *Cambs.* **PE27** 33 G1
Green End *Herts.* **SG12** 33 G6
Green End *Herts.* **SG9** 33 G5
Green End *Warks.* **CV7** 40 E7
Green Hammerton **YO26** 57 K4
Green Hill **SN4** 20 D3
Green Lane **B80** 30 B2
Green Moor **S35** 50 E3
Green Ore **BA5** 19 J6
Green Quarter **LA8** 61 F6
Green Street *E.Suss.* **TN38** 14 C6
Green Street *Herts.* **WD6** 22 E2
Green Street *Herts.* **SG11** 33 H6
Green Street *W.Suss.* **RH13** 12 E4
Green Street *Worcs.* **WR5** 29 H4
Green Street Green *Gt.Lon.* **BR6** 23 H5
Green Street Green *Kent* **DA2** 23 J4
Green Tye **SG10** 33 H7
Greenburn **DD5** 83 F3
Greencroft **DH7** 62 C2
Greendams **AB31** 90 E6
Greendykes **NE66** 71 F1
Greenend **OX7** 30 E6
Greenfaulds **G67** 75 F3
Greenfield *Beds.* **MK45** 32 D5
Greenfield (Maes-Glas) *Flints.* **CH8** 47 K5
Greenfield *Gt.Man.* **OL3** 50 C2
Greenfield *High.* **PH35** 87 J4
Greenfield *Lincs.* **LN13** 53 H5
Greenfield *Oxon.* **OX49** 22 A2
Greenford UB6 22 **E3**
Greengairs **ML6** 75 F3
Greengates **BD10** 57 G6
Greengill **CA7** 60 C3
Greenhalgh **PR4** 55 H6
Greenhall **AB52** 90 E2
Greenham **RG14** 21 H5
Greenhaugh **NE48** 70 C5
Greenhead **CA8** 70 B7
Greenheads **AB42** 91 J1
Greenheys **BL5** 49 G2
Greenhill *Gt.Lon.* **HA1** 22 E3
Greenhill *High.* **KW9** 97 G1
Greenhill *S.Yorks.* **S8** 51 F4
Greenhithe DA9 23 **J4**
Greenholm **KA16** 74 D7
Greenholme **CA10** 61 G6
Greenhow Hill **HG3** 57 G3
Greenigo **KW15** 106 D7
Greenland **KW14** 105 H2
Greenlands **RG9** 22 A3
Greenlaw *Aber.* **AB45** 98 E5
Greenlaw *Sc.Bord.* **TD10** 77 F6
Greenloaning **FK15** 81 K7
Greenmeadow **NP44** 19 F2
Greenmoor Hill **RG8** 21 K3
Greenmount **BL8** 49 G1
Greenmyre **AB53** 91 G1
Greenock PA16 74 **A3**
Greenodd **LA12** 55 G1
Greens Norton **NN12** 31 H4
Greenscares **FK15** 81 J6
Greenside *T. & W.* **NE40** 71 G7
Greenside *W.Yorks.* **HD5** 50 D1
Greenstead **CO4** 34 E6
Greenstead Green **CO9** 34 C6
Greensted **CM5** 23 J1
Greensted Green **CM5** 23 J1
Greenway *Pembs.* **SA66** 16 D2
Greenway *Som.* **TA3** 8 C2
Greenwell **CA8** 61 G1
Greenwich **SE10** 23 G4
Greet **GL54** 30 B5
Greete **SY8** 28 E1
Greetham *Lincs.* **LN9** 53 G5
Greetham *Rut.* **LE15** 42 C4
Greetland **HX4** 57 F7
Gregson Lane **PR5** 55 J7
Greinetobht (Grenitote) **HS6** 92 D4
Greinton **TA7** 8 D1
Grenaby **IM9** 54 B6
Grendon *Northants.* **NN7** 32 B2
Grendon *Warks.* **CV9** 40 E6
Grendon Common **CV9** 40 E6
Grendon Green **HR6** 28 E3
Grendon Underwood **HP18** 31 H6
Grenitote (Greinetobht) **HS6** 92 D4
Grenofen **PL19** 4 E3
Grenoside **S35** 51 F3
Greosabhagh **HS3** 93 G2
Gresford **LL12** 48 C7
Gresham **NR11** 45 F2
Greshornish **IV51** 93 J6
Gress (Griais) **HS2** 101 G3
Gressenhall **NR20** 44 D4
Gressingham **LA2** 55 J3
Greta Bridge **DL12** 62 B5
Gretna DG16 69 **J7**
Gretna Green **DG16** 69 J7
Gretton *Glos.* **GL54** 30 B5
Gretton *Northants.* **NN17** 42 C6
Gretton *Shrop.* **SY6** 38 E6
Grewelthorpe **HG4** 57 H2
Greygarth **HG4** 57 G2
Greylake **TA7** 8 C1
Greys Green **RG9** 22 A3
Greysouthen **CA13** 60 B4
Greystead **NE48** 70 C5
Greystoke **CA11** 60 F3
Greystone *Aber.* **AB35** 89 K5
Greystone *Angus* **DD11** 83 G3
Greystone *Lancs.* **BB9** 56 D5
Greystones **S11** 51 F4
Greywell **RG29** 22 A6
Griais (Gress) **HS2** 101 G3
Gribthorpe **DN14** 58 D6
Gribton **DG2** 68 E5
Griff **CV10** 41 F7
Griffithstown **NP4** 19 F2
Grigadale **PH36** 79 F1
Grigghall **LA8** 61 F7
Grimeford Village **PR6** 49 F1
Grimesthorpe **S4** 51 F3
Grimethorpe **S72** 51 G2
Griminis (Griminish) **HS7** 92 C6
Griminish (Griminis) **HS7** 92 C6
Grimister **ZE2** 107 N3
Grimley **WR2** 29 H2
Grimmet **KA19** 67 H2
Grimness **KW17** 106 D8
Grimoldby **LN11** 53 G4
Grimpo **SY11** 38 C3
Grimsargh **PR2** 55 J6
Grimsay (Griomsaigh) **HS6** 92 D6
Grimsbury **OX16** 31 F4
Grimsby DN32 53 **F2**
Grimscote **NN12** 31 H3
Grimscott **EX23** 6 A5
Grimshader (Griomsiadar) **HS2** 101 G5
Grimsthorpe **PE10** 42 D3
Grimston *E.Riding* **HU11** 59 J6
Grimston *Leics.* **LE14** 41 J3
Grimston *Norf.* **PE32** 44 B3
Grimstone **DT2** 9 F5
Grimstone End **IP31** 34 D2
Grindale **YO16** 59 H2
Grindiscol **ZE2** 107 N9
Grindle **TF11** 39 G5
Grindleford **S32** 50 E5
Grindleton **BB7** 56 C5
Grindley **ST14** 40 C3
Grindley Brook **SY13** 38 E1
Grindlow **SK17** 50 D5
Grindon *Northumb.* **TD15** 77 H6
Grindon *Staffs.* **ST13** 50 C7
Grindon *Stock.* **TS21** 62 E4
Grindon *T. & W.* **SR4** 62 E1
Gringley on the Hill **DN10** 51 K3
Grinsdale **CA5** 60 E1
Grinshill **SY4** 38 E3
Grinton **DL11** 62 B7
Griomarstaidh **HS2** 100 E4
Griomsaigh (Grimsay) **HS6** 92 D6
Griomsiadar (Grimshader) **HS2** 101 G5
Grisdale **LA10** 61 J7
Grishipoll **PA78** 78 C2
Gristhorpe **YO14** 59 G1
Griston **IP25** 44 D6
Gritley **KW17** 106 E7
Grittenham **SN15** 20 D3
Grittleton **SN14** 20 B4
Grizebeck **LA17** 55 F1
Grizedale **LA22** 60 E7
Grobister **KW17** 106 F5
Groby **LE6** 41 H5
Groes **LL16** 47 J6
Groes-faen **CF72** 18 D3
Groesffordd **LL53** 36 B2
Groesffordd Marli **LL22** 47 J5
Groeslon *Gwyn.* **LL54** 46 C7
Groeslon *Gwyn.* **LL55** 46 D6
Groes-lwyd **SY21** 38 B4
Groes-wen **CF15** 18 E3
Grogport **PA28** 73 G6
Groigearraidh **HS8** 84 C1
Gromford **IP17** 35 H3
Gronant **LL19** 47 J4
Groombridge **TN3** 13 J3
Grosmont *Mon.* **NP7** 28 D6
Grosmont *N.Yorks.* **YO22** 63 K6
Grotaig **IV63** 88 B2
Groton **CO10** 34 D4
Groundistone Heights **TD9** 69 K2
Grouville **JE3** 3 K7
Grove *Bucks.* **LU7** 32 C6
Grove *Dorset* **DT5** 9 F7
Grove *Kent* **CT3** 25 J5
Grove *Notts.* **DN22** 51 K5
Grove *Oxon.* **OX12** 21 H2
Grove End **ME9** 24 E5
Grove Green **ME14** 14 C2
Grove Park **SE12** 23 H4
Grove Town **WF8** 57 K7
Grovehill **HP2** 22 D1
Grovesend *S.Glos.* **BS35** 19 K3
Grovesend *Swan.* **SA4** 17 J5
Gruids **IV27** 96 C1
Grula **IV47** 85 J2
Gruline **PA71** 79 G3
Grumbla **TR20** 2 B6
Grundcruie **PH1** 82 B5
Grundisburgh **IP13** 35 G3
Gruting **ZE2** 107 L8
Grutness **ZE3** 107 N11
Gualachulain **PH49** 80 C3
Guardbridge **KY16** 83 F6
Guarlford **WR13** 29 H4
Guay **PH9** 82 B3
Gubbergill **CA19** 60 B7
Gubblecote **HP23** 32 C7
GUERNSEY GY 3 **J5**
Guernsey Airport **GY8** 3 H5
Guestling Green **TN35** 14 D6
Guestling Thorn **TN35** 14 D6
Guestwick **NR20** 44 E3
Guestwick Green **NR20** 44 E3
Guide **BB1** 56 C7
Guide Post **NE62** 71 H5
Guilden Down **SY7** 38 C7
Guilden Morden **SG8** 33 F4
Guilden Sutton **CH3** 48 D6
GUILDFORD GU 22 **C7**
Guildtown **PH2** 82 C4
Guilsborough **NN6** 31 H1
Guilsfield (Cegidfa) **SY21** 38 B4
Guilthwaite **S60** 51 G4
Guisborough TS14 63 **H5**
Guiseley **LS20** 57 G5
Guist **NR20** 44 E3
Guith **KW17** 106 E4
Guiting Power **GL54** 30 B6
Gulberwick **ZE2** 107 N9
Gullane EH31 76 **C2**
Gulval **TR18** 2 B5
Gulworthy **PL19** 4 E3
Gumfreston **SA70** 16 E5
Gumley **LE16** 41 J6
Gunby *Lincs.* **NG33** 42 C3
Gunby *Lincs.* **PE23** 53 H6
Gundleton **SO24** 11 H1
Gunn **EX32** 6 E2
Gunnersbury **W4** 22 E4
Gunnerside **DL11** 62 A7
Gunnerton **NE48** 70 E6
Gunness **DN15** 52 B1
Gunnislake PL18 4 **E3**
Gunnista **ZE2** 107 P8
Gunnister **ZE2** 107 M5
Gunstone **WV8** 40 A5
Gunter's Bridge **GU28** 12 C4
Gunthorpe *Norf.* **NR24** 44 E2
Gunthorpe *Notts.* **NG14** 41 J1
Gunthorpe *Rut.* **LE15** 42 B5
Gunville **PO30** 11 F6
Gunwalloe **TR12** 2 D6
Gupworthy **TA24** 7 H2
Gurnard **PO31** 11 F5
Gurnett **SK11** 49 J5
Gurney Slade **BA3** 19 K7
Gurnos *M.Tyd.* **CF47** 18 D1
Gurnos *Powys* **SA9** 18 A1
Gushmere **ME13** 15 F2
Gussage All Saints **BH21** 10 B3
Gussage St. Andrew **DT11** 9 J3
Gussage St. Michael **BH21** 9 J3
Guston **CT15** 15 J3
Gutcher **ZE2** 107 P3
Guthram Gowt **PE11** 42 E3
Guthrie **DD8** 83 G2
Guyhirn **PE13** 43 G5
Guynd **DD11** 83 G3
Guy's Head **PE12** 43 H3
Guy's Marsh **SP7** 9 H2
Guyzance **NE65** 71 H3
Gwaelod-y-garth **CF15** 18 E3
Gwaenysgor **LL18** 47 J4
Gwaithla **HR5** 28 B3
Gwalchmai **LL65** 46 B5
Gwastad **SA63** 16 D3
Gwastadnant **LL55** 46 E7
Gwaun-Cae-Gurwen **SA18** 27 G7
Gwaynynog **LL16** 47 J6
Gwbert **SA43** 16 E1
Gweek **TR12** 2 E6
Gwehelog **NP15** 19 G1
Gwenddwr **LD2** 27 K4
Gwendreath **TR12** 2 E7
Gwennap **TR16** 2 E4
Gwenter **TR12** 2 E7
Gwernaffield **CH7** 48 B6
Gwernesney **NP15** 19 H1
Gwernogle **SA32** 17 J2
Gwernymynydd **CH7** 48 B6
Gwern-y-Steeple **CF5** 18 D4
Gwersyllt **LL11** 48 C7
Gwespyr **CH8** 47 K4
Gwinear **TR27** 2 C5
Gwithian **TR27** 2 C4
Gwredog **LL71** 46 C4
Gwrhay **NP12** 18 E2
Gwyddelwern **LL21** 37 K1
Gwyddgrug **SA39** 17 H2
Gwynfryn **LL11** 48 B7
Gwystre **LD1** 27 K2
Gwytherin **LL22** 47 G6
Gyfelia **LL13** 38 C1
Gyre **KW17** 106 C7
Gyrn Goch **LL54** 36 C1

H

Habberley **SY5** 38 C5
Habin **GU31** 12 B4
Habrough **DN40** 52 E1
Haccombe **TQ12** 5 J3
Hacconby **PE10** 42 E3
Haceby **NG34** 42 D2
Hacheston **IP13** 35 H3
Hackbridge **SM6** 23 F5
Hackenthorpe **S12** 51 G4
Hackford **NR18** 44 E5
Hackforth **DL8** 62 D7
Hackland **KW17** 106 C5
Hacklet (Haclait) **HS7** 92 D7
Hacklete (Tacleit) **HS2** 100 D4
Hackleton **NN7** 32 B3
Hacklinge **CT14** 15 J2
Hackness *N.Yorks.* **YO13** 63 J3
Hackness *Ork.* **KW16** 106 C8
Hackney **E9** 23 G3
Hackthorn **LN2** 52 C4
Hackthorpe **CA10** 61 G4
Haclait (Hacklet) **HS7** 92 D7
Hacton **RM14** 23 J3
Hadden **TD5** 77 F7
Haddenham *Bucks.* **HP17** 22 A1
Haddenham *Cambs.* **CB6** 33 H1
Haddington *E.Loth.* EH41 76 **D3**
Haddington *Lincs.* **LN5** 52 C6
Haddiscoe **NR14** 45 J6
Haddon **PE7** 42 E6
Hade Edge **HD9** 50 D2
Hademore **WS14** 40 D5
Hadfield **SK13** 50 C3
Hadham Cross **SG10** 33 H7
Hadham Ford **SG11** 33 H6
Hadleigh *Essex* **SS7** 24 E3
Hadleigh *Suff.* **IP7** 34 E4
Hadleigh Heath **IP7** 34 D4
Hadley *Tel. & W.* **TF1** 39 F4
Hadley *Worcs.* **WR9** 29 H2
Hadley End **DE13** 40 D3
Hadley Wood **EN4** 23 F2
Hadlow **TN11** 23 K7
Hadlow Down **TN22** 13 J4
Hadnall **SY4** 38 E3
Hadspen **BA7** 9 F1
Hadstock **CB1** 33 J4
Hadston **NE65** 71 H4
Hadzor **WR9** 29 J2
Haffenden Quarter **TN27** 14 D3
Hafod Bridge **SA19** 17 K2
Hafod-Dinbych **LL24** 47 G7
Hafodunos **LL22** 47 G6
Hafodyrynys **NP11** 19 F2
Haggate **BB10** 56 D6
Haggbeck **CA6** 69 K6
Haggersta **ZE2** 107 M8
Haggerston *Gt.Lon.* **E2** 23 G3
Haggerston *Northumb.* **TD15** 77 J6
Haggrister **ZE2** 107 M5
Haggs **FK4** 75 F3
Hagley *Here.* **HR1** 28 E4
Hagley *Worcs.* **DY9** 40 B7
Hagnaby *Lincs.* **PE23** 53 G6
Hagnaby *Lincs.* **LN13** 53 H5
Hague Bar **SK22** 49 J4
Hagworthingham **PE23** 53 G6
Haigh **WN2** 49 F2
Haighton Green **PR2** 55 J6
Hail Weston **PE19** 32 E2
Haile **CA22** 60 B6
Hailes **GL54** 30 B5
Hailey *Herts.* **SG13** 33 G7
Hailey *Oxon.* **OX10** 21 K3
Hailey *Oxon.* **OX29** 30 E7
Hailsham BN27 13 **J6**
Haimer **KW14** 105 G2
Hainault **IG6** 23 H2
Haine **CT12** 25 K5
Hainford **NR10** 45 G4
Hainton **LN8** 52 E4
Haisthorpe **YO25** 59 H3
Hakin **SA73** 16 B5
Halam **NG22** 51 J7
Halbeath **KY11** 75 K2
Halberton **EX16** 7 J4
Halcro **KW1** 105 H2
Hale *Cumb.* **LA7** 55 J2
Hale *Gt.Man.* **WA15** 49 G4
Hale *Halton* **L24** 48 D4
Hale *Hants.* **SP6** 10 C3
Hale *Surr.* **GU9** 22 B7
Hale Bank **WA8** 48 D4
Hale Barns **WA15** 49 G4
Hale Nook **PR3** 55 G5
Hale Street **TN12** 23 K7
Hales *Norf.* **NR14** 45 H6
Hales *Staffs.* **TF9** 39 G2
Hales Green **DE6** 40 D1
Hales Place **CT2** 15 G2
Halesgate **PE12** 43 G3
Halesowen B63 40 **B7**
Halesworth IP19 35 **H1**
Halewood **L26** 48 D4
Half Way Inn **EX5** 7 J6
Halford *Devon* **TQ12** 5 J3
Halford *Shrop.* **SY7** 38 D7
Halford *Warks.* **CV36** 30 D4
Halfpenny **LA8** 55 J1
Halfpenny Green **DY7** 40 A6
Halfway *Carmar.* **SA19** 17 K2
Halfway *Carmar.* **SA15** 17 J5
Halfway *Powys* **SA20** 27 H5
Halfway *S.Yorks.* **S20** 51 G4
Halfway *W.Berks.* **RG20** 21 H5
Halfway Bridge **GU28** 12 C4
Halfway House **SY5** 38 C4
Halfway Houses *Kent* **ME12** 25 F4
Halfway Houses *Lincs.* **LN6** 52 B6
Halghton Mill **LL13** 38 D1
HALIFAX HX 57 **F7**
Halistra **IV55** 93 H6
Halket **KA3** 74 C5
Halkirk KW12 105 **G3**
Halkyn **CH8** 48 B5
Hall **G78** 74 C5
Hall Cross **PR4** 55 H7
Hall Dunnerdale **LA20** 60 D7
Hall Green *Ches.* **ST7** 49 H7
Hall Green *Lancs.* **PR4** 55 H7
Hall Green *W.Mid.* **B28** 40 D7
Hall Grove **AL7** 33 F7
Hall of the Forest **SY7** 38 B7
Halland **BN8** 13 J5
Hallaton **LE16** 42 A6
Hallatrow **BS39** 19 K6
Hallbankgate **CA8** 61 G1
Hallen **BS10** 19 J3
Hallfield Gate **DE55** 51 F7
Hallglen **FK1** 75 G3
Hallin **IV55** 93 H6
Halling **ME2** 24 D5
Hallington *Lincs.* **LN11** 53 G4
Hallington *Northumb.* **NE19** 70 E6
Halliwell **BL1** 49 F1
Halloughton **NG25** 51 J7
Hallow **WR2** 29 H3
Hallow Heath **WR2** 29 H3
Hallrule **TD9** 70 A2
Halls **EH42** 76 E3
Halls Green *Essex* **CM19** 23 H1
Hall's Green *Herts.* **SG4** 33 F6
Hallsands **TQ7** 5 J7
Hallthwaites **LA18** 54 E1
Hallwood Green **GL18** 29 F5
Hallworthy **PL32** 4 B2
Hallyne **EH45** 75 K6
Halmer End **ST7** 39 G1
Halmond's Frome **WR6** 29 F4
Halmore **GL13** 19 K1
Halmyre Mains **EH46** 75 K6
Halnaker **PO18** 12 C6
Halsall **L39** 48 C1
Halse *Northants.* **NN13** 31 G4
Halse *Som.* **TA4** 7 K3
Halsetown **TR26** 2 C5
Halsham **HU12** 59 J7
Halsinger **EX33** 6 D2
Halstead *Essex* CO9 34 **C5**
Halstead *Kent* **TN14** 23 H5
Halstead *Leics.* **LE7** 42 A5
Halstock **BA22** 8 E4
Halsway **TA4** 7 K2
Haltemprice Farm **HU10** 59 G6
Haltham **LN9** 53 F6
Haltoft End **PE22** 43 G1
Halton *Bucks.* **HP22** 32 B7
Halton *Halton* **WA7** 48 E4
Halton *Lancs.* **LA2** 55 J3
Halton *Northumb.* **NE45** 70 E7
Halton *Wrex.* **LL14** 38 C2
Halton East **BD23** 57 F4
Halton Gill **BD23** 56 D2
Halton Green **LA2** 55 J3
Halton Holegate **PE23** 53 H6
Halton Lea Gate **CA8** 61 H1
Halton Park **LA2** 55 J3
Halton West **BD23** 56 D4
Haltwhistle NE49 70 **C7**
Halvergate **NR13** 45 J5
Halwell **TQ9** 5 H5
Halwill **EX21** 6 C6
Halwill Junction **EX21** 6 C6
Ham *Devon* **EX13** 8 B4
Ham *Glos.* **GL13** 19 K2
Ham *Glos.* **GL52** 29 J6
Ham *Gt.Lon.* **TW10** 22 E4
Ham *High.* **KW14** 105 H1
Ham *Kent* **CT14** 15 J2
Ham *Plym.* **PL2** 4 E5
Ham *Shet.* **ZE2** 107 L2
Ham *Som.* **TA3** 8 B2
Ham *Som.* **TA20** 8 B3
Ham *Wilts.* **SN8** 21 G5
Ham Common **SP8** 9 H2
Ham Green *Here.* **WR13** 29 G4
Ham Green *Kent* **ME9** 24 E5
Ham Green *Kent* **TN30** 14 D5
Ham Green *N.Som.* **BS20** 19 J4

Ham Green *Worcs.* **B97** 30 B2
Ham Hill **ME6** 24 C5
Ham Street **BA6** 8 E1
Hambleden **RG9** 22 A3
Hambledon *Hants.* **PO7** 11 H3
Hambledon *Surr.* **GU8** 12 C3
Hamble-le-Rice **SO31** 11 F4
Hambleton *Lancs.* **FY6** 55 G5
Hambleton *N.Yorks.* **YO8** 58 B6
Hambridge **TA10** 8 C2
Hambrook *S.Glos.* **BS16** 19 K4
Hambrook *W.Suss.* **PO18** 11 J4
Hameringham **LN9** 53 G6
Hamerton **PE28** 32 E1
Hamilton ML3 75 **F5**
Hamlet *Devon* **EX14** 7 K6
Hamlet *Dorset* **DT9** 8 E4
Hammer **GU27** 12 B3
Hammerpot **BN16** 12 D6
Hammersmith **W6** 23 F4
Hammerwich **WS7** 40 C5
Hammerwood **RH19** 13 H3
Hammond Street **EN7** 23 G1
Hammoon **DT10** 9 H3
Hamnavoe *Shet.* **ZE2** 107 M9
Hamnavoe *Shet.* **ZE2** 107 N4
Hamnavoe *Shet.* **ZE2** 107 L4
Hamnavoe *Shet.* **ZE2** 107 N5
Hamnish Clifford **HR6** 28 E3
Hamp **TA6** 8 B1
Hampden Park **BN22** 13 K6
Hamperden End **CB11** 33 J5
Hampnett **GL54** 30 C7
Hampole **DN6** 51 H2
Hampreston **BH21** 10 B5
Hampstead **NW3** 23 F3
Hampstead Norreys **RG18** 21 J4
Hampsthwaite **HG3** 57 H4
Hampton *Devon* **EX13** 8 B5
Hampton *Gt.Lon.* TW12 22 **E5**
Hampton *Kent* **CT6** 25 H5
Hampton *Peter.* **PE7** 42 E6
Hampton *Shrop.* **WV16** 39 G7
Hampton *Swin.* **SN6** 20 E2
Hampton *Worcs.* **WR11** 30 B4
Hampton Bishop **HR1** 28 E5
Hampton Fields **GL6** 20 B2
Hampton Heath **SY14** 38 D1
Hampton in Arden **B92** 40 E7
Hampton Loade **WV15** 39 G7
Hampton Lovett **WR9** 29 H2
Hampton Lucy **CV35** 30 D3
Hampton on the Hill **CV35** 30 D2
Hampton Poyle **OX5** 31 G7
Hampton Wick **KT1** 22 E5
Hamptworth **SP5** 10 D3
Hamsey **BN8** 13 H5
Hamstall Ridware **WS15** 40 D4
Hamstead **PO41** 10 E5
Hamstead Marshall **RG20** 21 H5
Hamsteels **DH7** 62 C2
Hamsterley *Dur.* **DL13** 62 C3
Hamsterley *Dur.* **NE17** 62 C1
Hamstreet **TN26** 15 F4
Hamworthy **BH15** 9 J5
Hanbury *Staffs.* **DE13** 40 D3
Hanbury *Worcs.* **B60** 29 J2
Hanbury Woodend **DE13** 40 D3
Hanby **NG33** 42 D2
Hanchurch **ST4** 40 A1
Handa Island **IV27** 102 D4
Handale **TS13** 63 J5
Handbridge **CH4** 48 D6
Handcross **RH17** 13 F3
Handforth **SK9** 49 H4
Handley *Ches.* **CH3** 48 D7
Handley *Derbys.* **DE55** 51 F6
Handley Green **CM4** 24 C1
Handsacre **WS15** 40 C4
Handside **AL8** 33 F7
Handsworth *S.Yorks.* **S13** 51 G4
Handsworth *W.Mid.* **B21** 40 C6
Handwoodbank **SY5** 38 D4
Handy Cross **SL7** 22 B2
Hanford *Dorset* **DT11** 9 H3
Hanford *Stoke* **ST4** 40 A1
Hanging Bridge **DE6** 40 D1
Hanging Houghton **NN6** 31 J1
Hanging Langford **SP3** 10 B1
Hangingshaw **DG11** 69 G5
Hanham **BS15** 19 K4
Hankelow **CW3** 39 F1
Hankerton **SN16** 20 C2
Hankham **BN24** 13 K6
Hanley **ST1** 40 A1
Hanley Castle **WR8** 29 H4
Hanley Child **WR15** 29 F2
Hanley Swan **WR8** 29 H4
Hanley William **WR15** 29 F2
Hanlith **BD23** 56 E3
Hanmer **SY13** 38 D2
Hannah **LN13** 53 H5
Hannington *Hants.* **RG26** 21 J6
Hannington *Northants.* **NN6** 32 B1
Hannington *Swin.* **SN6** 20 E2
Hannington Wick **SN6** 20 E2
Hanslope **MK19** 32 B4
Hanthorpe **PE10** 42 D3
Hanwell *Gt.Lon.* **W7** 22 E3
Hanwell *Oxon.* **OX17** 31 F4
Hanwood **SY5** 38 D5
Hanworth *Gt.Lon.* **TW13** 22 E4
Hanworth *Norf.* **NR11** 45 F2
Happisburgh **NR12** 45 H2
Happisburgh Common **NR12** 45 H3
Hapsford **WA6** 48 D5
Hapton *Lancs.* **BB11** 56 C6
Hapton *Norf.* **NR15** 45 F6
Harberton **TQ9** 5 H5
Harbertonford **TQ9** 5 H5
Harbledown **CT2** 15 G2
Harborne **B17** 40 C7
Harborough Magna **CV23** 31 F1
Harbost (Tabost) **HS2** 101 H1
Harbottle **NE65** 70 E3
Harbourneford **TQ10** 5 H4
Harbridge **BH24** 10 C3
Harbridge Green **BH24** 10 C3
Harburn **EH55** 75 J4
Harbury **CV33** 30 E3
Harby *Leics.* **LE14** 42 A2
Harby *Notts.* **NG23** 52 B5
Harcombe **EX10** 7 K6
Harcombe Bottom **DT7** 8 C5
Harden *W.Mid.* **WS3** 40 C5
Harden *W.Yorks.* **BD16** 57 F6
Hardendale **CA10** 61 G5
Hardenhuish **SN14** 20 C4
Hardgate *Aber.* **AB31** 91 F4
Hardgate *N.Yorks.* **HG3** 57 H3
Hardham **RH20** 12 D5
Hardhorn **FY6** 55 G6
Hardingham **NR9** 44 E5
Hardingstone **NN4** 31 J3
Hardington **BA11** 20 A6
Hardington Mandeville **BA22** 8 E3
Hardington Marsh **BA22** 8 E4
Hardington Moor **BA22** 8 E3
Hardley **SO45** 11 F4
Hardley Street **NR14** 45 H5
Hardmead **MK16** 32 C4
Hardraw **DL8** 61 K7
Hardstoft **S45** 51 G6
Hardway *Hants.* **PO12** 11 H4
Hardway *Som.* **BA10** 9 G1
Hardwick *Bucks.* **HP22** 32 B7
Hardwick *Cambs.* **CB3** 33 G3
Hardwick *Lincs.* **LN1** 52 B5
Hardwick *Norf.* **NR15** 45 G6
Hardwick *Northants.* **NN9** 32 B2
Hardwick *Oxon.* **OX29** 21 G1
Hardwick *Oxon.* **OX27** 31 G6
Hardwick *S.Yorks.* **S26** 51 G4
Hardwick *W.Mid.* **B74** 40 C6
Hardwick Village **S80** 51 J5
Hardwicke *Glos.* **GL51** 29 J6
Hardwicke *Glos.* **GL2** 29 G7
Hardwicke *Here.* **HR3** 28 B4
Hardy's Green **CO2** 34 D6
Hare Green **CO7** 34 E6
Hare Hatch **RG10** 22 B4
Hare Street *Herts.* **SG2** 33 G6
Hare Street *Herts.* **SG9** 33 G6
Hareby **PE23** 53 G6
Harecroft **BD15** 57 F6
Hareden **BB7** 56 B4
Harefield **UB9** 22 D2
Harehill **DE6** 40 D2
Harehills **LS9** 57 J6
Harehope **NE66** 71 F1
Harelaw **ML11** 75 H6
Hareplain **TN27** 14 D4
Haresceugh **CA10** 61 H2
Harescombe **GL4** 29 H7
Haresfield **GL10** 29 H7
Hareshaw *N.Lan.* **ML1** 75 G4
Hareshaw *S.Lan.* **ML10** 74 E6
Harestock **SO22** 11 F1
Harewood **LS17** 57 J5
Harewood End **HR2** 28 E6
Harford *Devon* **PL21** 5 G5
Harford *Devon* **EX6** 7 G6
Hargate **NR16** 45 F6
Hargatewall **SK17** 50 D5
Hargrave *Ches.* **CH3** 48 D6
Hargrave *Northants.* **NN9** 32 D1
Hargrave *Suff.* **IP29** 34 B3
Hargrave Green **IP29** 34 B3
Harker **CA6** 69 J7
Harkstead **IP9** 35 F5
Harlaston **B79** 40 E4
Harlaxton **NG32** 42 B2
Harle Syke **BB10** 56 D6
Harlech LL46 36 **E2**
Harlequin **NG12** 41 J2
Harlescott **SY1** 38 E4
Harlesden **NW10** 23 F3
Harleston *Devon* **TQ7** 5 H6
Harleston *Norf.* IP20 45 **G7**
Harleston *Suff.* **IP14** 34 E2
Harlestone **NN7** 31 J2
Harley *S.Yorks.* **S62** 51 F3
Harley *Shrop.* **SY5** 38 E5
Harleyholm **ML12** 75 H7
Harlington *Beds.* **LU5** 32 D5
Harlington *Gt.Lon.* **UB3** 22 D4
Harlosh **IV55** 93 H7
Harlow CM17 33 **H7**
Harlow Hill **NE15** 71 F7
Harlthorpe **YO8** 58 D6
Harlton **CB3** 33 G3
Harlyn **PL28** 3 F1
Harman's Cross **BH19** 9 J6
Harmby **DL8** 57 G1
Harmer Green **AL6** 33 F7
Harmer Hill **SY4** 38 D3
Harmondsworth **UB7** 22 D4
Harmston **LN5** 52 C6
Harnage **SY5** 38 E5
Harnham **SP2** 10 C2
Harnhill **GL7** 20 D1
Harold Hill **RM3** 23 J2
Harold Park **RM3** 23 J2
Harold Wood **RM3** 23 J2
Haroldston West **SA62** 16 B4
Haroldswick **ZE2** 107 Q1
Harome **YO62** 58 C1
Harpenden AL5 32 **E7**
Harpford **EX10** 7 J6
Harpham **YO25** 59 G3
Harpley *Norf.* **PE31** 44 B3
Harpley *Worcs.* **WR6** 29 F2
Harpole **NN7** 31 H2
Harprigg **LA6** 56 B1
Harpsdale **KW12** 105 G3
Harpsden **RG9** 22 A3
Harpswell **DN21** 52 C4
Harpur Hill **SK17** 50 C5
Harpurhey **M9** 49 H2
Harracott **EX31** 6 D3
Harrapool **IV49** 86 C2
Harrietfield **PH1** 82 A5
Harrietsham **ME17** 14 D2
Harringay **N8** 23 G3
Harrington *Cumb.* **CA14** 60 A4
Harrington *Lincs.* **PE23** 53 G5
Harrington *Northants.* **NN6** 31 J1
Harringworth **NN17** 42 C6
Harris **PH43** 85 J5
Harris Green **NR15** 45 G6
Harriseahead **ST7** 49 H7
Harriston **CA7** 60 C2
HARROGATE HG 57 **J4**
Harrold **MK43** 32 C3
Harrop Fold **BB7** 56 C5
HARROW *Gt.Lon.* HA 22 **E3**
Harrow *High.* **KW14** 105 H1
Harrow Green **IP29** 34 C3
Harrow on the Hill **HA1** 22 E3
Harrow Weald **HA3** 22 E2
Harrowbarrow **PL17** 4 E3
Harrowden **MK42** 32 D4
Harrowgate Hill **DL3** 62 D5
Harry Stoke **BS34** 19 K4
Harston *Cambs.* **CB2** 33 H3
Harston *Leics.* **NG32** 42 B2
Harswell **YO42** 58 E5
Hart **TS27** 63 F3
Hartburn **NE61** 71 F5
Hartest **IP29** 34 C3
Hartfield *E.Suss.* TN7 13 **H3**
Hartfield *High.* **IV54** 94 D7
Hartford *Cambs.* **PE29** 33 F1
Hartford *Ches.* **CW8** 49 F5
Hartford *Som.* **TA22** 7 H3
Hartford End **CM3** 33 K7
Hartfordbridge **RG27** 22 A6
Hartforth **DL10** 62 C6
Hartgrove **SP7** 9 H3
Harthill *Ches.* **CH3** 48 E7
Harthill *N.Lan.* **ML7** 75 H4
Harthill *S.Yorks.* **S26** 51 G4
Hartington **SK17** 50 D6
Hartington Hall **NE61** 71 F5
Hartland **EX39** 6 A3
Hartland Quay **EX39** 6 A3
Hartlebury **DY11** 29 H1
Hartlepool TS24 63 **G3**
Hartley *Cumb.* **CA17** 61 J6
Hartley *Kent* **DA3** 24 C5
Hartley *Kent* **TN17** 14 C4
Hartley *Northumb.* **NE26** 71 J6
Hartley Green **ST18** 40 B3
Hartley Mauditt **GU34** 11 J1
Hartley Wespall **RG27** 21 K6
Hartley Wintney **RG27** 22 A6
Hartlington **BD23** 57 F3
Hartlip **ME9** 24 E5
Hartoft End **YO18** 63 J7
Harton *N.Yorks.* **YO60** 58 D3
Harton *Shrop.* **SY6** 38 D7
Harton *T.& W.* **NE34** 71 J7
Hartpury **GL19** 29 H6
Hartrigge **TD8** 70 B1
Hartshead **WF15** 57 G7
Hartshill **CV10** 41 F6
Hartshorne **DE11** 41 F3
Hartsop **CA10** 60 F5
Hartwell *Bucks.* **HP17** 31 J7
Hartwell *E.Suss.* **TN7** 13 H3
Hartwell *Northants.* **NN7** 31 J3
Hartwith **HG3** 57 H3
Hartwood **ML7** 75 G5
Harvel **DA13** 24 C5
Harvington *Worcs.* **WR11** 30 B4
Harvington *Worcs.* **DY10** 29 H1
Harwell *Notts.* **DN10** 51 J3
Harwell *Oxon.* **OX11** 21 H3
Harwich CO12 35 **G5**
Harwood *Dur.* **DL12** 61 K3
Harwood *Gt.Man.* **BL2** 49 G1
Harwood *Northumb.* **NE61** 71 F4
Harwood Dale **YO13** 63 J3
Harwood on Teviot **TD9** 69 K3
Harworth **DN11** 51 J3
Hasbury **B63** 40 B7
Hascombe **GU8** 22 D7
Haselbech **NN6** 31 J1
Haselbury Plucknett **TA18** 8 D3
Haseley **CV35** 30 D2
Haseley Knob **CV35** 30 D1
Haselor **B49** 30 C3
Hasfield **GL19** 29 H6
Hasguard **SA62** 16 B5
Haskayne **L39** 48 C2
Hasketon **IP13** 35 G3
Hasland **S41** 51 F6
Hasland Green **S41** 51 F6
Haslemere GU27 12 **C3**
Haslingden **BB4** 56 C7
Haslingden Grane **BB4** 56 C7
Haslingfield **CB3** 33 H3
Haslington **CW1** 49 G7
Hassall **CW11** 49 G7
Hassall Green **CW11** 49 G7
Hassell Street **TN25** 15 F3
Hassendean **TD9** 70 A1
Hassingham **NR13** 45 H5
Hassocks BN6 13 **G5**
Hassop **DE45** 50 E5
Haster **KW1** 105 J3
Hasthorpe **LN13** 53 H6
Hastigrow **KW1** 105 H2
Hastingleigh **TN25** 15 F3
Hastings *E.Suss.* TN34 14 **D7**
Hastings *Som.* **TA19** 8 C3
Hastingwood **CM17** 23 H1
Hastoe **HP23** 22 C1
Haswell **DH6** 62 E2
Haswell Plough **DH6** 62 E2
Hatch *Beds.* **SG19** 32 E4
Hatch *Hants.* **RG24** 21 K6
Hatch Beauchamp **TA3** 8 C2
Hatch End **HA5** 22 E2
Hatch Green **TA3** 8 C3
Hatching Green **AL5** 32 E7
Hatchmere **WA6** 48 E5
Hatcliffe **DN37** 53 F2
Hatfield *Here.* **HR6** 28 E3
Hatfield *Herts.* AL10 23 **F1**
Hatfield *S.Yorks.* **DN7** 51 J2
Hatfield Broad Oak **CM22** 33 J7
Hatfield Heath **CM22** 33 J7
Hatfield Peverel **CM3** 34 B7
Hatfield Woodhouse **DN7** 51 J2
Hatford **SN7** 21 G2
Hatherden **SP11** 21 G6
Hatherleigh **EX20** 6 D5
Hathern **LE12** 41 G3
Hatherop **GL7** 20 E1
Hathersage **S32** 50 E4
Hathersage Booths **S32** 50 E4
Hathershaw **OL8** 49 J2
Hatherton *Ches.* **CW5** 39 F1
Hatherton *Staffs.* **WS11** 40 B4
Hatley St. George **SG19** 33 F3
Hatt **PL12** 4 D4
Hattingley **GU34** 11 H1
Hatton *Aber.* **AB42** 91 J1
Hatton *Derbys.* **DE65** 40 E3
Hatton *Gt.Lon.* **TW14** 22 E4
Hatton *Lincs.* **LN8** 52 E5
Hatton *Shrop.* **SY6** 38 D6
Hatton *Warks.* **CV35** 30 D2
Hatton *Warr.* **WA4** 48 E4
Hatton Castle **AB53** 99 F6
Hatton Heath **CH3** 48 D6
Hatton of Fintray **AB21** 91 G3
Hattoncrook **AB21** 91 G2
Haugh **LN13** 53 H5
Haugh Head **NE71** 71 F1
Haugh of Glass **AB54** 90 C1
Haugh of Urr **DG7** 65 J4
Haugham **LN11** 53 G4
Haughhead **G66** 74 E3
Haughley **IP14** 34 E2
Haughley Green **IP14** 34 E2
Haughley New Street **IP14** 34 E2
Haughs **AB54** 98 D6
Haughton *Ches.* **CW6** 48 E7
Haughton *Notts.* **DN22** 51 J5
Haughton *Powys* **SY22** 38 C4
Haughton *Shrop.* **WV16** 39 F6
Haughton *Shrop.* **SY4** 38 E4
Haughton *Shrop.* **SY11** 38 C3
Haughton *Staffs.* **ST18** 40 A3
Haughton Green **M34** 49 J3
Haughton Le Skerne **DL1** 62 E5
Haultwick **SG11** 33 G6
Haunn **HS8** 84 C3
Haunton **B79** 40 E4
Hauxton **CB2** 33 H3
Havannah **CW12** 49 H6
Havant PO9 11 **J4**
Haven **HR4** 28 D3
Havenstreet **PO33** 11 G5
Havercroft **WF4** 51 F1
Haverfordwest (Hwlffordd) SA61 16 **C4**
Haverhill CB9 33 **K4**
Haverigg **LA18** 54 E2
Havering Park **RM5** 23 H2
Havering-atte-Bower **RM4** 23 J2
Haversham **MK19** 32 B4
Haverthwaite **LA12** 55 G1
Haverton Hill **TS23** 63 F4
Haviker Street **TN12** 14 C3
Havyat **BA6** 8 E1
Hawarden (Penarlâg) **CH5** 48 C6
Hawbridge **WR8** 29 J4
Hawbush Green **CM77** 34 B6
Hawcoat **LA14** 55 F2
Hawes DL8 56 **D1**
Hawe's Green **NR15** 45 G6
Hawick TD9 70 **A2**
Hawkchurch **EX13** 8 C4
Hawkedon **IP29** 34 B3
Hawkenbury *Kent* **TN2** 13 J3
Hawkenbury *Kent* **TN12** 14 D3
Hawkeridge **BA13** 20 B6
Hawkerland **EX10** 7 J7
Hawkes End **CV5** 40 E7
Hawkesbury **GL9** 20 A3
Hawkesbury Upton **GL9** 20 A3
Hawkhill **NE66** 71 H2
Hawkhurst **TN18** 14 C4
Hawkinge **CT18** 15 H3
Hawkley **GU33** 11 J2
Hawkridge **TA22** 7 G2
Hawkshead **LA22** 60 E7
Hawkshead Hill **LA22** 60 E7
Hawksheads **LA5** 55 H3
Hawksland **ML11** 75 G6
Hawkswick **BD23** 56 E2
Hawksworth *Notts.* **NG13** 42 A1
Hawksworth *W.Yorks.* **LS20** 57 G5
Hawksworth *W.Yorks.* **LS18** 57 H6
Hawkwell *Essex* **SS5** 24 E2
Hawkwell *Northumb.* **NE18** 71 F6
Hawley *Hants.* **GU17** 22 B6
Hawley *Kent* **DA2** 23 J4
Hawley's Corner **TN16** 23 H6
Hawling **GL54** 30 B6
Hawnby **YO62** 58 B1
Haworth **BD22** 57 F6
Hawstead **IP29** 34 C3
Hawstead Green **IP29** 34 C3
Hawthorn *Dur.* **SR7** 63 F2
Hawthorn *Hants.* **GU34** 11 H1
Hawthorn *R.C.T.* **CF37** 18 D3
Hawthorn *Wilts.* **SN13** 20 B5
Hawthorn Hill *Brack.F.* **RG42** 22 B4
Hawthorn Hill *Lincs.* **LN4** 53 F7
Hawthorpe **PE10** 42 D3
Hawton **NG24** 51 K7
Haxby **YO32** 58 C4
Haxey **DN9** 51 K2
Haxted **TN8** 23 H7
Haxton **SP4** 20 E7
Hay Green **PE34** 43 J4
Hay Mills **B25** 40 D7
Hay Street **SG11** 33 G6
Haydock **WA11** 48 E3
Haydon *Dorset* **DT9** 9 F3
Haydon *Swin.* **SN25** 20 E3
Haydon Bridge **NE47** 70 D7
Haydon Wick **SN25** 20 E3
Hayes *Gt.Lon.* UB3 22 **D3**
Hayes *Gt.Lon.* **BR2** 23 H5
Hayes End **UB4** 22 D3
Hayfield *Arg. & B.* **PA35** 80 B5
Hayfield *Derbys.* **SK22** 50 C4
Hayfield *Fife* **KY2** 76 A1
Hayfield *High.* **KW14** 105 G2
Haygrove **TA6** 8 B1
Hayhillock **DD11** 83 G3
Hayle TR27 2 **C5**
Hayling Island PO11 11 **J4**
Haymoor Green **CW5** 49 F7
Hayne **EX16** 7 H4
Haynes **MK45** 32 E4
Haynes Church End **MK45** 32 D4
Haynes West End **MK45** 32 D4
Hay-on-Wye (Y Gelli Gandryll) **HR3** 28 B4
Hayscastle **SA62** 16 B3
Hayscastle Cross **SA62** 16 C3
Hayton *Cumb.* **CA8** 61 G1
Hayton *Cumb.* **CA7** 60 C2
Hayton *E.Riding* **YO42** 58 E5
Hayton *Notts.* **DN22** 51 K4
Hayton's Bent **SY8** 38 E7
Haytor Vale **TQ13** 5 H3
Haytown **EX22** 6 B4
Haywards Heath RH16 13 **G4**
Haywood Oaks **NG21** 51 J7
Hazel End **CM23** 33 H6
Hazel Grove **SK7** 49 J4
Hazel Street **TN12** 13 K3
Hazelbank *Arg. & B.* **PA25** 80 B7
Hazelbank *S.Lan.* **ML11** 75 G6
Hazelbury Bryan **DT10** 9 G4
Hazeleigh **CM3** 24 E1
Hazeley **RG27** 22 A6
Hazelhurst **BL8** 49 G1
Hazelside **ML11** 68 D1
Hazelslack **LA7** 55 H2
Hazelslade **WS12** 40 C4
Hazelton Walls **KY15** 82 E5
Hazelwood *Derbys.* **DE56** 41 F1
Hazelwood *Gt.Lon.* **TN14** 23 H5
Hazlefield **DG7** 65 H6
Hazlehead *Aberdeen* **AB15** 91 G4
Hazlehead *S.Yorks.* **S36** 50 D2
Hazlemere **HP15** 22 B2
Hazlerigg **NE13** 71 H6
Hazleton **GL54** 30 B7
Hazon **NE65** 71 G3
Heacham **PE31** 44 A2
Head Bridge **EX37** 6 E4
Headbourne Worthy **SO23** 11 F1
Headcorn **TN27** 14 D3
Headingley **LS6** 57 H6
Headington **OX3** 21 J1
Headlam **DL2** 62 C5
Headless Cross **B97** 30 B2
Headley *Hants.* **GU35** 12 B3
Headley *Hants.* **RG19** 21 J5
Headley *Surr.* **KT18** 23 F6
Headley Down **GU35** 12 B3
Headley Heath **B38** 30 B1
Headon **DN22** 51 K5
Heads Nook **CA8** 61 F1
Heady Hill **OL10** 49 H1
Heage **DE56** 51 F7
Healaugh *N.Yorks.* **DL11** 62 B7
Healaugh *N.Yorks.* **LS24** 58 B5
Heald Green **SK8** 49 H4
Heale *Devon* **EX31** 6 E1
Heale *Som.* **TA10** 8 C2
Healey *Lancs.* **OL12** 49 H1
Healey *N.Yorks.* **HG4** 57 G1
Healey *Northumb.* **NE44** 62 B1
Healey *W.Yorks.* **WF17** 57 H7
Healeyfield **DH8** 62 B2
Healing **DN41** 53 F1
Heamoor **TR18** 2 B5
Heaning **LA23** 60 F7
Heanish **PA77** 78 B3
Heanor DE75 41 **G1**
Heanton Punchardon **EX31** 6 D2

Heanton Satchville EX20 6 D4
Heap Bridge BL9 49 H1
Heapey PR6 56 B7
Heapham DN21 52 B4
Hearn GU35 12 B3
Hearthstane ML12 69 G1
Heasley Mill EX36 7 F2
Heast IV49 86 C3
Heath Cardiff CF14 18 E3
Heath Derbys. S44 51 G6
Heath W.Yorks. WF1 51 F1
Heath and Reach LU7 32 C6
Heath End Derbys. LE65 41 F3
Heath End Hants. RG26 21 J5
Heath End Hants. RG20 21 H5
Heath End Surr. GU9 22 B7
Heath Hayes WS12 40 C4
Heath Hill TF11 39 G4
Heath House BS28 19 H7
Heath Town WV10 40 B6
Heathbrook TF9 39 F3
Heathcot AB12 91 G4
Heathcote Derbys. SK17 50 D6
Heathcote Shrop. TF9 39 F3
Heathencote NN12 31 J4
Heather LE67 41 F4
Heathfield Devon TQ12 5 J3
Heathfield E.Suss. TN21 13 J4
Heathfield N.Yorks. HG3 57 G3
Heathfield Som. TA4 7 K3
Heathrow Airport TW6 22 D4
Heathton WV5 40 A6
Heatley WA13 49 G4
Heaton Lancs. LA3 55 H3
Heaton Staffs. SK11 49 J6
Heaton T.& W. NE6 71 H7
Heaton W.Yorks. BD9 57 G6
Heaton Moor SK4 49 H3
Heaton's Bridge L40 48 D1
Heaverham TN15 23 J6
Heaviley SK2 49 J4
Heavitree EX1 7 H6
Hebburn NE31 71 J7
Hebden BD23 57 F3
Hebden Bridge HX7 56 E7
Hebden Green CW7 49 F6
Hebing End SG2 33 G6
Hebron Carmar. SA34 16 E3
Hebron Northumb. NE61 71 G5
Heck DG11 69 F5
Heckfield RG27 22 A5
Heckfield Green IP21 35 F1
Heckfordbridge CO3 34 D6
Heckingham NR14 45 H6
Heckington NG34 42 E1
Heckmondwike WF16 57 H7
Heddington SN11 20 C5
Heddle KW17 106 C6
Heddon-on-the-Wall NE15 71 G7
Hedenham NR35 45 H6
Hedge End SO30 11 F3
Hedgerley SL2 22 C3
Hedging TA7 8 C2
Hedley on the Hill NE43 62 B1
Hednesford WS12 40 C4
Hedon HU12 59 H7
Hedsor HP10 22 C3
Heeley S8 51 F4
Heglibister ZE2 107 M7
Heighington Darl. DL5 62 D4
Heighington Lincs. LN4 52 D6
Heightington DY12 29 G1
Heights of Brae IV14 96 C5
Heilam IV27 103 G3
Heisker Islands (Monach Islands) HS6 92 B5
Heithat DG11 69 G5
Heiton TD5 77 F7
Hele Devon EX34 6 D1
Hele Devon EX5 7 H5
Hele Devon PL15 6 B6
Hele Devon TQ13 5 H3
Hele Som. TA4 7 K3
Hele Torbay TQ1 5 K4
Hele Bridge EX20 6 D5
Hele Lane EX17 7 F4
Helebridge EX23 6 A5
Helensburgh G84 74 A2
Helford TR12 2 E6
Helhoughton NR21 44 C3
Helions Bumpstead CB9 33 K4
Hell Corner RG17 21 G5
Hellaby S66 51 H3
Helland Cornw. PL30 4 A3
Helland Som. TA3 8 C2
Hellandbridge PL30 4 A3
Hellesdon NR6 45 G4
Hellidon NN11 31 G3
Hellifield BD23 56 D4
Hellingly BN27 13 J5
Hellington NR14 45 H5
Hellister ZE2 107 M8
Helmdon NN13 31 G4
Helmingham IP14 35 F3
Helmington Row DL15 62 C3
Helmsdale KW8 105 F7
Helmshore BB4 56 C7
Helmsley YO62 58 C1
Helperby YO61 57 K3
Helperthorpe YO17 59 F2
Helpringham NG34 42 E1
Helpston PE6 42 E5
Helsby WA6 48 D5
Helsey PE24 53 J5
Helston TR13 2 D6
Helstone PL32 4 A2
Helton CA10 61 G4
Helwith DL11 62 B6
Helwith Bridge BD24 56 D3
Hem SY21 38 B5
Hemborough Post TQ9 5 J5
HEMEL HEMPSTEAD HP 22 D1
Hemerdon PL7 5 F5
Hemingbrough YO8 58 C6
Hemingby LN9 53 F5
Hemingfield S73 51 F2
Hemingford Abbots PE28 33 F1
Hemingford Grey PE28 33 F1
Hemingstone IP6 35 F3
Hemington Leics. DE74 41 G3
Hemington Northants. PE8 42 D7
Hemington Som. BA3 20 A6
Hemley IP12 35 G4
Hemlington TS8 63 F5
Hemp Green IP17 35 H2
Hempholme YO25 59 G4
Hempnall NR15 45 G6
Hempnall Green NR15 45 G6
Hempriggs IV36 97 J5
Hempriggs House KW1 105 J4
Hempstead Essex CB10 33 K5
Hempstead Med. ME7 24 D5
Hempstead Norf. NR12 45 J3
Hempstead Norf. NR25 45 F2
Hempsted GL2 29 H7
Hempton Norf. NR21 44 D3
Hempton Oxon. OX15 31 F5
Hemsby NR29 45 J4
Hemswell DN21 52 C3
Hemswell Cliff DN21 52 C4
Hemsworth WF9 51 G1
Hemyock EX15 7 K4
Henbury Bristol BS10 19 J4
Henbury Ches. SK10 49 H5
Henderland DG2 65 J3
Hendersyde Park TD5 77 F7
Hendham TQ7 5 H5
Hendon Gt.Lon. NW4 23 F3
Hendon T.& W. SR2 62 E1
Hendraburnick PL32 4 B2
Hendre Bridgend CF35 18 C3
Hendre Gwyn. LL53 36 C2
Hendreforgan CF39 18 C3
Hendy SA4 17 J5
Hendy-Gwyn (Whitland) SA34 17 F4
Heneglwys LL77 46 C5
Henfield S.Glos. BS36 19 K4
Henfield W.Suss. BN5 13 F5
Henford EX21 6 B6
Henghurst TN26 14 E4
Hengoed Caerp. CF82 18 E2
Hengoed Powys HR5 28 B3
Hengoed Shrop. SY10 38 B2
Hengrave IP28 34 C2
Henham CM22 33 J6
Heniarth SY21 38 A5
Henlade TA3 8 B2
Henley Dorset DT2 9 F4
Henley Shrop. SY8 28 E1
Henley Som. TA10 8 D1
Henley Som. TA18 8 D4
Henley Suff. IP6 35 F3
Henley W.Suss. GU27 12 B4
Henley Corner TA10 8 D1
Henley Park GU3 22 C6
Henley-in-Arden B95 30 C2
Henley-on-Thames RG9 22 A3
Henley's Down TN33 14 C6
Henllan Carmar. SA44 17 G1
Henllan Denb. LL16 47 J6
Henllan Amgoed SA34 16 E3
Henllys NP44 19 F2
Henlow SG16 32 E5
Hennock TQ13 7 G7
Henny Street CO10 34 C5
Henryd LL32 47 F5
Henry's Moat SA63 16 D3
Hensall DN14 58 B7
Henshaw NE47 70 C7
Hensingham CA28 60 A5
Henstead NR34 45 J7
Hensting SO21 11 F2
Henstridge BA8 9 G3
Henstridge Ash BA8 9 G3
Henstridge Bowden BA8 9 F2
Henstridge Marsh BA8 9 G2
Henton Oxon. OX39 22 A1
Henton Som. BA5 19 H7
Henwood PL14 4 C3
Heogan ZE2 107 N8
Heol Senni LD3 27 J6
Heolgerrig CF48 18 D1
Heol-y-Cyw CF35 18 C3
Hepburn NE66 71 F1
Hepburn Bell NE66 71 F1
Hepple NE65 70 E3
Hepscott NE61 71 H5
Hepthorne Lane S42 51 G6
Heptonstall HX7 56 E7
Hepworth Suff. IP22 34 D1
Hepworth W.Yorks. HD9 50 D2
Hepworth South Common IP22 34 D1
Herbrandston SA73 16 B5
HEREFORD HR 28 E4
Heriot EH38 76 B5
Herm GY1 3 J5
Hermiston EH14 75 K3
Hermitage D.& G. DG7 65 H4
Hermitage Dorset DT2 9 F4
Hermitage Sc.Bord. TD9 70 A4
Hermitage W.Berks. RG18 21 J4
Hermitage W.Suss. PO10 11 J4
Hermitage Green WA2 49 F3
Hermon Carmar. SA33 17 G2
Hermon I.o.A. LL62 46 B6
Hermon Pembs. SA36 17 F2
Herne CT6 25 H5
Herne Bay CT6 25 H5
Herne Common CT6 25 H5
Herne Pound ME18 23 K6
Herner EX32 6 D3
Hernhill ME13 25 G5
Herodsfoot PL14 4 C4
Herongate CM13 24 C2
Heron's Ghyll TN22 13 H4
Heronsgate WD3 22 D2
Herriard RG25 21 K7
Herringfleet NR32 45 J6
Herring's Green MK45 32 D4
Herringswell IP28 34 B2
Herringthorpe S65 51 G3
Hersden CT3 25 H5
Hersham Cornw. EX23 6 A5
Hersham Surr. KT12 22 E5
Herstmonceux BN27 13 K5
Herston KW17 106 D8
Hertford SG14 33 G7
Hertford Heath SG13 33 G7
Hertingfordbury SG14 33 G7
Hesket Newmarket CA7 60 E3
Hesketh Bank PR4 55 H7
Hesketh Lane PR3 56 B5
Heskin Green PR7 48 E1
Hesleden TS27 63 F3
Hesleyside NE48 70 D5
Heslington YO10 58 C4
Hessay YO26 58 B4
Hessenford PL11 4 D5
Hessett IP30 34 D2
Hessle HU13 59 G7
Hest Bank LA2 55 H3
Hester's Way GL51 29 J6
Hestley Green IP23 35 F2
Heston TW5 22 E4
Heswall CH60 48 B4
Hethe OX27 31 G6
Hethelpit Cross GL19 29 G6
Hetherington NE48 70 D6
Hethersett NR9 45 F5
Hethersgill CA6 69 K7
Hethpool NE71 70 D1
Hett DH6 62 D3
Hetton BD23 56 E4
Hetton-le-Hole DH5 62 E2
Heugh NE18 71 F6
Heugh-head Aber. AB36 90 B3
Heugh-head Aber. AB34 90 D5
Heveningham IP19 35 H1
Hever TN8 23 H7
Heversham LA7 55 H1
Hevingham NR10 45 F3
Hewas Water PL26 3 G4
Hewell Grange B97 30 B2
Hewell Lane B60 30 B2
Hewelsfield GL15 19 J1
Hewelsfield Common GL15 19 J1
Hewish N.Som. BS24 19 H5
Hewish Som. TA18 8 D4
Hewood TA20 8 C4
Heworth YO31 58 C4
Hewton EX20 6 D6
Hexham NE46 70 E7
Hextable BR8 23 J4
Hexthorpe DN4 51 H2
Hexton SG5 32 E5
Hexworthy PL20 5 G3
Hey BB8 56 D5
Hey Houses FY8 55 G7
Heybridge Essex CM4 24 C2
Heybridge Essex CM9 24 E1
Heybridge Basin CM9 24 E1
Heybrook Bay PL9 4 E6
Heydon Cambs. SG8 33 H4
Heydon Norf. NR11 45 F3
Heydour NG32 42 D2
Heylipoll PA77 78 A3
Heylor ZE2 107 L4
Heyop LD7 28 B1
Heysham LA3 55 H3
Heyshaw HG3 57 G3
Heyshott GU29 12 B5
Heyside OL2 49 J2
Heytesbury BA12 20 C7
Heythrop OX7 30 E6
Heywood Gt.Man. OL10 49 H1
Heywood Wilts. BA13 20 B6
Hibaldstow DN20 52 C2
Hibb's Green IP29 34 C3
Hickleton DN5 51 G2
Hickling Norf. NR12 45 J3
Hickling Notts. LE14 41 J3
Hickling Green NR12 45 J3
Hickling Heath NR12 45 J3
Hickstead RH17 13 F4
Hidcote Bartrim GL55 30 C4
Hidcote Boyce GL55 30 C4
High Ackworth WF7 51 G1
High Angerton NE61 71 F5
High Balantyre PA32 80 B6
High Bankhill CA10 61 G2
High Beach IG10 23 H2
High Bentham (Higher Bentham) LA2 56 B3
High Bickington EX37 6 D3
High Birkwith BD24 56 C2
High Blantyre G72 74 E5
High Bonnybridge FK4 75 G3
High Borgue DG6 65 G5
High Borve HS2 101 G2
High Bradfield S6 50 E3
High Bradley BD20 57 F5
High Bransholme HU7 59 H6
High Bray EX32 6 E2
High Bridge CA5 60 E2
High Brooms TN4 23 J7
High Bullen EX38 6 D3
High Burton HG4 57 H1
High Buston NE66 71 H3
High Callerton NE20 71 G6
High Casterton LA6 56 B2
High Catton YO41 58 D4
High Close DL11 62 C5
High Cogges OX29 21 G1
High Common IP21 45 F7
High Coniscliffe DL2 62 D5
High Crompton OL2 49 J2
High Cross Hants. GU32 11 J2
High Cross Herts. SG11 33 G7
High Cross W.Suss. BN6 13 F5
High Easter CM1 33 K7
High Ellington HG4 57 G1
High Entercommon DL6 62 E6
High Ercall TF6 38 E4
High Etherley DL14 62 C4
High Ferry PE22 43 G1
High Flatts HD8 50 E2
High Garrett CM7 34 B6
High Gate HX7 56 E7
High Grange DL15 62 C3
High Green Norf. NR9 45 F5
High Green Norf. NR19 44 D4
High Green Norf. IP25 44 D5
High Green S.Yorks. S35 51 F3
High Green Suff. IP29 34 C2
High Green Worcs. WR8 29 H4
High Halden TN26 14 D4
High Halstow ME3 24 D4
High Ham TA10 8 D1
High Harrington CA14 60 B4
High Harrogate HG2 57 J4
High Hatton SY4 39 F3
High Hauxley NE65 71 H3
High Hawsker YO22 63 J2
High Heath Shrop. TF9 39 F3
High Heath W.Mid. WS4 40 C5
High Hesket CA4 61 F2
High Hesleden TS27 63 F3
High Hoyland S75 50 E1
High Hunsley YO43 59 F6
High Hurstwood TN22 13 H4
High Hutton YO60 58 D3
High Ireby CA7 60 D3
High Kelling NR25 44 E2
High Kilburn YO61 58 B2
High Kingthorpe YO18 58 E1
High Knipe CA10 61 G5
High Lane Derbys. DE7 41 G1
High Lane Gt.Man. SK6 49 J4
High Lane Worcs. WR6 29 F2
High Laver CM5 23 J1
High Legh WA16 49 G4
High Leven TS15 63 F5
High Littleton BS39 19 K6
High Lorton CA13 60 C4
High Marishes YO17 58 E2
High Marnham NG23 52 B5
High Melton DN5 51 H2
High Moor S21 51 G4
High Newton LA11 55 H1
High Newton-by-the-Sea NE66 71 H1
High Nibthwaite LA12 60 D7
High Offley ST20 39 G3
High Ongar CM5 23 J1
High Onn ST20 40 A4
High Park Corner CO5 34 E6
High Roding CM6 33 K7
High Shaw DL8 61 K7
High Spen NE39 71 G7
High Stoop DL13 62 C2
High Street Cornw. PL26 3 G3
High Street Kent TN18 14 C4
High Street Suff. IP12 35 J3
High Street Suff. NR35 45 H7
High Street Suff. IP17 35 J1
High Street Suff. CO10 34 C4
High Street Green IP14 34 E3
High Throston TS26 63 F3
High Town WS11 40 B4
High Toynton LN9 53 F6
High Trewhitt NE65 71 F3
High Wham DL13 62 C4
High Wigsell TN32 14 C5
High Woolaston GL15 19 J2
High Worsall TS15 62 E6
High Wray LA22 60 E7
High Wych CM21 33 H7
High Wycombe HP13 22 B2
Higham Derbys. DE55 51 F7
Higham Kent ME3 24 D4
Higham Lancs. BB12 56 D6
Higham S.Yorks. S75 51 F2
Higham Suff. IP28 34 B2
Higham Suff. CO7 34 E5
Higham Dykes NE20 71 G6
Higham Ferrers NN10 32 C2
Higham Gobion SG5 32 E5
Higham on the Hill CV13 41 F6
Higham Wood TN10 23 K7
Highampton EX21 6 C5
Highams Park E4 23 G2
Highbridge Hants. SO50 11 F2
Highbridge Som. TA9 19 G7
Highbrook RH17 13 G3
Highburton HD8 50 D1
Highbury BA3 19 K7
Highclere RG20 21 H5
Highcliffe BH23 10 D5
Higher Alham BA4 19 K7
Higher Ansty DT2 9 G4
Higher Ashton EX6 7 G7
Higher Ballam FY8 55 G6
Higher Bentham (High Bentham) LA2 56 B3
Higher Blackley M9 49 H2
Higher Brixham TQ5 5 K5
Higher Cheriton EX14 7 K5
Higher Combe TA22 7 H2
Higher Folds WN7 49 F2
Higher Gabwell TQ1 5 K4
Higher Green M29 49 G3
Higher Halstock Leigh BA22 8 E4
Higher Kingcombe DT2 8 E5
Higher Kinnerton CH4 48 C6
Higher Muddiford EX31 6 D2
Higher Nyland SP8 9 G2
Higher Prestacott EX21 6 B6
Higher Standen BB7 56 C5
Higher Tale EX14 7 J5
Higher Thrushgill LA2 56 B3
Higher Town Cornw. PL26 4 A4
Higher Town I.o.S. TR25 2 C1
Higher Walreddon PL19 4 E3
Higher Walton Lancs. PR5 55 J7
Higher Walton Warr. WA4 48 E4
Higher Wambrook TA20 8 B4
Higher Whatcombe DT11 9 H4
Higher Wheelton PR6 56 B7
Higher Whiteleigh EX22 4 C1
Higher Whitley WA4 49 F4
Higher Wincham CW9 49 F5
Higher Woodhill BL8 49 G1
Higher Woodsford DT2 9 G6
Higher Wraxall DT2 8 E4
Higher Wych SY14 38 D1
Highfield E.Riding YO8 58 D6
Highfield N.Ayr. KA24 74 B5
Highfield Oxon. OX26 31 G6
Highfield S.Yorks. S2 51 F4
Highfield T.& W. NE39 62 C1
Highfields Cambs. CB3 33 G3
Highfields Northumb. TD15 77 H5
Highgate E.Suss. RH18 13 H3
Highgate Gt.Lon. N6 23 F3
Highgreen Manor NE48 70 D4
Highlane Ches. SK11 49 H6
Highlane Derbys. S12 51 G4
Highlaws CA7 60 C2
Highleadon GL18 29 G6
Highleigh Devon TA22 7 H3
Highleigh W.Suss. PO20 12 B7
Highley WV16 39 G7
Highmead SA40 17 J1
Highmoor Cross RG9 21 K3
Highmoor Hill NP26 19 H3
Highnam GL2 29 G7
Highstead CT3 25 J5
Highsted ME9 25 F5
Highstreet ME13 25 G5
Highstreet Green Essex CO9 34 B5
Highstreet Green Surr. GU8 12 C3
Hightae DG11 69 F6
Highter's Heath B14 30 B1
Hightown Hants. BH24 10 C4
Hightown Mersey. L38 48 B2
Hightown Green IP30 34 D3
Highway SN11 20 D4
Highweek TQ12 5 J3
Highwood WR15 29 F2
Highwood Hill NW7 23 F2
Highworth SN6 21 F2
Hilborough IP26 44 C5
Hilcote DE55 51 G7
Hilcott SN9 20 E6
Hilden Park TN11 23 J7
Hildenborough TN11 23 J7
Hildenley YO17 58 D2
Hildersham CB1 33 J4
Hilderstone ST15 40 B2
Hilderthorpe YO15 59 H3
Hilfield DT2 9 F4
Hilgay PE38 44 A6
Hill S.Glos. GL13 19 K2
Hill Warks. CV23 31 F2
Hill Worcs. WR10 29 J4
Hill Brow GU33 11 J2
Hill Chorlton ST5 39 G2
Hill Common NR12 45 J3
Hill Cottages YO18 63 J7
Hill Croome WR8 29 H4
Hill Deverill BA12 20 B7
Hill Dyke PE22 43 G1
Hill End Dur. DL13 62 B3
Hill End Fife KY12 75 J1
Hill End Glos. GL20 29 H5
Hill End Gt.Lon. UB9 22 D2
Hill End N.Yorks. BD23 57 F4
Hill Green CB11 33 H5
Hill Head PO14 11 G4
Hill Houses DY14 29 F1
Hill Mountain SA62 16 C5
Hill of Beath KY4 75 K2
Hill of Fearn IV20 97 F4
Hill Ridware WS15 40 C4
Hill Row CB6 33 H1
Hill Side HD5 50 D1
Hill Street SO40 10 E3
Hill Top Hants. SO42 11 F4
Hill Top S.Yorks. DN12 51 G3
Hill Top S.Yorks. S6 50 E4
Hill View BH21 9 J5
Hill Wootton CV35 30 E2
Hillam LS25 58 B7
Hillbeck CA17 61 J5
Hillberry IM4 54 C6
Hillborough CT6 25 J5
Hillbrae Aber. AB54 98 E6
Hillbrae Aber. AB51 91 F2
Hillbrae Aber. AB51 91 G1
Hillbutts BH21 9 J4
Hillclifflane DE56 40 E1
Hillend Aber. AB55 98 C6
Hillend Fife KY11 75 K2
Hillend Midloth. EH10 76 A4
Hillend N.Lan. ML6 75 G4

Hillend Swan. SA3 17 H6
Hillend Green GL18 29 G6
Hillersland GL16 28 E7
Hillesden MK18 31 H6
Hillesley GL12 20 A3
Hillfarrance TA4 7 K3
Hillfoot End SG5 32 E5
Hillhead Devon TQ5 5 K5
Hillhead S.Ayr. KA6 67 J1
Hillhead of Auchentumb AB43 99 H5
Hillhead of Cocklaw AB42 99 J6
Hilliard's Cross WS13 40 D4
Hilliclay KW14 105 G2
Hillingdon UB10 22 D3
Hillington Glas. G52 74 D4
Hillington Norf. PE31 44 B3
Hillmorton CV21 31 G1
Hillockhead Aber. AB36 90 B4
Hillockhead Aber. AB33 90 C3
Hillowton DG7 65 H4
Hillpound SO32 11 G3
Hill's End MK17 32 C5
Hills Town S44 51 G6
Hillsborough S6 51 F3
Hillsford Bridge EX35 7 F1
Hillside Aber. AB12 91 H5
Hillside Angus DD10 83 J1
Hillside Moray IV30 97 J5
Hillside Shet. ZE2 107 N6
Hillside Worcs. WR6 29 G2
Hillswick ZE2 107 L5
Hillway PO35 11 H6
Hillwell ZE2 107 M11
Hillyfields SO16 10 E3
Hilmarton SN11 20 D4
Hilperton BA14 20 B6
Hilsea PO3 11 H4
Hilston HU11 59 J6
Hilton Cambs. PE28 33 F2
Hilton Cumb. CA16 61 J4
Hilton Derbys. DE65 40 E2
Hilton Dorset DT11 9 G4
Hilton Dur. DL2 62 C4
Hilton High. IV20 97 G3
Hilton Shrop. WV15 39 G6
Hilton Staffs. WS14 40 C5
Hilton Stock. TS15 63 F5
Hilton Croft AB41 91 H1
Hilton of Cadboll IV20 97 F4
Hilton of Delnies IV12 97 F6
Himbleton WR9 29 J3
Himley DY3 40 A6
Hincaster LA7 55 J1
Hinchley Wood KT10 22 E5
Hinckley LE10 41 G6
Hinderclay IP22 34 E1
Hinderton CH64 48 C5
Hinderwell TS13 63 J5
Hindford SY11 38 C2
Hindhead GU26 12 B3
Hindley Gt.Man. WN2 49 F2
Hindley Northumb. NE43 62 B1
Hindley Green WN2 49 F2
Hindlip WR3 29 H3
Hindolveston NR20 44 E3
Hindon Som. TA24 7 H1
Hindon Wilts. SP3 9 J1
Hindringham NR21 44 D2
Hingham NR9 44 E5
Hinksford DY3 40 A7
Hinstock TF9 39 F3
Hintlesham IP8 34 E4
Hinton Glos. GL13 19 K1
Hinton Hants. BH23 10 D5
Hinton Here. HR2 28 C5
Hinton Northants. NN11 31 G3
Hinton S.Glos. SN14 20 A4
Hinton Shrop. SY5 38 D5
Hinton Admiral BH23 10 D5
Hinton Ampner SO24 11 G2
Hinton Blewett BS39 19 J6
Hinton Charterhouse BA2 20 A6
Hinton Martell BH21 10 B4
Hinton on the Green WR11 30 B4
Hinton Parva Dorset BH21 9 J4
Hinton Parva Swin. SN4 21 F3
Hinton St. George TA17 8 D3
Hinton St. Mary DT10 9 G3
Hinton Waldrist SN7 21 G2
Hinton-in-the-Hedges NN13 31 G5
Hints Shrop. SY8 29 F1
Hints Staffs. B78 40 D5
Hinwick NN29 32 C2
Hinxhill TN25 15 F3
Hinxton CB10 33 H4
Hinxworth SG7 33 F4
Hipperholme HX3 57 G7
Hipsburn NE66 71 H2
Hipswell DL9 62 C7
Hirn AB31 91 F4
Hirnant SY10 37 K3
Hirst NE63 71 H5
Hirst Courtney YO8 58 C7
Hirwaen LL15 47 K6
Hirwaun CF44 18 C1
Hiscott EX31 6 D3
Histon CB4 33 H2
Hitcham Bucks. SL1 22 C3
Hitcham Suff. IP7 34 D3
Hitchin SG5 32 E6
Hither Green SE13 23 G4
Hittisleigh EX6 7 F6
Hittisleigh Barton EX6 7 F6
Hive HU15 58 E6
Hixon ST18 40 C3
Hoaden CT3 15 H2
Hoaldalbert NP7 28 C6
Hoar Cross DE13 40 D3
Hoarwithy HR2 28 E6
Hoath CT3 25 J5
Hobarris SY7 28 C1
Hobbister KW17 106 C7
Hobbles Green CB8 34 B3
Hobbs Cross CM16 23 H2
Hobbs Lots Bridge PE15 43 G5
Hobkirk TD9 70 A2
Hobland Hall NR31 45 K5
Hobson NE16 62 C1
Hoby LE14 41 J4
Hockerill CM23 33 H6
Hockering NR20 44 E4
Hockerton NG25 51 K7
Hockley SS5 24 E2
Hockley Heath B94 30 C1
Hockliffe LU7 32 C6
Hockwold cum Wilton IP26 44 B7
Hockworthy TA21 7 J4
Hoddesdon EN11 23 G1
Hoddlesden BB3 56 C7
Hodgehill SK11 49 H6
Hodgeston SA71 16 D6
Hodnet TF9 39 F3
Hodnetheath TF9 39 F3
Hodsoll Street TN15 24 C5
Hodson SN4 20 E3
Hodthorpe S80 51 H5
Hoe NR20 44 D4
Hoe Gate PO7 11 H3
Hoff CA16 61 H5
Hoffleet Stow PE20 43 F2
Hoggard's Green IP29 34 C3
Hoggeston MK18 32 B6
Hoggie AB56 98 D5
Hoggrill's End B46 40 E6
Hogha Gearraidh HS6 92 C4
Hoghton PR5 56 B7
Hognaston DE6 50 E7
Hogsthorpe PE24 53 J5
Holbeach PE12 43 G3
Holbeach Bank PE12 43 G3
Holbeach Clough PE12 43 G3
Holbeach Drove PE12 43 G4
Holbeach Hurn PE12 43 G3
Holbeach St. Johns PE12 43 G4
Holbeach St. Marks PE12 43 G2
Holbeach St. Matthew PE12 43 H2
Holbeck S80 51 H5
Holbeck Woodhouse S80 51 H5
Holberrow Green B96 30 B3
Holbeton PL8 5 G5
Holborough ME2 24 D5
Holbrook Derbys. DE56 41 F1
Holbrook Suff. IP9 35 F5
Holbrooks CV6 41 F7
Holburn TD15 77 J7
Holbury SO45 11 F4
Holcombe Devon EX7 5 K3
Holcombe Gt.Man. BL8 49 G1
Holcombe Som. BA3 19 K7
Holcombe Burnell Barton EX6 7 G6
Holcombe Rogus TA21 7 J4
Holcot NN6 31 J2
Holden BB7 56 C5
Holden Gate OL14 56 D7
Holdenby NN6 31 H2
Holdenhurst BH8 10 C5
Holder's Green CM6 33 K6
Holders Hill NW4 23 F3
Holdgate TF13 38 E7
Holdingham NG34 42 D1
Holditch TA20 8 C4
Hole EX15 7 K4
Hole Park TN17 14 D4
Hole Street BN44 12 E5
Holehouse SK13 50 C3
Hole-in-the-Wall HR9 29 F6
Holford TA5 7 K1
Holgate YO26 58 B4
Holker LA11 55 G2
Holkham NR23 44 C1
Hollacombe Devon EX22 6 B5
Hollacombe Devon EX17 7 G5
Hollacombe Town EX18 6 E4
Holland Ork. KW17 106 D2
Holland Ork. KW17 106 F5
Holland Surr. RH8 23 H6
Holland Fen LN4 43 F1
Holland-on-Sea CO15 35 F7
Hollandstoun KW17 106 G2
Hollee DG11 69 H7
Hollesley IP12 35 H4
Hollicombe TQ2 5 K4
Hollingbourne ME17 14 D2
Hollingbury BN1 13 G6
Hollingrove TN32 13 K4
Hollington Derbys. DE6 40 E2
Hollington E.Suss. TN38 14 C6
Hollington Staffs. ST10 40 C2
Hollingworth SK14 50 C3
Hollins S42 51 F5
Hollins Green WA3 49 F3
Hollins Lane PR3 55 H4
Hollinsclough SK17 50 C6
Hollinwood Gt.Man. OL9 49 J2
Hollinwood Shrop. SY13 38 E2
Hollocombe EX18 6 E4
Hollow Meadows S6 50 E4
Holloway DE4 51 F7
Hollowell NN6 31 H1
Holly Bush LL13 38 D1
Holly End PE14 43 H5
Holly Green HP27 22 A1
Hollybush Caerp. NP12 18 E1
Hollybush E.Ayr. KA6 67 H2
Hollybush Worcs. HR8 29 G5
Hollyhurst SY13 38 E1
Hollym HU19 59 K7
Hollywater GU35 12 B3
Hollywood B47 30 B1
Holm D. & G. DG13 69 H4
Holm (Tolm) W.Isles HS2 101 G4
Holm of Drumlanrig DG3 68 D4
Holmbridge HD9 50 D2
Holmbury St. Mary RH5 22 E7
Holmbush RH12 13 F3
Holme Cambs. PE7 42 E7
Holme Cumb. LA6 55 J2
Holme N.Lincs. DN16 52 C2
Holme N.Yorks. YO7 57 J1
Holme Notts. NG23 52 B7
Holme W.Yorks. HD9 50 D2
Holme Chapel BB10 56 D7
Holme Hale IP25 44 C5
Holme Lacy HR2 28 E5
Holme Marsh HR5 28 C3
Holme next the Sea PE36 44 B1
Holme on the Wolds HU17 59 F5
Holme Pierrepont NG12 41 J2
Holme St. Cuthbert CA15 60 C2
Holme-on-Spalding-Moor YO43 58 E6
Holmer HR1 28 E4
Holmer Green HP15 22 C2
Holmes PR4 48 D1
Holmes Chapel CW4 49 G6
Holme's Hill BN8 13 J5
Holmesfield S18 51 F5
Holmeswood L40 48 D1
Holmewood S42 51 G6
Holmfield HX2 57 F7
Holmfirth HD9 50 D2
Holmhead D. & G. DG7 68 C5
Holmhead E.Ayr. KA18 67 K1
Holmpton HU19 59 K7
Holmrook CA19 60 B6
Holmsgarth ZE1 107 N8
Holmside DH7 62 D2
Holmsleigh Green EX14 8 B4
Holmston KA7 67 H1
Holmwrangle CA4 61 G2
Holne TQ13 5 H4
Holnest DT9 9 F4
Holnicote TA24 7 H1
Holsworthy EX22 6 B5
Holsworthy Beacon EX22 6 B5
Holt Dorset BH21 10 B4
Holt Norf. NR25 44 E2
Holt Wilts. BA14 20 B5
Holt Worcs. WR6 29 H2
Holt Wrex. LL13 48 D7
Holt End Hants. GU34 11 H1
Holt End Worcs. B98 30 B2
Holt Fleet WR6 29 H2
Holt Heath Dorset BH21 10 B4
Holt Heath Worcs. WR6 29 H2
Holt Wood BH21 10 B4
Holtby YO19 58 C4
Holton Oxon. OX33 21 K1
Holton Som. BA9 9 F2
Holton Suff. IP19 35 J1
Holton cum Beckering LN8 52 E4
Holton Heath BH16 9 J5
Holton le Clay DN36 53 F2
Holton le Moor LN7 52 D3
Holton St. Mary CO7 34 E5
Holtspur HP9 22 C3
Holtye TN8 13 H3
Holtye Common TN8 13 H3
Holway TA1 8 B2
Holwell Dorset DT9 9 F3
Holwell Herts. SG5 32 E5
Holwell Leics. LE14 42 A3
Holwell Oxon. OX18 21 F1
Holwell Som. BA11 20 A7
Holwick DL12 62 A4
Holworth DT2 9 G6
Holy Cross DY9 29 J1
Holy Island I.o.A. LL65 46 A5
Holy Island Northumb. TD15 77 K6
Holybourne GU34 22 A7
Holyfield EN9 23 G1
Holyhead (Caergybi) LL65 46 A4
Holymoorside S42 51 F6
Holyport SL6 22 B4
Holystone NE65 70 E3
Holytown ML1 75 F4
Holywell Cambs. PE27 33 G1
Holywell Cornw. TR8 2 E3
Holywell Dorset DT2 8 E4
Holywell E.Suss. BN20 13 K7
Holywell (Treffynnon) Flints. CH8 47 K5
Holywell Northumb. NE25 71 J6
Holywell Green HX4 50 C1
Holywell Lake TA21 7 K3
Holywell Row IP28 34 B1
Holywood DG2 68 E5
Hom Green HR9 28 E6
Homer TF13 39 F5
Homersfield IP20 45 G7
Homington SP5 10 C2
Homore (Tobha Mòr) HS8 84 C1
Honey Hill CT2 25 H5
Honey Street SN9 20 E5
Honey Tye CO6 34 D5
Honeyborough SA73 16 C5
Honeybourne WR11 30 C4
Honeychurch EX20 6 E5
Honicknowle PL5 4 E5
Honiley CV8 30 D1
Honing NR28 45 H3
Honingham NR9 45 F4
Honington Lincs. NG32 42 C1
Honington Suff. IP31 34 D1
Honington Warks. CV36 30 D4
Honiton EX14 7 K5
Honkley LL12 48 C7
Honley HD9 50 D1
Hoo Med. ME3 24 D4
Hoo Suff. IP13 35 G3
Hoo Green WA16 49 G4
Hoo Meavy PL20 5 F4
Hood Green S75 51 F2
Hood Hill S35 51 F3
Hooe E.Suss. TN33 13 K6
Hooe Plym. PL9 5 F5
Hooe Common TN33 13 K5
Hook Cambs. PE15 43 H6
Hook E.Riding DN14 58 D7
Hook Gt.Lon. KT9 22 E5
Hook Hants. RG27 22 A6
Hook Hants. SO31 11 G4
Hook Pembs. SA62 16 C4
Hook Wilts. SN4 20 D3
Hook Green Kent TN3 13 K3
Hook Green Kent DA13 24 C5
Hook Green Kent DA13 24 C4
Hook Green Kent DA2 23 J4
Hook Norton OX15 30 E5
Hook-a-Gate SY5 38 D5
Hooke DT8 8 E4
Hookgate TF9 39 G2
Hookway EX17 7 G6
Hookwood RH6 23 F7
Hoole CH3 48 D6
Hooley CR5 23 F6
Hoop NP25 19 J1
Hooton CH66 48 C5
Hooton Levitt S66 51 H3
Hooton Pagnell DN5 51 G2
Hooton Roberts S65 51 G3
Hop Pole PE11 42 E4
Hopcrofts Holt OX25 31 F6
Hope Derbys. S33 50 D4
Hope Devon TQ7 5 G7
Hope Flints. LL12 48 C7
Hope Powys SY21 38 B5
Hope Shrop. SY5 38 C5
Hope Staffs. DE6 50 D7
Hope Bagot SY8 28 E1
Hope Bowdler SY6 38 D6
Hope End Green CM22 33 J6
Hope Mansell HR9 29 F7
Hope under Dinmore HR6 28 E3
Hopehouse TD7 69 H2
Hopeman IV30 97 J5
Hope's Green SS7 24 D3
Hopesay SY7 38 C7
Hopkinstown CF37 18 D2
Hopley's Green HR3 28 C3
Hopperton HG5 57 K4
Hopsford CV7 41 G7
Hopstone WV5 39 G6
Hopton Derbys. DE4 50 E7
Hopton Norf. NR31 45 K6
Hopton Shrop. TF9 38 E3
Hopton Shrop. SY4 38 C3
Hopton Staffs. ST18 40 B3
Hopton Suff. IP22 34 D1
Hopton Cangeford SY8 38 E7
Hopton Castle SY7 28 C1
Hopton Wafers DY14 29 F1
Hoptonheath SY7 28 C1
Hopwas B78 40 D5
Hopwood B48 30 B1
Horam TN21 13 J5
Horbling NG34 42 E2
Horbury WF4 50 E1
Horden SR8 63 F2
Horderley SY7 38 D7
Hordle SO41 10 D5
Hordley SY12 38 C2
Horeb Carmar. SA15 17 H5
Horeb Cere. SA44 17 G1
Horeb Flints. LL12 48 B7
Horfield BS7 19 J4
Horham IP21 35 G1
Horkesley Heath CO6 34 D6
Horkstow DN18 52 C1
Horley Oxon. OX15 31 F4
Horley Surr. RH6 23 F7
Horn Hill SL9 22 D2
Hornblotton BA4 8 E1
Hornblotton Green BA4 8 E1
Hornby Lancs. LA2 55 J3
Hornby N.Yorks. DL8 62 D7
Hornby N.Yorks. DL6 62 E6
Horncastle LN9 53 F6
Hornchurch RM11 23 J3
Horncliffe TD15 77 H6
Horndean Hants. PO8 11 J3
Horndean Sc.Bord. TD15 77 H6
Horndon PL19 6 D7
Horndon on the Hill SS17 24 C3
Horne RH6 23 G7
Horne Row CM3 24 D1
Horner TA24 7 G1
Horniehaugh DD8 83 F1
Horning NR12 45 H4
Horninghold LE16 42 B6
Horninglow DE13 40 E3
Horningsea CB5 33 H2
Horningsham BA12 20 B7
Horningtoft NR20 44 D3
Horningtops PL14 4 C4
Horns Cross Devon EX39 6 B3
Horns Cross E.Suss. TN31 14 D5
Horns Green TN14 23 H6
Hornsbury TA20 8 C3
Hornsby CA8 61 G2
Hornsby Gate CA8 61 G1
Hornsea HU18 59 J5
Hornsey N8 23 G3
Hornton OX15 30 E4
Horrabridge PL20 5 F4
Horridge TQ13 5 H3
Horringer IP29 34 C2
Horrocks Fold BL1 49 G1
Horse Bridge ST9 49 J7
Horsebridge Devon PL19 4 E3
Horsebridge Hants. SO20 10 E1
Horsebrook ST19 40 A4
Horsecastle BS49 19 H5
Horsehay TF4 39 F5
Horseheath CB1 33 K4
Horsehouse DL8 57 F1
Horsell GU21 22 C6
Horseman's Green SY13 38 D1
Horsenden HP27 22 A1
Horseshoe Green TN8 23 H7
Horseway PE16 43 H7
Horsey NR29 45 J3
Horsey Corner NR29 45 J3
Horsford NR10 45 F4
Horsforth LS18 57 H6
Horsham W.Suss. RH12 12 E3
Horsham Worcs. WR6 29 G3
Horsham St. Faith NR10 45 G4
Horsington Lincs. LN10 52 E6
Horsington Som. BA8 9 G2
Horsington Marsh BA8 9 G2
Horsley Derbys. DE21 41 F1
Horsley Glos. GL6 20 B2
Horsley Northumb. NE15 71 F7
Horsley Northumb. NE19 70 D4
Horsley Cross CO11 35 F6
Horsley Woodhouse DE7 41 F1
Horsleycross Street CO11 35 F6
Horsleygate S18 51 F5
Horsleyhill TD9 70 A2
Horsmonden TN12 23 K7
Horspath OX33 21 J1
Horstead NR12 45 G4
Horsted Keynes RH17 13 G4
Horton Bucks. LU7 32 C7
Horton Dorset BH21 10 B4
Horton Lancs. BD23 56 D4
Horton Northants. NN7 32 B3
Horton S.Glos. BS37 20 A3
Horton Shrop. SY4 38 D3
Horton Som. TA19 8 C3
Horton Staffs. ST13 49 J7
Horton Swan. SA3 17 H7
Horton Tel. & W. TF6 39 F4
Horton W. & M. SL3 22 D4
Horton Wilts. SN10 20 D5
Horton Cross TA19 8 C3
Horton Grange NE13 71 H6
Horton Green SY14 38 D1
Horton Heath SO50 11 F3
Horton in Ribblesdale BD24 56 D2
Horton Inn BH21 10 B4
Horton Kirby DA4 23 J5
Horton-cum-Studley OX33 31 H7
Horwich BL6 49 F1
Horwich End SK23 50 C4
Horwood EX39 6 D3
Hoscar L40 48 D1
Hose LE14 42 A3
Hoses LA20 60 D7
Hosh PH7 81 K5
Hosta HS6 92 C4
Hoswick ZE2 107 N10
Hotham YO43 58 E6
Hothfield TN26 14 E3
Hoton LE12 41 H3
Houbie ZE2 107 Q3
Houdston KA26 67 F4
Hough CW2 49 G7
Hough Green WA8 48 D4
Hougham NG32 42 B1
Hough-on-the-Hill NG32 42 C1
Houghton Cambs. PE28 33 F1
Houghton Cumb. CA3 60 F1
Houghton Devon TQ7 5 G6
Houghton Hants. SO20 10 E1
Houghton Pembs. SA73 16 C5
Houghton W.Suss. BN18 12 D5
Houghton Bank DL2 62 D4
Houghton Conquest MK45 32 D4
Houghton le Spring DH4 62 E2
Houghton on the Hill LE7 41 J5
Houghton Regis LU5 32 D6
Houghton St. Giles NR22 44 D2
Houghton-le-Side DL2 62 D4
Houlsyke YO21 63 J6
Hound SO31 11 F4
Hound Green RG27 22 A6
Houndslow TD3 76 E6
Houndsmoor TA4 7 K3
Houndwood TD14 77 G4
Hounsdown SO40 10 E3
Hounslow TW3 22 E4
Housebay KW17 106 F5
Househill IV12 97 F6
Houses Hill HD5 50 D1
Housetter ZE2 107 M4
Housham Tye CM17 33 J7
Houss ZE2 107 M9
Houston PA6 74 C4
Houstry KW6 105 G5
Houstry of Dunn KW1 105 H3
Houton KW17 106 C7
Hove BN3 13 F6
Hove Edge HD6 57 G7
Hoveringham NG14 41 J1
Hoveton NR12 45 H4
Hovingham YO62 58 C2
How CA8 61 G1
How Caple HR1 29 F5
How End MK45 32 D4
How Green TN8 23 H7
How Man CA22 60 A5
Howbrook S35 51 F3

Howden DN14 58 D7
Howden Clough WF17 57 H7
Howden-le-Wear DL15 62 C3
Howe *Cumb.* LA8 55 H1
Howe *High.* KW1 105 J2
Howe *N.Yorks.* YO7 57 J1
Howe *Norf.* NR15 45 G6
Howe Green CM2 24 D1
Howe of Teuchar AB53 99 F6
Howe Street *Essex* CM3 33 K7
Howe Street *Essex* CM7 33 K5
Howegreen CM3 24 E1
Howell NG34 42 E1
Howey LD1 27 K3
Howgate *Cumb.* CA28 60 A4
Howgate *Midloth.* EH26 76 A5
Howgill *Lancs.* BB7 56 D5
Howgill *N.Yorks.* BD23 57 F4
Howick NE66 71 H2
Howle TF10 39 F3
Howle Hill HR9 29 F6
Howlett End CB10 33 J5
Howley TA20 8 B4
Hownam TD5 70 C2
Hownam Mains TD5 70 C1
Howpasley TD9 69 J3
Howsham *N.Lincs.* LN7 52 D2
Howsham *N.Yorks.* YO60 58 D3
Howt Green ME9 24 E5
Howtel TD12 77 G7
Howton HR2 28 D6
Howwood PA9 74 C4
Hoxa KW17 106 D8
Hoxne IP21 35 F1
Hoy *High.* KW14 105 H2
Hoy *Ork.* KW16 106 B8
Hoylake CH47 48 B4
Hoyland S74 51 F2
Hoylandswaine S36 50 E2
Hoyle GU29 12 C5
Hubberholme BD23 56 E2
Hubberston SA73 16 B5
Hubbert's Bridge PE20 43 F1
Huby *N.Yorks.* YO61 58 B3
Huby *N.Yorks.* LS17 57 H5
Hucclecote GL3 29 H7
Hucking ME17 14 D2
Hucknall NG15 41 H1
HUDDERSFIELD HD 50 D1
Huddington WR9 29 J3
Huddlesford WS13 40 D5
Hudnall HP4 32 D7
Hudscott EX37 6 E3
Hudswell DL11 62 C7
Huggate YO42 58 E4
Hugglescote LE67 41 G4
Hugh Town TR21 2 C1
Hughenden Valley HP14 22 B2
Hughley SY5 38 E6
Hugmore LL13 48 C7
Hugus TR3 2 E4
Huish *Devon* EX20 6 D4
Huish *Wilts.* SN8 20 E5
Huish Champflower TA4 7 J3
Huish Episcopi TA10 8 D2
Huisinis HS3 100 B6
Hulcote MK17 32 C5
Hulcott HP22 32 B7
HULL HU 59 H7
Hulland DE6 40 E1
Hulland Ward DE6 40 E1
Hullavington SN14 20 B3
Hullbridge SS5 24 E2
Hulme ST3 40 B1
Hulme End SK17 50 D7
Hulme Walfield CW12 49 H6
Hulver Street NR34 45 J7
Hulverstone PO30 10 E6
Humber *Devon* TQ14 5 J3
Humber *Here.* HR6 28 E3
Humberside Airport DN39 52 D1
Humberston DN36 53 G2
Humberstone LE5 41 J5
Humberton YO61 57 K3
Humbie EH36 76 C4
Humbleton *Dur.* DL2 62 B5
Humbleton *E.Riding* HU11 59 J6
Humbleton *Northumb.* NE71 70 E1
Humby NG33 42 D2
Hume TD5 77 F6
Humehall TD5 77 F6
Hummer DT9 8 E3
Humshaugh NE46 70 E6
Huna KW1 105 J1
Huncoat BB5 56 C6
Huncote LE9 41 H6
Hundalee TD8 70 B2
Hundall S18 51 F5
Hunderthwaite DL12 62 A4
Hundleby PE23 53 G6
Hundleton SA71 16 C5
Hundon CO10 34 B4
Hundred Acres PO17 11 G3
Hundred End PR4 55 H7
Hundred House LD1 28 A3
Hungarton LE7 41 J5
Hungate End MK19 31 J4
Hungerford *Hants.* SP6 10 C3
Hungerford *Shrop.* SY7 38 E7
Hungerford *W.Berks.* RG17 21 G5
Hungerford Newtown RG17 21 G4
Hungerton NG32 42 B3
Hunglader IV51 93 J4
Hunmanby YO14 59 G2
Hunningham CV33 30 E2
Hunningham Hill CV33 30 E2
Hunny Hill PO30 11 F6
Hunsdon SG12 33 H7
Hunsingore LS22 57 K4
Hunslet LS10 57 J6
Hunsonby CA10 61 G3
Hunspow KW14 105 H1
Hunstanton PE36 44 A1
Hunstanworth DH8 62 A2
Hunston *Suff.* IP31 34 D2
Hunston *W.Suss.* PO20 12 B6
Hunsworth BD19 57 G7
Hunt End B97 30 B2
Hunt House YO22 63 K7
Huntercombe End RG9 21 K3
Hunters Forstal CT6 25 H5
Hunter's Inn EX31 6 E1
Hunter's Quay PA23 73 K3
Hunterston KA23 73 K5
Huntford TD8 70 B3
Huntham TA3 8 C2
Huntingdon PE29 33 F1
Huntingfield IP19 35 H1
Huntingford SP8 9 H1
Huntington *Here.* HR5 28 B3
Huntington *Here.* HR4 28 D4
Huntington *Staffs.* WS12 40 B4
Huntington *Tel. & W.* TF6 39 F5
Huntington *York* YO32 58 C4
Huntingtower PH1 82 B5
Huntley GL19 29 G7
Huntly AB54 90 D1
Huntlywood TD4 76 E6
Hunton *Hants.* SO21 21 H7
Hunton *Kent* ME15 14 C3
Hunton *N.Yorks.* DL8 62 C7
Hunton Bridge WD4 22 D1
Hunt's Cross L25 48 D4
Huntscott TA24 7 H1
Huntsham EX16 7 J3
Huntshaw EX38 6 D3
Huntshaw Cross EX31 6 D3
Huntshaw Water EX38 6 D3
Huntspill TA9 19 G7
Huntworth TA7 8 C1
Hunwick DL15 62 C3
Hunworth NR24 44 E2
Hurcott *Som.* TA11 8 E2
Hurcott *Som.* TA19 8 C3
Hurdley SY15 38 B6
Hurdsfield SK10 49 J5
Hurley *W. & M.* SL6 22 B3
Hurley *Warks.* CV9 40 E6
Hurley Bottom SL6 22 B3
Hurlford KA1 74 C7
Hurliness KW16 106 B9
Hurlston Green L40 48 C1
Hurn BH23 10 C5
Hursley SO21 11 F2
Hurst *N.Yorks.* DL11 62 B6
Hurst *W'ham* RG10 22 A4
Hurst Green *E.Suss.* TN19 14 C5
Hurst Green *Essex* CO7 34 E7
Hurst Green *Lancs.* BB7 56 B6
Hurst Green *Surr.* RH8 23 G6
Hurst Wickham BN6 13 F5
Hurstbourne Priors RG28 21 H7
Hurstbourne Tarrant SP11 21 G6
Hurstpierpoint BN6 13 F5
Hurstwood BB10 56 D6
Hurtmore GU7 22 C7
Hurworth-on-Tees DL2 62 E5
Hury DL12 62 A4
Husabost IV55 93 G6
Husbands Bosworth LE17 41 J7
Husborne Crawley MK43 32 C5
Husthwaite YO61 58 B2
Hutcherleigh TQ9 5 H5
Huthwaite NG17 51 G7
Huttoft LN13 53 J5
Hutton *Cumb.* CA11 60 F4
Hutton *Essex* CM13 24 C2
Hutton *Lancs.* PR4 55 H7
Hutton *N.Som.* BS24 19 G6
Hutton *Sc.Bord.* TD15 77 H5
Hutton Bonville DL7 62 E6
Hutton Buscel YO13 59 F1
Hutton Conyers HG4 57 J2
Hutton Cranswick YO25 59 G4
Hutton End CA11 60 F3
Hutton Hang DL8 57 G1
Hutton Henry TS27 63 F3
Hutton Magna DL11 62 C5
Hutton Mount CM13 24 C2
Hutton Mulgrave YO21 63 K6
Hutton Roof *Cumb.* LA6 55 J2
Hutton Roof *Cumb.* CA11 60 E3
Hutton Rudby TS15 63 F6
Hutton Sessay YO7 57 K2
Hutton Wandesley YO26 58 B4
Hutton-le-Hole YO62 63 J7
Huxham EX5 7 H6
Huxham Green BA4 8 E1
Huxley CH3 48 E6
Huxter *Shet.* ZE2 107 M7
Huxter *Shet.* ZE2 107 P6
Huyton L36 48 D3
Hwlffordd (Haverfordwest) SA61 16 C4
Hycemoor LA19 54 D1
Hyde *Glos.* GL6 20 B1
Hyde *Gt.Man.* SK14 49 J3
Hyde End *W'ham* RG7 22 A5
Hyde End *W.Berks.* RG7 21 J5
Hyde Heath HP6 22 C1
Hyde Lea ST18 40 B4
Hydestile GU8 22 C7
Hyndford Bridge ML11 75 H6
Hyndlee TD9 70 A3
Hynish PA77 78 A4
Hyssington SY15 38 C6
Hythe *Hants.* SO45 11 F4
Hythe *Kent* CT21 15 G4
Hythe End TW19 22 D4
Hythie AB42 99 J5
Hyton LA19 54 D1

I

Ianstown AB56 98 C4
Iarsiadar HS2 100 D4
Ibberton DT11 9 G4
Ible DE4 50 E7
Ibsley BH24 10 C4
Ibstock LE67 41 G4
Ibstone HP14 22 A2
Ibthorpe SP11 21 G6
Ibworth RG26 21 J6
Icelton BS22 19 G5
Ickburgh IP26 44 C6
Ickenham UB10 22 D3
Ickford HP18 21 K1
Ickham CT3 15 H2
Ickleford SG5 32 E5
Icklesham TN36 14 D6
Ickleton CB10 33 H4
Icklingham IP28 34 B1
Ickwell Green SG18 32 E4
Icomb GL54 30 D6
Idbury OX7 30 D6
Iddesleigh EX19 6 D5
Ide EX2 7 H6
Ide Hill TN14 23 H6
Ideford TQ13 5 J3
Iden TN31 14 E5
Iden Green *Kent* TN17 14 C4
Iden Green *Kent* TN17 14 D4
Idle BD10 57 G6
Idless TR4 3 F4
Idlicote CV36 30 D4
Idmiston SP4 10 C1
Idridgehay DE56 40 E1
Idridgehay Green DE56 40 E1
Idrigil IV51 93 J5
Idstone SN6 21 F3
Idvies DD8 83 G3
Iffley OX4 21 J1
Ifield RH11 13 F3
Ifieldwood RH11 13 F3
Ifold RH14 12 D3
Iford *Bourne.* BH7 10 C5
Iford *E.Suss.* BN7 13 H6
Ifton NP26 19 H3
Ifton Heath SY11 38 C2
Ightfield SY13 38 E2
Ightham TN15 23 J6
Iken IP12 35 J3
Ilam DE6 50 D7
Ilchester BA22 8 E2
Ilderton NE66 71 F1
ILFORD IG 23 H3
Ilfracombe EX34 6 D1
Ilkeston DE7 41 G1
Ilketshall St. Andrew NR34 45 H7
Ilketshall St. Lawrence NR34 45 H7
Ilketshall St. Margaret NR35 45 H7
Ilkley LS29 57 G5
Illey B62 40 B7
Illidge Green CW11 49 G6
Illington IP24 44 D7
Illingworth HX2 57 F7
Illogan TR16 2 D4
Illston on the Hill LE7 42 A6
Ilmer HP27 22 A1
Ilmington CV36 30 D4
Ilminster TA19 8 C3
Ilsington *Devon* TQ13 5 H3
Ilsington *Dorset* DT2 9 G5
Ilston SA2 17 J6
Ilton *N.Yorks.* HG4 57 G2
Ilton *Som.* TA19 8 C3
Imachar KA27 73 G6
Imber BA12 20 C7
Immeroin FK19 81 G6
Immingham DN40 52 E1
Immingham Dock DN40 53 F1
Impington CB4 33 H2
Ince CH2 48 D5
Ince Blundell L38 48 C2
Ince-in-Makerfield WN3 48 E2
Inch Kenneth PA68 79 F4
Inch of Arnhall DD9 90 E7
Inchbae Lodge IV23 96 B5
Inchbare DD9 83 H1
Inchberry IV32 98 B5
Inchbraoch DD10 83 J2
Inchgrundle DD9 90 C7
Inchindown IV18 96 D4
Inchinnan PA4 74 C4
Inchkinloch IV27 103 J4
Inchlaggan PH35 87 H4
Inchlumpie IV17 96 C4
Inchmarlo AB31 90 E5
Inchmarnock PA20 73 J5
Inchnabobart AB35 90 B6
Inchnacardoch Hotel PH32 87 K3
Inchnadamph IV27 102 E6
Inchock DD11 83 H3
Inchrory AB37 89 J4
Inchture PH14 82 D5
Inchvuilt IV4 87 J1
Inchyra PH2 82 C5
Indian Queens TR9 3 G3
Inerval PA42 72 B6
Ingatestone CM4 24 C2
Ingbirchworth S36 50 E2
Ingerthorpe HG3 57 H3
Ingestre ST18 40 B3
Ingham *Lincs.* LN1 52 C4
Ingham *Norf.* NR12 45 H3
Ingham *Suff.* IP31 34 C1
Ingham Corner NR12 45 H3
Ingleborough PE14 43 H4
Ingleby *Derbys.* DE73 41 F3
Ingleby *Lincs.* LN1 52 B5
Ingleby Arncliffe DL6 63 F6
Ingleby Barwick TS17 63 F5
Ingleby Cross DL6 63 F6
Ingleby Greenhow TS9 63 G6
Ingleigh Green EX19 6 E5
Inglesbatch BA2 20 A5
Inglesham SN6 21 F2
Ingleton *Dur.* DL2 62 C4
Ingleton *N.Yorks.* LA6 56 B2
Inglewhite PR3 55 J6
Ingliston EH28 75 K3
Ingmire Hall LA10 61 H7
Ingoe NE20 71 F6
Ingoldisthorpe PE31 44 A2
Ingoldmells PE25 53 J6
Ingoldsby NG33 42 D2
Ingon CV37 30 D3
Ingram NE66 71 F2
Ingrave CM13 24 C2
Ingrow BD21 57 F6
Ings LA8 60 F7
Ingst BS35 19 J3
Ingworth NR11 45 F3
Inhurst RG26 21 J5
Inistrynich PA33 80 C5
Injebreck IM4 54 C5
Inkberrow WR7 30 B3
Inkersall S43 51 G5
Inkersall Green S43 51 G5
Inkhorn AB41 91 H1
Inkpen RG17 21 G5
Inkstack KW14 105 H1
Inmarsh SN12 20 C5
Innellan PA23 73 K4
Innergellie KY10 83 G7
Innerhadden PH16 81 H2
Innerleithen EH44 76 B7
Innerleven KY8 82 E7
Innermessan DG9 64 A4
Innerwick *E.Loth.* EH42 77 F3
Innerwick *P. & K.* PH15 81 G3
Inninbeg PA34 79 H3
Innsworth GL3 29 H6
Insch AB52 90 E2
Insh PH21 89 F4
Inshore IV27 103 F2
Inskip PR4 55 H6
Instow EX39 6 C2
Intake DN2 51 H2
Intwood NR4 45 F5
Inver *Aber.* AB35 89 K5
Inver *Arg. & B.* PA38 80 A3
Inver *High.* IV20 97 F3
Inver *High.* KW6 105 G5
Inver *P. & K.* PH8 82 B3
Inver Mallie PH34 87 H6
Inverailort PH38 86 D6
Inveralligin IV22 94 E6
Inverallochy AB43 99 J4
Inveran IV27 96 C2
Inveraray PA32 80 B7
Inverardoch Mains FK15 81 J7
Inverardran FK20 80 E5
Inverarish IV40 86 B1
Inverarity DD8 83 F3
Inverarnan G83 80 E6
Inverasdale IV22 94 E3
Inverbain IV54 94 D6
Inverbeg G83 74 B1
Inverbervie DD10 91 G7
Inverbroom IV23 95 H3
Inverbrough IV13 89 F2
Invercassley IV27 96 B1
Inverchaolain PA23 73 J3
Invercharnan PH49 80 C3
Inverchorachan PA26 80 D6
Inverchoran IV6 95 J6
Invercreran PA38 80 B3
Inverdruie PH22 89 G3
Inverebrie AB41 91 H1
Invereen IV13 88 E1
Invererne IV36 97 H5
Inveresk EH21 76 B3
Inverey AB35 89 H6
Inverfarigaig IV2 88 C2
Invergarry PH35 87 K4
Invergelder AB35 89 K5
Invergeldie PH6 81 J5
Invergloy PH34 87 J6
Invergordon IV18 96 E5
Invergowrie DD2 82 E4
Inverguseran PH41 86 D4
Inverharroch Farm AB54 90 B1
Inverherive FK20 80 E5
Inverhope IV27 103 G2
Inverie PH41 86 D4
Inverinan PA35 80 A6
Inverinate IV40 87 F2
Inverkeilor DD11 83 H3
Inverkeithing KY11 75 K2
Inverkeithny AB54 98 E6
Inverkip PA16 74 A3
Inverkirkaig IV27 102 C7
Inverlael IV23 95 H3
Inverlauren G84 74 B2
Inverliever PA31 79 K7
Inverliver PA35 80 B4
Inverlochlarig FK19 81 F6
Inverlochy PA33 80 C5
Inverlussa PA60 72 E2
Invermay PH2 82 B6
Invermoriston IV63 88 B3
Invernaver KW14 104 C2
Inverneil PA30 73 G2
INVERNESS IV 96 D7
Inverness Airport IV2 96 E6
Invernettie AB42 99 K6
Invernoaden PA27 73 K1
Inveroran Hotel PA36 80 D3
Inverquharity DD8 83 F2
Inverquhomery AB42 99 J6
Inverroy PH31 87 J6
Inversanda PH33 80 A2
Invershiel IV40 87 F3
Invershore KW3 105 H5
Inversnaid Hotel FK8 80 E7
Invertrossachs FK17 81 G7
Inverugie AB42 99 K6
Inveruglas G83 80 E7
Inveruglass PH21 89 F4
Inverurie AB51 91 F2
Invervar PH15 81 H3
Invervegain PA23 73 J3
Invery House AB31 90 E5
Inverythan AB53 99 F6
Inwardleigh EX20 6 D6
Inworth CO5 34 C7
Iochdar HS8 92 C7
Iona PA76 78 D5
Iping GU29 12 B4
Ipplepen TQ12 5 J4
Ipsden OX10 21 K3
Ipstones ST10 40 C1
IPSWICH IP 35 F4
Irby CH61 48 B4
Irby Hill CH61 48 B4
Irby in the Marsh PE24 53 H6
Irby upon Humber DN37 52 E2
Irchester NN29 32 C2
Ireby *Cumb.* CA7 60 D3
Ireby *Lancs.* LA6 56 B2
Ireland *Ork.* KW16 106 C7
Ireland *Shet.* ZE2 107 M10
Ireland's Cross CW3 39 G1
Ireleth LA16 55 F2
Ireshopeburn DL13 61 K3
Irlam M44 49 G3
Irnham NG33 42 D3
Iron Acton BS37 19 K3
Iron Cross WR11 30 B3
Ironbridge TF8 39 F5
Irons Bottom RH2 23 F7
Ironside AB53 99 G5
Ironville NG16 51 G7
Irstead NR12 45 H3
Irthington CA6 69 K7
Irthlingborough NN9 32 C1
Irton YO12 59 G1
Irvine KA12 74 B7
Isauld KW14 104 E2
Isbister *Ork.* KW17 106 C6
Isbister *Ork.* KW17 106 B5
Isbister *Shet.* ZE2 107 P6
Isbister *Shet.* ZE2 107 M3
Isfield TN22 13 H5
Isham NN14 32 B1
Ishriff PA65 79 H4
Isington GU34 22 A7
Island of Stroma KW1 105 J1
Islawr-dref LL40 37 F4
Islay PA 72 A4
Islay Airport PA42 72 B5
Islay House PA44 72 B4
Isle Abbotts TA3 8 C2
Isle Brewers TA3 8 C2
Isle of Lewis (Eilean Leodhais) HS 101 F3
ISLE OF MAN IM 54 C5
Isle of Man Airport IM9 54 B7
Isle of May KY10 76 E1
Isle of Noss ZE2 107 P8
Isle of Sheppey ME12 25 F4
Isle of Walney LA14 54 E3
Isle of Whithorn DG8 64 E7
Isle of Wight PO 11 F6
Isleham CB7 33 K1
Isleornsay (Eilean Iarmain) IV43 86 C3
Isles of Scilly (Scilly Isles) TR 2 C1
Islesburgh ZE2 107 M6
Isleworth TW7 22 E4
Isley Walton DE74 41 G3
Islibhig HS2 100 B5
Islip *Northants.* NN14 32 C1
Islip *Oxon.* OX5 31 G7
Isombridge TF6 39 F4
Istead Rise DA13 24 C5
Itchen SO19 11 F3
Itchen Abbas SO21 11 G1
Itchen Stoke SO24 11 G1
Itchingfield RH13 12 E4
Itchington BS35 19 K3
Itteringham NR11 45 F2
Itton *Devon* EX20 6 E6
Itton *Mon.* NP16 19 H2
Itton Common NP16 19 H2
Ivegill CA4 60 F2
Ivelet DL11 62 A7
Iver SL0 22 D3
Iver Heath SL0 22 D3
Iveston DH8 62 C1
Ivetsey Bank ST19 40 A4
Ivinghoe LU7 32 C7
Ivinghoe Aston LU7 32 C7
Ivington HR6 28 D3
Ivington Green HR6 28 D3
Ivy Hatch TN15 23 J6
Ivy Todd PE37 44 C5
Ivybridge PL21 5 G5
Ivychurch TN29 15 F5
Iwade ME9 25 F5
Iwerne Courtney (Shroton) DT11 9 H3

Iwerne Minster DT11 9 H3
Ixworth IP31 34 D1
Ixworth Thorpe IP31 34 D1

J

Jack Hill LS21 57 G4
Jackfield TF8 39 F5
Jacksdale NG16 51 G7
Jackstown AB51 91 F1
Jackton G75 74 D5
Jacobstow EX23 4 B1
Jacobstowe EX20 6 D5
Jacobswell GU4 22 C6
Jameston SA70 16 D6
Jamestown *D. & G.* DG13 69 J4
Jamestown *High.* IV14 96 B6
Jamestown *W.Dun.* G83 74 B2
Janefield IV10 96 E6
Janetstown *High.* KW14 105 F2
Janetstown *High.* KW1 105 J3
Jarrow NE32 71 J7
Jarvis Brook TN6 13 J3
Jasper's Green CM7 34 B6
Jawcraig FK1 75 G3
Jayes Park RH5 22 E7
Jaywick CO15 35 F7
Jealott's Hill RG42 22 B4
Jeater Houses DL6 63 F7
Jedburgh TD8 70 B1
Jeffreyston SA68 16 D5
Jemimaville IV7 96 E5
Jericho BL9 49 H1
Jersay ML7 75 G4
JERSEY JE 3 J7
Jersey Airport JE3 3 J7
Jersey Marine SA1 18 A2
Jerviswood ML11 75 G6
Jesmond NE2 71 H7
Jevington BN26 13 J6
Jockey End HP2 32 D7
Jodrell Bank SK11 49 G5
John o' Groats KW1 105 J1
Johnby CA11 60 F3
John's Cross TN32 14 C5
Johnshaven DD10 83 J1
Johnson Street NR29 45 H4
Johnston SA62 16 C4
Johnston Mains AB30 91 F7
Johnstone PA5 74 C4
Johnstone Castle PA5 74 C4
Johnstonebridge DG11 69 F4
Johnstown *Carmar.* SA31 17 G4
Johnstown *Wrex.* LL14 38 C1
Joppa KA6 67 J2
Jordans HP9 22 C2
Jordanston SA62 16 C2
Jordanstone PH11 82 D3
Joy's Green GL17 29 F7
Jumpers Common BH23 10 C5
Juniper Hill NN13 31 G5
Jura PA60 72 D2
Jura House PA60 72 C4
Jurby East IM7 54 C4
Jurby West IM7 54 C4

K

Kaber CA17 61 J5
Kaimes EH17 76 A4
Kames *Arg. & B.* PA21 73 H3
Kames *Arg. & B.* PA34 79 K6
Kames *E.Ayr.* KA18 68 B1
Kea TR3 3 F4
Keadby DN17 52 B1
Keal Cotes PE23 53 G6
Kearsley BL4 49 G2
Kearstwick LA6 56 B2
Kearton DL11 62 B7
Kearvaig IV27 102 E1
Keasden LA2 56 C3
Kebholes AB45 98 E5
Keckwick WA4 48 E4
Keddington LN11 53 G4
Keddington Corner LN11 53 G4
Kedington CB9 34 B4
Kedleston DE22 40 E1
Keelby DN41 52 E1
Keele ST5 40 A1
Keeley Green MK43 32 D4
Keelham BD13 57 F6
Keeres Green CM6 33 J7
Keeston SA62 16 B4
Keevil BA14 20 C6
Kegworth DE74 41 G3
Kehelland TR14 2 D4
Keig AB33 90 E3
Keighley BD21 57 F5
Keil *Arg. & B.* PA28 66 A3
Keil *High.* PA38 80 A2
Keilhill AB45 99 F5
Keillmore PA31 72 E2
Keillor PH13 82 D3
Keillour PH1 82 A5
Keills PA46 72 C4
Keils PA60 72 D4
Keinton Mandeville TA11 8 E1
Keir House FK15 75 F1
Keir Mill DG3 68 D4
Keisby PE10 42 D3
Keisley CA16 61 J4
Keiss KW1 105 J2
Keith AB55 98 C5
Keithick PH13 82 D4
Keithmore AB55 90 B1
Keithock DD9 83 H1
Kelbrook BB18 56 E5
Kelby NG32 42 D1
Keld *Cumb.* CA10 61 G5
Keld *N.Yorks.* DL11 61 K6
Keldholme YO62 58 D1
Keldy Castle YO18 63 J7
Kelfield *N.Lincs.* DN9 52 B2
Kelfield *N.Yorks.* YO19 58 B6
Kelham NG23 51 K7
Kella IM7 54 C4
Kellacott PL15 6 C7
Kellan PA72 79 G3
Kellas *Angus* DD5 83 F4
Kellas *Moray* IV30 97 J6
Kellaton TQ7 5 H7
Kellaways SN15 20 C4
Kelleth CA10 61 H6
Kelleythorpe YO25 59 G4
Kelling NR25 44 E1
Kellington DN14 58 B7
Kelloe DH6 62 E3
Kelloholm DG4 68 C2
Kelly *Cornw.* PL27 4 A3
Kelly *Devon* PL16 6 B7
Kelly Bray PL17 4 D3
Kelmarsh NN6 31 J1
Kelmscott GL7 21 F2
Kelsale IP17 35 H2
Kelsall CW6 48 E6
Kelsay PA47 72 A5
Kelshall SG8 33 G5
Kelsick CA7 60 D1
Kelso TD5 77 F7
Kelstedge S45 51 F6
Kelstern LN11 53 F3
Kelston BA1 20 A5
Keltneyburn PH15 81 J3
Kelton DG1 65 K3
Kelton Hill (Rhonehouse) DG7 65 H5
Kelty KY4 75 K1
Kelvedon CO5 34 C7
Kelvedon Hatch CM15 23 J2
Kelvinside G12 74 D4
Kelynack TR19 2 A6
Kemacott EX31 6 E1
Kemback KY15 83 F6
Kemberton TF11 39 G5
Kemble GL7 20 C2
Kemerton GL20 29 J5
Kemeys Commander NP15 19 G1
Kemeys Inferior NP18 19 G2
Kemnay AB51 91 F3
Kemp Town BN2 13 G6
Kempe's Corner TN25 15 F3
Kempley GL18 29 F6
Kempley Green GL18 29 F6
Kemps Green B94 30 C1
Kempsey WR5 29 H4
Kempsford GL7 20 E2
Kempshott RG22 21 J7
Kempston MK42 32 D4
Kempston Hardwick MK45 32 D4
Kempston West End MK43 32 C4
Kempton SY7 38 C7
Kemsing TN15 23 J6
Kemsley ME10 25 F5
Kenardington TN26 14 E4
Kenchester HR4 28 D4
Kencot GL7 21 F1
Kendal LA9 61 G7
Kenderchurch HR2 28 D6
Kendleshire BS36 19 K4
Kenfig CF33 18 A3
Kenfig Hill CF33 18 B3
Kenidjack TR19 2 A5
Kenilworth CV8 30 D1
Kenknock *P. & K.* PH15 81 G3
Kenknock *Stir.* FK21 81 F4
Kenley *Gt.Lon.* CR8 23 G5
Kenley *Shrop.* SY5 39 E5
Kenmore *Arg. & B.* PA32 80 B7
Kenmore *High.* IV54 94 D6
Kenmore *P. & K.* PH15 81 J3
Kenmore *W.Isles* HS2 100 E7
Kenn *Devon* EX6 7 H7
Kenn *N.Som.* BS21 19 H5
Kennacley HS3 93 G2
Kennacraig PA29 73 G4
Kennards House PL15 4 C2
Kennavay HS4 93 H2
Kenneggy Downs TR20 2 C6
Kennerleigh EX17 7 G5
Kennerty AB31 90 E5
Kennet FK10 75 H1
Kennethmont AB54 90 D2
Kennett CB8 33 K2
Kennford EX6 7 H7
Kenninghall NR16 44 E7
Kennington *Kent* TN24 15 F3
Kennington *Oxon.* OX1 21 J1
Kennoway KY8 82 E7
Kenny TA19 8 C3
Kennyhill IP28 33 K1
Kennythorpe YO17 58 D3
Kenovay PA77 78 A3
Kensaleyre IV51 93 K6
Kensington W8 23 F3
Kenstone TF9 38 E3
Kensworth LU6 32 D7
Kent International Airport CT12 25 K5
Kent Street *E.Suss.* TN33 14 C6
Kent Street *Kent* ME18 23 K6
Kentallen PA38 80 B2
Kentchurch HR2 28 D6
Kentford CB8 34 B2
Kentisbeare EX15 7 J5
Kentisbury EX31 6 E1
Kentisbury Ford EX31 6 E1
Kentish Town NW5 23 F3
Kentmere LA8 61 F6
Kenton *Devon* EX6 7 H7
Kenton *Suff.* IP14 35 F2
Kenton *T. & W.* NE3 71 H7
Kenton Corner IP14 35 G2
Kentra PH36 79 H1
Kents Bank LA11 55 G2
Kent's Green GL18 29 G6
Kent's Oak SO51 10 E2
Kenwick SY12 38 D2
Kenwyn TR1 3 F4
Kenyon WA3 49 F3
Keoldale IV27 103 F2
Keose (Ceos) HS2 101 F5
Keppanach PH33 80 B1
Keppoch *Arg. & B.* G82 74 B3
Keppoch *High.* IV40 86 E2
Keprigan PA28 66 A2
Kepwick YO7 63 F7
Keresley CV6 41 F7
Kernborough TQ7 5 H6
Kerrera PA34 79 K5
Kerridge SK10 49 J5
Kerris TR19 2 B6
Kerry (Ceri) SY16 38 A6
Kerrycroy PA20 73 K4
Kerry's Gate HR2 28 C5
Kerrysdale IV21 94 E4
Kersall NG22 51 K6
Kersey IP7 34 E4
Kersey Vale IP7 34 E4
Kershopefoot TD9 69 K5
Kerswell EX15 7 J5
Kerswell Green WR5 29 H4
Kerthen Wood TR27 2 C5
Kesgrave IP5 35 G4
Kessingland NR33 45 K7
Kessingland Beach NR33 45 K7
Kestle PL26 3 G4
Kestle Mill TR8 3 F3
Keston BR2 23 H5
Keswick *Cumb.* CA12 60 D4
Keswick *Norf.* NR4 45 G5
Keswick *Norf.* NR12 45 H2
Ketley Bank TF2 39 F4
Ketsby LN11 53 G5
Kettering NN16 32 B1
Ketteringham NR18 45 F5
Kettins PH13 82 D4
Kettle Corner ME15 14 C2
Kettlebaston IP7 34 D3
Kettlebridge KY15 82 E7
Kettlebrook B77 40 E5
Kettleburgh IP13 35 G2
Kettlehill KY15 82 E7
Kettleholm DG11 69 G6
Kettleness YO21 63 K5
Kettleshulme SK23 49 J5
Kettlesing HG3 57 H4
Kettlesing Bottom HG3 57 H4
Kettlesing Head HG3 57 H4
Kettlestone NR21 44 D2
Kettlethorpe LN1 52 B5
Kettletoft KW17 106 F4
Kettlewell BD23 56 E2
Ketton PE9 42 C5
Kevingtown BR5 23 H5
Kew TW9 22 E4
Kewstoke BS22 19 G5
Kexbrough S75 51 F2
Kexby *Lincs.* DN21 52 B4
Kexby *York* YO41 58 D4
Key Green CW12 49 H6
Keyham LE7 41 J5
Keyhaven SO41 10 E5
Keyingham HU12 59 J7
Keymer BN6 13 G5
Keynsham BS31 19 K5
Key's Toft PE24 53 H7
Keysoe MK44 32 D2
Keysoe Row MK44 32 D2
Keyston PE28 32 D1
Keyworth NG12 41 J2
Kibblesworth NE11 62 D1
Kibworth Beauchamp LE8 41 J6
Kibworth Harcourt LE8 41 J6
Kidbrooke SE3 23 H4
Kiddemore Green ST19 40 A5
Kidderminster DY10 29 H1
Kiddington OX20 31 F6
Kidlington OX5 31 F7
Kidmore End RG4 21 K4
Kidnal SY14 38 D1
Kidsdale DG8 64 E7
Kidsgrove ST7 49 H7
Kidstones DL8 56 E1
Kidwelly (Cydweli) SA17 17 H5
Kiel Crofts PA37 79 K4
Kielder NE48 70 B4
Kilbarchan PA10 74 C4
Kilbeg IV44 86 C4
Kilberry PA29 73 F4
Kilbirnie KA25 74 B5
Kilblaan PA32 80 C6
Kilbraur KW9 104 D7
Kilbrennan PA73 79 F3
Kilbride *Arg. & B.* PA34 79 K5
Kilbride *Arg. & B.* PA20 73 J4
Kilbride *High.* IV49 86 B2
Kilbride Farm PA21 73 H4
Kilbridemore PA22 73 J1
Kilburn *Derbys.* DE56 41 F1
Kilburn *Gt.Lon.* NW6 23 F3
Kilburn *N.Yorks.* YO61 58 B2
Kilby LE18 41 J6
Kilchattan Bay PA20 73 K5
Kilchenzie PA28 66 A1
Kilcheran PA34 79 K4
Kilchiaran PA48 72 A4
Kilchoan *Arg. & B.* PA34 79 J6
Kilchoan *High.* PH36 79 F1
Kilchoman PA49 72 A4
Kilchrenan PA35 80 B5
Kilchrist PA28 66 A2
Kilconquhar KY9 83 F7
Kilcot GL18 29 F6
Kilcoy IV6 96 C6
Kilcreggan G84 74 A2
Kildale YO21 63 H6
Kildary IV18 96 E4
Kildavie PA28 66 B2
Kildermorie Lodge IV17 96 C4
Kildonan *N.Ayr.* KA27 66 E1
Kildonan (Cilldonnain) *W.Isles* HS8 84 C2
Kildonan Lodge KW8 104 E6
Kildonnan PH42 85 K6
Kildrochet House DG9 64 A5
Kildrummy AB33 90 C3
Kildwick BD20 57 F5
Kilfinan PA21 73 H3
Kilfinnan PH34 87 J5
Kilgetty SA68 16 E5
Kilgwrrwg Common NP16 19 H2
Kilham *E.Riding* YO25 59 G3
Kilham *Northumb.* TD12 77 G7
Kilkenneth PA77 78 A3
Kilkenny GL54 30 B7
Kilkerran *Arg. & B.* PA28 66 B2
Kilkerran *S.Ayr.* KA19 67 H3
Kilkhampton EX23 6 A4
Killamarsh S21 51 G4
Killay SA2 17 K6
Killbeg PA72 79 H3
Killean *Arg. & B.* PA29 72 E6
Killean *Arg. & B.* PA32 80 B7
Killearn G63 74 D2
Killellan PA28 66 A2
Killen IV9 96 D6
Killerby DL2 62 C4
Killerton EX5 7 H5
Killichonan PH17 81 G2
Killiechonate PH34 87 J6
Killiechronan PA72 79 G3
Killiecrankie PH16 82 A1
Killiehuntly PH21 88 E5
Killiemor PA72 79 F4
Killilan IV40 87 F1
Killimster KW1 105 J3
Killin *High.* KW9 97 F1
Killin *Stir.* FK21 81 G4
Killinallan PA44 72 B3
Killinghall HG3 57 H4
Killington *Cumb.* LA6 56 B1
Killington *Devon* EX31 6 E1
Killingworth NE12 71 H6
Killochyett TD1 76 C6
Killocraw PA28 72 E7
Killunaig PA70 79 F5
Killundine PA34 79 G3
Kilmacolm PA13 74 B4
Kilmaha PA35 80 A7
Kilmahog FK17 81 H7
Kilmalieu PH33 79 K2
Kilmaluag IV51 93 K4
Kilmany KY15 82 E5
Kilmarie IV49 86 B3
KILMARNOCK KA 74 C7
Kilmartin PA31 73 G1
Kilmaurs KA3 74 C6
Kilmelford PA34 79 K6
Kilmeny PA45 72 B4
Kilmersdon BA3 19 K6
Kilmeston SO24 11 G2
Kilmichael PA28 66 A1
Kilmichael Glassary PA31 73 G1
Kilmichael of Inverlussa PA31 73 F2
Kilmington *Devon* EX13 8 B5
Kilmington *Wilts.* BA12 9 G1
Kilmington Common BA12 9 G1
Kilmorack IV4 96 B7
Kilmore *Arg. & B.* PA34 79 K5
Kilmore *High.* IV44 86 C4
Kilmory *Arg. & B.* PA31 73 F2
Kilmory *Arg. & B.* PA31 73 F3
Kilmory *High.* PH43 85 J4
Kilmory *High.* PH36 86 B7
Kilmory *N.Ayr.* KA27 66 D1
Kilmote KW8 104 E7
Kilmuir *High.* IV55 93 H7
Kilmuir *High.* IV1 96 D7
Kilmuir *High.* IV18 96 E4
Kilmuir *High.* IV51 93 J4
Kilmun PA23 73 K2
Kilmux KY8 82 E7
Kiln Green *Here.* HR9 29 F7
Kiln Green *W'ham* RG10 22 B4
Kiln Pit Hill DH8 62 B1
Kilnave PA44 72 A3
Kilncadzow ML8 75 G6
Kilndown TN17 14 C4
Kilnhurst S64 51 G3
Kilninian PA74 79 F3
Kilninver PA34 79 K5
Kilnsea HU12 53 H1
Kilnsey BD23 56 E3
Kilnwick YO25 59 F5
Kilnwick Percy YO42 58 E4
Kiloran PA61 72 B1
Kilpatrick KA27 66 D1
Kilpeck HR2 28 D5
Kilphedir KW8 104 E7
Kilpin DN14 58 D7
Kilpin Pike DN14 58 D7
Kilrenny KY10 83 G7
Kilsby CV23 31 G1
Kilspindie PH2 82 D5
Kilstay DG9 64 B7
Kilsyth G65 75 F3
Kiltarlity IV4 96 C7
Kilton *Notts.* S81 51 H5
Kilton *R. & C.* TS13 63 H5
Kilton *Som.* TA5 7 K1
Kilton Thorpe TS12 63 H5
Kiltyrie FK21 81 H4
Kilvaxter IV51 93 J5
Kilve TA5 7 K1
Kilverstone IP24 44 C7
Kilvington NG13 42 B1
Kilwinning KA13 74 B6
Kimberley *Norf.* NR18 44 E5
Kimberley *Notts.* NG16 41 H1
Kimberworth S61 51 G3
Kimble Wick HP17 22 B1
Kimblesworth DH2 62 D2
Kimbolton *Cambs.* PE28 32 D2
Kimbolton *Here.* HR6 28 E2
Kimbridge SO51 10 E2
Kimcote LE17 41 H7
Kimmeridge BH20 9 J7
Kimmerston NE71 77 H7
Kimpton *Hants.* SP11 21 F7
Kimpton *Herts.* SG4 32 E7
Kinaldy KY16 83 G6
Kinblethmont DD11 83 H3
Kinbrace KW11 104 D5
Kinbreack PH34 87 G5
Kinbuck FK15 81 J7
Kincaldrum DD8 83 F3
Kincaple KY16 83 F6
Kincardine *Fife* FK10 75 H2
Kincardine *High.* IV24 96 D3
Kincardine O'Neil AB34 90 D5
Kinclaven PH1 82 C4
Kincorth AB12 91 H4
Kincraig *Aber.* AB41 91 H2
Kincraig *High.* PH21 89 F4
Kincraigie PH8 82 A3
Kindallachan PH9 82 A2
Kindrogan Field Centre PH10 82 B1
Kinellar AB21 91 G3
Kineton *Glos.* GL54 30 B6
Kineton *Warks.* CV35 30 E3
Kineton Green B92 40 D7
Kinfauns PH2 82 C5
King Sterndale SK17 50 C5
Kingarth PA20 73 J5
Kingcoed NP15 19 H1
Kingerby LN8 52 D3
Kingham OX7 30 D6
Kingholm Quay DG1 65 K3
Kinghorn KY3 76 A2
Kinglassie KY5 76 A1
Kingoodie DD2 82 E5
King's Acre HR4 28 D4
King's Bank TN31 14 D5
King's Bromley DE13 40 D4
Kings Caple HR1 28 E6
King's Cliffe PE8 42 D6
King's Coughton B49 30 B3
King's Green WR13 29 G5
King's Heath B14 40 C7
Kings Hill *Kent* ME19 23 K6
King's Hill *W.Mid.* WS10 40 B6
Kings Hill *Warks.* CV3 30 E1
Kings Langley WD4 22 D1
King's Lynn PE30 44 A3
King's Meaburn CA10 61 H4
Kings Mills GY5 3 H5
King's Moss WA11 48 E2
Kings Muir EH45 76 A7
King's Newnham CV23 31 F1
King's Newton DE73 41 F3
King's Norton *Leics.* LE7 41 J5
King's Norton *W.Mid.* B30 30 B1
Kings Nympton EX37 6 E4
King's Pyon HR4 28 D3
Kings Ripton PE28 33 F1
King's Somborne SO20 10 E1
King's Stag DT10 9 G3
King's Stanley GL10 20 B1
King's Sutton OX17 31 F5
King's Tamerton PL5 4 E5
King's Walden SG4 32 E6
Kings Worthy SO23 11 F1
Kingsand PL10 4 E5
Kingsbarns KY16 83 G6
Kingsbridge *Devon* TQ7 5 H6
Kingsbridge *Som.* TA23 7 H2
Kingsburgh IV51 93 J6
Kingsbury *Gt.Lon.* HA3 22 E3
Kingsbury *Warks.* B78 40 E6
Kingsbury Episcopi TA12 8 D2
Kingscavil EH49 75 J3
Kingsclere RG20 21 J6
Kingscote GL8 20 B2
Kingscott EX38 6 D4
Kingscross KA27 66 E1
Kingsdale KY8 82 E7
Kingsdon TA11 8 E2
Kingsdown *Kent* CT14 15 J3
Kingsdown *Swin.* SN2 20 E3
Kingsdown *Wilts.* SN13 20 B5
Kingseat KY12 75 K1
Kingsey HP17 22 A1
Kingsfold *Pembs.* SA71 16 C6
Kingsfold *W.Suss.* RH12 12 E3
Kingsford *Aber.* AB53 99 F6
Kingsford *Aber.* AB33 90 D3
Kingsford *Aberdeen* AB15 91 G4
Kingsford *E.Ayr.* KA3 74 C6
Kingsford *Worcs.* DY11 40 A7
Kingsgate CT10 25 K4
Kingshall Street IP30 34 D2
Kingsheanton EX31 6 D2
Kingshouse FK19 81 G5
Kingshouse Hotel PH49 80 D2
Kingshurst B37 40 D7
Kingskerswell TQ12 5 J4
Kingskettle KY15 82 E7
Kingsland *Here.* HR6 28 D2

Kingsland *I.o.A.* **LL65** 46 A4
Kingsley *Ches.* **WA6** 48 E5
Kingsley *Hants.* **GU35** 11 J1
Kingsley *Staffs.* **ST10** 40 C1
Kingsley Green **GU27** 12 B3
Kingsley Holt **ST10** 40 C1
Kingslow **WV6** 39 G6
Kingsmoor **CM19** 23 H1
Kingsmuir *Angus* **DD8** 83 F3
Kingsmuir *Fife* **KY16** 83 G7
Kingsnorth **TN23** 15 F4
Kingsnorth Power Station **ME3** 24 E4
Kingstanding **B44** 40 C6
Kingsteignton **TQ12** 5 J3
Kingsteps **IV12** 97 G6
Kingsthorne **HR2** 28 D5
Kingsthorpe **NN2** 31 J2
Kingston *Cambs.* **CB3** 33 G3
Kingston *Cornw.* **PL17** 4 D3
Kingston *Devon* **TQ7** 5 G6
Kingston *Devon* **EX10** 7 J7
Kingston *Dorset* **DT10** 9 G4
Kingston *Dorset* **BH20** 9 J7
Kingston *E.Loth.* **EH39** 76 D2
Kingston *Gt.Man.* **SK14** 49 J3
Kingston *Hants.* **BH24** 10 C4
Kingston *I.o.W.* **PO38** 11 F6
Kingston *Kent* **CT4** 15 G2
Kingston *M.K.* **MK10** 32 C5
Kingston *Moray* **IV32** 98 B4
Kingston *W.Suss.* **BN16** 12 D6
Kingston Bagpuize **OX13** 21 G2
Kingston Blount **OX39** 22 A2
Kingston by Sea **BN43** 13 F6
Kingston Deverill **BA12** 9 H1
Kingston Gorse **BN16** 12 D6
Kingston Lisle **OX12** 21 G3
Kingston Maurward **DT2** 9 G5
Kingston near Lewes **BN7** 13 G6
Kingston on Soar **NG11** 41 H3
Kingston Russell **DT2** 8 E5
Kingston St. Mary **TA2** 8 B2
Kingston Seymour **BS21** 19 H5
Kingston Stert **OX39** 22 A1
KINGSTON UPON HULL HU 59 H7
KINGSTON UPON THAMES KT 22 E5
Kingston Warren **OX12** 21 G3
Kingstone *Here.* **HR2** 28 D5
Kingstone *Here.* **HR9** 29 F6
Kingstone *Som.* **TA19** 8 C3
Kingstone *Staffs.* **ST14** 40 C3
Kingstone Winslow **SN6** 21 F3
Kingstown **CA3** 60 E1
Kingswear **TQ6** 5 J5
Kingswell **KA3** 74 D6
Kingswells **AB15** 91 G4
Kingswinford DY6 40 A7
Kingswood *Bucks.* **HP18** 31 H7
Kingswood *Glos.* **GL12** 20 A2
Kingswood *Here.* **HR5** 28 B3
Kingswood *Kent* **ME17** 14 D2
Kingswood *Powys* **SY21** 38 B5
Kingswood *S.Glos.* **BS15** 19 K4
Kingswood *Som.* **TA4** 7 K2
Kingswood *Surr.* **KT20** 23 F6
Kingswood *Warks.* **B94** 30 C1
Kingthorpe **LN8** 52 E5
Kington *Here.* HR5 28 B3
Kington *Worcs.* **WR7** 29 J3
Kington Langley **SN15** 20 C4
Kington Magna **SP8** 9 G2
Kington St. Michael **SN14** 20 C4
Kingussie PH21 88 E4
Kingweston **TA11** 8 E1
Kinharrachie **AB41** 91 H1
Kinharvie **DG2** 65 K4
Kinkell **G66** 74 E3
Kinkell Bridge **PH3** 82 A6
Kinknockie **AB42** 99 J6
Kinlet **DY12** 39 G7
Kinloch *Fife* **KY15** 82 D6
Kinloch *High.* **IV27** 103 F5
Kinloch *High.* **PA34** 79 H2
Kinloch *High.* **PH43** 85 K5
Kinloch *High.* **IV16** 96 C4
Kinloch *P. & K.* **PH12** 82 D3
Kinloch *P. & K.* **PH10** 82 C3
Kinloch Hourn **PH35** 87 F4
Kinloch Laggan **PH20** 88 C6
Kinloch Rannoch **PH16** 81 H2
Kinlochan **PH37** 79 K1
Kinlochard **FK8** 81 F7
Kinlocharkaig **PH34** 87 F5
Kinlochbeoraid **PH38** 86 E6
Kinlochbervie **IV27** 102 E3
Kinlocheil **PH33** 87 F7
Kinlochetive **PH49** 80 C3
Kinlochewe **IV22** 95 G5
Kinlochlaich **PA38** 80 A3
Kinlochleven PH50 80 C1
Kinlochmoidart **PH38** 86 D7
Kinlochmorar **PH41** 86 E5
Kinlochmore **PH50** 80 C1
Kinlochroag (Ceann Lochroag) **HS2** 100 D5
Kinlochspelve **PA63** 79 H5
Kinloss **IV36** 97 H5
Kinmel Bay (Bae Cinmel) **LL18** 47 H4
Kinmuck **AB51** 91 G3
Kinnaber **DD10** 83 J1
Kinnadie **AB41** 99 H6
Kinnaird **PH14** 82 D5
Kinneff **DD10** 91 G7
Kinnelhead **DG10** 69 F3
Kinnell *Angus* **DD11** 83 H2
Kinnell *Stir.* **FK21** 81 G4
Kinnerley **SY10** 38 C3
Kinnersley *Here.* **HR3** 28 C4
Kinnersley *Worcs.* **WR8** 29 H4
Kinnerton **LD8** 28 B2
Kinnerton Green **CH4** 48 C6
Kinnesswood **KY13** 82 C7
Kinnettles **DD8** 83 F3
Kinninvie **DL12** 62 B4
Kinnordy **DD8** 82 E2
Kinoulton **NG12** 41 J2
Kinrara **PH22** 89 F4
Kinross KY13 82 C7
Kinrossie **PH2** 82 C4
Kinsbourne Green **AL5** 32 E7
Kinsham *Here.* **LD8** 28 C2
Kinsham *Worcs.* **GL20** 29 J5
Kinsley **WF9** 51 G1
Kinson **BH10** 10 B5
Kintarvie **HS2** 100 E6
Kintbury **RG17** 21 G5
Kintessack **IV36** 97 G5
Kintillo **PH2** 82 C6
Kintocher **AB33** 90 D4
Kinton *Here.* **SY7** 28 D1
Kinton *Shrop.* **SY4** 38 C4
Kintore **AB51** 91 F3
Kintour **PA42** 72 C5
Kintra *Arg. & B.* **PA42** 72 B6
Kintra *Arg. & B.* **PA66** 78 E5
Kintradwell **KW9** 97 G1
Kintraw **PA31** 79 K7
Kinuachdrachd **PA60** 73 F1
Kinveachy **PH24** 89 G3
Kinver **DY7** 40 A7
Kinwarton **B49** 30 C3
Kiplaw Croft **AB42** 91 J1
Kipp **FK18** 81 G6
Kippax **LS25** 57 K6
Kippen *P. & K.* **PH2** 82 B6
Kippen *Stir.* **FK8** 74 E1
Kippenross House **FK15** 81 J7
Kippford (Scaur) **DG5** 65 J5
Kipping's Cross **TN12** 23 K7
Kippington **TN13** 23 J6
Kirbister *Ork.* **KW17** 106 C7
Kirbister *Ork.* **KW17** 106 F5
Kirbuster **KW17** 106 B5
Kirby Bedon **NR14** 45 G5
Kirby Bellars **LE14** 42 A4
Kirby Cane **NR35** 45 H6
Kirby Corner **CV4** 30 D1
Kirby Cross **CO13** 35 G6
Kirby Fields **LE9** 41 H5
Kirby Green **NR35** 45 H6
Kirby Grindalythe **YO17** 59 F3
Kirby Hill *N.Yorks.* **DL11** 62 C6
Kirby Hill *N.Yorks.* **YO51** 57 J3
Kirby Knowle **YO7** 57 K1
Kirby le Soken **CO13** 35 G6
Kirby Misperton **YO17** 58 D2
Kirby Muxloe **LE9** 41 H5
Kirby Row **NR35** 45 H6
Kirby Sigston **DL6** 63 F7
Kirby Underdale **YO41** 58 E4
Kirby Wiske **YO7** 57 J1
Kirdford **RH14** 12 D4
Kirk **KW1** 105 H3
Kirk Bramwith **DN7** 51 J1
Kirk Deighton **LS22** 57 J4
Kirk Ella **HU10** 59 G7
Kirk Hallam **DE7** 41 G1
Kirk Hammerton **YO26** 57 K4
Kirk Ireton **DE6** 50 E7
Kirk Langley **DE6** 40 E2
Kirk Merrington **DL16** 62 D3
Kirk Michael **IM6** 54 C4
Kirk of Shotts **ML7** 75 G4
Kirk Sandall **DN3** 51 J2
Kirk Smeaton **WF8** 51 H1
Kirk Yetholm **TD5** 70 D1
Kirkabister **ZE2** 107 N9
Kirkandrews **DG6** 65 G6
Kirkandrews-upon-Eden **CA5** 60 E1
Kirkbampton **CA5** 60 E1
Kirkbean **DG2** 65 K5
Kirkbride **CA7** 60 D1
Kirkbuddo **DD8** 83 G3
Kirkburn *E.Riding* **YO25** 59 F4
Kirkburn *Sc.Bord.* **EH45** 76 A7
Kirkburton **HD8** 50 D1
Kirkby *Lincs.* **LN8** 52 D3
Kirkby *Mersey.* **L32** 48 D3
Kirkby *N.Yorks.* **TS9** 63 G6
Kirkby Fleetham **DL7** 62 D7
Kirkby Green **LN4** 52 D7
Kirkby in Ashfield **NG17** 51 G7
Kirkby la Thorpe **NG34** 42 D1
Kirkby Lonsdale **LA6** 56 B2
Kirkby Malham **BD23** 56 D3
Kirkby Mallory **LE9** 41 G5
Kirkby Malzeard **HG4** 57 H2
Kirkby on Bain **LN10** 53 F6
Kirkby Overblow **HG3** 57 J5
Kirkby Stephen CA17 61 J6
Kirkby Thore **CA10** 61 H4
Kirkby Underwood **PE10** 42 D3
Kirkby Wharfe **LS24** 58 B5
Kirkby Woodhouse **NG17** 51 G7
Kirkby-in-Furness LA17 55 F1
Kirkbymoorside **YO62** 58 C1
KIRKCALDY KY 76 A1
Kirkcambeck **CA8** 70 A7
Kirkcolm **DG9** 64 A4
Kirkconnel **DG4** 68 C2
Kirkconnell **DG2** 65 K4
Kirkcowan **DG8** 64 D4
Kirkcudbright DG6 65 G5
Kirkdale House **DG8** 65 F5
Kirkdean **EH46** 75 K6
Kirkfieldbank **ML11** 75 G6
Kirkgunzeon **DG2** 65 J4
Kirkham *Lancs.* **PR4** 55 H6
Kirkham *N.Yorks.* **YO60** 58 D3
Kirkhamgate **WF2** 57 J7
Kirkharle **NE19** 71 F5
Kirkhaugh **CA9** 61 H2
Kirkheaton *Northumb.* **NE19** 71 F6
Kirkheaton *W.Yorks.* **HD5** 50 D1
Kirkhill *Angus* **DD10** 83 H1
Kirkhill *High.* **IV5** 96 C7
Kirkhill *Moray* **AB38** 98 B5
Kirkhope **TD7** 69 J1
Kirkibost *High.* **IV49** 86 B3
Kirkibost (Circebost) *W.Isles* **HS2** 100 D4
Kirkinch **PH12** 82 E3
Kirkinner **DG8** 64 E5
Kirkintilloch **G66** 74 E3
Kirkland *Cumb.* **CA10** 61 H3
Kirkland *Cumb.* **CA26** 60 B5
Kirkland *D. & G.* **DG3** 68 D4
Kirkland *D. & G.* **DG4** 68 C2
Kirkland *D. & G.* **DG11** 69 F5
Kirkland of Longcastle **DG8** 64 D6
Kirkleatham **TS10** 63 G4
Kirklevington **TS15** 63 F5
Kirkley **NR33** 45 K6
Kirklington *N.Yorks.* **DL8** 57 J1
Kirklington *Notts.* **NG22** 51 J7
Kirklinton **CA6** 69 K7
Kirkliston EH29 75 K3
Kirkmaiden **DG9** 64 B7
Kirkmichael *P. & K.* **PH10** 82 B1
Kirkmichael *S.Ayr.* **KA19** 67 H3
Kirkmuirhill **ML11** 75 F6
Kirknewton *Northumb.* **NE71** 77 H7
Kirknewton *W.Loth.* EH27 75 K4
Kirkney **AB54** 90 D1
Kirkoswald *Cumb.* **CA10** 61 G2
Kirkoswald *S.Ayr.* **KA19** 67 G3
Kirkpatrick Durham **DG7** 65 H3
Kirkpatrick-Fleming **DG11** 69 H6
Kirksanton **LA18** 54 E1
Kirkstall **LS5** 57 H6
Kirkstead **LN10** 52 E6
Kirkstile *Aber.* **AB54** 90 D1
Kirkstile *D. & G.* **DG13** 69 J4
Kirkstyle **KW1** 105 J1
Kirkthorpe **WF1** 57 J7
Kirkton *Aber.* **AB52** 90 E2
Kirkton *Aber.* **AB53** 98 E5
Kirkton *Aber.* **AB33** 90 E3
Kirkton *Angus* **DD8** 83 F3
Kirkton *Arg. & B.* **PA31** 79 J7
Kirkton *D. & G.* **DG1** 68 E5
Kirkton *Fife* **DD6** 82 E5
Kirkton *High.* **IV3** 88 D1
Kirkton *High.* **KW10** 96 E2
Kirkton *High.* **IV2** 96 E6
Kirkton *High.* **KW13** 104 D2
Kirkton *High.* **IV40** 86 E2
Kirkton *P. & K.* **PH3** 82 A6
Kirkton *Sc.Bord.* **TD9** 70 A2
Kirkton Manor **EH45** 76 A7
Kirkton of Airlie **DD8** 82 E2
Kirkton of Auchterhouse **DD3** 82 E4
Kirkton of Barevan **IV12** 97 F7
Kirkton of Bourtie **AB51** 91 G2
Kirkton of Collace **PH2** 82 C4
Kirkton of Craig **DD10** 83 J2
Kirkton of Culsalmond **AB52** 90 E1
Kirkton of Durris **AB31** 91 F5
Kirkton of Glenbuchat **AB36** 90 B3
Kirkton of Glenisla **PH11** 82 D1
Kirkton of Kingoldrum **DD8** 82 E2
Kirkton of Lethendy **PH2** 82 C3
Kirkton of Logie Buchan **AB41** 91 H2
Kirkton of Maryculter **AB12** 91 G5
Kirkton of Menmuir **DD9** 83 G1
Kirkton of Monikie **DD5** 83 G4
Kirkton of Rayne **AB51** 90 E1
Kirkton of Skene **AB32** 91 G4
Kirkton of Tealing **DD4** 83 F4
Kirktonhill *Aber.* **AB30** 83 H1
Kirktonhill *W.Dun.* **G82** 74 B3
Kirktown **AB42** 99 J5
Kirktown of Alvah **AB45** 98 E4
Kirktown of Auchterless **AB53** 99 F6
Kirktown of Deskford **AB56** 98 D4
Kirktown of Fetteresso **AB39** 91 G6
Kirktown of Slains **AB41** 91 J2
KIRKWALL KW 106 D6
Kirkwall Airport **KW15** 106 D7
Kirkwhelpington **NE19** 70 E5
Kirmington **DN39** 52 E1
Kirmond le Mire **LN8** 52 E3
Kirn **PA23** 73 K3
Kirriemuir DD8 82 E2
Kirstead Green **NR15** 45 G6
Kirtlebridge **DG11** 69 H6
Kirtleton **DG11** 69 H5
Kirtling **CB8** 33 K3
Kirtling Green **CB8** 33 K3
Kirtlington **OX5** 31 G7
Kirtomy **KW14** 104 C2
Kirton *Lincs.* **PE20** 43 G2
Kirton *Notts.* **NG22** 51 J6
Kirton *Suff.* **IP10** 35 G5
Kirton End **PE20** 43 F1
Kirton Holme **PE20** 43 F1
Kirton in Lindsey **DN21** 52 C3
Kiscadale **KA27** 66 E1
Kislingbury **NN7** 31 H3
Kismeldon Bridge **EX22** 6 B4
Kites Hardwick **CV23** 31 F2
Kitley **PL8** 5 F5
Kittisford **TA21** 7 J3
Kittisford Barton **TA21** 7 J3
Kittle **SA3** 17 J7
Kitt's End **EN5** 23 F2
Kitt's Green **B33** 40 D7
Kitwood **SO24** 11 H1
Kivernoll **HR2** 28 D5
Kiveton Park **S26** 51 G4
Klibreck **IV27** 103 H5
Knabbygates **AB54** 98 D5
Knaith **DN21** 52 B4
Knaith Park **DN21** 52 B4
Knap Corner **SP8** 9 H2
Knaphill **GU21** 22 C6
Knaplock **TA22** 7 G2
Knapp *P. & K.* **PH14** 82 D4
Knapp *Som.* **TA3** 8 C2
Knapthorpe **NG23** 51 K7
Knaptoft **LE17** 41 J7
Knapton *Norf.* **NR28** 45 H2
Knapton *York* **YO26** 58 B4
Knapton Green **HR4** 28 D3
Knapwell **CB3** 33 G2
Knaresborough HG5 57 J4
Knarsdale **CA8** 61 H1
Knarston **KW17** 106 C5
Knaven **AB42** 99 G6
Knayton **YO7** 57 K1
Knebworth SG3 33 F6
Knedlington **DN14** 58 D7
Kneesall **NG22** 51 K6
Kneesworth **SG8** 33 G4
Kneeton **NG13** 42 A1
Knelston **SA3** 17 H7
Knenhall **ST15** 40 B2
Knettishall **IP22** 44 D7
Knightacott **EX31** 6 E2
Knightcote **CV47** 31 F3
Knightley **ST20** 40 A3
Knightley Dale **ST20** 40 A3
Knighton *Devon* **PL9** 5 F6
Knighton *Dorset* **DT9** 9 F3
Knighton *Leic.* **LE2** 41 J5
Knighton *Poole* **BH21** 10 B5
Knighton (Tref-y-clawdd) *Powys* LD7 28 B1
Knighton *Som.* **TA5** 7 K1
Knighton *Staffs.* **ST20** 39 G3
Knighton *Staffs.* **TF9** 39 G1
Knighton *Wilts.* **SN8** 21 F4
Knighton on Teme **WR15** 29 F1
Knightswood **G15** 74 D4
Knightwick **WR6** 29 G3
Knill **LD8** 28 B2
Knipoch **PA34** 79 K5
Knipton **NG32** 42 B2
Knitsley **DH8** 62 C2
Kniveton **DE6** 50 E7
Knock *Arg. & B.* **PA71** 79 G4
Knock *Cumb.* **CA16** 61 H4
Knock *High.* **IV44** 86 C4
Knock *Moray* **AB54** 98 D5
Knock of Auchnahannet **PH26** 89 H1
Knockalava **PA31** 73 H1
Knockally **KW6** 105 G6
Knockaloe Moar **IM5** 54 B5
Knockan **IV27** 102 E7
Knockandhu **AB37** 89 K2
Knockando **AB38** 97 J7
Knockarthur **IV28** 96 E1
Knockbain **IV8** 96 D6
Knockban **IV23** 95 J5
Knockbreck **IV19** 96 E3
Knockbrex **DG6** 65 F6
Knockdamph **IV26** 95 J2
Knockdee **KW12** 105 G2
Knockdow **PA23** 73 K3
Knockdown **GL8** 20 B3
Knockenkelly **KA27** 66 E1
Knockentiber **KA2** 74 B7
Knockfin **IV4** 87 K2
Knockgray **DG7** 67 K4
Knockholt **TN14** 23 H6
Knockholt Pound **TN14** 23 H6
Knockin **SY10** 38 C3
Knockinlaw **KA3** 74 C7
Knockintorran (Cnoc an Torrain) **HS6** 92 C5
Knocklearn **DG7** 65 H3
Knockmill **TN15** 23 J5
Knocknaha **PA28** 66 A2
Knocknain **DG9** 66 D7
Knocknalling **DG7** 67 K5
Knockrome **PA60** 72 D3
Knocksharry **IM5** 54 B5
Knockville **DG8** 64 D3
Knockvologan **PA66** 78 E6
Knodishall **IP17** 35 J2
Knodishall Common **IP17** 35 J2
Knodishall Green **IP17** 35 J2
Knole **TA10** 8 D2
Knolls Green **WA16** 49 H5
Knolton **LL13** 38 C2
Knook **BA12** 20 C7
Knossington **LE15** 42 B5
Knott End-on-Sea **FY6** 55 G5
Knotting **MK44** 32 D2
Knotting Green **MK44** 32 D2
Knottingley WF11 58 B7
Knotts **BD23** 56 C4
Knotty Green **HP9** 22 C2
Knowbury **SY8** 28 E1
Knowe **DG8** 64 D3
Knowes of Elrick **AB54** 98 E5
Knowesgate **NE19** 70 E5
Knoweside **KA19** 67 G2
Knowetownhead **TD9** 70 A2
Knowhead **AB43** 99 H5
Knowl Green **CO10** 34 B4
Knowl Hill **RG10** 22 B4
Knowl Wall **ST4** 40 A2
Knowle *Bristol* **BS4** 19 K4
Knowle *Devon* **EX17** 7 F5
Knowle *Devon* **EX33** 6 C2
Knowle *Devon* **EX9** 7 J7
Knowle *Shrop.* **SY8** 28 E1
Knowle *Som.* **TA24** 7 H1
Knowle *W.Mid.* **B93** 30 C1
Knowle Cross **EX5** 7 J6
Knowle Green **PR3** 56 B6
Knowle Hall **TA7** 19 G7
Knowle St. Giles **TA20** 8 C3
Knowlton *Dorset* **BH21** 10 B3
Knowlton *Kent* **CT3** 15 H2
Knowsley **L34** 48 D3
Knowstone **EX36** 7 G3
Knox Bridge **TN17** 14 C3
Knucklas **LD7** 28 B1
Knutsford WA16 49 G5
Knypersley **ST8** 49 H7
Krumlin **HX4** 50 C1
Kuggar **TR12** 2 E7
Kyle of Lochalsh **IV40** 86 D2
Kyleakin **IV41** 86 D2
Kylerhea **IV40** 86 D2
Kyles Scalpay (Caolas Scalpaigh) **HS3** 93 H2
Kylesbeg **PH38** 86 C7
Kylesknoydart **PH41** 86 E5
Kylesku **IV27** 102 E5
Kylesmorar **PH41** 86 E5
Kylestrome **IV27** 102 E5
Kyloag **IV24** 96 D2
Kynaston **SY10** 38 C3
Kynnersley **TF6** 39 F4
Kyre Park **WR15** 29 F2

L

Labost **HS2** 100 E3
Lacasaigh **HS2** 101 F5
Lacasdal (Laxdale) **HS2** 101 G4
Laceby **DN37** 53 F2
Lacey Green **HP27** 22 B1
Lach Dennis **CW9** 49 G5
Lacharn (Laugharne) **SA33** 17 G4
Lackford **IP28** 34 B1
Lacklee (Leac a' Li) **HS3** 93 G2
Lacock **SN15** 20 C5
Ladbroke **CV47** 31 F3
Laddingford **ME18** 23 K7
Lade Bank **PE22** 53 G7
Ladies Hill **PR3** 55 H5
Ladock **TR2** 3 F3
Lady Hall **LA18** 54 E1
Ladybank **KY15** 82 E6
Ladycross **PL15** 6 B7
Ladyfield **PA32** 80 B6
Ladykirk **TD15** 77 G6
Ladysford **AB43** 99 H4
Ladywood **WR9** 29 H2
Laga **PH36** 79 H1
Lagalochan **PA35** 79 K6
Lagavulin **PA42** 72 C6
Lagg *Arg. & B.* **PA60** 72 D3
Lagg *N.Ayr.* **KA27** 66 D1
Lagg *S.Ayr.* **KA7** 67 G2
Laggan *Arg. & B.* **PA43** 72 A5
Laggan *High.* **PH34** 87 J5
Laggan *High.* **PH20** 88 D5
Laggan *Moray* **AB55** 90 B1
Laggan *Stir.* **FK18** 81 G6
Lagganulva **PA73** 79 F3
Lagganvoulin **AB37** 89 J3
Laglingarten **PA25** 80 C7
Lagnalean **IV3** 96 D7
Lagrae **DG4** 68 C2
Laguna **PH1** 82 C4
Laid **IV27** 103 G3
Laide **IV22** 95 F2
Laig **PH42** 85 K6
Laight **KA18** 68 B2
Lainchoil **PH25** 89 H3
Laindon **SS15** 24 C3
Lair **PH10** 82 C1
Lairg IV27 96 C1
Lairg Lodge **IV27** 96 C1
Lairigmor **PH33** 80 C1
Laisterdyke **BD4** 57 G6
Laithers **AB53** 98 E6
Laithes **CA11** 61 F3
Lake *Devon* **EX31** 6 D2
Lake *Devon* **PL20** 5 F4
Lake *I.o.W.* **PO36** 11 G6
Lake *Wilts.* **SP4** 10 C1
Lakenham **NR1** 45 G5
Lakenheath **IP27** 44 B7
Lakesend **PE14** 43 J6
Lakeside *Cumb.* **LA12** 55 G1
Lakeside *S.Yorks.* **DN4** 51 H2
Lakeside *Thur.* **RM20** 23 J4
Laleham **TW18** 22 D5
Laleston **CF32** 18 B4
Lamancha **EH46** 76 A5
Lamarsh **CO8** 34 C5
Lamas **NR10** 45 G3
Lamb Corner **CO7** 34 E5
Lamb Roe **BB7** 56 C6
Lambden **TD10** 77 F6
Lamberhurst **TN3** 13 K3
Lamberhurst Quarter **TN3** 13 K3

Lamberton TD15 77 H5
Lambfell Moar IM4 54 B5
Lambley Northumb. CA8 61 H1
Lambley Notts. NG4 41 J1
Lambourn RG17 21 G4
Lambourn Woodlands RG17 21 G4
Lambourne End RM4 23 H2
Lambs Green RH12 13 F3
Lambston SA62 16 C4
Lambton NE38 62 D1
Lamellion PL14 4 C4
Lamerton PL19 4 E3
Lamesley NE11 62 D1
Lamington High. IV18 96 E4
Lamington S.Lan. ML12 75 H7
Lamlash KA27 73 J7
Lamloch DG7 67 K4
Lamonby CA11 60 F3
Lamorna TR19 2 B6
Lamorran TR2 3 F4
Lampert NE48 70 B6
Lampeter (Llanbedr Pont Steffan) SA48 17 J1
Lampeter Velfrey SA67 16 E4
Lamphey SA71 16 D5
Lamplugh CA14 60 B4
Lamport NN6 31 J1
Lamyatt BA4 9 F1
Lana Devon EX22 6 B6
Lana Devon EX22 6 B5
Lanark ML11 75 G6
Lanarth TR12 2 E6
LANCASTER LA 55 H3
Lanchester DH7 62 C2
Lancing BN15 12 E6
Landbeach CB4 33 H2
Landcross EX39 6 C3
Landerberry AB32 91 F4
Landewednack TR12 2 E7
Landford SP5 10 D3
Landhallow KW5 105 G5
Landican CH49 48 B4
Landimore SA3 17 H6
Landkey EX32 6 D2
Landmoth DL6 63 F7
Landore SA1 17 K6
Landrake PL12 4 D4
Landscove TQ13 5 H4
Landshipping SA67 16 D4
Landulph PL12 4 E4
Landwade CB8 33 K2
Landywood WS6 40 B5
Lane Bottom BB10 56 D6
Lane End Bucks. HP14 22 B2
Lane End Cumb. LA19 60 C7
Lane End Derbys. DE55 51 G6
Lane End Dorset BH20 9 H5
Lane End Hants. SO21 11 G2
Lane End Here. HR9 29 F7
Lane End Kent DA2 23 J4
Lane End Wilts. BA12 20 B7
Lane Ends Derbys. DE6 40 E2
Lane Ends Gt.Man. SK6 49 J3
Lane Ends Lancs. BB11 56 C6
Lane Ends N.Yorks. BD22 56 E5
Lane Green WV8 40 A5
Lane Head Dur. DL11 62 C5
Lane Head Dur. DL13 62 B4
Lane Head Gt.Man. WA3 49 F3
Lane Head W.Yorks. HD8 50 D2
Lane Heads PR3 55 H6
Lane Side BB4 56 C7
Laneast PL15 4 C2
Lane-end PL30 4 A4
Laneham DN22 52 B5
Lanehead Dur. DL13 61 K2
Lanehead Northumb. NE48 70 C5
Lanesend SA68 16 D5
Lanesfield WV4 40 B6
Laneshawbridge BB8 56 E5
Langais HS6 92 D5
Langamull PA75 78 E2
Langar NG13 42 A2
Langbank PA14 74 B3
Langbar LS29 57 F4
Langbaurgh TS9 63 G5
Langcliffe BD24 56 D3
Langdale End YO13 63 J3
Langdon Cornw. EX23 4 C1
Langdon Cornw. PL15 6 B7
Langdon Beck DL12 61 K3
Langdon Hills SS16 24 C3
Langdon House EX7 5 K3
Langdyke KY8 82 E7
Langford Beds. SG18 32 E4
Langford Essex CM9 24 E1
Langford Notts. NG23 52 B7
Langford Oxon. GL7 21 F1
Langford Budville TA21 7 K3
Langham Essex CO4 34 E5
Langham Norf. NR25 44 E1
Langham Rut. LE15 42 B4
Langham Suff. IP31 34 D2
Langham Moor CO4 34 E5
Langho BB6 56 B6
Langholm DG13 69 J5
Langland SA3 17 K7
Langlands DG6 65 G5
Langlee TD8 70 B2
Langleeford NE71 70 E1
Langley Ches. SK11 49 J5
Langley Derbys. NG16 41 G1
Langley Essex CB11 33 H5
Langley Glos. GL54 30 B6
Langley Gt.Man. M24 49 H2
Langley Hants. SO45 11 F4
Langley Herts. SG4 33 F6
Langley Kent ME17 14 C2
Langley Northumb. NE47 70 D7
Langley Oxon. OX29 30 E7
Langley Slo. SL3 22 D4
Langley Som. TA4 7 J3
Langley W.Suss. GU33 12 B4
Langley Warks. CV37 30 C2
Langley Burrell SN15 20 C4
Langley Corner SL3 22 D3
Langley Green Derbys. DE6 40 E2
Langley Green W.Suss. RH11 13 F3
Langley Green Warks. CV35 30 D2
Langley Heath ME17 14 D2
Langley Marsh TA4 7 J3
Langley Mill NG16 41 G1
Langley Moor DH7 62 D2
Langley Park DH7 62 D2
Langley Street NR14 45 H5
Langney BN23 13 K6
Langold S81 51 H4
Langore PL15 4 C2
Langport TA10 8 D2
Langrick PE22 43 F1
Langrick Bridge PE22 43 F1
Langridge B. & N.E.Som. BA1 20 A5
Langridge Devon EX37 6 D3
Langridgeford EX37 6 D3
Langrigg CA7 60 C2
Langrish GU32 11 J2
Langsett S36 50 E2
Langshaw TD1 76 D7
Langshawburn DG13 69 H3
Langside Glas. G43 74 D4
Langside P. & K. PH6 81 J6
Langskaill KW17 106 D3
Langstone Hants. PO9 11 J4
Langstone Newport NP18 19 G2
Langthorne DL8 62 D7
Langthorpe YO51 57 J3
Langthwaite DL11 62 B6
Langtoft E.Riding YO25 59 G3
Langtoft Lincs. PE6 42 E4
Langton Dur. DL2 62 C5
Langton Lincs. PE23 53 G5
Langton Lincs. LN9 53 F6
Langton N.Yorks. YO17 58 D3
Langton by Wragby LN8 52 E5
Langton Green Kent TN3 13 J3
Langton Green Suff. IP23 35 F1
Langton Herring DT3 9 F6
Langton Long Blandford DT11 9 H4
Langton Matravers BH19 9 J7
Langtree EX38 6 C4
Langtree Week EX38 6 C4
Langwathby CA10 61 G3
Langwell IV27 96 B1
Langwell House KW7 105 G6
Langwith NG20 51 H5
Langworth LN3 52 D5
Lanivet PL30 4 A4
Lank PL30 4 A3
Lanlivery PL30 4 A5
Lanner TR16 2 E4
Lanoy PL15 4 C3
Lanreath PL13 4 B5
Lansallos PL13 4 B5
Lansdown BA1 20 A5
Lanteglos PL32 4 A2
Lanteglos Highway PL23 4 B5
Lanton Northumb. NE71 77 H7
Lanton Sc.Bord. TD8 70 B1
Lanvean TR8 3 F2
Lapford EX17 7 F5
Laphroaig PA42 72 B6
Lapley ST19 40 A4
Lapworth B94 30 C1
Larach na Gaibhre PA31 73 F3
Larachbeg PA34 79 H3
Larbert FK5 75 G2
Larbreck PR3 55 H5
Larden Green CW5 48 E7
Larg DG8 64 D3
Largie AB52 90 E1
Largiemore PA21 73 H2
Largoward KY9 83 F7
Largs KA30 74 A5
Largue AB54 98 E6
Largybaan PA28 66 A2
Largybeg KA27 66 E1
Largymore KA27 66 E1
Lark Hall CB1 33 J3
Larkfield PA16 74 A3
Larkhall ML9 75 F5
Larkhill SP4 20 E7
Larklands DE7 41 G1
Larling NR16 44 D7
Larriston TD9 70 A4
Lartington DL12 62 B5
Lary AB35 90 B4
Lasborough GL8 20 B2
Lasham GU34 21 K7
Lashbrook EX22 6 C5
Lashenden TN27 14 D3
Lassington GL2 29 G6
Lassintullich PH16 81 J2
Lassodie KY12 75 K1
Lasswade EH18 76 B4
Lastingham YO62 63 J7
Latchford WA4 49 F4
Latchingdon CM3 24 E1
Latchley PL18 4 E3
Lately Common WN7 49 F3
Lathallan Mill KY9 83 F7
Lathbury MK16 32 B4
Latheron KW5 105 G5
Latheronwheel KW5 105 G5
Lathockar KY16 83 F6
Lathones KY15 83 F7
Lathrisk KY15 82 D7
Latimer HP5 22 D2
Latteridge BS37 19 K3
Lattiford BA9 9 F2
Latton SN6 20 D2
Lauchentyre DG7 65 F5
Lauchintilly AB51 91 F3
Lauder TD2 76 D6
Laugharne (Lacharn) SA33 17 G4
Laughterton LN1 52 B5
Laughton E.Suss. BN8 13 J5
Laughton Leics. LE17 41 J7
Laughton Lincs. NG34 42 D2
Laughton Lincs. DN21 52 B3
Laughton en le Morthen S25 51 H4
Launcells EX23 6 A5
Launcells Cross EX23 6 A5
Launceston PL15 6 B7
Launde Abbey LE7 42 A5
Launton OX26 31 H6
Laurencekirk AB30 91 F7
Laurieston D. & G. DG7 65 G4
Laurieston Falk. FK2 75 H3
Lavendon MK46 32 C3
Lavenham CO10 34 D4
Laverhay DG10 69 G4
Lavernock CF64 18 E5
Laversdale CA6 69 K7
Laverstock SP1 10 C1
Laverstoke RG28 21 H7
Laverton Glos. WR12 30 B5
Laverton N.Yorks. HG4 57 H2
Laverton Som. BA2 20 A6
Lavister LL12 48 C7
Law ML8 75 G5
Lawers P. & K. PH6 81 J5
Lawers P. & K. PH15 81 H4
Lawford Essex CO11 34 E5
Lawford Som. TA4 7 K2
Lawhitton PL15 6 B7
Lawkland LA2 56 C3
Lawkland Green LA2 56 C3
Lawley TF4 39 F5
Lawnhead ST20 40 A3
Lawrence Weston BS11 19 J4
Lawrenny SA68 16 D5
Laws DD5 83 F4
Lawshall IP29 34 C3
Lawshall Green IP30 34 C3
Lawton HR6 28 D3
Laxdale (Lacasdal) HS2 101 G4
Laxey IM4 54 D5
Laxfield IP13 35 G1
Laxfirth Shet. ZE2 107 N7
Laxfirth Shet. ZE2 107 N8
Laxford Bridge IV27 102 E4
Laxo ZE2 107 N6
Laxton E.Riding DN14 58 D7
Laxton Northants. NN17 42 C6
Laxton Notts. NG22 51 K6
Laycock BD22 57 F5
Layer Breton CO2 34 D7
Layer de la Haye CO2 34 D7
Layer Marney CO5 34 D7
Layham IP7 34 E4
Laymore TA20 8 C4
Layter's Green SL9 22 C2
Laytham YO42 58 D6
Layton FY3 55 G6
Lazenby TS6 63 G4
Lazonby CA10 61 G3
Lea Derbys. DE4 51 F7
Lea Here. HR9 29 F6
Lea Lincs. DN21 52 B4
Lea Shrop. SY9 38 C7
Lea Shrop. SY5 38 D5
Lea Wilts. SN16 20 C3
Lea Bridge DE4 51 F7
Lea Green WR6 29 F2
Lea Marston B76 40 E6
Lea Town PR4 55 H6
Lea Yeat LA10 56 C1
Leac a' Li (Lacklee) HS3 93 G2
Leachd PA27 73 J1
Leachkin IV3 96 D7
Leadburn EH46 76 A5
Leaden Roding CM6 33 J7
Leadenham LN5 52 C7
Leaderfoot TD6 76 D7
Leadgate Cumb. CA9 61 J2
Leadgate Dur. DH8 62 C1
Leadgate Northumb. NE17 62 C1
Leadhills ML12 68 D2
Leadingcross Green ME17 14 D2
Leafield OX29 30 E7
Leagrave LU4 32 D6
Leake Commonside PE22 53 G7
Leake Hurn's End PE22 43 H1
Lealands BN27 13 J5
Lealholm YO21 63 J6
Lealt Arg. & B. PA60 72 E1
Lealt High. IV51 94 B5
Leam S32 50 E5
Leamington Hastings CV23 31 F2
Leamington Spa CV32 30 E2
Leamoor Common SY7 38 D7
Leanach Arg. & B. PA27 73 J1
Leanach High. IV2 96 E7
Leanaig IV7 96 C6
Leanoch IV30 97 J6
Leargybreck PA60 72 D3
Leasgill LA7 55 H1
Leasingham NG34 42 D1
Leask AB41 91 J1
Leason SA3 17 H6
Leasowe CH46 48 B3
Leat PL15 6 B7
Leatherhead KT22 22 E6
Leathley LS21 57 H5
Leaton Shrop. SY4 38 D4
Leaton Tel. & W. TF6 39 F4
Leaveland ME13 15 F2
Leavenheath CO6 34 D5
Leavening YO17 58 D3
Leaves Green BR2 23 H5
Leavesden Green WD25 22 E1
Lebberston YO11 59 G1
Lechlade GL7 21 F2
Leck LA6 56 B2
Leckford SO20 10 E1
Leckfurin KW14 104 C3
Leckgruinart PA44 72 A4
Leckhampstead Bucks. MK18 31 J5
Leckhampstead W.Berks. RG20 21 H4
Leckhampstead Thicket RG20 21 H4
Leckhampton GL53 29 J7
Leckie High. IV22 95 G5
Leckie Stir. FK8 74 E1
Leckmelm IV23 95 H3
Leckroy PH31 87 K5
Leckuary PA31 73 G1
Leckwith CF11 18 E4
Leconfield HU17 59 G5
Ledaig PA37 80 A4
Ledard FK8 81 F7
Ledbeg IV27 102 E7
Ledburn LU7 32 B6
Ledbury HR8 29 G5
Ledcharrie FK20 81 G5
Ledgemoor HR4 28 D3
Ledicot HR6 28 D2
Ledmore Arg. & B. PA72 79 G3
Ledmore High. IV27 102 E7
Lednagullin KW14 104 D2
Ledsham Ches. CH66 48 C5
Ledsham W.Yorks. LS25 57 K7
Ledston WF10 57 K7
Ledstone TQ7 5 H6
Ledwell OX7 31 F6
Lee Arg. & B. PA67 79 F5
Lee Devon EX34 6 C1
Lee Hants. SO51 10 E3
Lee Lancs. LA2 55 J4
Lee Shrop. SY12 38 D2
Lee Brockhurst SY4 38 E3
Lee Chapel SS15 24 C3
Lee Clump HP16 22 C1
Lee Mill Bridge PL21 5 F5
Lee Moor PL7 5 F4
Leebotten ZE2 107 N10
Leebotwood SY6 38 D6
Leece LA12 55 F3
Leeds Kent ME17 14 D2
LEEDS W.Yorks. LS 57 H6
Leeds Bradford International Airport LS19 57 H5
Leedstown TR27 2 D5
Leegomery TF1 39 F4
Leek ST13 49 J7
Leek Wootton CV35 30 D2
Leekbrook ST13 49 J7
Leeming N.Yorks. DL7 57 H1
Leeming W.Yorks. BD22 57 F6
Leeming Bar DL7 57 H1
Lee-on-the-Solent PO13 11 G4
Lees Derbys. DE6 40 E2
Lees Gt.Man. OL4 49 J2
Leeswood CH7 48 B7
Leftwich CW9 49 F5
Legars TD5 77 F6
Legbourne LN11 53 G4
Legerwood TD4 76 D6
Legsby LN8 52 E4
LEICESTER LE 41 H5
Leicester Forest East LE3 41 H5
Leideag HS9 84 B5
Leigh Dorset DT9 9 F4
Leigh Dorset BH21 10 B5
Leigh Gt.Man. WN7 49 F2
Leigh Kent TN11 23 J7
Leigh Shrop. SY5 38 C5
Leigh Surr. RH2 23 F7
Leigh Wilts. SN6 20 D2
Leigh Worcs. WR6 29 G3
Leigh Beck SS8 24 E3
Leigh Common BA9 9 G2
Leigh Delamere SN14 20 B4
Leigh Green TN30 14 E4
Leigh Park PO9 11 J4
Leigh Sinton WR13 29 G3
Leigh upon Mendip BA3 19 K7
Leigh Woods BS8 19 J4
Leigham PL6 5 F5
Leighland Chapel TA23 7 J2
Leigh-on-Sea SS9 24 E3
Leighterton GL8 20 B2
Leighton N.Yorks. HG4 57 G2
Leighton (Tre'r Llai) Powys SY21 38 B5
Leighton Shrop. SY5 39 F5
Leighton Som. BA11 20 A7
Leighton Bromswold PE28 32 E1
Leighton Buzzard LU7 32 C6
Leinthall Earls HR6 28 D2
Leinthall Starkes SY8 28 D2
Leintwardine SY7 28 D1
Leire LE17 41 H7
Leirinmore IV27 103 G2
Leiston IP16 35 J2
Leitfie PH11 82 D3
Leith EH6 76 A3
Leitholm TD12 77 F6
Lelant TR26 2 C5
Lelley HU12 59 J6
Lemington NE15 71 G7
Lemnas AB43 99 G4
Lempitlaw TD5 77 F7
Lemsford AL8 33 F7
Lenchwick WR11 30 B4
Lendalfoot KA26 67 F4
Lendrick Lodge FK17 81 G7
Lenham ME17 14 D2
Lenham Heath ME17 14 E3
Lenie IV63 88 C2
Lenimore KA27 73 G6
Lennel TD12 77 G6
Lennox Plunton DG6 65 G5
Lennoxtown G66 74 E3
Lent Rise SL6 22 C3
Lenton Lincs. NG33 42 D2
Lenton Nott. NG7 41 H2
Lenton Abbey NG7 41 H2
Lenwade NR9 44 E4
Lenzie G66 74 E3
Leoch DD3 82 E4
Leochel-Cushnie AB33 90 D3
Leominster HR6 28 D3
Leonard Stanley GL10 20 B1
Leorin PA42 72 B6
Lepe SO45 11 F5
Lephin IV55 93 G7
Lephinchapel PA27 73 H1
Lephinmore PA27 73 H1
Leppington YO17 58 D3
Lepton HD8 50 E1
Lerags PA34 79 K5
Lerryn PL22 4 B5
Lerwick ZE1 107 N8
Lesbury NE66 71 H2
Leschangie AB51 91 F3
Leslie Aber. AB52 90 D2
Leslie Fife KY6 82 D7
Lesmahagow ML11 75 G7
Lesnewth PL35 4 B1
Lessendrum AB54 98 D6
Lessingham NR12 45 H3
Lessness Heath DA8 23 H4
Lessonhall CA7 60 D1
Leswalt DG9 64 A4
Letchmore Heath WD25 22 E2
Letchworth Garden City SG6 33 F5
Letcombe Bassett OX12 21 G3
Letcombe Regis OX12 21 G3
Leth Meadhanach HS8 84 C3
Letham Angus DD8 83 G3
Letham Falk. FK2 75 G2
Letham Fife KY15 82 E6
Lethanhill KA6 67 J2
Lethenty AB53 99 G6
Letheringham IP13 35 G3
Letheringsett NR25 44 E2
Lettaford TQ13 7 F7
Letter Finlay PH34 87 J5
Letterewe IV22 95 F4
Letterfearn IV40 86 E2
Lettermorar PH40 86 D6
Lettermore Arg. & B. PA72 79 F3
Lettermore High. IV27 103 J4
Letters IV23 95 H3
Lettershaws ML12 68 D1
Letterston SA62 16 C3
Lettoch High. PH25 89 H3
Lettoch High. PH26 89 J1
Letton Here. SY7 28 C1
Letton Here. HR3 28 C4
Letty Green SG14 33 F7
Letwell S81 51 H4
Leuchars KY16 83 F5
Leumrabhagh HS2 101 F6
Leurbost (Liurbost) HS2 101 F5
Leusdon TQ13 5 H3
Levedale ST18 40 A4
Level's Green CM23 33 H6
Leven E.Riding HU17 59 H5
Leven Fife KY8 82 E7
Levencorroch KA27 66 E1
Levenhall EH21 76 B3
Levens LA8 55 H1
Levens Green SG11 33 G6
Levenshulme M12 49 H3
Levenwick ZE2 107 N10
Leverburgh (An T-Òb) HS5 93 F3
Leverington PE13 43 H4
Leverstock Green HP3 22 D1
Leverton PE22 43 G1
Leverton Lucasgate PE22 43 H1
Leverton Outgate PE22 43 H1
Levington IP10 35 G5
Levisham YO18 63 K7
Levishie IV63 88 B3
Lew OX18 21 G1
Lewannick PL15 4 C2
Lewcombe DT2 8 E4
Lewdown EX20 6 C7
Lewes BN7 13 H5
Leweston SA62 16 C3
Lewisham SE13 23 G4
Lewiston IV63 88 C2
Lewistown CF32 18 C3
Lewknor OX49 22 A2
Leworthy EX32 6 E2
Lewson Street ME9 25 F5
Lewth PR4 55 H6
Lewtrenchard EX20 6 C7
Ley Aber. AB33 90 D3
Ley Cornw. PL14 4 B4
Ley Green SG4 32 E6
Leybourne ME19 23 K6
Leyburn DL8 62 C7
Leyland PR25 55 J7
Leylodge AB51 91 F3
Leymoor HD3 50 D1
Leys Aber. AB42 99 J5

Leys *Aber.* **AB34** 90 C4
Leys *P. & K.* **PH13** 82 D4
Leys of Cossans **DD8** 82 E3
Leysdown-on-Sea **ME12** 25 G4
Leysmill **DD11** 83 H3
Leysters **HR6** 28 E2
Leyton **E10** 23 G3
Leytonstone **E11** 23 G3
Lezant **PL15** 4 D3
Lezerea **TR13** 2 D5
Lhanbryde **IV30** 97 K5
Liatrie **IV4** 87 J1
Libanus **LD3** 27 J6
Libberton **ML11** 75 H6
Libbery **WR7** 29 J3
Liberton **EH16** 76 A4
Liceasto **HS3** 93 G2
Lichfield WS13 40 D5
Lickey **B60** 29 J1
Lickey End **B60** 29 J1
Lickfold **GU28** 12 C4
Liddaton Green **EX20** 6 C7
Liddel **KW17** 106 D9
Liddesdale **PH33** 79 J2
Liddington **SN4** 21 F3
Lidgate *Derbys.* **S18** 51 F5
Lidgate *Suff.* **CB8** 34 B3
Lidgett **NG21** 51 J6
Lidlington **MK43** 32 C5
Lidsey **PO22** 12 C6
Lidsing **ME7** 24 D5
Lidstone **OX7** 30 E6
Lienassie **IV40** 87 F2
Lieurary **KW14** 105 F2
Liff **DD2** 82 E4
Lifton PL16 6 B7
Liftondown **PL15** 6 B7
Lightcliffe **HX3** 57 G7
Lighthorne **CV35** 30 E3
Lighthorne Heath **CV33** 30 E3
Lightwater GU18 22 C5
Lightwood **ST3** 40 B1
Lightwood Green *Ches.* **CW3** 39 F1
Lightwood Green *Wrex.* **LL13** 38 C1
Lilbourne **CV23** 31 G1
Lilburn Tower **NE66** 71 F1
Lillesdon **TA3** 8 C2
Lilleshall **TF10** 39 G4
Lilley *Herts.* **LU2** 32 E6
Lilley *W.Berks.* **RG20** 21 H4
Lilliesleaf **TD6** 70 A1
Lilling Green **YO32** 58 C3
Lillingstone Dayrell **MK18** 31 J5
Lillingstone Lovell **MK18** 31 J4
Lillington *Dorset* **DT9** 9 F3
Lillington *Warks.* **CV32** 30 E2
Lilliput **BH14** 10 B6
Lilly **EX32** 6 D2
Lilstock **TA5** 7 K1
Lilyhurst **TF11** 39 G4
Limbury **LU3** 32 D6
Lime Side **OL8** 49 J2
Limefield **BL9** 49 H1
Limehillock **AB54** 98 D5
Limehurst **OL8** 49 J2
Limekilnburn **ML3** 75 F5
Limekilns **KY11** 75 J2
Limerigg **FK1** 75 G3
Limerstone **PO30** 11 F6
Limington **BA22** 8 E2
Limpenhoe **NR13** 45 H5
Limpley Stoke **BA2** 20 A5
Limpsfield **RH8** 23 H6
Limpsfield Chart **TN8** 23 H6
Linaclate (Lionacleit) **HS7** 92 C7
Linbriggs **NE65** 70 D3
Linby **NG15** 51 H7
Linchmere **GU27** 12 B3
Lincluden **DG2** 65 K3
LINCOLN LN 52 C5
Lincomb **DY13** 29 H2
Lincombe *Devon* **TQ9** 5 H5
Lincombe *Devon* **TQ7** 5 H6
Lindal in Furness **LA12** 55 F2
Lindale **LA11** 55 H1
Lindean **TD7** 76 C7
Lindertis **DD8** 82 E2
Lindfield **RH16** 13 G4
Lindford **GU35** 12 B3
Lindifferon **KY15** 82 E6
Lindisfarne (Holy Island) **TD15** 77 K6
Lindley **LS21** 57 H5
Lindores **KY14** 82 D6
Lindow End **WA16** 49 H5
Lindridge **WR15** 29 F2
Lindsaig **PA21** 73 H3
Lindsell **CM6** 33 K6
Lindsey **IP7** 34 D4
Lindsey Tye **IP7** 34 D4
Linfitts **OL3** 49 J2
Linford *Hants.* **BH24** 10 C4
Linford *Thur.* **SS17** 24 C4
Linford Wood **MK13** 32 B4
Lingague **IM9** 54 B6
Lingards Wood **HD7** 50 C1
Lingdale **TS12** 63 H5
Lingen **SY7** 28 C2
Lingfield RH7 23 G7
Lingley Green **WA5** 48 E4
Lingwood **NR13** 45 H5
Linhead **AB45** 98 E5
Linhope **TD9** 69 K3
Linicro **IV51** 93 J5
Linkend **GL19** 29 H5
Linkenholt **SP11** 21 G6
Linkhill **TN18** 14 D5
Linkinhorne **PL17** 4 D3
Linklater **KW17** 106 D9
Linksness *Ork.* **KW16** 106 B7
Linksness *Ork.* **KW17** 106 E6
Linktown **KY1** 76 A1
Linley *Shrop.* **SY9** 38 C6
Linley *Shrop.* **TF12** 39 F6
Linley Green **WR6** 29 F3
Linlithgow EH49 75 J3
Linlithgow Bridge **EH49** 75 H3
Linn of Muick Cottage **AB35** 90 B6
Linnels **NE46** 70 E7
Linney **SA71** 16 B6
Linshiels **NE65** 70 D3
Linsiadar **HS2** 100 E4
Linsidemore **IV27** 96 C2
Linslade **LU7** 32 C6
Linstead Parva **IP19** 35 H1
Linstock **CA6** 60 F1
Linthwaite **HD7** 50 D1
Lintlaw **TD11** 77 G5
Lintmill **AB56** 98 D4
Linton *Cambs.* **CB1** 33 J4
Linton *Derbys.* **DE12** 40 E4
Linton *Here.* **HR9** 29 F6
Linton *Kent* **ME17** 14 C2
Linton *N.Yorks.* **BD23** 56 E3
Linton *Sc.Bord.* **TD5** 70 C1
Linton *W.Yorks.* **LS22** 57 J5
Linton-on-Ouse **YO30** 57 K3
Lintzford **NE39** 62 C1
Linwood *Hants.* **BH24** 10 C4
Linwood *Lincs.* **LN8** 52 E4
Linwood *Renf.* **PA3** 74 C4
Lionacleit (Linaclate) **HS7** 92 C7
Lional (Lionel) **HS2** 101 H1
Lionel (Lional) **HS2** 101 H1
Liphook GU30 12 B3
Lipley **TF9** 39 G2
Liscard **CH45** 48 C3
Liscombe **TA22** 7 G2
Liskeard PL14 4 C4
L'Islet **GY2** 3 J5
Lismore **PA34** 79 K4
Liss GU33 11 J2
Liss Forest **GU33** 11 J2
Lissett **YO25** 59 H4
Lissington **LN3** 52 E4
Liston **CO10** 34 C4
Lisvane **CF14** 18 E3
Liswerry **NP19** 19 G3
Litcham **PE32** 44 C4
Litchborough **NN12** 31 H3
Litchfield **RG28** 21 H6
Litherland **L21** 48 C3
Litlington *Cambs.* **SG8** 33 G4
Litlington *E.Suss.* **BN26** 13 J6
Little Abington **CB1** 33 J4
Little Addington **NN14** 32 C1
Little Alne **B95** 30 C2
Little Altcar **L37** 48 C2
Little Amwell **SG13** 33 G7
Little Ann **SP11** 21 G7
Little Asby **CA16** 61 H6
Little Assynt **IV27** 102 D6
Little Aston **B74** 40 C6
Little Atherfield **PO38** 11 F7
Little Ayton **TS9** 63 G5
Little Baddow **CM3** 24 D1
Little Badminton **GL9** 20 B3
Little Ballinluig **PH15** 82 A2
Little Bampton **CA7** 60 D1
Little Bardfield **CM7** 33 K5
Little Barford **PE19** 32 E3
Little Barningham **NR11** 45 F2
Little Barrington **OX18** 30 D7
Little Barrow **CH3** 48 D6
Little Barugh **YO17** 58 D2
Little Bavington **NE19** 70 E6
Little Bealings **IP13** 35 G4
Little Bedwyn **SN8** 21 F5
Little Beeby **LE7** 41 J5
Little Bentley **CO7** 35 F6
Little Berkhamsted **SG13** 23 F1
Little Billing **NN3** 32 B2
Little Birch **HR2** 28 E5
Little Bispham **FY5** 55 G5
Little Blakenham **IP8** 35 F4
Little Bloxwich **WS3** 40 C5
Little Bollington **WA14** 49 G4
Little Bookham **KT23** 22 E6
Little Bourton **OX17** 31 F4
Little Bowden **LE16** 42 A7
Little Bradley **CB9** 33 K3
Little Brampton **SY7** 38 C7
Little Braxted **CM8** 34 C7
Little Brechin **DD9** 83 G1
Little Brickhill **MK17** 32 C5
Little Bridgeford **ST18** 40 A3
Little Brington **NN7** 31 H2
Little Bromley **CO11** 34 E6
Little Broughton **CA13** 60 B3
Little Budworth **CW6** 48 E6
Little Burdon **DL1** 62 E5
Little Burstead **CM12** 24 C2
Little Burton **YO25** 59 H5
Little Bytham **NG33** 42 D4
Little Canford **BH21** 10 B5
Little Carlton *Lincs.* **LN11** 53 G4
Little Carlton *Notts.* **NG23** 51 K7
Little Casterton **PE9** 42 D4
Little Catwick **HU17** 59 H5
Little Catworth **PE28** 32 D1
Little Cawthorpe **LN11** 53 G4
Little Chalfield **SN12** 20 B5
Little Chalfont **HP6** 22 C2
Little Chart **TN27** 14 E3
Little Chesterford **CB10** 33 J4
Little Chesterton **OX26** 31 G6
Little Cheverell **SN10** 20 C6
Little Clacton **CO16** 35 F7
Little Clanfield **OX18** 21 F1
Little Clifton **CA14** 60 B4
Little Coates **DN34** 53 F2
Little Comberton **WR10** 29 J4
Little Common **TN39** 14 C7
Little Compton **GL56** 30 D5
Little Corby **CA4** 61 F1
Little Cornard **CO10** 34 C5
Little Cowarne **HR7** 29 F3
Little Coxwell **SN7** 21 F2
Little Crakehall **DL8** 62 D7
Little Cransley **NN14** 32 B1
Little Crawley **MK16** 32 C4
Little Creaton **NN6** 31 J1
Little Creich **IV24** 96 D3
Little Cressingham **IP25** 44 C6
Little Crosby **L23** 48 C2
Little Crosthwaite **CA12** 60 D4
Little Cubley **DE6** 40 D2
Little Dalby **LE14** 42 A4
Little Dens **AB42** 99 J6
Little Dewchurch **HR2** 28 E5
Little Ditton **CB8** 33 K3
Little Doward **HR9** 28 E7
Little Down **SP11** 21 G6
Little Downham **CB6** 43 J7
Little Drayton **TF9** 39 F2
Little Driffield **YO25** 59 G4
Little Dunham **PE32** 44 C4
Little Dunkeld **PH8** 82 B3
Little Dunmow **CM6** 33 K6
Little Durnford **SP4** 10 C1
Little Easton **CM6** 33 K6
Little Eaton **DE21** 41 F1
Little Eccleston **PR3** 55 H6
Little Ellingham **NR17** 44 E6
Little End **CM5** 23 J1
Little Everdon **NN11** 31 G3
Little Eversden **CB3** 33 G3
Little Fakenham **IP24** 34 D1
Little Faringdon **GL7** 21 F1
Little Fencote **DL7** 62 D7
Little Fenton **LS25** 58 B6
Little Finborough **IP14** 34 E3
Little Fransham **NR19** 44 D4
Little Gaddesden **HP4** 32 C7
Little Garway **HR2** 28 D6
Little Gidding **PE28** 42 E7
Little Glemham **IP13** 35 H3
Little Glenshee **PH1** 82 A4
Little Gorsley **HR9** 29 F6
Little Gransden **SG19** 33 F3
Little Green *Cambs.* **SG8** 33 F4
Little Green *Notts.* **NG13** 42 A1
Little Green *Suff.* **IP23** 34 E1
Little Green *Suff.* **IP22** 34 E1
Little Green *Wrex.* **SY13** 38 D1
Little Grimsby **LN11** 53 G3
Little Gringley **DN22** 51 K4
Little Gruinard **IV22** 95 F3
Little Habton **YO17** 58 D2
Little Hadham **SG11** 33 H6
Little Hale **NG34** 42 E1
Little Hallingbury **CM22** 33 H7
Little Hampden **HP16** 22 B1
Little Haresfield **GL10** 20 B1
Little Harrowden **NN9** 32 B1
Little Haseley **OX44** 21 K1
Little Hatfield **HU11** 59 H5
Little Hautbois **NR12** 45 G3
Little Haven *Pembs.* **SA62** 16 B4
Little Haven *W.Suss.* **RH12** 12 E3
Little Hay **WS14** 40 D5
Little Hayfield **SK22** 50 C4
Little Haywood **ST18** 40 C3
Little Heath **CV6** 41 F7
Little Hereford **SY8** 28 E2
Little Hockham **IP24** 44 D6
Little Horkesley **CO6** 34 D5
Little Hormead **SG9** 33 H6
Little Horsted **TN22** 13 H5
Little Horton **SN10** 20 D5
Little Horwood **MK17** 31 J5
Little Houghton **NN7** 32 B3
Little Hucklow **SK17** 50 D5
Little Hulton **M38** 49 G2
Little Hungerford **RG18** 21 J4
Little Hutton **YO7** 57 K2
Little Irchester **NN8** 32 C2
Little Keyford **BA11** 20 A7
Little Kimble **HP17** 22 B1
Little Kineton **CV35** 30 E3
Little Kingshill **HP16** 22 B2
Little Langdale **LA22** 60 E6
Little Langford **SP3** 10 B1
Little Laver **CM5** 23 J1
Little Lawford **CV23** 31 F1
Little Leigh **CW8** 49 F5
Little Leighs **CM3** 34 B7
Little Lever **BL3** 49 G2
Little Ley **AB51** 90 E3
Little Linford **MK19** 32 B4
Little Linton **CB1** 33 J4
Little London *Bucks.* **HP18** 31 H7
Little London *E.Suss.* **TN21** 13 J5
Little London *Essex* **CM23** 33 H6
Little London *Hants.* **SP11** 21 G7
Little London *Hants.* **RG26** 21 K6
Little London *I.o.M.* **IM6** 54 C5
Little London *Lincs.* **PE12** 43 H3
Little London *Lincs.* **PE11** 43 F3
Little London *Lincs.* **LN9** 53 G5
Little London *Lincs.* **LN8** 52 E4
Little London *Norf.* **PE34** 43 J3
Little London *Norf.* **IP26** 44 B6
Little London *Oxon.* **OX14** 21 J1
Little London *Powys* **SY17** 37 K7
Little London *Suff.* **IP14** 34 E3
Little London *W.Yorks.* **LS19** 57 H6
Little Longstone **DE45** 50 D5
Little Lyth **SY3** 38 D5
Little Malvern **WR14** 29 G4
Little Maplestead **CO9** 34 C5
Little Marcle **HR8** 29 F5
Little Marland **EX20** 6 D4
Little Marlow **SL7** 22 B3
Little Marsden **BB9** 56 D6
Little Massingham **PE32** 44 B3
Little Melton **NR9** 45 F5
Little Milford **SA62** 16 C4
Little Mill **NP4** 19 G1
Little Milton **OX44** 21 K1
Little Missenden **HP7** 22 C2
Little Musgrave **CA17** 61 J5
Little Ness **SY4** 38 D4
Little Neston **CH64** 48 B5
Little Newcastle **SA62** 16 C3
Little Newsham **DL2** 62 C5
Little Oakley *Essex* **CO12** 35 G6
Little Oakley *Northants.* **NN18** 42 B7
Little Odell **MK43** 32 C3
Little Offley **SG5** 32 E6
Little Onn **ST20** 40 A4
Little Orton *Cumb.* **CA5** 60 E1
Little Orton *Leics.* **CV9** 41 F5
Little Ouse **CB7** 44 A7
Little Ouseburn **YO26** 57 K3
Little Overton **LL13** 38 C1
Little Packington **CV7** 40 E7
Little Parndon **CM20** 33 H7
Little Paxton **PE19** 32 E2
Little Petherick **PL27** 3 G1
Little Plumpton **PR4** 55 G6
Little Plumstead **NR13** 45 H4
Little Ponton **NG33** 42 C2
Little Posbrook **PO14** 11 G4
Little Potheridge **EX20** 6 D4
Little Preston **NN11** 31 G3
Little Raveley **PE28** 43 F7
Little Ribston **LS22** 57 J4
Little Rissington **GL54** 30 C7
Little Rogart **IV28** 96 E1
Little Rollright **OX7** 30 D5
Little Ryburgh **NR21** 44 D3
Little Ryle **NE66** 71 F2
Little Ryton **SY5** 38 D5
Little Salkeld **CA10** 61 G3
Little Sampford **CB10** 33 K5
Little Saxham **IP29** 34 C2
Little Scatwell **IV14** 95 K6
Little Shelford **CB2** 33 H3
Little Shrawardine **SY5** 38 C4
Little Silver **EX16** 7 H5
Little Singleton **FY6** 55 G6
Little Smeaton *N.Yorks.* **WF8** 51 H1
Little Smeaton *N.Yorks.* **DL6** 62 E6
Little Snoring **NR21** 44 D2
Little Sodbury **BS37** 20 A3
Little Sodbury End **BS37** 20 A3
Little Somborne **SO20** 10 E1
Little Somerford **SN15** 20 C3
Little Soudley **TF9** 39 G3
Little Stainforth **BD24** 56 D3
Little Stainton **TS21** 62 E5
Little Stanney **CH2** 48 D5
Little Staughton **MK44** 32 E2
Little Steeping **PE23** 53 H6
Little Stoke **ST15** 40 B2
Little Stonham **IP14** 35 F3
Little Street **CB6** 43 J7
Little Stretton *Leics.* **LE2** 41 J6
Little Stretton *Shrop.* **SY6** 38 D6
Little Strickland **CA10** 61 G5
Little Stukeley **PE28** 33 F1
Little Sugnall **ST21** 40 A2
Little Sutton **CH66** 48 C5
Little Swinburne **NE46** 70 E6
Little Tarrington **HR1** 29 F4
Little Tew **OX7** 30 E6
Little Tey **CO6** 34 C6
Little Thetford **CB6** 33 J1
Little Thornage **NR25** 44 E2
Little Thornton **FY5** 55 G5
Little Thorpe **SR8** 63 F2
Little Thurlow **CB9** 33 K3
Little Thurlow Green **CB9** 33 K3
Little Thurrock **RM17** 24 C4
Little Torboll **IV25** 96 E2
Little Torrington **EX38** 6 C4
Little Tosson **NE65** 71 F3
Little Totham **CM9** 34 C7
Little Town *Cumb.* **CA12** 60 D5
Little Town *Lancs.* **PR3** 56 B6
Little Town *Warr.* **WA3** 49 F3
Little Twycross **CV9** 41 F5
Little Urswick **LA12** 55 F2
Little Wakering **SS3** 25 F3
Little Walden **CB10** 33 J4
Little Waldingfield **CO10** 34 D4
Little Walsingham **NR22** 44 D2
Little Waltham **CM3** 34 B7
Little Warley **CM13** 24 C2
Little Washbourne **GL20** 29 J5
Little Weighton **HU20** 59 F6
Little Welland **WR13** 29 H5
Little Welnetham **IP30** 34 C2
Little Wenham **CO7** 34 E5
Little Wenlock **TF6** 39 F5
Little Whittington **NE19** 70 E7
Little Wilbraham **CB1** 33 J3
Little Wishford **SP2** 10 B1
Little Witcombe **GL3** 29 J7
Little Witley **WR6** 29 G2
Little Wittenham **OX14** 21 J2
Little Wittingham Green **IP21** 35 G1
Little Wolford **CV36** 30 D5
Little Woodcote **SM5** 23 F5
Little Wratting **CB9** 33 K4
Little Wymington **NN10** 32 C2
Little Wymondley **SG4** 33 F6
Little Wyrley **WS3** 40 C5
Little Wytheford **SY4** 38 E4
Little Yeldham **CO9** 34 B5
Littlebeck **YO22** 63 K6
Littleborough *Devon* **EX17** 7 G4
Littleborough *Gt.Man.* OL15 49 J1
Littleborough *Notts.* **DN22** 52 B4
Littlebourne **CT3** 15 H2
Littlebredy **DT2** 8 E6
Littlebury **CB11** 33 J5
Littlebury Green **CB11** 33 H5
Littledean **GL14** 29 F7
Littleferry **KW10** 97 F2
Littleham *Devon* **EX39** 6 C3
Littleham *Devon* **EX8** 7 J7
Littlehampton BN17 12 D6
Littlehempston **TQ9** 5 J4
Littlehoughton **NE66** 71 H2
Littlemill *E.Ayr.* **KA6** 67 J2
Littlemill *High.* **IV12** 97 G6
Littlemoor *Derbys.* **S45** 51 F6
Littlemoor *Dorset* **DT3** 9 F6
Littlemore **OX4** 21 J1
Littlemoss **M43** 49 J3
Littleover **DE23** 41 F2
Littleport **CB6** 43 J7
Littlestead Green **RG4** 22 A4
Littlestone-on-Sea **TN28** 15 F5
Littlethorpe **HG4** 57 J3
Littleton *Ches.* **CH3** 48 D6
Littleton *Hants.* **SO22** 11 F1
Littleton *P. & K.* **PH14** 82 D4
Littleton *Som.* **TA11** 8 D1
Littleton *Surr.* **TW17** 22 D5
Littleton Drew **SN14** 20 B3
Littleton Panell **SN10** 20 D6
Littleton-on-Severn **BS35** 19 J2
Littletown *Dur.* **DH6** 62 E2
Littletown *I.o.W.* **PO33** 11 G5
Littlewick Green **SL6** 22 B4
Littlewindsor **DT8** 8 D4
Littleworth *Glos.* **GL55** 30 C5
Littleworth *Oxon.* **SN7** 21 G2
Littleworth *S.Yorks.* **DN11** 51 J3
Littleworth *Staffs.* **WS12** 40 C4
Littleworth *Worcs.* **WR5** 29 H4
Littley Green **CM3** 33 K7
Litton *Derbys.* **SK17** 50 D5
Litton *N.Yorks.* **BD23** 56 E2
Litton *Som.* **BA3** 19 J6
Litton Cheney **DT2** 8 E5
Liurbost (Leurbost) **HS2** 101 F5
LIVERPOOL L 48 C3
Liverpool John Lennon Airport **L24** 48 D4
Liversedge WF15 57 H7
Liverton *Devon* **TQ12** 5 J3
Liverton *R. & C.* **TS13** 63 J5
Liverton Street **ME17** 14 D3
Livingston EH54 75 J4
Livingston Village **EH54** 75 J4
Lixwm **CH8** 47 K5
Lizard **TR12** 2 E7
Llaingarreglwyd **SA47** 26 D3
Llaingoch **LL65** 46 A4
Llaithddu **LD1** 37 K7
Llampha **CF35** 18 C4
Llan **SY19** 37 H5
Llan Ffestiniog (Ffestiniog) **LL41** 37 G1
Llanaber **LL42** 37 F4
Llanaelhaearn **LL54** 36 C1
Llanaeron **SA48** 26 D2
Llanafan **SY23** 27 F1
Llanafan-fawr **LD2** 27 J3
Llanafan-fechan **LD4** 27 J3
Llanallgo **LL72** 46 D4
Llanandras (Presteigne) LD8 28 C2
Llanarmon **LL53** 36 D2
Llanarmon Dyffryn Ceiriog **LL20** 38 A2
Llanarmon-yn-Ial **CH7** 47 K7
Llanarth *Cere.* SA47 26 D3
Llanarth *Mon.* **NP15** 28 C7
Llanarthney **SA32** 17 J3
Llanasa **CH8** 47 K4
Llanbabo **LL68** 46 B4
Llanbadarn Fawr **SY23** 36 E7
Llanbadarn Fynydd **LD1** 27 K1
Llanbadarn-y-garreg **LD2** 28 A4
Llanbadoc **NP15** 19 G1
Llanbadrig **LL67** 46 B3
Llanbeder **NP18** 19 G2
Llanbedr *Gwyn.* LL45 36 E3
Llanbedr *Powys* **NP8** 28 B6
Llanbedr *Powys* **LD2** 28 A4
Llanbedr Pont Steffan (Lampeter) SA48 17 J1
Llanbedr-Dyffryn-Clwyd **LL15** 47 K7
Llanbedrgoch LL76 46 D4
Llanbedrog **LL53** 36 C2
Llanbedr-y-cennin **LL32** 47 F6
Llanberis **LL55** 46 D7
Llanbethery **CF62** 18 D5
Llanbister **LD1** 28 A1
Llanblethian **CF71** 18 C4
Llanboidy **SA34** 17 F3
Llanbradach **CF83** 18 E2
Llanbryn-mair SY19 37 H5
Llancadle **CF62** 18 D5
Llancarfan **CF62** 18 D4
Llancayo **NP15** 19 G1

Llancynfelyn SY20 37 F6
Llandafal NP13 18 E1
Llandaff CF5 18 E4
Llandaff North CF14 18 E4
Llandanwg LL45 36 E3
Llandawke SA33 17 F4
Llanddaniel Fab LL60 46 C5
Llanddarog SA32 17 H4
Llanddeiniol SY23 26 E1
Llanddeiniolen LL55 46 D6
Llandderfel LL23 37 J2
Llanddeusant *Carmar.* SA19 27 G6
Llanddeusant *I.o.A.* LL65 46 B4
Llanddew LD3 27 K5
Llanddewi SA3 17 H7
Llanddewi Rhydderch NP7 28 C7
Llanddewi Skirrid NP7 28 C7
Llanddewi Velfrey SA67 16 E4
Llanddewi Ystradenni LD1 28 A2
Llanddewi-Brefi SY25 27 F3
Llanddewi'r Cwm LD2 27 K4
Llanddoged LL26 47 G6
Llanddona LL58 46 D5
Llanddowror SA33 17 F4
Llanddulas LL22 47 H5
Llanddwywe LL44 36 E3
Llanddyfnan LL78 46 D5
Llandefaelog Fach LD3 27 K5
Llandefaelog-tre'r-graig LD3 28 A6
Llandefalle LD3 28 A5
Llandegfan LL59 46 D5
Llandegla LL11 47 K7
Llandegley LD1 28 A2
Llandegveth NP18 19 G2
Llandegwning LL53 36 B2
Llandeilo SA19 17 K3
Llandeilo Abercywyn SA33 17 G4
Llandeilo Graban LD2 27 K4
Llandeilo'r-Fan LD3 27 H5
Llandeloy SA62 16 B3
Llandenny NP15 19 H1
Llandevaud NP18 19 H2
Llandevenny NP26 19 H3
Llandinabo HR2 28 E6
Llandinam SY17 37 K7
Llandissilio SA66 16 E3
Llandogo NP25 19 J1
Llandough *V. of Glam.* CF11 18 E4
Llandough *V. of Glam.* CF71 18 C4
Llandovery (Llanymddyfri) SA20 27 G5
Llandow CF71 18 C4
Llandre *Carmar.* SA19 17 K1
Llandre *Carmar.* SA34 16 E3
Llandre *Cere.* SY24 37 F7
Llandrillo LL21 37 K2
LLANDRINDOD WELLS LD 27 K2
Llandrinio SY22 38 B4
LLANDUDNO LL 47 F4
Llandudno Junction LL31 47 F5
Llandudoch (St. Dogmaels) SA43 16 E1
Llandwrog LL54 46 C7
Llandybie SA18 17 K4
Llandyfaelog SA17 17 H4
Llandyfan SA18 17 K4
Llandyfriog SA38 17 G1
Llandyfrydog LL71 46 C4
Llandygai LL57 46 D5
Llandygwydd SA43 17 F1
Llandyrnog LL16 47 K6
Llandyry SA17 17 H5
Llandysilio SY22 38 B4
Llandyssil SY15 38 A6
Llandysul SA44 17 H1
Llanedeyrn CF23 19 F3
Llanedy SA4 17 J5
Llaneglwys LD2 27 K5
Llanegryn LL36 37 F5
Llanegwad SA32 17 J3
Llaneilian LL68 46 C3
Llanelian-yn-Rhos LL29 47 G5
Llanelidan LL15 47 K7
Llanelieu LD3 28 A5
Llanellen NP7 28 C7
Llanelli SA15 17 J5
Llanelltyd LL40 37 G4
Llanelly NP7 28 B7
Llanelly Hill NP7 28 B7
Llanelwedd LD2 27 K3
Llanelwy (St. Asaph) LL17 47 J5
Llanenddwyn LL44 36 E3
Llanengan LL53 36 B3
Llanerfyl SY21 37 K5
Llaneuddog LL70 46 C4
Llaneurgain (Northop) CH7 48 B6
Llanfachraeth LL65 46 B4
Llanfachreth LL40 37 G3
Llanfaelog LL63 46 B5
Llanfaelrhys LL53 36 B3
Llanfaenor NP25 28 D7
Llan-faes *I.o.A.* LL58 46 E5
Llanfaes *Powys* LD3 27 K6
Llanfaethlu LL65 46 B4
Llanfaglan LL54 46 C6
Llanfair LL46 36 E3
Llanfair Caereinion SY21 38 A5
Llanfair Clydogau SA48 27 F3
Llanfair Dyffryn Clwyd LL15 47 K7
Llanfair Talhaiarn LL22 47 H5
Llanfair Waterdine LD7 28 B1
Llanfairfechan LL33 46 E5
Llanfair-Nant-Gwyn SA37 16 E2
Llanfair-Orllwyn SA44 17 G1
Llanfairpwllgwyngyll LL61 46 D5
Llanfair-ym-Muallt (Builth Wells) LD2 27 K3
Llanfairynghornwy LL65 46 B3
Llanfair-yn-neubwll LL65 46 B5
Llanfallteg SA34 16 E4
Llanfaredd LD2 27 K3
Llanfarian SY23 26 E1
Llanfechain SY22 38 A3
Llanfechell LL68 46 B3
Llanfendigaid LL36 36 E5
Llanferres CH7 47 K6
Llanfflewyn LL68 46 B4
Llanfigael LL65 46 B4
Llanfihangel Crucornau (Llanvihangel Crucorney) NP7 28 C6
Llanfihangel Glyn Myfyr LL21 37 J1
Llanfihangel Nant Bran LD3 27 J5
Llanfihangel Rhydithon LD1 28 A2
Llanfihangel Rogiet NP26 19 H3
Llanfihangel Tal-y-llyn LD3 28 A6
Llanfihangel-ar-arth SA39 17 H1
Llanfihangel-nant-Melan LD8 28 A3
Llanfihangel-uwch-Gwili SA32 17 H3
Llanfihangel-y-Creuddyn SY23 27 F1
Llanfihangel-yng-Ngwynfa SY22 37 K4
Llanfihangel-yn-Nhywyn LL65 46 B5
Llanfihangel-y-pennant *Gwyn.* LL51 36 E1
Llanfihangel-y-pennant *Gwyn.* LL36 37 F5
Llanfilo LD3 28 A5
Llanfoist NP7 28 B7
Llanfor LL23 37 J2
Llanfrechfa NP44 19 G2
Llanfrothen LL48 37 F1
Llanfrynach LD3 27 K6
Llanfwrog *Denb.* LL15 47 K7
Llanfwrog *I.o.A.* LL65 46 A4
Llanfyllin SY22 38 A4
Llanfynydd *Carmar.* SA32 17 J3
Llanfynydd *Flints.* LL11 48 B7
Llanfyrnach SA35 17 F2
Llangadfan SY21 37 K4
Llangadog SA19 27 G6
Llangadwaladr *I.o.A.* LL62 46 B6
Llangadwaladr *Powys* SY10 38 A2
Llangaffo LL60 46 C6
Llangain SA33 17 G4
Llangammarch Wells LD4 27 J4
Llangan CF35 18 C4
Llangarron HR9 28 E6
Llangasty-Talyllyn LD3 28 A6
Llangathen SA32 17 J3
Llangattock NP8 28 B7
Llangattock Lingoed NP7 28 C7
Llangattock-Vibon-Avel NP25 28 D7
Llangedwyn SY10 38 A3
Llangefni LL77 46 C5
Llangeinor CF32 18 C3
Llangeitho SY25 27 F3
Llangeler SA44 17 G2
Llangelynin LL36 36 E5
Llangendeirne SA17 17 H4
Llangennech SA14 17 J5
Llangennith SA3 17 H6
Llangenny NP8 28 B7
Llangernyw LL22 47 G6
Llangian LL53 36 B3
Llangiwg SA8 18 A1
Llangloffan SA62 16 C2
Llanglydwen SA34 16 E3
Llangoed LL58 46 E5
Llangoedmor SA43 16 E1
Llangollen LL20 38 B1
Llangolman SA66 16 E3
Llangorse LD3 28 A6
Llangorwen SY23 37 F7
Llangovan NP25 19 H1
Llangower LL23 37 J2
Llangrannog SA44 26 C3
Llangristiolus LL62 46 C5
Llangrove HR9 28 E7
Llangua NP7 28 C6
Llangunllo LD7 28 B1
Llangunnor SA31 17 H3
Llangurig SY18 27 J1
Llangwm *Conwy* LL21 37 J1
Llangwm *Mon.* NP15 19 H1
Llangwm *Pembs.* SA62 16 C5
Llangwnnadl LL53 36 B2
Llangwyfan LL16 47 K6
Llangwyllog LL77 46 C5
Llangwyryfon SY23 27 F1
Llangybi *Cere.* SA48 27 F3
Llangybi *Gwyn.* LL53 36 D1
Llangybi *Mon.* NP15 19 G2
Llangyfelach SA5 17 K6
Llangynhafal LL16 47 K6
Llangynidr NP8 28 A7
Llangyniew SY21 38 A5
Llangynin SA33 17 F4
Llangynllo SA44 17 G1
Llangynog *Carmar.* SA33 17 G4
Llangynog *Powys* SY10 37 K3
Llangynwyd CF34 18 B3
Llanhamlach LD3 27 K6
Llanharan CF72 18 D3
Llanharry CF72 18 D3
Llanhennock NP18 19 G2
Llanhilleth NP13 19 F1
Llanidloes SY18 37 J7
Llaniestyn LL53 36 B2
Llanigon HR3 28 B5
Llanilar SY23 27 F1
Llanilid CF35 18 C3
Llanishen *Cardiff* CF14 18 E3
Llanishen *Mon.* NP16 19 H1
Llanllawddog SA32 17 H3
Llanllechid LL57 46 E6
Llanlleonfel LD4 27 J3
Llanllugan SY21 37 K5
Llanllwch SA31 17 G4
Llanllwchaiarn SY16 38 A6
Llanllwni SA39 17 H1
Llanllyfni LL54 46 C7
Llanllywel NP15 19 G2
Llanmadoc SA3 17 H6
Llanmaes CF61 18 C5
Llanmartin NP18 19 G3
Llanmerewig SY15 38 A6
Llanmihangel CF71 18 C4
Llan-mill SA67 16 E4
Llanmiloe SA33 17 F5
Llanmorlais SA4 17 J6
Llannefydd LL16 47 H5
Llannerch Hall LL17 47 J5
Llannerch-y-medd LL71 46 C4
Llannerch-y-Môr CH8 47 K5
Llannon *Carmar.* SA14 17 J5
Llan-non *Cere.* SY23 26 E2
Llannor LL53 36 C2
Llanover NP7 19 G1
Llanpumsaint SA33 17 H3
Llanreithan SA62 16 B3
Llanrhaeadr LL16 47 J6
Llanrhaeadr-ym-Mochnant SY10 38 A3
Llanrhian SA62 16 B2
Llanrhidian SA3 17 H6
Llanrhyddlad LL65 46 B4
Llanrhystud SY23 26 E2
Llanrothal NP25 28 D7
Llanrug LL55 46 D6
Llanrumney CF3 19 F3
Llanrwst LL26 47 F6
Llansadurnen SA33 17 F5
Llansadwrn *Carmar.* SA19 17 K2
Llansadwrn *I.o.A.* LL59 46 D5
Llansaint SA17 17 G5
Llansamlet SA7 17 K6
Llansanffraid SY23 26 E2
Llansanffraid Glan Conwy LL28 47 G5
Llansannan LL16 47 H6
Llansannor CF71 18 C4
Llansantffraed LD3 28 A6
Llansantffraed-Cwmdeuddwr LD6 27 J2
Llansantffraed-in-Elwel LD1 27 K3
Llansantffraid-ym-Mechain SY22 38 B3
Llansawel *Carmar.* SA19 17 K2
Llansawel (Briton Ferry) *N.P.T.* SA11 18 A2
Llansilin SY10 38 B3
Llansoy NP15 19 H1
Llanspyddid LD3 27 K6
Llanstadwell SA73 16 C5
Llansteffan SA33 17 G4
Llanstephan LD3 28 A4
Llantarnam NP44 19 G2
Llanteg SA67 16 E4
Llanthony NP7 28 B6
Llantilio Crossenny NP7 28 C7
Llantilio Pertholey NP7 28 C7
Llantood SA43 16 E1
Llantrisant *I.o.A.* LL65 46 B4
Llantrisant *Mon.* NP15 19 G2
Llantrisant *R.C.T.* CF72 18 D3
Llantrithyd CF71 18 D4
Llantwit Fardre CF38 18 D3
Llantwit Major CF61 18 C5
Llantysilio LL20 38 A1
Llanuwchllyn LL23 37 H3
Llanvaches NP26 19 H2
Llanvair-Discoed NP16 19 H2
Llanvapley NP7 28 C7
Llanvetherine NP7 28 C7
Llanveynoe HR2 28 C5
Llanvihangel Crucorney (Llanfihangel Crucornau) NP7 28 C6
Llanvihangel Gobion NP7 19 G1
Llanvihangel-Ystern-Llewern NP25 28 D7
Llanvithyn CF62 18 D4
Llanwarne HR2 28 E6
Llanwddyn SY10 37 K4
Llanwenog SA40 17 H1
Llanwern NP18 19 G3
Llanwinio SA34 17 F3
Llanwnda *Gwyn.* LL54 46 C7
Llanwnda *Pembs.* SA64 16 C2
Llanwnnen SA48 17 J1
Llanwnog SY17 37 K6
Llanwonno CF37 18 D2
Llanwrda SA19 27 G5
Llanwrin SY20 37 G5
Llanwrthwl LD1 27 J2
Llanwrtyd LD5 27 H4
Llanwrtyd Wells LD5 27 H4
Llanwyddelan SY16 37 K5
Llanyblodwel SY10 38 B3
Llanybri SA33 17 G4
Llanybydder SA40 17 J1
Llanycefn SA66 16 E3
Llanychaer Bridge SA65 16 C2
Llanycil LL23 37 J2
Llanycrwys SA19 17 K1
Llanymawddwy SY20 37 H4
Llanymddyfri (Llandovery) SA20 27 G5
Llanymynech SY22 38 B3
Llanynghenedl LL65 46 B4
Llanynys LL16 47 K6
Llan-y-pwll LL13 48 C7
Llanyre LD1 27 K2
Llanystumdwy LL52 36 D2
Llanywern LD3 28 A6
Llawhaden SA67 16 D4
Llawndy CH8 47 K4
Llawnt SY10 38 B2
Llawr-y-dref LL53 36 B3
Llawryglyn SY17 37 J6
Llay LL12 48 C7
Llechcynfarwy LL71 46 B4
Llecheiddior LL51 36 D1
Llechfaen LD3 27 K6
Llechryd *Caerp.* NP22 18 E1
Llechryd *Cere.* SA43 17 F1
Llechrydau SY10 38 B2
Lledrod *Cere.* SY23 27 F1
Lledrod *Powys* SY10 38 B3
Llethrid SA2 17 J6
Llidiad-Nenog SA32 17 J2
Llidiardau LL23 37 H2
Llithfaen LL53 36 C1
Lloc CH8 47 K5
Llong CH7 48 B6
Llowes HR3 28 A4
Lloyney LD7 28 B1
Llundain-fach SA48 26 E3
Llwydcoed CF44 18 C1
Llwydiarth SY21 37 K4
Llwyn *M.Tyd.* CF48 27 K7
Llwyn *Shrop.* SY7 38 B7
Llwyncelyn SA46 26 D3
Llwyn-croes SA33 17 H3
Llwyndafydd SA44 26 C3
Llwynderw SY21 38 B5
Llwyndyrys LL53 36 C1
Llwyneinion LL14 38 B1
Llwyngwril LL37 36 E5
Llwynhendy SA14 17 J6
Llwyn-Madoc LD5 27 J3
Llwynmawr LL20 38 B2
Llwyn-onn SA45 26 D3
Llwyn-y-brain *Carmar.* SA34 16 E4
Llwyn-y-brain *Carmar.* SA20 27 G5
Llwyn-y-groes SY25 26 E3
Llwynypia CF40 18 C2
Llyn Penmaen (Penmaenpool) LL40 37 F4
Llynclys SY10 38 B3
Llynfaes LL65 46 C5
Llysfaen LL29 47 G5
Llyswen LD3 28 A5
Llysworney CF71 18 C4
Llys-y-frân SA63 16 D3
Llywel LD3 27 H5
Load Brook S6 50 E4
Loandhu IV20 97 F4
Loanhead *Aber.* AB41 91 H1
Loanhead *Midloth.* EH20 76 A4
Loans KA10 74 B7
Lobb EX33 6 C2
Lobhillcross EX20 6 C7
Loch a Charnain HS8 92 D7
Loch Baghasdail (Lochboisdale) HS8 84 C3
Loch Choire Lodge KW11 103 J5
Loch Eil Outward Bound PH33 87 G7
Loch Head *D. & G.* DG8 64 D6
Loch Head *D. & G.* KA6 67 J4
Loch na Madadh (Lochmaddy) HS6 92 E5
Loch Sgioport HS8 84 D1
Lochailort PH38 86 D6
Lochaline PA34 79 H3
Lochans DG9 64 A5
Locharbriggs DG1 68 E5
Lochawe PA33 80 C5
Lochboisdale (Loch Baghasdail) HS8 84 C3
Lochbuie PA62 79 H5
Lochcarron IV54 94 E7
Lochdhu Hotel KW12 105 F4
Lochdon PA64 79 J4
Lochdrum IV23 95 J4
Lochearnhead FK19 81 G5
Lochee DD2 82 E4
Lochend *High.* KW14 105 H2
Lochend *High.* IV3 88 C1
Locheport (Locheuphort) HS6 92 D5
Locheuphort (Locheport) HS6 92 D5
Lochfoot DG2 65 K3
Lochgair PA31 73 H1
Lochgarthside IV2 88 C3
Lochgelly KY5 75 K1
Lochgilphead PA31 73 G2
Lochgoilhead PA24 80 D7
Lochgoyn KA3 74 D6
Lochhill *E.Ayr.* KA18 67 K2
Lochhill *Moray* IV30 97 K5
Lochinch Castle DG9 64 B4
Lochinver IV27 102 C6
Lochlair DD8 83 G3
Lochlane PH7 81 K5
Lochlea KA1 74 C7
Lochluichart IV23 95 K5
Lochmaben DG11 69 F5
Lochmaddy (Loch na Madadh) HS6 92 E5
Lochore KY5 75 K1
Lochportain HS6 92 E4
Lochranza KA27 73 H5
Lochside *Aber.* DD10 83 J1
Lochside *High.* IV27 103 G3
Lochside *High.* KW11 104 D5
Lochside *High.* KW14 105 H2
Lochslin IV20 97 F3
Lochton KA26 67 G5
Lochty KY10 83 G7
Lochuisge PH33 79 J2
Lochurr DG3 68 C5
Lochussie IV7 96 B6
Lochwinnoch PA12 74 B5
Lockengate PL26 4 A4
Lockerbie DG11 69 G5
Lockeridge SN8 20 E5
Lockerley SO51 10 D2
Lockhills CA4 61 G2
Locking BS24 19 G6
Lockington *E.Riding* YO25 59 F5
Lockington *Leics.* DE74 41 G3
Lockleywood TF9 39 F3
Locks Heath SO31 11 G4
Locksbottom BR6 23 H5
Locksgreen PO30 11 F5
Lockton YO18 58 E1
Loddington *Leics.* LE7 42 A5
Loddington *Northants.* NN14 32 B1
Loddiswell TQ7 5 H6
Loddon NR14 45 H6
Lode CB5 33 J2
Loders DT6 8 D5
Lodsworth GU28 12 C4
Lofthouse *N.Yorks.* HG3 57 G2
Lofthouse *W.Yorks.* WF3 57 J7
Loftus TS13 63 J5
Logan *D. & G.* DG9 64 A6
Logan *E.Ayr.* KA18 67 K1
Loganlea EH55 75 H4
Loggerheads TF9 39 G2
Loggie IV23 95 H2
Logie *Angus* DD10 83 H1
Logie *Angus* DD8 82 E2
Logie *Fife* KY15 83 F5
Logie *Moray* IV36 97 H6
Logie Coldstone AB34 90 C4
Logie Hill IV18 96 E4
Logie Newton AB54 90 E1
Logie Pert DD10 83 H1
Logierait PH9 82 A2
Login SA34 16 E3
Lolworth CB3 33 G2
Lonbain IV54 94 C6
Londesborough YO43 58 E5
LONDON E, EC, N, NW, SE, SW, W, WC 23 G3
London Apprentice PL26 4 A6
London Ashford Airport TN29 15 F5
London Beach TN30 14 D4
London City Airport E16 23 H3
London Colney AL2 22 E1
London Gatwick Airport (Gatwick Airport) RH6 23 F7
London Heathrow Airport TW6 22 D4
London Luton Airport (Luton Airport) LU2 32 E6
London Minstead SO43 10 D3
London Southend Airport SS2 24 E3
London Stansted Airport (Stansted Airport) CM24 33 J6
Londonderry DL7 57 H1
Londonthorpe NG31 42 C2
Londubh IV22 94 E3
Lonemore IV25 96 E3
Long Ashton BS41 19 J4
Long Bank DY12 29 G1
Long Bennington NG23 42 B1
Long Bredy DT2 8 E5
Long Buckby NN6 31 H2
Long Clawson LE14 42 A3
Long Compton *Staffs.* ST18 40 A3
Long Compton *Warks.* CV36 30 D5
Long Crendon HP18 21 K1
Long Crichel BH21 9 J3
Long Dean SN14 20 B4
Long Downs TR10 2 E5
Long Drax YO8 58 C7
Long Duckmanton S44 51 G5
Long Eaton NG10 41 G2
Long Gill BD23 56 C4
Long Green *Ches.* CH3 48 D5
Long Green *Essex* CO6 34 D6
Long Green *Worcs.* GL19 29 H5
Long Hanborough OX29 31 F7
Long Itchington CV47 31 F2
Long Lane TF6 39 F4
Long Lawford CV23 31 F1
Long Load TA10 8 D2
Long Marston *Herts.* HP23 32 B7
Long Marston *N.Yorks.* YO26 58 B4
Long Marston *Warks.* CV37 30 C4
Long Marton CA16 61 H4
Long Meadowend SY7 38 D7
Long Melford CO10 34 C4
Long Newnton GL8 20 C2
Long Preston BD23 56 D4
Long Riston HU11 59 H5
Long Stratton NR15 45 F6
Long Street MK19 31 J4
Long Sutton *Hants.* RG29 22 A7
Long Sutton *Lincs.* PE12 43 H3
Long Sutton *Som.* TA10 8 D2

Long Thurlow **IP31** 34 E2
Long Whatton **LE12** 41 G3
Long Wittenham **OX14** 21 J2
Longbenton **NE7** 71 H7
Longborough **GL56** 30 C6
Longbridge *Plym.* **PL6** 5 F5
Longbridge *W.Mid.* **B31** 30 B1
Longbridge *Warks.* **CV34** 30 D2
Longbridge Deverill **BA12** 20 B7
Longburgh **CA5** 60 E1
Longburton **DT9** 9 F3
Longcliffe **DE4** 50 E7
Longcombe **TQ9** 5 J5
Longcot **SN7** 21 F2
Longcroft **FK4** 75 F3
Longcross *Devon* **PL19** 4 E3
Longcross *Surr.* **KT16** 22 C5
Longden **SY5** 38 D5
Longdon *Staffs.* **WS15** 40 C4
Longdon *Worcs.* **GL20** 29 H5
Longdon Green **WS15** 40 C4
Longdon upon Tern **TF6** 39 F4
Longdown **EX6** 7 G6
Longdrum **AB23** 91 H3
Longfield DA3 24 C5
Longfield Hill **DA3** 24 C5
Longfleet **BH15** 10 B5
Longford *Derbys.* **DE6** 40 E2
Longford *Glos.* **GL2** 29 H6
Longford *Gt.Lon.* **UB7** 22 D4
Longford *Shrop.* **TF9** 39 F2
Longford *Tel. & W.* **TF10** 39 G4
Longford *W.Mid.* **CV6** 41 F7
Longforgan **DD2** 82 E5
Longformacus **TD11** 76 E5
Longframlington **NE65** 71 G3
Longham *Dorset* **BH22** 10 B5
Longham *Norf.* **NR19** 44 D4
Longhill **AB42** 99 H5
Longhirst **NE61** 71 H5
Longhope *Glos.* GL17 29 F7
Longhope *Ork.* **KW16** 106 C8
Longhorsley **NE65** 71 G4
Longhoughton **NE66** 71 H2
Longlands *Aber.* **AB54** 90 C2
Longlands *Cumb.* **CA7** 60 D3
Longlands *Gt.Lon.* **SE9** 23 H4
Longlane *Derbys.* **DE6** 40 E2
Longlane *W.Berks.* **RG18** 21 H4
Longlevens **GL2** 29 H7
Longley **HD9** 50 D2
Longley Green **WR6** 29 G3
Longmanhill **AB45** 99 F4
Longmoor Camp **GU33** 11 J1
Longmorn **IV30** 97 K6
Longnewton *Sc.Bord.* **TD6** 70 A1
Longnewton *Stock.* **TS21** 62 E5
Longney **GL2** 29 G7
Longniddry EH32 76 C3
Longnor *Shrop.* **SY5** 38 D5
Longnor *Staffs.* **SK17** 50 C6
Longparish **SP11** 21 H7
Longridge *Lancs.* **PR3** 56 B6
Longridge *Staffs.* **ST18** 40 B4
Longridge *W.Loth.* **EH47** 75 H4
Longridge End **GL19** 29 H6
Longridge Towers **TD15** 77 H5
Longriggend **ML6** 75 G3
Longrock **TR20** 2 C5
Longsdon **ST9** 49 J7
Longshaw **WN5** 48 E2
Longside **AB42** 99 J6
Longslow **TF9** 39 F2
Longsowerby **CA2** 60 E1
Longstanton **CB4** 33 H2
Longstock **SO20** 10 E1
Longstone **TR26** 2 C5
Longstowe **CB3** 33 G3
Longstreet **SN9** 20 E6
Longthorpe **PE3** 42 E6
Longton *Lancs.* **PR4** 55 H7
Longton *Stoke* **ST3** 40 B1
Longtown *Cumb.* **CA6** 69 J7
Longtown *Here.* **HR2** 28 C6
Longville in the Dale **TF13** 38 E6
Longwell Green **BS30** 19 K4
Longwick **HP27** 22 A1
Longwitton **NE61** 71 F5
Longworth **OX13** 21 G2
Longyester **EH41** 76 D4
Lonmay **AB43** 99 J5
Lonmore **IV55** 93 H7
Looe PL13 4 C5
Loose **ME15** 14 C2
Loosebeare **EX17** 7 F5
Loosegate **PE12** 43 G3
Loosley Row **HP27** 22 B1
Lopcombe Corner **SP5** 10 D1
Lopen **TA13** 8 D3
Loppington **SY4** 38 D3
Lorbottle **NE65** 71 F3
Lorbottle Hall **NE66** 71 F3
Lordington **PO18** 11 J4
Lord's Hill **SO16** 10 E3
Lorgill **IV55** 93 G7
Lorn **G83** 74 B2
Lornty **PH10** 82 C3
Loscoe **DE75** 41 G1
Loscombe **DT6** 8 D5
Losgaintir **HS3** 93 F2
Lossiemouth IV31 97 K4
Lossit **PA47** 72 A5
Lostock Gralam **CW9** 49 F5
Lostock Green **CW9** 49 F5
Lostock Junction **BL6** 49 F2
Lostwithiel PL22 4 B5
Loth **KW17** 106 F4
Lothbeg **KW8** 104 E7
Lothersdale **BD20** 56 E5
Lothmore **KW8** 104 E7
Loudwater **HP10** 22 C2
Loughborough LE11 41 H4
Loughor **SA4** 17 J6
Loughton *Essex* IG10 23 H2
Loughton *M.K.* **MK5** 32 B5
Loughton *Shrop.* **WV16** 39 F7
Lound *Lincs.* **PE10** 42 D4
Lound *Notts.* **DN22** 51 J4
Lound *Suff.* **NR32** 45 K6
Lount **LE65** 41 F4
Lour **DD8** 83 F3
Louth LN11 53 G4
Love Clough **BB4** 56 D7
Lovedean **PO8** 11 H3
Lover **SP5** 10 D3
Loversall **DN11** 51 H3
Loves Green **CM1** 24 C1
Lovesome Hill **DL6** 62 E7
Loveston **SA68** 16 D5
Lovington **BA7** 8 E1
Low Ackworth **WF7** 51 G1
Low Angerton **NE61** 71 F5
Low Ballevain **PA28** 66 A1
Low Barlay **DG7** 65 F5
Low Barlings **LN3** 52 D5
Low Bentham (Lower Bentham) **LA2** 56 B3
Low Bolton **DL8** 62 B7
Low Bradfield **S6** 50 E3
Low Bradley (Bradley) **BD20** 57 F5
Low Braithwaite **CA4** 60 F2
Low Brunton **NE46** 70 E6
Low Burnham **DN9** 51 K2
Low Burton **HG4** 57 H1
Low Buston **NE65** 71 H3
Low Catton **YO41** 58 D4
Low Coniscliffe **DL2** 62 D5
Low Craighead **KA26** 67 G3
Low Dinsdale **DL2** 62 E5
Low Ellington **HG4** 57 H1
Low Entercommon **DL6** 62 E6
Low Etherley **DL14** 62 C4
Low Fell **NE11** 62 D1
Low Gate **NE46** 70 E7
Low Grantley **HG4** 57 H2
Low Green **IP29** 34 C2
Low Habberley **DY11** 29 H1
Low Ham **TA10** 8 D2
Low Hawsker **YO22** 63 J2
Low Haygarth **LA10** 61 H7
Low Hesket **CA4** 61 F2
Low Hesleyhurst **NE65** 71 F4
Low Hutton **YO60** 58 D3
Low Kingthorpe **YO18** 58 E1
Low Laithe **HG3** 57 G3
Low Langton **LN8** 52 E5
Low Leighton **SK22** 50 C4
Low Lorton **CA13** 60 C4
Low Marishes **YO17** 58 E2
Low Marnham **NG23** 52 B6
Low Middleton **NE70** 77 K7
Low Mill **YO62** 63 H7
Low Moor *Lancs.* **BB7** 56 C5
Low Moor *W.Yorks.* **BD12** 57 G7
Low Moorsley **DH5** 62 E2
Low Moresby **CA28** 60 A4
Low Newton-by-the-Sea **NE66** 71 H1
Low Row *Cumb.* **CA8** 70 A7
Low Row *N.Yorks.* **DL11** 62 A7
Low Stillaig **PA21** 73 H4
Low Street **NR9** 44 E5
Low Tharston **NR15** 45 F6
Low Torry **KY12** 75 J2
Low Town **NE65** 71 G3
Low Toynton **LN9** 53 F5
Low Wood **LA12** 55 G1
Low Worsall **TS15** 62 E6
Lowbands **GL19** 29 G5
Lowdham **NG14** 41 J1
Lowe **SY4** 38 E2
Lowe Hill **ST13** 49 J7
Lower Achachenna **PA35** 80 B5
Lower Aisholt **TA5** 8 B1
Lower Apperley **GL19** 29 H6
Lower Arncott **OX25** 31 H7
Lower Ashtead **KT21** 22 E6
Lower Ashton **EX6** 7 G7
Lower Assendon **RG9** 22 A3
Lower Auchalick **PA21** 73 H3
Lower Ballam **PR4** 55 G6
Lower Barewood **HR6** 28 C3
Lower Bartle **PR4** 55 H6
Lower Bayble (Pabail Iarach) **HS2** 101 H4
Lower Beeding **RH13** 13 F4
Lower Benefield **PE8** 42 C7
Lower Bentham (Low Bentham) **LA2** 56 B3
Lower Bentley **B60** 29 J2
Lower Berry Hill **GL16** 28 E7
Lower Birchwood **DE55** 51 G7
Lower Boddington **NN11** 31 F3
Lower Boscaswell **TR19** 2 A5
Lower Bourne **GU10** 22 B7
Lower Brailes **OX15** 30 E5
Lower Breakish **IV42** 86 C2
Lower Bredbury **SK6** 49 J3
Lower Broadheath **WR2** 29 H3
Lower Brynamman **SA18** 27 G7
Lower Bullingham **HR2** 28 E5
Lower Bullington **SO21** 21 H7
Lower Burgate **SP6** 10 C3
Lower Burrow **TA12** 8 D2
Lower Burton **HR6** 28 D3
Lower Caldecote **SG18** 32 E4
Lower Cam **GL11** 20 A1
Lower Cambourne **CB3** 33 G3
Lower Camster **KW3** 105 H4
Lower Chapel **LD3** 27 K5
Lower Cheriton **EX14** 7 K5
Lower Chicksgrove **SP3** 9 J1
Lower Chute **SP11** 21 G6
Lower Clent **DY9** 40 B7
Lower Creedy **EX17** 7 G5
Lower Cumberworth **HD8** 50 E2
Lower Darwen **BB3** 56 B7
Lower Dean **PE28** 32 D2
Lower Diabaig **IV22** 94 D5
Lower Dicker **BN27** 13 J5
Lower Dinchope **SY7** 38 D7
Lower Down **SY7** 38 C7
Lower Drift **TR19** 2 B6
Lower Dunsforth **YO26** 57 K3
Lower Earley **RG6** 22 A4
Lower Edmonton **N9** 23 G2
Lower Elkstone **SK17** 50 C7
Lower End *Bucks.* **HP18** 21 K1
Lower End *M.K.* **MK17** 32 C5
Lower End *Northants.* **NN7** 32 B2
Lower Everleigh **SN8** 20 E6
Lower Eythorne **CT15** 15 H3
Lower Failand **BS8** 19 J4
Lower Farringdon **GU34** 11 J1
Lower Fittleworth **RH20** 12 D5
Lower Foxdale **IM4** 54 B6
Lower Freystrop **SA62** 16 C4
Lower Froyle **GU34** 22 A7
Lower Gabwell **TQ12** 5 K4
Lower Gledfield **IV24** 96 C2
Lower Godney **BA5** 19 H7
Lower Gravenhurst **MK45** 32 E5
Lower Green *Essex* **CB11** 33 H5
Lower Green *Herts.* **SG5** 32 E5
Lower Green *Kent* **TN2** 23 K7
Lower Green *Norf.* **NR21** 44 D2
Lower Green *Staffs.* **WV9** 40 B5
Lower Green Bank **LA2** 55 J4
Lower Halstock Leigh **BA22** 8 E4
Lower Halstow **ME9** 24 E5
Lower Hardres **CT4** 15 G2
Lower Harpton **LD8** 28 B2
Lower Hartshay **DE5** 51 F7
Lower Hartwell **HP17** 31 J7
Lower Hawthwaite **LA20** 55 F1
Lower Haysden **TN11** 23 J7
Lower Hayton **SY8** 38 E7
Lower Heath **CW12** 49 H6
Lower Hergest **HR5** 28 B3
Lower Heyford **OX25** 31 F6
Lower Higham **ME3** 24 D4
Lower Holbrook **IP9** 35 F5
Lower Hopton **WF14** 50 D1
Lower Hordley **SY12** 38 C3
Lower Horncroft **RH20** 12 D5
Lower Horsebridge **BN27** 13 J5
Lower Houses **HD5** 50 D1
Lower Howsell **WR14** 29 G4
Lower Kersal **M25** 49 H2
Lower Kilchattan **PA61** 72 B1
Lower Kilcott **GL12** 20 A3
Lower Killeyan **PA42** 72 A6
Lower Kingcombe **DT2** 8 E5
Lower Kingswood **KT20** 23 F6
Lower Kinnerton **CH4** 48 C6
Lower Langford **BS40** 19 H5
Lower Largo **KY8** 83 F7
Lower Leigh **ST10** 40 C2
Lower Lemington **GL56** 30 D5
Lower Lovacott **EX31** 6 D3
Lower Loxhore **EX31** 6 E2
Lower Lydbrook **GL17** 28 E7
Lower Lye **HR6** 28 D2
Lower Machen **NP10** 19 F3
Lower Maes-coed **HR2** 28 C5
Lower Mannington **BH21** 10 B4
Lower Middleton Cheney **OX17** 31 G4
Lower Milton **BA5** 19 J7
Lower Moor **WR10** 29 J4
Lower Morton **BS35** 19 K2
Lower Nash **SA72** 16 D5
Lower Nazeing **EN9** 23 G1
Lower Netchwood **WV16** 39 F6
Lower Nyland **SP8** 9 G2
Lower Oddington **GL56** 30 D6
Lower Ollach **IV51** 86 B1
Lower Penarth **CF64** 18 E4
Lower Penn **WV4** 40 A6
Lower Pennington **SO41** 10 E5
Lower Peover **WA16** 49 G5
Lower Pollicott **HP18** 31 J7
Lower Quinton **CV37** 30 C4
Lower Race **NP4** 19 F1
Lower Rainham **ME8** 24 E5
Lower Roadwater **TA23** 7 J2
Lower Sapey **WR6** 29 F2
Lower Seagry **SN15** 20 C3
Lower Shelton **MK43** 32 C4
Lower Shiplake **RG9** 22 A4
Lower Shuckburgh **NN11** 31 F2
Lower Slaughter **GL54** 30 C6
Lower Soothill **WF17** 57 H7
Lower Stanton St. Quintin **SN14** 20 C3
Lower Stoke **ME3** 24 E4
Lower Stondon **SG16** 32 E5
Lower Stone **GL13** 19 K2
Lower Stonnall **WS9** 40 C5
Lower Stow Bedon **NR17** 44 D6
Lower Street *Dorset* **DT11** 9 H5
Lower Street *E.Suss.* **TN33** 14 C6
Lower Street *Norf.* **NR11** 45 G2
Lower Street *Norf.* **NR11** 45 F2
Lower Street *Suff.* **IP6** 35 F3
Lower Stretton **WA4** 49 F4
Lower Sundon **LU3** 32 D6
Lower Swanwick **SO31** 11 F4
Lower Swell **GL54** 30 C6
Lower Tadmarton **OX15** 31 F5
Lower Tale **EX14** 7 J5
Lower Tean **ST10** 40 C2
Lower Thurlton **NR14** 45 J6
Lower Thurnham **LA2** 55 H4
Lower Town *Cornw.* **TR13** 2 D6
Lower Town *Devon* **TQ13** 5 H3
Lower Town *I.o.S.* **TR25** 2 C1
Lower Town *Pembs.* **SA65** 16 C2
Lower Trebullett **PL15** 4 D3
Lower Tysoe **CV35** 30 E4
Lower Upcott **TQ13** 7 G7
Lower Upham **SO32** 11 G3
Lower Upnor **ME2** 24 D4
Lower Vexford **TA4** 7 K2
Lower Wallop **SY5** 38 C5
Lower Walton **WA4** 49 F4
Lower Waterhay **SN6** 20 D2
Lower Weald **MK19** 31 J5
Lower Wear **EX2** 7 H7
Lower Weare **BS26** 19 H6
Lower Welson **HR3** 28 B3
Lower Whatley **BA11** 20 A7
Lower Whitley **WA4** 49 F5
Lower Wick **WR2** 29 H3
Lower Wield **SO24** 21 K7
Lower Winchendon (Nether Winchendon) **HP18** 31 J7
Lower Withington **SK11** 49 H6
Lower Woodend **SL7** 22 B3
Lower Woodford **SP4** 10 C1
Lower Wyche **WR14** 29 G4
Lowerhouse **BB12** 56 D6
Lowertown **KW17** 106 D8
Lowesby **LE7** 42 A5
Lowestoft NR32 45 K6
Loweswater **CA13** 60 C4
Lowfield Heath **RH11** 23 F7
Lowgill *Cumb.* **LA8** 61 H7
Lowgill *Lancs.* **LA2** 56 B3
Lowick *Cumb.* **LA12** 55 F1
Lowick *Northants.* **NN14** 42 C7
Lowick *Northumb.* **TD15** 77 J7
Lowick Bridge **LA12** 55 F1
Lowick Green **LA12** 55 F1
Lownie Moor **DD8** 83 F3
Lowsonford **B95** 30 C2
Lowther **CA10** 61 G4
Lowther Castle **CA10** 61 G4
Lowthorpe **YO25** 59 G3
Lowton *Devon* **EX20** 6 E5
Lowton *Gt.Man.* **WA3** 49 F3
Lowton *Som.* **TA3** 7 K4
Lowton Common **WA3** 49 F3
Loxbeare **EX16** 7 H4
Loxhill **GU8** 12 D3
Loxhore **EX31** 6 E2
Loxley **CV35** 30 D3
Loxley Green **ST14** 40 C2
Loxton **BS26** 19 G6
Loxwood **RH14** 12 D3
Lubachoinnich **IV24** 96 B2
Lubcroy **IV27** 95 K1
Lubenham **LE16** 42 A7
Lubfearn **IV23** 95 K4
Lubmore **IV22** 95 G6
Lubreoch **PH15** 81 F3
Luccombe **TA24** 7 H1
Luccombe Village **PO37** 11 G6
Lucker **NE70** 77 K7
Luckett **PL17** 4 D3
Luckington **SN14** 20 B3
Lucklawhill **KY16** 83 F5
Luckwell Bridge **TA24** 7 H2
Lucton **HR6** 28 D2
Lucy Cross **DL11** 62 D5
Ludag **HS8** 84 C3
Ludborough **DN36** 53 F3
Ludbrook **PL21** 5 G5
Ludchurch **SA67** 16 E4
Luddenden **HX2** 57 F7
Luddenden Foot **HX2** 57 F7
Luddenham Court **ME13** 25 F5
Luddesdown **DA13** 24 C5
Luddington *N.Lincs.* **DN17** 52 B1
Luddington *Warks.* **CV37** 30 C3
Luddington in the Brook **PE8** 42 E7
Ludford *Lincs.* **LN8** 52 E4
Ludford *Shrop.* **SY8** 28 E1
Ludgershall *Bucks.* **HP18** 31 H7
Ludgershall *Wilts.* **SP11** 21 F6
Ludgvan **TR20** 2 C5
Ludham **NR29** 45 H4
Ludlow SY8 28 E1
Ludney **LN11** 53 G3
Ludstock **HR8** 29 F5
Ludstone **WV5** 40 A6
Ludwell **SP7** 9 J2
Ludworth **DH6** 62 E2
Luffincott **EX22** 6 B6
Luffness **EH32** 76 C2
Lufton **BA22** 8 E3
Lugar **KA18** 67 K1
Luggate **EH41** 76 D3
Luggate Burn **EH41** 76 E3
Luggiebank **G67** 75 F3
Lugton **KA3** 74 C5
Lugwardine **HR1** 28 E4
Luib **IV49** 86 B2
Luibeilt **PH30** 80 D1
Luing **PA34** 79 J6
Lulham **HR2** 28 D4
Lullington *Derbys.* **DE12** 40 E4
Lullington *Som.* **BA11** 20 A6
Lulsgate Bottom **BS40** 19 J5
Lulsley **WR6** 29 G3
Lulworth Camp **BH20** 9 H6
Lumb *Lancs.* **BB4** 56 D7
Lumb *W.Yorks.* **HX6** 57 F7
Lumbutts **OL14** 56 E7
Lumby **LS25** 57 K6
Lumphanan **AB31** 90 D4
Lumphinnans **KY4** 75 K1
Lumsdaine **TD14** 77 G4
Lumsdale **DE4** 51 F6
Lumsden **AB54** 90 C2
Lunan **DD11** 83 H2
Lunanhead **DD8** 83 F2
Luncarty **PH1** 82 B5
Lund *E.Riding* **YO25** 59 F5
Lund *N.Yorks.* **YO8** 58 C6
Lund *Shet.* **ZE2** 107 P2
Lundale **HS2** 100 D4
Lundavra **PH33** 80 B1
Lunderton **AB42** 99 K6
Lundie *Angus* **DD2** 82 D4
Lundie *High.* **IV63** 87 H3
Lundin Links **KY8** 83 F7
Lundwood **S71** 51 F2
Lundy **EX34** 6 A1
Lunga **PA31** 79 K7
Lunna **ZE2** 107 N6
Lunning **ZE2** 107 P6
Lunnon **SA3** 17 J7
Lunsford's Cross **TN39** 14 C6
Lunt **L29** 48 C2
Luntley **HR6** 28 C3
Luppitt **EX14** 7 K5
Lupset **WF2** 51 F1
Lupton **LA6** 55 J1
Lurgashall **GU28** 12 C4
Lurignich **PA38** 80 A2
Lusby **PE23** 53 G6
Luss **G83** 74 B1
Lussagiven **PA60** 72 E2
Lusta **IV55** 93 H6
Lustleigh **TQ13** 7 F7
Luston **HR6** 28 D2
Luthermuir **AB30** 83 H1
Luthrie **KY15** 82 E6
Luton *Devon* **EX14** 7 J5
Luton *Devon* **TQ13** 5 K3
LUTON *Luton* LU 32 D6
Luton *Med.* **ME5** 24 D5
Luton Airport (London Luton Airport) **LU2** 32 E6
Lutterworth LE17 41 H7
Lutton *Devon* **PL21** 5 F5
Lutton *Dorset* **BH20** 9 J6
Lutton *Lincs.* **PE12** 43 H3
Lutton *Northants.* **PE8** 42 E7
Luxborough **TA23** 7 H2
Luxulyan **PL30** 4 A5
Lybster *High.* **KW14** 105 F2
Lybster *High.* KW3 105 H5
Lydacott **EX21** 6 C5
Lydbury North SY7 38 C7
Lydcott **EX32** 6 E2
Lydd **TN29** 15 F5
Lydden **CT15** 15 H3
Lyddington **LE15** 42 B6
Lydd-on-Sea **TN29** 15 F5
Lyde Green **BS16** 19 K4
Lydeard St. Lawrence **TA4** 7 K2
Lydford **EX20** 6 D7
Lydford-on-Fosse **TA11** 8 E1
Lydgate *Gt.Man.* **OL15** 49 J1
Lydgate *Gt.Man.* **OL4** 49 J2
Lydgate *W.Yorks.* **OL14** 56 E7
Lydham **SY9** 38 C6
Lydiard Millicent **SN5** 20 D3
Lydiard Tregoze **SN5** 20 E3
Lydiate **L31** 48 C2
Lydlinch **DT10** 9 G3
Lydney GL15 19 K1
Lydstep **SA70** 16 D6
Lye **DY9** 40 B7
Lye Cross **BS40** 19 H5
Lye Green *Bucks.* **HP5** 22 C1
Lye Green *E.Suss.* **TN6** 13 J3
Lye Green *Warks.* **CV35** 30 C2
Lye's Green **BA12** 20 B7
Lyford **OX12** 21 G2
Lymbridge Green **TN25** 15 G3
Lyme Regis DT7 8 C5
Lymekilns **G74** 74 E5
Lyminge **CT18** 15 G3
Lymington SO41 10 E5
Lyminster **BN17** 12 D6
Lymm WA13 49 F4
Lymore **SO41** 10 D5
Lympne **CT21** 15 G4
Lympsham **BS24** 19 G6
Lympstone **EX8** 7 H7
Lynaberack **PH21** 88 E5
Lynch **TA24** 7 G1
Lynch Green **NR9** 45 F5
Lynchat **PH21** 88 E4
Lyndale House **IV51** 93 J6
Lyndhurst SO43 10 D4
Lyndon **LE15** 42 C5
Lyne *Aber.* **AB51** 91 F4
Lyne *Sc.Bord.* **EH45** 76 A6
Lyne *Surr.* **KT16** 22 D5
Lyne Down **HR8** 29 F5
Lyne of Gorthleck **IV2** 88 C2
Lyne of Skene **AB32** 91 F3
Lyne Station **EH45** 76 A6
Lyneal **SY12** 38 D2
Lynegar **KW1** 105 H3
Lyneham *Oxon.* **OX7** 30 D6
Lyneham *Wilts.* **SN15** 20 D4
Lyneholmeford **CA6** 70 A6
Lynemore *High.* **PH26** 89 H2
Lynemore *Moray* **AB37** 89 J1
Lynemouth **NE61** 71 H4
Lyness **KW16** 106 C8

Lynford IP26 44 C6
Lyng Norf. NR9 44 E4
Lyng Som. TA3 8 C2
Lyngate NR28 45 H3
Lynmouth EX35 7 F1
Lynn TF10 39 G4
Lynsted ME9 25 F5
Lynstone EX23 6 A5
Lynton EX35 7 F1
Lyon's Gate DT2 9 F4
Lyonshall HR5 28 C3
Lyrabus PA44 72 A4
Lytchett Matravers BH16 9 J5
Lytchett Minster BH16 9 J5
Lyth KW1 105 H2
Lytham FY8 55 G7
Lytham St. Anne's FY8 55 G7
Lythe YO21 63 K5
Lythe Hill GU27 12 C3
Lythes KW17 106 D9
Lythmore KW14 105 F2

M

Maaruig (Maraig) HS3 100 E7
Mabe Burnthouse TR10 2 E5
Mabie DG2 65 K3
Mablethorpe LN12 53 J4
Macclesfield SK11 49 J5
Macclesfield Forest SK11 49 J5
Macduff AB44 99 F4
Macedonia KY6 82 D7
Machan ML9 75 F5
Machany PH3 81 K6
Macharioch PA28 66 B3
Machen CF83 19 F3
Machrie Arg. & B. PA49 72 A4
Machrie Arg. & B. PA42 72 B6
Machrie N.Ayr. KA27 73 G7
Machrihanish PA28 66 A1
Machrins PA61 72 B1
Machynlleth SY20 37 G5
McInroy's Point PA19 74 A3
Mackerye End AL4 32 E7
Mackworth DE22 41 F2
Macmerry EH33 76 C3
Macterry AB53 99 F6
Madderty PH7 82 A5
Maddiston FK2 75 H3
Madehurst BN18 12 C5
Madeley Staffs. CW3 39 G1
Madeley Tel. & W. TF7 39 G5
Madeley Heath CW3 39 G1
Maders PL17 4 D3
Madford EX15 7 K4
Madingley CB3 33 G2
Madjeston SP8 9 H2
Madley HR2 28 D5
Madresfield WR13 29 H4
Madron TR20 2 B5
Maenaddwyn LL71 46 C4
Maenclochog SA66 16 D3
Maendy Cardiff CF14 18 E4
Maendy V. of Glam. CF71 18 D4
Maenporth TR11 2 E6
Maentwrog LL41 37 F1
Maen-y-groes SA45 26 C3
Maer Cornw. EX23 6 A5
Maer Staffs. ST5 39 G2
Maerdy Carmar. SA19 17 K3
Maerdy Carmar. SA19 17 K3
Maerdy Conwy LL21 37 K1
Maerdy R.C.T. CF43 18 C2
Maesbrook SY10 38 B3
Maesbury Marsh SY10 38 C3
Maes-Glas (Greenfield) Flints. CH8 47 K5
Maes-glas Newport NP20 19 F3
Maesgwynne SA34 17 F3
Maeshafn CH7 48 B6
Maesllyn SA44 17 G1
Maesmynis LD2 27 K4
Maesteg CF34 18 B2
Maes-Treylow LD8 28 B2
Maesybont SA14 17 J4
Maesycrugiau SA39 17 H1
Maesycwmmer CF82 18 E2
Maesyfed (New Radnor) LD8 28 B2
Magdalen Laver CM5 23 J1
Maggieknockater AB38 98 B6
Maggots End CM23 33 H6
Magham Down BN27 13 K5
Maghull L31 48 C2
Magna Park LE17 41 H7
Magor NP26 19 H3
Magpie Green IP22 34 E1
Maiden Bradley BA12 9 G1
Maiden Head BS41 19 J5
Maiden Law DH7 62 C2
Maiden Newton DT2 8 E5
Maiden Wells SA71 16 C6
Maidencombe TQ1 5 K4
Maidenhayne EX13 8 B5
Maidenhead SL6 22 B3
Maidens KA26 67 G3
Maiden's Green RG42 22 B4
Maidensgrove RG9 22 A3
Maidenwell Cornw. PL30 4 B3
Maidenwell Lincs. LN11 53 G5
Maidford NN12 31 H3
Maids' Moreton MK18 31 J5
Maidstone ME14 14 C2
Maidwell NN6 31 J1
Mail ZE2 107 N10
Maindee NP19 19 G3
Mainland Ork. KW 106 B6
Mainland Shet. ZE 107 M7
Mains of Ardestie DD5 83 G4
Mains of Balgavies DD8 83 G2
Mains of Balhall DD9 83 G1
Mains of Ballindarg DD8 83 F2
Mains of Burgie IV36 97 H6
Mains of Culsh AB53 99 G6
Mains of Dillavaird AB30 91 F6
Mains of Drum AB31 91 G4
Mains of Dudwick AB41 91 H1
Mains of Faillie IV2 88 E1
Mains of Fedderate AB42 99 G6
Mains of Glack AB51 91 F2
Mains of Glassaugh AB45 98 D4
Mains of Glenbuchat AB36 90 B3
Mains of Linton AB51 91 F3
Mains of Melgund DD9 83 G2
Mains of Pitfour AB42 99 H6
Mains of Pittrichie AB21 91 G2
Mains of Sluie IV36 97 H6
Mains of Tannachy AB56 98 B4
Mains of Thornton AB30 90 E7
Mains of Tig KA26 67 F5
Mains of Watten KW1 105 H3
Mainsforth DL17 62 E3
Mainsriddle DG2 65 K5
Mainstone SY9 38 B7
Maisemore GL2 29 H6
Major's Green B90 30 C1
Makendon NE65 70 D3
Makeney DE56 41 F1
Makerstoun TD5 76 E7
Malacleit HS6 92 C4
Malborough TQ7 5 H7
Malden Rushett KT9 22 E5
Maldon CM9 24 E1
Malham BD23 56 E3
Maligar IV51 93 K5
Malinbridge S6 51 F4
Mallaig PH41 86 C5
Mallaigmore PH41 86 C5
Mallaigvaig PH41 86 C5
Malleny Mills EH14 75 K4
Malletsheugh G77 74 D5
Malling FK8 81 G7
Mallows Green CM23 33 H6
Malltraeth LL62 46 C6
Mallwyd SY20 37 H4
Malmesbury SN16 20 C3
Malmsmead EX35 7 F1
Malpas Ches. SY14 38 D1
Malpas Cornw. TR1 3 F4
Malpas Newport NP20 19 G2
Maltby Lincs. LN11 53 G4
Maltby S.Yorks. S66 51 H3
Maltby Stock. TS8 63 F5
Maltby le Marsh LN13 53 H4
Malting End CB8 34 B3
Malting Green CO2 34 D7
Maltman's Hill TN27 14 D3
Malton YO17 58 D2
Malvern Link WR14 29 G4
Malvern Wells WR14 29 G4
Mambeg G84 74 A2
Mamble DY14 29 F1
Mamhead EX6 7 H7
Mamhilad NP4 19 G1
Manaccan TR12 2 E6
Manadon PL5 4 E5
Manafon SY21 38 A5
Manais (Manish) HS3 93 G3
Manaton TQ13 7 F7
Manby LN11 53 G4
Mancetter CV9 41 F6
MANCHESTER M 49 H3
Manchester Airport M90 49 H4
Mancot Royal CH5 48 C6
Mandally PH35 87 J4
Manea PE15 43 H7
Maneight KA18 67 K3
Manfield DL2 62 D5
Mangaster ZE2 107 M5
Mangerton DT6 8 D5
Mangotsfield BS16 19 K4
Mangrove Green LU2 32 E6
Mangurstadh HS2 100 C4
Manish (Manais) HS3 93 G3
Mankinholes OL14 56 E7
Manley WA6 48 E5
Manmoel NP12 18 E1
Mannal PA77 78 A3
Manningford Abbots SN9 20 E6
Manningford Bohune SN9 20 E6
Manningford Bruce SN9 20 E6
Manningham BD8 57 G6
Mannings Heath RH13 13 F4
Mannington BH21 10 B4
Manningtree CO11 35 F5
Mannofield AB15 91 H4
Manor Park SL2 22 C3
Manorbier SA70 16 D6
Manorbier Newton SA70 16 D5
Manordeifi SA43 17 F1
Manordeilo SA19 17 K3
Manorowen SA65 16 C2
Mansell Gamage HR4 28 C4
Mansell Lacy HR4 28 D4
Mansergh LA6 56 B1
Mansfield NG18 51 H6
Mansfield Woodhouse NG19 51 H6
Manson Green NR9 44 E5
Mansriggs LA12 55 F1
Manston Dorset DT10 9 H3
Manston Kent CT12 25 K5
Manston W.Yorks. LS15 57 J6
Manswood BH21 9 J4
Manthorpe Lincs. PE10 42 D4
Manthorpe Lincs. NG31 42 C2
Manton N.Lincs. DN21 52 C2
Manton Notts. S80 51 H5
Manton Rut. LE15 42 B5
Manton Wilts. SN8 20 E5
Manuden CM23 33 H6
Manwood Green CM5 33 J7
Maolachy PA35 79 K6
Maperton BA9 9 F2
Maple Cross WD3 22 D2
Maplebeck NG22 51 K6
Mapledurham RG4 21 K4
Mapledurwell RG25 21 K6
Maplehurst RH13 12 E4
Maplescombe DA4 23 J5
Mapleton DE6 40 D1
Mapperley Derbys. DE7 41 G1
Mapperley Notts. NG5 41 H1
Mapperton Dorset DT8 8 E5
Mapperton Dorset DT11 9 J5
Mappleborough Green B80 30 B2
Mappleton HU18 59 J5
Mapplewell S75 51 F2
Mappowder DT10 9 G4
Mar Lodge AB35 89 H5
Maraig (Maaruig) HS3 100 E7
Marazion TR17 2 C5
Marbhig HS2 101 G6
Marbury SY13 38 E1
March PE15 43 H6
Marcham OX13 21 H2
Marchamley SY4 38 E3
Marchamley Wood SY4 38 E2
Marchington ST14 40 D2
Marchington Woodlands ST14 40 D3
Marchwiel LL13 38 C1
Marchwood SO40 10 E3
Marcross CF61 18 C5
Marcus DD8 83 G2
Marden Here. HR1 28 E4
Marden Kent TN12 14 C3
Marden T. & W. NE30 71 J6
Marden Wilts. SN10 20 D6
Marden Ash CM5 23 J1
Marden Beech TN12 14 C3
Marden Thorn TN12 14 C3
Marden's Hill TN6 13 H3
Mardon TD12 77 H7
Mardy NP7 28 C7
Mare Green TA3 8 C2
Marefield LE7 42 A5
Mareham le Fen PE22 53 F6
Mareham on the Hill LN9 53 F6
Maresfield TN22 13 H4
Marfleet HU9 59 H6
Marford LL12 48 C7
Margam SA13 18 A3
Margaret Marsh SP7 9 H3
Margaret Roding CM6 33 J7
Margaretting CM4 24 C1
Margaretting Tye CM4 24 C1
Margate CT9 25 K4
Margnaheglish KA27 73 J7
Margreig DG2 65 J3
Margrove Park TS12 63 H5
Marham PE33 44 B5
Marhamchurch EX23 6 A5
Marholm PE6 42 E5
Marian Cwm LL18 47 J5
Mariandyrys LL58 46 E4
Marian-glas LL73 46 D4
Mariansleigh EX36 7 F3
Marine Town ME12 25 F4
Marishader IV51 93 K5
Maristow House PL6 4 E4
Mark TA9 19 G7
Mark Causeway TA9 19 G7
Mark Cross TN6 13 J3
Markbeech TN8 23 H7
Markby LN13 53 H5
Markdhu DG8 64 B3
Markeaton DE22 41 F2
Market Bosworth CV13 41 G5
Market Deeping PE6 42 E4
Market Drayton TF9 39 F2
Market Harborough LE16 42 A7
Market Lavington SN10 20 D6
Market Overton LE15 42 B4
Market Rasen LN8 52 E4
Market Stainton LN8 53 F5
Market Street NR12 45 G3
Market Warsop NG20 51 H6
Market Weighton YO43 58 E5
Market Weston IP22 34 D1
Markethill PH13 82 D4
Markfield LE67 41 G4
Markham NP12 18 E1
Markham Moor DN22 51 K5
Markinch KY7 82 D7
Markington HG3 57 H3
Marks Gate RM6 23 H2
Marks Tey CO6 34 D6
Marksbury BA2 19 K5
Markwell PL12 4 D5
Markyate AL3 32 D7
Marl Bank WR14 29 G4
Marland OL11 49 H1
Marlborough SN8 20 E5
Marlbrook B60 29 J1
Marlcliff B50 30 B3
Marldon TQ3 5 J4
Marle Green TN21 13 J5
Marlesford IP13 35 H3
Marley Green SY13 38 E1
Marley Hill NE16 62 D1
Marlingford NR9 45 F5
Marloes SA62 16 A5
Marlow Bucks. SL7 22 B3
Marlow Here. SY7 28 D1
Marlpit Hill TN8 23 H7
Marlpool DE75 41 G1
Marnhull DT10 9 G3
Marnoch AB54 98 D5
Marple SK6 49 J4
Marple Bridge SK6 49 J4
Marr DN5 51 H2
Marrel KW8 105 F7
Marrick DL11 62 B7
Marrister ZE2 107 P6
Marros SA33 17 F5
Marsden T. & W. NE34 71 J7
Marsden W.Yorks. HD7 50 C1
Marsett DL8 56 E1
Marsh EX14 8 B3
Marsh Baldon OX44 21 J2
Marsh Benham RG20 21 H5
Marsh Gibbon OX27 31 H6
Marsh Green Devon EX5 7 J6
Marsh Green Gt.Man. WN5 48 E2
Marsh Green Kent TN8 23 H7
Marsh Green Tel. & W. TF6 39 F4
Marsh Lane S21 51 G5
Marsh Street TA24 7 H1
Marshall Meadows TD15 77 H5
Marshalsea DT6 8 C4
Marshalswick AL1 22 E1
Marsham NR10 45 F3
Marshaw LA2 55 J4
Marshborough CT13 15 J2
Marshbrook SY6 38 D7
Marshchapel DN36 53 G3
Marshfield Newport CF3 19 F3
Marshfield S.Glos. SN14 20 A4
Marshgate PL32 4 B1
Marshland St. James PE14 43 J5
Marshside PR9 48 C1
Marshwood DT6 8 C5
Marske DL11 62 C6
Marske-by-the-Sea TS11 63 H4
Marsland Green M29 49 F3
Marston Ches. CW9 49 F5
Marston Here. HR6 28 C3
Marston Lincs. NG32 42 B1
Marston Oxon. OX3 21 J1
Marston Staffs. ST18 40 B3
Marston Staffs. ST20 40 A4
Marston Warks. B76 40 E6
Marston Wilts. SN10 20 C6
Marston Doles CV47 31 F3
Marston Green B37 40 D7
Marston Magna BA22 8 E2
Marston Meysey SN6 20 E2
Marston Montgomery DE6 40 D2
Marston Moretaine MK43 32 C4
Marston on Dove DE65 40 E3
Marston St. Lawrence OX17 31 G4
Marston Stannett HR6 28 E3
Marston Trussell LE16 41 J7
Marstow HR9 28 E7
Marsworth HP23 32 C7
Marten SN8 21 F5
Marthall WA16 49 G5
Martham NR29 45 J4
Martin Hants. SP6 10 B3
Martin Lincs. LN4 52 E7
Martin Lincs. LN9 53 F6
Martin Drove End SP6 10 B2
Martin Hussingtree WR3 29 H2
Martinhoe EX31 6 E1
Martinscroft WA1 49 F4
Martinstown DT2 9 F6
Martlesham IP12 35 G4
Martlesham Heath IP5 35 G4
Martletwy SA67 16 D4
Martley WR6 29 G2
Martock TA12 8 D3
Marton Ches. SK11 49 H6
Marton Cumb. LA12 55 F2
Marton E.Riding HU11 59 H6
Marton E.Riding YO15 59 J3
Marton Lincs. DN21 52 B4
Marton Middbro. TS7 63 G5
Marton N.Yorks. YO51 57 K3
Marton N.Yorks. YO62 58 D1
Marton Shrop. SY21 38 B5
Marton Shrop. SY4 38 D3
Marton Warks. CV23 31 F2
Marton Abbey YO61 58 B3
Marton-in-the-Forest YO61 58 B3
Marton-le-Moor HG4 57 J2
Martyr Worthy SO21 11 G1
Martyr's Green KT11 22 D6
Marwick KW17 106 B5
Marwood EX31 6 D2
Mary Tavy PL19 5 F3
Marybank High. IV6 96 B6
Marybank W.Isles HS2 101 G4
Maryburgh IV7 96 C6
Maryfield Cornw. PL11 4 E5
Maryfield Shet. ZE2 107 N8
Marygold TD11 77 G5
Maryhill Aber. AB53 99 G6
Maryhill Glas. G20 74 D4
Marykirk AB30 83 H1
Marylebone Gt.Lon. W1G 23 F3
Marylebone Gt.Man. WN1 48 E2
Marypark AB37 89 J1
Maryport Cumb. CA15 60 B3
Maryport D. & G. DG9 64 B7
Marystow PL16 6 C7
Maryton DD10 83 H2
Marywell Aber. AB12 91 H5
Marywell Aber. AB34 90 D5
Marywell Angus DD11 83 H3
Masham HG4 57 H1
Mashbury CM1 33 K7
Masongill LA6 56 B2
Mastin Moor S43 51 G5
Mastrick AB16 91 H4
Matchborough B98 30 B2
Matching CM17 33 J7
Matching Green CM17 33 J7
Matching Tye CM17 33 J7
Matfen NE20 71 F6
Matfield TN12 23 K7
Mathern NP16 19 J2
Mathon WR13 29 G4
Mathry SA62 16 B2
Matlaske NR11 45 F2
Matlock DE4 51 F6
Matlock Bank DE4 51 F6
Matlock Bath DE4 50 E7
Matson GL4 29 H7
Matterdale End CA11 60 E4
Mattersey DN10 51 J4
Mattersey Thorpe DN10 51 J4
Mattingley RG27 22 A6
Mattishall NR20 44 E4
Mattishall Burgh NR20 44 E4
Mauchline KA5 67 J1
Maud AB42 99 H6
Maufant JE2 3 K7
Maugersbury GL54 30 C6
Maughold IM7 54 D4
Mauld IV4 87 K1
Maulden MK45 32 D5
Maulds Meaburn CA10 61 H5
Maunby YO7 57 J1
Maund Bryan HR1 28 E3
Maundown TA4 7 J3
Mautby NR29 45 J4
Mavesyn Ridware WS15 40 C4
Mavis Enderby PE23 53 G6
Maw Green CW1 49 G7
Mawbray CA15 60 B2
Mawdesley L40 48 D1
Mawdlam CF33 18 B3
Mawgan TR12 2 E6
Mawgan Porth TR8 3 F2
Mawla TR16 2 E4
Mawnan TR11 2 E6
Mawnan Smith TR11 2 E6
Mawsley NN14 32 B1
Mawthorpe LN13 53 H5
Maxey PE6 42 E5
Maxstoke B46 40 E7
Maxted Street CT4 15 G3
Maxton Kent CT17 15 J3
Maxton Sc.Bord. TD6 76 E7
Maxwellheugh TD5 77 F7
Maxwelltown DG2 65 K3
Maxworthy PL15 4 C1
May Hill GL17 29 G6
Mayals SA3 17 K6
Maybole KA19 67 H3
Maybury GU22 22 D6
Mayen AB54 98 D6
Mayfair W1J 23 F3
Mayfield E.Suss. TN20 13 J4
Mayfield Midloth. EH22 76 B4
Mayfield Staffs. DE6 40 D1
Mayford GU22 22 C6
Mayland CM3 25 F1
Maylandsea CM3 25 F1
Maynard's Green TN21 13 J5
Maypole I.o.S. TR21 2 C1
Maypole Kent CT3 25 H5
Maypole Mon. NP25 28 D7
Maypole Green Essex CO2 34 D6
Maypole Green Norf. NR14 45 J6
Maypole Green Suff. IP13 35 G2
Maypole Green Suff. IP30 34 D3
May's Green N.Som. BS24 19 G5
Mays Green Oxon. RG9 22 A3
Maywick ZE2 107 M10
Mead EX39 6 A4
Mead End SP5 10 B2
Meadgate BA2 19 K6
Meadle HP17 22 B1
Meadow Green WR6 29 G3
Meadowhall S9 51 F3
Meadowmill EH33 76 C3
Meadowtown SY5 38 C5
Meadwell PL16 6 C7
Meaford ST15 40 A2
Meal Bank LA9 61 G7
Mealabost (Melbost Borve) HS2 101 G2
Mealasta HS2 100 B5
Meals LN11 53 H3
Mealsgate CA7 60 D2
Meanley BB7 56 C5
Meanwood LS6 57 H6
Mearbeck BD23 56 D3
Meare BA6 19 H7
Meare Green TA3 8 B2
Mearns G77 74 D5
Mears Ashby NN6 32 B2
Measham DE12 41 F4
Meathop LA11 55 H1
Meavy PL20 5 F4
Medbourne LE16 42 B6
Meddon EX39 6 A4
Meden Vale NG20 51 H6
Medlar PR4 55 H6
Medmenham SL7 22 B3
Medomsley DH8 62 C1
Medstead GU34 11 H1
Meer Common HR3 28 C3
Meer End CV8 30 D1
Meerbrook ST13 49 J6
Meesden SG9 33 H5
Meeson TF6 39 F3
Meeth EX20 6 D5
Meeting House Hill NR28 45 H3
Meggethead TD7 69 G1
Meidrim SA33 17 F3
Meifod Denb. LL16 47 J7
Meifod Powys SY22 38 A4

Meigle PH12 82 D3
Meikle Earnock ML3 75 F5
Meikle Grenach PA20 73 J4
Meikle Kilmory PA20 73 J4
Meikle Rahane G84 74 A2
Meikle Strath AB30 90 E7
Meikle Tarty AB41 91 H2
Meikle Wartle AB51 91 F1
Meikleour PH2 82 C4
Meikleyard KA4 74 D7
Meinciau SA17 17 H4
Meir ST3 40 B1
Meirheath ST3 40 B2
Melbost HS2 101 G4
Melbost Borve (Mealabost) HS2 101 G2
Melbourn SG8 33 G4
Melbourne Derbys. DE73 41 F3
Melbourne E.Riding YO42 58 D5
Melbury EX39 6 B4
Melbury Abbas SP7 9 H3
Melbury Bubb DT2 8 E4
Melbury Osmond DT2 8 E4
Melbury Sampford DT2 8 E4
Melby ZE2 107 K7
Melchbourne MK44 32 D2
Melcombe Bingham DT2 9 G4
Melcombe Regis DT4 9 F6
Meldon Devon EX20 6 D6
Meldon Northumb. NE61 71 G5
Meldreth SG8 33 G4
Meledor PL26 3 G3
Melfort PA34 79 K6
Melgarve PH20 88 B5
Melgum AB34 90 C4
Meliden (Gallt Melyd) LL19 47 J4
Melincourt SA11 18 B1
Melin-y-coed LL26 47 G6
Melin-y-ddol SY21 37 K5
Melin-y-grug SY21 37 K5
Melin-y-Wig LL21 37 K1
Melkinthorpe CA10 61 G4
Melkridge NE49 70 C7
Melksham SN12 20 C5
Melksham Forest SN12 20 C5
Melldalloch PA21 73 H3
Melling Lancs. LA6 55 J2
Melling Mersey. L31 48 C2
Melling Mount L31 48 D2
Mellis IP23 34 E1
Mellon Charles IV22 94 E2
Mellon Udrigle IV22 94 E2
Mellor Gt.Man. SK6 49 J4
Mellor Lancs. BB2 56 B6
Mellor Brook BB2 56 B6
Mells BA11 20 A7
Melmerby Cumb. CA10 61 H3
Melmerby N.Yorks. DL8 57 F1
Melmerby N.Yorks. HG4 57 J2
Melplash DT6 8 D5
Melrose Aber. AB45 99 F4
Melrose Sc.Bord. TD6 76 D7
Melsetter KW16 106 B9
Melsonby DL10 62 C6
Meltham HD9 50 C1
Melton E.Riding HU15 59 F7
Melton Suff. IP12 35 G3
Melton Constable NR24 44 E2
Melton Mowbray LE13 42 A4
Melton Ross DN38 52 D1
Meltonby YO42 58 D4
Melvaig IV21 94 D3
Melverley SY10 38 C4
Melverley Green SY10 38 C4
Melvich KW14 104 D2
Membury EX13 8 B4
Memsie AB43 99 H4
Memus DD8 83 F2
Menabilly PL24 4 A5
Menai Bridge (Porthaethwy) LL59 46 D5
Mendham IP20 45 G7
Mendlesham IP14 35 F2
Mendlesham Green IP14 34 E2
Menethorpe YO17 58 D3
Menheniot PL14 4 C4
Menie House AB23 91 H2
Menithwood WR6 29 G2
Mennock DG4 68 D3
Menston LS29 57 G5
Menstrie FK11 75 G1
Mentmore LU7 32 C7
Meoble PH40 86 D6
Meole Brace SY3 38 D4
Meon PO14 11 G4
Meonstoke SO32 11 H3
Meopham DA13 24 C5
Meopham Green DA13 24 C5
Mepal CB6 43 H7
Meppershall SG17 32 E5
Merbach HR3 28 C4
Mercaston DE6 40 E1
Mere Ches. WA16 49 G4
Mere Wilts. BA12 9 H1
Mere Brow PR9 48 D1
Mere Green B75 40 D6
Mere Heath CW9 49 F5
Mereclough BB10 56 D6
Mereside FY4 55 G6
Meretown TF10 39 G3
Mereworth ME18 23 K6
Mergie AB39 91 F6
Meriden CV7 40 E7
Merkadale IV47 85 J1
Merkinch IV3 96 D7
Merkland DG7 65 H3
Merley BH21 10 B5
Merlin's Bridge SA61 16 C4
Merridge TA5 8 B1
Merrifield TQ7 5 J6
Merrington SY4 38 D3
Merrion SA71 16 C6
Merriott TA16 8 D3
Merrivale PL19 5 F3
Merrow GU1 22 D6
Merry Hill Herts. WD23 22 E2
Merry Hill W.Mid. DY5 40 B7
Merry Hill W.Mid. WV3 40 A6
Merrymeet PL14 4 C4
Mersea Island CO5 34 E7
Mersham TN25 15 F4
Merstham RH1 23 F6
Merston PO20 12 B6
Merstone PO30 11 G6
Merther TR2 3 F4
Merthyr SA33 17 G3
Merthyr Cynog LD3 27 J5
Merthyr Dyfan CF62 18 E5
Merthyr Mawr CF32 18 B4
Merthyr Tydfil CF47 18 D1
Merthyr Vale CF48 18 D2
Merton Devon EX20 6 D4
Merton Norf. IP25 44 D6
Merton Oxon. OX25 31 G7
Mervinslaw TD8 70 B2
Meshaw EX36 7 F4
Messing CO5 34 D7
Messingham DN17 52 B2
Metcombe EX11 7 J6
Metfield IP20 45 G7
Metheringham LN4 52 D6
Metherwell PL17 4 E4
Methil KY8 76 B1
Methlem LL53 36 A2
Methley LS26 57 J7
Methley Junction LS26 57 J7
Methlick AB41 91 G1
Methven PH1 82 B5
Methwold IP26 44 B6
Methwold Hythe IP26 44 B6
MetroCentre NE11 71 H7
Mettingham NR35 45 H7
Metton NR11 45 F2
Mevagissey PL26 4 A6
Mewith Head LA2 56 C3
Mexborough S64 51 G3
Mey KW14 105 H1
Meysey Hampton GL7 20 E1
Miabhag W.Isles HS3 93 G2
Miabhag W.Isles HS3 100 C7
Miabhaig (Miavaig) HS2 100 C4
Mial IV21 94 D4
Miavaig (Miabhaig) HS2 100 C4
Michaelchurch HR2 28 E6
Michaelchurch Escley HR2 28 C5
Michaelchurch-on-Arrow HR5 28 B3
Michaelston-le-Pit CF64 18 E4
Michaelston-super-Ely CF5 18 E4
Michaelston-y-Fedw CF3 19 F3
Michaelstow PL30 4 A3
Michelcombe TQ13 5 G4
Micheldever SO21 11 G1
Michelmersh SO51 10 E2
Mickfield IP14 35 F2
Mickle Trafford CH2 48 D6
Micklebring S66 51 H3
Mickleby TS13 63 K5
Micklefield LS25 57 K6
Micklefield Green WD3 22 D2
Mickleham RH5 22 E6
Micklehurst OL5 49 J2
Mickleover DE3 41 F2
Micklethwaite Cumb. CA7 60 D1
Micklethwaite W.Yorks. BD20 57 F5
Mickleton Dur. DL12 62 A4
Mickleton Glos. GL55 30 C4
Mickletown LS26 57 J7
Mickley Derbys. S18 51 F5
Mickley N.Yorks. HG4 57 H2
Mickley Green IP29 34 C3
Mickley Square NE43 71 F7
Mid Ardlaw AB43 99 H4
Mid Beltie AB31 90 E4
Mid Calder EH53 75 J4
Mid Clyth KW3 105 H5
Mid Lambrook TA13 8 D3
Mid Lavant PO18 12 B6
Mid Letter PA27 80 B7
Mid Lix FK21 81 G4
Mid Mossdale DL8 61 K7
Mid Yell ZE2 107 P3
Midbea KW17 106 D3
Middle Assendon RG9 22 A3
Middle Aston OX25 31 F6
Middle Barton OX7 31 F6
Middle Bickenhill B92 40 E7
Middle Bockhampton BH23 10 C5
Middle Claydon MK18 31 J6
Middle Drift PL14 4 B4
Middle Drums DD9 83 G2
Middle Duntisbourne GL7 20 C1
Middle Handley S21 51 G5
Middle Harling NR16 44 D7
Middle Kames PA31 73 H2
Middle Littleton WR11 30 B4
Middle Maes-coed HR2 28 C5
Middle Marwood EX31 6 D2
Middle Mill SA62 16 B3
Middle Quarter TN26 14 D4
Middle Rasen LN8 52 D4
Middle Rigg PH2 82 B7
Middle Salter LA2 56 B3
Middle Sontley LL13 38 C1
Middle Stoford TA21 7 K3
Middle Taphouse PL14 4 B4
Middle Town TR25 2 C1
Middle Tysoe CV35 30 E4
Middle Wallop SO20 10 D1
Middle Winterslow SP5 10 D1
Middle Woodford SP4 10 C1
Middlebie DG11 69 H6
Middlecliff S72 51 G2
Middlecott EX22 6 C5
Middleham DL8 57 G1
Middlehill Aber. AB53 99 G6
Middlehill Cornw. PL14 4 C4
Middlehope SY7 38 E7
Middlemarsh DT9 9 F4
Middlemoor PL19 4 E3
Middlequarter (Ceathramh Meadhanach) HS6 92 D4
Middlesbrough TS1 63 F4
Middlesceugh CA4 60 F2
Middleshaw LA8 55 J1
Middlesmoor HG3 57 F2
Middlestone DL16 62 D3
Middlestone Moor DL16 62 D3
Middlestown WF4 50 E1
Middleton Aber. AB21 91 G3
Middleton Angus DD11 83 G3
Middleton Cumb. LA6 56 B1
Middleton Derbys. DE4 50 E7
Middleton Derbys. DE45 50 D6
Middleton Essex CO10 34 C4
Middleton Gt.Man. M24 49 H2
Middleton Hants. SP11 21 H7
Middleton Here. SY8 28 E2
Middleton Lancs. LA3 55 H4
Middleton Midloth. EH23 76 B5
Middleton N.Yorks. YO18 58 D1
Middleton Norf. PE32 44 A4
Middleton Northants. LE16 42 B7
Middleton Northumb. NE61 71 F5
Middleton Northumb. NE70 77 J7
Middleton P.& K. KY13 82 C7
Middleton P.& K. PH10 82 C3
Middleton Shrop. SY15 38 B6
Middleton Shrop. SY8 28 E1
Middleton Shrop. SY11 38 C3
Middleton Suff. IP17 35 J2
Middleton Swan. SA3 17 H7
Middleton W.Yorks. LS29 57 G5
Middleton W.Yorks. LS10 57 J7
Middleton Warks. B78 40 D6
Middleton Baggot WV16 39 F6
Middleton Bank Top NE61 71 F5
Middleton Cheney OX17 31 F4
Middleton Green ST10 40 B2
Middleton Hall NE71 70 E1
Middleton Moor IP17 35 J2
Middleton of Potterton AB23 91 H3
Middleton on the Hill SY8 28 E2
Middleton One Row DL2 62 E5
Middleton Park AB22 91 H3
Middleton Priors WV16 39 F7
Middleton Quernhow HG4 57 J2
Middleton St. George DL2 62 E5
Middleton Scriven WV16 39 F7
Middleton Stoney OX25 31 G6
Middleton Tyas DL10 62 D6
Middleton-in-Teesdale DL12 62 A4
Middleton-on-Leven TS15 63 F5
Middleton-on-Sea PO22 12 C6
Middleton-on-the-Wolds YO25 59 F5
Middletown Cumb. CA22 60 A6
Middletown Powys SY21 38 C4
Middlewich CW10 49 G6
Middlewood Ches. SK12 49 J4
Middlewood S.Yorks. S6 51 F3
Middlewood Green IP14 34 E2
Middlezoy TA7 8 C1
Middridge DL4 62 D4
Midfield IV27 103 H2
Midford BA2 20 A5
Midge Hall PR26 55 J7
Midgeholme CA8 61 H1
Midgham RG7 21 J5
Midgley W.Yorks. WF4 50 E1
Midgley W.Yorks. HX2 57 F7
Midhopestones S36 50 E3
Midhurst GU29 12 B4
Midlem TD7 70 A1
Midloe Grange PE19 32 E2
Midpark PA20 73 J5
Midsomer Norton BA3 19 K6
Midthorpe LN9 53 F5
Midtown High. IV27 103 H2
Midtown High. IV22 94 E3
Midtown of Barras AB39 91 G6
Midville PE22 53 G7
Midway DE11 41 F3
Migdale IV24 96 D2
Migvie AB34 90 C4
Milarrochy G63 74 C1
Milber TQ12 5 J3
Milbethill AB54 98 E5
Milborne Port DT9 9 F3
Milborne St. Andrew DT11 9 G5
Milborne Wick DT9 9 F2
Milbourne Northumb. NE20 71 G6
Milbourne Wilts. SN16 20 C3
Milburn CA10 61 H4
Milbury Heath GL12 19 K2
Milcombe OX15 31 F5
Milden IP7 34 D4
Mildenhall Suff. IP28 34 B1
Mildenhall Wilts. SN8 21 F5
Mile Elm SN11 20 C5
Mile End Essex CO4 34 D6
Mile End Glos. GL16 28 E7
Mile Oak TN12 23 K7
Mile Town ME12 25 F4
Milebrook LD7 28 C1
Milebush TN12 14 C3
Mileham PE32 44 D4
Miles Green ST7 40 A1
Miles Hope WR15 28 E2
Milesmark KY12 75 J2
Miles's Green RG7 21 J5
Milfield NE71 77 H7
Milford Derbys. DE56 41 F1
Milford Devon EX39 6 A3
Milford Shrop. SY4 38 D3
Milford Staffs. ST17 40 B3
Milford Surr. GU8 22 C7
Milford Haven (Aberdaugleddau) SA73 16 B5
Milford on Sea SO41 10 D5
Milkwall GL16 19 J1
Mill Bank HX6 57 F7
Mill Brow SK6 49 J4
Mill End Bucks. RG9 22 A3
Mill End Cambs. CB8 33 K3
Mill End Herts. SG9 33 G5
Mill End Green CM6 33 K6
Mill Green Cambs. CB1 33 K4
Mill Green Essex CM4 24 C1
Mill Green Herts. AL9 23 F1
Mill Green Norf. IP22 45 F7
Mill Green Shrop. TF9 39 F3
Mill Green Staffs. WS15 40 C3
Mill Green Suff. IP13 35 H2
Mill Green Suff. IP14 35 F3
Mill Green Suff. IP14 34 D3
Mill Green W.Mid. WS9 40 C5
Mill Hill B'burn. BB2 56 B7
Mill Hill Cambs. SG19 33 F3
Mill Hill Gt.Lon. NW7 23 F2
Mill Houses LA2 56 B3
Mill Lane GU10 22 A6
Mill of Camsail G84 74 A2
Mill of Colp AB53 99 F6
Mill of Elrick AB41 99 H6
Mill of Fortune PH6 81 J5
Mill of Kingoodie AB21 91 G2
Mill of Monquich AB39 91 G5
Mill of Uras AB39 91 G6
Mill Side LA11 55 H1
Mill Street Kent ME19 23 K6
Mill Street Norf. NR20 44 E4
Milland GU30 12 B4
Millbank AB42 99 J6
Millbeck CA12 60 D4
Millbounds KW17 106 E4
Millbreck AB42 99 J6
Millbridge GU10 22 B7
Millbrook Beds. MK45 32 D5
Millbrook Cornw. PL10 4 E5
Millbrook Devon EX13 8 C5
Millbrook S'ham. SO15 10 E3
Millburn Aber. AB33 90 D2
Millburn Aber. AB54 90 E1
Millcombe TQ9 5 J6
Millcorner TN31 14 D5
Milldale DE6 50 D7
Millden AB23 91 H3
Milldens DD8 83 G2
Millearne PH7 82 A6
Millend OX7 30 E6
Millenheath SY13 38 E2
Millerhill EH22 76 B4
Miller's Dale SK17 50 D5
Millers Green Derbys. DE4 50 E7
Miller's Green Essex CM5 23 J1
Millgate OL12 56 D7
Millhalf HR3 28 B4
Millhayes Devon EX15 7 K4
Millhayes Devon EX14 8 B4
Millholme LA8 61 G7
Millhouse Arg. & B. PA21 73 H3
Millhouse Cumb. CA7 60 E3
Millhouse Green S36 50 E2
Millhousebridge DG11 69 G5
Millikenpark PA10 74 C4
Millin Cross SA62 16 C4
Millington YO42 58 E4
Millington Green DE6 40 E1
Millmeece ST21 40 A2
Millness IV63 87 K1
Millom LA18 54 E1
Millow SG18 33 F4
Millpool PL30 4 B3
Millport KA28 73 K5
Millthorpe S18 51 F5
Millthrop LA10 61 H7
Milltimber AB13 91 G4
Milltown Aber. AB36 89 K4
Milltown Cornw. PL22 4 B5
Milltown D.& G. DG14 69 J6
Milltown Derbys. S45 51 F6
Milltown Devon EX31 6 D2
Milltown High. IV12 97 G7
Milltown of Aberdalgie PH2 82 B5
Milltown of Auchindoun AB55 90 B1
Milltown of Craigston AB53 99 F5
Milltown of Edinvillie AB38 97 K7
Milltown of Kildrummy AB33 90 C3
Milltown of Rothiemay AB54 98 D6
Milltown of Towie AB33 90 C3
Milnathort KY13 82 C7
Milners Heath CH3 48 D6
Milngavie G62 74 D3
Milnrow OL16 49 J1
Milnsbridge HD3 50 D1
Milnthorpe LA7 55 H1
Milovaig IV55 93 G6
Milrig KA4 74 D7
Milson DY14 29 F1
Milstead ME9 14 E2
Milston SP4 20 E7
Milton Angus DD8 82 E3
Milton Cambs. CB4 33 H2
Milton Cumb. CA8 70 A7
Milton D.& G. DG2 68 D5
Milton D.& G. DG2 65 J3
Milton D.& G. DG8 64 C5
Milton Derbys. DE65 41 F3
Milton High. IV6 95 K6
Milton High. IV18 96 E4
Milton High. IV12 97 G6
Milton High. IV54 94 D7
Milton High. IV6 96 C7
Milton High. KW1 105 J3
Milton High. IV63 88 B1
Milton Moray AB56 98 D4
Milton N.Som. BS22 19 G5
Milton Newport NP19 19 G3
Milton Notts. NG22 51 K5
Milton Oxon. OX15 31 F5
Milton Oxon. OX14 21 H2
Milton P.& K. PH8 82 A4
Milton Pembs. SA70 16 D5
Milton Ports. PO4 11 H5
Milton Som. TA12 8 D2
Milton Stir. FK8 81 G7
Milton Stoke ST2 49 J7
Milton W.Dun. G82 74 C3
Milton Abbas DT11 9 H4
Milton Abbot PL19 4 E3
Milton Bridge EH26 76 A4
Milton Bryan MK17 32 C5
Milton Clevedon BA4 9 F1
Milton Combe PL20 4 E4
Milton Damerel EX22 6 B4
Milton End GL2 29 G7
Milton Ernest MK44 32 D3
Milton Green CH3 48 D7
Milton Hill OX13 21 H2
MILTON KEYNES MK 32 B5
Milton Keynes Village MK10 32 B5
Milton Lilbourne SN9 20 E5
Milton Malsor NN7 31 J3
Milton Morenish FK21 81 H4
Milton of Auchinhove AB31 90 D4
Milton of Balgonie KY7 82 E7
Milton of Buchanan G63 74 C1
Milton of Cairnborrow AB54 98 C6
Milton of Callander FK17 81 G7
Milton of Campfield AB31 90 E4
Milton of Campsie G66 74 E3
Milton of Coldwells AB41 91 H1
Milton of Cullerlie AB32 91 F4
Milton of Cushnie AB33 90 D3
Milton of Dalcapon PH9 82 A2
Milton of Inveramsay AB51 91 F2
Milton of Noth AB54 90 D2
Milton of Tullich AB35 90 B5
Milton on Stour SP8 9 G2
Milton Regis ME10 24 E5
Milton Street BN26 13 J6
Miltonduff IV30 97 J5
Miltonhill IV36 97 H5
Miltonise DG8 64 B3
Milton-Lockhart ML8 75 G6
Milton-under-Wychwood OX7 30 D7
Milverton Som. TA4 7 K3
Milverton Warks. CV32 30 E2
Milwich ST18 40 B2
Mimbridge GU24 22 C5
Minard PA32 73 H1
Minard Castle PA32 73 H1
Minchington DT11 9 J3
Minchinhampton GL6 20 B1
Mindrum TD12 77 G7
Mindrummill TD12 77 G7
Minehead TA24 7 H1
Minera LL11 48 B7
Minety SN16 20 D2
Minety Lower Moor SN16 20 D2
Minffordd Gwyn. LL40 37 G4
Minffordd Gwyn. LL48 36 E2
Minffordd Gwyn. LL57 46 D5
Miningsby PE22 53 G6
Minions PL14 4 C3
Minishant KA19 67 H2
Minley Manor GU17 22 B6
Minllyn SY20 37 H4
Minnes AB41 91 H2
Minngearraidh HS8 84 C2
Minnigaff DG8 64 E4
Minnonie AB45 99 F4
Minskip YO51 57 J3
Minstead SO43 10 D3
Minsted GU29 12 B4
Minster Kent ME12 25 F4
Minster Kent CT12 25 K5
Minster Lovell OX29 30 E7
Minsteracres NE44 62 B1
Minsterley SY5 38 C5
Minsterworth GL2 29 G7
Minterne Magna DT2 9 F4
Minterne Parva DT2 9 F4
Minting LN9 52 E5
Mintlaw AB42 99 J6
Minto TD9 70 A1
Minton SY6 38 D6
Minwear SA67 16 D4
Minworth B76 40 D6
Miodar PA77 78 B2

Mirbister KW17 106 C6
Mirehouse CA28 60 A5
Mireland KW1 105 J2
Mirfield WF14 57 H7
Miserden GL6 20 C1
Miskin *R.C.T.* CF72 18 D3
Miskin *R.C.T.* CF45 18 D2
Misselfore SP5 10 B2
Misson DN10 51 J3
Misterton *Leics.* LE17 41 H7
Misterton *Notts.* DN10 51 K3
Misterton *Som.* TA18 8 D4
Mistley CO11 35 F5
Mitcham CR4 23 F5
Mitchel Troy NP25 28 D7
Mitcheldean GL17 29 F7
Mitchell TR8 3 F3
Mitchelland LA8 60 F7
Mitcheltroy Common NP25 19 H1
Mitford NE61 71 G5
Mithian TR5 2 E3
Mitton ST19 40 A4
Mixbury NN13 31 H5
Mixenden HX2 57 F7
Moar PH15 81 G3
Moat CA6 69 K6
Moats Tye IP14 34 E3
Mobberley *Ches.* WA16 49 G5
Mobberley *Staffs.* ST10 40 C1
Moccas HR2 28 C4
Mochdre *Conwy* LL28 47 G5
Mochdre *Powys* SY16 37 K7
Mochrum DG8 64 D6
Mockbeggar *Hants.* BH24 10 C4
Mockbeggar *Kent* TN12 14 C3
Mockerkin CA13 60 B4
Modbury PL21 5 G5
Moddershall ST15 40 B2
Modsarie KW14 103 J2
Moelfre *I.o.A.* LL72 46 D4
Moelfre *Powys* SY10 38 A3
Moffat DG10 69 F3
Mogerhanger MK44 32 E4
Moin'a'choire PA44 72 B4
Moine House IV27 103 H3
Moira DE12 41 F4
Molash CT4 15 F2
Mol-chlach PH41 85 K3
Mold (Yr Wyddgrug) CH7 48 B6
Molehill Green *Essex* CM6 33 J6
Molehill Green *Essex* CM6 34 B6
Molescroft HU17 59 G5
Molesden NE61 71 G5
Molesworth PE28 32 D1
Mollance DG7 65 H4
Molland EX36 7 G3
Mollington *Ches.* CH1 48 C5
Mollington *Oxon.* OX17 31 F4
Mollinsburn G67 75 F3
Monach Islands (Heisker Islands) HS6 92 B5
Monachty SY23 26 E2
Monachyle FK19 81 F6
Monevechadan PA24 80 C7
Monewden IP13 35 G3
Moneydie PH1 82 B5
Moneyrow Green SL6 22 B4
Moniaive DG3 68 C4
Monifieth DD5 83 G4
Monikie DD5 83 G4
Monimail KY15 82 D6
Monington SA43 16 E1
Monk Bretton S71 51 F2
Monk Fryston LS25 58 B7
Monk Hesleden TS27 63 F3
Monk Sherborne RG26 21 K6
Monk Soham IP13 35 G2
Monk Soham Green IP13 35 G2
Monk Street CM6 33 K6
Monken Hadley EN5 23 F2
Monkerton EX1 7 H6
Monkhide HR8 29 F4
Monkhill CA5 60 E1
Monkhopton WV16 39 F6
Monkland HR6 28 D3
Monkleigh EX39 6 C3
Monknash CF71 18 C4
Monkokehampton EX19 6 D5
Monks Eleigh IP7 34 D4
Monks Eleigh Tye IP7 34 D4
Monk's Gate RH13 13 F4
Monks' Heath SK10 49 H5
Monk's Hill TN27 14 D3
Monks Kirby CV23 41 G7
Monks Risborough HP27 22 B1
Monkscross PL17 4 D3
Monkseaton NE25 71 J6
Monkshill AB53 99 F6
Monksilver TA4 7 J2
Monkstadt IV51 93 J5
Monkswood NP15 19 G1
Monkton *Devon* EX14 7 K5
Monkton *Kent* CT12 25 J5
Monkton *Pembs.* SA71 16 C5
Monkton *S.Ayr.* KA9 67 H1
Monkton *T. & W.* NE32 71 J7
Monkton *V. of Glam.* CF71 18 C4
Monkton Combe BA2 20 A5
Monkton Deverill BA12 9 H1
Monkton Farleigh BA15 20 B5
Monkton Heathfield TA2 8 B2
Monkton Up Wimborne BH21 10 B3
Monkton Wyld DT6 8 C5
Monkwearmouth SR6 62 E1
Monkwood SO24 11 H1
Monmouth (Trefynwy) NP25 28 E7
Monnington Court HR2 28 C5
Monnington on Wye HR4 28 C4
Monreith DG8 64 D6
Montacute TA15 8 E3
Monteach AB41 99 G6
Montford SY4 38 D4
Montford Bridge SY4 38 D4
Montgarrie AB33 90 D3
Montgomery (Trefaldwyn) SY15 38 B6
Montgreenan KA13 74 B6
Montrave KY8 82 E7
Montrose DD10 83 J2
Monxton SP11 21 G7
Monyash DE45 50 D6
Monymusk AB51 90 E3
Monzie PH7 81 K5
Moodiesburn G69 74 E3
Moons Moat North B98 30 B2
Moonzie KY15 82 E6
Moor Allerton LS17 57 J6
Moor Cock LA2 56 B3
Moor Crichel BH21 9 J4
Moor End *Beds.* MK43 32 D3
Moor End *Beds.* LU6 32 C6
Moor End *Cumb.* LA6 55 J2
Moor End *E.Riding* YO43 58 E6
Moor End *Lancs.* FY6 55 G5
Moor End *N.Yorks.* YO19 58 B6
Moor End *W.Yorks.* HX2 57 F7
Moor Green *W.Mid.* B13 40 C7
Moor Green *Wilts.* SN13 20 B5
Moor Head BD18 57 G6
Moor Monkton YO26 58 B4
Moor Row CA24 60 B5
Moor Side *Cumb.* LA16 55 F2
Moor Side *Lancs.* PR4 55 H6
Moor Side *Lancs.* PR4 55 H6
Moor Side *Lincs.* PE22 53 F7
Moor Street ME8 24 E5
Moorby PE22 53 F6
Moorcot HR5 28 C3
Moordown BH9 10 B5
Moore WA4 48 E4
Moorend CA5 60 E1
Moorends DN8 51 J1
Moorfield SK13 50 C3
Moorgreen *Hants.* SO30 11 F3
Moorgreen *Notts.* NG16 41 G1
Moorhall S18 51 F5
Moorhampton HR4 28 C4
Moorhouse *Cumb.* CA5 60 E1
Moorhouse *Notts.* NG23 51 K6
Moorland (Northmoor Green) TA7 8 C1
Moorlinch TA7 8 C1
Moorsholm TS12 63 H5
Moorside *Dorset* DT10 9 G3
Moorside *Gt.Man.* OL1 49 J2
Moorside *W.Yorks.* LS13 57 H6
Moorthorpe WF9 51 G1
Moortown *I.o.W.* PO30 11 F6
Moortown *Lincs.* LN7 52 D3
Moortown *Tel. & W.* TF6 39 F4
Morangie IV19 96 E3
Morar PH40 86 C5
Morborne PE7 42 E6
Morchard Bishop EX17 7 F5
Morcombelake DT6 8 D5
Morcott LE15 42 C5
Morda SY10 38 B3
Morden *Dorset* BH20 9 J5
Morden *Gt.Lon.* SM4 23 F5
Morden Park SM4 23 F5
Mordiford HR1 28 E5
Mordington Holdings TD15 77 H5
Mordon TS21 62 E4
More SY9 38 C6
Morebath EX16 7 H3
Morebattle TD5 70 C1
Morecambe LA4 55 H3
Morefield IV26 95 H2
Moreleigh TQ9 5 H5
Morenish FK21 81 H4
Moresby Parks CA28 60 A5
Morestead SO21 11 G2
Moreton *Dorset* DT2 9 H6
Moreton *Essex* CM5 23 J1
Moreton *Here.* HR6 28 E2
Moreton *Mersey.* CH46 48 B4
Moreton *Oxon.* OX9 21 K1
Moreton *Staffs.* DE6 40 D2
Moreton *Staffs.* TF10 39 G4
Moreton Corbet SY4 38 E3
Moreton Jeffries HR1 29 F4
Moreton Mill SY4 38 E3
Moreton Morrell CV35 30 E3
Moreton on Lugg HR4 28 E4
Moreton Paddox CV35 30 E3
Moreton Pinkney NN11 31 G4
Moreton Say TF9 39 F2
Moreton Valence GL2 20 A1
Moretonhampstead TQ13 7 F7
Moreton-in-Marsh GL56 30 D5
Morfa *Carmar.* SA14 17 J4
Morfa *Cere.* SA44 26 C3
Morfa Bychan LL49 36 E2
Morfa Glas SA11 18 B1
Morfa Nefyn LL53 36 B1
Morgan's Vale SP5 10 C2
Morganstown CF15 18 E3
Mork GL15 19 J1
Morland CA10 61 G4
Morley *Derbys.* DE7 41 F1
Morley *Dur.* DL14 62 C4
Morley *W.Yorks.* LS27 57 H7
Morley Green SK9 49 H4
Morley St. Botolph NR18 44 E6
Mornick PL17 4 D3
Morningside *Edin.* EH10 76 A3
Morningside *N.Lan.* ML2 75 G5
Morningthorpe NR15 45 G6
Morpeth NE61 71 H5
Morphie DD10 83 J1
Morrey DE13 40 D4
Morridge Side ST13 50 C7
Morrilow Heath ST10 40 B2
Morriston *S.Ayr.* KA19 67 G3
Morriston *Swan.* SA6 17 K6
Morristown CF64 18 E4
Morroch PH39 86 C6
Morston NR25 44 E1
Mortehoe EX34 6 C1
Morthen S66 51 G4
Mortimer RG7 21 K5
Mortimer West End RG7 21 K5
Mortimer's Cross HR6 28 D2
Mortlake SW14 23 F4
Morton *Derbys.* DE55 51 G6
Morton *Lincs.* PE10 42 D3
Morton *Lincs.* DN21 52 B3
Morton *Lincs.* LN6 52 B6
Morton *Notts.* NG25 51 K7
Morton *S.Glos.* BS35 19 K2
Morton *Shrop.* SY10 38 B3
Morton Bagot B80 30 C2
Morton on the Hill NR9 45 F4
Morton Tinmouth DL2 62 C4
Morton-on-Swale DL7 62 E7
Morvah TR20 2 B5
Morval PL13 4 C5
Morvich *High.* IV40 87 F2
Morvich *High.* IV28 96 E1
Morvil SA66 16 D2
Morville WV16 39 F6
Morwellham PL19 4 E4
Morwenstow EX23 6 A4
Morwick Hall NE65 71 H3
Mosborough S20 51 G4
Moscow KA4 74 C6
Mosedale CA11 60 E3
Moselden Height HD3 50 C1
Moseley *W.Mid.* B13 40 C7
Moseley *W.Mid.* WV1 40 B6
Moseley *Worcs.* WR2 29 H3
Moses Gate BL3 49 G2
Moss *Arg. & B.* PA77 78 A3
Moss *S.Yorks.* DN6 51 H1
Moss *Wrex.* LL11 48 C7
Moss Bank WA11 48 E3
Moss Houses SK11 49 H5
Moss Nook M22 49 H4
Moss of Barmuckity IV30 97 K5
Moss Side *Gt.Man.* M14 49 H3
Moss Side *Lancs.* FY8 55 G6
Moss Side *Mersey.* L31 48 C2
Mossat AB33 90 C3
Mossbank ZE2 107 N5
Mossblown KA6 67 J1
Mossburnford TD8 70 B2
Mossdale DG7 65 G3
Mossend ML4 75 F4
Mossgiel KA5 67 J1
Mosshead AB54 90 D1
Mosside of Ballinshoe DD8 83 F2
Mossley *Ches.* CW12 49 H6
Mossley *Gt.Man.* OL5 49 J2
Mossley Hill L18 48 C4
Mosspaul Hotel TD9 69 J4
Moss-side *High.* IV12 97 F6
Moss-side *Moray* AB54 98 D5
Mosstodloch IV32 98 B4
Mosston DD11 83 G3
Mossy Lea WN6 48 E1
Mosterton DT8 8 D4
Moston *Gt.Man.* M40 49 H2
Moston *Shrop.* SY4 38 E3
Moston Green CW11 49 G6
Mostyn CH8 47 K4
Motcombe SP7 9 H2
Mothecombe PL8 5 G6
Motherby CA11 60 F4
MOTHERWELL ML 75 F5
Mottingham SE9 23 H4
Mottisfont SO51 10 E2
Mottistone PO30 11 F6
Mottram in Longdendale SK14 49 J3
Mottram St. Andrew SK10 49 H5
Mouldsworth WA6 48 E5
Moulin PH16 82 A2
Moulsecoomb BN2 13 G6
Moulsford OX10 21 J3
Moulsham CM2 24 D1
Moulsoe MK16 32 C4
Moulton *Ches.* CW9 49 F6
Moulton *Lincs.* PE12 43 G3
Moulton *N.Yorks.* DL10 62 D6
Moulton *Northants.* NN3 31 J2
Moulton *Suff.* CB8 33 K2
Moulton *V. of Glam.* CF62 18 D4
Moulton Chapel PE12 43 F4
Moulton St. Mary NR13 45 J5
Moulton Seas End PE12 43 G3
Mounie Castle AB51 91 F2
Mount *Cornw.* TR8 2 E3
Mount *Cornw.* PL30 4 B4
Mount *High.* IV12 97 G7
Mount *Kent* CT4 15 G3
Mount *W.Yorks.* HD3 50 D1
Mount Ambrose TR16 2 E4
Mount Bures CO8 34 D5
Mount Charles PL25 4 A5
Mount Hawke TR4 2 E4
Mount Manisty CH65 48 C5
Mount Oliphant KA6 67 H2
Mount Pleasant *Ches.* ST7 49 H7
Mount Pleasant *Derbys.* DE56 41 F1
Mount Pleasant *Derbys.* DE11 40 E4
Mount Pleasant *E.Suss.* BN8 13 H5
Mount Pleasant *Flints.* CH6 48 B5
Mount Pleasant *Gt.Lon.* UB9 22 D2
Mount Pleasant *Hants.* SO41 10 E5
Mount Pleasant *Norf.* NR17 44 D6
Mount Pleasant *Suff.* CO10 34 B4
Mount Sorrel SP5 10 B2
Mount Tabor HX2 57 F7
Mountain HX2 57 F6
Mountain Ash (Aberpennar) CF45 18 D2
Mountain Cross EH46 75 K6
Mountain Water SA62 16 C3
Mountbenger TD7 69 J1
Mountblairy AB53 98 E5
Mountblow G60 74 C3
Mountfield TN32 14 C5
Mountgerald IV15 96 C5
Mountjoy TR8 3 F2
Mountnessing CM15 24 C2
Mounton NP16 19 J2
Mountsorrel LE12 41 H4
Mousa ZE2 107 N10
Mousehole TR19 2 B6
Mouswald DG1 69 F6
Mow Cop ST7 49 H7
Mowden DL3 62 D5
Mowhaugh TD5 70 D1
Mowsley LE17 41 J7
Mowtie AB39 91 G6
Moxley WS10 40 B6
Moy *High.* PH33 87 H6
Moy *High.* PH31 88 B6
Moy *High.* IV13 88 E1
Moy House IV36 97 H6
Moylgrove SA43 16 E1
Muasdale PA29 72 E6
Much Birch HR2 28 E5
Much Cowarne HR7 29 F4
Much Dewchurch HR2 28 D5
Much Hadham SG10 33 H7
Much Hoole PR4 55 H7
Much Hoole Town PR4 55 H7
Much Marcle HR8 29 F5
Much Wenlock TF13 39 F5
Muchalls AB39 91 H5
Muchelney TA10 8 D2
Muchelney Ham TA10 8 D2
Muchlarnick PL13 4 C5
Muchra TD7 69 H2
Muchrachd IV4 87 J1
Muck PH41 85 K7
Mucking SS17 24 C3
Muckle Roe ZE2 107 M6
Muckleford DT2 9 F5
Mucklestone TF9 39 G2
Muckleton TF6 38 E3
Muckletown AB33 90 D2
Muckley WV16 39 F6
Muckley Corner WS14 40 C5
Muckton LN11 53 G4
Mudale IV27 103 H5
Muddiford EX31 6 D2
Muddles Green BN8 13 J5
Muddleswood BN6 13 F5
Mudeford BH23 10 C5
Mudford BA21 8 E3
Mudgley BS28 19 H7
Mugdock G62 74 D3
Mugeary IV51 85 K1
Mugginton DE6 40 E1
Muggintonlane End DE6 40 E1
Muggleswick DH8 62 B2
Mugswell KT20 23 F6
Muie IV28 96 D1
Muir AB35 89 H6
Muir of Fowlis AB33 90 D3
Muir of Lochs IV32 98 B4
Muir of Ord IV6 96 C6
Muirden AB53 99 F5
Muirdrum DD7 83 G4
Muiredge KY8 76 B1
Muirhead *Aber.* AB33 90 D3
Muirhead *Angus* DD2 82 E4
Muirhead *Fife* KY15 82 D7
Muirhead *Moray* IV36 97 H5
Muirhead *N.Lan.* G69 74 E4
Muirhouses EH51 75 J2
Muirkirk KA18 68 B1
Muirmill FK6 75 F2
Muirtack *Aber.* AB41 91 H1
Muirtack *Aber.* AB53 99 G6
Muirton *High.* IV11 96 E5
Muirton *P. & K.* PH3 82 A6
Muirton *P. & K.* PH1 82 C5
Muirton of Ardblair PH10 82 C3
Muirton of Ballochy DD10 83 H1
Muirtown IV36 97 G6
Muiryfold AB53 99 F5
Muker DL11 62 A7
Mulbarton NR14 45 F5
Mulben AB55 98 B5
Mulhagery HS2 101 F7
Mull PA 79 G4
Mullach Charlabhaigh HS2 100 E3
Mullacott Cross EX34 6 D1
Mullion TR12 2 D7
Mullion Cove TR12 2 D7
Mumby LN13 53 J5
Munderfield Row HR7 29 F3
Munderfield Stocks HR7 29 F3
Mundesley NR11 45 H2
Mundford IP26 44 C6
Mundham NR14 45 H6
Mundon CM9 24 E1
Mundurno AB23 91 H3
Munerigie PH35 87 J4
Mungasdale IV22 95 F2
Mungoswells EH39 76 C3
Mungrisdale CA11 60 E3
Munlochy IV8 96 D6
Munnoch KA22 74 A6
Munsley HR8 29 F4
Munslow SY7 38 E7
Murchington TQ13 6 E7
Murcott *Oxon.* OX5 31 G7
Murcott *Wilts.* SN16 20 C2
Murdostoun ML2 75 G5
Murieston EH54 75 J4
Murkle KW14 105 G2
Murlaganmore FK21 81 G4
Murlaggan *High.* PH34 87 G5
Murlaggan *High.* PH31 87 K6
Murra KW16 106 B7
Murrell Green RG27 22 A6
Murroes DD5 83 F4
Murrow PE13 43 G5
Mursley MK17 32 B6
Murston ME10 25 F5
Murthill DD8 83 F2
Murthly PH1 82 B4
Murton *Cumb.* CA16 61 J4
Murton *Dur.* SR7 62 E2
Murton *Northumb.* TD15 77 H6
Murton *Swan.* SA3 17 J7
Murton *York* YO19 58 C4
Musbury EX13 8 B5
Muscliff BH9 10 B5
Musdale PA34 80 A5
Musselburgh EH21 76 B3
Mustard Hyrn NR29 45 J4
Muston *Leics.* NG13 42 B2
Muston *N.Yorks.* YO14 59 G2
Mustow Green DY10 29 H1
Mutford NR34 45 J7
Muthill PH5 81 K6
Mutley PL3 4 E5
Mutterton EX15 7 J5
Muxton TF2 39 G4
Mybster KW1 105 G3
Myddfai SA20 27 G5
Myddle SY4 38 D3
Myddlewood SY4 38 D3
Mydroilyn SA48 26 D3
Myerscough College PR3 55 H6
Myerscough Smithy PR5 56 B6
Mylor TR11 3 F5
Mylor Bridge TR11 3 F5
Mynachdy CF14 18 E4
Mynachlog-ddu SA66 16 E2
Myndtown SY7 38 C7
Mynydd Llandygai LL57 46 E6
Mynydd-bach *Mon.* NP16 19 H2
Mynydd-bach *Swan.* SA5 17 K6
Mynyddmechell LL68 46 B3
Mynyddygarreg SA17 17 H5
Mynytho LL53 36 C2
Myrebird AB31 91 F5
Mytchett GU16 22 B6
Mytholm HX7 56 E7
Mytholmroyd HX7 57 F7
Mythop FY4 55 G6
Myton-on-Swale YO61 57 K3
Mytton SY4 38 D4

N

Naast IV22 94 E3
Nab's Head PR5 56 B7
Na-Buirgh HS3 93 F2
Naburn YO19 58 B5
Nackington CT4 15 G2
Nacton IP10 35 G4
Nadderwater EX4 7 G6
Nafferton YO25 59 G4
Nailbridge GL17 29 F7
Nailsbourne TA2 8 B2
Nailsea BS48 19 H4
Nailstone CV13 41 G5
Nailsworth GL6 20 B2
Nairn IV12 97 F6
Nancegollan TR13 2 D5
Nancekuke TR16 2 D4
Nancledra TR20 2 B5
Nanhoron LL53 36 B2
Nannau LL40 37 G3
Nannerch CH7 47 K6
Nanpantan LE11 41 H4
Nanpean PL26 3 G3
Nanstallon PL30 4 A4
Nant Peris LL55 46 E7
Nant-ddu CF48 27 K7
Nanternis SA45 26 C3
Nantgaredig SA32 17 H3
Nantgarw CF15 18 E3
Nant-glas LD1 27 J2
Nantglyn LL16 47 J6
Nantgwyn LD6 27 J1
Nantlle LL54 46 D7
Nantmawr SY10 38 B3
Nantmel LD1 27 K2
Nantmor LL55 37 F1
Nantwich CW5 49 F7
Nantycaws SA32 17 H4
Nant-y-derry NP7 19 G1
Nant-y-dugoed SY21 37 J4
Nantyffyllon CF34 18 B2
Nantyglo NP23 28 A7
Nant-y-Gollen SY10 38 B3
Nant-y-groes LD1 27 K2
Nant-y-moel CF32 18 C2
Nant-y-Pandy LL33 46 E5
Naphill HP14 22 B2

Napley Heath TF9 39 G2
Nappa BD23 56 D4
Napton on the Hill CV47 31 F2
Narberth (Arberth) SA67 16 E4
Narborough Leics. LE19 41 H6
Narborough Norf. PE32 44 B4
Narkurs PL11 4 D5
Narrachan PA35 80 A6
Nasareth LL54 36 D1
Naseby NN6 31 H1
Nash Bucks. MK17 31 J5
Nash Here. LD8 28 C2
Nash Newport NP18 19 G3
Nash Shrop. SY8 29 F1
Nash V. of Glam. CF71 18 C4
Nash Street DA13 24 C5
Nassington PE8 42 D6
Nasty SG11 33 G6
Nateby Cumb. CA17 61 J6
Nateby Lancs. PR3 55 H5
Nately Scures RG27 22 A6
Natland LA9 55 J1
Naughton IP7 34 E4
Naunton Glos. GL54 30 C6
Naunton Worcs. WR8 29 H5
Naunton Beauchamp WR10 29 J3
Navenby LN5 52 C7
Navestock RM4 23 J2
Navestock Side CM14 23 J2
Navidale KW8 105 F7
Navity IV11 96 E5
Nawton YO62 58 C1
Nayland CO6 34 D5
Nazeing EN9 23 H1
Neacroft BH23 10 C5
Neal's Green CV7 41 F7
Neap ZE2 107 P7
Neap House DN15 52 B1
Near Sawrey LA22 60 E7
Nearton End MK17 32 B6
Neasden NW10 23 F3
Neasham DL2 62 E5
Neat Enstone OX7 30 E6
Neath (Castell-nedd) SA11 18 A2
Neatham GU34 22 A7
Neatishead NR12 45 H3
Nebo Cere. SY23 26 E2
Nebo Conwy LL26 47 G7
Nebo Gwyn. LL54 46 C7
Nebo I.o.A. LL68 46 C3
Necton PE37 44 C5
Nedd IV27 102 D5
Nedderton NE22 71 H5
Nedging IP7 34 D4
Nedging Tye IP7 34 E4
Needham IP20 45 G7
Needham Market IP6 34 E3
Needham Street CB8 34 B2
Needingworth PE27 33 G1
Needwood DE13 40 D3
Neen Savage DY14 29 F1
Neen Sollars DY14 29 F1
Neenton WV16 39 F7
Nefyn LL53 36 C1
Neighbourne BA3 19 K7
Neilston G78 74 C5
Neithrop OX16 31 F4
Nelson Caerp. CF46 18 E2
Nelson Lancs. BB9 56 D6
Nelson Village NE23 71 H6
Nemphlar ML11 75 G6
Nempnett Thrubwell BS40 19 J5
Nenthall CA9 61 J2
Nenthead CA9 61 J2
Nenthorn TD5 76 E7
Neopardy EX17 7 F6
Nerabus PA48 72 A5
Nercwys CH7 48 B6
Neriby PA44 72 B4
Nerston G74 74 E5
Nesbit NE71 77 H7
Nesfield LS29 57 F5
Ness CH64 48 C5
Ness of Tenston KW16 106 B6
Nesscliffe SY4 38 C4
Neston Ches. CH64 48 B5
Neston Wilts. SN13 20 B5
Nether Alderley SK10 49 H5
Nether Auchendrane KA7 67 H2
Nether Barr DG8 64 E4
Nether Blainslie TD1 76 D6
Nether Broughton LE14 41 J3
Nether Burrow LA6 56 B2
Nether Cerne DT2 9 F5
Nether Compton DT9 8 E3
Nether Crimond AB51 91 G2
Nether Dalgliesh TD7 69 H3
Nether Dallachy IV32 98 B4
Nether Edge S7 51 F4
Nether End DE45 50 E5
Nether Exe EX5 7 H6
Nether Glasslaw AB43 99 G5
Nether Handwick DD8 82 E3
Nether Haugh S62 51 G3
Nether Heage DE56 51 F7
Nether Heselden BD23 56 D2
Nether Heyford NN7 31 H3
Nether Kellet LA6 55 J3
Nether Kinmundy AB42 99 J6
Nether Langwith NG20 51 H5
Nether Lenshie AB51 98 E6
Nether Loads S42 51 F6
Nether Moor S42 51 F6
Nether Padley S32 50 E5
Nether Pitforthie AB30 91 G7
Nether Poppleton YO26 58 B4
Nether Silton YO7 63 F7
Nether Skyborry LD7 28 B1
Nether Stowey TA5 7 K2
Nether Urquhart KY14 82 C7
Nether Wallop SO20 10 E1
Nether Wasdale CA20 60 C6
Nether Wellwood KA18 68 B1
Nether Welton CA5 60 E2
Nether Westcote OX7 30 D6
Nether Whitacre B46 40 E6
Nether Winchendon (Lower Winchendon) HP18 31 J7
Nether Worton OX7 31 F6
Netheravon SP4 20 E7
Netherbrae AB53 99 F5
Netherbrough KW17 106 C6
Netherburn ML9 75 G6
Netherbury DT6 8 D5
Netherby Cumb. CA6 69 J6
Netherby N.Yorks. HG3 57 J5
Nethercott OX5 31 F6
Netherfield E.Suss. TN33 14 C6
Netherfield Notts. NG4 41 J1
Netherfield S.Lan. ML10 75 F6
Netherhall KA30 74 A4
Netherhampton SP2 10 C2
Netherhay DT8 8 D4
Netherland Green ST14 40 D2
Netherley AB39 91 G5
Nethermill DG1 69 F5
Nethermuir AB42 99 H6
Netherseal DE12 40 E4
Nethershield KA5 67 K1
Netherstreet SN15 20 C5
Netherthird D. & G. DG7 65 H5
Netherthird E.Ayr. KA18 67 K2
Netherthong HD9 50 D2
Netherthorpe S80 51 H4
Netherton Angus DD9 83 G2
Netherton Ches. WA6 48 E5
Netherton Devon TQ12 5 J3
Netherton Hants. SP11 21 G6
Netherton Mersey. L30 48 C2
Netherton N.Lan. ML2 75 F5
Netherton Northumb. NE65 70 E3
Netherton Oxon. OX13 21 H1
Netherton P. & K. PH10 82 C2
Netherton S.Lan. ML11 75 H5
Netherton W.Mid. DY2 40 B7
Netherton W.Yorks. WF4 50 E1
Netherton W.Yorks. HD4 50 D1
Netherton Worcs. WR10 29 J4
Netherton Burnfoot NE65 70 E3
Netherton Northside NE65 70 E3
Nethertown Cumb. CA22 60 A6
Nethertown Ork. KW1 105 J1
Nethertown Staffs. WS15 40 D4
Netherwitton NE61 71 G4
Netherwood D. & G. DG1 65 K3
Netherwood E.Ayr. KA18 68 B1
Nethy Bridge PH25 89 H2
Netley Abbey SO31 11 F4
Netley Marsh SO40 10 E3
Nettlebed RG9 21 K3
Nettlebridge BA3 19 K7
Nettlecombe Dorset DT6 8 E5
Nettlecombe I.o.W. PO38 11 G7
Nettlecombe Som. TA4 7 J2
Nettleden HP1 32 D7
Nettleham LN2 52 D5
Nettlestead Kent ME18 23 K6
Nettlestead Suff. IP8 34 E4
Nettlestead Green ME18 23 K6
Nettlestone PO34 11 H5
Nettlesworth DH2 62 D2
Nettleton Lincs. LN7 52 E2
Nettleton Wilts. SN14 20 B4
Nettleton Hill HD7 50 C1
Netton Devon PL8 5 F6
Netton Wilts. SP4 10 C1
Neuadd Cere. SA47 26 D3
Neuadd I.o.A. LL67 46 B3
Neuadd Powys LD2 27 J4
Nevendon SS12 24 D2
Nevern SA42 16 D2
Nevill Holt LE16 42 B6
New Abbey DG2 65 K4
New Aberdour AB43 99 G4
New Addington CR0 23 G5
New Alresford SO24 11 G1
New Alyth PH11 82 D3
New Arley CV7 40 E6
New Arram HU17 59 G5
New Ash Green DA3 24 C5
New Balderton NG24 52 B7
New Barn DA3 24 C5
New Belses TD8 70 A1
New Bewick NE66 71 F1
New Bolingbroke PE22 53 G7
New Boultham LN6 52 C5
New Bradwell MK13 32 B4
New Brancepeth DH7 62 D2
New Bridge D. & G. DG2 65 K3
New Bridge Devon TQ13 5 H3
New Brighton Flints. CH7 48 B6
New Brighton Hants. PO10 11 J4
New Brighton Mersey. CH45 48 C3
New Brighton W.Yorks. LS27 57 H7
New Brighton Wrex. LL11 48 B7
New Brinsley NG16 51 G7
New Broughton LL11 48 C7
New Buckenham NR16 44 E6
New Byth AB53 99 G5
New Cheriton SO24 11 G2
New Cross Cere. SY23 27 F1
New Cross Gt.Lon. SE14 23 G4
New Cumnock KA18 68 B2
New Deer AB53 99 G6
New Duston NN5 31 J2
New Earswick YO31 58 C4
New Edlington DN12 51 H3
New Elgin IV30 97 K5
New Ellerby HU11 59 H6
New Eltham SE9 23 H4
New End B96 30 B2
New England PE1 42 E5
New Farnley LS12 57 H6
New Ferry CH62 48 C4
New Galloway DG7 65 G3
New Gilston KY8 83 F7
New Greens AL3 22 E1
New Grimsby TR24 2 B1
New Hartley NE25 71 J6
New Haw KT15 22 D5
New Heaton TD12 77 G7
New Hedges SA70 16 E5
New Herrington DH4 62 E1
New Hinksey OX1 21 J1
New Holland DN19 59 G7
New Houghton Derbys. NG19 51 H6
New Houghton Norf. PE31 44 B3
New Houses BD24 56 D2
New Hunwick DL15 62 C3
New Hutton LA8 61 G7
New Hythe ME20 14 C2
New Inn Carmar. SA39 17 H2
New Inn Fife KY7 82 D7
New Inn Mon. NP16 19 H1
New Inn Torfaen NP4 19 F2
New Invention Shrop. SY7 28 B1
New Invention W.Mid. WV12 40 B5
New Kelso IV54 95 F7
New Lanark ML11 75 G6
New Lane L40 48 D1
New Lane End WA3 49 F3
New Leake PE22 53 H7
New Leeds AB42 99 H5
New Leslie AB52 90 D2
New Lodge S75 51 F2
New Longton PR4 55 J7
New Luce DG8 64 B4
New Mains ML11 75 G7
New Mains of Ury AB39 91 G6
New Malden KT3 23 F5
New Marske TS11 63 H4
New Marton SY11 38 C2
New Mill Cornw. TR20 2 B5
New Mill Herts. HP23 32 C7
New Mill W.Yorks. HD9 50 D2
New Mill End LU1 32 E7
New Mills Cornw. TR2 3 F3
New Mills Derbys. SK22 50 C4
New Mills Glos. GL15 19 K1
New Mills Mon. NP25 19 J1
New Mills (Y Felin Newydd) Powys SY16 37 K5
New Milton BH25 10 D5
New Mistley CO11 35 F5
New Moat SA63 16 D3
New Ollerton NG22 51 J6
New Orleans PA28 66 B2
New Oscott B44 40 C6
New Park Cornw. PL15 4 B2
New Park N.Yorks. HG1 57 H4
New Pitsligo AB43 99 G5
New Polzeath PL27 3 G1
New Quay (Ceinewydd) SA45 26 C2
New Rackheath NR13 45 G4
New Radnor (Maesyfed) LD8 28 B2
New Rent CA11 61 F3
New Ridley NE43 71 F7
New Road Side BD22 56 E5
New Romney TN28 15 F5
New Rossington DN11 51 J3
New Row Cere. SY25 27 G1
New Row Lancs. PR3 56 B6
New Sawley NG10 41 G2
New Shoreston NE69 77 K7
New Silksworth SR3 62 E1
New Stevenston ML1 75 F5
New Swannington LE67 41 G4
New Totley S17 51 F5
New Town Beds. SG18 32 E4
New Town Cere. SA43 16 E1
New Town Dorset SP5 9 J3
New Town Dorset BH21 9 J4
New Town E.Loth. EH34 76 C3
New Town E.Suss. TN22 13 H4
New Town Glos. GL54 30 B5
New Tredegar NP24 18 E1
New Tupton S42 51 F6
New Ulva PA31 73 F2
New Valley HS2 101 G4
New Village DN5 51 H2
New Walsoken PE13 43 H5
New Waltham DN36 53 F2
New Winton EH33 76 C3
New World PE15 43 G6
New Yatt OX29 30 E7
New York Lincs. LN4 53 F7
New York T. & W. NE27 71 J6
Newall LS21 57 H5
Newark Ork. KW17 106 G3
Newark Peter. PE1 43 F5
Newark-on-Trent NG24 52 B7
Newarthill ML1 75 F5
Newball LN3 52 D5
Newbarn CT18 15 G4
Newbarns LA14 55 F2
Newbattle EH22 76 B4
Newbiggin Cumb. CA11 61 F4
Newbiggin Cumb. CA10 61 H4
Newbiggin Cumb. CA8 61 G2
Newbiggin Cumb. LA12 55 F3
Newbiggin Cumb. LA19 60 B7
Newbiggin Dur. DL12 62 A4
Newbiggin N.Yorks. DL8 57 F1
Newbiggin N.Yorks. DL8 62 A7
Newbiggin Northumb. NE46 70 E7
Newbiggin-by-the-Sea NE64 71 J5
Newbigging Aber. AB39 91 G5
Newbigging Aber. AB35 89 J6
Newbigging Angus DD4 83 F4
Newbigging Angus DD5 83 F4
Newbigging Angus PH12 82 D3
Newbigging S.Lan. ML11 75 J6
Newbiggin-on-Lune CA17 61 J6
Newbold Derbys. S41 51 F5
Newbold Leics. LE67 41 G4
Newbold on Avon CV21 31 F1
Newbold on Stour CV37 30 D4
Newbold Pacey CV35 30 D3
Newbold Verdon LE9 41 G5
Newborough (Niwbwrch) I.o.A. LL61 46 C6
Newborough Peter. PE6 43 F5
Newborough Staffs. DE13 40 D3
Newbottle Northants. OX17 31 G5
Newbottle T. & W. DH4 62 E1
Newbourne IP12 35 G4
Newbridge (Cefn Bychan) Caerp. NP11 19 F2
Newbridge Cornw. TR20 2 B5
Newbridge Cornw. PL17 4 D4
Newbridge E.Suss. TN7 13 H3
Newbridge Edin. EH28 75 K3
Newbridge Hants. SO40 10 D3
Newbridge I.o.W. PO41 11 F6
Newbridge N.Yorks. YO18 58 E1
Newbridge Oxon. OX29 21 H1
Newbridge Pembs. SA62 16 C2
Newbridge Wrex. LL14 38 B1
Newbridge Green WR8 29 H5
Newbridge on Wye LD1 27 K3
Newbridge-on-Usk NP15 19 G2
Newbrough NE47 70 D7
Newbuildings EX17 7 F5
Newburgh Aber. AB43 99 H5
Newburgh Aber. AB41 91 H2
Newburgh Fife KY14 82 D6
Newburgh Lancs. WN8 48 D1
Newburgh Sc.Bord. TD7 69 J1
Newburn NE15 71 G7
Newbury Som. BA11 19 K6
Newbury W.Berks. RG14 21 H5
Newbury Wilts. BA12 20 B7
Newbury Park IG2 23 H3
Newby Cumb. CA10 61 G4
Newby Lancs. BB7 56 D5
Newby N.Yorks. TS8 63 G5
Newby N.Yorks. LA2 56 C3
Newby N.Yorks. YO12 59 G1
Newby Bridge LA12 55 G1
Newby Cote LA2 56 C2
Newby Cross CA5 60 E1
Newby East CA4 61 F1
Newby West CA2 60 E1
Newby Wiske DL7 57 J1
Newcastle Bridgend CF31 18 B4
Newcastle Mon. NP25 28 D7
Newcastle Shrop. SY7 38 B7
Newcastle Emlyn (Castell Newydd Emlyn) SA38 17 G1
Newcastle International Airport NE13 71 G6
NEWCASTLE UPON TYNE NE 71 H7
Newcastleton TD9 69 K5
Newcastle-under-Lyme ST5 40 A1
Newchapel Pembs. SA37 17 F2
Newchapel Stoke ST7 49 H7
Newchapel Surr. RH7 23 G7
Newchurch Carmar. SA33 17 G3
Newchurch I.o.W. PO36 11 G6
Newchurch Kent TN29 15 F4
Newchurch Lancs. BB4 56 D7
Newchurch Lancs. BB12 56 D6
Newchurch Mon. NP16 19 H2
Newchurch Powys HR5 28 B3
Newchurch Staffs. DE13 40 D3
Newcott EX14 8 B4
Newcraighall EH21 76 B3
Newdigate RH5 22 E7
Newell Green RG42 22 B4
Newenden TN18 14 D5
Newent GL18 29 G6
Newerne GL15 19 K1
Newfield Dur. DL14 62 D3
Newfield Dur. DH2 62 D1
Newfield High. IV19 96 E4
Newfound RG23 21 J6
Newgale SA62 16 B3
Newgate NR25 44 E1
Newgate Street SG13 23 G1
Newgord ZE2 107 P2
Newhall Ches. CW5 39 F1
Newhall Derbys. DE11 40 E3
Newham NE67 71 G1
Newham Hall NE67 71 G1
Newhaven BN9 13 H6
Newhey OL16 49 J1
Newholm YO21 63 K5
Newhouse ML1 75 F4
Newick BN8 13 H4
Newingreen CT21 15 G4
Newington Edin. EH9 76 A3
Newington Kent CT18 15 G4
Newington Kent ME9 24 E5
Newington Notts. DN10 51 J3
Newington Oxon. OX10 21 K2
Newington Bagpath GL8 20 B2
Newland Cumb. LA12 55 G2
Newland Glos. GL16 19 J1
Newland Hull HU6 59 G6
Newland N.Yorks. YO8 58 C7
Newland Oxon. OX28 30 E7
Newland Worcs. WR13 29 G4
Newlandrig EH23 76 B4
Newlands Cumb. CA7 60 E3
Newlands Essex SS8 24 E3
Newlands Northumb. DH8 62 B1
Newlands Sc.Bord. TD9 70 A4
Newland's Corner GU4 22 D7
Newlands of Geise KW14 105 F2
Newlands of Tynet IV32 98 B4
Newlyn TR18 2 B6
Newmachar AB21 91 G3
Newmains ML2 75 G5
Newman's End CM22 33 J7
Newman's Green CO10 34 C4
Newmarket Suff. CB8 33 K2
Newmarket W.Isles HS2 101 G4
Newmill Aber. AB39 91 F6
Newmill Aber. AB41 99 G6
Newmill Aber. AB51 91 G2
Newmill Moray AB55 98 C5
Newmill Sc.Bord. TD9 69 K2
Newmill of Inshewan DD8 83 F1
Newmillerdam WF2 51 F1
Newmills IV7 96 D5
Newmiln P. & K. PH2 82 C4
Newmiln P. & K. PH1 82 B5
Newmilns KA16 74 D7
Newney Green CM1 24 C1
Newnham Glos. GL14 29 F7
Newnham Hants. RG27 22 A6
Newnham Herts. SG7 33 F5
Newnham Kent ME9 14 E2
Newnham Northants. NN11 31 G3
Newnham Bridge WR15 29 F2
Newnham Paddox CV23 41 G7
Newnoth AB54 90 D1
Newport Cornw. PL15 6 B7
Newport Devon EX32 6 D2
Newport E.Riding HU15 58 E6
Newport Essex CB11 33 J5
Newport Glos. GL13 19 K2
Newport High. KW7 105 G6
Newport I.o.W. PO30 11 G6
NEWPORT (CASNEWYDD) Newport NP 19 G3
Newport Norf. NR29 45 K4
Newport (Trefdraeth) Pembs. SA42 16 D2
Newport Som. TA3 8 C2
Newport Tel. & W. TF10 39 G4
Newport Pagnell MK16 32 B4
Newport-on-Tay DD6 83 F5
Newpound Common RH14 12 D4
Newquay TR7 3 F2
Newquay Cornwall International Airport TR8 3 F2
Newsbank CW12 49 H6
Newseat AB51 91 F1
Newsells SG8 33 G5
Newsham Lancs. PR3 55 J6
Newsham N.Yorks. DL11 62 C5
Newsham N.Yorks. YO7 57 J1
Newsham Northumb. NE24 71 H6
Newsholme E.Riding DN14 58 D7
Newsholme Lancs. BB7 56 D4
Newsome HD4 50 D1
Newstead Northumb. NE67 71 G1
Newstead Notts. NG15 51 H7
Newstead Sc.Bord. TD6 76 D7
Newthorpe N.Yorks. LS25 57 K6
Newthorpe Notts. NG16 41 G1
Newtoft LN8 52 D4
Newton Aber. AB54 98 C6
Newton Aber. AB42 99 J6
Newton Arg. & B. PA27 73 J1
Newton Bridgend CF36 18 B4
Newton Cambs. PE13 43 H4
Newton Cambs. CB2 33 H4
Newton Cardiff CF3 19 F4
Newton Ches. CH3 48 E7
Newton Ches. WA6 48 E5
Newton Cumb. LA13 55 F2
Newton D. & G. DG10 69 G4
Newton Derbys. DE55 51 G7
Newton Gt.Man. SK14 49 J3
Newton Here. SY7 28 C2
Newton Here. HR6 28 E3
Newton Here. HR2 28 C5
Newton High. KW1 105 J3
Newton High. IV2 96 E7
Newton High. KW1 105 H3
Newton High. IV27 102 E5
Newton High. IV6 96 C6
Newton High. IV11 96 E5
Newton Lancs. BB7 56 B4
Newton Lancs. LA6 55 J2
Newton Lancs. FY3 55 G6
Newton Lincs. NG34 42 D2
Newton Moray IV32 98 B4
Newton N.Ayr. KA27 73 H5
Newton Norf. PE32 44 C4
Newton Northants. NN14 42 B7
Newton Northumb. NE43 71 F7
Newton Northumb. NE65 70 E3
Newton Notts. NG13 41 J1
Newton P. & K. PH8 81 K4
Newton Pembs. SA62 16 B3
Newton Pembs. SA71 16 C5
Newton S.Glos. BS35 19 K2
Newton S.Lan. ML12 75 H7
Newton Sc.Bord. TD8 70 B1
Newton Shrop. SY12 38 D2

Newton *Som.* **TA4** 7 K2
Newton *Staffs.* **WS15** 40 C3
Newton *Suff.* **CO10** 34 D4
Newton *Swan.* **SA3** 17 K7
Newton *W.Loth.* **EH52** 75 J3
Newton *W.Yorks.* **WF10** 57 K7
Newton *Warks.* **CV23** 31 G1
Newton *Wilts.* **SP5** 10 D2
Newton Abbot TQ12 5 J3
Newton Arlosh **CA7** 60 D1
Newton Aycliffe DL5 62 D4
Newton Bewley **TS22** 63 F4
Newton Blossomville **MK43** 32 C3
Newton Bromswold **MK44** 32 C2
Newton Burgoland **LE67** 41 F5
Newton by Toft **LN8** 52 D4
Newton Ferrers **PL8** 5 F6
Newton Flotman **NR15** 45 G6
Newton Green **NP16** 19 J2
Newton Harcourt **LE8** 41 J6
Newton Kyme **LS24** 57 K5
Newton Longville **MK17** 32 B5
Newton Mearns **G77** 74 D5
Newton Morrell *N.Yorks.* **DL10** 62 D6
Newton Morrell *Oxon.* **OX27** 31 H6
Newton Mountain **SA73** 16 C5
Newton Mulgrave **TS13** 63 J5
Newton of Affleck **DD5** 83 F4
Newton of Ardtoe **PH36** 86 C7
Newton of Balcanquhal **PH2** 82 C6
Newton of Dalvey **IV36** 97 H6
Newton of Falkland **KY15** 82 D7
Newton of Leys **IV2** 88 D1
Newton on the Hill **SY4** 38 D3
Newton on Trent **LN1** 52 B5
Newton Poppleford **EX10** 7 J7
Newton Purcell **MK18** 31 H5
Newton Regis **B79** 40 E5
Newton Reigny **CA11** 61 F3
Newton St. Cyres **EX5** 7 G6
Newton St. Faith **NR10** 45 G4
Newton St. Loe **BA2** 20 A5
Newton St. Petrock **EX22** 6 C4
Newton Solney **DE15** 40 E3
Newton Stacey **SO20** 21 H7
Newton Stewart DG8 64 E4
Newton Tony **SP4** 21 F7
Newton Tracey **EX31** 6 D3
Newton under Roseberry **TS9** 63 G5
Newton Underwood **NE61** 71 G5
Newton upon Derwent **YO41** 58 D5
Newton Valence **GU34** 11 J1
Newton with Scales **PR4** 55 H6
Newtonairds **DG2** 68 D5
Newtongrange **EH22** 76 B4
Newtonhill **AB39** 91 H5
Newton-le-Willows *Mersey.* WA12 48 E3
Newton-le-Willows *N.Yorks.* **DL8** 57 H1
Newtonmill **DD9** 83 H1
Newtonmore PH20 88 E5
Newton-on-Ouse **YO30** 58 B4
Newton-on-Rawcliffe **YO18** 63 K7
Newton-on-the-Moor **NE65** 71 G3
Newtown *Bucks.* **HP5** 22 C1
Newtown *Ches.* **CH3** 48 E7
Newtown *Cornw.* **PL15** 4 C3
Newtown *Cornw.* **TR20** 2 C6
Newtown *Cumb.* **CA6** 70 A7
Newtown *Derbys.* **SK22** 49 J4
Newtown *Devon* **EX36** 7 F3
Newtown *Devon* **EX5** 7 J6
Newtown *Dorset* **DT8** 8 D4
Newtown *Glos.* **GL13** 19 K1
Newtown *Gt.Man.* **WN5** 48 E2
Newtown *Gt.Man.* **M27** 49 G2
Newtown *Hants.* **PO17** 11 H3
Newtown *Hants.* **RG20** 21 H5
Newtown *Hants.* **SO43** 10 D3
Newtown *Hants.* **SO51** 10 E2
Newtown *Hants.* **SO32** 11 G3
Newtown *Here.* **HR8** 29 F4
Newtown *Here.* **HR6** 28 D3
Newtown *High.* **PH35** 87 K4
Newtown *I.o.M.* **IM4** 54 C6
Newtown *I.o.W.* **PO30** 11 F5
Newtown *Northumb.* **NE65** 71 F3
Newtown *Northumb.* **NE66** 71 F1
Newtown *Oxon.* **RG9** 22 A3
Newtown (Y Drenewydd) *Powys* SY16 38 A6
Newtown *R.C.T.* **CF45** 18 D2
Newtown *Shrop.* **SY4** 38 D2
Newtown *Som.* **TA6** 8 B1
Newtown *Som.* **TA20** 8 B3
Newtown *Staffs.* **ST8** 49 J6
Newtown *Staffs.* **SK17** 50 C6
Newtown *Staffs.* **WS6** 40 B5
Newtown *Wilts.* **SP3** 9 J2
Newtown *Wilts.* **SN8** 21 G5
Newtown Linford **LE6** 41 H5
Newtown St. Boswells **TD6** 76 D7
Newtown Unthank **LE9** 41 G5
Newtown-in-Saint-Martin **TR12** 2 E6
Newtyle **PH12** 82 D3
Newyears Green **UB9** 22 D3
Neyland **SA73** 16 C5
Nibley *Glos.* **GL15** 19 K1
Nibley *S.Glos.* **BS37** 19 K3
Nibley Green **GL11** 20 A2
Nicholashayne **TA21** 7 K4
Nicholaston **SA3** 17 J7
Nidd **HG3** 57 J3
Nigg *Aberdeen* **AB12** 91 H4
Nigg *High.* **IV19** 97 F4
Nightcott **TA22** 7 G3
Nilig **LL15** 47 J7
Nilston Rigg **NE47** 70 D7
Nimlet **SN14** 20 A4
Nine Ashes **CM4** 23 J1
Nine Elms **SN5** 20 E3
Nine Mile Burn **EH26** 75 K5
Ninebanks **NE47** 61 J1
Ninemile Bar (Crocketford) **DG2** 65 J3
Nineveh **WR15** 29 F2
Ninfield **TN33** 14 C6
Ningwood **PO30** 11 F6
Nisbet **TD8** 70 B1
Niton **PO38** 11 G7
Nitshill **G53** 74 D4
Niwbwrch (Newborough) **LL61** 46 C6
Nizels **TN11** 23 J6
No Man's Heath *Ches.* **SY14** 38 E1
No Man's Heath *Warks.* **B79** 40 E5
No Man's Land **PL13** 4 C5
Noah's Ark **TN15** 23 J6
Noak Hill **RM4** 23 J2
Noblehill **DG1** 65 K3
Noblethorpe **S75** 50 E2
Nobottle **NN7** 31 H2
Nocton **LN4** 52 D6
Noddsdale **KA30** 74 A4
Nogdam End **NR14** 45 H5
Noke **OX3** 31 G7
Nolton **SA62** 16 B4
Nolton Haven **SA62** 16 B4
Nomansland *Devon* **EX16** 7 G4
Nomansland *Wilts.* **SP5** 10 D3
Noneley **SY4** 38 D3
Nonington **CT15** 15 H2
Nook *Cumb.* **CA6** 69 K6
Nook *Cumb.* **LA6** 55 J1
Noonsbrough **ZE2** 107 L7
Noranside **DD8** 83 F1
Norbreck **FY5** 55 G5
Norbury *Ches.* **SY13** 38 E1
Norbury *Derbys.* **DE6** 40 D1
Norbury *Gt.Lon.* **SW16** 23 G4
Norbury *Shrop.* **SY9** 38 C6
Norbury *Staffs.* **ST20** 39 G3
Norbury Common **SY13** 38 E1
Norbury Junction **ST20** 39 G3
Norchard **SA70** 16 D6
Norcott Brook **WA4** 49 F4
Nordelph **PE38** 43 J5
Norden *Dorset* **BH20** 9 J6
Norden *Gt.Man.* **OL11** 49 H1
Nordley **WV16** 39 F6
Norham **TD15** 77 H6
Norland Town **HX6** 57 F7
Norley **WA6** 48 E5
Norleywood **SO41** 10 E5
Norlington **BN8** 13 H5
Norman Cross **PE7** 42 E6
Normanby *N.Lincs.* **DN15** 52 B1
Normanby *N.Yorks.* **YO62** 58 D1
Normanby *R. & C.* **TS6** 63 G5
Normanby by Stow **DN21** 52 B4
Normanby le Wold **LN7** 52 E3
Normanby-by-Spital **LN8** 52 D4
Normandy **GU3** 22 C6
Normann's Ruh **PA74** 79 F3
Norman's Bay **BN24** 13 K6
Norman's Green **EX15** 7 J5
Normanston **NR32** 45 K6
Normanton *Derby* **DE23** 41 F2
Normanton *Leics.* **NG13** 42 B1
Normanton *Lincs.* **NG32** 42 C1
Normanton *Notts.* **NG25** 51 K7
Normanton *Rut.* **LE15** 42 C5
Normanton *W.Yorks.* WF6 57 J7
Normanton le Heath **LE67** 41 F4
Normanton on Soar **LE12** 41 H3
Normanton on Trent **NG23** 51 K6
Normanton-on-the-Wolds **NG12** 41 J2
Normoss **FY3** 55 G6
Norrington Common **SN12** 20 B5
Norris Green **PL17** 4 E4
Norris Hill **DE12** 41 F4
Norristhorpe **WF15** 57 H7
North Acton **W3** 23 F3
North Anston **S25** 51 H4
North Ascot **SL5** 22 C5
North Aston **OX25** 31 F6
North Baddesley **SO52** 10 E3
North Ballachulish **PH33** 80 B1
North Balloch **KA26** 67 H4
North Barrow **BA22** 9 F2
North Barsham **NR22** 44 D2
North Benfleet **SS12** 24 D3
North Bersted **PO21** 12 C6
North Berwick EH39 76 D2
North Boarhunt **PO17** 11 H3
North Bogbain **AB55** 98 B5
North Bovey **TQ13** 7 F7
North Bradley **BA14** 20 B6
North Brentor **PL19** 6 C7
North Brewham **BA10** 9 G1
North Bridge **GU8** 12 C3
North Buckland **EX33** 6 C1
North Burlingham **NR13** 45 H4
North Cadbury **BA22** 9 F2
North Cairn **DG9** 66 D6
North Camp **GU14** 22 B6
North Carlton *Lincs.* **LN1** 52 C5
North Carlton *Notts.* **S81** 51 H4
North Cave **HU15** 58 E6
North Cerney **GL7** 20 D1
North Chailey **BN8** 13 G4
North Charford **SP6** 10 C3
North Charlton **NE67** 71 G1
North Cheriton **BA8** 9 F2
North Chideock **DT6** 8 D5
North Cliffe **YO43** 58 E6
North Clifton **NG23** 52 B5
North Cockerington **LN11** 53 G3
North Coker **BA22** 8 E3
North Collafirth **ZE2** 107 M4
North Common *S.Glos.* **BS30** 19 K4
North Common *Suff.* **IP22** 34 D1
North Commonty **AB53** 99 G6
North Connel **PA37** 80 A4
North Coombe **EX17** 7 G5
North Cornelly **CF33** 18 B3
North Corner **BS36** 19 K3
North Cotes **DN36** 53 G2
North Cove **NR34** 45 J7
North Cowton **DL7** 62 D6
North Crawley **MK16** 32 C4
North Cray **DA14** 23 H4
North Creake **NR21** 44 C2
North Curry **TA3** 8 C2
North Dallens **PA38** 80 A3
North Dalton **YO25** 59 F4
North Dawn **KW17** 106 D7
North Deighton **LS22** 57 J4
North Dell (Dail Bho Thuath) **HS2** 101 G1
North Duffield **YO8** 58 C6
North Elkington **LN11** 53 F3
North Elmham **NR20** 44 D3
North Elmsall **WF9** 51 G1
North End *Bucks.* **LU7** 32 B6
North End *Dorset* **SP7** 9 H2
North End *E.Riding* **YO25** 59 H4
North End *E.Riding* **HU11** 59 H5
North End *E.Riding* **HU12** 59 J6
North End *Essex* **CM6** 33 K7
North End *Hants.* **SO24** 11 G2
North End *Hants.* **SP6** 10 C3
North End *Leics.* **LE12** 41 H4
North End *N.Som.* **BS49** 19 H5
North End *Norf.* **NR16** 44 E6
North End *Northumb.* **NE65** 71 G3
North End *Ports.* **PO2** 11 H4
North End *W.Suss.* **BN14** 12 E5
North End *W.Suss.* **BN18** 12 C6
North Erradale **IV21** 94 D3
North Essie **AB42** 99 J5
North Fambridge **CM3** 24 E2
North Ferriby HU14 59 F7
North Frodingham **YO25** 59 H4
North Gorley **SP6** 10 C3
North Green *Norf.* **IP21** 45 G7
North Green *Suff.* **IP19** 35 H1
North Green *Suff.* **IP17** 35 H2
North Green *Suff.* **IP17** 35 H2
North Grimston **YO17** 58 E3
North Halling **ME2** 24 D5
North Harby **NG23** 52 B5
North Hayling **PO11** 11 J4
North Hazelrigg **NE66** 77 J7
North Heasley **EX36** 7 F2
North Heath *W.Berks.* **RG20** 21 H4
North Heath *W.Suss.* **RH20** 12 D4
North Hill **PL15** 4 C3
North Hillingdon **UB10** 22 D3
North Hinksey **OX2** 21 H1
North Holmwood **RH5** 22 E7
North Houghton **SO20** 10 E1
North Huish **TQ10** 5 H5
North Hykeham **LN6** 52 C6
North Johnston **SA62** 16 C4
North Kelsey **LN7** 52 D2
North Kessock **IV1** 96 D7
North Killingholme **DN40** 52 E1
North Kilvington **YO7** 57 K1
North Kilworth **LE17** 41 J7
North Kingston **BH24** 10 C4
North Kyme **LN4** 52 E7
North Lancing **BN15** 12 E6
North Lee **HP22** 22 B1
North Lees **HG4** 57 J2
North Leigh **OX29** 30 E7
North Leverton with Habblesthorpe **DN22** 51 K4
North Littleton **WR11** 30 B4
North Lopham **IP22** 44 E7
North Luffenham **LE15** 42 C5
North Marden **PO18** 12 B5
North Marston **MK18** 31 J6
North Middleton *Midloth.* **EH23** 76 B5
North Middleton *Northumb.* **NE71** 71 F1
North Millbrex **AB53** 99 G6
North Molton **EX36** 7 F3
North Moreton **OX11** 21 J3
North Mundham **PO20** 12 B6
North Muskham **NG23** 51 K7
North Newbald **YO43** 59 F6
North Newington **OX15** 31 F5
North Newnton **SN9** 20 E6
North Newton **TA7** 8 B1
North Nibley **GL11** 20 A2
North Oakley **RG26** 21 J6
North Ockendon **RM14** 23 J3
North Ormesby **TS3** 63 G5
North Ormsby **LN11** 53 F3
North Otterington **DL7** 57 J1
North Owersby **LN8** 52 D3
North Perrott **TA18** 8 D4
North Petherton **TA6** 8 B1
North Petherwin **PL15** 4 C2
North Pickenham **PE37** 44 C5
North Piddle **WR7** 29 J3
North Plain **CA7** 69 G7
North Pool **TQ7** 5 H6
North Poorton **DT6** 8 E5
North Quarme **TA24** 7 H2
North Queensferry **KY11** 75 K2
North Radworthy **EX36** 7 F2
North Rauceby **NG34** 42 D1
North Reston **LN11** 53 G4
North Rigton **LS17** 57 H5
North Rode **CW12** 49 H6
North Roe **ZE2** 107 M4
North Ronaldsay **KW17** 106 G2
North Ronaldsay Airfield **KW17** 106 G2
North Runcton **PE33** 44 A4
North Sandwick **ZE2** 107 P3
North Scale **LA14** 54 E3
North Scarle **LN6** 52 B6
North Seaton **NE63** 71 H5
North Shian **PA38** 80 A3
North Shields NE30 71 J7
North Shoebury **SS3** 25 F3
North Side **PE6** 43 F6
North Skelton **TS12** 63 H5
North Somercotes **LN11** 53 H3
North Stainley **HG4** 57 H2
North Stainmore **CA17** 61 K5
North Stifford **RM16** 24 C3
North Stoke *B. & N.E.Som.* **BA1** 20 A5
North Stoke *Oxon.* **OX10** 21 K3
North Stoke *W.Suss.* **BN18** 12 D5
North Stoneham **SO50** 11 F3
North Street *Hants.* **SO24** 11 H1
North Street *Kent* **ME13** 15 F2
North Street *Med.* **ME3** 24 E4
North Street *W.Berks.* **RG7** 21 K4
North Sunderland **NE68** 77 K4
North Tamerton **EX22** 6 B6
North Tarbothill **AB23** 91 H3
North Tawton EX20 6 E5
North Third **FK7** 75 F2
North Thoresby **DN36** 53 F3
North Tidworth **SP9** 21 F7
North Togston **NE65** 71 H3
North Town *Devon* **EX20** 6 D5
North Town *Hants.* **GU12** 22 B6
North Town *W. & M.* **SL6** 22 B3
North Tuddenham **NR20** 44 E4
North Uist (Uibhist a Tuath) HS6 92 D4
North Walsham NR28 45 G2
North Waltham **RG25** 21 J7
North Warnborough **RG29** 22 A6
North Water Bridge **AB30** 83 H1
North Watten **KW1** 105 H3
North Weald Bassett **CM16** 23 H1
North Wembley **HA0** 22 E3
North Wheatley **DN22** 51 K4
North Whilborough **TQ12** 5 J4
North Wick **BS41** 19 J5
North Widcombe **BS40** 19 J6
North Willingham **LN8** 52 E4
North Wingfield **S42** 51 G6
North Witham **NG33** 42 C3
North Wootton *Dorset* **DT9** 9 F3
North Wootton *Norf.* **PE30** 44 A3
North Wootton *Som.* **BA4** 19 J7
North Wraxall **SN14** 20 B4
North Wroughton **SN4** 20 E3
North Yardhope **NE65** 70 E3
Northacre **NR17** 44 D6
Northall **LU6** 32 C6
Northall Green **NR20** 44 D4
Northallerton DL6 62 E7
Northam *Devon* **EX39** 6 C3
Northam *S'ham.* **SO14** 11 F3
NORTHAMPTON NN 31 J2
Northaw **EN6** 23 F1
Northay *Devon* **EX13** 8 C4
Northay *Som.* **TA20** 8 B3
Northbay **HS9** 84 C4
Northbeck **NG34** 42 D1
Northborough **PE6** 42 E5
Northbourne *Kent* **CT14** 15 J2
Northbourne *Oxon.* **OX11** 21 J3
Northbridge Street **TN32** 14 C5
Northbrook *Hants.* **SO21** 11 G1
Northbrook *Oxon.* **OX5** 31 F6
Northburnhill **AB53** 99 G6
Northchapel **GU28** 12 C4
Northchurch **HP4** 22 C1
Northcote Manor **EX37** 6 E4
Northcott **PL15** 6 B6
Northcourt **OX14** 21 J2
Northdyke **KW16** 106 B5
Northedge **S42** 51 F6
Northend *B. & N.E.Som.* **BA1** 20 A5
Northend *Bucks.* **RG9** 22 A2
Northend *Warks.* **CV47** 30 E3
Northfield *Aber.* **AB45** 99 G4
Northfield *Aberdeen* **AB16** 91 H4
Northfield *High.* **KW1** 105 J4
Northfield *Hull* **HU4** 59 G7
Northfield *Sc.Bord.* **TD14** 77 H4
Northfield *Som.* **TA6** 8 B1
Northfield *W.Mid.* **B31** 30 B1
Northfields **PE9** 42 D5
Northfleet **DA11** 24 C4
Northhouse **TD9** 69 K3
Northiam **TN31** 14 D5
Northill **SG18** 32 E4
Northington *Glos.* **GL14** 20 A1
Northington *Hants.* **SO24** 11 G1
Northlands **PE22** 53 G7
Northleach **GL54** 30 C7
Northleigh *Devon* **EX24** 7 K6
Northleigh *Devon* **EX32** 6 E2
Northlew **EX20** 6 D6
Northmoor **OX29** 21 H1
Northmoor Green (Moorland) **TA7** 8 C1
Northmuir **DD8** 82 E2
Northney **PO11** 11 J4
Northolt UB5 22 E3
Northop (Llaneurgain) **CH7** 48 B6
Northop Hall **CH7** 48 B6
Northorpe *Lincs.* **PE11** 43 F2
Northorpe *Lincs.* **DN21** 52 B3
Northorpe *Lincs.* **PE10** 42 D4
Northover *Som.* **BA22** 8 E2
Northover *Som.* **BA6** 8 D1
Northowram **HX3** 57 G7
Northport **BH20** 9 J6
Northpunds **ZE2** 107 N10
Northrepps **NR27** 45 G2
Northton (Taobh Tuath) **HS3** 92 E3
Northtown **KW17** 106 D8
Northway *Glos.* **GL20** 29 J5
Northway *Som.* **TA4** 7 K3
Northwich CW8 49 F5
Northwick *S.Glos.* **BS35** 19 J3
Northwick *Som.* **TA9** 19 G7
Northwick *Worcs.* **WR3** 29 H3
Northwold **IP26** 44 B6
Northwood *Gt.Lon.* HA6 22 D2
Northwood *I.o.W.* **PO31** 11 F5
Northwood *Kent* **CT12** 25 K5
Northwood *Mersey.* **L33** 48 D3
Northwood *Shrop.* **SY4** 38 D2
Northwood Green **GL14** 29 G7
Northwood Hills **HA6** 22 E2
Norton *Glos.* **GL2** 29 H6
Norton *Halton* **WA7** 48 E4
Norton *Herts.* **SG6** 33 F5
Norton *I.o.W.* **PO41** 10 E6
Norton *Mon.* **NP7** 28 D6
Norton *N.Som.* **BS22** 19 G5
Norton *N.Yorks.* **YO17** 58 D2
Norton *Northants.* **NN11** 31 H2
Norton *Notts.* **NG20** 51 H5
Norton *Powys* **LD8** 28 C2
Norton *S.Yorks.* **DN6** 51 H1
Norton *S.Yorks.* **S8** 51 F4
Norton *Shrop.* **SY4** 38 E5
Norton *Shrop.* **TF11** 39 G5
Norton *Shrop.* **SY7** 38 D7
Norton *Stock.* **TS20** 63 F4
Norton *Suff.* **IP31** 34 D2
Norton *Swan.* **SA3** 17 K7
Norton *V. of Glam.* **CF32** 18 B4
Norton *W.Mid.* **DY8** 40 A7
Norton *W.Suss.* **PO20** 12 C6
Norton *W.Suss.* **PO20** 12 B7
Norton *Wilts.* **SN16** 20 B3
Norton *Worcs.* **WR5** 29 H3
Norton *Worcs.* **WR11** 30 B4
Norton Bavant **BA12** 20 C7
Norton Bridge **ST15** 40 A2
Norton Canes **WS11** 40 C5
Norton Canon **HR4** 28 C4
Norton Disney **LN6** 52 B7
Norton Ferris **BA12** 9 G1
Norton Fitzwarren **TA2** 7 K3
Norton Green *Herts.* **SG1** 33 F6
Norton Green *I.o.W.* **PO40** 10 E6
Norton Green *Stoke* **ST6** 49 J7
Norton Hawkfield **BS40** 19 J5
Norton Heath **CM4** 24 C1
Norton in Hales **TF9** 39 G2
Norton in the Moors **ST6** 49 H7
Norton Lindsey **CV35** 30 D2
Norton Little Green **IP31** 34 D2
Norton Malreward **BS39** 19 K5
Norton Mandeville **CM5** 23 J1
Norton St. Philip **BA2** 20 A6
Norton Subcourse **NR14** 45 J6
Norton Wood **HR4** 28 C4
Norton Woodseats **S8** 51 F4
Norton-Juxta-Twycross **CV9** 41 F5
Norton-le-Clay **YO61** 57 K2
Norton-sub-Hamdon **TA14** 8 D3
Norwell **NG23** 51 K6
Norwell Woodhouse **NG23** 51 K6
NORWICH NR 45 G5
Norwich International Airport **NR6** 45 G4
Norwick **ZE2** 107 Q1
Norwood End **CM5** 23 J1
Norwood Green *Gt.Lon.* **UB2** 22 E4
Norwood Green *W.Yorks.* **HX3** 57 G7
Norwood Hill **RH6** 23 F7
Norwood Park **BA6** 8 E1
Noseley **LE7** 42 A6
Noss Mayo **PL8** 5 F6
Nosterfield **DL8** 57 H1
Nosterfield End **CB1** 33 K4
Nostie **IV40** 86 E2
Notgrove **GL54** 30 C6
Nottage **CF36** 18 B4
Notting Hill **W11** 23 F3
Nottingham *High.* **KW5** 105 H5
NOTTINGHAM *Nott.* NG 41 H1
Nottingham East Midlands Airport **DE74** 41 G3
Nottington **DT3** 9 F6
Notton *W.Yorks.* **WF4** 51 F1
Notton *Wilts.* **SN15** 20 C5
Nottswood Hill **GL17** 29 G7
Nounsley **CM3** 34 B7
Noutard's Green **WR6** 29 G2

Nowton **IP29** 34 C2
Nox **SY5** 38 D4
Noyadd Trefawr **SA43** 17 F1
Nuffield **RG9** 21 K3
Nun Monkton **YO26** 58 B4
Nunburnholme **YO42** 58 E5
Nuneaton CV11 41 F6
Nuneham Courtenay **OX44** 21 J2
Nunney **BA11** 20 A7
Nunnington *Here.* **HR1** 28 E4
Nunnington *N.Yorks.* **YO62** 58 C2
Nunnington Park **TA4** 7 J3
Nunnykirk **NE61** 71 F4
Nunsthorpe **DN32** 53 F2
Nunthorpe *Middbro.* **TS7** 63 G5
Nunthorpe *York* **YO23** 58 B4
Nunton **SP5** 10 C2
Nunwick *N.Yorks.* **HG4** 57 J2
Nunwick *Northumb.* **NE48** 70 D6
Nup End **SG4** 33 F7
Nupend **GL10** 20 A1
Nursling **SO16** 10 E3
Nursted **GU31** 11 J2
Nurton **WV6** 40 A6
Nutbourne *W.Suss.* **RH20** 12 D5
Nutbourne *W.Suss.* **PO18** 11 J4
Nutfield **RH1** 23 G6
Nuthall **NG16** 41 H1
Nuthampstead **SG8** 33 H5
Nuthurst *W.Suss.* **RH13** 12 E4
Nuthurst *Warks.* **B94** 30 C1
Nutley *E.Suss.* **TN22** 13 H4
Nutley *Hants.* **RG25** 21 K7
Nutwell **DN3** 51 J2
Nyadd **FK9** 75 F1
Nybster **KW1** 105 J2
Nyetimber **PO21** 12 B7
Nyewood **GU31** 11 J2
Nymet Rowland **EX17** 7 F5
Nymet Tracey **EX17** 7 F5
Nympsfield **GL10** 20 B1
Nynehead **TA21** 7 K3
Nythe **TA7** 8 D1
Nyton **PO20** 12 C6

O

Oad Street **ME9** 24 E5
Oadby **LE2** 41 J5
Oak Cross **EX20** 6 D6
Oak Tree **DL2** 62 E5
Oakamoor **ST10** 40 C1
Oakbank *Arg. & B.* **PA64** 79 J4
Oakbank *W.Loth.* **EH53** 75 J4
Oakdale *Caerp.* **NP12** 18 E2
Oakdale *Poole* **BH15** 10 B5
Oake **TA4** 7 K3
Oaken **WV8** 40 A5
Oakenclough **PR3** 55 J5
Oakengates **TF2** 39 G4
Oakenhead **IV31** 97 K5
Oakenholt **CH6** 48 B5
Oakenshaw *Dur.* **DL15** 62 D3
Oakenshaw *W.Yorks.* **BD12** 57 G7
Oakerthorpe **DE55** 51 F7
Oakes **HD3** 50 D1
Oakfield *I.o.W.* **PO33** 11 G5
Oakfield *Torfaen* **NP44** 19 F2
Oakford *Cere.* **SA47** 26 D3
Oakford *Devon* **EX16** 7 H3
Oakfordbridge **EX16** 7 H3
Oakgrove **SK11** 49 J6
Oakham LE15 42 B5
Oakhanger **GU35** 11 J1
Oakhill **BA3** 19 K7
Oakington **CB4** 33 H2
Oaklands *Conwy* **LL26** 47 G7
Oaklands *Herts.* **AL6** 33 F7
Oakle Street **GL2** 29 G7
Oakley *Beds.* **MK43** 32 D3
Oakley *Bucks.* **HP18** 31 H7
Oakley *Fife* **KY12** 75 J2
Oakley *Hants.* **RG23** 21 J6
Oakley *Oxon.* **OX39** 22 A1
Oakley *Poole* **BH21** 10 B5
Oakley *Suff.* **IP21** 35 F1
Oakley Green **SL4** 22 C4
Oakley Park **SY17** 37 J7
Oakridge Lynch **GL6** 20 C1
Oaks **SY5** 38 D5
Oaks Green **DE6** 40 D2
Oaksey **SN16** 20 C2
Oakshaw Ford **CA6** 70 A6
Oakshott **GU33** 11 J2
Oakthorpe **DE12** 41 F4
Oaktree Hill **DL6** 62 E7
Oakwoodhill **RH5** 12 E3
Oakworth **BD22** 57 F6
Oare *Kent* **ME13** 25 G5
Oare *Som.* **EX35** 7 G1
Oare *Wilts.* **SN8** 20 E5
Oasby **NG32** 42 D2
Oatfield **PA28** 66 A2
Oath **TA7** 8 C2
Oathlaw **DD8** 83 F2
Oatlands **HG2** 57 J4
Oban PA34 79 K5
Obley **SY7** 28 C1
Oborne **DT9** 9 F3
Obthorpe **PE10** 42 D4
Occlestone Green **CW10** 49 F6
Occold **IP23** 35 F1
Occumster **KW3** 105 H5
Ochiltree **KA18** 67 K1
Ochr-y-foel **LL18** 47 J5
Ochtermuthill **PH5** 81 K6
Ochtertyre *P. & K.* **PH7** 81 K5
Ochtertyre *Stir.* **FK9** 75 F1
Ockbrook **DE72** 41 G2
Ockeridge **WR6** 29 G2
Ockham **GU23** 22 D6
Ockle **PH36** 86 B7
Ockley **RH5** 12 E3
Ocle Pychard **HR1** 28 E4
Octon **YO25** 59 G2
Odcombe **BA22** 8 E3
Odd Down **BA2** 20 A5
Oddendale **CA10** 61 H5
Oddingley **WR9** 29 J3
Oddington **OX5** 31 G7
Oddsta **ZE2** 107 P3
Odell **MK43** 32 C3
Odham **EX21** 6 C5
Odie **KW17** 106 F5
Odiham **RG29** 22 A6
Odsey **SG7** 33 F5
Odstock **SP5** 10 C2
Odstone **CV13** 41 F5
Offchurch **CV33** 30 E2
Offenham **WR11** 30 B4
Offerton **SK2** 49 J4
Offham *E.Suss.* **BN8** 13 G5
Offham *Kent* **ME19** 23 K6
Offham *W.Suss.* **BN18** 12 D6
Offley Hoo **SG5** 32 E6
Offleymarsh **ST21** 39 G3
Offord Cluny **PE19** 33 F2
Offord D'Arcy **PE19** 33 F2
Offton **IP8** 34 E4
Offwell **EX14** 7 K6
Ogbourne Maizey **SN8** 20 E4
Ogbourne St. Andrew **SN8** 20 E4
Ogbourne St. George **SN8** 20 E4
Ogil **DD8** 83 F1
Ogle **NE20** 71 G6
Oglet **L24** 48 D4
Ogmore **CF32** 18 B4
Ogmore Vale **CF32** 18 C2
Ogmore-by-Sea **CF32** 18 B4
Oil Terminal **KW16** 106 C8
Okeford Fitzpaine **DT11** 9 H3
Okehampton EX20 6 D6
Okehampton Camp **EX20** 6 D6
Okraquoy **ZE2** 107 N9
Olchard **TQ13** 5 J3
Olchfa **SA2** 17 K6
Old **NN6** 31 J1
Old Aberdeen **AB24** 91 H4
Old Alresford **SO24** 11 G1
Old Arley **CV7** 40 E6
Old Basford **NG6** 41 H1
Old Basing **RG24** 21 K6
Old Belses **TD6** 70 A1
Old Bewick **NE66** 71 F1
Old Blair **PH18** 81 K1
Old Bolingbroke **PE23** 53 G6
Old Bramhope **LS16** 57 H5
Old Brampton **S42** 51 F5
Old Bridge of Urr **DG7** 65 H4
Old Buckenham **NR17** 44 E6
Old Burdon **SR7** 62 E1
Old Burghclere **RG20** 21 H6
Old Byland **YO62** 58 B1
Old Cassop **DH6** 62 E3
Old Church Stoke **SY15** 38 B6
Old Cleeve **TA24** 7 J1
Old Clipstone **NG21** 51 J6
Old Colwyn **LL29** 47 G5
Old Craig **AB41** 91 H2
Old Craighall **EH21** 76 B3
Old Crombie **AB54** 98 D5
Old Dailly **KA26** 67 G4
Old Dalby **LE14** 41 J3
Old Dam **SK17** 50 D5
Old Deer **AB42** 99 H6
Old Dilton **BA13** 20 B7
Old Down *S.Glos.* **BS32** 19 K3
Old Down *Som.* **BA3** 19 K6
Old Edlington **DN12** 51 H3
Old Eldon **DL4** 62 D4
Old Ellerby **HU11** 59 H6
Old Felixstowe **IP11** 35 H5
Old Fletton **PE2** 42 E6
Old Ford **E3** 23 G3
Old Glossop **SK13** 50 C3
Old Goginan **SY23** 37 F7
Old Goole **DN14** 58 D7
Old Gore **HR9** 29 F6
Old Grimsby **TR24** 2 B1
Old Hall **HU12** 53 F1
Old Hall Green **SG11** 33 G6
Old Hall Street **NR28** 45 H2
Old Harlow **CM20** 33 H7
Old Heath **CO2** 34 E6
Old Heathfield **TN21** 13 J4
Old Hill **B64** 40 B7
Old Hurst **PE28** 33 G1
Old Hutton **LA8** 55 J1
Old Kea **TR3** 3 F4
Old Kilpatrick **G60** 74 C3
Old Kinnernie **AB32** 91 F4
Old Knebworth **SG3** 33 F6
Old Leake **PE22** 53 H7
Old Leslie **AB52** 90 D2
Old Malton **YO17** 58 E2
Old Milton **BH25** 10 D5
Old Milverton **CV32** 30 D2
Old Montsale **CM0** 25 G2
Old Netley **SO31** 11 F3
Old Newton **IP14** 34 E2
Old Philpstoun **EH49** 75 J3
Old Poltalloch **PA31** 79 K7
Old Radnor (Pencraig) **LD8** 28 B3
Old Rattray **AB42** 99 J5
Old Rayne **AB52** 90 E2
Old Romney **TN29** 15 F5
Old Scone **PH2** 82 C5
Old Shields **G67** 75 G3
Old Sodbury **BS37** 20 A3
Old Somerby **NG33** 42 C2
Old Stratford **MK19** 31 J4
Old Sunderlandwick **YO25** 59 G4
Old Swarland **NE65** 71 G3
Old Swinford **DY8** 40 B7
Old Thirsk **YO7** 57 K1
Old Town *Cumb.* **LA6** 55 J1
Old Town *I.o.S.* **TR21** 2 C1
Old Town Farm **NE19** 70 D4
Old Tupton **S42** 51 F6
Old Warden **SG18** 32 E4
Old Weston **PE28** 32 D1
Old Windsor **SL4** 22 C4
Old Wives Lees **CT4** 15 F2
Old Woking **GU22** 22 D6
Old Woodhall **LN9** 53 F6
Old Woods **SY4** 38 D3
Oldberrow **B95** 30 C2
Oldborough **EX17** 7 F5
Oldbury *Kent* **TN15** 23 J6
Oldbury *Shrop.* **WV16** 39 G6
Oldbury *W.Mid.* B69 40 B7
Oldbury *Warks.* **CV10** 41 F6
Oldbury Naite **BS35** 19 K2
Oldbury on the Hill **GL9** 20 B3
Oldbury-on-Severn **BS35** 19 K2
Oldcastle *Bridgend* **CF31** 18 C4
Oldcastle *Mon.* **NP7** 28 C6
Oldcastle Heath **SY14** 38 D1
Oldcotes **S81** 51 H4
Oldcroft **GL15** 19 K1
Oldeamere **PE7** 43 G6
Oldfield **WR9** 29 H2
Oldford **BA11** 20 A6
Oldhall *Aber.* **AB34** 90 C5
Oldhall *High.* **KW1** 105 H3
OLDHAM OL 49 J2
Oldham Edge **OL1** 49 J2
Oldhamstocks **TD13** 77 F3
Oldland **BS30** 19 K4
Oldmeldrum **AB51** 91 G2
Oldmill **AB31** 90 D4
Oldpark **TF3** 39 F5
Oldridge **EX4** 7 G6
Oldshore Beg **IV27** 102 D3
Oldshoremore **IV27** 102 E3
Oldstead **YO61** 58 B2
Oldtown **IV24** 96 C3
Oldtown of Aigas **IV4** 96 B7
Oldtown of Ord **AB45** 98 E5
Oldwalls **SA3** 17 H6
Oldways End **EX16** 7 G3
Oldwhat **AB53** 99 G5
Oldwich Lane **B93** 30 D1
Olgrinmore **KW12** 105 G3
Oliver **ML12** 69 G1
Oliver's Battery **SO22** 11 F2
Ollaberry **ZE2** 107 M4
Ollerton *Ches.* **WA16** 49 G5
Ollerton *Notts.* **NG22** 51 J6
Ollerton *Shrop.* **TF9** 39 F3
Olmstead Green **CB1** 33 K4
Olney MK46 32 B3
Olrig House **KW14** 105 G2
Olton **B92** 40 D7
Olveston **BS35** 19 K3
Ombersley **WR9** 29 H2
Ompton **NG22** 51 J6
Onchan **IM3** 54 C6
Onecote **ST13** 50 C7
Onehouse **IP14** 34 E3
Ongar Hill **PE34** 43 J3
Ongar Street **HR6** 28 C2
Onibury **SY7** 28 D1
Onich **PH33** 80 B1
Onllwyn **SA10** 27 H7
Onneley **CW3** 39 G1
Onslow Green **CM6** 33 K7
Onslow Village **GU2** 22 C7
Opinan *High.* **IV22** 94 E2
Opinan *High.* **IV21** 94 D4
Orange Lane **TD12** 77 F6
Orasaigh **HS2** 101 F6
Orbliston **IV32** 98 B5
Orbost **IV55** 93 H7
Orby **PE24** 53 H6
Orcadia **PA20** 73 K4
Orchard **PA23** 73 K2
Orchard Portman **TA3** 8 B2
Orcheston **SP3** 20 D7
Orcop **HR2** 28 D6
Orcop Hill **HR2** 28 D6
Ord **IV46** 86 C3
Ordhead **AB51** 90 E3
Ordie **AB34** 90 C4
Ordiequish **IV32** 98 B5
Ordsall **DN22** 51 J5
Ore **TN35** 14 D6
Oreham Common **BN5** 13 F5
Oreston **PL9** 5 F5
Oreton **DY14** 29 F1
Orford *Suff.* **IP12** 35 J4
Orford *Warr.* **WA2** 49 F3
Organford **BH16** 9 J5
Orgreave **DE13** 40 D4
Orkney Islands KW 106 B6
Orlestone **TN26** 14 E4
Orleton *Here.* **SY8** 28 D2
Orleton *Worcs.* **WR6** 29 F2
Orleton Common **SY8** 28 D2
Orlingbury **NN14** 32 B1
Ormacleit **HS8** 84 C1
Ormesby **TS3** 63 G5
Ormesby St. Margaret **NR29** 45 J4
Ormesby St. Michael **NR29** 45 J4
Ormidale **PA22** 73 J2
Ormiscaig **IV22** 94 E2
Ormiston **EH35** 76 C4
Ormlie **KW14** 105 G2
Ormsaigmore **PH36** 79 F1
Ormsary **PA31** 73 F3
Ormskirk L39 48 D2
Oronsay **PA61** 72 B2
Orphir **KW17** 106 C7
Orpington BR6 23 H5
Orrell *Gt.Man.* **WN5** 48 E2
Orrell *Mersey.* **L20** 48 C3
Orrisdale **IM6** 54 C4
Orrok House **AB23** 91 H3
Orroland **DG6** 65 H6
Orsett **RM16** 24 C3
Orsett Heath **RM16** 24 C3
Orslow **TF10** 40 A4
Orston **NG13** 42 A1
Orton *Cumb.* **CA10** 61 H6
Orton *Northants.* **NN14** 32 B1
Orton Longueville **PE2** 42 E6
Orton Rigg **CA5** 60 E1
Orton Waterville **PE2** 42 E6
Orton-on-the-Hill **CV9** 41 F5
Orwell **SG8** 33 G3
Osbaldeston **BB2** 56 B6
Osbaldwick **YO10** 58 C4
Osbaston *Leics.* **CV13** 41 G5
Osbaston *Shrop.* **SY10** 38 C3
Osbaston *Tel. & W.* **TF6** 38 E4
Osbaston Hollow **CV13** 41 G5
Osborne **PO32** 11 G5
Osbournby **NG34** 42 D2
Oscroft **CH3** 48 E6
Ose **IV56** 93 J7
Osgathorpe **LE12** 41 G4
Osgodby *Lincs.* **LN8** 52 D3
Osgodby *N.Yorks.* **YO8** 58 C6
Osgodby *N.Yorks.* **YO11** 59 G1
Oskaig **IV40** 86 B1
Osleston **DE6** 40 E2
Osmaston *Derby* **DE24** 41 F2
Osmaston *Derbys.* **DE6** 40 D1
Osmington **DT3** 9 G6
Osmington Mills **DT3** 9 G6
Osmondthorpe **LS9** 57 J6
Osmotherley **DL6** 63 F7
Osnaburgh (Dairsie) **KY15** 83 F6
Ospringe **ME13** 25 G5
Ossett WF5 57 H7
Ossett Street Side **WF5** 57 H7
Ossington **NG23** 51 K6
Ostend **CM0** 25 F2
Osterley **TW7** 22 E4
Oswaldkirk **YO62** 58 C2
Oswaldtwistle **BB5** 56 C7
Oswestry SY11 38 B3
Oteley **SY12** 38 D2
Otford **TN14** 23 J6
Otham **ME15** 14 C2
Otherton **ST19** 40 B4
Othery **TA7** 8 C1
Otley *Suff.* **IP6** 35 G3
Otley *W.Yorks.* LS21 57 H5
Otter **PA21** 73 H3
Otter Ferry **PA21** 73 H2
Otterbourne **SO21** 11 F2
Otterburn *N.Yorks.* **BD23** 56 D4
Otterburn *Northumb.* **NE19** 70 D4
Otterburn Camp **NE19** 70 D4
Otterden Place **ME13** 14 E2
Otterham **PL32** 4 B1
Otterham Quay **ME8** 24 E5
Otterhampton **TA5** 19 F7
Otternish **HS6** 92 E4
Ottershaw **KT16** 22 D5
Otterswick **ZE2** 107 P4
Otterton **EX9** 7 J7
Otterwood **SO42** 11 F4
Ottery St. Mary EX11 7 J6
Ottinge **CT4** 15 G3
Ottringham **HU12** 59 J7
Oughterby **CA5** 60 D1
Oughtershaw **BD23** 56 D1
Oughterside **CA7** 60 C2
Oughtibridge **S35** 51 F3
Oulston **YO61** 58 B2
Oulton *Cumb.* **CA7** 60 D1
Oulton *Norf.* **NR11** 45 F3
Oulton *Staffs.* **ST15** 40 B2
Oulton *Staffs.* **ST20** 39 G3
Oulton *Suff.* **NR32** 45 K6
Oulton *W.Yorks.* **LS26** 57 J7
Oulton Broad **NR33** 45 K6
Oulton Grange **ST15** 40 B2
Oulton Street **NR11** 45 F3
Oultoncross **ST15** 40 B2
Oundle **PE8** 42 D7
Ousby **CA10** 61 H3
Ousdale **KW7** 105 F6
Ousden **CB8** 34 B3
Ousefleet **DN14** 58 E7
Ouston *Dur.* **DH2** 62 D1
Ouston *Northumb.* **NE18** 71 F6
Out Newton **HU19** 59 K7
Out Rawcliffe **PR3** 55 H5
Out Skerries Airstrip **ZE2** 107 Q5
Outcast **LA12** 55 G2
Outchester **NE70** 77 K7
Outertown **KW16** 106 B7
Outgate **LA22** 60 E7
Outhgill **CA17** 61 J6
Outlands **ST20** 39 G3
Outlane **HD3** 50 C1
Outwell **PE14** 43 J5
Outwood *Surr.* **RH1** 23 G7
Outwood *W.Yorks.* **WF1** 57 J7
Outwoods **TF10** 39 G4
Ouzlewell Green **WF3** 57 J7
Ovenden **HX3** 57 F7
Over *Cambs.* **CB4** 33 G1
Over *Ches.* **CW7** 49 F6
Over *Glos.* **GL2** 29 H7
Over *S.Glos.* **BS32** 19 J3
Over Burrows **DE6** 40 E2
Over Compton **DT9** 8 E3
Over Dinsdale **DL2** 62 E5
Over End **DE45** 50 E5
Over Green **B76** 40 D6
Over Haddon **DE45** 50 E6
Over Hulton **BL5** 49 F2
Over Kellet **LA6** 55 J3
Over Kiddington **OX20** 31 F6
Over Monnow **NP25** 28 D7
Over Norton **OX7** 30 E6
Over Peover **WA16** 49 G5
Over Rankeilour **KY15** 82 E6
Over Silton **YO7** 63 F7
Over Stowey **TA5** 7 K2
Over Stratton **TA13** 8 D3
Over Tabley **WA16** 49 G4
Over Wallop **SO20** 10 D1
Over Whitacre **B46** 40 E6
Over Winchendon (Upper Winchendon) **HP18** 31 J7
Over Worton **OX7** 31 F6
Overbister **KW17** 106 F3
Overbrae **AB53** 99 G5
Overbury **GL20** 29 J5
Overcombe **DT3** 9 F6
Overgreen **S42** 51 F5
Overleigh **BA16** 8 D1
Overpool **CH66** 48 C5
Overscaig Hotel **IV27** 103 G6
Overseal **DE12** 40 E4
Overslade **CV22** 31 F1
Oversland **ME13** 15 F2
Oversley Green **B49** 30 B3
Overstone **NN6** 32 B2
Overstrand **NR27** 45 G1
Overthorpe **OX17** 31 F4
Overton *Aber.* **AB51** 91 F3
Overton *Aberdeen* **AB21** 91 G3
Overton *Ches.* **WA6** 48 E5
Overton *Hants.* **RG25** 21 J7
Overton *Lancs.* **LA3** 55 H4
Overton *N.Yorks.* **YO30** 58 B4
Overton *Shrop.* **SY8** 28 E1
Overton *Swan.* **SA3** 17 H7
Overton *W.Yorks.* **WF4** 50 E1
Overton (Owrtyn) *Wrex.* **LL13** 38 C1
Overton Bridge **LL13** 38 C1
Overtown *Lancs.* **LA6** 56 B2
Overtown *N.Lan.* **ML2** 75 G5
Overtown *Swin.* **SN4** 20 E4
Overy **OX10** 21 J2
Oving *Bucks.* **HP22** 31 J6
Oving *W.Suss.* **PO20** 12 C6
Ovingdean **BN2** 13 G6
Ovingham **NE42** 71 F7
Ovington *Dur.* **DL11** 62 C5
Ovington *Essex* **CO10** 34 B4
Ovington *Hants.* **SO24** 11 G1
Ovington *Norf.* **IP25** 44 D5
Ovington *Northumb.* **NE42** 71 F7
Ower *Hants.* **SO51** 10 E3
Ower *Hants.* **SO45** 11 F4
Owermoigne **DT2** 9 G6
Owler Bar **S17** 50 E5
Owlpen **GL11** 20 A2
Owl's Green **IP13** 35 G2
Owlswick **HP27** 22 A1
Owmby **DN38** 52 D2
Owmby-by-Spital **LN8** 52 D4
Owrtyn (Overton) **LL13** 38 C1
Owslebury **SO21** 11 G2
Owston **LE15** 42 A5
Owston Ferry **DN9** 52 B2
Owstwick **HU12** 59 J6
Owthorpe **NG12** 41 J2
Oxborough **PE33** 44 B5
Oxcliffe Hill **LA3** 55 H3
Oxcombe **LN9** 53 G5
Oxen End **CM7** 33 K6
Oxen Park **LA12** 55 G1
Oxencombe **TQ13** 7 G7
Oxenhall **GL18** 29 G6
Oxenholme **LA9** 61 G7
Oxenhope **BD22** 57 F6
Oxenpill **BA6** 19 H7
Oxenton **GL52** 29 J5
Oxenwood **SN8** 21 G6
OXFORD OX 21 J1
Oxhey **WD17** 22 E2
Oxhill **CV35** 30 E4
Oxley **WV10** 40 B5
Oxley Green **CM9** 34 D7
Oxley's Green **TN32** 13 K4
Oxnam **TD8** 70 C2
Oxnead **NR10** 45 G3
Oxnop Ghyll **DL8** 62 A7
Oxshott **KT22** 22 E5
Oxspring **S36** 50 E2
Oxted RH8 23 G6
Oxton *Mersey.* **CH43** 48 C4
Oxton *Notts.* **NG25** 51 J7
Oxton *Sc.Bord.* **TD2** 76 C5
Oxwich **SA3** 17 H7
Oxwich Green **SA3** 17 H7
Oxwick **NR21** 44 D3
Oykel Bridge **IV27** 95 K1
Oyne **AB52** 90 E2
Ozleworth **GL12** 20 A2

P

Pabail Iarach (Lower Bayble) **HS2** 101 H4
Pabail Uarach (Upper Bayble) **HS2** 101 H4
Pabbay **HS6** 92 E3

Packington LE65 41 F4
Packwood B94 30 C1
Padanaram DD8 83 F2
Padbury MK18 31 J5
Paddington W2 23 F3
Paddlesworth CT18 15 G3
Paddock TN25 14 E2
Paddock Wood TN12 23 K7
Paddockhaugh IV30 97 K6
Paddockhole DG11 69 H5
Paddolgreen SY4 38 E2
Padeswood CH7 48 B6
Padfield SK13 50 C3
Padiham BB12 56 C6
Padside HG3 57 G4
Padstow PL28 3 G1
Padworth RG7 21 K5
Paganhill GL5 20 B1
Pagham PO21 12 B7
Paglesham Churchend SS4 25 F2
Paglesham Eastend SS4 25 F2
Paible HS3 93 F2
Paignton TQ3 5 J4
Pailton CV23 41 G7
Paine's Corner TN21 13 K4
Painscastle LD2 28 A4
Painshawfield NE43 71 F7
Painswick GL6 20 B1
Pairc HS2 100 E3
PAISLEY PA 74 C4
Pakefield NR33 45 K6
Pakenham IP31 34 D2
Pale LL23 37 J2
Palehouse Common TN22 13 H5
Palestine SP11 21 F7
Paley Street SL6 22 B4
Palgowan DG8 67 H5
Palgrave IP22 35 F1
Pallinsburn House TD12 77 G7
Palmarsh CT21 15 G4
Palmers Cross GU5 22 D7
Palmers Green N13 23 G2
Palmerscross IV30 97 K5
Palmerstown CF63 18 E4
Palnackie DG7 65 J5
Palnure DG8 64 E4
Palterton S44 51 G6
Pamber End RG26 21 K6
Pamber Green RG26 21 K6
Pamber Heath RG26 21 K5
Pamington GL20 29 J5
Pamphill BH21 9 J4
Pampisford CB2 33 H4
Pan KW16 106 C8
Panborough BA5 19 H7
Panbride DD7 83 G4
Pancrasweek EX22 6 A5
Pancross CF62 18 D5
Pandy Gwyn. LL36 37 F5
Pandy Mon. NP7 28 C6
Pandy Powys SY19 37 J5
Pandy Wrex. LL20 38 A2
Pandy Tudur LL22 47 G6
Pandy'r Capel LL21 47 J7
Panfield CM7 34 B6
Pangbourne RG8 21 K4
Pannal HG3 57 J4
Pannal Ash HG3 57 H4
Panshanger AL7 33 F7
Pant SY10 38 B3
Pant Glas LL54 36 D1
Pant Gwyn LL40 37 H3
Pant Mawr SY18 37 H7
Pantasaph CH8 47 K5
Panteg NP4 19 G2
Pantglas SY20 37 G6
Pantgwyn Carmar. SA19 17 J3
Pantgwyn Cere. SA43 17 F1
Pant-lasau SA6 17 K5
Panton LN8 52 E5
Pant-pastynog LL16 47 J6
Pantperthog SY20 37 G5
Pant-y-dwr LD6 27 J1
Pantyffordd CH7 48 B7
Pant-y-ffridd SY21 38 A5
Pantyffynnon SA18 17 K4
Pantygasseg NP4 19 F2
Pantygelli NP7 28 C7
Pantymwyn CH7 47 K6
Panxworth NR13 45 H4
Papa Stour ZE2 107 K6
Papa Stour Airstrip ZE2 107 K6
Papa Westray KW17 106 D2
Papa Westray Airfield KW17 106 D2
Papcastle CA13 60 C3
Papil ZE2 107 M9
Papple EH41 76 D3
Papplewick NG15 51 H7
Papworth Everard CB3 33 F2
Papworth St. Agnes CB3 33 F2
Par PL24 4 A5
Parbold WN8 48 D1
Parbrook Som. BA6 8 E1
Parbrook W.Suss. RH14 12 D4
Parc LL23 37 H2
Parcllyn SA43 26 B3
Parcrhydderch SY25 27 F3
Parc-Seymour NP26 19 H2
Parc-y-rhôs SA48 17 J1
Pardshaw CA13 60 B4
Parham IP13 35 H2
Parish Holm ML11 68 C1
Park AB45 98 D5
Park Close BB18 56 D5
Park Corner E.Suss. TN3 13 J3
Park Corner Oxon. RG9 21 K3
Park End Northumb. NE48 70 D6
Park End Staffs. ST7 49 G7
Park End Worcs. DY12 29 G1
Park Gate Hants. SO31 11 G4
Park Gate W.Yorks. LS20 57 G5
Park Gate W.Yorks. HD8 50 E1
Park Gate Worcs. B61 29 J1
Park Green IP14 35 F2
Park Hill S2 51 F4
Park Lane LL13 38 D2
Park Langley BR4 23 G5
Park Street AL2 22 E1
Parkend Cumb. CA7 60 E3
Parkend Glos. GL15 19 K1
Parker's Green TN10 23 K7
Parkeston CO12 35 G5
Parkfield Cornw. PL14 4 D4
Parkfield S.Glos. BS16 19 K4
Parkfield W.Mid. WV4 40 B6
Parkford DD8 83 F2
Parkgate Ches. CH64 48 B5
Parkgate D. & G. DG1 69 F5
Parkgate Kent TN30 14 D4
Parkgate S.Yorks. S62 51 G3
Parkgate Surr. RH5 23 F7
Parkham EX39 6 B3
Parkham Ash EX39 6 B3
Parkhead G31 74 E4
Parkhill Angus DD11 83 H3
Parkhill P. & K. PH10 82 C3
Parkhouse NP25 19 H1
Parkhurst PO30 11 F5
Parkmill SA3 17 J7
Parkmore AB55 97 B6
Parkneuk AB30 91 F7
Parkside LL12 48 C7
Parkstone BH14 10 B5
Parkway BA22 8 E2
Parley Cross BH22 10 B5
Parley Green BH23 10 C5
Parlington LS25 57 K6
Parracombe EX31 6 E1
Parrog SA42 16 D2
Parson Cross S5 51 F3
Parson Drove PE13 43 G5
Parsonage Green CM1 33 K7
Parsonby CA7 60 C3
Partick G11 74 D4
Partington M31 49 G3
Partney PE23 53 H6
Parton Cumb. CA28 60 A4
Parton D. & G. DG7 65 G3
Partridge Green RH13 12 E5
Parwich DE6 50 D7
Paslow Wood Common CM4 23 J1
Passenham MK19 31 J5
Passfield GU30 12 B3
Passingford Bridge RM4 23 J2
Paston NR28 45 H2
Paston Street NR28 45 H2
Pasturefields ST18 40 B3
Patchacott EX21 6 C6
Patcham BN1 13 G6
Patchetts Green WD25 22 E2
Patching BN13 12 D6
Patchole EX31 6 E1
Patchway BS34 19 K3
Pateley Bridge HG3 57 G3
Path of Condie PH2 82 B6
Pathe TA7 8 C1
Pathfinder Village EX6 7 G6
Pathhead Aber. DD10 83 J1
Pathhead E.Ayr. KA18 68 B2
Pathhead Fife KY1 76 A1
Pathhead Midloth. EH37 76 B4
Pathlow CV37 30 C3
Patmore Heath SG11 33 H6
Patna KA6 67 J2
Patney SN10 20 D6
Patrick IM5 54 B5
Patrick Brompton DL8 62 D7
Patrington HU12 59 K7
Patrington Haven HU12 59 K7
Patrishow NP7 28 B6
Patrixbourne CT4 15 G2
Patterdale CA11 60 E5
Pattingham WV6 40 A6
Pattishall NN12 31 H3
Pattiswick CM77 34 C6
Paul TR19 2 B6
Paulerspury NN12 31 J4
Paull HU12 59 H7
Paull Holme HU12 59 H7
Paul's Green TR27 2 D5
Paulton BS39 19 K6
Pauperhaugh NE65 71 F4
Pave Lane TF10 39 G4
Pavenham MK43 32 C3
Pawlett TA6 19 G7
Pawston TD12 77 G7
Paxford GL55 30 C5
Paxhill Park RH16 13 G4
Paxton TD15 77 H5
Payden Street ME17 14 E2
Payhembury EX14 7 J5
Paythorne BB7 56 D4
Peacehaven BN10 13 H6
Peacemarsh SP8 9 H2
Peachley WR2 29 H3
Peak Dale SK17 50 C5
Peak Forest SK17 50 D5
Peakirk PE6 42 E5
Pean Hill CT5 25 H5
Pear Tree DE23 41 F2
Pearsie DD8 82 E2
Pearson's Green TN12 23 K7
Peartree AL7 33 F7
Peartree Green Essex CM15 23 J2
Peartree Green Here. HR1 29 F5
Pease Pottage RH11 13 F3
Peasedown St. John BA2 20 A6
Peasehill DE5 41 G1
Peaseland Green NR20 44 E4
Peasemore RG20 21 H4
Peasenhall IP17 35 H2
Peaslake GU5 22 D7
Peasley Cross WA9 48 E3
Peasmarsh E.Suss. TN31 14 D5
Peasmarsh Surr. GU3 22 C7
Peaston EH35 76 C4
Peastonbank EH34 76 C4
Peat Inn KY15 83 F7
Peathill AB43 99 H4
Peathrow DL13 62 C4
Peatling Magna LE8 41 H6
Peatling Parva LE17 41 H7
Peaton SY7 38 E7
Pebble Coombe KT20 23 F6
Pebmarsh CO9 34 C5
Pebworth CV37 30 C4
Pecket Well HX7 56 E7
Peckforton CW6 48 E7
Peckham SE15 23 G4
Peckleton LE9 41 G5
Pedham NR13 45 H4
Pedmore DY9 40 B7
Pedwell TA7 8 D1
Peebles EH45 76 A6
Peel I.o.M. IM5 54 B5
Peel Lancs. FY4 55 G6
Peening Quarter TN30 14 D5
Peggs Green LE67 41 G4
Pegsdon SG5 32 E5
Pegswood NE61 71 H5
Pegwell CT11 25 K5
Peighinn nan Aoireann HS8 84 C1
Peinchorran IV51 86 B1
Peinlich IV51 93 K6
Pelaw NE10 71 H7
Pelcomb SA62 16 C4
Pelcomb Bridge SA62 16 C4
Pelcomb Cross SA62 16 C4
Peldon CO5 34 D7
Pellon HX2 57 F7
Pelsall WS3 40 C5
Pelton DH2 62 D1
Pelutho CA7 60 C2
Pelynt PL13 4 C5
Pemberton WN5 48 E2
Pembrey (Pen-bre) SA16 17 H5
Pembridge HR6 28 C3
Pembroke (Penfro) SA71 16 C5
Pembroke Dock (Doc Penfro) SA72 16 C5
Pembury TN2 23 K7
Penallt NP25 28 E7
Penally SA70 16 E6
Penalt HR1 28 E6
Penare PL26 3 G4
Penarlâg (Hawarden) CH5 48 C6
Penarran SY16 38 A7
Penarth CF64 18 E4
Pen-bont Rhydybeddau SY23 37 F7
Penboyr SA44 17 G2
Pen-bre (Pembrey) SA16 17 H5
Penbryn SA44 26 B3
Pencader SA39 17 H2
Pen-cae SA47 26 D3
Pen-cae-cwm LL16 47 H6
Pencaenewydd LL53 36 D1
Pencaitland EH34 76 C4
Pencarnisiog LL63 46 B5
Pencarreg SA40 17 J1
Pencarrow PL32 4 B2
Pencelli LD3 27 K6
Pen-clawdd SA4 17 J6
Pencoed CF35 18 C3
Pencombe HR7 28 E3
Pencoyd HR2 28 E6
Pencraig Here. HR9 28 E6
Pencraig Powys SY10 37 K3
Pencraig (Old Radnor) Powys LD8 28 B3
Pendeen TR19 2 A5
Penderyn CF44 18 C1
Pendine (Pentywyn) SA33 17 F5
Pendlebury M27 49 G2
Pendleton BB7 56 C6
Pendock GL19 29 G5
Pendoggett PL29 4 A3
Pendomer BA22 8 E3
Pendoylan CF71 18 D4
Penegoes SY20 37 G5
Penelewey TR3 3 F4
Pen-ffordd SA66 16 D3
Penffordd-las (Staylittle) SY19 37 H6
Penfro (Pembroke) SA71 16 C5
Pengam NP12 18 E2
Penge SE20 23 G4
Pengenffordd LD3 28 A6
Pengorffwysfa LL68 46 C3
Pengover Green PL14 4 C4
Pen-groes-oped NP7 19 G1
Pengwern LL18 47 J5
Penhale TR12 2 D7
Penhallow TR4 2 E3
Penhalvean TR16 2 E5
Penhelig LL35 37 F6
Penhill SN2 20 E3
Penhow NP26 19 H2
Penhurst TN33 13 K5
Peniarth LL36 37 F5
Penicuik EH26 76 A4
Peniel SA32 17 H3
Penifiler IV51 93 K7
Peninver PA28 66 B1
Penisa'r Waun LL55 46 D6
Penisarcwm SY10 37 K4
Penishawain LD3 27 K5
Penistone S36 50 E2
Penjerrick TR11 2 E5
Penketh WA5 48 E4
Penkill KA26 67 G4
Penkridge ST19 40 B4
Penlean EX23 4 C1
Penley LL13 38 D2
Penllech LL53 36 B2
Penllergaer SA4 17 K6
Pen-llyn I.o.A. LL65 46 B4
Penllyn V. of Glam. CF71 18 C4
Pen-lôn LL61 46 C6
Penmachno LL24 47 F7
Penmaen SA3 17 J7
Penmaenan LL34 47 F5
Penmaenmawr LL34 47 F5
Penmaenpool (Llyn Penmaen) LL40 37 F4
Penmaen-Rhôs LL29 47 G5
Penmark CF62 18 D5
Penmon LL58 46 E4
Penmorfa LL49 36 E1
Penmynydd LL61 46 D5
Penn Bucks. HP10 22 C2
Penn W.Mid. WV4 40 A6
Penn Street HP7 22 C2
Pennal SY20 37 F5
Pennal-isaf SY20 37 G5
Pennan AB43 99 G4
Pennance TR16 2 E4
Pennant Cere. SY23 26 E2
Pennant Powys SY19 37 H6
Pennant Melangell SY10 37 K3
Pennar SA72 16 C5
Pennard SA3 17 J7
Pennerley SY5 38 C6
Penninghame DG8 64 D4
Pennington Cumb. LA12 55 F2
Pennington Hants. SO41 10 E5
Pennington Green WN2 49 F2
Pennorth LD3 28 A6
Pennsylvania SN14 20 A4
Penny Bridge LA12 55 G1
Pennycross PL5 4 E5
Pennyfuir PA34 79 K4
Pennygate NR12 45 H3
Pennyghael PA70 79 G5
Pennyglen KA19 67 G2
Pennygown PA72 79 H3
Pennymoor EX16 7 G4
Penny's Green NR16 45 F6
Pennyvenie KA6 67 J3
Penparc Cere. SA43 17 F1
Penparc Pembs. SA62 16 B2
Penparcau SY23 36 E7
Penpedairheol NP15 19 G1
Penpethy PL34 4 A2
Penpillick PL24 4 A5
Penpol TR3 3 F5
Penpoll PL22 4 B5
Penponds TR14 2 D5
Penpont D. & G. DG3 68 D4
Penpont Powys LD3 27 J6
Penprysg CF35 18 C3
Penquit PL21 5 G5
Penrherber SA38 17 F2
Penrhiw SA37 17 F1
Penrhiwceiber CF45 18 D2
Penrhiwgoch SA32 17 J4
Penrhiw-llan SA44 17 G1
Penrhiw-pâl SA44 17 G1
Penrhiwtyn SA11 18 A2
Penrhos Gwyn. LL53 36 C2
Penrhos I.o.A. LL65 46 A4
Penrhos Mon. NP15 28 D7
Penrhos Powys SA9 27 H7
Penrhos-garnedd LL57 46 D5
Penrhyn Bay (Bae Penrhyn) LL30 47 G4
Penrhyn-coch SY23 37 F7
Penrhyndeudraeth LL48 37 F2
Penrhyn-side LL30 47 G4
Penrhys CF43 18 D2
Penrice SA3 17 H7
Penrith CA11 61 G4
Penrose Cornw. PL27 3 F1
Penrose Cornw. PL15 4 C2
Penruddock CA11 60 F4
Penryn TR10 2 E5
Pensarn Carmar. SA31 17 H4
Pensarn Conwy LL22 47 H5
Pen-sarn Gwyn. LL45 36 E3
Pen-sarn Gwyn. LL54 36 D1
Pensax WR6 29 G2
Pensby CH61 48 B4
Penselwood BA9 9 G1
Pensford BS39 19 K5
Pensham WR10 29 J4
Penshaw DH4 62 E1
Penshurst TN11 23 J7
Pensilva PL14 4 C4
Pensnett DY5 40 B7
Penston EH33 76 C3
Pentewan PL26 4 A6
Pentir LL57 46 D6
Pentire TR7 2 E2
Pentireglaze PL27 3 G1
Pentlepoir SA69 16 E5
Pentlow CO10 34 C4
Pentlow Street CO10 34 C4
Pentney PE32 44 B4
Penton Mewsey SP11 21 G7
Pentonville N1 23 G3
Pentraeth LL75 46 D5
Pentre Powys SY10 37 K3
Pentre Powys SY16 37 K7
Pentre Powys LD8 28 B2
Pentre Powys SY15 38 B6
Pentre Powys SY16 38 A7
Pentre R.C.T. CF41 18 C2
Pentre Shrop. SY4 38 C4
Pentre Shrop. SY7 28 C1
Pentre Wrex. LL14 38 B1
Pentre Wrex. LL14 38 C1
Pentre Berw LL60 46 C5
Pentre Ffwrndan CH6 48 B5
Pentre Galar SA41 16 E2
Pentre Gwenlais SA18 17 K4
Pentre Gwynfryn LL45 36 E3
Pentre Halkyn CH8 48 B5
Pentre Isaf LL22 47 G6
Pentre Llanrhaeadr LL16 47 J6
Pentre Maelor LL13 38 C1
Pentre Meyrick CF71 18 C4
Pentre Poeth SA6 17 K6
Pentre Saron LL16 47 J6
Pentre-bach Cere. SA48 17 J1
Pentrebach M.Tyd. CF48 18 D1
Pentre-bach Powys LD3 27 J5
Pentrebach R.C.T. CF37 18 D3
Pentrebach Swan. SA4 17 J5
Pentre-bont LL25 47 F7
Pentre-bwlch LL11 38 A1
Pentrecagal SA38 17 G1
Pentre-celyn Denb. LL15 47 K7
Pentre-celyn Powys SY19 37 H5
Pentre-chwyth SA1 17 K6
Pentreclwydau SA11 18 B1
Pentre-cwrt SA44 17 G2
Pentre-Dolau-Honddu LD3 27 J4
Pentredwr Denb. LL20 38 A1
Pentre-dwr Swan. SA7 17 K6
Pentrefelin Carmar. SA19 17 K3
Pentrefelin Cere. SA48 17 K1
Pentrefelin Conwy LL28 47 G5
Pentrefelin Gwyn. LL52 36 E2
Pentrefelin Powys SY10 38 A3
Pentrefoelas LL24 47 G7
Pentregat SA44 26 C3
Pentreheyling SY15 38 B6
Pentre-llwyn-llŵyd LD2 27 J3
Pentre-llyn SY23 27 F1
Pentre-llyn-cymmer LL21 47 H7
Pentre-piod LL23 37 H2
Pentre-poeth NP10 19 F3
Pentre'r beirdd SY21 38 A4
Pentre'r Felin LL28 47 G6
Pentre'r-felin LD3 27 J5
Pentre-tafarn-y-fedw LL26 47 G6
Pentre-ty-gwyn SA20 27 H5
Pentrich DE5 51 F7
Pentridge SP5 10 B3
Pentwyn Caerp. CF81 18 E1
Pen-twyn Caerp. NP13 19 F1
Pentwyn Cardiff CF23 19 F3
Pen-twyn Mon. NP25 19 J1
Pentwyn-mawr NP11 18 E2
Pentyrch CF15 18 E3
Pentywyn (Pendine) SA33 17 F5
Penuwch SY25 26 E2
Penwithick PL26 4 A5
Penwood RG20 21 H5
Penwortham PR1 55 J7
Penwortham Lane PR1 55 J7
Penwyllt SA9 27 H7
Pen-y-banc SA19 17 K3
Pen-y-bont Carmar. SA20 27 G5
Pen-y-bont Carmar. SA33 17 G3
Pen-y-bont Powys SY21 37 K4
Pen-y-bont Powys SY10 38 B3
Penybont Powys LD1 28 A2
Pen-y-bont ar Ogwr (Bridgend) CF31 18 C4
Penybontfawr SY10 37 K3
Penybryn Caerp. CF82 18 E2
Pen-y-bryn Gwyn. LL40 37 F4
Pen-y-bryn Pembs. SA43 16 E1
Pen-y-bryn Wrex. LL14 38 B1
Pen-y-cae Powys SA9 27 H7
Penycae Wrex. LL14 38 B1
Pen-y-cae-mawr NP15 19 H2
Pen-y-cefn CH7 47 K5
Pen-y-clawdd NP25 19 H1
Pen-y-coedcae CF37 18 D3
Penycwm SA62 16 B3
Pen-y-Darren CF47 18 D1
Pen-y-fai CF31 18 B3
Penyffordd Flints. CH4 48 C6
Pen-y-ffordd Flints. CH8 47 K4
Penyffridd LL54 46 D7
Pen-y-gaer NP8 28 A6
Pen-y-garn Carmar. SA32 17 J2
Pen-y-garn Cere. SY24 37 F7
Penygarn Torfaen NP4 19 F1
Penygarnedd SY10 38 A3
Pen-y-garreg LD2 27 K4
Pen-y-Graig Gwyn. LL53 36 B2
Penygraig R.C.T. CF40 18 D2
Penygroes Carmar. SA14 17 J4
Penygroes Gwyn. LL54 46 C7
Pen-y-Gwryd Hotel LL55 46 E7
Pen-y-lan CF23 18 E4
Penymynydd CH4 48 C6
Pen-y-parc CH7 48 B6
Pen-y-Park HR3 28 B4
Pen-yr-englyn CF42 18 C2
Pen-yr-heol Mon. NP25 28 D7
Penyrheol Swan. SA4 17 J6
Pen-y-sarn LL69 46 C3
Pen-y-stryt LL11 47 K7
Penywaun CF44 18 C1
Penzance TR18 2 B5
Penzance Heliport TR18 2 B5
Peopleton WR10 29 J3
Peover Heath WA16 49 G5
Peper Harow GU8 22 C7
Peplow TF9 39 F3
Pepper Arden DL7 62 D6
Pepper's Green CM1 33 K7

Perceton KA11 74 B6
Percie AB31 90 D5
Percyhorner AB43 99 H4
Perham Down SP11 21 F7
Periton TA24 7 H1
Perivale UB6 22 E3
Perkhill AB31 90 D4
Perkins Beach SY5 38 C5
Perkin's Village EX5 7 J6
Perlethorpe NG22 51 J5
Perran Downs TR20 2 C5
Perranarworthal TR3 2 E5
Perranporth TR6 2 E3
Perranuthnoe TR20 2 C6
Perranzabuloe TR4 2 E3
Perrott's Brook GL7 20 D1
Perry Barr B42 40 C6
Perry Crofts B79 40 E5
Perry Green *Essex* CM77 34 C6
Perry Green *Herts.* SG10 33 H7
Perry Green *Wilts.* SN16 20 C3
Perry Street DA11 24 C4
Perrymead BA2 20 A5
Pershall ST21 40 A3
Pershore WR10 29 J4
Persie House PH10 82 C2
Pert AB30 83 H1
Pertenhall MK44 32 D2
PERTH PH 82 C5
Perthcelyn CF45 18 D2
Perthy SY12 38 C2
Perton WV6 40 A6
Pestalozzi Children's Village TN33 14 C6
Peter Tavy PL19 5 F3
PETERBOROUGH PE 42 E6
Peterburn IV21 94 D3
Peterchurch HR2 28 C5
Peterculter AB14 91 G4
Peterhead AB42 99 K6
Peterlee SR8 63 F2
Peter's Green LU2 32 E7
Peters Marland EX38 6 C4
Peters Port (Port Pheadair) HS7 92 D7
Petersfield GU32 11 J2
Petersfinger SP5 10 C2
Peterstone Wentlooge CF3 19 F3
Peterston-super-Ely CF5 18 D4
Peterstow HR9 28 E6
Petham CT4 15 G2
Petrockstowe EX20 6 D5
Pett TN35 14 D6
Pettaugh IP14 35 F3
Petteril Green CA11 61 F2
Pettinain ML11 75 H6
Pettistree IP13 35 G3
Petton *Devon* EX16 7 J3
Petton *Shrop.* SY4 38 D3
Petts Wood BR5 23 H5
Petty AB53 91 F1
Pettycur KY3 76 A2
Pettymuick AB41 91 H2
Petworth GU28 12 C4
Pevensey BN24 13 K6
Pevensey Bay BN24 13 K6
Peverell PL2 4 E5
Pewsey SN9 20 E5
Pheasant's Hill RG9 22 A3
Phesdo AB30 90 E7
Philham EX39 6 A3
Philiphaugh TD7 69 K1
Phillack TR27 2 C5
Philleigh TR2 3 F5
Philpstoun EH49 75 J3
Phocle Green HR9 29 F6
Phoenix Green RG27 22 A6
Phones PH20 88 E5
Phorp IV36 97 H6
Pibsbury TA10 8 D2
Pica CA14 60 B4
Piccadilly Corner IP20 45 G7
Pickerells CM5 23 J1
Pickering YO18 58 D1
Pickering Nook NE16 62 C1
Picket Piece SP11 21 G7
Picket Post BH24 10 C4
Pickford Green CV5 40 E7
Pickhill YO7 57 J1
Picklescott SY6 38 D6
Pickletillem KY16 83 F5
Pickmere WA16 49 F5
Pickney TA2 7 K3
Pickstock TF10 39 G3
Pickston PH1 82 A5
Pickup Bank BB3 56 C7
Pickwell *Devon* EX33 6 C1
Pickwell *Leics.* LE14 42 A4
Pickworth *Lincs.* NG34 42 D2
Pickworth *Rut.* PE9 42 C4
Picton *Ches.* CH2 48 D5
Picton *N.Yorks.* TS15 63 F6
Piddinghoe BN9 13 H6
Piddington *Bucks.* HP14 22 B2
Piddington *Northants.* NN7 32 B3
Piddington *Oxon.* OX25 31 H7
Piddlehinton DT2 9 G5
Piddletrenthide DT2 9 G5
Pidley PE28 33 G1
Piercebridge DL2 62 D5
Pierowall KW17 106 D3
Pigdon NE61 71 G5
Pike Hill BB10 56 D6
Pikehall DE4 50 D7
Pikeshill SO43 10 D4
Pilgrims Hatch CM15 23 J2
Pilham DN21 52 B3
Pill BS20 19 J4
Pillaton *Cornw.* PL12 4 D4
Pillaton *Staffs.* ST19 40 B4
Pillerton Hersey CV35 30 D4
Pillerton Priors CV35 30 D4
Pilleth LD7 28 B2
Pilley *Hants.* SO41 10 E5
Pilley *S.Yorks.* S75 51 F2
Pilling PR3 55 H5
Pilling Lane FY6 55 G5
Pillowell GL15 19 K1
Pilning BS35 19 J3
Pilsbury SK17 50 D6
Pilsdon DT6 8 D5
Pilsgate PE9 42 D5
Pilsley *Derbys.* S45 51 G6
Pilsley *Derbys.* DE45 50 E5
Pilson Green NR13 45 H4
Piltdown TN22 13 H4
Pilton *Devon* EX31 6 D2
Pilton *Northants.* PE8 42 D7
Pilton *Rut.* LE15 42 C5
Pilton *Som.* BA4 19 J7
Pilton *Swan.* SA3 17 H7
Pilton Green SA3 17 H7
Pimhole BL9 49 H1
Pimlico HP3 22 D1
Pimperne DT11 9 J4
Pin Mill IP9 35 G5
Pinchbeck PE11 43 F3
Pinchbeck Bars PE11 43 F3
Pinchbeck West PE11 43 F3
Pincheon Green DN14 51 J1
Pinchinthorpe TS14 63 G5
Pindon End MK19 31 J4
Pinehurst SN25 20 E3
Pinfold L40 48 C1
Pinged SA16 17 H5
Pinhay DT7 8 C5
Pinhoe EX1 7 H6
Pinkneys Green SL6 22 B3
Pinley Green CV35 30 D2
Pinminnoch KA26 67 F4
Pinmore KA26 67 G4
Pinn EX10 7 K7
Pinner HA5 22 E3
Pinner Green HA5 22 E2
Pinvin WR10 29 J4
Pinwherry KA26 67 F5
Pinxton NG16 51 G7
Pipe and Lyde HR1 28 E4
Pipe Gate TF9 39 G1
Pipe Ridware WS15 40 C4
Pipehill WS13 40 C5
Piperhall PA20 73 J5
Piperhill IV12 97 F6
Pipers Pool PL15 4 C2
Pipewell NN14 42 B7
Pippacott EX31 6 D2
Pipton LD3 28 A5
Pirbright GU24 22 C6
Pirnmill KA27 73 G6
Pirton *Herts.* SG5 32 E5
Pirton *Worcs.* WR8 29 H4
Pisgah FK15 81 J7
Pishill RG9 22 A3
Pistyll LL53 36 C1
Pitagowan PH18 81 K1
Pitblae AB43 99 H4
Pitcairngreen PH1 82 B5
Pitcairns PH2 82 B6
Pitcaple AB51 91 F2
Pitch Green HP27 22 A1
Pitch Place *Surr.* GU3 22 C6
Pitch Place *Surr.* GU8 12 B3
Pitchcombe GL6 20 B1
Pitchcott HP22 31 J6
Pitchford SY5 38 E5
Pitcombe BA10 9 F1
Pitcot CF32 18 B4
Pitcox EH42 76 E3
Pitcur PH13 82 D4
Pitfichie AB51 90 E3
Pitgrudy IV25 96 E2
Pitinnan AB51 91 F1
Pitkennedy DD8 83 G2
Pitkevy KY6 82 D7
Pitlessie KY15 82 E7
Pitlochry PH16 82 A2
Pitman's Corner IP14 35 F2
Pitmedden AB41 91 G2
Pitminster TA3 8 B3
Pitmuies DD8 83 G3
Pitmunie AB51 90 E3
Pitnacree PH9 82 A2
Pitney TA10 8 D2
Pitroddie PH2 82 D5
Pitscottie KY15 83 F6
Pitsea SS13 24 D3
Pitsford NN6 31 J2
Pitsford Hill TA4 7 J2
Pitstone LU7 32 C7
Pitt *Devon* EX16 7 J4
Pitt *Hants.* SO22 11 F2
Pittendreich IV30 97 J5
Pittentrail IV28 96 E1
Pittenweem KY10 83 G7
Pitteuchar KY7 76 A1
Pittington DH6 62 E2
Pittodrie House AB51 90 E2
Pitton *Swan.* SA3 17 H7
Pitton *Wilts.* SP5 10 D1
Pittulie AB43 99 H4
Pittville GL52 29 J6
Pity Me DH1 62 D2
Pityme PL27 3 G1
Pixey Green IP21 35 G1
Pixley HR8 29 F5
Place Newton YO17 58 E2
Plaidy AB53 99 F5
Plain Dealings SA67 16 D4
Plainfield NE65 70 E3
Plains ML6 75 F4
Plainsfield TA5 7 K2
Plaish SY6 38 E6
Plaistow *Gt.Lon.* E13 23 G3
Plaistow *W.Suss.* RH14 12 D3
Plaitford SO51 10 D3
Plaitford Green SO51 10 D2
Plas SA32 17 H3
Plas Gwynant LL55 46 E7
Plas Isaf LL21 37 K1
Plas Llwyd LL18 47 H5
Plas Llwyngwern SY20 37 G5
Plas Llysyn SY17 37 J6
Plas Nantyr LL20 38 A2
Plashett SA33 17 F5
Plasisaf LL16 47 H6
Plas-rhiw-Saeson SY19 37 J5
Plastow Green RG19 21 J5
Plas-yn-Cefn LL17 47 J5
Platt TN15 23 K6
Platt Bridge WN2 49 F2
Platt Lane SY13 38 E2
Platt's Heath ME17 14 D2
Plawsworth DH2 62 D2
Plaxtol TN15 23 K6
Play Hatch RG4 22 A4
Playden TN31 14 E5
Playford IP6 35 G4
Playing Place TR3 3 F4
Playley Green GL19 29 G5
Plealey SY5 38 D5
Plean FK7 75 G2
Pleasance KY14 82 D6
Pleasant Valley CB11 33 J5
Pleasington BB2 56 B7
Pleasley NG19 51 H6
Pleasleyhill NG19 51 H6
Pleck *Dorset* DT9 9 G3
Pleck *W.Mid.* WS2 40 B6
Pledgdon Green CM22 33 J6
Pledwick WF2 51 F1
Plemstall CH2 48 D5
Plenmeller NE49 70 C7
Pleshey CM3 33 K7
Plockton IV52 86 E1
Plocropol HS3 93 G2
Plomer's Hill HP13 22 B2
Plot Gate TA11 8 E1
Plough Hill CV10 41 F6
Plowden SY7 38 C7
Ploxgreen SY5 38 C5
Pluckley TN27 14 E3
Pluckley Thorne TN27 14 E3
Plucks Gutter CT3 25 J5
Plumbland CA7 60 C3
Plumbley S20 51 G4
Plumley WA16 49 G5
Plumpton *Cumb.* CA11 61 F3
Plumpton *E.Suss.* BN7 13 G5
Plumpton *Northants.* NN12 31 H4
Plumpton Green BN7 13 G5
Plumpton Head CA11 61 G3
Plumstead *Gt.Lon.* SE18 23 H4
Plumstead *Norf.* NR11 45 F2
Plumtree NG12 41 J2
Plungar NG13 42 A2
Plush DT2 9 G4
Plusha PL15 4 C2
Plushabridge PL14 4 D3
Plwmp SA44 26 C3
Plym Bridge PL7 5 F5
PLYMOUTH PL 4 E5
Plymouth City Airport PL6 5 F4
Plympton PL7 5 F5
Plymstock PL9 5 F5
Plymtree EX15 7 J5
Pockley YO62 58 C1
Pocklington YO42 58 E5
Pockthorpe NR20 44 E3
Pocombe Bridge EX2 7 G6
Pode Hole PE11 43 F3
Podimore BA22 8 E2
Podington NN29 32 C2
Podmore ST21 39 G2
Podsmead GL2 29 H7
Poffley End OX29 30 E7
Point Clear CO16 34 E7
Pointon NG34 42 E2
Polanach PA38 80 A2
Polapit Tamar PL15 6 B7
Polbae DG8 64 C3
Polbain IV26 102 B7
Polbathic PL11 4 D5
Polbeth EH55 75 J4
Poldean DG10 69 G4
Pole Moor HD3 50 C1
Polebrook PE8 42 D7
Polegate BN26 13 J6
Poles IV25 96 E2
Polesworth B78 40 E5
Polglass IV26 95 G1
Polgooth PL26 3 G3
Polgown DG3 68 C3
Poling BN18 12 D6
Poling Corner BN18 12 D6
Polkerris PL24 4 A5
Poll a' Charra HS8 84 C3
Polla IV27 103 F3
Pollardras TR13 2 D5
Polldubh PH33 80 C1
Pollie IV28 104 C7
Pollington DN14 51 J1
Polloch PH37 79 J1
Pollok G53 74 D4
Pollokshaws G43 74 D4
Pollokshields G41 74 D4
Polmassick PL26 3 G4
Polmont FK2 75 H3
Polnoon G76 74 D5
Polperro PL13 4 C5
Polruan PL23 4 B5
Polsham BA5 19 J7
Polstead CO6 34 D5
Polstead Heath CO6 34 D4
Poltalloch PA31 73 G1
Poltimore EX4 7 H6
Polton EH18 76 A4
Polwarth TD10 77 F5
Polyphant PL15 4 C2
Polzeath PL27 3 G1
Pomphlett PL9 5 F5
Pond Street CB11 33 H5
Ponders End EN3 23 G2
Pondersbridge PE26 43 F6
Ponsanooth TR3 2 E5
Ponsonby CA20 60 B6
Ponsongath TR12 2 E7
Ponsworthy TQ13 5 H3
Pont Aber SA19 27 G6
Pont Aberglaslyn LL55 36 E1
Pont ar Hydfer LD3 27 H6
Pont Crugnant SY19 37 H6
Pont Cyfyng LL24 47 F7
Pont Dolgarrog LL32 47 F6
Pont Pen-y-benglog LL57 46 E6
Pont Rhyd-sarn LL23 37 H3
Pont Rhyd-y-cyff CF34 18 B3
Pont Walby SA11 18 B1
Pont yr Alwen LL21 47 H7
Pontamman SA18 17 K4
Pontantwn SA17 17 H4
Pontardawe SA8 18 A1
Pontarddulais SA4 17 J5
Pontarfynach (Devil's Bridge) SY23 27 G1
Pontargothi SA32 17 J3
Pont-ar-llechau SA19 27 G6
Pontarsais SA32 17 H3
Pontblyddyn CH7 48 B6
Pontbren Llwyd CF44 18 C1
Pontefract WF8 57 K7
Ponteland NE20 71 G6
Ponterwyd SY23 37 G7
Pontesbury SY5 38 D5
Pontesbury Hill SY5 38 C5
Pontesford SY5 38 D5
Pontfadog LL20 38 B2
Pontfaen *Pembs.* SA65 16 D2
Pont-faen *Powys* LD3 27 J5
Pontgarreg SA44 26 C3
Pont-Henri SA15 17 H5
Ponthir NP18 19 G2
Ponthirwaun SA43 17 F1
Pont-iets (Pontyates) SA15 17 H5
Pontllanfraith NP12 18 E2
Pontlliw SA4 17 K5
Pontllyfni LL54 46 C7
Pontlottyn CF81 18 E1
Pontneddfechan SA11 18 C1
Pontrhydfendigaid SY25 27 G2
Pontrhydyfen SA12 18 A2
Pont-rhyd-y-groes SY25 27 G1
Pontrhydyrun NP44 19 F2
Pontrilas HR2 28 C6
Pontrobert SY22 38 A4
Pont-rug LL55 46 D6
Ponts Green TN33 13 K5
Pontshill HR9 29 F6
Pont-siân SA44 17 H1
Pontsticill CF48 27 K7
Pontwelly SA44 17 H2
Pontyates (Pont-iets) SA15 17 H5
Pontyberem SA15 17 J4
Pont-y-blew LL14 38 C2
Pontybodkin CH7 48 B7
Pontyclun CF72 18 D3
Pontycymer CF32 18 C2
Pontygwaith CF43 18 D2
Pontymister NP11 19 F2
Pontymoel NP4 19 F1
Pont-y-pant LL25 47 F7
Pontypool NP4 19 F1
Pontypridd CF37 18 D2
Pont-y-rhyl CF32 18 C3
Pontywaun NP11 19 F2
Pooksgreen SO40 10 E3
Pool *Cornw.* TR15 2 D4
Pool *W.Yorks.* LS21 57 H5
Pool Bank LA11 55 H1
Pool Green WS9 40 C5
Pool Head HR1 28 E3
Pool of Muckhart FK14 82 B7
Pool Quay SY21 38 B4
Pool Street CO9 34 B5
Poole BH15 10 B5
Poole Keynes GL7 20 C2
Poolend ST13 49 J7
Poolewe IV22 94 E3
Pooley Bridge CA10 61 F4
Pooley Street IP22 44 E7
Poolfold ST8 49 H7
Poolhill GL18 29 G6
Poolsbrook S43 51 G5
Poolthorne Farm DN20 52 D2
Pope Hill SA62 16 C4
Popeswood RG42 22 B5
Popham SO21 21 J7
Poplar E14 23 G3
Porchfield PO30 11 F5
Porin IV6 95 K6
Poringland NR14 45 G5
Porkellis TR13 2 D5
Porlock TA24 7 G1
Porlock Weir TA24 7 G1
Port Allen PH2 82 D5
Port Appin PA38 80 A3
Port Askaig PA46 72 C4
Port Bannatyne PA20 73 J4
Port Carlisle CA7 69 H7
Port Charlotte PA48 72 A5
Port Clarence TS2 63 G4
Port Driseach PA21 73 H3
Port e Vullen IM7 54 D4
Port Ellen PA42 72 B6
Port Elphinstone AB51 91 F3
Port Erin IM9 54 A7
Port Erroll AB42 91 J1
Port Eynon SA3 17 H7
Port Gaverne PL29 4 A2
Port Glasgow PA14 74 B3
Port Henderson IV21 94 D4
Port Isaac PL29 4 A2
Port Logan DG9 64 A6
Port Mòr PH41 85 K7
Port Mulgrave TS13 63 J5
Port na Craig PH16 82 A2
Port nan Giùran (Portnaguran) HS2 101 H4
Port nan Long HS6 92 D4
Port Nis (Port of Ness) HS2 101 H1
Port of Menteith FK8 81 G7
Port of Ness (Port Nis) HS2 101 H1
Port o'Warren DG5 65 J5
Port Penrhyn LL57 46 D5
Port Pheadair (Peters Port) HS7 92 D7
Port Quin PL29 3 G1
Port Ramsay PA34 79 K3
Port St. Mary IM9 54 B7
Port Solent PO6 11 H4
Port Sunlight CH62 48 C4
Port Talbot SA12 18 A2
Port Tennant SA1 17 K6
Port Wemyss PA47 72 A5
Port William DG8 64 D6
Portachoillan PA29 73 F5
Portavadie PA21 73 H4
Portbury BS20 19 J4
Portchester PO16 11 H4
Portencross KA23 73 K6
Portesham DT3 9 F6
Portessie AB56 98 C4
Portfield *Arg. & B.* PA63 79 J5
Portfield *W.Suss.* PO19 12 B6
Portfield Gate SA62 16 C4
Portgate EX20 6 C7
Portgordon AB56 98 B4
Portgower KW8 105 F7
Porth *Cornw.* TR7 3 F2
Porth *R.C.T.* CF39 18 D2
Porth Colmon LL53 36 A2
Porth Llechog (Bull Bay) LL68 46 C3
Porth Navas TR11 2 E6
Porthaethwy (Menai Bridge) LL59 46 D5
Porthallow *Cornw.* TR12 2 E6
Porthallow *Cornw.* PL13 4 C5
Porthcawl CF36 18 B4
Porthcothan PL28 3 F1
Porthcurno TR19 2 A6
Porthgain SA62 16 B2
Porthill ST5 40 A1
Porthkerry CF62 18 D5
Porthleven TR13 2 D6
Porthmadog LL49 36 E2
Porthmeor TR20 2 B5
Portholland PL26 3 G4
Porthoustock TR12 3 F6
Porthpean PL26 4 A5
Porthtowan TR4 2 D4
Porthyrhyd *Carmar.* SA19 27 G5
Porthyrhyd *Carmar.* SA32 17 J4
Porth-y-waen SY10 38 B3
Portincaple G84 74 A1
Portington DN14 58 D6
Portinnisherrich PA33 80 A6
Portinscale CA12 60 D4
Portishead BS20 19 H4
Portknockie AB56 98 C4
Portlethen AB12 91 H5
Portlethen Village AB12 91 H5
Portloe TR2 3 G5
Portlooe PL13 4 C5
Portmahomack IV20 97 G3
Portmeirion LL48 36 E2
Portmellon PL26 4 A6
Portmore SO41 10 E5
Port-na-Con IV27 103 G2
Portnacroish PA38 80 A3
Portnaguran (Port nan Giùran) HS2 101 H4
Portnahaven PA47 72 A5
Portnalong IV47 85 J1
Portnaluchaig PH39 86 C6
Portobello EH15 76 B3
Porton SP4 10 C1
Portpatrick DG9 64 A5
Portreath TR16 2 D4
Portree IV51 93 K7
Portscatho TR2 3 F5
Portsea PO1 11 H4
Portskerra KW14 104 D2
Portskewett NP26 19 J3
Portslade BN41 13 F6
Portslade-by-Sea BN41 13 F6
Portslogan DG9 64 A5
PORTSMOUTH PO 11 H5
Portsonachan PA33 80 B5
Portsoy AB45 98 D4
Portuairk PH36 79 F1
Portvoller HS2 101 H4
Portway *Here.* HR4 28 C4
Portway *Here.* HR4 28 D4
Portway *Here.* HR2 28 D5
Portway *Worcs.* B48 30 B1
Portwrinkle PL11 4 D5

Portyerrock DG8 64 E7
Posenhall TF12 39 F5
Poslingford CO10 34 B4
Postbridge PL20 5 G3
Postcombe OX9 22 A2
Postling CT21 15 G4
Post-mawr (Synod Inn) SA44 26 D3
Postwick NR13 45 G5
Potarch AB31 90 E5
Potsgrove MK17 32 C6
Pott Row PE32 44 B3
Pott Shrigley SK10 49 J5
Potten End HP4 22 D1
Potter Brompton YO12 59 F2
Potter Heigham NR29 45 J4
Potter Street CM17 23 H1
Pottergate Street NR16 45 F6
Potterhanworth LN4 52 D6
Potterhanworth Booths LN4 52 D6
Potterne SN10 20 C6
Potterne Wick SN10 20 D6
Potternewton LS7 57 J6
Potters Bar EN6 23 F1
Potters Crouch AL2 22 E1
Potter's Green CV2 41 F7
Potters Marston LE9 41 G6
Potterspury NN12 31 J4
Potterton *Aber.* AB23 91 H3
Potterton *W.Yorks.* LS15 57 K6
Pottle Street BA12 20 B7
Potto DL6 63 F6
Potton SG19 33 F4
Pott's Green CO6 34 D6
Poughill *Cornw.* EX23 6 A5
Poughill *Devon* EX17 7 G5
Poulshot SN10 20 C6
Poulton GL7 20 E1
Poulton-le-Fylde FY6 55 G6
Pound Bank WR14 29 G4
Pound Green *E.Suss.* TN22 13 J4
Pound Green *Suff.* CB8 34 B3
Pound Green *Worcs.* DY12 29 G1
Pound Hill RH10 13 F3
Pound Street RG20 21 H5
Poundbury DT1 9 F5
Poundffald SA4 17 J6
Poundfield TN6 13 J3
Poundgate TN6 13 H4
Poundland KA26 67 F5
Poundon OX27 31 H6
Poundsbridge TN11 23 J7
Poundsgate TQ13 5 H3
Poundstock EX23 4 C1
Povey Cross RH6 23 F7
Pow Green HR8 29 G4
Powburn NE66 71 F2
Powderham EX6 7 H7
Powerstock DT6 8 E5
Powfoot DG12 69 G7
Powick WR2 29 H3
Powler's Piece EX22 6 B4
Powmill FK14 75 J1
Poxwell DT2 9 G6
Poyle SL3 22 D4
Poynings BN45 13 F5
Poyntington DT9 9 F2
Poynton *Ches.* SK12 49 J4
Poynton *Tel. & W.* TF6 38 E4
Poynton Green SY4 38 E4
Poyntzfield IV7 96 E5
Poys Street IP17 35 H1
Poyston SA62 16 C4
Poyston Cross SA62 16 C4
Poystreet Green IP30 34 D3
Praa Sands TR13 2 C6
Pratis KY8 82 E7
Pratt's Bottom BR6 23 H5
Praze-an-Beeble TR14 2 D5
Predannack Wollas TR12 2 D7
Prees SY13 38 E2
Prees Green SY13 38 E2
Prees Heath SY13 38 E2
Prees Higher Heath SY13 38 E2
Prees Lower Heath SY13 38 E2
Preesall FY6 55 G5
Preesgweene SY10 38 B2
Prenbrigog CH7 48 B6
Prendergast SA61 16 C4
Prendwick NE66 71 F2
Pren-gwyn SA44 17 H1
Prenteg LL49 36 E1
Prenton CH42 48 C4
Prescot L34 48 D3
Prescott *Devon* EX15 7 J4
Prescott *Shrop.* SY4 38 D3
Presley IV36 97 H6
Pressen TD12 77 G7
Prestatyn LL19 47 J4
Prestbury *Ches.* SK10 49 J5
Prestbury *Glos.* GL52 29 J6
Presteigne (Llanandras) LD8 28 C2
Presthope TF13 38 E6
Prestleigh BA4 19 K7
Prestolee M26 49 G2
Preston *B. & H.* BN1 13 G6
Preston *Devon* TQ12 5 J3
Preston *Dorset* DT3 9 G6
Preston *E.Loth.* EH40 76 D3
Preston *E.Riding* HU12 59 H6
Preston *Glos.* HR8 29 F5
Preston *Glos.* GL7 20 D1
Preston *Herts.* SG4 32 E6
Preston *Kent* ME13 25 G5
Preston *Kent* CT3 25 J5
PRESTON *Lancs.* PR 55 J7
Preston *Northumb.* NE67 71 G1
Preston *Rut.* LE15 42 B5
Preston *Sc.Bord.* TD11 77 F5
Preston *Shrop.* SY4 38 E4
Preston *Som.* TA4 7 J2
Preston *Suff.* CO10 34 D3
Preston *Torbay* TQ3 5 J4
Preston *Wilts.* SN15 20 D4
Preston Bagot B95 30 C2
Preston Bissett MK18 31 H5
Preston Bowyer TA4 7 K3
Preston Brockhurst SY4 38 E3
Preston Brook WA7 48 E4
Preston Candover RG25 21 K7
Preston Capes NN11 31 G3
Preston Deanery NN7 31 J3
Preston Gubbals SY4 38 D4
Preston on Stour CV37 30 D4
Preston on the Hill WA4 48 E4
Preston on Wye HR2 28 C4
Preston Plucknett BA20 8 E3
Preston upon the Weald Moors TF6 39 F4
Preston Wynne HR1 28 E4
Preston-le-Skerne DL5 62 E4
Prestonpans EH32 76 B3
Preston-under-Scar DL8 62 B7
Prestwich M25 49 H2
Prestwick *Northumb.* NE20 71 G6
Prestwick *S.Ayr.* KA9 67 H1
Prestwold LE12 41 H3
Prestwood *Bucks.* HP16 22 B1
Prestwood *Staffs.* ST14 40 D1
Price Town CF32 18 C2
Prickwillow CB7 43 J7
Priddy BA5 19 J6
Priest Hill PR3 56 B6
Priest Hutton LA6 55 J2
Priest Weston SY15 38 B6
Priestcliffe SK17 50 D5
Priestland KA17 74 D7
Priestwood DA13 24 C5
Primethorpe LE9 41 H6
Primrose Green NR9 44 E4
Primrose Hill NW1 23 F3
Princes End DY4 40 B6
Princes Gate SA67 16 E4
Princes Risborough HP27 22 B1
Princethorpe CV23 31 F1
Princetown *Caerp.* NP22 28 A7
Princetown *Devon* PL20 5 F3
Prior Muir KY16 83 G6
Prior's Frome HR1 28 E5
Priors Halton SY8 28 D1
Priors Hardwick CV47 31 F3
Priors Marston CV47 31 F3
Prior's Norton GL2 29 H6
Priors Park GL20 29 H5
Priorslee TF2 39 G4
Priory Wood HR3 28 B4
Priston BA2 19 K5
Pristow Green NR16 45 F7
Prittlewell SS0 24 E3
Privett GU34 11 H2
Prixford EX31 6 D2
Proaig PA44 72 C5
Probus TR2 3 F4
Protstonhill AB45 99 G4
Prudhoe NE42 71 F7
Prussia Cove TR20 2 C6
Pubil PH15 81 F3
Publow BS39 19 K5
Puckeridge SG11 33 G6
Puckington TA19 8 C3
Pucklechurch BS16 19 K4
Pucknall SO51 10 E2
Puckrup GL20 29 H5
Puddinglake CW10 49 G6
Puddington *Ches.* CH64 48 C5
Puddington *Devon* EX16 7 G4
Puddlebrook GL17 29 F7
Puddledock NR17 44 E6
Puddletown DT2 9 G5
Pudleston HR6 28 E3
Pudsey LS28 57 H6
Pulborough RH20 12 D5
Puldagon KW1 105 J4
Puleston TF10 39 G3
Pulford CH4 48 C7
Pulham DT2 9 G4
Pulham Market IP21 45 F7
Pulham St. Mary IP21 45 G7
Pulley SY3 38 D5
Pulloxhill MK45 32 D5
Pulrossie IV25 96 E3
Pulverbatch SY5 38 D5
Pumpherston EH53 75 J4
Pumsaint SA19 17 K1
Puncheston SA62 16 D3
Puncknowle DT2 8 E6
Punnett's Town TN21 13 K4
Purbrook PO7 11 H4
Purewell BH23 10 C5
Purfleet RM19 23 J4
Puriton TA7 19 G7
Purleigh CM3 24 E1
Purley CR8 23 G5
Purley on Thames RG8 21 K4
Purlogue SY7 28 B1
Purlpit SN12 20 B5
Purls Bridge PE15 43 H7
Purse Caundle DT9 9 F3
Purslow SY7 38 C7
Purston Jaglin WF7 51 G1
Purtington TA20 8 C4
Purton *Glos.* GL13 19 K1
Purton *Glos.* GL15 19 K1
Purton *Wilts.* SN5 20 D3
Purton Stoke SN5 20 D2
Purves Hall TD10 77 F6
Pury End NN12 31 J4
Pusey SN7 21 G2
Putley HR8 29 F5
Putley Green HR8 29 F5
Putney SW15 23 F4
Putsborough EX33 6 C1
Puttenham *Herts.* HP23 32 B7
Puttenham *Surr.* GU3 22 C7
Puttock End CO10 34 C4
Putts Corner EX10 7 K6
Puxton BS24 19 H5
Pwll SA15 17 H5
Pwllcrochan SA71 16 C5
Pwlldefaid LL53 36 A3
Pwll-glas LL15 47 K7
Pwllgloyw LD3 27 K5
Pwllheli LL53 36 C2
Pwll-Mawr CF3 19 F4
Pwllmeyric NP16 19 J2
Pwll-trap SA33 17 F4
Pwll-y-glaw SA12 18 A2
Pye Corner *Herts.* CM20 33 H7
Pye Corner *Kent* ME17 14 D3
Pye Corner *Newport* NP18 19 G3
Pye Green WS12 40 B4
Pyecombe BN45 13 F5
Pyle *Bridgend* CF33 18 B3
Pyle *I.o.W.* PO38 11 F7
Pyleigh TA4 7 K2
Pylle BA4 9 F1
Pymoor (Pymore) CB6 43 H7
Pymore (Pymoor) *Cambs.* CB6 43 H7
Pymore *Dorset* DT6 8 D5
Pyrford GU22 22 D6
Pyrford Green GU22 22 D6
Pyrton OX49 21 K2
Pytchley NN14 32 B1
Pyworthy EX22 6 B5

Q

Quabbs LD7 38 B7
Quadring PE11 43 F2
Quadring Eaudike PE11 43 F2
Quainton HP22 31 J6
Quarff ZE2 107 N9
Quarley SP11 21 F7
Quarndon DE22 41 F1
Quarr Hill PO33 11 G5
Quarrier's Village PA11 74 B4
Quarrington NG34 42 D1
Quarrington Hill DH6 62 E3
Quarry Bank DY5 40 B7
Quarrybank CW6 48 E6
Quarrywood IV30 97 J5
Quarter ML3 75 F5
Quatford WV15 39 G6
Quatt WV15 39 G7
Quebec DH7 62 C2
Quedgeley GL2 29 H7
Queen Adelaide CB7 43 J7
Queen Camel BA22 8 E2
Queen Charlton BS31 19 K5
Queen Dart EX16 7 G4
Queen Oak SP8 9 G1
Queen Street TN12 23 K7
Queenborough ME11 25 F4
Queen's Bower PO36 11 G6
Queen's Head SY11 38 C3
Queensbury *Gt.Lon.* HA3 22 E3
Queensbury *W.Yorks.* BD13 57 G6
Queensferry (South Queensferry) *Edin.* EH30 75 K3
Queensferry *Flints.* CH5 48 C6
Queenzieburn G65 74 E3
Quemerford SN11 20 D5
Quendale ZE2 107 M11
Quendon CB11 33 J5
Queniborough LE7 41 J4
Quenington GL7 20 E1
Quernmore LA2 55 J3
Queslett B43 40 C6
Quethiock PL14 4 D4
Quholm KW16 106 B6
Quick's Green RG8 21 J4
Quidenham NR16 44 E7
Quidhampton RG25 21 J6
Quidinish (Cuidhtinis) HS3 93 F3
Quilquox AB41 91 H1
Quina Brook SY4 38 E2
Quindry KW17 106 D8
Quine's Hill IM4 54 C6
Quinhill PA29 73 F5
Quinton *Northants.* NN7 31 J3
Quinton *W.Mid.* B32 40 B7
Quinton Green NN7 31 J3
Quintrell Downs TR8 3 F2
Quixhill ST14 40 D1
Quoditch EX21 6 C6
Quoig PH7 81 K5
Quoiggs House FK15 81 K7
Quoisley SY13 38 E1
Quorn (Quorndon) LE12 41 H4
Quorndon (Quorn) LE12 41 H4
Quothquan ML12 75 H7
Quoyloo KW16 106 B5
Quoys ZE2 107 Q1
Quoys of Reiss KW1 105 J3

R

Raasay IV40 94 B7
Raby CH63 48 C5
Rachan ML12 75 K7
Rachub LL57 46 E6
Rackenford EX16 7 G4
Rackham RH20 12 D5
Rackheath NR13 45 G4
Racks DG1 69 F6
Rackwick *Ork.* KW16 106 B8
Rackwick *Ork.* KW17 106 D3
Radbourne DE6 40 E2
Radcliffe *Gt.Man.* M26 49 G2
Radcliffe *Northumb.* NE65 71 H3
Radcliffe on Trent NG12 41 J2
Radclive MK18 31 H5
Radcot OX18 21 F2
Raddington TA4 7 J3
Radernie KY15 83 F7
Radford *B. & N.E.Som.* BA2 19 K6
Radford *Nott.* NG7 41 H1
Radford *Oxon.* OX7 31 F6
Radford *W.Mid.* CV6 41 F7
Radford Semele CV31 30 E2
Radipole DT3 9 F6
Radlett WD7 22 E1
Radley OX14 21 J2
Radley Green CM4 24 C1
Radmore Green CW6 48 E7
Radnage HP14 22 A2
Radstock BA3 19 K6
Radstone NN13 31 G4
Radway CV35 30 E4
Radway Green CW1 49 G7
Radwell *Beds.* MK43 32 D3
Radwell *Herts.* SG7 33 F5
Radwinter CB10 33 K5
Radyr CF15 18 E3
Raechester NE19 70 E5
Raemoir House AB31 90 E5
Raffin IV27 102 C5
Rafford IV36 97 H6
Ragdale LE14 41 J3
Ragged Appleshaw SP11 21 G7
Raglan NP15 19 H1
Ragnall NG22 52 B5
Rahoy PA34 79 H2
Rain Shore OL12 49 H1
Rainford WA11 48 D2
Rainham *Gt.Lon.* RM13 23 J3
Rainham *Med.* ME8 24 E5
Rainhill L35 48 D3
Rainhill Stoops L35 48 E3
Rainow SK10 49 J5
Rainsough M27 49 G2
Rainton YO7 57 J2
Rainworth NG21 51 H7
Raisbeck CA10 61 H6
Raise CA9 61 J2
Rait PH2 82 D5
Raithby *Lincs.* PE23 53 G6
Raithby *Lincs.* LN11 53 G4
Rake GU33 12 B4
Raleigh's Cross TA23 7 J2
Ram SA48 17 J1
Ram Alley SN8 21 F5
Ram Lane TN26 14 E3
Ramasaig IV55 93 G7
Rame *Cornw.* TR10 2 E5
Rame *Cornw.* PL10 4 E6
Rampisham DT2 8 E4
Rampside LA13 55 F3
Rampton *Cambs.* CB4 33 H2
Rampton *Notts.* DN22 52 B5
Ramsbottom BL0 49 G1
Ramsbury SN8 21 F4
Ramscraigs KW6 105 G6
Ramsdean GU32 11 J2
Ramsdell RG26 21 J6
Ramsden OX7 30 E7
Ramsden Bellhouse CM11 24 D2
Ramsden Heath CM11 24 D2
Ramsey *Cambs.* PE26 43 F7
Ramsey *Essex* CO12 35 G5
Ramsey *I.o.M.* IM8 54 D4
Ramsey Forty Foot PE26 43 G7
Ramsey Heights PE26 43 F7
Ramsey Island *Essex* CM0 25 F1
Ramsey Island *Pembs.* SA62 16 A3
Ramsey Mereside PE26 43 F7
Ramsey St. Mary's PE26 43 F7
Ramsgate CT11 25 K5
Ramsgate Street NR24 44 E2
Ramsgill HG3 57 G2
Ramsholt IP12 35 H4
Ramshorn ST10 40 C1
Ramsnest Common GU8 12 C3
Ranachan PH36 79 J1
Ranais (Ranish) HS2 101 G5
Ranby *Lincs.* LN8 53 F5
Ranby *Notts.* DN22 51 J4
Rand LN8 52 E5
Randwick GL6 20 B1
Rangemore DE13 40 D3
Rangeworthy BS37 19 K3
Ranish (Ranais) HS2 101 G5
Rankinston KA6 67 J2
Rank's Green CM3 34 B7
Ranmoor S10 51 F4
Rannoch School PH17 81 G2
Ranochan PH38 86 E6
Ranscombe TA24 7 H1
Ranskill DN22 51 J4
Ranton ST18 40 A3
Ranton Green ST18 40 A3
Ranworth NR13 45 H4
Rapness KW17 106 E3
Rapps TA19 8 C3
Rascarrel DG7 65 H6
Rash LA10 56 B1
Rashwood WR9 29 J2
Raskelf YO61 57 K2
Rassau NP23 28 A7
Rastrick HD6 57 G7
Ratagan IV40 87 F3
Ratby LE6 41 H5
Ratcliffe Culey CV9 41 F6
Ratcliffe on Soar NG11 41 G3
Ratcliffe on the Wreake LE7 41 J4
Ratford Bridge SA62 16 B4
Ratfyn SP4 20 E7
Rathen AB43 99 H4
Rathillet KY15 82 E5
Rathliesbeag PH34 87 J6
Rathmell BD24 56 D3
Ratho EH28 75 K3
Ratho Station EH28 75 K3
Rathven AB56 98 C4
Ratley OX15 30 E4
Ratling CT3 15 H2
Ratlinghope SY5 38 D6
Ratsloe EX4 7 H6
Rattar KW14 105 H1
Ratten Row *Cumb.* CA5 60 E2
Ratten Row *Lancs.* PR3 55 H5
Rattery TQ10 5 H4
Rattlesden IP30 34 D3
Rattray PH10 82 C3
Raughton Head CA5 60 E2
Raunds NN9 32 C1
Ravenfield S65 51 G3
Ravenglass CA18 60 B7
Raveningham NR14 45 H6
Raven's Green CO7 35 F6
Ravenscar YO13 63 J2
Ravensdale IM7 54 C4
Ravensden MK44 32 D3
Ravenshaw BD23 56 E5
Ravenshayes EX5 7 H5
Ravenshead NG15 51 H7
Ravensmoor CW5 49 F7
Ravensthorpe *Northants.* NN6 31 H1
Ravensthorpe *W.Yorks.* WF13 57 H7
Ravenstone *Leics.* LE67 41 G4
Ravenstone *M.K.* MK46 32 B3
Ravenstonedale CA17 61 J6
Ravenstruther ML11 75 H6
Ravensworth DL11 62 C6
Raw YO22 63 J2
Rawcliffe *E.Riding* DN14 58 C7
Rawcliffe *York* YO30 58 B4
Rawcliffe Bridge DN14 58 C7
Rawdon LS19 57 H6
Rawmarsh S62 51 G3
Rawnsley WS12 40 C4
Rawreth SS11 24 D2
Rawridge EX14 8 B4
Rawson Green DE56 41 F1
Rawtenstall BB4 56 D7
Rawyards ML6 75 F4
Raxton AB41 91 G1
Raydon IP7 34 E5
Raylees NE19 70 E4
Rayleigh SS6 24 E2
Raymond's Hill EX13 8 C5
Rayne CM77 34 B6
Rayners Lane HA5 22 E3
Raynes Park SW20 23 F5
Reach CB5 33 J2
Read BB12 56 C6
READING RG 22 A4
Reading Green IP21 35 F1
Reading Street TN30 14 E4
Reagill CA10 61 H5
Rearquhar IV25 96 E2
Rearsby LE7 41 J4
Rease Heath CW5 49 F7
Reaster KW1 105 H2
Reaveley NE66 71 F2
Reawick ZE2 107 M8
Reay KW14 104 E2
Reculver CT6 25 J5
Red Ball EX16 7 J4
Red Bull ST7 49 H7
Red Dial CA7 60 D2
Red Hill *Hants.* PO9 11 J3
Red Hill *Warks.* B49 30 C3
Red Lodge IP28 33 K1
Red Lumb OL11 49 H1
Red Oaks Hill CB10 33 J5
Red Point IV21 94 D5
Red Post *Cornw.* EX23 6 A5
Red Post *Devon* TQ9 5 J4
Red Rail HR2 28 E6
Red Rock WN2 48 E2
Red Roses SA34 17 F4
Red Row NE61 71 H4
Red Street ST5 49 H7
Red Wharf Bay (Traeth Coch) LL75 46 D4
Redberth SA70 16 D5
Redbourn AL3 32 E7
Redbourne DN21 52 C3
Redbrook *Glos.* NP25 28 E7
Redbrook *Wrex.* SY13 38 E1
Redbrook Street TN26 14 E4
Redburn *High.* IV16 96 C5
Redburn *High.* IV12 97 G7
Redburn *Northumb.* NE47 70 C7
Redcar TS10 63 H4
Redcastle *Angus* DD11 83 H2
Redcastle *High.* IV6 96 C7
Redcliff Bay BS20 19 H4
Redcloak AB39 91 G6
Reddingmuirhead FK2 75 H3
Reddish SK5 49 H3
Redditch B97 30 B2
Rede IP29 34 C3
Redenhall IP20 45 G7
Redesmouth NE48 70 D5
Redford *Aber.* AB30 91 F7
Redford *Angus* DD11 83 G3
Redford *Dur.* DL13 62 B3

Redford W.Suss. GU29 12 B4
Redgrave IP22 34 E1
Redheugh DD8 83 F1
Redhill Aber. AB51 90 E1
Redhill Aber. AB32 91 F4
Redhill Moray AB54 98 D6
Redhill N.Som. BS40 19 H5
Redhill Notts. NG5 41 H1
REDHILL Surr. RH 23 F6
Redhill Aerodrome & Heliport RH1 23 F7
Redhouse Aber. AB33 90 D2
Redhouse Arg. & B. PA29 73 G4
Redhouses PA44 72 B4
Redisham NR34 45 J7
Redland Bristol BS6 19 J4
Redland Ork. KW17 106 C5
Redlingfield IP23 35 F1
Redlynch Som. BA10 9 G1
Redlynch Wilts. SP5 10 D2
Redmarley D'Abitot GL19 29 G5
Redmarshall TS21 62 E4
Redmile NG13 42 A2
Redmire DL8 62 B7
Redmoor PL30 4 A4
Rednal SY11 38 C3
Redpath TD4 76 D7
Redruth TR15 2 D4
Redscarhead EH45 76 A6
Redshaw ML11 68 D1
Redstone Bank SA67 16 E4
Redwick Newport NP26 19 H3
Redwick S.Glos. BS35 19 J3
Redworth DL5 62 D4
Reed SG8 33 G5
Reed End SG8 33 G5
Reedham NR13 45 J5
Reedley BB10 56 D6
Reedness DN14 58 D7
Reef (Riof) HS2 100 D4
Reepham Lincs. LN3 52 D5
Reepham Norf. NR10 44 E3
Reeth DL11 62 B7
Regaby IM7 54 D4
Regil BS40 19 J5
Regoul IV12 97 F6
Reiff IV26 102 B7
Reigate RH2 23 F6
Reighton YO14 59 H2
Reinigeadal (Rhenigidale) HS3 100 E7
Reisgill KW3 105 H5
Reiss KW1 105 J3
Rejerrah TR8 3 F3
Releath TR14 2 D5
Relubbus TR20 2 C5
Relugas IV36 97 G7
Remenham RG9 22 A3
Remenham Hill RG9 22 A3
Remony PH15 81 J3
Rempstone LE12 41 H3
Rendcomb GL7 30 B7
Rendham IP17 35 H2
Rendlesham IP12 35 H3
Renfrew PA4 74 D4
Renhold MK41 32 D3
Renishaw S21 51 G5
Rennington NE66 71 H2
Renton G82 74 B3
Renwick CA10 61 G2
Repps NR29 45 J4
Repton DE65 41 F3
Rescobie DD8 83 G2
Rescorla PL26 4 A5
Resipole PH36 79 J1
Resolis IV7 96 D5
Resolven SA11 18 B1
Resourie PH37 86 E7
Respryn PL30 4 B4
Reston TD14 77 G4
Restormel PL22 4 B4
Reswallie DD8 83 G2
Reterth TR9 3 G2
Retew PL26 3 G3
Retford (East Retford) DN22 51 K4
Rettendon CM3 24 D2
Rettendon Place CM3 24 D2
Retyn TR8 3 F3
Revesby PE22 53 F6
Revesby Bridge PE22 53 G6
Rew TQ13 5 H3
Rew Street PO31 11 F5
Rewe Devon EX5 7 H6
Rewe Devon EX5 7 G6
Reybridge SN15 20 C5
Reydon IP18 35 J1
Reydon Smear IP18 35 K1
Reymerston NR9 44 E5
Reynalton SA68 16 D5
Reynoldston SA3 17 H7
Rezare PL15 4 D3
Rhadyr NP15 19 G1
Rhaeadr Gwy (Rhaeadr) LD6 27 J2
Rhandirmwyn SA20 27 G4
Rhaoine IV28 96 D1
Rhayader (Rhaeadr Gwy) LD6 27 J2
Rhedyn LL53 36 B2
Rhegreanoch IV27 102 C7
Rheindown IV4 96 C7
Rhelonie IV24 96 C2
Rhemore PA34 79 G2
Rhenigidale (Reinigeadal) HS3 100 E7
Rheola SA11 18 B1
Rhes-y-cae CH8 47 K6
Rhewl Denb. LL20 38 A1
Rhewl Denb. LL15 47 K6
Rhewl Shrop. SY10 38 C2
Rhian IV27 103 H7
Rhicarn IV27 102 C6
Rhiconich IV27 102 E3
Rhicullen IV18 96 D4
Rhidorroch IV26 95 H2
Rhifail KW11 104 C4
Rhigos CF44 18 C1
Rhilochan IV28 96 E1
Rhinduie IV3 96 C7
Rhireavach IV23 95 G2
Rhiroy IV23 95 H3
Rhiston SY15 38 B6
Rhiw LL53 36 B3
Rhiwabon (Ruabon) LL14 38 C1
Rhiwargor SY10 37 J3
Rhiwbina CF14 18 E3
Rhiwbryfdir LL41 37 F1
Rhiwderin NP10 19 F3
Rhiwinder CF39 18 D3
Rhiwlas Gwyn. LL57 46 D6
Rhiwlas Gwyn. LL23 37 J2
Rhiwlas Powys SY10 38 B2
Rhode TA5 8 B1
Rhodes Minnis CT4 15 G3
Rhodesia S80 51 H5
Rhodiad-y-brenin SA62 16 A3
Rhodmad SY23 26 E1
Rhonadale PA28 73 F7
Rhonehouse (Kelton Hill) DG7 65 H5
Rhoose CF62 18 D5
Rhos Carmar. SA44 17 G2
Rhos N.P.T. SA8 18 A1
Rhos Common SY22 38 B4
Rhosaman SA18 27 G7
Rhoscolyn LL65 46 A5
Rhoscrowther SA71 16 C5
Rhosesmor CH7 48 B6
Rhos-fawr LL53 36 C2
Rhosgadfan LL54 46 D7
Rhos-goch I.o.A. LL66 46 C4
Rhosgoch Powys LD2 28 A4
Rhos-hill SA43 16 E1
Rhoshirwaun LL53 36 A3
Rhoslan LL52 36 D1
Rhoslefain LL36 36 E5
Rhosllanerchrugog LL14 38 B1
Rhoslligwy LL70 46 C4
Rhosmaen SA19 17 K3
Rhosmeirch LL77 46 C5
Rhosneigr LL64 46 B5
Rhosnesni LL13 48 C7
Rhôs-on-Sea LL28 47 G4
Rhossili SA3 17 H7
Rhosson SA62 16 A3
Rhostrehwfa LL77 46 C5
Rhostryfan LL54 46 C7
Rhostyllen LL14 38 C1
Rhos-y-bol LL68 46 C4
Rhos-y-brithdir SY22 38 A3
Rhosycaerau SA64 16 C2
Rhos-y-garth SY23 27 F1
Rhos-y-gwaliau LL23 37 J2
Rhos-y-llan LL53 36 B2
Rhos-y-mawn LL22 47 G6
Rhos-y-Meirch LD7 28 B2
Rhu G84 74 A2
Rhuallt LL17 47 J5
Rhubodach PA20 73 J3
Rhuddall Heath CW6 48 E6
Rhuddlan LL18 47 J5
Rhue IV26 95 H2
Rhulen LD2 28 A4
Rhumach PH39 86 C6
Rhunahaorine PA29 73 F6
Rhuthun (Ruthin) LL15 47 K7
Rhyd Gwyn. LL48 37 F1
Rhyd Powys SY17 37 J5
Rhydaman (Ammanford) SA18 17 K4
Rhydargaeau SA32 17 H3
Rhydcymerau SA19 17 J2
Rhyd-Ddu LL54 46 D7
Rhydding SA10 18 A2
Rhydgaled LL16 47 H6
Rhydlanfair LL24 47 G7
Rhydlewis SA44 17 G1
Rhydlios LL53 36 A2
Rhydlydan Conwy LL24 47 G7
Rhydlydan Powys SY16 37 K6
Rhydolion LL53 36 B3
Rhydowen SA44 17 H1
Rhyd-Rosser SY23 26 E2
Rhydspence HR3 28 B4
Rhydtalog CH7 48 B7
Rhyd-uchaf LL23 37 H2
Rhyd-wen LL23 37 J3
Rhyd-wyn LL65 46 B4
Rhyd-y-ceirw CH7 48 B7
Rhyd-y-clafdy LL53 36 C2
Rhydycroesau SY10 38 B2
Rhydyfelin Cere. SY23 26 E1
Rhydyfelin R.C.T. CF37 18 D3
Rhyd-y-foel LL22 47 H5
Rhyd-y-fro SA8 18 A1
Rhyd-y-groes LL57 46 D6
Rhydymain LL40 37 H3
Rhydymwyn CH7 48 B6
Rhyd-yr-onnen LL36 37 F5
Rhyd-y-sarn LL41 37 F1
Rhydywrach SA34 16 E4
Rhyl LL18 47 J4
Rhymney NP22 18 E1
Rhyn SY11 38 C2
Rhynd PH2 82 C5
Rhynie Aber. AB54 90 C2
Rhynie High. IV20 97 F4
Ribbesford DY12 29 G1
Ribchester PR3 56 B6
Ribigill IV27 103 H3
Riby DN37 52 E2
Riccall YO19 58 C6
Riccarton KA1 74 C7
Richards Castle SY8 28 D2
Richings Park SL0 22 D4
Richmond Gt.Lon. TW9 22 E4
Richmond N.Yorks. DL10 62 C6
Richmond S.Yorks. S13 51 G4
Rich's Holford TA4 7 K2
Rickarton AB39 91 G6
Rickerscote ST17 40 B3
Rickford BS40 19 H6
Rickinghall IP22 34 E1
Rickleton NE38 62 D1
Rickling CB11 33 H5
Rickling Green CB11 33 J6
Rickmansworth WD3 22 D2
Riddell TD6 70 A1
Riddings DE55 51 G7
Riddlecombe EX18 6 E4
Riddlesden BD20 57 F5
Ridge Dorset BH20 9 J6
Ridge Herts. EN6 23 F1
Ridge Wilts. SP3 9 J1
Ridge Green RH1 23 G7
Ridge Lane CV10 40 E6
Ridgebourne LD1 27 K2
Ridgeway S12 51 G4
Ridgeway Cross WR13 29 G4
Ridgeway Moor S12 51 G4
Ridgewell CO9 34 B4
Ridgewood TN22 13 H4
Ridgmont MK43 32 C5
Riding Gate BA9 9 G2
Riding Mill NE44 71 F7
Ridley TN15 24 C5
Ridleywood LL13 48 C7
Ridlington Norf. NR28 45 H2
Ridlington Rut. LE15 42 B5
Ridsdale NE48 70 E5
Riechip PH8 82 B3
Rievaulx YO62 58 B1
Rift House TS25 63 F3
Rigg D. & G. DG16 69 H7
Rigg High. IV51 94 B6
Riggend ML6 75 F4
Rigifa KW1 105 J1
Rigmaden Park LA6 56 B1
Rigsby LN13 53 H5
Rigside ML11 75 G7
Riley Green PR5 56 B7
Rileyhill WS13 40 D4
Rilla Mill PL17 4 C3
Rillaton PL17 4 C3
Rillington YO17 58 E2
Rimington BB7 56 D5
Rimpton BA22 9 F2
Rimswell HU19 59 K7
Rinaston SA62 16 C3
Ring o' Bells L40 48 D1
Ringford DG7 65 G5
Ringinglow S11 50 E4
Ringland NR8 45 F4
Ringles Cross TN22 13 H4
Ringmer BN8 13 H5
Ringmore Devon TQ7 5 G6
Ringmore Devon TQ14 5 K3
Ringorm AB38 97 K7
Ring's End PE13 43 G5
Ringsfield NR34 45 J7
Ringsfield Corner NR34 45 J7
Ringshall Herts. HP4 32 C7
Ringshall Suff. IP14 34 E3
Ringshall Stocks IP14 34 E3
Ringstead Norf. PE36 44 B1
Ringstead Northants. NN14 32 C1
Ringwood BH24 10 C4
Ringwould CT14 15 J3
Rinloan AB35 89 K4
Rinmore AB33 90 C3
Rinnigill KW16 106 C8
Rinsey TR13 2 C6
Riof (Reef) HS2 100 D4
Ripe BN8 13 J6
Ripley Derbys. DE5 51 F7
Ripley Hants. BH23 10 C5
Ripley N.Yorks. HG3 57 H3
Ripley Surr. GU23 22 D6
Riplingham HU15 59 F6
Ripon HG4 57 J2
Rippingale PE10 42 E3
Ripple Kent CT14 15 J3
Ripple Worcs. GL20 29 H5
Ripponden HX6 50 C1
Risabus PA42 72 B6
Risbury HR6 28 E3
Risby E.Riding HU17 59 G6
Risby Suff. IP28 34 B2
Risca NP11 19 F2
Rise HU11 59 H5
Riseden TN17 14 C4
Risegate PE11 43 F3
Riseholme LN2 52 C5
Riseley Beds. MK44 32 D2
Riseley W'ham RG7 22 A5
Rishangles IP23 35 F2
Rishton BB1 56 C6
Rishworth HX6 50 C1
Risinghurst OX3 21 J1
Risley Derbys. DE72 41 G2
Risley Warr. WA3 49 F3
Risplith HG4 57 H3
Rispond IV27 103 G2
Rivar SN8 21 G5
Rivenhall CM8 34 C7
Rivenhall End CM8 34 C7
River Kent CT17 15 H3
River W.Suss. GU28 12 C4
River Bank CB7 33 J2
River Bridge TA7 19 G7
Riverford Bridge TQ9 5 H4
Riverhead TN13 23 J6
Riverside CF11 18 E4
Riverton EX32 6 E2
Riverview Park DA12 24 C4
Rivington BL6 49 F1
Roa Island LA13 55 F3
Roach Bridge PR5 55 J7
Road Green NR15 45 G6
Road Weedon NN7 31 H3
Roade NN7 31 J3
Roadhead CA6 70 A6
Roadside High. KW12 105 G2
Roadside Ork. KW17 106 F3
Roadside of Kinneff DD10 91 G7
Roadwater TA23 7 J2
Roag IV55 93 H7
Roast Green CB11 33 H5
Roath CF24 18 E4
Roberton S.Lan. ML12 68 E1
Roberton Sc.Bord. TD9 69 K2
Robertsbridge TN32 14 C5
Robertstown Moray AB38 97 K7
Robertstown R.C.T. CF44 18 D1
Roberttown WF15 57 G7
Robeston Cross SA73 16 B5
Robeston Wathen SA67 16 D4
Robeston West SA73 16 B5
Robin Hood Derbys. DE45 50 E5
Robin Hood Lancs. WN6 48 E1
Robin Hood W.Yorks. LS26 57 J7
Robin Hood Doncaster Sheffield Airport DN10 51 J3
Robin Hood's Bay YO22 63 J2
Robinhood End CO9 34 B5
Robins GU29 12 B4
Roborough Devon EX19 6 D4
Roborough Plym. PL6 5 F4
Roby L36 48 D3
Roby Mill WN8 48 E2
Rocester ST14 40 D2
Roch SA62 16 B3
Roch Bridge SA62 16 B3
Roch Gate SA62 16 B3
Rochallie PH10 82 C2
Rochdale OL16 49 H1
Roche PL26 3 G2
Rochester Med. ME1 24 D5
Rochester Northumb. NE19 70 D4
Rochford Essex SS4 24 E2
Rochford Worcs. WR15 29 F2
Rock Cornw. PL27 3 G1
Rock Northumb. NE66 71 H2
Rock Worcs. DY14 29 G1
Rock Ferry CH42 48 C4
Rockbeare EX5 7 J6
Rockbourne SP6 10 C3
Rockcliffe Cumb. CA6 69 J7
Rockcliffe D. & G. DG5 65 J5
Rockcliffe Cross CA6 69 J7
Rockfield Arg. & B. PA29 73 G5
Rockfield High. IV20 97 G3
Rockfield Mon. NP25 28 D7
Rockford BH24 10 C4
Rockhampton GL13 19 K2
Rockhead PL33 4 A2
Rockingham LE16 42 B6
Rockland All Saints NR17 44 D6
Rockland St. Mary NR14 45 H5
Rockland St. Peter NR17 44 D6
Rockley SN8 20 E4
Rockside PA49 72 A4
Rockwell End RG9 22 A3
Rockwell Green TA21 7 K4
Rodborough GL5 20 B1
Rodbourne SN16 20 C3
Rodbridge Corner CO10 34 C4
Rodd LD8 28 C2
Roddam NE66 71 F1
Rodden DT3 9 F6
Rode BA11 20 B6
Rode Heath ST7 49 H7
Rodeheath SK11 49 H6
Rodel (Roghadal) HS5 93 F3
Roden TF6 38 E4
Rodhuish TA24 7 J2
Rodington SY4 38 E4
Rodington Heath SY4 38 E4
Rodley GL14 29 G7
Rodmarton GL7 20 C2
Rodmell BN7 13 H6
Rodmersham ME9 25 F5
Rodmersham Green ME9 25 F5
Rodney Stoke BS27 19 H6
Rodsley DE6 40 E1
Rodway TA5 19 F7
Roe Cross SK14 49 J3
Roe Green SG9 33 G5
Roecliffe YO51 57 J3
Roehampton SW15 23 F4
Roesound ZE2 107 M6
Roffey RH12 12 E3
Rogart IV28 96 E1
Rogate GU31 12 B4
Rogerstone NP10 19 F3
Roghadal (Rodel) HS5 93 F3
Rogiet NP26 19 H3
Rokemarsh OX10 21 K2
Roker SR6 63 F1
Rollesby NR29 45 J4
Rolleston Leics. LE7 42 A5
Rolleston Notts. NG23 51 K7
Rollestone SP3 20 D7
Rolleston-on-Dove DE13 40 E3
Rolston HU18 59 J5
Rolstone BS24 19 G5
Rolvenden TN17 14 D4
Rolvenden Layne TN17 14 D4
Romaldkirk DL12 62 A4
Romanby DL7 62 E7
Romannobridge EH46 75 K6
Romansleigh EX36 7 F3
Romesdal IV51 93 K6
Romford Dorset BH31 10 B4
ROMFORD Gt.Lon. RM 23 J3
Romiley SK6 49 J3
Romney Street TN15 23 J5
Romsey SO51 10 E2
Romsley Shrop. WV15 39 G7
Romsley Worcs. B62 29 J1
Rona IV40 94 C6
Ronachan PA29 73 F5
Ronague IM9 54 B6
Ronnachmore PA43 72 B5
Rood End B67 40 C7
Rookhope DL13 62 A2
Rookley PO38 11 G6
Rookley Green PO38 11 G6
Rooks Bridge BS26 19 G6
Rook's Nest TA4 7 J2
Rookwith HG4 57 H1
Roos HU12 59 J6
Roose LA13 55 F3
Roosebeck LA12 55 F3
Roosecote LA13 55 F3
Rootham's Green MK44 32 D3
Rootpark ML11 75 H5
Ropley SO24 11 H1
Ropley Dean SO24 11 H1
Ropley Soke SO24 11 H1
Ropsley NG33 42 C2
Rora AB42 99 J5
Rorandle AB51 90 E3
Rorrington SY15 38 C5
Rosarie AB55 98 B6
Rose TR4 2 E3
Rose Ash EX36 7 F3
Rose Green Essex CO6 34 D6
Rose Green W.Suss. PO21 12 C7
Rose Hill TN22 13 H5
Roseacre Kent ME14 14 C2
Roseacre Lancs. PR4 55 H6
Rosebank ML8 75 G6
Rosebrough NE67 71 G1
Rosebush SA66 16 D3
Rosecare EX23 4 B1
Rosecliston TR8 3 F3
Rosedale Abbey YO18 63 J7
Roseden NE66 71 F1
Rosehall IV27 96 B1
Rosehearty AB43 99 H4
Rosehill Aber. AB34 90 D5
Rosehill Shrop. SY4 38 D4
Roseisle IV30 97 J5
Roselands BN22 13 K6
Rosemarket SA73 16 C5
Rosemarkie IV10 96 E6
Rosemary Lane EX15 7 K4
Rosemount P. & K. PH10 82 C3
Rosemount S.Ayr. KA9 67 H1
Rosenannon PL30 3 G2
Rosenithon TR12 3 F6
Rosepool SA62 16 B4
Rosevean PL26 4 A5
Roseville WV14 40 B6
Rosewell EH24 76 A4
Roseworth TS19 63 F4
Rosgill CA10 61 G5
Roshven PH38 86 D7
Roskhill IV55 93 H7
Roskorwell TR12 2 E6
Rosley CA7 60 E2
Roslin EH25 76 A4
Rosliston DE12 40 E4
Rosneath G84 74 A2
Ross D. & G. DG6 65 G6
Ross Northumb. NE70 77 K7
Ross P. & K. PH6 81 J5
Ross Priory G83 74 C2
Rossdhu House G83 74 B2
Rossett LL12 48 C7
Rossett Green HG2 57 J4
Rosside LA12 55 F2
Rossie Farm School DD10 83 H2
Rossie Ochill PH2 82 B6
Rossie Priory PH14 82 D4
Rossington DN11 51 J3
Rosskeen IV18 96 D5
Rossmore BH12 10 B5
Ross-on-Wye HR9 29 F6
Roster KW3 105 H5
Rostherne WA16 49 G4
Rosthwaite Cumb. CA12 60 D5
Rosthwaite Cumb. LA20 55 F1
Roston DE6 40 D1
Rosudgeon TR20 2 C6
Rosyth KY11 75 K2
Rothbury NE65 71 F3
Rotherby LE14 41 J4
Rotherfield TN6 13 J3
Rotherfield Greys RG9 22 A3
Rotherfield Peppard RG9 22 A3
Rotherham S60 51 G3
Rothersthorpe NN7 31 J3
Rotherwick RG27 22 A6
Rothes AB38 97 K7
Rothesay PA20 73 J4
Rothiebrisbane AB53 91 F1
Rothienorman AB51 91 F1
Rothiesholm KW17 106 F5
Rothley Leics. LE7 41 H4
Rothley Northumb. NE61 71 F5
Rothney AB52 90 E2
Rothwell Lincs. LN7 52 E3
Rothwell Northants. NN14 42 B7
Rothwell W.Yorks. LS26 57 J7
Rotsea YO25 59 G4

Rottal **DD8** 82 E1
Rotten Row *Bucks.* **RG9** 22 A3
Rotten Row *W.Mid.* **B93** 30 C1
Rottingdean **BN2** 13 G6
Rottington **CA28** 60 A5
Roud **PO38** 11 G6
Roudham **NR16** 44 D7
Rough Close **ST3** 40 B2
Rough Common **CT2** 15 G2
Rougham *Norf.* **PE32** 44 C3
Rougham *Suff.* **IP30** 34 D2
Rougham Green **IP30** 34 D2
Roughburn **PH31** 87 K6
Roughlee **BB9** 56 D5
Roughley **B75** 40 D6
Roughton *Lincs.* **LN10** 53 F6
Roughton *Norf.* **NR11** 45 G2
Roughton *Shrop.* **WV15** 39 G6
Round Bush **WD25** 22 E2
Roundbush Green **CM6** 33 J7
Roundham **TA18** 8 D4
Roundhay **LS8** 57 J6
Roundstreet Common **RH14** 12 D4
Roundway **SN10** 20 D5
Rous Lench **WR11** 30 B3
Rousay **KW17** 106 C4
Rousdon **DT7** 8 B5
Rousham **OX25** 31 F6
Rousham Gap **OX25** 31 F6
Routenburn **KA30** 73 K4
Routh **HU17** 59 G5
Rout's Green **HP14** 22 A2
Row *Cornw.* **PL30** 4 A3
Row *Cumb.* **LA8** 55 H1
Row *Cumb.* **CA10** 61 H3
Row Heath **CO16** 35 F7
Row Town **KT15** 22 D5
Rowanburn **DG14** 69 K6
Rowardennan Lodge **G63** 74 B1
Rowarth **SK22** 50 C4
Rowbarton **TA2** 8 B2
Rowberrow **BS25** 19 H6
Rowchoish **G63** 80 E7
Rowde **SN10** 20 C5
Rowden **EX20** 6 E6
Rowen **LL32** 47 F5
Rowfields **DE6** 40 D1
Rowfoot **NE49** 70 B7
Rowhedge **CO5** 34 E6
Rowhook **RH12** 12 E3
Rowington **CV35** 30 D2
Rowland **DE45** 50 E5
Rowland's Castle PO9 11 **J3**
Rowlands Gill NE39 62 **C1**
Rowledge **GU10** 22 B7
Rowlestone **HR2** 28 C6
Rowley *Devon* **EX36** 7 F4
Rowley *Dur.* **DH8** 62 B2
Rowley *Shrop.* **SY5** 38 C5
Rowley Park **ST17** 40 B3
Rowley Regis B65 40 **B7**
Rowly **GU5** 22 D7
Rowner **PO13** 11 G4
Rowney Green **B48** 30 B1
Rownhams **SO16** 10 E3
Rowrah **CA26** 60 B5
Rowsham **HP22** 32 B7
Rowsley **DE4** 50 E6
Rowstock **OX11** 21 H3
Rowston **LN4** 52 D7
Rowthorne **S44** 51 G6
Rowton *Ches.* **CH3** 48 D6
Rowton *Shrop.* **SY5** 38 C4
Rowton *Tel. & W.* **TF6** 39 F4
Roxburgh **TD5** 77 F7
Roxby *N.Lincs.* **DN15** 52 C1
Roxby *N.Yorks.* **TS13** 63 J5
Roxton **MK44** 32 E3
Roxwell **CM1** 24 C1
Royal British Legion Village **ME20** 14 C2
Royal Leamington Spa CV32 30 **E2**
Royal Oak **L39** 48 D2
ROYAL TUNBRIDGE WELLS TN 13 **J3**
Roybridge PH31 87 **J6**
Roydon *Essex* **CM19** 33 H7
Roydon *Norf.* **IP22** 44 E7
Roydon *Norf.* **PE32** 44 B3
Roydon Hamlet **CM19** 23 H1
Royston *Herts.* SG8 33 **G4**
Royston *S.Yorks.* **S71** 51 F1
Royton **OL2** 49 J2
Rozel **JE3** 3 K6
Ruabon (Rhiwabon) **LL14** 38 C1
Ruaig **PA77** 78 B3
Ruan Lanihorne **TR2** 3 F4
Ruan Major **TR12** 2 D7
Ruan Minor **TR12** 2 E7
Ruanaich **PA76** 78 D5
Ruardean GL17 29 **F7**
Ruardean Hill **GL17** 29 F7
Ruardean Woodside **GL17** 29 F7
Rubery **B45** 29 J1
Ruckcroft **CA4** 61 G2
Ruckinge **TN26** 15 F4
Ruckland **LN11** 53 G5
Rucklers Lane **HP3** 22 D1
Ruckley **SY5** 38 E5
Rudbaxton **SA62** 16 C3
Rudby **TS15** 63 F6
Rudchester **NE15** 71 G7
Ruddington **NG11** 41 H2
Ruddlemoor **PL26** 4 A5
Rudford **GL2** 29 G6
Rudge **BA11** 20 B6
Rudgeway **BS35** 19 K3
Rudgwick **RH12** 12 D3
Rudhall **HR9** 29 F6
Rudheath **CW9** 49 F5
Rudley Green **CM3** 24 E1
Rudloe **SN13** 20 B5
Rudry **CF83** 18 E3
Rudston **YO25** 59 G3
Rudyard **ST13** 49 J7
Rufford **L40** 48 D1
Rufforth **YO23** 58 B4
Ruffside **DH8** 62 A1
Rugby CV21 31 **G1**
Rugeley WS15 40 **C4**
Ruilick **IV4** 96 C7
Ruishton **TA3** 8 B2
Ruisigearraidh **HS6** 92 E3
Ruislip HA4 22 **D3**
Ruislip Gardens **HA4** 22 D3
Ruislip Manor **HA4** 22 E3
Rum PH43 85 **J5**
Rumbling Bridge **KY13** 75 J1
Rumburgh **IP19** 45 H7
Rumford **PL27** 3 F1
Rumleigh **PL20** 4 E4
Rumney **CF3** 19 F4
Rumwell **TA4** 7 K3
Runacraig **FK18** 81 G6
Runcorn WA7 48 **E4**
Runcton **PO20** 12 B6
Runcton Holme **PE33** 44 A5
Rundlestone **PL20** 5 F3
Runfold **GU10** 22 B7
Runhall **NR9** 44 E5
Runham *Norf.* **NR29** 45 J4
Runham *Norf.* **NR30** 45 K5
Runnington **TA21** 7 K3
Runsell Green **CM3** 24 D1
Runshaw Moor **PR7** 48 E1
Runswick Bay **TS13** 63 K5
Runtaleave **DD8** 82 D1
Runwell **SS11** 24 D2
Ruscombe *Glos.* **GL6** 20 B1
Ruscombe *W'ham* **RG10** 22 A4
Rush Green *Gt.Lon.* **RM7** 23 J3
Rush Green *Herts.* **SG4** 33 F6
Rushall *Here.* **HR8** 29 F5
Rushall *Norf.* **IP21** 45 F7
Rushall *W.Mid.* **WS4** 40 C5
Rushall *Wilts.* **SN9** 20 E6
Rushbrooke **IP30** 34 C2
Rushbury **SY6** 38 E6
Rushden *Herts.* **SG9** 33 G5
Rushden *Northants.* NN10 32 **C2**
Rushford *Devon* **PL19** 4 E3
Rushford *Norf.* **IP24** 44 D7
Rushgreen **WA13** 49 F4
Rushlake Green **TN21** 13 K5
Rushmere **NR33** 45 J7
Rushmere St. Andrew **IP5** 35 G4
Rushmoor **GU10** 22 B7
Rushock **WR9** 29 H1
Rusholme **M13** 49 H3
Rushton *Ches.* **CW6** 48 E6
Rushton *Northants.* **NN14** 42 B7
Rushton *Shrop.* **TF6** 39 F5
Rushton Spencer **SK11** 49 J6
Rushwick **WR2** 29 H3
Rushy Green **BN8** 13 H5
Rushyford **DL17** 62 D4
Ruskie **FK8** 81 H7
Ruskington **NG34** 52 D7
Rusko **DG7** 65 F5
Rusland **LA12** 55 G1
Rusper **RH12** 13 F3
Ruspidge **GL14** 29 F7
Russ Hill **RH6** 23 F7
Russel **IV54** 94 E7
Russell Green **CM3** 34 B7
Russell's Green **TN33** 14 C6
Russell's Water **RG9** 22 A2
Russel's Green **IP21** 35 G1
Rusthall **TN4** 13 J3
Rustington **BN16** 12 D6
Ruston **YO13** 59 F1
Ruston Parva **YO25** 59 G3
Ruswarp **YO21** 63 K6
Rutherend **ML10** 74 E5
Rutherford **TD5** 76 E7
Rutherglen **G73** 74 E4
Ruthernbridge **PL30** 4 A4
Ruthin (Rhuthun) *Denb.* LL15 47 **K7**
Ruthin *V. of Glam.* **CF35** 18 C4
Ruthrieston **AB10** 91 H4
Ruthven *Aber.* **AB54** 98 D6
Ruthven *Angus* **PH12** 82 D3
Ruthven *High.* **IV13** 89 F1
Ruthven *High.* **PH21** 88 E5
Ruthvoes **TR9** 3 G2
Ruthwaite **CA7** 60 D3
Ruthwell **DG1** 69 F7
Ruyton-XI-Towns **SY4** 38 C3
Ryal **NE20** 71 F6
Ryal Fold **BB3** 56 B7
Ryall *Dorset* **DT6** 8 D5
Ryall *Worcs.* **WR8** 29 H4
Ryarsh **ME19** 23 K6
Rydal **LA22** 60 E6
Ryde PO33 11 **G5**
Rydon **EX22** 6 B5
Rye TN31 14 **E5**
Rye Foreign **TN31** 14 D5
Rye Harbour **TN31** 14 E6
Rye Park **EN11** 23 G1
Rye Street **WR13** 29 G5
Ryebank **SY4** 38 E2
Ryeford **HR9** 29 F6
Ryehill *Aber.* **AB52** 90 E2
Ryehill *E.Riding* **HU12** 59 J7
Ryhall **PE9** 42 D4
Ryhill **WF4** 51 F1
Ryhope **SR2** 63 F1
Rylands **NG9** 41 H2
Rylstone **BD23** 56 E4
Ryme Intrinseca **DT9** 8 E3
Ryther **LS24** 58 B6
Ryton *Glos.* **GL18** 29 G5
Ryton *N.Yorks.* **YO17** 58 D2
Ryton *Shrop.* **TF11** 39 G5
Ryton *T. & W.* NE40 71 **G7**
Ryton-on-Dunsmore **CV8** 30 E1

S

Saasaig **IV44** 86 C4
Sabden **BB7** 56 C6
Sabden Fold **BB12** 56 D6
Sackers Green **CO10** 34 D5
Sacombe **SG12** 33 G7
Sacombe Green **SG12** 33 G7
Sacriston **DH7** 62 D2
Sadberge **DL2** 62 E5
Saddell **PA28** 73 F7
Saddington **LE8** 41 J6
Saddle Bow **PE34** 44 A4
Sadgill **LA8** 61 F6
Saffron Walden CB10 33 **J5**
Sageston **SA70** 16 D5
Saham Hills **IP25** 44 D5
Saham Toney **IP25** 44 C5
Saighdinis **HS6** 92 D5
Saighton **CH3** 48 D6
St. Abbs **TD14** 77 H4
St. Agnes TR5 2 **E3**
ST. ALBANS AL 22 **E1**
St. Allen **TR4** 3 F3
St. Andrews KY16 83 **G6**
St. Andrews Major **CF64** 18 E4
St. Anne **GY9** 3 K4
St. Anne's **FY8** 55 G7
St. Ann's **DG11** 69 F4
St. Ann's Chapel *Cornw.* **PL18** 4 E3
St. Ann's Chapel *Devon* **TQ7** 5 G6
St. Anthony **TR2** 3 F5
St. Anthony-in-Meneage **TR12** 2 E6
St. Anthony's Hill **BN23** 13 K6
St. Arvans **NP16** 19 J2
St. Asaph (Llanelwy) LL17 47 **J5**
St. Athan **CF62** 18 D5
St. Aubin **JE3** 3 J7
St. Audries **TA4** 7 K1
St. Austell PL25 4 **A5**
St. Bees CA27 60 **A5**
St. Blazey **PL24** 4 A5
St. Blazey Gate **PL24** 4 A5
St. Boswells **TD6** 76 D7
St. Brelade **JE3** 3 J7
St. Breock **PL27** 3 G1
St. Breward **PL30** 4 A3
St. Briavels **GL15** 19 J1
St. Brides **SA62** 16 B4
St. Brides Major **CF32** 18 B4
St. Bride's Netherwent **NP26** 19 H3
St. Brides Wentlooge **NP10** 19 F3
St. Bride's-super-Ely **CF5** 18 D4
St. Budeaux **PL5** 4 E5
St. Buryan **TR19** 2 B6
St. Catherine **BA1** 20 A5
St. Catherines **PA25** 80 C7
St. Clears (Sanclêr) **SA33** 17 F4
St. Cleer **PL14** 4 C4
St. Clement *Chan.I.* **JE2** 3 K7
St. Clement *Cornw.* **TR1** 3 F4
St. Clether **PL15** 4 C2
St. Colmac **PA20** 73 J4
St. Columb Major TR9 3 **G2**
St. Columb Minor **TR7** 3 F2
St. Columb Road **TR9** 3 G3
St. Combs **AB43** 99 J4
St. Cross South Elmham **IP20** 45 G7
St. Cyrus **DD10** 83 J1
St. Davids *Fife* **KY11** 75 K2
St. David's *P. & K.* **PH7** 82 A5
St. David's (Tyddewi) *Pembs.* **SA62** 16 A3
St. Day **TR16** 2 E4
St. Decumans **TA23** 7 J1
St. Dennis **PL26** 3 G3
St. Denys **SO17** 11 F3
St. Dogmaels (Llandudoch) **SA43** 16 E1
St. Dogwells **SA62** 16 C3
St. Dominick **PL12** 4 E4
St. Donats **CF61** 18 C5
St. Edith's Marsh **SN15** 20 C5
St. Endellion **PL29** 3 G1
St. Enoder **TR8** 3 F3
St. Erme **TR4** 3 F4
St. Erney **PL12** 4 D5
St. Erth **TR27** 2 C5
St. Erth Praze **TR27** 2 C5
St. Ervan **PL27** 3 F1
St. Eval **PL27** 3 F2
St. Ewe **PL26** 3 G4
St. Fagans **CF5** 18 E4
St. Fergus **AB42** 99 J5
St. Fillans **PH6** 81 H5
St. Florence **SA70** 16 D5
St. Gennys **EX23** 4 B1
St. George *Bristol* **BS5** 19 K4
St. George *Conwy* **LL22** 47 H5
St. Georges *N.Som.* **BS22** 19 G5
St. George's *Tel. & W.* **TF2** 39 G4
St. George's *V. of Glam.* **CF5** 18 D4
St. Germans **PL12** 4 D5
St. Giles in the Wood **EX38** 6 D4
St. Giles on the Heath **PL15** 6 B6
St. Harmon **LD6** 27 J1
St. Helen Auckland **DL14** 62 C4
St. Helena **NR10** 45 F4
St. Helen's *E.Suss.* **TN34** 14 D6
St. Helens *I.o.W.* **PO33** 11 H6
St. Helens *Mersey.* WA10 48 **E3**
St. Helier *Chan.I.* **JE2** 3 J7
St. Helier *Gt.Lon.* **SM5** 23 F5
St. Hilary *Cornw.* **TR20** 2 C5
St. Hilary *V. of Glam.* **CF71** 18 D4
St. Hill **RH19** 13 G3
St. Ibbs **SG4** 32 E6
St. Illtyd **NP13** 19 F1
St. Ippollitts **SG4** 32 E6
St. Ishmael **SA17** 17 G5
St. Ishmael's **SA62** 16 B5
St. Issey **PL27** 3 G1
St. Ive **PL14** 4 D4
St. Ives *Cambs.* PE27 33 **G1**
St. Ives *Cornw.* TR26 2 **C4**
St. Ives *Dorset* **BH24** 10 C4
St. James South Elmham **IP19** 45 H7
St. John *Chan.I.* **JE3** 3 J6
St. John *Cornw.* **PL11** 4 E5
St. John's *Gt.Lon.* **SE4** 23 G4
St. John's *I.o.M.* **IM4** 54 B5
St. John's *Surr.* **GU21** 22 C6
St. John's *Worcs.* **WR2** 29 H3
St. John's Chapel *Devon* **EX31** 6 D3
St. John's Chapel *Dur.* **DL13** 61 K3
St. John's Fen End **PE14** 43 J4
St. John's Hall **DL13** 62 B3
St. John's Highway **PE14** 43 J4
St. John's Kirk **ML12** 75 H7
St. John's Town of Dalry **DG7** 68 B5
St. Judes **IM7** 54 C4
St. Just **TR19** 2 A5
St. Just in Roseland **TR2** 3 F5
St. Katherines **AB51** 91 F1
St. Keverne **TR12** 2 E6
St. Kew **PL30** 4 A3
St. Kew Highway **PL30** 4 A3
St. Keyne **PL14** 4 C4
St. Lawrence *Cornw.* **PL30** 4 A4
St. Lawrence *Essex* **CM0** 25 F1
St. Lawrence *I.o.W.* **PO38** 11 G7
St. Leonards *Bucks.* **HP23** 22 C1
St. Leonards *Dorset* **BH24** 10 C4
St. Leonards *E.Suss.* TN37 14 **D7**
St. Leonards Grange **SO42** 11 F5
St. Leonard's Street **ME19** 23 K6
St. Levan **TR19** 2 A6
St. Lythans **CF5** 18 E4
St. Mabyn **PL30** 4 A3
St. Madoes **PH2** 82 C5
St. Margaret South Elmham **IP20** 45 H7
St. Margarets *Here.* **HR2** 28 C5
St. Margarets *Herts.* **SG12** 33 G7
St. Margarets *Wilts.* **SN8** 21 F5
St. Margaret's at Cliffe **CT15** 15 J3
St. Margaret's Hope **KW17** 106 D8
St. Mark's **IM9** 54 B6
St. Martin *Chan.I.* **GY4** 3 J5
St. Martin *Chan.I.* **JE3** 3 K7
St. Martin *Cornw.* **PL13** 4 C5
St. Martin *Cornw.* **TR12** 2 E6
St. Martin's *I.o.S.* **TR25** 2 C1
St. Martins *P. & K.* **PH2** 82 C4
St. Martin's *Shrop.* **SY11** 38 C2
St. Mary **JE3** 3 J6
St. Mary Bourne **SP11** 21 H6
St. Mary Church **CF71** 18 D4
St. Mary Cray **BR5** 23 H5
St. Mary Hill **CF35** 18 C4
St. Mary Hoo **ME3** 24 D4
St. Mary in the Marsh **TN29** 15 F5
St. Marychurch **TQ1** 5 K4
St. Mary's *I.o.S.* **TR21** 2 C1
St. Mary's *Ork.* **KW17** 106 D7
St. Mary's Airport **TR21** 2 C1
St. Mary's Bay **TN29** 15 F5
St. Mary's Croft **DG9** 64 A4
St. Mary's Grove **BS48** 19 H5
St. Maughans Green **NP25** 28 D7
St. Mawes **TR2** 3 F5
St. Mawgan **TR8** 3 F2
St. Mellion **PL12** 4 D4
St. Mellons **CF3** 19 F3
St. Merryn **PL28** 3 F1
St. Mewan **PL26** 3 G3
St. Michael Caerhays **PL26** 3 G4
St. Michael Church **TA7** 8 C1
St. Michael Penkevil **TR2** 3 F4
St. Michael South Elmham **NR35** 45 H7
St. Michaels *Fife* **KY16** 83 F5
St. Michaels *Kent* **TN30** 14 D4
St. Michaels *Worcs.* **WR15** 28 E2
St. Michael's on Wyre **PR3** 55 H5
St. Minver **PL27** 3 G1
St. Monans **KY10** 83 G7
St. Neot **PL14** 4 B4
St. Neots PE19 32 **E2**
St. Newlyn East **TR8** 3 F3
St. Nicholas *Pembs.* **SA64** 16 C2
St. Nicholas *V. of Glam.* **CF5** 18 D4
St. Nicholas at Wade **CT7** 25 J5
St. Ninians **FK7** 75 F1
St. Osyth **CO16** 35 F7
St. Ouen **JE3** 3 J6
St. Owen's Cross **HR2** 28 E6
St. Paul's Cray **BR5** 23 H5
St. Paul's Walden **SG4** 32 E6
St. Peter **JE3** 3 J7
St. Peter Port **GY1** 3 J5
St. Peter's **CT10** 25 K5
St. Petrox **SA71** 16 C6
St. Pinnock **PL14** 4 C4
St. Quivox **KA6** 67 H1
St. Ruan **TR12** 2 E7
St. Sampson **GY2** 3 J5
St. Saviour *Chan.I.* **GY7** 3 H5
St. Saviour *Chan.I.* **JE2** 3 K7
St. Stephen **PL26** 3 G3
St. Stephens *Cornw.* **PL12** 4 E5
St. Stephens *Cornw.* **PL15** 6 B7
St. Stephens *Herts.* **AL1** 22 E1
St. Teath **PL30** 4 A2
St. Thomas **EX2** 7 H6
St. Tudy **PL30** 4 A3
St. Twynnells **SA71** 16 C6
St. Veep **PL22** 4 B5
St. Vigeans **DD11** 83 H3
St. Wenn **PL30** 3 G2
St. Weonards **HR2** 28 D6
St. Winnow **PL22** 4 B5
Saintbury **WR12** 30 C5
Salachail **PA38** 80 B2
Salcombe TQ8 5 **H7**
Salcombe Regis **EX10** 7 K7
Salcott **CM9** 34 D7
Sale M33 49 **G3**
Sale Green **WR9** 29 J3
Saleby **LN13** 53 H5
Salehurst **TN32** 14 C5
Salem *Carmar.* **SA19** 17 K3
Salem *Cere.* **SY23** 37 F7
Salem *Gwyn.* **LL54** 46 D7
Salen *Arg. & B.* **PA72** 79 G3
Salen *High.* **PH36** 79 H1
Salendine Nook **HD3** 50 D1
Salesbury **BB1** 56 B6
Saleway **WR9** 29 J3
Salford *Beds.* **MK17** 32 C5
Salford *Gt.Man.* M5 49 **H3**
Salford *Oxon.* **OX7** 30 D6
Salford Priors **WR11** 30 B3
Salfords **RH1** 23 F7
Salhouse **NR13** 45 H4
Saline **KY12** 75 J1
SALISBURY SP 10 **C2**
Salkeld Dykes **CA11** 61 G3
Sallachan **PH33** 80 A1
Sallachry **PA32** 80 B6
Sallachy *High.* **IV27** 96 C1
Sallachy *High.* **IV40** 87 F1
Salle **NR10** 45 F3
Salmonby **LN9** 53 G5
Salmond's Muir **DD11** 83 G4
Salperton **GL54** 30 B6
Salph End **MK41** 32 D3
Salsburgh **ML7** 75 G4
Salt **ST18** 40 B3
Salt Hill **SL1** 22 C3
Salt Holme **TS2** 63 F4
Saltaire **BD18** 57 G6
Saltash PL12 4 **E5**
Saltburn **IV18** 96 E4
Saltburn-by-the-Sea TS12 63 **H4**
Saltby **LE14** 42 B3
Saltcoats *Cumb.* **CA19** 60 B7
Saltcoats *N.Ayr.* KA21 74 **A6**
Saltcotes **FY8** 55 G7
Saltdean **BN2** 13 G6
Salterbeck **CA14** 60 A4
Salterforth **BB18** 56 D5
Saltergate **YO18** 63 K7
Salterhill **IV30** 97 K5
Salterswall **CW7** 49 F6
Saltfleet **LN11** 53 H3
Saltfleetby All Saints **LN11** 53 H3
Saltfleetby St. Clements **LN11** 53 H3
Saltfleetby St. Peter **LN11** 53 H4
Saltford **BS31** 19 K5
Salthaugh Grange **HU12** 59 J7
Salthouse **NR25** 44 E1
Saltley **B8** 40 C7
Saltmarshe **DN14** 58 D7
Saltness **KW16** 106 B8
Saltney **CH4** 48 C6
Salton **YO62** 58 D1
Saltrens **EX39** 6 C3
Saltwick **NE61** 71 G6
Saltwood **CT21** 15 G4
Salum **PA77** 78 B3
Salvington **BN13** 12 E6
Salwarpe **WR9** 29 H2
Salwayash **DT6** 8 D5
Sambourne **B96** 30 B2
Sambrook **TF10** 39 G3
Samhla **HS6** 92 C5
Samlesbury **PR5** 56 B6
Sampford Arundel **TA21** 7 K4
Sampford Brett **TA4** 7 J1
Sampford Courtenay **EX20** 6 E5
Sampford Moor **TA21** 7 K4
Sampford Peverell **EX16** 7 J4
Sampford Spiney **PL20** 5 F3
Samuelston **EH41** 76 C3
Sanaigmore **PA44** 72 A3
Sanclêr (St. Clears) **SA33** 17 F4
Sancreed **TR20** 2 B6
Sancton **YO43** 59 F6
Sand *Shet.* **ZE2** 107 M8
Sand *Som.* **BS28** 19 H7
Sand Hutton **YO41** 58 C4
Sandaig *Arg. & B.* **PA77** 78 A3

Sandaig *High.* **PH41** 86 D4
Sandaig *High.* **IV40** 86 D3
Sandal Magna **WF2** 51 F1
Sanday **KW17** 106 G3
Sanday Airfield **KW17** 106 F3
Sandbach CW11 49 G6
Sandbank **PA23** 73 K2
Sandbanks **BH13** 10 B6
Sandend **AB45** 98 D4
Sanderstead **CR2** 23 G5
Sandford *Cumb.* **CA16** 61 J5
Sandford *Devon* **EX17** 7 G5
Sandford *Dorset* **BH20** 9 J6
Sandford *I.o.W.* **PO38** 11 G6
Sandford *N.Som.* **BS25** 19 H6
Sandford *S.Lan.* **ML10** 75 F6
Sandford *Shrop.* **SY13** 38 E2
Sandford *Shrop.* **SY11** 38 C3
Sandford Orcas **DT9** 9 F2
Sandford St. Martin **OX7** 31 F6
Sandfordhill **AB42** 99 K6
Sandford-on-Thames **OX4** 21 J1
Sandgarth **KW17** 106 E6
Sandgate **CT20** 15 H4
Sandgreen **DG7** 65 F5
Sandhaven **AB43** 99 H4
Sandhead **DG9** 64 A5
Sandhills *Dorset* **DT9** 9 F3
Sandhills *Dorset* **DT2** 8 E4
Sandhills *Surr.* **GU8** 12 C3
Sandhills *W.Yorks.* **LS14** 57 J6
Sandhoe **NE46** 70 E7
Sandholme *E.Riding* **HU15** 58 E6
Sandholme *Lincs.* **PE20** 43 G2
Sandhurst *Brack.F.* GU47 22 B5
Sandhurst *Glos.* **GL2** 29 H6
Sandhurst *Kent* **TN18** 14 C5
Sandhurst Cross **TN18** 14 C5
Sandhutton **YO7** 57 J1
Sandiacre **NG10** 41 G2
Sandilands **LN12** 53 J4
Sandiway **CW8** 49 F5
Sandleheath **SP6** 10 C3
Sandleigh **OX13** 21 H1
Sandling **ME14** 14 C2
Sandlow Green **CW4** 49 G6
Sandness **ZE2** 107 K7
Sandon *Essex* **CM2** 24 D1
Sandon *Herts.* **SG9** 33 G5
Sandon *Staffs.* **ST18** 40 B3
Sandown PO36 11 H6
Sandplace **PL13** 4 C5
Sandquoy **KW17** 106 G3
Sandridge *Devon* **TQ9** 5 J5
Sandridge *Herts.* **AL4** 32 E7
Sandridge *Wilts.* **SN12** 20 C5
Sandringham PE35 44 A3
Sandrocks **RH16** 13 G4
Sandsend **YO21** 63 K5
Sandside **LA7** 55 H1
Sandside House **KW14** 104 E2
Sandsound **ZE2** 107 M8
Sandtoft **DN8** 51 K2
Sanduck **TQ13** 7 F7
Sandway **ME17** 14 D2
Sandwell **B66** 40 C7
Sandwich CT13 15 J2
Sandwick *Cumb.* **CA10** 60 F5
Sandwick *Shet.* **ZE2** 107 N10
Sandwick (Sanndabhaig) *W.Isles* **HS1** 101 G4
Sandwith **CA28** 60 A5
Sandy *Beds.* SG19 32 E4
Sandy *Carmar.* **SA15** 17 H5
Sandy Bank **LN4** 53 F7
Sandy Haven **SA62** 16 B5
Sandy Lane *W.Yorks.* **BD15** 57 G6
Sandy Lane *Wilts.* **SN15** 20 C5
Sandy Lane *Wrex.* **LL13** 38 D1
Sandy Way **PO30** 11 F6
Sandycroft **CH5** 48 C6
Sandygate *Devon* **TQ12** 5 J3
Sandygate *I.o.M.* **IM7** 54 C4
Sandyhills **DG5** 65 J5
Sandylands **LA3** 55 H3
Sandypark **TQ13** 7 F7
Sandyway **HR2** 28 D6
Sangobeg **IV27** 103 G2
Sankyn's Green **WR6** 29 G2
Sanna **PH36** 79 F1
Sannaig **PA60** 72 D4
Sanndabhaig (Sandwick) **HS1** 101 G4
Sannox **KA27** 73 J6
Sanquhar DG4 68 C3
Santon Bridge **CA19** 60 C6
Santon Downham **IP27** 44 C7
Sant-y-Nyll **CF5** 18 D4
Sapcote **LE9** 41 G6
Sapey Common **WR6** 29 G2
Sapiston **IP31** 34 D1
Sapperton *Derbys.* **DE65** 40 D2
Sapperton *Glos.* **GL7** 20 C1
Sapperton *Lincs.* **NG34** 42 D2
Saracen's Head **PE12** 43 G3
Sarclet **KW1** 105 J4
Sardis **SA73** 16 C5
Sarisbury **SO31** 11 G4
Sark **GY9** 3 K6
Sarn *Bridgend* **CF32** 18 C3
Sarn *Powys* **SY16** 38 B6
Sarn Bach **LL53** 36 C3
Sarn Meyllteyrn **LL53** 36 B2
Sarnau *Carmar.* **SA33** 17 G4
Sarnau *Cere.* **SA44** 26 C3
Sarnau *Gwyn.* **LL23** 37 J2
Sarnau *Powys* **SY22** 38 B4
Sarnau *Powys* **LD3** 27 K5
Sarnesfield **HR4** 28 C3
Saron *Carmar.* **SA18** 17 K4
Saron *Carmar.* **SA44** 17 G2
Saron *Gwyn.* **LL55** 46 D6
Saron *Gwyn.* **LL54** 46 C7
Sarratt **WD3** 22 D2
Sarre **CT7** 25 J5
Sarsden **OX7** 30 D6
Sarsgrum **IV27** 103 F2
Sartfield **IM7** 54 C4
Satley **DL13** 62 C2
Satron **DL11** 62 A7
Satterleigh **EX37** 6 E3
Satterthwaite **LA12** 60 E7
Sauchen **AB51** 90 E3
Saucher **PH2** 82 C4
Sauchie **FK10** 75 G1
Sauchieburn **AB30** 83 H1
Sauchrie **KA19** 67 H2
Saughall **CH1** 48 C5
Saughall Massie **CH46** 48 B4
Saughtree **TD9** 70 A4
Saul **GL2** 20 A1
Saundby **DN22** 51 K4
Saundersfoot SA69 16 E5
Saunderton **HP27** 22 A1
Saunton **EX33** 6 C2
Sausthorpe **PE23** 53 G6
Saval **IV27** 96 C1
Savalbeg **IV27** 96 C1
Saverley Green **ST11** 40 B2
Savile Town **WF12** 57 H7
Sawbridge **CV23** 31 G2
Sawbridgeworth CM21 33 H7
Sawdon **YO13** 59 F1
Sawley *Derbys.* **NG10** 41 G2
Sawley *Lancs.* **BB7** 56 C5
Sawley *N.Yorks.* **HG4** 57 H3
Sawston **CB2** 33 H4
Sawtry **PE28** 42 E7
Saxby *Leics.* **LE14** 42 B4
Saxby *Lincs.* **LN8** 52 D4
Saxby All Saints **DN20** 52 C1
Saxelbye **LE14** 41 J3
Saxham Street **IP14** 34 E2
Saxilby **LN1** 52 B5
Saxlingham **NR25** 44 E2
Saxlingham Green **NR15** 45 G6
Saxlingham Nethergate **NR15** 45 G6
Saxlingham Thorpe **NR15** 45 G6
Saxmundham IP17 35 H2
Saxon Street **CB8** 33 K3
Saxondale **NG13** 41 J2
Saxtead **IP13** 35 G2
Saxtead Green **IP13** 35 G2
Saxtead Little Green **IP13** 35 G2
Saxthorpe **NR11** 45 F2
Saxton **LS24** 57 K6
Sayers Common **BN6** 13 F5
Scackleton **YO62** 58 C2
Scadabhagh **HS3** 93 G2
Scaftworth **DN10** 51 J3
Scagglethorpe **YO17** 58 E2
Scaitcliffe **BB5** 56 C7
Scalasaig **PA61** 72 B1
Scalby *E.Riding* **HU15** 58 E7
Scalby *N.Yorks.* **YO13** 63 K3
Scaldwell **NN6** 31 J1
Scale Houses **CA10** 61 G2
Scaleby **CA6** 69 K7
Scalebyhill **CA6** 69 K7
Scales *Cumb.* **CA12** 60 E4
Scales *Cumb.* **LA12** 55 F2
Scalford **LE14** 42 A3
Scaling **TS13** 63 J5
Scallasaig **IV40** 86 E3
Scallastle **PA65** 79 J4
Scalloway **ZE1** 107 M9
Scalpay (Eilean Scalpaigh) HS4 93 H2
Scamblesby **LN11** 53 F5
Scammadale **PA34** 79 K5
Scamodale **PH37** 86 F7
Scampston **YO17** 58 E2
Scampton **LN1** 52 C5
Scaniport **IV2** 88 D1
Scapa **KW15** 106 D7
Scapegoat Hill **HD7** 50 C1
Scar **KW17** 106 F3
Scarborough YO11 59 G1
Scarcewater **TR2** 3 G3
Scarcliffe **S44** 51 G6
Scarcroft **LS14** 57 J5
Scardroy **IV6** 95 J6
Scarff **ZE2** 107 L4
Scarfskerry **KW14** 105 H1
Scargill **DL12** 62 B5
Scarinish **PA77** 78 B3
Scarisbrick **L40** 48 C1
Scarning **NR19** 44 D4
Scarrington **NG13** 42 A1
Scarrowhill **CA8** 61 G1
Scarth Hill **L39** 48 D2
Scarthingwell **LS24** 57 K6
Scartho **DN33** 53 F2
Scarwell **KW16** 106 B5
Scatraig **IV2** 88 E1
Scaur *D. & G.* **DG2** 65 J3
Scaur (Kippford) *D. & G.* **DG5** 65 J5
Scawby **DN20** 52 C2
Scawby Brook **DN20** 52 C2
Scawton **YO7** 58 B1
Scayne's Hill **RH17** 13 G4
Scealascro **HS2** 100 D5
Scethrog **LD3** 28 A6
Schaw **KA5** 67 J1
Scholar Green **ST7** 49 H7
Scholes *S.Yorks.* **S61** 51 F3
Scholes *W.Yorks.* **LS15** 57 J6
Scholes *W.Yorks.* **HD9** 50 D2
Scholes *W.Yorks.* **BD19** 57 G7
School Green **CW7** 49 F6
School House **TA20** 8 C4
Schoose **CA14** 60 B4
Sciberscross **IV28** 96 E1
Scilly Isles (Isles of Scilly) **TR** 2 C1
Scissett **HD8** 50 E1
Scleddau **SA65** 16 C2
Sco Ruston **NR12** 45 G3
Scofton **S81** 51 J4
Scole **IP21** 35 F1
Scolpaig **HS6** 92 C4
Scone **PH2** 82 C5
Scones Lethendy **PH2** 82 C5
Sconser **IV48** 86 B1
Scoor **PA67** 79 F6
Scopwick **LN4** 52 D7
Scoraig **IV23** 95 G2
Scorborough **YO25** 59 G5
Scorrier **TR16** 2 E4
Scorriton **TQ11** 5 H4
Scorton *Lancs.* **PR3** 55 J5
Scorton *N.Yorks.* **DL10** 62 D6
Scot Hay **ST5** 40 A1
Scotby **CA4** 60 F1
Scotch Corner **DL10** 62 D6
Scotforth **LA1** 55 H4
Scothern **LN2** 52 D5
Scotland **NG33** 42 D2
Scotland End **OX15** 30 E5
Scotland Street **CO6** 34 D5
Scotlandwell **KY13** 82 C7
Scotnish **PA31** 73 F2
Scots' Gap **NE61** 71 F5
Scotsburn **IV18** 96 E4
Scotston *Aber.* **AB30** 91 F7
Scotston *P. & K.* **PH8** 82 A3
Scotstoun **G14** 74 D4
Scotstown **PH36** 79 K1
Scott Willoughby **NG34** 42 D2
Scotter **DN21** 52 B2
Scotterthorpe **DN21** 52 B2
Scottlethorpe **PE10** 42 D3
Scotton *Lincs.* **DN21** 52 B3
Scotton *N.Yorks.* **DL9** 62 C7
Scotton *N.Yorks.* **HG5** 57 J4
Scottow **NR10** 45 G3
Scoughall **EH39** 76 E2
Scoulton **NR9** 44 D5
Scounslow Green **ST14** 40 C3
Scourie **IV27** 102 D4
Scourie More **IV27** 102 D4
Scousburgh **ZE2** 107 M11
Scouthead **OL4** 49 J2
Scrabster **KW14** 105 G1
Scrafield **LN9** 53 G6
Scrainwood **NE66** 70 E3
Scrane End **PE22** 43 G1
Scraptoft **LE7** 41 J5
Scratby **NR29** 45 K4
Scrayingham **YO41** 58 D4
Scredington **NG34** 42 D1
Scremby **PE23** 53 H6
Scremerston **TD15** 77 J6
Screveton **NG13** 42 A1
Scriven **HG5** 57 J4
Scronkey **PR3** 55 H5
Scrooby **DN10** 51 J3
Scropton **DE65** 40 D2
Scrub Hill **LN4** 53 F7
Scruton **DL7** 62 E7
Sculthorpe **NR21** 44 C2
Scunthorpe DN15 52 B1
Scurlage **SA3** 17 H7
Sea **TA19** 8 C3
Sea Mills **BS9** 19 J4
Sea Palling **NR12** 45 J3
Seabank **PA37** 80 A3
Seaborough **DT8** 8 D4
Seaburn **SR6** 71 K7
Seacombe **CH41** 48 B3
Seacroft *Lincs.* **PE25** 53 J6
Seacroft *W.Yorks.* **LS14** 57 J6
Seadyke **PE20** 43 G2
Seafield *Arg. & B.* **PA31** 73 F2
Seafield *S.Ayr.* **KA7** 67 H1
Seafield *W.Loth.* **EH47** 75 J4
Seaford BN25 13 H7
Seaforth **L21** 48 C3
Seagrave **LE12** 41 J4
Seagry Heath **SN15** 20 C3
Seaham SR7 63 F2
Seaham Grange **SR7** 63 F1
Seahouses NE68 77 K4
Seal **TN15** 23 J6
Sealand **CH1** 48 C6
Seale **GU10** 22 B7
Sealyham **SA62** 16 C3
Seamer *N.Yorks.* **TS9** 63 F5
Seamer *N.Yorks.* **YO12** 59 G1
Seamill **KA23** 73 K6
Searby **DN38** 52 D2
Seasalter **CT5** 25 G5
Seascale CA20 60 B6
Seathorne **PE25** 53 J6
Seathwaite *Cumb.* **CA12** 60 D5
Seathwaite *Cumb.* **LA20** 60 D7
Seatle **LA11** 55 G1
Seatoller **CA12** 60 D5
Seaton *Cornw.* **PL11** 4 D5
Seaton *Cumb.* **CA14** 60 B3
Seaton *Devon* EX12 8 B5
Seaton *Dur.* **SR7** 62 E1
Seaton *E.Riding* **HU11** 59 H5
Seaton *Northumb.* **NE26** 71 J6
Seaton *Rut.* **LE15** 42 C6
Seaton Burn **NE13** 71 H6
Seaton Carew **TS25** 63 G4
Seaton Delaval **NE25** 71 J6
Seaton Junction **EX13** 8 B5
Seaton Ross **YO42** 58 D5
Seaton Sluice **NE26** 71 J6
Seatown *Aber.* **AB42** 99 J5
Seatown *Dorset* **DT6** 8 D5
Seatown *Moray* **AB56** 98 D4
Seave Green **TS9** 63 G6
Seaview PO34 11 H5
Seaville **CA7** 60 C1
Seavington St. Mary **TA19** 8 D3
Seavington St. Michael **TA19** 8 D3
Seawick **CO16** 35 F7
Sebastopol **NP4** 19 F2
Sebergham **CA5** 60 E2
Seckington **B79** 40 E5
Second Coast **IV22** 95 F2
Sedbergh LA10 61 H7
Sedbury **NP16** 19 J2
Sedbusk **DL8** 61 K7
Seddington **SG19** 32 E4
Sedgeberrow **WR11** 30 B5
Sedgebrook **NG32** 42 B2
Sedgefield **TS21** 62 E4
Sedgeford **PE36** 44 B2
Sedgehill **SP7** 9 H2
Sedgemere **CV8** 30 D1
Sedgley **DY3** 40 B6
Sedgwick **LA8** 55 J1
Sedlescombe **TN33** 14 C6
Sedlescombe Street **TN33** 14 C6
Seend **SN12** 20 C5
Seend Cleeve **SN12** 20 C5
Seer Green **HP9** 22 C2
Seething **NR15** 45 H6
Sefton **L29** 48 C2
Seghill **NE23** 71 H6
Seifton **SY8** 38 D7
Seighford **ST18** 40 A3
Seil **PA34** 79 J6
Seilebost **HS3** 93 F2
Seion **LL55** 46 D6
Seisdon **WV5** 40 A6
Seisiadar **HS2** 101 H4
Selattyn **SY10** 38 B2
Selborne **GU34** 11 J1
Selby YO8 58 C6
Selham **GU28** 12 C4
Selhurst **SE25** 23 G5
Selkirk TD7 69 K1
Sellack **HR9** 28 E6
Sellafield **CA20** 60 B6
Sellafirth **ZE2** 107 P3
Sellindge **TN25** 15 G4
Selling **ME13** 15 F2
Sells Green **SN12** 20 C5
Selly Oak **B29** 40 C7
Selmeston **BN26** 13 J6
Selsdon **CR2** 23 G5
Selsey **PO20** 12 B7
Selsfield Common **RH19** 13 G3
Selside *Cumb.* **LA8** 61 G7
Selside *N.Yorks.* **BD24** 56 C2
Selsley **GL5** 20 B1
Selstead **CT15** 15 H3
Selston **NG16** 51 G7
Selworthy **TA24** 7 H1
Semblister **ZE2** 107 M7
Semer **IP7** 34 D4
Semington **BA14** 20 B5
Semley **SP7** 9 H2
Send **GU23** 22 D6
Send Marsh **GU23** 22 D6
Senghenydd **CF83** 18 E2
Sennen **TR19** 2 A6
Sennen Cove **TR19** 2 A6
Sennybridge **LD3** 27 J6
Senwick **DG6** 65 G6
Sequer's Bridge **PL21** 5 G5
Serlby **DN10** 51 J4
Serrington **SP3** 10 B1
Sessay **YO7** 57 K2
Setchey **PE33** 44 A4
Setley **SO42** 10 E4
Setter *Shet.* **ZE2** 107 P8
Setter *Shet.* **ZE2** 107 M7
Settiscarth **KW17** 106 C6
Settle BD24 56 D3
Settrington **YO17** 58 E2
Seven Ash **TA4** 7 K2
Seven Bridges **SN6** 20 E2
Seven Kings **IG3** 23 H3
Seven Sisters **SA10** 18 B1
Seven Springs **GL53** 29 J7
Sevenhampton *Glos.* **GL54** 30 B6
Sevenhampton *Swin.* **SN6** 21 F2
Sevenoaks TN13 23 J6
Sevenoaks Weald **TN14** 23 J6
Severn Beach **BS35** 19 J3
Severn Stoke **WR8** 29 H4
Sevick End **MK44** 32 D3
Sevington **TN24** 15 F3
Sewards End **CB10** 33 J5
Sewardstone **E4** 23 G2
Sewerby **YO15** 59 H3
Seworgan **TR11** 2 E5
Sewstern **NG33** 42 B3
Seymour Villas **EX34** 6 C1
Sezincote **GL56** 30 C5
Sgarasta Mhòr **HS3** 93 F2
Sgiogarstaigh **HS2** 101 H1
Sgodachail **IV24** 96 B2
Shabbington **HP18** 21 K1
Shackerley **WV7** 40 A5
Shackerstone **CV13** 41 F5
Shackleford **GU8** 22 C7
Shadfen **NE61** 71 H5
Shadforth **DH6** 62 E2
Shadingfield **NR34** 45 J7
Shadoxhurst **TN26** 14 E4
Shadsworth **BB1** 56 C7
Shadwell *Norf.* **IP24** 44 D7
Shadwell *W.Yorks.* **LS17** 57 J5
Shaftenhoe End **SG8** 33 H5
Shaftesbury SP7 9 H2
Shafton **S72** 51 F1
Shalbourne **SN8** 21 G5
Shalcombe **PO41** 10 E6
Shalden **GU34** 21 K7
Shalden Green **GU34** 22 A7
Shaldon **TQ14** 5 K3
Shalfleet **PO30** 11 F6
Shalford *Essex* **CM7** 34 B6
Shalford *Surr.* **GU4** 22 D7
Shalford Green **CM7** 34 B6
Shallowford *Devon* **EX31** 7 F1
Shallowford *Staffs.* **ST15** 40 A3
Shalmsford Street **CT4** 15 F2
Shalmstry **KW14** 105 G2
Shalstone **MK18** 31 H5
Shalunt **PA20** 73 J3
Shambellie **DG2** 65 K4
Shamley Green **GU5** 22 D7
Shandon **G84** 74 A2
Shandwick **IV20** 97 F4
Shangton **LE8** 42 A6
Shankend **TD9** 70 A3
Shankhouse **NE23** 71 H6
Shanklin PO37 11 G6
Shannochie **KA27** 66 D1
Shantron **G83** 74 B2
Shantullich **IV8** 96 D6
Shanzie **PH11** 82 D2
Shap **CA10** 61 G5
Shapinsay **KW17** 106 E6
Shapwick *Dorset* **DT11** 9 J4
Shapwick *Som.* **TA7** 8 D1
Sharcott **SN9** 20 E6
Shard End **B34** 40 D7
Shardlow **DE72** 41 G2
Shareshill **WV10** 40 B5
Sharlston **WF4** 51 F1
Sharlston Common **WF4** 51 F1
Sharnal Street **ME3** 24 D4
Sharnbrook **MK44** 32 C3
Sharneyford **OL13** 56 D7
Sharnford **LE10** 41 G6
Sharnhill Green **DT2** 9 G4
Sharow **HG4** 57 J2
Sharp Street **NR29** 45 H3
Sharpenhoe **MK45** 32 D5
Sharperton **NE65** 70 E3
Sharpham House **TQ9** 5 J5
Sharpness **GL13** 19 K1
Sharpthorne **RH19** 13 G3
Sharrington **NR24** 44 E2
Shatterford **DY12** 39 G7
Shatterling **CT3** 15 H2
Shaugh Prior **PL7** 5 F4
Shave Cross **DT6** 8 D5
Shavington **CW2** 49 G7
Shaw *Gt.Man.* **OL2** 49 J2
Shaw *Swin.* **SN5** 20 E3
Shaw *W.Berks.* **RG14** 21 H5
Shaw *Wilts.* **SN12** 20 B5
Shaw Green *Herts.* **SG7** 33 F5
Shaw Green *N.Yorks.* **HG3** 57 H4
Shaw Mills **HG3** 57 H3
Shaw Side **OL2** 49 J2
Shawbost (Siabost) **HS2** 100 E3
Shawbury **SY4** 38 E3
Shawell **LE17** 41 H7
Shawfield *Gt.Man.* **OL12** 49 H1
Shawfield *Staffs.* **SK17** 50 C6
Shawford **SO21** 11 F2
Shawforth **OL12** 56 D7
Shawhead **DG2** 65 J3
Shawtonhill **ML10** 74 E6
Sheanachie **PA28** 66 B2
Sheandow **AB38** 89 K1
Shearington **DG1** 69 F7
Shearsby **LE17** 41 J6
Shebbear **EX21** 6 C5
Shebdon **ST20** 39 G3
Shebster **KW14** 105 F2
Shedfield **SO32** 11 G3
Sheen **SK17** 50 D6
Sheepridge **HD2** 50 D1
Sheepscombe **GL6** 29 H7
Sheepstor **PL20** 5 F4
Sheepwash *Devon* **EX21** 6 C5
Sheepwash *Northumb.* **NE62** 71 H5
Sheepway **BS20** 19 H4
Sheepy Magna **CV9** 41 F5
Sheepy Parva **CV9** 41 F5
Sheering **CM22** 33 J7
Sheerness ME12 25 F4
Sheet **GU32** 11 J2
SHEFFIELD S 51 F4
Sheffield Bottom **RG7** 21 K5
Sheffield Green **TN22** 13 H4
Shefford SG17 32 E5
Shefford Woodlands **RG17** 21 G4
Sheigra **IV27** 102 D2
Sheinton **SY5** 39 F5
Shelderton **SY7** 28 D1
Sheldon *Derbys.* **DE45** 50 D6
Sheldon *Devon* **EX14** 7 K5
Sheldon *W.Mid.* **B26** 40 D7
Sheldwich **ME13** 15 F2
Sheldwich Lees **ME13** 15 F2
Shelf *Bridgend* **CF35** 18 C3
Shelf *W.Yorks.* **HX3** 57 G7
Shelfanger **IP22** 45 F7
Shelfield *W.Mid.* **WS4** 40 C5
Shelfield *Warks.* **B49** 30 C2
Shelfield Green **B49** 30 C2
Shelford **NG12** 41 J1

Shellachan Arg. & B. PA34 79 K5
Shellachan Arg. & B. PA35 80 B5
Shellbrook LE65 41 F4
Shellbrook Hill SY12 38 C1
Shelley Essex CM5 23 J1
Shelley Suff. IP7 34 E5
Shelley W.Yorks. HD8 50 E1
Shellingford SN7 21 G2
Shellow Bowells CM5 24 C1
Shelsley Beauchamp WR6 29 G2
Shelsley Walsh WR6 29 G2
Shelswell MK18 31 H5
Shelthorpe LE11 41 H4
Shelton Beds. PE28 32 D2
Shelton Norf. NR15 45 G6
Shelton Notts. NG23 42 A1
Shelton Shrop. SY3 38 D4
Shelve SY5 38 C6
Shelwick HR1 28 E4
Shelwick Green HR1 28 E4
Shenfield CM15 24 C2
Shenington OX15 30 E4
Shenley WD7 22 E1
Shenley Brook End MK5 32 B5
Shenley Church End MK5 32 B5
Shenleybury WD7 22 E1
Shenmore HR2 28 C5
Shennanton DG8 64 D4
Shenstone Staffs. WS14 40 D5
Shenstone Worcs. DY10 29 H1
Shenstone Woodend WS14 40 D5
Shenton CV13 41 F5
Shenval AB37 89 K2
Shepeau Stow PE12 43 G4
Shephall SG2 33 F6
Shepherd's Bush W12 23 F4
Shepherd's Green RG9 22 A3
Shepherd's Patch GL2 20 A1
Shepherdswell (Sibertswold) CT15 15 H3
Shepley HD8 50 D2
Sheppardstown KW3 105 H5
Shepperdine BS35 19 K2
Shepperton TW17 22 D5
Shepreth SG8 33 G4
Shepshed LE12 41 G4
Shepton Beauchamp TA19 8 D3
Shepton Mallet BA4 19 K7
Shepton Montague BA9 9 F1
Shepway ME15 14 C2
Sheraton TS27 63 F3
Sherborne Dorset DT9 9 F3
Sherborne Glos. GL54 30 C7
Sherborne St. John RG24 21 K6
Sherbourne CV35 30 D2
Sherbourne Street CO10 34 D4
Sherburn Dur. DH6 62 E2
Sherburn N.Yorks. YO17 59 F2
Sherburn Hill DH6 62 E2
Sherburn in Elmet LS25 57 K6
Shere GU5 22 D7
Shereford NR21 44 C3
Sherfield English SO51 10 D2
Sherfield on Loddon RG27 21 K6
Sherford Devon TQ7 5 H6
Sherford Som. TA1 8 B2
Sheriff Hutton YO60 58 C3
Sheriffhales TF11 39 G4
Sheringham NR26 45 F1
Sherington MK16 32 B4
Shernal Green WR9 29 J2
Shernborne PE31 44 B2
Sherramore PH20 88 C5
Sherrington BA12 9 J1
Sherston SN16 20 B3
Sherwood NG5 41 H1
Sherwood Green EX31 6 D3
SHETLAND ISLANDS ZE 107 M7
Shettleston G32 74 E4
Shevington WN6 48 E2
Shevington Moor WN6 48 E1
Sheviock PL11 4 D5
Shide PO30 11 G6
Shiel Bridge IV40 87 F3
Shieldaig High. IV54 94 E6
Shieldaig High. IV21 94 E4
Shieldhill FK1 75 G3
Shielfoot PH36 86 C7
Shielhill DD8 83 F2
Shiels AB51 90 E4
Shifford OX29 21 G1
Shifnal TF11 39 G5
Shilbottle NE66 71 G3
Shildon DL4 62 D4
Shillingford Devon EX16 7 H3
Shillingford Oxon. OX10 21 J2
Shillingford Abbot EX2 7 H7
Shillingford St. George EX2 7 H7
Shillingstone DT11 9 H3
Shillington SG5 32 E5
Shillmoor NE65 70 D3
Shilstone EX20 6 D5
Shilton Oxon. OX18 21 F1
Shilton Warks. CV7 41 G7
Shimpling Norf. IP21 45 F7
Shimpling Suff. IP29 34 C3
Shimpling Street IP29 34 C3
Shincliffe DH1 62 D2
Shiney Row DH4 62 E1
Shinfield RG2 22 A5
Shingay SG8 33 G4
Shingham PE37 44 B5
Shingle Street IP12 35 H4
Shinness Lodge IV27 103 H7
Shipbourne TN11 23 J6
Shipbrookhill CW9 49 F5
Shipdham IP25 44 D5
Shipham BS25 19 H6
Shiphay TQ2 5 J4
Shiplake RG9 22 A4
Shiplake Row RG9 22 A4
Shipley Northumb. NE66 71 G2
Shipley Shrop. WV6 40 A6
Shipley W.Suss. RH13 12 E4
Shipley W.Yorks. BD18 57 G6
Shipley Bridge Devon TQ10 5 G4
Shipley Bridge Surr. RH6 23 G7
Shipley Common DE7 41 G1
Shipmeadow NR34 45 H6
Shippea Hill CB7 44 A7
Shippon OX13 21 H2
Shipston on Stour CV36 30 D4
Shipton Glos. GL54 30 B7
Shipton N.Yorks. YO30 58 B4
Shipton Shrop. TF13 38 E6
Shipton Bellinger SP9 21 F7
Shipton Gorge DT6 8 D5
Shipton Green PO20 12 B6
Shipton Moyne GL8 20 B3
Shipton Oliffe GL54 30 B7
Shipton Solers GL54 30 B7
Shipton-on-Cherwell OX5 31 F7
Shiptonthorpe YO43 58 E5
Shipton-under-Wychwood OX7 30 D7
Shira PA32 80 C6
Shirburn OX49 21 K2
Shirdley Hill L39 48 C1
Shire Oak WS8 40 C5
Shirebrook NG20 51 H6
Shirecliffe S5 51 F3
Shiregreen S5 51 F3
Shirehampton BS11 19 J4
Shiremoor NE27 71 J6
Shirenewton NP16 19 H2
Shireoaks S81 51 H4
Shirl Heath HR6 28 D3
Shirland DE55 51 F7
Shirley Derbys. DE6 40 E1
Shirley Gt.Lon. CR0 23 G5
Shirley Hants. BH23 10 C5
Shirley S'ham. SO15 11 F3
Shirley W.Mid. B90 30 C1
Shirley Heath B90 30 C1
Shirley Warren SO16 10 E3
Shirleywich ST18 40 B3
Shirrell Heath SO32 11 G3
Shirwell EX31 6 D2
Shirwell Cross EX31 6 D2
Shiskine KA27 66 D1
Shittlehope DL13 62 B3
Shobdon HR6 28 C2
Shobley BH24 10 C4
Shobrooke EX17 7 G5
Shocklach SY14 38 D1
Shocklach Green SY14 38 D1
Shoeburyness SS3 25 F3
Sholden CT14 15 J2
Sholing SO19 11 F3
Shoot Hill SY5 38 D4
Shooter's Hill DA16 23 H4
Shop Cornw. PL28 3 F1
Shop Cornw. EX23 6 A4
Shop Corner IP9 35 G5
Shopnoller TA4 7 K2
Shore OL15 49 J1
Shoreditch N1 23 G3
Shoreham TN14 23 J5
Shoreham Airport BN15 12 E6
Shoreham-by-Sea BN43 13 F6
Shoremill IV11 96 E5
Shoresdean TD15 77 H6
Shoreswood TD15 77 H6
Shoreton IV7 96 D5
Shorley SO24 11 G2
Shorncote GL7 20 D2
Shorne DA12 24 C4
Shorne Ridgeway DA12 24 C4
Short Cross SY21 38 B5
Short Green IP22 44 E7
Short Heath Derbys. DE12 41 F4
Short Heath W.Mid. B23 40 C6
Shortacombe EX20 6 D7
Shortbridge TN22 13 H4
Shortfield Common GU10 22 B7
Shortgate BN8 13 H5
Shortgrove CB11 33 J5
Shorthampton OX7 30 E6
Shortlands BR2 23 G5
Shortlanesend TR4 3 F4
Shorton TQ3 5 J4
Shorwell PO30 11 F6
Shoscombe BA2 20 A6
Shotatton SY4 38 C3
Shotesham NR15 45 G6
Shotgate SS11 24 D2
Shotley Northants. NN17 42 C6
Shotley Suff. IP9 35 G5
Shotley Bridge DH8 62 B1
Shotley Gate IP9 35 G5
Shotleyfield DH8 62 B1
Shottenden CT4 15 F2
Shottermill GU27 12 B3
Shottery CV37 30 C3
Shotteswell OX17 31 F4
Shottisham IP12 35 H4
Shottle DE56 41 F1
Shottlegate DE56 41 F1
Shotton Dur. SR8 63 F3
Shotton Dur. TS21 62 E4
Shotton Flints. CH5 48 C6
Shotton Northumb. NE13 71 H6
Shotton Colliery DH6 62 E2
Shotts ML7 75 G4
Shotwick CH1 48 C5
Shouldham PE33 44 A5
Shouldham Thorpe PE33 44 A5
Shoulton WR2 29 H3
Shover's Green TN5 13 K3
Shrawardine SY4 38 C4
Shrawley WR6 29 H2
Shreding Green SL0 22 D3
Shrewley CV35 30 D2
SHREWSBURY SY 38 D4
Shrewton SP3 20 D7
Shripney PO22 12 C6
Shrivenham SN6 21 F3
Shropham NR17 44 D6
Shroton (Iwerne Courtney) DT11 9 H3
Shrub End CO2 34 D6
Shucknall HR1 28 E4
Shudy Camps CB1 33 K4
Shurdington GL51 29 J7
Shurlock Row RG10 22 B4
Shurnock B96 30 B2
Shurrery KW14 105 F3
Shurrery Lodge KW14 105 F3
Shurton TA5 19 F7
Shustoke B46 40 E6
Shut Heath ST18 40 A3
Shute Devon EX13 8 B5
Shute Devon EX17 7 G5
Shutford OX15 30 E4
Shuthonger GL20 29 H5
Shutlanger NN12 31 J4
Shutt Green ST19 40 A5
Shuttington B79 40 E5
Shuttlewood S44 51 G5
Shuttleworth BL0 49 G1
Siabost (Shawbost) HS2 100 E3
Siabost Bho Dheas HS2 100 E3
Siabost Bho Thuath HS2 100 E3
Siadar Iarach HS2 101 F2
Siadar Uarach HS2 101 F2
Sibbaldbie DG11 69 G5
Sibbertoft LE16 41 J7
Sibdon Carwood SY7 38 D7
Sibertswold (Shepherdswell) CT15 15 H3
Sibford Ferris OX15 30 E5
Sibford Gower OX15 30 E5
Sible Hedingham CO9 34 B5
Sibley's Green CM6 33 K6
Sibsey PE22 53 G7
Sibson Cambs. PE8 42 D6
Sibson Leics. CV13 41 F5
Sibster KW1 105 J3
Sibthorpe NG23 42 A1
Sibton IP17 35 H2
Sibton Green IP17 35 H1
Sicklesmere IP30 34 C2
Sicklinghall LS22 57 J5
Sidbury Devon EX10 7 K6
Sidbury Shrop. WV16 39 F7
Sidcot BS25 19 H6
Sidcup DA14 23 H4
Siddal HX3 57 G7
Siddington Ches. SK11 49 H5
Siddington Glos. GL7 20 D2
Sidemoor B61 29 J1
Sidestrand NR27 45 G2
Sidford EX10 7 K6
Sidlesham PO20 12 B7
Sidley TN39 14 C7
Sidlow RH2 23 F7
Sidmouth EX10 7 K7
Sigford TQ12 5 H3
Sigglesthorne HU11 59 H5
Sigingstone CF71 18 C4
Signet OX18 30 D7
Silchester RG7 21 K5
Sildinis HS2 100 E6
Sileby LE12 41 J4
Silecroft LA18 54 E1
Silfield NR18 45 F6
Silian SA48 26 E3
Silk Willoughby NG34 42 D1
Silkstead SO21 11 F2
Silkstone S75 50 E2
Silkstone Common S75 50 E2
Sill Field LA8 55 J1
Silloth CA7 60 C1
Sills NE19 70 D3
Sillyearn AB55 98 D5
Silpho YO13 63 J3
Silsden BD20 57 F5
Silsoe MK45 32 D5
Silver End Beds. MK45 32 E4
Silver End Essex CM8 34 C6
Silver Green NR15 45 G6
Silver Street Kent ME9 24 E5
Silver Street Som. TA11 8 E1
Silverburn EH26 76 A4
Silvercraigs PA31 73 G2
Silverdale Lancs. LA5 55 H2
Silverdale Staffs. ST5 40 A1
Silvergate NR11 45 F3
Silverhill TN37 14 C6
Silverlace Green IP13 35 H3
Silverley's Green IP19 35 G1
Silvermoss AB51 91 G1
Silverstone NN12 31 H4
Silverton EX5 7 H5
Silvington DY14 29 F1
Silwick ZE2 107 L8
Simister M25 49 H2
Simmondley SK13 50 C3
Simonburn NE48 70 D6
Simonsbath TA24 7 F2
Simonside NE34 71 J7
Simonstone Bridgend CF35 18 C3
Simonstone Lancs. BB12 56 C6
Simprim TD12 77 G6
Simpson MK6 32 B5
Sinclair's Hill TD11 77 G5
Sinclairston KA18 67 J2
Sinderby YO7 57 J1
Sinderhope NE47 61 K1
Sindlesham RG41 22 A5
Sinfin DE24 41 F2
Singdean TD9 70 A3
Singleton Lancs. FY6 55 G6
Singleton W.Suss. PO18 12 B5
Singlewell DA12 24 C4
Singret LL12 48 C7
Sinkhurst Green TN12 14 D3
Sinnahard AB33 90 C3
Sinnington YO62 58 D1
Sinton Green WR2 29 H2
Sipson UB7 22 D4
Sirhowy NP22 28 A7
Sisland NR14 45 H6
Sissinghurst TN17 14 C4
Siston BS16 19 K4
Sithney TR13 2 D6
Sittingbourne ME10 25 F5
Siulaisiadar HS2 101 H4
Six Ashes WV15 39 G7
Six Hills LE14 41 J3
Six Mile Bottom CB8 33 J3
Six Roads End DE6 40 D3
Sixhills LN8 52 E4
Sixmile CT4 15 G3
Sixpenny Handley SP5 10 B3
Sizewell IP16 35 J2
Skail KW11 104 C4
Skaill Ork. KW16 106 B6
Skaill Ork. KW17 106 E7
Skaill Ork. KW17 106 D4
Skares Aber. AB54 90 E1
Skares E.Ayr. KA18 67 K2
Skarpigarth ZE2 107 K7
Skateraw EH42 77 F3
Skaw ZE2 107 P6
Skeabost IV51 93 K7
Skeabrae KW17 106 B5
Skeeby DL10 62 D6
Skeffington LE7 42 A5
Skeffling HU12 53 G1
Skegby NG17 51 H6
Skegness PE25 53 J6
Skelberry Shet. ZE2 107 M11
Skelberry Shet. ZE2 107 N6
Skelbo IV25 96 E2
Skelbo Street IV25 96 E2
Skelbrooke DN6 51 H1
Skeld (Easter Skeld) ZE2 107 M8
Skeldon KA6 67 H2
Skeldyke PE20 43 G2
Skellingthorpe LN6 52 C5
Skellister ZE2 107 N7
Skellow DN6 51 H1
Skelmanthorpe HD8 50 E1
Skelmersdale WN8 48 D2
Skelmonae AB41 91 G1
Skelmorlie PA17 73 K4
Skelmuir AB42 99 H6
Skelpick KW14 104 C3
Skelton Cumb. CA11 60 F3
Skelton E.Riding DN14 58 D7
Skelton N.Yorks. DL11 62 B6
Skelton (Skelton-in-Cleveland) R. & C. TS12 63 H5
Skelton York YO30 58 B4
Skelton-in-Cleveland (Skelton) TS12 63 H5
Skelton-on-Ure HG4 57 J3
Skelwick KW17 106 D3
Skelwith Bridge LA22 60 E6
Skendleby PE23 53 H6
Skendleby Psalter LN13 53 H5
Skenfrith NP7 28 D6
Skerne YO25 59 G4
Skeroblingarry PA28 66 B1
Skerray KW14 103 J2
Skerton LA1 55 H3
Sketchley LE10 41 G6
Sketty SA2 17 K6
Skewen SA10 18 A2
Skewsby YO61 58 C2
Skeyton NR10 45 G3
Skeyton Corner NR10 45 G3
Skidbrooke LN11 53 H3
Skidbrooke North End LN11 53 H3
Skidby HU16 59 G6
Skilgate TA4 7 H3
Skillington NG33 42 B3
Skinburness CA7 60 C1
Skinflats FK2 75 H2
Skinidin IV55 93 H7
Skinnet KW12 105 G2
Skinningrove TS13 63 J5
Skipness PA29 73 G5
Skippool FY5 55 G5
Skipsea YO25 59 H4
Skipsea Brough YO25 59 H4
Skipton BD23 56 E4
Skipton-on-Swale YO7 57 J2
Skipwith YO8 58 C6
Skirbeck PE21 43 G1
Skirbeck Quarter PE21 43 G1
Skirethorns BD23 56 E3
Skirlaugh HU11 59 H6
Skirling ML12 75 J7
Skirmett RG9 22 A3
Skirpenbeck YO41 58 D4
Skirwith Cumb. CA10 61 H3
Skirwith N.Yorks. LA6 56 C2
Skirza KW1 105 J2
Skittle Green HP27 22 A1
Skomer Island SA62 16 A5
Skulamus IV42 86 C2
Skullomie IV27 103 J2
Skyborry Green LD7 28 B1
Skye IV 85 K1
Skye Green CO5 34 C6
Skye of Curr PH26 89 G2
Skyreholme BD23 57 F3
Slack Aber. AB52 90 D1
Slack Derbys. S45 51 F6
Slack W.Yorks. HX7 56 E7
Slackhall SK23 50 C4
Slackhead AB56 98 C4
Slad GL6 20 B1
Slade Devon EX34 6 D1
Slade Devon EX14 7 K5
Slade Pembs. SA61 16 C4
Slade Swan. SA3 17 H7
Slade Green DA8 23 J4
Slade Hooton S25 51 H4
Sladesbridge PL27 4 A3
Slaggyford CA8 61 H1
Slaidburn BB7 56 C4
Slains Park DD10 91 G7
Slaithwaite HD7 50 C1
Slaley NE47 62 A1
Slamannan FK1 75 G3
Slapton Bucks. LU7 32 C6
Slapton Devon TQ7 5 J6
Slapton Northants. NN12 31 H4
Slate Haugh AB56 98 C4
Slatepit Dale S42 51 F6
Slattadale IV22 94 E4
Slaugham RH17 13 F4
Slaughden IP15 35 J3
Slaughterford SN14 20 B4
Slawston LE16 42 A6
Sleaford Hants. GU35 12 B3
Sleaford Lincs. NG34 42 D1
Sleagill CA10 61 G5
Sleap SY4 38 D3
Sledge Green WR13 29 H5
Sledmere YO25 59 F3
Sleights YO22 63 K6
Slepe BH16 9 J5
Slerra EX39 6 B3
Slickly KW1 105 H2
Sliddery KA27 66 D1
Sliemore PH25 89 H2
Sligachan IV47 85 K2
Slimbridge GL2 20 A1
Slindon Staffs. ST21 40 A2
Slindon W.Suss. BN18 12 C6
Slinfold RH13 12 E3
Sling GL16 19 J1
Slingsby YO62 58 C2
Slioch AB54 90 D1
Slip End Beds. LU1 32 D7
Slip End Herts. SG7 33 F5
Slipton NN14 32 C1
Slitting Mill WS15 40 C4
Slochd PH23 89 F2
Slockavullin PA31 73 G1
Slogarie DG7 65 G4
Sloley NR12 45 G3
Slongaber DG2 65 J3
Sloothby LN13 53 H5
SLOUGH SL 22 C3
Slough Green Som. TA3 8 B2
Slough Green W.Suss. RH17 13 F4
Sluggan PH23 89 F2
Slyne LA2 55 H3
Smailholm TD5 76 E7
Small Dole BN5 13 F5
Small Hythe TN30 14 D4
Smallbridge OL16 49 J1
Smallbrook EX5 7 G6
Smallburgh NR12 45 H3
Smallburn Aber. AB42 99 J6
Smallburn E.Ayr. KA18 68 B1
Smalldale SK17 50 C5
Smalley DE7 41 G1
Smallfield RH6 23 G7
Smallford AL4 22 E1
Smallridge EX13 8 B4
Smallthorne ST6 49 H7
Smallworth IP22 44 E7
Smannell SP11 21 G7
Smardale CA17 61 J6
Smarden TN27 14 D3
Smaull PA44 72 A4
Smeatharpe EX14 7 K4
Smeeth TN25 15 F4
Smeeton Westerby LE8 41 J6
Smerclet HS8 84 C3
Smerral KW5 105 G5
Smestow DY3 40 A6
Smethwick B66 40 C7
Smethwick Green CW11 49 H6
Smirisary PH38 86 C7
Smisby LE65 41 F4
Smith End Green WR13 29 G3
Smithfield CA6 69 K7
Smithies S71 51 F2
Smithincott EX15 7 J4
Smith's End SG8 33 G5
Smith's Green Essex CM22 33 J6
Smith's Green Essex CB9 33 K4
Smithstown IV21 94 D4
Smithton IV2 96 E7
Smithy Green WA16 49 G5
Smockington LE10 41 G7
Smyrton KA26 67 F5
Smythe's Green CO5 34 D7
Snailbeach SY5 38 C5
Snailwell CB8 33 K2
Snainton YO13 59 F1
Snaith DN14 58 C7
Snape N.Yorks. DL8 57 H1
Snape Suff. IP17 35 H3
Snape Green PR8 48 C1
Snape Watering IP17 35 H3
Snarestone DE12 41 F5

Snarford **LN8** 52 D4
Snargate **TN29** 14 E5
Snave **TN29** 15 F5
Sneachill **WR7** 29 J3
Snead **SY15** 38 C6
Snead's Green **DY13** 29 H2
Sneath Common **NR15** 45 F7
Sneaton **YO22** 63 K6
Sneatonthorpe **YO22** 63 J2
Snelland **LN3** 52 D4
Snellings **CA22** 60 A6
Snelston **DE6** 40 D1
Snetterton **NR16** 44 D6
Snettisham **PE31** 44 A2
Snipeshill **ME10** 25 F5
Sniseabhal (Snishival) **HS8** 84 C1
Snishival (Sniseabhal) **HS8** 84 C1
Snitter **NE65** 71 F3
Snitterby **DN21** 52 C3
Snitterfield **CV37** 30 D3
Snitterton **DE4** 50 E6
Snittlegarth **CA7** 60 D3
Snitton **SY8** 28 E1
Snodhill **HR3** 28 C4
Snodland ME6 **24 D5**
Snow End **SG9** 33 H5
Snow Street **IP22** 44 E7
Snowden Hill **S35** 50 E2
Snowshill **WR12** 30 B5
Soar *Cardiff* **CF15** 18 D3
Soar *Carmar.* **SA19** 17 K3
Soar *Devon* **TQ7** 5 H7
Soay **PH41** 85 K3
Soberton **SO32** 11 H3
Soberton Heath **SO32** 11 H3
Sockbridge **CA10** 61 G4
Sockburn **DL2** 62 E6
Sodom **LL16** 47 J5
Sodylt Bank **SY12** 38 C2
Softley **DL13** 62 B4
Soham **CB7** 33 J1
Soham Cotes **CB7** 33 J1
Solas (Sollas) **HS6** 92 D4
Soldon **EX22** 6 B4
Soldon Cross **EX22** 6 B4
Soldridge **GU34** 11 H1
Sole Street *Kent* **CT4** 15 F3
Sole Street *Kent* **DA12** 24 C5
Soleburn **DG9** 64 A4
Solihull B91 **30 C1**
Solihull Lodge **B90** 30 B1
Sollas (Solas) **HS6** 92 D4
Sollers Dilwyn **HR4** 28 D3
Sollers Hope **HR1** 29 F5
Sollom **PR4** 48 D1
Solomon's Tump **GL19** 29 G7
Solsgirth **FK14** 75 H1
Solva **SA62** 16 A3
Solwaybank **DG14** 69 J6
Somerby *Leics.* **LE14** 42 A4
Somerby *Lincs.* **DN38** 52 D2
Somercotes **DE55** 51 G7
Somerford **ST19** 40 B5
Somerford Keynes **GL7** 20 D2
Somerley **PO20** 12 B7
Somerleyton **NR32** 45 J6
Somersal Herbert **DE6** 40 D2
Somersby **PE23** 53 G5
Somersham *Cambs.* **PE28** 33 G1
Somersham *Suff.* **IP8** 34 E4
Somerton *Newport* **NP19** 19 G3
Somerton *Oxon.* **OX25** 31 F6
Somerton *Som.* TA11 **8 D2**
Somerton *Suff.* **IP29** 34 C3
Sompting **BN15** 12 E6
Sompting Abbotts **BN15** 12 E6
Sonning **RG4** 22 A4
Sonning Common **RG4** 22 A3
Sonning Eye **RG4** 22 A4
Sontley **LL13** 38 C1
Sookholme **NG19** 51 H6
Sopley **BH23** 10 C5
Sopworth **SN14** 20 B3
Sorbie **DG8** 64 E6
Sordale **KW12** 105 G2
Sorisdale **PA78** 78 D1
Sorn **KA5** 67 K1
Sornhill **KA4** 74 D7
Soroba **PA34** 79 K5
Sortat **KW1** 105 H2
Sotby **LN8** 53 F5
Sots Hole **LN4** 52 E6
Sotterley **NR34** 45 J7
Soudley **TF9** 39 G3
Soughton **CH7** 48 B6
Soulbury **LU7** 32 B6
Soulby **CA17** 61 J5
Souldern **OX27** 31 G5
Souldrop **MK44** 32 C2
Sound *Ches.* **CW5** 39 F1
Sound *Shet.* **ZE1** 107 N8
Sound *Shet.* **ZE2** 107 M7
Sourhope **TD5** 70 D1
Sourin **KW17** 106 D4
Sourton **EX20** 6 D6
Soutergate **LA17** 55 F1
South Acre **PE32** 44 C4
South Acton **W5** 22 E4
South Alkham **CT15** 15 H3
South Allington **TQ7** 5 H7
South Alloa **FK7** 75 G1
South Ambersham **GU29** 12 C4
South Anston **S25** 51 H4
South Ascot **SL5** 22 C5
South Baddesley **SO41** 10 E5
South Ballachulish **PH49** 80 B2
South Balloch **KA26** 67 H4
South Bank **TS6** 63 G4
South Barrow **BA22** 9 F2
South Bellsdyke **FK2** 75 H2
South Benfleet SS7 **24 D3**
South Bersted **PO22** 12 C6
South Blackbog **AB51** 91 F1
South Bockhampton **BH23** 10 C5
South Bowood **DT6** 8 D5
South Brent TQ10 **5 G4**
South Brentor **PL19** 6 C7
South Brewham **BA10** 9 G1
South Broomhill **NE61** 71 H4
South Burlingham **NR13** 45 H5
South Cadbury **BA22** 9 F2
South Cairn **DG9** 66 D7
South Carlton **LN1** 52 C5
South Cave **HU15** 59 F6
South Cerney **GL7** 20 D2
South Chard **TA20** 8 C4
South Charlton **NE66** 71 G1
South Cheriton **BA8** 9 F2
South Church **DL14** 62 D4
South Cliffe **YO43** 58 E6
South Clifton **NG23** 52 B5
South Cockerington **LN11** 53 G4
South Collafirth **ZE2** 107 M4
South Common **BN8** 13 G5
South Cornelly **CF33** 18 B3
South Corriegills **KA27** 73 J7
South Cove **NR34** 45 J7
South Creagan **PA37** 80 A3
South Creake **NR21** 44 C2
South Crosland **HD4** 50 D1
South Croxton **LE7** 41 J4
South Dalton **HU17** 59 F5
South Darenth **DA4** 23 J4
South Dell
(Dail Bho Dheas) **HS2** 101 G1
South Duffield **YO8** 58 C6
South Elkington **LN11** 53 F4
South Elmsall **WF9** 51 G1
South End *Bucks.* **LU7** 32 B6
South End *Cumb.* **LA14** 55 F3
South End *Hants.* **SP6** 10 C3
South End *N.Lincs.* **DN19** 59 H7
South Erradale **IV21** 94 D4
South Fambridge **SS4** 24 E2
South Fawley **OX12** 21 G3
South Ferriby **DN18** 59 F7
South Field **HU13** 59 G7
South Flobbets **AB51** 91 F1
South Garth **ZE2** 107 P3
South Godstone **RH9** 23 G7
South Gorley **SP6** 10 C3
South Green *Essex* **CM11** 24 C2
South Green *Essex* **CO5** 34 E7
South Green *Norf.* **NR20** 44 E4
South Green *Suff.* **IP23** 35 F1
South Gyle **EH12** 75 K3
South Hall **PA22** 73 J3
South Hanningfield **CM3** 24 D2
South Harefield **UB9** 22 D3
South Harting **GU31** 11 J3
South Hayling **PO11** 11 J5
South Hazelrigg **NE66** 77 J7
South Heath **HP16** 22 C1
South Heighton **BN9** 13 H6
South Hetton **DH6** 62 E2
South Hiendley **S72** 51 F1
South Hill **PL17** 4 D3
South Hinksey **OX1** 21 J1
South Hole **EX39** 6 A4
South Holme **YO62** 58 C2
South Holmwood **RH5** 22 E7
South Hornchurch **RM13** 23 J3
South Hourat **KA24** 74 A5
South Huish **TQ7** 5 G6
South Hykeham **LN6** 52 C6
South Hylton **SR4** 62 E1
South Kelsey **LN7** 52 D3
South Kessock **IV3** 96 D7
South Killingholme **DN40** 52 E1
South Kilvington **YO7** 57 K1
South Kilworth **LE17** 41 J7
South Kirkby **WF9** 51 G1
South Kirkton **AB32** 91 F4
South Knighton **TQ12** 5 J3
South Kyme **LN4** 42 E1
South Lancing **BN15** 12 E6
South Ledaig **PA37** 80 A4
South Leigh **OX29** 21 G1
South Leverton **DN22** 51 K4
South Littleton **WR11** 30 B4
South Lopham **IP22** 44 E7
South Luffenham **LE15** 42 C5
South Malling **BN7** 13 H5
South Marston **SN3** 20 E3
South Middleton **NE71** 70 E1
South Milford **LS25** 57 K6
South Milton **TQ7** 5 G6
South Mimms **EN6** 23 F1
South Molton EX36 **7 F3**
South Moor **DH9** 62 C1
South Moreton **OX11** 21 J3
South Mundham **PO20** 12 B6
South Muskham **NG23** 51 K7
South Newbald **YO43** 59 F6
South Newington **OX15** 31 F5
South Newton **SP2** 10 B1
South Normanton **DE55** 51 G7
South Norwood **SE25** 23 G5
South Nutfield **RH1** 23 G7
South Ockendon RM15 **23 J3**
South Ormsby **LN11** 53 G5
South Ossett **WF5** 50 E1
South Otterington **DL7** 57 J1
South Owersby **LN8** 52 D3
South Oxhey **WD19** 22 E2
South Park **RH2** 23 F7
South Parks **KY6** 82 D7
South Perrott **DT8** 8 D4
South Petherton TA13 **8 D3**
South Petherwin **PL15** 6 B7
South Pickenham **PE37** 44 C5
South Pool **TQ7** 5 H6
South Queensferry
(Queensferry) EH30 **75 K3**
South Radworthy **EX36** 7 F2
South Rauceby **NG34** 42 D1
South Raynham **NR21** 44 C3
South Redbriggs **AB53** 99 F6
South Reston **LN11** 53 H4
South Ronaldsay **KW17** 106 D9
South Ruislip **HA4** 22 E3
South Runcton **PE33** 44 A5
South Scarle **NG23** 52 B6
South Shian **PA37** 80 A3
South Shields NE33 **71 J7**
South Somercotes **LN11** 53 H3
South Somercotes
Fen Houses **LN11** 53 H3
South Stainley **HG3** 57 J3
South Stoke *Oxon.* **RG8** 21 K3
South Stoke *W.Suss.* **BN18** 12 D6
South Street *E.Suss.* **BN8** 13 G5
South Street *Gt.Lon.* **TN16** 23 H6
South Street *Kent* **DA13** 24 C5
South Street *Kent* **CT5** 25 H5
South Street *Kent* **ME9** 24 E5
South Tawton **EX20** 6 E6
South Thoresby **LN13** 53 H5
South Tidworth **SP9** 21 F7
South Tottenham **N15** 23 G3
South Town *Devon* **EX6** 7 H7
South Town *Hants.* **GU34** 11 H1
South Uist
(Uibhist a Deas) HS8 **84 C1**
South Upper Barrack **AB41** 99 H6
South View **RG21** 21 K6
South Walsham **NR13** 45 H4
South Warnborough **RG29** 22 A7
South Weald **CM14** 23 J2
South Weston **OX9** 22 A2
South Wheatley *Cornw.*
PL15 4 C1
South Wheatley *Notts.*
DN22 51 K4
South Whiteness **ZE2** 107 M8
South Wigston **LE18** 41 H6
South Willingham **LN8** 52 E4
South Wingfield **DE55** 51 F7
South Witham **NG33** 42 C4
South Wonston **SO21** 11 F1
South Woodham Ferrers
CM3 24 E2
South Wootton **PE30** 44 A3
South Wraxall **BA15** 20 B5
South Yardley **B26** 40 D7
South Zeal **EX20** 6 E6
SOUTHALL UB **22 E3**
Southam *Glos.* **GL52** 29 J6
Southam *Warks.* CV47 **31 F2**
SOUTHAMPTON SO **11 F3**
Southampton Airport **SO18** 11 F3
Southbar **PA4** 74 C4
Southborough *Gt.Lon.*
BR2 23 H5
Southborough *Kent* **TN4** 23 J7
Southbourne *Bourne.* **BH6** 10 C5
Southbourne *W.Suss.*
PO10 11 J4
Southbrook **EX5** 7 J6
Southburgh **IP25** 44 E5
Southburn **YO25** 59 F4
Southchurch **SS1** 25 F3
Southcott *Devon* **EX20** 6 D6
Southcott *Wilts.* **SN9** 20 E6
Southcourt **HP21** 32 B7
Southdean **TD9** 70 B3
Southdene **L32** 48 D3
Southease **BN7** 13 H6
Southend *Aber.* **AB53** 99 F6
Southend *Arg. & B.* **PA28** 66 A3
Southend *Bucks.* **RG9** 22 A3
Southend *W.Berks.* **RG7** 21 J4
Southend *Wilts.* **SN8** 20 E4
Southend Airport **SS2** 24 E3
SOUTHEND-ON-SEA SS **24 E3**
Southerfield **CA7** 60 C2
Southerly **EX20** 6 D7
Southern Green **SG9** 33 G5
Southerndown **CF32** 18 B4
Southerness **DG2** 65 K5
Southery **PE38** 44 A6
Southfield **KY6** 76 A1
Southfields **SW18** 23 F4
Southfleet **DA13** 24 C4
Southgate *Cere.* **SY23** 36 E7
Southgate *Gt.Lon.* **N14** 23 G2
Southgate *Norf.* **NR10** 45 F3
Southgate *Norf.* **PE31** 44 A2
Southgate *Swan.* **SA3** 17 J7
Southill **SG18** 32 E4
Southington **RG25** 21 J7
Southleigh **EX24** 8 B5
Southmarsh **BA9** 9 G1
Southminster CM0 **25 F2**
Southmuir **DD8** 82 E2
Southoe **PE19** 32 E2
Southolt **IP23** 35 F2
Southorpe **PE9** 42 D5
Southowram **HX3** 57 G7
Southport PR8 **48 C1**
Southrepps **NR11** 45 G2
Southrey **LN3** 52 E6
Southrop **GL7** 20 E1
Southrope **RG25** 21 K7
Southsea *Ports.* PO4 **11 H5**
Southsea *Wrex.* **LL11** 48 B7
Southstoke **BA2** 20 A5
Southtown *Norf.* **NR31** 45 K5
Southtown *Ork.* **KW17** 106 D8
Southwaite *Cumb.* **CA17** 61 J6
Southwaite *Cumb.* **CA4** 61 F2
Southwater **RH13** 12 E4
Southwater Street **RH13** 12 E4
Southway **BA5** 19 J7
Southwell *Dorset* **DT5** 9 F7
Southwell *Notts.* NG25 **51 J7**
Southwick *D. & G.* **DG2** 65 K5
Southwick *Hants.* **PO17** 11 H4
Southwick *Northants.* **PE8** 42 D6
Southwick *Som.* **TA9** 19 G7
Southwick *T. & W.* **SR5** 62 E1
Southwick *W.Suss.* **BN42** 13 F6
Southwick *Wilts.* **BA14** 20 B6
Southwold IP18 **35 K1**
Southwood **BA6** 8 E1
Sowden **EX8** 7 H7
Sower Carr **FY6** 55 G5
Sowerby *N.Yorks.* **YO7** 57 K1
Sowerby *W.Yorks.* **HX6** 57 F7
Sowerby Bridge HX6 **57 F7**
Sowerby Row **CA4** 60 E2
Sowerhill **TA22** 7 G3
Sowley Green **CB9** 34 B3
Sowood **HX4** 50 C1
Sowton **EX5** 7 H6
Soyal **IV24** 96 C2
Spa Common **NR28** 45 G2
Spadeadam **CA8** 70 A6
Spalding PE11 **43 F3**
Spaldington **DN14** 58 D6
Spaldwick **PE28** 32 E1
Spalefield **KY10** 83 G7
Spalford **NG23** 52 B6
Spanby **NG34** 42 D2
Sparham **NR9** 44 E4
Spark Bridge **LA12** 55 G1
Sparkford **BA22** 9 F2
Sparkhill **B11** 40 C7
Sparkwell **PL7** 5 F5
Sparrow Green **NR19** 44 D4
Sparrowpit **SK17** 50 C4
Sparrow's Green **TN5** 13 K3
Sparsholt *Hants.* **SO21** 11 F1
Sparsholt *Oxon.* **OX12** 21 G3
Spartylea **NE47** 61 K2
Spath **ST14** 40 C2
Spaunton **YO62** 58 D1
Spaxton **TA5** 8 B1
Spean Bridge PH34 **87 J6**
Spear Hill **RH20** 12 E5
Speddoch **DG2** 68 D5
Speedwell **BS16** 19 K4
Speen *Bucks.* **HP27** 22 B1
Speen *W.Berks.* **RG14** 21 H5
Speeton **YO14** 59 H2
Speke **L24** 48 D4
Speldhurst **TN3** 23 J7
Spellbrook **CM23** 33 H7
Spelsbury **OX7** 30 E6
Spen Green **CW11** 49 H6
Spencers Wood **RG7** 22 A5
Spennithorne **DL8** 57 G1
Spennymoor DL16 **62 D3**
Spernall **B80** 30 B2
Spetchley **WR5** 29 H3
Spetisbury **DT11** 9 J4
Spexhall **IP19** 45 H7
Spey Bay **IV32** 98 B4
Speybridge **PH26** 89 H2
Speyview **AB38** 97 K7
Spilsby PE23 **53 G6**
Spindlestone **NE70** 77 K7
Spinkhill **S21** 51 G5
Spinningdale **IV24** 96 D3
Spirthill **SN11** 20 C4
Spital *High.* **KW1** 105 G3
Spital *W. & M.* **SL4** 22 C4
Spital in the Street **LN8** 52 C3
Spitalbrook **EN11** 23 G1
Spithurst **BN8** 13 H5
Spittal *D. & G.* **DG8** 64 E4
Spittal *D. & G.* **DG8** 64 D5
Spittal *E.Loth.* **EH32** 76 C3
Spittal *Northumb.* **TD15** 77 J5
Spittal *Pembs.* **SA62** 16 C3
Spittal of Glenmuick **AB35** 90 B6
Spittal of Glenshee **PH10** 82 C1
Spittalfield **PH1** 82 C3
Spixworth **NR10** 45 G4
Splayne's Green **TN22** 13 H4
Splott **CF24** 19 F4
Spofforth **HG3** 57 J4
Spondon **DE21** 41 G2
Spooner Row **NR18** 44 E6
Spoonley **TF9** 39 F2
Sporle **PE32** 44 C4
Sportsman's Arms **LL16** 47 H7
Spott **EH42** 76 E3
Spratton **NN6** 31 J1
Spreakley **GU10** 22 B7
Spreyton **EX17** 6 E6
Spriddlestone **PL9** 5 F5
Spridlington **LN8** 52 D4
Spring Grove **TW7** 22 E4
Spring Vale **PO34** 11 H5
Springburn **G21** 74 E4
Springfield *Arg. & B.* **PA22** 73 J3
Springfield *D. & G.* **DG16** 69 J7
Springfield *Fife* **KY15** 82 E6
Springfield *Moray* **IV36** 97 H6
Springfield *P. & K.* **PH13** 82 C4
Springfield *W.Mid.* **B13** 40 C7
Springfields Outlet
Village **PE12** 43 F3
Springhill *Staffs.* **WS14** 40 C5
Springhill *Staffs.* **WV11** 40 B5
Springholm **DG7** 65 J4
Springkell **DG11** 69 H6
Springleys **AB51** 91 F1
Springside **KA11** 74 B7
Springthorpe **DN21** 52 B4
Springwell **NE9** 62 D1
Sproatley **HU11** 59 H6
Sproston Green **CW4** 49 G6
Sprotbrough **DN5** 51 H2
Sproughton **IP8** 35 F4
Sprouston **TD5** 77 F7
Sprowston **NR7** 45 G4
Sproxton *Leics.* **LE14** 42 B3
Sproxton *N.Yorks.* **YO62** 58 C1
Sprytown **PL16** 6 C7
Spurlands End **HP15** 22 B2
Spurstow **CW6** 48 E7
Spyway **DT2** 8 E5
Square Point **DG7** 65 H3
Squires Gate **FY4** 55 G6
Sròndoire **PA30** 73 G3
Sronphadruig Lodge **PH18** 88 E7
Stableford *Shrop.* **WV15** 39 G6
Stableford *Staffs.* **ST5** 40 A2
Stacey Bank **S6** 50 E3
Stackhouse **BD24** 56 D3
Stackpole **SA71** 16 C6
Stacksteads **OL13** 56 D7
Staddiscombe **PL9** 5 F5
Staddlethorpe **HU15** 58 E7
Staden **SK17** 50 C5
Stadhampton **OX44** 21 K2
Stadhlaigearraidh
(Stilligarry) **HS8** 84 C1
Staffield **CA10** 61 G2
Staffin **IV51** 93 K5
Stafford ST16 **40 B3**
Stagden Cross **CM1** 33 K7
Stagsden **MK43** 32 C4
Stagshaw Bank **NE46** 70 E7
Stain **KW1** 105 J2
Stainburn *Cumb.* **CA14** 60 B4
Stainburn *N.Yorks.* **LS21** 57 H5
Stainby **NG33** 42 C3
Staincross **S75** 51 F1
Staindrop **DL2** 62 C4
Staines TW18 **22 D4**
Stainfield *Lincs.* **PE10** 42 D3
Stainfield *Lincs.* **LN3** 52 E5
Stainforth *N.Yorks.* **BD24** 56 D3
Stainforth *S.Yorks.* **DN7** 51 J1
Staining **FY3** 55 G6
Stainland **HX4** 50 C1
Stainsacre **YO22** 63 J2
Stainsby *Derbys.* **S44** 51 G6
Stainsby *Lincs.* **LN9** 53 G5
Stainton *Cumb.* **LA8** 55 J1
Stainton *Cumb.* **CA11** 61 F4
Stainton *Dur.* **DL12** 62 B5
Stainton *Middbro.* **TS8** 63 F5
Stainton *N.Yorks.* **DL11** 62 C7
Stainton *S.Yorks.* **S66** 51 H3
Stainton by Langworth
LN3 52 D5
Stainton le Vale **LN8** 52 E3
Stainton with Adgarley
LA13 55 F2
Staintondale **YO13** 63 J3
Stair *Cumb.* **CA12** 60 D4
Stair *E.Ayr.* **KA5** 67 J1
Stairfoot **S70** 51 F2
Staithes **TS13** 63 J5
Stake Pool **PR3** 55 H5
Stakeford **NE62** 71 H5
Stakes **PO7** 11 H4
Stalbridge **DT10** 9 G3
Stalbridge Weston **DT10** 9 G3
Stalham **NR12** 45 H3
Stalham Green **NR12** 45 H3
Stalisfield Green **ME13** 14 E2
Stalling Busk **DL8** 56 E1
Stallingborough **DN41** 52 E1
Stallington **ST11** 40 B2
Stalmine **FY6** 55 G5
Stalybridge SK15 **49 J3**
Stambourne **CO9** 34 B5
Stamford *Lincs.* PE9 **42 D5**
Stamford *Northumb.*
NE66 71 H2
Stamford Bridge *Ches.*
CH3 48 D6
Stamford Bridge *E.Riding*
YO41 58 D4
Stamfordham **NE18** 71 F6
Stanah **FY5** 55 G5
Stanborough **AL8** 33 F7
Stanbridge *Beds.* **LU7** 32 C6
Stanbridge *Dorset* **BH21** 10 B4
Stanbridge Earls **SO51** 10 E2
Stanbury **BD22** 57 F6
Stand **ML6** 75 F4
Standburn **FK1** 75 H3
Standeford **WV10** 40 B5
Standen **TN27** 14 D4
Standen Street **TN17** 14 D4
Standerwick **BA11** 20 B6
Standford **GU35** 12 B3
Standford Bridge **TF10** 39 G3
Standish *Glos.* **GL10** 20 B1
Standish *Gt.Man.* **WN6** 48 E1
Standlake **OX29** 21 G1
Standon *Hants.* **SO21** 11 F2
Standon *Herts.* **SG11** 33 G6
Standon *Staffs.* **ST21** 40 A2
Standon Green End **SG11** 33 G7
Stane **ML7** 75 G5
Stanecastle **KA11** 74 B7
Stanfield **NR20** 44 D3
Stanford *Beds.* **SG18** 32 E4
Stanford *Kent* **TN25** 15 G4
Stanford *Shrop.* **SY5** 38 C4
Stanford Bishop **WR6** 29 F3
Stanford Bridge **WR6** 29 G2
Stanford Dingley **RG7** 21 J4

Stanford End RG7 22 A5
Stanford in the Vale SN7 21 G2
Stanford on Avon NN6 31 G1
Stanford on Soar LE12 41 H3
Stanford on Teme WR6 29 G2
Stanford Rivers CM5 23 J1
Stanford-le-Hope SS17 24 C3
Stanfree S44 51 G5
Stanghow TS12 63 H5
Stanground PE2 43 F6
Stanhoe PE31 44 C2
Stanhope *Dur.* DL13 62 A3
Stanhope *Sc.Bord.* ML12 69 G1
Stanion NN14 42 C7
Stanklyn DY10 29 H1
Stanley *Derbys.* DE7 41 G1
Stanley *Dur.* DH9 62 C1
Stanley *Notts.* NG17 51 G6
Stanley *P. & K.* PH1 82 C4
Stanley *Staffs.* ST9 49 J7
Stanley *W.Yorks.* WF3 57 J7
Stanley *Wilts.* SN15 20 C4
Stanley Common DE7 41 G1
Stanley Crook DL15 62 C3
Stanley Gate L39 48 D2
Stanley Green BH15 10 B5
Stanley Hill HR8 29 F4
Stanleygreen SY13 38 E2
Stanlow *Ches.* CH65 48 D5
Stanlow *Shrop.* WV6 39 G6
Stanmer BN1 13 G5
Stanmore *Gt.Lon.* HA7 22 E2
Stanmore *W.Berks.* RG20 21 H4
Stannersburn NE48 70 C5
Stanningfield IP29 34 C3
Stannington *Northumb.* NE61 71 H6
Stannington *S.Yorks.* S6 51 F4
Stansbatch HR6 28 C2
Stansfield CO10 34 B3
Stanshope DE6 50 D7
Stanstead CO10 34 C4
Stanstead Abbotts SG12 33 G7
Stansted TN15 24 C5
Stansted Airport (London Stansted Airport) CM24 33 J6
Stansted Mountfitchet CM24 33 J6
Stanton *Derbys.* DE15 40 E4
Stanton *Glos.* WR12 30 B5
Stanton *Northumb.* NE65 71 G4
Stanton *Staffs.* DE6 40 D1
Stanton *Suff.* IP31 34 D1
Stanton by Bridge DE73 41 F3
Stanton by Dale DE7 41 G2
Stanton Drew BS39 19 J5
Stanton Fitzwarren SN6 20 E2
Stanton Harcourt OX29 21 H1
Stanton Hill NG17 51 G6
Stanton in Peak DE4 50 E6
Stanton Lacy SY8 28 D1
Stanton Lees DE4 50 E6
Stanton Long TF13 38 E6
Stanton Prior BA2 19 K5
Stanton St. Bernard SN8 20 D5
Stanton St. John OX33 21 J1
Stanton St. Quintin SN14 20 C4
Stanton Street IP31 34 D2
Stanton under Bardon LE67 41 G4
Stanton upon Hine Heath SY4 38 E3
Stanton Wick BS39 19 K5
Stanton-on-the-Wolds NG12 41 J2
Stanwardine in the Fields SY4 38 D3
Stanwardine in the Wood SY12 38 D3
Stanway *Essex* CO3 34 D6
Stanway *Glos.* GL54 30 B5
Stanway Green *Essex* CO3 34 D6
Stanway Green *Suff.* IP13 35 G1
Stanwell TW19 22 D4
Stanwell Moor TW19 22 D4
Stanwick NN9 32 C1
Stanwix CA3 60 F1
Stanydale ZE2 107 L7
Staoinebrig HS8 84 C1
Stapeley CW5 39 F1
Stapenhill DE15 40 E3
Staple *Kent* CT3 15 H2
Staple *Som.* TA4 7 K1
Staple Cross TA21 7 J3
Staple Fitzpaine TA3 8 B3
Staplecross TN32 14 C5
Staplefield RH17 13 F4
Stapleford *Cambs.* CB2 33 H3
Stapleford *Herts.* SG14 33 G7
Stapleford *Leics.* LE14 42 B4
Stapleford *Lincs.* LN6 52 B7
Stapleford *Notts.* NG9 41 G2
Stapleford *Wilts.* SP3 10 B1
Stapleford Abbotts RM4 23 H2
Stapleford Tawney RM4 23 J2
Staplegrove TA2 8 B2
Staplehay TA3 8 B2
Staplehurst TN12 14 C3
Staplers PO30 11 G6
Staplestreet ME13 25 G5
Stapleton *Cumb.* CA6 70 A6
Stapleton *Here.* LD8 28 C2
Stapleton *Leics.* LE9 41 G6
Stapleton *N.Yorks.* DL2 62 D5
Stapleton *Shrop.* SY5 38 D5
Stapleton *Som.* TA12 8 D2
Stapley TA3 7 K4
Staploe PE19 32 E2
Staplow HR8 29 F4
Star *Fife* KY7 82 E7
Star *Pembs.* SA35 17 F2
Star *Som.* BS25 19 H6
Starbotton BD23 56 E2
Starcross EX6 7 H7
Stareton CV8 30 E1
Starkholmes DE4 51 F7
Starling BL8 49 G1
Starling's Green CB11 33 H5
Starr KA6 67 J4
Starston IP20 45 G7
Startforth DL12 62 B5
Startley SN15 20 C3
Statham WA13 49 F4
Stathe TA7 8 C2
Stathern LE14 42 A2
Station Town TS28 63 F3
Staughton Green PE19 32 E2
Staughton Highway PE19 32 E2
Staunton *Glos.* GL16 28 E7
Staunton *Glos.* GL19 29 G6
Staunton Harold Hall LE65 41 F3
Staunton in the Vale NG13 42 B1
Staunton on Arrow HR6 28 C2
Staunton on Wye HR4 28 C4
Staveley *Cumb.* LA8 61 F7
Staveley *Derbys.* S43 51 G5
Staveley *N.Yorks.* HG5 57 J3
Staveley-in-Cartmel LA12 55 G1
Staverton *Devon* TQ9 5 H4
Staverton *Glos.* GL51 29 H6
Staverton *Northants.* NN11 31 G2
Staverton *Wilts.* BA14 20 B5
Staverton Bridge GL51 29 H6
Stawell TA7 8 C1
Stawley TA21 7 J3
Staxigoe KW1 105 J3
Staxton YO12 59 G2
Staylittle (Penffordd-las) SY19 37 H6
Staynall FY6 55 G5
Staythorpe NG23 51 K7
Stean HG3 57 F2
Steane NN13 31 G5
Stearsby YO61 58 C2
Steart TA5 19 F7
Stebbing CM6 33 K6
Stebbing Green CM6 33 K6
Stechford B33 40 D7
Stedham GU29 12 B4
Steel Cross TN6 13 J3
Steel Green LA18 54 E2
Steele Road TD9 70 A4
Steen's Bridge HR6 28 E3
Steep GU32 11 J2
Steep Marsh GU32 11 J2
Steeple *Dorset* BH20 9 J6
Steeple *Essex* CM0 25 F1
Steeple Ashton BA14 20 C6
Steeple Aston OX25 31 F6
Steeple Barton OX25 31 F6
Steeple Bumpstead CB9 33 K4
Steeple Claydon MK18 31 H6
Steeple Gidding PE28 42 E7
Steeple Langford SP3 10 B1
Steeple Morden SG8 33 F4
Steeraway TF1 39 F5
Steeton BD20 57 F5
Stein IV55 93 H6
Steinmanhill AB53 99 F6
Stella NE21 71 G7
Stelling Minnis CT4 15 G3
Stembridge TA12 8 D2
Stemster *High.* KW12 105 G2
Stemster *High.* KW5 105 G4
Stemster House KW12 105 G2
Stenalees PL26 4 A5
Stenhill EX15 7 J4
Stenhousemuir FK5 75 G2
Stenigot LN11 53 F4
Stenis HS1 101 G4
Stenness ZE2 107 L5
Stenscholl IV51 93 K5
Stenson DE73 41 F3
Stenton *E.Loth.* EH42 76 E3
Stenton *P. & K.* PH8 82 B3
Steornabhagh (Stornoway) HS1 101 G4
Stepaside *Pembs.* SA67 16 E5
Stepaside *Powys* SY16 37 K7
Stepney E1 23 G3
Steppingley MK45 32 D5
Stepps G33 74 E4
Sternfield IP17 35 H2
Sterridge EX34 6 D1
Stert SN10 20 D6
Stetchworth CB8 33 K3
STEVENAGE SG 33 F6
Stevenston KA20 74 A6
Steventon *Hants.* RG25 21 J7
Steventon *Oxon.* OX13 21 H2
Steventon End CB10 33 K4
Stevington MK43 32 C3
Stewartby MK43 32 D4
Stewarton *D. & G.* DG8 64 E6
Stewarton *E.Ayr.* KA3 74 C6
Stewkley LU7 32 B6
Stewley TA19 8 C3
Stewton LN11 53 G4
Steyning BN44 12 E5
Steynton SA73 16 C5
Stibb EX23 6 A4
Stibb Cross EX38 6 C4
Stibb Green SN8 21 F5
Stibbard NR21 44 D3
Stibbington PE8 42 D6
Stichill TD5 77 F7
Sticker PL26 3 G3
Stickford PE22 53 G6
Sticklepath *Devon* EX20 6 E6
Sticklepath *Som.* TA20 8 C3
Stickling Green CB11 33 H5
Stickney PE22 53 G7
Stiff Street ME9 24 E5
Stiffkey NR23 44 D1
Stifford's Bridge WR13 29 G4
Stileway BA6 19 H7
Stilligarry (Stadhlaigearraidh) HS8 84 C1
Stillingfleet YO19 58 B5
Stillington *N.Yorks.* YO61 58 B3
Stillington *Stock.* TS21 62 E4
Stilton PE7 42 E7
Stinchcombe GL11 20 A2
Stinsford DT2 9 G5
Stirchley *Tel. & W.* TF3 39 G5
Stirchley *W.Mid.* B30 40 C7
Stirkoke House KW1 105 J3
Stirling *Aber.* AB42 99 K6
Stirling *Stir.* FK8 75 F1
Stirton BD23 56 E4
Stisted CM77 34 C6
Stitchcombe SN8 21 F5
Stithians TR3 2 E5
Stittenham IV17 96 D4
Stivichall CV3 30 E1
Stix PH15 81 J3
Stixwould LN10 52 E6
Stoak CH2 48 D5
Stobo EH45 75 K7
Stoborough BH20 9 J6
Stoborough Green BH20 9 J6
Stobwood ML11 75 H5
Stocinis (Stockinish) HS3 93 G2
Stock CM4 24 C2
Stock Green B96 29 J3
Stock Lane SN8 21 F4
Stock Wood B96 30 B3
Stockbridge *Hants.* SO20 10 E1
Stockbridge *Stir.* FK15 81 J7
Stockbridge *W.Suss.* PO19 12 B6
Stockbury ME9 24 E5
Stockcross RG20 21 H5
Stockdale TR11 2 E5
Stockdalewath CA5 60 E2
Stockerston LE15 42 B6
Stocking Green *Essex* CB10 33 J5
Stocking Green *M.K.* MK19 32 B4
Stocking Pelham SG9 33 H6
Stockingford CV10 41 F6
Stockinish (Stocinis) HS3 93 G2
Stockland *Cardiff* CF5 18 E4
Stockland *Devon* EX14 8 B4
Stockland Bristol TA5 19 F7
Stockleigh English EX17 7 G5
Stockleigh Pomeroy EX17 7 G5
Stockley SN11 20 D5
Stocklinch TA19 8 C3
STOCKPORT SK 49 H3
Stocksbridge S36 50 E3
Stocksfield NE43 71 F7
Stockton *Here.* HR6 28 E2
Stockton *Norf.* NR34 45 H6
Stockton *Shrop.* TF11 39 G6
Stockton *Shrop.* SY21 38 B5
Stockton *Tel. & W.* TF10 39 G4
Stockton *Warks.* CV47 31 F2
Stockton *Wilts.* BA12 9 J1
Stockton Heath WA4 49 F4
Stockton on Teme WR6 29 G2
Stockton on the Forest YO32 58 C4
Stockton-on-Tees TS19 63 F5
Stockwell GL4 29 J7
Stockwell Heath WS15 40 C3
Stockwood *Bristol* BS14 19 K5
Stockwood *Dorset* DT2 8 E4
Stodday LA2 55 H4
Stodmarsh CT3 25 J5
Stody NR24 44 E2
Stoer IV27 102 C6
Stoford *Som.* BA22 8 E3
Stoford *Wilts.* SP2 10 B1
Stogumber TA4 7 J2
Stogursey TA5 19 F7
Stoke *Devon* EX39 6 A3
Stoke *Hants.* SP11 21 H6
Stoke *Hants.* PO11 11 J4
Stoke *Med.* ME3 24 E4
Stoke *Plym.* PL3 4 E5
Stoke *W.Mid.* CV2 30 E1
Stoke Abbott DT8 8 D4
Stoke Albany LE16 42 B7
Stoke Ash IP23 35 F1
Stoke Bardolph NG14 41 J1
Stoke Bishop BS9 19 J4
Stoke Bliss WR15 29 F2
Stoke Bruerne NN12 31 J3
Stoke by Clare CO10 34 B4
Stoke Canon EX5 7 H6
Stoke Charity SO21 11 F1
Stoke Climsland PL17 4 D3
Stoke D'Abernon KT11 22 E6
Stoke Doyle PE8 42 D7
Stoke Dry LE15 42 B6
Stoke Edith HR1 29 F4
Stoke Farthing SP5 10 B2
Stoke Ferry PE33 44 B6
Stoke Fleming TQ6 5 J6
Stoke Gabriel TQ9 5 J5
Stoke Gifford BS34 19 K4
Stoke Golding CV13 41 F6
Stoke Goldington MK16 32 B4
Stoke Green SL2 22 C3
Stoke Hammond MK17 32 B6
Stoke Heath *Shrop.* TF9 39 F3
Stoke Heath *Worcs.* B60 29 J2
Stoke Holy Cross NR14 45 G5
Stoke Lacy HR7 29 F4
Stoke Lyne OX27 31 G6
Stoke Mandeville HP22 32 B7
Stoke Newington N16 23 G3
Stoke on Tern TF9 39 F3
Stoke Orchard GL52 29 J6
Stoke Pero TA24 7 G1
Stoke Poges SL2 22 C3
Stoke Pound B60 29 J2
Stoke Prior *Here.* HR6 28 E3
Stoke Prior *Worcs.* B60 29 J2
Stoke Rivers EX32 6 E2
Stoke Rochford NG33 42 C3
Stoke Row RG9 21 K3
Stoke St. Gregory TA3 8 C2
Stoke St. Mary TA3 8 B2
Stoke St. Michael BA3 19 K7
Stoke St. Milborough SY8 38 E7
Stoke sub Hamdon TA14 8 D3
Stoke Talmage OX9 21 K2
Stoke Trister BA9 9 G2
Stoke Villice BS40 19 J5
Stoke Wake DT11 9 G4
Stoke-by-Nayland CO6 34 D5
Stokeford BH20 9 H6
Stokeham DN22 51 K5
Stokeinteignhead TQ12 5 K3
Stokenchurch HP14 22 A2
Stokenham TQ7 5 J6
STOKE-ON-TRENT ST 40 A1
Stokesay SY7 38 D7
Stokesby NR29 45 J4
Stokesley TS9 63 G6
Stolford TA5 19 F7
Ston Easton BA3 19 K6
Stonar Cut CT13 25 K5
Stondon Massey CM15 23 J1
Stone *Bucks.* HP17 31 J7
Stone *Glos.* GL13 19 K2
Stone *Kent* DA9 23 J4
Stone *Kent* TN30 14 E5
Stone *S.Yorks.* S66 51 H4
Stone *Som.* BA4 8 E1
Stone *Staffs.* ST15 40 B2
Stone *Worcs.* DY10 29 H1
Stone Allerton BS26 19 H6
Stone Cross *Dur.* DL12 62 B5
Stone Cross *E.Suss.* BN24 13 K6
Stone Cross *E.Suss.* TN6 13 J4
Stone Cross *Kent* TN25 15 F4
Stone Cross *Kent* TN3 13 J3
Stone House LA10 56 C1
Stone Street *Kent* TN15 23 J6
Stone Street *Suff.* IP19 45 H7
Stone Street *Suff.* CO10 34 D5
Stonea PE15 43 H6
Stonebridge *E.Suss.* TN22 13 J4
Stonebridge *N.Som.* BS29 19 G6
Stonebridge *Warks.* CV7 40 E7
Stonebroom DE55 51 G7
Stonecross Green IP29 34 C3
Stonefield *Arg. & B.* PA29 73 G3
Stonefield *Staffs.* ST15 40 B2
Stonegate *E.Suss.* TN5 13 K4
Stonegate *N.Yorks.* YO21 63 J6
Stonegrave YO62 58 C2
Stonehaugh NE48 70 C6
Stonehaven AB39 91 G6
Stonehill KT16 22 C5
Stonehouse *Ches.* CH3 48 E5
Stonehouse *D. & G.* DG2 65 J4
Stonehouse *Glos.* GL10 20 B1
Stonehouse *Northumb.* NE49 61 H1
Stonehouse *Plym.* PL1 4 E5
Stonehouse *S.Lan.* ML9 75 F6
Stoneleigh *Surr.* KT17 23 F5
Stoneleigh *Warks.* CV8 30 E1
Stoneley Green CW5 49 F7
Stonely PE19 32 E2
Stoner Hill GU32 11 J2
Stones OL14 56 E7
Stones Green CO12 35 F6
Stonesby LE14 42 B3
Stonesfield OX29 30 E7
Stonestreet Green TN25 15 F4
Stonethwaite CA12 60 D5
Stoney Cross SO43 10 D3
Stoney Middleton S32 50 E5
Stoney Stanton LE9 41 G6
Stoney Stoke BA9 9 G1
Stoney Stratton BA4 9 F1
Stoney Stretton SY5 38 C5
Stoneyburn EH47 75 H4
Stoneyford EX10 7 J7
Stoneygate LE2 41 J5
Stoneyhills CM0 25 F2
Stoneykirk DG9 64 A5
Stoneywood AB21 91 G3
Stonganess ZE2 107 P2
Stonham Aspal IP14 35 F3
Stonnall WS9 40 C5
Stonor RG9 22 A3
Stonton Wyville LE16 42 A6
Stony Houghton NG19 51 G6
Stony Stratford MK11 31 J4
Stonybreck ZE2 107 K2
Stoodleigh *Devon* EX16 7 H4
Stoodleigh *Devon* EX32 6 E2
Stopham RH20 12 D5
Stopsley LU2 32 E6
Stoptide PL27 3 G1
Storeton CH63 48 C4
Stormontfield PH2 82 C5
Stornoway (Steornabhagh) HS1 101 G4
Stornoway Airport HS2 101 G4
Storridge WR13 29 G4
Storrington RH20 12 D5
Storrs S6 50 E4
Storth LA7 55 H1
Storwood YO42 58 D5
Stotfield IV31 97 K4
Stotfold SG5 33 F5
Stottesdon DY14 39 F7
Stoughton *Leics.* LE2 41 J5
Stoughton *Surr.* GU2 22 C6
Stoughton *W.Suss.* PO18 11 J3
Stoughton Cross BS28 19 H7
Stoul PH41 86 D5
Stoulton WR7 29 J4
Stour Provost SP8 9 G2
Stour Row SP7 9 H2
Stourbridge DY8 40 A7
Stourpaine DT11 9 H4
Stourport-on-Severn DY13 29 H1
Stourton *Staffs.* DY7 40 A7
Stourton *Warks.* CV36 30 D5
Stourton *Wilts.* BA12 9 G1
Stourton Caundle DT10 9 G3
Stove KW17 106 F4
Stoven NR34 45 J7
Stow *Lincs.* LN1 52 B4
Stow *Sc.Bord.* TD1 76 C6
Stow Bardolph PE34 44 A5
Stow Bedon NR17 44 D6
Stow cum Quy CB5 33 J2
Stow Longa PE28 32 E1
Stow Maries CM3 24 E2
Stow Pasture LN1 52 B4
Stowbridge PE34 43 J5
Stowe *Glos.* GL15 19 J1
Stowe *Shrop.* LD7 28 C1
Stowe *Staffs.* WS13 40 D4
Stowe-by-Chartley ST18 40 C3
Stowehill NN7 31 H3
Stowell *Glos.* GL54 30 B7
Stowell *Som.* DT9 9 F2
Stowey BS39 19 J6
Stowford *Devon* EX20 6 C7
Stowford *Devon* EX37 6 E3
Stowford *Devon* EX10 7 K7
Stowlangtoft IP31 34 D2
Stowmarket IP14 34 E3
Stow-on-the-Wold GL54 30 C6
Stowting TN25 15 G3
Stowupland IP14 34 E3
Straad PA20 73 J4
Stracathro DD9 83 H1
Strachan AB31 90 E5
Strachur (Clachan Strachur) PA27 80 B7
Stradbroke IP21 35 G1
Stradishall CB8 34 B3
Stradsett PE33 44 A5
Stragglethorpe LN5 52 C7
Straight Soley RG17 21 G4
Straiton *Edin.* EH20 76 A4
Straiton *S.Ayr.* KA19 67 H3
Straloch *Aber.* AB21 91 G2
Straloch *P. & K.* PH10 82 B1
Stramshall ST14 40 C2
Strands LA18 54 E1
Strang IM4 54 C6
Strangford HR9 28 E6
Strannda HS5 93 F3
Stranraer DG9 64 A4
Strata Florida SY25 27 G2
Stratfield Mortimer RG7 21 K5
Stratfield Saye RG7 21 K5
Stratfield Turgis RG27 21 K6
Stratford *Beds.* SG19 32 E4
Stratford *Glos.* GL20 29 H5
Stratford *Gt.Lon.* E15 23 G3
Stratford St. Andrew IP17 35 H3
Stratford St. Mary CO7 34 E5
Stratford sub Castle SP1 10 C1
Stratford Tony SP5 10 B2
Stratford-upon-Avon CV37 30 D3
Strath KW1 105 H3
Strathan *High.* IV27 102 C6
Strathan *High.* PH34 87 F5
Strathaven ML10 75 F6
Strathblane G63 74 D3
Strathcanaird IV26 95 H1
Strathcarron IV54 95 F7
Strathdon AB36 90 B3
Strathgirnock AB35 90 B5
Strathkinness KY16 83 F6
Strathmiglo KY14 82 D6
Strathpeffer IV14 96 B6
Strathrannoch IV23 95 K4
Strathtay PH9 82 A2
Strathwhillan KA27 73 J7
Strathy KW14 104 D2
Strathyre FK18 81 G6
Stratton *Cornw.* EX23 6 A5
Stratton *Dorset* DT2 9 F5
Stratton *Glos.* GL7 20 D1
Stratton Audley OX27 31 H6
Stratton Hall IP10 35 G5
Stratton St. Margaret SN3 20 E3
Stratton St. Michael NR15 45 G6
Stratton Strawless NR10 45 G3
Stratton-on-the-Fosse BA3 19 K6
Stravanan PA20 73 J5
Stravithie KY16 83 G6
Strawberry Hill TW2 22 E4
Stream TA4 7 J2
Streat BN6 13 G5
Streatham SW16 23 F4
Streatham Vale SW16 23 F4
Streatley *Beds.* LU3 32 D6
Streatley *W.Berks.* RG8 21 J3
Street *Devon* EX12 7 K7
Street *Lancs.* PR3 55 J4
Street *N.Yorks.* YO21 63 J6
Street *Som.* BA16 8 D1
Street *Som.* TA20 8 C4
Street Ashton CV23 41 G7

Street Dinas SY11 38 C2
Street End PO20 12 B7
Street Gate NE16 62 D1
Street Houses LS24 58 B5
Street Lane DE5 41 F1
Street on the Fosse BA4 9 F1
Streethay WS13 40 D4
Streethouse WF7 57 J7
Streetlam DL7 62 E7
Streetly B74 40 C6
Streetly End CB1 33 K4
Strefford SY7 38 D7
Strelley NG8 41 H1
Strensall YO32 58 C3
Strensham WR8 29 J4
Stretcholt TA6 19 F7
Strete TQ6 5 J6
Stretford Gt.Man. M32 49 G3
Stretford Here. HR6 28 D3
Stretford Here. HR6 28 E3
Strethall CB11 33 H5
Stretham CB6 33 J1
Strettington PO18 12 B6
Stretton Ches. SY14 48 D7
Stretton Derbys. DE55 51 F6
Stretton Rut. LE15 42 C4
Stretton Staffs. ST19 40 A4
Stretton Staffs. DE13 40 E3
Stretton Warr. WA4 49 F4
Stretton en le Field DE12 41 F4
Stretton Grandison HR8 29 F4
Stretton Heath SY5 38 C4
Stretton Sugwas HR4 28 D4
Stretton under Fosse CV23 41 G7
Stretton Westwood TF13 38 E6
Stretton-on-Dunsmore CV23 31 F1
Stretton-on-Fosse GL56 30 D5
Stribers LA12 55 G1
Strichen AB43 99 H5
Strines SK6 49 J4
Stringston TA5 7 K1
Strixton NN29 32 C2
Stroat NP16 19 J2
Stromeferry IV53 86 E1
Stromemore IV54 86 E1
Stromness KW16 106 B7
Stronaba PH34 87 J6
Stronachlachar FK8 81 F6
Strone Arg. & B. PA23 73 K2
Strone High. IV63 88 C2
Strone High. PH33 87 H6
Strone Stir. FK17 81 F6
Stronechrubie IV27 102 E7
Stronlonag PA23 73 K2
Stronmilchan PA33 80 C5
Stronsay KW17 106 F5
Stronsay Airfield KW17 106 F5
Strontian PH36 79 K1
Strontoiller PA34 80 A5
Stronvar FK19 81 G5
Strood ME2 24 D5
Strood Green Surr. RH3 23 F7
Strood Green W.Suss. RH14 12 D4
Strood Green W.Suss. RH12 12 E3
Stroquhan DG2 68 D5
Stroud Glos. GL5 20 B1
Stroud Hants. GU32 11 J2
Stroud Common GU5 22 D7
Stroud Green Essex SS4 24 E2
Stroud Green Glos. GL10 20 B1
Stroude GU25 22 D5
Stroul G84 74 A2
Stroxton NG33 42 C2
Struan High. IV56 85 J1
Struan P. & K. PH18 81 J1
Strubby Lincs. LN13 53 H4
Strubby Lincs. LN8 52 E5
Strumpshaw NR13 45 H5
Struthers KY15 82 E7
Struy IV4 88 B1
Stryd y Facsen LL65 46 B4
Stryt-cae-rhedyn CH7 48 B6
Stryt-issa LL14 38 B1
Stuartfield AB42 99 H6
Stub Place LA19 60 B7
Stubber's Green WS9 40 C5
Stubbington PO14 11 G4
Stubbins BL0 49 G1
Stubbs Green NR14 45 H6
Stubhampton DT11 9 J3
Stubley S18 51 F5
Stubshaw Cross WN4 48 E2
Stubton NG23 42 B1
Stuck Arg. & B. PA20 73 J4
Stuck Arg. & B. PA23 73 K1
Stuckbeg PA24 74 A1
Stuckgowan G83 80 E7
Stuckindroin G83 80 E6
Stuckreoch PA27 73 J1
Stuckton SP6 10 C3
Stud Green SL6 22 B4
Studdon NE47 61 K1
Studfold BD24 56 D2
Studham LU6 32 D7
Studholme CA7 60 D1
Studland BH19 10 B6
Studley Warks. B80 30 B2
Studley Wilts. SN11 20 C4
Studley Common B80 30 B2
Studley Green HP14 22 A2
Studley Roger HG4 57 H2
Stuggadhoo IM4 54 C6
Stump Cross Essex CB10 33 J4
Stump Cross Lancs. PR3 55 J6
Stuntney CB7 33 J1
Stunts Green BN27 13 K5
Sturbridge ST21 40 A2
Sturgate DN21 52 B4
Sturmer CB9 33 K4
Sturminster Common DT10 9 G3
Sturminster Marshall BH21 9 J4
Sturminster Newton DT10 9 G3
Sturry CT2 25 H5
Sturton by Stow LN1 52 B4
Sturton le Steeple DN22 51 K4
Stuston IP21 35 F1
Stutton N.Yorks. LS24 57 K5
Stutton Suff. IP9 35 F5
Styal SK9 49 H4
Styrrup DN11 51 J3
Suainebost (Swainbost) HS2 101 H1
Suardail HS2 101 G4
Succoth Aber. AB54 90 C1
Succoth Arg. & B. G83 80 D7
Succothmore PA27 80 C7
Suckley WR6 29 G3
Suckley Green WR6 29 G3
Suckley Knowl WR6 29 G3
Sudborough NN14 42 C7
Sudbourne IP12 35 J3
Sudbrook Lincs. NG32 42 C1
Sudbrook Mon. NP26 19 J3
Sudbrooke LN2 52 D5
Sudbury Derbys. DE6 40 D2
Sudbury Gt.Lon. HA0 22 E3
Sudbury Suff. CO10 34 C4
Sudden OL11 49 H1
Sudgrove GL6 20 C1
Suffield N.Yorks. YO13 63 J3
Suffield Norf. NR11 45 G2
Sugarloaf TN26 14 E4
Sugnall ST21 39 G2
Sugwas Pool HR4 28 D4
Suie Lodge Hotel FK20 81 F5
Suisnish IV49 86 B3
Sulby I.o.M. IM7 54 C4
Sulby I.o.M. IM4 54 C5
Sulgrave OX17 31 G4
Sulham RG8 21 K4
Sulhamstead RG7 21 K5
Sullington RH20 12 D5
Sullom ZE2 107 M5
Sullom Voe Oil Terminal ZE2 107 M5
Sully CF64 18 E5
Sumburgh ZE3 107 M11
Sumburgh Airport ZE3 107 M11
Summer Bridge HG3 57 H3
Summer Isles IV26 95 F1
Summer Lodge DL8 62 A7
Summercourt TR8 3 F3
Summerfield Norf. PE31 44 B2
Summerfield Worcs. DY11 29 H1
Summerhill LL11 48 C7
Summerhouse DL2 62 D5
Summerlands LA8 55 J1
Summerleaze NP26 19 H3
Summertown OX2 21 J1
Summit OL15 49 J1
Sun Green SK15 49 J3
Sunadale PA28 73 G6
Sunbiggin CA10 61 H6
Sunbury TW16 22 E5
Sundaywell DG2 68 D5
Sunderland Cumb. CA13 60 C3
Sunderland Lancs. LA3 55 H4
SUNDERLAND T. & W. SR 62 E1
Sunderland Bridge DH6 62 D3
Sundhope TD7 69 J1
Sundon Park LU3 32 D6
Sundridge TN14 23 H6
Sundrum Mains KA6 67 J1
Sunhill GL7 20 E1
Sunipol PA75 78 E2
Sunk Island HU12 53 F1
Sunningdale SL5 22 C5
Sunninghill SL5 22 C5
Sunningwell OX13 21 H1
Sunniside Dur. DL13 62 C3
Sunniside T. & W. NE16 62 D1
Sunny Bank LA21 60 D7
Sunny Brow DL15 62 C3
Sunnylaw FK9 75 F1
Sunnyside Aber. AB12 91 G5
Sunnyside Northumb. NE46 70 E7
Sunnyside S.Yorks. S65 51 G3
Sunnyside W.Suss. RH19 13 G3
Sunton SN8 21 F6
Sunwick TD15 77 G5
Surbiton KT6 22 E5
Surfleet PE11 43 F3
Surfleet Seas End PE11 43 F3
Surlingham NR14 45 H5
Sustead NR11 45 F2
Susworth DN17 52 B2
Sutcombe EX22 6 B4
Sutcombemill EX22 6 B4
Suton NR18 44 E6
Sutors of Cromarty IV11 97 F5
Sutterby LN13 53 G5
Sutterton PE20 43 F2
Sutton Beds. SG19 33 F4
Sutton Cambs. CB6 33 H1
Sutton Devon EX17 7 F5
Sutton Devon TQ7 5 H6
SUTTON Gt.Lon. SM 23 F5
Sutton Kent CT15 15 J3
Sutton Lincs. LN5 52 B7
Sutton Norf. NR12 45 H3
Sutton Notts. NG13 42 A2
Sutton Notts. DN22 51 J4
Sutton Oxon. OX29 21 H1
Sutton Pembs. SA62 16 C4
Sutton Peter. PE5 42 D6
Sutton S.Yorks. DN6 51 H1
Sutton Shrop. WV16 39 G7
Sutton Shrop. TF9 39 F2
Sutton Shrop. SY2 38 E4
Sutton Shrop. SY11 38 C3
Sutton Staffs. TF10 39 G3
Sutton Suff. IP12 35 H4
Sutton W.Suss. RH20 12 C5
Sutton Abinger RH5 22 E7
Sutton at Hone DA4 23 J4
Sutton Bassett LE16 42 A7
Sutton Benger SN15 20 C4
Sutton Bingham BA22 8 E3
Sutton Bonington LE12 41 H3
Sutton Bridge PE12 43 H3
Sutton Cheney CV13 41 G5
Sutton Coldfield B74 40 D6
Sutton Courtenay OX14 21 J2
Sutton Crosses PE12 43 H3
Sutton Grange HG4 57 H2
Sutton Green Oxon. OX29 21 H1
Sutton Green Surr. GU4 22 D6
Sutton Green Wrex. LL13 38 D1
Sutton Holms BH21 10 B4
Sutton Howgrave DL8 57 J2
Sutton in Ashfield NG17 51 G7
Sutton in the Elms LE9 41 H6
Sutton Ings HU8 59 H6
Sutton Lane Ends SK11 49 J5
Sutton le Marsh LN12 53 J4
Sutton Leach WA9 48 E3
Sutton Maddock TF11 39 G5
Sutton Mallet TA7 8 C1
Sutton Mandeville SP3 9 J2
Sutton Montis BA22 9 F2
Sutton on Sea LN12 53 J4
Sutton on the Hill DE6 40 E2
Sutton on Trent NG23 51 K6
Sutton Poyntz DT3 9 G6
Sutton St. Edmund PE12 43 G4
Sutton St. James PE12 43 H4
Sutton St. Nicholas HR1 28 E4
Sutton Scarsdale S44 51 G6
Sutton Scotney SO21 11 F1
Sutton upon Derwent YO41 58 D5
Sutton Valence ME17 14 D3
Sutton Veny BA12 20 B7
Sutton Waldron DT11 9 H3
Sutton Weaver WA7 48 E5
Sutton Wick B. & N.E.Som. BS40 19 J6
Sutton Wick Oxon. OX14 21 H2
Sutton-in-Craven BD20 57 F5
Sutton-on-Hull HU7 59 H6
Sutton-on-the-Forest YO61 58 B3
Sutton-under-Brailes CV36 30 E5
Sutton-under-Whitestonecliffe YO7 57 K1
Swaby LN13 53 G5
Swadlincote DE11 41 F4
Swaffham PE37 44 C5
Swaffham Bulbeck CB5 33 J2
Swaffham Prior CB5 33 J2
Swafield NR28 45 G2
Swainbost (Suainebost) HS2 101 H1
Swainby DL6 63 F6
Swainsthorpe NR14 45 G5
Swainswick BA1 20 A5
Swalcliffe OX15 30 E5
Swalecliffe CT5 25 H5
Swallow LN7 52 E2
Swallow Beck LN6 52 C6
Swallowcliffe SP3 9 J2
Swallowfield RG7 22 A5
Swallows Cross CM15 24 C2
Swampton SP11 21 H6
Swan Green Ches. WA16 49 G5
Swan Green Suff. IP19 35 G1
Swan Street CO6 34 C6
Swanage BH19 10 B7
Swanbach CW3 39 F1
Swanbourne MK17 32 B6
Swanbridge CF64 18 E5
Swancote WV15 39 G6
Swanland HU14 59 F7
Swanlaws TD8 70 C2
Swanley BR8 23 J5
Swanley Village BR8 23 J5
Swanmore Hants. SO32 11 G3
Swanmore I.o.W. PO33 11 G5
Swannington Leics. LE67 41 G4
Swannington Norf. NR9 45 F4
Swanscombe DA10 24 C4
SWANSEA (ABERTAWE) SA 17 K6
Swanston EH10 76 A4
Swanton Abbot NR10 45 G3
Swanton Morley NR20 44 E4
Swanton Novers NR24 44 E2
Swanton Street ME9 14 D2
Swanwick Derbys. DE55 51 G7
Swanwick Hants. SO31 11 G4
Swanwick Green SY13 38 E1
Swarby NG34 42 D1
Swardeston NR14 45 G5
Swarkestone DE73 41 F3
Swarland NE65 71 G3
Swarraton SO24 11 G1
Swarthmoor LA12 55 F2
Swaton NG34 42 E2
Swavesey CB4 33 G2
Sway SO41 10 D5
Swayfield NG33 42 C3
Swaythling SO18 11 F3
Swaythorpe YO25 59 G3
Sweetham EX5 7 G6
Sweethay TA3 8 B2
Sweetshouse PL30 4 A4
Swefling IP17 35 H2
Swell TA3 8 C2
Swepstone LE67 41 F4
Swerford OX7 30 E5
Swettenham CW12 49 H6
Swffryd NP11 19 F2
Swift's Green TN27 14 D3
Swiftsden TN19 14 C5
Swilland IP6 35 F3
Swillington LS26 57 J6
Swimbridge EX32 6 E3
Swimbridge Newland EX32 6 D2
Swinbrook OX18 30 D7
Swincliffe HG3 57 H4
Swincombe EX31 6 E1
Swinden BD23 56 D4
Swinderby LN6 52 B6
Swindon Staffs. DY3 40 A6
SWINDON Swin. SN 20 E3
Swindon Village GL51 29 J6
Swine HU11 59 H6
Swinefleet DN14 58 D7
Swineford BS30 19 K5
Swineshead Beds. MK44 32 D2
Swineshead Lincs. PE20 43 F1
Swineshead Bridge PE20 43 F1
Swineside DL8 57 F1
Swiney KW3 105 H5
Swinford Leics. LE17 31 G1
Swinford Oxon. OX29 21 H1
Swingate NG16 41 H1
Swingfield Minnis CT15 15 H3
Swingleton Green IP7 34 D4
Swinhoe NE67 71 H1
Swinhope LN8 53 F3
Swining ZE2 107 N6
Swinithwaite DL8 57 F1
Swinscoe DE6 40 D1
Swinside Hall TD8 70 C2
Swinstead NG33 42 D3
Swinton Gt.Man. M27 49 G2
Swinton N.Yorks. YO17 58 D2
Swinton N.Yorks. HG4 57 H2
Swinton S.Yorks. S64 51 G3
Swinton Sc.Bord. TD11 77 G6
Swinton Quarter TD11 77 G6
Swintonmill TD12 77 G6
Swithland LE12 41 H4
Swordale IV16 96 C5
Swordland PH41 86 D5
Swordle PH36 86 B7
Swordly KW14 104 C2
Sworton Heath WA16 49 F4
Swyddffynnon SY25 27 F2
Swyncombe RG9 21 K2
Swynnerton ST15 40 A2
Swyre DT2 8 E6
Sychnant LD6 27 J1
Syde GL53 29 J7
Sydenham Gt.Lon. SE26 23 G4
Sydenham Oxon. OX39 22 A1
Sydenham Damerel PL19 4 E3
Syderstone PE31 44 C2
Sydling St. Nicholas DT2 9 F5
Sydmonton RG20 21 H6
Sydney CW1 49 G7
Syerston NG23 42 A1
Sykehouse DN14 51 J1
Sykes BB7 56 B4
Sylen SA15 17 J5
Symbister ZE2 107 P6
Symington S.Ayr. KA1 74 B7
Symington S.Lan. ML12 75 H7
Symonds Yat HR9 28 E7
Symondsbury DT6 8 D5
Synod Inn (Post-mawr) SA44 26 D3
Syre KW11 103 J4
Syreford GL54 30 B6
Syresham NN13 31 H4
Syston Leics. LE7 41 J4
Syston Lincs. NG32 42 C1
Sytchampton DY13 29 H2
Sywell NN6 32 B2

T

Taagan IV22 95 G5
Tableyhill WA16 49 G5
Tabost W.Isles HS2 101 F6
Tabost (Harbost) W.Isles HS2 101 H1
Tachbrook Mallory CV33 30 E2
Tacher KW5 105 G4
Tackley OX5 31 F6
Tacleit (Hacklete) HS2 100 D4
Tacolneston NR16 45 F6
Tadcaster LS24 57 K5
Tadden BH21 9 J4
Taddington Derbys. SK17 50 D5
Taddington Glos. GL54 30 B5
Taddiport EX38 6 C4
Tadley RG26 21 K5
Tadlow SG8 33 F4
Tadmarton OX15 30 E5
Tadpole Bridge SN7 21 G1
Tadworth KT20 23 F6
Tafarnaubach NP22 28 A7
Tafarn-y-bwlch SA41 16 D2
Tafarn-y-Gelyn CH7 47 K6
Taff Merthyr Garden Village CF46 18 E2
Taff's Well (Ffynnon Taf) CF15 18 E3
Tafolwern SY19 37 H5
Taibach N.P.T. SA13 18 A3
Tai-bach Powys SY10 38 A3
Taicynhaeaf LL40 37 F4
Tain High. KW14 105 H2
Tain High. IV19 96 E3
Tai'n Lôn LL54 46 C7
Tai'r Bull LD3 27 J6
Tairbeart (Tarbert) HS3 100 D7
Tairgwaith SA18 27 G7
Tai'r-heol CF46 18 E2
Tairlaw KA19 67 J3
Tai'r-ysgol SA7 17 K6
Takeley CM22 33 J6
Takeley Street CM22 33 J6
Talachddu LD3 27 K5
Talacre CH8 47 K4
Talardd LL23 37 H3
Talaton EX5 7 J6
Talbenny SA62 16 B4
Talbot Green CF72 18 D3
Talbot Village BH10 10 B5
Talerddig SY19 37 J5
Talgarreg SA44 26 D3
Talgarth LD3 28 A5
Taliesin SY20 37 F6
Talisker IV47 85 J1
Talke Pits ST7 49 H7
Talkin CA8 61 G1
Talla Linnfoots ML12 69 G1
Talladale IV22 95 F4
Talladh-a-Bheithe PH17 81 G2
Talland PL13 4 C5
Tallarn Green SY14 38 D1
Tallentire CA13 60 C3
Talley (Talyllychau) SA19 17 K2
Tallington PE9 42 D5
Talmine IV27 103 H2
Talog SA33 17 G3
Tal-sarn SA48 26 E3
Talsarnau LL47 37 F2
Talskiddy TR9 3 G2
Talwrn I.o.A. LL77 46 C5
Talwrn Wrex. LL14 38 B1
Talwrn Wrex. LL13 38 C1
Talybont Cere. SY24 37 F7
Tal-y-bont Conwy LL32 47 F6
Tal-y-bont Gwyn. LL43 36 E3
Tal-y-bont Gwyn. LL57 46 E5
Talybont-on-Usk LD3 28 A6
Tal-y-Cae LL57 46 E6
Tal-y-cafn LL28 47 F5
Tal-y-coed NP7 28 D7
Talygarn CF72 18 D3
Talyllychau (Talley) SA19 17 K2
Tal-y-llyn Gwyn. LL36 37 G5
Talyllyn Powys LD3 28 A6
Talysarn LL54 46 C7
Tal-y-wern SY20 37 H5
Tamavoid FK8 74 D1
Tamerton Foliot PL5 4 E4
Tamworth B79 40 E5
Tamworth Green PE22 43 G1
Tan Office Green IP29 34 B3
Tandem HD5 50 D1
Tandridge RH8 23 G6
Tanerdy SA31 17 H3
Tanfield DH9 62 C1
Tanfield Lea DH9 62 C1
Tang HG3 57 H4
Tang Hall YO10 58 C4
Tangiers SA62 16 C4
Tanglandford AB41 91 G1
Tangley SP11 21 G6
Tangmere PO20 12 C6
Tangwick ZE2 107 L5
Tangy PA28 66 A1
Tankerness KW17 106 E7
Tankersley S75 51 F2
Tankerton CT5 25 H5
Tan-lan LL48 37 F1
Tannach KW1 105 J4
Tannachie AB39 91 F6
Tannachy IV28 96 E1
Tannadice DD8 83 F2
Tannington IP13 35 G2
Tannochside G71 74 E4
Tansley DE4 51 F7
Tansley Knoll DE4 51 F7
Tansor PE8 42 D6
Tantobie DH9 62 C1
Tanton TS9 63 G5
Tanworth in Arden B94 30 C1
Tan-y-fron LL16 47 H6
Tan-y-graig LL53 36 C2
Tanygrisiau LL41 37 F1
Tan-y-groes SA43 17 F1
Tan-y-pistyll SY10 37 K3
Tan-yr-allt LL19 47 J4
Taobh a' Deas Loch Baghasdail HS8 84 C3
Taobh Siar HS3 100 D7
Taobh Tuath (Northton) HS3 92 E3
Tapeley EX39 6 C3
Taplow SL6 22 C3
Tapton Grove S43 51 G5
Taransay (Tarasaigh) HS3 100 C7
Taraphocain PA38 80 B3
Tarasaigh (Taransay) HS3 100 C7
Tarbat House IV18 96 E4
Tarbert Arg. & B. PA29 73 G4
Tarbert Arg. & B. PA41 72 E5
Tarbert Arg. & B. PA60 72 E2
Tarbert High. PH36 79 H1
Tarbert (Tairbeart) W.Isles HS3 100 D7
Tarbet Arg. & B. G83 80 E7
Tarbet High. PH41 86 D5
Tarbet High. IV27 102 D4
Tarbock Green L35 48 D4
Tarbolton KA5 67 J1
Tarbrax EH55 75 J5
Tardebigge B60 29 J2
Tardy Gate PR5 55 J7
Tarfside DD9 90 C7
Tarland AB34 90 C4

Tarleton PR4 55 H7
Tarlscough L40 48 D1
Tarlton GL7 20 C2
Tarnbrook LA2 55 J4
Tarnock BS26 19 G6
Tarporley CW6 48 E6
Tarr TA4 7 K2
Tarrant Crawford DT11 9 J4
Tarrant Gunville DT11 9 J3
Tarrant Hinton DT11 9 J3
Tarrant Keyneston DT11 9 J4
Tarrant Launceston DT11 9 J4
Tarrant Monkton DT11 9 J4
Tarrant Rawston DT11 9 J4
Tarrant Rushton DT11 9 J4
Tarrel IV20 97 F3
Tarring Neville BN9 13 H6
Tarrington HR1 29 F4
Tarrnacraig KA27 73 H7
Tarsappie PH2 82 C5
Tarskavaig IV46 86 B4
Tarves AB41 91 G1
Tarvie High. IV14 96 B6
Tarvie P. & K. PH10 82 B1
Tarvin CH3 48 D6
Tarvin Sands CH3 48 D6
Tasburgh NR15 45 G6
Tasley WV16 39 F6
Taston OX7 30 E6
Tatenhill DE13 40 E3
Tathall End MK19 32 B4
Tatham LA2 56 B3
Tathwell LN11 53 G4
Tatsfield TN16 23 H6
Tattenhall CH3 48 D7
Tattenhoe MK4 32 B5
Tatterford NR21 44 C3
Tattersett PE31 44 C2
Tattershall LN4 53 F7
Tattershall Bridge LN4 52 E7
Tattershall Thorpe LN4 53 F7
Tattingstone IP9 35 F5
Tatworth TA20 8 C4
Tauchers AB55 98 B6
TAUNTON TA 8 B2
Tavelty AB51 91 F3
Taverham NR8 45 F4
Tavernspite SA34 16 E4
Tavistock PL19 4 E3
Taw Bridge EX18 6 E5
Taw Green EX20 6 E6
Tawstock EX31 6 D3
Taxal SK23 50 C5
Tayburn KA3 74 D6
Taychreggan PA35 80 B5
Tayinloan PA29 72 E6
Taylors Cross EX23 6 A4
Taynafead PA33 80 B6
Taynish PA31 73 F2
Taynton Glos. GL19 29 G6
Taynton Oxon. OX18 30 D7
Taynuilt PA35 80 B4
Tayock DD10 83 H2
Tayovullin PA44 72 A3
Tayport DD6 83 F5
Tayvallich PA31 73 F2
Tea Green LU2 32 E6
Tealby LN8 52 E3
Tealing DD4 83 F4
Team Valley NE11 71 H7
Teanamachar HS6 92 C5
Teangue IV44 86 C4
Teasses KY8 83 F7
Tebay CA10 61 H6
Tebworth LU7 32 C6
Tedburn St. Mary EX6 7 G6
Teddington Glos. GL20 29 J5
Teddington Gt.Lon. TW11 22 E4
Tedstone Delamere HR7 29 F3
Tedstone Wafre HR7 29 F3
Teeton NN6 31 H1
Teffont Evias SP3 9 J1
Teffont Magna SP3 9 J1
Tegryn SA35 17 F2
Teigh LE15 42 B4
Teign Village TQ13 7 G7
Teigngrace TQ12 5 J3
Teignmouth TQ14 5 K3
TELFORD TF 39 F5
Telham TN33 14 C6
Tellisford BA2 20 B6
Telscombe BN7 13 H6
Telscombe Cliffs BN10 13 H6
Tempar PH16 81 H2
Templand DG11 69 F5
Temple Cornw. PL30 4 B3
Temple Midloth. EH23 76 B5
Temple Balsall B93 30 D1
Temple Bar SA48 26 E3
Temple Cloud BS39 19 K6
Temple End CB9 33 K3
Temple Ewell CT16 15 H3
Temple Grafton B49 30 C3
Temple Guiting GL54 30 B6
Temple Herdewyke CV47 30 E3
Temple Hirst YO8 58 C7
Temple Normanton S42 51 G6
Temple Sowerby CA10 61 H4
Templecombe BA8 9 G2
Templeton Devon EX16 7 G4
Templeton Pembs. SA67 16 E4
Templeton Bridge EX16 7 G4
Templewood DD9 83 H1
Tempsford SG19 32 E3
Ten Mile Bank PE38 44 A6
Tenbury Wells WR15 28 E2
Tenby (Dinbych-y-pysgod) SA70 16 E5
Tendring CO16 35 F6
Tendring Green CO16 35 F6
Tenga PA72 79 G3
Tenterden TN30 14 D4
Tepersie Castle AB33 90 D2
Terally DG9 64 B6
Terling CM3 34 B7
Tern TF6 39 F4
Ternhill TF9 39 F2
Terregles DG2 65 K3
Terriers HP13 22 B2
Terrington YO60 58 C2
Terrington St. Clement PE34 43 J3
Terrington St. John PE14 43 J4
Terry's Green B94 30 C1
Tervieside AB37 89 K1
Teston ME18 14 C2
Testwood SO40 10 E3
Tetbury GL8 20 B2
Tetbury Upton GL8 20 B2
Tetchill SY12 38 C2
Tetcott EX22 6 B6
Tetford LN9 53 G5
Tetney DN36 53 G2
Tetney Lock DN36 53 G2
Tetsworth OX9 21 K1
Tettenhall WV6 40 A5
Tettenhall Wood WV6 40 A6
Tetworth SG19 33 F3
Teuchan AB42 91 J1
Teversal NG17 51 G6
Teversham CB1 33 H3
Teviothead TD9 69 K3
Tewel AB39 91 G6
Tewin AL6 33 F7
Tewkesbury GL20 29 H5
Teynham ME9 25 F5
Thackley BD10 57 G6
Thainston AB30 90 E7
Thainstone AB51 91 F3
Thakeham RH20 12 E5
Thame OX9 22 A1
Thames Ditton KT7 22 E5
Thames Haven SS17 24 D3
Thamesmead SE28 23 H3
Thanington CT1 15 G2
Thankerton ML12 75 H7
Tharston NR15 45 F6
Thatcham RG18 21 J5
Thatto Heath WA9 48 E3
Thaxted CM6 33 K5
The Apes Hall CB6 43 J6
The Bage HR3 28 B4
The Balloch PH7 81 K6
The Banking AB51 91 F1
The Bar RH13 12 E4
The Birks AB32 91 F4
The Bog SY5 38 C6
The Bourne GU9 22 B7
The Bratch WV5 40 A6
The Broad HR6 28 D2
The Bryn NP7 19 G1
The Burf DY13 29 H2
The Burn DD9 90 D7
The Butts BA11 20 A7
The Camp GL6 20 C1
The Chequer SY13 38 D1
The City Bucks. HP14 22 A2
The City Suff. NR34 45 H7
The Common Wilts. SP5 10 D1
The Common Wilts. SN15 20 D3
The Craigs IV24 96 B2
The Cronk IM7 54 C4
The Delves WS5 40 C6
The Den KA24 74 B5
The Dicker BN27 13 J6
The Down WV16 39 F6
The Drums DD8 82 E1
The Eaves GL15 19 K1
The Flatt CA6 70 A6
The Folly AL4 32 E7
The Forge HR5 28 C3
The Forstal E.Suss. TN3 13 J3
The Forstal Kent TN25 15 F4
The Grange Lincs. LN13 53 J5
The Grange Shrop. SY12 38 C2
The Grange Surr. RH9 23 G7
The Green Arg. & B. PA77 78 A3
The Green Cumb. LA18 54 E1
The Green Essex CM8 34 B7
The Green Flints. CH7 48 B6
The Green Wilts. SP3 9 H1
The Grove WR8 29 H4
The Haven RH14 12 D3
The Headland TS24 63 G3
The Heath ST14 40 C2
The Herberts CF71 18 C4
The Hermitage KT20 23 F6
The Hill LA18 54 E1
The Holme HG3 57 H4
The Howe IM9 54 A7
The Isle SY3 38 D4
The Laurels NR14 45 H6
The Leacon TN26 14 E4
The Lee HP16 22 B1
The Leigh GL19 29 H6
The Lhen IM7 54 C3
The Lodge PA24 73 K1
The Marsh SY5 38 C6
The Moor E.Suss. TN35 14 D6
The Moor Kent TN18 14 C5
The Mumbles SA3 17 K7
The Murray G75 74 E5
The Mythe GL20 29 H5
The Narth NP25 19 J1
The Neuk AB31 91 F5
The Node SG4 33 F7
The Oval BA2 20 A5
The Polchar PH22 89 G4
The Quarter TN27 14 D3
The Reddings GL51 29 J6
The Rhos SA62 16 D4
The Rookery ST7 49 H7
The Rowe ST5 40 A2
The Sale DE13 40 D4
The Sands GU10 22 B7
The Shoe SN14 20 B4
The Slade RG7 21 J4
The Smithies WV16 39 F6
The Stocks TN30 14 E5
The Swillett WD3 22 D2
The Thrift SG8 33 G5
The Vauld HR1 28 E4
The Wern LL14 48 B7
The Wyke TF11 39 G5
Theakston DL8 57 J1
Thealby DN15 52 B1
Theale Som. BS28 19 H7
Theale W.Berks. RG7 21 K4
Thearne HU17 59 G6
Theberton IP16 35 J2
Thedden Grange GU34 11 H1
Theddingworth LE17 41 J7
Theddlethorpe All Saints LN12 53 H4
Theddlethorpe St. Helen LN12 53 H4
Thelbridge Barton EX17 7 F4
Thelbridge Cross EX17 7 F4
Thelnetham IP22 34 E1
Thelveton IP21 45 F7
Thelwall WA4 49 F4
Themelthorpe NR20 44 E3
Thenford OX17 31 G4
Therfield SG8 33 G5
Thetford Lincs. PE6 42 E4
Thetford Norf. IP24 44 C7
Thethwaite CA5 60 E2
Theydon Bois CM16 23 H2
Theydon Garnon CM16 23 H2
Theydon Mount CM16 23 H2
Thickwood SN14 20 B4
Thimbleby Lincs. LN9 53 F6
Thimbleby N.Yorks. DL6 63 F7
Thingley SN13 20 B5
Thirkleby YO7 57 K2
Thirlby YO7 57 K1
Thirlestane TD2 76 D6
Thirn HG4 57 H1
Thirsk YO7 57 K1
Thirston New Houses NE65 71 G4
Thirtleby HU11 59 H6
Thistleton Lancs. PR4 55 H6
Thistleton Rut. LE15 42 C4
Thistley Green IP28 33 K1
Thixendale YO17 58 E3
Thockrington NE48 70 E6
Tholomas Drove PE13 43 G5
Tholthorpe YO61 57 K3
Thomas Chapel SA68 16 E5
Thomas Close CA11 60 F2
Thomastown AB54 90 D1
Thompson IP24 44 D6
Thomshill IV30 97 K6
Thong DA12 24 C4
Thongsbridge HD9 50 D2
Thoralby DL8 57 F1
Thoresby NG22 51 J5
Thoresthorpe LN13 53 H5
Thoresway LN8 52 E3
Thorganby Lincs. DN37 53 F3
Thorganby N.Yorks. YO19 58 C5
Thorgill YO18 63 J7
Thorington IP19 35 J1
Thorington Street CO6 34 E5
Thorley CM23 33 H7
Thorley Houses CM23 33 H6
Thorley Street Herts. CM23 33 H7
Thorley Street I.o.W. PO41 10 E6
Thormanby YO61 57 K2
Thornaby-on-Tees TS17 63 F5
Thornage NR25 44 E2
Thornborough Bucks. MK18 31 J5
Thornborough N.Yorks. DL8 57 H2
Thornbury Devon EX22 6 B5
Thornbury Here. HR7 29 F3
Thornbury S.Glos. BS35 19 K2
Thornbury W.Yorks. BD3 57 G6
Thornby NN6 31 H1
Thorncliff HD8 50 E1
Thorncliffe ST13 50 C7
Thorncombe TA20 8 C4
Thorncombe Street GU5 22 D7
Thorncote Green SG19 32 E4
Thorncross PO30 11 F6
Thorndon IP23 35 F2
Thorndon Cross EX20 6 D6
Thorne DN8 51 J1
Thorne St. Margaret TA21 7 J3
Thorner LS14 57 J6
Thorney Bucks. SL0 22 D4
Thorney Notts. NG23 52 B5
Thorney Peter. PE6 43 F5
Thorney Som. TA10 8 D2
Thorney Close SR4 62 E1
Thorney Hill BH23 10 D5
Thornfalcon TA3 8 B2
Thornford DT9 9 F3
Thorngrafton NE47 70 C7
Thorngrove TA7 8 C1
Thorngumbald HU12 59 J7
Thornham PE36 44 B1
Thornham Magna IP23 35 F1
Thornham Parva IP23 35 F1
Thornhaugh PE8 42 D5
Thornhill Cardiff CF83 18 E3
Thornhill Cumb. CA22 60 B6
Thornhill D. & G. DG3 68 D4
Thornhill Derbys. S33 50 D4
Thornhill S'ham. SO19 11 F3
Thornhill Stir. FK8 81 H7
Thornhill W.Yorks. WF12 50 E1
Thornhill Lees WF12 50 E1
Thornholme YO25 59 H3
Thornicombe DT11 9 H4
Thornley Dur. DH6 62 E3
Thornley Dur. DL13 62 C3
Thornley Gate NE47 61 K1
Thornliebank G46 74 D5
Thornroan AB41 91 G1
Thorns CB8 34 B3
Thorns Green WA15 49 G4
Thornsett SK22 50 C4
Thornthwaite Cumb. CA12 60 D4
Thornthwaite N.Yorks. HG3 57 G4
Thornton Angus DD8 82 E3
Thornton Bucks. MK17 31 J5
Thornton E.Riding YO42 58 D5
Thornton Fife KY1 76 A1
Thornton Lancs. FY5 55 G5
Thornton Leics. LE67 41 G5
Thornton Lincs. LN9 53 F6
Thornton Mersey. L23 48 C2
Thornton Middbro. TS8 63 F5
Thornton Northumb. TD15 77 H6
Thornton P. & K. PH8 82 B3
Thornton Pembs. SA73 16 C5
Thornton W.Yorks. BD13 57 G6
Thornton Bridge YO61 57 K2
Thornton Curtis DN39 52 D1
Thornton Heath CR7 23 G5
Thornton Hough CH63 48 C4
Thornton in Lonsdale LA6 56 B2
Thornton le Moor LN7 52 D3
Thornton Park TD15 77 H6
Thornton Rust DL8 56 E1
Thornton Steward HG4 57 G1
Thornton Watlass HG4 57 H1
Thorntonhall G74 74 D5
Thornton-in-Craven BD23 56 E5
Thornton-le-Beans DL6 63 F7
Thornton-le-Clay YO60 58 C3
Thornton-le-Dale YO18 58 E1
Thornton-le-Moor DL7 57 J1
Thornton-le-Moors CH2 48 D5
Thornton-le-Street YO7 57 K1
Thorntonloch EH42 77 F3
Thornwood CM16 23 H1
Thornyhill AB30 90 E7
Thornylee TD1 76 C7
Thoroton NG13 42 A1
Thorp Arch LS23 57 K5
Thorpe Derbys. DE6 50 D7
Thorpe E.Riding YO25 59 F5
Thorpe Lincs. LN12 53 H4
Thorpe N.Yorks. BD23 57 F3
Thorpe Norf. NR14 45 J6
Thorpe Notts. NG23 51 K7
Thorpe Surr. TW20 22 D5
Thorpe Abbotts IP21 45 F7
Thorpe Acre LE11 41 H4
Thorpe Arnold LE14 42 A3
Thorpe Audlin WF8 51 G1
Thorpe Bassett YO17 58 E2
Thorpe Bay SS1 25 F3
Thorpe by Water LE15 42 B6
Thorpe Constantine B79 40 E5
Thorpe Culvert PE24 53 H6
Thorpe End NR13 45 G4
Thorpe Green Essex CO16 35 F6
Thorpe Green Lancs. PR6 55 J7
Thorpe Green Suff. IP30 34 D3
Thorpe Hall YO62 58 B2
Thorpe Hesley S61 51 F3
Thorpe in Balne DN6 51 H1
Thorpe in the Fallows LN1 52 C4
Thorpe Langton LE16 42 A6
Thorpe Larches TS21 62 E4
Thorpe le Street YO42 58 E5
Thorpe Malsor NN14 32 B1
Thorpe Mandeville OX17 31 G4
Thorpe Market NR11 45 G2
Thorpe Morieux IP30 34 D3
Thorpe on the Hill Lincs. LN6 52 C6
Thorpe on the Hill W.Yorks. WF3 57 J7
Thorpe Row IP25 44 D5
Thorpe St. Andrew NR7 45 G5
Thorpe St. Peter PE24 53 H6
Thorpe Salvin S80 51 H4
Thorpe Satchville LE14 42 A4
Thorpe Street IP22 34 E1
Thorpe Thewles TS21 63 F4
Thorpe Tilney Dales LN4 52 E7
Thorpe Underwood N.Yorks. YO26 57 K4
Thorpe Underwood Northants. NN6 42 A7
Thorpe Waterville NN14 42 D7
Thorpe Willoughby YO8 58 B6
Thorpefield YO7 57 K2
Thorpe-le-Soken CO16 35 F6
Thorpeness IP16 35 J2
Thorpland PE33 44 A5
Thorrington CO7 34 E6
Thorverton EX5 7 H5
Thrandeston IP21 35 F1
Thrapston NN14 32 C1
Threapland BD23 56 E3
Threapwood SY14 38 D1
Threapwood Head ST10 40 C1
Three Ashes BA3 19 K7
Three Bridges RH10 13 F3
Three Burrows TR4 2 E4
Three Chimneys TN27 14 D4
Three Cocks (Aberllynfi) LD3 28 A5
Three Crosses SA4 17 J6
Three Cups Corner TN21 13 K4
Three Hammers PL15 4 C2
Three Holes PE14 43 J5
Three Leg Cross TN5 13 K3
Three Legged Cross BH21 10 B4
Three Mile Cross RG7 22 A5
Three Oaks TN35 14 D6
Threehammer Common NR12 45 H4
Threekingham NG34 42 D2
Threemilestone TR3 2 E4
Threlkeld CA12 60 E4
Threshfield BD23 56 E3
Threxton Hill IP25 44 C5
Thriepley DD2 82 E4
Thrigby NR29 45 J4
Thringarth DL12 62 A4
Thringstone LE67 41 G4
Thrintoft DL7 62 E7
Thriplow SG8 33 H4
Throapham S25 51 H4
Throckenholt PE12 43 G5
Throcking SG9 33 G5
Throckley NE15 71 G7
Throckmorton WR10 29 J4
Throop DT2 9 H5
Throphill NE61 71 G5
Thropton NE65 71 F3
Througham GL6 20 C1
Throwleigh EX20 6 E6
Throwley ME13 14 E2
Throws CM6 33 K6
Thrumpton Notts. NG11 41 H2
Thrumpton Notts. DN22 51 K5
Thrumster KW1 105 J4
Thrunton NE66 71 F2
Thrupp Glos. GL5 20 B1
Thrupp Oxon. OX5 31 F7
Thrupp Oxon. SN7 21 F2
Thruscross HG3 57 G4
Thrushelton EX20 6 C7
Thrussington LE7 41 J4
Thruxton Hants. SP11 21 F7
Thruxton Here. HR2 28 D5
Thrybergh S65 51 G3
Thulston DE72 41 G2
Thunder Bridge HD8 50 D1
Thundergay KA27 73 G6
Thundersley SS7 24 E3
Thunderton AB42 99 J6
Thundridge SG12 33 G7
Thurcaston LE7 41 H4
Thurcroft S66 51 G4
Thurdistoft KW14 105 H2
Thurdon EX23 6 A4
Thurgarton Norf. NR11 45 F2
Thurgarton Notts. NG14 41 J1
Thurgoland S35 50 E2
Thurlaston Leics. LE9 41 H6
Thurlaston Warks. CV23 31 F1
Thurlbear TA3 8 B2
Thurlby Lincs. PE10 42 E4
Thurlby Lincs. LN5 52 C6
Thurlby Lincs. LN13 53 H5
Thurleigh MK44 32 D3
Thurlestone TQ7 5 G6
Thurloxton TA2 8 B1
Thurlstone S36 50 E2
Thurlton NR14 45 J6
Thurlwood ST7 49 H7
Thurmaston LE4 41 J5
Thurnby LE7 41 J5
Thurne NR29 45 J4
Thurnham ME14 14 D2
Thurning Norf. NR20 44 E3
Thurning Northants. PE8 42 D7
Thurnscoe S63 51 G2
Thursby CA5 60 E1
Thursden BB10 56 E6
Thursford NR21 44 D2
Thursley GU8 12 C3
Thurso KW14 105 G2
Thurstaston CH61 48 B4
Thurston IP31 34 D2
Thurston Clough OL3 49 J2
Thurstonfield CA5 60 E1
Thurstonland HD4 50 D1
Thurton NR14 45 H5
Thurvaston Derbys. DE6 40 E2
Thurvaston Derbys. DE6 40 D2
Thuster KW1 105 H3
Thuxton NR9 44 E5
Thwaite N.Yorks. DL11 61 K7
Thwaite Suff. IP23 35 F2
Thwaite Head LA12 60 E7
Thwaite St. Mary NR35 45 H6
Thwaites BD21 57 F5
Thwaites Brow BD21 57 F5
Thwing YO25 59 G2
Tibbermore PH1 82 B5
Tibberton Glos. GL19 29 G6
Tibberton Tel. & W. TF10 39 F3
Tibberton Worcs. WR9 29 J3
Tibbie Shiels Inn TD7 69 H1
Tibenham NR16 45 F6
Tibertich PA31 79 K7
Tibshelf DE55 51 G6
Tibthorpe YO25 59 F4
Ticehurst TN5 13 K3
Tichborne SO24 11 G1
Tickencote PE9 42 C5
Tickenham BS21 19 H4
Tickford End MK16 32 B4
Tickhill DN11 51 H3
Ticklerton SY6 38 D6

Ticknall DE73 41 F3
Tickton HU17 59 G5
Tidbury Green B90 30 C1
Tidcombe SN8 21 F6
Tiddington *Oxon.* OX9 21 K1
Tiddington *Warks.* CV37 30 D3
Tiddleywink SN14 20 B4
Tidebrook TN5 13 K4
Tideford PL12 4 D5
Tideford Cross PL12 4 D4
Tidenham NP16 19 J2
Tidenham Chase NP16 19 J2
Tideswell SK17 50 D5
Tidmarsh RG8 21 K4
Tidmington CV36 30 D5
Tidpit SP6 10 B3
Tidworth SP9 21 F7
Tiers Cross SA62 16 C4
Tiffield NN12 31 H3
Tifty AB53 99 F6
Tigerton DD9 83 G1
Tigh a' Gearraidh HS6 92 C4
Tighachnoic PA34 79 H3
Tighnablair PH6 81 J6
Tighnabruaich PA21 73 H3
Tighnacomaire PH33 80 A1
Tigley TQ9 5 H4
Tilbrook PE28 32 D2
Tilbury RM18 24 C4
Tilbury Green CO9 34 B4
Tile Hill CV4 30 D1
Tilehurst RG31 21 K4
Tilford GU10 22 B7
Tilgate RH10 13 F3
Tilgate Forest Row RH10 13 F3
Tillathrowie AB54 90 C1
Tillers' Green GL18 29 F5
Tillery AB41 91 H2
Tilley SY4 38 E3
Tillicoultry FK13 75 H1
Tillingham CM0 25 F1
Tillington *Here.* HR4 28 D4
Tillington *W.Suss.* GU28 12 C4
Tillington Common HR4 28 D4
Tillyarblet DD9 83 G1
Tillybirloch AB51 90 E4
Tillycairn Castle AB51 90 E3
Tillycorthie AB41 91 H2
Tillydrine AB34 90 E5
Tillyfar AB53 99 G6
Tillyfour AB33 90 D3
Tillyfourie AB51 90 E3
Tillygreig AB41 91 G2
Tillypronie AB34 90 C4
Tilmanstone CT14 15 J2
Tiln DN22 51 K4
Tilney All Saints PE34 43 J4
Tilney Fen End PE14 43 J4
Tilney High End PE34 43 J4
Tilney St. Lawrence PE34 43 J4
Tilshead SP3 20 D7
Tilstock SY13 38 E2
Tilston SY14 48 D7
Tilstone Fearnall CW6 48 E6
Tilsworth LU7 32 C6
Tilton on the Hill LE7 42 A5
Tiltups End GL6 20 B2
Timberland LN4 52 E7
Timberland Dales LN10 52 E6
Timbersbrook CW12 49 H6
Timberscombe TA24 7 H1
Timble LS21 57 G4
Timewell EX16 7 H3
Timperley WA15 49 G4
Timsbury *B. & N.E.Som.* BA2 19 K6
Timsbury *Hants.* SO51 10 E2
Timsgearraidh HS2 100 C4
Timworth IP31 34 C2
Timworth Green IP31 34 C2
Tincleton DT2 9 G5
Tindale CA8 61 H1
Tindon End CB10 33 K5
Tingewick MK18 31 H5
Tingley WF3 57 H7
Tingrith MK17 32 D5
Tingwall KW17 106 D5
Tingwall (Lerwick) Airport ZE2 107 N8
Tinhay PL16 6 B7
Tinney EX22 4 C1
Tinshill LS16 57 H6
Tinsley S9 51 G3
Tinsley Green RH10 13 F3
Tintagel PL34 4 A2
Tintern Parva NP16 19 J1
Tintinhull BA22 8 D3
Tintwistle SK13 50 C3
Tinwald DG1 69 F5
Tinwell PE9 42 D5
Tippacott EX35 7 F1
Tipperty *Aber.* AB30 91 F6
Tipperty *Aber.* AB41 91 H2
Tipps End PE14 43 H6
Tiptoe SO41 10 D5
Tipton DY4 40 B6
Tipton St. John EX10 7 J6
Tiptree CO5 34 C7
Tiptree Heath CO5 34 C7
Tirabad LD4 27 H4
Tiree PA77 78 A3
Tiree Airport PA77 78 B3
Tirindrish PH34 87 J6
Tirley GL19 29 H6
Tirphil NP24 18 E1
Tirril CA10 61 G4
Tir-y-dail SA18 17 K4
Tisbury SP3 9 J2
Tisman's Common RH12 12 D3
Tissington DE6 50 D7
Tister KW12 105 G2
Titchberry EX39 6 A3
Titchfield PO14 11 G4
Titchmarsh NN14 32 D1
Titchwell PE31 44 B1
Tithby NG13 41 J2
Titley HR5 28 C2
Titlington NE66 71 G2
Titmore Green SG4 33 F6
Titsey RH8 23 H6
Titson EX23 6 A5
Tittensor ST12 40 A2
Tittleshall PE32 44 C3
Tiverton *Ches.* CW6 48 E6
Tiverton *Devon* EX16 7 H4
Tivetshall St. Margaret NR15 45 F7
Tivetshall St. Mary NR15 45 F7
Tivington TA24 7 H1
Tixall ST18 40 B3
Tixover PE9 42 C5
Toab *Ork.* KW17 106 E7
Toab *Shet.* ZE3 107 M11
Tobermory PA75 79 G2
Toberonochy PA34 79 J7
Tobha Mòr (Homore) HS8 84 C1
Tobson HS2 100 D4
Tocher AB51 90 E1
Tockenham SN4 20 D4
Tockenham Wick SN4 20 D3
Tockholes BB3 56 B7
Tockington BS32 19 K3
Tockwith YO26 57 K4
Todber DT10 9 G2
Toddington *Beds.* LU5 32 D6
Toddington *Glos.* GL54 30 B5
Todenham GL56 30 D5
Todhills *Angus* DD4 83 F4
Todhills *Cumb.* CA6 69 J7
Todlachie AB51 90 E3
Todmorden OL14 56 E7
Todwick S26 51 G4
Toft *Cambs.* CB3 33 G3
Toft *Lincs.* PE10 42 D4
Toft *Shet.* ZE2 107 N5
Toft Hill DL14 62 C4
Toft Monks NR34 45 J6
Toft next Newton LN8 52 D4
Toftcarl KW1 105 J4
Toftrees NR21 44 C3
Tofts KW1 105 J2
Toftwood NR19 44 D4
Togston NE65 71 H3
Tokavaig IV46 86 C3
Tokers Green RG4 21 K4
Tolastadh HS2 101 H3
Tolastadh a' Chaolais HS2 100 D4
Tolastadh Ùr HS2 101 H3
Toll Bar DN5 51 H2
Toll of Birness AB41 91 J1
Tolland TA4 7 K2
Tollard Farnham DT11 9 J3
Tollard Royal SP5 9 J3
Tollcross G32 74 E4
Toller Down Gate DT2 8 E4
Toller Fratrum DT2 8 E5
Toller Porcorum DT2 8 E5
Toller Whelme DT8 8 E4
Tollerton *N.Yorks.* YO61 58 B3
Tollerton *Notts.* NG12 41 J2
Tollesbury CM9 34 D7
Tollesby TS4 63 G5
Tolleshunt D'Arcy CM9 34 D7
Tolleshunt Knights CM9 34 D7
Tolleshunt Major CM9 34 C7
Tolm (Holm) HS2 101 G4
Tolmachan HS3 100 C7
Tolpuddle DT2 9 G5
Tolvah PH21 89 F5
Tolworth KT6 22 E5
Tom an Fhuadain HS2 101 F6
Tomatin IV13 89 F2
Tombreck IV2 88 D1
Tomchrasky IV63 87 J3
Tomdoun PH35 87 H4
Tomdow IV36 97 H7
Tomich *High.* IV4 87 K2
Tomich *High.* IV18 96 E4
Tomich *High.* IV27 96 D1
Tomintoul AB37 89 J3
Tomnacross IV4 96 C7
Tomnamoon IV36 97 H6
Tomnaven AB54 90 C1
Tomnavoulin AB37 89 K2
Tomvaich PH26 89 H1
Ton Pentre CF41 18 C2
Tonbridge TN9 23 J7
Tondu CF32 18 B3
Tonedale TA21 7 K3
Tonfanau LL36 36 E5
Tong *Kent* TN27 14 D3
Tong *Shrop.* TF11 39 G5
Tong *W.Yorks.* BD4 57 H6
Tong Norton TF11 39 G5
Tong Street BD4 57 G6
Tonge DE73 41 G3
Tongham GU10 22 B7
Tongland DG6 65 G5
Tongue IV27 103 H3
Tongue House IV27 103 H3
Tongwynlais CF15 18 E3
Tonmawr SA12 18 B2
Tonna SA11 18 A2
Tonwell SG12 33 G7
Tonypandy CF40 18 C2
Tonyrefail CF39 18 D3
Toot Baldon OX44 21 J1
Toot Hill CM5 23 J1
Toothill *Hants.* SO51 10 E3
Toothill *Swin.* SN5 20 E3
Tooting Graveney SW17 23 F4
Top End MK44 32 D2
Top of Hebers M24 49 H2
Topcliffe YO7 57 K2
Topcroft NR35 45 G6
Topcroft Street NR35 45 G6
Toppesfield CO9 34 B5
Toppings BL7 49 G1
Toprow NR16 45 F6
Topsham EX3 7 H7
Topsham Bridge TQ7 5 H5
Torastan PA78 78 D1
Torbain AB37 89 J3
Torbeg *Aber.* AB35 90 B5
Torbeg *N.Ayr.* KA27 66 D1
Torbothie ML7 75 G5
Torbryan TQ12 5 J4
Torcastle PH33 87 H7
Torcross TQ7 5 J6
Tordarroch IV2 88 D1
Tore IV6 96 D6
Toreduff IV36 97 J5
Toremore *High.* PH26 89 J1
Toremore *High.* KW6 105 G5
Torfrey PL23 4 B5
Torgyle IV63 87 K3
Torksey LN1 52 B5
Torlum HS7 92 C6
Torlundy PH33 87 H7
Tormarton GL9 20 A4
Tormisdale PA47 72 A5
Tormore KA27 73 G7
Tornagrain IV2 96 E6
Tornahaish AB36 89 K4
Tornaveen AB31 90 E4
Torness IV2 88 C2
Toronto DL14 62 C3
Torpenhow CA7 60 D3
Torphichen EH48 75 H3
Torphins AB31 90 E4
Torpoint PL11 4 E5
TORQUAY TQ 5 K4
Torquhan TD1 76 C6
Torr PL8 5 F5
Torran *Arg. & B.* PA31 79 K7
Torran *High.* IV18 96 E4
Torran *High.* IV40 94 B7
Torrance G64 74 E3
Torrance House G75 74 E5
Torrancroy AB36 90 B3
Torre *Som.* TA23 7 J1
Torre *Torbay* TQ1 5 K4
Torrich IV12 97 F6
Torridon IV22 94 E6
Torrin IV49 86 B2
Torrisdale *Arg. & B.* PA28 73 F7
Torrisdale *High.* KW14 103 J2
Torrish KW8 104 E7
Torrisholme LA4 55 H3
Torroble IV27 96 C1
Torry *Aber.* AB54 98 C6
Torry *Aberdeen* AB11 91 H4
Torryburn KY12 75 J2
Torsonce TD1 76 C6
Torterston AB42 99 J6
Torthorwald DG1 69 F6
Tortington BN18 12 C6
Torton DY10 29 H1
Tortworth GL12 20 A2
Torvaig IV51 93 K7
Torver LA21 60 D7
Torwood FK5 75 G2
Torworth DN22 51 J4
Tosberry EX39 6 A3
Toscaig IV54 86 D1
Toseland PE19 33 F2
Tosside BD23 56 C4
Tostarie PA74 78 E3
Tostock IP30 34 D2
Totaig IV55 93 G6
Totamore PA78 78 C2
Tote IV51 93 K7
Tote Hill GU29 12 B4
Totegan KW14 104 D2
Totford SO24 11 G1
Totham Hill CM9 34 C7
Tothill LN13 53 H4
Totland PO39 10 E6
Totley S17 51 F5
Totnes TQ9 5 J4
Toton NG9 41 H2
Totronald PA78 78 C2
Totscore IV51 93 J5
Tottenham N17 23 G2
Tottenhill PE33 44 A4
Tottenhill Row PE33 44 A4
Totteridge *Bucks.* HP13 22 B2
Totteridge *Gt.Lon.* N20 23 F2
Totternhoe LU6 32 C6
Tottington *Gt.Man.* BL8 49 G1
Tottington *Norf.* IP24 44 C6
Totton SO40 10 E3
Toulton TA4 7 K2
Tournaig IV22 94 E3
Toux AB42 99 H5
Tovil ME15 14 C2
Tow Law DL13 62 C3
Towan Cross TR4 2 E4
Toward PA23 73 K4
Towcester NN12 31 H4
Towednack TR26 2 B5
Tower End PE32 44 A4
Towersey OX9 22 A1
Towie *Aber.* AB43 99 G4
Towie *Aber.* AB54 90 D2
Towie *Aber.* AB33 90 C3
Towiemore AB55 98 B6
Town End *Cambs.* PE15 43 H6
Town End *Cumb.* LA11 55 H1
Town End *Mersey.* WA8 48 D4
Town Green *Lancs.* L39 48 D2
Town Green *Norf.* NR13 45 H4
Town of Lowton WA3 49 F3
Town Row TN6 13 J3
Town Street IP27 44 B7
Town Yetholm TD5 70 D1
Townfield DH8 62 A2
Townhead *D. & G.* DG6 65 G6
Townhead *S.Yorks.* S36 50 D2
Townhead of Greenlaw DG7 65 H4
Townhill *Fife* KY12 75 K2
Townhill *Swan.* SA1 17 K6
Towns End RG26 21 J6
Towns Green CW6 49 F6
Townshend TR27 2 C5
Towthorpe *E.Riding* YO25 59 F3
Towthorpe *York* YO32 58 C4
Towton LS24 57 K6
Towyn LL22 47 H5
Toynton All Saints PE23 53 G6
Toynton Fen Side PE23 53 G6
Toynton St. Peter PE23 53 H6
Toy's Hill TN16 23 H6
Trabboch KA5 67 J1
Traboe TR12 2 E6
Tradespark *High.* IV12 97 F6
Tradespark *Ork.* KW15 106 D7
Traeth Coch (Red Wharf Bay) LL75 46 D4
Trafford Centre M17 49 G3
Trafford Park M17 49 G3
Trallong LD3 27 J6
Trallwn SA7 17 K6
Tram Inn HR2 28 D5
Tranent EH33 76 C3
Tranmere CH42 48 C4
Trantlebeg KW13 104 D3
Trantlemore KW13 104 D3
Tranwell NE61 71 G5
Trap SA19 17 K4
Trap Street SK11 49 H6
Traprain EH41 76 D3
Trap's Green B94 30 C2
Traquair EH44 76 B7
Trawden BB8 56 E6
Trawsfynydd LL41 37 G2
Trealaw CF40 18 D2
Treales PR4 55 H6
Trearddur LL65 46 A5
Treaslane IV51 93 J6
Tre-Aubrey CF71 18 D4
Trebanog CF39 18 D2
Trebanos SA8 18 A1
Trebarrow EX22 4 C1
Trebartha PL15 4 C3
Trebarvah TR11 2 E5
Trebarwith PL33 4 A2
Trebeath PL15 4 C2
Trebetherick PL27 3 G1
Trebister ZE1 107 N9
Tre-boeth SA5 17 K6
Treborough TA23 7 J2
Trebudannon TR8 3 F2
Trebullett PL15 4 D3
Treburley PL15 4 D3
Treburrick PL27 3 F1
Trebyan PL30 4 A4
Trecastle LD3 27 H6
Trecott EX20 6 E5
Trecrogo PL15 6 B7
Trecwn SA62 16 C2
Trecynon CF44 18 C1
Tredaule PL15 4 C2
Tredavoe TR20 2 B6
Treddiog SA62 16 B3
Tredegar NP22 18 E1
Tredington *Glos.* GL20 29 J6
Tredington *Warks.* CV36 30 D4
Tredinnick *Cornw.* PL27 3 G2
Tredinnick *Cornw.* PL14 4 C5
Tredogan CF62 18 D5
Tredomen LD3 28 A5
Tredrissi SA42 16 D1
Tredunnock NP15 19 G2
Tredustan LD3 28 A5
Tredworth GL1 29 H7
Treen *Cornw.* TR19 2 A6
Treen *Cornw.* TR20 2 B5
Treesmill PL24 4 A5
Treeton S60 51 G4
Trefaldwyn (Montgomery) SY15 38 B6
Trefasser SA64 16 B2
Trefdraeth *I.o.A.* LL62 46 C5
Trefdraeth (Newport) *Pembs.* SA42 16 D2
Trefecca LD3 28 A5
Trefechan CF48 18 D1
Trefeglwys SY17 37 J6
Trefenter SY23 27 F2
Treffgarne SA62 16 C3
Treffynnon (Holywell) *Flints.* CH8 47 K5
Treffynnon *Pembs.* SA62 16 B3
Trefgarn Owen SA62 16 B3
Trefil NP22 28 A7
Trefilan SA48 26 E3
Trefin SA62 16 B2
Treflach SY10 38 B3
Trefnanney SY22 38 B4
Trefnant LL16 47 J5
Trefonen SY10 38 B3
Trefor *Gwyn.* LL54 36 C1
Trefor *I.o.A.* LL65 46 B4
Treforest CF37 18 D3
Treforest Industrial Estate CF37 18 E3
Trefriw LL27 47 F6
Tref-y-clawdd (Knighton) LD7 28 B1
Trefynwy (Monmouth) NP25 28 E7
Tregadillett PL15 4 C2
Tregaian LL77 46 C5
Tregare NP15 28 D7
Tregarland PL13 4 C5
Tregarne TR12 2 E6
Tregaron SY25 27 F3
Tregarth LL57 46 E6
Tregaswith TR8 3 F2
Tregavethan TR4 2 E4
Tregear TR2 3 F3
Tregeare PL15 4 C2
Tregeiriog LL20 38 A2
Tregele LL67 46 B3
Tregidden TR12 2 E6
Tregiskey PL26 4 A6
Treglemais SA62 16 B3
Tregolds PL28 3 F1
Tregole EX23 4 B1
Tregonetha TR9 3 G2
Tregony TR2 3 G4
Tregoodwell PL32 4 B2
Tregoss PL26 3 G2
Tregowris TR12 2 E6
Tregoyd LD3 28 A5
Tregrehan Mills PL25 4 A5
Tre-groes SA44 17 H1
Treguff CF71 18 D4
Tregullon PL30 4 A4
Tregunnon PL15 4 C2
Tregurrian TR8 3 F2
Tregynon SY16 37 K6
Trehafod CF37 18 D2
Trehan PL12 4 E5
Treharris CF46 18 D2
Treherbert CF42 18 C2
Tre-hill CF5 18 D4
Trekenner PL15 4 D3
Treknow PL34 4 A2
Trelan TR12 2 E7
Trelash PL15 4 B1
Trelassick TR2 3 F3
Trelawnyd LL18 47 J5
Trelech SA33 17 F2
Treleddyd-fawr SA62 16 A3
Trelewis CF46 18 E2
Treligga PL33 4 A2
Trelights PL29 3 G1
Trelill PL30 4 A3
Trelissick TR3 3 F5
Trelleck NP25 19 J1
Trelleck Grange NP16 19 H1
Trelogan CH8 47 K4
Trelowla PL13 4 C5
Trelystan SY21 38 B5
Tremadog LL49 36 E1
Tremail PL32 4 B2
Tremain SA43 17 F1
Tremaine PL15 4 C2
Tremar PL14 4 C4
Trematon PL12 4 D5
Tremeirchion LL17 47 J5
Tremethick Cross TR20 2 B5
Tremore PL30 4 A4
Trenance *Cornw.* TR8 3 F2
Trenance *Cornw.* PL27 3 G1
Trenarren PL26 4 A6
Trench *Tel. & W.* TF2 39 F4
Trench *Wrex.* LL13 38 C2
Trencreek TR7 3 F2
Trenear TR13 2 D5
Treneglos PL15 4 C2
Trenewan PL13 4 B5
Trengune EX23 4 B1
Trent DT9 8 E3
Trent Port DN21 52 B4
Trent Vale ST4 40 A1
Trentham ST4 40 A1
Trentishoe EX31 6 E1
Trenwheal TR27 2 D5
Treoes CF35 18 C4
Treorchy CF42 18 C2
Treowen NP11 19 F2
Trequite PL30 4 A3
Tre'r Llai (Leighton) SY21 38 B5
Tre'r-ddol SY20 37 F6
Trerhyngyll CF71 18 D4
Tre-Rhys SA43 16 E1
Trerulefoot PL12 4 D5
Tresaith SA43 26 B3
Tresco TR24 2 B1
Trescott WV6 40 A6
Trescowe TR20 2 C5
Tresean TR8 2 E3
Tresham GL12 20 A2
Treshnish PA75 78 E3
Tresillian TR2 3 F4
Tresinney PL32 4 B2
Tresinwen SA64 16 B1
Treskinnick Cross EX23 4 C1
Treslea PL30 4 B4
Tresmeer PL15 4 C2
Tresowes Green TR13 2 D6
Tresparrett PL32 4 B1
Tresparrett Posts PL32 4 B1
Tressait PH16 81 K1
Tresta *Shet.* ZE2 107 Q3
Tresta *Shet.* ZE2 107 M7
Treswell DN22 51 K5
Trethewey TR19 2 A6
Trethomas CF83 18 E3
Trethurgy PL26 4 A5
Tretio SA62 16 A3
Tretire HR2 28 E6
Tretower NP8 28 A6
Treuddyn CH7 48 B7
Trevadlock PL15 4 C3

Trevalga PL35 4 A1
Trevalyn LL12 48 C7
Trevanson PL27 3 G1
Trevarnon TR27 2 C5
Trevarrack TR18 2 B5
Trevarren TR9 3 G2
Trevarrian TR8 3 F2
Trevarrick PL26 3 G4
Tre-vaughan *Carmar.* SA31 17 G3
Trevaughan *Carmar.* SA34 16 E4
Treveighan PL30 4 A3
Trevellas TR5 2 E3
Trevelmond PL14 4 C4
Trevenen TR13 2 D6
Treverva TR10 2 E5
Trevescan TR19 2 A6
Trevethin NP4 19 F1
Trevigro PL17 4 D4
Trevine PA35 80 B5
Treviscoe PL26 3 G3
Trevivian PL32 4 B2
Trevone PL28 3 F1
Trevor LL20 38 B1
Trewalder PL33 4 A2
Trewarmett PL34 4 A2
Trewarthenick TR2 3 G4
Trewassa PL32 4 B2
Trewellard TR19 2 A5
Trewen *Cornw.* PL15 4 C2
Trewen *Here.* HR9 28 E7
Trewennack TR13 2 D6
Trewent SA71 16 D6
Trewern SY21 38 B4
Trewethern PL27 4 A3
Trewidland PL14 4 C5
Trewilym SA41 16 E1
Trewint *Cornw.* EX23 4 B1
Trewint *Cornw.* PL15 4 C2
Trewithian TR2 3 F5
Trewoon PL25 3 G3
Treworga TR2 3 F4
Treworlas TR2 3 F5
Trewornan PL27 3 G1
Treworthal TR2 3 F5
Tre-wyn NP7 28 C6
Treyarnon PL28 3 F1
Treyford GU29 12 B5
Trezaise PL26 3 G3
Triangle HX6 57 F7
Trickett's Cross BH22 10 B4
Triermain CA8 70 A7
Trimdon TS29 62 E3
Trimdon Colliery TS29 62 E3
Trimdon Grange TS29 62 E3
Trimingham NR11 45 G2
Trimley Lower Street IP11 35 G5
Trimley St. Martin IP11 35 G5
Trimley St. Mary IP11 35 G5
Trimpley DY12 29 G1
Trimsaran SA17 17 H5
Trimstone EX34 6 C1
Trinafour PH18 81 J1
Trinant NP11 19 F2
Tring HP23 32 C7
Trinity *Angus* DD9 83 H1
Trinity *Chan.I.* JE3 3 K6
Trinity *Edin.* EH5 76 A3
Trisant SY23 27 G1
Triscombe *Som.* TA24 7 H2
Triscombe *Som.* TA4 7 K2
Trislaig PH33 87 G7
Trispen TR4 3 F3
Tritlington NE61 71 H4
Trochry PH8 82 A4
Troedyraur SA38 17 G1
Troedyrhiw CF48 18 D1
Trofarth LL22 47 G5
Trondavoe ZE2 107 M5
Troon *Cornw.* TR14 2 D5
Troon *S.Ayr.* KA10 74 B7
Trosairidh HS8 84 C3
Troston IP31 34 C1
Troswell PL15 4 C1
Trottick DD4 83 F4
Trottiscliffe ME19 24 C5
Trotton GU31 12 B4
Trough Gate OL13 56 D7
Troughend NE19 70 D4
Troustan PA22 73 J3
Troutbeck *Cumb.* LA23 60 F6
Troutbeck *Cumb.* CA11 60 E4
Troutbeck Bridge LA23 60 F6
Trow Green GL15 19 J1
Troway S21 51 F5
Trowbridge *Cardiff* CF3 19 F3
Trowbridge *Wilts.* BA14 20 B6
Trowell NG9 41 G2
Trowle Common BA14 20 B6
Trowley Bottom AL3 32 D7
Trows TD5 76 E7
Trowse Newton NR14 45 G5
Troy LS18 57 H6
Trudernish PA42 72 C5
Trudoxhill BA11 20 A7
Trull TA3 8 B2
Trumaisgearraidh HS6 92 D4
Trumpan IV55 93 H5
Trumpet HR8 29 F5
Trumpington CB2 33 H3
Trumps Green GU25 22 C5
Trunch NR28 45 G2
Trunnah FY5 55 G5
TRURO TR 3 F4
Truscott PL15 6 B7
Trusham TQ13 7 G7
Trusley DE6 40 E2
Trusthorpe LN12 53 J4
Truthan TR4 3 F3
Trysull WV5 40 A6
Tubney OX13 21 H2
Tuckenhay TQ9 5 J5
Tuckhill WV15 39 G7
Tuckingmill TR14 2 D4
Tuddenham *Suff.* IP6 35 F4
Tuddenham *Suff.* IP28 34 B1
Tudeley TN11 23 K7
Tudeley Hale TN11 23 K7
Tudhoe DL16 62 D3
Tudweiliog LL53 36 B2
Tuesley GU7 22 C7
Tuffley GL4 29 H7
Tufton *Hants.* RG28 21 H7
Tufton *Pembs.* SA63 16 D3
Tugby LE7 42 A5
Tugford SY7 38 E7
Tughall NE67 71 H1
Tulchan PH1 82 A5
Tullibody FK10 75 G1
Tullich *Arg. & B.* PA32 80 B6
Tullich *Arg. & B.* PA34 79 K6
Tullich *High.* IV20 97 F4
Tullich *High.* IV2 88 D2
Tullich *Moray* AB55 98 B6
Tullich *Stir.* FK21 81 G4
Tullich Muir IV18 96 E4
Tulliemet PH9 82 B2
Tulloch *Aber.* AB51 91 G1
Tulloch *High.* IV24 96 D2
Tulloch *Moray* IV36 97 H6
Tullochgorm PA32 73 H1
Tullochgribban High PH26 89 G2
Tullochvenus AB31 90 D4
Tulloes DD8 83 G3
Tullybannocher PH6 81 J5
Tullybelton PH1 82 B4
Tullyfergus PH11 82 D3
Tullymurdoch PH11 82 C2
Tullynessle AB33 90 D3
Tulse Hill SE21 23 G4
Tumble (Y Tymbl) SA14 17 J4
Tumby PE22 53 F7
Tumby Woodside PE22 53 F7
Tummel Bridge PH16 81 J2
TUNBRIDGE WELLS TN 13 J3
Tundergarth Mains DG11 69 G5
Tunga HS2 101 G4
Tungate NR28 45 G3
Tunley BA2 19 K6
Tunstall *E.Riding* HU12 59 K6
Tunstall *Kent* ME10 24 E5
Tunstall *Lancs.* LA6 56 B2
Tunstall *N.Yorks.* DL10 62 D7
Tunstall *Norf.* NR13 45 J5
Tunstall *Stoke* ST6 49 H7
Tunstall *Suff.* IP12 35 H3
Tunstall *T. & W.* SR2 62 E1
Tunstead *Gt.Man.* OL3 50 C2
Tunstead *Norf.* NR12 45 H3
Tunstead Milton SK23 50 C4
Tunworth RG25 21 K7
Tupholme LN3 52 E6
Tupsley HR1 28 E5
Tupton S42 51 F6
Tur Langton LE8 42 A6
Turbiskill PA31 73 F2
Turclossie AB43 99 G5
Turgis Green RG27 21 K6
Turin DD8 83 G2
Turkdean GL54 30 C7
Turleigh BA15 20 B5
Turn BL0 49 H1
Turnastone HR2 28 C5
Turnberry KA26 67 G3
Turnchapel PL9 4 E5
Turnditch DE56 40 E1
Turner's Green CV35 30 C2
Turners Hill RH10 13 G3
Turners Puddle DT2 9 H5
Turnford EN10 23 G1
Turnworth DT11 9 H4
Turret Bridge PH31 87 K5
Turriff AB53 99 F6
Turton Bottoms BL7 49 G1
Turvey MK43 32 C3
Turville RG9 22 A2
Turville Heath RG9 22 A2
Turweston NN13 31 H5
Tutbury DE13 40 E3
Tutnall B60 29 J1
Tutshill NP16 19 J2
Tuttington NR11 45 G3
Tutts Clump RG7 21 J4
Tutwell PL17 4 D3
Tuxford NG22 51 K5
Twatt *Ork.* KW17 106 B5
Twatt *Shet.* ZE2 107 M7
Twechar G65 75 F3
Tweedmouth TD15 77 H5
Tweedsmuir ML12 69 F1
Twelve Oaks TN32 13 K4
Twelveheads TR4 2 E4
Twemlow Green CW4 49 G6
Twenty PE10 42 E3
TWICKENHAM TW 22 E4
Twigworth GL2 29 H6
Twineham RH17 13 F4
Twineham Green RH17 13 F4
Twinhoe BA2 20 A6
Twinstead CO10 34 C5
Twiss Green WA3 49 F3
Twiston BB7 56 D5
Twitchen *Devon* EX36 7 F2
Twitchen *Shrop.* SY7 28 C1
Twitton TN14 23 J6
Twizell House NE70 71 G1
Two Bridges *Devon* PL20 5 G3
Two Bridges *Glos.* GL14 19 K1
Two Dales DE4 50 E6
Two Gates B77 40 E5
Two Mills CH1 48 C5
Twycross CV9 41 F5
Twyford *Bucks.* MK18 31 H6
Twyford *Derbys.* DE73 41 F3
Twyford *Dorset* SP7 9 H3
Twyford *Hants.* SO21 11 F2
Twyford *Leics.* LE14 42 A4
Twyford *Norf.* NR20 44 E3
Twyford *Oxon.* OX17 31 F5
Twyford *W'ham* RG10 22 A4
Twyford Common HR2 28 E5
Twyn Shôn-Ifan CF82 18 E2
Twynholm DG6 65 G5
Twyning GL20 29 H5
Twynllanan SA19 27 G6
Twyn-yr-odyn CF5 18 E4
Twyn-y-Sheriff NP15 19 H1
Twywell NN14 32 C1
Tyberton HR2 28 C5
Tycroes SA18 17 K4
Tycrwyn SY22 38 A4
Tydd Gote PE13 43 H4
Tydd St. Giles PE13 43 H4
Tydd St. Mary PE13 43 H4
Tyddewi (St. David's) SA62 16 A3
Tye Common CM12 24 C2
Tye Green *Essex* CM77 34 B6
Tye Green *Essex* CM22 33 J6
Tye Green *Essex* CM1 33 K7
Tye Green *Essex* CM18 23 H1
Tyersal BD4 57 G6
Ty-hen LL53 36 A2
Tyldesley M29 49 F2
Tyle-garw CF72 18 D3
Tyler Hill CT2 25 H5
Tylers Green *Bucks.* HP10 22 C2
Tyler's Green *Essex* CM16 23 J1
Tylorstown CF43 18 D2
Tylwch LD6 27 J1
Ty-Mawr *Conwy* LL21 37 J1
Ty-mawr *Denb.* LL21 38 A1
Ty-nant *Conwy* LL21 37 J1
Ty-nant *Gwyn.* LL23 37 J3
Tyndrum FK20 80 E4
Tyneham BH20 9 H6
Tynehead EH37 76 B5
Tynemouth NE30 71 J7
Tynewydd CF42 18 C2
Tyninghame EH42 76 E3
Tynron DG3 68 D4
Tyntesfield BS48 19 J4
Tyn-y-cefn LL21 37 K1
Ty'n-y-coedcae CF83 18 E3
Tyn-y-cwm SY18 37 H7
Tyn-y-ffridd SY10 38 A2
Ty'n-y-garn CF31 18 B3
Tyn-y-gongl LL74 46 D4
Tynygraig *Cere.* SY25 27 F2
Tyn-y-graig *Powys* LD2 27 K4
Ty'n-y-groes LL32 47 F5
Tyrie AB43 99 H4
Tyringham MK16 32 B4
Tyseley B11 40 D7
Tythegston CF32 18 B4
Tytherington *Ches.* SK10 49 J5
Tytherington *S.Glos.* GL12 19 K3
Tytherington *Som.* BA11 20 A7
Tytherington *Wilts.* BA12 20 C7
Tytherton Lucas SN15 20 C4
Tyttenhanger AL4 22 E1
Ty-uchaf SY10 37 J3
Tywardreath PL24 4 A5
Tywardreath Highway PL24 4 A5
Tywyn LL36 36 E5

U

Uachdar HS7 92 D6
Uags IV54 86 D1
Ubberley ST2 40 B1
Ubbeston Green IP19 35 H1
Ubley BS40 19 J6
Uckerby DL10 62 D6
Uckfield TN22 13 H4
Uckinghall GL20 29 H5
Uckington GL51 29 J6
Uddingston G71 74 E4
Uddington ML11 75 G7
Udimore TN31 14 D6
Udley BS40 19 H5
Udny Green AB41 91 G2
Udny Station AB41 91 H2
Udston ML3 75 F5
Udstonhead ML10 75 F6
Uffcott SN4 20 E4
Uffculme EX15 7 J4
Uffington *Lincs.* PE9 42 D5
Uffington *Oxon.* SN7 21 G3
Uffington *Shrop.* SY4 38 E4
Ufford *Peter.* PE9 42 D5
Ufford *Suff.* IP13 35 G3
Ufton CV33 30 E2
Ufton Green RG7 21 K5
Ufton Nervet RG7 21 K5
Ugborough PL21 5 G5
Ugford SP2 10 B1
Uggeshall NR34 45 J7
Ugglebarnby YO22 63 K6
Ugley CM22 33 J6
Ugley Green CM22 33 J6
Ugthorpe YO21 63 J5
Uibhist a Deas (South Uist) HS8 84 C1
Uibhist a Tuath (North Uist) HS6 92 D4
Uidh HS9 84 B5
Uig *Arg. & B.* PA78 78 C2
Uig *Arg. & B.* PA23 73 K2
Uig *High.* IV51 93 J5
Uig *High.* IV55 93 G6
Uigen HS2 100 C4
Uiginish IV55 93 H7
Uigshader IV51 93 K7
Uisgebhagh (Uiskevagh) HS7 92 D6
Uisken PA67 78 E6
Uiskevagh (Uisgebhagh) HS7 92 D6
Ulbster KW2 105 J4
Ulcat Row CA11 60 F4
Ulceby *Lincs.* LN13 53 H5
Ulceby *N.Lincs.* DN39 52 E1
Ulceby Cross LN13 53 H5
Ulceby Skitter DN39 52 E1
Ulcombe ME17 14 D3
Uldale CA7 60 D3
Uldale House CA17 61 J7
Uley GL11 20 A2
Ulgham NE61 71 H4
Ullapool IV26 95 H2
Ullenhall B95 30 C2
Ullenwood GL53 29 J7
Ulleskelf LS24 58 B6
Ullesthorpe LE17 41 H7
Ulley S26 51 G4
Ullingswick HR1 28 E4
Ullinish IV56 85 J1
Ullock CA14 60 B4
Ulpha *Cumb.* LA20 60 C7
Ulpha *Cumb.* LA11 55 H1
Ulrome YO25 59 H4
Ulsta ZE2 107 N4
Ulting CM9 24 E1
Uluvalt PA70 79 G4
Ulva PA73 79 F4
Ulverston LA12 55 F2
Ulwell BH19 10 B6
Ulzieside DG4 68 C3
Umberleigh EX37 6 E3
Unapool IV27 102 E5
Underbarrow LA8 61 F7
Undercliffe BD2 57 G6
Underhill EN5 23 F2
Underhoull ZE2 107 P2
Underling Green TN12 14 C3
Underriver TN15 23 J6
Underwood *Newport* NP18 19 G3
Underwood *Notts.* NG16 51 G7
Underwood *Plym.* PL7 5 F5
Undley IP27 44 A7
Undy NP26 19 H3
Ungisiadar HS2 100 D5
Unifirth ZE2 107 L7
Union Croft AB39 91 G5
Union Mills IM4 54 C6
Union Street TN5 14 C4
Unst ZE2 107 Q1
Unst Airport ZE2 107 Q2
Unstone S18 51 F5
Unstone Green S18 51 F5
Unsworth BL9 49 H2
Unthank *Cumb.* CA11 61 F3
Unthank *Derbys.* S18 51 F5
Up Cerne DT2 9 F4
Up Exe EX5 7 H5
Up Hatherley GL51 29 J6
Up Holland WN8 48 E2
Up Marden PO18 11 J3
Up Mudford BA21 8 E3
Up Nately RG27 21 K6
Up Somborne SO20 10 E1
Up Sydling DT2 9 F4
Upavon SN9 20 E6
Upchurch ME9 24 E5
Upcott *Devon* EX21 6 C6
Upcott *Devon* EX31 6 D2
Upcott *Here.* HR3 28 C3
Upcott *Som.* TA22 7 H3
Upend CB8 33 K3
Upgate NR9 45 F4
Upgate Street *Norf.* NR16 44 E6
Upgate Street *Norf.* NR35 45 G6
Uphall *Dorset* DT2 8 E4
Uphall *W.Loth.* EH52 75 J3
Uphall Station EH54 75 J4
Upham *Devon* EX17 7 G5
Upham *Hants.* SO32 11 G2
Uphampton *Here.* HR6 28 C2
Uphampton *Worcs.* WR9 29 H2
Uphempston TQ9 5 J4
Uphill BS23 19 G6
Uplands *Glos.* GL5 20 B1
Uplands *Swan.* SA2 17 K6
Uplawmoor G78 74 C5
Upleadon GL18 29 G6
Upleatham TS11 63 H5
Uplees ME13 25 G5
Uploders DT6 8 E5
Uplowman EX16 7 J4
Uplyme DT7 8 C5
Upminster RM14 23 J3
Upottery EX14 8 B4
Upper Affcot SY6 38 D7
Upper Ardroscadale PA20 73 J4
Upper Arley DY12 39 G7
Upper Arncott OX25 31 H7
Upper Astley SY4 38 E4
Upper Aston WV5 40 A6
Upper Astrop OX17 31 G5
Upper Barvas HS2 101 F2
Upper Basildon RG8 21 K4
Upper Bayble (Pabail Uarach) HS2 101 H4
Upper Beeding BN44 12 E5
Upper Benefield PE8 42 C7
Upper Bentley B97 29 J2
Upper Berwick SY4 38 D4
Upper Bighouse KW13 104 D3
Upper Boat CF37 18 E3
Upper Boddam AB52 90 E1
Upper Boddington NN11 31 F3
Upper Borth SY24 37 F7
Upper Boyndlie AB43 99 H4
Upper Brailes OX15 30 E5
Upper Breakish IV42 86 C2
Upper Breinton HR4 28 D4
Upper Broadheath WR2 29 H3
Upper Broughton LE14 41 J3
Upper Brynamman SA18 27 G7
Upper Bucklebury RG7 21 J5
Upper Burgate SP6 10 C3
Upper Burnhaugh AB39 91 G5
Upper Caldecote SG18 32 E4
Upper Camster KW3 105 H4
Upper Canada BS24 19 G6
Upper Catesby NN11 31 G3
Upper Catshill B61 29 J1
Upper Chapel LD3 27 K4
Upper Cheddon TA2 8 B2
Upper Chicksgrove SP3 9 J1
Upper Chute SP11 21 F6
Upper Clatford SP11 21 G7
Upper Coberley GL53 29 J7
Upper Colwall WR13 29 G4
Upper Cotton ST10 40 C1
Upper Cound SY5 38 E5
Upper Cumberworth HD8 50 E2
Upper Cwmbran NP44 19 F2
Upper Dallachy IV32 98 B4
Upper Dean PE28 32 D2
Upper Denby HD8 50 E2
Upper Denton CA8 70 B7
Upper Derraid PH26 89 H1
Upper Diabaig IV22 94 E5
Upper Dicker BN27 13 J5
Upper Dovercourt CO12 35 G5
Upper Dunsforth YO26 57 K3
Upper Dunsley HP23 32 C7
Upper Eastern Green CV5 40 E7
Upper Eathie IV11 96 E5
Upper Egleton HR8 29 F4
Upper Elkstone SK17 50 C7
Upper End SK17 50 C5
Upper Enham SP11 21 G7
Upper Farringdon GU34 11 J1
Upper Framilode GL2 29 G7
Upper Froyle GU34 22 A7
Upper Gills KW1 105 J1
Upper Glendessarry PH34 87 F5
Upper Godney BA5 19 H7
Upper Gornal DY3 40 B6
Upper Gravenhurst MK45 32 E5
Upper Green *Essex* CB11 33 H5
Upper Green *Essex* CB10 33 J5
Upper Green *Mon.* NP7 28 C7
Upper Green *W.Berks.* RG17 21 G5
Upper Grove Common HR9 28 E6
Upper Gylen PA34 79 K5
Upper Hackney DE4 50 E6
Upper Halliford TW17 22 D5
Upper Halling ME2 24 C5
Upper Hambleton LE15 42 C5
Upper Harbledown CT2 15 G2
Upper Hardres Court CT4 15 G2
Upper Hartfield TN7 13 H3
Upper Hatton ST21 40 A2
Upper Hawkhillock AB42 91 J1
Upper Hayesden TN11 23 J7
Upper Hayton SY8 38 E7
Upper Heath SY7 38 E7
Upper Heaton HD5 50 D1
Upper Hellesdon NR3 45 G4
Upper Helmsley YO41 58 C4
Upper Hengoed SY10 38 B2
Upper Hergest HR5 28 B3
Upper Heyford *Northants.* NN7 31 H3
Upper Heyford *Oxon.* OX25 31 F6
Upper Hill *Here.* HR6 28 D3
Upper Hill *S.Glos.* GL13 19 K2
Upper Horsebridge BN27 13 J5
Upper Howsell WR14 29 G4
Upper Hulme ST13 50 C6
Upper Inglesham SN6 21 F2
Upper Kilchattan PA61 72 B1
Upper Killay SA2 17 J6
Upper Knockando AB38 97 J7
Upper Lambourn RG17 21 G3
Upper Langford BS40 19 H6
Upper Langwith NG20 51 H6
Upper Largo KY8 83 F7
Upper Leigh ST10 40 C2
Upper Ley GL14 29 G7
Upper Llandwrog (Y Fron) LL54 46 D7
Upper Loads S42 51 F6
Upper Lochton AB31 90 E5
Upper Longdon WS15 40 C4
Upper Longwood SY5 39 F5
Upper Ludstone WV5 40 A6
Upper Lybster KW3 105 H5
Upper Lydbrook GL17 29 F7
Upper Lyde HR4 28 D4
Upper Lye HR6 28 C2
Upper Maes-coed HR2 28 C5
Upper Midhope S36 50 E3
Upper Milovaig IV55 93 G7
Upper Milton OX7 30 D7
Upper Minety SN16 20 D2
Upper Moor WR10 29 J4
Upper Morton BS35 19 K2
Upper Muirskie AB12 91 G5

Upper Nash SA71 16 D5
Upper Newbold S41 51 F5
Upper North Dean HP14 22 B2
Upper Norwood SE19 23 G4
Upper Obney PH1 82 B4
Upper Oddington GL56 30 D6
Upper Ollach IV51 86 B1
Upper Padley S32 50 E5
Upper Pennington SO41 10 D5
Upper Pollicott HP18 31 J7
Upper Poppleton YO26 58 B4
Upper Quinton CV37 30 C4
Upper Ratley SO51 10 E2
Upper Ridinghill AB43 99 J5
Upper Rissington GL54 30 D6
Upper Rochford WR15 29 F2
Upper Sanday KW17 106 E7
Upper Sapey WR6 29 F2
Upper Scolton SA62 16 C3
Upper Seagry SN15 20 C3
Upper Shelton MK43 32 C4
Upper Sheringham NR26 45 F1
Upper Shuckburgh NN11 31 F2
Upper Siddington GL7 20 D2
Upper Skelmorlie PA17 74 A4
Upper Slaughter GL54 30 C6
Upper Sonachan PA33 80 B5
Upper Soudley GL14 29 F7
Upper Staploe PE19 32 E3
Upper Stoke NR14 45 G5
Upper Stondon SG16 32 E5
Upper Stowe NN7 31 H3
Upper Street *Hants.* SP6 10 C3
Upper Street *Norf.* NR12 45 H4
Upper Street *Norf.* IP21 35 F1
Upper Street *Suff.* IP9 35 F5
Upper Street *Suff.* IP6 35 F3
Upper Strensham WR8 29 J5
Upper Sundon LU5 32 D6
Upper Swanmore SO32 11 G3
Upper Swell GL54 30 C6
Upper Tean ST10 40 C2
Upper Thurnham LA2 55 H4
Upper Tillyrie KY13 82 C7
Upper Tooting SW17 23 F4
Upper Town *Derbys.* DE4 50 E6
Upper Town *Derbys.* DE4 50 E7
Upper Town *Derbys.* DE6 50 E7
Upper Town *Here.* HR1 28 E4
Upper Town *N.Som.* BS40 19 J5
Upper Tysoe CV35 30 E4
Upper Upham SN8 21 F4
Upper Upnor ME2 24 D4
Upper Victoria DD7 83 G4
Upper Vobster BA3 20 A7
Upper Wardington OX17 31 F4
Upper Waterhay SN6 20 D2
Upper Weald MK19 32 B5
Upper Weedon NN7 31 H3
Upper Welson HR3 28 B3
Upper Weston BA1 20 A5
Upper Whiston S60 51 G4
Upper Wick WR2 29 H3
Upper Wield SO24 11 H1
Upper Winchendon (Over Winchendon) HP18 31 J7
Upper Witton B23 40 C6
Upper Woodford SP4 10 C1
Upper Woolhampton RG7 21 J5
Upper Wootton RG26 21 J6
Upper Wraxall SN14 20 B4
Upper Wyche WR13 29 G4
Upperby CA2 60 F1
Uppermill OL3 49 J2
Upperthong HD9 50 D2
Upperton GU28 12 C4
Uppertown *Derbys.* S45 51 F6
Uppertown *Ork.* KW1 105 J1
Uppingham LE15 42 B5
Uppington TF6 38 E5
Upsall YO7 57 K1
Upsettlington TD15 77 G6
Upshire EN9 23 H1
Upstreet CT3 25 J5
Upthorpe IP31 34 D1
Upton *Bucks.* HP17 31 J7
Upton *Cambs.* PE28 32 E1
Upton *Ches.* CH2 48 D6
Upton *Cornw.* PL14 4 C3
Upton *Cornw.* EX23 6 A5
Upton *Devon* EX14 7 J5
Upton *Devon* TQ7 5 H6
Upton *Dorset* BH16 9 J5
Upton *Dorset* DT2 9 G6
Upton *E.Riding* YO25 59 H4
Upton *Hants.* SP11 21 G6
Upton *Hants.* SO16 10 E3
Upton *Leics.* CV13 41 F6
Upton *Lincs.* DN21 52 B4
Upton *Mersey.* CH49 48 B4
Upton *Norf.* NR13 45 H4
Upton *Northants.* NN5 31 J2
Upton *Notts.* DN22 51 K5
Upton *Notts.* NG23 51 K7
Upton *Oxon.* OX11 21 J3
Upton *Oxon.* OX18 30 D7
Upton *Pembs.* SA72 16 D5
Upton *Peter.* PE5 42 E5
Upton *Slo.* SL1 22 C4
Upton *Som.* TA4 7 H3
Upton *Som.* TA10 8 D2
Upton *W.Yorks.* WF9 51 G1
Upton *Wilts.* SP3 9 H1
Upton Bishop HR9 29 F6
Upton Cheyney BS30 19 K5
Upton Cressett WV16 39 F6
Upton Crews HR9 29 F6
Upton Cross PL14 4 C3
Upton End SG5 32 E5
Upton Grey RG25 21 K7
Upton Hellions EX17 7 G5
Upton Lovell BA12 20 C7
Upton Magna SY4 38 E4
Upton Noble BA4 9 G1
Upton Park E13 23 H3
Upton Pyne EX5 7 H6
Upton St. Leonards GL4 29 H7
Upton Scudamore BA12 20 B7
Upton Snodsbury WR7 29 J3
Upton upon Severn WR8 29 H4
Upton Warren B61 29 J2
Upwaltham GU28 12 C5
Upware CB7 33 J1
Upwell PE14 43 J5
Upwey DT3 9 F6
Upwick Green SG11 33 H6
Upwood PE26 43 F7
Uradale ZE1 107 N9
Urafirth ZE2 107 M5
Urchany IV12 97 F7
Urchfont SN10 20 D6
Urdimarsh HR1 28 E4
Ure ZE2 107 L5
Urgha HS3 93 G2
Urlay Nook TS16 63 F5
Urmston M41 49 G3
Urpeth DH2 62 D1
Urquhart *High.* IV7 96 C6
Urquhart *Moray* IV30 97 K5
Urra TS9 63 G6
Urray IV6 96 C6
Ushaw Moor DH7 62 D2
Usk (Brynbuga) NP15 19 G1
Usselby LN8 52 D3
Usworth NE37 62 E1
Utley BD20 57 F5
Uton EX17 7 G6
Utterby LN11 53 G3
Uttoxeter ST14 40 C2
Uwchmynydd LL53 36 A3
Uxbridge UB8 22 D3
Uyeasound ZE2 107 P2
Uzmaston SA62 16 C4

V

Valley (Y Fali) LL65 46 A5
Valley Truckle PL32 4 B2
Valleyfield *D. & G.* DG6 65 G5
Valleyfield *Fife* KY12 75 J2
Valsgarth ZE2 107 Q1
Vange SS16 24 D3
Vardre SA6 17 K5
Varteg NP4 19 F1
Vatersay (Bhatarsaigh) HS9 84 B5
Vatsetter ZE2 107 P4
Vatten IV55 93 H7
Vaul PA77 78 B3
Vaynor CF48 27 K7
Vaynor Park SY21 38 A5
Veaullt HR5 28 A3
Veensgarth ZE2 107 N8
Velindre *Pembs.* SA41 16 D2
Velindre *Powys* LD3 28 A5
Vellow TA4 7 J2
Veness KW17 106 E5
Venn TQ7 5 H6
Venn Ottery EX11 7 J6
Venngreen EX22 6 B4
Vennington SY5 38 C5
Venny Tedburn EX17 7 G6
Venterdon PL17 4 D3
Ventnor PO38 11 G7
Venton PL7 5 F5
Vernham Dean SP11 21 G6
Vernham Street SP11 21 G6
Vernolds Common SY7 38 D7
Verwood BH31 10 B4
Veryan TR2 3 G5
Veryan Green TR2 3 G4
Vickerstown LA14 54 E3
Victoria PL26 3 G2
Vidlin ZE2 107 N6
Viewfield KW14 105 F2
Viewpark G71 75 F4
Vigo WS9 40 C5
Vigo Village DA13 24 C5
Villavin EX19 6 D4
Vinehall Street TN32 14 C5
Vine's Cross TN21 13 J5
Viney Hill GL15 19 K1
Virginia Water GU25 22 C5
Virginstow EX21 6 B6
Virley CM9 34 D7
Vobster BA3 20 A7
Voe *Shet.* ZE2 107 N6
Voe *Shet.* ZE2 107 M4
Vowchurch HR2 28 C5
Voy KW16 106 B6
Vron Gate SY5 38 C5

W

Waberthwaite CA18 60 C7
Wackerfield DL2 62 C4
Wacton NR15 45 F6
Wadbister ZE2 107 N8
Wadborough WR8 29 J4
Waddesdon HP18 31 J7
Waddeton TQ5 5 J5
Waddicar L31 48 C3
Waddingham DN21 52 C3
Waddington *Lancs.* BB7 56 C5
Waddington *Lincs.* LN5 52 C6
Waddingworth LN10 52 E5
Waddon *Devon* TQ13 5 J3
Waddon *Gt.Lon.* CR0 23 G5
Wadebridge PL27 3 G1
Wadeford TA20 8 C3
Wadenhoe PE8 42 D7
Wadesmill SG12 33 G7
Wadhurst TN5 13 K3
Wadshelf S42 51 F5
Wadworth DN11 51 H3
Wadworth Hill HU12 59 J7
Waen *Denb.* LL16 47 K6
Waen *Denb.* LL16 47 H6
Waen Aberwheeler LL16 47 J6
Waen-fâch SY22 38 B4
Waen-wen LL57 46 D6
Wag KW7 105 F6
Wainfleet All Saints PE24 53 H7
Wainfleet Bank PE24 53 H7
Wainfleet St. Mary PE24 53 H7
Wainford NR35 45 H6
Waingroves DE5 41 G1
Wainhouse Corner EX23 4 B1
Wainscott ME2 24 D4
Wainstalls HX2 57 F7
Waitby CA17 61 J6
WAKEFIELD WF 57 J7
Wakerley LE15 42 C6
Wakes Colne CO6 34 C6
Walberswick IP18 35 J1
Walberton BN18 12 C6
Walbottle NE15 71 G7
Walcot *Lincs.* NG34 42 D2
Walcot *Lincs.* LN4 52 E7
Walcot *N.Lincs.* DN15 58 E7
Walcot *Shrop.* SY7 38 C7
Walcot *Tel. & W.* TF6 38 E4
Walcot Green IP22 45 F7
Walcote *Leics.* LE17 41 H7
Walcote *Warks.* B49 30 C3
Walcott NR12 45 H2
Walcott Dales LN4 52 E7
Walden DL8 57 F1
Walden Head DL8 56 E1
Walden Stubbs DN6 51 H1
Walderslade ME5 24 D5
Walderton PO18 11 J3
Walditch DT6 8 D5
Waldley DE6 40 D2
Waldridge DH2 62 D2
Waldringfield IP12 35 G4
Waldron TN21 13 J5
Wales S26 51 G4
Walesby *Lincs.* LN8 52 E3
Walesby *Notts.* NG22 51 J5
Waleswood S26 51 G4
Walford *Here.* SY7 28 C1
Walford *Here.* HR9 28 E6
Walford *Shrop.* SY4 38 D3
Walford *Staffs.* ST21 40 A2
Walford Heath SY4 38 D4
Walgherton CW5 39 F1
Walgrave NN6 32 B1
Walhampton SO41 10 E5
Walk Mill BB10 56 D6
Walkden M28 49 G2
Walker NE6 71 H7
Walker Fold BB7 56 B5
Walkerburn EH43 76 B7
Walkeringham DN10 51 K3
Walkerith DN21 51 K3
Walkern SG2 33 F6
Walker's Green HR1 28 E4
Walkford BH23 10 D5
Walkhampton PL20 5 F4
Walkingham Hill HG3 57 J3
Walkington HU17 59 F6
Walkwood B97 30 B2
Wall *Cornw.* TR27 2 D5
Wall *Northumb.* NE46 70 E7
Wall *Staffs.* WS14 40 D5
Wall End LA17 55 F1
Wall Heath DY6 40 A7
Wall Houses NE45 71 F7
Wall under Heywood SY6 38 E6
Wallacehall DG11 69 H6
Wallacetown KA19 67 G3
Wallasey CH45 48 B3
Wallaston Green SA71 16 C5
Wallend ME3 24 E4
Waller's Green HR8 29 F5
Wallingford OX10 21 K3
Wallington *Gt.Lon.* SM6 23 F5
Wallington *Hants.* PO16 11 G4
Wallington *Herts.* SG7 33 F5
Wallington *Wrex.* LL13 38 D1
Wallingwells S81 51 H4
Wallis SA62 16 D3
Wallisdown BH12 10 B5
Walliswood RH5 12 E3
Walls ZE2 107 L8
Wallsend NE28 71 J7
Wallyford EH21 76 B3
Walmer CT14 15 J2
Walmer Bridge PR4 55 H7
Walmersley BL9 49 H1
Walmley B76 40 D6
Walmsgate LN11 53 G5
Walpole IP19 35 H1
Walpole Cross Keys PE34 43 J4
Walpole Highway PE14 43 J4
Walpole Marsh PE14 43 H4
Walpole St. Andrew PE14 43 J4
Walpole St. Peter PE14 43 J4
Walrond's Park TA3 8 C2
Walrow TA9 19 G7
WALSALL WS 40 C6
Walsall Wood WS9 40 C5
Walsden OL14 56 E7
Walsgrave on Sowe CV2 41 F7
Walsham le Willows IP31 34 E1
Walshford LS22 57 K4
Walsoken PE13 43 H4
Walston ML11 75 J6
Walsworth SG4 32 E5
Walter's Ash HP14 22 B2
Walterston CF62 18 D4
Walterstone HR2 28 C6
Waltham *Kent* CT4 15 G3
Waltham *N.E.Lincs.* DN37 53 F2
Waltham Abbey EN9 23 G1
Waltham Chase SO32 11 G3
Waltham Cross EN8 23 G1
Waltham on the Wolds LE14 42 A3
Waltham St. Lawrence RG10 22 B4
Walthamstow E17 23 G3
Walton *Bucks.* HP21 32 B7
Walton *Cumb.* CA8 70 A7
Walton *Derbys.* S42 51 F6
Walton *Leics.* LE17 41 H7
Walton *M.K.* MK7 32 B5
Walton *Mersey.* L9 48 C3
Walton *Peter.* PE4 42 E5
Walton *Powys* LD8 28 B3
Walton *Shrop.* SY7 28 D1
Walton *Som.* BA16 8 D1
Walton *Staffs.* ST15 40 A2
Walton *Suff.* IP11 35 H5
Walton *Tel. & W.* TF6 38 E4
Walton *W.Yorks.* WF2 51 F1
Walton *W.Yorks.* LS23 57 K5
Walton *Warks.* CV35 30 D3
Walton Cardiff GL20 29 J5
Walton East SA63 16 D3
Walton Elm DT10 9 G3
Walton Highway PE14 43 H4
Walton Lower Street IP11 35 G5
Walton on the Hill KT20 23 F6
Walton on the Naze CO14 35 G6
Walton on the Wolds LE12 41 H4
Walton Park *D. & G.* DG7 65 H3
Walton Park *N.Som.* BS21 19 H4
Walton West SA62 16 B4
Walton-in-Gordano BS21 19 H4
Walton-le-Dale PR5 55 J7
Walton-on-Thames KT12 22 E5
Walton-on-the-Hill ST17 40 B3
Walton-on-Trent DE12 40 E4
Walwen *Flints.* CH8 47 K5
Walwen *Flints.* CH6 48 B5
Walwick NE46 70 E6
Walworth DL2 62 D5
Walworth Gate DL2 62 D4
Walwyn's Castle SA62 16 B4
Wambrook TA20 8 B4
Wanborough *Surr.* GU3 22 C7
Wanborough *Swin.* SN4 21 F3
Wandel ML12 68 E1
Wandon NE71 71 F1
Wandon End LU2 32 E6
Wandsworth SW15 23 F4
Wandylaw NE67 71 G1
Wangford *Suff.* NR34 35 J1
Wangford *Suff.* IP27 44 B7
Wanlip LE7 41 J4
Wanlockhead ML12 68 D2
Wannock BN26 13 J6
Wansford *E.Riding* YO25 59 G4
Wansford *Peter.* PE8 42 D6
Wanshurst Green TN12 14 C3
Wanstrow BA4 20 A7
Wanswell GL13 19 K1
Wantage OX12 21 G3
Wapley BS37 20 A4
Wappenbury CV33 30 E2
Wappenham NN12 31 H4
Warblebank CA7 60 D2
Warbleton TN21 13 K5
Warblington PO9 11 J4
Warborough OX10 21 J2
Warboys PE28 43 G7
Warbreck FY2 55 G6
Warbstow PL15 4 C1
Warburton WA13 49 F4
Warcop CA16 61 J5
Ward End B8 40 D7
Ward Green IP14 34 E2
Warden *Kent* ME12 25 G4
Warden *Northumb.* NE46 70 E7
Warden Hill GL51 29 J6
Warden Street SG18 32 E4
Wardhouse AB52 90 D1
Wardington OX17 31 F4
Wardle *Ches.* CW5 49 F7
Wardle *Gt.Man.* OL12 49 J1
Wardley *Gt.Man.* M27 49 G2
Wardley *Rut.* LE15 42 B5
Wardley *T. & W.* NE10 71 J7
Wardlow SK17 50 D5
Wardsend SK10 49 J4
Wardy Hill CB6 43 H7
Ware *Herts.* SG12 33 G7
Ware *Kent* CT3 25 J5
Wareham BH20 9 J6
Warehorne TN26 14 E4
Waren Mill NE70 77 K7
Warenford NE70 71 G1
Warenton NE70 77 K7
Wareside SG12 33 G7
Waresley *Cambs.* SG19 33 F3
Waresley *Worcs.* DY11 29 H1
Warfield RG42 22 B4
Wargrave *Mersey.* WA12 48 E3
Wargrave *W'ham* RG10 22 A4
Warham *Here.* HR4 28 D5
Warham *Norf.* NR23 44 D1
Wark *Northumb.* NE48 70 D6
Wark *Northumb.* TD12 77 G7
Warkleigh EX37 6 E3
Warkton NN16 32 B1
Warkworth *Northants.* OX17 31 F4
Warkworth *Northumb.* NE65 71 H3
Warland OL14 56 E7
Warleggan PL30 4 B4
Warley *Essex* CM14 23 J2
Warley *W.Mid.* B68 40 C7
Warley Town HX2 57 F7
Warlingham CR6 23 G6
Warmfield WF1 57 J7
Warmingham CW11 49 G6
Warminghurst RH20 12 E5
Warmington *Northants.* PE8 42 D6
Warmington *Warks.* OX17 31 F4
Warminster BA12 20 B7
Warmlake ME17 14 D3
Warmley BS30 19 K4
Warmley Hill BS15 19 K4
Warmsworth DN4 51 H2
Warmwell DT2 9 G6
Warndon WR4 29 H3
Warners End HP1 22 D1
Warnford SO32 11 H2
Warnham RH12 12 E3
Warningcamp BN18 12 D6
Warninglid RH17 13 F4
Warren *Ches.* SK11 49 H5
Warren *Pembs.* SA71 16 C6
Warren House PL20 6 E7
Warren Row RG10 22 B3
Warren Street ME17 14 E2
Warrenby TS10 63 G4
Warren's Green SG4 33 F6
Warrington *M.K.* MK46 32 B3
WARRINGTON *Warr.* WA 49 F4
Warroch KY13 82 B7
Warsash SO31 11 F4
Warslow SK17 50 C7
Warsop Vale NG20 51 H6
Warter YO42 58 E4
Warthill YO19 58 C4
Wartle AB31 90 D4
Wartling BN27 13 K6
Wartnaby LE14 42 A3
Warton *Lancs.* LA5 55 J2
Warton *Lancs.* PR4 55 H7
Warton *Northumb.* NE65 71 F3
Warton *Warks.* B79 40 E5
Warton Bank PR4 55 H7
Warwick CV34 30 D2
Warwick Bridge CA4 61 F1
Warwick Wold RH1 23 G6
Warwick-on-Eden CA4 61 F1
Wasbister KW17 106 C4
Wasdale Head CA20 60 C6
Wash SK23 50 C4
Wash Common RG14 21 H5
Washall Green SG9 33 H5
Washaway PL30 4 A4
Washbourne TQ9 5 H5
Washbrook BS28 19 H7
Washfield EX16 7 H4
Washfold DL11 62 B6
Washford *Som.* TA23 7 J1
Washford *Warks.* B98 30 B2
Washford Pyne EX17 7 G4
Washingborough LN4 52 D5
Washington *T. & W.* NE38 62 E1
Washington *W.Suss.* RH20 12 E5
Washmere Green CO10 34 D4
Wasing RG7 21 J5
Waskerley DH8 62 B2
Wasperton CV35 30 D3
Wasps Nest LN4 52 D6
Wass YO61 58 B2
Watchet TA23 7 J1
Watchfield *Oxon.* SN6 21 F2
Watchfield *Som.* TA9 19 G7
Watchgate LA8 61 G7
Watcombe TQ1 5 K4
Watendlath CA12 60 D5
Water BB4 56 D7
Water Eaton *M.K.* MK2 32 B5
Water Eaton *Oxon.* OX2 31 G7
Water End *Beds.* MK44 32 E4
Water End *Beds.* MK45 32 D5
Water End *E.Riding* YO43 58 D6
Water End *Essex* CB10 33 J4
Water End *Herts.* AL9 23 F1
Water End *Herts.* HP1 32 D7
Water Newton PE8 42 E6
Water Orton B46 40 D6
Water Stratford MK18 31 H5
Water Yeat LA12 55 F1
Waterbeach CB5 33 H2
Waterbeck DG11 69 H6
Watercombe DT2 9 G6
Waterend HP14 22 A2
Waterfall ST10 50 C7
Waterfoot *E.Renf.* G76 74 D5
Waterfoot *Lancs.* BB4 56 D7
Waterford SG14 33 G7
Watergate PL32 4 B2
Waterhead *Cumb.* LA22 60 E6
Waterhead *D. & G.* DG7 68 C5
Waterheath NR34 45 J6
Waterhill of Bruxie AB42 99 H6
Waterhouses *Dur.* DH7 62 C2
Waterhouses *Staffs.* ST10 50 C7
Wateringbury ME18 23 K6
Waterlane GL6 20 C1
Waterloo *Aber.* AB42 91 J1
Waterloo *Derbys.* S45 51 G6
Waterloo *Gt.Man.* OL7 49 J2
Waterloo *High.* IV42 86 C2
Waterloo *Mersey.* L22 48 C3
Waterloo *N.Lan.* ML2 75 G5
Waterloo *Norf.* NR10 45 G4
Waterloo *P. & K.* PH1 82 B4
Waterloo *Pembs.* SA72 16 C5

Waterloo Poole BH17 10 B5
Waterloo Cross EX15 7 J4
Waterloo Port LL55 46 C6
Waterlooville PO7 11 H3
Watermeetings ML12 68 E2
Watermillock CA11 60 F4
Waterperry OX33 21 K1
Waterrow TA4 7 J3
Waters Upton TF6 39 F4
Watersfield RH20 12 D5
Watersheddings OL4 49 J2
Waterside Aber. AB36 90 B3
Waterside Aber. AB41 91 J2
Waterside B'burn. BB3 56 C7
Waterside Bucks. HP5 22 C1
Waterside E.Ayr. KA6 67 J3
Waterside E.Ayr. KA3 74 C6
Waterside E.Dun. G66 74 E3
Waterstock OX33 21 K1
Waterston SA73 16 C5
Waterthorpe S20 51 G4
WATFORD Herts. WD 22 E2
Watford Northants. NN6 31 H2
Watford Park CF83 18 E3
Wath N.Yorks. HG4 57 J2
Wath N.Yorks. HG3 57 G3
Wath Brow CA25 60 B5
Wath upon Dearne S63 51 G2
Watley's End BS36 19 K3
Watlington Norf. PE33 44 A4
Watlington Oxon. OX49 21 K2
Watnall NG16 41 H1
Watten KW1 105 H3
Wattisfield IP22 34 E1
Wattisham IP7 34 E3
Watton Dorset DT6 8 D5
Watton E.Riding YO25 59 G5
Watton Norf. IP25 44 D5
Watton at Stone SG14 33 G7
Watton Green IP25 44 D5
Watton's Green CM14 23 J2
Wattston ML6 75 F4
Wattstown CF39 18 D2
Wattsville NP11 19 F2
Waughtonhill AB43 99 H5
Waun Fawr SY23 37 F7
Waun y Clyn SA17 17 H5
Waunarlwydd SA5 17 K6
Waunclunda SA19 17 K2
Waunfawr LL55 46 D7
Waun-Lwyd NP23 18 E1
Wavendon MK17 32 C5
Waverbridge CA7 60 D2
Waverton Ches. CH3 48 D6
Waverton Cumb. CA7 60 D2
Wavertree L15 48 C4
Wawne HU7 59 G6
Waxham NR12 45 J3
Waxholme HU19 59 K7
Way Gill BD23 56 E3
Way Village EX16 7 G4
Way Wick BS24 19 G5
Wayford TA18 8 D4
Waytown DT6 8 D5
Wdig (Goodwick) SA64 16 C2
Weachyburn AB45 98 E5
Weacombe TA4 7 K1
Weald OX18 21 G1
Wealdstone HA3 22 E2
Weardley LS17 57 H5
Weare BS26 19 H6
Weare Giffard EX39 6 C3
Wearhead DL13 61 K3
Wearne TA10 8 D2
Weasenham All Saints PE32 44 C3
Weasenham St. Peter PE32 44 C3
Weathercote LA6 56 C2
Weatheroak Hill B48 30 B1
Weaverham CW8 49 F5
Weaverthorpe YO17 59 F2
Webheath B97 30 B2
Webton HR2 28 D5
Wedderlairs AB41 91 G1
Weddington CV10 41 F6
Wedhampton SN10 20 D6
Wedmore BS28 19 H7
Wednesbury WS10 40 B6
Wednesfield WV11 40 B6
Weedon HP22 32 B7
Weedon Bec NN7 31 H3
Weedon Lois NN12 31 H4
Weeford WS14 40 D5
Week Devon EX18 7 F4
Week Devon TQ9 5 H4
Week Som. TA22 7 H2
Week Orchard EX23 6 A5
Week St. Mary EX22 4 C1
Weeke SO22 11 F1
Weekley NN16 42 B7
Weel HU17 59 G6
Weeley CO16 35 F6
Weeley Heath CO16 35 F6
Weem PH15 81 K2
Weeping Cross ST17 40 B3
Weethley B49 30 B3
Weeting IP27 44 B7
Weeton E.Riding HU12 59 K7
Weeton Lancs. PR4 55 G6
Weeton N.Yorks. LS17 57 H5
Weetwood LS16 57 H6
Weir Essex SS6 24 E3
Weir Lancs. OL13 56 D7
Weir Quay PL20 4 E4
Weirbrook SY11 38 C3
Weisdale ZE2 107 M7
Welbeck Abbey S80 51 H5
Welborne NR20 44 E5
Welbourn LN5 52 C7
Welburn N.Yorks. YO60 58 D3
Welburn N.Yorks. YO62 58 C1
Welbury DL6 62 E6
Welby NG32 42 C2
Welches Dam PE16 43 H7
Welcombe EX39 6 A4
Weldon NN17 42 C7
Welford Northants. NN6 41 J7
Welford W.Berks. RG20 21 H4
Welford-on-Avon CV37 30 C3
Welham Leics. LE16 42 A6
Welham Notts. DN22 51 K4
Welham Green AL9 23 F1
Well Hants. RG29 22 A7
Well Lincs. LN13 53 H5
Well N.Yorks. DL8 57 H1
Well End Bucks. SL8 22 B3
Well End Herts. WD6 23 F2
Well Hill BR6 23 H5
Well Street ME19 23 K6
Well Town EX16 7 H5
Welland WR13 29 G4
Wellbank DD5 83 F4
Wellesbourne CV35 30 D3
Wellhill IV36 97 G5
Wellhouse W.Berks. RG18 21 J4
Wellhouse W.Yorks. HD7 50 C1
Welling DA16 23 H4
Wellingborough NN8 32 B2
Wellingham PE32 44 C3
Wellingore LN5 52 C7
Wellington Cumb. CA20 60 B6
Wellington Here. HR4 28 D4
Wellington Som. TA21 7 K3
Wellington Tel. & W. TF1 39 F4
Wellington Heath HR8 29 G4
Wellington Marsh HR4 28 D4
Wellow B. & N.E.Som. BA2 20 A6
Wellow I.o.W. PO41 10 E6
Wellow Notts. NG22 51 J6
Wells BA5 19 J7
Wells Green B92 40 D7
Wellsborough CV13 41 F5
Wells-next-the-Sea NR23 44 D1
Wellstyle Green CM6 33 K7
Wellwood KY12 75 J2
Welney PE14 43 J6
Welsh Bicknor HR9 28 E7
Welsh End SY13 38 E2
Welsh Frankton SY11 38 C2
Welsh Hook SA62 16 C3
Welsh Newton NP25 28 D7
Welsh St. Donats CF71 18 D4
Welshampton SY12 38 D2
Welshpool (Y Trallwng) SY21 38 B5
Welton B. & N.E.Som. BA3 19 K6
Welton Cumb. CA5 60 E2
Welton E.Riding HU15 59 F7
Welton Lincs. LN2 52 D4
Welton Northants. NN11 31 G2
Welton le Marsh PE23 53 H6
Welton le Wold LN11 53 F4
Welwick HU12 59 K7
Welwyn AL6 33 F7
Welwyn Garden City AL8 33 F7
Wem SY4 38 E3
Wembdon TA6 8 B1
Wembley HA0 22 E3
Wembley Park HA9 22 E3
Wembury PL9 5 F6
Wembworthy EX18 6 E4
Wemyss Bay PA18 73 K4
Wenallt Cere. SY23 27 F1
Wenallt Gwyn. LL21 37 J1
Wendens Ambo CB11 33 J5
Wendlebury OX25 31 G7
Wendling NR19 44 D4
Wendover HP22 22 B1
Wendover Dean HP22 22 B1
Wendron TR13 2 D5
Wendy SG8 33 G4
Wenfordbridge PL30 4 A3
Wenhaston IP19 35 J1
Wenlli LL22 47 G6
Wennington Cambs. PE28 33 F1
Wennington Gt.Lon. RM13 23 J3
Wennington Lancs. LA2 56 B2
Wensley Derbys. DE4 50 E6
Wensley N.Yorks. DL8 57 F1
Wentbridge WF8 51 G1
Wentnor SY9 38 C6
Wentworth Cambs. CB6 33 H1
Wentworth S.Yorks. S62 51 F3
Wenvoe CF5 18 E4
Weobley HR4 28 C3
Weobley Marsh HR4 28 D3
Weoley Castle B29 40 C7
Wepham BN18 12 D6
Wepre CH5 48 B6
Wereham PE33 44 A5
Wergs WV6 40 A5
Wern Gwyn. LL49 36 E2
Wern Powys SY21 38 B4
Wern Powys NP8 28 A7
Wern Shrop. SY10 38 B2
Wernffrwd SA4 17 J6
Wern-olau SA4 17 J6
Wernrheolydd NP15 28 C7
Wern-y-cwrt NP15 19 G1
Werrington Cornw. PL15 6 B7
Werrington Peter. PE4 42 E5
Werrington Staffs. ST9 40 B1
Wervil Grange SA44 26 C3
Wervin CH2 48 D5
Wesham PR4 55 H6
Wessington DE55 51 F7
West Aberthaw CF62 18 D5
West Acre PE32 44 B4
West Acton W3 22 E3
West Allerdean TD15 77 H6
West Alvington TQ7 5 H6
West Amesbury SP4 20 E7
West Anstey EX36 7 G3
West Ashby LN9 53 F5
West Ashford EX31 6 D2
West Ashling PO18 12 B6
West Ashton BA14 20 B6
West Auckland DL14 62 C4
West Ayton YO13 59 F1
West Bagborough TA4 7 K2
West Barkwith LN8 52 E4
West Barnby YO21 63 K5
West Barns EH42 76 E3
West Barsham NR21 44 D2
West Bay DT6 8 D5
West Beckham NR25 45 F2
West Benhar ML7 75 G4
West Bergholt CO6 34 D6
West Bexington DT2 8 E6
West Bilney PE32 44 B4
West Blatchington BN3 13 F6
West Boldon NE36 71 J7
West Bourton SP8 9 G2
West Bowling BD5 57 G6
West Brabourne TN25 15 F3
West Bradford BB7 56 C5
West Bradley BA6 8 E1
West Bretton WF4 50 E1
West Bridgford NG2 41 H2
West Bromwich B70 40 C6
West Buckland Devon EX32 6 E2
West Buckland Som. TA21 7 K3
West Burrafirth ZE2 107 L7
West Burton N.Yorks. DL8 57 F1
West Burton W.Suss. RH20 12 C5
West Butsfield DL13 62 B2
West Butterwick DN17 52 B2
West Byfleet KT14 22 D5
West Cairncake AB53 99 G6
West Caister NR30 45 K4
West Calder EH55 75 J4
West Camel BA22 8 E2
West Carbeth G63 74 D3
West Carr Houses DN9 51 K2
West Cauldcoats ML10 74 E6
West Chaldon DT2 9 G6
West Challow OX12 21 G3
West Charleton TQ7 5 H6
West Chevington NE61 71 H4
West Chiltington RH20 12 D5
West Chiltington Common RH20 12 D5
West Chinnock TA18 8 D3
West Chisenbury SN9 20 E6
West Clandon GU4 22 D6
West Cliffe CT15 15 J3
West Clyne KW9 97 F1
West Coker BA22 8 E3
West Compton Dorset DT2 8 E5
West Compton Som. BA4 19 J7
West Cowick DN14 58 C7
West Cross SA3 17 K7
West Crudwell SN16 20 C2
West Curry PL15 4 C1
West Curthwaite CA7 60 E2
West Dean W.Suss. PO18 12 B5
West Dean Wilts. SP5 10 D2
West Deeping PE6 42 E5
West Derby L12 48 C3
West Dereham PE33 44 A5
West Ditchburn NE66 71 G1
West Down EX34 6 D1
West Drayton Gt.Lon. UB7 22 D4
West Drayton Notts. DN22 51 K5
West Dullater FK17 81 G7
West Dunnet KW14 105 H1
West Edington NE61 71 G5
West Ella HU10 59 G7
West End Beds. MK43 32 C3
West End Brack.F. RG42 22 B4
West End Caerp. NP11 19 F2
West End Cambs. PE15 43 H6
West End E.Riding YO25 59 G3
West End Hants. SO30 11 F3
West End Herts. AL9 23 F1
West End Kent CT6 25 H5
West End Lancs. LA4 55 H3
West End Lincs. DN36 53 G3
West End N.Som. BS48 19 H5
West End N.Yorks. HG3 57 G4
West End Norf. NR30 45 J4
West End Norf. IP25 44 D5
West End Oxon. OX29 21 H1
West End Oxon. OX10 21 J3
West End S.Lan. ML11 75 H6
West End Suff. NR34 45 J7
West End Surr. KT10 22 E5
West End Surr. GU24 22 C5
West End Wilts. SN15 20 C4
West End Wilts. SP7 9 J2
West End Wilts. SP5 9 J2
West End Green RG7 21 K5
West Farleigh ME15 14 C2
West Farndon NN11 31 G3
West Felton SY11 38 C3
West Firle BN8 13 H6
West Fleetham NE67 71 G1
West Flotmanby YO14 59 G2
West Garforth LS25 57 J6
West Ginge OX12 21 H3
West Glen PA21 73 H3
West Grafton SN8 21 F5
West Green Gt.Lon. N15 23 G3
West Green Hants. RG27 22 A6
West Grimstead SP5 10 D2
West Grinstead RH13 12 E4
West Haddlesey YO8 58 B7
West Haddon NN6 31 H1
West Hagbourne OX11 21 J3
West Hagley DY9 40 B7
West Hall CA8 70 A7
West Hallam DE7 41 G1
West Halton DN15 59 F7
West Ham E15 23 G3
West Handley S21 51 F5
West Hanney OX12 21 H2
West Hanningfield CM2 24 D2
West Hardwick WF4 51 G1
West Harnham SP2 10 C2
West Harptree BS40 19 J6
West Harrow HA1 22 E3
West Harting GU31 11 J2
West Hatch Som. TA3 8 B2
West Hatch Wilts. SP3 9 J2
West Head PE34 43 J5
West Heath Ches. CW12 49 H6
West Heath Gt.Lon. SE2 23 H4
West Heath Hants. GU14 22 B6
West Heath Hants. RG26 21 J6
West Heath W.Mid. B31 30 B1
West Helmsdale KW8 105 F7
West Hendon NW9 23 F3
West Hendred OX12 21 H3
West Heslerton YO17 59 F2
West Hewish BS24 19 G5
West Hill Devon EX11 7 J6
West Hill E.Riding YO16 59 H3
West Hill N.Som. BS20 19 H4
West Hoathly RH19 13 G3
West Holme BH20 9 H6
West Horndon CM13 24 C3
West Horrington BA5 19 J7
West Horsley KT24 22 D6
West Horton NE71 77 J7
West Hougham CT15 15 H4
West Howe BH11 10 B5
West Howetown TA24 7 H2
West Huntspill TA9 19 G7
West Hyde WD3 22 D2
West Hythe CT21 15 G4
West Ilsley RG20 21 H3
West Itchenor PO20 11 J4
West Keal PE23 53 G6
West Kennett SN8 20 E5
West Kilbride KA23 74 A6
West Kingsdown TN15 23 J5
West Kington SN14 20 B4
West Kington Wick SN14 20 B4
West Kirby CH48 48 B4
West Knapton YO17 58 E2
West Knighton DT2 9 G6
West Knoyle BA12 9 H1
West Kyloe TD15 77 J6
West Lambrook TA13 8 D3
West Langdon CT15 15 J3
West Langwell IV28 96 D1
West Lavington W.Suss. GU29 12 B4
West Lavington Wilts. SN10 20 D6
West Layton DL11 62 C6
West Leake LE12 41 H3
West Learmouth TD12 77 G7
West Lees DL6 63 F6
West Leigh Devon EX17 6 E5
West Leigh Devon TQ9 5 H5
West Leigh Som. TA4 7 K2
West Leith HP23 32 C7
West Lexham PE32 44 C4
West Lilling YO60 58 C3
West Lingo KY9 83 F7
West Linton EH46 75 K5
West Liss GU33 11 J2
West Littleton SN14 20 A4
West Lockinge OX12 21 H3
West Looe PL13 4 C5
West Lulworth BH20 9 H6
West Lutton YO17 59 F3
West Lydford TA11 8 E1
West Lyn EX35 7 F1
West Lyng TA3 8 C2
West Lynn PE34 44 A4
West Mains TD15 77 J6
West Malling ME19 23 K6
West Malvern WR14 29 G4
West Marden PO18 11 J3
West Markham NG22 51 K5
West Marsh DN31 53 F2
West Marton BD23 56 D4
West Melbury SP7 9 H2
West Melton S63 51 G2
West Meon GU32 11 H2
West Meon Hut GU32 11 H2
West Mersea CO5 34 E7
West Milton DT6 8 D5
West Minster ME12 25 F4
West Molesey KT8 22 E5
West Monkton TA2 8 B2
West Moors BH22 10 B4
West Morden BH20 9 J5
West Morriston TD4 76 E6
West Morton BD20 57 F5
West Mostard LA10 61 J7
West Mudford BA21 8 E2
West Muir DD9 83 G1
West Ness YO62 58 C2
West Newbiggin DL2 62 E5
West Newton E.Riding HU11 59 H6
West Newton Norf. PE31 44 A3
West Norwood SE27 23 G4
West Ogwell TQ12 5 J4
West Orchard SP7 9 H3
West Overton SN8 20 E5
West Panson PL15 6 B6
West Park Aber. AB31 91 F5
West Park Mersey. WA10 48 E3
West Parley BH22 10 B5
West Peckham ME18 23 K6
West Pelton DH9 62 D1
West Pennard BA6 8 E1
West Pentire TR8 2 E2
West Perry PE28 32 E2
West Porlock TA24 7 G1
West Prawle TQ8 5 H7
West Preston BN16 12 D6
West Pulham DT2 9 G4
West Putford EX22 6 B4
West Quantoxhead TA4 7 K1
West Raddon EX17 7 G5
West Rainton DH4 62 E2
West Rasen LN8 52 D4
West Raynham NR21 44 C3
West Retford DN22 51 J4
West Rounton DL6 63 F6
West Row IP28 33 K1
West Rudham PE31 44 C3
West Runton NR27 45 F1
West Saltoun EH34 76 C4
West Sandford EX17 7 G5
West Sandwick ZE2 107 N4
West Scrafton DL8 57 F1
West Shepton BA4 19 K7
West Shinness Lodge IV27 103 H7
West Somerton NR29 45 J4
West Stafford DT2 9 G6
West Stockwith DN10 51 K3
West Stoke PO18 12 B6
West Stonesdale DL11 61 K6
West Stoughton BS28 19 H7
West Stour SP8 9 G2
West Stourmouth CT3 25 J5
West Stow IP28 34 C1
West Stowell SN8 20 E5
West Stratton SO21 21 J7
West Street Kent ME17 14 E2
West Street Med. ME3 24 D4
West Street Suff. IP31 34 D1
West Tanfield HG4 57 H2
West Taphouse PL22 4 B4
West Tarbert PA29 73 G4
West Tarring BN13 12 E6
West Thirston NE65 71 G3
West Thorney PO10 11 J4
West Thurrock RM20 23 J4
West Tilbury RM18 24 C4
West Tisted SO24 11 H2
West Tofts Norf. IP26 44 C6
West Tofts P. & K. PH1 82 C4
West Torrington LN8 52 E4
West Town B. & N.E.Som. BS40 19 J5
West Town Hants. PO11 11 J5
West Town N.Som. BS48 19 H5
West Town Som. BA6 8 E1
West Tytherley SP5 10 D2
West Walton PE14 43 H4
West Wellow SO51 10 D3
West Wembury PL9 5 F6
West Wemyss KY1 76 B1
West Wick BS24 19 G5
West Wickham Cambs. CB1 33 K4
West Wickham Gt.Lon. BR4 23 G5
West Williamston SA68 16 D5
West Winch PE33 44 A4
West Winterslow SP5 10 D1
West Wittering PO20 11 J5
West Witton DL8 57 F1
West Woodburn NE48 70 D5
West Woodhay RG20 21 G5
West Woodlands BA11 20 A7
West Worldham GU34 11 J1
West Worlington EX17 7 F4
West Worthing BN11 12 E6
West Wratting CB1 33 K3
West Wycombe HP14 22 B2
West Yatton SN14 20 B4
West Yell ZE2 107 N4
West Youlstone EX23 6 A4
Westbere CT2 25 H5
Westborough NG23 42 B1
Westbourne Bourne. BH4 10 B5
Westbourne W.Suss. PO10 11 J4
Westbourne Green W2 23 F3
Westbrook Kent CT9 25 K4
Westbrook W.Berks. RG20 21 H4
Westbrook Wilts. SN15 20 C5
Westbury Bucks. NN13 31 H5
Westbury Shrop. SY5 38 C5
Westbury Wilts. BA13 20 B6
Westbury Leigh BA13 20 B6
Westbury on Trym BS9 19 J4
Westbury-on-Severn GL14 29 G7
Westbury-sub-Mendip BA5 19 J7
Westby Lancs. PR4 55 G6
Westby Lincs. NG33 42 C3
Westcliff-on-Sea SS0 24 E3
Westcombe BA4 9 F1
Westcot OX12 21 G3
Westcott Bucks. HP18 31 J7
Westcott Devon EX15 7 J5
Westcott Surr. RH4 22 E7
Westcott Barton OX7 31 F6
Westcourt SN8 21 F5
Westcroft MK4 32 B5
Westdean BN25 13 J7
Westdowns PL33 4 A2
Westend Town SN14 20 A4
Wester Aberchalder IV2 88 C2
Wester Badentyre AB53 99 F5
Wester Balgedie KY13 82 C7
Wester Culbeuchly AB45 98 E4
Wester Dechmont EH52 75 J3
Wester Fintray AB51 91 G3
Wester Foffarty DD8 83 F3
Wester Greenskares AB45 99 F4
Wester Gruinards IV24 96 C2
Wester Hailes EH14 76 A4

Wester Lealty IV17 96 D4
Wester Lonvine IV18 96 E4
Wester Newburn KY8 83 F7
Wester Ord AB32 91 G4
Wester Quarff ZE2 107 N9
Wester Skeld ZE2 107 L8
Westerdale High. KW12 105 G3
Westerdale N.Yorks. YO21 63 H6
Westerfield Shet. ZE2 107 M7
Westerfield Suff. IP6 35 F4
Westergate PO20 12 C6
Westerham TN16 23 H6
Westerhope NE5 71 G7
Westerleigh BS37 19 K4
Westerloch KW1 105 J3
Westerton Aber. AB31 91 F5
Westerton Angus DD10 83 H2
Westerton Dur. DL14 62 D3
Westerton P. & K. PH5 81 K6
Westerwick ZE2 107 L8
Westfield Cumb. CA14 60 A4
Westfield E.Suss. TN35 14 D6
Westfield High. KW14 105 F2
Westfield N.Lan. G68 75 F3
Westfield Norf. NR19 44 D5
Westfield W.Loth. EH48 75 H3
Westfield W.Yorks. WF16 57 H7
Westfield Sole ME14 24 D5
Westgate Dur. DL13 62 A3
Westgate N.Lincs. DN9 51 K2
Westgate Norf. NR21 44 D1
Westgate Northumb. NE20 71 G6
Westgate Hill BD4 57 H7
Westgate on Sea CT8 25 K4
Westhall Aber. AB52 90 E2
Westhall Suff. IP19 45 J7
Westham Dorset DT4 9 F7
Westham E.Suss. BN24 13 K6
Westham Som. TA7 19 H7
Westhampnett PO18 12 B6
Westhay Devon EX13 8 C4
Westhay Som. BA6 19 H7
Westhead L40 48 D2
Westhide HR1 28 E4
Westhill Aber. AB32 91 G4
Westhill High. IV2 96 E7
Westhope Here. HR4 28 D3
Westhope Shrop. SY7 38 D7
Westhorp NN11 31 G3
Westhorpe Lincs. PE11 43 F2
Westhorpe Notts. NG25 51 J7
Westhorpe Suff. IP14 34 E2
Westhoughton BL5 49 F2
Westhouse LA6 56 B2
Westhouses DE55 51 G7
Westhumble RH5 22 E6
Westing ZE2 107 P2
Westlake PL21 5 G5
Westlands ST5 40 A1
Westlea SN5 20 E3
Westleigh Devon EX39 6 C3
Westleigh Devon EX16 7 J4
Westleigh Gt.Man. WN7 49 F2
Westleton IP17 35 J2
Westley Shrop. SY5 38 C5
Westley Suff. IP33 34 C2
Westley Heights SS16 24 C3
Westley Waterless CB8 33 K3
Westlington HP17 31 J7
Westlinton CA6 69 J7
Westloch EH45 76 A5
Westmancote GL20 29 J5
Westmarsh CT3 25 J5
Westmeston BN6 13 G5
Westmill SG9 33 G6
Westminster SW1H 23 F4
Westmuir DD8 82 E2
Westness KW17 106 C5
Westnewton Cumb. CA7 60 C2
Westnewton Northumb. NE71 77 H7
Westoe NE33 71 J7
Weston B. & N.E.Som. BA1 20 A5
Weston Ches. CW2 49 G7
Weston Devon EX12 7 K7
Weston Devon EX14 7 K5
Weston Dorset DT5 9 F7
Weston Halton WA7 48 E4
Weston Hants. GU32 11 J2
Weston Here. HR6 28 C3
Weston Herts. SG4 33 F5
Weston Lincs. PE12 43 F3
Weston Moray AB56 98 C4
Weston N.Yorks. LS21 57 G5
Weston Northants. NN12 31 G4
Weston Notts. NG23 51 K6
Weston S'ham. SO19 11 F3
Weston Shrop. SY4 38 E3
Weston Shrop. TF13 38 E6
Weston Shrop. SY7 28 C1
Weston Staffs. ST18 40 B3
Weston W.Berks. RG20 21 H4
Weston Bampfylde BA22 9 F2
Weston Beggard HR1 28 E4
Weston by Welland LE16 42 A6
Weston Colville CB1 33 K3
Weston Corbett RG25 21 K7
Weston Coyney ST3 40 B1
Weston Favell NN3 31 J2
Weston Green Cambs. CB1 33 K3
Weston Green Norf. NR9 45 F4
Weston Heath TF11 39 G4
Weston Hills PE12 43 F3
Weston in Arden CV12 41 F7
Weston Jones TF10 39 G3
Weston Longville NR9 45 F4
Weston Lullingfields SY4 38 D3
Weston Patrick RG25 21 K7
Weston Point WA7 48 D4
Weston Rhyn SY10 38 B2
Weston Subedge GL55 30 C4
Weston Town BA4 20 A7
Weston Turville HP22 32 B7
Weston under Penyard HR9 29 F6
Weston under Wetherley CV33 30 E2
Weston Underwood Derbys. DE6 40 E1
Weston Underwood M.K. MK46 32 B3
Westonbirt GL8 20 B3
Westoning MK45 32 D5
Weston-in-Gordano BS20 19 H4
Weston-on-Avon CV37 30 C3
Weston-on-the-Green OX25 31 G7
Weston-on-Trent DE72 41 G3
Weston-super-Mare BS23 19 G5
Weston-under-Lizard TF11 40 A4
Westonzoyland TA7 8 C1
Westow YO60 58 D3
Westport Arg. & B. PA28 66 A1
Westport Som. TA10 8 C2
Westra CF64 18 E4
Westray KW17 106 D3
Westray Airfield KW17 106 D2
Westridge Green RG8 21 J4
Westrigg EH48 75 H4
Westruther TD3 76 E6
Westry PE15 43 G6
Westside AB12 91 G5
Westvale L32 48 D3
Westville NG15 41 H1
Westward CA7 60 D2
Westward Ho! EX39 6 C3
Westwell Kent TN25 14 E3
Westwell Oxon. OX18 21 F1
Westwell Leacon TN27 14 E3
Westwick Cambs. CB4 33 H2
Westwick Dur. DL12 62 B5
Westwick N.Yorks. YO51 57 J3
Westwick Norf. NR10 45 G3
Westwood Devon EX5 7 J6
Westwood Peter. PE3 42 E6
Westwood S.Lan. G75 74 E5
Westwood Wilts. BA15 20 B6
Westwood Heath CV4 30 D1
Westwoodside DN9 51 K3
Wetham Green ME9 24 E5
Wetheral CA4 61 F1
Wetherby LS22 57 K5
Wetherden IP14 34 E2
Wetherden Upper Town IP14 34 E2
Wetheringsett IP14 35 F2
Wethersfield CM7 34 B5
Wethersta ZE2 107 M6
Wetherup Street IP14 35 F2
Wetley Abbey ST9 40 B1
Wetley Rocks ST9 40 B1
Wettenhall CW7 49 F6
Wettenhall Green CW7 49 F6
Wetton DE6 50 D7
Wetwang YO25 59 F4
Wetwood ST21 39 G2
Wexcombe SN8 21 F6
Wexham Street SL3 22 C3
Weybourne Norf. NR25 45 F1
Weybourne Surr. GU9 22 B7
Weybread IP21 45 G7
Weybread Street IP21 35 G1
Weybridge KT13 22 D5
Weycroft EX13 8 C4
Weydale KW14 105 G2
Weyhill SP11 21 G7
Weymouth DT4 9 F7
Whaddon Bucks. MK17 32 B5
Whaddon Cambs. SG8 33 G4
Whaddon Glos. GL4 29 H7
Whaddon Glos. GL52 29 J6
Whaddon Wilts. SP5 10 C2
Whaddon Wilts. BA14 20 B5
Whaddon Gap SG8 33 G4
Whale CA10 61 G4
Whaley NG20 51 H5
Whaley Bridge SK23 50 C4
Whaley Thorns NG20 51 H5
Whaligoe KW2 105 J4
Whalley BB7 56 C6
Whalsay ZE2 107 P6
Whalsay Airport ZE2 107 P6
Whalton NE61 71 G5
Wham BD24 56 C3
Whaplode PE12 43 G3
Whaplode Drove PE12 43 G4
Whaplode St. Catherine PE12 43 G4
Wharfe LA2 56 C3
Wharles PR4 55 H6
Wharley End MK43 32 C4
Wharncliffe Side S35 50 E3
Wharram le Street YO17 58 E3
Wharram Percy YO17 58 E3
Wharton Ches. CW7 49 F6
Wharton Here. HR6 28 E3
Whashton DL11 62 C6
Whatcote CV36 30 E4
Whateley B78 40 E6
Whatfield IP7 34 E4
Whatley BA11 20 A7
Whatlington TN33 14 C6
Whatsole Street TN25 15 G3
Whatstandwell DE4 51 F7
Whatton NG13 42 A2
Whauphill DG8 64 E6
Whaw DL11 62 A6
Wheatacre NR34 45 J6
Wheatcroft DE4 51 F7
Wheatenhurst GL2 20 A1
Wheatfield OX9 21 K2
Wheathampstead AL4 32 E7
Wheathill Shrop. WV16 39 F7
Wheathill Som. TA11 8 E1
Wheatley Hants. GU34 11 J1
Wheatley Oxon. OX33 21 K1
Wheatley W.Yorks. HX3 57 F7
Wheatley Hill DH6 62 E3
Wheatley Lane BB12 56 D6
Wheatley Park DN2 51 H2
Wheaton Aston ST19 40 A4
Wheddon Cross TA24 7 H2
Wheedlemont AB54 90 C2
Wheelerstreet GU8 22 C7
Wheelock CW11 49 G7
Wheelock Heath CW11 49 G7
Wheelton PR6 56 B7
Wheen DD8 90 B7
Wheldale WF10 57 K7
Wheldrake YO19 58 C5
Whelford GL7 20 E2
Whelley WN1 48 E2
Whelpley Hill HP5 22 C1
Whelpo CA7 60 E3
Whelston CH6 48 B5
Whenby YO61 58 C3
Whepstead IP29 34 C3
Wherstead IP9 35 F4
Wherwell SP11 21 G7
Wheston SK17 50 D5
Whetley Cross DT8 8 D4
Whetsted TN12 23 K7
Whetstone Gt.Lon. N20 23 F2
Whetstone Leics. LE8 41 H6
Whicham LA18 54 E1
Whichford CV36 30 E5
Whickham NE16 71 H7
Whiddon EX21 6 C5
Whiddon Down EX6 6 E6
Whifflet ML5 75 F4
Whigstreet DD8 83 F3
Whilton NN11 31 H2
Whim EH46 76 A5
Whimble EX22 6 B5
Whimple EX5 7 J6
Whimpwell Green NR12 45 H3
Whin Lane End PR3 55 G5
Whinburgh NR19 44 E5
Whinny Hill TS21 62 E5
Whinnyfold AB42 91 J1
Whippingham PO32 11 G5
Whipsnade LU6 32 D7
Whipton EX1 7 H6
Whirlow S11 51 F4
Whisby LN6 52 C6
Whissendine LE15 42 B4
Whissonsett NR20 44 D3
Whisterfield SK11 49 H5
Whistley Green RG10 22 A4
Whiston Mersey. L35 48 D3
Whiston Northants. NN7 32 B2
Whiston S.Yorks. S60 51 G3
Whiston Staffs. ST10 40 C1
Whiston Staffs. ST19 40 A4
Whiston Cross WV7 39 G5
Whiston Eaves ST10 40 C1
Whitacre Fields B46 40 E6
Whitacre Heath B46 40 E6
Whitbeck LA19 54 E1
Whitbourne WR6 29 G3
Whitburn T. & W. SR6 71 K7
Whitburn W.Loth. EH47 75 H4
Whitby Ches. CH65 48 C5
Whitby N.Yorks. YO21 63 K5
Whitbyheath CH65 48 C5
Whitchurch B. & N.E.Som. BS14 19 K5
Whitchurch Bucks. HP22 32 B6
Whitchurch Cardiff CF14 18 E3
Whitchurch Devon PL19 4 E3
Whitchurch Hants. RG28 21 H7
Whitchurch Here. HR9 28 E7
Whitchurch Pembs. SA62 16 A3
Whitchurch Shrop. SY13 38 E1
Whitchurch Warks. CV37 30 D4
Whitchurch Canonicorum DT6 8 C5
Whitchurch Hill RG8 21 K4
Whitchurch-on-Thames RG8 21 K4
Whitcombe DT2 9 G6
Whitcott Keysett SY7 38 B7
White Ball TA21 7 J4
White Colne CO6 34 C6
White Coppice PR6 49 F1
White Cross Cornw. TR8 3 F3
White Cross Devon EX5 7 J6
White Cross Here. HR4 28 D4
White Cross Wilts. BA12 9 G1
White End GL19 29 H6
White Hill BA12 9 H1
White Houses DN22 51 K5
White Kirkley DL13 62 B3
White Lackington DT2 9 G5
White Ladies Aston WR7 29 J3
White Lund LA3 55 H3
White Mill SA32 17 H3
White Moor DE56 41 F1
White Notley CM8 34 B7
White Ox Mead BA2 20 A6
White Pit LN13 53 G5
White Rocks HR2 28 D6
White Roding CM6 33 J7
White Waltham SL6 22 B4
Whiteacen AB38 97 K7
Whiteash Green CO9 34 B5
Whitebirk BB1 56 C7
Whitebog AB43 99 H5
Whitebridge High. KW14 105 H1
Whitebridge High. IV2 88 B3
Whitebrook NP25 19 J1
Whiteburn TD2 76 D6
Whitecairn DG8 64 C5
Whitecairns AB23 91 H3
Whitecastle ML12 75 J6
Whitechapel PR3 55 J5
Whitechurch SA41 16 E2
Whitecote LS13 57 H6
Whitecraig EH21 76 B3
Whitecroft GL15 19 K1
Whitecrook DG9 64 B5
Whitecross Cornw. TR20 2 C5
Whitecross Cornw. PL27 3 G1
Whitecross Dorset DT6 8 D5
Whitecross Falk. EH49 75 H3
Whiteface IV25 96 E3
Whitefield Aber. AB51 91 F2
Whitefield Devon EX32 7 F2
Whitefield Dorset BH20 9 J5
Whitefield Gt.Man. M45 49 H2
Whitefield High. IV2 88 C2
Whitefield High. KW1 105 H3
Whitefield P. & K. PH13 82 C4
Whiteford AB51 91 F2
Whitegate CW8 49 F6
Whitehall Devon EX15 7 K4
Whitehall Hants. RG29 22 A6
Whitehall Ork. KW17 106 F5
Whitehall W.Suss. RH13 12 E4
Whitehaven CA28 60 A5
Whitehill Aber. AB42 99 H5
Whitehill Hants. GU35 11 J1
Whitehill Kent ME13 14 E2
Whitehill Midloth. EH22 76 B4
Whitehill N.Ayr. KA24 74 A5
Whitehills AB45 98 E4
Whitehouse Aber. AB33 90 E3
Whitehouse Arg. & B. PA29 73 G4
Whitehouse Common B75 40 D6
Whitekirk EH42 76 D2
Whitelackington TA19 8 C3
Whitelaw TD11 77 G5
Whiteleen KW2 105 J4
Whitelees KA1 74 B7
Whiteley PO15 11 G4
Whiteley Bank PO38 11 G6
Whiteley Green SK10 49 J5
Whiteley Village KT12 22 D5
Whiteleys DG9 64 A5
Whitemans Green RH17 13 G4
Whitemire IV36 97 G6
Whitemoor PL26 3 G3
Whiteness ZE2 107 M8
Whiteoak Green OX29 30 E7
Whiteparish SP5 10 D2
Whiterashes AB21 91 G2
Whiterow KW1 105 J4
Whiteshill GL6 20 B1
Whiteside Northumb. NE49 70 C7
Whiteside W.Loth. EH48 75 H4
Whitesmith BN8 13 J5
Whitestaunton TA20 8 B3
Whitestone Aber. AB31 90 E5
Whitestone Arg. & B. PA28 73 F7
Whitestone Devon EX4 7 G6
Whitestreet Green CO10 34 D5
Whitestripe AB43 99 H5
Whiteway GL6 29 J7
Whitewell Aber. AB43 99 H4
Whitewell Lancs. BB7 56 B5
Whitewell Wrex. SY13 38 D1
Whiteworks PL20 5 G3
Whitewreath IV30 97 K6
Whitfield Here. HR2 28 D5
Whitfield Kent CT16 15 J3
Whitfield Northants. NN13 31 H5
Whitfield Northumb. NE47 61 J1
Whitfield S.Glos. GL12 19 K2
Whitford Devon EX13 8 B5
Whitford (Chwitffordd) Flints. CH8 47 K5
Whitgift DN14 58 E7
Whitgreave ST18 40 A3
Whithorn DG8 64 E6
Whiting Bay KA27 66 E1
Whitkirk LS15 57 J6
Whitlam AB21 91 G2
Whitland (Hendy-Gwyn) SA34 17 F4
Whitland Abbey SA34 17 F4
Whitleigh PL5 4 E4
Whitletts KA8 67 H1
Whitley N.Yorks. DN14 58 B7
Whitley Read. RG2 22 A5
Whitley W.Mid. CV3 30 E1
Whitley Wilts. SN12 20 B5
Whitley Bay NE26 71 J6
Whitley Chapel NE47 62 A1
Whitley Heath ST21 40 A3
Whitley Lower WF12 50 E1
Whitley Row TN14 23 H6
Whitlock's End B90 30 C1
Whitminster GL2 20 A1
Whitmore Dorset BH21 10 B4
Whitmore Staffs. ST5 40 A1
Whitnage EX16 7 J4
Whitnash CV31 30 E2
Whitnell TA5 19 F7
Whitney-on-Wye HR3 28 B4
Whitrigg Cumb. CA7 60 D1
Whitrigg Cumb. CA7 60 D3
Whitsbury SP6 10 C3
Whitsome TD11 77 G5
Whitson NP18 19 G3
Whitstable CT5 25 H5
Whitstone EX22 4 C1
Whittingham NE66 71 F2
Whittingslow SY6 38 D7
Whittington Derbys. S41 51 F5
Whittington Glos. GL54 30 B6
Whittington Lancs. LA6 56 B2
Whittington Norf. PE33 44 B6
Whittington Shrop. SY11 38 C2
Whittington Staffs. DY7 40 A7
Whittington Staffs. WS14 40 D5
Whittington Worcs. WR5 29 H3
Whittlebury NN12 31 H4
Whittle-le-Woods PR6 55 J7
Whittlesey PE7 43 F6
Whittlesford CB2 33 H4
Whittlestone Head BL7 49 G1
Whitton Gt.Lon. TW2 22 E4
Whitton N.Lincs. DN15 59 F7
Whitton Northumb. NE65 71 F3
Whitton Powys LD7 28 B2
Whitton Shrop. SY8 28 E1
Whitton Stock. TS21 62 E4
Whitton Suff. IP1 35 F4
Whittonditch SN8 21 F4
Whittonstall DH8 62 B1
Whitway RG20 21 H6
Whitwell Derbys. S80 51 H5
Whitwell Herts. SG4 32 E6
Whitwell I.o.W. PO38 11 G7
Whitwell N.Yorks. DL10 62 D7
Whitwell Rut. LE15 42 C5
Whitwell Street NR10 45 F3
Whitwell-on-the-Hill YO60 58 D3
Whitwick LE67 41 G4
Whitwood WF10 57 K7
Whitworth OL12 49 H1
Whixall SY13 38 E2
Whixley YO26 57 K4
Whorlton Dur. DL12 62 C5
Whorlton N.Yorks. DL6 63 F6
Whygate NE48 70 C6
Whyle HR6 28 E2
Whyteleafe CR3 23 G6
Wibdon NP16 19 J2
Wibsey BD6 57 G6
Wibtoft LE17 41 G7
Wichenford WR6 29 G2
Wichling ME9 14 E2
Wick Bourne. BH6 10 C5
Wick Devon EX14 7 K5
Wick High. KW1 105 J3
Wick S.Glos. BS30 20 A4
Wick Som. TA5 19 F7
Wick Som. BA6 8 E1
Wick V. of Glam. CF71 18 C4
Wick W.Suss. BN17 12 D6
Wick Wilts. SP5 10 C2
Wick Worcs. WR10 29 J4
Wick Airport KW1 105 J3
Wick Hill Kent TN27 14 D3
Wick Hill W'ham RG40 22 A5
Wick St. Lawrence BS22 19 G5
Wicken Cambs. CB7 33 J1
Wicken Northants. MK19 31 J5
Wicken Bonhunt CB11 33 H5
Wickenby LN3 52 D4
Wicker Street Green CO10 34 D4
Wickerslack CA10 61 H5
Wickersley S66 51 G3
Wicketwood Hill NG4 41 J1
Wickford SS12 24 D2
Wickham Hants. PO17 11 G3
Wickham W.Berks. RG20 21 G4
Wickham Bishops CM8 34 C7
Wickham Heath RG20 21 H5
Wickham Market IP13 35 H3
Wickham St. Paul CO9 34 C5
Wickham Skeith IP23 34 E2
Wickham Street Suff. CB8 34 B3
Wickham Street Suff. IP23 34 E2
Wickhambreaux CT3 15 H2
Wickhambrook CB8 34 B3
Wickhamford WR11 30 B4
Wickhampton NR13 45 J5
Wicklewood NR18 44 E5
Wickmere NR11 45 F2
Wickstreet BN26 13 J6
Wickwar GL12 20 A3
Widcombe BA2 20 A5
Widdington CB11 33 J5
Widdop HX7 56 E6
Widdrington NE61 71 H4
Widdrington Station NE61 71 H4
Wide Open NE13 71 H6
Widecombe in the Moor TQ13 5 H3
Widegates PL13 4 C5
Widemouth Bay EX23 6 A5
Widewall KW17 106 D8
Widford Essex CM2 24 C1
Widford Herts. SG12 33 H7
Widford Oxon. OX18 30 D7
Widgham Green CB8 33 K3
Widmer End HP15 22 B2
Widmerpool NG12 41 J3
Widnes WA8 48 E4
WIGAN WN 48 E2
Wiganthorpe YO60 58 C2
Wigborough TA13 8 D3
Wiggaton EX11 7 K6
Wiggenhall St. Germans PE34 43 J4
Wiggenhall St. Mary Magdalen PE34 43 J4
Wiggenhall St. Mary the Virgin PE34 43 J4
Wiggenhall St. Peter PE34 44 A4
Wiggens Green CB9 33 K4
Wigginton Herts. HP23 32 C7
Wigginton Oxon. OX15 30 E5

Wigginton *Shrop.* **SY11** 38 C2
Wigginton *Staffs.* **B79** 40 E5
Wigginton *York* **YO32** 58 C4
Wigglesworth **BD23** 56 D4
Wiggonby **CA7** 60 E1
Wiggonholt **RH20** 12 D5
Wighill **LS24** 57 K5
Wighton **NR23** 44 D2
Wightwizzle **S36** 50 E3
Wigley **SO51** 10 E3
Wigmore *Here.* **HR6** 28 D2
Wigmore *Med.* **ME8** 24 E5
Wigsley **NG23** 52 B5
Wigsthorpe **NN14** 42 D7
Wigston LE18 41 J6
Wigston Parva **LE10** 41 G7
Wigthorpe **S81** 51 H4
Wigtoft **PE20** 43 F2
Wigton CA7 60 D2
Wigtown **DG8** 64 E5
Wike **LS17** 57 J5
Wilbarston **LE16** 42 B7
Wilberfoss **YO41** 58 D4
Wilburton **CB6** 33 H1
Wilby *Norf.* **NR16** 44 E6
Wilby *Northants.* **NN8** 32 B2
Wilby *Suff.* **IP21** 35 G1
Wilcot **SN9** 20 E5
Wilcott **SY4** 38 C4
Wilcrick **NP26** 19 H3
Wilday Green **S18** 51 F5
Wildboarclough **SK11** 49 J6
Wilde Street **IP28** 34 B1
Wilden *Beds.* **MK44** 32 D3
Wilden *Worcs.* **DY13** 29 H1
Wildhern **SP11** 21 G6
Wildhill **AL9** 23 F1
Wildmoor **B61** 29 J1
Wildsworth **DN21** 52 B3
Wilford **NG11** 41 H2
Wilkesley **SY13** 39 F1
Wilkhaven **IV20** 97 G3
Wilkieston **EH27** 75 K4
Wilksby **PE22** 53 F6
Willand *Devon* **EX15** 7 J4
Willand *Som.* **TA3** 7 K4
Willaston *Ches.* **CH64** 48 C5
Willaston *Ches.* **CW5** 49 F7
Willaston *Shrop.* **SY13** 38 E2
Willen **MK15** 32 B4
Willenhall *W.Mid.* WV13 40 B6
Willenhall *W.Mid.* **CV3** 30 E1
Willerby *E.Riding* **HU10** 59 G6
Willerby *N.Yorks.* **YO12** 59 G2
Willersey **WR12** 30 C5
Willersley **HR3** 28 C4
Willesborough **TN24** 15 F3
Willesborough Lees **TN24** 15 F3
Willesden **NW10** 23 F3
Willesleigh **EX32** 6 D2
Willesley **GL8** 20 B3
Willett **TA4** 7 K2
Willey *Shrop.* **TF12** 39 F6
Willey *Warks.* **CV23** 41 G7
Willey Green **GU3** 22 C6
William's Green **IP7** 34 D4
Williamscot **OX17** 31 F4
Williamthorpe **S42** 51 G6
Willian **SG6** 33 F5
Willimontswick **NE47** 70 C7
Willingale **CM5** 23 J1
Willingdon **BN20** 13 J6
Willingham **CB4** 33 H1
Willingham by Stow **DN21** 52 B4
Willingham Green **CB8** 33 K3
Willington *Beds.* **MK44** 32 E3
Willington *Derbys.* **DE65** 40 E3
Willington *Dur.* **DL15** 62 C3
Willington *Kent* **ME15** 14 C2
Willington *T. & W.* **NE28** 71 J7
Willington *Warks.* **CV36** 30 D5
Willington Corner **CW6** 48 E6
Willisham **IP8** 34 E3
Willitoft **YO8** 58 D6
Williton **TA4** 7 J1
Willoughbridge **TF9** 39 G1
Willoughby *Lincs.* **LN13** 53 H5
Willoughby *Warks.* **CV23** 31 G2
Willoughby Waterleys **LE8** 41 H6
Willoughby-on-the-Wolds **LE12** 41 J3
Willoughton **DN21** 52 C3
Willow Green **CW8** 49 F5
Willows Green **CM3** 34 B7
Willsbridge **BS30** 19 K4
Willslock **ST14** 40 C2
Willsworthy **PL19** 6 D7
Willtown **TA10** 8 C2
Wilmcote **CV37** 30 C3
Wilmington *B. & N.E.Som.* **BA2** 19 K5
Wilmington *Devon* **EX14** 8 B4
Wilmington *E.Suss.* **BN26** 13 J6
Wilmington *Kent* **DA2** 23 J4
Wilmslow SK9 49 H4
Wilnecote **B77** 40 E5
Wilney Green **IP22** 44 E7
Wilpshire **BB1** 56 B6
Wilsden **BD15** 57 F6
Wilsford *Lincs.* **NG32** 42 D1
Wilsford *Wilts.* **SP4** 10 C1
Wilsford *Wilts.* **SN9** 20 E6
Wilsham **EX35** 7 F1
Wilshaw **HD9** 50 D2
Wilsill **HG3** 57 G3
Wilsley Green **TN17** 14 C4
Wilsley Pound **TN17** 14 C4
Wilson **DE73** 41 G3
Wilstead **MK45** 32 D4
Wilsthorpe *E.Riding* **YO15** 59 H3
Wilsthorpe *Lincs.* **PE9** 42 D4
Wilstone **HP23** 32 C7
Wilton *Cumb.* **CA22** 60 B5
Wilton *Here.* **HR9** 28 E6
Wilton *N.Yorks.* **YO18** 58 E1
Wilton *R. & C.* **TS10** 63 G5
Wilton *Sc.Bord.* **TD9** 69 K2
Wilton *Wilts.* **SN8** 21 F5
Wilton *Wilts.* **SP2** 10 B1
Wiltown **EX15** 7 K4
Wimbish **CB10** 33 J5
Wimbish Green **CB10** 33 K5
Wimblebury **WS12** 40 C4
Wimbledon **SW19** 23 F4
Wimblington **PE15** 43 H6
Wimborne Minster BH21 10 B4
Wimborne St. Giles **BH21** 10 B3
Wimbotsham **PE34** 44 A5
Wimpole **SG8** 33 G3
Wimpole Lodge **SG8** 33 G4
Wimpstone **CV37** 30 D4
Wincanton BA9 9 G2
Winceby **LN9** 53 G6
Wincham **CW9** 49 F5
Winchburgh **EH52** 75 J3
Winchcombe **GL54** 30 B6
Winchelsea TN36 14 E6
Winchelsea Beach **TN36** 14 E6
Winchester SO23 11 F2
Winchet Hill **TN17** 14 C3
Winchfield **RG27** 22 A6
Winchmore Hill *Bucks.* **HP7** 22 C2
Winchmore Hill *Gt.Lon.* **N21** 23 G2
Wincle **SK11** 49 J6
Wincobank **S9** 51 F3
Windermere LA23 60 F7
Winderton **OX15** 30 E4
Windhill **IV4** 96 C7
Windle Hill **CH64** 48 C5
Windlehurst **SK6** 49 J4
Windlesham GU20 22 C5
Windley **DE56** 41 F1
Windmill **SK17** 50 D5
Windmill Hill *E.Suss.* **BN27** 13 K5
Windmill Hill *Som.* **TA19** 8 C3
Windmill Hill *Worcs.* **WR7** 29 J4
Windrush **OX18** 30 C7
Windsor SL4 22 C4
Windsor Green **IP30** 34 C3
Windy Nook **NE10** 71 H7
Windygates **KY8** 82 E7
Windy-Yett **KA3** 74 C5
Wineham **BN5** 13 F4
Winestead **HU12** 59 J7
Winewall **BB8** 56 E6
Winfarthing **IP22** 45 F7
Winford *I.o.W.* **PO36** 11 G6
Winford *N.Som.* **BS40** 19 J5
Winforton **HR3** 28 B4
Winfrith Newburgh **DT2** 9 H6
Wing *Bucks.* **LU7** 32 B6
Wing *Rut.* **LE15** 42 B5
Wingate TS28 62 E3
Wingates *Gt.Man.* **BL5** 49 F2
Wingates *Northumb.* **NE65** 71 F4
Wingerworth **S42** 51 F6
Wingfield *Beds.* **LU7** 32 D6
Wingfield *Suff.* **IP21** 35 G1
Wingfield *Wilts.* **BA14** 20 B6
Wingfield Green **IP21** 35 G1
Wingham **CT3** 15 H2
Wingham Well **CT3** 15 H2
Wingmore **CT4** 15 G3
Wingrave **HP22** 32 B7
Winkburn **NG22** 51 K7
Winkfield **SL4** 22 C4
Winkfield Row **RG42** 22 B4
Winkhill **ST13** 50 C7
Winkleigh EX19 6 E5
Winksley **HG4** 57 H2
Winkton **BH23** 10 C5
Winlaton **NE21** 71 G7
Winlaton Mill **NE21** 71 G7
Winless **KW1** 105 J3
Winmarleigh **PR3** 55 H5
Winnard's Perch **TR9** 3 G2
Winnersh **RG41** 22 A4
Winnington **CW8** 49 F5
Winscombe BS25 19 H6
Winsford *Ches.* CW7 49 F6
Winsford *Som.* **TA24** 7 H2
Winsham *Devon* **EX33** 6 C2
Winsham *Som.* **TA20** 8 C4
Winshill **DE15** 40 E3
Winsh-wen **SA7** 17 K6
Winskill **CA10** 61 G3
Winslade **RG25** 21 K7
Winsley **BA15** 20 B5
Winslow **MK18** 31 J6
Winson **GL7** 20 D1
Winsor **SO40** 10 E3
Winster *Cumb.* **LA23** 60 F7
Winster *Derbys.* **DE4** 50 E6
Winston *Dur.* **DL2** 62 C5
Winston *Suff.* **IP14** 35 F2
Winston Green **IP14** 35 F2
Winstone **GL7** 20 C1
Winswell **EX38** 6 C4
Winterborne Came **DT2** 9 G6
Winterborne Clenston **DT11** 9 H4
Winterborne Herringston **DT2** 9 F6
Winterborne Houghton **DT11** 9 H4
Winterborne Kingston **DT11** 9 H5
Winterborne Monkton **DT2** 9 F6
Winterborne Stickland **DT11** 9 H4
Winterborne Whitechurch **DT11** 9 H4
Winterborne Zelston **DT11** 9 H5
Winterbourne *S.Glos.* **BS36** 19 K3
Winterbourne *W.Berks.* **RG20** 21 H4
Winterbourne Abbas **DT2** 9 F5
Winterbourne Bassett **SN4** 20 E4
Winterbourne Dauntsey **SP4** 10 C1
Winterbourne Earls **SP4** 10 C1
Winterbourne Gunner **SP4** 10 C1
Winterbourne Monkton **SN4** 20 E4
Winterbourne Steepleton **DT2** 9 F6
Winterbourne Stoke **SP3** 20 D7
Winterbrook **OX10** 21 K3
Winterburn **BD23** 56 E4
Wintercleugh **ML12** 68 E2
Winteringham **DN15** 59 F7
Winterley **CW11** 49 G7
Wintersett **WF4** 51 F1
Wintershill **SO32** 11 G3
Winterslow **SP5** 10 D1
Winterton **DN15** 52 C1
Winterton-on-Sea **NR29** 45 J4
Winthorpe *Lincs.* **PE25** 53 J6
Winthorpe *Notts.* **NG24** 52 B7
Winton *Bourne.* **BH9** 10 B5
Winton *Cumb.* **CA17** 61 J5
Wintringham **YO17** 58 E2
Winwick *Cambs.* **PE28** 42 E7
Winwick *Northants.* **NN6** 31 H1
Winwick *Warr.* **WA2** 49 F3
Wirksworth **DE4** 50 E7
Wirksworth Moor **DE4** 51 F7
Wirswall **SY13** 38 E1
Wisbech PE13 43 H5
Wisbech St. Mary **PE13** 43 H5
Wisborough Green **RH14** 12 D4
Wiseton **DN10** 51 K4
Wishaw *N.Lan.* ML2 75 F5
Wishaw *Warks.* **B76** 40 D6
Wisley **GU23** 22 D6
Wispington **LN9** 53 F5
Wissett **IP19** 35 H1
Wissington **CO6** 34 D5
Wistanstow **SY7** 38 D7
Wistanswick **TF9** 39 F3
Wistaston **CW2** 49 F7
Wiston *Pembs.* **SA62** 16 D4
Wiston *S.Lan.* **ML12** 75 H7
Wistow *Cambs.* **PE28** 43 F7
Wistow *N.Yorks.* **YO8** 58 B6
Wiswell **BB7** 56 C6
Witcham **CB6** 33 H1
Witchampton **BH21** 9 J4
Witchburn **PA28** 66 B1
Witchford **CB6** 33 J1
Witcombe **TA12** 8 D2
Witham CM8 34 C7
Witham Friary **BA11** 20 A7
Witham on the Hill **PE10** 42 D4
Withcall **LN11** 53 F4
Withcote **LE15** 42 A5
Withdean **BN1** 13 G6
Witherenden Hill **TN19** 13 K4
Witherhurst **TN19** 13 K4
Witheridge **EX16** 7 G4
Witherley **CV9** 41 F6
Withern **LN13** 53 H4
Withernsea HU19 59 K7
Withernwick **HU11** 59 H5
Withersdale Street **IP20** 45 G7
Withersfield **CB9** 33 K4
Witherslack **LA11** 55 H1
Witherslack Hall **LA11** 55 H1
Withiel **PL30** 3 G2
Withiel Florey **TA24** 7 H2
Withielgoose **PL30** 4 A4
Withington *Glos.* **GL54** 30 B7
Withington *Gt.Man.* **M20** 49 H3
Withington *Here.* **HR1** 28 E4
Withington *Shrop.* **SY4** 38 E4
Withington *Staffs.* **ST10** 40 C2
Withington Green **SK11** 49 H5
Withington Marsh **HR1** 28 E4
Withleigh **EX16** 7 H4
Withnell **PR6** 56 B7
Withnell Fold **PR6** 56 B7
Withybrook *Som.* **BA3** 19 K7
Withybrook *Warks.* **CV7** 41 G7
Withycombe **TA24** 7 J1
Withycombe Raleigh **EX8** 7 J7
Withyham **TN7** 13 H3
Withypool **TA24** 7 G2
Witley **GU8** 12 C3
Witnesham **IP6** 35 F3
Witney OX28 21 G1
Wittering **PE8** 42 D5
Wittersham **TN30** 14 D5
Witton *Angus* **DD9** 90 D7
Witton *Norf.* **NR13** 45 H5
Witton *Worcs.* **WR9** 29 H2
Witton Bridge **NR28** 45 H2
Witton Gilbert **DH7** 62 D2
Witton Park **DL14** 62 C3
Witton-le-Wear **DL14** 62 C3
Wiveliscombe **TA4** 7 J3
Wivelsfield **RH17** 13 G4
Wivelsfield Green **RH17** 13 G5
Wivenhoe **CO7** 34 E6
Wiveton **NR25** 44 E1
Wix **CO11** 35 F6
Wixford **B49** 30 B3
Wixhill **SY4** 38 E3
Wixoe **CO10** 34 B4
Woburn **MK17** 32 C5
Woburn Sands **MK17** 32 C5
Wokefield Park **RG7** 21 K5
Woking GU22 22 D6
Wokingham RG40 22 B5
Wolborough **TQ12** 5 J3
Wold Newton *E.Riding* **YO25** 59 G2
Wold Newton *N.E.Lincs.* **LN8** 53 F3
Woldingham **CR3** 23 G6
Wolfelee **TD9** 70 A3
Wolferlow **HR7** 29 F2
Wolferton **PE31** 44 A3
Wolfhampcote **CV23** 31 G2
Wolfhill **PH2** 82 C4
Wolfpits **LD8** 28 B3
Wolf's Castle **SA62** 16 C3
Wolfsdale **SA62** 16 C3
Woll **TD7** 69 K1
Wollaston *Northants.* **NN29** 32 C2
Wollaston *Shrop.* **SY5** 38 C4
Wollaston *W.Mid.* **DY8** 40 A7
Wollaton **NG8** 41 H2
Wollerton **TF9** 39 F3
Wollescote **DY9** 40 B7
Wolsingham **DL13** 62 B3
Wolston **CV8** 31 F1
Wolsty **CA7** 60 C1
Wolvercote **OX2** 21 J1
WOLVERHAMPTON WV 40 B6
Wolverley *Shrop.* **SY4** 38 D2
Wolverley *Worcs.* **DY11** 29 H1
Wolvers Hill **BS29** 19 G5
Wolverton *Hants.* **RG26** 21 J6
Wolverton *M.K.* **MK12** 32 B4
Wolverton *Warks.* **CV35** 30 D2
Wolverton *Wilts.* **BA12** 9 G1
Wolverton Common **RG26** 21 J6
Wolvesnewton **NP16** 19 H2
Wolvey **LE10** 41 G7
Wolvey Heath **LE10** 41 G7
Wolviston **TS22** 63 F4
Womaston **LD8** 28 B2
Wombleton **YO62** 58 C1
Wombourne **WV5** 40 A6
Wombwell **S73** 51 F2
Womenswold **CT4** 15 H2
Womersley **DN6** 51 H1
Wonastow **NP25** 28 D7
Wonersh **GU5** 22 D7
Wonford **EX2** 7 H6
Wonson **EX20** 6 E7
Wonston **SO21** 11 F1
Wooburn **HP10** 22 C3
Wooburn Green **HP10** 22 C3
Wood Bevington **B49** 30 B3
Wood Burcote **NN12** 31 H4
Wood Dalling **NR11** 44 E3
Wood Eaton **ST20** 40 A4
Wood End *Beds.* **MK43** 32 D4
Wood End *Beds.* **MK44** 32 D2
Wood End *Bucks.* **MK17** 31 J5
Wood End *Herts.* **SG2** 33 G6
Wood End *W.Mid.* **WV11** 40 B5
Wood End *Warks.* **CV9** 40 E6
Wood End *Warks.* **B94** 30 C1
Wood End *Warks.* **CV7** 40 E7
Wood Enderby **PE22** 53 F6
Wood Green *Essex* **EN9** 23 H1
Wood Green *Gt.Lon.* **N22** 23 G2
Wood Green *Norf.* **NR15** 45 G6
Wood Lane **SY12** 38 D2
Wood Norton **NR20** 44 E3
Wood Seats **S35** 51 F3
Wood Stanway **GL54** 30 B5
Wood Street **NR29** 45 H3
Wood Street Village **GU3** 22 C6
Woodacott **EX22** 6 B5
Woodale **DL8** 57 F2
Woodall **S26** 51 G4
Woodbastwick **NR13** 45 H4
Woodbeck **DN22** 51 K5
Woodborough *Notts.* **NG14** 41 J1
Woodborough *Wilts.* **SN9** 20 E6
Woodbridge *Devon* **EX24** 7 K6
Woodbridge *Dorset* **DT10** 9 G3
Woodbridge *Suff.* IP12 35 G4
Woodbury *Devon* **EX5** 7 J7
Woodbury *Som.* **BA5** 19 J7
Woodbury Salterton **EX5** 7 J7
Woodchester **GL5** 20 B1
Woodchurch *Kent* **TN26** 14 E4
Woodchurch *Mersey.* **CH49** 48 B4
Woodcombe **TA24** 7 H1
Woodcote *Oxon.* **RG8** 21 K3
Woodcote *Tel. & W.* **TF10** 39 G4
Woodcote Green **B61** 29 J1
Woodcott **RG28** 21 H6
Woodcroft **NP16** 19 J2
Woodcutts **SP5** 9 J3
Wodditton **CB8** 33 K3
Woodeaton **OX3** 31 G7
Woodend *Aber.* **AB51** 90 E3
Woodend *Cumb.* **CA18** 60 C7
Woodend *High.* **IV13** 88 E2
Woodend *High.* **PH36** 79 J1
Woodend *Northants.* **NN12** 31 H4
Woodend *P. & K.* **PH15** 81 J3
Woodend *W.Suss.* **PO18** 12 B6
Woodend Green **CM22** 33 J6
Woodfalls **SP5** 10 C2
Woodfield *Oxon.* **OX26** 31 G6
Woodfield *S.Ayr.* **KA8** 67 H1
Woodfoot **CA10** 61 H5
Woodford *Cornw.* **EX23** 6 A4
Woodford *Devon* **TQ9** 5 H5
Woodford *Glos.* **GL13** 19 K2
Woodford *Gt.Lon.* **IG8** 23 H2
Woodford *Gt.Man.* **SK7** 49 H4
Woodford *Northants.* **NN14** 32 C1
Woodford *Som.* **TA4** 7 J2
Woodford Bridge **IG8** 23 H2
Woodford Green IG8 23 H2
Woodford Halse **NN11** 31 G3
Woodgate *Devon* **EX15** 7 K4
Woodgate *Norf.* **NR20** 44 E4
Woodgate *W.Mid.* **B32** 40 B7
Woodgate *W.Suss.* **PO20** 12 C6
Woodgate *Worcs.* **B60** 29 J2
Woodgreen **SP6** 10 C3
Woodhall *Inclyde* **PA14** 74 B3
Woodhall *N.Yorks.* **DL8** 62 A7
Woodhall Hills **LS28** 57 G6
Woodhall Spa LN10 52 E6
Woodham *Bucks.* **HP18** 31 H7
Woodham *Dur.* **DL17** 62 D4
Woodham *Surr.* **KT15** 22 D5
Woodham Ferrers **CM3** 24 D2
Woodham Mortimer **CM9** 24 E1
Woodham Walter **CM9** 24 E1
Woodhaven **DD6** 83 F5
Woodhead *Aber.* **AB53** 91 F1
Woodhead *Staffs.* **ST10** 40 C1
Woodhey **CH42** 48 C4
Woodhey Green **CW5** 48 E7
Woodhill *Shrop.* **WV16** 39 G7
Woodhill *Som.* **TA3** 8 C2
Woodhorn **NE63** 71 H5
Woodhouse *Cumb.* **LA7** 55 J1
Woodhouse *Leics.* **LE12** 41 H4
Woodhouse *S.Yorks.* **S13** 51 G4
Woodhouse *W.Yorks.* **LS2** 57 H6
Woodhouse *W.Yorks.* **WF6** 57 J7
Woodhouse *W.Yorks.* **HD6** 57 G7
Woodhouse Down **BS32** 19 K3
Woodhouse Eaves **LE12** 41 H4
Woodhouse Green **SK11** 49 J6
Woodhouses *Gt.Man.* **M35** 49 H2
Woodhouses *Staffs.* **DE13** 40 D4
Woodhouses *Staffs.* **WS7** 40 C5
Woodhuish **TQ6** 5 K5
Woodhurst **PE28** 33 G1
Woodingdean **BN2** 13 G6
Woodington **SO51** 10 E2
Woodland *Devon* **TQ13** 5 H4
Woodland *Dur.* **DL13** 62 B4
Woodland *Kent* **CT18** 15 G3
Woodland Head **EX17** 7 F6
Woodlands *Dorset* **BH21** 10 B4
Woodlands *Hants.* **SO40** 10 E3
Woodlands *N.Yorks.* **HG2** 57 J4
Woodlands *Shrop.* **WV16** 39 G7
Woodlands *Som.* **TA5** 7 K1
Woodlands Park **SL6** 22 B4
Woodlands St. Mary **RG17** 21 G4
Woodlane **DE13** 40 D3
Woodleigh **TQ7** 5 H6
Woodlesford **LS26** 57 J7
Woodley *Gt.Man.* **SK6** 49 J3
Woodley *W'ham* **RG5** 22 A4
Woodmancote *Glos.* **GL7** 20 D1
Woodmancote *Glos.* **GL52** 29 J6
Woodmancote *Glos.* **GL11** 20 A2
Woodmancote *W.Suss.* **BN5** 13 F5
Woodmancote *W.Suss.* **PO10** 11 J4
Woodmancott **SO21** 21 J7
Woodmansey **HU17** 59 G6
Woodmansterne **SM7** 23 F6
Woodmanton **EX5** 7 J7
Woodmill **DE13** 40 D3
Woodminton **SP5** 10 B2
Woodmoor **SY15** 38 B5
Woodnesborough **CT13** 15 J2
Woodnewton **PE8** 42 D6
Woodperry **OX33** 31 G7
Woodplumpton **PR4** 55 J6
Woodrising **NR9** 44 D5
Woodrow **DT10** 9 G3
Wood's Corner **TN21** 13 K5
Woods Eaves **HR3** 28 B4
Wood's Green **TN5** 13 K3
Woodseaves *Shrop.* **TF9** 39 F2
Woodseaves *Staffs.* **ST20** 39 G3
Woodsend **SN8** 21 F4
Woodsetts **S81** 51 H4
Woodsford **DT2** 9 G5
Woodside *Aberdeen* **AB24** 91 H4
Woodside *Beds.* **LU1** 32 D7
Woodside *Brack.F.* **SL4** 22 C4
Woodside *Cumb.* **CA15** 60 B3
Woodside *D. & G.* **DG1** 69 F6
Woodside *Fife* **KY8** 83 F7
Woodside *Fife* **KY7** 82 D7
Woodside *Gt.Lon.* **SE25** 23 G5
Woodside *Hants.* **SO41** 10 E5
Woodside *Herts.* **AL9** 23 F1
Woodside *N.Ayr.* **KA15** 74 B5
Woodside *P. & K.* **PH13** 82 C4
Woodside *Shrop.* **SY7** 38 C7
Woodside *W.Mid.* **DY5** 40 B7
Woodside Green **ME17** 14 E2
Woodstock *Oxon.* OX20 31 F7
Woodstock *Pembs.* **SA63** 16 D3
Woodthorpe *Derbys.* **S43** 51 G5
Woodthorpe *Leics.* **LE12** 41 H4
Woodthorpe *Lincs.* **LN13** 53 H4
Woodthorpe *S.Yorks.* **S2** 51 F4
Woodton **NR35** 45 G6
Woodtown **EX39** 6 C3

Woodvale **PR8** 48 C1
Woodville **DE11** 41 F4
Woodwall Green **ST21** 39 G2
Woodwalton **PE28** 43 F7
Woodwick **KW17** 106 C5
Woodworth Green **CW6** 48 E7
Woodyates **SP5** 10 B3
Woofferton **SY8** 28 E2
Wookey **BA5** 19 J7
Wookey Hole **BA5** 19 J7
Wool **BH20** 9 H6
Woolacombe EX34 6 **C1**
Woolage Green **CT4** 15 H3
Woolage Village **CT4** 15 H2
Woolaston **GL15** 19 J1
Woolaston Slade **GL15** 19 J1
Woolavington **TA7** 19 G7
Woolbeding **GU29** 12 B4
Woolcotts **TA22** 7 H2
Wooldale **HD9** 50 D2
Wooler NE71 70 **E1**
Woolfardisworthy *Devon* **EX17** 7 G5
Woolfardisworthy *Devon* **EX39** 6 B3
Woolfold **BL8** 49 G1
Woolfords Cottages **EH55** 75 J5
Woolgarston **BH20** 9 J6
Woolgreaves **WF2** 51 F1
Woolhampton **RG7** 21 J5
Woolhope **HR1** 29 F5
Woolland **DT11** 9 G4
Woollard **BS39** 19 K5
Woollaton **EX38** 6 C4
Woollensbrook **EN11** 23 G1
Woolley *B. & N.E.Som.* **BA1** 20 A5
Woolley *Cambs.* **PE28** 32 E1
Woolley *Cornw.* **EX23** 6 A4
Woolley *Derbys.* **DE55** 51 F6
Woolley *W.Yorks.* **WF4** 51 F1
Woolley Green *W. & M.* **SL6** 22 B4
Woolley Green *Wilts.* **BA15** 20 B5
Woolmer Green **SG3** 33 F7
Woolmere Green **B60** 29 J2
Woolmersdon **TA5** 8 B1
Woolpit **IP30** 34 D2
Woolpit Green **IP30** 34 D2
Woolscott **CV23** 31 F2
Woolsgrove **EX17** 7 F5
Woolstaston **SY6** 38 D6
Woolsthorpe **NG32** 42 B2
Woolsthorpe by Colsterworth **NG33** 42 C3
Woolston *Devon* **TQ7** 5 H6
Woolston *S'ham.* **SO19** 11 F3
Woolston *Shrop.* **SY10** 38 C3
Woolston *Shrop.* **SY6** 38 D7
Woolston *Warr.* **WA1** 49 F4
Woolston Green **TQ13** 5 H4
Woolstone *Glos.* **GL52** 29 J5
Woolstone *M.K.* **MK15** 32 B5
Woolstone *Oxon.* **SN7** 21 F3
Woolton **L25** 48 D4
Woolton Hill **RG20** 21 H5
Woolverstone **IP9** 35 F5
Woolverton **BA2** 20 A6
Woolwich **SE18** 23 H4
Woonton **HR3** 28 C3
Wooperton **NE66** 71 F2
Woore **CW3** 39 G1
Wootten Green **IP21** 35 G1
Wootton *Beds.* **MK43** 32 D4
Wootton *Hants.* **BH25** 10 D5
Wootton *I.o.W.* **PO33** 11 G5
Wootton *Kent* **CT4** 15 H3
Wootton *N.Lincs.* **DN39** 52 D1
Wootton *Northants.* **NN4** 31 J3
Wootton *Oxon.* **OX20** 31 F7
Wootton *Oxon.* **OX1** 21 H1
Wootton *Shrop.* **SY7** 28 D1
Wootton *Shrop.* **SY11** 38 C3
Wootton *Staffs.* **ST21** 40 A3
Wootton *Staffs.* **DE6** 40 D1
Wootton Bassett **SN4** 20 D3
Wootton Bridge **PO33** 11 G5
Wootton Common **PO33** 11 G5
Wootton Courtenay **TA24** 7 H1
Wootton Fitzpaine **DT6** 8 C5
Wootton Green **MK43** 32 D4
Wootton Rivers **SN8** 20 E5
Wootton St. Lawrence **RG23** 21 J6
Wootton Wawen **B95** 30 C2
WORCESTER WR 29 **H3**
Worcester Park KT4 23 **F5**
Wordsley **DY8** 40 A7
Wordwell **IP28** 34 C1
Worfield **WV15** 39 G6
Worgret **BH20** 9 J6
Work **KW15** 106 D6
Workhouse End **MK41** 32 E3
Workington CA14 60 **B4**
Worksop S80 51 **H5**
Worlaby *Lincs.* **LN11** 53 G5
Worlaby *N.Lincs.* **DN20** 52 D1
World's End *Bucks.* **HP22** 22 B1
Worlds End *Hants.* **PO7** 11 H3
World's End *W.Berks.* **RG20** 21 H4
Worlds End *W.Mid.* **B91** 40 D7
Worle **BS22** 19 G5
Worleston **CW5** 49 F7
Worlingham **NR34** 45 J7
Worlington **IP28** 33 K1
Worlingworth **IP13** 35 G2
Wormald Green **HG3** 57 J3
Wormbridge **HR2** 28 D5
Wormegay **PE33** 44 A4
Wormelow Tump **HR2** 28 D5
Wormhill **SK17** 50 D5
Wormiehills **DD11** 83 H4
Wormingford **CO6** 34 D5
Worminghall **HP18** 21 K1
Wormington **WR12** 30 B5
Worminster **BA4** 19 J7
Wormiston **KY10** 83 H7
Wormit **DD6** 82 E5
Wormleighton **CV47** 31 F3
Wormley *Herts.* **EN10** 23 G1
Wormley *Surr.* **GU8** 12 C3
Wormley West End **EN10** 23 G1
Wormshill **ME9** 14 D2
Wormsley **HR4** 28 D4
Worplesdon **GU3** 22 C6
Worrall **S35** 51 F3
Worsbrough **S70** 51 F2
Worsley **M28** 49 G2
Worstead **NR28** 45 H3
Worsted Lodge **CB1** 33 J3
Worsthorne **BB10** 56 D6
Worston **BB7** 56 C5
Worswell **PL8** 5 F6
Worth *Kent* **CT14** 15 J2
Worth *W.Suss.* **RH10** 13 F3
Worth Matravers **BH19** 9 J7
Wortham **IP22** 34 E1
Worthen **SY5** 38 C5
Worthenbury **LL13** 38 D1
Worthing *Norf.* **NR20** 44 D4
Worthing *W.Suss.* BN11 12 **E6**
Worthington **LE65** 41 G3
Worting **RG23** 21 K6
Wortley *Glos.* **GL12** 20 A2
Wortley *S.Yorks.* **S35** 51 F3
Wortley *W.Yorks.* **LS12** 57 H6
Worton *N.Yorks.* **DL8** 56 E1
Worton *Wilts.* **SN10** 20 C6
Wortwell **IP20** 45 G7
Wothersome **LS23** 57 K5
Wotherton **SY15** 38 B5
Wotter **PL7** 5 F4
Wotton **RH5** 22 E7
Wotton Underwood **HP18** 31 H7
Wotton-under-Edge GL12 20 **A2**
Woughton on the Green **MK6** 32 B5
Wouldham **ME1** 24 D5
Wrabness **CO11** 35 F5
Wrae **AB53** 99 F5
Wrafton **EX33** 6 C2
Wragby **LN8** 52 E5
Wragholme **LN11** 53 G3
Wramplingham **NR18** 45 F5
Wrangaton **PL21** 5 G5
Wrangham **AB52** 90 E1
Wrangle **PE22** 53 H7
Wrangle Lowgate **PE22** 53 H7
Wrangway **TA21** 7 K4
Wrantage **TA3** 8 C2
Wrawby **DN20** 52 D2
Wraxall *N.Som.* **BS48** 19 H4
Wraxall *Som.* **BA4** 9 F1
Wray **LA2** 56 B3
Wray Castle **LA22** 60 E6
Wrays **RH6** 23 F7
Wraysbury **TW19** 22 D4
Wrayton **LA6** 56 B2
Wrea Green **PR4** 55 G6
Wreay *Cumb.* **CA11** 60 F4
Wreay *Cumb.* **CA4** 60 F2
Wrecclesham **GU10** 22 B7
Wrecsam (Wrexham) LL13 38 **C1**
Wrekenton **NE9** 62 D1
Wrelton **YO18** 58 D1
Wrenbury **CW5** 38 E1
Wrench Green **YO13** 59 F1
Wreningham **NR16** 45 F6
Wrentham **NR34** 45 J7
Wrenthorpe **WF2** 57 J7
Wrentnall **SY5** 38 D5
Wressle *E.Riding* **YO8** 58 D6
Wressle *N.Lincs.* **DN20** 52 C2
Wrestlingworth **SG19** 33 F4
Wretham **IP24** 44 D6
Wretton **PE33** 44 A5
Wrexham (Wrecsam) LL13 38 **C1**
Wrexham Industrial Estate **LL13** 38 C1
Wribbenhall **DY12** 29 G1
Wrightington Bar **WN6** 48 E1
Wrightpark **FK8** 74 E1
Wright's Green **CM22** 33 J7
Wrinehill **CW3** 39 G1
Wrington **BS40** 19 H5
Writhlington **BA3** 19 K6
Writtle **CM1** 24 C1
Wrockwardine **TF6** 39 F4
Wroot **DN9** 51 K2
Wrose **BD18** 57 G6
Wrotham **TN15** 23 K6
Wrotham Heath **TN15** 23 K6
Wrotham Hill Park **TN15** 24 C5
Wrottesley **WV8** 40 A5
Wroughton **SN4** 20 E3
Wroxall *I.o.W.* **PO38** 11 G7
Wroxall *Warks.* **CV35** 30 D1
Wroxeter **SY5** 38 E5
Wroxham **NR12** 45 H4
Wroxton **OX15** 31 F4
Wstrws **SA44** 17 G1
Wyaston **DE6** 40 D1
Wyberton **PE21** 43 G1
Wyboston **MK44** 32 E3
Wybunbury **CW5** 39 F1
Wych Cross **RH18** 13 H3
Wychbold **WR9** 29 J2
Wychnor **DE13** 40 D4
Wychnor Bridges **DE13** 40 D4
Wyck **GU34** 11 J1
Wyck Rissington **GL54** 30 C6
Wycliffe **DL12** 62 C5
Wycoller **BB8** 56 E6
Wycomb **LE14** 42 A3
Wycombe Marsh **HP11** 22 B2
Wyddial **SG9** 33 G5
Wye **TN25** 15 F3
Wyesham **NP25** 28 E7
Wyfordby **LE14** 42 A4
Wyke *Devon* **EX17** 7 G6
Wyke *Dorset* **SP8** 9 G2
Wyke *Shrop.* **TF13** 39 F5
Wyke *Surr.* **GU3** 22 C6
Wyke *W.Yorks.* **BD12** 57 G7
Wyke Champflower **BA10** 9 F1
Wyke Regis **DT4** 9 F7
Wykeham *N.Yorks.* **YO13** 59 F1
Wykeham *N.Yorks.* **YO17** 58 E2
Wyken *Shrop.* **WV15** 39 G6
Wyken *W.Mid.* **CV2** 41 F7
Wykey **SY4** 38 C3
Wylam NE41 71 **G7**
Wylde Green **B72** 40 D6
Wyllie **NP12** 18 E2
Wylye **BA12** 10 B1
Wymering **PO6** 11 H4
Wymeswold **LE12** 41 J3
Wymington **NN10** 32 C2
Wymondham *Leics.* **LE14** 42 B4
Wymondham *Norf.* NR18 45 **F5**
Wyndham **CF32** 18 C2
Wynford Eagle **DT2** 8 E5
Wynnstay Park **LL14** 38 C1
Wynyard **TS22** 63 F4
Wyre Piddle **WR10** 29 J4
Wyresdale Tower **LA2** 56 B4
Wysall **NG12** 41 J3
Wyson **SY8** 28 E2
Wythall **B47** 30 B1
Wytham **OX2** 21 H1
Wythburn **CA12** 60 E5
Wythenshawe **M22** 49 H4
Wyton *Cambs.* **PE28** 33 F1
Wyton *E.Riding* **HU11** 59 H6
Wyverstone **IP14** 34 E2
Wyverstone Street **IP14** 34 E2
Wyville **NG32** 42 B3
Wyvis Lodge **IV16** 96 B4

Y

Y Bala (Bala) LL23 37 **J2**
Y Bryn **LL23** 37 H3
Y Drenewydd (Newtown) SY16 38 **A6**
Y Fali (Valley) **LL65** 46 A5
Y Fan **SY18** 37 J7
Y Felin Newydd (New Mills) **SY16** 37 K5
Y Felinheli LL56 46 **D6**
Y Fenni (Abergavenny) NP7 28 **B7**
Y Fflint (Flint) CH6 48 **B5**
Y Ffôr **LL53** 36 C2
Y Fron (Upper Llandwrog) **LL54** 46 D7
Y Gelli Gandryll (Hay-on-Wye) **HR3** 28 B4
Y Trallwng (Welshpool) SY21 38 **B5**
Y Tymbl (Tumble) **SA14** 17 J4
Y Waun (Chirk) **LL14** 38 B2
Yaddlethorpe **DN17** 52 B2
Yafford **PO30** 11 F6
Yafforth **DL7** 62 E7
Yalberton **TQ4** 5 J5
Yalding **ME18** 23 K7
Yanley **BS41** 19 J5
Yanwath **CA10** 61 G4
Yanworth **GL54** 30 B7
Yapham **YO42** 58 D4
Yapton **BN18** 12 C6
Yarburgh **LN11** 53 G3
Yarcombe **EX14** 8 B4
Yardley **B25** 40 D7
Yardley Gobion **NN12** 31 J4
Yardley Hastings **NN7** 32 B3
Yardro **LD8** 28 B3
Yarford **TA2** 8 B2
Yarkhill **HR1** 29 F4
Yarlet **ST18** 40 B3
Yarley **BA5** 19 J7
Yarlington **BA9** 9 F2
Yarm TS15 63 **F5**
Yarmouth PO41 10 **E6**
Yarnacott **EX32** 6 E2
Yarnbrook **BA14** 20 B6
Yarnfield **ST15** 40 A2
Yarnscombe **EX31** 6 D3
Yarnton **OX5** 31 F7
Yarpole **HR6** 28 D2
Yarrow *Sc.Bord.* **TD7** 69 J1
Yarrow *Som.* **TA9** 19 G7
Yarrow Feus **TD7** 69 J1
Yarrowford **TD7** 69 K1
Yarsop **HR4** 28 D4
Yarwell **PE8** 42 D6
Yate **BS37** 20 A3
Yatehouse Green **CW10** 49 G6
Yateley GU46 22 **B5**
Yatesbury **SN11** 20 D4
Yattendon **RG18** 21 J4
Yatton *Here.* **HR6** 28 D2
Yatton *N.Som.* **BS49** 19 H5
Yatton Keynell **SN14** 20 B4
Yaverland **PO36** 11 H6
Yawl **DT7** 8 C5
Yaxham **NR19** 44 E4
Yaxley *Cambs.* **PE7** 42 E6
Yaxley *Suff.* **IP23** 35 F1
Yazor **HR4** 28 D4
Yeabridge **TA13** 8 D3
Yeading **UB4** 22 E3
Yeadon **LS19** 57 H5
Yealand Conyers **LA5** 55 J2
Yealand Redmayne **LA5** 55 J2
Yealand Storrs **LA5** 55 J2
Yealmbridge **PL8** 5 F5
Yealmpton **PL8** 5 F5
Yearby **TS11** 63 H4
Yearsley **YO61** 58 B2
Yeaton **SY4** 38 D4
Yeaveley **DE6** 40 D1
Yeavering **NE71** 77 H7
Yedingham **YO17** 58 E2
Yelford **OX29** 21 G1
Yell **ZE2** 107 N4
Yelland *Devon* **EX31** 6 C2
Yelland *Devon* **EX20** 6 D6
Yelling **PE19** 33 F2
Yelvertoft **NN6** 31 G1
Yelverton *Devon* PL20 5 **F4**
Yelverton *Norf.* **NR14** 45 G5
Yenston **BA8** 9 G2
Yeo Mill **EX36** 7 G3
Yeo Vale **EX39** 6 C3
Yeoford **EX17** 7 F6
Yeolmbridge **PL15** 6 B7
Yeomadon **EX22** 6 B5
Yeovil BA20 8 **E3**
Yeovil Marsh **BA21** 8 E3
Yeovilton **BA22** 8 E2
Yerbeston **SA68** 16 D5
Yesnaby **KW16** 106 B6
Yetholm Mains **TD5** 70 D1
Yetlington **NE66** 71 F2
Yetminster **DT9** 8 E3
Yettington **EX9** 7 J7
Yetts o'Muckhart **FK14** 82 B7
Yew Green **CV35** 30 D2
Yielden **MK44** 32 D2
Yieldshields **ML8** 75 G5
Ynys **LL47** 36 E2
Ynys Enlli (Bardsey Island) **LL53** 36 A3
Ynys Môn (Anglesey) **LL** 46 B4
Ynys Tachwedd **SY24** 37 F6
Ynysboeth **CF45** 18 D2
Ynysddu **NP11** 18 E2
Ynyshir **CF39** 18 D2
Ynyslas **SY24** 37 F6
Ynysmaerdy **CF72** 18 D3
Ynysmeudwy **SA8** 18 A1
Ynystawe **SA6** 17 K5
Ynyswen **CF42** 18 C2
Ynysybwl **CF37** 18 D2
Yockenthwaite **BD23** 56 E2
Yockleton **SY5** 38 C4
Yokefleet **DN14** 58 E7
Yoker **G14** 74 D4
Yonder Bognie **AB54** 98 E6
YORK YO 58 **C4**
Yorkletts **CT5** 25 G5
Yorkley **GL15** 19 K1
Yorton **SY4** 38 E3
Yorton Heath **SY4** 38 E3
Youldon **EX22** 6 B5
Youldonmoor Cross **EX22** 6 B5
Youlgreave **DE45** 50 E6
Youlthorpe **YO41** 58 D4
Youlton **YO61** 57 K3
Young's End **CM3** 34 B7
Yoxall **DE13** 40 D4
Yoxford **IP17** 35 H2
Yr Wyddgrug (Mold) CH7 48 **B6**
Ysbyty Cynfyn **SY23** 27 G1
Ysbyty Ifan **LL24** 37 H1
Ysbyty Ystwyth **SY25** 27 G1
Ysceifiog **CH8** 47 K5
Ysgubor-y-coed **SY20** 37 F6
Ystalyfera **SA9** 18 A1
Ystrad **CF41** 18 C2
Ystrad Aeron **SA48** 26 E3
Ystrad Meurig SY25 27 **G2**
Ystrad Mynach **CF82** 18 E2
Ystradfellte **CF44** 27 J7
Ystradffin **SA20** 27 G4
Ystradgynlais **SA9** 27 G7
Ystradowen *N.P.T.* **SA9** 27 G7
Ystradowen *V. of Glam.* **CF71** 18 D4
Ystumtuen **SY23** 27 G1
Ythanwells **AB54** 90 E1
Ythsie **AB41** 91 G1

Z

Zeal Monachorum **EX17** 7 F5
Zeals **BA12** 9 G1
Zelah **TR4** 3 F3
Zennor **TR26** 2 B5
Zouch **LE12** 41 H3

INDEX TO NORTHERN IRELAND

Administrative area abbreviations

B'mena	Ballymena	*Cooks.*	Cookstown	*Dungan.*	Dungannon	*Maghera.*	Magherafelt	*Newtown.*	Newtownabbey
Banbr.	Banbridge	*Craig.*	Craigavon	*Ferm.*	Fermanagh	*New. & M.*	Newry & Mourne	*Strab.*	Strabane

A

Acton BT35 109 G6
Aghadowey BT51 109 F2
Aghagallon BT67 109 G5
Aghalee BT67 109 G5
Aghanloo BT49 108 E2
Ahoghill BT42 109 G3
Aldergrove BT29 109 G5
Annaclone BT32 109 G6
Annahilt BT26 109 H6
Annalong BT34 109 H8
Annsborough BT31 109 H7
Antrim BT41 109 G4
Ardboe BT80 109 F5
Ardglass BT30 109 J7
Ardmillan BT23 109 J5
Ardstraw BT78 108 C4
Armagh BT60 109 F6
Armoy BT53 109 G2
Arney BT92 108 C7
Articlave BT51 108 E2
Artigarvan BT82 108 C3
Attical BT34 109 H8
Aughamullan BT71 109 F5
Augher BT77 108 D6
Aughnacloy BT69 108 E6

B

Ballinamallard BT94 108 C6
Ballintoy BT54 109 G1
Ballybogy BT53 109 F2
Ballycarry BT38 109 J4
Ballycassidy BT94 108 C6
Ballycastle BT54 109 G1
Ballyclare BT39 109 H4
Ballyeaston BT39 109 H4
Ballygalley BT40 109 H3
Ballygawley BT70 108 E6
Ballygowan BT23 109 J5
Ballyhalbert BT22 109 K5
Ballyhoe Bridge BT53 109 G2
Ballyholme BT20 109 J4
Ballyhornan BT30 109 J6
Ballykeel BT25 109 H6
Ballykelly BT49 108 E2
Ballykinler BT30 109 J7
Ballyleny BT61 109 F6
Ballyloughbeg BT57 109 F2
Ballymackilroy BT70 108 E6
Ballymagorry BT82 108 C3
Ballymartin BT34 109 H8
Ballymena BT43 109 G3
Ballymoney BT53 109 F2
Ballynahatty BT78 108 D5
Ballynahinch BT24 109 H6
Ballynakilly BT71 109 F5
Ballynamallaght BT82 108 D4
Ballyneaner BT82 108 D3
Ballynoe BT30 109 J7
Ballynure BT39 109 H4
Ballyrobert BT39 109 H4
Ballyronan BT45 109 F4
Ballyroney BT32 109 H7
Ballystrudder BT40 109 J4
Ballyvoy BT54 109 G1
Ballywalter BT22 109 K5
Ballyward BT31 109 H7
Balnamore BT53 109 F2
Banbridge BT32 109 G6
Bangor BT20 109 J4
Bannfoot BT66 109 F5
Belcoo BT93 108 B7
BELFAST BT 109 H5
Belfast City Airport BT3 109 H5
Belfast International Airport BT29 109 G4
Bellaghy BT45 109 F4
Bellanaleck BT92 108 C7
Belleek *Ferm.* BT93 108 A6
Belleek *New. & M.* BT35 109 F7
Belmont BT38 109 J4
Benburb BT71 109 F6
Bendooragh BT53 109 F2
Beragh BT79 108 D5
Bessbrook BT35 109 G7
Blackwatertown BT71 109 F6
Blaney BT93 108 B6
Bleary BT63 109 G6
Boho BT74 108 B6
Bolea BT49 108 E2
Bovedy BT51 109 F3
Boviel BT47 108 E3
Bready BT82 108 C3
Brookeborough BT94 108 C6
Broughshane BT42 109 G3
Bryansford BT33 109 H7
Burnside BT39 109 H4
Burren BT34 109 G7
Bushmills BT57 109 F1
Butterlope BT79 108 D4

C

Caddy BT41 109 G4
Caledon BT68 108 E6
Camlough BT35 109 G7
Cappagh BT70 108 E5
Cargan BT43 109 G3
Carland BT71 108 E5
Carncastle BT40 109 H3
Carnduff BT54 109 G1
Carnlough BT44 109 H3
Carnteel BT69 108 E6
Carrickfergus BT38 109 J4
Carrickmore BT79 108 E5
Carryduff BT8 109 H5
Castlecaulfield BT70 108 E5
Castledawson BT45 109 F4
Castlederg BT81 108 C4
Castlereagh BT6 109 H5
Castlerock BT51 108 E2
Castleroe BT51 109 F2
Castlewellan BT31 109 H7
Chapeltown BT41 109 G4
Charlemont BT71 109 F6
Church Ballee BT30 109 J6
Church Hill BT93 108 B6
Churchtown BT30 109 J6
City of Derry Airport BT47 108 D2
Clabby BT75 108 D6
Clady *Maghera.* BT44 109 F3
Clady *Strab.* BT82 108 C4
Clady Milltown BT60 109 F7
Clanabogan BT78 108 D5
Clare BT62 109 G6
Claudy BT47 108 D3
Clogh BT44 109 G3
Cloghcor BT82 108 C3
Clogher BT76 108 D6
Cloghy BT22 109 K6
Clonelly BT93 108 B5
Clonoe BT71 109 F5
Clough BT30 109 J6
Cloughmills BT44 109 G3
Cloughreagh BT35 109 G7
Cloyfin BT52 109 F2
Coagh BT80 109 F5
Coalisland BT71 109 F5
Coleraine BT52 109 F2
Comber BT23 109 J5
Conlig BT23 109 J5
Cookstown BT80 109 F5
Cooneen BT75 108 D6
Corkey BT44 109 G2
Cox's Hill BT62 109 F6
Craig BT47 108 D4
Craigantlet BT23 109 J5
Craigavole BT51 109 F3
Craigavon BT65 109 G6
Craigdarragh BT47 108 D3
Craigs BT42 109 G3
Cranagh BT79 108 D4
Creagh BT94 108 C6
Creggan *New. & M.* BT35 109 F8
Creggan *Omagh* BT79 108 E5
Crilly BT69 108 E6
Cromkill BT42 109 G4
Crossgar BT30 109 J6
Crossmaglen BT35 109 F8
Crumlin BT29 109 G5
Culcavy BT26 109 H5
Culkey BT92 108 C6
Cullaville BT35 109 F8
Cullybackey BT42 109 G3
Cullyhanna BT35 109 F7
Culmore BT48 108 D2
Culnady BT46 109 F3
Curragh BT23 109 J6
Curran BT45 109 F4
Cushendall BT44 109 H2
Cushendun BT44 109 H2

D

Damhead BT52 109 F2
Darkley BT60 109 F7
Darragh Cross BT30 109 J6
Derry (Londonderry) BT48 108 D3
Derrychrin BT80 109 F5
Derrygonnelly BT93 108 B6
Derrylin BT92 108 C7
Derrymacash BT66 109 G5
Derrytrasna BT66 109 F5
Dervock BT53 109 F2
Desertmartin BT45 109 F4
Doagh BT39 109 H4
Dollingstown BT66 109 G6
Donagh BT92 108 C7
Donaghadee BT21 109 J5
Donaghcloney BT66 109 G6
Donaghmore BT70 108 E5
Donemana BT82 108 D3
Downhill BT51 108 E2
Downpatrick BT30 109 J6
Draperstown BT45 108 E4
Dromara BT25 109 H6
Dromore *Banbr.* BT25 109 H6
Dromore *Omagh* BT78 108 C5
Drumahoe BT47 108 D3
Drumaness BT24 109 H6
Drumaroad BT31 109 H6
Drumbo BT27 109 H5
Drumcard BT92 108 B7
Drumduff BT94 108 C6
Drumlegagh BT78 108 C4
Drummacabranagher BT92 108 C7
Drumnakilly BT79 108 D5
Drumquin BT78 108 C5
Drumsurn BT49 108 E3
Dunaghy BT53 109 F2
Dundonald BT16 109 J5
Dundrod BT29 109 H5
Dundrum BT33 109 J7
Dungannon BT70 108 E5
Dungiven BT47 108 E3
Dunloy BT44 109 G3
Dunmurry BT17 109 H5
Dunnamore BT80 108 E4
Dyan BT68 108 E6

E

Eden BT38 109 J4
Ederny BT93 108 C5
Eglinton BT47 108 D2
Eglish BT70 108 E6
Enniskillen BT74 108 C6
Ervey Cross Roads BT47 108 D3
Eshnadarragh BT92 108 D7
Eskragh BT78 108 D6

F

Feeny BT47 108 E3
Fintona BT78 108 D5
Finvoy BT53 109 F3
Fivemiletown BT75 108 D6
Foreglen BT47 108 E3
Forkhill BT35 109 G8

G

Gamblestown BT66 109 G6
Garrison BT93 108 A6
Garvagh BT51 109 F3
Garvaghy BT70 108 D5
Garvary BT74 108 C6
Gilford BT63 109 G6
Glarryford BT44 109 G3
Glebe BT82 108 C4
Glenanne BT60 109 F7
Glenariff BT44 109 H2
Glenarm BT44 109 H3
Glenavy BT29 109 G5
Glengormley BT36 109 H4
Glenhead BT49 108 E3
Glenhull BT79 108 E4
Glenoe BT40 109 H4
Glynn BT40 109 J4
Gortaclare BT79 108 D5
Gortin BT79 108 D4
Gortnahey BT47 108 E3
Gracehill BT42 109 G3
Grange Corner BT41 109 G4
Granville BT70 108 E5
Greencastle BT79 108 D4
Greenisland BT38 109 H4
Greyabbey BT22 109 J5
Greysteel BT47 108 D2
Groomsport BT19 109 J4
Gulladuff BT45 109 F4

H

Hamilton's Bawn BT60 109 F6
Hannahstown BT17 109 H5
Helen's Bay BT19 109 J4
Hillhall BT27 109 H5
Hillsborough BT26 109 H6
Hilltown BT34 109 H7
Holywell BT93 108 B7
Holywood BT18 109 J5

I

Inishrush BT44 109 F3
Irvinestown BT94 108 C6

J

Jonesborough BT35 109 G8

K

Katesbridge BT32 109 H6
Keady BT60 109 F7
Kearney BT22 109 K6
Keeran BT93 108 C5
Kells BT42 109 G4
Kesh BT93 108 B5
Kilcoo BT34 109 H7
Kilkeel BT34 109 H8
Killadeas BT94 108 C6
Killagan Bridge BT44 109 G2
Killen BT81 108 C4
Killeter BT81 108 C4
Killinchy BT23 109 J5
Killough BT30 109 J7
Killowen BT34 109 G8
Killyclogher BT79 108 D5
Killylea BT60 108 E6
Killyleagh BT30 109 J6
Kilmood BT23 109 J5
Kilmore BT30 109 J6
Kilraghts BT53 109 G2
Kilrea BT51 109 F3
Kilskeery BT78 108 C6
Kilwaughter BT40 109 H3
Kinallen BT25 109 H6
Kircubbin BT22 109 J5
Kirkistown BT22 109 K6
Knockcloghrim BT45 109 F4
Knocknacarry BT44 109 H2

L

Lack BT93 108 C5
Lackagh BT49 108 E3
Lagavara BT54 109 G1
Laghy Corner BT71 109 F5
Larne BT40 109 H3
Laurelvale BT62 109 G6
Lawrencetown BT63 109 G6
Leggs BT93 108 B5
Leitrim BT31 109 H7
Letter BT93 108 B5
Letterbreen BT74 108 B6
Lettershendony BT47 108 D3
Ligoniel BT14 109 H5
Limavady BT49 108 E2
Lisbane BT23 109 J5
Lisbellaw BT94 108 C6
Lisburn BT28 109 H5
Liscloon BT82 108 D3
Liscolman BT53 109 F2
Lislea BT44 109 F3
Lisnarrick BT94 108 B6
Lisnaskea BT92 108 C7
Lissan BT80 108 E4
Listooder BT30 109 J6
Loanends BT29 109 H4
Londonderry (Derry) BT48 108 D3
Loughbrickland BT32 109 G6
Loughgall BT61 109 F6
Loughguile BT44 109 G2
Loughinisland BT30 109 J6
Loughmacrory BT79 108 D5
Lower Ballinderry BT28 109 G5
Lurgan BT66 109 G6
Lurganare BT34 109 G7

M

McGregor's Corner BT43 109 G3
Mackan BT92 108 C7
Macosquin BT51 109 F2
Maghaberry BT67 109 G5
Maghera *Down* BT31 109 H7
Maghera *Maghera.* BT46 109 F3
Magherafelt BT45 109 F4
Magheralin BT67 109 G6
Magheramason BT47 108 C3
Magheraveely BT92 108 D7
Maghery BT71 109 F5
Magilligan BT49 108 E2
Maguiresbridge BT94 108 C7
Mallusk BT36 109 H4
Markethill BT60 109 F7
Martinstown BT43 109 G3
Mayobridge BT34 109 G7
May's Corner BT32 109 G7
Mazetown BT28 109 H5
Meigh BT35 109 G7
Middletown BT60 108 E7
Mill Town BT41 109 G4
Millbay BT40 109 J4
Millbrook BT40 109 H3
Millford BT60 109 F6
Millisle BT22 109 J5
Milltown *Banbr.* BT32 109 G7
Milltown *Craig.* BT62 109 F5
Minerstown BT30 109 J7
Moira BT67 109 G5
Monea BT74 108 B6
Moneydig BT51 109 F3
Moneyglass BT41 109 G4
Moneymore BT45 109 F4
Moneyneany BT45 108 E4
Moneyreagh BT23 109 J5
Moneyslane BT31 109 H7
Monteith BT32 109 G6
Moorfields BT42 109 G4
Moortown BT80 109 F5
Mossley BT36 109 H4
Moss-side BT53 109 G2
Mount Hamilton BT79 108 E4
Mount Norris BT60 109 F7
Mountfield BT79 108 D5
Mountjoy *Dungan.* BT71 109 F5
Mountjoy *Omagh* BT78 108 D5
Moy BT71 109 F6
Moyarget BT54 109 G2
Moygashel BT71 109 F5
Mullaghbane BT35 109 F8
Mullaghmassa BT79 108 D5
Mullan BT92 108 B7
Murley BT75 108 D6

N

New Buildings BT47 108 D3
New Ferry BT45 109 F4
Newcastle BT33 109 H7
Newmill BT39 109 H4
Newmills BT71 109 F5
Newry BT34 109 G7
Newtown Crommelin BT43 109 G3
Newtownabbey BT36 109 H4
Newtownards BT23 109 J5
Newtownbutler BT92 108 D7
Newtownhamilton BT35 109 F7
Newtownstewart BT78 108 D4
Nutt's Corner BT29 109 H5

O

Omagh BT79 108 D5
Oritor BT80 108 E5

P

Park BT47 108 D3
Parkgate BT39 109 H4
Pettigo BT93 108 B5
Plumbridge BT79 108 D4
Pomeroy BT70 108 E5
Portadown BT62 109 G6
Portaferry BT22 109 J6
Portavogie BT22 109 K6
Portballintrae BT57 109 F1
Portglenone BT44 109 F3
Portrush BT56 109 F1
Portstewart BT55 109 F2
Poyntz Pass BT35 109 G7
Prehen BT47 108 D3

R

Raffrey BT30 109 J6
Raholp BT30 109 J6
Randalstown BT41 109 G4
Rathfriland BT34 109 G7
Ravernet BT27 109 H5
Richhill BT61 109 F6
Ringboy BT22 109 K6
Ringsend BT51 109 F2
Riverside BT34 109 H8
Rosscor BT93 108 A6
Rosslea BT92 108 D7
Rostrevor BT34 109 G8
Rousky BT79 108 D4
Roxhill BT41 109 G4
Rubane BT22 109 K5

S

Saintfield BT24 109 J6
Sandholes BT80 108 E5
Saul BT30 109 J6
Scarva BT63 109 G6
Scollogstown BT30 109 J7
Scotch Street BT62 109 F6
Scribbagh BT93 108 A6
Seaforde BT30 109 J6
Seapatrick BT32 109 G6
Seskinore BT78 108 D5
Shoptown BT42 109 H4
Shrigley BT30 109 J6
Sion Mills BT82 108 C4
Sixmilecross BT79 108 D5
Soldierstown BT67 109 G5
Spamount BT81 108 C4
Springfield BT74 108 B6
Staffordstown BT41 109 G4
Stewartstown BT71 109 F5
Stonyford BT28 109 H5
Strabane BT82 108 C4
Straid *B'mena* BT42 109 G4
Straid *Newtown.* BT39 109 H4
Strangford BT30 109 J6
Stranocum BT53 109 G2
Swatragh BT46 109 F3

T

Tamlaght BT74 108 C6
Tamlaght O'Crilly BT46 109 F3
Tamnamore BT71 109 F5
Tandragee BT62 109 G6
Tassagh BT60 109 F7
Teemore BT92 108 C7
Templepatrick BT39 109 H4
Tempo BT94 108 C6
The Bush BT71 109 F5
The Diamond *Cooks.* BT71 109 F5
The Diamond *Omagh* BT78 108 D5
The Drones BT53 109 G2
The Loup BT45 109 F4
The Rock BT70 108 E5
The Sheddings BT42 109 H3
The Six Towns BT45 108 E4
The Spa BT24 109 H6
The Temple BT27 109 H5
Tobermore BT45 109 F4
Toome BT41 109 F4
Trillick BT78 108 C6
Trory BT94 108 C6
Tully BT92 108 C7
Tullyhogue BT80 109 F5
Tynan BT60 108 E6

U

Upper Ballinderry BT28 109 G5
Upperlands BT46 109 F3

V

Victoria Bridge BT82 108 C4
Vow BT53 109 F3

W

Waringsford BT25 109 H6
Waringstown BT66 109 G6
Warrenpoint BT34 109 G8
Whitecross BT60 109 F7
Whitehead BT38 109 J4